ISLAM IN THE SCHOOL OF MADINA

ISLAM IN THE SCHOOL OF MADINA

A COMMENTARY ON THE MURSHID AL-MU'IN

The Helping Guide to the Necessary Knowledge of the Deen

Ibn 'Ashir's work on Ash'ari Kalam,

Maliki Fiqh and Junaydi Tasawwuf

Shaykh Ahmad ibn al-Bashir al-Qalawi ash-Shinqiti

d. 1272 AH (1851 CE)

TRANSLATED BY ASADULLAH YATE

Classical and Contemporary Books on Islam and Sufism

Copyright © Asadullah Yate, 2013 CE/1434 AH

Islam in the School of Madina

Published by:	Diwan Press Ltd.
	6 Terrace Walk,
	Norwich
	NR1 3JD
	UK
Website:	www.diwanpress.com
E-mail:	info@diwanpress.com

All rights reserved. No part of this publication may be reproduced, stored in any retrieval system or transmitted in any form or by any means, electronic, mechanical, photocopying, recording or otherwise without the prior permission of the publishers.

Author:	Ahmad ibn al-Bashir al-Qalawi ash-Shinqiti
Translation:	Asadullah Yate
Typesetting and cover design by:	
	Abdassamad Clarke

A catalogue record of this book is available from the British Library.

ISBN-13:	978-1-908892-06-5 (hardback)
	978-1-908892-04-1 (paperback)
	978-1-908892-10-2 (epub)
	978-1-908892-12-6 (Kindle)

Printed and bound by:	Lightning Source

To my teacher, the Master of the Habibiyya-Shadhiliyya Tariqa,
Shaykh Dr Abdalqadir as-Sufi

Thanks are due to Ustadh Abu Sayf Kharkhashi

In the name of Allah, All-Merciful, Most Merciful
And may Allah bless His noble Prophet.
O Allah bless our Master Muhammad and the Family of Muhammad

Contents

INTRODUCTION	1
'Abd al-Wahid ibn 'Ashir	8
Hamd – Praise	8
Knowledge	10
Salat an-Nabi – Asking for blessings on the Prophet	31
Issue	33
The Name "Muhammad"	36
His Family	38
The Poem's Subject Matter	39

IMAN – 'AQIDA

INTRODUCTION TO THE BOOK OF 'AQIDA	41
WHICH IS AN AID TO ACTS OF OBEDIENCE AND ATTAINING THE DESIRED GOAL	41
The Necessarily True, the Inconceivable and the Conceivable	45
Reflection	47
Taqlid in Matters of *'Aqida*	48
THE BOOK OF BASIC PRINCIPLES REGARDING *'AQIDA*	69
Wujud – existence	71
Qidam – Existence from before time	72
Baqa' – Going on	72

Ghina' mutlaq – Absolute independence	72
Mukhalafa – His being different from His Creation	73
Wahda – Oneness	75
Qudra – Power	77
Irada – Will	77
'Ilm – Knowledge	79
As-Sam' wa'l-Basar – Hearing and Sight	80
Kalam – Speech	81
What attributes are impossible for Allah	95
What is conceivable for Allah	98
THE PROOFS	103
Wujud – Existence	103
Timelessness	113
Baqa' – Going On	114
Ghina – Independence	120
Wahda – Oneness	121
Hayat – Life	128
Unwavering Trust	167
The Books	180
The Messengers	181
The Angels	182
The Raising up	182
The Decree	182
The *Sirat*	183
The Balance	184
The Basin of the Prophet	187
The Garden	188
The Fire	188

Contents   xiii

ISLAM – FIQH

INTRODUCTORY MATTERS
– FROM THE ROOTS – WHOSE BRANCHES ARE AN AID TO ARRIVAL   193
   Wajib – incumbent   198
   Mandub – recommended actions   200
   Ja'iz – permissible   202
   Makruh – reprehensible actions   205
   Haram – forbidden   209

THE BOOK OF PURIFICATION   227
   Pure Water   229

Section: Concerning *Wudu'*   249

The Obligations of *Wudu'*   253
   INTENTION   257

That which Breaks *Wudu'*   285

Section concerning *ghusl*   311

The *Fard* Obligations of the *Ghusl*   319

Section regarding *tayammum*   351

THE BOOK OF *SALAT*   381
Obligations of the *Salat*   387

The Adhan   449
   Makruh Acts in the *Salat*   477
   Fard 'Ayn and *Fard Kifaya Salats*   488
   The *Fard* of *Janaza*   492
   Sunna *Salats*: Witr, Eclipse and *Salats* for Rain   500
   Qada' of Fajr and Subh   503
   Nafila Salats: greeting the mosque, Duha and Tarawih   507

Nafila Salats: Witr, before Dhuhr and 'Asr, after Maghrib and Dhuhr	511
A Muslim does not say 'The Prophet said…' without a chain of narration lest he falsely ascribe something to him	513
Prostrations for Forgetfulness	515
Blowing out or Speaking	518
Distractions	522
Voiding *Wudu'*, Forgetting, Laughing or Eating and Drinking Deliberately	524
LAWS GOVERNING THE JUMU'A	537
The *Khutbah*	539
The *Jami'*	543
Hastening to the Jumu'ah	548
The *Ghusl*	549
The *Jama'a*	550
The Imam	558
Things Makruh in the Imam such as Incontinence	572
THE BOOK OF ZAKAT	595
Zakat of Livestock	613
ZAKAT AL-FITR	659
BOOK OF FASTING	673
THE BOOK OF HAJJ	721
A description of his hajj, may the peace and blessings of Allah be upon him, from *Zad al-Ma'ad fi Hady Khayr il-'Ibad* of Ibn al-Qayyim al-Jawziyya	730
Hajj	735
The pillars of Hajj	736

The kinds of *ihram* of the Hajj	747
1. *Ifrad*	747
Being prevented from making the hajj	748
2. *Tamattu'*	750
3. *Qiran*	751
Ihram	752
The period of the *miqat*	753
Tawaf	755
The time of the *tawaf*	759
The *Sa'y* between Safa and Marwa	761
The Day of Tarwiya (watering) and 'Arafa	766
Moving off from Muzdalifa, that is, Jam' the 'Place of Gathering', and the Mash'ar al-Haram	773
'Umra	795
Visiting our Chief and Master, Muhammad ibn 'Abdallah, the Messenger of Allah, may the peace and blessings of Allah be upon him	803
The superiority of Madina al-Munawwara over every city in every other land, may the best blessings and peace be on the one who resides there	816

APPENDIX CONSISTING OF FORTY HADITH REGARDING THE HAJJ — 827

The *Talbiya*	827
The time of his entering the *ihram*, may the peace and blessings of Allah be upon him	827
Cupping	830
Marriage while in a state of *ihram*	830
The obligation to perform the hajj immediately (it becomes possible)	830
Having someone else perform the hajj	830

Fulfilling one's promise to a person who has died	831
The capacity to perform it: provision and the mount	831
A woman journeying without a *mahram* (that is, someone closely related to her)	831
Whoever makes the hajj on behalf of someone else when he himself has not performed it	831
The hajj in the case of a minor	832
His entering *ihram*, may the peace and blessings of Allah be upon him	832
His 'umra, may the peace and blessings of Allah be upon him	832
What the person who intends to enter the state of *ihram* should do	833
Greeting the Black Stone and kissing it	833

IHSAN – TASAWWUF

THE PRINCIPLES OF TASAWWUF AND THE GUIDES TO REALISATION	837
First Section	840
Second section	844
Third Section	847
INDEX	971

Introduction

O Allah grant peace and blessings to our Master Muhammad and his Family and Companions

A BLESSED BEGINNING, A BLESSED END

P RAISE belongs to Allah Who granted us the gift of iman and Islam, Who from His generosity granted us knowledge of the halal and the haram and purified the hearts of whomever He wishes from sickness and disease.

And may Allah bless Muhammad, the best of creation, who made clear His law, both what is obligatory and recommended, and bless his Family and Companions and those who follow in his footsteps.

The needy slave, dependent upon the mercy of his Lord, Ahmad ibn al-Bashir al-Qalawi ash-Shinqiti says: Seeking knowledge is the most important of all matters of concern, the best act of obedience and the quickest way of coming close to one's Lord, in particular in this age when people have almost come to differ about the indispensable aspects of the deen. As the poem of Shaykh Ibn 'Ashir[1] has indicated many of the sciences of the practice of the deen concisely, I want to write down some comments on it which might be of benefit, Allah, exalted is He, willing. In doing so, I shall rely on the (previous)

---

1 The great imam, the sea of knowledge, he who made the hajj from the most distant land (*abarr*), the *mujahid*, Abu Muhammad, 'Abd al-Wahid ibn 'Ali ibn 'Ashir, of the Ansari line, originally from Andalusia, brought up in Fez which he made his home. He has compositions on various different sciences, amongst them the poem entitled *al-Murshid al-mu'in 'ala daruri min 'ulum ad-deen* about Maliki *fiqh*. It parallels the *Mukhtasar* of Khalil in that it combines both the roots and branches of the deen such that whoever reads it and understands its points is able to abandon once and for all *taqleed* – imitation – for the soundness of the iman (of the people of *taqleed*) is disputed. He is thus able to learn what Allah has made incumbent on him of the sciences necessary for each and every Muslim to know. He died in Dhu'l-Hijja 1040 AH. (*Ash-Shajara* p.299, No. 1161)

commentators of this work, although an analysis of the text was not my actual aim but rather an imitation in the manner of al-Mawwaq's commentary of (the *Mukhtasar* of) Khalil, seeking help from Allah, glorious is He, and holding fast to His rope, His strength and His power, absolving myself of any strength or power on my part. In undertaking all my actions, I bear witness that there is no salvation or refuge from Him except by turning to Him. I am certain that He is the One Who disposes the right outcome of my affair and that it is up to Him if He punishes me for my wrong actions or forgives me.

I have referred to the commentator Mayyara,[1] and Ibn 'Abd as-Sadiq.[2] Likewise, I have referred to the *'alim* of the age, Muhammad ibn Marzuq,[3] to al-Mawwaq,[4] to Ibn al-Hattab,[5] to Ahmad Zarruq,[6] to Shaykh as-Sanusi,[7] to 'Abd

---

1   The *faqih*, Abu 'Abdallah Muhammad ibn Ahmad Mayyara, known for his eloquence, an imam, a man of exceedingly vast knowledge, known for his scrupulousness and his adherence to the deen. He has written various works, among them, *The Greater Commentary* and *The Lesser Commentary* on *al-Murshid al-Mu'een*. He was born in 999 AH and died in 1070. He was the student of Ibn 'Ashir. (*Ash-Shajara* p.309, No. 1200)

2   Abu'l-Hasan 'Ali ibn 'Abd as-Sadiq, one of the great men of knowledge and action, an accomplished author who sought and taught the truth, a man of *tasawwuf*. He has written a number of works, among them a commentary on *al-Murshid al-Mu'een*. I have not been able to find out when he died. (*Ash-Shajara* p.351, No. 1397)

3   Abu 'Abdallah Shams ad-Deen, Muhammad ibn Marzuq at-Tilimsani, known as al-*Khateeb* and known for his acquisition and teaching of knowledge. Born 710 AH, died 781, and buried between Ibn al-Qasim and Ashhab, may Allah have mercy on all of them. Author of many works. (*Ash-Shajara* p.236, No. 849)

4   Muhammad ibn Yusuf ibn Abu'l-Qasim al-'Abdari, known as al-Mawwaq, from Granada in Andalusia. Author of many works, among them two commentaries on the *Mukhtasar* of Khalil. Died Sha'ban, 897 AH. (*Nayl al-Ibtihaj* p.242)

5   Abu 'Abdallah Muhammad ibn al-Hattab, born and resided in Makka. Among his most famous works is the excellent and renowned commentary of great benefit on the *Mukhtasar* of Khalil, the like of which has not been surpassed. Born Ramadan 902 AH, died Rabi' ath-Thani 945. (*Ash-Shajara* p.270, No. 998)

6   The great *'alim*, the *faqih*, the *muhaddith*, the sufi, the *wali*, the *salih*, the hajji, a person of praiseworthy qualities and author of many works, Ahmad ibn Ahmad ibn 'Isa al-Barnissi, al-Fasi, known as Zarruq, born Thursday, 28th Muharram 846 AH, died 899. He has written two commentaries on *ar-Risala* and a commentary of *al-Mukhtasar* and many other works. (*Nayl al-Ibtihaj, Ash-Shajara* p.267-8, No. 988)

7   Abu 'Abdallah Muhammad ibn Yusuf as-Sanusi. At-Tilimsani, after informing us that he acquired a great deal of knowledge, that he composed various works and took on the qualities of a *wali*, mentions *The Greater and Lesser 'Aqidas* as being the most quoted from amongst his writings. Born 830 AH, died Jumada al-Akheera, 895AH. (*Ash-Shajara* p.266, No. 984)

al-Baqi,[1] to al-Khurshi – with respect to his *Greater and Lesser Commentaries*,[2] to *al-Mi'yar*,[3] to an-Nafarawi,[4] to al-Lubnani,[5] to at-Tawudi,[6] to al-Ubbi,[7] to

1   Abu Muhammad 'Abd al-Baqi ibn Yusuf ibn Ahmad az-Zurqani. Noted for his knowledge, teaching and composition. Wrote a commentary on the *Mukhtasar* of Khalil in which he seeks to encompass the widest depth and breadth of meanings. Born in Egypt, 1020 AH, died Ramadan 1099. (*Ash-Shajara* p.204, No. 1177)

2   The leading *'alim* of his age, Abu 'Abdallah al-Khurshi, one of the most brilliant of the Maliki *'ulama* of his time, composed the *Greater and Lesser commentaries* on the *Mukhtasar* of Khalil, died in Egypt 1101 AH. (*Ash-Shajara* p.317, No. 1234)

3   Referring to the book *al-Mi'yar al-mu'rib wa'l-jami' al-mughrib 'an fatawi ahl Ifriqiyya wa'l-Andalus wa'l-Maghrib*, (*The Measure that makes clear, and the Compendium that goes furthest, on the fatwas of the people of Tunisia, Andalusia and the Maghrib*), 13 volumes, a work which may be described as an encyclopaedia of Maliki *fiqh*; its author – Abu'l-'Abbas Ahmad ibn Yahya ibn Muhammad ibn 'Abd al-Wahid al-Wansharisi. The Shaykh of the community in al-Maghrib, the Imam Muhammad ibn Ghazi said: "If a man were to swear to divorce his wife, swearing that Abu'l-'Abbas Ahmad al-Wansharisi had mastered the Maliki *madhhab*, both in its roots and branches, then he would be keeping to his oath but his wife would not be divorced on the basis of this oath." (*Nayl al-Ibtihaj* p.87-88, and his biographical notice is in the first volume of the published edition of the *Mi'yar*)

4   Abu'l-'Abbas Ahmad ibn Ghaneem Salim an-Nafarawi, the *faqih*, the *'alim*, the support and pillar, the one who seeks and teaches the truth, the towering intellect, the author and paragon; leadership of the *madhhab* came to him; among his writings, a famous commentary on the *Risala*; died 1125 AH at the age of 82 years. (*Ash-Shajara* p.318, No. 1239)

5   The *'alim* of his age Abu 'Abdallah Muhammah ibn al-Hasan al-Bannani, unequalled in his time; he composed many finely executed writings of benefit, among them the gloss on the commentary of Shaykh 'Abd al-Baqi on the *Mukhtasar* of Khalil on which his fame and acceptance as an *'alim* rests; born 1113 AH, died 1194. (*Ash-Shajara* p.357, No. 1426)

The *'ulama* have stipulated that in order for az-Zurqani's view to be accepted, it must first conform to the way of at-Tawudi or al-Bannani. The talented poet al-Qalawi ash-Shinqiti said:

> Az-Zurqani's view is not complete
> Except together with at-Tawudi or al-Bannani

6   At-Tawudi whom we also know under the name of at-Tudi – although that is a grammatical mistake; his full name was Abu 'Abdallah at-Tawudi ibn Muhammad at-Talib ibn Suda al-Mazzi al-Fasi al-Qurashi; he has composed works of great conciseness and accuracy and of great benefit, among them a gloss on the commentary of az-Zurqani on the *Mukhtasar* which he named the *Tali' al-Amani* (*Fortunate Desires*); born in 1111 AH, died 1193. (*Ash-Shajara* p.372, No. 1486)

7   Abu 'Abdallah Muhammad ibn Khalaf known as al-Ubbi, a skilled writer, author of *Ikmal al-Ikmal* (*Completion of the Completion*), a commentary on Muslim, the student of the great *'alim* of his age, Ibn 'Arafa; died 828 AH. (*Ash-Shajara* p.244, No. 874)

his shaykh Ibn 'Arafa,¹ to the shaykh of Ibn 'Arafa, Ibn 'Abd as-Salam,² to his student Ibn Naji,³ to *at-Tawdih*,⁴ and finally to al-Munawi's great commentary on *al-Jami' as-Saghir* (*The Lesser Compendium*).⁵

Know that the aim of this commentary – may Allah accept it by His overflowing generosity and by the rank and glory of Muhammad, His Prophet, may the peace and blessings of Allah be upon him, and on his Family and Companions – is to remove any confusion, to explain any strange terms in ordinary language, but not to transmit things of common knowledge or well known matters, except in questions of *'aqida*.

The nature of this commentary is such that with regard to recommended matters, I have tended to indulgence and tolerance whereas with regard to the laws, I have taken special pains to explain exactly, concisely and exhaustively – and help in all of this has been from Allah, glorious is He. Part of the character of this work, too, is that when I have transmitted an unfamiliar matter from the books of the later writers, like al-Amir⁶ and an-Nafarawi and then found

---

1   Abu 'Abdallah Muhammad ibn ash-Shaykh – who was blessed with him – Muhammad ibn 'Arafa al-Waraghmi at-Tunisi, imam and *khateeb* at the main *jami'* mosque for fifty years; composed many works, among them his *Mukhtasar*, a compendium of *fiqh*, a commentary on the *hudud* and others; he was unique as a Shaykh, imam, in passing *fatwas* and in acceptance throughout his life; born 716 AH, died 803 AH. (*Ash-Shajara* p.227, No. 817) Among his most famous students were al-Ubbi and al-Barzali.

2   The judge of the community in Tunis, Abu 'Abdallah, Muhammad ibn 'Abd as-Salam al-Hawwari, at-Tunisi; he was the Shaykh of the above-mentioned Ibn 'Arafa; he excelled in both transmitted (*naqli*) and intellectual (*'aqli*) sciences; he has an accomplished commentary on the *Mukhtasar* of Ibn Hajib; died 749 AH of the plague. (*Ash-Shajara* p.210, No. 731)

3   Abu'l-Fadl Qasim ibn 'Isa ibn Naji at-Tanukhi al-Qayrawani, an imam, *faqih*, sharp sighted and sagacious, a pillar of generosity, a just judge, author and master of the revealed laws; he has a commentary on the *Risala* and two commentaries on the *Mudawwana* and other writings; died at Qayrawan 838 AH. (*Ash-Shajara* p.244-5, No. 878). He is the pupil of Ibn 'Arafa as the author mentions.

4   Commentary by Khalil ibn Ishaq al-Maliki, the author of the famous *Mukhtasar*, on the *Mukhtasar* of Ibn al-Hajib; Khalil died 767 AH. (*Ash-Shajara* p.223, No. 794)

5   The major ommentary (called *al-Fayd al-Kabir*) of Muhammad 'Abd ar-Ra'uf al-Munawi on the *Lesser Compendium* (*al-Jami' as-Saghir*) of as-Suyuti, six volumes; born in 952 AH/1545 CE, died 1030 AH/1621 CE.

6   Abu 'Abdallah Muhammad, known as al-Amir, the nickname of his closest grandfather, the family originally being from the Maghrib, but then settled in Egypt, noted for his learning and teaching and his profound research into all branches of knowledge, author of many works, amongst which the *Compendium, commentary and gloss on Shaykh az-Zurqani's commentary on the Mukhtasar* of Khalil; born 1154 AH, died Dhu'l-Qa'da 1232. (*Ash-Shajara* p.262-3, No. 1446)

it in reliable books like those of al-Munawi and Ibn 'Arafa and the like, then I have nevertheless transmitted it so that it might serve as a proof.

The reason I have called this work by the title of *The Book of Benefit for both the beginners and the learned among the slaves*[1] is that someone came to one of the brothers in a dream and advised him to name it by this name.

And beware – O reader, who examine this work – lest shaytan say to you "This is a new work and its author was not someone of knowledge, nor someone who held to the pure deen" such that it leads you to desist altogether from the book or to criticise it without any foundation. Rather study and reflect upon it: anything you find to have sprung from my own imagination or to be a product of my mind then it is up to you whether you accept or reject it. However, you must be equitable, for dealing with this subject is a noble profession and you will not – insha'Allah glorious is He, – encounter it very often. Whatever I have found from the 'ulama – and you find it correct – then it will save you from having to look it up in the original; if you do not find it correct, then the onus is on them not on me. Therefore look, may Allah have mercy on you, with the intention of finding instruction and hopefully you will be guided thereby. As-Sanusi said in his *Middle Commentary* that it has been said: "No one listens with the intention of finding instruction but that he is guided and no one intends to disobey but that Allah prohibits him from being guided." Indeed I state, as al-Munawi said at the beginning of his *Commentary*: "O you who investigate, do so by looking into the matter exhaustively with the eye of solicitousness and perfect understanding. Do not pervert the words or meanings merely because you look down upon the author and do not allow the veil of your self to prevent you from attaining the truth. If you do chance upon a mistake or mistakes, or I have committed an error or errors then know that I do not shrink from recognising such faults and I am not exempt from such lapses." Then he goes on: "Allah, glorious is He, has mercy on someone who conquers his desires, on someone who heeds the call of justice and makes justice his goal, on someone who is not inclined to obduracy – but not on someone who when he intends a thing and sees good in it, conceals it or who when he sees a fault, manifests it and spreads it abroad. So let him ponder the matter in a fair manner, without envy or deviousness. Know that whoever seeks faults will find them and perfection is ascribed only to the Majestic."

---

1   This is a literal rendering of the original title of the work in Arabic which is based on an *ayat* of Qur'an (See *"equally for those who live near it and those who come from far away"*. Al-Hajj – The Pilgrimage: 23). Trans.

'Abd al-Wahid ibn 'Ashir

The author of the poem, Ibn 'Ashir, says:

$$يَقُولُ عَبْدُ الْوَاحِدِ بْنُ عَاشِرِ$$

$$مُبْتَدِئاً بِاسْمِ الْإِلَهِ الْقَادِرِ$$

1   'Abd al-Wahid ibn 'Ashir says, beginning with the name of the Powerful God

Mayyara says: "The author, may Allah, exalted is He, have mercy on him, begins by naming himself because it is of the utmost importance in this situation: it is well known that working from or taking *fatwas* from books is not permitted if one does not know their author or one is unsure of the soundness of their contents."

Imam al-Qarafi said: "Taking *fatwas* from books written recently is not permitted if what is transmitted in them cannot be clearly traced to reputable books; unless it is known that their author is from amongst those one can rely on for the soundness of their knowledge, because documents are valid only by their integrity and probity. Likewise, it is prohibited to take *fatwas* from unfamiliar books or books which have no reputation until people have had time to consider them properly and to assess whether the knowledge contained in them is correct or not. Likewise, it is prohibited to take them from the (hand-written) margins or glosses of books because one cannot rely on them absolutely."

Ibn Farhun said: "What he refers to here is if the gloss has been transmitted by an unfamiliar author. However, if what is written is to be found in the well-accepted source books or its source is acknowledged and it is in the handwriting of someone who can be trusted then there is no difference between this and any other book."

Hamd – Praise

$$اَلْحَمْدُ لِلَّهِ الَّذِي عَلَّمَنَا$$

$$مِنَ الْعُلُومِ مَا بِهِ كَلَّفَنَا$$

2   Praise belongs to Allah Who has taught us the sciences which He has made incumbent upon us.

Al-Munawi said: "Praise belongs to Allah – i.e. The description of beauty is either owned by or is deserved by Allah, exalted is He. It does not extend from Him to any other than Him. He did not suffice himself with naming (Him with the *bismillah*) because of who He is and because of what people have agreed upon as customary, namely that this (beginning) point (in the work) should be one of magnifying Him. Therefore it is fitting that there be a clear mention of praise. The person who restricts himself to the *bismillah* – despite its containing an aspect of praise (*hamd*) within it – is not normally known as someone who praises (*hamid*). For this reason there arises a kind of manifest contention between the two hadiths referring to beginning (affairs with the *bismillah* or with praise) and it is necessary to harmonise the two in the following manner: the beginning of something is either a literal beginning – in which the thing (under discussion) is mentioned explicitly from the outset, or it is relative, in which case it is mentioned relative to something rather than some other thing. This latter corresponds to the mention of *hamd*, which does not refer to the actual essence of the matter. Thus, the literal beginning is specific to the *bismillah* in which mention of the essence is made, while in the *hamd* mention of the attribute is made. The *bismillah*, then, must come before the *hamd* insofar as the one should precede the other in rank when beginning a work.

"Some have plagiarised what he stated and ascribed it to themselves after producing far-fetched, doubtful arguments and incorrect suppositions. Some have claimed that the aim of every introductory word or phrase is achieved by (just) one of the two or whatever fulfils this function in their stead. Thus one may be used to express the other such that sometimes the *bismillah* is used, sometimes the *al-hamdulillah*, sometimes even neither of the two. Some have argued that when treating a disease it is necessary to begin with one of the affected parts rather than (the simultaneous treatment of) all of them. It has also been said that the two phrases of the *bismillah* and *al-hamdulillah* are mutually incompatible in this instance and mentioning both of them ceases to be necessary as in the case of (mentioning both) when making (repeated) washings of (something sullied by the licking of a) dog. However, (Ibn 'Ashir) is referring to the more general meaning, that is the general meaning of the *dhikr* (of His name) and the (mention of) *hamd* rather than any particular meaning. Do you not see that the Legislator does not begin most of the actions of the *shari'ah* specifically with *al-hamd* – like the *salat*, the *adhan*, the hajj, for example. Rather, He indicates that what is intended is the manifestation of an aspect of perfection and this is achieved, for example, in the *salat* by the *takbir* and on the hajj by the required *dhikrs* when putting on the *ihram*. This does not apply to what has been said above. A general resolution (of the matter) is difficult to obtain from (the example to be had in) the outward form of the *salat* and the *adhan*. This is the result of my collecting together the answers which have satisfied the *'ulama*. There are also many famous responses and many explanations which are weak in nature. They have been analysed critically in the commentary entitled *Al-Bahja*, a work unparalleled in its contents."

In the *Lesser Compendium* there is another tradition (indicating the saying of a formula at the outset of an event which is other than *bismillah* or *al-hamdulillah*): "Whatever blessings (*ni'ma*) – be it with respect to family, wealth or children – Allah bestows on a slave who then says

$$\text{مَا شَاءَ اللَّهُ لَا قُوَّةَ إِلَّا بِاللَّهِ}$$

'That which Allah wills (happens), (there is) no power except by Allah', and then he will see no harm or loss to this (blessing) but death...." There is also: "Allah, exalted is He does not bestow a blessing on a slave – who then says '*al-hamdulillah*' – but that (in doing so) he makes (fitting) thanks for it. If he says it a second time, then Allah will renew his reward for it. If he says it a third time, then Allah will forgive him his wrong actions."

KNOWLEDGE

Commenting on Ibn 'Ashir's saying: "Who has taught us" Mayyara said "Who" refers to the majestic name (Allah)[1] and "the sciences which He has made incumbent upon us" refer to the knowledge which is obligatory on each and every *mukallaf* – (the person who is fully responsible and legally capable) – that is, the knowledge needed to carry out an obligatory action, without which the action in question would not be properly completed."

It is necessary at this point to make an introduction which makes mention of some important points even if this means making a lengthy explanation which might bore the reader – and which would be a shortcoming and lack of attention on the part of the author. But, *insha'Allah*, you will find precious things which will make up for or compensate most generously for any deficiency.

He[2] said in *Nur al-Basar*: "The seeker of knowledge should intend (to obtain) detailed knowledge if he is able; if not, then a general understanding such that

---

1 i.e. the One Who has taught us is Allah. Ed.
2 Ahmad ibn 'Abd al-'Aziz al-Filali al-Hilali as-Sijilmasi. *Nur al-Basar* is a commentary on the *Mukhtasar Khalil*. Ed.

he is in a position to carry out what is personally binding on him; whatever goes beyond this, then he should make the intention of acquiring knowledge, on behalf of people, of what is obligatory on the community as a whole (*fard kifaya*). He should not restrict himself to making the intention to undertake something which is (merely) recommended (*nadb*) as the reward for what is obligatory is far greater. He should also make the intention to put into action whatever Allah has apprised him of personally and to hope and expect that Allah teaches him everything that it is possible to learn; to be successful in teaching it for the benefit of (various) ranks and grades (of people) by means of (both) knowledge and action until the Day of Rising; to busy himself with obedience to Allah and turning from acts of disobedience – such that his obedience prevents him from superfluities, which if there was nothing else but that they would be a waste of one's life which is one's capital that would be sufficient in itself to drive any person of intellect away from them. How could this come about? he would be occupying the Noble Scribes (recording one's actions) with something containing no good. He would have to relate (these acts of) arrogance to the witnessing angels on the Day of Rising when they say to him: "*Read your Book! Today your own self is reckoner enough against you!*"[1].

And he will be covered in shame in the place of terror and calamity, he will be hungry, thirsty and naked, his despair will increase in the knowledge that he did not busy himself with correct actions during his time of superfluity, actions of which he stands in profound need at this particular time and place. He will be reprimanded in this tremendous place and will be asked: 'Why did you do this? Why did you say this?' All argument in his favour will cease before the Knower of Unseen Realities and he will fall into confusion, unable to reply. If this then is his state after mere superfluities then what would it be if he had been guilty of disobedience? I ask Allah, glorious is He, for forgiveness and mercy."

He has also indicated, the noble hadith: "Surely actions are by intentions…" – that actions are only valid by the intention such that whoever intends good by an action then he has good (written) for him and whoever intends bad by it then bad is (written) against him; whoever intends a thing which is licit but of no obvious merit (*mubah*), then it is without profit. If the form of such an (action) is one of worship then, at times, it can be worship, at other times disobedience and sometimes purely superfluous – like the prostration, for example, which is an act of worship if made to Allah, exalted is He, and *kufr* if made to an idol, and an act of disobedience – without attaining the rank of

---

1   Al-Isra, The Night Journey: 14

kufr – if made in order to extol the Sultan without actually believing that he is the Lord. Occupying oneself with knowledge is the best of all good actions if one intends thereby to follow the command of Allah, exalted is He, and to put it into action. It is disobedience if one intends thereby to set oneself proudly over one's peers or to obtain wealth via haram means like bribery or take what is granted of ill-gotten gains.

A person may also be described as exaggerated in his behaviour if he makes the intention to avoid something which is licit but of which he has no specific need – if he is aware of this. The most important thing for the person of intellect and in particular for the one given to the learning and teaching of knowledge is first to correct his intention and secondly to cause it to grow. As for correcting (the intention), it is that he turns it away from corrupt aims and turns it towards goals which are good. Thus he makes the intention to do whatever he has been commanded to do and to abandon what he has been prohibited from doing. This would then be accordance with the command of Allah, exalted is He, to perform or to abandon what is *mubah* while seeking thereby only help in remaining obedient – so that all his movements and times of rest are acts of obedience. As for causing his intention to grow, it is that he examines whatever he is determined to do or not to do: if he finds that such-and-such an undertaking most probably contains aspects of good, then he intends (not just one but) all the aspects."

Then he continues after a lengthy discussion: "In short, every movement or moment of rest which a person is subject to is necessarily either commanded – as an obligation or recommendation – or prohibited – as totally illicit (haram) or disliked; or thirdly, that which is (merely) licit – *mubah*. The least a person of intellect should make the intention for is to undertake the first of the two divisions, that is, to follow the command of Allah in doing it and in the second of the divisions to follow the command of Allah in abandoning it. In the third division, his intention in the matter is his being aware that Allah, exalted is He, has been generous to him in making it licit for him and that had He prohibited him from it he would not have done it. If he is able to cause these intentions to grow, then to him belongs the reward in accordance with whatever he intends." (Here ends the text of *Nur al-Basar*).

Muhammad ibn Abu'l-Hasan, the author of *Majma' al-Ahbab*, may Allah grant us benefit by him, says – after talking of the need to intensify one's search for sincerity: "What one needs to be aware of is that the intention – if one is sincere in seeking after knowledge – is not impeded in this by the passion of the self for imparting and teaching knowledge. The self has its tricks and it commands to what is evil and shaytan has power over man – if he despairs of attacking him by way of acts of disobedience, then he approaches him by the door of good actions in another, incognito, form by giving good advice to him saying: 'Avoid that as you desire it.' This argument, as we have said, is invalidated by the mere act of determining this causality: the joy experienced by the self when possessing power is an inborn thing which cannot be rejected as power is a quality of excellence. Likewise, pre-eminence in knowledge and the inclination of the self to such a thing is a help and aid to acquiring knowledge, especially at the beginning – in the sense that if such a thing did not exist in human nature, then knowledge would not be acquired. It is not possible to remove the trace of these things from the self – anyone who imagines that he can have sexual intercourse without pleasure or that he can hold a conversation without delighting in dominating the talk then he is imagining the inconceivable. Indeed, there is nothing in any of this which can harm the deen in any way. What one must strive after however, as we have said above, is to avoid excessive dominance in conversation, conceit and pride and other bad qualities which prevent one from achieving one's goal."

Then after speaking at some length he says: "Rely on five principles: the halal, sincerity, intention, truthfulness and whatever contains what is right for the heart – for the actions (of those mentioned above) depend on these (five). In this way one may discern the nature of the excuse of those who abstain from imparting and teaching knowledge as well as recognising the pure aim of those who act according to these five principles. And why should it not be like this? There is no rank above that of the *'alim* who acts upon his knowledge, other than prophethood, especially if he puts this knowledge into action, propagates it and has as his goal the face of Allah, glorious is He. He may rejoice a thousand times if the matter is as we have mentioned – for surely this joy is not detrimental to his deen in any way, and neither is it reprehensible. Indeed, more than one of the former and latter imams have described that this kind of joy is to be sought after, that it is one branch of iman and that there is no doubt in this. Look at the Imams of the deen, the Companions, the Followers and the Followers of the Followers and all those *fuqaha* of the major cities who came after them, may Allah be pleased with all of them. Were there any amongst them who prevented the spreading of knowledge or its teaching for the purpose mentioned above? Imam Malik and others of the Imams before him and after him, may Allah, glorious is He, be pleased with them, would sit for the sake of hadith and none of them would turn his attention to what was termed "a worldly subject." If they had attached importance to this, knowledge would have vanished and people would have remained in their blindness and would have destroyed each other.

Jussous said in his commentary on the words of the *ar-Risala* "They stop at the limit set for them" that this is an indication that part of the good behaviour of the *muminun* whose hearts have been illuminated by knowledge is their stopping at the limits (*hudud*) of the *shari'ah* and desisting from anything prohibited them by the people of knowledge. The stopping of the slave at the limits means not going outside what his Lord has prescribed as limits for him – for surely Allah has addressed him with the five (types of) prescription, saying: "This you may do or not do, and this you must do, and this you must desist from doing, and this has a reward in it for you although there is no punishment if you desist from doing it and the opposite to this (i.e. this has a punishment...)." Thus if the slave acts in accordance with what his Lord has prescribed for him, then he is fulfilling the contract Allah, exalted is He, has made binding on him. This in turn means he is being grateful and this gratitude is the gratitude which is incumbent on all the responsible slaves (*mukallifun*), and which manifests in obedience to everything contained in the *shari'ah*. Thus what He has made obligatory, we have made obligatory for ourselves, what He has made haram we have made haram, what He has permitted we have permitted and so on for everything else. This applies in a similar manner to the oath of allegiance to the Messenger of Allah, may the peace and blessings of Allah be upon him. Action with knowledge is its aim and its purpose. Knowledge is the means to action, like *wudu'* in relation to the *salat*.

Know that knowledge is a blessing and action is another blessing. The slave should ask his Lord, glorious is He, for each one of them separately saying: "O Allah, show me the truth as the truth and grant me the gift of being able to follow it, and show me the false as the false and grant me the gift of being able to avoid it." The imam, Shihab ad-Deen al-Qarafi said: "Whoever acts in accordance with what he knows has obeyed Allah twice over, whoever does not know and does not act has disobeyed Allah twice over and whoever knows but does not act has obeyed Allah once and disobeyed him once."

Knowledge without action is a blessing and a mercy for those who do not study this (knowledge) with a corrupt intention. If he does study it with a sound and perfect intention or with an intention which is not devoid of perfect sincerity then it is as if he has studied it in order to purify his self from the darkness which affects others and to obtain a rank by virtue of which he is raised above his own self (*nafs*). In other words he should not study in order to remove from the *nafs* something that it has already no need of; or study without an intention from the outset. As for those who study it with the intention of collecting and storing it, who imagine they are free of self deception and who harbour no fear or anxiety, being content with their *nafs* – such persons are flawed in their understanding and they will enjoy no mercy, unless *tawba* comes to them. Our Shaykh, the seeker after and teacher of the truth, says in the commentary on the *Hikam*: "By this he restricts the general import of al-Qarafi's words 'whoever has knowledge but does not act upon it.' The stopping at the limits with respect to the people of incorruptibility is not allowing oneself to fall into wrongdoing at all. With respect to other than them, it is not persisting in wrongdoing. This is the result of knowledge and its benefit. His fatigue is not from striving after what is false and he does not waste the precious moments of his life for something without profit or wealth. It is in this way that the *'alim* obtains the honour and esteem of this world and the next – as the poet said:

Knowledge is only obtained through action,
   understand al-'Ubayd's word
If, in knowledge, there were a weapon for the young man,
   Iblis would have been the equal of al-Junayd

It is by action that knowledge is fixed in the world and persists. It is as has been said: 'Knowledge calls for action: if it finds it, it stays and if not it moves on.' It is by action that the *zakat* – purification – of knowledge is made and thereby grows. It is by action that one may perceive the secrets and gifts of divine knowledge 'from *ladun*', that is from His presence – all of which one has no access to by acquired learning.

Allah, exalted is He, says: '*Have taqwa of Allah and Allah will give you knowledge*'[1] and he, may peace and blessings be upon him, said: 'Whoever acts on what he knows, Allah, exalted is He, will transmit to him a knowledge that he did not have'[2] or words to this effect. There is also a distinction made between knowledge which is useful for its people – about which many *ayats* have been mentioned in the Book and innumerable references in the sunna – and knowledge which is not useful from which the Messenger of Allah, may the peace and blessings of Allah be upon him, sought refuge and which he mentioned as being a threat to its people.

As for what has been recorded of the first, the saying of Allah, exalted is He: '*He gives wisdom to whomever He wills*'[3] in which 'wisdom' refers to knowledge.

---

1   al-Baqara – The Cow: 282
2   The hadith of Muslim also supports this: "Whoever goes along a path seeking by it knowledge, then Allah will cause him to take a path to the Garden."
3   al-Baqara – The Cow: 269

There is also the saying of Allah, exalted is He: '*Only those of His slaves with knowledge have fear of Allah*'[1] indicating that fear is restricted to such slaves. This fear is also the characteristic of the Prophets and the Angels in the heavens. Likewise there is His saying: '*Allah will raise in rank those of you who have iman and those who have been given knowledge*'[2], the hadith: 'The best of actions is the seeking knowledge' and 'One '*alim* is harder on shaytan than a thousand worshipping slaves and the angels lower their wings over the seeker of knowledge, content with what he is seeking.' The Prophet, peace and blessings upon him, said: 'Be either someone of knowledge or someone who learns, or who listens (to knowledge) or who loves (knowledge) and do not be a fifth and so perish.' This latter person is detested by the '*ulama*." Here end the words of Jussous.

Then after continuing for a while he says: "As for what has been mentioned of the second type – 'The person who will be punished the most severely will be the '*alim* who has not put his knowledge to good use for Allah, exalted is He.' It has also been reported: 'Woe to the person who has not acquired knowledge once and woe to the person who has acquired knowledge and has not acted (upon it) a thousand times.' Al-Fudail ibn 'Iyad and Asad ibn al-Furat have said: 'It has come to our notice that the corrupt of the '*ulama* and those who have learnt the Qur'an will be dealt with before the worshippers of idols.' The Prophet, peace and blessings be upon him, said: 'There are three (types of) judges: two judges in the Fire and one in the Garden. As for the one in the Garden, it is the man who knew the truth and judged according to it; as for the two in the Fire, it is the man who knew the truth but deliberately acted unjustly in (giving his) judgement and the man who based his judgements on other than (the basis of) knowledge and who was ashamed of saying 'I do not know.'" Here ends the point he is making.

Then he says after a while that al-Qalshani said of the saying: 'The most important of knowledges is the best knowledge' – "know, O brother, may Allah grant us and you success in being obedient to Him, that knowledge – wherever it may occur in the speech of Allah, glorious is He, and the speech of the Messenger of Allah, may Allah grant him peace and blessings, is an occasion of ennobling and conferring honour. What is meant by this is useful knowledge, one which curbs and stifles desire. What bears testimony to the existence of knowledge which is sought for the sake of Allah is fear (*khashya*) and what testifies to the existence of fear is that one is successful (in acquiring

---

1 Fatir – The Bringer into Being: 28
2 al-Mujadila – The Disputer: 11

knowledge). As for knowledge which is accompanied by a longing after this world, by flattering its people and directing one's enthusiasm towards acquiring it, towards collecting it and storing it up, by vying with each other in vain and boastful pursuits, gathering more and more (things of this world), by challenging those in a position and leadership, by opposition to one's peers, competing with them, by drawing out one's hopes (with respect to things of this world), corrupt actions, being hard of heart, committing actions which incur the anger of the Lord, preferring this world and forgetting the next – how far removed is such knowledge, how far away is the person of such a character from being judged as being amongst the 'heirs of the Prophets.' Is it not true that what is inherited can only be transferred to someone when he possesses a character similar to that possessed by the one making the inheritance? The likeness of these characteristics, that is characteristics of the *'ulama*, is the likeness of a candle which lights up that which is other than it while it itself burns up. Allah has made the knowledge He has taught to a person of this other type a proof against him and a reason for an intensifying of the punishment against him. However, do not be in any doubt that both the experienced person and the beginner will benefit by it for the Messenger of Allah, may the peace and blessings of Allah be upon him, said: 'Allah will surely support this deen by means of a corrupt man.'

The likeness of someone who acquires knowledge in order to obtain (something of) this world and to get high rank and standing in it is like someone who clears away filth with a ruby spoon: What a noble instrument and how contemptible that which is obtained!

The likeness of someone who devotes his time to seeking knowledge, spending forty years acquiring it, but who does not act according to it is like the person who sits for this same length of time cleaning himself and renewing his *wudu'* but does not pray a single *salat*. Thus the object of knowledge is action just as the object of purification is *salat*."

All this has been transmitted by Sayyidi Ibn 'Abbad from the *Lata'if al-Minan* and *at-Tanweer* and likewise from Shaykh Zarruq. And following his words: "Is it not true that what is inherited can only be transferred…?" he says: "In it there is an indication that the *'alim* without *taqwa* is not an heir. However, this should be examined because corrupting what is inherited and acting upon it for (a purpose) other than what is true does not undo the fact that the heir (of this knowledge) actually inherits. Disobedience does not undo the ties (of the deen). Rather one says of him that he is an evil heir and the like. Allah, exalted is He, has confirmed that knowledge belongs to those who have *taqwa* of Him but at the same time He has not denied its existence in someone who has no *taqwa* – so take note." Here end the words of Zarruq in the eleventh chapter of this commentary on the *Hikam*.

Our Shaykh, the *muhaqqiq* (the verifier of true knowledge), says in his commentary on the *Hikam*: "And the answer is to be found in his words: 'Disobedience does not undo the ties (of the deen)' that there are two ties: firstly, the general one and that is Islam by which a general matter is inherited, that is to be comprised in the ummah which has answered [the call of the Prophet] which is dependent on a general matter, which is one's belief and articulation [of it]; as for the special tie, it is the tie of proximity and election by which a particular matter is inherited, that is, to be comprised in the sons of the deen and the successors of the messengers. This particularity is based on good action and it is annulled by disobedience although proximity in itself and election are not annulled merely by disobedience but rather disobedience is utterly shameless. Sheer disobedience annuls the perfection of a person's [proximity] and what is spoken about in *at-Tanweer* is with regard to shameless disobedience – up to his words 'As for knowledge....' This then is what he said and Allah knows best." With the omission of some of it.

There is no doubt that there is no good in knowledge which is not accompanied by a deep rooted fear – anyone, for example, who imagines he is safe from self-deception and who does not take care about what he does, who believes that his acquisition of knowledge is enough for him in all respects and that he has no longer any need of acquiring (rewards through good actions) or avoiding (punishment through bad actions); who believes people are as cows, or sheep and goats to be watched over by him, and who treats them as if they have only been created to serve the likes of him and to humble themselves to those like him, who considers that he himself is of great importance, that the harmony of the world is dependent upon his existence and that he is from among the imams and ʽulama in whose hands rests the correctness of the deen and the *dunya*. Such a person reckons that Allah, glorious is He, will transform his evil actions into good ones. Anyone of this type, then, possesses nothing but evil and his knowledge becomes a curse on him. It results only in an increase in *fitna* around him and this is referred to in the words of the *Hikam*: "What knowledge does an ʽalim have who is content with his *nafs*." This is what the words of *at-Tanweer* are referring to, and Allah, exalted is He, knows best. There are other, similar things mentioned about evil ʽulama together with harsh threats to them contained in the texts above and others.

He also says in *at-Tanweer*: 'Useful knowledge is that which is used to help towards obedience of Allah, exalted is He, and which binds you to fear of Allah, glorious is He: knowledge of Allah and knowledge of that which He has commanded as long as this has been acquired for the sake of Allah. Sayyidi Ibn 'Abbad, may Allah be pleased with him, said: 'Know that (the definition of) useful knowledge – about which the earliest generations and those following them are all in agreement – is that it is knowledge which guides the one who possesses it to fear and awe; to taking on humility and humbleness, taking on a character steeped in iman, to a harmonisation of the secret and the public and all that is implied in this, namely, hatred of this world and doing without in it, preferring the next world to it, being constant in one's relationship to Allah glorious is He, vying with each other in it, taking care to reflect upon the reasons for acting correctly and always acting with *adab* before Allah. Such a person naturally inclines to all these qualities, indeed actively seeks them and endeavours to preserve them. He is aware of the reasons and causes which may prevent him from attaining them, transforming them rather – through his rejection of them – into sublime attributes whose only aim and purpose is the establishment of the sunna. All this enables him to acquire the benefits of knowledge and its fruits in this world and the next. If the seeker, after knowledge, is void of this or even part of this, then if what he was seeking after was knowledge of (inner) realities, this becomes an argument against him; and if he sought after formal knowledge then it becomes a curse clinging to him, may we be granted refuge with Allah glorious is He, from that.'

Al-Hasan said: "As for the man who seeks knowledge, it is not long before this begins to show in his taking on the attribute of fear in his dress, his glance, his speech, his mode and manner, and his doing without. If a man acquires an aspect of knowledge and he acts upon it, then it is better for him than everything in the world – if, that is, he invests it in the next world. But there will surely come a time upon people in which truth and falsehood becomes confused for them. When this is so, then only *du'a* will be of benefit, like the *du'a* of the person drowning."

Al-Fudail ibn 'Iyad said: "The *'ulama* were a source of joy, as welcome as the spring-time for the people; if the sick person saw them, recovering his health would cease to preoccupy him and if the poor person caught sight of them, he would have no desire to become wealthy. However, today they have become a *fitna* for people."

Sayyidi Ibn 'Abbad said: "This applied to his time when behaviour was correct – what if he were to experience this time of ours? *'surely we belong to Allah and surely to Him we are returning.'*"

What these imams have said, may Allah be pleased with them and may Allah benefit us by them, is true by its very nature, of this there is no doubt. However, it is not fitting that it be taken as a general rule but rather it is an indication of the path of the *'arifun* and the way of *salikun*. If however, it is taken as a general rule, this may lead to the abandonment of knowledge and its people and to a bad opinion of those who transmit it because those of the description mentioned above are exceedingly rare. They are individuals of limited numbers throughout the centuries, several thousands of them, such as al-Fudhail, al-Junayd, Ma'ruf and ad-Darani – may He be praised Who gave them gifts, Who helped and strengthened them. However, it is not permitted to look down on or despise others who are not of their ilk. Al-Mawwaq said in his *Sunan al-Muhtadeen*: "In the search for knowledge do not let the saying that 'knowledge, if unaccompanied by fear, becomes a punishment for the one who has acquired it' of Taj ad-Deen or the like in *al-Ihya'* make you give up. This is not how things are. In this instance, the *'ulama* say that it is confusing the beginning with the end. Whoever confuses the beginning with the end, then his path is closer to going astray than being guided. Thus I say: his saying 'If fear accompanies it, then...' is said with respect to someone who does not make it a means [to earn or worldly advancement] in itself and it refers to the *sabiqun* (forerunners). Others, however, like someone who a *muqtasid* (that is someone who strives to do what is right and is moderate in action but who through circumstances beyond his control is compelled to use his knowledge of the deen for worldly purposes) or someone who is clearly doing an injustice to his self (*dhalim linafsihi*) without rendering his actions invalid (*idh lam takun fihi jurha*), that is – for such persons, then, the knowledge they have is a mercy. Even if he has no fear, an *'alim* who just possesses knowledge is not equal to someone who has no knowledge." Then he transmits what al-Qarafi said above and goes on to say:

"What is clear from *fiqh* is that artisanal work, trade, and occupying oneself with knowledge beyond what is *fard al-'ayn* (obligatory on oneself alone), and knowledge of medicine are all (valid) means [of livelihood] (*asbab*) within the *shari'ah*. Thus whoever occupies himself with any of these things without intention, then he is doing an injustice to himself; and if he does something without understanding (*la dark 'alayhi*) then he will have lost the reward; if he does occupy himself with one of these things intending however to abstain from (begging) then he is a *muqtasid*. Ibn 'Arafa said: "Whoever is unable to provide for himself and for his family except by the provision afforded by his taking on the post of a judge, then he should strive to gain this post." It has been related from Ibn Yunus: "Someone ought not to make the hajj for another, but if it should occur then the payment (agreed upon) should be made." 'Abd al-Wahhab said: "This is by analogy with being paid for being a judge."

Al-Mawwaq has also said on another occasion: "The *muqtasid* is he who considers it [knowledge] a means to acquiring the *dunya*. One man says: 'It is the best of means while another says: 'I prefer seeking the *dunya* with a drum and a flute than seeking after it by means of knowledge and the deen.'"

Our Shaykh, the verifier of knowledge, said in his commentary on *al-Hikam*: "Al-Mawwaq's words are valid, especially in this time when knowledge has become a strange thing and its people rare, and when people have almost come to differ on the '*dharuriyat*' (the indispensable, necessary aspects of the deen). The study of knowledge is the most important of matters and striving to teach and acquire it is the greatest of acts of worship. Even if fear (*khashya*) may not come easily to the one studying, it may well be that the foundations of iman and islam are preserved in him and the deen is established in him – for knowledge of the manner in which the Lord of the worlds is to be worshipped is secured by means of the very existence of the people of knowledge amongst the multitude of Muslims." Then he transmitted *hadith* and sayings of the imams which support what he had discussed, namely that occupying oneself with knowledge – teaching and acquiring it – is better than occupying oneself with any other recommended good act, be it fasting, *salat*, glorification and other acts of obedience. He said: "and the saying of al-Mawwaq 'a means to the *dunya*' refers to (something in) the *dunya* which is needed and which is halal, for example, when, he speaks of the person who seeks after the post of judge in order to provide for himself and his family." Here end the words of Jussous.

Then after speaking at length he also says: "Know that, whatever the circumstances, occupying oneself with knowledge is better then being idle or being ignorant. This is, because of the greater number of calamities which occur through lack of knowledge than those occurring when knowledge is present. The person who is ignorant cannot perceive truths and realities as long as he himself is caught up in misdeeds and is unaware of his being submerged in worldly affairs. Indeed, he considers acts of disobedience to be acts of obedience and in believing so confuses *mubahat* (acts which are merely licit) or *qurubat* (acts which bring him close to Allah) with such acts of disobedience. This is a great disaster which leads to the ruin of this world and the next: it causes the door of *tawba* to be closed for the person of this description – as, in his view, what he is doing is not an offence. This applies to the person who does not occupy himself with knowledges, especially the knowledge of *tasawwuf*

– a necessary quality and attribute which must be embedded and fixed in a person on account of the *nafs*' trickery, its deception of the *'alim* who acts upon his knowledge and its ability to make flawed action look perfectly sound and correct. The saying of Shaykh Abu'l-Hasan has already been mentioned: "Whoever does not strive to acquire a profound knowledge of our sciences dies persisting in committing major wrong actions even though he is unaware of it." Our Shaykh has expressed this same meaning in the commentary on *an-Naseeha*.

He has also said in his commentary on *al-Hikam*: "Everything the Shaykhs have mentioned regarding the prohibition of studying this knowledge with a corrupt intention and regarding their warning against it does not mean that they want people to abandon this study and to turn their backs on it. How could this be when it is required both of the individual person and of the community in general? Rather, they intend it is as admonition to awaken people so that they might purify their intention for study and strive to obtain sincerity. If they did not mean this it would lead to people leaving off this study but this would be absolute ignorance and the root of corruption. Rather, obtaining sincerity is by means of the study of the above mentioned masters, by reading their works, by examining the hadith and traditions which inspire one to avoid acts of showing off, of pride, or being content with the *nafs*, or vying with each other in this world. It encourages instead desire for the opposite of this and keeping the company of the people of good actions and the deen. All these things help one in attaining an intention and purifying it." Then he mentions narrations and sayings which testify to what the Shaykhs actually mean, namely awakening the desire to correct one's action not to abandon it. Here ends the saying of Jussous.

What he meant by his Shaykh the verifier of knowledge was Ibn Zakari, and what he mentioned of his words: "There is no doubt that there is no good in knowledge which is entirely unaccompanied by fear" to his words: "what knowledge belongs to an *'alim* who is content with his *nafs*?" has been transmitted word for word by Abu'l-Qasim ibn Ahmad ibn Muhammad ibn 'Abd al-Qadir al-Fasi in the commentary on *The Aqida* of his grandfather 'Abd al-Qadir. His saying that "occupying oneself with knowledge is better than ignorance whatever the circumstances..." is like what Zarruq said, may Allah grant us benefit by him – and I think it is in the book *An-Nush al-Anfa*': "The disobedient *'alim* is better than the ignorant worshipper." It has also been transmitted that: "Sleeping based on knowledge is better than worship based on ignorance."

The benefit of this is contained in what Bashir ibn al-Harith, may Allah be pleased with him, said in *Majma' al-Ahbab*, may He make us die upon love of our Master Muhammad, may the peace and blessings of Allah be upon him, and then love of him: "The likeness of those who consume the *dunya* by means of the deen is the likeness of those who try to wash their hands of a putrid smell using fish." Ibrahim al-Harbi said. "My father took me to Bashir ibn al-Harith saying: 'This son of mine likes to write down hadith and knowledge.' Then Bashir said to me: 'Son, one ought to act upon this knowledge, but if you do not act upon all of it, then for every two hundred hadith (act upon) five of them, as one does with dirhams¹.' Then my father said to him: 'Abu Nasr make a *du'a* for him' and he replied: 'Your *du'a* is more likely to be answered than mine. The *du'a* of the father for his son is like the *du'a* of the Prophet for his *umma*.'" Here ends the text from *Majma' al-Ahbab*.

Jussous said: "Know that seeking knowledge is an action which is exposed to health and sickness. People who seek after it are in ranks and some are higher than others, just as in any other action. Thus there are those who seek after it purely for their *akhira* and those who seek after it purely for their *dunya* and between these two there are ranks. This can be ascertained by examining what has been discussed above. The highest rank is seeking after it for the sake of Allah, no other." Shaykh Ibn 'Abbad said: "And the soundness of his intention in this matter is that his aim is to seek the pleasure of Allah, to put it to use for the benefit of those around him and to prefer leaving the darkness of ignorance for the light of knowledge – such an intention is sound: its outcome, manifest in the next world, is praiseworthy and, through obedience to Allah, its fruits are harvested in this world. The Messenger of Allah, may the peace and blessings of Allah be upon him, said: 'There is no blessing for me in the rising of the sun on any day in which I do not obtain an increase in knowledge which brings me closer to Allah, exalted is He.' Sufyan ath-Thawri said, may Allah be pleased with him, 'Knowledge is acquired in order to have *taqwa* of Allah and knowledge is superior to other things because by it one has *taqwa* of Allah.' If this aim is flawed and the intention of the student is corrupted such that he deliberately intends thereby to obtain some of the *dunya*, be it wealth or position, then his reward is annulled, his action is rendered useless and he is reduced to clear loss. Allah, exalted is He, said: '*If anyone desires to cultivate the akhira, we will increase him in his cultivation.*'"²

He has also said in *Tanbih al-Ghafil*: "The person seeking knowledge ought

---

1 For every 200 dirhams one gives away 5 in *zakat*. Translator.
2 ash-Shura – Counsel: 18.

to desire the pleasure of Allah, exalted is He, and desire the abode of the *akhira*, the ridding himself and others of ignorance, reviving the deen and the preservation of Islam – for surely its preservation is by means of knowledge, by means of gratitude for the blessing of the intellect and by means of the health of the body."

Know that the sure sign which bears witness to the soundness of a person's claim to be teaching and acquiring knowledge for the sake of Allah is that he measures the arrival of death in terms of the importance of this knowledge – if he is happy to be occupied with knowledge at this moment, then he is on the right path and if not, then he is on the wrong path.

He said in the *Lata'if al-Minan*: "During a conversation between myself and someone who was preoccupied with knowledge – on the subject of the necessity of having a sincere intention in it and of not occupying oneself with it other than for the sake of Allah – I said: 'The one who studies knowledge for the sake of Allah is the one who if you said to him "tomorrow you will die" he would not put down his book.'"

Sayyidi ibn 'Abbad said: "This is a clear statement and utterly correct: one cannot imagine other than right action from a slave in this state – one who is freed from the flaws of showing off, who has left his portion of the *nafs* and the pursuing of desires. This is what is required of the slave." Here ends the text of Jussous. Then he says after a while: "He is referring, in what he says, to people seeking after knowledge who are of the highest rank."

Al-Mawwaq said in the *Sunan al-Muhtadeen*: "It is clear that the *'alim* is one of the forerunners in his relation (to the deen) is the one of whom they have said: 'He is the one who if you said to him "tomorrow you will die", then he would not lay down his book. As for the one who is *muqtasid* (who strives to do what is right and is moderate in action), who consider it a means to (obtaining something of) the *dunya* ...'" – to the end of what he says above. Here ends the text of Jussous.

In Abu Mutafannin's commentary on Muslim with respect to the hadith about the three (types of persons) who will be the first to burn in the Fire – "'...but you acquired knowledge and taught it and studied the Qur'an in order that it be said: "He is a reciter" and indeed it has been said.' Then the order is given concerning this person and he is dragged on his face until he is thrown in the Fire" – he says: 'There is no meaning to "in order that it be said" unless one understands that what the person intends thereby is boasting and showing off.' Al-Qarafi said: 'The recitation aloud (of the sincere person) is not done in order to become famous – but he may well be celebrated in order that people should not shrink from learning from him.' 'Izz ad-Deen said: '(The sincere reciter) is rewarded for his recitation aloud' and our Shaykh (that is Ibn 'Arafa) used to say: 'He liked to recite aloud and this is not reprehensible: it is not unlikely that he will be rewarded for this as it is way of honouring and attaching importance to a quality of perfection.' He said: 'This recitation aloud is done in order to free himself of ignorance and is one of the (various ways of) recitation performed out of love for Allah.'

In refutation of as-Safadi when he says "Muhammad is the Messenger of Allah…" there is: "There is no difference of opinion that knowledge ennobles. Whoever says 'There is no superiority of the *'alim* over the ignorant person' is put to death as he has violated the consensus (*ijma'*) and has denied the Qur'an and sunna. If one asks whether the father may say to the child: 'Study in order to become superior to your peers'? then the reply would be that it is permitted. However when he grows up, he should change his intention. As for the person who is already grown up, however, this is not permitted for him. Rather, he should study knowledge on condition that he become free of ignorance, that he revive the sunna of the Prophet, may the peace and blessings of Allah be upon him, that he teach it to people and act upon it.' Ibn al-Faris said: 'It is permitted to study knowledge in order to exalt oneself over others.' Ibn al-'Arabi said: 'It is permitted for him to study in order that he may be exempted from taking office (*wadha'if*).'

Jussous said: 'Al-Qalshani said in his commentary on his words in the *Risala*: "Knowledge guides to good things, and leads to them" – "this is an indication that man is required to strive in his seeking after knowledge even if he has not made the best of intentions – for knowledge will draw him to the good." It has been narrated from one of the earlier men of knowledge: "We sought knowledge for other than the sake of Allah and it drove us back to Allah" – that is it showed us the excellence of correcting one's intention, the punishment awaiting the one who corrupts his intention and the greatness and majesty of having knowledge as one's goal."'

Ad-Darimi has related from al-Hasan: "Some people sought after knowledge not wanting it for the sake of Allah and what is with Him – then this knowledge stayed with them until they wanted it for the sake of Allah and what is with Him." It is also narrated that Mujahid said: "We sought this knowledge without having a strong intention in it, but then Allah granted us this intention afterwards." Al-Hasan said: "We used to seek after knowledge for the *dunya* but this drew us to the next world" and Sufyan ath-Thawri said it, may Allah be pleased with him. Al-Baji said, however, in *Sunan as-Saliheen* in the chapter on knowledge: "Know that the knowledge indicated by Sufyan ibn 'Uyayna with his words 'We sought to acquire knowledge for other than the sake of Allah ...' refers to knowledge of hadith, *tafsir* and the biographies of the Prophets and the *Salihun* – for such knowledge contains teachings which invoke fear and serve as a warning. Such knowledge causes one to realise the importance of fear of Allah, exalted is He, and even if it does not have an immediate effect it will have an effect on his end in life. As for *kalam* and legal discussion merely connected with *fatwas* based on the commercial and social aspects of the deen (*mu'amalat*) and the settling of disputes, such things only increase one's desire for the *dunya* and only increase covetousness until the end of one's days.' Then he said: 'Look to the final actions of many of the *fuqaha* who sought to acquire knowledge for other than Allah take admonition from them. They died and they were doomed in their search for the *dunya*, snarling at each other like dogs. And news (of something) is not the same as direct experience (of this thing).'" Jussous

He also said: "Sayyidi ibn 'Abbad, may Allah be pleased with him, said in the commentary on the *Hikam*: 'The teacher should examine the state of the person acquiring knowledge from him. He should only give of his knowledge to someone who has the signs of goodness and correctness, for it is by means of them that his intention and goal will be upright. He should not give of his knowledge to someone else whose state and ignorance are well known.' Then he said: 'And the words of Allah, exalted is He "*Do not hand over to the simple-minded any property of theirs*"[1] draw attention to the fact that it is more appropriate to preserve knowledge from someone who might corrupt it and blether about it – as has been expressed in the following verse:

Whoever gives the ignorant knowledge has squandered it
    and whoever prevents someone capable of understanding it from obtaining it has acted unjustly

"It has been related from some of the earlier nations that they would first test the behaviour of the person seeking to acquire knowledge: if they found that it was low and mean, they would use every means to prevent him from acquiring knowledge. They would say: 'Knowledge would help him to further contemptible behaviour. Thus knowledge, in his case, would become an evil instrument.'

"Wise men (*hukama'*) have said: 'A lot of knowledge in an evil man is like a lot of water in the roots of the colocynth – the more you water it, the more bitter it becomes. This is something which is tried and tested by experience.'

---

[1] An-Nisa' – Women: 5

Then he said: 'One of them said: "I saw Sufyan ath-Thawri in a sad state. I asked him about it and he replied in irritation: 'We have become nothing but a shop for the sons of this world.' I asked: 'And how is that?' 'One of them keeps our company until he becomes acquainted with us and takes the wages of a worker, a door-keeper, a chamberlain or a tax collector by saying "Sufyan ath-Thawri has related to us."' Then he, may Allah, exalted is He, have mercy on him, mentioned in his teaching the causes of corruption which especially affect such people, and further causes of corruption which spread from them to others. Of the former there is the intensification of their despicable qualities because they are aware that all their worldly desires, without exception, may be obtained by the knowledge they possess.

"Thus their *nafs* become so exited that the effect of this is visible in their outward appearance because of their vying with each other like dogs after the *dunya* and their having recourse to those of its children who have it living in ease and comfort, seeking thereby their favour, and use every trick to make sure that such people respond to them. In doing so, they inevitably take on ostentatious and affected behaviour, hypocrisy, flattery and other forms of disobedience, and all kinds of servile and humiliating actions. One of the acknowledged causes of corruption is their deceiving ignorant persons who see how they have obtained all they desire of the world and they imagine that they have obtained the honour of the next world by the help they have given others and the profit they themselves have derived. This causes them to imitate them and so they fall victim to what those they imitate have fallen victim to; or it leads them to have love for them and to consider their states commendable. This, in turn, causes a hidden illness in them, namely, their imperceptibly taking on the vileness of character of these ignorant people. Thus the purpose for which the Messengers were sent is lost for them, that is, encouragement of *zuhd* in this world and of desire for the next world, of love for poverty and destitution, of preferring humility and going low, and of taking on the characteristics of Iman and Islam, and their intense warnings against committing anything which is forbidden or evil. This, then, causes them to commit hidden and open *shirk*, and evil deceit takes hold of them. This curse may be attributed to the teacher who facilitated the causes of what happened." Here ends the section and some parts have been omitted – he spent a long time discussing the *nafs*, so examine it further." Jussous

Ibn Zakari has transmitted something similar or even more forceful in *Sharh an-Nasiha* from al-Ghazali, may Allah grant us benefit by them all and there is no power and no strength except by Allah, the Sublime, the Vast.

In *Tanbih al-Ghafil* Jussous has transmitted the following text from al-Fakihani in *Sharh ar-Risala* which contradicts this: "It is not fitting for the *'alim* that he refuse to teach anyone just because he does not have the correct intention – for it is hoped that he will acquire a good intention. Often it is difficult for many beginners to concern themselves with correcting their intention because of the weakness of their *nafs* and their lack of familiarity with what is needed to correct their intention. Refusing to teach them leads to the loss of a great deal of knowledge; although – by the very blessed nature of knowledge – it is to be hoped that one purifies one's intention if one has an intimate relationship to knowledge, and they have said: 'We sought knowledge for other than Allah but it refused to belong to other than Allah' – meaning that in the end the intention (of even the person without a correct intention) comes to be for Allah."

Our Shaykh the verifier of knowledge said in *Sharh al-Hikam*: "What they mean – and Allah knows best – when they say that the teacher should not dispense his knowledge except to good and correct people is that when it is known that someone's intention is corrupt, that his very being is depraved, that his heart has become hardened, that counsel would be of no avail and that reminding him would be of no use, then one must keep one's distance, avoid him and withhold one's knowledge from him whoever he may be because it would only increase his evil if the possibility presented itself to him – without there being any specific cause of corruption. If, however, this is not the case then they have stated that one should not refuse to teach a student just because his intention is not sincere." Then he has transmitted from *Sharh al-Muhadhdhab* what has been mentioned above from al-Fakihani, and Allah, exalted is He is the one who gives success.

I say: "And this is what may be understood from the saying of the author: 'Knowledge is a guide to good things, a pointer to them.' Allah, exalted is He, said: "*Remind, then, if the reminder benefits*"[1], that is, the admonition is for the *muminun* and not the *kafirun*. This is like His saying: "*So remind, with the Qur'an, whoever fears My threat*"[2] Here end the words of Jussous.

I say: "Ash-Sha'rani says the following: 'It is part of their character that if they come to know from some evidence about a lack of sincerity on the part of those seeking to acquire knowledge from them, then they carry on with the instruction but turn to Allah, exalted is He, making *du'a* that the intention of the person concerned become sincere. In this way, both they and the person in question receive a reward. They do not abandon instructing the person – for this would be ignorance on their part with respect to what the Legislator

1 al-A'la – The Most High: 9
2 Qaf: 45

intended, may the peace and blessings of Allah be upon him. Knowledge is only obtained for two reasons: in order to act by it and in order to revive the *shari'ah* by means of it. So the person of knowledge is rewarded whatever happens – be it with a partial or a full reward."

Sayyidi 'Ali al-Khawwas, may Allah be content with him, used to say: "There is no one who possesses knowledge but that he acts upon it – even if only with respect to himself when he commits acts of disobedience and then turns in *tawba* and regrets his action – for if it were not for his knowledge of the judgement, he would not have been guided to the awareness that the action was wrong and he would not have turned in *tawba* away from it, for if it had not been because of his knowledge of the legal considerations he would not have been guided to the fact that it was a wrong action, even if the one who does disobey has not acted by his knowledge according to the technical usage of the term – so understand this. So knowledge is of benefit to the one who possesses it whatever the circumstances, and the knowledge of each person is always more than his action – in every age. And praise belongs to Allah for Iman and Islam." Here ends the text taken from *Tanbeeh al-Mughtarreen*.

The first benefit: In *Kifayat al-Muhtaj*, in the section on the biography of ash-Shareef at-Tilimsani, he says: "In his time, students were the most noble of people and those with the most abundant provision. No others excelled them or equalled them in rank. Their words were understood in the best possible light. They were all left to study those knowledges which interested them and all knowledge was regarded as a source of ultimate happiness. They used to say: 'Whoever is granted knowledge in one domain, then he should keep to it.'"

Then he said: "The *'ulama* would not dispute in their gatherings, they would not accuse others of mistakes, they would not seek to dominate for the sake of their *nafs*, they would respond to the one who envied them their knowledge in the most polite and fitting manner and they would persist in reading a *hizb* (of the Qur'an)."

On another occasion he related from Ibn Marzuq that according to the consensus of the *'ulama* – amongst them Ibn 'Arafa – ash-Shareef at-Tilimsani was the most knowledgeable of the people of his time.

2. The author of the book *an-Nurayn* mentioned that "Everyone is either in the Garden or the Fire except for the people of the *A'raf* – the wall separating the two – who are: the *'alim* who did not act according to his knowledge, the illegitimate child and someone who goes on a military expedition (*ghazwa*) without the permission of his parents." The quotation ends here and the responsibility is his.

3. Muhammad ibn al-Hasan, the author of *Majma' al-Ahbab* relates: "A man laughed in the gathering of 'Abd ar-Rahman ibn Mahdi. On hearing him he said: 'Who is laughing?' And he repeated his question several times until some of those present pointed a man out. He went up to him saying: 'You seek knowledge and you are laughing? I shall not narrate to you for two months.' Then the people got up and left."

4. The following has been recorded in *Sahih Muslim*: "Whoever removes one of the afflictions of this world from a *mumin*, then Allah will remove for him one of the afflictions of the Day of Rising, and whoever makes it easy for someone in difficulty, then Allah will make it easy for him in this world and the next, and whoever shields a Muslim then Allah will shield him in this world and the next and Allah, exalted is He, will assist the slave as long as the slave assists his brother. Whoever takes a path seeking thereby knowledge, then Allah will make the path to the Garden easy for him" – in the form narrated by an-Nawawi in his *Sharh al-Arba'in*, or in whatever its wording is.

I SAY: "It has been narrated in al-Bukhari that the Messenger of Allah, may the peace and blessings of Allah be upon him, said: 'A Muslim is a brother to a Muslim, so he should neither oppress him nor surrender him to oppression. Whoever fulfils the needs of his brother, Allah will fulfil his needs and whoever alleviates an affliction from a Muslim Allah will alleviate an affliction of his on the day of Rising and whoever shields a Muslim Allah will shield him on the Day of Rising." Or however its wording is.

Ibn Hajar al-Haytami said in the *Sharh al-Arba'in* – with respect to his words "Whoever removes one of the afflictions of this world from a *mumin*" – "the *mumin* takes preference because of his nobility and inviolability and the reward for whatever good treatment he shows him. If this were not the case (and there were no distinctions), the *dhimmi* would be the same – here and in the following – if we understand the (general) nature of the reward as mentioned in the tradition quoted above (in the *Arba'in* of an-Nawawi), namely that: 'Allah has prescribed good treatment for everything' and in the tradition 'In every hot liver there is a reward.' (However, in terms of rank), a *dhimmi* granted safety (*adh-dhimmi al-musta'min*) comes after a *mumin*, and a non-Muslim from a people at war with the Muslims (*harbi*) comes after this. The reward for (helping) each of the above declines the more (their varying degrees of) nobility and respect decrease."

He also said with respect to his words "whoever makes it easy for someone in difficulty…" that "these words may be correctly taken to comprise referring to solving a question of law for a common person regarding some predicament he may have fallen into." He also said with respect to his saying "and whoever takes a path seeking thereby knowledge" – [meaning, knowledge] of the *shari'ah* or one of its instruments (like *tafsir*) intending thereby the face of Allah, exalted is He, that others said: "Even if this is a condition for every act of worship, the practice of the *'ulama* is to stipulate this specifically regarding the matter (of seeking knowledge) because some people are very lax in this respect or are negligent." Here ends the text. It is as if what he means is that ostentatious behaviour affects knowledge more than it effects other acts of worship so special notice of the necessity of sincerity is needed – sincerity in being meticulous when dealing with the *shari'ah* and the methods and instruments used in understanding the law, for example *tafsir*, hadith, *fiqh*. As for logic, which is used by people today, it is useful and not prohibited – from one point of view. What is prohibited are the philosophical aspects opposed to the *shari'ah* which used to be mixed up with it."

With respect to the words "Allah will make a path to the Garden easy for him", means that his seeking and acquisition of knowledge direct him towards seeking guidance and obedience which will take him to the Garden; but this is only possible when Allah, exalted is He, makes this easy for him for without His kindness and His granting of success neither knowledge or anything else will be of use. Or it means that He will reward his seeking and his acquisition of knowledge by making it easy for him to enter the Garden such that he will not experience any of the difficulties when standing (before Allah on the Day of Judgement) which others will experience – and this latter meaning is closer to the literal meaning of the hadith." Here end his words.

O Allah shield us by our Master Muhammad, the Messenger of Allah, may the peace and blessing of Allah be upon him, from the difficulties of this standing (before Allah).

SALAT AN-NABI – ASKING FOR BLESSINGS ON THE PROPHET

صَلَّى وَسَلَّمَ عَلَى مُحَمَّدٍ

وَآلِهِ وَصَحْبِهِ وَالْمُقْتَدِي

3   Then blessings and peace on Muhammad, his Family, Companions and those who follow his example

Mayyara has explained this formula in *Sharh al-Wadhifa* with reference to our saying 'O Allah bless Muhammad' saying it means 'honour Muhammad' and this means – in this world – exalt his fame, manifest his deen , establish his *shari'ah* and – with respect to the next world – make his reward profuse and abundant, appoint him intercessor for his *umma* and increase his excellence in the Praiseworthy Station (Maqam al-Mahmud). What is meant by the words of, exalted is He, "*Bless him*"¹ is, "Call on your Lord for blessings [for him]."

He said in *Nur al-Basar*: "*Salat* – blessings – from Allah are *in'am* – the granting of favour and grace. From the slave, *salat* is his requesting that from Allah, whether it is for the Prophet or someone else, whether it issues from an angel or someone else, and everything they mentioned about it is based on what I have mentioned – so take notice. And *salam* – peace – from Allah, exalted is He, is His granting safety from what is hateful (to Allah), and from the slave, it is his requesting this from Him, glorious is He."

USEFUL POINT: Al-Aqdamisi said in the commentary on *al-Idha'a* when going into the legal judgement regarding *salat* – blessings – on the Prophet, may the peace and blessings of Allah be upon him: "As for when it is forbidden, it is when impurities are present along with the intention of belittling him, since that is one of the prohibited actions which renders the person guilty of *kufr*, may Allah grant us refuge from this by the rank of Muhammad, may the peace and blessings of Allah be upon him" Here end the words of Al-Aqdamisi. Al-Khurshi was his Shaykh and the Shaykh of an-Nafarawi.

In the *Mi'yar* of the *'alim* of the Maghrib Muhammad ibn Marzooq during his discussion – to come – insha'Allah, exalted is He, – of the statement of the author [Ibn 'Ashir]: "... and the use of stones to wipe oneself [after defecating or urinating] is permitted" ... "and for this reason *dhikr* is permitted in a place which is not clean, but it is not permitted to call for blessings on the Prophet, may the peace and blessings of Allah be upon him."

In the commentary on *Al-Hisn al-Hasin* of Muhammad ibn 'Abd al-Qadir al-Fasi it says: "As-Sanusi was asked about calling for blessings on the Prophet, may the peace and blessings of Allah be upon him, in an unclean bed and he replied that there is no harm in this if the place for the head is clean."

The first benefit: Ibn al-Hattab said that ibn Naji said in the commentary on the *Mudawwana*: "One of them made a *fatwa* saying that books of hadith which do not contain the words of *salat* on the Prophet, may the peace and blessings of Allah be upon him, are to be rejected." As-Sakhawi has mentioned that "a copyist of the *at-Tamheed* of Ibn 'Abd al-Barr deliberately omitted the *salat* on the Prophet, may the peace and blessings of Allah be upon him, whenever his name was mentioned and this greatly reduced the value of it, and he sold it very

---

1 al-Ahzab – The Confederates: 56

cheaply. Moreover, Allah did not honour the work of the copyist with esteem and acceptance after his death despite his knowing one section of knowledge well."

ISSUE

Al-Qadi Abu Bakr ibn al 'Arabi said an extraordinary thing in *al-'Arida*: "What I believe is that his saying, may the peace and blessings of Allah be upon him 'Whoever calls for blessings on me, then Allah will bless him ten times' does not simply refer to the person who says 'The Messenger of Allah, may the peace and blessings of Allah be upon him, was …' but rather these blessings are for the person who calls for blessings on him in a manner which is well known and which we have stated explicitly." As-Sakhawi mentioned many dreams which indicate how great a reward is to be gained from making this *dhikr*.'" Here end the words of Ibn al-Hattab.

2. I have seen a text of one of the people of knowledge which reads: "What is the point of worship by means of invocations without knowing their meaning – this is ineffectual. The person making *salat* on our Master Muhammad, may the peace and blessings of Allah be upon him, and on all the other Prophets of Allah, exalted is He, should have the intention of making a *du'a* for them, and should have as his goal an act of worship, a coming closer to Allah glorious is He, a coming closer to His elevated Majesty."

3. Ash-Sha'rani narrated in *Tabaqat al-Awliya* from one of the people of knowledge: "I saw the Prophet, may the peace and blessings of Allah be upon him, and I said: 'Messenger of Allah (may the peace and blessings of Allah be upon him) the ten blessings for whoever calls, just once, for blessings on you, does this refer to someone whose heart is present?' He replied: 'No, it refers to anyone, even a distracted person, who calls for blessings on me and Allah will give him the like of mountains which will make *du'a* and ask forgiveness for him. If his heart is present during his call for blessings then only Allah, exalted is He, knows that.'"

Al-Aqdamisi said: "Know that no invocations are of benefit to the person doing them and they are not accepted of him unless his heart is present – except for the recitation of the Qur'an and making *salat* on the Prophet, may the peace and blessings of Allah be upon him, for these two are accepted without a person's heart being present."

4. He also narrated from one of the *awliya* who are *shareef* in the *Tabaqat*: "I saw the Prophet, may the peace and blessings of Allah be upon him, and he said: 'Son, backbiting is haram but if it is not possible to avoid listening to

people's backbiting, then recite sura Ikhlas three times and give the *thawab* (reward) for it to the person being talked about for surely backbiting and the *thawab* will inherit from each other, insha'Allah.'" He also said: "I said on one occasion in a gathering:

Muhammad is human but yet not like a human
    Rather he is like a ruby amongst stones.

Then I saw the Prophet, may the peace and blessings of Allah be upon him, and he said: 'Allah will forgive you and everyone who recites this on your behalf'" – and he would recite this, may Allah be pleased with him, during every gathering until he died.

5. The author of the *Mukhtasar* of as-Suyuti's *Hawi* said, explaining the hadith: 'There is no one who calls for peace on me but that Allah restores my *ruh* to me so that I may answer with a call for peace on him' – "what is meant by the *ruh* is the mercy for his *umma* which is in his heart, may the peace and blessings of Allah be upon him, and the kindness on which he was created, even though he did become angered at times by those whose wrong actions were many and who violated the prohibitions of Allah. *Salat* on the Prophet, may the peace and blessings of Allah be upon him, brings about forgiveness of wrong actions as is narrated in the hadith: '…then your worries will be dispelled and your wrong actions will be forgiven.' Thus the Prophet, may the peace and blessings of Allah be upon him, has informed us that there is no one who calls for peace on him – however great his wrong actions may be – but that his mercy (*rahma*) on which he was created returns to him in order that he may answer the call in person – and a person's wrong actions before this do not prevent him from answering the call. This is something of precious benefit and news of great import. The particular emphasis of the phrase "there is no one … but" with its combination of negation and exception, points clearly to an all inclusive statement rather than a general one with a specific, limited meaning." Here ends the statement in *al-Hawi*.

I SAY: "This is a clear statement, namely, that no single individual from amongst the disobedient calls for peace on the Prophet, may the peace and blessings of Allah be upon him, but that he, on him be peace and blessings, returns this call for peace, and this – by the everlasting life of Allah – is news of great import – as as-Suyuti said. However al-Bayhaqi's explanation in the *Sharh al-Arba'in* stipulates that what is meant here is whoever calls for peace on him at his grave. This interpretation supports al-Aqdamisi who draws attention to the hadith: 'It has been narrated that Jibril, peace be upon him, said to the Prophet, may the peace and blessings of Allah be upon him: "Muhammad shall

I not give you some good news?" He replied: "What is it, my beloved Jibril?" He said: "Every action undertaken by the son of Adam and everything he says is suspended between acceptance and non-acceptance, except for the calling of blessings on you, for this is accepted without condition from everyone." The 'ulama have gone very far with this matter, even as far as saying: "It is accepted of the thief and the disobedient person even if they are in the middle of committing their deeds." If you have understood that, then know, too, that our calling for blessings on him, may the peace and blessings of Allah be upon him, is meant in two ways, one way regarding the relation between the slave who calls for blessings and his Lord, and one between the Prophet, may the peace and blessings of Allah be upon him, and his Lord because when the slave says: 'O Allah bless him' once, then Allah blesses him ten times, as is narrated: "That when he slave asks for blessings for him once, then Allah blesses him ten times, and when he asks for blessings for him ten times, He blesses him one hundred times," as has been reported in the hadith. Know, too, that the slave's calling for blessings on the Prophet, may the peace and blessings of Allah be upon him, is an act of worship because it is obedience to the words of Allah, exalted is He: *'You who have* iman! *call down blessings on him and ask for complete peace and safety for him.'*[1] Know, too, that the 'ulama have differed as to the opinion of the earlier generations with respect to whether it is accepted of the disobedient person even if he is in the middle of acting disobediently. Some of them said that the two intentions (referred to above) are accepted of such a person, while others have said that what is accepted in this case is rather in the sense of the relation between the Prophet, may the peace and blessings of Allah be upon him, and his Lord. As for it referring to the relation between the slave and his Lord, this is subject to the same conditions as any other *du'a*. However, one ought to trust in the reality of the first way as the overflowing generosity of Allah, exalted is He, and the excellence of our Prophet, may the peace and blessings of Allah be upon him, are more worthy of this meaning." Here end the words of al-Aqdamisi.

I SAY: "I saw that one of the *Salihun* said that calling for blessings is better for the disobedient than reciting Qur'an. I saw that another said that the person calling for blessings on him, may the peace and blessings of Allah be upon him, cannot be considered to be someone (truly) calling for blessings if he is not following his sunna while the person who is following the sunna may be considered to be someone who is calling for blessings even if he does not ask for blessings. What the person who said this meant is clear."

1   al-Ahzab – The Confederates 56

6. Ibn al-Hattab said that Ahmad Zarruq said that the Prophet's saying, may the peace and blessings of Allah be upon him: "Whoever calls for blessings on me in a book, then the angels continually call for blessings on him as long as my name remains in that book" refers either to the writing down of the Prophet's name, may the peace and blessings of Allah be upon him, and calling for blessings on him – and this is the literal meaning – and the saying of these words out loud – and this is preferred."

I heard one of my Shaykhs stipulate that in order to obtain the reward mentioned, the calling for blessings should be spoken out loud while writing them down, although I have not come across this from anyone other then him. Rather the literal meaning of the hadith and the sayings of the ʿulama indicate that this is not a condition. Hafidh as-Sakhawi said: "The student should take care to write the formula calling for blessings and peace on the Messenger of Allah, may the peace and blessings of Allah be upon him, every time his name is mentioned – in its full form, not by a mere sign as the lazy do. Moreover one should not tire of repeating it, irrespective of whether it is written in its full and proper form in the original. Whoever neglects to call for blessings and peace upon him, may the peace and blessings of Allah be upon him, will be deprived of a vast blessing. It is narrated of him, may the peace and blessings of Allah be upon him, that he said: 'Whoever calls for blessings on me....' The literal meaning of this is that the above mentioned reward is obtained merely by writing it and that the speaking of it out loud is another (separate) matter, which is recommended."

The Name "Muhammad"

The word "Muhammad" is a sign and mark indicating his noble essence, may the peace and blessings of Allah be upon him. Naming people with this or the name Ahmad contains great benefit. In *al-Jamiʿ as-Saghir* is to be found: "No one amongst you will suffer harm if there is a Muhammad, two Muhammads or three in his household" – or words to this effect.

Al-Munawi said: "In this there is a recommendation to name people after him. Malik said: 'The name Muhammad is not to be found amongst a household but that its blessing increases.' Abu Tahir as-Salafi has narrated from a *marfuʿ* hadith (with a chain of narration reaching to the Prophet, may the peace and blessings be upon him) of Humayd at-Taweel from Anas: "Two slaves are standing before Allah, exalted is He and Allah says to them both: 'Enter both of you into the Garden for I have made a promise to myself that no one with the name Muhammad or Ahmad will enter the Fire.'"

I say: "One of the people of our time said: 'Perhaps this refers to someone who names the person out of love for him and for the blessing contained in it from him. This is indicated by what as-Suyuti mentions in *al-Hawi*: Ibn Bakir reported the excellence in the name Muhammad or Ahmad from a hadith of Abu Umama: "Whoever has a new born child and calls him Muhammad out of love for me and for the blessing in my name then he and his child will be in the Garden" – or words to this effect. He said: 'In my view the chain of narration is the rank of *hasan* (good).'" I say that the meaning of "reported" is "narrated."

Al-Bayjuri said in explanation of the hadith: "The Prophet, may the peace and blessings of Allah be upon him, would take off his ring before going to the toilet" that it indicates that entering the toilet with something on which a noble name has been engraved is disliked lest it become contaminated – although it has also been said that it is forbidden. If a noble name like Muhammad has been engraved on it – and nobility and glory in the name are intended – then it is disliked to take it with one into the toilet. This is the opinion preferred by Ibn Jama'a. If, however, he does not have in mind this meaning but rather merely the name of his friend, then it is not disliked." This for me indicates the above mentioned restriction. What is also an indication of this is that we have seen many naming their children Muhammad and they have only been involved in mischief throughout their lives. This is because they did not name their sons seeking his blessing, may the peace and blessings of Allah be upon him, but rather they named him after their father or brother or someone else whom they held to be important."

The author of *as-Sira al-Halabiya* said: "Whoever wants their wife to bear a male child should lay their hand on her belly and say: 'If this child is born a male, then I name him Muhammad' – and he will be born a male. It has also been narrated from 'Ata': 'No child still in the womb of its mother is named Muhammad but that he will be a boy.' It is narrated from al-Husayn ibn 'Ali, may Allah be pleased with them both: 'Whoever is expecting a child and intends to call it Muhammad, then Allah will turn it into a male child even if it is a female.' One of the narrators of this hadith added: 'Then I made the intention to do this and I was blessed with seven children all of whom I named Muhammad.'"

It is reported from Ibn Abi Hamza, may Allah, exalted is He, grant us benefit by him, and others like him: "His allowing, may the peace and blessings of Allah be upon him, to call people by his name, may the peace and blessings of Allah be upon him, is because of the good and benefit in it: he has reminded us that if on the Day of Rising the name 'Muhammad!' is called out then those who hear this and raise their heads in response will have success and happiness and there are many narrations to this effect."

"I have seen one of the people of *baraka* who had mastered a portion of the language of knowledge and he had a number of children all of whom he named Muhammad – only differentiating them with honorifics – because of the good he had heard which, in general, comes with this blessed name and, in particular, to the person who names his child by this name. For this reason, I never saw him and them but that they were enjoying great good – and although he was a poor man and had a large family he did not have to rely on anyone or have to leave any part of the deen which was of particular importance to him." The end of his words.

His Family

The word "Family" in his saying "And on his Family and Companions…" refers to his relations who were *muminun* from amongst Bani Hashim. The "Companions" refer to those of the *muminun* who were with him, may the peace and blessings of Allah be upon him – even if they did not narrate – and even if only for a very short time, and who died in this state.

The first benefit: He said in the *Sharh al-Wadhifa* that the commentator on the *Dala'il al-Khayrat* said: "There are many narrations regarding the excellence of the progeny of the Prophet, may the peace and blessings of Allah be upon him, and that they will be the lords of the people of the Garden, that they will be in its highest abode, that every single one of them possesses the power of intercession and that Allah, exalted is He, promised him that none of them will enter the Fire."

2. Al-Munawi said in his *Kabeer* in commentary on the *Jami'*, regarding his saying "I asked my Lord that I would not marry into a family of my *umma* and that no one from my *umma* would marry into my family except that they would be with me in the Garden and He granted me this" – or words to this effect: "The literal meaning of this is that it includes whoever gets married to or marries (one of his children) to one of his progeny, may the peace and blessings of Allah be upon him. This is indeed good news of great import for whoever becomes related by marriage to a *shareef* who is a man or woman from the Prophet's family, may the peace and blessings of Allah be upon him."

3. I asked the *'alim*, the *salih*, the seeker of knowledge, Ahmad ibn Atweer al-Jinna, as to who was the most noble of the *shareefs* of our land and he replied: "The family of Mawlayi az-Zayn" and he related a story which had happened

to him concerning this family: he gave one of them presents and the people imitated him by also giving him presents. Then a child whom he loved was afflicted by something painful in his throat and the following came to him:

The love of Muhammad protects us from ruin and calamity …

He interpreted this as proof that he loved the Prophet, may the peace and blessings be upon him, that the nobility of Mawlayi as-Zayn's family was genuine and that Allah, exalted is He, would remove the misfortune that had befallen him. Indeed, by the overflowing generosity of Allah, exalted is He, He removed this affliction from the child by the *baraka* of Muhammad, may the peace and blessings of Allah be upon him.

In the commentary of Abu'l-Qasim ibn Muhammad ibn 'Abd al-Qadir al-Fasi on the *Aqida* composed by his grandfather 'Abd al-Qadir it reads: "Al-Maqrizi has related from one of the *'ulama* that he harboured a hatred for some of the *shareefs* of Madina because of some innovations they were making a show of. Then he saw Mustafa, may the peace and blessings of Allah be upon him, in a dream and he berated him. He said: 'O Messenger of Allah (may the peace and blessings of Allah be upon him) I seek protection from Allah for disliking them – but I only dislike their harsh treatment of the people of the sunna' He replied: 'A legal question: is not the disobedient son still related to the family (despite his disobedience)? – they are like the disobedient son.'"

Ibn Zakari said in the *Sharh an-Naseeha*: "And in the *Mukhtasar al-Futuhat* there is: 'A man from Makka who we regard as reliable informed us that he strongly disliked what the *shareefs* used to do with the people in Makka and then he saw Fatima, may Allah be content with her, in a dream. She was facing away from him. He greeted her and asked her why she was facing away from him and she told him: 'You are attacking the *shareefs*.' He said, 'I replied to her: "Have you not seen what they are doing with the people?" She replied: "Are they not my children?" I replied: "I turn in *tawba* from this moment on"' and then she turned to face him."

THE POEM'S SUBJECT MATTER

وَبَعْدُ فَالْعَوْنُ مِنَ اللَّهِ الْمَجِيدِ

فِي نَظْمِ أَبْيَاتٍ لِلْأُمِّيِّ تُفِيدْ

4   And then, help is from Allah, the Glorious, in the composition of verses which will be of benefit to the unlettered person…

فِي عَقْدِ الْأَشْعَرِي وَفِقْهِ مَالِكْ

وَفِي طَرِيقَةِ الْجُنَيْدِ السَّالِكْ

5   ...on the subject of the *'aqida* of al-Ash'ari, the *fiqh* of Malik and the *tariqa* of al-Junayd, the wayfarer.

"And then" the preceding lines praising Allah and calling for blessings on His Messenger, or "after" this introductory passage, and since this extra material is implicit because of the evidence of what he mentioned beforehand, then he omitted it here in order to be brief. He ended the word "then" with a *u* because of having cut off the genitive relation textually along with his intending it in the meaning.

Thus he says the word *'awn* – help from Allah – which refers to His enabling or strengthening a person to master a subject; then *al-Majid* – the Glorious – is the One Who has the furthest limit of nobility, the perfection of kingship, and His expansiveness to a degree beyond which nothing more is possible nor is it possible to reach anything of it.

Then he uses the words *fi nadhm* – meaning (this help has been given) "in the composition" – instead of *'ala nadhm* which would be the normal prepositional form in Arabic here. The word *nadhm* is in the plural and it refers to the arranging of the jewels on a necklace to achieve the most beautiful effect. When used as a linguistic term it refers to a harmonious phrase, written in a metre which seeks to combine meaning and rhyme. The word *ummi* – unlettered – refers linguistically to the female slave (of Allah) whose status when born is that of her mother's, and who is unable to read or write.

As for his saying *fi 'aqd al-Ash'ari* – the *'aqida* of al-Ash'ari – this use of the shorter word *'aqd* rather than the more usual form (*'aqida*) is necessary here to permit the ordered metre of the couplet; yet at the same time the formation of a proper meaningful phrase is assured. Al-Ash'ari is mentioned as he formulated the science of *'aqida* – see his biography in *al-Madarik* if you wish.

His mention of *wa fiqh Malik* – regarding the *fiqh* of Malik – refers to what the latter said, or to what those of his followers said or to what the trustworthy men of knowledge after them said who were well versed in Malik's foundations and methods. See the biography of our Imam Malik in Ahmad al-Mayyara's work or in *al-Madarik*.

As for al-Junayd, may Allah be content with him, he is the famous imam, the Master of the Sufis who died, may Allah benefit us by him, in 296.

Introduction to the Book of 'Aqida

which is an aid to acts of obedience and attaining the desired goal

Introduction to the Book of 'Aqida

Which is an Aid to Acts of Obedience and Attaining the Desired Goal

وَحُكْمُنَا الْعَقْلِي قَضِيَّةٌ بِلاَ

وَقْفٍ عَلَى عَادَةٍ أَوْ وَضْعٍ جَلاَ

6   Our (pure) intellectual judgement is a proposition which is independent of anything learned by repeated experience or from customary usage[1] which is clear (from the *shari'ah*).

AHMAD al-Mayyara said: "Know that whoever understands a certain matter but only conceives of its meaning and does not come to a judgement as to its confirmation or as to its refutation based on acknowledgement of something actual or specific, then this kind of understanding is termed imagination – like, for example, our understanding that the meaning of origination (*huduth*) is the coming into existence (of creational realities) after their non-existence, without our having attested to this or our having refuted it through something specific (in creation itself); if however, one imagines along with that the confirmation of that matter for something specific or its refutation, then this kind of understanding is termed judgement or affirmation, like our attesting to the coming into existence after having conceived of this fact for the worlds – and [the worlds] comprise everything which is other than Allah, blessed is He and exalted. Thus we conclude: 'Our Lord, exalted is He, is not of these creational realities.' Thus the attesting to

---

1   *Wad'* is a customary usage, but what is referred to here is usage derived from revelation. The author therefore outlines three types of knowledge: those derived from experience such as medicine, those derived from revelation such as the number of *rak'ahs* of Maghrib, and those which are completely rational such as mathematics and the core elements of the *'aqida*. Ed.

or the refuting of something through something else is called judgement and this is what is intended by the author by the word 'proposition' in the above-mentioned line of the poem. Know, then, that the judgement in itself may be divided into three parts: that which relates to the *shari'ah*, that which is learned by repeated experience and that which is disclosed by the intellect. Thus as for the attesting to or refutation of anything pertaining to a judgement – if it is based on the *shari'ah* such that it is not possible to know this matter except by means of it, then this is (termed) a legal judgement, connected to the *shari'ah*, like our saying: 'The five *salats* are obligatory but the fasting on the day of 'Ashura is not.' If, however, the matter is not dependent on the *shari'ah*, and the intellect suffices to understand it without having to resort to repeated probing or experiment, then this is an intellectual judgement. It is termed intellectual because the intellect has reached this judgement without resorting to anything else, like our saying: 'The number ten is even and seven is odd.' If the refutation or attestation which are in the judgement are not dependent upon the *shari'ah* to arrive at a judgement regarding either of the two, and the intellect does not suffice to arrive at [refutation or attestation] but rather repeated probing or experiment is necessary to determine a refutation or attestation, then it is termed a customary judgement by ascription to custom because by means of it one has arrived not through the *shari'ah* nor the intellect.

أَقْسَامُ مُقْتَضَاهُ بِالْحَصْرِ ثَمَازُ

وَهْيَ الْوُجُوبُ الِاسْتِحَالَةُ الْجَوَازُ

7   The requisite divisions encompassing the judgement as a whole are differentiated into the necessarily true, the inconceivable and the conceivable.

فَوَاجِبٌ لَا يَقْبَلُ النَّفْيَ بِحَالٍ

وَمَا أَبَى الثُّبُوتَ عَقْلًا الْمُحَالُ

8   The 'necessarily true' refers to that which does not admit of negation whatsoever, and that which the intellect refuses to attest to is the 'inconceivable.'

$$\text{وَجَائِزاً مَاقَبِلَ الأَمْرَيْنِ سِمْ}$$

$$\text{لِلضَّرُورِي وَالنَّظَرِي كُلٌّ قُسِمْ}$$

9   'Conceivable' is a term applied to that which admits of the two (aforementioned) terms, and the description *daruri* (i.e. a necessarily true judgement immediately apparent to all) or *nadhari* (a judgement only apparent upon reflection) may be (further) applied to each of the (three) divisions.

$$\text{أَوَّلُ وَاجِبٍ عَلَى مَنْ كُلِّفَا}$$

$$\text{مُمَكَّناً مِنْ نَظَرٍ أَنْ يَعْرِفَا}$$

10   The first thing which is incumbent upon the legally capable person – as long as he is capable of reflection – is that he know…

$$\text{اللَّهَ وَالرُّسُلَ بِالصِّفَاتِ}$$

$$\text{مِمَّا عَلَيْهِ نَصَبَ الْآيَاتِ}$$

11   …Allah and the Messengers by the attributes set out in the *ayats*

THE NECESSARILY TRUE, THE INCONCEIVABLE AND THE CONCEIVABLE

Ahmad al-Mayyara said: "He informed us that what is required for an intellectual judgement may be understood as comprising three divisions or kinds, namely that which is necessarily true, inconceivable or conceivable. This in turn may be explained by saying that whenever the intellect arrives at a judgement, it may either be regarding something which admits of both affirmation or rejection, or admits of only affirmation, or of only rejection. The first, then, is the conceivable and it is also termed the possible, the second is the necessarily true and the third is the inconceivable. He said 'the requisite divisions encompassing the judgement as a whole' rather than simply 'its divisions or kinds' because an intellectual judgement is not the same as the three above mentioned divisions – so therefore they are not 'its' divisions or kinds. This is because one of the conditions of such a division into 'kind' (logically speaking) is that the name of 'that which has been divided' (*maqsoum*) must also hold true for each of its different kinds. However, the word 'judgement' does not fit or hold true for the words 'necessarily true', 'inconceivable' or 'conceivable' – rather what holds true of these words is that they refer to 'that whereby a judgement is arrived at.'"

As-Sanusi said in *al-Wusta*: "Know that intellectual judgement comprises three divisions or kinds: the necessarily true, inconceivable or conceivable, and these three form the basis upon which investigation of *'ilm al-kalam* – the science pertaining to Allah, exalted is He, and the unseen – takes place. The 'necessarily true' is that whose non-existence cannot be imagined in the intellect, such as a body occupying space; the 'inconceivable' is what cannot be conceived of as existing, like a body devoid of movement or rest; the 'conceivable' is that whose existence and non-existence are both conceivable for the intellect, like the death of one of us today or tomorrow."

He said in its commentary: "The predisposition of substance, that is, its taking up a specific amount of space. This is an example of a necessarily true judgement immediately apparent to all. An example of the necessarily true that is known after reflection is the *qidam* – the before-endless-timelessness – of Allah, exalted is He, because this is a notion which is understood by the intellect through reflection. An example of the inconceivable that is immediately apparent to all is a body's being devoid of movement or rest. An example of something inconceivable that is only known after reflection is Allah's 'being', exalted is He, having material substance [which is impossible] because the judgement as to the inconceivability of this notion with respect to Him, exalted is He, is perceived by the intellect by means of two things: the first of these, the proof that bodies are originated; the second, by means of the proof that Allah's being, exalted is He, is necessarily existent from before endless time (*qidam*). Thus if these two propositions are true, it would be correct to state the following: If our Lord, exalted is He, were a body then His coming into existence would be necessarily true because of what has been determined as to the necessity of bodies coming into existence; however, it is inconceivable for Allah, exalted is He, to come into existence because it has been established that His being is from before endless time. Therefore, it follows that it is inconceivable for Allah, exalted is He, to be a substance or body. Thus the first proposition which we have known through the proof – namely, the necessity for all bodies to (first) come into existence – provides the first part of this demonstration. This proposition is of the type which is based on an inseparable (or inherent) condition. The second proposition, namely His necessarily being from before endless time, exalted is He, forms the second part of the demonstration, and this is known as the proposition of exception.

As for the conceivable – an example of the conceivable which is immediately evident to everyone is what he gave as an example in the original *'aqida*. An example of what is known to be conceivable after reflection is Allah's being able to reward the obedient (slave) – for this is conceivable for Him but not incumbent upon Him."

REFLECTION

Ahmad al-Mayyara said: "He informed us that the first thing which is obligatory on the *mukallaf* – the legally capable person – who is that person of sound mind, of age (having reached puberty), possessing the capacity to reflect, is that he have knowledge of Allah, exalted is He, and knowledge of His Messengers, on whom be peace and blessing, with respect to the attributes upon which Allah set up the *ayats* – that is, He established the proofs and evidence on them, since ignorance of an attribute would be the same as ignorance of the thing to which the attribute is ascribed. He uses the words 'possessing the capacity to reflect' in order to exclude the *mukallaf* who is not capable of reflection because of his sudden death immediately after puberty – for knowledge is not incumbent on him as it can only be obtained by reflection, and one assumes, in his case, that he was not in a position to do this."

Then after a while he said that Ibn al-'Arabi said: "Reflection is ordered thinking in a person in such a manner that it leads to the knowledge whoever undertakes it seeks, a knowledge of things which can be known or to what is most probable in cases of doubt, and whenever certainty cannot be obtained absolutely."

He goes on to say after a passage: "As for his using the word *sifat* – the plural of *sifa* (attribute or quality), this term has (basically) the same meaning as the word of the same root *wasf* – which indicates a description or property (of something). However for the *mutakallimun*, *wasf* specifically refers to what the person describing something says, i.e. the description (itself) whereas *sifa* relates to the quality inherent in the thing described, and this is what is meant here.

"His saying 'set out in the *ayats*' is connected to an omission of *sifa* or it is adverbial with respect to the attributes and what is understood from it is that knowledge of the attributes for which no proof or evidence is set up is not incumbent, and it is thus. This is like the saying of as-Sanusi in the commentary on the *Sughra* (*Lesser*): 'The attributes of our Lord, exalted is He, are not limited to these twenty for His perfections are without number. However, Allah, exalted is He, by his generosity, will not call us to account because of our incapacity to know something for which no proof – by way of the intellect or tradition – has been set out.'" Here ends the text of Mayyara.

I SAY: "What as-Sanusi has asserted authoritatively here, may Allah benefit us by him, is one of three opinions related by the author, the *'alim*, the verifier, Ibn ash-Shat in *Hashiya al-Farouq*: 'People have differed regarding this matter: there are those who teach that there is no attribute beyond those that we know, while from others we understand that there are attributes of which we have no knowledge and still others from whom we must draw the conclusion that the matter is open to reflection and investigation and this is the correct position.'" This is the sense of his words.

Taqlid in Matters of 'Aqida

NOTE: The *'ulama* differ, in four ways, as to whether it suffices to make *taqlid* in matters of *'aqida*:

1. That it is not correct to make *taqlid* (i.e. to merely imitate others) in this matter. As-Sanusi states in *Sharh al-Qaseed*: "And this is the *madhhab* of the *jumhur* (the majority). Some relate that this is the *ijma'* (the consensus) too. The proof of this is that we are charged to acquire *ma'rifa* (knowledge) of Allah, exalted is He, and *ma'rifa* of His Messengers but what is acquired by the *muqallid* (the person who imitates) is not called *'ilm* or *ma'rifa* – and *'ilm* and *ma'rifa* both have the same meaning, that is the certainty in which there is no possibility of contradiction whatsoever. However, *taqlid*, in the realm of *'aqida* does contain the possibility of contradiction, and of incompatibility when those who cause doubts do so. The command to reflect upon and investigate that which will produce knowledge of Allah, exalted is He, occurs many times in the Book and the sunna, and the making of *taqlid* of one's parents and ancestors or others in matters of the roots of the deen has been criticised many times. It is for this reason that the teacher Abu Ishaq, may Allah be pleased with him, said: "The *mukallaf* has no alternative – regarding any of the *'aqidas* of iman – but to acquire at least one proof or more. The hadith – which attests to the torment in the grave of whoever replies "I do not know, I heard people saying something or other and I have (simply) repeated it" when asked (by the angels) about any of the *'aqidas* of iman – is also proof of the obligation to acquire knowledge in matters of iman and the prohibition of settling for mere *taqlid*. This is the opinion preferred by most of the people of sunna, like the Imam of the Haramayn (al-Juwaini), Shaykh al-Ash'ari, al-Qadi and al-Ustadh. Al-Qadi has added that it is not correct to command (someone to practice) *taqlid* using the proof of intellectual investigation because either the

mukallaf is commanded to make *taqlid* of whomever he wishes, or of someone with whom – according to his estimation – the truth in all probability lies, or of someone who is acting according to the truth in the eyes of Allah, exalted is He. However, all three possibilities are invalid. The first and second are invalid because he cannot know who is acting according to the truth in the eyes of Allah except after correct investigation. If he did come to know the truth through correct investigation then he would have no need of making *taqlid* for its sake. Thus none of this results in *taqlid* whatever the circumstances." Here end the words of as-Sanusi.

He has given absolute preference to this opinion in the commentary on *al-Kubra* and *al-Wusta*. In the commentary on *al-Wusta* he said: "Ibn Dihaq, may Allah, exalted is He, have mercy on him, said in the commentary on *al-Irshad* when speaking about the trial of the grave and its torment: 'No one who learns his deen by means of *taqlid* or who abandons examination of the proof afforded by the (divine) message or (the doctrine of) *tawhid* is saved from this trial.' For this reason it is said that hypocrisy is of two kinds: one which the person is aware of himself and another which he is unaware of. The first refers to the hypocrisy of those who used to worship idols in secret while at the same time showing signs of the deen outwardly – for example, in their speech or *salat*. As for the hypocrisy of which one is unaware, it occurs in a man or a woman born to parents who are *muminun* who say *la ilaha illa'llah muhammadur-rasoolullah* (There is no god but Allah, Muhammad is the Messenger of Allah) and they repeat whatever they hear from them in such a manner that had they been born of Christian parents they would have repeated and followed whatever they say without examining (the nature of) their creation or what they have been created from or (the miracle of) how they grow and develop in different stages. It may well be that sometimes thoughts as to Allah's creation, exalted is He, do come into his mind but then a shaytan from amongst the jinn or mankind responds and says to him: 'If you think, then you will only have doubts and illusions' and so he turns away from reflection until his death. Then, when his *ruh* reaches the throat, shaytan comes to him in this moment of constriction when no further reflection is possible and causes him to have doubts about his deen, and so he dies in a state of doubt. We seek refuge with Allah, exalted is He. Then, when he is in the grave a seal is placed on his lips and he will only be able to speak from his own knowledge. If he is a gnostic, he will speak about what is true, and if he is a doubter and not a person of knowledge, he will say: 'I do not know.' This was how he was during his life, that is, he used to say in his heart: 'I do not know.' Shaytan used to fall upon him unawares at times but he would not search for the reason and did not treat the sickness of his innermost being. So when he dies he is overcome with remorse at a time when remorse is of no further benefit, and he makes excuses to someone who does not hear him and so he perishes – may Allah protect us from such an end." Here ends the gist of what as-Sanusi said on this matter.

Then after a long discussion in support of the above subject he says that Ustadh Abu Ishaq, may Allah be pleased with him, related that the scholars who verify said: "No one may be described as having the attribute of iman unless they have a proof for each of the essential points (*arkan*) of the deen." He has also said: "The Dhahiri *madhhab* accepts *taqlid* but Ibn al-Qasar has transmitted from Malik, may Allah be pleased with him, that it is obligatory to reflect and that *taqlid* in matters of *'aqida* is not enough." The *Shareef* Abu Yahya said in *Sharh al-Irshad*: "I am of the opinion that *'aqida* is of two types: firstly, believing that something which is well known is contrary to what it really is, and this is true ignorance and the person who is ignorant of Allah is a *kafir*; secondly, believing something which is well known to be as it is. If this is acquired through reflection, then this is the *'aqida* which is desired. If it is through *taqlid*, however, then either the *mukallaf* in question possesses ample capacity for reflection and seeking appropriate proofs or he does not: if, he is among the former, then he is a *mumin* who is in a state of disobedience; if of the latter, then he is a *mumin*, but not of the disobedient – otherwise it would mean the imposition of an obligation which could not be discharged and this would be inconceivable, both by the intellect, according to one group, or by virtue of the *shari'ah*, according to others. The *taqlid* they forbade was only with respect to those able to reflect and seek proofs – otherwise, without this capacity, the imposition of a task that is impossible would be obligatory as we have stated.'"

I say: He made mention of the incapacity to reflect in a person – but this is extremely rare, or indeed it does not exist at all. It would appear that anyone who possesses the basic intellect that makes him responsible has the capacity for knowledge and reflection. In short, correct reflection is difficult for some and easy for others. However, difficulty does not cause one's obligations to be annulled in many of the branches of the deen so how could this be with respect to the roots? As for accepting that incapacity does exist, as the Shareef claims, and that the obligation of the *mukallaf* to reflect would be an unbearable burden in his case, we do not accept that an unbearable obligation can occur in the roots of the deen. What the Shareef claims, namely that this capacity to reflect might not exist at all – this is sheer *ijtihad* which contradicts what al-Qarafi has transmitted contrary to that.

Al-Qarafi said: "The Possessor of the law laid extreme emphasis on matters of *'aqida* regarding the roots of the deen to such an extent that if a person exerts himself to the utmost to remove his ignorance of some attributes of Allah, exalted is He, or of some matter he is obliged to hold to regarding his *'aqida* in the roots of the deen but the ignorance is not removed from him then he is guilty of wrong action and a *kafir* according to the most well known opinion in this *madhhab*. Despite his having striven to make *ijtihad* and despite this ignorance remaining with him through his incapacity to get rid of it, he is not excused. One cannot simply conclude that his state is such that this obligation is impossible to fulfil – even the obligation of a foolish woman of corrupt temperament from a land far beyond those climates where the intellect can function properly, like the furthest parts of the Sudan, or of a man from the most outlying, incompatible lands of the Turks (for in such places the intellect does not possess illumination of any significance, and for this reason Allah, exalted is He, said of the land of the Turks: "...*until he arrived between the two mountains where he found a people scarcely able to understand speech*"[1]) – they are still, despite all this, *mukallafun* with the obligation to understand the intricacies and implications of the roots of the deen and the proofs pointing to *tawhid*, and because of their ignorance, they will remain forever in the fire."

As for the Shareef's restricting what he said to just the act of disobedience in the case of the person who is capable of reflection, this claim of his has no proof and it is not possible to find evidence for it – for reflection is an obligation from the branches of the deen in the same way that the *salat* is an obligation. To throw obstacles in the way of reflection, as he does, is not correct. Rather the truth of the matter is that reflection is a means to obtaining the iman which is itself knowledge (*ma'rifa*), or to obtaining premonitions or impulses (*hadith an-nafs*) from one's self which are a part of knowledge. If iman can only be obtained by a certain means then this means becomes a fundamental obligation, like iman." Here ends the discussion of as-Sanusi, may Allah, exalted is He, benefit us by him.

I SAY: "What ash-Shareef says after this is accepted by his contemporary Ibn Zakari, as stated by al-Manjouri in *Hashiya al-Kubra*, and what al-Qarafi has mentioned, and as-Sanusi accepts – regarding the obligations of the weak-minded woman of corrupt temperament even if in that there is the imposition of a charge that cannot be borne. It is, in my view – and Allah, exalted is He, knows best – best answered by the words of Qadi 'Iyad in the *Shifa*: 'Al-Jahidh and Thumama have said that Allah, exalted is He, has no argument against

[1] al-Kahf – The Cave: 89

many of the common people, women, the weak-minded, the imitators of the Jews and the Christians if they do not have the inherent capacity to arrive at and establish proof and evidence. Those who say such things reject (are *kafir* of) the consensus that those who do not treat the Christians and Jews as *kuffar* are themselves *kuffar*, together with all those who separate themselves from the deen of Islam, or who hesitate to treat them as *kuffar* or have doubts.' Here end the words of Qadi 'Iyad. I am not certain as to his being in accord with what al-Qarafi says. Moreover Ibn ash-Shat in his *Hashiya* on the *Qawa'id* of al-Qarafi does not approve of al-Qarafi's discussion in general whose text is: "If by women with corrupt temperament he means they do not understand anything, then I do not consider that this is correct – for there is no obligation for the likes of such women. However, if he means that they do understand – but only after tiring themselves and with extreme difficulty – then this is correct." Here end his words.

There is something similar to his saying: "There is no obligation for the likes of such women" from Ibn 'Arafa, and at-Tartushi in *Siraj al-Muluk*. The first text, cited by Abu Mutafannin in his *Ikmal al-Ikmal* is: "Just as having been reached by the call to Islam is a precondition, so too is understanding the being charged with responsibility. If there is someone from among the non-Arabs (being called to Islam by means of Arabic) who does not understand (the Arabic) then he is treated in the same manner as any other person who had not heard the call to Islam."

The second text: "Whoever has the capacity to draw conclusions from what he witnesses of the visible about what is invisible to him, then such a person (may be said to) possess an intellect and is called 'of sound mind', according to the people of *tawhid* – and it is on this that (the legal judgement as to whether there exists an) obligation (*takleef*) is based." Here end the words of at-Tartushi and he is one of the chiefs of the *'ulama*, according to Ibn ash-Shat.

CONCLUSION: The person of weak mind and corrupt temperament who is unable to comprehend proof or evidence is legally obliged (*mukallaf*) to hold to the roots of the deen even if there is an obligation which he cannot fulfil – according to al-Qarafi, and those with him, – while he is excused and is under no obligation – according to Ibn 'Arafa and those with him.

Ibn ash-Shat has made the following distinction: "If he is unable to comprehend at all, then he is under no obligation (*ghayr mukallaf*) while if he is able to comprehend only after tiring himself and difficulty then he is responsible." It is possible that this distinction of Ibn Shat is what Ibn 'Arafa is referring to and this is the more evident of the meanings. So reflect whether it is possible to reconcile the two views or not – and Allah, exalted is He, knows best and is the better judge – and examine the matter fairly, without overstepping the bounds.

Following this discussion I concentrated my investigation on the last section of the *Shifa* and I found it impervious to all controversy. The text in question is to be found after his saying "or who hesitates to treat them as *kuffar*, or has doubts": "Qadi Abu Bakr says: '…because the opinion established through the text of the Qur'an (*tawqeef*) and the consensus (*ijma'*) both concur that such persons are to be treated as *kuffar* and that whoever wavers or has doubts in this is denying the text on the subject and the opinion established through the text of the Qur'an, and because such a denial or harbouring doubts on the matter can only arise in a *kafir*.' Ash-Shihab said: '…this is because it is a famous matter in the deen which is necessarily well known.'"

Then as-Sanusi says – after the above words: "How great is the need of the aspirants to *fiqh* of our time to learn the roots of the deen, to occupy themselves with what concerns them and to leave aside much of what does not concern them – and how great, then, must be the need of the ordinary people! Where is the truth and its people? and where are those who can accept the truth according to it its proper worth – they are rare! Whoever has been granted the gift of knowledge of the truth in this age and then is able to put it into practice should endeavour to increase his thanks to Allah, exalted is He, as much as he is able. Let him consider that to be a miracle. Allah, exalted is He, is the One Who aids the slave to this, and there is no power, and no strength but by Allah.

"In short, if Allah wishes good for someone, He shows him the path leading to his own salvation and opens up for him knowledge of this science which is the best knowledge, the most obligatory of them and the first appropriate that the *mukallaf* should occupy himself with. Contentment with the business of *taqlid* is a lowering of *himma* and the deen. It is also exposing oneself to the horror of the tremendous torment of the grave and the terror of remaining forever in the Fire, and we seek refuge with Allah, exalted is He, from this. What is required, as far as iman is concerned, is certainty and knowledge, and this is only possible by correct investigation. Examine the hadith of Abu Hurayra, may Allah be content with him: 'Whoever you meet behind this wall[1] who bears witness that there is no god but Allah and whose heart has certainty, then give him good news of the Garden' and in Muslim: 'Whoever dies knowing that there is no god but Allah, and his heart has certainty then

---

1 The wall of an orchard belonging to the Ansar. See: *Sahih Muslim, Sharh an-Nawawi*, vol. 1, p. 235.

give him good news of the Garden' and in Muslim: 'Whoever dies knowing that there is no god but Allah, will enter the Garden.' Just look at how certainty and knowledge are stipulated in these two hadith – and they are the opposite of *taqlid*!"

Then after a long discussion in support of this statement he says: "Shaikh Abu'l-Qasim 'Abd al-Jalil al-Qasri said in his *'Aqida*: 'Know that many people occupy themselves only with the science of grammar and arithmetic, with analysis of and perfecting pronunciation and the improving of handwriting because they hope to rely on such skills to obtain things and find employment. You see them exhibiting themselves in a haughty and extravagant fashion, regarding people with contempt and looking down on them. When such a person is asked 'What is the first obligation? When does one become fully responsible before the law? What is the proof that the path he is on is the correct one? And what is the corruption which a person should want to avoid?' he remains more silent than the grave and more terrified than a bird caught in a trap. His zeal which had been great is reduced to nought and all that seemed powerful, weighty and momentous in his *nafs* is humbled. He becomes wrapped in his own silence and timorousness. What a calamity has befallen him! What a disaster has struck him!"

I say: Would that he had scrutinised the disaster that strikes him in this world, and had considered how the questioning of (the angels) Munkir and Nakeer about *tawhid* will be in the grave after his death; how the terrors of the next world – from which no one will be saved but those whom Allah has blessed with excellent knowledge of Allah, exalted is He – await each and every person; and how the good and the bad will be separated from each other; how the secrets of those who are ignorant regarding the roots of the deen will be revealed; how the extravagant and haughty will reap only the regret whose causes they have sown in this abode because of their turning away from examining *tawhid*, by their occupying themselves with what does not concern them; and how all grief and sorrow will cease at this moment but that will not avail him."

Ibn Rahal stated in *Sharh al-Buni* in the section on 'knowledge of the proofs and the (necessity for) proper examination': "Know that this (knowledge and readiness to examine) is the heart of the deen and (the basis of) worship of the Prophets, the Messengers, the rightly guided Imams and all the other *'ulama* of the Muslims; all the various ranks and circles of the earlier generations held to this and they were followed in this by those that came after them. However, when the great masters disappeared and those possessing oceans of knowledge perished, they were followed by generations who found great difficulty and hardship in the acquiring of knowledge of proofs and methods of examination. They preferred to remain in places of ease and to board the ship of ignorance. They took upon themselves the lowliness of *taqlid* [in *'aqida*] – which is the domain of the weak-minded and foolish. Allah, exalted is He, has condemned those people who imitate their fathers without any proof or evidence. Such people say: "*We found our fathers following a religion and we are simply following in their footsteps.*"[1]

Let us limit ourselves to this criticism of *taqlid* and of those who encourage others to make *taqlid* and of those who belittle study of the science of *tawhid* or who forbid it completely. They cut off the path of knowledge of Allah, exalted is He, for the slaves of Allah, exalted is He. Sometimes they deceive the slaves of Allah into believing their knowledge is correct, and at other times that their *tawhid* is sound and presents no danger to them. Allah glorious is He, will bring the shaytans amongst mankind to account those who prevent the poor and destitute from living their way of life correctly in the deen. The complete discussion of this is contained in the *Sharh al-'Aqida al-Kubra.*" Here end the words of as-Sanusi, may Allah be content with him, and with us through him.

All that is contrary to this, he has commented on in his *Sharh al-Kubra*. In it he says that amongst the *fuqaha* of his time were those who were corrupt in their *'aqida,* how then must the common people have been? Investigate what he has to say and you will see the greatest of wonders.

In the second of the four statements in *Sharh al-Qaseed* he says: "Unwavering *taqlid* by which one holds to and trusts in the various aspects of iman (*'aqa'id al-iman*) is enough even if it is devoid of any proof. This view is preferred by Ibn Rushd who adds that investigation is recommended not obligatory. The Proof of Islam, al-Ghazali, inclines to this view also, as does the Shaykh, the *wali*, the gnostic of Allah, exalted is He, Ibn Abi Jamra.

"The third statement discriminates between those who have the capacity to understand such investigation, in which case *taqlid* is forbidden them and they must undertake a proper examination of the matter – and if they abandon it they are considered to be disobedient – and between those who have no capacity to understand investigation – in which case there is no obligation for them to undertake such an examination and *taqlid* is enough for them: to oblige someone who has no capacity for investigation is the same as obliging someone to take on responsibility for something he has no capacity to undertake. Allah has relieved this *umma* of such a burden saying: '*Allah does not impose on any self*

---

1 az-Zukhruf – The Gold Ornaments: 22

any more than it can stand.'[1] A group of the imams of the people of sunna have also inclined to this view.

"The fourth statement discriminates between the sources of knowledge which the *muqallid* relies on: there is that which is necessarily free of mistakes like the Qur'an for '*falsehood cannot reach it from before it or behind it*'[2], or that which is classed with a similar rank like the knowledge which issues from the Messengers, may blessings and peace be upon them, for they are secure from any mistake through the infallibility which is necessarily inherent in them. It is correct to imitate them – for through reliance on them one is assured of arrival at the absolute truth demanded by intellectual proof. On the other hand, there are sources which are not free from mistakes, like individual *'ulama*. It is not correct to rely on such persons in matters of *'aqida*, but rather one must undertake a correct examination of the matter because one can never be sure that their *'aqida* is free of mistakes or innovations. Indeed it would be open *kufr* to do so because of the inevitable lack of infallibility in individual *'ulama*'s words and deeds. This statement, however, is very weak as one cannot know the truth of the Qur'an and the Messengers – such that one might follow and imitate them – until one has undertaken a correct examination leading to knowledge of Allah, exalted is He, and knowledge of the Messenger of Allah, may the peace and blessings of Allah be upon him, and this is contrary to *taqlid*. Moreover in the Qur'an and the sayings of the Messenger, may the peace and blessings of Allah be upon him, there are statements concerning the roots of *'aqida* which are of a literal nature and which must be interpreted – for to retain their literal meaning would inevitably lead to *shirk*, the attributing of corporeal reality to Allah and to all kinds of *kufr* and innovations, may Allah protect us from this. Interpretation of such literal statements can only be done through correct examination of them."

Then after a discussion he says: "… and the author – that is al-Jaza'iri – has indicated with his saying: 'There is no basis or proof for a *tawhid* which does not lead to an answer to any question, that is, which does not reject the statement that *taqlid* is enough. They argue that: "If *taqlid* is wrong and instead examination and investigation are necessary, then most people would be excused the obligation to do this because of their difficulty in undertaking a proper examination whereas the tolerant, forbearing *shari'ah* has judged otherwise; Allah, exalted is He, says: '*He has not placed any constraint upon you*

---

1 al-Baqara – The Cow: 285
2 Fussilat – Made Plain: 42

in the deen'[1] and *'Allah does not impose on any self any more than it can stand'*[2]." Sometimes people presume that this statement (i.e. *taqlid* is not enough) leads to an unbearable burden for many people and they point to the difficulty of correct examination for most people during the time before the mission of our Prophet, may the peace and blessings of Allah be upon him. Despite their numbers and the existence of many people of intellect at that time – like the philosophers who were occupied with the sciences of logic, the analysis of proof and evidence and investigation into the numerous intricacies of the sciences – they were not guided to the truth and they were not able to know it. Indeed, most of them went astray, worshipped other than Allah, exalted is He, and leaned to heretical beliefs with regard to His essence and attributes. They spoke nonsense unacceptable to anyone of intellect.' The author, may Allah, exalted is He, be pleased with him, then answers this question saying that 'There would be no difficulty in investigation, according to this statement, except if the evidence and proof of the *'aqida* of *tawhid* had not been explained in the clearest terms by the Law or if the intellect, on its own, had been charged with finding guidance to this *'aqida*. How could this be when there is not a single proof in support of the *'aqida* of *tawhid* that has not been transmitted in the Book and the sunna in a great variety of forms such that both the ignorant and the clever, the strong and the weak are all equally able to understand them. So there is no excuse for anyone to abandon this obligatory examination – because this is the easiest thing in the world for every person of sound mind.'" Here end the words of as-Sanusi.

After a while, he goes on to say: "If you were to say: 'When one has recourse to the proofs of *tawhid* which are transmitted in the Book, the sunna and the like, then this is in itself *taqlid* because the *mukallaf* is following something which comes not from his own judgement but from another source' – a view close in nature to the fourth statement which holds that *taqlid* should be made of the Qur'an and nothing else – then I would reply: 'I will give you an example which will explain to you the difference between this statement and the fourth statement: if we were to imagine an astronomer who looks at the sky on the first night of the month, then he will know from the science of the stars and their aspects the distance of the crescent moon from the (setting) sun and will know its position. He will be able to sight it despite its extreme thinness. Were it not for his knowledge of the appropriate science he would not have been able to see it. Then someone comes without any knowledge of astronomy

1   al-Hajj – The Pilgrimage: 76
2   al-Baqara – The Cow: 285

and begins to search for the crescent moon in an incorrect way because of his lack of knowledge of the exact location of the crescent. This prevents him from looking in the right direction. For this reason there is no doubt that it is difficult for him to catch sight of the crescent and so he will mostly end up by looking haphazardly about like the weak sighted person without any result. However were this ignorant person to go to the man of knowledge – who had seen the crescent with this own eyes – in order to obtain from him knowledge of how to sight it, then he would find himself in one of two positions:

'First, that he is content with the man of knowledge informing him that the crescent has appeared, that he has seen it with his own eyes and that he has no need to ask him to let him see with his own eyes what the astronomer has already seen. In this case there is no doubt that he is a *muqallid* of the astronomer with respect to the appearance of the crescent moon and it would not be true to say of him that he has knowledge of its appearance. For this reason, if he were asked as to the appearance of the moon on that night then his reply would be: "I have heard such-and-such a person say that it has appeared although I have no knowledge as to the reality of what he said. However, what this means for me is that I am absolutely certain of what the scientist said because of my trust in his knowledge and in his being a truthful person."

'Second, that he is not content merely with the astronomer's telling him of the appearance of the moon and so he asks him to let him see for himself what the other has seen. Thus the astronomer shows him the particular position of the crescent moon and he is able to see it clearly and without difficulty. The appearance of the moon is shown to him by actual observation of what was obvious to the astronomer. There is no doubt, therefore, that even though he relied on the astronomer in the beginning for the sighting, it would not be correct to say that he is a *muqallid* with respect to the appearance of the moon that night. Likewise, it would not be correct for him to reply in the same manner as the first replied, saying that such-and-such an astronomer said this. Rather, he would reply that he has actually seen it, that he had proof that it was a fact and that he had reached certainty. His reply in this matter would be exactly the same as the reply of the astronomer. The difference, then, between these two positions will have made clear to you the difference between what he said in the first statement and the fourth.'" Here ends his discussion.

Then he says with respect to the statement of the *Qasida*: "...meaning that some Shaykhs restrict the difference of opinion of earlier generations regarding *taqlid* saying that what was at issue was a *taqlid* in accordance with the truth – a *taqlid* so absolutely certain that one's self rested assured whatever the circumstances. Thus, even if one were to imagine the *muqallid* following a person of truth who then changed in the *'aqida* he was holding to (and which the *muqallid* had imitated him in) then the *muqallid* would not go back on what he held to. Rather he would keep firm to the truth of what he had imitated him in. However, if his heart had no absolute confidence regarding the *'aqida* he had imitated from the other person but rather his state was such that if the person he was imitating changed what he held to for something else – even to the point of open *kufr*, may Allah protect us from this – then he too would turn his back on what the other had turned his back on. In this case, there is no difference that his *taqlid* of the other is unreliable. There is also agreement that his iman is not reliable. There is no doubt that the majority of those purely making *taqlid* are in the second state – that is, they would turn their back on what they hold to if the person they are imitating goes back on what he holds to and would hold fast to their belief when he holds fast. It is rare that the first state occurs. Only the person who rises above pure *taqlid* to an understanding of some of the correct and fitting examinations which serve to set the heart at rest is successful. In short, the way of sheer *taqlid* is a difficult and obscure way. It is not fitting for the person of *himma* who takes care to preserve his deen and who desires to have mercy on his self by avoiding such a path, for it is a way without safety. We ask Him glorious is He, by His overflowing generosity and His goodness, to guide us to a correct examination of all of our affairs and to establish us firmly in what we say in this world and the next." Here ends as-Sanusi's discussion may Allah benefit us by him and his knowledge, may He cause us to die on his love and the like of him and may He raise us up in their company.

I SAY: "There is no harm in mentioning whatever is evidence for the second statement when intending thereby to relieve the hardship and distress of those who lack the capacity to attain to an understanding of correct examination. Sa'd ad-Deen said in *al-Maqasid*: 'The majority are of the opinion that the iman of a *muqallid* is sound because affirmation is in itself certainty. What I am referring to is holding to something with certainty when it conforms with the truth. Indeed often this acceptance of what conforms to the truth is enough – that is, whatever is most likely to be true is treated as a certainty as long as no contradiction arises in one's mind.'" Here end the words of Sa'd ad-Deen.

Ibn Hajar al-Haytami said in his *Sharh al-Arba'in*: "Know that the obligation to have iman in Allah, His angels, His Books, His Messengers and the Last Day is not conditional upon it being based on examination and the establishing of evidence. Rather having certainty in one's *'aqida* regarding them is enough.

What is preferred by the early generations, the imams of *fatwa* and the *fuqaha* in general is that the iman of the *muqallid* is valid. However, what has been transmitted from the imam of the sunna, Shaykh Abu'l-Hasan al-Ash'ari in prohibition of it is falsely attributed to him as Ustadh Abu'l-Qasim al-Qushayri said, because a *muqallid* in iman in Allah is rarely seen, since we see the speech of the ordinary people full of proofs for the existence of Allah and His attributes – like knowledge, will and power – by means of the existence of this world, and this is not *taqlid*. *Taqlid* is when someone who was raised on top of a mountain hears people say 'people have a Lord Who created them and has created everything without a partner and deserves worship frmo them' and such a person arrives at certainty in his decision by considering them far removed from mistakes and by having a good opinion of them. Thus if he is quite certain that what they told him cannot be contradicted then he will have attained the necessary iman even if he omitted to search for evidence and proof. This is because the establishment of proof is not what is intended in itself rather it is merely a means to obtaining absolute certainty and this he obtained (by *taqlid*). The purpose of this argument is to demonstrate that he is not committing an act of disobedience by abandoning the search for evidence and proof as it has been shown that the goal itself has been attained without it. However, one of the people of knowledge has transmitted that there is a consensus of opinion which condemns this lack of examination as a wrong action and which claims that his absolute certainty in this case cannot be trusted. If he were exposed to doubt, it is argued, then his certainty would disappear and he would be full of hesitation and wavering – as opposed to an absolute certainty arrived at through seeking out evidence – for such a certainty would not disappear if exposed to this doubt. Another matter which also refutes the claim that the iman of the *muqallid* is invalid is that the Companions, may Allah be pleased with them, opened up most of the non-Arab countries to Islam and accepted the iman of the ordinary people, just as they had done in the case of the rude and uncivilised Arabs, even though their iman was acquired under the shadow of the sword or because they were following a chief from amongst them who had accepted Islam. The Companions did not command any of those who became Muslim to make any further examination or investigation (of the matter of *'aqida*) and they did not ask them for the evidence for their affirmation nor did they desire that they be commanded to make this investigation. Moreover any intellectual enquiry, in this case, would certainly conclude that no search for proof on their part was undertaken because it would have been impossible at the time. Thus what the

Companions and the people agreed upon is proof (in itself), that is, proof of the validity of the iman of the *muqallid*. As for the difference of opinion of al-Baqillani, al-Asfarayni and Abu'l-Ma'ali — in the first of his two opinions — they have followed in this matter what the Mu'tazila innovated and have invented this view following the era of the imams of the first generations. It would be impossible and foolish to make stipulations concerning the correctness of someone's iman of things they did not recognise, when they were who they were, in their understanding from Allah, mighty is He and majestic, and in their learning from His Messenger, may the peace and blessings of Allah be upon him, their striving to deliver the news of his *shari'ah* to others and to follow his sunna and his path. As for the proofs which the *mutakallimun* have set down and which the people of logical argument (*jadaliyun*) have arranged in order, these have been invented by later generations. The earlier generations of rightly acting persons did not preoccupy themselves with any of this. For this reason, al-Ghazali and others have preferred that the common people without any capacity to understand such proofs should not preoccupy themselves with them — indeed that it is forbidden for them if they fear that doubt might arise on encountering some difficulty when investigating such proofs because of the difficulty of removing such doubts from their hearts." Here ends the discussion of al-Haytami.

His saying: "... if someone who was raised on top of a mountain" is similar to that of as-Sa'd in *Sharh al-Qasida* where it reads: "If it is said that most of the people of Islam held to *taqlid*, confined themselves to Islam and that the Companions and those imams and Khalifs after them were content with this of them and they applied the laws of the Muslims to them, then what reason can there be for this difference of opinion? and what reason can there be for many of the *'ulama* and the *mujtahids* being of the view that the iman of the *muqallid* is not sound? — then we would reply: 'The difference of opinion is not concerning those who grew up in the territories of Islam — in the towns, villages and deserts where the life and teachings of the Prophet, may the peace and blessings of Allah be upon him, and what he brought of miracles had been transmitted in an uninterrupted succession; nor is it concerning those who reflect on the creation of the heavens and the earth and the alternation of the night and the day — because all such people are used to investigate and seek proofs — but rather it refers to someone who lives high up in the mountains, who has not reflected on the realms of the heavens and the earth and who is then informed by someone of his obligation to have an *'aqida*. It refers to such a person when he affirms what he is told just on the strength of having heard it without thinking or reflecting upon it.'" Here end the words of as-Sa'd.

In *Ikhtisar Hawi as-Suyuti* he says: "As-Suyuti was asked, may Allah, exalted is He, be content with him, in the following lines of verse:

O you who are alone as the *mujtahid* of the age

O source of the utmost clarity, honesty, knowledge and action.

What is the definition of our *tawhid* of Allah, Who created us

He, exalted is He, Who is exalted above any 'where' or 'likeness'?

He replied: "It has been transmitted to us with a sound chain of narration by way of al-Muzani that a man asked him about something to do with knowledge of *kalam* and he replied: 'I strongly dislike this, indeed I forbid this just as ash-Shafi'i forbade it for I heard ash-Shafi'i say: "Malik was asked about *kalam* and *tawhid* and he replied: 'It is inconceivable that the Prophet, may the peace and blessings of Allah be upon him, taught his *umma* how to clean themselves after going to the toilet but did not teach them *tawhid* – since he said, may the peace and blessings of Allah be upon him, "I have been commanded to fight people until they say there is no god but Allah" – in other words that which prevents blood from being shed or wealth from being appropriated is the reality of *tawhid*.'"[1] This, then, is the reply of Imam Malik, may Allah be pleased with him, and this is what I also replied."

Also in *al-Hawi* there is what as-Suyuti says in refutation of those who claim that logic is obligatory on every person and that the *tawhid* of someone who has no knowledge of it is not correct: "If they do not intend the establishment of proof based on the principles of logic but rather the kind of unconditional proof which is contained in the nature of every person, even the elderly, the desert Arabs and children – like the proof obtained by way of the stars which affirms the stars must have a Creator or the proofs afforded by the very existence of the heavens, the earth, the rivers and fruits and others things – then all this does not need logic or any other means, and the common people and uncivilised tribes may all become *muminun* by this method."

In al-Munawi's commentary on the narration, "When the end of time comes and the views (of the various sects) differ, then hold to the deen of the people of the countryside and women," he says: "In other words, hold to their *'aqida* and proceed using their way and methods by obtaining a very basic iman and holding to the manifest aspect of *'aqida* by means of *taqlid* and by busying oneself with good actions – for the danger in abandoning this way is great, as al-Ghazali has noted. Whoever has not heard of the differences of the *madhhabs* and the

---

[1] The full hadith indicates that the blood and wealth of all those (i.e. the Muslims) who pronounce the *shahadas* are inviolate.

manner in which people lead each other astray has an easier time than people who have heard of such things. For this reason Imam ar-Razi – as transmitted by Hafidh Ibn Hajar – has made this penetrating comment: "Whoever holds on to the deen of the old women will be successful." As-Sam'ani said in the supplement to al-Hamdani: "I heard the Imam of the Haramayn [al-Juwayni] say: '[I read] fifty thousand in fifty thousand (i.e. absolutely incontrovertible transmissions), then I left the people of Islam with their Islam and their outward knowledge. I set out on the wide sea of knowledge and I dived into that which the people of Islam had forbidden – all in my search for truth and my flight from *taqlid*. Now I have returned from the action I undertook to the word of truth "You must take on the deen of the old women," for if the Real does not reach me with His kindness and I do not die on the deen of the old women, and if the end of my affair is not sealed with truth and the words of sincerity 'There is no god but Allah' then woe to al-Juwayni's son." Here end the words of al-Munawi.

Ahmad Zarruq said in *Sharh al-Waghleesiya*: "Iman is attesting to what has to be attested to, irrespective of whether it is by means of *taqlid* or *ijtihad* – as long as the person being imitated is a man of knowledge and the person following him does not go back on what he holds to if the person he is imitating abandons what is correct."

He also said: "Expertise in matters of *'aqida* is not necessary but rather a knowledge of its principles. Indeed it is not permitted for the common people to delve beyond the above mentioned principles for this would cause confusion in their *'aqida*."

Imam al-Ghazali said, may Allah, exalted is He, be content with him: "The ordinary people are harmed by inner truths just as the dung beetle is harmed by rose water and musk. The Prophet, may the peace and blessings of Allah be upon him, said: 'Speak to the people in a language they understand – do you want them to deny Allah and His Messenger?' He also said, may peace and blessings be upon him: 'I have been commanded to address people in accordance with the capacity of their intellects.'" Here end his words, may Allah be content with him.

He explained the principles which hehas mentioned by saying: "They refer to those matter which one is under an obligation to attest to and confirm. Hafidh Ibn Hajar said: 'The Imam of the Haramayn said: "The *'ulama* are in agreement that it is obligatory to have knowledge of Allah, exalted is He, while they differ as to what constitutes the first portion of this obligation. Some say it is knowledge while others that it is examination of and reflection upon the evidence.'" Al-Muqtarih said: 'There is no difference of opinion that the first of obligations to be addressed and intended is knowledge, and the first of obligations – with respect to the capacity it affords to carry out one's individual immediate obligation – is the intention to examine evidence and proof.' However, there is a serious difference of opinion and a very lengthy discussion about transmitting it as the, so much so that one group of *'ulama* have transmitted the opposite of this consensus and have supported their claim by evidence from the people of the first generation who were in accord as to the acceptability of the Islam of those who came into the deen without inquiry. The narrations on this subject are very numerous. The people of the first generations responded to this by arguing that the *kuffar* used to defend and fight for their deen but then their abandoning it was proof for them that the truth had manifested to the *kuffar*. All this means that the least amount of investigation and reflection is enough with respect to the knowledge mentioned above – contrary to what others have determined. Moreover, the words of Allah, exalted is He: 'So set your face firmly towards the Deen, as a pure natural believer, Allah's natural pattern on which He has made mankind'[1] and the hadith 'Every child is born in *fitra* – Allah's natural pattern for mankind' – are both manifest proofs which basically support this matter. More will be said about this later in the Book of *Tawhid*, insha'Allah, exalted is He. The model and example, Abu Muhammad ibn Abi *Jamra*, has transmitted from Abu'l-Waleed al-Baji from Abu Ja'far as-Samani, one of the leading Ash'aris, that he heard him say: 'This is one of the matters of the Mu'tazilis which has remained in the *madhhab* and there is only Allah, exalted is He, upon whom one can call upon for help.'" Here ends the discussion of Ibn Hajar.

There is also the following in the Commentary on *The Book of Iman* of al-Bukhari and in the Commentary on *The Book of Tawhid* during as-Sam'ani's discussion in which he criticises the way of the scholars of *kalam*: "It suffices to say when you hear what is necessary of their way and method that were we to put what they say into practice and demand of people what they make mention of, one would have to declare that the ordinary people are all *kuffar* because they only make simple deductions and inferences. If this way were shown them most of them would not understand let alone become capable of examining any proofs. The aim of their *tawhid* is to hold to what they find their imams holding to with regard to matters of *'aqida* in the deen, to cling fast to them and to persevere in the duties of worship and the regular practice of *dhikr* with a heart at peace, purified of any ambiguity and doubt. For this reason, you

1   ar-Rum – The Romans: 29

see them unswerving in their *'aqida* even if their limbs were to be severed from their bodies, one after the other. What a blessing is this certainty! What better thing is there than this peace of mind?! If these people were to be declared *kuffar* – and they are the vast majority, the very body of the *umma* – then it would mean the end of Islam and the destruction of the lighthouse of the deen. And Allah it is Whom one must ask for help."

وَكُلُّ تَكْلِيفٍ بِشَرْطِ الْعَقْلِ

مَعَ الْبُلُوغِ بِدَمٍ أَوْ حَمْلٍ

12 Every imposition of a duty is conditional upon the person being of sane mind, having reached puberty – recognised by the onset of menstruation or pregnancy (in the case of young women)

أَوْ بِمَنِيٍّ أَوْ بِإِنْبَاتِ الشَّعَرِ

أَوْ بِثَمَانِ عَشْرَةَ حَوْلاً ظَهَرْ

13 or by the presence of sperm, or the growth of (pubic) hair or (in the absence of any of these signs), the completion of eighteen years.

Mayyara said: "There is a difference of opinion as to (the nature of) imposition of responsibility (*takleef*) – some have said that it means the compulsion or coercion of that for which there is responsibility, while others have said it is seeking the performance of that for which there is responsibility. Both views are valid although the second as an obligation is recommended."

There are three conditions to such an obligation:

1. Intellect (*'aql*), that is that one is of sane mind, and it refers to the capacity to receive knowledge. It is also said that it is the capacity to be able to discriminate between what is beautiful and ugly. According to the *Qamous*, "it is a spiritual light by means of which the self recognises both actual (*daruri*) and theoretical (*nadhari*) matters. The beginning of its coming into being is when the child forms (in the womb) and then it continues to grow until it reaches perfection at puberty." This is what he intended in speaking about this condition. Then he said:

2. The second condition of *takleef* is maturity (*bulough*) which is as Imam al-Mazari said: "It is a capacity which appears in the child by means of which the child leaves its state of childhood for the state of manhood. Not many people

are knowledgeable of the nature of this faculty and so the Legislator has placed signs by which the attainment of such a capacity may be ascertained."

There are five signs – three of which are common to both male and females – first, is dreaming of sexual intercourse, and it is the (capacity for) emission of seminal fluids. Ibn Shas said: "The capacity for emission of sperm (from the man) or fluid (from the woman) is established by their attesting to this, as long, that is, as this appears at all possible, that is, unless the existence of any doubt contradicts this; second, the growth of hair, that is, course hair, not fine, downy hair (about the private parts)." Ibn al-'Arabi said: "This can be ascertained by looking in the mirror and carefully examining the usual place of growth."

Muhammad ibn 'Arafa said: "This is refuted by 'Izz ad-Deen who said that this is the same as looking directly at the private parts [which is not allowed], and likewise Ibn al-Qattan."

3. Age – there is a difference opinion as to how many years. The well known view is that it is eighteen, while others have said seventeen, others fifteen.

Two of these signs are particular to females, and they are pregnancy and menstruation. Ibn Naji said that the inclusion of pregnancy is disputable as it can only take place after the emission of fluid on the woman's part, in which case it thus depends on her capacity to produce this fluid. Shihab al-Qarafi has added the smell of the armpits to these signs while others have added the distinguishing feature of the splaying of the lobules of the nose; according to al-Barzali, one should take a thread and draw it around the neck joining the two ends between his teeth: if one's head can pass through it then one has reached puberty, otherwise one has not. Sayyidi 'Abd ar-Rahman 'Abd al-Qadir al-Fasi said: "There is no justification for the use of this thread according to the *fuqaha*." Using what he said above as an example, Mayyara said: "The third of the conditions of obligation is that the *da'wa* of the Prophet, may the peace and blessings of Allah be upon him, has reached the person in question." Here end the words of Mayyara.

The immediate meaning of what he says is that this is conditional upon the *da'wa* of the Prophet but not the miracles having reached the person in question, – this is what Ibn 'Arafa holds to as does Abu Mutafannin in his commentary on the hadith in Muslim: "By the One in whose hand is the *nafs* of Muhammad, there is no Christian or Jew from this *umma* who hears of me and then dies – without having iman in what I was sent with – but that he will be among the companions of the Fire." The text of it is; "'Iyad said: 'This indicates that those whom the call to Islam and the command of the Prophet, may the peace and blessings of Allah be upon him, have not reached are excused because the way of attaining iman in these two matters is, for those who were present at the time, by witnessing a miracle and, for those who did not witness it, the correct transmission of this miracle – as opposed to iman in Allah, exalted is He, whose way is investigation and examination.'

"I say: The gist of his words is that iman in Him is conditional firstly upon the *da'wa* having reached the person concerned. He considers that this iman then actually comes about when news of the miracle reaches the person. The first part of this, namely the *da'wa* reaching the person, is the literal meaning of the hadith. However, some have interpreted the hadith saying that the words mean 'there is no one who hears of me and my miracles are clear to him and who dies but that ....' It is as if the Shaykh is saying that 'this is conditional upon the *da'wa* reaching him not that the miracles have been transmitted to him.' Indeed it is not unlikely that on the frontiers of civilisation or on some isolated island there are people whom the *da'wa* has not reached. The judgement regarding them is that they are under no imposition (to perform any of the obligations), this being a basic legal principle, about which there is consensus, and which is founded on the saying of, exalted is He: '*We never punish until We have sent a Messenger*'[1] – as well as other *ayats*. On the basis of this hadith and this principle we can conclude with certainty that the *da'wa* had reached Yajuj and Majuj because of what has come to us in the *sahih* hadith regarding their being sent, as people of the Fire, to be tormented.

"It has also been said that he, may the peace and blessings of Allah be upon him, warned them during the Night Journey. Just as iman is conditional upon the call to Islam reaching a person so too is an understanding of one's obligation. Thus if one of the non-Arabs does not understand (what he is being called to) then he is treated as someone whom the *da'wa* has not reached." The words of Abu Mutafannin.

'Ali ibn 'Abd as-Sadiq said that the meaning of (Ibn 'Ashir's words) "the completion of eighteen years" is that it means it is completed and does not mean having begun the second year.

---

1 al-Isra' – The Night Journey: 15

The Book of Basic Principles Regarding 'Aqida

The Book of Basic Principles Regarding 'Aqida

يَجِبُ لِلَّهِ الْوُجُودُ وَالْقِدَمْ

كَذَا الْبَقَاءُ وَالْغِنَى الْمُطْلَقُ عَمْ

14   It is necessarily true that Allah have existence and that this existence is from before endless time, and likewise that He possess going-on, and absolute independence universally

Wujud – existence

'Ali ibn 'Abd as-Sadiq said: "He has begun with it as others have done as it is a root and foundation underlying conceiving something (*ta'aqqul*) – since the judgement regarding the obligatory nature of the things that are necessarily true of Allah and the impossibility of what He kept Himself aloof from, exalted is He, is derived from His existence, exalted is He. His mention of His existence at the beginning is analogous to giving precedence to conceptualising (*tasawwur*) over confirmation or attestation (*tasdeeq*) as His existence denotes a quality corresponding to the Essence itself (*sifa nafsiyya*)[1] [which indicates the very substance and reality (of Allah)], according to al-Ash'ari and his followers. Its essential reality is that it is necessarily true of the essence as long, that is, as the essence is not considered to be caused by a cause or reason, like ascribing a space to a corporeal body for it must necessarily be true as long as the body exists – for one is not ascribing any cause or reason to the constancy and immutability of this space in relation to the body. Thus he has treated it – that is existence – as an attribute of the essence since it is described by it verbally when one says: 'the essence of our Lord exists.' As for

---

1   It is called essential (*nafsiyya*) since it indicates the essence itself (*nafs adh-dhat*), rather than any meaning in addition to it. And it is one attribute only: existence. *Tahdheeb sharh as-Sanusiyya – Umm al-Barahin*, Sa'd 'Abd al-Lateef Fouda.

the view that it is additional to the essence, as Imam ar-Razi and the majority hold, this is based on their treating it as an attribute manifest in the outward (*sifa zahir*)."

Qidam – Existence from before time

"Ibn as-Subki and al-Jalal al-Mahalli said: 'The truth of the matter is what al-Ash'ari declared, that is: "Existence from before endless time (*qidam*) necessarily belongs to Him, exalted is He, and this means denying any non-existence prior to (His) existence." If you wish, you may say: "It is an expression of a lack of any beginning to existence" and if you wish, you may say: "It is an expression of lack of any inception to existence" and all three expressions convey the same meaning.' As-Sanusi said it.

"Is it permitted to ascribe the name *al-Qadeem* to Him or not? One says of him: 'Existence from before endless time (*qidam*) necessarily belongs to Him' and other similar expressions. Various Shaykhs have differed about that. Al-'Iraqi said, commenting on the words of as-Subki: 'Al-Haleemi has counted it as one of the names (of Allah) although there is no specific mention of it in the Book but it does occur in the sunna.'" Here end the words of 'Ali ibn 'Abd as-Sadiq.

Baqa' – Going on

Then he says: "And likewise it is necessarily true that Allah, exalted is He, possesses going on, that is the denial of any non-existence to come with respect to existence. There is a difference of opinion as to the nature of existence from before endless time (*qidam*)[1] and going on. Those who have investigated the matter thoroughly are of the opinion that they are two negative attributes, that is that each of them divests our Lord of something which it is not fitting He be ascribed with – and this is the truth and neither refer to any meaning other then mental concepts. And Allah knows best.

Ghina' mutlaq – Absolute independence

As for his saying "absolute independence", as-Sanusi said in *al-Wusta*: "It is also necessarily true that He, exalted is He, exist by Himself – is self-existent – (*qa'im binafsihi*), that is, in essence, such that He is in no need of place and it is inconceivable that He be an attribute. There are those who have interpreted His existence by Himself as his total lack of need of place or one

---

1 The text has *'adam* (non-existence) which I have taken to be a mistake since it is *qidam* pre-existence that is a negative attribute like *baqa'* and not *'adam*. Ed.

who particularises – and this is more specific than the first interpretation and it excludes substance's sharing with Him in this attribute."

Ahmad Mayyara said: "his mention of 'universally' – *'amm* at the end of the first verse is an adverb emphasising the absoluteness the independence and freedom from need. The word was originally *'amma* in Arabic and then the first *alif* was omitted just as it may be omitted in the word *barr*, which was originally *barr*. Then the second *alif* was omitted, a *sukun* (the sign for vowellessness) was added in accordance with the dialect of Rabi'a and the second *mim* removed.

وَخُلْقُهُ لِخَلْقِهِ بِلاَ مِثَالٍ

وَوَحْدَةُ الذَّاتِ وَوَصْفٍ وَالْفِعَالُ

15   And His being different from His creation without resemblance, And His Oneness of essence, of attribute and action

MUKHALAFA – HIS BEING DIFFERENT FROM HIS CREATION

'Ali ibn 'Abd as-Sadiq said: "This means that there is absolutely no resemblance between the creation and Him, not with respect to His essence, or attributes or actions. The reality of this negation is the denying of any corporeality or accidental, inessential nature – or everything pertaining to these two. Allah, exalted is He, says: '*Nothing is like Him. He is the All-Hearing, the All-Seeing*'[1] – meaning there is no essence like His essence, no name like His name, no action like His action, and no attribute like His attribute except through a linguistic correspondence. The essence from before endless time is too illustrious that it possess an attribute of an in-time creational nature (*haditha*) just as it is inconceivable for an in-time creational essence to possess an attribute of beyond endless time. His saying, may the peace and blessings of Allah be upon him: 'Allah created Adam on his form' was uttered for a (specific) reason – as al-Jalal as-Suyuti explained – namely "that the Messenger of Allah, may the peace and blessings of Allah be upon him, on seeing a person strike a slave of his on the face, addressed him saying: 'Do not do that for Allah has created Adam on his form' that is He created Adam on the form of that slave so you should respect that form", and this is a fitting answer.

"However the word 'form' may also refer to affair, judgement and business, that is, he may do with his affair what Allah wants, such as commanding (to

---

1   ash-Shura – Counsel: 9

the good) and forbidding (evil), acting justly, with mercy and the like because of the fact that he is Khalifa on earth – this the meaning of 'form' he transmits in *al-Yawaqeet* from Muhyiddeen – and it is also a fitting answer.

"Ustadh Abu Ishaq al-Isfarayni, may Allah have mercy on him said: 'Everything the *mutakallimun* have said regarding *tawhid*, the people of truth have encompassed in two phrases: the first – the belief that Allah is unlike anything that can be imagined by the mind and the second – the belief that His essence, exalted is He, is not like any other essence and is not separated from or cut off from the attributes. This they have emphasised by quoting the words of, exalted is He: *"And no one is comparable to Him*[1].*"*'"

"Shaykh Muhyiddeen said: 'Nothing veils men except the existence of likenesses, and for this reason the Creator, exalted is He, has rejected any likeness for Himself in order to distance His purity (*tanzeehan li-qudsihi*) (from anything other than Him). Whenever you imagine Him, represent or picture Him in your mind, then Allah, exalted is He, is contrary to this, and this is the conviction of the community of the Muslims until the Final Hour.'" Here end the words of 'Ali ibn 'Abd as-Sadiq.

ISSUE: Ahmad Mayyara said: "The Imam, the *'alim* Abu 'Abdallah Sayyidi Muhammad ibn Jalal was asked: 'May one say: "The Lord, blessed is He and exalted, is neither inside the world nor outside it?"' The questioner said, 'This I have heard from one of our Shaykhs although someone objected to this, saying this is declaring two contradictory statements.' One of our *fuqaha'* has commented on this issue saying: 'He is the whole by means of which every thing exists', and has claimed that it is from Imam al-Ghazali. Some have responded that this question is extremely difficult and that it is not permitted to pose this question. Some have claimed that Ibn Miqlash responded in his commentary on the *Risala* by saying: 'This is what we say, what we are convinced of and what we hold to, that is, that He is not in the world and not outside it, and the (very) incapacity to comprehend is itself understanding, because of the establishment of clear proofs of that, both with regard to the intellect and to what has been transmitted (of the divine teaching).'

"As for what has been transmitted, there is the Book, the sunna and the consensus of the *'ulama*. As for the Book, then there are His words, exalted is He: '*Nothing is like Him. He is the All-Hearing, the All-Seeing*'[2] for if He were in the world or outside of it, some kind of resemblance or correspondence to Him would exist, and an explanation of any such correspondence would be

---

1 al-Ikhlas – Sincerity: 4
2 ash-Shura – Counsel: 9

clear. As for the first (part of the statement), this is because if He were in it, He would be of the same genus or kind as it and what would be necessarily true for the one would be necessarily true for the other. As for the second, if He were outside of it, then this would necessarily entail either that He were connected to it or separated from it, either by a finite distance or an infinite distance – all of which would lead to His need of a being who particularised him. As for the sunna, it is the saying of the Prophet, may the peace and blessings of Allah be upon him: 'Allah was and there was nothing with Him and He is now as He was.' As for the *ijma'*, it is that the people of truth are all agreed that Allah, exalted is He, has no direction or locus, that is, no above, no beneath, no right side, no left side, no before and no behind. As for the intellect, this has been explained completely in the above discussion of the question of inseparability – with respect to the words of Allah, exalted is He: *'Nothing is like Him. He is the All-Hearing, the All-Seeing.'*[1]

"As for the objection that he is making two contradictory statements, this does not hold true: a contradiction may be said to apply when something is described with one of two contrary qualities and then with the other, but when it is incorrect to assert that both apply in this manner, and when it is not possible to describe it with either of the two, then there is in fact no (real) contradiction – like when one were to say, 'A wall is neither blind nor seeing.' Here there is no contradiction despite the truth of the two contrasting assertions because the wall cannot be described with the one rather than the other (as both are true). This is similar to saying with regard to the Creator: '(There is) no above and no below (in His regard)' – so reckon on this basis!

"As for the one who said: 'He is the whole' claiming that this is from al-Ghazali, his argument tends in the direction of that of the philosophers – adopted by some of the people of *tasawwuf*. But this is an improbable expression. The reply given by one of them, namely that 'this question is extremely difficult and that it is not permitted to pose this question' is not correct – because of the manifest clarity of the proofs available. Moreover, if it is correctly transmitted from Ibn Miqlash, then it should be disregarded in this matter because of his lack of expertise in the methods of the *mutakallimun* and because most of the *fuqaha*' have no experience of this, let alone expertise in it." Here end the words of Mayyara.

Wahdah – Oneness

As for Ibn 'Ashir's saying 'Oneness of essence', Mayyara said: "Sixth: This

---

1   ash-Shura – Counsel: 9

'Oneness' means He, exalted is He, has no second in His essence, or in His attributes or in His actions. There are therefore three aspects to this Oneness: the oneness of the essence, the oneness of the attributes and the oneness of the actions.

"Oneness of the essence refutes the notion that His essence, exalted is He, is composite or that there is another essence similar to the sublime essence. It refutes plurality or multiplicity with respect to the reality of this essence, both with respect to anything (that might be imagined to be) connected to it or disconnected to it. The oneness of the attributes refutes multiplicity in the reality of each and every attribute, again both with respect to anything connected or disconnected to it. So the knowledge belonging to our Lord, majestic is He and mighty, has no second resembling it, neither a knowledge (which might be imagined to be) connected, that is existent by virtue of the supreme essence, nor disconnected, that is existent by some other essence. Thus He knows everything there is to be known (*ma'lumat*) of which there is no end, by one knowledge which has no multiplicity and no second to it whatsoever – and compare all the other attributes of our Lord, mighty is He and majestic, in this manner.

"The oneness of actions refutes that (one could imagine) there be anywhere else a bringing into being by anything which is other than from Allah, exalted is He, in any actions – for our Lord, He alone, is the Bringer into being of everything in creation without any mediator. In short, the oneness of actions refutes the existence of any rival of Allah, exalted is He, in His divinity and refutes any partner with Him in the whole of creation – there is no one other than Him who acts upon any of it.

"This Oneness which is firmly established for His essence, exalted is He, does not mean that it reaches such a fine and minute degree that it is not to be subdivided – for otherwise it would necessarily follow that He be a single, unique substance (*jawhar fard* – atom); nor in the sense that He is a meaning which does not accept subdivision – for otherwise it would necessarily follow that He be an attribute which is not self existent, and this is inconceivable."

وَقُدْرَةٌ إِرَادَةٌ عِلْمٌ حَيَاةٌ

سَمْعٌ كَلَامٌ بَصَرٌ ذِي وَاجِبَاتُ

16 and power, will, knowledge, life, hearing, speech, sight; these are necessarily true (for Him)

QUDRA – POWER

Mayyara said: "Power is an attribute by means of which that which is potential or latent is brought into or out of being in accordance with (His) will, that is, by means of which is facilitated the bringing out of that which is potential from non-existence into existence and the bringing it out of existence into non-existence, irrespective of whether that which is potential has corporeality or is a property [of something], whether it is acquired or not, possesses life or not."

'Ali ibn 'Abd as-Sadiq said: "Power is a timeless attribute which acts upon all that is predestined (*muqaddarat*) when it comes into contact with them – and what is meant by *muqaddarat* is anything that is potential and possible. His saying 'when this power comes into contact with anything that is predetermined' is an indication that these comings into contact with power are events within creational time (*haditha*), and this is a matter for those who are able to investigate closely." Ibn Naji at-Tanoukhi said it.

IRADA – WILL

Ahmad Mayyara said: "The will is an attribute by which the particularisation of the potential with some of that which is conceivable for it is facilitated, and that means that all potentialities have an equal relationship to His power, exalted is He, – thus if this (will) were to connect itself in particular to one of them rather than another then incapacity would necessarily follow (with respect to the other potentialities). It is therefore necessary to specify some of the potentialities as occurring without anything corresponding from another attribute – and this is nothing other than (the effect of) the attribute of will since we would not be wrong in saying that Allah, exalted is He, willed the existence of this potentiality (for example) and He did not will this other potentiality, rather He willed its non-existence. Indeed, this is proof of the utmost perfection (of Allah) because His disposing, exalted is He, with respect to the potentialities, is purely by virtue of (His) will and choosing, and there is no cause (to which His disposing is subject) with respect to any one of these potentialities and there is no coercion or force as Allah, exalted is He, said: "*And your Lord creates and chooses whatever He wills.*"[1]

If you were to say: "Allah has been able to determine, decree (and apportion – *qaddara*) this existent potentiality but not its opposite, then this would be false because it implies a shortcoming, namely that of incapacity. However, with respect to all the rest of the attributes, like knowledge, speech, hearing and sight, it would not be correct to designate particularisation to them

---

1 al-Qasas – The Story: 68

for particularisation denotes an influencing (over something) while these attributes do not exert an influence." Here end the words of Mayyara from *Sharh al-Muqaddimat*.

'Ali ibn 'Abd as-Sadiq said: "There is a difference of opinion as to whether 'will' (*irada*) may be designated as 'wish' (*mashee'a*) or vice versa, or whether they express the particular and the general in regard to each other. In *al-Yawaqeet* he said that what the majority hold to is that 'will' may be termed 'wish' and vice versa. Another said however that *irada* is more specific than *mashee'a* and that *mashee'a* is more general because it refers to both the bringing into being (of something) and sending (it) to non-existence and 'will' only refers to the bringing into being of all potentialities (*al-mumkinat*) – which are connected to relative (*idafi*) non-existence – and so this (will) is directed at non-existence and brings it into existence. The correct view is the first. The word *al-irada al-azaliya* (the will pertaining to before endless time) is also used to refer to the decree (*qada'*). As for the terms *rida* (Allah's good pleasure) and *mahabba* (Allah's love) they both denote the same thing as he has made clear in *al-Yawaqeet*.

"Yet another (Ibn Naji at-Tanoukhi) said: 'The *'ulama'* differ as to whether it is permitted to say that Allah, exalted is He, wills *kufr* and disobedience or not.' Some are of the opinion that this is not permitted (of Him) – even if this is correct in the domain of *'aqida* – because to say such a thing is to have bad *adab* with Allah, exalted is He, and might lead some to imagine that disobedience is a good thing and that man is commanded to it. Others have said that it is permitted – and this is correct.

"Shaykh Abu'l-Hasan ash-Shadhili, may Allah be content with him, used to say: 'Shaytan is like the male and the *nafs* is like the female, and the origin of a wrong action between them is like the birth of a child from the mother and father for (in reality) it is not they who brought it into being although it appeared from them.' Taj ad-Deen ibn 'Ata'ullah said: 'The meaning of these words of the Shaykh is that the person of intellect has no doubt that the child is not the (real) creation of the father and the mother, and that it was not them who brought it into being but rather that it is related to them by the fact that it appeared from them. Likewise the *muminun* have no doubt that disobedience is not from Shaytan and the *nafs* but rather it was by way of them, and because its appearance was by means of them it is ascribed to them. So the relationship of disobedience to Shaytan is a secondary connection, and its relation to Allah, exalted is He, is a relation of justice and bringing into being – just as He created obedience by His generosity so He has created disobedience by virtue of His justice: "*Say, everything comes from Allah.*"[1]

"One of the gnostics said: 'The secret in the bringing into being of Shaytan is the wiping clean of the impurities of relativity by means of him: he has been made into the 'cleaning cloth' of this world and it is to him that are ascribed the causes of disobedience and the existence of *kufr*, negligence and forgetfulness. Have you not heard the words of Allah, exalted is He: "*No one made me forget it except Shaytan*"[2] and the words of Allah, exalted is He: "*This is part of Shaytan's handiwork*"[3] and other *ayats*.'

"Reflect upon this for it is a precious statement." Here end the words of 'Ali ibn 'Abd as-Sadiq.

'Ilm – Knowledge

Of his mention of the word 'knowledge', the commentator said: "And this is an attribute by means of which that which is known (*ma'lum*) – in whatever form it might be – is discovered in such a way as which does not admit of contradiction in any way whatsoever. He said in *Sharh al-Muqaddimat*: "... what he means by 'the known' is everything it is valid to know, that is, every thing that is necessarily true, everything which is inconceivable and everything which is conceivable."

'Ali ibn 'Abd as-Sadiq said: "Al-Jalal al-Mahalli said: 'He, exalted is He, knows every potentiality but stands aloof from the general, universal matters or particulars. As for the general things, He has an absolute knowledge of them, and as for the particulars, the consensus of the people of penetrating understanding is that He also knows them. The Jews, Christians, fire-worshippers and the Samaritans were asked about this in the land of Egypt and all replied: "Nothing escapes the knowledge of our Lord" – so I do not know what those who transmit the following from them can be thinking of when they say: "Allah, exalted is He, does not know the particulars." It may well be that those who relate this from them have taken it by inferring it from their *madhhab* – but an inference from a *madhhab* is not a *madhhab* itself, according to the preferred opinion.' Here end the words from *al-Yawaqeet*.

"In *Sharh ar-Risala* of Zarruq there is: 'They say: "He knows them in detail" while one does not say: "as a whole" (*jumlatan*) which would imply (a degree of) ignorance; nor is it said "both as a whole and in detail" because this would be a contradiction in terms.' So reflect upon this together with what precedes

---

1 al-Nisa' – Women:77
2 al-Kahf – The Cave: 62
3 al-Qasas – The Story: 14

it." Here end 'Ali ibn 'Abd as-Sadiq's words.

May I mention a subtle point: In one of the works of as-Suyuti I read the following: "A Fire-worshipper asked Abu Muhammad as-Sahri, may Allah, exalted is He, have mercy on him, 'Does Allah perceive an end to the Garden?' thinking that he would reply with a 'yes' or a 'no'[1] whereupon he answered: 'Allah knows the Garden with no end', and the person who questioned became confused and filled with astonishment."

As-Sam' wa'l-Basar – Hearing and Sight

Regarding Ibn 'Ashir's mention of 'hearing and sight', Mayyara said in *al-Muqaddimat*: "(His) hearing from before endless time is an attribute by which each existent is revealed as it is, manifest in such a way that it is necessarily distinct from each other thing; this holds true, likewise, for sight; and perception (*al-idrak*) – for those who are of the opinion (that it is one of His attributes) – is also similar to these two[2]." In his commentary on them, he says: "These attributes are shared in their connection with what exists, whether eternal or in-time, except that in the evident world they are particular to some beings because He, exalted is He, has particularised the [beings] for that. And if Allah, glorious is He, had broken the norm respecting that it would have been valid for them to be connected to all other beings. For this reason it is conceivable for created beings to see our Lord, blessed is He and exalted, according to the *madhhab* of the people of the truth, and it is conceivable for them to hear His ancient speech which subsists by His exalted essence, along with the fact that vision in the evident world is ordinarily connected to bodies and their beings, and hearing in the evident world is ordinarily connected to letters and sounds. Since it is inconceivable for there to be particularisation in the attributes of our Lord, blessed is He and exalted, because that would necessarily require the need of one who particularises, who would necessarily be originated, then it is necessarily true that His attributes be connected with everything that is fitting for it. Since the [attributes] are necessarily true, it is not possible that they be described with anything which would necessitate their origination in time. So the principle is that everything which our Master, blessed is He and exalted, accepts of essential attributes and their perfections, then they are necessarily true because of the impossibility of Him, mighty is He and majestic, being described with things that are merely conceivable."

---

1 The 'no' would have been to ascribe lack of knowledge to Him. Ed.
2 al-An'am – Livestock: 104 – *"Eyesight cannot perceive Him but He perceives eyesight."*

Kalam – Speech

Of Ibn 'Ashir's mention of the word 'speech', Mayyara said that as-Sanusi said in al-Muqaddimat: "Speech from before endless time refers to a self-existent meaning, expressed by various terms ('ibarat), and which is distinct from the nature of the letters and exalted above the part and the whole, from bringing earlier [in the syntactical order] or putting back, from silence, from melody, from inflections in word endings and from all the other kinds of modifications, and connection with what relates to knowledge of anything which is connected, conditional or related (al-muta'alliqat) – rather than absolute and necessary."

In explaining this he said: "There is no doubt that the Book, the sunna and ijma' are explicit in their attesting to the speech of our Lord, majestic is He and mighty, with respect to (His) command, promise, threat, His giving of the good news (of the Garden), (His) warning (of the Fire), and His informing (mankind). Moreover, intellectual proof indicates by way of the intellect that anyone who has knowledge of something may validly speak of it. Our Lord, blessed is He and exalted, has knowledge of all things that may be known and so it would be correct to assert that speech – with respect to all these things which may be known – belongs to Him. And every time it would be correct to assert that our Lord, mighty is He and majestic, may be described as possessing this (knowledge), then this assertion would be an absolutely necessary ascription to Him because of the impossibility that He be described with a quality that is (merely) a possibility or (merely) permitted. Therefore, that speech is possessed by Him, exalted is He, is necessarily true." Then he says: "It follows clearly that the truth upon which the people of the sunna are agreed is the conviction that speech belongs to our Lord, blessed is He and exalted, and that it is not of a kind composed of letters and sounds, that it is free of (any notion) that (one utterance of His) precedes or follows (chronologically another), free of the particular or the general, of melody or vowel inflections at the end of words, or of silence and anything else pertaining to the characteristics of our speech in creational time – irrespective of whether orally or mentally – since all of that would necessarily mean shortcoming and dumbness and origination in time, whereas His speech, majestic is He and exalted, is a necessary attribute like the necessary attribute of (His being) before endless time or (His) going on; and it is an attribute which is connected to everything to which His knowledge connects, and its essential nature is veiled from creation, having no likeness, intellectually speaking, nor can it even be imagined or supposed; neither is there a likeness in existence, nor in estimation. That is like His sublime essence and all the other noble attributes."

In short, this is an attestation that (His) speech is from before endless time and that it is inconceivable that there exist in it any attribute from among the attributes of speech belonging to this in-time world – that is, that there be any letters or sounds or anything else which he mentions afterwards (in the above description). Rather, it is an attribute of a meaning which is existent from before endless time and which is self existent by His sublime essence and which is referred to by various terms such as the Tawrah (revealed to Musa), the Injil (to 'Isa), the Zabur (to Dawud, upon all of them be peace) and the Furqan (the Discrimination, i.e. the Qur'an) without, however, these names denoting His very speech, exalted is He, for they all consist of letters and sounds. Rather, these letters point to or indicate the speech – belonging to before endless time – of Allah, exalted is He, while the actual speech of Allah, exalted is He, is not to be found in books but rather it exists by virtue of His supreme essence; nor is it to be separated from Him and no one or nothing else may be described as possessing it. However, because the letters of the Qur'an indicate His speech, exalted is He, the Qur'an is said to be the speech of Allah, exalted is He, from the point of view that that which indicates is (sometimes) given the name of the thing indicated, and this is as the saying of 'A'isha, may Allah, exalted is He, be pleased with her (when she said): 'That which is between the two covers of the book (*mus-haf*) is the speech of Allah.'"

In *Sharh al-Muqaddimat,* after what has been mentioned above, he says: "And if you know the teaching (*madhhab*) of the people of truth regarding the speech of Allah, exalted is He, you would know that the first generations, may Allah be pleased with them, characterised the speech of Allah as that which was recited by the tongues, written in the copies (of the Qur'an), known by heart – and this, as a reality not in any metaphorical way. However, they do not mean by this that the speech of Allah – from before endless time – comes to be located in these things, may Allah be exalted above this. What they want to express is that His speech, exalted is He, is remembered and indicated by means of the recitation on the tongues, the language of the hearts of men and in its hand-written form, so it exists in both of them both in understanding and in knowledge but not incarnate, because a thing may have four (possible modes of) existence: an existence in its original source-form (*al-'iyan*), an existence in the minds (of people), an existence on the tongue and an existence in the fingers, i.e. in a written form.

"As for the first existence, it refers to the essential, true existence and the remaining forms of existence are (merely) an expression of that which indicates or makes comprehensible (this original form). From this you will realise that the recitation is not the actual thing recited, the reading is not the actual thing read and the writing is not the actual thing written because the first of each of these divisions is incidental and in time, and the second of them is from before endless time, without end." Here end Mayyara's words.

His explanation that these letters and sounds indicate a meaning pertaining to before endless time that is self existent by His essence is the opinion of the majority, and it is to this that the pioneer of this art restricted himself in his works, although one of the later writers has disputed this saying: "The words which have been revealed do not denote a meaning pertaining to before endless time but rather indicate that which this meaning from before endless time indicates, and Sayyidi Ahmad ibn 'Abd al-'Aziz al-Hilali asserts this with conviction in the commentary on the poem of his Shaykh, Ibn at-Teebi, as does al-Aqdamisi in his commentary on *al-Idha'a*. After his explanation of indication, Sayyidi Ahmad ibn 'Abd al-'Aziz says: 'If you are aware of the three kinds of meanings ascribed to utterances, that is the conventional signification, the inherent signification and the signification of the intellect then you will know that none of the Vast Qur'an, that is this inimitable, miraculous composition (*an-nadhm al-mu'jiz*), indicates the speech of Allah, exalted is He, that is the meaning from before endless time, self existent by the noble essence. As for its non-indication of it in the realm of conventional understanding, this is because complex meanings are informational and stylistic relationships and relationships – as has been determined in its proper place (i.e. in grammatical and linguistic rules) – are relative concepts which have no outward reality, whereas, speech which contains existential meaning materialises in reality and speech from before endless time also exists in outward reality, and so what results from the second of the second is that there is nothing of relationships with the speech from before endless time.

Second, all that is indicated by the inimitable text has a widely varying range of reference, and changes clearly and unmistakably in relation to what is being referred to. No one of any intellect would doubt that what is being referred to by the words of Allah, exalted is He, "*We have sent you to mankind as a Messenger*"[1] is not exactly the same sphere of reference denoted by Him, exalted is He in His majesty, in "*We send forth the pollinating winds*",[2] and that referred to in His words, exalted is He, "*And we revealed to Ibrahim*",[3] is other than what is referred

---

1 an-Nisa' – Women: 78
2 al-Hijr – 22
3 an-Nisa' – Women: 162

to with His words, exalted is He, "*Your Lord revealed to the bees*"[1]. If the various changes in reference are clear in these examples, then examine too His words, exalted is He, "*As for those who are glad, they will be in the Garden remaining in it timelessly, for ever, as long as the heavens and earth endure, except as your Lord wills: an uninterrupted gift*"[2] as opposed to His words, exalted is He: "*As for those who are wretched, they will be in the Fire, where they will sigh and gasp, remaining in it timelessly, for ever, as long as the heavens and the earth endure, except as your Lord wills. Your Lord is the Doer of what He wills*"[3]. Examine too His words, exalted is He, "*Enter them in peace, in complete security*"[4] as opposed to His words, exalted is He: "*(He said) 'Get out of it, reviled and driven out'*"[5]. If then it has become clear to you that there exist these changes despite the fact that they are all from one and the same kind (of communication, namely speech) which differentiates the form – as to whether it is imperative, optative (*insha'iya*) or rather indicative so that despite the difference of modes, it is clearer and more manifest. Moreover, the speech of Allah, exalted is He, is one meaning and is an attribute which does not possess multiplicity – as is the case regarding all the other meanings according to us, that is, the Ash'aris. Those of the people of sunna who hold to multiplicity (of meanings), like Ibn Sa'd, do not say that this (speech) is as many in number as the phrases of the Qur'an but rather consider it to have seven modes – although this is not approved of by the people who verify exactly (*muhaqqiqun*). What we say is that these (different) relations and references indicated by the expressions of the Qur'an are in reality many in number while the speech of Allah, exalted is He, is not multiple in number in reality. Thus the (different) references indicated by the Qur'anic words and which result from the first of the two (categories) are not Allah's (actual) speech.

So if you were to say: "We accept what you say about the individual words' significations being different from speech, and likewise the composite sentences – based on the understanding that the signification of the predicate is an affirmation of a relation to a divine decree (*an-nisba al-hukmiyya*), as al-Qarafi asserts; however, as for (the assertion that) what is referred to by a judgement is the (mere) proof of a relation (*thubut an-nisba*) as ar-Razi holds, then we do not accept this because our understanding is that the divine decree is One – despite the fact that the references and connections depending upon

---

[1] an-Nahl – The Bee: 68
[2] Hud: 108
[3] Hud: 106
[4] al-Hijr: 46
[5] al-A'raf: The Ramparts: 17

and conditional upon these relations differ – and that the composition, in turn, is based on what is being said (*turji' ila al-ikhbar*). Thus that which is indicated by the Qur'an is of one meaning but possessing various dependent (utterances), and this one meaning is the essential speech (*al-kalam an-nafsi*)."

I would reply: "What do you mean by 'decree' or 'judgement' (*al-hukm*)? If what is meant by it is knowledge of the enduring connection of something in relation to something else or the refutation of this (connection), then the difference between knowledge as opposed to speech is obvious. However, if what is meant is the affirmation of an action, that is, the link and connection of one of two sides to the other, then this would denote a meaning which is in-time and created while the speech of Allah, exalted is He, is from before endless time. Thus it would not be correct to say that the decree (*al-hukm*) is speech (itself). After writing this, I reflected upon a similar (statement) of the imam, the respected Sayyidi Abu 'Abdallah ash-Shareef at-Tilimsani, may Allah be pleased with him, and may we benefit by him, in his replies to the questions which one of the Imams of Toozar had asked him, according that is to what is contained in the *Jami' al-Mi'yar*. He found the reasons adduced from the principle behind Ibn al-Hajib's saying difficult to support – that is, that essential speech is a relation between two individual things, self existent by virtue of the speaker (*al-mutakallim*) – because a relation, according to the people of truth, is non-existent (*'adamiyya*): if it did exist then its occurrence would exist in its (own particular) place and would form a link – and so would necessitate that essential speech (*al-kalam an-nafsi*) exist (in time, in creation); moreover its being a relation (*nisba*) necessarily presupposes change but His speech, exalted is He, is from before endless time and not subject to change."

Part of the reply of the above mentioned Shareef was his saying: "What you have mentioned, namely that speech is not the relation or reference itself is true, there is no dispute as to this, according to what has been demonstrated in the (relevant) place (in discussion of such matters). Rather speech is an attribute which is dependant upon this relation just as knowledge is an attribute which is connected to it. Therefore in the author's words – that is Ibn al-Hajib – there is something implied, which is that he meant to refer to in-time speech which has already been established to be the bringing about of a relation between two single (words) or a judgement regarding the relation between two separate (words).[1] However, as for (his estimation) regarding speech from before endless time, then the occasioning and the decree or judgement are

---

1 In most cases speech does not occur when single words are uttered, but is a meaning that arises when two or more words are connected in a syntactical relationship.

two acts pertaining to the speaker. This fact thus prevents it from being an attribute pertaining to 'the before endless time.'" Then he goes on to say: "And what you have mentioned, namely, that if speech were the very relation itself, then it would be subject to change – this is indeed true, understanding what is implicit in the words of *alif-lam-mim-sad* saves us from this consequence." Here ends what he has to say, and there is similar to this in the *Mahsal al-Maqasid* of Ibn Zakariyya. Ibn al-Hajib said: "That essential speech is a relation must be refuted even if one does not refute that it has relationship." Here ends the gist of what he has to say (on this subject). The author of *al-Marasid* has explained (it) as an implied ascription (*al-mudhaf al-muqaddar*):

And say, 'a description of speech pertaining to the essence
is that it is ascribed to Pure Majesty (*Janab al-Quds*),
(that is) an attribute of meaning self existent in the essence,
possessing a relation contrary to and incompatible with the attributes (*an-nafsiyya* – i.e. attributes of the essence itself).'

Because the Qur'an neither indicates nor is based on an attribute from before endless time, one often sees – especially from amongst those who are taken as sources of knowledge regarding the Arabic language, like al-Jahidh, al-Farsi, ad-Damameeni, az-Zamakhshari, as-Sakaki and al-Jurjani, as well as countless others – many who deny 'essential speech' (*al-kalam an-nafsi*) despite their being in agreement with the people regarding the positive, conventional sense (*madlul al-wad'i*) indicated by the inimitable text (*an-nadhm al-mu'jiz*) – with respect to the obligations of the *shari'ah* and other matters concerning outward meanings. The scholars who carefully verify do not have recourse to such people when demonstrating the validity of this speech (*kalam*) – that is, with respect to their acceptance of it and their affirming it in the positive, conventional sense indicated. If you understand that speech from before endless time is an (additional) attribute of meaning which is dependant upon a relation – but not the source – then you will realise, by means of the *muhaqqiqun* who have explained this, that an *interpretation* of speech is necessarily true, like the Shaykh of Shaykhs Abu 'Ali al-Yousi in his refutation of al-Qarafi – who has indicated this in his famous classification containing the divisions of meanings referred to by the various expressions of the Qur'an. What is meant by this is that speech from before endless time constitutes a perfect relation, both in content and form (*ikhbariyatan wa insha'iyyatan*), but that al-Manjouri's point of view regarding what al-Qarafi says, namely his remaining with the literal, manifest meaning – and indicated in Ibn Hajib's above mentioned explanation – is not well founded; and the replies his student, as-Sijistani, chose to make regarding the nature of these positivistic, conventional references – based on his argument that essential speech is itself the very relation – are not undisputed. Moreover, you will have become aware, by now, of the refutation of this. The reason for denying that the inimitable expression (*al-lafdh al-mu'jiz*) inherently indicates – that is, directly, of its very nature – the meanings of before endless time is because understanding whatever is indicated by the nature inherent in the expression is understanding a matter (directly) from the expression itself, by means of the character which the speaker has endowed it with. However, the speaker of the inimitable, miraculous expression is himself created from the created world (*mulk*), that is a prophet, or someone else and no one would doubt for a minute that this nature, this character on which this speaker is created, is itself a means to attaining an understanding of the High, Self-existent (Being) from the words which are recited to him.

That the text does not directly indicate the meanings from before endless time – intellectually speaking – is because it is not necessary, from the point of view of the intellect, that the Bringer into being of the letters on the tablet (of forms – *al-lawh* – in the unseen), or on the tongue of the Angel (Jibril) on whom be peace or on the tongue of the Prophet, may the peace and blessings of Allah be upon him, possesses a (form of) speech which indicates (directly) their meanings because if it were necessary, then every time a created being were to make a mistake in speaking, then it would be an indication that the Creator, may He be recognised in His elevation and purity, had spoken by means of the speech of creation – which may contain mistakes or nonsense – thereby relating to that which the speech of created beings relates to. However, Allah, exalted is He, is independent and absolute in His action of bringing into being any of the letters in use on the tongues of creation, without intermediary, and so there would be no difference (for Him, exalted is He) between (bringing) them (into being) or (bringing) the letters of the Qur'an (into being) – that is, from the point of view of their both being a creation of Allah, exalted is He. Thus proof afforded by the intellect demands that this (lack of differentiation) be rejected: such an inseparable, necessary consequence is absolutely invalid because of the absence of proof for such an act. Some have relied on gathering narrated evidence (*naql*) for their affirmation of (the manner of) His bringing into being of words; those who have tried to affirm this by way of the intellect have done so by way of *tanzih* – the distancing of Him from any imperfection – not from the point of view of His bringing into being of speech and words.

So if you were to say: "We do not accept the invalidity of this inseparable, necessary consequence or the invalidity of the argument supporting the assertion that His speech, exalted is He, is connected to every necessity, possibility or impossibility, or likewise that His knowledge is connected to these", I would reply: "It is necessary that you know that when a meaning connects the speech of Allah, exalted is He, with what is inconceivable, then this inconceivability is one of two sides of a relation which is indicated by the speech of Allah, exalted is He, – not, definitely not, that the occurrence of an impossible relation is an indication of His speech, exalted is He. His cognisance as to the extent of His knowledge of divine utterances, like His saying for example: '*Those who say that Allah is the third of three are kafirun*' – to the end of the *ayat*[1] does not indicate that it is itself, His speech, exalted is He, for the sense here is contrary to what is in the knowledge of Allah; rather what is indicated by the speech of Allah, exalted is He, is the relation inferred in the above words of His, '*Those who say Allah is third ...*', namely, that this is rather an attestation of *kufr* in those who assert such a thing or who judge thereby, and that this saying of theirs is connected to one of the two sides of the relation only, that is, to the subject, namely to those to which it (specifically) refers. The same holds true regarding Allah's words, exalted is He: '*The Jews say "Uzayr is the son of Allah*'[2] which although (as Qur'an) is an indication of (Allah's) speech from before endless time is nevertheless spoken by and pertains (specifically) to the Jews. As for their (actual) saying of this, then it is that which is connected to (just) one of the two ends of this relation – that is to the subject – may Allah, exalted is He, be exalted far above any idea indicated by His Speech that is invalid (in relation to Him) – so be aware of this."

If you were to say: "If the inimitable, miraculous text (of the Qur'an) does not indicate speech from before endless time by means of one of the three ways then what is the difference between this and other kinds of expression – such that it might be deemed immeasurably superior? What is the reason for calling it the 'speech of Allah, exalted is He,'? and what does it mean when the imams say, 'it is that which has been given the name of "that which indicates" (*ad-dal*) but which in fact is itself the "indicated" (*al-madlul*)?"

Then I would answer: "The difference between the two divisions is clear for the composition of the Qur'an is not something that may be 'acquired' by of the slaves and it is not something which is in their capacity to create – whereas other compositions may be acquired and mastered by them. Indeed this inimitable, miraculous expression has been set out to indicate (just) a part of the meanings indicated in the speech of Allah, exalted is He; it is as if it were

1 al-Ma'ida – The Table: 73
2 at-Tawba – Repentance: 30

a quotation from Him, rather than being (of the same nature as) our speech. So its being called 'the speech of Allah, exalted is He,' is either by way of its being revealed from Allah, exalted is He, that is, not of the composition of created beings and not included as part of that which may be acquired by them, in which case its ascription to Him is the ascription on the part of created beings vis-à-vis the Creator, out of honour and respect for Him, in the same way as one might say of the Garden that it is 'The House of Allah, exalted is He,' even though (in reality) all houses belong to Him – the building of this (Garden) being neither of the handiwork of created beings, nor of the kind or type to be found among their buildings which they are able to acquire. So on the basis of this example, the calling of it by the name 'the speech of Allah, exalted is He,', in the light of the above mentioned justification, refers rather to an interpretation of its meaning – in order to designate its specificity as an ascription or attribution to Allah, exalted is He, only. Or, (its being called the 'speech of Allah, exalted is He,') is because its purpose is to indicate some of the sense of the attributes from before endless time – which are self existent by His Essence, glorious is He, – just as one would speak, for example, of a translation of the Sultan's speech for the benefit of the person who does not understand his language or has not heard his speech. And to Allah belongs the highest likeness (*al-mithal al-'ala*). This (translated) speech of the Sultan, by its nature, indicates the meanings inferred by the (original) speech of the Sultan, and just as we say of the speech reported in the Qur'an from the prophets and their ummas who do not speak Arabic that it is their speech – despite this not being the case, for it rather *refers* to their original speech – we do so because what it refers to in whole is the sense inferred in their speech and because the translation serves in place of their speech. So in this light the above mentioned calling by this name is metaphorical (*majaz*), its connection being two consecutive indications which happen to coincide with and be identical with (just) one indicated thing. If this is understood, then their saying: "the naming of the inimitable, miraculous expression by (the phrase) 'the speech of Allah'" is an example of calling 'that which indicates' by the term 'the indicated.' Alternatively one might say that in fact, there is an omission in this term and it should be called "the indicator of the indicated (*dal al-madlul*)" because any attribute from before endless time is an indicator of that which is indicated in the inimitable, miraculous expression, just as it indicates that which is indicated in other contexts, such as the Tawrat for example.

One of the true seekers and teachers of knowledge, a contemporary of our Shaykhs, the great *'alim*, the verifier of knowledge, Sayyidi Abu Madyan, the commentator of *as-Sullam*, the Qadi of Meknes in his time, has explained this omission in a composition of his in which he speaks of His words, exalted is He: "*Muhammad is only a Messenger*"[1]. I had it for a long time although it is not with me at the moment. The Shaykh of our Shaykhs, the great *'alim* and seeker after true knowledge, Sayyidi Ahmad, the son of Ya'qoub agreed with him saying: "This naming is one which indicates with a name which refers to the act of indicating." The imam, the verifier of knowledge, Sayyidi Muhammad, the son of 'Abd al-Qadir al-Fasi also inclined to this (understanding), and this also corresponds to what has been transmitted from Shaykh Yaseen via al-'Ibadi, where he says in the gloss of *Sharh as-Sughra*: "...and this is what is referred to by the term inimitable, miraculous expression." What first comes to mind is that the pronoun 'this' refers to self existent speech which is an attribute of eternity in the past, without a beginning in time (*sifa azaliya*), and so this speech is self existent and is inferred from the spoken, articulated expression – this, then, is what the author is describing here and in all his writings, as as-Sa'd has also explained and others of the verifiers of knowlege. However, there is extreme confusion in the matter. What accords with the intellect is the explanation given by ash-Shihab al-Qasimi, namely that the meanings referred to are its relationships or connections (*ta'alluqatuhu*). Thus he explains that the speech of Allah, exalted is He, is one single attribute belonging to which are connections which in turn may be divided into commands, prohibitions and statements (*khabar*); and any multiplying of those connections exists without (any multiplication in) this (attribute); and then these connections are divided in accordance with the expressions which indicate them into Qur'an and all the other (divine) Books. These connections may be termed 'the Qur'an' by virtue of their specific, particular expression in the Arabic language, and so in this way the sense indicated (by the word) 'Qur'an' is not (one and the same as) the attribute existent by His essence but rather refers to matters which are indicated and inferred (*madlulatuhu*). Thus it becomes clear that the meaning indicated by the Qur'an is other that that indicated by the Injil – and it follows necessarily that the connections referred to by the Qur'an are other than those referred to in the other Books for in it are judgements which do not exist in other Books and matters which are dissimilar to or which refute judgements in the other Books, – so be aware of this.

It is obvious that what he means by *ta'alluqat* (a becoming connected, dependent or related) is in fact *muta'llaqat* (that which is already connected, related or dependent) thus using the *masdar* form (verbal noun) in place of the

---

[1] Ali 'Imran – The Family of 'Imran: 144

maf'ul form (the 'object' which suffers the action). It is for this reason that he uses above the term *madlulat* (matters indicated or inferred). In the gloss on the *Sharh al-Kubra* of the Muhaqqiq al-Yousi he indicates (something similar to what) we have mentioned: 'Sahib Qutb al-'Arifin said regarding the hearing of speech: "Allah, exalted is He, said: *'If any of the mushrikun ask you for protection, give them protection until they have heard the speech of Allah'*[1]. The meaning of this is like, for example, the case where an interpreter explains to a man the words of another in order that he may understand what has been indicated by the words expressed by the other – and this is proof that one may understand speech which has been interpreted – so be aware of this."

He has also said in *Fadl al-Nuzul*: "glorious is He, said, *'Say: "The purest Ruh has brought it down from your Lord with truth"*.'[2] The purest Ruh is Jibril. The words imply that Jibril's position, on whom be peace, was above and then he heard the words of Allah, exalted is He, from Allah or by revelation (*wahy*). However, Allah glorious is He, is not in a position above nor is He in any specific place. Jibril declares to Muhammad, may the peace and blessings of Allah be upon him, on the tongue, that which he has understood of the words of Allah, mighty is He and majestic, and then Muhammad, may the peace and blessings of Allah be upon him, expresses this in the Arabic language to his *umma* based on what he had understood from the expression of Jibril, from the words of Allah, exalted is He." Here ends his words.

His mention of what Jibril relates to our Lord Muhammad, may the peace and blessing of Allah be upon him, and then, in turn, that it was his understanding of the words of Allah, exalted is He, – indicate the two (forms of transmission) we have touched upon above, namely, that the meaning of the utterances is the meaning of the (utterance from) before endless time not the original utterance itself. Here end the words of Sayyidi Ahmad ibn al-'Aziz

I SAY: "I have heard that one of our contemporaries of penetrating vision has refuted this although he has retained the explanation of the majority in its manifest literal sense. Al-Aqdamisi, the student of Khurshi, in *Sharh al-Ida'a* is of the same opinion as Ibn 'Abd al-'Aziz, saying: 'Know, may Allah give us and you success, that *kalam Allah*, exalted is He, (the speech or words of Allah, exalted is He,) and the Qur'an have been named in this way for six reasons. Each of these two terms refers to an attribute which is eternal in the past, without beginning, self existent with the supreme essence, like our saying: "The Qur'an is an attribute of Allah, exalted is He, and *kalam* is an

---

1   at-Tawba – Repentance: 6
2   an-Nahl – The Bee: 102

attribute from among the attributes of Allah, exalted is He." It also applies to the meanings which are indicated by the attribute of before endless time which is self existent with the supreme essence, like our saying: "The Qur'an is divided into commands, prohibitions, threats, promises and the like." What is intended is the meanings indicated by the *kalam* not the attribute *kalam* itself. It also refers to the four proofs by which we nowadays furnish evidence for the meanings which indicate the attribute *kalam*: these are the proof and evidence which may be written, namely, the letters written in the copies of the Qur'an (*mus-hafs*) and the writing boards of the students *(alwah)* and which are referred to as the words of Allah, exalted is He, like our saying: "What is between the two covers of the *mus-haf* is the *kalam* of Allah, exalted is He," or "You have written the *kalam* of Allah." So what is meant by *kalam* of Allah is these letters since it can only be written with the letters and there is nothing else between the two covers of the *mus-haf* but letters; and the proofs which may be read (aloud), and these refer to the inimitable, miraculous text and the reading of the Book of Allah. So what is meant by the *kalam* of Allah, exalted is He, is the words of the text *(alfadh)* since there can be no reading except by means of these *alfadh*; and the proofs – which may be heard – are those referring to the voice of the reciter. So if you were to say: "I have heard the '*kalam* of Allah'" then what is meant by *kalam* of Allah, exalted is He, is the voice of the reciter since nothing may be heard – in one's normal state – except sounds or voices; and finally the proofs which may be preserved (in the breast), and this refers to the light which Allah, exalted is He, creates in the heart of the memoriser, usually when he is in a state of being obliterated (to the outside world) during the recitation itself or study of it: that is, as he vocalises its words, Allah, exalted is He, creates from this vocalisation an understanding of the meanings which indicate the attribute of *kalam*.

If you have understood all this, and are aware that the *kalam* of Allah, exalted is He, is a name for these six things, then you will realise that the attribute which is existent by His essence, exalted is He, which is among the seven attributes, and which is called *kalam* from the point of view of an investigation of this art – is in fact the knowledge of *tawhid*. This is explained by the people of this art in the following manner: "*kalam* which is eternal and from before endless time is the meaning which is existent by His supreme essence, exalted is He, expressed in various kinds of ways. It is different from the nature (*jins*) of the letters and the sound, unaffected by (such concepts as) the general or the particular, or by a coming before or coming after, by mispronunciation or grammatical modifications and all the other changes connected with everything which is necessarily true, conceivable or inconceivable (of existence)." What they mean by this is that the attribute which is existent by the eternal, from the before-endless-time attribute of His essence, blessed is He and exalted, is expressed by various kinds of expressions, which are called by a number of names although what these names denote is one (and the same thing).

Their saying: "different from the nature of letters and the sounds" means that His *kalam*, exalted is He, is one attribute from among His attributes of existence (*as-sifat al-wujudiyya*). It is not (the same as) the sound emitted from someone's mouth, that is, composed of letters and sounds – far be Allah, exalted is He, from possessing attributes like those of created beings! Their saying: "unaffected by (such concepts as) the general or the particular" means that the attribute of Allah, exalted is He, which is called the attribute of *kalam* is unaffected and distant from any description to do with generality or particularity – because something can only be described with generality and particularity if it has parts or is composed from dimensions like physical bodies. But the attribute of Allah, exalted is He, is not like this. Moreover, only that which is in time and in creation may be described as preceding or coming after (something else). Thus the *kalam* of Allah, exalted is He, is not *lafdh* – expression (in the sense pertaining to man)."

Their saying: "and all the other modifications" refers to matters like silence, alterations, copies, forgetfulness, revelation and other things. If you were to say, 'How is it that the *kalam* of Allah is unaffected by the *descent* (*nuzul* – of the revelation) when one says: "Jibril brought *down* (the revelation) of the Prophet, may the peace and blessings of Allah be upon him, and all the other revealed Books?" Then I would reply: "There is no difficulty and no contradiction in this for the person who has understood what we have mentioned first of all in the above discussion – namely that the Qur'an and the *kalam* are two names for six things. It has all been explained above: what the descent (of the revelation) on the Prophet, may the peace and blessings of Allah be upon him, refers to is the words which indicate the meanings, which in turn contain the meaning of the attribute of *kalam* – not the attribute of *kalam* itself, – how very distant Allah is from that the attribute existent in Him be subject to alteration and descent!"

And if you were to say also: "What is the meaning of your saying: 'the *kalam* of Allah is not subject to division into parts, nor subject to partition' given that you have not rejected the statement of the one who says: 'The Qur'an is divided into commands, prohibitions, threats and promises' and your saying: 'Such-and-such a person has memorised a part of the Qur'an and such-and-such a person has written down some of the Qur'an', I would answer:

'There is no contradiction or difficulty for the person who has understood what we have explained above regarding the fact that the Qur'an is a name for six things. What is intended by their saying, 'The Qur'an is divided into commands, prohibitions, threats and promises' is the meanings from which may be inferred the attribute of *kalam*, not the attribute of *kalam* (itself).

As for their saying, 'The Qur'an is divided into *suras*, *ayats*, *hizbs* and the like' the word 'Qur'an' refers here to the words which indicate the meanings from which may be inferred the attribute of *kalam*, not the attribute *kalam* (itself). As for their saying: 'memorisation of some of the Qur'an' — what is being referred to here by the words 'Qur'an is the light which He creates in the heart of the slave' is the light which indicates the meanings — from which, in turn, may be inferred the attribute of *kalam*, not the attribute of *kalam* itself. If you study all this, you will realise that they amount to six matters which are known as the Qur'an and the *kalam*, the speech of Allah, exalted is He: contained in these terms is that which is absolutely *qadeem*, that is, from before endless time and which may not be separated into parts — and this is the attribute existent with His essence, blessed is He and exalted; also contained in them is that which is partially *qadeem* — from before endless time — and partially *hadith*, that is, in time and creation, — and all these are the meanings from which may be inferred the attribute of *kalam*." Here ends this discussion of what is intended by the words of al-Aqdamisi.

I would like to draw the reader's attention to two things: the first, what he said in *Ghayat al-Ma'ani*, when mentioning the words, 'and that the Qur'an is the *kalam* of Allah from the text of *ar-Risala* (of Ibn Abi Zayd al-Qayrawani): "The investigation of the difference of opinion between us and them, that is, the Mu'tazilis, who deny that the *kalam* is from before endless time and existent by the supreme essence — is based on two things: the assertion that *kalam* is either essential (in nature) or a rejection of this, and the understanding that we do not hold to the opinion that the words and the letters (themselves) are from before endless time — although they too do not hold to the in-time occurrence of the essential *kalam* (of Allah). Our proof — namely that which we have mentioned above — is that it is established by consensus and by multiple chains of narration from the Prophets, on whom be peace and blessing, that He, exalted is He, is the One Who speaks (*Mutakallim*). There is no meaning to this other than that He is to be described as possessing *kalam* — speech. It is not possible that words in time and in creation be existent by His essence, exalted is He, be designated as essential (*nafsi*) or from before endless time (*qadeem*). But as for their adducing that the Qur'an may be described as having the attribute of created beings and characteristics of in-time occurrence, namely of composition, arrangement, the 'coming down' (as revelation) and its being in the Arabic language, capable of being heard (by man), eloquent, inimitable and miraculous, etc., then this is an argument against the Hanbalis not against us because we say that the (actual) arrangement (*nadhm*) (of the Qur'an) is in time and that *kalam* is the meaning of that which is from before endless time. When the Mu'tazilis were unable to deny, His being, exalted is He, the *Mutakallim* – the One Who speaks – they formed the opinion that He is *Mutakallim* in the sense of bringing into existence the letters and the sounds in their (appropriate) places and the bringing into existence of the formation of the writing on the preserved tablet of (revelation and the divine decrees) (*lawh al-mahfudh*)." Here ends his words.

2. he said in *Fath al-Bari*: "The safe and secure (teaching transmitted) from the majority of the *salaf* is that one should desist from delving (too deeply) into this (matter), that one should restrict oneself to saying that the Noble Qur'an is the speech of Allah, exalted is He, that it is not created (*makhluq*) and remain silent about anything else beyond this." Here ends his words.

WHAT ATTRIBUTES ARE IMPOSSIBLE FOR ALLAH

وَيَسْتَحِيلُ ضِدُّ هَذِهِ الصِّفَاتْ

الْعَدَمُ الْحُدُوثُ ذَا لِلْحَادِثَاتْ

17 And the opposite of these attributes are inconceivable (for Him – like) non-existence, coming into being in time (*hudouth*); that is for originated things.

كَذَا الْفَنَا وَالِافْتِقَارُ عُدَّهْ

وَأَنْ يُمَاثَلَ وَنَفْيُ الْوَحْدَةْ

18 Likewise, annihilation, being in need of other than Him, count them! and that He be like (anything else) or His oneness be negated,

عَجْزٌ كَرَاهَةٌ وَجَهْلٌ وَمَاتْ

وَصَمَمْ وَبَكَمْ عَمَى صُمَاتْ

19 Incapacity, unwillingness, ignorance, death, deafness, dumbness,

blindness or silence

Mayyara said: "This then is the second (of the three) sections (i.e regarding the necessarily true, inconceivable and conceivable) namely that with which it is inconceivable to describe Allah, exalted is He, and these attributes are thirteen in number, like the number of necessarily true attributes, as they are their opposite, as mentioned above. The author, may Allah have mercy on him, has based (by way of comparison) this section (of what is inconceivable) on the first (i.e. what is necessarily true): thus non-existence is the opposite of existence and coming into being (*hudouth*) is the opposite of pre-endless existence (*qidam*) and coming to an end (*fana*) the opposite of going on (*baqa*). Deeming that non-existence is not conceivable for Him necessarily implies that coming into being (*hudouth*) and disappearance (*fana*) are also inconceivable because if non-existence is inconceivable for Him, exalted is He, then it cannot be conceived of neither before or after; likewise the necessity of His existence, exalted is He and glorified, necessarily requires (His) existence from before endless time and (His) going on forever. Thus the adjunction of the second attribute (of the thirteen, i.e. *hudouth* and *qidam*) and the third (*fana* and *baqa*) in the two sections regarding what is necessarily true (*wujub*) and what is inconceivable (*mustaheel*) with the first (i.e. *wujoud* and *'adam*) in each section is by way of adjoining the particular to the general or 'the necessary consequence' (attribute) (*lazim*) to 'that to which it is a consequence' (*malzoum*). He does not deem it sufficient (to merely mention) the first of the two sections as the goal is to enumerate the necessarily true and inconceivable attributes in detail. To do without the particular and settle for the general or to settle for 'that which is a necessary consequence' without 'that to which it is a consequence' would lead to much ignorance in this matter because of the subtle nature of 'that which is a necessary consequence' and the difficulty of containing details in general categories. Ignorance in this science is a major matter and one should take care to explain the matter carefully."

Being in need (*iftiqar*) is the opposite of being free of need (*ghina*). Resembling (*mumathala*) originated beings is the opposite of being different from them (*mukhalafa*). There are many aspects of this resemblance (which is inconceivable for Him). In *as-Sughra* there is mentioned the example of His being a (physical) body, that His supreme essence takes up (and therefore is in need of) an amount of space, or that He be some contingent, non-essential characteristic pertaining to a body, or that He be in some direction with respect to the body or that He Himself have direction, or that He is bound to a place or a time, or that His higher essence be described as being subject to in-time occurrences, or that it has the qualities of being small or big, or that it possess the quality of being subject to contingent non-essential characteristics or laws. Know that a mass (*jurm*) is (defined as being) more general than a substance (*jawhar*) or a body (*jism*) because a mass refers to the amount of space taken up by its essential nature, be it a composite (mass) or not; the substance (*jawhar*) is an expression referring to that which is not composite or complex and it is that which attains such fineness that the intellect cannot imagine any (further) division is possible;[1] and a body (*jism*) is a term referring to that which is composed of two or more substances.

To negate oneness would be to contradict the unity of essence, attributes and actions, incapacity is the opposite of power, and unwillingness (*karaha*) is the opposite of will. What is intended here is not the dislike or compulsion (i.e. the '*makruh*') which is one of the divisions of legal judgement (*al-hukum ash-shar'i*) – which is requiring that one desist from an action either in an absolute manner or otherwise – for it would be valid to assert the existence (of such abhorrence) together with (His) bringing (of something) into being: Allah may bring into existence an act together with an abhorrence or revulsion for it, that is a prohibition against it, just as Allah, exalted is He, has led astray many of His creation while at the same time prohibiting them from this going astray.

As for unwillingness (*karaha*), meaning the absence of the will of Allah, exalted is He, it is inconceivable that it coexist with the bringing into being (of something) since it is inconceivable that something occur in His creation, majestic is He and mighty, that He does not will to occur. As for ignorance, it is the opposite of knowledge and included in (the term) 'ignorance' is (all manner of) surmise, illusion, forgetfulness, sleep and knowledge in its theoretical or speculative form when it is incompatible with (real) knowledge just like the incompatibility or contradiction that exists in the relation of ignorance to knowledge. As for death, it is the opposite of life; deafness, the opposite of hearing; dumbness, the opposite of speech and blindness the opposite of sight." Here end the words of Mayyara.

'Ali ibn 'Abd as-Sadiq said: "*Sumat* (silence) is a variant of *sumt* because whenever the speaker expresses one letter he is (necessarily) silent with regard to another (which follows) – although he is nevertheless described as 'talking' throughout (the whole of) the sentence."

What is Conceivable for Allah

[1] Thus it is a term for the 'atom' in the original Greek sense of that which is incapable of further division.

$$\text{يَجُوزُ فِي حَقِّهِ فِعْلُ الْمُمْكِنَاتُ}$$
$$\text{بِأَسْرِهَا وَتَرْكُهَا فِي الْعَدَمَاتُ}$$

20 It is conceivable with respect to Him that He carry out anything that is possible or leave (all) that is possible in (a state of) non-existence.

As-Sanusi said in *al-Kubra*: "Among the conceivable matters with respect to Him, exalted is He, is the creation of the slaves, the creation of their actions, the creation of reward and punishment for them. However, nothing of this is obligatory for Him, nor undertaken in consideration or compliance with (the dictates of) goodness or usefulness, or because something is more correct or more suitable – for otherwise it would necessarily follow that man were not responsible for his actions, that there be no testing in this world or the next. All actions, the good and the bad, the useful and the harmful are equal in indicating the splendour of His power, mighty is He and majestic, the breadth of His knowledge and the influence of His will – while nothing of that perfection or imperfection penetrates to His supreme essence for Allah, exalted is He, was and there was nothing with Him and He is now as He was (before). Thus glorious is He and exalted is He, ennobles whom He wishes, by means of a generosity which encompasses all kinds of blessings beyond description – and this, solely by his overflowing bounty for He does not incline to it in order to fulfil any right or obligation that (one might imagine) is incumbent on Him; and He exercises requital with regard to whomever He wishes by an unbearable punishment by means of the various degrees of Gehannam; nor on account of the raging Fire or on account of gratification of His anger or for any harm (one might imagine) He has suffered at this person's hand. These two types (of requital) indicate the extent of His knowledge, the subjection of all created beings to His will and the absence of any (possibility of) escape from His power – each of the two (modes of requital) coming to pass in accordance with the course fitting for it, in harmony with His knowledge and His will, without this adding anew any perfection or imperfection, neither in the present or any time in the future. Thus, His being obliged (to something) or being capable of an injustice are both inconceivable in relation to Him since obligation implies (the possibility that) some (aspects) of the possible might be able to escape submission (to His will), and oppression or injustice would require His acting in a way contrary to what is fitting. It follows from this too that it is inconceivable that any action of Allah, exalted is He, be for a purpose because if He were acting for a purpose this would be obliging Him (to something), and would mean the 'reason' (for His acting) were not His (alone) and that He Himself were subject to and overcome by irresistible might. How could this be? – (when) *"Your Lord creates and chooses whatever He wills."*[1] Here end the words of as-Sanusi.

'Ali ibn 'Abd as-Sadiq said: "(the word) *haqq* (in the above mentioned text of as-Sanusi, and in Ibn 'Ashir's text) has various meanings, among them 'he who is entitled to or deserves' or 'the word or action (which is true).' What is fitting here is the first, that is, the word refers to what is permitted with regard to His reality, that is His essence. The addition of *hi* in *haqqihi* is for clarification, and the word *fi* has the sense of *li* (on account of), like for example in the tradition: "A woman entered the Fire on account of (her abuse of) the cat (*li hirratin*)." However, this use of *fi* is unusual (grammatically speaking), connected as it is to the (word) *yajuz* (it is permitted), and is used for emphasis according to some. He has used this expression *fi haqqihi* rather than *'ala haqqihi* following what is mentioned by as-Sanusi in his *Aqa'id*. However, this is strange because both expressions imply a certain lack of courtesy by the suggestion that He, exalted is He, may be described as possessing a possible attribute. He, however, is necessary (of existence) and may only be described with necessary attributes. Any mention of possibility refers to His actions in the sense that they are connected to one or more of His attributes – and possibility in no way pertains or attains to His essence, and neither does it extend to an attribute by which is sustained in some manner or other (along with that attribute)." And this as-Sanusi said in his *Sharh al-Wusta*.

As for (his mention of) 'the doing of *the* possible' (*fi'l al-mumkinat*), this means 'a bringing into being' and the *al* (*the*) – means the generality of what is conceivable, that is, *all* that is conceivable because this form of the 'sound' plural (*al-jam' as-salim,* i.e. a plural which is not 'broken' by the introduction of other letters between the root letters of the verb) in Arabic – when it is preceded by the (*al*) – serves to express generality, and so nothing is excluded from this. For this reason, he says: 'as a whole' (*bi'asrihi*), thus including within it the actions of living creatures whether they possess intellect or not, and likewise all that which is brought about through a cause and which may be linked to such a cause – be it (demonstrably through the proof afforded by repeated experiment or experience (*'adatan*), or by virtue of a legal premise (*shar'an*), which includes the sending of the Messenger, may the peace and blessings of Allah be upon him, and what they brought (as a good news and a

[1] al-Qasas – The Story: 68

warning) of the events of the next world in general and in particular.

His saying: "or may leave all that (is conceivable in a state of non-existence)' refers to His leaving off, His desisting from the making of conceivable things non existent after their being existent and making them remain in (a state of) non existence, in the sense that His leaving off doing this is desisting from bringing them into being – as opposed to doing it. This includes the bringing into being of that which is non-existent and the bringing into non-existence of what is existent; and the gathering of the non-existent things in accordance with each individual possible thing in order to achieve a balance with what precedes it – for otherwise 'non-existence' would be a single entity. Ibn 'Ashir's mention of 'or (He) may leave' means that what is permitted – with respect to Allah's either carrying out the possible things or desisting from them – (occurs) alternately. As for the carrying out of all of them in one moment, this would be inconceivable – and is not conceivable – for this would necessarily entail the entry of an infinite number (of events or things) into existence. We have interpreted this leaving off or desisting from (bringing into being) as a destruction or bringing into non-existence (*i'dam*) which are actions – as leaving off or desisting from (something) must refer to an action. All this is based on the fact that that which validates or attests to the connection of the power and decree from before endless time is only the (existence of the) possibility. Thus, on this basis, each possibility, be it existent or non-existent, prior to (something else) or an inherent part (of it) is subject to the absolute might of our Lord, blessed and exalted is He. As for the bringing into existence of what is non existent or the bringing about the non-existence of what is existent – this is clear and obvious. As for the bringing into non-existence of what is (already) non-existent, this means that it is within His grasp, within His power and decree, exalted is He, to cause it to go on. That something is subject to another's power, in a lesser domain (than that of Allah's) is conceivable both grammatically (*lughatan*) and in ordinary language (*'urfan*) – thus one says: 'The king has power over the people but they do not have power over him' meaning that he disposes metaphorically over the changing of some of their states, for example his being able to raise them up or bring them low and the like. So how could it be that this possible non-existence (*al-'adam al-mumkin*) is not subject to the power and decree of Allah, exalted is He? for He, exalted is He and glorified, has the power to cause it to go on or to change it by whatever means He wills, however He wills – that is, in reality and not just metaphorically. Thus making statements (to the effect that) it is not subject to the power of the Lord, blessed is He and exalted, – given that (what He wills in) reality is neither by means of existence or something that occurs unexpectedly (but by Him) – is a lack of courtesy because of the alleged incapacity with respect to His power, exalted is He, as some of the *muhaqqiqun* have indicated." Here ends what as-Sanusi said in *Sharh al-Muqaddimat*. Here ends, too, the words of 'Ali ibn 'Abd as-Sadiq.

He has also said in *Sharh al-Wusta*, "If it is asked how, if He has influence in the world by His power and decree – and therefore is either in a state of acting or desisting from something (for he who has power is he who, if he wills, does (it) and, if he wills, desists from it) – how is it conceivable that (the act of) desisting from (something) be determined through the influence of a power (*maqdouran*) for it is a negation and pure non existence: (the nature of) power necessarily entails influence while non-existence is not an exerting of influence (over anything) – if it were, then it would necessarily entail the existence of the world from before endless time; moreover desisting from something is a continuing non-existence but if it did exert an influence (over anything) it would necessitate the fulfilment of whatever occurrence (it disposed over in its influence)?" This question, then, may be answered in two ways:

The first: "We do not accept that (the act of) desisting is not subject to the power of the One Who has power – your saying the act of desisting is pure negation and a continual non-existence is, as we have said, not permitted. This is because leaving off doing (something) is abstaining from action – and in this sense may be termed an action – and it is a matter pertaining to existence; however, what we say is that your saying 'this would necessitate the existence of the world from before endless time and the fulfilment of whatever occurrence (it disposed over in its influence) (*tahseel al-hasil*)' – is not permitted for action, as action, is incompatible with eternal pre-endless time. Reality exists by that which is eternal, of pre-endless time, and if the 'desisting' is 'renewed' after its not having existed, then what you have said is invalidated – with regard to it being the fulfilment of whatever occurrence (it disposed over in its influence) (*tahseel al-hasil*). From this you will understand that the saying of some of the *fuqaha*, 'desisting is an act' should not be spurned, as some people of restricted understanding think – indeed some of them, unrestricted by any feeling of shame or bonds of the deen go so far as to declare that those who say this are *kuffar*.

2. and this is the truth (of the matter) – we say: "What you have mentioned indicates that the wielder of influence is not the actor in his desisting or bringing into being; nor does it necessitate from this a refutation that he has power over this because the one who possesses power is the one who may

rightly (be said to) do something or not do it. What we mean by saying, 'or not do it' is that he does not bring the action out into existence but rather causes it to remain in non-existence – not that he brings about non-existence and causes a desisting. If one accepts this, then it would not be farfetched to think it connected to an actor, an agent who may freely choose (al-mukhtar) and it would not necessitate – (merely) from its being subject to the power of the actor – that this (remaining in non-existence) be tangible or visible (atharan), that is that it have (some kind of actual) existence."

PROOFS

EXISTENCE

وُجُودُهُ لَهُ دَلِيلٌ قَاطِعٌ

حَاجَةُ كُلِّ مُحْدَثٍ لِلصَّانِعْ

21 His existence has an absolute proof: every in-time, creational occurrence needs a Creator

لَوْ حَدَثَتْ بِنَفْسِهَا الْأَكْوَانُ

لَاجْتَمَعَ التَّسَاوِي وَالرُّجْحَانُ

22 If beings had originated of themselves, then the equal probability [of existence and non-existence]¹ and the [fact of] the preponderance [of existence, in that beings do exist] would be united –

As-Sanusi said in his *al-Kubra* after his words criticising *taqlid*: "If you realise this – O you of *taqlid*! and you want to look at your self with the eye of mercy, then the quickest thing which will take you out of the darkness of *taqlid*, with the help of Allah, is that you examine that which is the nearest thing to you, and that is your self. Allah, exalted is He, said: *"(There are certainly Signs in the earth for people with certainty;) and in yourselves as well."*² By doing so you will

1 The author considers the possibility of existence and non-existence being two equal probabilities, but then says that existence has preponderance since beings do exist, and that to claim that beings originate of themselves is to unite these two ideas which are impossible to reconcile. He shows later that non-existence needs no cause but existence needs a cause, so that they are not equal probabilities. Trans.
2 adh-Dhariyat – The Scatterers: 20-21

necessarily realise that (at one time) you did not exist and then you did exist; realise that you are present bodily, that you have been created – because it would have been impossible for you to create yourself. If this were conceivable, then it would mean that you could bring into being something more feeble than yourself from yourself – that is an essence other than yourself – by virtue of this (other essence) being equal to you in its possibility (of being). We have said 'something more feeble than yourself' just to emphasise the absurdity of bringing your own self into being and the fact that it would be a combining of two contradictory things, that is the making your own self precede yourself and your causing yourself to come after your self – because of the (necessary) precedence of the actor in relation to the action. It follows then that if the essence (of the self in question) is the same as his action, then it necessarily entails one be on one's guard (against such a statement).

And if you were to say: "How do I know that I was necessarily non-existent beforehand – since I was sperm in the loins of my father and likewise my father in the loins of his father and so on. All I can really say is that I have a knowledge of my necessary transformation from one form to another – not (of my necessary transformation) from non-existence to existence, as you have mentioned?"

Then I would answer that your essence now is decidedly bigger than the sperm from which it evolved. This will necessarily bring you to the realisation that what has been added (to this sperm) was non-existent and that it then (came into) being. Thus if it was non-existent and then existent, then there must have been something that brought it into existence. (In this, then,) there is a complete and absolute proof for you – based on a cognisance of this addition to your essence – of the existence of a creator, without the need for (proof) other than this. Moreover, if you examine this addition, you will find that it is a body which fills a space, that it is of a particular size and has a particular quality – although it is also possible that it be the opposite of this. Thus you will know for certain that your Creator possesses the choice in (His) particularisation of your essence by means of a certain number of (the characteristics and qualities) which it is possible for it (to possess). This (fact) will afford you decisive proof that it is impossible that the sperm from which you originated be that which brings your essence into existence. This is because this (sperm) does not dispose of a choice (in the matter) such that it may allot particular characteristics to your essence, that is (by selecting) some of (those qualities) it is permitted (to have); nor does it determine the natural characteristic (*tab'*) of the existence of your essence for if it did you would be rounded in form following the uniformity and regularity of the shape of the sperm; nor its growth, for otherwise you would grow for ever. Because of the necessary similarity of this example and that (of the sperm) you also realise that this sperm and the rest of creation were not existent, and then became (existent), and that all of creation is like you in that each (created reality) is a body which fills a space whose existence or non-existence is possible, which possesses specific dimensions, certain characteristics and other (qualities); and therefore, that this (body) stands in (a state of) need, in the same manner as it needs that which qualifies and characterises it to designate or define what it is – in everything which is necessarily true, conceivable or is inconceivable. That non-existence precedes its essence is a necessary fact, and this likewise is also necessarily true by analogy with regard to the rest of the world. This is so because if it is permitted that some of the world is from before endless time – and the attribute of before endless time applies, necessarily, only to that which is from before endless time, as we shall explain below – then it is inevitable that one of the two examples (of the sperm and the body) will be differentiated from the other by a necessary (rather than contingent) quality. This, however, is impossible because this would necessarily entail a coming together of two contrary aspects. Rather, the existence of a correspondence and likeness between you and the rest of possible things is a definitive proof for the in-time, coming into being of all the world, from the high to the low, from the throne to the footstool, in its roots and branches; and that the whole is incapable of bringing into being its self or the bringing into other than itself – like your own incapacity (in this respect); and that the whole is dependent upon an actor who is free to choose, just like your own dependency.

In the *Siraj al-Mulouk* of at-Tartushi it reads: "Whoever has the capacity to furnish proofs for what he cannot see (in the Unseen) by what he can see (in the visible world), then he possesses an intellect, is recognised as being a sane person, according to the people of *tawhid* (*muwahhidun*) and fully responsible (regarding the fulfilment of the duties contained in the *shari'ah*). An illustration of this would be a palace whose building has been perfected and whose pillars have been fortified, equipped with all the furnishings sufficient (for the needs of) those living there. Then a person comes to oversee it and notices the various rooms, the doorways, elevated couches, spread carpets, laid tables, raised sofas, veiled bridal chambers, basins, cisterns, pipes channelling water and beneath, drains funnelling off the water, sees the windows letting in the light of the day, chimneys carrying the smoke outside and ventilators and wind-towers capturing the breezes and wind and all the other things that sane people install to make life easier. Then he wonders whether someone of power and knowledge has constructed this palace and all it contains or whether it came to be of its own (volition), that is, took on a form without a creator. (He will) surely conclude that it must have had a creator who created it. This knowledge is strikingly clear to all who have intellect and does not need to be examined or proved with arguments and evidence.

"Moreover one may find many other similar examples. The nature of the limbs and their subtle physical formations is many times more astonishing than what is contained in the palace. If one were to examine one's own self, one would see wonders it in: the composition and the use to which each organ is devoted, for example, the particular capacity of each organ to benefit (the body) and repel any harm from it. Let him examine just one organ, the mouth and he will see first of all the teeth, set in a circular formation, like the arc of bow, specially suited to grinding; will see the power of its jaws, grinding like two millstones and witness how the teeth prevent the food from spilling out of the mouth, how the tongue pushes any food which might escape from the mouth back on to the grinding molar teeth; the mouth, in turn, is connected to a gullet which is perfectly adapted to swallow this masticated food. Thus it is manifestly clear and all are agreed upon this point – even after the slightest reflection – that this creation has not made itself, that it is dependent upon the design of a designer and upon its being given a form by someone with the capacity to form. If we were to continue in this manner describing the benefit and utility of each organ, you would certainly come to share our astonishment. However, we have refrained from doing this lest it become too lengthy a description. This very meaning is transmitted in the Book *'which inspires trust'* (*kitab al-muhaymin*) when Allah, exalted is He, says, *"(There are certainly Signs in the earth for people with certainty;) and in yourselves as well."*[1] Indeed this (*ayat* alone) is enough for the intellect to establish proof of (the existence of) the Creator: it has no further need to examine the essences and contingent events or qualities (contained in creation). Such beneficial knowledge, which serves to affirm the Creator in the visible world (*ash-shahid*) is like that which one necessarily acquires after examination of the handiwork of a builder, carpenter, tailor and the like. It is a knowledge that proves the existence of the Creator, glorious is He, that is, a knowledge based on examination of the coming into being of the world, which in turn is based on inferring conclusions and affirming the validity of the unseen from the seen world: from the point of view of the intellect, there is no difference between one created thing and another, each

---

1 adh-Dhariyat – The Scatterers: 20-21

thing necessarily standing in need of a creator; and knowledge regarding the seen world is necessarily always available: one can always observe the builder building, the tailor making the clothes or the carpenter fashioning the table. Although the people of intellect have not been able to see how Allah, exalted is He, has invented creation from before endless time they have been able to infer it from an examination of the visible realm." Here ends his discussion of at-Tartushi, and it is very precious.

As-Sanusi said in his *al-Wusta* in the chapter regarding the decisive proof on the existence of, exalted is He, and an explanation of how the world is in need of Him, mighty is He and majestic: "If the world is a created in-time occurrence – after its non-existence that is – then there must necessarily be a reason for this occurrence: the intellect cannot conceive of its transfer from the state of non-existence it was in to a state of contingent, incidental existence without their being a reason for this. If it were not for the actor, who is free to choose its existence – at a moment in time and with the dimensions and attributes of his willing – then it would have to have stayed in the state of non-existence it had been in for ever and ever, given the lack of differentiation regarding the dimensions, attributes and moments in time which necessarily exist in relation to its essence. Existence and non-existence, it is argued, are equal in relation to the essence (of the thing in question). So it is inconceivable that contingent existence – equal in its potential to be existent or non existent – move without a reason. It is also argued that it is more likely that non-existence precedes (existence, rather than vice versa) because of (a sense that) the former is the primal or natural origin (*li isalatihi fihi*), and the fact that non-existence does not stand in need of a reason. Given that preferring or according predominance or superiority to one of two equal things without a reason is inconceivable, then giving preference to existence, that is giving precedence to it in relation to non-existence – on this basis – is even more unlikely.

He said in his commentary: "...and this is because the coming into being of in time occurrences at a particular moment does not inevitably necessitate – from the aspect of the essence – this particular time. Indeed the relation of its existence to this time and to any other moments in time is equal (in potentiality) – the proof of this may be seen in all the other similar occurrences which have come into being before this time and after it. Likewise, that its existence possesses a particular dimension rather than another (which it might have acquired) from all the other (possible) dimensions or a particular attribute rather than another from all the other attributes – none of this particularity is inevitable or necessary from the aspect of its essence. So there must inevitably be something which determines this specificity for otherwise it would necessarily entail the combining of two contrary things, namely that one of two matters, each equal in its potentiality, would be both equal to its essence and yet at the same time predominant with respect to its essence (regarding its manifestation of particularity), and this is inconceivable.

He said in his *Sharh al-Qaseed*: "They are all in agreement as to the existence of the actor, all races and peoples, both the *muminun* and the *kuffar* except a small group of the philosophers who claim that the coming into being of the world is an incidental matter without the agency of an actor – however such a statement from people of intellect is most strange. Among the greatest of proofs of His existence, exalted is He and glorified is that He, glorious is He, has chosen, to place the hearts of such people behind a veil of ignorance with the result that they have become blind, unable to see this manifest matter – manifest, necessarily, because of the amount of evidence available to them to understand clearly this matter just as it has become clear for the rest of the people of intellect."

In *al-Jawahir* of ash-Sha'rani it reads: "It has been narrated that a man denied (the existence of) a creator in the presence of Ja'afar as-Sadiq. The latter then began to speak to him using demonstrations and proofs. However, the man did not pay attention to these proofs and Ja'far as-Sadiq said to him: 'Have you ever been on a ship' to which he replied 'yes, once our ship began to break up and I managed to get onto to a piece of wood which took me towards the shore. However, the piece of wood slipped from me as I came ashore.' Then Ja'far said to him, 'When you lost the piece of wood – in whom did your hope for safety and salvation lie when your reliance on reasons disappeared?' The man became silent, and then Ja'far said: 'The one that you hoped would save you was the One Who created you', and the man accepted Islam.'" Here ends his words. There is also the poem describing the Bedouin Arab who saw a fox urinate on an idol which he used to worship and then exclaimed

Is it a Lord that the fox may urinate on its head?
   Low and mean has become that on which the fox has urinated
I have freed myself of all idols and *shirk*
   And am certain that Allah without doubt is the Conquering Force."
Here ends the text from *al-Jawahir*.
Ibn 'Ashir continues:

$$\text{وَذَا مُحَالٌ وَحُدُوثُ الْعَالَمِ}$$

مِنْ حَدَثِ الْأَعْرَاضِ مَعْ تَلَازُمٍ

23 and this is inconceivable, and the coming into existence of the world is necessarily a coming into being of contingent, incidental occurrence.

As-Sanusi said in the *Sharh al-Wusta*: "Know that knowledge of the contingent nature of the coming into being of the world is a vast foundation on which rests knowledge of all the other matters of 'aqida. And it is a firm basis for an examination of the various benefits to be discussed below. The proof which leads to this foundation of 'aqida is a decisive proof which is easy for people's comprehension. The form of it is to establish proof of the in-time occurrence of one of two matters, which are equal (in nature and potential), and which share common (*mutalaziman*) attributes in order to demonstrate by analogy the coming into being in time of the other. Thus one may argue that the whole world is (composed of various) bodies, which are without intellect, and inherently without movement and rest (of their own volition)..." Then he goes on to say, after discussing matters connected with the language used to express 'aqida, "This serves as a proof with them, that is, proof of the in-time occurrence of the world, and this proof is based on the affirmation of four pillars:

First: affirmation of an addition with which the bodies may be described;

Second: affirmation of the in-time occurrence of this addition;

Third: affirmation that the bodies themselves may not be separated from this addition;

Fourth: the impossibility of any in time occurrence that does not have a beginning to it.

The manner in which one may base one's understanding – of the in-time occurrence of the world – on these four roots is the following: that you realise that its proof is based on the establishing of proof for the in-time occurrence of one of two inseparable aspects (belonging to a body) in order (to establish proof) for the coming into being in time of the other. This, in turn, requires the affirmation of an addition (having come about) to the bodies in order that one may judge this (addition) as an inseparable, inherent (part of the whole). It is after all clear that a thing cannot adhere to or be inherent to itself. It is then necessary to affirm the coming into being in time of this addition since, by way of this coming into being, one may then establish a proof for the coming into being of the world. It is also necessary to demonstrate the nature of these bodies as being incapable of separation from this addition – in order to prove the indissoluble connection to each other such that the occurrence of this addition necessitates inevitably the occurrence of these bodies. It is also necessary to establish the inconceivability of any occurrence which does not have a beginning: the reason for this is that after we had confirmed to our satisfaction these three principles and we intended to use their in-time occurrence as proof for the occurrence of the bodies which are an inseparably, inherent part (of the addition), the argument was put to us that this does not necessarily follow unless the individual (aspect) of this addition — which has come into being in creation in time — possesses a beginning. The person making the argument said: "We accept that it has come into being in time but we say that there is no beginning to it. Thus even if a celestial sphere, for example, is inseparably associated with movements which are in time and of creational occurrence — this does not necessitate its own coming into creation as an in-time occurrence unless the beginning was for all these movements. If this were not so, then it would necessitate an impossibility regarding the past existence of the sphere, namely that it was at one time devoid of any movement or rest. However if there was no beginning to the movements, then this does not follow of necessity." This then is the reason why the four divisions are needed to establish the proof.

The second principle of these (four) is the coming into being in time of the addition, and this too is dependent upon knowledge of four principles: the first, the invalidation of the existence of this addition of its own volition; secondly, invalidation of its change (of location); thirdly, invalidation of its being hidden or manifest; fourthly, the inconceivability of non-existence in pre-endless time. The way in which the occurrence of this contingent addition depends upon the four principles is demonstrated either by adducing the coming into existence occurred after non-existence or the onset of non-existence after existence. Establishing proof of the onset of existence requires three matters, namely, all (three principles) except the affirmation of the impossibility of non-existence from before endless time — for then, coming into being in time follows of necessity. Establishing proof for the onset of non-existence requires those (same) three matters — for then non-existence is confirmed. Moreover when non-existence is followed immediately by existence, then this in itself is an occurrence since the occurrence (of something) refers to (its) existence after non-existence — not existence which is followed by non-existence which would necessitate an explanation of the impossibility of non-existence pertaining to 'before endless time' because the onset of non-existence upon existence necessitates that non-existence preceded it, and this in any case would in itself be (yet) an(other) occurrence. By way of explanation of this we would say: 'to establish proof for the onset of existence by way of an incidental occurrence, like movement and rest for example, one must argue that if the onset of this (existence) did not come about, then it must have been in existence before the state in which we witnessed this new occurrence. And if it had been existent before this (new state) then of necessity it must either have happened in a location or not happened in a location. If it had been in a location then it was either this visible event which took place in it or something else. If it was this one, then it was concealed and latent in it, and if it was other than this, then it could only have reached it or connect to it by means of a change of locality from other than it to this (place). If it was in another place before its coming about in this one, then it must have come into being of its own volition. Thus here is proof for the in time occurrence of a contingent, incidental event, for its onset (after non existence) is dependent on the invalidation of these three divisions. It will now be clear that the onset of this visible, in time occurrence is a renewal after non-existence, and this is the meaning of *huduth* – the coming into being in time and in creation.'

Likewise we say, regarding the establishment of proof for the onset of non-existence of an incidental occurrence after its existence, that if it had not been non-existent then it would have been in a state of going on. This going on must necessarily either take place in a location or not take place in a location. If its going on does take place in a location, then it is either in this location or another – and if in another, then it can only arrive at the other by moving from this to it. If it is not in any location, then it has come into existence of itself. Thus, if these three divisions are invalidated, then the onset of non-existence is realised. However someone may ask after this: 'Why did you say the occurrence of non-existence after existence necessitates an occurrence which is prior to non-existence in its existence, and why do you not say that this incidence, this contingent occurring, is from before endless time and that the onset of non-existence came about onto it?'

Then we would reply that if it were from before endless time, then its non-existence would not be permitted, and we would inform the questioner of this. If by the onset of non-existence, it is demonstrated that it was not from before endless time, then it follows of necessity that it is an in time occurrence and this is what we are seeking for (in our argument). So it will also be clear that confirmation of the second principle is dependent on these four principles, and in effect encompasses them into the rest of the principles upon which proof for the in time occurrence of the world is established. Thus the complete number of principles on which proof for the (in time occurrence of the) world are seven:

First: affirmation of an addition to the (physical) bodies;

Second: invalidation of its coming into existence by itself;

Third: invalidation of its change of locality or movement;

Fourth: invalidation of its concealment or manifestation;

Fifth: the inconceivability of non-existence from before endless time;

Sixth: affirmation that (physical) bodies are, by their nature, inseparable from this addition;

Seventh: the inconceivability that in-time occurrences have no beginning.

The manner in which these seven principles may be proved is in short as follows:

As for the first, that is affirmation of an addition to the bodies and that they take on the characteristics of this (addition), like movement or rest, for example – this is an inevitable, necessary (matter for which there is no need of proof): there is no sane person but that he feels that in his own essence there exist meanings in addition to it. For this reason, one of the astute among the 'ulama said in reply to those who deny the existence of incidental, contingent occurrences: 'As for your contesting the proof regarding contingent occurrences – that is your questioning whether such proof exists or not – if you were to say: "It does not exist", then you would be stepping outside the bounds of the manner (of valid argument) practised by persons of intellect: you would thereby invalidate your statement as the (irrational) assertion on your part that it does not exist is an argument in our favour (for the rationality of our proof).'

As for the second, that is the invalidation of the coming into existence of incidental occurrence by itself and the third, that is the invalidation of its movement or change of locality, the proof for these two is that if incidental occurrence came into being by itself and changed location, it would necessitate the transformation of the reality of the occurrence. This is because the reality of movement, for example, is the change of locality of the essence from one area to another: if it had come into existence by itself or had moved then it would necessitate a carrying out of this movement on its behalf – and this execution of the movement is itself also a moving, bringing into being another change (of location). All this necessitates a chain (of events), and the establishing of a meaning by means of another meaning.

As for the fourth, that is the invalidation of concealment and manifestation, the reason for this is that concealment and manifestation lead to the combining of two contradictions in one location: if a single substance moves, for example, and rest is concealed or latent in it during the movement, then it would necessitate the combining of two opposites in this (substance), that is, movement and rest necessarily. This also leads to the existence of an incidental, contingent occurrence without its own essential attribute — so movement, for example, is itself an attribute by means of which the essence moves; if it is concealed then its reality is transformed and an attribute essential to it separates itself from it. Moreover, concealment and manifestation which come into being in relation to the occurrence, alternate in their relation to it, that is, according to them: it necessarily follows that they are both also contingent occurrences in themselves, like movement and rest, which alternate in their existence vis-à-vis the substance. Thus if one of them is non-existent during the existence of the other, then they contradict their principles regarding concealment of the contingent occurrences and they are obliged to accept what they would avoid accepting regarding inseparability of the substance from the contingent occurrences. If what they are holding to is a (kind of) concealment and manifestation other than the (original) concealment and manifestation, then this would necessarily entail a sequence (of occurrences).

As for the fifth, that is the inconceivability that non-existence be from before endless time, the reason for this is that if it were non-existent then its existence would be conceivable, not necessarily true, and what is possible only exists with respect to what is contingent and in time. So this before endless timelessness would then be an in time, creational occurrence, and thus a contradiction in terms.

As for the sixth, that is the affirmation of the bodies being such that they are inseparable from this addition: this is a necessary, inevitable fact for the intellect cannot imagine a body being separated from its being in movement or at rest, for example.

As for the seventh, that is the inconceivability of in time occurrences having no beginning: there are many proofs for this and we have mentioned them in our *al-Aqida al-Kubra* and its commentary. The most pertinent of them is the following: if each individual occurrence was a coming into being which happens by itself, and then each of these individual occurrences were to become non-existent and fixed in pre-endless time, then it must inevitable be either that this non-existence is united with or associated with one of these individual occurrences, or not associated with it. If it is associated with it, then this necessarily entails the coming together of the existence of something and its non-existence. This is because this individual (occurrence) is one from among all the other individual (occurrences) whose non-existence has been determined in pre-existent time, and the coming together of the existence of something and its non-existence is inconceivable – as an intellectual imperative. If, however, this non-existence is not associated with any of these individual occurrences, it necessarily follows that it does not have a beginning because of the absence of pre-existent time with respect to the whole of this supposition.

So, having determined these seven principles by way of their proofs you will have now understood that both movement and rest are in time, contingent occurrences, that is, by means of the proof of the onset of its existence some times and its non-existence at others, and the fact that they both have a beginning – because of the impossibility that any occurrence be without a beginning. Thus, it necessarily follows that bodies which are inseparable from these two (aspects of movement and rest) are in time, contingent occurrences and that they possess a beginning like these two (aspects). We have therefore arrived at the required (result of the discussion)."

TIMELESSNESS

لَوْ لَمْ يَكُ الْقِدَمُ وَصْفَهُ لَزِمْ

حُدُوثُهُ دَوْرٌ تَسَلْسُلٌ حُتِمْ

24   If His attribute were not timelessness then His coming into being in time as a chain of events would be necessarily true

As-Sanusi said in his *Kubra*: "Then you say: 'It is necessarily true that He who has brought the world into being be timeless, that is not preceded by non-existence for otherwise He would have had to have had someone to bring Him into existence and that would lead to a chain (of events) – if that which had brought Him into existence has no effect on him – or a cycke (of events) if it does; however both a chain (of events) or a cycle (of events) are inconceivable: because of the gaps in the first which are infinite in number, and in the second because of its being a single thing preceded by itself and also followed by it. It must also necessarily be that the Bringer into Being (of the world) possesses going on, that is that its existence is not followed by non-existence for otherwise its essence would admit of the two (i.e. going on and non-existence) and this in turn would necessitate – in giving preference to the existence (of the world over its non-existence) – that there be an agent which gives specificity and so this (essence) would (necessarily) be an in time occurrence. There has been ample proof given above of the necessity of His being from before endless time, and from this you will realise that everytime the timelessness of His existence is proven, His non-existence is also inconceivable.'"

He has also said in *al-Wusta*: "Then it is necessarily true that the Bringer into Being of the world be timeless, that is there is no firstness to His existence for otherwise He would be in need of something to bring Him into being, and a chain of events would be necessarily true which would lead to a infinite number of gaps, or a cycle which would lead to something preceding itself – and both of these are inconceivable and incomprehensible for the intellect. It is also necessarily true that the Bringer into Being be ongoing, that is, nothing comes after His existence for if it were acceptable that non-existence be associated with Him, His existence would be (merely) conceivable, rather than necessarily true because, by definition, the reality of the necessary is that it is inconceivable for the intellect to imagine its non-existence – and as for this existence it has been supposed that it admit of non-existence and so it is possible (rather than necessarily true) since that which is possible is that for which existence and non-existence are both correct. Moreover, with respect to that which is possible, it is inconceivable that it occur without reason and so this possible existence is in need of a reason and so would necessarily be of this world and in time – and proof has been given above that His existence necessarily be from before endless time. Moreover if one supposes the absence of the existence of going on with respect to everything which has been proved timeless, then this is a contradiction and unacceptable to the intellect."

BAQA' – GOING ON

$$\text{لَوْ أَمْكَنَ الْفَنَاءُ لَانْتَفَى الْقِدَمُ}$$

$$\text{لَوْ مَاثَلَ الْخَلْقَ حُدُوثُهُ انْحَتَمْ}$$

25   If annihilation were possible, then timelessness would be nullified. If He resembled creation, His coming-into-being would be necessarily true

As-Sanusi said in his *al-Wusta*: "It is necessarily true that the Bringer into Being of the world is not corporeal and that He does not have the attributes of a body because, by definition, all bodies and their attributes have been created necessarily in time." Then after some further dicussion he continues: "And He does not exist in any location because location is only occupied by bodies; He also does not have direction because this is one of the accidents of a body

– thus aboveness is one of the accidents pertaining to the head, belowness a quality pertaining to the legs, being on the right pertains to the limbs on the right (of the body), leftness is a quality possessed by the limbs on the left of the body, being in front is inherent to the part of the body called the belly and behindness pertains to the back. Thus it is inconceivable that He be a body, inconceivable that He be described as possessing these limbs and all the other adjoining parts (of the body) which necessarily possess these characteristics (of being above or below for example)."

He has also said in *ash-Sharh*: "His saying 'because location is only occupied by bodies' means that the occupying of direction and location necessitates that a space be occupied and every space which is occupied presupposes a body. However, it is inconceivable that Allah, mighty is He and majestic, be a body for if He were in a location He would either be bigger than it or smaller than it and He would need an agent of particularisation. Moreover, if He were in a location, then He would necessarily either be in a state of movement in it or at rest, and both movement and rest are in-time occurrences. Moreover, if He were in a location, He would be necessary there be an agent which specifies one particular location rather than another and this (in turn) necessitates an in-time occurrence and none of the people of sunna are of the opinion that (He has) location; rather a group of innovators hold to this, namely the Hashwiyya and the Karamiyya and they are all of the opinion – may Allah be far above any opinion of theirs – that of the (various) directions or locations above-ness is specific to Him; and then they have differed after this: some of them saying that He is tangential to the throne – may He be elevated far above this; others claim that He is removed by an infinite distance, while yet others that He is removed by a finite distance. The Hashwiyyas have infected some of the Imams of the people of sunna with this disgraceful *madhhab*: thus sometimes they have attributed this *madhhab* to Ahmad ibn Hanbal, may Allah be pleased with him, since they make *taqlid* of him with respect to the branches of the deen and they are under the illusion that just as they follow him in the branches they also follow him in matters of *'aqida* – and Allah forbid that his *'aqida*, may Allah have mercy on him, be like their *'aqida*: his precedence in knowledge of *tawhid* in accordance with the way of the people of sunna is agreed upon by all and his disputation with the people of *bid'a* and his being put to the test at their hands on the subject of the essence of Allah is well known all over (the *umma*), may Allah be pleased with him, and may he and the Muslims be rewarded with the best of rewards. Even if it were possible that this (teaching) had occurred at his hand, may Allah, exalted is

He, be pleased with him – for the sake of argument, and there is no power no strength but by Allah, the High, the Vast – they would have no excuse and no basis for following him since *taqlid* regarding matters of *'aqida*, even when there is general agreement as to the correctness of these matters, is of of no use according to many of the *muhaqqiqun*. How much less true then is their stand when it is a question of *taqlid* about which there is definitive proof and consensus as to its invalidity; as for some passages in certain books containing the blemishes in the teachings of Shaykh Ibn Abi Zayd (see, for example, his interpretation of the 'location' of Allah's essence '*above* His glorious Throne' – see *Risala*, Book of Iman, Section 10), Abu 'Umar Ibn 'Abd al-Barr and some (of the *'ulama*) of the earlier generations before him they are invalid and should be disregarded. The reason for this illusion on the part of those who have transmitted it from some of the earlier generations is their well known habit of desisting, may Allah be pleased with them, from making *ta'wil* – interpretation – of texts whose literal meanings are inconceivable, like for example, '*established firmly upon the Throne*'[1] and similar *ayats*. Thus they have imagined that their desisting from making *ta'wil* of such *ayats* is because of their holding to the literal meaning of them, and Allah forbid that they should have done this; rather they have desisted from making *ta'wil* of these *ayats* because of the existence of a number of correct interpretations without, however, their knowing what is exactly intended by them – despite their being certain that inconceivable interpretations are definitely not meant. And what is more ugly than thinking something evil of someone who does not merit it."

His saying: 'that He also has no location or direction… ' etc, to the end of his discussion, is obvious and does not need any explanation. Moreover, this can also not be imagined of His supreme essence since it is not a body and is not existent by means of a body, and it may not be described with smallness or bigness, nor is it in a location or possesses location, this being a negation of the existence of this (essence) – any such supposition belongs rather to the realities one supposes existent in bodies or anything else which supports these (bodies). You find this erroneous supposition because of his combining the qualities existent in bodies or that which lends these (bodies) existence with his claim that the existence of other than these is inconceivable. On occasion, the intellect may affirm that in time occurrences necessarily stand in need of an agent which brings them into being; however, this is in opposition to the intellect when one wants to prove the necessity of His contrariety, exalted is

---

1   Ta Ha: 4

He, to all in-time occurrences. Thus there are those who are not in agreement in order to be in a position to reject what they experience as this untrue illusion, so they are convinced – and may refuge be found in Allah, exalted is He – that the Bringer into Being of the world is a body among other bodies, although none of these bodies resembles His goodness and beauty. And this is meaning of the words of Allah, exalted is He: "*Nothing is like Him. He is the All-Hearing, the All-Seeing*"[1] according to (the teachings of) such persons – who are rejected (by the sunnis) and upon whom is Allah's anger, may Allah be far removed from this. The reason for their going astray is that they have made a comparison between what they have not seen with what they have seen without integrating them, and so brought ruin on himself and refuge is only to be found with Allah, exalted is He and there is no strength and no power except by Allah the High, the Vast.

And amongst those (above mentioned sects) may be found some for whom it has become evident that if the existence of the world is a body then it would necessarily entail its having come into existence in time and in this it would necessitate a cycle or chain (of events) Thus they have decided upon (the matter) on account of this, together with what has become firmly fixed in his heart of the untrue illusion, namely that every existent reality must be a body or subsistent by it and that the world came into being of itself without an agent which brought it into being. This disaster came upon both parties because they have been deprived of success (from Allah) – the absence of Allah's assistance has deprived them of the capacity for a correct examination. So people have listened to the lies of illusion and supposition, plunging into what he does not understand of the laws of the Possessor of Majesty, He who is not contained by limits and who may not be known by any comparison. Those who heed this illusion do not realise that this illusion arises only through a lack of awareness of the essence – not of the body, nor of incidental, contingent event – but just because there is a lack of awareness of something, it does not necessarily follow that this thing does not exist. Does not the person of intellect realise that the person of intellect is only capable of comprehending physical realities and the Sustainer of them – if Allah, exalted is He, opens up knowledge for him at the moment of his perception of something. Indeed, if He does not open up for him a cognizance in his own essence, he would have no perception of these (corporeal realities) at all. Let him examine the mineral and animal kingdoms which are an image and representation (of meanings) for the man of intellect; let him reflect how

---

1 ash-Shura – Counsel: 9

these (inanimate objects and animals) are incapable of comprehending as long as they are not given an opening (by Allah) to a perception of this (knowledge) – even if this is clear to other (creational realities, like man). The existence of the supreme essence is unquestionable, necessarily existent and more manifest than any other manifestation. Every part of the world and each one of its attributes speaks of this (truth) by the language of hal – of states – and declares it with the clearest and most eloquent of speech. However despite this there is no access to knowledge of its reality except if we have an opening to comprehending the nature and truth of creational, in time realities since He, exalted is He, has no likeness to them, may His splendour be exalted. Moreover He, exalted is He, has not created for us a knowledge of the reality of His essence, that is, that which is necessary of existence, just as He has not created the mineral or plant kingdoms with a capacity to perceive certain things which without doubt belong to them as a type or class and which are so close in nature and form to them – or indeed any other thing more distant in its relationship to them. None of the creational realities has any knowledge except by virtue of what has been taught it by our Lord, mighty and majestic is He, and which He has opened up to it by His overflowing generosity. It is by His overflowing generosity that He, glorious is He, has opened up (our intellects to) our knowledge of His existence and His attributes, and this, by His having differentiated our intellects from all other (forms of awareness)." This then is the gist of as-Sanusi's discussion.

I SAY: "I have seen the following text by one of the people of knowledge who verify knowledge carefully (*muhaqqiqun*): 'If our Lord came to be in a location then He would be in need of the location and if He were in need of it then He would be dependent upon an agent to determine that place for Him rather than another place; and if He were in need of an agent to specify this then He would be in time and contingent. Through this you realise the impossibility of His being bound by time for if He were bound by time He would be in need of an agent to specify one particular time rather than another.'"

USEFUL POINT: 'Ayn Jeem[1] said in the gloss on the *Risala*: "The *madhhab* of the four imams is the same as that of the earlier generations regarding the matter of Allah's likeness (to anything) for ash-Shafi'i was asked about – *al-istawa'* – " (His firm) establishment (upon the Throne)" and he replied: 'It is an establishing without likeness (to anything) and I affirm the truth of

---

1 This commentator of the *Risala* I have not been able to identify – the letters he uses to indicate the various commentators are explained at the beginning of the work but not *'Ayn Jeem*.

this without metaphor or similarity; I suspect my *nafs* (of wrongly trying to) comprehend this and so I refrain absolutely from delving into this.' When imam Malik was asked about it he replied: 'The establishment (of Allah on the Throne) is known, the manner (in which it came to be) is not, trusting (this to be so) is obligatory and asking about it is a *bid'a*.' Ahmad ibn Hanbal was asked about it and he replied: 'The establishment (of Allah on His Throne) is as has been narrated (in the Qur'an) not as people imagine it to be.' Abu Hanifa said: 'Whoever says: "I do not know whether Allah is in the heavens or on the earth has committed an act of *kufr* because this statement presupposes that Allah, the Real, has a location and whoever imagines that the Real has location is conceiving of a likeness (for Him with regard to creational realities)."' Here ends the discussion of *'Ayn-Jeem*. Zarruq said: "'Izz ad-Deen ibn 'Abd as-Salam said: 'The correct opinion is that someone who ascribes location (to Him) does not commit an act of *kufr*.'"

ANOTHER BENEFIT: al-Munawi said: "As-Siddeeq, may Allah, exalted is He, be pleased with him, was asked: 'How do you recognise your Lord?' and he replied: 'I recognise my Lord by my Lord.' Then he was asked: 'Is it possible for a man to perceive of Him?' and he replied: 'The very incapacity to perceive Him is itself perception.' The Lantern of Tawhid, the Light of Devotion, 'Ali, may Allah, exalted is He, ennoble his face, was asked: 'By what have you come to know your Lord?' and he replied: 'By that which he has made known Himself: He is not perceived by the senses, He is not to be compared with people and (He is) near in His distance, distant in His nearness.'"

Another useful point: Sayyidi Ahmad Bab said in *Kifayat al-Muhtaj*: "One day someone related the saying of Ibn Abi Zayd to 'Abd ar-Rahman ibn Muhammad ibn Ahmad al-Hajj al-Magribi, known as at-Tajouri, namely that 'He is above the Illustrious Throne in His essence' and he mentioned that among the responses given were that the words 'in His essence' had been interpolated into his book but one of them refuted it and said: 'Any expression to which an objection is made may be responded to in this fashion then no objection remains to any expression.' The Shaykh got angry and said: 'People are agreed as to the sublime rank of this imam – he has not been described as possessing any (false *'aqida*) that might be imagined from the expression.' Then he said to the questioner: 'Be quiet or otherwise I will not speak.' Then the student said: 'For the sake of Allah, exalted is He, do not speak', and then the Shaykh went off angrily. The student was asked (about the incident) after this and he said: 'I feared that I would miss a lesson because I was in a state of *janaba* – ritual impurity. I came to the mosque and I was in a state of *janaba* and the Shaikh rebuked me as you have seen.'"

Ghina – Independence

لَوْ لَمْ يَجِبْ وَصْفُ الْغِنَى لَهُ افْتَقَرْ

26 If the attribute of independence were not necessarily true (with respect to Him) He would be in need ...

As-Sanusi said in his *Wusta*: "It is necessarily true that He, exalted is He, be self subsistent, that is, self-subsistent in essence and that He not be in need of location. It is inconceivable that He be an attribute. There are those who interpret His self-subsistence as His being independent of location and of any agent of particularisation. This is more specific than the first interpretation: the association of a substance (*jawhar*) belonging to Him is absent from this attribute. Proof of His being independent of any agent of particularisation is that mentioned above, namely regarding His timelessness and His going on. Proof of His being independent of location is that if this were an attribute then it would be inconceivable to describe Him with the attributes of meaning or attributes indicating meaning[1] because one attribute cannot subsist by another and because in addition if this were an attribute then it would be in need of a location in which to be existent. If then the location were a god like the attribute it would necessitate there be more than one god; if the attribute alone took on the aspect of divinity and (all this implies of) its laws and judgements (relative to divinity) then it would require the possibility of the attribute occupying a location while the location does not take on the attribute of its law and judgement. Moreover, that the attribute should be a divinity is not more likely than its location be a divinity."

He said in explanation of this: "This means that the need for an agent of particularisation necessarily entails in-time occurrence because the effect of the agent of particularisation only manifests as an in-time occurrence. This is because that which is from before endess time is that which is and remains existent (when superfluities are gone) and that which necessitates this (existence). Moreover to obtain what has already been obtained is inconceivable and the occurrence of

---

1 Arabic: *sifat al-Ma'ani wa'l-ma'nawiyya*, the first referring for example to His names like 'the Living', 'the Hearer', 'the All-Powerful' and the second to the actual attribute contained in the name, like life, hearing or power

an in-time event within the essence of our Lord – majestic is He and mighty – and within His attributes is inconceivable because timelessness and on-goingness necessarily pertain to the supreme essence and its attributes. Again, that He, exalted is He, should be in need of an agent of particularisation is inconceivable.

Wahda – Oneness

لَوْ لَمْ يَكُنْ بِوَاحِدٍ آَا قَدَرْ

... if He were not One, He would have no power.

As-Sanusi said in his *Kubra*: "This Creator must be One for if there were a second with Him it would necessarily entail the incapacity of both of them or the incapacity of one of them in the case of a difference (of opinion or will); also, the overpowering of them both or the overpowering of one of them in the case of necessary agreement along with the inconceivability of what is known to possible for each one of them with respect to their individual uniqueness and singularity – making them independent of each other – precludes necessary existence for each one of the two. Thus if their agreeing does not have to happen but rather their differing is conceivable – then they must both necessarily accept incapacity, and the first (argument mentioned at the beginning of our discussion) reoccurs. Moreover, absolutely incapacity necessarily follows, in the case of agreement, because one act cannot possible be divided up: they both mutually prevent the other from this; the incapacity of both or the incapacity of one of them necessarily follows, as in the case of a difference between them. Incapacity for Allah, exalted is He, is inconceivable because this would contradict (His) power: if He is of before endless time, it necessarily entails the impossibility of His non-existence. It must necessarily be that this God has power over something all the time. If this God were in time, then the opposite of this (is true), that is, power from before endless time: (if power from before endless time is presupposed then) non-existence of this (power) is inconceivable and so incapacity also does not exist (in this case), and thus it is inconceivable for God, exalted is He, to be described as possessing the attributes of in-time, contingent occurrence.""

If you were to say: "Why is it not conceivable for the world to be divided between them into two parts such that one of them has power over one of the parts and the other over the other – and a mutual restricting by the one of the other would not necessarily follow?" – then the answer would be that the impossibility of finiteness with regard to God's power to determine and decree things and His willing whatever He wills has already been expounded above: the supposition contained in the question is thus inconceivable. Moreover, if the two parts existed together in their substance, then power must necessarily be attached to one (part) of the two substances; for if it were attached to all of it then – by virtue of their simularity – a mutual restricting of the one by the other would follow; and if one of the two parts were substance (itself) and the other incidental or contigent then this would not be acceptable from the point of view of the intellect since power over a substance cannot be conceived of intellectually without that power also disposing of that which is incidental or contigent to it; likewise the opposite is true because of the inherent association between them. This would also not remove the (above mentioned) mutual restriction on the part of the one by the other – that is, should one of the two want to cause the substance to have existence while the other does not wish to bring that which is incidental to it into existence. Then they claim that by this proof, I mean the proof of mutual restriction, we can establish proof that, exalted is He, is the Bringer into Being of the acts of the slaves and that there is no (actual) influence or effect as a result of their in-time contingent power in these (actions of theirs); rather this (power) is existent, adjoined to these (actions). We have already mentioned that we hold to (the notion of) adjoined, associate power – in the sense that it is to be found in the inevitable difference between movement which occurs out of necessity (that is determined by Allah) and movement out of choice (that is determined by the slave), and in the attachment of this in-time, contingent power to that which has been determined by Allah's power in its place of occurrence, that is, by association or by adjoining – without it being of any (actual) influence in (a person's capacity for) acquisition (of good or bad), according to the people of sunna, may Allah, exalted is He, be pleased with them. This '(capacity for) acquisition' refers to (the necessary understanding of) legal responsibility of every sane person who is of age (*at-takleef ash-shar'i*) and all this implies of reward and punishment. Thus (with this argument) is the *madhhab* of the Jabariya rendered invalid, namely, the teaching which rejects in-time contigent power because of the implied refutation of necessity and the invalidation of the role of legal responsibility (takleef) and the notion of reward and punishment. It was on account of this latter teaching that the *bid'a* and *madhhab* of the Qadariyya evolved (as a response), namely (the claim) that the slave invents his actions in accordance with his will by means of the power which Allah, exalted is He, has created – (the true teaching) of which you are aware – and the proof of oneness and the impossibility of a partner with Allah, exalted is

He, in whatever form (that may be conceived of)."

He has also said in *al-Wusta* in a discussion about the proof for oneness: "By means of this proof you will be aware of the impossibility of their being any influence whatsoever on the part of anything of this world on any other (in-time) manifestion because of what this would necessarily entail of this manifestation being outside the orbit of the power and will of our Lord, majestic is He and mighty; and this would necessitate in-time, contingent occurrence having hegemony over timelessness, and this would be inconceivable. Thus there is no influence (over that which is other than it) belonging to the power of the creation neither in movement or rest, neither in obedience or disobedience – neither with respect to an influence in general, nor a direct (influence) or any other (indirect influence) through generation. Reward and punishment, then, are both without cause or reason and obedience and disobedience are two indications, which are created in nature and which belong to Allah, exalted is He, but which are subject to no specific agency of the slave; rather they both indicate, within a *shari'ah* sense, that which glorious is He, has selected of reward and punishment: if He, glorious is He, were to reverse what these two things refer to, or reward or punish spontaneously without prior indication (of the reasons for His action) then it would (necessarily) be an acceptable action on His part, majestic is He and mighty: "*He will not be questioned about what He does, but they will be questioned.*"[1] As for the acquisition (of reward or punishment) on behalf of the slave this refers to the bringing into being on the part of Allah, exalted is He, that which is subject to His irresistible power, like movement and rest, for example, and which accompagnies the in-time power. This in-time power, in turn, is connected to and dependent upon that which is subject to irresistible force – without, however, exerting any influence over it in any way. This acquisition (of power on behalf of the slave) is connected to (his responsibility regarding) the obligations of the *shari'ah* and characterises the reward and punishment – from the point of view of the *shari'ah* not of the intellect. That which indicates the association of this action with this power – even though we do not perceive any effect of the former on the latter at all – is (the example afforded by) our perception of the difference between the movement occasioned by the trembling (of the limbs) or other involuntary movements, and movements determined by (our) free choice. However, on thorough examination, there is no (actual) difference between the two – other than that fact that the movements which have been consciously chosen are accompanied by the in-time, incidental power in the slave who experiences

1   al-Anbiya – The Prophets: 22

thereby the sensation of ease (in the execution) of the act, in opposition to the aforementioned involuntary, necessary movement.

So you will realise from this that our saying that 'the action which is not experienced by the person performing it as involuntary is an in-time incidental power in the slave' refers to one among the (numerous) incidental occurrences (of existence), like knowledge and similar non-essential aspects, for example, which may be connected to an action even if we do not see any influence whatsoever on its part over the action in question. Thus we distinguish ourselves from the *madhhab* of the Jabariyya which refutes in-time, incidental power in the slave under all circumstances. Furthermore by means of our saying that this in-time incidental power does not possess any influence over the action at all but rather is connected to and associated with it, we separate ourselves from the *madbhab* of the Qadariyya, the Zarathustrians of this *umma*, who say that by means of this power a person may initiate his actions in accordance with his own will.

They have also said: "by this, acts of obedience or disobedience are carried out and acts are rewarded or punished" – however, we have already explained to you above that reward and punishment do not have a cause or reason from the point of view of the intellect, according to the people of truth; rather acts of obedience or disobedience are indications of an artificial nature which have no intellectual basis. Thus we have been able to discriminate between this (correct way) and these other two – something which is a subject of misunderstanding for many people."

He has also said in his commentary: "In general, that which the people of truth hold to – that is those who are free of any kind of *shirk* with respect to Allah, exalted is He, and whose hearts, by the reality of their *tawhid*, have been saved by the overflowing generosity of Allah, exalted is He, from remaining in intense torment – is that creation, whatever its form, possesses no influence over any manifestation (in creation), whatever it may be, neither in a general manner, nor in a specific or direct manner, or indirectly, through generation, that is neither without the agency or means (of something else) or by means (of something else): whatever actions exist by the power or strength of a created reality, irrespective of whether they exist in their essence like the movements or moments of rest, for example, or they accompany that which exists in the essence like the movements of a stone, a lance or an arrow when being propelled forward and the movements of a sword and the wounds associated with it and the like – all this occurs only by the creation of Allah, exalted is He, and His invention and His choosing it, without mediation or cause. He, mighty is He and majestic, brings together what ever He wishes of His creation and separates whatever He wishes of His creation, blessed and exalted is He."

After a while he also says: "As for the *madhhab* of the people of truth, may Allah be pleased with them, they have joined the haqiqat and the *shari'ah* and are free of the *bid'a* of the two sects, by the overflowing generosity of Allah, exalted is He. This is because they have avoided the Jabariyya sect which divides actions into two modes, those which are freely chosen and those which are inevitable or involuntary, that is, (they claim) the former is decreed for the slave in the sense that he possesses in-time incidental power which accompanies those actions chosen (by him) but is connected to them without exerting any influence (over them). Thus these actions are those normally in the capacity of the *mukallaf*; and it is in them that occur the obligations, in accordance with what is indicated in the *shari'ah*. They have avoided the (false teaching of the) Qadariyya by the fact that they do not ascribe any influence whatsoever to that incidental, in-time occurrence, that is be it of either (a deliberately chosen or involuntary nature) in general; rather, according to them, the slave and his incidental power and that (occurence) decreed (by Allah) which is subject to this power is all a creation belonging to Allah, exalted is He, without mediation and no associate whatsoever – in accordance with what is indicated in this matter by the truth of the intellect. In short, the nature of the empowered slave, according to the people of truth, is that he is compelled within a framework or setting which is chosen such that in general he exerts no influence at all over any manifestation (in creation). Rather he is a container for the occurrences and incidents such that Allah creates what He wishes of them within it. Allah chooses in the sense that the practice of our Lord, exalted is He in His majesty, with regard to what prevails with this (person), is the absence of continuity or constancy of a (particular) action (in question) in his regard, especially when He, exalted is He, creates a disliked action in him, to which he is compelled. However He, exalted is He, continues an action in his regard on some occasions in accordance with the need – in particular when He creates for him a state in which the (person) is determined and resolved to undertake a (particular) action and by virtue of this extraordinary state – an indication in itself of the power of the One Who is not preoccupied by one event from neglecting another – he may attain to the furthest limits. His knowledge extends to all things by His choosing; He is capable of (carrying out) an action or desisting from it in outward appearance, and so glorious is Allah, He who subjects (to His will) and overpowers, who has softened some of His overwhelming force such that many intellects fail to perceive this, let alone those of idle thoughts and illusion. Because of their ignorance, the latter hold to the inner meaning of the matter, despite the vastness of their incapacity and the intensity of their need – that they are excluded in some of their actions from the control of the might of the One, the Subduer, the King, the Knower of all things. How on earth could this be when he is allied to general incapacity and always in a real state of need! For this reason some of the imams have said: 'The thing which most resembles the slave who is free to choose is the instrument of the imagination which toys (with him) in the sense that from the outward (appearance of things the slave is coerced) and this contradicts his inner (freedom of movement): it appears to the one who is ignorant of the nature (of the imagination) in the first instance that he may cause it to moves, be at rest or to strives (after something); the (slave) brings one part of this (imagination) to bear on another, or imputes or ascribes one thing to another by selecting of it (what he wishes); but if he is aware of its nature he finds this (imagination) coercing him into (undertaking) those actions which manifest from it, incapable (at the same time) through the utmost incapacity of initiating anything of it (of his own volition).

From this you will realise that the meaning of coercion (*jabr*) from the point of view of the intellect is a power (the notion of which is) shared amongst the people of sunna and the group whose name (in Arabic) is coloured by the term 'coercion', namely the word al-Jabariyya. It is for this reason that the Mu'tazilis also call the people of sunna al-Jabariyya – i.e. those of *jabr* – those under the force of fate. These two groups are '*jabariyya*' in an intellectual sense – that is with respect to the inner truth. The difference, however, between the two *jabariyya* groups is that the jabr that the people of truth hold to with respect to the voluntary, freely chosen actions are only perceived by the intellect, rather than the senses and the *jabr* which those we designate as the *jabariyya* hold to – according to (its definition in) their principles – is perceived by the senses and the intellect in all actions. There is no doubt that their opinion is false, both according to the *shari'ah* and according to what has been set out in the above (discussion). According to the people of truth, the freely choosing slave is not coerced in outward appearance and Allah, glorious is He, creates in him the fundamental elements of the action from an in-time power – dependent upon two kinds of connection – but not the connection capable of exerting an influence (over something else). Will is present in this in general: (thus) it is correct linguistically, in practice and in accordance with the *shari'ah* that this (person) be (either) exhorted to perform the action, or forbidden from it, that he be praised (for this action) or rebuked and censured (for it), that astonishment at the person's *kufr* be expressed, as in the words of, exalted is He: *"People of the Book! Why do you reject"*[1] and the like of this, of which there are many (*ayats*). As for what all this indicates according to the intellect alone – it is that certain actions are characterised by reward, like the obligations and the recommendations, while others by punishment, like the forbidden things; while others are not characterised by any of these things, like permitted or disliked things. As for the judgement as to happiness or unhappiness, it is (determined from) timelessness, without cause or reason, and Allah judges as He wishes and he does what He wills." Here end the words of as-Sanusi, may Allah be pleased with him, and may we benefit by him.

USEFUL POINT: Zarruq said in his *Naseeha*: "One of our Shaykhs said: 'There is no problem in *tawhid* other than *kalam*, the (question as to whether one can attain to) seeing Allah (on the Last Day) and the power acquired (by man). In all of these things one should hold to what is true in them and not expose oneself to matters of dubiety beyond this."

Ibn Zakari said in his commentary: "His words 'what is true' mean that the actions of the slave are subject to the power of Allah, exalted is He, – that is regarding their being brought into being – and to the power of the slave from another point of connection – expressed by the term 'acquisition.' It is not inevitable or necessary that power be connected to the thing or event subject to and determined by this power because the power of Allah, exalted is He, is in timelessness, connected to knowledge without (necessarily) a bringing into being. However, on its being brought into into being another kind of connection then becomes connected to it: this movement into being, by virtue of its connection to the power (of the slave) is called 'acquired', and by virtue of its relation to the power of Allah, exalted is He, it is called 'created.' Thus it is a creation belonging to the Lord yet ascribed to the slave and acquired by him: his power is a creation belonging to the Lord while ascribed to him, and is not acquired by him." This is the gist of the discussion on the matter contained in the *Sharh al-Maqasid* from al-imam Hujjat al-Islam.

Then he says: "(One must) stay free of dispute regarding dubious matters and desist from investigation of them – despite the fact that the people of the sunna have responded to the matter – because sometimes the matter may get a hold on the *nafs* of the person investigating and the answer may not satisfy him because of his lack of understanding. Thus there is a danger and risk in investigation."

USEFUL POINT: Abu'l-Qasim ibn Muhammad ibn 'Abd al-Qadir al-Fasi in

---

[1] Ali 'Imran – The Family of 'Imran: 69

the commentary on *Sharh al-'Aqida* of his grandfather 'Abd al-Qadir, may Allah benefit us by it, says: "He is the Creator of creation and the Creator of the actions of creation, of their movements, their moments of rest and all their states: thus there is no one other than Him who has influence (over others) in any action whatsoever and in any manner whatsoever. The effect and influence (of one thing on another) on the occassion of the coming together of one thing with another like the existence of combustion when fire comes into contact with wood or satiation after eating is the visible manifestation of the fire, for example, coming in contact with the wood but the fact that it is the fire which is doing the burning is not visible; and nor does any proof of the intellect point to this. Rather it is the action of Allah, and those who say that it is the action of the fire are bearing false witness." The *'ulama* have recognised that this (state of) incapacity in arriving at the reality and truth of this acquisition (of divine power on behalf of the slave) is in fact the aim of every equitable person and is the *madhhab* of the people of sunna and the *jama'a* – and what Khalil[1] holds to.

Ibn Hajar in *Fath al-Bari* said at the point where al-Bukhari says in the chapter entitled '*Do not make others equal to Allah*'[2] during his discussion on the matter of acquisition: "So if it is asserted that the action of the slave is necessarily either by virtue of a power from him or not from him – since there is no half-way point or connection between negation and affirmation – then, according to the assertion, the power which the Mu'tazilis claim is affirmed, while according to the negation *jabr*, 'coercion and fate', which is claimed by the Jabariyya is affirmed.

To this one may respond by saying: "Indeed the slave possesses a power by which he can discriminate between the person who is descending from the minaret and the person who is falling from it although he has no influence over this (occurrence) but rather his action occurs by the power of Allah, exalted is He. Thus the influence of His power in it (comes into being) after the power of the slave over it, and this is what is called 'acquisition.' In short that which is known as the power of the slave is an attribute from which are derived the action and the desisting in general, and this occurs in accordance with the will."

Hayat – Life, Irada – Will, 'Ilm – Knowledge, Qudra – Power

---

[1] In the text is only the abbreviation *alif-lam-mim-sad* which is not mentioned in the index at the beginning but which appears to refer to the *Mukhtasar* of Khalil. The Arabic letter *Kha'* – which is also not mentioned in the index appears to refer to Khalil himself.

[2] Al-Baqara – The Cow: 21

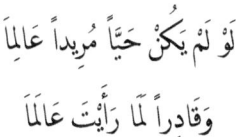

27 If He were not Living, Willing, Knowing, and and Powerful you would not see the universe –

As-Sanusi said in *al-Wusta*: "It is necessarily true that the Bringer into being of the world is living for otherwise he could not be described as having knowledge, or power or will, hearing, sight or speech, or as possessing life from before endless time. This is because of what has been explained above, namely the necessarily true aspects which have been stipulated as conditions of timelessness: it is inconceivable that a condition come after that aspect which has been qualified by a condition when that aspect is necessarily 'on going' for otherwise its timelessness would be negated. You will have understood its necessity through this.

He has also said in *Fasl al-Irada*: "It is necessarily true that the Bringer into Being of the world wills this, that is have the aim to do this for if He did not have the aim to determine an action with existence, in a specific time with specific dimensions and specific attributes then it would be necessarily true that this (action) remain in the state it was in without any of the aforementioned occurring – for ever and ever." He has also said in *Fasl al-Qudra*: "It is also necessarily true that the Bringer into Being of the world be powerful for otherwise nothing of the world would have come into existence."

Reminder: Know that just as before-endless-time and going on necessarily belong to His supreme essence, exalted is He, likewise before endless time and going on also necessarily belong to the rest of the attributes which are existent by His supreme essence, exalted is He. He said in *al-Wusta*: "Likewise before-endless-time and going on necessarily belong to the rest of the attributes existent with the supreme essence, exalted is He, for if they were to admit of non-existence they would be in-time and contingent. This is because, as you are aware, before-endless-time does not admit of non-existence, and it is inconceivable to ascribe an in-time contingent attribute to Him, exalted is He, for otherwise His essence would have had to have accepted it in eternity without beginning. This is because His acceptance of this would (necessarily) be essential in nature (*nafsiy*), and if this acceptance were also incidental to the essence then the essence would also necessarily need to accept other (incidental qualities) in addition to the first – and this would result in a chain (of events). Moreover, if it is necessarily true that His acceptance of those attributes – assumed to be incidental and in time – be existent in eternity then it would be correct to describe Him with those incidental attributes in eternity – for 'acceptance' (of these attributes) would be meaningless other than this. However, this is inconceivable because an in-time occurrence cannot possibly be of before endless time for one of the inherent features of before endless time is that its does not admit of non-existence – and incidental occurrence necessarily accepts non-existence and is described by means of it. Thus they are mutually incompatible. One may conclude from this that any of the attributes accepted by the supreme essence must be eternal and obligatory of existence in relation to it: the intellect cannot conceive that they be in-time or incidental; and that which is not accepted by the supreme essence in eternity is unaccepted for ever and ever for it is clear that it is inconceivable that acceptance may come about on behalf of the essence after this has not been so." Commenting on this, he said: "Since he has explained with proof and evidence the necessity of timelessness, going on and life, and since he has accepted those of the attributes that we know by way of the intellect and the *shari'ah* that Allah, exalted is He, may be ascribed with, he wanted to explain here the necessarily true nature of before endless time and going on with respect to the rest of the attributes which are existent in general by His essence, exalted is He – what we know of them and what we do not – such that one may conclude definitely that it is inconceivable for the supreme essence to be a locus for incidental events and that it may only be described with necessarily true attributes like before endless time and going on. He has given three proofs for this matter:

The first that if it were permitted to ascribe an incidental attribute to Allah, exalted is He, then it would necessarily follow that His supreme essence would also have to be ascribed with this in-time incidental attribute – in eternity. That this is inherently so may be explained in that the acceptance and reception of the essence, as essence, of anything that may be ascribed to it is necessarily that which has always pertained to it essentially (nafsiy): it is not possible that it come into being upon the essence after not having existed. This is because if the acceptance of the attributes came about after they had not existed then the essence would necessarily have to be described as not possessing (at a particular moment in time) the coming into being of this acceptance (of the attributes) in order for this coming into being to happen – and this too would necessarily require a chain of events, which is inconceivable. Thus it is necessarily true that the receptiion on behalf of any essence of that which is ascribed to it is inherent to it and that it is inconceivable that it have come into being anew on it after it had not belonged to it. You will be aware by this proof that if it had been possible for the supreme essence to take on an attribute of a contingent in-time nature it would have had to have taken it on in eternity, and to have taken it on in eternity necessarily requires the validity of the existence of this contingent attribute in eternity since there is no meaning to the essence having taken on this attribute in eternity unless it is valid that it take on this attribute in eternity. This, in turn, necessarily requires that both contingent occurrence and before endless time both be possible with respect to this attribute and this is inconceivable since before endless time is inherently necessarily true by nature and cannot accept non-existence, neither preceding (creational time) nor coming after it. Part of the inherent nature of in-time occurrence is that it must have been preceded by non-existence and it must be possible that it join to this (non-existence). Thus they are incompatible according to the nature of the description of each and what may be described to the one cannot be described to the other: this attribute which is necessarily incidental and in time in nature is not applicable to the supreme essence in eternity because of the impossibility that timelessness be ascribed to anything which has the capacity to take on in time occurrence. If the supreme essence cannot admit of it in eternity then it must necessarily not admit of it for ever and ever because of what is already known, namely the impossibility that the essence accept anew the attribute given that this (attribute) did not originally belong to the (essence). Thus if it is necessarily true that the supreme essence should not admit of any in-time attribute for ever and ever then it is also necessarily true that it not be described as possessing it for ever and ever – because of the impossibility of describing His essence with (such) an attribute and because this (essence) does not admit of it (anyway). It will have become clear to you through this that every time the supreme essence admits of any attributes then they are eternal and obligatory (of existence) with respect to this (essence), and by the law of corresponding opposites anything which is not eternal will not be admitted by the supreme essence.

If you were to say: "What you have mentioned demands – with respect to anything that admits of an attribute, irrespective of whether this disposition to acceptance is from before endless time or an in time occurrence – that the existene of this attribute which is accepted accompany the existence of this (essence which admits of it) and not come after it (chronologically)" – then this would be invalid. Proof (of this invalidation) is that a body has the disposition to accept (attributes) in the first moments of its existence although it may not described with possessing them originally. Thus it does not follow from the essence's acceptance of such-and-such an attribute that it be described as possessing it (originally) – much less that this attribute belong to it in an obligatory manner.

I SAY: "On the basis of what we have mentioned it necessarily follows that in the case of anything which admits of an attribute the possession of this (attribute) be such that it accompany the existence of this (accepting agent) – because acceptance by definition is only by way of the essence of the accepting agent: it is not possible that it come into being anew with respect to it after not having been (there); rather, it is necessarily true, with respect to every attribute which the supreme essence accepts, that it be obligatory (of existence) in relation to this (essence); also that it be eternal. This latter is true because since the supreme essence's taking on this attribute in eternity is necessarily true – by definition, because this disposition to acceptance cannot come into being anew onto the essence after not having been there (in the first place) – then it is also necessarily true that this attribute be obligatory (of existence in nature) since everything which may validly be termed 'of before endless time' cannot admit of incidental occurrence. This may be explained in that this attribute – accepted by 'the before endless time' in an eternal way must necessarily either be obligatory of existence, inconceivable of existence or conceivable of existence. Its being inconceivable of existence is clearly invalid for if it were like this, then 'the before endless time' would not admit of taking on this attribute or anything else; and likewise its being possible of existence is invalid for otherwise 'before endless time' would not have accepted this (attribute) in eternity – since that which is possible can only be contingent and an in-time occurrence. This is because it would need an agent to determine its specificity while (the nature of) eternity contradicts this need for an agent of specificity. Thus the reality of the (nature of that which is) possible contradicts (the nature of) eternity absolutely and so the two divisions (mentioned above) belonging to this attribute which is (supposedly) accepted by the supreme essence in eternity are invalidated. The third division, then, is necessarily true, that is, that this (attribute) be obligatory of existence – and this is the required result (of our argument). In other words, for the nature of the attribute to admit of existence in eternity it is necessarily true that this attribute be independent – in its essence – of an agent: anything that is in need in its essence of an agent cannot be existent in eternity and can only be incidental and in-time necessarily. Further, if it is obligatory that this attribute be independent of an agent in its essence then this necessarily means that it be obligatory of existence and this is the required result (of our argument).

In short, the coming after of the attribute in relation to eternity necessarily entails its possibility and everything possible is necessarily in time and contingent, and so does not admit of existence in eternity. Thus the juxtaposition of the nature of the attribute as being accepted by the supreme essence in eternity and the nature of this attribute accepting a coming after eternity is without doubt contradictory. What we have mentioned (above) will have become clear to you by means of this definitive proof, namely, that every time the supreme essence admits of any of the attributes, then it is necessarily true that they be eternal and obligatory of existence for this (essence) cannot admit of any(thing) coming after the existence of itself. As for a contingent in-time essence (such as man) admitting of qualities then it does not follow that they must be necessary of existence with respect to this essence. This is because there is nothing to stop this essence – as it is in-time – from admitting the coming into existence of attributes after the existence of the essence. This is so since this (created existence) remains possible and in need of an agent – whether or not the (in-time, contingent) essence took on these attributes at the moment of its existence or not – and our Lord, majestic is He and mighty, is the Doer who chooses freely, is the Muqaddim – He Who draws others near – and the Mu'akhkhir – He Who puts back and defers. He does in this whatever He wishes and he causes that which He wishes to go before or to come after.

In short, there is no contradiction with respect to in-time, contingent occurrence between our saying that it may be described with such-and-such an attribute at the moment of its existence and between our saying that it is correct to assert that this attribute comes after it in relation to it since there is no inherent inevitability regarding the validity of what is possible and its actual happening. However, as for timelessness, our saying that it is correct to descibe it with such-and-such an attribute in eternity contradicts the validity of the coming after of this attribute with respect to eternity because of what it contains of a turning upside down of the reality of things: the validity of the existence of an attribute necessarily entails its being necessary and obligatory of existence because of what we have explained above, and the validity of its coming after eternity necessarily entails its being conceivable (rather than necessarily true) and this explanation has also been made above. Combining or juxtaposing these two is contradictory and an inverting of the reality and truth (of things) by making the necessarily true conceivable and the conceivable necessarily true. Take care to understand the examination of this matter for many go astray and you will never find – and Allah knows best – a more satisfying explanation with respect to this proof than the one we have set out above. And to Allah belongs all praise and success, and there is no Lord other than Him."

USEFUL POINT: He has also said in *Ghayat al-Amani*: "Whoever intentionally describes Allah, exalted is He, with other than what He himself has described himself then he is a *kafir*; if this is by way of interpretation – *ta'weel* – then he is an innovator; and if out of ignorance then there is no excuse for ignorance and it is incumbent upon the fathers, the masters and the husbands to teach the deen of Allah, exalted is He, His *shari'ah*, and the branches of the law, including the fasting and all the other matters to those who fall under their jurisdiction since knowledge comes before action, action without knowledge being invalid."

وَالتَّالِ فِي السِّتِّ الْقَضَايَا بَاطِلُ

قَطْعاً مُقَدَّمٌ إِذاً مُمَاثِلُ

28 Any consequence of these six (propositions) is absolutely false; thus any such proposition is likewise false

"Any consequence of these" refers to Ibn 'Ashir's enumeration of "you would not have seen the world" and the like. Thus "any consequence" with respect to the first (of the six) matters namely Ibn 'Ashir's statement 'If timelessness were not His attribute …' (see above line 24), means that anything beyond or other than this (state of affairs) would as a consequence imply His coming into existence (*hadouthihi*): this is inconceivable because it would necessitate of a cycle or chain of events. Thus the proposition – namely His, exalted is He, *not* being ascribed with the attribute of timelessness – is like the consequent term in the conditional proposition of invalidity. The second consequence in the second matter (discussed by Ibn 'Ashir) is the negation of going on for Him, exalted is He. This (consequence) is (as the first term or proposition, also) invalid because the first term, namely the possibility of the onset of annihilation on Him, resembles it, that is, in its invalidity. This applies likewise to the (following four) other matters. So reflect on this and understand.

وَالسَّمْعُ وَالْبَصَرُ وَالْكَلَامُ

بِالنَّقْلِ مَعْ كَمَالِهِ تُرَامُ

29 and (proof of His) hearing, seeing, and speech (is afforded) by

transmission – and also (by deduction from) His perfection

Mayyara said: "It has been stated that there are two proofs in the *shari'ah* for the necessity of Allah, exalted is He, possessing the attribute of hearing, seeing and speech – either that which is termed *naqli* (transmitted/traditional) or (secondly) *sam'i* (that 'which is heard') – and this is what is meant by (Ibn 'Ashir's use of the word) 'transmission' and the *'aqli* he indicates by his words 'with His perfection.' As for (the proof of) *sam'i* transmission, there is the words of, exalted is He: "*He is the All-Hearing the All-Seeing*",[1] and His words, exalted is He: "*and Allah spoke directly to Musa*"[2]; (there are also) the *hadith* about this, which are many in number. The *ijma'* are united in the obligation of ascribing, exalted is He, in this way. As for the way of the intellect – it is that one refute those attributes that ascribe, exalted is He, as possessing attributes opposite to these, namely those which indicate lack or defect – for imperfection is inconceivable for Allah."

In conclusion: as-Sanusi said in *Sharh as-Qaseed*: "According to Shihab ad-Deen al-Qarafi in his *Qawa'id* ignorance is divided into ten parts:

1. (that kind of ignorance about which) there is absolutely no command to remove it or (concerning which) there is no punishment for allowing it to remain because it is inherent in us and there is no possibility of separating ourselves from it: such (ignorance on our part) is (part of) the majesty of Allah, exalted is He, and (in the nature of) His attributes which are not indicated by any manifest act or event in creation. The slave cannot therefore attain to comprension of them by investigation and so is excused because of his incapacity. This is indicated by his words, may the peace and blessings of Allah be upon him: "I am not able to praise you as You have praised yourself" and the saying of the Siddiq, may Allah be pleased with him, "The incapacity to understand is itself an understanding."

2. Muslims are in accord that it is *kufr* to deny that Allah, exalted is He, is All-knowing, or the Possessor of Speech or All-Powerful or to deny the like of His essential attributes. If he is ignorant of this but does not deny it then he is guilty of *kufr* according to at-Tabari, and it has also been said that he is not guilty of *kufr*.

3. That about which there is a difference of opinion as to whether someone be designated as a *kafir*, namely, whether the person who affirms the judgements (regarding Allah, exalted is He,) without affirming the corresponding attributes, should be regarded as a *kafir*, that is when he says, for example:

---

1   ash-Shura – Counsel: 9
2   an-Nisa' – Women: 163

Allah is all-Knowing but is without knowledge, All-Powerful but without power — and likewise for all the other judgements (regarding Allah) in the realm of meaning. There are two (different) views ascribed to Malik, ash-Shafi'i and al-Qadi regarding whether a person should be regarded as a *kafir* in this case.

4. There is a difference of opinion as to whether ignorance is such that it must be removed or that it is a reality which must (necessarily be allowed to) remain. As for (permitting) this (ignorance) it is an act of disobedience but I am not aware of anyone who has accused anyone of *kufr* through this. An example of this is (the question as to) 'before endlesss time' and 'going on' — are they both (positive) attributes existent from the attribute of meanings, or are they attributes of negation (- that is the negation of the possibility of His non-existence)? In fact, this latter is the correct view which one must hold to.

5. Ignorance as to the connection of the attributes rather than with the attributes (themselves), like the Mu'tazilis' singling out (the connection of) power and will to some of the conceivable (rather than necessarily true) aspects. As to treating them as *kuffar*, there are two opinions, and the correct view is that they are not to be treated as *kuffar*.

6. Ignorance connected with the essence of, exalted is He, like holding to its corporeality, its having location and direction. As for treating them as *kuffar*, there are two opinions — the correct one that they should not be — other than those who hold that Allah has paternity or has sons, or that one may become one with Him (*al-ittihad wa'l-hulul*), for all are agreed that he who holds to this is a *kafir*.

7. Ignorance as to the timeless nature of the attributes while recognising their existence, like the saying of the Karamiyya that (His) will is contingent and in time and the like. As for treating them as *kuffar* for that, there is two opinions. The correct view is that they are not to be treated as *kuffar*.

8. Ignorance as what has occurred or will occur (as a result) of that which pertains to or is dependent on the attributes when decisive, necessary proof has been furnished as to their occurrence. This is ignorance, for example, of the will of Allah, exalted is He, and the sending of the Messengers or ignorance of the raising up of creation and the like. It is clear that this is *kufr* because it is ignorance as to the necessary knowledge of the deen. Here ends what he intends by his discussion. I SAY: "What he has transmitted in the second Section is that referred to by the Shaykh of the people of sunna Abu'l-Hasan al-Ash'ari — according to what Qadi 'Iyad says in the *Shifa*: "As for he who denies an attribute from among the essential attributes of Allah, exalted is He, or

rejects them while in full command of his intellect like his saying that He is not All Knowing, nor All Powerful, nor Possessor of Will, nor Possessor of Speech and any other attribute from amongst the attributes of perfection which are obligatory for Him, exalted is He, – then our imams have laid down, according to the *ijma'*, that those who deny His being ascribed with these (attributes) or strip Him of them should be treated as *kuffar*." This is the import also of the saying of Sahnun: 'Whoever says that He does not possess Speech is a *kafir*' – although he does not treat the muta'awalun (those who practise ta'weel) as *kuffar*. As for the person who is ignorant of one of these attributes, the *'ulama* have differed, some treating him as a *kafir*, and this is related from Abu Ja'afar at-Tabari and others. Abu al-Hasan al-Ash'ari has pronounced this view on one occasion. One group are of the opinion that it does not prevent the term 'Iman' being applied to him and this is what Ash'ari holds to – saying: 'This is because he does not hold to this having decided definitely as to its correctness and having considered it as part of the deen and the *shari'ah*. Rather one treats as a *kafir* he who believes that what he said is the (absolute) truth. Those who hold to this take as their proof the hadith of Sawda – when the Prophet, peace and blessings of Allah be upon him, only required of her an affirmation of *tawhid* and nothing else. They also cite as proof the saying of the person who said: "If Allah were to have power over me" and in the narration "it may well be (that I shall be able to hide such) that Allah will not be able to see me (and I will escape punishment)[1] He said: "so Allah forgave him." If most people were to be questioned as to the attributes and were to reveal (what they knew) of them, only a very few would have any knowledge of them.'" Here ends the discussion in the *Shifa*.

Take note: Ibn Shat said in the gloss to the *Qawa'id* of al-Qarafi, at the point where he says: 'The eighth: Ignorance as to what has occurred or will occur with respect to that which is connected to or dependent on the attributes when decisive, necessary proof has been furnished as to their occurrence …': "What he said in this eighth section is correct, however it could (be seen to) include the ignorance regarding the false teaching of the philosophers – for which there is no decisive proof – namely their certainty that the bodies will not be raised up (after death)." Here end the words of Ibn Shat.

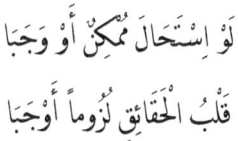

---

1 Vol.2, p.1082, *Bab ar-Ridda*

30 If the conceivable became inconceivable or necessarily true, realities and truths would necessarily be turned upside down.

His saying 'If the possible became impossible' – like, for example our own existence or the sending of the Messengers (being impossible), or other examples besides these two – and his words and 'become obligatory' – like if its reality (as a possibility) were to become an obligatory essence or substance in itself – then it would necessarily turn (the nature of) realities upside down and this is impossible, as he has made clear in the words 'would necessarily be turned upside down and become obligatory' for it would be impossible to affirm the existence of something without its (corresponding) reality. The words 'upside down' refer to the impossiblity of the possible, – possible here referring to that whose existence and non-existence are both correct; or refer to its being obligatory (of existence) and would necessarily entail the reversal of its reality – so understand." Here ends *"Ayn-Sad."*

يَجِبُ لِلرُّسْلِ الكِرَامِ الصِّدْقُ

أَمَانَةٌ تَبْلِيغُهُمْ يَحِقُّ

31 It is necessarily true that the noble Messengers are truthful, trustworthy and convey the message.

'Ayn-Sad said: "Sincerity refers to the belief that they are truthful regarding everything they convey from Allah, blessed is He and exalted, meaning that what they relate regarding this only corresponds to the matter itself, and that no falsehood on their part occurs in any of it, neither deliberately according to the *ijma'*, and nor out of forgetfulness according to the *muhaqqiqun*."

His saying: "Trustworthiness" is explained by as-Sanusi in his *al-Muqaddimat* as: "The preserving of the limbs outwardly and inwardly from getting involved in anything prohibited, be it forbidden absolutely (*tahrim*) or highly disliked (*makruh*), and their conveying of this prohibition This (in short) is the faithful fulfilment of everything which Allah has send them with and has commanded them to convey to the people, and in the manner they have been commanded to – regarding their conveyance to the common people and the elite amongst them."

NOTE: first, 'Abd al-Qadir al-Fasi said in his *'Aqida*: "The conditions of (conveyance of) the message are that (the Messenger be): male, perfect of intellect, in possession of mental acuteness and sagacity, sharp in judgement, noble of lineage, free of any loathsome aspect like their forefathers being tainted with adultery or madness, free of leprosy or anything which might impair manliness and nobility like practising low professions such as the job of cupping and scarification, or anything which might impair the wisdom of the Messengership, like blindness, according to the most correct view, or dumbness and blindness."

Second, 'Ali ibn 'Abd as-Sadiq has related from Muhammad ibn Marzouq the following: "What the people of truth hold to is that Prophethood is a miraculous act of generosity (*karama*) from, exalted is He, granted to whomever He wishes from His slaves and a blessing from Him upon whomever He has chosen from His creation; that none of them has a choice in the matter, but rather it is from the overflowing generosity of Allah which He grants to whomever He chooses: "Is it then they who allocate the mercy of your Lord?"[1] and "Allah knows best where to place His Message."[2]

مُحَالٌ الْكَذِبُ وَالْمَنْهِيُّ

كَكَدَمِ التَّبْلِيغِ يَا ذَكِيُّ

32   Impossible are lying, and what is forbidden, as well as not conveying the Message, O man of intellect!

As-Sanusi said in his *Kubra*: "And given that the truthfulness of the Messengers is known by means of the miraculous proof, then it is obligatory to affirm them with respect to everything they have brought from Allah, exalted is He. It is impossible, intellectually speaking, that any lie issue from them, nor that they commit any act of disobedience from the point of view of the *shari'ah* because we are commanded to follow them and if it were permitted for them to commit acts of disobedience then we too would be commanded to follow them in this: "Say: 'Allah does not command indecency.'"[3] From this you will understand that there is no occurrence of anything disliked from them also, neither indeed anything which is (merely) permitted – in the manner that it occurs in people other than the Messengers – and by Allah, exalted is He, is success.

يَجُوزُ فِي حَقِّهِمْ كُلُّ عَرَضْ

لَيْسَ مُؤَدِّيًا لِنَقْصٍ كَالْمَرَضْ

33   Every (human) contingency is conceivable with respect to them, like

---

1   az-Zukhruf – The Gold Ornaments: 31
2   al-An'am – Livestock: 125
3   al-'Araf – The Ramparts: 27

illness, as long as this does not imply any imperfection

This refers to lesser illnesses, not those which are loathsome, like the various kinds of leprosy and the like – for such are not permitted with respect to the prophets.

$$\text{لَوْ لَمْ يَكُونُوا صَادِقِينَ لَلَزِمَ}$$
$$\text{أَنْ يَكْذِبَ الإِلَهَ فِي تَصْدِيقِهِمْ}$$

34 If they were not truthful, it would necessarily follow that God had told a lie in confirming them:

$$\text{إِذْ مُعْجِزَاتُهُمْ كَقَوْلِهِ وَبَرَّ}$$
$$\text{صَدَقَ هَذَا الْعَبْدُ فِي كُلِّ خَبَرٍ}$$

35 Since their miracles are equivalent to Him saying, 'He is truthful! This slave has spoken the truth in everything he reports'

As-Sanusi said in *al-Wusta*: "The method of proof for the certainty of the Message of the Messengers, on whom be peace and blessings, in general, and on the certainty of the Message of our Prophet and Lord Muhammad, may the peace and blessings of Allah be upon him, and may he be ennobled and granted everything most generously, in particular, and the explanation of the aspect of proof for the miracle and making it comprehensible by way of metaphor is the following: Among the things which are possible (for Him) is His sending, glorious is He, His Messengers to the slaves in order to convey the command of Allah, exalted is He, His prohibition, those things which He has permitted and all that is connected with these things. He has corroborated and endorsed them out of His generosity, glorious is He, by indicating their truthfulness regarding whatever they have conveyed from Him. All this is contained in His words of revelation: 'My slave has told the truth regarding everything that he conveys from Me.' Our imams, may Allah be pleased with them, have illustrated this with the following story: a person, before a great audience, affected to be in the company of the king although all the people had been screened off from seeing him. The person declared: 'Do you know why the king has gathered you together in order to command you to such-and-such a thing and to prohibit you from such-and-such a thing? why he summons you to meet him, but not in person? why sometimes the people's hearts melt just on hearing him? and why sometimes those of intellect are prevented from sleeping out of worry and anxiety? and why no one will escape from him except the one who endeavours now to prepare himself for him before he assails them, except he who lends a keen ear and who attends with all his heart and mind to what the king indicates in this regard from the depths of his knowledge? He has commanded me to convey this to you now so – move! move! get on with it! – for nothing remains between you and this fearful matter but a short span of time. With respect to this matter I am a trustworthy adviser and a warner for you. I have now completed the message of the king for you: whoever obeys him and who takes good care of his self will free it and will attain the great satisfaction of the king; whoever disobeys and who is negligent in looking after his self then he will expose himself to the unbearable terror of the king's anger – no one will be able to save him from the great destruction wrought by the king. Know that my saying this you is by a knowledge from the king, that is, from seeing and hearing it from him (directly). Even if we are now shut off from him, he is not veiled from seeing us or from listening to what is going on between us. He it is who raises up whomever he wishes and brings low whomever he wishes, and he is capable of punishing me if I have lied about him. There is no refuge for me if I disobey him nor anywhere to escape to or any means of resistance. You have known me since my childhood, known that I will not permit myself to lie to those who are like me or to lie to my own intellect. Just because my childhood is now past, my hair has turned grey about my temples and in my beard would I lie about the king before his very ears and eyes, in the full knowledge of his force and power and the painful punishment awaiting anyone who opposes his majesty or who treats an important matter of his with disdain? What could possibly protect me from him if I were to lie about him just once. I know for sure that if I were to render his words falsely and give you to understand something other what he said, then he would take me by the right hand and sever my arteries. And none of you would be able to prevent this happening. and so if neither the truthfulness of what I say nor what you have learnt from me convinces you – despite your having had the benefit of such comprehensive advice on my part, despite my extreme kindness to you, my great trustworthiness, the nobility of my predecessors, despite my aloofness from any low or despicable thing, especially that of lying, despite what you witness of my good character – then here is something which will overcome the excuse of each and every one of you; here is something whereby you will attain to the suns of necessary knowledge on the horizons of the heart so that you will no longer be able to deny all this – except for those who expose themselves to the anger of the king by their rebellious and disobedient behaviour such that the judgement of torment falls upon him. And it is this: that I ask the king – just as he has granted my mission to you in order to explain to you, guide you and warn you before death comes upon you unawares and granted you the capacity to prepare for your final reckoning – to have the kindness also of announcing explicitly my truthfulness with respect to what I have conveyed from him, that I have not lied and that I have not slandered him by claiming he does something when it would be against his nature to do so; that he singles me out to declare how singular is my truthfulness without any of you having to get up to ask him about it – like, for example, the liar who would seek to oppose me through the king by his false claim and his denial of the validity of what I have said. Such a person does not possess this truthfulness which I possess. Then he said: "O king! if I have been truthful with regard to what I have conveyed from you then break your habit and do this thing (I have asked of you)." Then the king replied to him regarding this matter in accordance with what he had asked, and all realised that he would not have achieved such an action from the king by an act of trickery.' It is clear then that this act was from the king and it served as an example of his affirmation of the truthfulness of this person in all that he conveyed of him. Thus knowledge of this was necessary and inevitable for those present at this *majlis* or who were absent but who received news of it from numerous informants.

It is clear that this example corresponds to the state of the Messengers, on whom be peace and blessings, and it is clear that, with respect to their character and behavior, peace and blessings on them, their holding to truthfulness is necessarily known (by all, their being no possibility for doubt) – as is their rising above any lowness or meanness in their aspirations, their doing without the *dunya* completely such that its gold and clay are equal to them and their adhering to extreme humility with the poor and destitute; as in their lack of recognition of rank and honour in people but their demand for it with respect to the King, the Real; and their great kindness towards all of creation; their perfect counsel to the slaves of Allah, exalted is He, their intense fear of Him, exalted is He and their endeavour to fulfil whatever they have conveyed from Him before anyone else and their perseverance – right up to their deaths – in calling creation to Allah, exalted is He; their treating equally the people of low rank and those of high rank, the rich and the poor, those sharp of intellect and the stupid, those unable to communicate properly and the eloquent, their equity regarding both the free and the enslaved, the male and the female from amongst them, those present and those absent, to kings and subjects alike; then their being expansive in their breasts in order to tolerate the lack of courtesy and extremes of roughness or courseness in people's behaviour; and their being merciful to all of them – kinder to them even than to their own children, or to themselves – never expecting anything in return for this, nor any benefit of this world from them. Rather they, on whom be peace and blessings, expose themselves to the extremes of harshness and menaces on their part to such a degree that (it is evident that) only they (the Messengers) who are sustained by the very core of truth could possibly withstand such people; only those who are occupied with the delight of their contentment of their Lord could persevere in this – thus they are able to have awe and reverence for a matter (of the deen) such that they can bring it to fulfilment in accordance with His will and desire. It is established by numerous chains of narration just how much they were subject to the torment and molestation of people on account of their calling them to Allah, exalted is He, – so much so that people became bold and impudent towards the most excellent of creation, the most noble of them in the eyes of Allah, exalted is He, our Prophet Muhammad, may the peace and blessings of Allah be upon him: they caused harm to him, molested him and fought him so much so that they broke his tooth. Despite this, however, his noble and elevated face continued to shine resplendent while they were veiled by their gross ways from witnessing his excellence of character; and this, despite the fact that even the slightest understanding of the extraordinary, miraculous nature of that vast and graceful character should have been enough to arouse wonder in their minds, should have intoxicated their senses. How could a people have success who caused the face of our Prophet – who had showed such kindness and mercy to them – to bleed; who received them with the sun of his presence, with his beautiful and resplendent face and who gave them the good news by virtue of his elevated, pure essence; who persevered in protecting them from the Fire – so concerned was he that they should be averted from it – continuing in his efforts right up to the last minute, right up to the moment when the matter ceases to be in their hands – the moment of their entry into the Abode of Perdition.

All this indicates that they were truthful in everything which they conveyed from Allah, exalted is He. The very circumstances of their state is necessarily incompatible with the state of lying. How could this be otherwise when Allah has confirmed them through miracles which could certainly not have been worked by trickery, magic, delving into medicine or any other means – miracles like reviving the dead, causing the sea to split into two towering walls (of water) and the like. If this were something that he had had access to by trickery then it would mean a (a capacity to) alter normality which they alone had access to – to the exclusion of the rest of the people on earth. On the contrary, it is known with certainty that the Messengers we far removed from such knowledges, their causes and the practioners of such (trickery and magic): *"You never recited any Book before it nor did you write one down with your right hand. If you had, the purveyors of falsehood would have voiced their doubts."*[1] This (namely that they wrought miracles) is attested to both by those who supported (the Messengers) and opposed (them) – this despite there being amongst the enemies and enviers sufficient cause to motivate them into inquiry and investigation. Common sense precludes their having a relationship to anything (in the realm of magic) – for otherwise this (practice on their part) would be well known and hidden to no one. In short, the truthfulness of the Messengers, on whom be blessings and peace is something which is necessarily well known – accepted by all who meet with success through Divine guidance." Here ends the discussion of *al-Wusta*.

In the *Kubra* he says: "The excellence of our Prophet Muhammad, may the peace and blessings of Allah be upon him is known by a necessary knowledge (which does not admit of dubiety). His claim to the Message is clear and his challenges (to mankind) by way of his miracles are innumerable. The most excellent of these (miracles) is the Vast Qur'an whose *ayats* still address serious-minded people by their invalidation of all *deens* other than the deen of Islam; whose *ayats* incite those who are strong and impulsive in their opposition to compose prose and poetry in defiance of the inimitability (of the Qur'an), whose *ayats* challenge those profoundly versed in every art of eloquence, those who have mastered language in all its breadth and depth such that no word escapes them in their verbal attacks however intractible. And if they meet with no success – then how is one to be surprised when they themselves can hear of their own incapacity in the clear, unmistakable words of, exalted is He: *"Then produce ten invented suras like this."*[2] or *"Then produce a sura like it."*[3] He, exalted is He, then declares the incapacity of all creatures, both mankind and the jinn, whether gathered together or individually saying: *"Say: 'If both men and jinn banded together to produce the like of this Qur'an, they could never produce anything like it, even if they backed each other up.'"*[4] Despite this however, their conceit – on which their whole character is based – is not shaken: usually they can hardly

---

[1] al-'Ankabut – The Spider: 48
[2] Hud: 13
[3] Yunus – Jonah: 38
[4] al-Isra' – The Night Journey: 88

control themselves at the slightest criticism of their rank or dignity, even if it means risking their own life. But how can this be when this (challenge of Allah) is a kind of rhetoric which they themselves employ – so much so that it pervades their speech and they are to be found exclaiming such things in every corner of the earth. However, in the end it reduced such people to silence when they realised that it was impossible to stand up to this divine matter – either because it was not in their power, and this is the most correct view, or because, according to the second view, they were dissuaded or prevented from doing so (by Allah). Whoever felt no shame, who met the challenge and who took up a stand against this divine matter, like Musaylama the Liar, was exposed and reduced to shame; they produced a hocus pocus which will be ridiculed until the end of time. If this Qur'an had been transmitted to them like any other text, that is transmitted by isolated or single lines of transmission, then they would have had an excuse that the text had not reached them (in its original form). This however is not the case but rather the import of its words, its pages and commands have filled the whole earth, its plains and mountain ranges, have reached its nomadic folk and people of the cities, on the land and on the sea, both the *muminun* and the *kuffar*, both the jinn and mankind. This state of affairs has remained like this for almost 900 years – does the person of intellect have any doubt after all this that it is not from Allah, exalted is He, that His Prophet has not affirmed the truth of it? – despite the news it contains of corresponding unseen realities before their coming into being, despite the tremendous knowledges of the *shari'ah* contained in it, knowledges comprising things mankind has been incapable of mastering (himself) – matters of benefit in this world and the next; despite the exposition of proofs, the refutation of the rejectors by means of definitive proofs, the narration of stories of past peoples, counsel for the purification of the self and admonition so apt and pertinent that all the counsel and admonition ever given would be nothing in comparison to just one fragment of this divine admonition. All this from a Prophet who had never before laid eyes on a book and not had the opportunity to keep company with people of knowledge such that he might have acquired any of it from them; whose knowledge of all this was of a necessary kind (that did not admit of doubt or debate): "*You never recited any Book before it nor did you write one down with your right hand. If you had, the purveyors of falsehood would have voiced their doubts.*"[1] And this is affirmed both by those who agree and those who disagree (with his Message). Then there are all the innumerable miracles; and his character from which his noble essence has been formed

---

1   al-'Ankabut – The Spider: 48

– endowed with almost indescribable perfections, but which were already manifest in his behaviour and character before the onset of his mission. On top of all this Allah, exalted is He, has confirmed mention of his name and all his attributes (as a Prophet) in past (revealed) Books saying: "*...those who follow the Messenger, the Unlettered Prophet, whom they find written down with them in the Torah and the Gospel.*"[1] People even foretold of all this shortly before his mission. The indications (of his coming) were such that glorious is He, assured there be no doubt as to his Prophethood by forbidding the Arabs from using his name – except for just a few people who, on the basis of the rumours (of the coming of a Prophet) were called with this name just before his mission in the hope of their acquiring the Prophethood thereby. However, by the vast generosty of Allah, exalted is He, He removed all doubt by ensuring that none of those who had been called by this name uttered the claim of Prophethood.

USEFUL POINT: The author of *al-Mi'yar* has related from 'Ali ibn Rasheeq that there arose a long argument between the latter and some priests – during which a priest said – may Allah, exalted is He, be far removed from any of his words and may the noble revelation be far distant from any of his imaginings: "Listen now to what I have to say and do not think that I want to contest the Qur'an or to introduce anything of ambiguity in the matter – for by Allah this is not what I am saying: I am not claiming anything other than what has already been said by your people or others. But I would like to add something else: It is a point of concern formulated by myself – which none of your people has been able to remove from my mind, despite the great number of questions I have put about it to those who have distinguished themselves in knowledge from amongst you. It is to do with the book of your people entitled the *al-Maqamat* (of al-Hariri): your people are in accord that the men of letters are incapable of contesting it: all those who have tried are unable to come up with anything like it in rank or merit. Its author has challenged all those of eloquence to respond to any of it, being of the opinion that nothing comparable could be produced. Further he has declared the impossibility of producing the like of it in the future – in such a manner as to appear irrefutable. So they said: "Recite the two finely polished lines, in *mustabihi* metre, in the forty sixth *Maqama* which have silenced every sorcerer, lines so succinct that they are in no need of a third to support them" – and so he recited:

Coriander is praised for its beneficial effects
   so praise whoever gives, even it be a coriander seed,
wherever deceit manifests, do not even go near it –

---

1   al-A'raf – The Ramparts: 157

In order to safeguard your dominion and noble character

He said: "So I set about responding in my own words, my heart preoccupied with composing a third line to follow these two and then Allah inspired me and I said to him: 'I remember a third line – to these two – although I do not recall who said it. I do not want to ascribe it to myself at the moment for I fear that it would be disdained if I did, and it would have no effect.'" Then I recited:

The bride price is that of the houris of the Garden – namely *taqwa* of Allah

Endeavour to attain to it before youth and old age!

When he heard it from me – after I had explained it to him so he might understand – it was as if he swallowed a stone." Here end the words of *al-Mi'yar* from Ibn Rasheeq – although some of it is the original text of *al-Mi'yar* and some of it a rendering of the meaning of the original text.

I say: "What may be understood from his words: 'I do not recall now who said it' – if it is meant to convey that he had forgotten who said it – is the permissibility of lying in order to reject a falsehood. Ahmad ibn Abdal 'Azziz al-Hilali, on the basis of this permissibility, has explained this in the commentary on the poem of Ibn at-Tayyib. Thus I composed the following and I seek forgiveness from Allah, exalted is He:

Encounter falsehood with fitting truth,

prepare a corresponding requital for falsehood!

This, the illustrious al-Hilali the *'alim* of great understanding, Ahmad has declared

In his commentary – a poem of great eloquence – on the *'alim* Ibn at-Tayyib, a most perspicacious person of *taqwa*.

Useful point: 'Ayn-Jeem said in his commentary on the *'Aqida ar-Risala* – after his words "Then the seal of the Message": I was informed by someone I trust that a book had been found – buried beneath the ground – in Granada in which the following was written: 'There will come after me someone bearing a light into existence from Allah whose name is al-Mahi (the Destroyer). He will be the seal of the prophets by means of the Book (with him), and He will also be the seal of the deen. The people would have had no light without him, nor anyone in all the worlds. And in it – that is the Tablet – (it was stated) that the Messenger to Andalusia to him would be Maryam, the mother of 'Isa, on him be peace. It was found that the Book dated back one thousand and six hundred years from the time of its discovery. He also informed me that the *'alim*, the *faqih* – that is al-Akbar – when he learnt of this said to those of their *'ulama* who were present: 'What do you say regarding the person who informed the Messiah, 'Isa that he would come after him?' They replied: 'This is the Pure Ruh,' and he said: 'The Pure Ruh will not bring a Book and his name is not al-Mahi, the destroyer. Moreover it will not be said of him that he is the seal of Prophets.' They were filled with a great unease. The the Book was then seized and hidden, and they counselled people to keep silent about it. The informant came by knowledge of this because it appeared he was on the same deen as them, like the rest of those in Andalusia."

$$\text{لَوِ انْتَفَى التَّبْلِيغُ أَوْ خَانُوا حُتِمْ}$$

$$\text{أَنْ يُقْلَبَ الْمَنْهِيُّ طَاعَةً لَهُمْ}$$

36 If the conveyance of the Message went unfulfilled or they were to betray the trust (Allah had placed in them), then (the judgement regarding) something forbidden (by Allah) would be reversed – by the act of obedience to their (disobedience).

"Unfulfilled" refers to omission of the Message by the Messengers, on whom be peace and blessings – that is, their concealing or suppressing some of what they had been commanded to convey. "Betray the trust" refers to their committing something forbidden or disliked such that it would inevitably lead to this forbidden or disliked action being followed out of obedience to them – because we have been commanded to imitate them in their actions and words. However there is no one of the people of sunna, who holds to this (omission or betrayal).

$$\text{جَوَازُ الْأَعْرَاضِ عَلَيْهِمْ حُجَّتُهُ}$$

$$\text{وُقُوعُهَا بِهِمْ تَسَلِّ حِكْمَتُهُ}$$

37 The proof that contingencies can happen to them is that they occurred (and were witnessed); their patient endurance (of whatever occurred) was by His wisdom.

"Contingencies" here refer to any unforeseen, irregular occurrence – of a human nature – in the lives of the Prophets which is either witnessed by those (of the Companions) present or narrated in multiple chains to those not present. "They come upon them by His wisdom" refers to the benefit of such things happening to them: it is by means of such occurrences that the significance of the reward (in the Hereafter) is made clear, that the *shari'ah* is laid down – that is, the instruction and authorisation of the people (as to what they are permitted) in this matter (of the *shari'ah*). (By such occurrences) he has acquainted us also with the judgement concerning inadvertence (*sahw*) in the *salat* by means of his own inadvertence, may the peace and blessings of Allah be upon him. Ibn 'Ashir has not mentioned these two (i.e. making clear the significance of the reward and the laying down of the *shari'ah*) because they are well known. Other human occurrences (in the lives of the Prophets) also include doing without, and being patient with the *dunya* when its pleasures are present and remaining calm when they are gone; being alert too to how worthless it is in the esteem of Allah, exalted is He, and His lack of contentment with it. The requital for His Awliya is by virtue of the states of the Prophets in it, may Allah be pleased with them: Allah, exalted is He, has magnified their ranks but has not given them requital for their obedience in an abode of annihilation, doomed to be cut off and brought to an end. This is because anything which is in a state of annihilation – even if it lasts for a considerable period of time – is as if it were nothing; rather He has accorded them an eternity of blessings and a continual going on in the realm of lasting residence. Allah, exalted is He, says: "*For those who fear the station of their Lord there are two Gardens*"[1] that is, the Garden of here and now which is the sweetness of obedience, the delight of intimacy (with one's Lord) and acquainting oneself with the sciences of unveiling; and the Garden to come which is the science of requital for good actions and the raising in rank and station." Here ends the discussion of 'Ali ibn 'Abd as-Sadiq.

I say: "Among the accidents which may occur to them is people's harming them – either by killing them or otherwise. But this is in no way implies a belittling of their rank, rather it is an indication of an increase in their rank; likewise, for every *mumin* who is tested in this world. This has been mentioned by Ibn Naji in *Mu'alim al-Iman* from Ibn al-Lubad: 'The wife of Ibn al-Lubad used to criticise and insult him and he would suffer great hardship at her hand. The students would say to him: "Divorce her and we will return payment of her dowry" and he would reply to them: "I have kept her on account of her father – I had sought many (daughters) in marriage and their (fathers) rejected me saying 'we do not want to marry off (our daughters) to someone who earns his living with the pen.' Then, finally, I addressed her father, and he married off his daughter to me for the sake of Allah, mighty is He and majestic. He treated me well – should I in return divorce his daughter?'" It is also said that he added: 'I fear that if I were to divorce her that a(nother) Muslim would be put to the test by her. It may be that Allah, mighty is He and majestic – by my

---

1 ar-Rahman – The All-Merciful: 45

enduring of her (torment) — will remove a great poverty from me.' He would also say: 'Every *mumin* undergoes a test and this is my test.'"

وَقَوْلُ لَا إِلَهَ إِلَّا اللَّهُ

مُحَمَّدٌ أَرْسَلَهُ الْإِلَهُ

38   The declarations 'there is no god except Allah and Muhammad has been sent by God',

يَجْمَعُ كُلَّ هَذِهِ الْمَعَانِي

39   unites all these meanings ...

... which precede concerning the *'aqida* of *tawhid* regarding the right of Allah, exalted is He, and the right of the Messengers, may peace and blessings be upon them ...

كَانَتْ لِذَا عَلَامَةَ الْإِيمَانِ

... and for this reason it is the sign of Iman

It is by the outward aspect (of a person) that one may interpret whether Islam exists in the heart (of this person) and come to a corresponding judgement (of his status) according the *shari'ah*. (The declaration of) Iman is not accepted of anyone except by means of this (*shahada*). As-Sanusi has explained this by saying: "The preferred commentary on (the meaning of) God is that He is independent of all that is other than Him and that all that is other than Him is are need of Him." Thus the meaning of "There is no god other than Allah" is that only Allah is independent of all that is other than Him, and all that is other than Him is dependent on Him. By virtue of His independence of all other than Him, it necessarily follows that He, exalted is He, possess eight attributes which are necessary in nature and two which are possible in nature.

As for those which are necessary in nature, they are the following: (that He possess) timelessness, going on, (that His existence is such that it is) opposite of in-time, contingent occurrence, self subsistence, hearing, sight and speech — for the opposite of these necessarily entails a negation of independence.

As for the conceivable attributes — that it is not obligatory on Him to enact anything of the possible things or events) in creation or to desist from them — for if any of this were obligatory on Him, exalted is He, then He would not be independent of them. Moreover if He were to enact things for a reason then this reason for doing it would mean He were in need of this thing, and so He would not be independent. Further, His describing everything other than, exalted is He, as in need of Him necessarily entails that He possess five necessary attributes and two possible.

As for the necessarily true: (that He possess) oneness, power, will, knowledge, life – for the opposite of these would negate (the fact that other than Him was in) need of Him.

As for the conceivable attributes: that the occurrence of the world in its entirety be in-time, contingent – for if any of it were of before endless time then it would be independent of Him, exalted is He, and would not be in need of Him; secondly that none of the creational realities be capable of having an effect (on something else) whatever it may be – for otherwise this effect would necessary be independent of Him, tabarak was, exalted is He. This would also mean that something were not in need of Him – how could this be when everything, without exception, other than Him is in need of Him. In any case – as Shaikh as-Sanusi has explained in his *Sughra* – all of the necessary attributes are derived from (His) independence, and (all that is other than Him) from their being in need, that is, thirteen in number according to the teaching of the author (Ibn 'Ashir). Moreover, if the seven pertaining to meaning are added then they will amount to twenty. These seven relate to the realm of meaning in the manner outlined above. In short, if it is obligatory to describe, exalted is He, with these attributes then it is impossible to describe Him, exalted is He, with their opposite because of the (logical) impossibility of combining the two, and all of this is included in our saying "there is no god except Allah."

As for our saying "Muhammad is the Messenger of Allah", what is derived from it is that the truthfulness of the Messengers, on whom be peace and blessings, is necessarily true and the impossibility of their lying, on whom be peace and blessings – for otherwise they would not have become Messengers who trusted in our Lord, majestic is He and mighty, who is knowledgeable of all that is hidden. Their being entrusted (with the Message), the conveyance (of the Message) and the impossibility of their committing any forbidden action would all have remained hidden had not they, on whom be peace and blessings, been sent to teach creation by their words, their actions and (whatever of the actions of others they tacitly affirmed by) their silence. This necessarily requires that none of this be in opposition to the command of our Lord, majestic is He and mighty, who has chosen them from the whole of creation, who has entrusted them with the secret of revelation, in its entirety – including all of its subtlest details. And Muhammad, may the peace and blessings be upon him, came to affirm the truth of all of this. The possibility of (the occurrence of) untoward human accidents on him and the rest of the Prophets, on whom be peace and blessings is part of this secret of revelation for such accidents do not impair their Message in any way or compromise the elevation of their rank with Allah, exalted is He; indeed it only enhances their rank. Thus it will have become clear to you that an understanding of the word *tawhid* and a deep knowedge of it is based on a knowledge of that which befits God, the Real, with regard to the attributes. This is in order that the person of *tawhid* know exactly what is being confirmed by the statement of *tawhid* in relation to our Lord, majestic is He and mighty and what is being negated with respect to 'other than Him.' It will thus be clear to you from our remarks that the statement of *tawhid* comprises, in its summation, the whole of the *'aqida* of *tawhid*. It is for this reason that, in the *shari'ah*, it has been recognised as a outward measure of the (inner quality of) Iman, as the author has mentioned. So realise this, O brother! and learn it off by heart." Here ends the discussion of 'Ali ibn as-Sadiq.

Remarks: the first: The exception in the noble *shahada* (i.e. there is no god *but* Allah) is contiguous – the Muhaqqaq Sayyid Ahmad, the son of 'Abd al-'Aziz al-Hilali has written about its contiguous, uninterrupted nature and refuted those who have claimed otherwise.

2. He has mentioned the following in his commentary under the heading 'branch': "Among the writings of our Shaykh, al-Hafidh, al-Hujja Sayyidi Abu'l-'Abbas al-Maqqari at-Tlimsani there is the following: 'The Shaykh Abu Muhammad ibn Yusuf as-Sanusi, may Allah, exalted is He, benefit us by him, was asked: "Is Iman conditional upon the *mukallaf* knowing the meaning of *la ilaha illa'llah Muhammadar rasulu'llah* (there is no god other than Allah and Muhammad is the Messenger of Allah, may the peace and blessings of Allah be upon him), in all the detail outlined in *al-'Aqida as-Sughra*?" He replied that this was not a condition for the perfection of Iman but rather a condition for the correctness of knowledge of the meaning in general – not from the point of view of the details. There is no doubt that this is true of most of the *muminun*, both the common and the elite, as each of them knows that God is the Creator and not the created and that He is the Provider and not the provided for – and this necessarily implies that He independent of everything other than Him and that other than Him is in need of Him; they realise too that *salat* is only made to God, that fasting and hajj are only undertaken for

Him and that no other than Him is worshipped. This, then, is the meaning of their saying "God is He who merits worship and that no other than Him has a right to this." The person judged to be without Iman – in the *fatwa* – is extremely rare. It refers to the person who does not know the meaning of *la ilaha illa'llah*, neither in general or in detail and who does not discriminate between Him and the Messenger but rather imagines that the latter is similar to Allah, exalted is He. Such a (person) may be found in the deserts, far removed from civilisation where no knowledge or information has penetrated, and Allah knows best.'"

His words "the person judged to be without Iman in the *fatwa*" refers to his saying in *Sharh al-Wusta* in the chapter 'Proof of the necessity of Oneness for Allah, exalted is He.' The *fuqaha* of the town of Bijaya and other imams were asked at the beginning of this century or just before it regarding the person who declares the two parts of the *shahada* and prays, fasts makes the hajj but only performs the outer form of the actions or words as he sees others saying. Thus in declaring the two parts of the *shahada*, he does not know the meaning of it and does not know the meaning of God, nor the meaning of the Messenger. He does not know, as a general truth, that which is affirmed in the two parts of the *shahada* and that which is negated. Such people often imagine that the Messenger of Allah, may the peace and blessings of Allah be upon him, is equal to God because they see that He is mentioned together with the Messenger in the two parts of the *shahada*. As to the question of whether such a person, in the main, benefits by all that he says or does – apparently as a Muslim, and whether it is true to say of him that he is bound by a bond of real trust to his Lord – they have all replied that such a person is accorded no portion in Islam despite the outer manifestation of Iman in his words and actions.

This then is the *fatwa* they have given regarding such a person and all those who are clearly and manifestly in the same state as he, and no one can contest (the truth of) this.

3. Al-Haytami said: "It is a condition on someone entering Islam that he respects the order of the two *shahadas*. Thus it is not correct to have Iman in the Messenger before Iman in Allah, exalted is He. However, it is not a condition that they follow one another in (absolutely) unbroken succession, nor that it be said in Arabic – even if the person knows Arabic well. What is necessary is that the two *shahadas* be treated together.

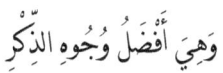

فَاشْغَلْ بِهَا الْعُمْرَ تَفُزْ بِالذُّخْرِ

40   And it is the best kind of *dhikr*, and so occupy your life with it and you will win a great treasure.

'Ali ibn 'Abd as-Sadiq said: "The excellence of it is mentioned in many *hadith*, among them the saying of his, may the peace and blessings of Allah be upon him: 'The best *dhikr* is *la ilaha illa'llah*.' This has been narrated by at-Tirmidhi and an-Nasa'i. Among these narrations is also the saying of his, may the peace and blessings of Allah be upon him: 'The best that I and the Prophets before me have said is *la ilaha illa'llah*. This is narrated by Malik in his *Muwatta'*.'" Here end the words of 'Ali ibn 'Abd as-Sadiq. I am not absolutely sure however that the text of the two *hadith* are like this.

REMARK: There is a difference of opinion amongst the *'ulama* as to what has been narrated as to the excellence of *la ilaha illa'llah* and other declarations and acts of obedience – does it apply both to the person of *taqwa* and others, or does it apply in particular to the person of *taqwa* who desists from the greater prohibited actions? Most of the discussion of Ghazali indicates that it has a particular reference, although for some acts of worship and declarations of submission and obedience he does refer to it as applicable to others. In Abu Mutafannin's commentary on Muslim there is the following: 'Iyad said: 'It has been said that the excellence of the *dhikrs* in this chapter are applicable to the people of noble behaviour in the deen and those who are purified of the greater wrong actions, and who do not persist in such actions' – although there is a difference of opinion as to what he said. However (we are are of the opinion that) it refers in general to all those who say such (*dhikrs*) with the intention of coming closer (to Allah, exalted is He), and Allah, exalted is He, knows best."

Muhammad ibn 'Abd al-Qadir in his commentary – following mention of *ashhadu an la ilaha illa'llah* and *anna muhammadar rasulu'llah*, may the peace and blessings of Allah be upon him – says that no one declares this but that Allah forbids him from (being touched by) the Fire. One group from amongst the people of knowledge are of the opinion that such declarations as "whoever says *la ilaha illa'llah* enters the Garden" and "Allah has forbidden the Fire from touching him" and the like were made at the beginning of Islam when the call (to Islam) was only to an affirmation of *tawhid*; but then when the obligations were imposed and the *hadd* punishments were established this was revoked. Proof and evidence for this are many and manifest and *hadith* have been mentioned more than once above which indicate this in the *salat*, *zakat* and the *hajj*. Various other *hadith* will follow insha'Allah, exalted is He, and this is the opinion of ad-Dahhak, az-Zuhri, Sufyan ath-Thawri and others. Qadi 'Iyad said: "There is nothing to prevent the *hadith* from being understood according to their manifest literal meaning – in other words, that we abstain from interpretation – for according to us the disobedient person is he (who is disobedient) in the desire (of the moment) and it may be that he is forgiven anew the next: thus he joins company with those who have not been disobedient and does not enter the Fire except for a moment at the beginning. Moreover it is possible that the threat (of punishment) is carried out and he does enter it but then he inevitably enters the Garden (on the strength of some later good action of his). Thus the *hadith* (in which mention of) "his entering the Garden" (is made) is a promise – according to its literal meaning – that he will inevitably enter the Garden; and the *hadith* in which it is mentioned that Allah has forbidden a person from being touched by the Fire mean that it is forbidden he stay there for ever. The hadith: "He whose final words are *la ilaha illa'llah* will enter the Garden" means – according to the manifest, literal meaning – that he will enter the Garden from the very beginning, either because the seal of his words causes his wrong actions to be covered up or his reward is increased such that his good qualities become superior to his bad.

Al-Munawi said in *Sharh al-Jami'*: "Allah's forbidding him to be touched by the Fire" means the Fire of eternity – as long as he avoids wrong actions, turns in *tawba* or is forgiven them. The manifest meaning of this implies that all who declare the two *shahadas* will not enter the Fire – thus its literal meaning has a general application; however, there is unequivocal evidence and proof that a group of those professing *tawhid* – but nevertheless disobedient – will be tormented although they will later be brought out (of the Fire) by intercession. So it is clear that the literal meaning of this is not what is meant; instead what he might have said is the following: "This is dependent upon the person acting correctly or the person turning in *tawba* or his dying on this (declaration of the two *shahadas*), or that this was before the revelation of the obligations, commands and prohibitions, or it was meant to apply to the majority of cases given that the majority of persons who profess *tawhid* do in fact perform the acts of submission and obedience and avoid committing the acts of disobedience. Hadiths have been related which refer to this with the words "those who say the *shahada* sincerely." Al-Hakeem said: "Sincerity is that you free your tongue until it is not corrupted by the lusts and passions of your self."

I say: "Among the *hadith* which mention this condition is that related by al-Hakim and at-Tirmidhi from Zayd ibn Arqam who said: 'The Messenger, may the peace and blessings of Allah be upon him, said: "Allah, mighty is He and majestic, has promised me that none of my *umma* will come to me with *la ilaha illa'llah*, – adding nothing to it – but that the Garden will be obligatory for him." They said: "O Messenger of Allah, what about the person who adds something to *la ilaha illa'llah*?" He replied: "Out of greed for this world, from their desire to hoard it or deprive and forbid (others) from it, they declare the saying of the Prophets but behave as tyrants".' Among such *hadith* is also that related from 'Umar, may Allah be pleased with him, who said: "The Messenger of Allah, may the peace and blessings of Allah be upon him, said: 'I know of a phrase which if declared with sincerity by a slave, then Allah will forbid the Fire from touching him: "*la ilaha illa'llah*."' This is related by Abu Nu'aym in *al-Hilya*. 'Uthman, may Allah be pleased with him, also said: "The Messenger of Allah, may the peace and blessings of Allah be upon him, said: 'I surely know a phrase which no slave will declare in truth from his heart and will die while still affirming it but that Allah will forbid him from being touched by the Fire.'" This is related by Ibn Hibban with a sound chain of transmission. At-Tabarani and Abu Nu'aym in *al-Hilya* from Zayd ibn Arqam have narrated that he, may the peace and blessings of Allah be upon him, said: "Whoever says *la ilaha illa'llah* sincerely will enter the Garden." They said: "O Messenger of Allah: 'and what is the sincerity referred to here?' He replied: "that which prevents him from everything which Allah has forbidden." This has been transmitted by al-*Khateeb*. All these *hadith* have been related by Shaykh Zayn al-'Abideen al-Bakri, may Allah be pleased with him, in a composition of his regarding the excellence of *la ilaha illa'llah* in which he says: "So if you were to say that this person entered the Garden by his being free of forbidden actions then what good does *la ilaha illa'llah* bring?" I replied: "By the blessing of his truthfulness in saying it and by his watching out for the Truth, the Real while declaring it, his entry into the Garden will be made easier." He added: "and this does not negate what we have affirmed before, namely that the forgiveness obtained by *la ilaha illa'llah* includes, insha'Allah, both the minor and the major wrong actions. So if the Legislator has made the entry into the Garden conditional upon it then by reason of this (declaration) too the slave should refrain from all prohibited actions – for what the slave desires by it is an entry which is perfect in its honour and resplendence and arrival at the highest stations of the Garden. If this were not the case it would imply a restriction of the generosity (on the part of Allah, exalted is He,) – that is, if the subject of the discussion were merely about those who enter by virtue of their striving and all that was understood from these *hadith* was that no one enters the Garden except those who (by their own efforts) avoid the smaller and greater wrong actions. However, the people of sunna are in agreement that Allah, exalted is He, will cause certain groups of persons to enter His Garden without tormenting them despite their having died persisting in the greater wrong actions – and this by Allah's generosity and mercy alone. In conclusion, the entry (into the Garden) which is conditional upon desisting from prohibited actions is a particular kind of entry and does not refer to entry in general, and the generosity (of Allah, exalted is He) is vast."

The discussion which the author referred to saying 'that he has mentioned it earlier' is the following: "Forgiveness – insha'Allah, exalted is He – is not particular to the minor wrong actions, and only those matters which are connected to the rights of one man over another are excluded from it; indeed it is to be hoped that Allah, exalted is He, by the *baraka* of *la ilaha illa'llah*, will give success in freeing oneself even from these – even if it is by way of (asking Allah that) the person – whose right it is – pardon him. The majority, however, are of the view that this does not extend beyond the minor wrong actions. Our proof for this is established practice of reading the basis text according to its original, literal meaning as long as there is nothing to cause one to interpret it otherwise. Thus if the condition that one should avoid the minor and major wrong actions is stipulated in (declarations or *dhikrs*) other than (the remembrance of) *la ilaha illa'llah* then this is specific to the particular narration in question; and it is part of the nature of reward that analogy has no part to play in this matter – and likewise in the subject of punishment. One does not say, for example – if an absolute (judgement) is expressed in one place while bound by a restriction in another that the general, unrestricted (judgement) dominates the conditional one as long as the context and import of the one is like the other; and that if they are not alike, then the one does not dominate the other. If, however, it is argued that one should practice analogy we would reiterate – as we have already mentioned above – that there is no room for analogy in this matter." Here end the words of Muhammad ibn 'Abd al-Qadir.

He has also said the following while commenting on the tradition "And if he remembers Me in a company, I remember him in a company which is better than it: 'Shaykh Ibn Abi Jamra said: "*Dhikr* (remembrance) may be with the tongue or with the heart or both of them; or by carrying out the command and avoiding what is forbidden. However, the traditions indicate that remembrance may be of two kinds, one of which excludes the person practising the *dhikr* from the benefit mentioned in the hadith; and in the second it is open to question because the proof and evidence regarding *dhikr* are contradictory: some indicate that he will be among all those who remember, as Allah, exalted is He, says: "*Whoever does an atom's weight of good will see it*," [1] while other evidence which precludes this like the saying of our Lord, glorious is He, to Musa, on whom be peace: "Say to the oppressors: 'Do not remember Me' for I have made it incumbent on Myself that whoever remembers Me I shall remember him but if they remember Me I shall remember them with anger"; and on account of the saying of our Prophet, may the peace and blessings of Allah be upon him – regarding the person who performs the *salat* but whose *salat* does not prevent him from evil and corrupt action: "This does not increase him with Allah but in distance" – so how (much less likely is the benefit in the case of someone whose practice is) just with *dhikr*. Moreover, He exalted is He has only mentioned *dhikr* in His Book after mention of those who have attained to Iman – namely when He says: "*Men and women who are Muslims, men and women who are muminun ... men and women who remember Allah much.*"[2] In fact this *ayat* clarifies perfectly what we are talking about. However, remembering Him, mighty and majestic is He, with actions is the best, and may the words of 'Umar, may Allah be pleased with him, be enough (to illustrate) this matter: "Remembrance of Allah by means of the (carrying out) of His command and His prohibition is better than remembrance of Allah with the tongue – unless a person is in a state of disobedience and he remembers Allah with fear and trembling during whatever (act of disobedience) he is committing: in this case one may hope for the generosity of the Lord for him."

Examine too what Shaikh Ibn Abi Jamra, may Allah be pleased with him, has mentioned regarding the incompatibility of proofs and what is required in the *madhhab* of the people of sunna – namely that there be no contradiction. Thus *ta'wil* – interpretation – must be done regarding the matter he mentions and research must be undertaken into the soundness of this (hadith). Hafidh Ibn Hajar has narrated what he says but has abbreviated it a great deal, restricting himself to the proof in support of the hadith "...but whose *salat* does not prevent him from evil and corrupt action..." rather than the other (hadith), namely the (above-mentioned) saying of Musa to the oppressors. It may well be that there is no basis for this (latter hadith) according to him. If we assume its correctness, however, then it may be that the oppressors are to be interpreted as referring to the *kuffar*. As for the other, it is narrated by at-Tabarani and Ibn Majah, and if we suppose it is correct then it may be interpreted as referring to the *salat* which has been performed defectively,

---

1 az-Zilzala – The Earthquake: 8
2 al-Ahzab – The Confederates: 35

that is one of its conditions (has not been fulfilled); or the statement is to be interpreted as an exaggeration which is meant as a rebuke – so this addition (to the hadith) is to be understood metaphorically: since performance (of the *salat*) does not cause him to desist from wrong action, he persists in this (wrong action) and this distance from the mercy of Allah, exalted is He, causes him not to perform the *salat* as it should be done. That which needs *ta'wil* is well known and established with the people of sunna. The actions of a *mumin* will not be overlooked or treated unjustly, and there are many proofs for this, like the *ayat*: "But anyone who does right actions, being a mumin, need fear no wrong or belittlement"[1] and the like – for leaving actions unrewarded would be an injustice and is not held to by the people of sunna; nor that people should be treated as *kuffar* because of some wrong action they have committed: that which (appears to) be clearly and precisely determined in particular case of law can have two aspects in the case of a specific person, that which is known and is rewarded from one point of view – even though he (in particular) may be punished from another point of view, as has been made clear in its proper place. In the *Tafseer* of Ibn 'Atiyya it is narrated from Ibn 'Abbas, may Allah be pleased with both of them, that if the slave remembers Allah but does not carry out the obligatory acts of worship then his saying (of the *dhikr*) is rejected. Ibn 'Atiyya said: "This saying is rejected by those who hold to the people of truth and sunna and what has been narrated from Ibn 'Abbas is not correct. The truth (of the matter) is that when an disobedient person – who abandons the obligatory acts of worship – makes *dhikr* of Allah and pronounces good words then this is recorded for him and accepted of him: to him belongs (the recompense) for his good actions and he will be held to account for his bad actions, and Allah, exalted is He, accepts (the good actions) from each person who protects himself from *shirk*. Moreover, pronouncing good words is a good and proper act." Here end the words of Ibn 'Atiyya as narrated by al-Mawwaq in *Sunan al-Muhtadeen*.

It has also been narrated of Ibn al-'Arabi: "Whoever indulges his passions and then curses his *nafs* then he is fearful of his Hereafter but if he is disobedient and thinks that he will be (automatically) forgiven then he is deceiving himself – as if someone were to seek protection of him and he were to abuse the trust of this person then he could hardly expect others to seek his protection. Rather he should say: "O He in whose hand is the dominion over everything, I have sought protection from my *nafs* and from the evil of every creature whose forelock is in Your hand" – it may be that his call is answered. Shaykh

---

1 Ta Ha: 109:

al-Mawwaq said: "He has in mind the saying of Taj ad-Deen in his *Hikam*: 'Whoever thinks it far fetched that Allah might save someone from his passions and that He cause him to leave his state of negligence then such a person will also consider His Power far fetched – and Allah has dominion over all things.'"

Al-Munawi has related that al-Ubbi said: "Attaining the promised reward is conditional upon this *dhikr* being accepted – the Shaykh used to say 'among the conditions of its acceptance is that he not occupy himself with it during the time when he should be doing something else – for example that his throat is full of *dhikr* at the time of an obligatory *salat* which he does not perform; so therefore *dhikr* is also not accepted of someone who has usurped (something), for such a person would be obliged at every moment to strive to return (this thing).' However it appears that the correct view is different than that mentioned and that it is correct to busy oneself with *dhikr* at a time of another act of worship – even though such a person is committing a wrong action by abandoning or delaying this act of worship."

In short, any *dhikr* which is performed as it should be done is inevitably accompanied by this mercy which the (expression) 'company of Allah, glorious is He,' (referred to above in the hadith) indicates; and the different degrees (of mercy) is conditional upon the different degrees of perfection – however what prejudices perfection does not (necessarily) invalidate its invalidity. Here ends the discussion of Muhammad ibn 'Abd al-Qadir.

In Munawi's *al-Kabir* is the following: "Note well: If a forbidden act is committed together with *dhikr* then its reward is not annulled as Ibn al-'Arabi has made clear when he says: 'Sometimes a person is successful in some of his actions and sometimes he meets with failure – like the one who makes *dhikr* of Allah, exalted is He, in his heart and tongue while he strikes someone with his hand whom he has no right to strike. However, this does not diminish the worth of the *dhikr* just as this *dhikr* does not remove the wrong action.'"

In the *Sunan al-Muhtadeen* of Imam al-Mawwaq it reads: "Take note! The first station is that of the person who violates his own self – that is, he who only holds to the words of *tawhid* (i.e. the *shahada*), and this is a dangerous (state to be in) for him. However the people of the sunna and the *jama'a* do not condemn as *kafir* anyone of the *qibla* on account of a wrong action of his. We must stay with him despite a (particular) state (he might have) for if we were to compare his state with that of a *kafir*'s we would realised the difference between the two: that his is (based on) love for Allah – which is obligatory on every Muslim. We would realise too that Allah does not accept the *kafir* under any circumstances irrespective of whether his behaviour is devious or just – as opposed to the (above mentioned Muslim). Thus his wrong action does not exclude him from Islam even if he commits great wrong for Allah will accept of him every atom's weight of good: Allah will accept every act of obedience from the person who protects himself from *shirk*.

In an-Nafrawi's commentary on the words of the *Risala* 'Allah glorious is He, has multiplied the reward for the *muminun* among His slaves' he says: "The literal meaning of *muminun* is that it includes the disobedient. This is so because the (degree and worth of the) *mumin* is (only) to be understood in comparison with the *kuffar*."

Muhammad ibn 'Abd al-Qadir al-Fasi, may Allah, exalted is He, benefit us by them both, said: "The performance of some of those things one has been commanded to does not negate one's obligation with respect to the rest of them just as the taking on of all the obligations does not preclude the acceptance of some – on account of both the general and particular evidence for this. This has been narrated by the commentator of the *'Aqida* of 'Abd al-Qadir. Al-Qarafi has mentioned in *al-Farouq* that the acceptance of actions is conditional upon *taqwa*. His evidence for this is the saying of the Prophet, may the peace and blessings of Allah be upon him: "Whoever becomes Muslim and his Islam is correct, then he will be rewarded for his actions both in the Jahiliyya and during his time in Islam" – or words to this effect. What he understands by *taqwa* is avoidance of acts of disobedience. However Ibn ash-Shat has contradicted him in his gloss saying: "I said: What he probably means by 'his Islam is correct' is that he fulfil the obligations of Iman rather than his avoidance of acts of disobedience. This fulfilling of the demands of Iman is a condition for the constancy of his actions, in fact there is no other condition for the firmness and sureness of actions. Everything else that is mentioned in the *ayats* and *hadith* from which one has stipulated additional conditions for the validity of an action or for the acquitting oneself of an obligation is (only) an interpretation of what is meant (without solid basis).

He said in the *Fath al-Bari*: "Even if the reciter (of the Qur'an) has committed an act of disobedience – other than one connected with the recitation of the Qur'an – he is rewarded for his recitation, according to the people of sunna." Al-'Alqami: "It does not follow that if a Muslim has committed an act of disobedience that he not be rewarded for an act of obedience – and may the words of, exalted is He, be enough proof for the validity of this: '*but others have mixed a right action with another which is wrong.*'[1]"

USEFUL POINT: al-Munawi said that Ibn al-'Arabi said: "I counsel you to

---

1 Repentance – at-Tawba: 103

ensure that you purchase your self from Allah, exalted is He, in return for freeing your neck from the Fire by saying *la ilaha illa'llah* seventy thousand times for surely Allah, exalted is He, will free your neck or free the neck of the person you say it for – and this (has been indicated) in a Prophetic tradition." Abul-'Abbas al-Qastallani in Egypt has informed me that the gnostic Abu'r-Rabi' al-Maliqi was at table and he mentioned this *dhikr*. There was also a young boy at the table who was from among the people of unveiling. When he stretched his hand out to the food, he began to weep and someone said to him: 'What's the matter?' to which he replied: 'I see Jahannam and my mother is in it.' Al-Maliqi then said to himself: 'O Allah may You cause his mother to be freed from the Fire by the saying of these *la ilaha illa'llah*s' whereupon the young boy laughed saying: 'Praise belongs to Allah who has brought my mother out of the Fire although I do not know the reason for here being taken out of it.' Then al-Maliqi said: 'Now the truth of the hadith has become manifest to me.' Ibn al-'Arabi said: "I used to practise this and I have seen its *baraka*."

He has also said: "Useful point: Hasan al-Basri sat at the burial of an-Nawwar, the wife of al-Farazdaq, wearing a black turban the end of which hung down his neck. The people around him were looking at him. Then al-Farazdaq stood in front of him saying: 'O Abu Sa'd, the people are claiming the best and most evil people have gathered for this burial – who might these two persons be?' He said: 'You and I.' He said: 'I am not the best of them and you are not the most evil of them. Besides, what have you prepared for that Day?' He replied: 'The saying of the *shahada* – *la ilaha illa'llah* – for the past seventy years.' He said: 'Yes and Allah, exalted is He, is the means.'

ANOTHER USEFUL POINT: Al-Haytami said that at-Tirmidhi has narrated that whoever enters a market and says '*la ilaha illa'llah* wahdahu la sharika la lahu'l-mulku wa lahu'l-hamd yuheey wa yumeet biyadihi'l-khayr wa huwa 'ala kulli shayin qadeer' – there is no god except Allah, the One without any associate, to Him belongs the creation and all praise, He gives life and brings death and all good is in His hand and He has power over all things – then Allah will write a reward of a thousand thousand good deeds and will raise him up a thousand thousand degrees." There is however a weakness in (the chain of narration of) this hadith.

A third benefit: ath-Tha'alabi has commented on the saying of Allah, exalted is He, "Anyone who does a good action will get something better"[1] saying: "It has been narrated that 'Ali ibn al-Hasan, may Allah, exalted is He, be pleased

---

1 Al-Qasas – The Story: 84

with him, said: 'On one occasion when I had retired into khalwa I raised my voice saying *la ilaha illa'llah* and then I heard someone saying 'these are the words about which Allah, exalted is He, said: "Anyone who does a good action will get something better."'

$$\text{فَضْلٌ وَطَاعَةُ الْجَوَارِحِ الْجَمِيعْ}$$

$$\text{قَوْلاً وَفِعْلاً هُوَ الْإِسْلَامُ الرَّفِيعْ}$$

41 Section: Obedience of all the limbs both in speech and action – this is elevated Islam.

$$\text{قَوَاعِدُ الْإِسْلَامِ خَمْسٌ وَاجِبَاتْ}$$

$$\text{وَهْيَ الشَّهَادَتَانِ شَرْطُ الْبَاقِيَاتْ}$$

42 The pillars of Islam are five obligations, the first being the two *shahadas* – which are prerequisite for the rest

$$\text{ثُمَّ الصَّلَاةُ والزَّكَاةُ فِي الْقِطَاعْ}$$

$$\text{والصَّوْمُ والْحَجُّ عَلَى مَنِ اسْتَطَاعْ}$$

43 then the *salat*, the *zakat* – on what is zakatable , the fasting and the hajj for the one who is able

These five are the basic foundations of Islam because they are the greatest in importance. He is indicating thereby the words of him, may Allah bless him and grant him peace, who said: "Islam is based on five things: bearing witness that there is no god except Allah and that Muhammad is the Messenger of Allah, the establishing of the *salat*, the payment of *zakat*, the fasting of ramadan and the making the hajj of the House if you are able." There is also another *sahih* hadith narrated from 'Umar ibn al-Khattab, may Allah be pleased with him, who said: "One day while we were sitting with the Messenger of Allah, may the peace and blessings of Allah be upon him, a man appeared wearing extremely white clothes, with intensely black hair. There was no trace of a journey on him and none of us knew him. Then he came to sit facing the Prophet, may the peace and blessings of Allah be upon him, placing his knees against his knees and resting his hands on his thighs and said: 'O Muhammad tell me about Islam?' and the Messenger of Allah, may the peace and blessings of Allah be upon him, replied 'Islam is that you bear witness that there is no god except Allah and that Muhammad is the Messenger of Allah, may the peace and blessings of Allah be upon him, that you pay *zakat*, fast Ramadan and make the hajj of the House if you are able.'" At this point I remember, insha'Allah, something said by al-Haytami with respect to another hadith – namely his words: "O Muhammad!" and the permissibility of calling an important *'alim* by his name, even if it is on the part of the student. However, this only refers to the person who is not aware that this is *makruh*; otherwise it may be used to express a lowering of one's esteem for someone – that is one's opposition to those who make a habit of calling them by (excessively) exalted names."

I SAY: "Ibn Hajar al-'Asqalani said in *Fath al-Bari* during a discussion on the subject of *waqf* and how it is registered: 'One of the benefits of this (above mentioned hadith) is that it is permissible for the son to address his father by his name only without mention of his family name or title.'"

Al-Haytami said regarding his saying "...that he bear witness that there is no god except Allah" that instead of 'god', it would be enough (to say) the Creator, the Merciful or the Provider; instead of (the word) 'Allah', 'the Giver of Life' or 'the Bringer of Death' – that is names which do not indicate qualities or characteristics like the above-mentioned three qualities, namely names pertaining to 'creating', or 'being merciful' or 'providing' or words which indicate 'He who is in the heavens' rather that 'He who inhabits the heavens', or 'He in whom the Muslims trust'; and instead of Muhammad, Ahmad or Abu'l-Qasim; and instead of 'no', 'other than' for example; and instead of 'Messenger', 'Prophet.'

Regarding his saying "and that you establish the *salat*" – this is joined to and follows on from "you bear witness" – as opposed to the one who claims that it and what is mentioned after this is a fresh statement. It is as if such a person has considered (the matter) on the basis that the carrying out of the commands (ahkam) (implicit) in the two *shahadas* alone is enough. In reply to this person it may be stated that submitting to and allowing oneself to be guided by this (first pillar, i.e. the two *shahadas*) is the lesser way, but the most perfect is (all) that which follows in the hadith. Thus that which is added to the words "that you bear witness to..." is to ensure this perfecting and bringing to completion, or to preserve its pillars and conditions.

He has commented on his saying 'that they pay the *zakat*' saying: "Among the things upon which payment is obligatory according to the *ijma'* are livestock, dates and raisins, grains considered staple foods – payment of wheat and barley, for example, being counted as similar grains such that payment may be made in the one for the other and alternatively, or silver and gold, and the *zakat al-fitr*. The difference of opinion regarding of one of our followers, Ibn al-Luban is foolish for he is not a *mujtahid* in matters other than the knowledge of the obligations. As for those things about which there is a difference of opinion, they include for example the *zakat* of trade and all the other fruits and vegetables and the like (not included in the general ordinance) – with respect to those who hold to its obligation on the basis of *ijtihad* or *taqlid*. Linguistically, the root of the word *zakat* means to grow and to purify; in the context of the *shari'ah*, it refers to that which is exacted on wealth, that is, taken from wealth which 'grows' to a *nisab* – a minimum amount – and which, in turn, grows by the *baraka* and good action of the person who pays it; or the meaning refers to the purification of the person and thus the *zakat* is testimony to the Iman of the person who makes its payment. Anyone who denies its obligatory nature is a *kafir* according to the *ijma'* for it is one of the well known matters of the deen which it is necessary (to hold to)."

As for his words 'that he make the hajj of the House if he is able' he comments by saying: "The going on hajj is made conditional upon the capacity of the person. Although the matters mentioned before this are also conditional (upon a person's capacity) explicit mention is made for the matter of hajj so as to accord with the wording of the Qur'anic text of the subject. It is an indication of the difficulty involved in this particular act of worship that the mention of this condition is made (in the Qur'an) – as opposed to other acts of worship."

He has commented on the text 'Islam is based on five pillars, bearing witness that there is no god except Allah and that Muhammad is His slave and Messenger, the establishing of the *salat* and the payment of *zakat*' saying: "These three matters have been placed together in all the other narrations as they are obligatory in this manner: thus the first of these obligations is the two *shahadas*, then the *salat*, then the *zakat*. Some have said: 'The obligation of these (three) preceded (the others), and that of the fast preceded the hajj.'"

However, one of the latter *'ulama* well versed in the *fiqh* and hadith said: "The time of the obligation of *zakat* is not precisely defined for me, nor is the giving precedence of one (pillar) on account of its (assumed) excellence over another, or its being more important." What may be derived from this is that whoever is unable to perform two (pillars), like for example the person who has hardly any time left to do the *salat* but who at the same time is under the obligation to pay *zakat* to someone in need who is entitled to it then he should give preference to the most important (of the two) which is the *salat*. This, however, is not an absolute judgement; rather it is by analogy for if the person entitled to the payment would be harmed by the person in question giving preference to the *salat*, then it is forbidden to give preference to the *salat*. Indeed it becomes obligatory to make the payment – based on their judging obligatory the payment in its time if (praying) would hinder the saving of a drowning person or one fears the onset of death or that the preparation (of the corpse) and its swathing (in cloth) be abandoned through its (performance) – for it it possible to make up (the *salat*) later while in the case of an accident or it is not possible (to make good the ensuing damage); if the *'Isha salat* and the performance of the hajj coincide with each other then it is obligatory to do the former first and leave the latter for it is not difficult to make this up later." Here ends his discussion. Then he goes on to say: "One may infer from the words 'Islam is based on' – as mentioned above – the obvious fact that a house will not stand firm without its supports, and that whoever abandons all these pillars is a *kafir*; likewise whoever abandons the two *shahadas* because they are the foundation of the whole thing – that which supports the whole building and all of these basic teachings. Likewise, One may also infer (this structure) from proofs and evidence like, for example, the *sahih* narration: 'The head of the matter is Islam, its support is the *salat* and the very peak of the matter is the *jihad*.' What is meant by Islam here is the two *shahadas* – and this is clear from the make up of the sentence; whoever abandons some (pillar) other than these two (*shahadas*) – such a person falls short of attaining the perfection of Islam to the extent by which he abandons the other pillars of the house. In doing so he enters into corruption but not the zone of *kufr* – except if he actively denies the obligation (of these other pillars). It is in this sense that most people interpret the narration of Muslim: 'Between a man and *kufr* is the abandonment of the *salat*.' However Ahmad and others are of a different opinion and treat as *kafir* any one who abandons any of the pillars.

Ishaq said 'This is what the *ijma'* of the people of knowledge hold to', while others have said: 'This is what the majority of the people of hadith hold to, although one group have extended the judgement to include as *kafir* the person who abandons any of the (remaining) three pillars – and this is a narration from Ahmad which has been given preference by a group of his followers and some of the Malikis. This (i.e. the treatment of such a person as *kafir*) is contrary to the (manifest) import of Iman (as defined) above in the hadith of Jibril." Here end the words of al-Haytami.

I say: "His words 'the (manifest) import of Iman' refer to the words in the hadith of Jibril: 'That you have Iman in Allah and His angels and His Books and His Messengers...'"

In conclusion: Al-Munawi said in his major commentary: "He has related in *al-Matali'* concerning the *ijma'* of the *umma* as to the (future) coming of 'Isa, on whom be peace, but as for the time of his descent on earth, this is unknown.

الْإِيمَانُ جَزْمٌ بِالْإِلَهِ وَالْكُتُبْ

وَالرُّسْلِ وَالْأَمْلَاكِ مَعَ بَعْثٍ قَرُبْ

44 Iman is unwavering trust in Allah, the Books, the Messengers, the Angels, the imminent Raising up (of mankind),

وَقَدَرٌ كَذَا الصِّرَاطُ فَالْمِيزَانْ

حَوْضُ النَّبِيِّ جَنَّةٌ وَنِيرَانْ

45 the Decree, the *Sirat*-bridge, the Balance, the Fountain of the Prophet, the Garden and the Fire

UNWAVERING TRUST

'Ali ibn 'Abd as-Sadiq said: "'Unwavering trust' means a sincere affirmation with the heart of all the clear unabiguous matters the Messenger has made known to mankind from Allah, exalted is He, – as has been made clear in Jibril's questionning (of the Prophet, may the peace and blessings of Allah be upon him) in the hadith contained in the two *Sahihs*, namely that Iman is 'that you trust in Allah and His angels, His Books, His Messengers, the Day of Raising Up and that you trust in the Decree of good and evil.' What is meant is the affirmation in one's heart of what the Messenger has brought, may the peace and blessings of Allah be upon him, obedience to what the Messengers have brought and acceptance of it."

Ash-Sha'rani said: "The *'ulama* knowledgeable of the roots of the deen have said: 'Taking on full responsibility (takleef) for this obligation is to become conscious of what it means – like applying one's mind, reflecting upon these matters, concentrating one's attention and removing any obstacles – for otherwise it would not be a voluntary conscious action which is the necessary prerequisite of responsibility or obligation."

Ibn Hajar al-'Asqalani said in his commentary on the *Sahih* of al-Bukhari – during his discussion in the Book of Iman: "Iman, linguistically speaking means affirmation based on trust; according to the *shari'ah*, it means the affirmation of the Messenger, may the peace and blessings of Allah be upon him, and what he has brought from His Lord – and this is agreed upon. However, there is a difference of opinion as to whether this is conditional upon anything else – like declaring this affirmation on the tongue in order to express (openly) what is (hidden) in the heart – since affirmation is (either hidden as) an action of the heart or a confirmation (of this inner state which is manifest) through the acting out of what has been commanded or through the avoidance of what has been prohibited. An explanation of this will follow insha'Allah.'" He then goes on to comment on (al-Bukhari's) words 'Iman is (manifest) both in words and actions and is subject to increase and decrease' by saying: "The people of the first generations have said that it is belief in the heart, the expression (of this) on the tongue and the carrying out of actions relating to the pillars (of the deen)." What they meant by this is that perfection in this (matter of Iman) is dependent upon these actions. Moreover, on this is based their view of increase and decrease – as we shall discuss below. The Murji'ites have said that it is only a question of belief and the expression of this (on the tongue). The Karamites have said that it is only the expression of this. The Mu'tazilis have said that it is action, expression and belief. The difference between the latter and the *salaf* is that they have made actions a condition of its validity while the *salaf* have made them a condition of its perfection. And all this, as we have said, is with respect to what is due to (and known only by) Allah, exalted is He; with respect to us, however, Iman is only (open) acknowledgement (iqrar) – and whoever acknowledges this (before witnesses) then the laws (of the *shari'ah*) are applied to him in this world and he is not judged to be a *kafir* unless he affirms an action of *kufr* like prostrating to an idol."

Al-Bannani has mentioned the following from one of the muhaqiqun: "Iman in the heart is one of the branches of knowledge and an effect and consequence of it, given that it is a science (*ma'rifa*); *hadith an-nafs* – the capacity of the self to persuade and convince is also part of iman."

Ibn Hajar al-Haytami also said: "Iman from the point of view of the *shari'ah* is only affirmation with the heart, that is acceptance and submission to what one knows to be necessary and to be indubitably of the deen of Muhammad, may the peace and blessings of Allah be upon him, – as we shall explain below in more detail. As for what is mentioned in general, like the Angels, the Books and the Messenger, (one's) Iman in them is general in nature; that which is mentioned in particular, like Jibril, Musa and the Injil, then an Iman which is specific in nature is stipulated – such that someone who does not affirm the particularity of these things is *kafir*. What I have set out here is the meaning of one commentator when he talks of an 'all embracing Iman': whoever is mentioned specifically by name like Jibril then it is necessary to have Iman in him specifically; whoever we do not know the name of, then we must have Iman in him in general, and likewise in the Books, the Prophets, the Messengers."

The negation or rejection of belief in something specific is not enough to comprise an act of *kufr* if this (affirmation of belief) is based on (mere acknowledgement of) its existence (*thubutuhu*). Rather, there must be a consensus (*tawatir*) (of learned opinion) as to its validity (as demonstrated) through various confirmatory channels – such that one arrives at absolute belief (*hatta yuqta'*) in this – (before someone who rejects it may be accused of *kufr*)."[1] Then al-Haytami continues – after relating the difference of opinion as to whether the declaration aloud of the *shahada* is a condition: "Those who hold that it is (a condition) say that the validity of the oral declaration does not depend on the absence of disobedience. (It is enough) that the person believes that whenever he is asked to declare it he does so, and that if he is asked but refuses out of disobedience then he has committed an act of *kufr*: for example, if he were to pray to an idol or he disdains a Prophet or the Ka'ba or any other of the things which render him *kafir*. There is doubt, however, regarding the judgement as to whether he is to be treated as a *kafir* (merely) on account of his having committed one of the above mentioned acts while (merely) affirming (belief) with his heart. The matter is complicated because when defining Iman as affirmation (of the heart) then it may well be that he makes an affirmation while lacking Iman in this (particular thing). The answer (to this problem) may be understood by determining the important matters about which it is obligatory to reflect. (Among these matters is that of) affirmation with the heart – about which the *'ulama* differ – which constitutes the complete meaning of Iman, according to the Ash'aris, or part of its meaning according to others. It is also said that it is a part of knowledge. It has also been reported that we may judge many of the people of the Book to be *kuffar* by their knowledge of the truth of his message, may the peace and blessings of Allah be upon him and what he brought (to mankind): Allah, exalted is He, said: '...*yet when what they*

---

[1] This is related to a condition necessary in all elements of Iman: that their existence (*thubut*) should be based on a multiple proof (*dalil qat'i* i.e. *mutawatir*). In other words: all the tenets of belief should be based on *qat'i* evidences. The *dhanni* evidences are not valid to be the bases for *'aqida*. They are only valid as the basis for *fiqh* injunctions not for *'aqida* injunctions.

recognise does come to them, they reject it'[1] and 'Those We have given the Book recognise it as they recognise their own sons'[2]; and by their knowledge that it is an obligation to believe in it and that this obligation is dependent upon conscious voluntary actions and upon the knowledge of the truthfulness of all that is claimed by prophecy because of the existence of a cause, namely the miracle (of revelation) which overwhelmed him. It has also been said that Iman is to be regarded as something one arrives at through conviction (*kalam an-nafs*) and this is held to by the Imam of the Haramayn and others. The literal meaning of the words of Shaykh Abu'l-Hasan al-Ash'ari is that it is a matter of convincing oneself (*kalam an-nafs*) and that knowledge is a necessary condition in this matter since what is meant by *kalam an-nafs* is an acceptance, that is an inner confirmation and allowing oneself to be guided in obedience to the commands and prohibitions; and what is meant by *ma'rifa* – knowledge – is that one realises how the call of the Prophet, may the peace and blessings of Allah be upon him, conforms with reality, that is, in the manner it manifests to the heart and reveals itself to it. This submission and acceptance is arrived at after attaining this *ma'rifa*. However, it is conceivable that both of the two above mentioned matters (i.e. acceptance as an inner confirmation and then allowing oneself to be guided in obedience to the commands and prohibitions) are basic elements (*ruknun*) and so it is necessary to include *ma'rifa* if we treat them as a basic elements or conditions. We also include acceptance and submission (*istislam*) with these two (matters) – because of (the possibility) we have mentioned above, namely that they can sometimes be affirmed at the same time as (the existence of an act of) *kufr* to which the *nafs* is compelled; or because of one's taking on these obligations (of the deen) under compulsion by the (mere outward) affirmation of Allah's, exalted is He, declaration: "*Know then that there is no god except Allah.*"[3] What I mean by this is (a submission based on) the attainment of the means to this – that is, the intention to examine the effects of (His) power which indicate the existence of, exalted is He, and his Oneness, the focusing of one's attention to this and the taking of the preliminary steps derived from this in such a way as to lead to that is being aimed for.

The literal meaning of the discussion in *Sharh al-Maqasid* is that knowledge which is accepted under compulsion (without submission to it) is not enough. Rather it must be acquired by establishing proof and evidence. He has responded (by saying) that the attainment of acceptance in the inward – after the obtaining

1   al-Baqara – The Cow: 88
2   al-Baqara – The Cow: 145
3   Muhammad: 20

of compelling compulsory knowledge – removes the need to seek to obtain it by producing means and reasons. Being satisfied with compelling compulsory (knowledge) may be justified by its being accompanied by submission and acceptance, and the taking on of the obligations by occupying oneself and pursuing the means and reasons. And this pertains to someone who has obtained this compelling compulsory knowledge. Some hold to the opinion that it is inevitable that one includes (the notion of) submission and acceptance to ma'rifa because the very meaning (of the word) 'Islam" is (based on the Arabic for) submission and acceptance and (as such) is (necessarily) part of what is understood by the term 'Iman.' Some even treat the two terms as synonymous. It is clear, as one of the *muhaqqiqun* said, that they are both interconnected in meaning and that Iman has no reality in the outward, according to the *shari'ah*, without Islam or vice versa; that affirmation is the expression of the *nafs* (*qawl an-nafs*) which is other than *ma'rifa* even if it derives from it – in the sense that it denotes the (quality of) sincerity linking the heart or tongue to the person who declares this. And the one, namely affirmation, is an action while the other, *ma'rifa*, is not. Rather the latter is a mode and all knowledge and submission lie outside the meaning of affirmation (tasdeeq), linguistically speaking, even if they are taken into consideration, according to the *shari'ah*, in the matter of Iman. The taking into consideration of submission and knowledge – according the *shari'ah* – is either because they constitute two elements of what is to be understood by the term 'Iman' according to the *shari'ah*, or because they constitute two conditions underlying its validity with respect to the different legal consequences (issuing from Iman) according to the *shari'ah*. The latter of these two opinions is the preferred one because the first implies having to alter (the word) 'Iman' from its linguistic meaning to what it means according to the *shari'ah* – and whatever has been altered is necessarily other than the original. Inclination to this (altered meaning) cannot be justified without proof and evidence – indeed the evidence points to its opposite since numerous are the occasions in the Book and sunna when the Arabs were asked (as to the nature of Iman) and their reply was not interpreted as referring to anything other than its linguistic meaning. Any interpretation that some of them may have made was of the nature of an appendage – based on the fact that when he, may the peace and bessings of Allah be upon him, asked Jibril, the latter replied by mentioning this explanatory addition: namely, when he said: "That you have Iman in ...." He interprets by means of this addition rather than interpreting the meaning of the word itself: thus he repeats (mention of) this (word) saying: "That you have Iman in ..." because this (word) was well known amongst them and there was no dispute that it meant, linguistically, 'absolute affirmation', and according to the *shari'ah*, 'affirmation of certain specific things' – namely the well known, necessary matters of the deen as mentioned above. This then refers to affirmation – in accordance with its linguistic meaning. An absence of this (latter form of affirmation) by virtue of an absence of knowledge and submission does not necessarily mean that these two (qualities) be detached from their meaning according to the *shari'ah* – because of the possibility of their both being prerequisite conditions to this (affirmation) according to the *shari'ah*. Thus it appears that affirmation (*tasdeeq*) can be said to exist – linguistically – without these two (qualities) and that the existence of this affirmation may be accompanied by *kufr* since, from the point of view of the intellect, there is nothing to preclude a tyrant from affirming a Prophet and (then) killing him out of sheer stupidity or in a moment when some whim overcomes him. His killing him does not indicate, in principle, an absence of affirmation of the Prophet – as some of the Imams think – but rather it indicates, in accordance with the *shari'ah*, that his affirmation is not of the kind that will save him from remaining for ever in the Fire. In short, Allah, exalted is He, has caused it to be that the taking on of and commitment to (this genuine) Iman will necessarily be accompanied by an inherent quality (*lazimun*) which is an inseparable part of it, namely, (the guarantee of) eternal bliss; that the opposite of this will be the unhappiness which is the inherent quality accompanying *kufr*, according to the *shari'ah*. Moreover, He has also considered that this inherent quality accompanying Iman must be accompanied by the existence of (further) matters – the absence of which necessarily result in the inherent quality of *kufr*, according to the *shari'ah*[1]. Among these matters is the (slave's) glorification of Him, the glorification of His Prophets, the abandoning of prostration to idols and the like and an inner submission leading to acceptance of His commands and prohibitions – which is the meaning of 'Islam' linguistically speaking. Furthermore, the people of truth, namely the two groups composed of the Ash'aris and the Hanafis, are agreed that there is no validity to Iman without Islam – and vice versa – since the one cannot be seperated from the other. It is known that the lack of one of these matters denotes a lack of Iman. However, the Hanafis are more pronounced in their respect for this glorification (of Allah and the Prophets). For this reason they treat many as *kafir* on account of the latter's words and actions – which they perceive as denigrating the deen – such as deliberately performing the *salat* without *wudu'*, continually leaving off doing the sunna (acts of worship) out of disdain for them or doing abhorred things

1 (This is an interpretation – the Arabic being garbled at this point.)

like excusing the drinker (of alcohol), or placing one end of the turban beneath the throat and other things explained mentioned below.

Having explained the reality of Iman and all that is connected to it then you should also have *ma'rifa* – knowledge – of all that is connected to it which is obligatory in its nature. This may be defined in the manner outlined above, namely, that which Muhammad may the peace and blessings of Allah be upon him, conveyed (to us of his sunna). It is obligatory to affirm all that he conveyed, both in the realm of *'aqida* and action. What is meant by affirmation is holding to the belief that what he, may the peace and blessings of Allah be upon him, brought is true. The details of these two matters (of *'aqida* and action) are very many, namely the total of what is contained in the books of *kalam* and the sunna. They may be summed up in a person's affirming that there is no god except Allah and that Muhammad is the Messenger of Allah, may the peace and blessings of Allah be upon him, that is an affirmation which is from the heart and to which he fully submits. As for the details which the author has mentioned, some are (inspired) by his insight – that is he was attracted by a (secondary) additional detail of this (matter of Iman); sometimes his rejection of one detail results in a rejection of a former detail but because the latter does not necessarily follow it effectively invalidates (the argument). I have written a copious book about this which is indispensable on this subject entitled "*Al-I'lam bima yuqta' al-Islam*" – The signs by which Islam is ascertained." In it I have explained most of the laws according to the four *madhhabs*. You should study it if you wish to take care of your deen.

What must be rejected is the denial of what is known in the deen of Muhammad, may the peace and blessings of Allah be upon him, as the *dharuri* matters. These are the necessary matters which are self-evident and common place, known by the great body of Muslims – like the Oneness (of Allah, exalted is He,), Prophethood, the Raising Up (of man on the Last Day), the reward and punishment (of actions); the obligatory, like the *salat*, the forbidden like wine; sexual relations with a woman who is menstruating; the permitted, like buying and selling, marriage in the rauda (- the tomb of the Prophet, may the peace and blessings of Allah be upon him, in Madina), the prohibition of sexual relations with a woman in the *'idda* (waiting period after divorce) – as opposed to those matters which are not known automatically (by the common people). This is a difficult matter, for what is the difference between this and the prohibition of sexual intercourse with a menstruating woman, indeed the latter is more apparent to the ordinary person than the former – as is obvious to someone who investigates their states. It is as if the excuse in the matter is the ignorance of most of them as to the details of the waiting period and what (activity) this (state) precludes – which in turn leads to ignorance as to the prohibition of intercourse with such a woman in many instances or to the prohibition of that about which there is agreement as to its being permitted; and the (person holding to the) opposite (of this) is also deemed a misbeliever.

If you were to say that there is no benefit in stipulating that knowledge (of this self evident kind only exists) on the condition that one has had intercourse with people as mentioned above given that when he does know and denies (this knowledge) then he is committing an act of *kufr*, and if he does not frequent society and does not know then he does not commit an act of *kufr* – if, when he does indeed mix with people, you argue 'He is like this (i.e. ignorant)' (then one would answer): the person who does mix with people is not believed on the face of it when he claims ignorance – in opposition to the person who does not. It may be that there is a matter which has been narrated by numerous chains of relation to one group and they may be deemed *kafir* (if they do not apply this knowledge) while another group (who has not heard this narration) is not. But as for what is agreed on by *ijma'* and which is known necessarily, like for example the right of the daughter of the son to a sixth (of the inheritance) together with the daughter of one's own loins – the person who denies this is not committing an act of *kufr*, according to us, although the Hanafis deem the person a *kafir* if he is aware with certainty of the validity of this, if the people of knowledge have mentioned to him that it is a matter about which there is certainty and if he continues to deny it out of disobedience." Here end the words of al-Haytami. Even if the discussion (of his) goes on at length and may cause the reader to tire there are many fine points which are of great interest.

First benefit: "Know that the greatest of blessings is Iman. As-Sakhawi said: 'Allah has not blessed a man with anything higher', and in his *Qasida* he says:

The foremost of blessings may not be computed

But the most resplendent is Iman in the Messengers

As-Sanusi said in his Commentary: "This is the most brilliant of blessings as it is a guarantee of eternal happiness in the next world."

Ibn Zakari as said in *Sharh an-Naseeha*: "The imam Hujjat al-Islam, our Lord Abu Muhammad al-Ghazali, may Allah, exalted is He, be pleased with him, said: 'The first of blessings is Islam, and the second is that you do not slacken during the night or the day in giving thanks for it and praising (Allah, exalted is He) for it: even if you are unable to understand the extent (of this blessing) then know in truth that if you had been created at the beginning of the world and you had started to give thanks for the blessing of Islam from that very first moment (and continued) right on to eternity you would be unable to do this let alone fulfil this (as it should be done).'"

I SAY: "Know that at this point (in the work) there is no room to mention the knowledge I have regarding some aspects of this blessing – even if I were to fill a thousand pages my knowledge would be more than this. However I admit that what I know in comparison to what I do not know is like a drop in the all the seas of the world – have you not heard the words of, exalted is He, to the Lord of the Messengers: 'You had no idea of what the Book was, nor faith'[1] and He said: 'It is Allah who has favoured you by guiding you to Iman if you are telling the truth.'"[2] Here end the words of Ibn Zakari.

Among the great benefits is that whoever dies with this (Iman) will not stay forever in the Fire, according to the *ijma'* of the people of truth. Al-Fakihani said in *Sharh al-'Umda*: "Whoever commits all of the prohibited things but dies with *tawhid*, affirming the Message, then he will go to the Garden, according to the *ijma'* of the *'ulama*. (This means that) either Allah will forgive him for what he has done and will not punish him for his disobedience, or He will punish him for it but then will cause him to enter the Garden." There is also something similar from as-Sanusi in *ash-Sharh al-Wusta*, and from al-Munawi and others. The narrations whose literal meaning appear to imply that the disobedient person will stay forever in the Fire are interpreted in various ways by the *ijma'* of the people of sunna. Al-Munawi, (for example,) has indicated such (a narration) in his Commentary – namely "Whoever claims that someone is his father while aware that that person is not his father then the Garden is forbidden him' saying that (what it means is that it) is forbidden him before his punishment, for if Allah wishes He will punish him (first); or that (it is forbidden him to be reckoned along) with the forerunners (amongst the Muslims) who will enter the Garden; or that it is conceivable (for such a person to enter the Fire) because to deem the haram halal when it does not admit of interpretation by the *mujtahid*een is *kufr* and this (particular) narration requires that one deem the Garden haram (for such a person); or it means that a specific garden has been made haram (for him), like the Garden of Eden; or that the narration is to be understood as (an example of the) use of harsh language in order to inspire fear (in people's hearts); or that this is his requital if punished but that then he will be pardoned; or that this is prescribed in the law by those who hold that those who commit a major wrong action are also committing an act of *kufr*."

1   ash-Shura – Counsel: 49
2   al-Hujarat – The Private Quarters: 17

The second benefit: As for mention of those actions which cause an unhappy sealing (of one's life), may Allah protect us from such an end, by the rank of the most noble of creation in the eyes of Allah, our Lord Muhammad may the peace and blessings of Allah be upon him – it includes, for example, the consuming of usury. Al-Munawi has related that Ibn Daqiq said that it is a cause of someone having an miserable seal (to the end of his life).

Among the further benefits is the guarantee that one's Iman will not taken away; likewise, (protection from) the false claim of *wilayat* or that one is capable of *karamat*. It is related in the *al-Ihya'*: "Abu ad-Darda' swore that anyone who has lost all fear that his Iman will be taken away will in fact have it taken from him" It is also said that a false claim to *wilayat* is a wrong action whose punishment is an unhappy seal (to one's life).

Mayyara said in his conclusion: "This may refer to the false claim on his own behalf or a claim on behalf of someone else." He has also said in *Majma'u'l-Ahbab*: "More than one of the 'arifun, from amongst them as-Sayyid as-Sirri, have said may Allah, exalted is He, be pleased with him: 'I do not know of anyone of whom I could say that I will have a better end than they.' It is also narrated in this (work) that the 'ulama of the first generations would say: 'Anyone who feels sure that his Iman will not be taken from him will in fact have it taken from him.' There is no doubt that the first and latter generations of 'ulama had an intense fear with respect to their Iman. They always sought refuge with Allah subanahu wa, exalted is He, that he preserve their Iman for them and that He have them die with Iman. We humbly petition Allah glorious and exalted is He, that He preserve our Iman for us, that He cause us to die with it, that He not cause it to be taken from us and that He not cause us to be removed from Him. Iman is something deposited for us with Him, glorious and exalted is He, and He surely does not have a thing deposited but that He takes good care of it, and Allah is the best of Protectors and and He is the Most Merciful of the Merciful."

As for disobedience of the Shaykhs, Shaykh Sayyidi al-Mukhtar said: "There is no punishment for someone (guilty of this) other than an unhappy end (at death)."

The harm which may befall the people of Iman, their lack of gratitude for their Iman and their lack of fear lest it be taken from them – all these matters have been mentioned by the Shaykh. The author of the book entitled *an-Nurayn* said: "The four things which are most likely to cause someone's Iman being taken from him are desisting from giving thanks for Islam, lack of fear that one's Iman disappear, oppression of the people of Islam and disobedience of one's parents. More than one of the *'ulama* have recorded that disobedience of them is cause of someone's having an unhappy end (to his life)." In the *adh-Dhahab al-Ibreez* in the Section regarding the qualities of 'Abd al-'Aziz: I have heard him, may Allah be pleased with him, relating from his Shaykh, Sayyidi 'Umar ibn Muhammad al-Hawari. He mentioned that he was seated with him at as-Sadr al-Muharara which is outside the grave of Sayyidi 'Ali ibn Harazahum when his son came to him seeking leave of him before going on Hajj. Sayyidi 'Umar refused the son permission and the son disobeyed his father leaving without the latter's assent. Sayyidi 'Umar told me: 'Disobedience of one's parents results in four things: 1) the *dunya* leaves him and hates him just as the *mumin* hates Jahannam; 2) when he sits down in a place and speaks about some matter with those present Allah, exalted is He, distracts their hearts from listening to his words, Allah removes the *baraka* and light from his words and he becomes hated by them; 3) the *awliya* of Allah, exalted is He, from amongst the people of the Diwan and in authority will not look with mercy or kindness to them under any circumstances; 4) the light of his Iman will become less and less, and if Allah has willed only difficulty for him – and we seek refuge in Allah, exalted is He, from this – his state will last until the light of his Iman becomes faint, then is extinguished completely and he dies a *kafir*. We ask Allah glorious is He, that we be saved (from such a fate); if Allah does not wish for him such (a fate) then he will die with (only) deficient Iman, and also we seek refuge with Allah, exalted is He, from this." He has also said: "The result of causing one's parents to be content are also four in number, that is the opposite of the above mentioned matters: the *dunya* loves him as much as the *mumin* loves the Garden, his words are as sweet as honey to people and the *awliya* of Allah, exalted is He, are in sympathy with him and his Iman never ceases to increase. And Allah, exalted is He, is the Granter of Success." Here end the words from *adh-Dhahab al-Ibreez*.

Another said: "There are some wrong actions whose punishment is delayed in this world. As for the one who disobeys (his parents) little will be his success with respect to his actions undertaken for worldly gain or for the next world." He then mentioned the incident of the young man whom the Messenger, may the peace and blessings of Allah be upon him, went to see (at his home) and who would not say the two *shahadas* until his mother was content with what he was doing.

Among such (wrong actions) too, is the breaking off of family relations – this has been mentioned by Shaykh Sayyidi.

Another example (of such actions) is being preoccupied with the whispering of Shaytan. In the *Ghayat al-Ma'ani* in the commentary on the words of *ar-Risala* (he says): "Whoever is beset by doubt should flee from this for preoccupation with this leads to doubt in *tawhid*."

Third benefit: as for the actions which guarantee a happy seal (to one's life), may Allah grant us and all you (readers) who are looking (for the truth) there is the example of good behaviour towards one's parents as has been mentioned above in *adh-Dhahab al-Ibreez*.

Another example, a resplendent benefit, is the one I have found in certain books only – as narrated from Sayyidi 'Abdal-Wahhab ash-Sha'rani from Sayyidi 'Ali al-Khawwas from Sayyidina Da'ud, may blessings be upon him and on our Prophet, who said: "Whoever says every day morning and evening:

سُبْحَانَ الْقَائِمِ الدَّائِمِ، سُبْحَانَ الدَّائِمِ الْقَائِمِ، سُبْحَانَ الْحَيِّ الْقَيُّومِ، سُبْحَانَ اللهِ وَبِحَمْدِهِ، سُبْحَانَ اللهِ الْعَظِيمِ، سُبْحَانَ الْمَلِكِ الْقُدُّوسِ، سُبْحَانَ اللهِ رَبِّ الْمَلَائِكَةِ وَالرُّوحِ.

"*Subhana* to the One Who maintains and Who exists for ever, *subhana* to the One Who maintains (creation) and exists for ever, *subhana* to the Living to the Sustainer, *subhan'Allah* and praise be to Him, *subhan'Allah* the Vast, *subhana* the King, the Most Pure, *subhan'Allah*, the Lord of the Angels and the *Ruh*,"

then he will without doubt die professing Islam without any hesitation (on his part)."

Here ends his words. This is how I found the text. What is well known amongst people is that it is said three times between the *salat* of *fajr* and *Subh*, but that '*subhan:Allah* the Vast' is not part of it.

Another version reads:

يَا حَيُّ يَا قَيُّومُ، يَا بَدِيعَ السَّمَاوَاتِ وَالْأَرْضِ، يَا ذَا الْجَلَالِ وَالْإِكْرَامِ، لَا إِلَهَ إِلَّا أَنْتَ، أَسْأَلُكَ أَنْ تُحْيِيَ قَلْبِي بِنُورِ مَعْرِفَتِكَ أَبَداً، يَا اَللَّهُ، يَا اَللَّهُ، يَا اَللَّهُ

"O Living, O Sustainer, O Originator of the heavens and earth, O Master of Majesty and Generosity, there is no god but You! I ask you that you revive my heart with the light of Your *ma'rifa* for ever and ever O Allah, O Allah"

(to be recited) forty times between *fajr* and *Subh* as Ahmad Zarruq has mentioned, as narrated from Hakim at-Tirmidhi.

Other examples of actions which bring about a happy seal (to one's life) are having fear lest Iman come to an end, giving thanks for Iman and being useful and helpful towards the people of Iman – this is mentioned by Shaykh al-Mukhtar.

Another example is that mentioned in the book entitled *an-Nurayn* concerning what befits the two abodes (of this world and the next): "What acts as a guarantee against one's Iman being taken from one at death is the praying of two *rak'ats* between *Maghrib* and *'Isha*, reciting in each *rak'a* the Fatiha and al-Qadr/Power' once, and Surat al-Ikhlas/Sincerity seven times and the two final surahs known as the *Mu'awudhatan* – (al-Falak and an-Nas). Then, when he says the *salam*, he should say three times:

اَللّٰهُمَّ إِنِّي أَسْتَوْدِعُكَ دِينِي وَإِيمَانِي، فَاحْفَظْهُمَا عَلَيَّ فِي حَيَاتِي وَعِنْدَ وَفَاتِي وَبَعْدَ مَمَاتِي

'O Allah I hand over my deen and my Iman to You for safe keeping and so protect them for me during my life and on my death and after my death.'"

I SAY: "Amongst the actions that should also be counted among them is the remaining awake (in *dhikr*) during the two 'Eid nights, as mentioned in *al-Jami' as-Saghir*: 'The heart of the person who stays awake for the two 'Eid nights striving to spend the time (in *dhikr*) will not die the day when the hearts die'" or words similar to this. Al-Munawi has explained this 'striving to spend the time in *dhikr*' in his commentary by saying that the person does not become infatuated with love of this world, or feel sure that he will not have an unhappy seal. this is obtained by spending the greater part of the night (in *dhikr*) although it has also been said by praying (just) the *'Isha* and *Subh salats* in *jama'a*." Here end the words of al-Munawi.

Another example is seeing to the needs of the destitute, as mentioned in *al-Jami' as-Saghir*: "Seeing to the needs of the destitute protects one from an unhappy death." Al-'Alqami said: "An unhappy death is that Shaytan causes him to go astray at the moment of death." Al-Munawi said: "It refers to someone dying while persisting in acts of disobedience, or despairing of (Allah's) mercy, or to drowning or being burnt alive or being stung (by a scorpion) or the like."

In the book entitled *al-Barakat* he comments on this saying: "An unhappy death is that someone dies persisting in wrong action or despairing of the mercy of Allah, exalted is He, or that death comes upon him unawares or that his seal is unhappy, or he dies crushed to death or stung by a scorpion or the like – this he has mentioned in *Nawadir al-Usul*."

Another example is the comforting of the grieved: in *Majma'u'l-Ahbab* it is related from Wahb ibn Munabbih from the Zabur of (the Prophet), Da'ud, may blessings be upon him and our Prophet: "O Allah, what is the reward for the one who comforts the person distressed by misfortune when he does it for Your sake?" He replied: "His reward is that I bestow upon him the cloak of iman and then never take it off him."

I SAY: "What should also be included (is the case) where someone says on seeing a *kafir*:

اَلْحَمْدُ لِلَّهِ الَّذِي عَافَانِي مِمَّا ابْتَلَاكَ بِهِ وَفَضَّلَنِي عَلَى كَثِيرٍ مِمَّنْ خَلَقَ تَفْضِيلاً

'Praise belongs to Allah who has spared me from the trial that He has afflicted you with and who has preferred me over many others whom He has created';

and in another narration:

اَلْحَمْدُ لِلَّهِ الَّذِي عَافَانِي مِمَّا ابْتَلَاكَ بِهِ وَفَضَّلَنِي عَلَى كَثِيرٍ مِنْ عِبَادِهِ تَفْضِيلاً

'Praise be to Allah who has spared me from the trial he has afflicted you with and who has preferred me over many other of His slaves'

– as recorded in *al-Jami' as-Saghir*. Whoever sees someone afflicted by some trial and says this, then he himself will never be afflicted by this trial. One of his commentators said that 'afflicted by some trial' means his deen is put to the test, although another said that it refers also to a trial of a worldly concern. I have seen some of the active *'ulama* like as-Sanusi, may Allah be content with him, say it when mentioning people of the misguided sects."

Al-Munawi has also said that [use of] the *siwak* tooth stick reminds of the *shahada* when someone dies and in *Ghayat al-Ma'ani* one of the 'Arifun said: 'Whoever wants to die with his tongue moist with the *dhikr* of Allah, exalted is He, then he should keep to six things: the saying of the *bismillah* when starting any action; the saying of *al-hamdu lillah* when finishing any action, the saying of *la hawla wa la quwwata ila billah* when faced with something disliked, thereby relinquishing his own power and strength; if afflicted by some trial, the saying of *inna lillah wa in inna ilayhi raji'un*; and if he commits a wrong action, the saying of *astaghfirullah*. Ash-Shabrakheeti said in his *Sharh al-'Ashmaweeya*: 'and if he is faced by some weighty matter, then he should say: *la ilaha illa'llah*.'"

In *Sharh an-Naseeha* Ibn Zakiri says: "Whoever fears the agony of death, then the key to forgiveness is prescribed for him, namely that his tongue recite *la ilaha illa'llah* – this is what Ibn Hajar says in *Sharh al-Bukhari*. He also says:

'Iman in Allah is affirming His existence and that He possess the attributes of perfection, far removed from any attribute of impefection.'"

THE BOOKS

As for Ibn 'Ashir's saying 'and the Books', Ibn Hajar al-Haytami says that they refer to the speech of Allah, exalted is He, from before endless time, that is (speech) disconnected from letters and sound: it refers to the fact that Allah, exalted is He, revealed these (Books) to His Messengers by way of in-time, contingent speech on the tablets or on the tongue of an angel; that all that they contained came into being and proved true; that some of the judgements contained in them were abrogated and some not. Az-Zamakhshari said: 'They comprise one hundred and four Books, fifty of which were revealed to Shayth, thirty to Idris, ten to Adam, ten to Ibrahim and then the Torah, the Injil, the Zabur and the Furqan (the Discrimination, i.e. the Qur'an).

THE MESSENGERS

As for Ibn 'Ashir's mention of 'the Messengers', al-Haytami said: "What he has indicated by this is that He sent them to creation in order to guide them and to perfect their manner of living and their end; that He assisted them by miracles which indicated their sincerity; that they delivered the Message from Him and so made clear to those charged with responsibility (*mukallafun*) what they had been commanded to explain; that it is obligatory to honour all of them, without discriminating between any of them; that He has removed from them any imperfection or shortcoming; that they are free of both the lesser and greater wrong actions both before their messengership and after it according to the preferred judgement, indeed it is the correct one; and that the incidents which happened (to the Prophets) are related by the commentators; that anything related in the books containing the stories of the Prophets contrary to what we have mentioned should not be relied on and no attention should be paid to such works even if the narrator is widely regarded, like al-Baghawi or al-Wahidi."

USEFUL POINT: in *Shu'ub al-Iman* al-Bayhaqi relates that Ibn 'Abbas, may Allah be pleased with him, said: "All the Prophets were from the tribe of Israel except for ten of them: Nuh, Hud, Salih, Shu'ayb, Ibrahim, Lut, Isma'il, Ishaq, Ya'qub and Muhammad, may the peace and blessings of Allah be upon him, and no Prophet had two names except 'Isa – who was also called al-Masih and Ya'qub, who was also called Isra'il."

Ibn Abi Hatim has narrated from Qatada who said: "Between Adam and

Nuh, a thousand years elapsed and between Nuh and Ibrahim a thousand, between Ibrahim and Musa a thousand; between Musa and 'Isa four hundred years and between 'Isa and Muhammad, may the peace and blessings of Allah be upon him, six hundred years."

The Angels

Ibn 'Ashir's mention of the 'angels' refers to the fact that they were slaves belonging to Him, not godly beings as the *mushrikun* claim; honoured and not defective as the Jews claim; and they do not disobey what Allah has commanded them to do but rather they carry out what they are ordered; and they are the ambassadors of Allah, exalted is He, between Him and His creation having the power to move and act among this creation; truthful in whatever they relate to creation from Him." Here end the words of Al-Haytami.

The Raising up

As for his saying 'the imminent Raising Up', 'Ali ibn 'Abd as-Sadiq said this implies affirmation (on behalf of the slave) that it will come to pass and that there is no escape from it; it refers also to the coming out of the graves to the place of standing. Its being described as 'imminent' is in the sense that its arrival is (necessarily, with the passing of time) always getting nearer; and all the different *shari'ahs* (of the various *deens*) are agreed upon this. It forms part of the necessary body of knowledge of the deen which has been narrated in both the Book and the sunna, and there is no need to go into detail regarding the proofs either from the point of view of the intellect or the narrations for the *ijma'* are agreed that anyone who denies this raising up – be it in a literal or metaphorical way – is committing *kufr*."

USEFUL POINT: Al-Munawi said: "Adh-Dhahabi said: 'Texts have come to us affirming the annihilation of this abode and its inhabitants and the razing and scattering of the mountains – and these reports are by way of multiple chains of uninterrupted narration which are incontestable; and no one knows when this will happen except Allah, exalted is He, and whoever claims that he knows this by way of calculation or by some manner of estimation or by way of unveiling or the like then he is astray and liable to lead others astray.'"

The Decree

As for his saying 'The Decree', al-Ubbi said that this refers to the way in which the knowledge of Allah, exalted is He, and His will from before endless time connects to the realities of creation before their coming into being: this is such that there is no in-time contingent event but that He, glorious is He, has determined and decreed it from before endless time; that His knowledge of it precedes it and His will is connected to it.

An-Nawawi: "'Iyad said: 'Many have claimed that the meaning of the Decree is Allah, exalted is He, compelling the slave to what He has decreed and decided upon. However, it is not like this. Rather He wills and (this willing) is that referred to above, namely (by way of a) connection between knowledge and will. Holding to this was the *'aqida* of all the people of sunna – until a group manifested at the end of the time of the Companions who said that there was no decree." Here end the words of al-Ubbi.

Al-Haytami said in *Sharh al-Arba'in*: "Know that Iman in the Decree is divided into two parts: Iman that He, exalted is He, has prior knowledge with respect to both the good and bad actions of the slaves – together with all that is possible or conceivable with respect to this knowledge; and that He has recorded this and accounted for it for Himself; that the actions of the slaves are carried out in accordance with His prior knowledge. Second, that He, exalted is He, has created the actions of His slaves, exalted is He from (any notion of) goodness, evil, *kufr* and Iman. This second part is denied by all the Qadiris, whereas the former is only denied by a fanatical sect from among them. Many treat them as *kuffar* on account of this denial. The point of dispute is that they do not deny knowledge from before endless time – for otherwise they would be *kuffar* (outright), as ash-Shafi'i has noted and al-imam Ahmad and others."

Al-Munawi in *Sharh al-Jami'* said: "There is a difference of opinion as to whether the Qadiris who hold to the belief that good is from Allah, exalted is He, and evil is from those who act on His behalf are to be regarded as *kuffar*; as for the Qadiris who deny that Allah, exalted is He, has decreed things from before endless time and who regard the event (of creation) as a (reality involving) constant renewal and fresh beginnings, there being no decree, that Allah, exalted is He, has no knowledge of it and that He comes to know of it after its occurrence, then they are *kuffar* – and regarding this matter there is no difference of opinion as an-Nawawi has related from 'Iyad.

The Sirat

As for Ibn 'Ashir's saying 'Likewise the *Sirat*', al-Fakihani is quoted as saying in *Ghayat al-Ma'ani*: "The Mu'tazilis differ as to their affirmation or rejection of this, although most of them reject it. They base their argument on the fact that a description of the *Sirat* has been narrated describing it as 'sharper than a sword, finer than a hair' and that people will 'walk over it on foot.' They argue that the placing of one's foot on something of this description is impossible and so it is necessary to interpret the literal expression of this in order to obtain the proper understanding of the deen which Allah blessed is He and exalted, has commanded us to hold firm to; moreover (they argue for the interpretation of the literal meaning) because such (a crossing on such a bridge) would necessarily entail exhaustion, pain and grief for the *mumin* in the next world – which is forbidden (him by his nature of being a *mumin*). This only goes to show their feeble mindedness and the shallowness of their understanding and that they pay no attention to the effect of the decree and its connection to all events which are possible of existence. One might say to them: why is it you can conceive of the birds (flying) in the air and walking on water but you cannot conceive of (someone) walking on the *Sirat*? What is preventing you from this?' One could also say to them: 'Examine his words, may the peace and blessings of Allah be upon him, 'The *kafir* will be raised on the Final Day on his face' to which someone responded: 'O Messenger of Allah – how will he be able to walk on his face?' to which he, may the peace and blessings of Allah be upon him, replied: 'Surely the One Who caused him to walk on his two legs is capable of causing him to walk on his face.' *Subhan'Allah!* – Who has closed the hearts of whichever of creation He wills: if He had wished He could have guided all people. A logical extension (of their argument) would have been their denial also of the turning of the staff into the serpent, the cleaving of the sea or the raising of the dead in this world. They must differentiate between such (incidents related in the Qur'an) and the walking (on the *Sirat*) and their refusal to accept that the *mumin* could possibly suffer any grief or exhaustion. However, we do not accept that this is impossible. One of them said: 'It is conceivable that the Prophets and *awliya* are affected by the terrors of the day of Raising up such that their confidence and trust is shaken for in the *Sahih* is recorded: "Truly Jahannam will moan with such a moaning that all of the angels most intimate with Allah and all of the Prophets sent by Allah will end up crouching down on their knees." This is confirmed by Allah, exalted is He, *"You will see every nation on its knees."*[1] They say: 'If this (understanding) is accepted then it is (also) conceivable that Allah, exalted is He, will protect whomever He wishes of His slaves from the terrors of the *Sirat* and beyond" and Allah is the One Who guarantees success and guidance there is no Lord other than Him.'"

Al-Aqfahasi has commented on one of the *hadith* saying: "The time needed to cover its (the *Sirat*'s) length is three thousand years, a thousand years in ascent,

---

1   al-Jathiyya – Kneeling: 27

a thousand years on the level and a thousand in descent." Here end the words of *Ghayat al-Ma'ani*.

THE BALANCE

As for his mention of the 'Balance' al-Haytami said: "It is said that the weighing up is of different kinds: that of the weighing up of Iman by assessing all the good actions together with that of *kufr* by means of all the bad actions – the *mumin* remaining forever in ease and happiness and the *kafir* in the Fire of Jaheem; then there is the weighing up of actions according to their precise weight (in importance) in order to make clear the amount of the reward – as the sura at the end of the Qur'an, 'The Earthquake' indicates; and there is also the weighing up of any wrong against a slave with respect to the one who committed this – based on what has been narrated in the *sahih* traditions, namely that the reward for good actions will be stripped from the person of wrong action in favour of the person wronged – in accordance with the degree of this wrong action; and that if he has no good actions, then bad actions of the (person wronged) will be added to his (account)." Here ends the discussion of Ibn Hajar al-Haytami.

Ibn Hajar al-'Asqalani in *Fath al-Bari* during his commentary of the words of al-Bukhari 'Whoever leaves off doing the *'Asr salat* will see his actions come to nothing' and his commentary on 'The Section regarding a *mumin*'s fear that his actions will come to nothing while not being aware of this' says: "Al-Qadi Abu Bakr ibn al-'Arabi has refuted the Murij'ites in his detailed discussion of this matter: …'there are two kinds of actions which are of no avail, the first when one thing is thwarted by another causing it to come to nothing, like *kufr* causing one's Iman and all one's good deeds to come to nothing; secondly, the coming to nothing of the weighing in the balance – when the good deeds are placed one side of the scale and the bad in the other. The person whose good deeds tip the balance will be saved but the one whose bad deeds weigh more will be suspended in a state subject to the will of Allah – either He will forgive him or He will punish him. This suspension represents the thwarting or inactivity (of his account) within two states: the suspension of benefit at a time when he has need of it and a suspension of any further punishment – that is of anything worse than this – until he comes out of the Fire. However, both of these (states) represent a relative invalidation (of his account) and terming it 'a coming to nothing' is metaphorical. In reality it is not a real coming to nothing for if he comes out of the Fire and enters the Garden, the reward for his actions will be returned to him. This is other than the coming to nothing and loss of those who lie outside these two states of loss: the disobedient will be judged by the judgment of *kufr*, and most of the Qadiris will be among them. And Allah, exalted is He, is the One Who grants success." Here end the words of Ibn Hajar regarding the chapter entitled 'Fear of the *mumin* that his good actions will come to nothing.

As for his mention of 'Whoever abandons doing the *'Asr salat* then his actions will come to nothing' he — that is Ibn al-'Arabi — says in his commentary on at-Tirmidhi: "This loss is of two types: firstly, the loss whereby *kufr* brings Iman and all one's good actions to nothing; secondly the loss at the weighing up whereby disobedience prevents a person benefitting from his good actions — as long, that is, as they are more (than his bad actions) — until he is saved (by Allah's intervention) and the reward for his good actions is returned to him."

I SAY: "Reflect upon his words: As for the person's whose good actions weigh more according to the compiler of the writings of 'Abd al-Qadir al-Fasi — and a similar saying of imam as-Sanusi from Ibn Dihaq — then even if the slave has performed countless good actions but has one wrong deed to his account then he will be held, as it were, in ransom by this deed until Allah, exalted is He, either forgives him (outright), or punishes him and then takes him out of the Fire."

Muhammad ibn 'Abd al-Qadir in *Sharh Hisn al-Hasin* said: "Shaykh Abu 'Abdallah al-Manoufi said in reply to him: 'The weighing up of deeds does not mean that the bad ones are set against the good such that the one wipes out the other and he benefits by whatever remain over of the good (actions) or is harmed by the bad — for this is the *madhhab* of some of the Mu'tazilis. None of the people of sunna hold to this. What the people of sunna have said is that whoever commits a major wrong action and does not turn in *tawba* from it, then even if he performs good actions as great in volume as the whole earth he is still held in ransom by this major wrong action, and nothing but the forgiveness of Allah will save him' For this reason Ibn Dihaq said: 'The benefit of the weighing up, for the people of sunna, is knowledge of the amount of the reward of the good actions and the amount of the punishment of the bad actions.' Shaykh as-Sanusi after a discussion says: 'Given this, it is not hard to believe that He, glorious is He, will make the sign of His forgiveness the greater weight of the good actions in relation to the bad and the sign of the execution of His threatened punishment the greater weight of the bad actions. (In the latter case) the good actions (of this person) which are accepted and the amount of the reward for them will be suspended for this slave until he comes out of the Fire. The reward is not annulled by the greater or lesser degree of wrong actions in comparison to it as the Mu'tazilis say. Rather the heaviness or lightness of good (in the scales) is merely an indication of the forgiveness or punishment. For this reason we assert that Allah, exalted is He, may cause one single good action to weigh more than major wrong actions as great in volume as the whole earth if Allah glorious is He, wants to forgive purely from His generosity; it may be too that Allah, exalted is He, will cause good actions as great in volume as the whole earth to be light in the balance and will cause one wrong action to outweigh them – if Allah, exalted is He, wills the carrying out of the threat of punishment purely by (virtue of) His (attribute of) justice. Thus, the affair of the *mumin* is that he should not disdain any of the good actions for it may well be that Our Lord, the Vast, will be content with the (good action); nor that he should treat lightly any single bad action for it may well be that the anger of our Lord, exalted is He, lies in this (one action).' Then he says: 'In short, the benefit of the weighing up is not confined to what Ibn Dihaq said. Rather one of its benefits is knowledge of whom our Generous Lord grants his forgiveness to and whom he takes to task by His justice. And Allah glorious is He, is more knowledgeable of what will be. What is incumbent upon the *mumin* is that he not believe what some of the Mu'tazilis have said, as we have explained above. However, he does not have to investigate further than this. He should refrain from going too deeply into the matter and hand over knowledge of the matter to Allah glorious is He." Here end the words of Muhammad ibn 'Abd al-Qadir al-Fasi.

The Basin of the Prophet

As for Ibn 'Ashir's mention of 'The Basin of the Prophet' as-Sanusi said in *al-Kubra*: "What the Prophet has come with, may the peace and blessings of Allah be upon him, and what it is necessary to believe in, is (Allah's) carrying out of the threat (of punishment) with regard to a group of the disobedient from his *umma* – but that they will be brought out by his intercession, may the peace and blessings of Allah be upon him. As for whether 'the Basin' is before the *Sirat* or after it or whether there are two Basin, one of them before the *Sirat* and the other after it – and this latter is the correct opinion (in my view) – there are various opinions."

Useful point: As for those who are driven from the Basin (*al-Hawd*) – among them are those who had a distaste for the sunna. He said in *Ghayat al-Ma'ani* that at-Tirmidi al-Hakim has narrated from the hadith of 'Uthman ibn Madh'un: "O 'Uthman do not be averse to my sunna for whoever is averse to my sunna and then dies before turning in *tawba*, then the angels will strike his face and cause him to turn away from my Basin."

It is also related in the *al-Jami' as-Saghir* that whoever comes to his brother excusing himself then he should accept his excuse: "Whoever comes to his brother then he should accept this excuse whether or not it is justified or not, and if he does not, then he will not come to drink at the Basin." Ash-Shabrakheeti has composed some verses whose worth one would not be able to do justice to – even if written down using tears as ink:

If a friend comes to you excusing himself one day
   Then forgive his many wrong actions
For ash-Shafi'i has narrated a hadith
   With a sound chain of transmission from Mughira
From the Chosen One that Allah will erase
   two thousand major wrong actions by one forgiveness.

The Garden

As for his mention of 'The Garden' the author of *Ghayat al-Ma'ani* in his commentary on the saying of the *Risala* 'and He has created the Fire' said: "There is no dispute among the people of the sunna as to what he has mentioned of the Garden and the Fire being two creations (which exist) now in the present time (rather than after time). Whoever claims that they are not created or has doubts about this is a *kafir* and there is no excuse for ignorance."

In al-Munawi there is a commentary on the hadith 'Whoever enters the Garden will enjoy ease and experience no hardship; his clothes will not wear out and his youth will not disappear' which reads: "This is clear proof that the Garden lasts for ever and does not come to an end, and that the Fire is likewise. Jahm ibn Safwan has claimed that they both come to an end as they are both in-time, contingent creations. However, none of the people of Islam follow him; rather, they treat him as a *kafir*. Some hold to the opinion that the Fire will come to an end but not the Garden."

Ibn al-Qayyim has composed a long explanation in support of his opinion and that of his Shaykh; Ibn Taymiyya as to the eventual coming to end of the Fire. He has also composed several essays on the subject. In these (writings) he comes closer to *kufr* than to Iman because of his opposition to the text of the Qur'an. In one of his works, he has concluded his description of the Gardens with the following (hadith): "One of you will perform the actions of the people of the Garden until there remains only an arm's span between him and it and then what has been written for him overtakes him and he performs the actions of the people of the Fire and he will enter the Fire." As-Subki said, regarding Ibn Taymiyya: "He is astray and leads others astray."

THE FIRE

As for his mention of "the Fire", this is something the existence of which one must also believe in, as well as that it will go on for ever. In his *al-Wusta* as-Sanusi has added the following to (the matters) one must believe in: "... the blessings and ease of the *muminun* and the torment of the *kafirun*."

After mentioning that the torment of the people of the Fire will be forever Al-Munawi said: "Take note of what I have mentioned repeatedly – namely, that the torment of the *kuffar* in Jahannam will be forever and that this is indicated by *ayats* and *hadith* and confirmed by the majority of the *umma*, both from the earlier and later generations. As for other statements on the subject which differ from the above they must be interpreted."

USEFUL POINT: al-Munawi has also commented on the hadith 'The last to enter the Garden will be a man known as Jaheena and the people of the Garden will say that Jaheena has certain knowledge as to the truth regarding whether anyone will remain in the Fire to be tormented or not' saying: "His being 'the last' is not contradicted by the hadith of Muslim 'The last person to enter the Garden will be a man who will walk on the *Sirat*, sometimes walking, sometimes stumbling and sometimes touched by the fire. When he gets past it he will turn round to it saying: "*Tabaraka* to the One Who has saved me from you"' because it is possible to regard them as compatible. (Thus one can argue) that Jaheena is the last to enter the Garden from among those who enter the Fire, who are tormented in it for a while (only) and who then come out of it; whereas the 'last person' (mentioned in the second hadith) to enter the Garden is from among those who set out on the journey (to the after-life), who then pass over the *Sirat* while on their way to the Garden and who do not end up entering into the Fire at all. This also does not contradict his saying 'and sometimes the Fire touches him' as what is meant is that its flames reach him while he remains outside of the limits of the Fire itself. I have also read a similar means of harmonising them by Ibn Abi Jamra who said: 'The person (in the first hadith) will be the last of those who come out of it after having entered it in reality while the other will be the last person to exit from among those who had remained (a brief moment in its outermost flames) while passing over the *Sirat*. Thus the expression indicates that the latter's exit from the Fire is metaphorical, that is, he will be affected by the heat and agony (of the Fire), thus sharing (to a degree the torment of) those who enter it (completely).' He did not, however, mention whether the name Jaheena occurred in this narration. Al-Qurtubi relates that as-Saheeli said: 'It has been narrated that his name is Hanad' and he harmonises the two (*hadith*) by treating one of the names as belonging to the person in the first (hadith) and the other as belonging to the second.'"

Another benefit: He has also said in *Ghayat al-Ma'ani*: "Know that the torment in the Fire of the people of *tawhid* will be of different kinds: some will be tormented for a day, some for a week, some for a month, some for a year, some for a thousand years and some for seven thousand years and this will be the last person to remain in the Fire. It has been recorded in some narrations the last person to remain in the Fire will be Hanad."

Two remarks: firstly, Muhammad Mayyara said: "The literal understanding of the wording (of the hadith of Jibril) implies that Iman is only accorded to the person who affirms all that has been mentioned (in the text). However, the *fuqaha* are of the opinion that it is acceptable to accord Iman to the person who trusts in Allah and in His Messenger (only). Moreover, there is no difference of opinion that what is meant by 'trust in the Messenger of Allah' is 'trust in his existence and in what he brought from His Lord.' Thus (one may assert) that this (understanding of trust) necessarily includes 'all of what has been mentioned' – and Allah knows best"; secondly al-Mayyara said: "As already mentioned above during the discussion of Ibn Hajar al-'Asqalani, Ibn Hajar al-Haytami has also narrated from one of the *'ulama* that one must have complete trust in all the Angels, the Books, the Messengers as well as in whatever has been mentioned specifically by name, like Jibril, the Injil and Musa: whoever does not affirm any of these specific realities then he is a *kafir*; whoever does not know their names should believe in them in general and this will be acceptable. Thus one must pay attention to these realities which are specifically mentioned by name in order that one may trust in them specifically. As for the Books, four are named, the Torah, the Injil, the Zabur and the Furqan and we have combined them all in our saying:

Then the Injil and the Torah, then the Zabur

And after them, the Furqan of Ahmad – which completed them

Then he mentioned a poem about the Messengers:

As for mention of the names of the Messengers and Prophets

There are twenty five – so take note of each of them

Adam, Nuh then Idris after him

And thereafter Ibrahim and his great and respected sons

And Ya'qub also, then Yusuf his offspring

Hud and Lut, Salih all were sent

Then Shu'ayb came, then Musa and his brother
And Da'ud, so be aware of this, together with Sulayman
And Ayyub, then Dhul Kifl
Then Yunus, Ilyas and al-Yasa'
As well as Zakariya and his son and the son of Maryam
And the seal of the Prophets of Allah who came to complete them all.

وَأَمَّا الْإِحْسَانُ فَقَالَ مَنْ دَرَاهُ

أَنْ تَعْبُدَ اللَّهَ كَأَنَّكَ تَرَاهُ

46   As for *Ihsan* the one who knows said that you should 'worship Allah as if you can see Him'

Al-Haytami said in *Sharh al-Arba'in*: "This is part of his all-encompassing capacity of speech, may the peace and blessings of Allah be upon him, for in it he has expressed, in the concisest of terms, through (this metaphor of) the slave's watchful, waking state vis-à-vis his Lord, how perfect submission, humility and other qualities besides these (should be present) in all his states and how sincerity (should accompany) all his actions; moreover the very formulation of this saying of his, may the peace and blessings of Allah be upon him, both encourages people to take this on and provides an explanation of the cause which brings about such (qualities) – if it were decreed that someone should worship his Lord while actually being able to see Him then he would not fail to be as humble as courteous as possible, both in his outward and inward, and to take pains to nurture these (qualities) in the best possible manner.

إِنْ لَمْ تَكُنْ تَرَاهُ إِنَّهُ يَرَاكَ

وَالدِّينُ ذِي الثَّلَاثِ خُذْ أَقْوَى عُرَاكَ

47   and that 'if you cannot see Him (then know that) He sees you.' The deen has three aspects – so take hold of the firmest of supports

Al-Haytami said: "The second aspect is that the slave does not necessarily end by seeing his Lord but rather he is overcome by the fact that the Real glorious and exalted is He, is cognisant of him. He, may the peace and blessings of Allah be upon him, has explained this saying: 'If you do not see him then He sees you' indicating thereby that the slave's state – even if he cannot see Him – should be the same as if he could see Him as He, exalted is He, is cognisant of him in both states. He watches over what each and every person earns for himself, witnesses each and every creational reality both in their movements and when they are at rest. Thus just as he would not have the audacity to fall short (in his worship) in the first state (in which Allah sees him) so he should not in the second – because, as the (hadith) has made clear, both are equal in that Allah has cognizance of both of them, has knowledge of him and witnesses him by the vastness of His perfection and brilliance of His majesty. The people of truths and realities have recommended that one should keep the company of the *Salihun* – out of respect for them and a sense of modesty in their presence, one does not dare to behave badly; also that the slave should worship his Lord like the weak, incapable person in the presence of a powerful person for in such a situation he strives not to behave badly, whatever the circumstances. These two states are the fruit of knowledge of Allah, exalted is He, and of fear of Him. These two (states) he designates metaphorically – by mention what one should do, that is 'that you should fear Allah as if you see Him' – in other words by indicating the result of one's action through the action itself."

Introductory matters
— from the roots — whose branches are an aid to arrival

Introductory matters
— from the roots —
whose branches are an aid to arrival

الْحُكْمُ فِي الشَّرْعِ خِطَابُ رَبِّنَا

الْمُقْتَضِي فِعْلَ الْمُكَلَّفِ افْطُنَا

48   The judgement in the Law is that our Lord's addressing us requires action on behalf of the *mukallaf* – O take note of this! –

بِطَلَبٍ أَوْ إِذْنٍ أَوْ بِوَضْعِ

لِسَبَبٍ أَوْ شَرْطٍ أَوْ ذِي مَنْعِ

49   action which is demanded, or permitted or set out by virtue of a reason, condition or prohibition

Muhammad Mayyara said: "He has informed us as to the general legal judgement (of Islam), and that it is dependent upon the *shariʻah* and is only known by means of the *shariʻah* – in other words not attained by the intellect, nor by anything learned by repeated experience. This judgement has been communicated to us by Allah, exalted is He, and applies to the action of the *mukallaf*, that is 'the person legally obliged to carry out the actions required in the *shariʻah*.' This requirement is either by way of demand, that is, demanded of him by Allah, exalted is He; or by way of permission, that is, 'permitted' a person in that he may do it or desist from it; or by way of an indication in the form of a demand or of authorisation – and, in turn, this indication may be accompanied by a causal premise, a condition or some impediment (restricting immediate execution). Know, too, that a demand can either be a demand for action, or demand to desist (from action), and both can be either a clear definitive demand or otherwise – thus there are four divisions to this communication (from Allah, exalted is He) addressed to the *mukallaf* regarding some action on his part: a clear, absolute demand such that he is not permitted to abandon doing it, like his belief in Allah, exalted is He, His Messengers, and the five pillars of Islam – that is, the obligatory; that which is demanded of him in a non-definitive manner such that he is permitted not to do it, like the *salat* of *fajr* and the like, i.e. those which are recommended; the demand to desist from something in a definitive absolute manner such that he is not permitted to do it, like drinking wine, committing fornication and the like, i.e that which is forbidden; and the demand that he desist from something – but which is not absolute and which he is nevertheless permitted to do, like the recitation (of the Qur'an) in the *ruku'* or the *sujud*, for example, i.e. that which is disliked. These various kinds of demand also include a permitting, that is the licence to perform or desist from something without any preference for the one or the other, like buying and selling and the like. Thus the divisions of action within the *shari'ah* are contained within these five, and this Section is called (Allah's) communication of responsibility (*khitab at-takleef*). The way in which this communication is actually connected to or related to the actions of the *mukallaf*, that is the manner in which it is laid down or indicated, by way of the reasons, conditions or prohibitions attached to any of these five judgements is known in the terminology of the *'ulama* as the communication through circumstance (*khitab al-wad'*)."

Ibn 'Ashir's mention of 'the judgement in the *shari'ah*' refers to the judgement regarding the affirmation of a command to do something, or negation of a command to do something according to the *shari'ah* – i.e. not (demanded) from the point of view of the intellect or because of one's experience gained as the result of repeating something over and over again. The reality of this 'communication' or 'address' is speech (on behalf of Allah) addressed to those who are capable of understanding. There is a difference of opinion as to whether its being called by the term 'communication' is conditional upon the person addressed being present. Likewise, there is a difference of opinion as to whether the speech of Allah, exalted is He, should be called "a communication" from before endless time, that is, before the existence of the person addressed. What, in fact, is meant by 'communication' here is the actual person being communicated with – thus in the Arabic the infinitive is being used to refer to the second person. Mention of Allah in relation to this communication (obviously) ensures that no other person is meant as the addressee.

Then his saying 'which is demanded…' means either absolutely or as a request, implying that it is permitted.

Al-Qarafi said: "The difference between the communication which is 'set out', i.e. through circumstance (*khitab al-wad'*) and the (direct) 'communication of responsibility' (*khitab al-takleef*) is an actual difference of form, that is, that the 'judgement through circumstance' is a ruling of the *shari'ah* derived from a property or characteristic deemed to be a cause, condition or prohibition. The (direct) 'communication of responsibility' (*khitab al-takleef*) refers to the (direct) demand to carry out what has been established through reasons, conditions or prohibitions." Then he goes on to say: "Know that the 'communication of responsibility' is conditional upon the *mukallaf* having knowledge of what is demanded of him and being able to do it, like the *salat*; but there are no such conditions in the 'communication through circumstance', like for example, holding a child or mad person responsible for damages done. For this reason the *fuqaha'* say: any action, whether deliberate or by mistake, which is prejuducial to someone's wealth, is treated alike. However knowledge is stipulated for some reasons or causes (resulting in a judgement), like the liability of fornication, blood money and retaliation."

أَقْسَامُ حُكْمِ الشَّرْعِ خَمْسَةٌ تُرَامْ

فَرْضٌ وَنَدْبٌ وَكَرَاهَةٌ حَرَامْ

50   The divisions of the judgements in the *shari'ah* are five: obligatory (*fard*), recommended (*nadb*), disliked (*makruh*), prohibited (*haram*) and

ثُمَّ إِبَاحَةٌ فَمَأْمُورٌ جُزِمْ

فَرْضٌ وَدُونَ الْجَزْمِ مَنْدُوبٌ وُسِمْ

51   permitted (*ibaha*). An absolute command is obligatory, and that which is other than absolute is recommended, so take note!

ذُو النَّهْيِ مَكْرُوهٌ وَمَعْ حَتْمٍ حَرَامْ

مَأْذُونٌ وَجْهَيْهِ مُبَاحٌ ذَا تَمَامْ

52   That which contains an interdiction (*nahy*) is disliked, and when absolute, then it is a prohibition. That which is permitted means one is allowed (either to do it or not to do it) – and this completes (the five).

$$\text{وَالْفَرْضُ قِسْمَانِ كِفَايَةٌ وَعَيْنٌ}$$

$$\text{وَيَشْمَلُ الْمَنْدُوبُ سُنَّةً بِذَيْنْ}$$

53 The obligatory is of two types, the collective and the individual and the 'recommended' (as a general term) includes (the more specific term) 'sunna' with respect to both (the latter).

He thus informs us that the obligatory is that which is commanded to absolutely, that is, it is rewarded if one does it and is punished if one abandons it. The recommended is that which is rewarded if one does it – but one is not punished for abandoning it. The prohibited is that which is punished for doing it and rewarded for not doing it. The reprehensible is that for which one is rewarded for desisting from, and one is not punished for doing it. The conceivable is that – the doing or not doing of which – is equal(ly valid)." His saying '(which) is punished' means that he *merits* punishment – because the punishment is not inevitable, except in the case of the *kafir*; his saying 'is rewarded' means on the condition that, or as long as, it is accepted from him. This is the gist of his discussion, and an explanation of the text we have left to the commentators. I shall mention, insha'Allah, exalted is He, lesser-known examples for each of the judgements – however they will be of more use than examples of necessary, well known matters of the deen.

Wajib – incumbent

An example of what is incumbent is the conveyance of greetings from someone who has entrusted you with conveying greetings to another – as long as one has taken it upon oneself as a duty; and the returning of these greetings immediately – (that is) even if the greetings come (conveyed) via a messenger or as a written message. In al-Bukhari from Abu Salma ibn 'Abd ar-Rahman from 'A'isha, may Allah be pleased with her, it is narrated that the Prophet, may the peace and blessings of Allah be upon him, said to her: 'Jibril sends his greetings to you' and she replied 'and I return greetings of peace and mercy to him.' Ibn Hajar has related that an-Nawawi said: 'This hadith contains the legal sanction for sending greetings. Moreover, it is obligatory on the Messenger to convey them for it is sunna. It follows, (as a consequence) that in the case of a deposit the case is analogous – on investigation, (it is clear) that the Messenger – whenever committing himself to something – likened this (responsibility) to something given to him for safekeeping, or if not for safekeeping as a deposit.

However if something (offered as a) deposit is not accepted then the person is under no duty to carry out (this responsibility)." He continued: .. "and all this applies if someone comes to another with greetings from a third party or a written message: one should reply to them immediately, and it is preferable to return the greetings (immediately) via the person who conveyed them."

Another example is the removal of pubic hair in the case of the woman if her husband asks it of her, according to the most correct version (of the two narrations) – this Ibn Hajar has narrated from an-Nawawi. (I realise) the latter are both Shafi'is, but I have found no text from the Malikis which contradicts what we have mentioned – and when one does not find a text on the matter from the people of our *madhhab*, then one must follow another. It is in this light that we have related in this commentary from the writings of the Shafi'is, like al-Ghazali, an-Nawawi, al-Munawi, Ibn Hajar and al-Qastallani.

Another example is the asking for permission (to enter people's houses). There is no difference of opinion as to its obligatory nature and it is agreed that the person who does not do it is corrupt (of character) – this has been stated by at-Tata'i in the *Sharh ar-Risala* from Ibn Rushd.

Another is the saying of '*tabarak'Allah...*' when one sees something wonderful in order to protect himself from danger or misfortune – this is stated by an-Nafrawi – that is by saying:

$$\text{تَبَارَكَ اللَّهُ أَحْسَنُ الْخَالِقِينَ، اَللَّهُمَّ بَارِكْ فِيهِ}$$

'to Allah belongs the *baraka*, the best of Creators, O Allah give us *baraka* in it.'

Another example (of the obligatory) is repelling harm from the Muslims as long as the person doing this does not cause himself physical hardship or exhaustion and it does not lead to loss with respect to his wealth or honour. He said in the *Ihya'*: "If you were to say that anyone who sees animals wandering freely over a person's planted field is obliged to turn them out or anyone who sees some article of wealth which is about to be exposed to loss should protect it – and if you say that this is obligatory (in both cases) then this would be such a wide ranging obligation that it would result in one becoming subject to others for the whole of his life. If you were to say that one is not obliged (to undertake anything in such circumstances) then it would not be obligatory to call another to account when he usurps the wealth of another even though his only intention in the matter is taking care of the wealth of another. We would respond by saying that this a delicate and complicated matter. However, in brief, we would say that as long as he is able to protect it from loss without suffering any physical hardship himself or loss to his own wealth or honour then he is obliged to do this – this much is obligatory with respect to the rights a Muslim has (over another). Indeed, this is the least of rights for there are numerous proofs attesting to the rights of the Muslims (which are greater). However it is more obligatory than the return of the greeting for the distress caused in this (latter case) is more than that caused by abandoning the return of the greeting. Moreover, if someone's wealth is at risk through the illicit action of some criminal – and one has evidence of this such that were one to speak out the criminal would return the other's property – then there is no difference of opinion that it would be obligatory (to speak out) and that it would an act of disobedience (towards Allah, exalted is He,) to remain silent about the evidence. In fact any action undertaken to repel harm (from someone else's wealth) – as long as no harm is incurred by the person repelling this harm – falls within this category of 'desisting from furnishing evidence.' If, however, a person were to incur physical difficulty or loss to his wealth or honour, then he is not bound to do this – as he also has a duty to take care of his body, of his own wealth and his honour just as he has a duty to others. Thus he is not under an obligation to benefit others to the detriment of his self. Of course, preferring others to oneself is recommended and undergoing hardship for the sake of the Muslims is an act of coming closer to Allah, exalted is He, but making or deeming it obligatory (legally) is not. If, then, he would have had to undergo physical hardship to get the animals out of the field, then he is under no obligation to do so. If there is no hardship involved in his warning the owner of the field – who is asleep, for example – then he is obliged to do so for neglecting to warn him would be like neglecting to let the *qadi* know of a piece of evidence; and this, no one is permitted to do." Here end the words of al-Ghazali. They are well founded, indeed, so rare that they should be written in gold – so reflect upon them, together with the words of Khalil: "kindness or giving treatment (to someone) is obligatory, like the stitching of a deep wound, the giving of food and drink to the one in need or preventing a wall from falling with wooden supports – for this is good if you find such (supports)." Indeed, there is a narration which affirms that it is obligatory to protect the wall of someone else using one's own wood (if necessary).

Mandub – recommended actions

An example of the recommended is the saying of *as-salamu 'alaykum* of the person who gets up from a gathering. Muhammad ibn al-Hattab said in *Hashiyat ar-Risala*: "It is recommended for the one who gets up from a gathering to say *as-salamu 'alaykum* to those still sitting? And is there a *sahih* tradition on the subject? The answer is that it is a sunna. Abu Hurayra, may Allah be pleased with him, has related that the Prophet, may the peace and blessings of Allah be upon him, said: 'When any of you arrives at a gathering then he should say *as-salamu 'alaykum* and if he intends to get up (to leave) then he should say *as-salamu 'alaykum*, and the first (of these *salams*) is not more obligatory then the second.' This is narrated by at-Tirmidhi who said it is a *sahih* tradition."

Another example is the saying of *as-salamu 'alaykum* to children. Muhammad ibn al-Hattab said in *Khashiyat al-Risala*: "The *'ulama* are in agreement that it is recommended to say *as-salamu 'alaykum* to children."

Another example is a married woman's dyeing (her hands and part of her arms beyond her wrists) up to the point (she normally wears) her bracelets. Muhammad ibn al-Hattab said that al-Burzuli said: "The dyeing of women's skin is permitted if she has no husband and she is not in the *'idda* waiting period (after divorce), and it is recommended for a married woman but prohibited in her *'idda* waiting period. It is recommended up to the place of her bracelets."

Another example (of the recommended) is the extinguishing of any fire in the house before going to sleep. In *al-Fath* in his commentary on the words of al-Bukhari in the chapter 'Do not leave (an open) fire in the house' he said: "At-Tabari said with respect to these *hadith* that if someone spends the night in a house and there is no one other than him there, then he should extinguish any fire before going to sleep or he should see that there is no danger of the fire spreading (from the hearth); likewise if there is a group in the house, this becomes obligatory on one of them – and the person who is most duty bound to do this is the person who last goes to sleep. Whoever neglects to do this is contravening the sunna, and abandoning its courtesies."

Another example is meeting the people of excellence with joy and welcoming words. In his commentary in *al-Fath* on the hadith of the 'Night Journey'[1], he says: "(Among the things) one understands from this hadith is that it is recommended to meet the people of excellence with joy and welcoming words, that it is permitted to praise the *mumin*, who is safe from the being corrupted (by such praise), to his face, and that it is more excellent to travel by night rather than during the day – and he, may the peace and blessings of Allah be upon him, usually travelled by night."

Another example is a teacher's being freed of any obligation towards a child whom he has hit when it (later) becomes clear that the (child) did not merit

---

1 See al-Bukhari, Vol.9, *K. al-Tawhid*, no.608, p.449

this. In the *al-Mi'yar* of al-Wanshareesi: "Ibn Abi Zayd[1] was asked whether the teacher who – intending to hit one child with his hand or stick, strikes another instead, or hits a child for something and then it becomes clear that he was not responsible – is absolved from (seeking the pardon of) the child or his father and his reply was: "If he did it by mistake then he is not liable (for anything) legally – as long as the child suffered no wound. From the point of his own sense of probity and honour, he should make amends to the child. This however is (considered as) an act of good will (on his behalf) for he is not bound to do this. It is said that this matter is analogous to the difference of opinion in the case of the *mujtahid* who commits a mistake – irrespective of whether his mistake is excused or not – and there are well known discussions on this matter." There is similar in the *Ikhtisar Nawazil* of al-Burzuli.

Ja'iz – permissible

There are examples of what is permissible which are not known to many people – for example, the employment of the orphan without payment: in *al-Fath al-Bari*, during the explanation of the the chapter in al-Bukhari entitled 'Whoever makes a military expedition taking an orphan to serve him' he says: "The hadith serves as permission to employ an orphan without making payment to him." The evidence for his mention of the permission to employ an orphan without paying him is clear, and the hadith commentators have written about this – although the author of *al-Madkhal* has recorded that it is prohibited to employ an orphan. And Allah is the One Who grants success.

Another example is the permissibility of three or more persons riding on a beast if the latter is able to bear it: in al-Bukhari, in the chapter entitled 'Three persons on a beast' it is narrated from Ibn 'Abbas: "…when he, may the peace and blessings of Allah, arrived in Makka, he was met by Agheelama, of the tribe of the Bani 'Abdul-Mutallib, (riding on a beast with) one of his tribe riding in front of him and one behind." In his commentary al-Qastallani said: "As for the *hadith* which forbid three persons from riding on a beast, there is a discussion as to the validity of their chains of relation. If one accepts however that they may be used as a proof, then the consensus of opinion is that this prohibition applies if the beast is not able to bear (three persons)." An-Nawawi said: "Our *madhhab* and the *madhhab* of all the *'ulama* is that it is permissible for three to ride on a beast as long as it is able to bear this." He has also related in *al-Fath* that at-Tabarani and Ibn Abi Shayba have narrated from ash-Sha'bi from Ibn 'Umar: "I do not mind if there are a dozen persons on a beast if it is

---

[1] See his work regarding the education of children

able to bear it" – and this has been interpreted to mean that it is forbidden if the beast cannot bear them, like a donkey, and the opposite (meaning) in the case of a camel. An-Nawawi said: "Our *madhhab* and that of all the *'ulama* is that it is permitted."

Another example is what he has mentioned in *al-Fath*, in his commentary on the chapter entitled 'The wearing of *qassi* (-a kind of Egyptian tissue of mixed flax and silk)': "The majority are of the opinion that it is permissible to wear cloth made of a mixture of mixed flax and silk, as long as the silk does not constitute a major part of it."

Another example is having the pubic hairs shaved by another in case of necessity – in *Fath al-Bari* he states: "Whoever is not good at shaving, then it is permitted for him – if he does not have a wife who is good at shaving – to seek help from someone else to the degree of his need. However this only applies if he has no *nura*[1] available; if available, then he does not need to shave, and this is acceptable."

Another example is seeking to warn, help or catching hold of a woman who is not related to you if she falls or is about to fall – that is to help prevent what one fears might befall her – this is related by Ibn Hajar in his commentary on the hadith of al-Bukhari, narrated by Anas, may Allah be pleased with him: "We were coming from Khaybar along with the Messenger of Allah, may the peace and blessings of Allah be upon him, while I was riding behind Abu Talha who was preceding me. One of the wives of the Messenger, may the peace and blessings of Allah be upon him, was riding behind him, may the peace and blessings of Allah be upon him, when the camel stumbled. I SAY: 'the woman!' and got down (off my camel). The Messenger of Allah may the peace and blessings of Allah be upon him, said: 'She is your mother.' So I made the saddle firm.'"

Another example is the kissing of a small child on any part of his body – that is including the grown-up child, as long as it is not on his private parts. Ibn Hajar said, commenting on the words of al-Bukhari in his chapter entitled 'The mercy of the father towards his child, and his kissing and embracing him' that "Thabit has related from Anas that the Prophet, may the peace and blessings of Allah be upon him, took hold of his child Ibrahim, on whom be peace, and kissed and smelled him. Ibn Battal said that it is permitted to kiss a small child anywhere on his body, and also the older child, according to most of the *'ulama*, as long as it is not in the region of the private parts. Mention

---

1 A depilatory of quicklime and arsenic; see also *Fath al-Bari*/al-Bukhari, *K. al-Libas, bab qass ash-sharib*.

has been made before of the qualities of Fatima, may Allah be pleased with her, and that he, may Allah bless him and grant him peace, would kiss her. Likewise, Abu Bakr would kiss 'A'isha, may Allah be pleased with them both."

Another example is the recitation of the Qur'an while on a beast – this is mentioned in the *Fath al-Bari* in the chapter entitled 'Recitation on a beast.'

Another example is the embracing of a small child. Muhammad ibn al-Hattab said in the *Hashiya ar-Risala*: "It is narrated from some of the commentators of Muslim – and there is no difference of opinion in the matter as far as I am aware – that it is permitted to embrace children as he did, may the peace and blessings of Allah be upon him. There is, however, a difference of opinion as to embracing older persons, and Malik disliked it while Ibn 'Uyayna permitted it."

Another example of the permitted is the imitating of the *kafir*, the small child and female by (reciprocating the giving of) presents and asking for permission (to enter their houses) – this has been said by al-Baqouri in *Ikhtisar Qawa'id al-Qarafi*: "Ibn al-Qasar said that Malik said: 'It is permitted to entrust a woman, a child and a *kafir* with presents and to authorise them to give permission (to a guest to enter the house). Ibn ash-Shat accepted this, saying: "He (i.e. Malik) has allowed persons who have not been (specifically) allowed in the narration, namely consenting to (the authorisation of) the child and the *kafir* in case of some necessity compelling one to this, that is, because of the difficulty of the circumstances; however, he esteems it to be not allowed if the circumstances are such that one is seldom free of doubt (as to their trustworthiness)."

Another example of what is permitted is making a *du'a* for the *dhimmi kafir* that he be granted much wealth, children, good health and strength – in al-Munawi he comments on the tradition 'If you make a *du'a* for one of the Jews or Christians, then say "may Allah increase your wealth and children" saying "…as (his) wealth will benefit us by their payment of the *jizya*, by his death without heirs, by his breaking his contract and gaining the territory of *dar al-harb* or by some other means; as for (any increase in) children, it may be they will become Muslim, or we will take their *jizya*, or – if they die before puberty – then they will be our servants in the Garden, or – if they die afterwards as *kuffar* – then they will redeem us (by the *baraka* of our *du'a*) from the Fire. The *du'a* for them is problematic for in doing so one is asking, in a way, for the continuing of *kufr*, and this is not permitted. It is also permitted to make *du'a* for the *kafir* for his guidance, health or strength – but not for his forgiveness: "*Allah does not forgive anything being associated with Him.*"[1]

Another example is someone joining in with others when he unexpectedly

---

1 an-Nisa' – Women: 115

comes across them eating – in the *Nawazil ibn Hilal* he is asked about this and he replied: "In the ninth *Book of Miscellanea* in outline of dividing up, it is related from 'Isa ibn al-'Utbiya from what he had himself heard, that Ibn al-Qasim and Ibn Wahb were asked about the person who comes across others eating, and they both replied: 'It is good that he accept if they invite him but if they do not, then he should not eat.'"

Ibn Rushd said: "A man should behave according to the situation: if it appears to him they they are pleased to see him and are happy for him to eat with them, then it is recommended that he accept their invitation; if however, it appears to him that they are disturbed by his sudden appearance while they are eating and that they have only invited him out of a sense of obligation, then it is disliked that he accept; if he is unclear as to which of these two situations (he finds himself in) it is permitted for him to accept – without it being (reckoned) either recommended or reprehensible for him."

Another example is what is explained in *al-Fath* regarding the chapter entitled *'Allah took Ibrahim as an intimate friend'*[1] when Ibn Hajar comments on the hadith in which Ibrahim says 'That is my sister' saying: "The hadith[2] demonstrates the legality of brother- and sisterhood through Islam, the permissibility of making petitions, the permission to submit to oppressive rulers, the acceptance of maintaining ties of kinship with an unjust king and the approval (for receiving) a present from a *mushrik*."

Another example of what is permitted is what al-Ubbi mentions regarding Muslim's words "concerning slave boys" namely: "'Iyad says that if adults have a screen such as a door or something else and he opens the door or raises the curtain for someone to come in then it does not require one to verbally ask permission to enter. It is similar in the case of a man in his own house with his servants and retinue: if he lowers the curtain then no one should enter without seeking his permission; if, however, it is pulled up, then it is permitted for someone to enter his room without his permission."

Makruh – reprehensible actions

As for what is *makruh* – reprehensible – here are some less well known examples: the hanging of garlands around the necks of animals – unless it is to ward off evil. Ibn Fa'ida said in *Sharh al-Mukhtasar* just before the chapter on 'Slaughter of animals for meat' that Malik narrated – in the Section regarding the oath when divorcing one's wife – from Ibn al-Qasim who heard it directly,

---

1 an-Nisa' – Women 124
2 al-Bukhari, vol. 4, *K. al-Anbiya'*, Chapter 9, p.578.

from the *Book of Miscellanea* that "..the reprehensibility of attaching bells is greater than the attaching of any garland to the necks of camels." Someone said: "Why are bells reprehensible?" He replied "What occurs to my heart is that it is on account of their sound."

Ibn Rushd said: "The attaching of something in which there is no mention of Allah, exalted is He, on the necks of camels is reprehensible because of what is recorded in the *Muwatta'*, namely that the Messenger of Allah, may the peace and blessings of Allah be upon him, sent a messenger during one of his campaigns while people were resting at midday (with the message): 'Do not keep garlands on the necks of the camels.' However, he did not single out bells. Malik has also narrated: 'Bells are worse than other things because of the nuisance caused by their sound.' There is no doubt then that the greater (the nuisance), the greater the reprehensibility, and it may be that its reprehensibility lies in its similarity to the bells of the Christians."

I SAY: "The literal meaning of Ibn Rushd's words is that it is reprehensible even when something is attached for ornamentation – but this contradicts Ibn Hajar's declaration that it is permitted. However they both [Ibn Hajar and his father] are Shafi'is. In the chapter 'What has been said concerning bells and the like attached to the necks of camels' Ibn Hajar said: 'Do not attach a chord or string of garlands to the necks of camels.' Ibn Jawzi said that there are three opinions as to what is meant by 'a chord' or 'string':

The first opinion, (refers to the *hadith* describing how) they would garland the camels with silken strings claiming it warded off the evil eye and how he ordered them to be cut off, indicating thereby that such silken strands would not repel anything if Allah had decreed something, and this is the opinion of Malik."

I SAY: "This refers to the *hadith* mentioned in the *Muwatta'*, in Muslim, Abu Dawud and others." Malik said: "I am of the opinion that it is on account of the evil eye and the hadith of 'Uqba ibn 'Amir supports this: 'Whoever hangs an amulet (*tamima*) then Allah will not protect him', and this has also been narrated by Abu Dawud." The *tamima* is a kind of garland which some believe can repel the Decree, and for this reason it is not permitted."

The second opinion refers to the prohibition against this – lest one suffocate the animal when moving at speed, and this is narrated of Muhammad ibn al-Hasan, the follower of Abu Hanifa. The explanation of Abu 'Ubayd is most excellent: "It is prohibited because animals suffer through (attaching the like) and are constricted in their breathing; sometimes they get caught up in a tree (through wearing such things) and are choked (to death) or prevented from moving."

The third opinion is that it refers to their custom of hanging bells on them. This is narrated by al-Khattabi and indicated in the Section on the subject in al-Bukhari. Abu Dawud and an-Nasa'i have also narrated the hadith of Umm Habiba, the Mother of the *muminun*, in a *marfu'* chain of narration: 'The angels do not keep the company of a group in which bells are (rung). Moreover, an-Nasa'i has also narrated from the hadith of Umm Salma. It appears that al-Bukhari has indicated what happened (in this incident) in one of his chains of narration while ad Daraqutni has narrated it in a chain of narration from 'Uthman ibn 'Umar in the following form: "Do not leave garlands of silken strands or bells unbroken on the necks of the camels."

I SAY: "Camels are not discriminated from other animals in this (matter) except with regard to the third statement. It was not, however, customary to hang bells around the necks of their horses. and it is narrated by Abu Dawud and an-Nasa'i from a hadith of Abu *Wahb* al-Hasani in a *marfu'* hadith: "Ride horses and garland them but do not hang them with silken strands." This is an indication that the (reprehensibility) specifically refers to camels, and it may well be that the particular restriction with reference to them in the commentary is based on what is customary." Here ends the discussion of Ibn Hajar

Then he continues after a while: "As for the linguistic root *jaras* in Arabic, 'Iyad has narrated that when written *jaras*, it refers to the (musical) instrument and when *jars*, then to the sound (of it). Muslim has narrated in the hadith of al-Ala' ibn 'Abd ar-Rahman from Abu Hurayra in a *marfu'* hadith: 'The bell is the musical instrument of Shaytan' and (here) he is indicating (in particular) the reprehensibility of its sound because it resembles the sound of the Christian bell – as well as its shape."

An-Nawawi and others have said: "The majority hold that the prohibition is of the order of reprehensibility, that is, that one should refrain from it if possible, although some have said that it is forbidden. Moreover, it is also said that it is forbidden if there is no need for it while it is permitted if a need arises." Malik has reported: "The reprehensibility applies to garlands with silk chords; it is permitted using something else as long as it is not intended to avert the evil eye by it – and all this refers to the attaching of amulets and other things which do not contain any Qur'an and the like. If, however, they do contain the word of Allah, then it is not prohibited – for (in this case) it is done for the blessing it brings and for seeking refuge in His names. Likewise what is attached for decoration is not prohibited as long as it is not done out of pride or conceit, or when it incurs extravagance." Here end the words of Ibn Hajar.

DIGRESSION: al-Munawi said in his commentary on the hadith 'Whoever attaches a cowry shell amulet (*wadi'a*) to protect himself, then Allah will not protect him, and whoever attaches a *tamima* amulet, then Allah will also not protect him': "The author of *al-Firdaws* said that the *wada'a* is a sea shell like mother of pearl which people wear to protect themselves with, and the *tamima* is a pierced bead or pearl attached to children to ward off the evil eye; and he, may the peace and blessings of Allah be upon him, refuted their validity."

REMARK: Ibn Hajar and others have said: "What is referred to in the narration is the attaching of something which does not contain the Qur'an and the like; as for what does contain mention of Allah, then there is no prohibition against it for it is done for the blessing it brings, to seek refuge in His names and in order to remember Him; likewise, there is no prohibition to attaching something for decoration as long as it is not done out of vanity and as long as it is not excessive." Here ends the discussion of al-Munawi.

Another example of a reprehensible act is shaving the head of slave boys and girls so as to leave only stray tufts of hair. Ibn Hajar has mentioned it in his commentary on the hadith of Ibn 'Umar, may Allah be pleased with him "I heard the Messenger of Allah, may the peace and blessings of Allah be upon him, prohibit such shaving" saying: "An-Nawawi said: 'They are in agreement as to its reprehensibility if done in separate places (on the head) – and for a purpose other than medical or the like. Its reprehensibility is such that one should refrain from it. There is no difference between a male and a female, and Malik disliked it in the case of slaves girls and boys. At-Tata'i has written about it in the commentary on *ar-Risala* from the point of view of the people of our *madhhab*, al-Qarafi has mentioned it in *adh-Dhakhira*, and as far as I know, the author of *al-Bayan* too.

Another example or reprehensibility is the piercing of the ears for earrings, according to the majority – the author of *al-Fath* in his commentary on the saying of al-Bukhari in the chapter 'Earrings for Women', narrates that Ibn 'Abbas, may Allah be pleased with him, said: '(One day), he, may the peace and blessings of Allah be upon him, commanded the women to give *sadaqa*, and I saw them reaching for their ears and (the ornaments around) their necks so as to take (them off)." Ibn al-Qayyim said: "The majority hold that it is reprehensible to pierce the ears of a child, while some have permitted this for a female."

I SAY: "Permissibility in the case of females is narrated from Ahmad as long as it is for ornamentation, while he found it reprehensible for children. Al-Ghazali said in *al-Ihya*': 'It is forbidden for a woman to have her ears pierced and it is forbidden to hire her in return for payment (with earrings) unless something in the law justifying this can be established.'"

Introductory matters   209

I SAY: "It is narrated from Ibn 'Abbas, as related by at-Tabarani in *al-Awsat*, that there are seven sunnas regarding children, and he mentioned them, the seventh being the piercing of their ears. However, this is taken from the sayings of one of the commentators and is not accepted by those of our *madhhab* as a sunna."

Another example is a woman not applying henna. Muhammad ibn al-Hattab said in *Hashiyat ar-Risala*: "It is reprehensible that a woman refrain from applying henna." Al Aqfahasi said: "A man should not dye his hands or feet because this is an ornament of women, and the Prophet, may the peace and blessings of Allah be upon him, has cursed those who imitate women – and this is what the common people do."

Another example is a man giving the greeting of *salam* to a girl who is not related to him. This has been narrated by more than one person.

Another example is praising someone to his face – lest the person praised be influenced adversely by this. Al-Munawi said: "As for praising someone who is absent or someone to his face, the first is not prohibited unless the person doing the praising oversteps the limits and tells lies – for it is the lying which is forbidden not the fact that he is praising someone, and anything which contains no lies is recommended if there is benefit to be found in it and it does not lead to corruption; as for the second, there are narrations which infer that it is permitted and others which infer it is prohibited – harmonisation (of this apparent difference) is (achieved by understanding) that if the person praised has a perfect Iman, clarity of conviction and the strength of character to withstand being tempted or seduced and there is no danger his *nafs* will get the better of him then it is not forbidden; if, however, it is feared that any of this (temptation) will befall him, then it is reprehensible to praise him."

Another example is the *salat* of a woman without a necklace – Ibn al-Bashir said: "The reason for this (being regarded as reprehensible) is (lest there should be any) resemblance to men. Anas ibn Malik al-Ansari has made a *fatwa* stating that a woman should not perform the *salat* without a necklace around her neck and if she does not find one, then a belt."

HARAM – FORBIDDEN

There are many examples of the forbidden – such as a woman increasing the volume of her hair either by using other hair or by something else, irrespective of whether the added (attachment) is (ritually) clean or not, whether done with the permission of her husband or not or whether it is attached with a fastener or simply placed on top (of her own hair). This is the *madhhab* of Malik and the majority; however, examine also *Fath al-Bari*, al-Munawi, al-'Alqami, al-Ubbi and an-Nawawi, in which *sahih hadith* are (given as) proof of its permissibility.

It is recorded in *al-Fath* that it is a major wrong action; it is also recorded that the narration from 'A'isha, may Allah be pleased with her, permitting this, is invalid – on the evidence in al-Bukhari in various places, for example in the 'Book of Marriage': "'A women should not obey her husband when it would mean disobeying (Allah)' – Khalid related to us: Ibrahim related to us from Hasan, that is Ibn Muslim, from Safiya from 'A'isha, may Allah be pleased with her, that a woman from the Ansar gave her daughter away in marriage and her hair fell out. She then came to the Prophet, may the peace and blessings of Allah be upon him, and mentioned it to him saying that her husband had commanded her to attach hair to her head, to which he replied: 'No those women who attach hair to their heads are cursed.'"

Al-Qastallani said: "This hadith is proof for the majority of the prohibitions regarding attaching anything to the hair, be it another hairpiece or something else. However some have made a distinction, permitting the placing of hair on the head without any kind of fixture and prohibiting the use of fixtures – however they have made up what he actually said." Al-Munawi said: "The distinction between the placing and the fixing (of hair) is purely superficial, and ignores the real sense (of the hadith)."

Another example of the prohibited is tattoos, marking of the skin and anything else which alters the creation of Allah, like the plucking of hair and having a tooth (which is deemed) superfluous extracted."

Another is making representations or images – for al-Bukhari narrates: "The people who will be tormented the most by Allah on the Day of Raising Up will be those who make images and representations." Ibn Hajar said in his commentary (taken) from at-Tabari: "…that is images which are worshipped rather than Allah while the person is aware of this and specifically intends to do this – for he is committing an act of *kufr*. It is not far fetched to suppose that he will suffer the same fate as Fir'awn. However, the person who makes images without this intention would only be committing an act of disobedience."

Another example is disobedience of one's parents. Al-Qastallani said in the *Fatawa* of Ibn as-Salah that the disobedience which is forbidden (referred to here) is any act which molests the parent in a significant way as long as it does not involve one of the obligatory actions (of the deen). He has (also) said: "Sometimes it is expressed by saying that obedience to parents is obligatory in everything which does not constitute disobedience of Allah."

Al-Qarafi in the last section, that is the 23rd – between (his explanation of) the principle governing what is obligatory on one man with respect to another and that governing what is obligatory to one's parents in particular – he says: "The general rule with respect to what is particular to the parent rather than people in general is that in the case of the former the son should avoid causing them any kind of harm whatsoever – as long, that is, as no harm comes to himself; then there is the obligation to obey both the mother and the father and (if necessary) to desist from supererogatory acts of worship (until their need is first fulfilled); to desist from performing those obligations whose nature is such that they may be delayed without invalidating them; and (finally) abstaining from the obligations of a communal nature if there is someone else who can perform them. There is no obligation to obey them in anything other than these, although it is (obviously) recommended to obey them and treat them well whatever the circumstances, just as it is recommended to treat all people – other than one's parents – well in all circumstances. However the recommendation (to obey) with respect to the parents is stronger with respect to supererogatory and non-obligatory acts of worship, and there is no recommendation to obey people who are not related when it comes to refraining from supererogatory acts of worship – indeed it would be reprehensible (to do so), although not forbidden. As for what is obligatory towards relatives other than parents, I have not been able to discover any details about the matter – as I have done in the above mentioned matters regarding parents. I have only managed to discover the basic principle of obligation in general, with respect to the way one discriminates in the matter; and in the past I have seen a great many people having difficulty in defining exactly this point." (All) this is affirmed by Ibn as-Shat in *Hashiyat al-Furuq*.

Another example is the breaking of family ties – in al-Bukhari, from Muhammad ibn Jubayr (it is related) that he heard the Prophet, may the peace and blessings of Allah be upon him, say: "Anyone who breaks off family ties will not enter the Garden." Al-Qastallani said in *al-Adab al-Mufrad*: "What is referred to by mention of 'the person who breaks off family ties' is his breaking off ties with close family members without reason or cause, while being aware that it is prohibited." In *al-Furuq*, he said that Shaykh Abu'l-Waleed at-Tartushi, may Allah have mercy on him, related that one of the *'ulama* said: "Keeping up family ties is obligatory if there is consanguinity, that is, the two parties in question are (so closely) related that if one is male and the other female they would not be permitted to marry, and this (definition) is accepted by Ibn ash-Shat."

Another example of what is forbidden is scaring a *mumin* – in *al-Jami' as-*

Saghir it is recorded: "Whoever causes fright in the *mumin*, then he has no Iman in Allah and his fright will occur on the Day of Raising Up." Al-Munawi said in his commentary: "…that is, he causes him fright by brandishing, for example, a sword or a knife – even if this in done in jest, or he shakes a rope in front of him causing him to imagine that it is a snake"; and he has added to the words 'It is not permitted for the Muslim to cause fear in another Muslim' in *al-Jami'* saying: "…by taking his belongings and making him fear that they have been lost." In the *Hashiya* of Muhammad ibn al-Khitab on the *Risala* it states: "SECTION: 'the prohibition of brandishing a weapon in front of a Muslim, either in jest or in earnest' – and it is forbidden to instil fear in him and this is stated by 'Iyad, al-Qurtubi and others."

Another example of what is forbidden is ignoring a Muslim for more than three nights – other than for a specific reason in which there is benefit, or out of necessity. He said in *ar-Risala*: "One should not ignore one's brother for more than three days – it is by giving the greetings of *salam* that one brings an end to this (separation); and one should not desist from speaking to him after greeting him." Ibn Hajar said in *Fath al-Bari* in the chapter entitled 'Ignoring someone': "…and there is no doubt that we should recognise two states, the greater and the lesser. The greater is the avoiding of any occasion leading to an exchange of greetings, to making conversation and or doing anything which might strengthen love and mutual friendship; and the lesser is restricting oneself to saying the greeting of *salam* rather than anything else. (Allah's) threat of serious (punishment) has been narrated with respect to the person who abandons the lesser state; as for the greater, then whoever desists from it regarding people outside his family relations, then he is not open to censure – however, regarding relatives, this would be classed as breaking off family relations."

Al-Munawi said in *Sharh al-Jami'* that an-Nawawi said in *Sharh Muslim*: "It is permitted to ignore the people of innovation and corruption continuously, and the prohibition of ignoring someone for more than three days refers to someone who ignores another for some personal reason or worldly gain."

Hafidh Ibn Hajar said: "They are in agreement that it is permissible to ignore someone for more than three days if one fears harm might come to one's deen or wordly interest by speaking to him: many a time it is beneficial to avoid someone rather than suffering injury by mixing with him. 'Umar, may Allah be pleased with him, said: 'Cutting someone is better that kindness towards him when there is rancour and malice.'"

Another example is that a man wear his waist wrap or the like such that it hangs below his ankles – when done out of haughtiness or vanity. Al-Munawi has commented on the words 'Pull up your waist wrap and have *taqwa* of Allah': "…that is, shorten it in obedience to Allah prohibiting you from trailing your waist wrap (on the ground) in pride and haughtiness – it is prohibited for a man to let his waist wrap hang below his ankles when done out of haughtiness, and it is reprehensible whatever (one's attitude)." Here end the words of al-Munawi.

I say: "An-Nafrawi in his commentary on the *Risala* is adamant as to the prohibition of letting one's waist wrap hang below one's ankles irrespective of whether done out of haughtiness or not while (Ibn Hajar) in *al-Fath* gives preference to this (judgement). There is, however, no difference of opinion that when done out of haughtiness it is a major wrong action."

Another example is to reply to someone's insult with two insults – in *al-Jami' as-Saghir*: "Among the major wrong actions, is to speak insolently regarding a Muslim man's honour; and also among the major wrong actions, is responding to someone's insult with two insults." Al-Munawi has commented: "That is, if a man abuses you once and you abuse him twice."

Anther example of the forbidden is that two persons who bear hatred towards each other meet each other in an equivocal, ambivalent manner. Al-Munawi said in his commentary on the words of the al-Jami 'Whoever has two tongues in this world will have two tongues in the Fire on the Day of Raising Up': "Al-'Iraqi said: 'They are in agreement that when two persons who bear hatred to each other meet in an equivocal, ambivalent manner, then this is hypocrisy, and hypocrisy has signs and this is one of them. If each is amiable and courteous to the other and each is genuine, then neither will (be deemed) as 'having two tongues.'" Here end the words of al-Munawi.

Another example is not accepting the excuse of the person excusing himself – because of what is related in the tradition: "If a brother comes with an excuse and one does not accept it then the wrong one commits is like that of the person who commits fraud in a bargain or contract." We have already mentioned above the text from *al-Jami' as-Saghir*: "Whoever comes to his brother with the intention of renewing his ties (after a break) then he should accept it of him irrespective of whether the other is justified in this or not; and if he does not accept, then he will not drink from the Fountain of the Prophet." See also al-Munawi's commentary (on the matter).

Another example is to interpret dreams based on what is in Ibn Sirin and the like. An-Nafrawi said, commenting on the words of the *Risala* 'No one should interpret dreams who has no knowledge of them': "It is not permitted for him to interpret them just by looking at books of interpretation – as some of the ignorant persons do after they have examined the like of Ibn Sirin when someone says to them: 'I have seen such-and-such a thing in a dream' – when he has no knowledge of the principles of interpretation. This is forbidden – for interpretion varies according to the different personalities (of those interpreting), to their (various) states, to the time (this takes place) and to the character of those who dream."

Another example is for a woman to imitate men in their appearance – based on the hadith: "There are three (kinds of) person who will not enter the Garden, whoever disobeys his parents, a procurer (of women) and women who imitates men." Commentating on this hadith, al-Munawi said: "…imitating them in their clothing and appearance, not in knowledge and judgement – for such things are praiseworthy." Adh-Dhahabi said: "Here is indication that they are (considered) among the major wrong actions – and whoever suspects shameless behaviour on behalf of his wife but ignores it out of love for her, then he is not someone who is attached to her or who really loves her. There is no good in someone who has no sense of jealousy (for his wife). As for the procuress, if she remains with a free woman until she turns her into a prostitute she will have two burdens weighing in the balance against her." Here end the words of al-Munawi.

Adh-Dhahabi also said: "Many major wrong actions, indeed the majority of them except for a very few, are unknown to a great many of the *umma* whether they are declared haram, are very thoroughly prohibited or there is a threat for someone doing them, and this type has some detail, so the *'alim* should not be too hasty in imposing them on the ignorant person; but rather should be kind in teaching him especially if he has only recently come from ignorance, like for example someone who has (recently) been made captive and been brought to the land of Islam. It is enough that he declare the two *shahadas*. There is no blame on someone until after he has acquired knowledge of his state and the proof has been established against him." Here ends the explanation of al-Munawi – and I am not responsible for copyist's mistakes[1].

Among the forbidden actions is opposing the will of the husband, that is recalcitrance on the part of the wife, or violation of marital duties. In *Sahih al-Bukhari*, it is narrated from Abu Hurayra, may Allah be please with him, that the Prophet, may the peace and blessings of Allah be upon him said: "If a man calls his wife to bed and she refuses, then the angels curse her until morning comes."

It is also narrated from Abu Hurayra, may Allah be pleased with him,

---

1   There is a lacuna in the Arabic, pointed out in the footnotes to this edition.

from the Prophet, may the peace and blessings of Allah be upon him: "It is not permitted for a woman to fast while her husband is present without his permission, and she should not give permission (to a visitor or guest) to enter the house without his permission."

It is narrated from Ibn Khuzayma and Ibn Hibban from the *marfu'* hadith of Jabir: "The *salat* is not accepted from three persons, nor does the reward for a (single) good action (of theirs) rise to the heavens for them: the runaway slave until he returns, the drunk person – until he becomes sober, and the woman whose husband is angry with her – until he is pleased with her again."

At-Tabarani narrates from the *marfu'* hadith of Ibn 'Umar: "There are two persons whose *salat* does not go beyond their heads: the runaway slave and the woman who disobeys her husband – until she returns (to obedience)."

In al-Bukhari, at the end of the chapter on ingratitude to husbands, is narrated (the hadith): "I saw the Fire, and I have never seen such a spectacle. I saw that most of its inhabitants are women. They said: 'Why, Messenger of Allah?' He replied: 'They are ungrateful (*kufr*).' He was then asked: 'Are they ungrateful in their denial of Allah?' He replied: 'They are ungrateful to their husbands and ungrateful for the kindness and benefits they had received. (Some women are such that) even if treat them kindly all their lives, then they notice something (bad) in you they say: 'I have never seen any good in you.'"

Note: "He said in *al-Fath* that Ibn al-Mundhir has narrated that the consensus of the *umma* is that a man should prevent his wife from going out on all journeys. However, there is a difference of opinion as to journeys which are obligatory (for her)."

Another example of the forbidden is giving hospitality and shelter to the disobedient woman, that is comforting her and helping her. Here, 'disobedience' – *nushuz* – refers to her stopping obeying her husband in what Allah, exalted is He, has made obligatory on her – regarding those matters she must obey him in, among them, her going out of the house without his permission. Thus, by 'disobedience' is not meant her hatred of her husband as many people think nowadays; rather something more general than this is intended: it refers to her opposition and disobedience of him – even though there is love for him. I have composed the following:

Praise belongs to the One Who in this time has increased
 The reward of those who seek what is true through the sunnas,
Who has indicated that the curse of a person who commits
 Major wrong actions is his removal from His mercy.
The anger of husbands and masters

Is one of the causes of this curse and blight.
So if the anger of a husband falls on his wife
Then her *salat* will never be accepted.
And whoever helps her, then he brings this (punishment)
Upon himself – say 'the anger of the Lord is more manifest!'
We seek refuge with Allah lest He abandon us
And (seek protection) from the evil of the *nafs* and shaytan.
Her being cursed has been made clear in the traditions
She will be cursed by the chosen angels
And it is incumbent upon those she comes to (for help)
To censure her and not make her welcome.

Also forbidden is a woman asking her husband for divorce without her being caused any harm in any of her rights – and this is based on the narration: "Any woman who asks her husband for a divorce without her being subject to any difficulty or injustice, then she will be prohibited from the fragrance of the Garden" – or words to this effect.

Al-'Alqami said: "In the narration of Ibn Majah from Ibn 'Abbas: 'A woman who asks her husband for divorce without true grounds (*kunh*) for it will not find the fragrance of the Garden, even though its fragrance will be experienced forty years distance (from the Garden itself)." He said in *an-Nihaya*, "The *kunh* (essence) of a matter – is its reality (or true grounds) but some say 'the right time' or 'the measure', and some say 'its limit', i.e. that the nuisance or harm caused her should reach the limit such that she is excused in asking for divorce because of it."

Ibn Ruslan said: "In this, there is (an indication of) the severe reprimand and threat (of punishment ensuing) a woman's asking for a divorce when there is no real need." Then he goes on to say: "However, the hadith also demonstrates the permissibility of asking for divorce if an injustice exists."

Another example is a man's being alone with a woman who is unrelated to him. Ibn Hajar, commenting on the words of al-Bukhari 'A man should not go into (the same place as) her unless (she is) accompanied by a *mahram* (that is, a man barred from marrying her by his consanguinity to her)' saying: "There is a consensus of opinion as to this although there is a difference of opinion as to whether someone other than a *mahram* is permitted, like the presence of some trustworthy women for example. This latter view is the correct as it is unlikely that any risk (exists in their presence)."

Another example is that a woman travel without her husband or a *mahram* companion, except when travelling within safety of a group – specifically when it is a journey of an obligatory nature. The gist of what al-Hattab has mentioned is that her travelling with her husband or *mahram* is permitted in all circumstances, while travelling without either of them is permitted if she is with a trusted travelling party as long as it is of an obligatory nature; but as for her travelling without her husband or *mahram* on a journey other than of an obligatory nature, then this is not permitted, according to the consensus – except in one case: if the journey is less than a day and a night. As for the permissibility of (travel) in the safety of a group, there are two opinions – the most preferred that one should abstain from this.

Then he goes on to examine the question in more detail: "There is a difference of wording in the *hadith* as to the length of the journey for which it is not permitted for a woman to journey except in the company of *mahram* or her husband – according to some, it is a distance of twelve miles, to some a day, to some two nights, while other have said three days and still others, that the woman should not travel unless accompanied by a *mahram* – unless it is a short journey and does not (last a) long (time) that is, less than twelve miles. This latter is the *madhhab* of the Dhahiris. While some have restricted it to twelve miles, others have defined it as a day, others two nights, still others three days – and this is the *madhhab* of Abu Hanifa. Also contained in his *madhhab* is (the judgement) that if a woman envisages a journey of three days or more between her and Makka and she has no husband or *mahram* with her, then she is released from the obligation of hajj. The evidence for this from Malik is mentioned above, and he is of the opinion that the distance is a day and a night – based on his narration of the hadith in the *Muwatta'*; he has also made this a principle underlying the judgement as to whether one can shorten the *salat*, just as Abu Hanifa has stipulated the distance as three days as the limit determining whether one shortens the *salat*."

In *al-Fath* he comments on the words of al-Bukhari 'A woman should not travel...' saying: "The prohibition of travel for a woman is not based on the distance in which the shortening of the *salat* is permitted – in opposition to the Hanafis whose evidence for the prohibition being three days is well established. Anything other than this is doubtful, and one should take what is certain. It is invalid to argue that each and every narration is absolute (in the way it is understood) and that every such (narration) applies to every journey. So one hold to their (judgement) and reject all others for they are doubtful."

He has also said that al-Baghawi said: "They have not differed as to (the judgement that) a woman should not travel for a purpose which is not obligatory, except that is with her husband or a *mahram*; rather, they differ in the case of the *kafir* woman who becomes Muslim in Dar al-Harb or a captive who escapes – and one (*'alim*) has included in this (judgement the case of) a woman who becomes separated from her company: if a trustworthy man encounters her, then it is permitted for him to accompany her back to her travelling company." Then he says after a discussion: "The well known judgement according to the Shafi'is is that (her journeying) is conditional upon (the presence of) her husband, *mahram* or trustworthy women; there is also an opinion that one trustworthy woman is enough. The opinion related by al-Kurasi, and accepted as *sahih* in the *madhhab* is that she may travel alone if the road is safe. All the (above) refers to what is obligatory regarding the hajj and *'umra*. Ibn Hajar treats the caravan as something exceptional and rejects the (judgement regarding it as applicable) in all journeys, while ar-Rouyani prefers it be taken (as an applicable example) as long as it is not contrary to the principle text (on the subject)." I say: "This, however, invalidates somewhat the claim that there is no difference of opinions – as reported by al-Baghawi on several occasions."

NOTICE: "It is permitted that she deduct (something) from the dowry (owed) her by her husband so as to able to travel. This is not to be considered an invalid transaction involving a debt for a debt. The author of *al-Mi'yar* answered this question in response to al-'Utayba who imagined (the transaction was) invalid (being) a debt for a debt saying – after mention of clear evidence for the prohibition of invalidating or rescinding one debt for another in many places in *al-Mudawwana* and other works: "...he said in the fourth matter, narrated from Asbagh, from the 'Book of Advanced Payment for Goods and of Delayed Payment': 'I asked Ibn al-Qasim about a woman who remits[1] (something) from her dowry (owed her) by her husband so that he may send her on hajj. He replied that "this is forbidden – it is not permitted as it is a debt for a debt", and this is what Asbagh said. Ibn Rushd has also said: "What he said is clear, namely that it is a debt for a debt for she rescinds her money owed by him for something not yet undertaken, namely his sending her on hajj from his (own) wealth, by (his) buying or renting out (something, for example,) and undertaking (any trade-contract) needed to (raise the amount for her) going there and returning. A matter has been related from the narrations of 'Isa from the 'Book of Gifts and *Sadaqa*' which is contrary to this in its literal meaning. Some of the Shaykhs (of outer knowledge) have understood it to be contrary to the above, but it cannot be correct that there be a difference of opinion in a matter like this: it should be interpreted in such a way as to harmonise with the principles (governing 'a debt for a debt')."' As for the (relevant) text (on

---

1 See al-Bukhari, vol.3, p.460 and Qur. 4:4

the subject): "Ibn al-Qasim was asked as to the (following case): a man asked his wife that she remit her dowry to him (which he still owed her) and she replied '…if you bear the cost of taking me to my family, then this will be a *sadaqa* on your part'; so she gave it to him as a *sadaqa* on condition that he take her to her sister who was ill; he, in turn, decided it would be good to take her – (that is) after she had released him from the dowry. However, she had already left without his permission and had gone to her sister's (house). Ibn al-Qasim was asked: 'Do you consider that the *sadaqa* (she had agreed to remit to him in the form of her postponed dowry) belongs to him?' He replied: 'If she went out with the aim of breaking off (the agreement as to) what she had made over to her husband then he is under no liability (to pay her dowry); and if he had decided he should convey her but then refused to travel with her and she was aware of this then she may claim restitution of that (dowry) from which she had released him. Therefore, we say the meaning in this matter is that she relieved him of the dowry obligation in return for his going out with her and that she should not have started out alone without him; not that he convey her at his expense or that he spend anything on her during the journey other than the minimum legal maintenance (*nafaqa*) which he would (normally be) obliged to make for her in her place of residence. If the matter is understood in this way it is correct and is in harmony with the principles. It may well be that she does not have a *mahram* to accompany her on her journey in this case and thus she spends her dowry on removing this difficulty from herself, (and) in order that he might leave with her – as the Messenger of Allah may the peace and blessings of Allah be upon him, said: 'A woman who has Iman in Allah and in the Last Day is not permitted to travel a distance (more than) a day and a night unless accompanied by a *mahram*.'" Here end the words of *al-Mi'yar*.

I SAY: "There are benefits regarding the sunna in this matter which any thinking person cannot do without."

Yet another prohibition is an unmarried man hiring a female unrelated to him for service in his house even if he is a trustworthy person – unless he is living with his family; but as for a woman who is majestic in bearing and who is not in need, or a young girl employed by a old man far advanced in years, then this is permitted." The like is narrated from al-Lakhmi. Here end the words of Ahmad Baba.

Also prohibited is excessive disputation. In *al-Ihya*, he says: "The definition of argumentativeness is any opposition to the words of another such that one reveals the other's faults – either regarding (his use of) the words themselves, or the meaning or with respect to the intention of the speaker; desisting from disputation is desisting from refuting or opposing the other. You should affirm any conversation you are a party to, if true; and if false – if unconnected with matters of the deen – then you should remain silent. (What is meant by) criticism of someone else's speech is by revealing mistakes in (his use of the) words – either from the point of view of grammar or with respect to the Arabic language, or from the point of view of syntax and the order of the phrases. The reason for such (mistakes) is sometimes through lack of knowledge and sometimes from a violation of the rules of the language. However, whatever (the manner) in which they occur, there is no reason to reveal the mistakes of another. As for (mistakes in the realm of) meaning, it is that one says (for example): 'It is not as you say – you are mistaken in (asserting) such-and-such a thing.' As for (seeking fault in) the intention of the speaker, it is that one says: 'These words are true but what you intend by them is not the truth – you have an ulterior motive' or the like." Here ends his discussion, and take note of the last part of it for there are valuable things in it!

Ibn Abi Jamra, may Allah benefit us by him, has illustrated (what is meant by) a sound intention and a corrupt intention (in the following manner): "For example, two persons are discussing some matter of *fiqh*. The intention of one is to explain the judgement of Allah, exalted is He, in it and to seek what is correct – based on (the dictates of) Iman and correct belief. He is not concerned whether it is he himself or his companion who arrives (first) at the truth (regarding the judgement). Such a person's action is accepted by virtue of his good intention – this being the highest level (of knowledge); and he will enter amongst those (reckoned as) possessing divine knowledge, those who are the inheritors of the Prophets, on whom be peace and blessings; however, the other's intention springs from vanity and pride: his aim is to get the better of his companion (merely) because the (latter) is reckoned amongst the *'ulama* of excellence. Thus the latter ends up with the worst of states even if he does get the better of his brother and even if his station is raised in this world. He will be the first to be burned by the Fire on the Day of Raising Up for the Messenger of Allah may the peace and blessings of Allah be upon him, said: 'The first to be burnt by the Fire will be three (kinds of persons)", and he includes mention of the *'alim* of this description."

I have written some verses regarding (the nature of) argument and dispute which are indispensable for those of intellect:

>Praise to Allah who has generously bestowed us knowledge
>>of what is forbidden in the company of those of excellence.
>I would remind you then, by the generosity of my Lord, of

Some of the things they find reprehensible or have prohibited.
They find those of idle talk reprehensible,
   And have forbidden disputation and argument
That is, objecting to what has been said, or
   finding fault and revealing it to the *ulama* for
It certainly leads to the breaking off of friendship
   And is the cause of hate and emnity -
Leaving the person devoid of blessing and subject to trial,
   Beset with difficulties, grief and affliction.
He who refrains from it, finds ease and mercy
   Intimacy, blessing and the Garden,
Especially if the other is telling the truth and he remains silent
   On account of (his awareness of) the blessing contained in this.
However, if keeping silent harms our worldly affairs
   And brings corruption upon us,
Then our responding with the truth is obligatory – in a friendly manner,
   by courteously encouraging the person to follow the Prophet.
Then we should only speak the truth
   Without importuning (the other), molesting (him) or exceeding the proper bounds
Whoever exceeds the bounds with us, then we are patient
   In face of his offence for overcoming him is not our aim.
And desisting from such – O person of intellect! -
   Is the path by which excellence is obtained
A path to good and success,
   A means to triumph and victory.
The one who acts in this manner
   Should perceive that this is from your Lord
And consider his action as an appeal (to the other's good will).
   Any one (who acts) other than (in) this (way) is committing *kufr* and is ungrateful.
Have fear – Oh our brother! – lest vanity
   Pride, then deceit and denial befall you.
His blessing encompasses every obligatory act of devotion,
   That is, when performed in the best manner – so be awake!
– this is what befits these times –
   And by it the *nafs* and shaytan are removed.
He has indicated with his words 'is committing *kufr* and is ungrateful' the

person who is unaware that blessings are from Allah, exalted is He, that is (their appearance is subject to) his making them present in his heart. Such a person conducts his (whole) affair between (the realm of) *kufr* – if he believes that these blessings are from other than Him, and (the realm of) denial of these blessings and corruption – if he is unaware of their being from Allah, exalted is He."

Also prohibited is a person claiming descent from other than his real father[1] out of preference for this (surrogate father) and repugnance for the (real father); or likewise, he claims to be the son of someone in order that he be honoured or granted wealth – in the manner explained by al-Ubbi; or the person claims someone as his father in jest – as Ibn Abi Jamra has explained, may Allah be pleased with him. Al-Ubbi's words are a comment on the hadith: 'Whoever claims descent from someone other than his real father, then the Garden is prohibited him.'"

I SAY: "Examine whether or not he is claiming to be related to other than his real father because of some necessity – for example, he is on a journey and something happens to make him afraid causing him to say: 'I am the son of such-and-such a man' – who is respected for his good actions, or to some other person. The most evident judgement is that the punishment threatening (those who disregard this prohibition) does not apply to such a person; as opposed to someone who claims someone as his father in order that he be honoured or that he be granted something. It is clear that in this latter case the threat of punishment does apply to such a person. Examine, (what the judgement is) if he is (in fact) related to this (person he claims as) father by an adulterous marriage. As-Shaykh said that this is not so serious for the (person whom he claims a relation to) is his father linguistically speaking – although not according to the *shari'ah*. The hadith of Jareej indicates that the person (in question) is his father linguistically – when the child said: 'My father is such-and-such a shepherd.'"

As for the opposite of what is contained in the hadith, that is, when a father claims someone other than his son (as his), this (matter) may possibly be included in the (above mentioned subject). However, it is possible that it does not belong here because disobedience or undutiful behaviour is (referred to) in the hadith and this is a major wrong action (as opposed to a person's false claim that someone is his son). A person of consequence had a foster son and he would call out 'O my son' and his fellow men were hostile to him on account of his invalid claim." Here ends the comment of al-Ubbi.

1 See al-Bukhari, *K. al-Muharibin*, chapter 17, p.537, vol.8.

Ibn Abi Jamra, may Allah, exalted is He, benefit us by him, has commented on the hadith 'Whoever claims that someone is his father when he is aware that he is not his father, then the Garden is prohibited him' saying: "There are various aspects to this condemnation of the (above mentioned) person: 'Is the person saying this serious (in his claim)? is he connected to him or not? The wording of the hadith expresses generality and probably refers to someone who is heedless. He, may the peace and blessings of Allah be upon him, said that ' the man who utters words of evil, making fun of his family and disparaging them will fall for forty years in the Fire' – or in words similar to this. From another aspect, from the point of view of the *fiqh*, (one may argue that) he is playing with the deen of Allah and is making fun of the words of the Legislator, may the peace and blessings of Allah be upon him, and this is the greatest of wrong actions."

Also prohibited, is feeding the guests before one's family if one's family is in need. Ash-Shabrakheeti has written about this in *Sharh al-Arba'in*. This (matter) is self evident for it would be giving preference to the sunna over the obligatory. Al-Haytami has also indicated this in his commentary on the forty hadith saying: "Whoever has Iman in Allah and the Last Day, then he should be generous to the guest – (that is) both to the rich and the poor, with joy in one's face, and by speaking kind words and by endeavouring to present whatever one can easily find in one's house – without causing hardship or difficulty to his family – unless the latter are content (with his going beyond this degree of hospitality) and they are of age and of sound intellect."

I have explained in the following book the well known discussion regarding one of the Ansar whom Allah, exalted is He, and the Messenger have praised, together with his wife, for their preferring the guest over themselves and their children. (In the incident the wife) put the (children) to bed (in obedience) to her (husband's) command so that the guest might eat. The response to the obvious question which arises regarding their giving preference to the guest rather than seeing to the needs of the children is that the children cannot have been in great need of food; and the (parents) were afraid that if they brought the food to the guest while the (children) were still awake then they would not have been able to refrain from eating with the (guest) despite their being full – as is the wont of children – and (as a result) would have disturbed him. It is for this reason that they put them to bed. This is the most obvious explanation." Here end the words of al-Haytami.

I say: "What may be understood from the discussion of al-Haytami is that the circumstances in which one should give preference to the children over the guests is when they are really in need of food; otherwise one should give preference to the guest. What is understood by his words 'unless they are content (with his going beyond this degree of hospitality) and they are of age and of sound intellect' is that the assent of someone who is not of age is of no consequence; and likewise in the case of the mad person. As for animals, one cannot imagine their being content, whatever the circumstances."

Also prohibited is (contributing to an) increase in the (numbers of) people of seditious (*fitna*) and unjust behaviour – even if those (contributing to this increase) do not fight and do not intend (to fight) – for al-Bukhari relates from al-Aswad: "A unit of soldiers was being recruited from the people of Madina and my name was registered among them. Then I met 'Ikrima and I informed him about it and he forbade me from doing so in the strongest possible terms."[1]

Ibn Hajar said: "The hadith of Ibn 'Ikrima which he relates demonstrates that if someone goes out in an army to fight the Muslims, then he is committing a wrong action even if he does not fight or does not (even) intend (to fight). This (fact) is also confirmed from (a narration which contains) a different (sense) to this, namely 'They are a people who have no difficulty in their company[2].'"

I SAY: "This is the clear proof that the person who sits with the people of *dhikr* is also rewarded even if he himself does no *dhikr* and does not intend (doing) this (*dhikr*). He has also said in *al-Fath*: "It has been reported in a *marfu'* hadith from Ibn Mas'ud: "Whoever lends support to a people, then he is of them, and whoever is pleased with the actions of a people, then he shares in their actions."

Also prohibited is making marks in the sand (*al-khatt bi'r-ramal*) in order to seek knowledge of the unseen. This may well refer to what is called in our language *Lakzana* – and this is asserted by Sayyidi Ibn al-Hajj Ibrahim al-'Alawi, and has also been indicated by Ibn al-Haytami at the point (in his work immediately) after his discusses the four kinds of person whose *salat* is not accepted for forty days, namely, the drinker of wine, the fortune teller, the runaway slave and the woman whose husband is angry with her.

Also prohibited is flattery and fawning. Al-Bayjuri has commented on the hadith (describing) how 'Uyayna ibn Hisn entered the room of the Messenger of Allah, may the peace and blessings of Allah be upon him, and the latter said: "He is an evil member of the tribe" (in an aside) – and when ('Uyayna actually

---

1   See *Fath al-Bari*, vol. 13, p.43, no.7085. The hadith continues with the latter's saying 'Ibn 'Abbas told me that there were some Muslims who were with the *mushrikun* to increase their numbers against the Messenger of Allah, may the peace and blessings of Allah be upon him...' – on the occasion on which Allah, exalted is He, revealed *ayat* 4, sura an-Nisa'.
2   See *K. ar-Riqaq*, Ibn Hajar

came in then (he said): "Let him speak (first)." Permission for dissimulation is taken from this, that is, acting kindly and courteously towards someone in order to set right some worldly matter. It is allowed, indeed, sometimes recommended – and one of the *'ulama* has narrated: "Whoever lives his life affecting kindness will die as a *shahid*." This is contrary to flattery and fawning in the deen – which is not allowed. The difference between them is that affecting kindness is expending (of oneself in) this world in the interest of the deen while flattery is expending the deen in the interest of the *dunya*. This often occurs (amongst people), and there is no strength and no power except by Allah. What he mentions of flattery (*al-mudahina*) refers to its specific meaning (in *fiqh*); and another (definition) is indicated by al-Bayjuri in *Ikhtisar Qawa'id al-Qarafi*, in the Section entitled 'the rule governing (the type of flattery) which is permitted and how to differentiate it from that which is not permitted.'

Flattery is basically telling someone what he wants to hear – but know that it varies (in kind) as much as the five legal judgements vary. Thus it can be prohibited, like, for example, when someone expresses gratitude for some unjust action – for this would be a means of increasing injustice; and sometimes it is obligatory – if by it there lies the means to prevent some forbidden action or actions, and it is only to be prevented by this means; and sometimes it is recommended – if it affords a means to what is recommended; and sometimes it is reprehensible – if done out of weakness and there are no compelling circumstances, or it is a means of protecting oneself from what is reprehensible; and sometimes it is merely allowed – for example when one expresses gratitude to someone one fears by mentioning some of the good qualities in him while one remains silent regarding others." Here ends the discussion of Bayjuri and his saying 'expressing gratitude for an injustice' is taken from the original text of al-Qarafi namely: "… and likewise whoever expresses gratitude to an unjust person for his act of injustice or to an innovator for his innovation or to a falsifier for his falsehoods, then this act of fawning is forbidden – for this would result in an increase in this injustice and these falsehoods and (a strengthening of) those guilty of such (acts)." Ibn ash-Shat said in *Ikhtisar al-Ubbi* that 'Iyad said: "The difference between affecting kindness and flattery is that the former is to expend (of oneself in) this world in the interest of the deen or the *dunya* while the latter is to sell the deen in the interest of the *dunya*."

Also prohibited is that a person causes someone else to curse his parents even if (done) in jest – for in the hadith: "One of the greatest of wrong actions is that a man curse his parents." (Then on hearing this) those (with him) said: "O Messenger of Allah and how does a man curse his parents?" He replied "(When) a person curses the father of someone and the latter in turn curses his father or a person curses another's mother and he in turn curses his mother" – or however the text reads, for I have not been able to check the exact wording of it. Ibn Abi Jamra, may Allah benefit us by his *baraka*, said: "In this there is proof of the great disparity and contrast in the kinds of major wrong actions, and in it is a proof that one of the greatest causes of good is knowledge of the sunna. One may conclude from this that whoever does not know the (sunna) is *jahil* – ignorant – just like the person (mentioned above) who commits the greatest of wrong actions while being unaware of them. There are certain ignorant people, nowadays, who take pleasure cursing the father of another in jest – thereby expressing enmity, but in an (apparently) friendly and social manner – and I seek refuge with Allah glorious is He, from ignorance, and going astray. For this reason it is said 'No one acts more disobediently to Allah than (someone who acts) out of his ignorance.' This is true – for the ignorant person is continually exposing himself to actions which bring about his ruin without even being aware of it."

Also prohibited is molesting one's neighbour – for in Muslim (is narrated): "A slave who does not protect his neighbour from his evil will not enter the Garden"; and in al-Bukhari: "By Allah he does not believe, by Allah he does not believe, by Allah he does not believe" and they asked: "Who O Messenger of Allah? and he replied "the one who does not protect his neighbour from his (own) evil." We have not gone into an account of the above mentioned lines of poetry for this would be too long.

The Book of Purification

The Book of Purification

$$\text{فَصْلٌ وَتَحْصُلُ الطَّهَارَةُ بِمَا}$$

$$\text{مِنَ التَّغَيُّرِ بِشَيْءٍ سَلِمَا}$$

54 Purification is obtained by means of water which has not been adulterated by anything.

$$\text{إِذَا تَغَيَّرَ بِنَجِسٍ طُرِحَا}$$

$$\text{أَوْ طَاهِرٍ لِعَادَةٍ قَدْ صَلُحَا}$$

55 If it has been adulterated with something impure, it is to be rejected; likewise (it is to be rejected), even if pure – although it may be used for day to day (non ritual) use –

$$\text{إِلَّا إِذَا لَازَمَهُ فِي الْغَالِبِ}$$

$$\text{كَمُغْرَةٍ فَمُطْلَقٌ كَالذَّائِبِ}$$

56 unless this pure thing is usually part of the water, like the red colouring (of turf) – in which case it is deemed good for all purposes, and likewise melted water (from snow).

Pure Water

These lines mean that (bodily) purity is obtained by (washing) with water which is free from adulteration – with respect to the three qualities of taste, colour and smell – by means of something which is not usually part of the water, irrespective of whether it be pure or impure.

If it changes by means of something impure then it is rejected (outright) and is not to be used – either for daily use or for (acts of worship). If it has not undergone any change, then there is no reprehensibility in using it if the amount of water is considerable; if (the amount is) small – like the amount contained in a receptacle used for doing *wudu'* or in a receptacle used for *ghusl* – and the impurity is slight – then it is reprehensible to use it when other water is available, according to the well known opinion; if it has undergone a change through some pure thing, then it is suitable for daily use but not for worship – unless that which has brought about the change is normally to be found in the water, in which case it is treated as good for all purposes, both for daily use and for worship." Here end the words of 'Ali ibn 'Abd as-Sadiq.

REMARK: Ahmad Zarruq said: "Some have added to his definition the adulteration which ensues through contact with a leathern water bag over a long period of time"; and Abu Muhammad ash-Shabeebi has noted that the water of a leathern carrier bag and water from a well which has undergone change from contact with water used in tanning or from contact with the tamarisk and the like is pure, although (using) other than it is better.

Al-Mawwaq al-Mazari said: "If there is doubt as to whether or not the thing which caused the change is of the kind which causes adulteration to the water, then the judgement is that it does not.' Malik said that if one does not know the cause of some foul smell in a well supplying houses then one should leave it; Ibn Rushd, (has added) but 'not in the case of a well or pool in the desert'; Ibn 'Arafa has narrated that Ibn Rushd judged the water of a well which had undergone change by contact with wood or grass concealed in it to be pure."

Ibn Ghazi has written in his *Hashiya*: "Ibn Rushd has mentioned that the opinion of one of the latter *'ulama* – (namely) one is not permitted to do *wudu'* or *ghusl* using water from river beds and pools which has undergone change by contact with leaves falling from trees growing on their banks or brought by the wind – is an isolated judgement (*shadhdh*), and falls outside the principle (governing this matter) in this *madhhab*; that one should therefore disregard this and not linger over (to long on the matter). These words of his demonstrate too that Ibn Rushd's *fatwa* is not to be restricted to what a well contains – of the like of this."

In *al-Mi'yar*: Abu 'Umran was asked – regarding a receptacle which had contained oil or fat but which is emptied out and then filled with water – as to whether one should do *wudu'* with it or not if droplets (of oil or fat) rise to the surface. He replied: "If negligible (in amount), then there is no harm."

Sahnun, when asked, with regard to this same subject, about houses which had been built using water which is not completely pure (*bi-ma' in bakhsin*) and whether one may pray on the roofs of such (houses) or do *wudu'* with the water that collects on the surface (of these roofs) replied: "Yes."

SECTION: Regarding water which is not harmed when changed by something adjacent to it – Khalil has added to the (definition of) what does not remove the purity (of water saying) "… (its purity is not removed) when it undergoes a change by means of something adjacent to it, even if there is oil clinging to the (water)." Al-Hattab said: "… this means that if the water changes because of something adjacent to it, then its purity is not removed, irrespective of whether the thing adjacent to it is separate from the water or sticking to it." As for the first (case) when for example, there is a dead body or excrement or something else at the side of the water and the wind carries the smell of this to the water and it undergoes a change – there is no difference of opinion in this (that its purity is not removed). One of the *'ulama* said: "(Also) included here is (the case) when the mouth of a receptacle is blocked off by a plant or the like and the water changes as a result – without (the water) actually coming into direct contact with the (plant)." As for the second, that is when the thing adjacent to it is clinging or sticking to it, Ibn al-Hajib has given the example of oil, and the author concurs with him in this – although stipulates that it must be clinging to it, thereby excluding what is admixed to it. He has also said in his *Tawdheeh*: "As for oil, he has rejected what the author has stated – for what is well known in the *madhhab* is that oil removes purity: among those who have mentioned this is Ibn Basheer. Thus on the basis of this, one understands his words as referring to something which is adjacent to the surface of the water. Ibn 'Ata'illah and Ibn Rushd have also indicated this. (If one argues) that this is tautological and he could have omitted mention of the notion of adjacent, then we would argue: "He wanted to make clear that whatever is adjacent and which does not adversely affect the (water) is of two types – that which does not adhere to it and that which does."

Here Ibn 'Arafa has objected to Ibn al-Hajib's saying that water changed by oil is pure; and he (also) rejects Ibn 'Abd as-Salam's assertion that one should desist from it by virtue of it being adjacent to it – that is, (precisely) because it is (only) adjacent and not (not because it is) mixed with it. This (rejection of his) is based on the manifest meaning of the narrations, namely that any change, whatever the conditions, counts, even if (the impure thing or substance in question) does not (directly) mix with the (water).

More than one of the *'ulama* has given preference to the words of Ibn 'Arafa; and al-Hattab has given priority to the words of Khalil and Ibn al-Hajib saying: "the matter is clear in that if the oil is adhering to the surface of the water and is not admixed with it then it does not affect it adversely" — as the author (of the Mukhtasar) said. Then he says after a while: "..and Ibn Farhoun has related that Ibn Rushd said: 'the above mentioned words of al-Hajib are to be understood, in my opinion, to refer to water which has become oily from contact with receptacles which are used for both eating and (drinking) water (from). The proof of this is that the Companions, may Allah, exalted is He, be content with them, used their receptacles for eating, drinking and *wudu'*. The (judgement therefore) varies in accordance with the greater or lesser amount of oil — if it is negligible and there is no food in the water, then the most literal judgement is that it does not harm (the purity of the water).

What Ibn 'Arafa holds to is supported by al-Marzouq — according to Ahmad ibn 'Abd al-'Aziz al-Hilali in his *Nawazil*. Al-Hattab has objected to his opinion but is alone in his objection.

SECTION: among things which do not adulterate water is the smell (given off by) tar contained in a receptacle. Khalil said adding to (his discussion of) that which does not remove purity: "...or changes by being adjacent to it even if it is oil clinging to it or the smell of tar in the receptacle of a traveller." Ibn al-Hattab said: "that is, that purity is not removed from the water which undergoes a change from the smell of tar which is in the receptacle of a traveller. The manifest meaning of Khalil's words is that this applies irrespective of whether the change comes about from the smell of the tar which lingers — even though none of the actual tar remains in the receptacle, or changes from the smell of the tar which still (actually) remains in the receptacle. However, if the change is from the smell lingering in the receptacle and nothing of the actual tar remains, then there is no doubt that this change has come about by 'being adjacent' — that is, by way of indirect contact and that this does not remove the purity (of the water) — and there is no obscurity in this (matter); if, however, the change has come about through the smell of the tar when there is still some of the actual tar remaining in the receptacle, then what appears to be the evident meaning of the ensuing words of the author is that he has decided that it does not adulterate (the water): as if he has treated it as being a change of the type which is (both) adjacent (and) adhering (to it) — this is the gist of what (Khalil) mentions (in his *Mukhtasar*). If we understand Khalil's discussion in this light, then his words '...or by the smell of the tar from the receptacle of the traveller' should be understood together with his words 'and if oil adheres to it.' This would mean that (mention of) 'the traveller' is a factor indicating what is normally done (in the circumstances) — because the traveller is usually in need of such a thing. But this would then not make sense and there would be no (alteration). One thus understands from this that if a change does take place in its colour or taste, then its purity is removed."

Then he continues after a while: "The gist of the above is that if it is only the smell of the water which changes from (the effect of) the tar then this is treated as a case of a change which comes about through contact with something adjacent – and it is permitted to use it. Moreover (in this case), there is no stipulation that the circumstances be those of necessity or that the person be a traveller or be resident, except that is, when the literal meaning is understood (as the valid judgement) – from what is narrated by Ibn Rushd from some of the later 'ulama, in which case travel and compelling circumstances are stipulated. However, this is not correct when other water is available." Here end the words of al-Hattab.

Ahmad ibn 'Abd al-'Aziz has justified the difference between the change which comes about through smell and something else by explaining that the change through smell may possibly have come about by something being adjacent, whereas colour and taste both indicate that some fragments of the tar have broken down and dissolved in the water.

Since Khalil has mentioned that what is changed by an impurity is itself impure and what is changed by something pure is itself pure, it occurred to me that I should mention some of the things which are impure and some which are pure.

Among these impure things is the (non-ritually slaughtered) carcass of wild, warm-blooded animals. Al-Mawwaq reports that Ibn 'Arafa said: "The carcass of terrestrial, warm or cold blooded animals, other than man himself, like for example the *wazag* lizard, are impure – even the louse." Ibn Bashir (said): "The flea does not have blood circulating in its veins so it is not impure when dead, unless it has sucked blood (of another), in which case there are two opinions, and the (difference in) judgement as to killing them in the mosque is based on these (two judgements); as opposed to a louse which should not be killed or discarded in a mosque."

In *al-Jami'* of al-'Utayba: "Sahnun said regarding a flea which falls into one's soup, that there is no harm in eating it. Al-Baji said that it may be rendered impure if there was blood in it. Al-Burzuli said that Ibn 'Arafa considered the dead remains of a flea of no significance while Ibn 'Abd as-Salam has related that it is impure."

The commentator on *Mayyara* said, regarding the *Sharh* of Ibn Marzouq on Khalil: "I have heard from one of the rightly-acting *fuqaha* from among his contemporaries that he used to say: "Whoever needs to kill a louse on his clothing or in the mosque, should intend to slaughter it ritually, in which case its dead remains will be pure and will not render anything impure for him." However, I do not know if he considers this as a tradition or whether it is a judgement of his based on legal principles, and even if it is probably based on investigative (judgement) on his behalf (rather than tradition) there is no harm in it. If it is permitted to eat lice, then this has not been mentioned in a clear, unequivocal text; if we suppose that it is among the things which are prohibited or reprehensible to eat then this (judgement of his) is based on the fact that ritual slaughter has an effect on what is prohibited or reprehensible, as well as what is allowed – and this is what is meant by his saying "based on the principles." And Allah, exalted is He, knows best.

Also impure is vomit which has changed (in consistency) from being food. Ibn 'Arafa (said): "Vomit which has changed from its state as food is impure"; at-Tunisi and al-Lakhmi: "…if it resembles one of the qualities of excrement (it is impure)"; Ibn Rushd: "…or resembles it."

Among impure things is flowing blood. Khalil said: "…and flowing blood, even if from a fish or fly," and also included, according to the strongest opinion, is blood which comes out from a slaughtered sheep after it has been skinned – in the *Ikhtisar Nawazil al-Burzuli* of al-Wansharisi: "…as for the question regarding blood which drips out of a slaughtered sheep after it has been skinned, there are two opinions." Al-Burzuli: "What we heed and what the Shaykhs have based their judgements on is that (this blood) is (considered) *masfuh* – flowing blood[1]."

Also impure is fluid and dampness from the vagina. Al-Hattab has related from Ibn 'Arafa that al-'Iyad said: "Water and dampness from the vagina is impure according to us." Ibn 'Arafa: "An-Nawawi's acceptance of a transmission of one of their followers – namely, that according to the consensus, a foetus ejected with moisture from the vagina of its mother is pure and that there is no disagreement (as to the purity of) vaginal fluid – may be dismissed (with the argument that) the principle (governing this case is) that a thing becomes impure on contact with something which is itself impure and wet, and also (with the argument) that this (case) is absent in the books on the subject of consensus. Ibn al-Qattan has understood this but he does not mention it."

What Ibn 'Arafa said is supported by what al-Burzuli has transmitted of the legal issues of Ibn Qudah: whoever lifts up the foetus of a cow at the moment of its birth – when moist – and he presses it against his clothing then their is no need for him to clean himself. Al-Burzuli said: "…as long as the dampness

---

1 (see al-An'am – Livestock: 145)

is not from blood – in which case it is (treated in the same manner) as when it is damp from its urine. If it is the foetus of a horse which he presses to his clothing, then his clothing becomes impure." Al-Burzuli (has added): "...this is with respect to what an-Nawawi has related, namely there is agreement that the dampness (on the skin) of a human new born when it emerges is pure – and our Shaykh would add: '...the nature of this example is more appropriate because of the difference of opinion as to (the permissibility of) eating horse (flesh).'"

In the *Ikhtisar Nawazil al-Burzuli* of al-Wansharisi, he says: "The dampness of a human new born is pure according to all (the *'ulama*) – and so all the more reason for the new born calf (to be pure)." Al-Burzuli (adds) "...as long as the dampness is not blood." However, it has also been said of the new born calf that it is impure. Ibn 'Arafa follows this by saying that it is more fitting to consider the human new born as impure given the difference of opinion as to whether one can eat horse flesh." Here end the words of al-Wansharisi.

I SAY: "One of the people of our time said: 'What has been related from Ibn 'Arafa is contradictory – examine it fairly for first of all it concerns his mention of the agreement as to its purity, and secondly it concerns the agreement as to the impurity of the dampness or fluid which is an inherent, inseparable part of the new born foal, and Allah, exalted is He, knows best.'"

Among the things which are pure is saliva: Khalil said: "Living creatures, their blood, sweat and saliva." Al-Hattab said: "Examine whether the fluid which comes out of the person who is sleeping is included in his what he says." Al-Mashdali said in his *Hashiya* of the *Mudawwana*, as related by an-Nawawi: "If it has changed (consistency) then it is impure, if not then pure – if we were to say that it is impure and it is part of the person, then it would be analogous to the blood of the flea." Al-Mashduli said: "There are two opinions on this – (which arise) from amongst the issues which resemble it. 'Isa Ibn Naji said in the commentary on the *Mudawwana*: "The customary practice in our *madhhab* if it changes (consistency), then it is treated as a fluid which is admixed but not impure"

I SAY: "There is no basis for this, rather the most obvious argument is that if it is from the mouth, then it is pure, even if from the stomach. It is as an-Nawawi said: 'If it has changed (from its normal consistency), then it is impure, if not then it is pure.'"

Ad-Dameeri said in his *Sharh al-Minhaj*: "One recognises if it is from the stomach or not by its offensive smell and yellow colour." It has also been said: "...as long as the head is on the pillow, then it is from this (normal saliva), otherwise it is from the stomach – however whatever the circumstances, it is an inherent, inseparable (part of the saliva) and as such excused (from being treated as something impure)."

Also pure is blood which is not flowing. Khalil said – regarding blood which is not flowing – that al-Mawwaq has related from al-Lakhmi: "If blood is not visible, then it is agreed that (the meat) may be eaten, for example, even when a sheep is roasted before being cut up and then blood appears when cut up. Malik, said on one occasion that it is haram, but has interpreted that it is permissible to (eat the meat) when (blood) is not visible – even when blood appears after cutting it up after it has been roasted whole – because determining from the veins if there is still blood (in them) is difficult; however, on another occasion he said that it is halal – based on the words of, exalted is He, "or flowing blood."[1] Thus if the meat is cut up on this basis, that is after the removal of the 'flowing blood', then it is not haram and it is permitted to eat it. In (Qadi Abu Bakr ibn al-'Arabi's) al-Qabas (fi sharh al-Muwatta' li-Malik ibn Anas) – his words 'and flowing blood' necessarily entails one consider as lawful the blood still in the veins and which flows when the meat is cut up.

Al-Hattab said – after mention of the difference of opinion mentioned by al-Mawwaq that Abu Hasan al-Mashdali related in his *Hashiya* on the *Mudawwana*: Abu 'Imran said: "As for blood which spurts out of the meat onto one's clothes and body when cutting it up, the best thing is to wash it out."

I SAY: "…and al-Mawwaq – as is clear from reading *al-Mi'yar* – tends to give preference to the opinion that it is impure. Al-Khurshi said: '…as for what still remains in the veins, then there is unanimity that it is not "flowing blood" – and this is also mentioned by Ibn Bashir and others. The difference of opinion in this matter is when the sheep is cut up and blood appears. However, if it is roasted before being cut up, then there is no difference of opinion that it is permissible to eat it – this has been stated by al-Lakhmi."

Ibn al-Hattab said: "As for whether what comes out of the heart of the sheep – when split open – is (to be considered as) 'flowing blood' or not, I have not seen a text on the subject. What may to be understood by the words of al-Burzuli and al-Lakhmi is that it is coagulated blood and as such, not flowing.

SECTION: In *al-Mi'yar* he says: "Sayyidi Muhammad ibn Marzouq was asked about a sheep which was slaughtered but not washed and whether or not its head, roasted together with the blood – without washing it – is impure, and so haram. He replied: "As for the head which is roasted but not washed, then it should be washed after the roasting and then eaten."

---

1 al-An'am – Livestock: 146

Also pure is vomit unless it has changed (in substance from its form as) food. Al-Ubbi said that al-Mazari said: "The eating of vomit is not haram unless it resembles one of the qualities of excrement."

Also pure is paper (acquired) from the Europeans – the *'alim* of the *Maghrib*, the Malik of his time and his land, al-Mawwaq, has investigated whether it is pure in (one of) his works and claimed that if it were impure it would contradict (Allah's, exalted is He, promise to) preserve the Qur'an: the Qur'an is copied down on to such (paper) and the copying down on something which is impure contradicts this (promise of) preservation. The following passage, as related in *al-Mi'yar*, occurs after a long discussion: "..and also Allah, exalted is He, said: 'It is We Who have sent down the Reminder and We Who will preserve it'[1] – if the roman paper were impure the Qur'an could not be said to be preserved as whatever is written on an impure thing is not preserved. Moreover, one cannot argue: 'You have judged that one should treat the person who throws a copy of the Qur'an into the dirt as *kafir* – but how is one to conceive of the judgement if such an outrage has not in fact not occurred?' What we say is that many a judgement may be conceived of but has not been applied: the intention (of the *'ulama*) is knowledge of the judgement by means of a hypothetical occurrence. For this reason they suppose the occurrence of what is normally impossible, like the occurrence of the 'Eid and the eclipse of the sun on the same day. You will be aware that (the supposition of) the impossible as habitual is classified by the logicians as a matter of logic, rather than one of the judgements of our *'ulama* – and praise belongs to Allah, exalted is He. We have not heard from any sound chain of narration of the occurrence of such an outrage – and refuge is only with Allah. If it were to occur, then it would be because of the anger of Allah, exalted is He, on the perpetrator: he would be judged to have deserted Islam, and either he would have to turn in *tawba* or be killed – if he is a Muslim; and if he is a *kafir*, then the argument would be otherwise. The whole matter is based on Allah's (promise of) preservation of it glorious is He, that is, that impurity will not come into contact with it – for no one will commit such an action when aware of the punishment (awaiting him). Even the rod which the Messenger of Allah, may the peace and blessings of Allah be upon him, used to hold was protected from abuse – for when the evil Jahjaha tried to break it over his knee, his leg was afflicted by gangrene; (a similar thing occurred regarding) the letter the Messenger of Allah, may the peace and blessings of Allah be upon him sent to Khosroes – when the latter tore it up he and the people of his deen were destroyed; but Heraklius preserved it,

1 al-Hijr: 243

and they will remain Christians during the centuries up to the Day of Raising Up. This preservation of the letter (on the part of, exalted is He,) was to ensure that it was not treated with disrespect – and how much greater must the degree of protection be in the case of the source of the letter (namely the Qur'an); again, (there is the example in) the story of al-Waleed who opened up the Qur'an to seek (guidance) by (divine) indication and the *ayat "and every obdurate tyrant failed"*[1] turned up: what he did with the copy of the Qur'an in that moment is well known. However the punishment of Allah, exalted is He, afflicted him after three years. Allah can thus delay the destruction of someone who has earned His punishment for such a time. This incident is the clearest of proofs that the Book of Allah, exalted is He, is protected from anything of the like happening to it. Despite it being unrelated directly to our topic, we have related at length what he said concerning the matter on account of the extraordinary benefits contained in it – and (the transmission of such benefits) is in fact the aim of this book.

LEGAL POINT: al-Hattab has related that Ibn 'Arafa and others have said: "There are two different opinions regarding creatures whose blood has been (sucked) from other (creatures), like fleas, lice and gnats – firstly, that, when dead, they are pure and secondly, that they are impure; likewise ticks and flies, as the author of *al-Jam'* from Ibn Harun has made clear. Khalil too has declared that they have flowing blood. What one understands from the *Iqtisar* of Khalil on the subject of lice is that he gives preference to the view that (creatures of this type) other than them are pure." A similar (judgement) may be understood from the discussion of *'ain-sin* on this subject – as he said: "Fleas do not have flowing blood, but as for lice, it is well known that they have flowing blood." Thus one understands from him that preference is given to (the opinion which) discriminates between lice and fleas, and this opinion he has narrated from one of the *'ulama* in the *Tawdih* (of Khalil on the *Mukhtasar* of Ibn al-Hajib). Another has given a judgement as to the impurity of lice on the basis that they originate from people – as opposed to fleas which are from the earth, that they are given to jumping – as well as the fact that they are difficult to guard against.

There is no doubt that gnats, flies and bedbugs are (treated) like fleas according to what he has mentioned. He has summed the matter up in *al-Jalab* (by stating) that flies and gnats do not have flowing blood, and (Khalil) is definitively of the opinion in *at-Tawdih* – in the discussion regarding dead creatures – when he says: "What is meant by 'flowing blood' is any (creature) that has blood, although sometimes the (*'ulama*) argue that it is not (flowing

---

1 Ibrahim: 18

blood) because of the fact that it is sucked (from the body of another organism) – thus flies do not have flowing blood, although blood is to be found in them." Moreover in the last part of the Section regarding the narrations of Ashhab – in the 'Book of Hunting and Slaughtering' – he is of the opinion that mites are not reckoned to be among creatures with flowing blood, (adding): "there is no doubt that ticks are like them."

The outcome of this is that the preferred judgement regarding creatures whose blood is sucked (from another organism) is that they do not have flowing blood – other than lice; and this does not contradict the judgement as to the impurity of the flowing blood in flies and the like. Do you not see that the flowing blood of fish is judged to be impure despite the agreement as to the purity of (its flesh) when dead. And Allah knows best.

LEGAL MATTER: Ibn 'Arafa said: "(It is stated) in the *Mudawwana* that if insects fall into a pot or a bowl, then one may still eat the food in it or do *wudu'* with the water in it." Ibn Yunus said: "It may be eaten irrespective of whether the insect may be discerned (in the food) and is removed, or cannot be discerned; and irrespective too of whether or not the (amount of) food is a lot or a little." It has also been said that food (in which such creatures have fallen) may be eaten in all circumstances – (this judgement being given) on the basis of the narration regarding the (permission to) eat of locusts. Al-Lakhmi said: "If a long time elapses such that something (of the creature) exudes from it or part of it becomes detached, then the food is (to be treated) as having been affected by some impurity and should be thrown away. There is a difference of opinion, however, regarding water as long as it has not changed – on condition that the locust or the like is killed ritually." This, however, may be rejected as the well known opinion is that such (a creature) is not impure when dead.

LEGAL MATTER: Ibn 'Arafa said: "The companion of Sahnun, Sulayman, discarded flour which had been adulterated by a louse – and he included the gnat in this (judgement); but someone else rejected his opinion – distinguishing in his argument between the latter which is like the fly and which consumes blood, and the louse which is from man." Ibn Rushd (has stated that) "discarding a lot of flour is an (unlawful) waste as the (creature) is not dissolved in it. Thus, (in this case,) a large amount (of flour) would not be forbidden (for consumption) – just as the mixing of a *mahram*, a near relation, with a lot of women (would not be considered an affront to her reputation) – for (as he argues) just as we assess with less severity the eating of a part of it because of the probability of the (louse) being in the rest of the (flour), then we may (likewise) adjudge with less severity the rest of the (flour) because of the probability of the (louse) having being in what we have just eaten."

I SAY: "It appears that there is no explicit text regarding the eating of it. (As for the narration) from 'Abd al-Haqq from Sahnun regarding a louse falling in the soup, it is not mentioned that he ate it. Ibn Rushd: 'The *fatwa* of Sa'd ibn Numayr relates how a pot overturned and burst when a rat fell in it – and then emerged alive from the same place. Others have narrated the same: (namely that) it should be thrown away; and the same incident is related by someone else from Ibn Wahb. In al-Baji's *shudhudh* – the *hadith* with isolated chains of narration (he states): "Sahnun considers there to be no great harm in using oil in which a dried out (carcass of a) mouse or the like is found. He bases (his judgement) on the fact that its dryness is an indication that oil was poured over it, and that it did not die in it."' Al-Baji (continues): "As for a large amount of oil in which a mouse or the like dies, or into which a dead animal falls, and it does not change (the nature of the oil), the well-known opinion is Malik's saying: 'I dislike it(s use).'"

Ibn Sahnun from Ibn Nafi': "Ibn Majishun does not alter this judgement, namely: 'If it dies in the (oil), then it is thrown away, otherwise it is halal.'"

I SAY: "I shall discuss shortly al-Hattab's estimation of what al-Baji has related from Sahnun as weak, as well as other opinions beside this. Al-Hattab also relates Ibn Rushd's discussion – as narrated by Ibn 'Arafa – then goes on to say: '...and it is clear from the words of Ibn Rushd that if something impure becomes mixed with a large amount of something pure which is not fluid – as long as the impurity is indistinguishable (from the rest) – then the whole of it is not discarded just because one may has doubts (as to its purity).' This is analogous to an impure apple or fresh-date or the like getting mixed up in a pile of apples or dates."

'Isa ibn Naji said in his commentary on the saying of the *Mudawwana*: "Whoever is certain that some impurity has got on to his clothes but does not know its exact whereabouts, then he should clean the whole of it; if he does know the precise spot then he should wash it out." The (ulama) have said: "What may be concluded from this is that if a piece of pork falls onto a pile of meat and one knows the precise spot (where it fell), then one should refrain from (using) this (part) and eat the rest of it; otherwise, one should throw all of it away." It is possible to harmonise between this (latter judgement) and the above-mentioned explanation of Ibn Rushd, may Allah have mercy on him, by (arguing that) the latter (judgement) refers to the case where the amount (of meat) is quite considerable – for this is the manifest meaning of his words – so study the matter. What is also clear from this is that whatever comes into direct contact with it is impure – as long as it does not dissolve or disintegrate, thereby causing (the rest to become) impure. Part of this (argument) has been mentioned above.

REMARK: the saying of Khalil "a lot of food in a fluid form is rendered impure by a little impurity" includes (such food) in which an animal with flowing blood has died, or in which (an animal) falls after having died, or (food) which is poured over a dead creature which does not have flowing blood – and this is the well known judgement.

Then he said: "Section: if a creature falls in and it comes out alive, then the food is not spoiled unless it is known that there is some impurity on its body. However, if it is not known to be so, then one may assume that it is pure even if it is usually considered to frequent filth(y places)."

LEGAL MATTER: al-Hattab said: "…and if the head has been scorched and the slaughtered animal has not be washed (previously) but then it is washed after the scorching, then there is no harm in this; and if it is not washed after the scorching but the fire reached such a degree that the blood which was on the surface of the slaughtered animal is removed, then there is also no harm in eating the whole of the head; and if there is any doubt as to the removal of all of it by the heat of the fire, then one should avoid eating the meat from the actual point (the neck) of the slaughtering and eat the rest."

LEGAL MATTER: an-Nafrawi said: "The impurity of oil which has been placed in a receptacle made of ivory has been the subject of discussion amongst the Shaykhs. What has been established from the discussion of the people of the (Maliki) *madhhab* is that if one is sure that nothing (of the ivory) has dissolved or broken off, then it retains its purity. The judgement is similar in the case of old bone from a donkey: it does not render impure whatever it falls into; if, however, there is a possibility that part of it has broken off or dissolved (in the food), then there is no doubt as to its impurity."

LEGAL MATTER: al-Hattab said: "Note: What Ibn 'Arafa said, namely, that the principle 'that anything that comes into contact with an impurity which is wet is rendered impure' is clear and there is no doubt in this. In the 'legal matters' of Ibn Qudah – regarding the person who puts on clean dry clothes on top of wet, impure clothes, and the former are affected by this impurity – (it is argued that) if the impurity is (known to be) in a specific place, then this place only is to be washed, otherwise the whole of it is washed; and if the person does not have any other (clothes) and the time (for the *salat*) is close, then he should pray in them." In the narrations of Ashhab (is stated): "If a person plucks his armpits, then he should wash his hands." Ibn Rushd has commented on this saying: "It is recommended" while al-Basati said in *al-Mughni* that: "it is obligatory when some impurity is attached to the hair" – and the (reasoning behind this case) is clear if the roots of the hair come into contact with his hands. (The following) is similar this case – (namely) if one blows one's nose on one's clothes or into one's hand and finds hair with its roots in the mucus, then it will render the (latter) impure, and Allah, exalted is He, knows best. However, the most evident meaning of their words is that the (judgement in such cases only applies) in the case where (a part of) the impurity (in question) breaks off or dissolves (in the mucus).

Al-Burzuli said: "Ibn Abi Zayd said, with respect to (the case where) someone makes *wudu'* on the bank of a river: if he washes his foot and it comes into contact with the bone of some dead animal covered by the water and mud and then his foot touches his clothes then his clothes do not become impure and he does not have to clean them."

Al-Burzuli said: "If the bone is old (and dry) then the (matter) is clear, and at-Tunisi has written about this in his commentary (saying): "…however, if there is any fat or meat (on it), then the correct judgement is that impurity will be transferred to his leg – unless, that is, he is sure that the wetness of the impurity has all gone and all that remains is the wetness from the water, in which case it is treated as (subject to the same judgement as) an old bone. Mention will be made below of (case of) the louse (with regard to this subject) – which supports this."

Also included in this (subject) is Ashhab's narration from Malik (regarding the case when) someone takes a *ghusl* and then dries himself with a towel on which is some blood: "If the (amount of blood) is insignificant, and none of it gets onto him as a result of his drying himself with the towel, then he is under no obligation (to clean himself once more); however, if he fears that in drying himself, the blood (on the towel) became wet and some of it detached itself and stuck to his body, then he should wash his body (once more). This (judgement) is accepted by Ibn Rushd." Here end the words of Muhammad ibn al-Hattab with respect to the words of Khalil "and the dampness of the vagina (*al-farj*)."

LEGAL MATTER: Ibn al-Hattab said: "SECTION: There is no difference between a fluid impurity or a non-fluid impurity – which is to be found on something solid – one looks rather to the possibility of the one (thing) spreading to or affecting the other. As for a fluid impurity which falls into solidified honey or the like – if it is seen at the moment of its falling into the (substance) and is removed together with the (substance) around it, then the rest of it is not adversely affected; likewise, a drop of blood which falls into yoghurt – as long as one removes it together with what is around it and makes sure that there is no trace of it remaining. However, if a long time elapses and the impurity affects the whole of it, then it should be thrown away and not eaten. Similarly, no distinction is made as to whether an impurity is in a liquid or solid state when it falls into a liquid. In al-Burzuli – from the legal matters related by Ibn Qudah – is narrated: 'If a feather from a bird which has not been slaughtered (ritually) falls into food which is fluid, then it should be thrown away.'"

LEGAL MATTER: Al-Bannani said regarding the words of Khalil 'oil mixed with an impurity, meat cooked with an impurity, olives salted with an impurity or eggs fried in an impurity cannot be rendered pure; nor an earthenware pot which has been penetrated deeply (by impurity)': "(here) he has delivered an absolute judgement regarding (all) earthenware pots – but the (most) evident judgement is that old pots or jugs can be rendered pure, as is stated in the *Nawazil* of as-Sayyid 'Abd al-Qadir al-Fasi – although there is also (the judgement) that such a receptacle cannot be purified based on the principle that it should not be carried on one's person when praying, for example. However, food or water may be placed in it for they are not rendered impure thereby as no visible, physical traces of the impurity remain. Shaykh Abu'l-Hasan ar-Rahali said, commenting on the words of the *Mudawwana* 'If a Muslim buys wine from a Christian, then the breaking of the (receptacle in which the wine is held) is the responsibility of the Muslim': "Reflect upon whether or not there is evidence enough here that it is not permitted to use the receptacles in which wine has been kept? – for there is a (clear) textual evidence that it is in fact permitted to use receptacles and skins used for wine after they have been washed and cleaned. Ibn 'Abd al-Hakam said: "Receptacles may be used, but not skins."

Al-Hattab said: "The author of *al-Akmal* has related a difference of opinion transmitted from Malik regarding receptacles used to hold wine: 'They are washed free (of wine) and may be used.' It has also been narrated from him: 'If water is boiled in them and they are (thoroughly) cleaned, then they may be used.' It has also been narrated from him, that they and vessels should be broken up. Thus it is said: 'The punishment for such a contract (i.e. the buying or selling of such vessels) results in punishment regarding one's wealth.' It has also been said: 'This is because they cannot be cleaned by washing as the (wine) has penetrated it (too) deeply.' Al-Ubbi said: 'The most evident judgement is that a receptacle in which wine has been kept is pure if it is washed – as it is established (as a principle) that any remaining colour (from the wine) is of no harm unless it can be argued that the water cannot penetrate as deeply as the wine can penetrate (and therefore cannot purify it thoroughly).'" Here end the words of al-Hattab.

Also regarding this (subject) – he said in *al-Jawahir*: "If the taste remains after the substance itself has disappeared to the naked eye, then the place is impure for its remaining is an indication that the substance is still there; and likewise if the colour and smell remain – and it is easy to get rid of them with water – (then it is also impure until the colour and smell are removed). If, however, it is difficult to get rid of the (colour and smell), then one is exempted (from the obligation of their removal), and the vessel is pure."

He has also said, commenting on the words of Khalil 'Water used in washing out an impurity is also impure': "there is no doubt as to its impurity if it has changed (in its qualities) – irrespective of whether it has changed in colour, taste or smell. Muhammad ibn 'Abd as-Salam said: 'But it is not the same judgement as the place of impurity itself, that is, if it has changed by means of an impurity or filth on the clothes (then it is impure); but if the change is from a dye in the clothes and the (water used) in the washing is affected such that one is convinced that the change is from the dye, then one should judge it to be pure; and if it has changed as mentioned above, then one should judge the clothes are pure. Likewise, if water – mixed with something and changed by means of something pure – is used to wash an impurity such that it removes the actual impure spot and its traces and (yet) the water (despite this) is as it was – then one should judge this water used for washing to be pure. This is in accordance with what Khalil (in his *Mukhtasar*) applies in the following branch (of the law) – namely his saying 'If the actual spot of the impurity is removed with water which is not absolutely pure then anything which touches this place (which has been cleaned) is not rendered impure.' This is because if the (jurists) do not judge the wetness on the clothing to be impure, then likewise the wetness which drops from it (is also not impure) – for the two are one thing even if part of it becomes separated and part remains. If this were not so it would conflict with the above mentioned branch (of the law)."

Then he says referring to the words of Khalil 'if the actual spot of the impurity is removed with water which is not absolutely pure, then whatever touches the place (which has been cleaned) is not rendered impure': "this refers to an impurity which is removed by means of water that is not absolutely pure – (that is) either by water to which something has been admixed or with some fluid extract, other than water, like vinegar or the like. However, (what) we have said (is that) this does not actually render the place of the impurity pure, (that) it is judged according to the law as impure and that *salat* is not permitted when it is on one's person. Moreover, if something touches this place when it is wet, or something wet touches it after it has dried or while it is wet – then there are two opinions as to whether that which touches it becomes impure or not."

'Ali ibn 'Abd as-Sadiq and Khalil and others have said: "Most (of the *'ulama*) are of the opinion that it does not render (that which touches it) impure, and in *al-Mukhtasar* he adds 'Non-permanent qualities do not affect (other things).' It is regarding this (latter) principle that there is a difference of opinion between the two Shaykhs, al-Qabisi and Ibn Abi Zayd: regarding a new (leathern) bucket which is rubbed with oil and when (water from) it is used to clean excrement from himself (after going to the toilet), they are of the opinion that this is not acceptable – but while Al-Qabisi said: "He should wash any clothing on which the water has fallen", Ibn Abi Zayd said: "He should repeat the cleaning (of himself) but not the washing of his clothes."

As for what we have mentioned, namely, that there is no difference between removing the actual spot of impurity with water (which is pure but) mixed with something or with an extract (like vinegar), this is the opinion of Ibn 'Arafa who said: "If the actual spot (of the impurity) is removed with water (which is pure but) mixed with something or with a liquid extract (like vinegar) then this fluid becomes impure by contact with this place – as narrated by 'Abd al-Haqq from one of the later (ulama) and Ibn 'Abd ar-Rahman from al-Qabisi, and Ibn al-'Arabi – (who made clear that they were) unaware of any difference of opinion. However, he has also lent support to the opinion of Shaykh Abi Ishaq at-Tunisi, Shaykh ibn Abi Zayd and Ibn Rushd, namely, that this does not render (such liquids) impure, stating that the (jurists) are all in agreement regarding this. Moreover this is also held to by 'Abd al-Haqq and al-Qabisi. Thus he has two opinions on this (matter), the well known being the second – in accordance with what 'Abd al-Haqq said. He said in *at-Tawdheeh* that the second opinion is the *madhhab* of the majority, and this has also been stated by Muhammad ibn 'Abd as-Salam." Here end the words of al-Hattab.

Al-Hattab has also said: "Section: if he puts his hand into (various) receptacles containing oil and then finds a dead mouse in the first, al-Burzuli has narrated from Ibn al-Harith that the consensus is that the first three are (rendered) impure, while there are two opinions as to the fourth and thereafter. Ibn 'Abd al-Hakam is of the opinion that they are impure – even if the (mouse) is dead. Ibn Muhriz has related that this was narrated to him from Malik and his followers. Asbagh said: 'The (mouse) is pure.' Ibn 'Arafa said: 'The question as to whether some impurity is rendered impure is dependent upon the question as to whether the original source of impurity can be removed by water which is not absolutely pure itself.' Al-Burzuli said: 'This is how the matter was dealt with by us: when the measurer measured out (the oil) from an (earthenware) jar he left some over in it. Then he measured out further jars and other containers and only then returned to the first and empty it, whereupon he found a dead mouse in it. A *fatwa* was given that the (receptacle used) immediately after the first was impure because the (traces of the) impurity remained in the measuring instrument, and that (oil taken from the receptacles) after the first could be sold – after informing (the buyer of what had happened). This is because nothing (of the actual physical impurity) remained and any judgement as to its impurity (would be theoretical). The most evident judgement regarding the two opinions mentioned by Ibn Harith is that it is pure because one would (normally – given the circumstances) suppose that the source of impurity has been removed. This is affirmed by the saying of Khalil (in *al-Mukhtasar*) which will be mentioned below, namely: 'If the source of the impurity is removed by means of (water) which is not absolutely pure that which comes into contact with the place (from which the impurity) was removed is not rendered impure.'"

CASE IN QUESTION: Al-Mawwaq said, regarding the saying of Khalil 'use of that which has been rendered impure is itself not impure': "Ashhab has narrated that Malik was asked – regarding the person who has an ulcerous sore – as to whether it may be washed with urine or wine and he replied: 'If it is cleaned with water, then this is the best for I strongly dislike wine (to be used in) any matter.' Someone then said to him: '(Does this mean that) urine is less reprehensible according to you?' He said: 'Yes.' He was then asked: 'What is your view of the person who drinks human urine to treat himself (medicinally) with it?' He replied: 'I do not consider this (to be a good thing) but there is no harm in drinking the urine of cows and camels.' Then I asked him: 'Is it permitted to drink the urine of any (animal) whose meat (one is permitted) to eat?' He replied: 'This (judgement) is from you and I have not said this to you – rather (I mentioned) the urine of cattle, sheep and goats (*al-an'am*).' Ibn Rushd considered the washing of wounds with urine as less reprehensible (than the drinking of urine) and he permitted the use of urine for washing wounds basing his analogy on the (fact that the) use of the skin of a dead animal is permitted in the sunna; and he forbids treatment by way of the drinking of urine – discriminating in this narration between the drinking of the urine of animals (in general) and those animals used as livestock whose meat may be consumed. (He adds that) if through the use of analogy equal weight may be accorded to the permissibility of drinking it medicinally or to its non-use then the judgement is that it is pure according to him. Al-Baji said: 'There is difference of opinion regarding the use of an impure thing externally – Malik has permitted it while Ibn Sahnun has forbidden it but as for eating or drinking an (impurity) this is forbidden from both aspects.'" Here ends the discussion of al-Mawwaq. In the *al-Mi'yar*, the following is narrated of Muhammad ibn Marzouq from *an-Nawadir*: "Sahnun said: 'The wounded person can treat his wound with the bone of animals if the latter have been ritually slaughtered but he is not to treat it with wine, human bone, or that of pig, or (with bone) from a carcass (of an animal not slaughtered ritually), nor with excrement of animals which are not permitted to be eaten. If he finds an old bone and he does not know whether it is the bone of a sheep or pig then there is no harm in it – unless it is (found in a) battleground and is known to contain a lot of human bones or a place known to contain a lot of pig bones, in which case it is not correct (to use them).'" Here ends the discussion in *al-Mi'yar*.

USEFUL POINT: Ibn 'Arafa said that Ibn Rushd said: "Washing with honey, (sour) milk and bran, and a woman brushing her hair with a sprinkling of perfumed water concocted with dates and raisins – the narrations detail the reprehensibility of their (use) not there prohibition." What is meant by 'washing one's hand with bran' is drying it with it, as one (of the *'ulama*) has explained).

USEFUL POINT: al-Ubbi said, commenting on Muslim where he relates 'If a morsel of solid food falls (to the ground), then one should pick it up, wipe off whatever dirt might be adhering to it and eat it – and not leave it for shaytan' saying: "Here is a recommendation to eat a morsel (of food) which falls (to the ground) as long as any dirt adhering to it is removed – even if it falls on a place which is ritually impure and it becomes itself impure; if it is not possible to clean it, then it should be fed to animals and not left for shaytan."

USEFUL POINT: al-Munawi narrates in his *Kabir* from *al-Jami' as-Saghir*: "Important benefit: Abu Ya'la has related from al-Hasan ibn 'Ali, may Allah be pleased with him, that he entered the place for doing *wudu'* and he came across a morsel (of food) lying on the ground – or he said 'a chunk of bread lying in a gutter used for excrement and urine.' He wiped the dirt from it, washed it clean and then handed it to his young slave boy saying: 'Remind me about it after I have made *wudu'*.' When he had made *wudu'* he said: 'Give it to me.' The young slave boy said: 'I have eaten it.' He said: 'Go, you are now free.' He said: 'How is this?' He said: 'I have heard Fatima relate from her father, the Messenger of Allah, may the peace and blessings of Allah be upon him, saying: "Whoever picks up a morsel (of food) or piece of bread from a gutter used for excrement or urine and wipes off the dirt, washes it well and eats it, then before it reaches his stomach he will be forgiven" and I was not (placed here) to employ a man of the Garden.'" Al-Bayhaqi said: 'The men he (cites in the chain of narration) are trustworthy.'

Section: Concerning *Wudu'*

The obligation of *wudu'* is an imperative and indispensable (part of) that which is known from the deen, and there is no difference of opinion (as to the fact that) anyone who denies this is *kafir* – although there is a difference of opinion as to those who abandon it (without actively denying it). The majority (of the *'ulama*) consider that such (a person) is a *fasiq* – corrupt – but not a *kafir*; however, the *madhhab* of Ahmad ibn Hanbal and the opinion of Ibn Habib and Ibn 'Abd al-Hakam from amongst the Malikis is that he is *kafir*. It is also the *madhhab* of a considerable number of the people of hadith – this is held to by Zarruq in both his commentaries, namely that on *al-Risala* and *al-Waghleesiya*. It is also related by Ibn Hajar al-Haytami in *Sharh al-Arba'in* from the Hanafis that they consider such a person as *kafir* although they do not consider the person who abandons the *salat* as *kafir*. On this basis it would thus be graver (to deny the obligation of *wudu'* than leave off doing the *salat*). The relevant text, that is from al-Haytami, occurs in (the Section) regarding matters which indicate (someone's) belittling of the Legislator of the *shari'ah*, on whom be peace and blessings – that is how persons commit *kufr* by many of the things they say or do for they reveal their denigration of the deen – like doing the *salat* deliberately without *wudu'*.

Regarding the *Sahih* hadith 'Allah does not accept the *salat* of someone who is ritually impure until he makes *wudu'* Ibn Hajar al-Haytami said in *Sharh al-Arba'in*: "Lack of acceptance implies a lack of correctness" as (demonstrated) in (the hadith) "Allah does not accept the *salat* of any of you if the state of impurity comes upon him (*ahdatha*) – until he does *wudu'*"; and one may interpret 'acceptance' here as the dependance of the desired goal (i.e. *salat*) upon something else (i.e. *wudu'*); however this is not always the case: in (the hadith which declares that) 'Allah does not accept the *salat* of the runaway slave, the wife whose husband is angry with her, the person who goes to a fortune teller and the drinker of wine for forty days' acceptance is understood as reward. There is also that related by Ahmad: 'Whoever prays in clothes which costing ten dirhams, one dirham of which is haram, then his *salat* is not accepted of him.' One differentiates between the two uses (to which the hadith may be put to) according to the outward evidence; but as for a basic acceptance of anything as such (*min haithu dhatihi*), then negation of it does not necessarily entail a negation of its correctness, even if (by the rules of logic) any affirmation of it, necessarily entails an affirmation of its correctness." Here end the words of al-Haytami

REMARK: al-Hattab said: "*Wudu'* in the *shari'ah* has four divisions: obligatory, recommended, permitted, and forbidden. Thus the *wudu'* of each individual is part of an act of worship: it is incorrect to perform any act (of worship) except in a state of purity, like the *salat* or the *tawwaf*, (for example), both with respect to the obligation and supererogatory aspects of these two (acts of worship); also with respect to the touching of a *mus-haf* of the Qur'an, although it is a sunna in the case of touching the Qur'an as it is not a (punishable) wrong action to omit the (*wudu'*) – and there is a consensus as to this. However, doing any of these things deliberately without ritual purification is an act of disobedience and the supererogatory (act in question) has no validity, although it is not necessary to make it up. However, Shaykh Sa'd ad-Deen considers as *kafir* the person who does the *salat* without being in a state of purification." Here end the words of Muhammad ibn al-Hattab.

Sa'd ad-Deen is in accord with what al-Haytami has transmitted from the Hanafis as to the *kufr* of the person who abandons *wudu'*; however, in *al-Mi'yar*, (he states that) ascribing (the narration) to Abu Hanifa – namely that he considers it *kufr* to abandon *wudu'* – is not correct; even if one were to accept it as correct, it must be interpreted so that it harmonises with the *sahih* (hadith) indicating (that such an act) does not entail *kufr*.

USEFUL POINT: the author of the *adh-Dhahab al-Ibreez* said, regarding the words of Allah, exalted is He, '*especially the middle salat*'[1] that the following hadith has been related by ath-Tha'labi from al-Qurtubi: "He commanded that one of the slaves of Allah be whipped a hundred times in the grave and the latter did not cease to ask Allah, exalted is He, and call on Him until the (whipping) was reduced to one (lash). When he and the grave were engulfed with fire he asked: 'Why did You have me whipped?' He replied: 'You prayed the *salat* without being in a state of purification and you passed by a person being wronged and did not help him."

In al-Munawi's *al-Kabir li'l-Jami' as-Saghir* there is something similar related at the point of his commentary on the following narration: "There is no man who abandons another Muslim in a place where his honour is being degraded

---

[1] Al-Baqara – the Cow: 236.

and his esteem is being violated but that Allah will abandon him in a place where he would wish for His help and there is no one who helps a Muslim in a place where his honour is being degraded and his esteem violated but that Allah, exalted is He, will help him in a place where he would wish for His help" – or however the exact wording of the hadith is.

Among the narrations regarding the threat (of punishment awaiting) the person who abandons helping the person being wronged is that in at-Ṭabarani from Ibn 'Umar in a *marfu'* tradition: "A man was buried in his grave and two angels came to him saying: 'We are going to hit you once' and he asked 'Why are you going to hit me?' Then they hit him one time and his grave filled with fire. They then left him and when he awoke his fear left him and he asked 'Why did you hit me?' and they replied: 'You performed the *salat* without being in a state of purity, and you passed by a man who was being wronged and you did not help him'" – or whatever the exact wording of the hadith. I do not guarantee that every hadith I relate in this book is recorded with the exact wording of the hadith.

The Obligations of Wudu'

$$\text{فَرَائِضُ الْوُضُوءِ سَبْعٌ وَهِي}$$

$$\text{دَلْكٌ وَفَوْرٌ نِيَّةٌ فِي بَدْئِهِ}$$

57 The obligations of the *wudu'* are seven in number and they are rubbing (the water over the skin), (performing the various acts of *wudu'*) one after the other without interruption, and intention at the beginning.

AHMAD Mayyara said: "It is said that the word *wudu'* refers to the action (of washing oneself) but that when spelled *wadu'* it refers to the water (used for this washing); but it has also been said that both have the same meaning. Ibn Daqeeq al-'Eid: "If we say that it is spelled *wadu'* and refers to the water (used), then there is a difference of opinion as to whether it refers to water in general or refers specifically to that with which one has made or will make *wudu'*.

In the text (of Ibn 'Ashir) it is spelled *wudu'* because what is intended here is the act (of washing) and the *hamza* has been omitted (in the Arabic) for the sake of the rhythm (of the metre in which Ibn 'Ashir's poem is composed); the *wa-hiya* (in the Arabic text) is pronounced *wa-hiy*, that is, with a *sukun* over the *ya'* (as it falls at the end of the line and can be shortened) as a stop (*li'l-waqf*). The (author) mentions that the obligations are seven (in number), the first of them, the rubbing (of the skin with water). (Khalil) said in his *Tawdih*: "There are three opinions regarding the rubbing – the well known of these that it is obligatory; the second (related) from Ibn 'Abd al-Hakam who rejects that it is absolutely necessary; the third, (that it is) indispensable – not in itself, but to ensure that the water reaches (all over) such that if the water does indeed reach (everywhere) – having remained for some time (on the skin by immersion) – it is acceptable. One (of the *'ulama*) considers that this (latter view) is based on (the opinion of those who hold) that the rubbing can be omitted.

Ibn al-'Arabi (said): "It is permitted to get someone else to pour the water on to the limbs (washed) in the *wudu'* but it is not permitted to have someone rub it in unless the person doing the *wudu'* is ill and unable to do it himself. Note that if one rubs one foot with the other and does not wipe it with one's hand, then according to the *madhhab* of Ibn al-Qasim this is acceptable; and the well-known (position) is that the rubbing is obligatory in itself. Ibn Abi Zayd: 'If a man in a state of *janaba* rubs himself after having completely immersed himself in water, then this is acceptable.' One of the Shaykhs of 'Abd al-Haqq said: 'If there is an impurity on his body then it is not accepted as the (impurity) is not removed unless the pouring of the water is directly accompanied by rubbing – (for otherwise) a patch (of skin) would remain (untouched by the water).'"

SECTION: al-Hattab said that Zarruq said in his *Sharh al-Irshad*: "What 'rubbing' actually means is passing one's hand (over the skin simultaneously) with water – according to the opinion of al-Qabisi, and following the (pouring of the water), according to Ibn Abi Zayd, and this is the well-known (opinion)."

Ibn Farhun, commenting on the words of Ibn Hajib 'secondly, the washing of one's face is done by applying water to it and rubbing': "this should be understood as dependent upon the application of the water – thus implying that the rubbing is conditional upon the simultaneous pouring of the water and that it is not acceptable if done following the pouring. This is the reasoning outlined in the *madhhab* of al-Qabisi – as opposed to the *madhhab* of Ibn Abi Zayd which states that it is enough if (done) following the pouring of the water – and this is the correct (teaching) for (otherwise) it would entail considerable difficulty."

SECTION: He has also said that Sayyidi Zarruq said in his commentary on the *Risala's* words regarding washing one's face 'He should apply the (water) to his face, performing the washing with both hands' that this means he should rub them firmly (*dalkan wasatan*) (over his face) together with the water or making use of the (water applied before the rubbing) which remains (on his face), ensuring that it reaches (the whole surface of the face); and it is not necessary that he remove insignificant (amounts of) dirt, but rather what is clearly manifest and which would prevent the water from having direct contact with the (surface of the) limb (in question) – that it is only necessary that he remove dirt which is of a definite, tangible nature (*mutajassid*)." Ibn Sha'ban said in *az-Zahi*: "(What is meant by) washing is passing both hands over one's face – not just applying water to it. He does not have to rub his face – even if he is able (to do so) for passing his hand over his face, however lightly, is acceptable as long as the word 'washing' applies. If he cleans his face of any dirt (beforehand), then this is all the better – as unlike the rest of the body, it is not usually protected (by clothing)."

SECTION: Muhammad ibn al-Hattab has also said – after a lengthy discussion regarding the (manner in which) water is applied to the face: "What is clear from this is that application of water to the limb, that is ensuring it reaches the (whole surface of the) limb is obligatory, according to the consensus; however, it is not obligatory that the water be brought (to the face) with one's hands. As for the person in a state of *junuba* who immerses himself in a river, there is a consensus (that this is permitted); as for when rainwater falls on those limbs which are washed for the *wudu'*, or on his body or he plunges his foot into water (and then does *wudu'* with it), then the prevalent opinion (is that it is permitted). This (latter) is the *madhhab* of Ibn al-Qasim as understood from the *Mudawwana* and other (sources) – except in the matter of wiping over one's head for it is not possible to wipe it with the wetness already on it for it would be as if the (head) were doing the wiping – rather than being the thing wiped, and Allah, exalted is He, knows best."

As for (Ibn 'Ashir's) saying 'one after the other without interruption', the commentator said: "The second obligation is – as Ibn Bashir said – that each action follows on from the other without a break; however, Ibn Hajib (said that) 'a minor break is excusable, even if it is deliberate.' The well-known opinion is that this (consecutiveness) is obligatory when one is aware (of this while performing the various actions) and when one is able. Ibn Rushd said: 'It is a sunna and is incumbent upon him; if, however, he interrupts the *wudu'* out of forgetfulness then this (lapse) is excused; if, (omitted) deliberately (however) then he remains under an obligation to repeat (the *wudu'*) – however much time elapses – because of his disparaging attitude.' Ibn al-Qasim said that Ibn 'Abd al-Hakam said[1]: 'He does not have to do this again.' If we assume this (consecutiveness) is an obligation, then there are three different opinions if it is interrupted: that the person's *wudu'* is annulled if the interruption is deliberate; that it is not annulled if out of forgetfulness; and thirdly, as stated in *al-Mudawwana* – and this is the well-known statement – that it is annulled if a deliberate decision was made, but not if out of forgetfulness or incapacity (through lack of water), and that if the interruption was out of forgetfulness then one should carry on where one left off irrespective of whether the time elapsed is long or not.'"

Khalil said: "One should always carry on where one has left off if one forgets

---

1 This is from the original text of the *Mayyara*: in Shinqeeti's text it reads 'Ibn al-Qasim and Ibn abd al-Hakam have said.'

(to do it consecutively); if incapable (of continuing one should carry on where one has left off), as long as the time elapsed is not long, that is, as long as the limbs have not dried and the temperature is moderate." Muhammad ibn al-Hattab, commenting on (Khalil's) words 'even if incapable (of continuing) as long as the time elapsed is not long' says: "After he mentions the judgement regarding the person who forgets (to perform the various actions of the *wudu'*) consecutively, he mentions the judgement regarding the person who leaves off (its performance) because of incapacity – for example, when one runs out of water and goes to find some (more) and then resumes from where one has left off. The most evident (judgement) in this case is that (this hold true) irrespective of whether he prepares enough water for his (*wudu'*) and then it is spilt (for example), or it is stolen (from him) or he commences his *wudu'* with an amount he thinks is enough and then it becomes clear that it is not in fact enough. This then is the manifest meaning of the *Mudawwana*, according to al-Baji and his followers." Then al-Hattab follows this with quotations from al-Lakhmi and others: "If he prepares water and is sure it is enough but then it is spilt or stolen then he should resume where he left off even if a long time elapses." Then he says, that is al-Hattab – after a long discussion on the matter: "The most evident judgement from this is that the person who cannot (complete the *wudu'*) but who had prepared enough water for it – water which was then stolen, or spilt, unintentionally by himself or a third party, or he is compelled to interrupt his *wudu'* – then he should resume where he left off even if a long time elapses, like in the case of the person who forgets. (There is) no difference (of opinion) in this, according to some of them – that is, as it appears from the discussion of al-Lakhmi and Ibn Rushd, although according to others, it is the preferred and prevalent opinion. However, it would have been more fitting if in the *Mukhtasar* he had made an exception of this way (of understanding the nature of consecutiveness), and had narrated a difference of opinion in the matter – if the words of al-Baji, and whoever concurs with him, are given preference, that is in their interpreting the discussion of *al-Mudawwana* in an absolute manner.

SECTION: al-Hattab has also said that Ibn Farhun said: "The assessment of dryness is a fine matter – is it reckoned from the last action performed (of the elements of *wudu'*) or from the first limb? – thus if one washes one's face, hands and forearms and an interruption occurs and then one wipes one's head before the water on one's hands and forearms dries but after the water on his face dries – does this impair his (*wudu'*) or not?" Taqi ud-Deen said: "The manifest meaning of their discussion is that all is excusable and that as long as (the limbs) are (still) wet, then it is permitted to resume from where one left off."

SECTION: al-Hattab has also said: "There is no harm in an insignificant break even if deliberate." Al-Qadi 'Abd al-Wahhab said: "There is no difference of opinion in the *madhhab* on this matter." Then, after a long discussion he transmits from Ibn Farhun saying that an insignificant time is deemed the time in which the limbs of the *wudu'* have not dried – in the same manner as he had explained (above), that is, when water is removed (from the person doing *wudu'*) such that it is not enough (to complete it). Al-Hattab (continues by) saying: "This difference of opinion has been related by the author of *al-Jam'* from Ibn Harun at the point where he comments on Ibn al-Hajib's words 'a short interruption is excused': 'In my opinion, the drying of the limbs is not the criterion as is in the case of the person unable to obtain water. Rather, the (time allowed to lapse) is less than this because of his lack of excuse.'" I SAY: "This is the most evident (judgement) from the discussion of the people of the *madhhab*. However, what Ibn Farhun said is not immediately evident as he has rendered the incapacity (to obtain water) an acceptable excuse in the case of an interruption in the *wudu'* as long as the limbs have not dried. But a small break is excusable even if one has no excuse – so reflect upon this." Here ends the discussion of al-Hattab, and al-Khurshi has examined exhaustively the discussion of Ibn Farhun.

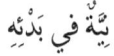

...and intention at the beginning

58 One makes the intention to remove an impurity, to perform an obligation, or to make permissible what was forbidden

INTENTION

Al-Hattab said that al-Qarafi said in *al-Dhakheera*: "It refers to a person's purpose or aim with his heart, that is, what he wants to do. It is a kind of resolution and will and is not classed as a branch of knowledge or *'aqida*. The difference between it and will is absolute in that will (*irada*) is connected to the action of someone else, for example, when a person wants forgiveness from Allah. It is also called appetite (*shahwa*) and is not called intention. The difference between intention and having resolve (*'azm*) is that the latter is having the determination to realise an action, while the former is a conscious perception on his part, is of a lesser intensity and precedes it. In *Kitab al-Umniyya* he said: "Will is connected to lending impetus to the action – that is towards that which will receive it – not to the action itself. Thus one may distinguish between our intent to *perform* the *salat* and our purpose regarding the same as an act of *qurba* (bringing us closer to Allah) or as a *fard* (obligation) or *ada'an* (carrying out any other kind of *salat*). Thus the part (of this consciousness) connected to the bringing into being and 'acquisition' (of the act) is called *irada* (will) while that which is connected to inclining the action to something that will accept it is called *niyya* (intention). Intention is also different from will from another aspect, namely the fact that intention is only connected to the action of the person making the intention while will is connected to the action of someone else – like when we desire the forgiveness of Allah and His *Ihsan*. As such (the will) is not of our doing.

Al-Munawi said that an-Nawawi said: "Intention is the purpose and determination of the heart" while al-Kirmani has refuted him saying: "It is the determination of the heart – for the mutakallamun say: 'The purpose and aim to perform an action is that which we find (already existing) within us at the moment of bringing it into being while determination and resolve precedes it. This latter is susceptible to becoming stronger or weaker – as opposed to aim and purpose. Thus the (mutakallimun) have distinguished between them from two aspects – and this interpretation of theirs is not correct."

SECTION: Al-Hattab said: "Neither the *wudu'* nor the *ghusl* of the *kafir* is correct, given the absence of real intention in his regard. However, this is not so in the case of the *dhimmi* woman who is compelled to perform the *ghusl* to purify from menstruation – given the right of her Muslim husband to this. This is because it is not permitted to have intercourse with a menstruating woman until after she has taken a *ghusl*, according to the well-known judgement." *At-Tawdih* (of Khalil): "If one should ask 'What is the benefit of compelling her make a *ghusl* when it is only acceptable when accompanied by intention – which in her case is not acceptable' then one answer which has been given is that the validity of the *ghusl* is only required if performed for the *salat* but when performed for intercourse – on account of the (Muslim) husband – then it is not. This is so because the husband is in a state of worship by means of the *ghusl* – undertaken on her part. This is not the case, however, regarding the acts of worship undertaken by the worshipper for someone else – for which the intention does not need to be made, like washing the dead, or washing the utensil which has been licked by a dog. The Muslim should not compel his *kafir* wife to make the *ghusl* to purify herself from her *janaba* as intercourse with a person in *janaba* is permitted."

BENEFITS: firstly he said in *al-Jami' as-Saghir*: "The best of actions is a genuine intention as hypocrisy cannot impinge upon this (genuine intention) and annul it. Malik ibn Dinar said: 'I saw a man making *tawaf* saying: "Just as you have accepted my four (previous) hajjs of me, so accept this hajj of me." I then said: 'How do you know that Allah has accepted them?' He replied: "For four years I used to make the intention each year to go on hajj and Allah knew of the (truth of the) intention on my part. I have now made the hajj this year but I fear lest it not be accepted of me. Then I realised that intention is the best of actions."

2. ash-Sha'rani said in *al-Mizan*: "I have heard Sayyidi 'Ali al-Khawwas, may Allah have mercy on him, say that the reality of intention is the resolve of the *mukallaf* to (perform) an action and (perform it) directly after (having the resolve). Whoever says that he can imagine the *mukallaf* performing an act of worship without an intention has not examined (the matter) properly – for if you were to say to a Hanafi while he is purifying himself 'What are you doing?' He would answer you: 'I am purifying myself.' Indeed if someone does not know what he was doing then he would not be (considered) a *mukallaf* by any means."

3. al-Hattab said that in the *Tawdih* he states: "Action is of three kinds. The first consists of pure worship, like the *salat* and there is a consensus that it is obligatory. The second includes exchange or compensation – like paying a debt, returning things entrusted or unlawfully taken – and the *ijma'* is that no intention is necessary, that is no intention of *taqarrub*, although if done there is more reward, like for example his making an intention to free himself of his liability, to fulfil Allah's, exalted is He, commands or to bring happiness to the person to whom the debt is owed; in this respect they have also said that an imam does not have to have the intention of being the imam but it is better for him so that he might obtain the excellence of this. The third is that which combines the two aspects, like the *zakat* or purification. Zakat has a meaning for the intellect, that is, acting kindly towards the poor and all the other categories (mentioned in *ayat* 60 of sura Tawba -Repentance). However, the fact that it becomes obligatory (when a) specific (minimum) amount (is reached) cannot be comprehended by the intellect. Likewise purification (*tahara*) can be comprehended by the intellect, namely the (aspect of) cleaning,

but the reason why it is done on specific limbs in a specific manner cannot be understood intellectually. Moreover there is a difference of opinion as to whether an intention is obligatory with respect to this (purification)."

4. ash-Shatibi said in *al-Muwafaqat*: "They are in agreement that customary acts (of daily life) do not need an intention. Actions undertaken (without this intention) in order to acquire something of this world are not diminished in value – such that if we suppose a man wants to marry in order to show off or in order that he be reckoned as one of the people of integrity (by his seeking sexual pleasure in marriage rather than outside it) or for some other purpose, then his marriage would be legitimate as the intention (to undertake it) for worship is not stipulated in the *shari'ah*."

5. al-Munawi said commenting on the hadith 'Actions are by intention...' – after having examined (other) matters extrapolated from this hadith: "Whoever expresses something which renders him thereby a *kafir* but then claims that this burst out of him impulsively then he is held responsible for it" – and this is the opinion of the majority, in opposition to some of the Malikis.

وَغَسْلُ وَجْهِ غَسْلُهُ الْيَدَيْنِ

وَمَسْحُ رَأْسٍ غَسْلُهُ الرِّجْلَيْنِ

59 (then) washes one's face, one's hands and forearms, wipes one's head, and washes one's feet

Mayyara said: "Washing the face is the fourth obligation. Ibn al-Hajib: 'The face is (taken to be) from where the hair normally grows until the end of the chin – the chin and the place where the turban sits being included but not the place where baldness (usually occurs); and from ear to ear, although it has also been said from cheek to cheek. It has also been said – with respect to the former – that this exclude the cheeks[1] while – with respect to the second – that it excludes what is covered in hair. 'Abd al-Wahhab is alone in (holding to the opinion) that what is between them is sunna."

In his *Tawdih* (Khalil) said: "The beard is the place where the two jawbones come together and the reason for our saying 'where the hair normally grows' is to convey that one should wash that (part) of the forehead covered in hair but that the bald headed (person) does not wash that (part of) his head which has become bald."

1 More correctly the part extending from the circuit of the eye to the part where the beard grows on either side of the face

By his words '...the face, from where the hair grows...' he has indicated the extent of the face length-wise, and by 'from ear to ear' the extent of the face in width. The author has (also) indicated its width by his words 'the obligation is to cover the place between of the ears' and Allah, exalted is He, knows best."

Ibn al-Hajib: "... and it is obligatory to rub (water into) the sparse hair – but not thick hair – of the beard or other places, even eye lashes. It is also said (that it is) (obligatory to rub water into) thick hair and that it is obligatory to wash the extended part of the beard, according to the most evident judgement. In the *Tawdih*: "Thin hair is that beneath which the skin may be seen while in the case of thick hair the skin cannot be seen. The beard is to be rubbed vigorously (*takhleel*) to ensure the water reaches the skin. According to the well-known opinion, it is not obligatory to rub water into thick hair during the *wudu'* as what is commanded to is 'the washing of the face' and the face (*wahj*) is 'what is (visible) in front of one' (*ma yuwajihu*).' However in the case of the *ghusl*, then particular attention should be taken – because Allah, exalted is He, says: '*If you are in a state of major impurity, then purify yourselves*'¹ and because the Messenger, may the peace and blessings of Allah be upon him, said: 'Under each hair, there is a major impurity, so wash the hair (thoroughly) and clean the skin.' The obligation, then, is to rub water into both sparse hair and thick hair (in the case of the *ghusl*). Ibn Yunus: 'He does not have to wash a wound which has healed or (a part of his body) covered by a fold of fat which has grown over it or because the person is by nature fat.'"

NOTICE: Zarruq said: "Among some general matters (one should know about) concerning *wudu'* is that pouring water over the face below the forehead invalidates (the *wudu'*) as does shaking one's hands before applying water to the face; striking the face with water – if done out of ignorance – is of no consequence." He has also said before this: "He should not splash water over his face with his hands, or sprinkle it – for both (indicate) ignorance."

Al-Hattab said: "What is meant by the 'skin being visible' is that it is visible to the person who addresses him; by *takhleel*, rubbing the water in so that it reaches the skin." I am narrating al-Hattab's explanation – although already mentioned above in the *Tawdih* – in order to stress it and fix it in the heart of the student.

After a long discussion, al-Hattab has also said regarding 'the face': "What may be understood from this is that the face extends lengthways from the place where the hair normally grows on the head, irrespective of whether this is on the forehead or the temples, to the end of the (beard on the) chin;

---

1 al-Ma'ida – The Table: 6

and in breadth, from ear to ear – excluding the two ligaments of the ears (*wataday al-udhun*); also (included in this definition of breadth is the area) of white (hairless skin) between the cheek and the ear and the lower part of the jawbone which juts out below the ears in the direction of the ears (*fi samt al-udhun*) – according to what one understands from the author of *at-Taraz*. However, al-Qadi 'Abd al-Wahhab excludes the white (hairless) patch between the temples and the ear as well as the outer jawbones below the ear and extending to the ear. However, it has already been explained above that the lower jaw bone is (accepted as) part of the face. Know too that the temples (*sudgh*) is the (area) between the eye and the ear – this is how he explains it in *al-Sihah*, and this is also how al-Fakihani also explains it in his *Sharh ar-Risala*. If this is so then what is below the protruding bone is part of the face and what is above it is part of the head. What they mean by saying that it is obligatory to wash the white (hairless) patch between the temples and the ear is the (area) below the protruding bone, and Allah knows best."

USEFUL POINT: in *al-Jami' as-Saghir* it says: "Allah has cursed the person who applies red colouring (to the skin of another) (*ghashira*) and the person who has this done (*maghshoura*)" and this is related by Ahmad from 'A'isha. Al-Haytami relates that "there are women (in the chain of narration) whom I do not recognise."

Al-Zamakhshari said: "*Al-ghashr* is that she treats her face with a red (powder) by crushing it on the skin and (leaving it) until it dries out to enhance the (natural) colour. There are (traditions relating) that it is absolutely forbidden."

Regarding his saying 'the washing of the hands and forearms' Mayyara said: "fifth: the hands and forearms should be washed up to the elbows, according to the well known opinion, and the author of the poem (Ibn 'Ashir) calls attention to the fact that the elbows are included in the washing." Khalil said, adding to his words 'the obligations of the *wudu*' are washing (the area) between one's ears': "...and his hands/forearms up to his elbows and what remains of his wrist if it has been amputated, likewise if the palm (of one's hand is attached) to the shoulder (because of a deformation) and rubbing water between the fingers, but not turning one's ring around."

Al-Mawwaq said that Ibn al-Qasim said: 'I do not consider that anyone should move his ring during the *wudu*'.' When he was asked: 'What if he cleans himself after defecating wearing it and Allah is mentioned on it?' he replied: 'It would be better were he to remove it. No one in the past used to be so cautious regarding such a thing and would not ask about it.' Ibn Rushd: 'There is no difference of opinion that whoever makes *wudu*' while a small amount of dough, tar or pitch adheres to his nails or to his forearms (then his *wudu'* is acceptable). In Zarruq's commentary on the *Risala* he says: "It is not necessary for the person making *wudu'* to remove a small amount of dirt, but rather whatever is clearly visible and which prevents the water from reaching the limb." Ibn 'Arafa has also related that one is excused a small patch of dough, pitch or tar which is adheres to the nail or forearms – transmitting this from Ibn Rushd, Abi Zayd and Ibn Abi Umaya, together with Muhammad ibn Dinar The literal meaning of the words of Ashhab together with the words of Ibn Qasim from his Shaykh is that (the *wudu'*) of the person who makes *wudu'* when he has ink on his hand is acceptable. This is supported by *at-Taraz* from the narration of Muhammad although he makes it conditional upon it (being permitted only in the case of) a writer. One of our Shaykhs has stipulated that (this is only permitted) when the (amount of ink is no more than a) fine (line or spot) and that it has not solidified (into a blob) – in the case of ink which has been (on his hand for) some time."

Mayyara said: "As for something other than a ring which prevents the water from reaching the limb, be it in connection with the hand, or the face or some other (part of the body), then this must be removed. If it is not, then the place (it covers) is (considered) a patch of unwashed skin (thereby invalidating the *wudu'*). Also included in this (legal) category, are the pieces of bone which archers and others place on their fingers, the (beauty) spots women adorn their faces and fingers with – when they are of definite thickness and consistency, the threads women use to braid their hair with, the henna, asafetida or other things (they use) on their hair which have a definite consistency, and dough, tar or wax or the like which sticks to their nails, forearms or elsewhere. If, however, the dough or the like is negligible, then there are two points of view. Ibn Rushd maintains that it is excusable. However both opinions are based on (cases where) it has already happened – as for commencing (application of such things), then they must be removed. Sulphate of ammonia (on the skin) is (considered) an unwashed patch (of skin) if it is seen to flake off; as to its being impure, there are differences of opinion based on whether or not its normal consistency has undergone an alteration. As for henna which has separated itself from the head and has not been washed out, one of the Shaykhs has related a contrary view to that permitting wiping over it. However he himself then tends to permit it saying: "Adding water after applying it to the limb is of no consequence."

USEFUL POINT: Mayyara has also said: "A person who from her navel downwards has the form of a woman and above the form of two persons should wash all four of her hands and forearms and should wipe her two heads; and it is permissible to have intercourse with her in marriage although 'Iyad has doubted this maintaining that they are sisters. Ibn 'Arafa said: 'The judgement should be that it is prohibited because of the conjoining of (two persons at) the place of intercourse.' 'Iyad has mentioned this in his *Mudarik* – at the point where he introduces (the section on) ash-Shafi'i saying: 'While I was travelling around searching for hadith in Yemen someone said to me: "Here there is a woman, from her middle downwards one person and above two separate bodies with four arms and two heads" and so I wanted to see her (for myself). However I did not deem it lawful so I asked her in marriage and had intercourse with her, and I found her as she had been described. I was able to witness how her two bodies[1] (coexisted), how it was that (the two pairs of hands) clapped each other, (how the two bodies) contended with each other and then reconciled each other; how both ate and both drank. Then I separated from her. When I returned after a period, I asked after her and was told that one of her bodies had died and her lower part had been bound with a strong chord and left until it withered away. Then it was cut off and buried. I then saw another person (like her) after this who was walking backwards and forwards on the road.' 'Iyad said: 'a legal uncertainty exists as to whether they are sisters.'"

NOTICE: One must be careful when making *wudu'* to wash the palms of the hand and make make sure one rubs the water in well for there are few who rub in as it should be done – out of absent mindedness or negligence.

As for his (Ibn 'Ashir) saying 'and the wiping of the head', Al-Hattab said: "Ibn al-Hajib said: 'Fourthly, the whole of the head – in the case of the man and woman – and whatever of her hair that hangs loosely should be wiped over. She does not have to undo her plaits. She should not wipe over henna or other than this. The commencement (of the wiping) is from where the face begins and its end is (when) the whole expanse of the skull (has been wiped). It has also been said (that one should wipe up) to the last place of normal hair growth on the nape of the neck and that if (only) part of it is wiped then it is unacceptable. (This latter opinion is) based on the (Qur'anic) text (which mentions the head – and therefore implies the whole of it). Ibn Maslama (said): 'Two thirds is acceptable' while Abu al-Faraj said: 'a third' and Ashhab said: 'the forelock', and it is also related of Ashhab (that) any (part of the head) whatsoever (is acceptable): 'If he does not cover the head all over it is acceptable if he cannot (reach) what there is no harm in leaving.' Al-Lakhmi and Muhammad ibn 'Abd as-Salam have said: 'There is no difference of opinion that one is instructed

---

1 Here the text reads 'two hands' and should read here two bodies in Mayyara's original

to (wipe) all the (head) in the first instance (*ibtadian*) and that the difference of opinion exists with respect to those who restrict (what should be wiped) to part of the head.' Muhammad ibn 'Abd as-Salam said: 'One of my Shaykhs used to relate from one of the Shaykhs of Andalusia that the difference of opinion is regarding which part (of the head) in the first instance (is being referred to), although I have not seen this (opinion) from other than him."

As for a (woman's) plaits, it is not obligatory for her to undo them – because of the difficulty involved were she to undertake this. In *at-Tawdih* (Khalil states): 'Plaits which may be wiped over are those (made) with a little thread; if a lot (is used) then it is not permitted to wipe (over them) because the threads would then be in the way.' Al-Baji: "Likewise, if she has increased her hair (in volume) by means of wool or (added other) hair (to it), it is not acceptable to wipe over it as these (things) would prevent (here from wiping it) properly." Ibn Yunus: "If a man plaits (the hair on) his head, it is permitted that he wipe over it like a woman (does) – although al-Balnasi has related in *Sharh ar-Risala* that is not permitted a man to plait the hair on his head." Ibn Abi Zayd: "She should insert her hands beneath her plaits of hair when bringing her hands back while wiping."

Then he says: "Notice: He has mentioned in *an-Nawadir* that the hair of the temples is included in the wiping – (and by this) he means what is above the bone."

NOTICE: It is obligatory to wipe the white (hairless) patch between the ears and the head. Whoever leaves it out has left out a part of the head. This has been stated by al-Hattab and az-Zurqani – and the latter has added (a further text) to this. "Benefits: included in (what counts as) the head is the bare patch above the ears, (that is) in addition to the bare patch (immediately) above the ligament. One should wipe all over the head with fresh water, and it is *makruh* to do it with other than this – like, for example, the wetness from his beard – for (what is required here is water) which has not changed by having been used to remove impurity. If he does wipe (with water already used for the beard, for example) or he does not wipe the whole (of his head) then it is preferred that he repeat (the action). If we were to instruct a woman to wipe all her head she would leave off doing the *salat*; and were she to pray – having wiped (only) part of it it – then this would be acceptable as performing an act of worship about which there is a difference of opinion is better than not doing it (at all) – this is what 'Uthman al-'Arabi has decided. In the discussion of Zarruq there is benefit. It may well be that imitation (*taqlid*) in this is better; or that one should regard (the wiping) as a matter in which it is permitted to forego all the (various) conditions. This is different from leaving off part of what is obligatory for a reason other than necessity – out of laziness, for example..".

In Ahmad az-Zarruq's commentary on the *Risala*, he said: "Our Shaykh 'Abdallah al-Qouri, may Allah have mercy on him, used to say: 'I do not give a *fatwa* to the women regarding the wiping over henna for if I were to forbid them this they would leave off doing the *salat* immediately. If it is a matter of either (having them) leaving off doing the *salat* or doing it on the basis of a point of dispute then accepting this difference of opinion takes priority – so examine this.'"

In an-Nafrawi's commentary on the *Risala* it reads: "Al-imam Ashhab said: 'It is enough to wipe over part of the head – even if it is only the forelock.' Ibn al-Faraj said: 'A third is acceptable.' Ibn Musalama said: 'Two thirds is acceptable and the difference of the *umma* is a mercy. A woman might leave off doing the *salat* because of the difficulty of wiping over the whole of her head but would perform it if we instruct her to wipe over part of it. It is obligatory for her husband to threaten her – even by striking her – if he thinks that this will result in her carrying it out. If she still does not do it; then she should follow one of those (above mentioned) Shaykhs as performance of an act of worship, even if based on a weak opinion, is better than leaving off doing it.'"

USEFUL POINT: It has been narrated in the *Sahih*: "Allah has cursed the woman who attaches (something to her hair), a woman who performs tattoos and the person who allows himself to be tattooed." Al-Munawi said: "Al-Qurtubi said: 'The word *wasal* means both to attach and to increase (volume of the hair).'"

Then he says after a discussion (of other matters): "Not included in the prohibition is binding the hair with coloured silk, anything which does not resemble hair and whatever does not increase it in volume." This has also been stated by al-Munawi in the first part of his commentary on the *al-Jami.*'

USEFUL POINT: In *al-Jami' as-Saghir* of as-Suyuti it related: "If you see those who stack up (their hair) on their heads like the humps of camels then inform them that their *salat* is not accepted of them as long as they are like this", and the narration: "They will not enter the Garden" or whatever the precise text is. I remember what al-Munawi says in his *Kabir* on this subject, regarding the words 'If you see those who stack up (their hair)' – namely: "…that is, who elevate their hair by means of wadding, bands and veils until it becomes like turbans or camels humps." Ibn al-'Arabi said: "This refers to her padding up her hair so that someone seeing her thinks it is all hair" and this is forbidden, and for this reason he said: 'Inform them that as long as they do this their *salat* will not be accepted.' To judge the (*salat* of the) person who prays in clothes which he has acquired unlawfully as valid is preferable than this (case regarding piled-up hair) – for the person who performs the (*salat* in this state) has committed one forbidden action, that is taking something unlawfully, but such (women) have committed several forbidden actions, namely imitating men, wastefulness, conceit and more besides. This (hadith) is among the signs of his prophecy, may the peace and blessings of Allah be upon him, as he informed of a (custom) not apparent (in the society of the day but) which came into being and became prevalent. As for the narration 'They will not enter the Garden' Qadi 'Iyad said: "This means that they will not enter it, and would not encounter its breezes if they were to enter it." Ibn al-'Arabi: "Women should flatten the (hair of their) heads, especially, when going out and if their hair is abundant they should wash it and not allow it to appear voluminous. If a woman has some pain in her head and she adds more veiling to it (for this reason), then this is not included in this prohibition and there is no harm in this for her. Rather there is harm for the person who looks at her and thinks this (of her)."

وَالْفَرْضُ عَمَّ مَجْمَعَ الأُذْنَيْنِ

وَالْمِرْفَقَيْنِ عَمَّ وَالْكَعْبَيْنِ

60 It is obligatory to cover up to the juncture (– with the face –) of one's ears (when washing), and up to (and including) the elbows and the ankles.

That is, the obligation mentioned above is to cover the whole of (the area of) the ears, and the (area) adjacent to the head and adjacent to the face, that is, the cheeks of the face, is included in this, according to the well known opinion – irrespective of whether the person is bearded or not. Regarding the hands and forearms, then this is understood (to mean) up to (and including) the elbows and the elbows (which he mentions explicitly), and the same applies for the ankles of the feet, according to the most well-known opinion.

خَلِّلْ أَصَابِعَ الْيَدَيْنِ وَشَعَرْ

وَجْهٍ إِذَا مِنْ تَحْتِهِ الْجِلْدُ ظَهَرْ

61 (and) to rub between the fingers and the hair of the face if the skin is visible beneath it

'Ali ibn 'Abd as-Sadiq: "It is obligatory to rub in water between the fingers, according to the well-known opinion. It is not obligatory for a woman to remove gold or silver signet-rings – or in the case of a man, his silver signet-rings. This (judgement) also applies to the *ghusl* as it is (stated) in *at-Tawdih*. Anything other than this annuls the (*wudu'*) if it prevents (water) reaching the hand or forearm, as do (things like) dough, candle wax, an (ordinary, non-signet) ring worn on the finger, bracelets or a gold signet ring in the case of a man – but not ink, although some have stipulated that (it is excusable) when it forms (only a) thin (film on the skin) and does not have the thick consistency (of ink which has dried on the hand) after some time has elapsed. In *at-Taraz* it is stipulated that this is (applicable only) in the case of the writer (who habitually uses ink)."

Examine his words: 'bracelets and signet rings' together with the words of al-Amir: "Included in the (term) 'rings' – which need not be removed – are women's bracelets." So examine which of the two sayings is the stronger. It may be that Ibn 'Abd as-Sadiq's saying '(in the case) of the man' refers to his saying 'bracelets and signet rings.' Then Ibn 'Abd as-Sadiq continues: "(There is a difference of opinion) as to whether a thorn in one's hand or forearm should be extracted or not and whether – if extracted – the place (it was in) should be washed. If one's nail folds over (and covers) part of the tip of the finger and prevents it (from being washed), then it is obligatory to wash what is beneath it – this Dawud al-Laqqani has stated in *Sharh al-'Ashmawiya*. As for any dirt beneath it, al-Jazuli said: 'I have not seen any text on the subject except that some have said that 'cutting one's nails is a part of *fitra* – lest it become a place where dirt gathers and becomes a place which remains unwashed.'"

'Abd al-Baqi az-Zurqani said, commenting on the words of Khalil 'and you should not repeat (the washing in the place where the) nails are clipped': "... (this applies) even if they are long such that they are not folded over (the skin) – as long as no dirt is attached to them which covers part of the fingers. If they are long and dirt is attached to them and this dirt covers (part of) the finger or the (nail) is folded over such that it covers part of the tip of the finger, then it is obligatory to cut them and wash what is beneath them." This is (stated) in Ibn 'Arafa (who argues that it is) because it covers up a part (of the finger) which it not usually (covered by the nail) – as opposed to the first which is covering the part (of the finger) it normally covers. Thus (in the former example) it is not necessary to clip the (nail) or to remove any dirt beneath it; indeed to remove would be (an indication that) one was (too) absorbed (in the matter) and would be (from the) whispering (of shaytan). Moreover it is contrary to what the majority of the right-acting *salaf* practice. However, this does not apply when the (nails) are inordinately long – in which case it is obligatory to remove any dirt beneath them – as al-Ubbi said. This is what is stipulated in the words of the poet in the *Muqaddima* of Ibn Rushd:

If you omit to remove the dirt from under your nails
   You are at liberty to do so – for it is not a fault.

Here end the words of az-Zurqani.

Al-Hattab said that al-Ubbi said in *Sharh Muslim* during the discussion of what determines whether the nails should be washed: "If there is something clinging to the nails – however much it may be – preventing the water from reaching the skin, then this is excused as long as they are not unusually long.

Az-Zarruq said, commenting on the words of the *Risala* 'one must rub water into the fingers and whatever (dirt) is beneath the ends of the nails acting as a barrier (to the water reaching the skin) if they are long': "…that is, if they are unusually long."

He has also said: "As for ink, the author of *at-Taraz* has considered it an exception – with respect to the question of 'that which prevents (water from reaching the skin)': 'SECTION: the question poses itself that if it is not acceptable to wipe over something which prevents (water from reaching the skin) and it is something which cannot be avoided or removed – then is it excusable (to wipe over it)? And is the obligation (to wipe over) transferred to this thing preventing (the water reaching the skin) as in the case of a (finger) nail which is covered in necessity? Malik said in *al-Mudawwana* – regarding someone who does *wudu'* when he has ink on his hand and only notices this after doing the *salat* – that there is no harm in this if he had passed water over the ink.' Then he has added: '…if it was the person who was writing' – as if the person writing could not avoid this, which is not so in the case of someone who is not a scribe. His saying 'if he had passed water over the ink' is clear proof that he accords ink the (same) status as the (skin) beneath it. If he had said 'ink is not something which prevents (water from reaching the skin)' then it would have the same legal status as something used to dye like henna – in which case we would argue that this is not so for henna may be removed while its effect remains – as opposed to ink. If it were not a barrier then it would have no meaning to stipulate that that the person (doing *wudu'*) be a scribe. This he has transmitted from *an-Nawadir* from Ibn al-Qasim in *al-Majmu'a* in the following text: 'Ibn al-Qasim said that whoever does *wudu'* with ink on his hand then there is no harm in this.' Then he transmits the above discussion of Ibn 'Arafa where he describes washing one's hands – namely: 'One of our

Shaykhs has stipulated that it be a thin (film of ink) and that it should not have become thick in consistency, that is (that it not be) ink (which has been) used some time before.' Then he said: 'It appears that what is stipulated by one of the Shaykhs mentioned by Ibn 'Arafa is different from what is mentioned by the author of *at-Taraz*.'"

NOTICE: He said in *Ghayat al-Amani*: "Al-Aqfahisi said: 'The nature of *takhleel*, according to the *fuqaha*', is rubbing in water between the fingers from the back (of the hands) – as doing it from the (side of the) palm would be (considered) *tashbeek* – an inserting the fingers into one another – (which is) disliked; however, in the case of the feet (it is done) from below (that is from the soles of the feet).' Yusuf ibn 'Umar said: '*Takhleel* is inserting the fingers together and in the case of the feet, from below (that is from the soles).'"

سُنَنُهُ السَّبْعُ ابْتَدَا غَسْلِ الْيَدَيْنْ

وَرَدُّ مَسْحِ الرَّأْسِ مَسْحُ الْأُذُنَيْنْ

62   The sunnas are seven in number: one begins by washing each hand, (then) one wipes one's head from the back (to the front) and ears

Having finished with the obligations (of *wudu*'), he goes on to state that the sunnas are seven in number.

1. One begins by washing the hands three times before immersing them in the receptacle (containing the water) – and this is the well-known opinion, although it has also been said that it is (only) recommended. As for it being an act of worship the wisdom of which we are not able to discern – and this is the opinion of Ibn al-Qasim – or an (act containing) rational meaning, (namely, for reasons of) cleanliness – and this view is that of Ashhab – there are two views. In *at-Tawdih* he says: "If (treated as) an act of worship then one should wash one's hands if one becomes impure (again – *man ahdatha*) while making the *wudu*'; if one's body is clean, he requires an intention and should wash them separately. If (it is considered the act is) for reasons of cleanliness, then the opposite to all this (is required)."

The principle upon which the washing of one's hands is based is that saying of the Prophet, may the peace and blessings of Allah be upon him: "If one of you awakens from sleep, then he should wash his hands three times before immersing them in the receptacle for none of you knows where his hands have been while asleep." This stipulation of three times indicates an act of worship and the giving of the reason that 'none of you knows where his hands have been while asleep' indicates cleanliness. The instruction in the hadith is not meant as an obligation because the Prophet, may the peace and blessings of Allah be upon him, replied to the person who asked him about *wudu'*: 'Do *wudu'* as Allah has commanded', thereby referring him to the *ayat* 'When you get up to do salat, wash your faces…'¹ in which there is no mention of washing the hands (prior to beginning the *wudu'*), or rinsing out the mouth, or inhaling water into the nostrils. Thus the nature of the *ayat* is one of instruction, and if something obligatory is not mentioned in an *ayat*, the Prophet, may the peace and blessings of Allah be upon him, would have informed (us) of it for it is not permitted to delay explanation (of something) once the obligation exists.'

2. The wiping – from the back of the head to the front – Ibn 'Arafa: "Among the sunna of the wiping is returning the hands from the (first wiping from the front to back) by bringing them back from the back to where one began." 'Abd al-Baqi az-Zurqani: "This is sunna as long as it is done with the wetness remaining from the obligatory wiping (from front to back) – otherwise it is not prescribed as a sunna." Al-Hattab: "It is disliked that one do it again with new water as Ibn al-Hajib and others have made clear."

3. The wiping of the ears both externally and internally – such that one wipes the external (part) with the thumb and the internal part with his two index fingers, placing them in the cavity of the ear. Ibn Habib: "He does not need to wipe over every fold of the (ears)." Al-Lakhmi: "The wiping of the cavity of the ear is an agreed sunna." 'Abd al-Baqi az-Zurqani has stated that this means – as al-Mawwaq said: "The wiping of the ear cavities is a separate sunna, in addition to the wiping of both sides of the ears."

مَضْمَضَةٌ اسْتِنْشَاقٌ اسْتِنْثَارُ

تَرْتِيبُ فَرْضِهِ وَذَا الْمُخْتَارُ

63 (then) one rinses one's mouth, sniffing up water into the nose, blowing out (and) performs the obligatory elements in order – this is the preferred (judgement)

4. Rinsing of the mouth: water is introduced into the mouth, rolled from side to side and spat out. 'Abd al-Baqi az-Zurqani: "If he swallows it, then he is not fulfilling the sunna, according to the preferred opinion of two; and likewise if he opens his mouth and discharges it without the appearance or sound of spitting – as if silently chewing food – for this is a *bid'a*."

1 Ma'da – the Table:

5 & 6. Sniffing up water and blowing out – that is, drawing up water into his nose and then ejecting it with his breath while holding (his nose) with his fingers. One should exert oneself in doing this – although not in the case of the fasting person. Malik disliked it if a person did not place (the fingers of) his hand on his nose – as recorded by Ibn Rushd: "(He disliked it) because, by placing the (fingers of his) hand (on his nose) he prevents the water he has sniffed up from running over his nose and beard."

SECTION: al-Hattab said: "As for the person who leaves off doing these two things deliberately, that is the sniffing up water and blowing it out (again), and who prays with this *wudu'*, then there are three opinions regarding his *salat*: it is said he does not have to repeat it during the time (of that *salat*) nor after the permitted period (has elapsed) – and in the discussion of Ibn Rushd this is (considered) the correct opinion; it is also said that he should repeat it during the time, and this is transmitted from Ibn al-Qasim – and al-Basati said that this is the well known opinion; and it is also said that (responsibility) to repeat it remains (with him) for ever (until it is done), and this is transmitted by the author of *at-Taraz* – but who has esteemed it weak."

7. The order of the obligations: the face is done before the hands, and the latter before the head and the latter before the feet – according to the preferred opinion, and this is referred to by Ibn al-Hajib as the well known opinion. It is also said that the order is obligatory – this is related by 'Ali according to Malik; the third opinion is that it is obligatory when one remembers this (order) but not, when forgotten. If the order is broken, then as Khalil said: "one repeats only the thing missed out in the order if the time which has elapsed is such that the limbs have dried, otherwise (the thing done out of order) should be done – together with the other elements – in their order." 'Abd al-Baqi az-Zurqani said commenting on his words 'one repeats only the thing missed out in the order': "that is, an obligatory action – not the sunna – which is done before the place assigned to it by the *shari'ah*, irrespective of whether it is a matter of the (whole) limb or part of it: like, for example, if someone misses out the washing of his hands – but not his forearms up to the elbows – when performing his *wudu'* with the intention of obligation, then only his hands are considered as having been washed out of turn."

His saying '…if such a long time has elapsed such that it has dried' is with respect to the last washing of the last limb: here one must take into account a normal limb, in normal conditions and circumstances, and the fact that he is repeating it because a long time has elapsed – that is, he performed the wrong order out of forgetfulness; if, however, he has deliberately performed the wrong order, he must repeat the *wudu'* preferably (*nadaban*), as is related by Ibn Zarqoun from the *Mudawwana*, and this is also the opinion of Ibn al-Qasim. In *al-Muqaddimat*: "It is not to be repeated, nor the *salat*, and this he corroborates from Malik in the *Mudawwana*." Al-Mawwaq has narrated that the *wudu'* and the *salat* should be repeated however much time has elapsed, that is within the time (allotted for the *salat*) and after it.

He has commented on his saying. 'otherwise (the thing done out of order) together with the other elements in their order': "If there is not the above mentioned time-lapse then he repeats the element done in the wrong order three times as a sunna, together with the following elements (in sequence) as stipulated by the *shari'ah* – but not as a recommended act; or just once when it is easy to do so because of how short a time has elapsed. As for this distinction – namely, regarding something made up within a short space of time – it does not matter whether he inverted the order out of forgetfulness or deliberately. Indeed, whether the distinction made is regarding (a short lapse or long lapse of time) in both cases the person either wants to stay in a state of purification or perform that which is dependent upon the state of purification. If, however, he wants to interrupt and discontinue his *wudu'* (completely), then he is not commanded to repeat what he remembers (he has forgotten to do) because if this (potential) means (of correcting his *wudu'*) is not based on the appropriate intention, then it is not stipulated in the *shari'ah*. Among the possible combinations of doing something in the wrong order is washing the face first, then one's head, then washing one's feet, then washing one's forearms – in which case the head and feet have been done before their (proper) order. Thus it is required that (only) they be repeated – not the hands. This is because, given that they were done afterwards, it is as if the person did them after the face; he should repeat the head and feet, irrespective of whether he has done the wiping of the head, in second place, before the feet or vice versa. Thus order with respect to these two is not stipulated when repeating because this inversion of order occurred between them."

SECTION: al-Hattab said that Ibn Rushd said: "If he leaves off the sunna deliberately in the *salat*, then there are two opinions regarding repeating it – and so it is here. However, the difference of opinion here is weaker because the sunnas of the *salat* are stronger, and the opinion which affirms the correctness (of the judgements) in both places is the most correct one as the sunna does not reprimand the one who leaves off doing a sunna."

وَأَحَدَ عَشَرَ الْفَضَائِلُ أَتَتْ

تَسْمِيَةٌ وَبُقْعَةٌ قَدْ طَهُرَتْ

64 There are eleven praiseworthy aspects: saying *bismillah*, a clean place,

That is there are eleven recommended elements:

1. The *bismillah*. It has been narrated both that it is allowed (*ibaha*) and that it is preferred.

2. Al-Aqdamisi said in *Sharh al-Idha'a*: "saying the *bismillah* in a place containing dirt and filth – if done with the aim of belittling it – is a forbidden act rendering the person responsible guilty of *kufr*, may Allah protect us from this; if he does not intend it disparagingly, then there are two opinions – that it is permitted, and forbidden."

3. As-Sijistani has mentioned in his *Nawazil* that the saying of the *bismillah* while drinking wine or committing adultery is *kufr*. When he was asked whether the person who deliberately changes the documented form of the *mus-haf* is guilty of *kufr* he replied: "As for the question of the writing (*rasm*), if he adds something which is not there or leaves out something which is then, I am of the opinion that he is not (a *kafir*) – the most extreme (judgement) in his case is that he has violated the sunna of writing the *mus-haf*. (This only applies) however as long as it does not detract from its meaning and does not transgress the manner of its recitation – as long as there is nothing in this (kind of) written (alteration) which indicates *kufr*, that is a denial, a belittling or a making a mockery of the Qur'an. In short, he has committed a *bid'a* with respect to a sunna, like the *adhan* for example or a sunna *salat*: his *bid'a* is not something which is related to *'aqida*; rather it is purely an act of disobedience which does not point to a defect in *'aqida* – as would the throwing of the *mus-haf* into dirt or rubbish, besmearing it with impurity, saying the *bismillah* while drinking wine, or committing adultery and the like. In short, the justification for (judging) *kufr* is denial of the Messengers and Prophets."

3. Ahmad ibn 'Abd al-'Aziz: "If you recite the *bismillah* twenty one times before sleeping, then you will be safe from the accursed Shaytan, from being robbed, from sudden death that night. It is also a protection from all evil and if you recite it in front of a tyrant fifty times Allah will abase him, glorious and exalted is He, and will inspire fear in his heart; and if you recite it in the ear of an epileptic forty one times he will awake (from his dementia); and if one recites it three hundred times at sunrise while facing the sun and

sends blessings on the Prophet, may the peace and blessings of Allah be upon him, a hundred times, then Allah will provide for him from where he has not reckoned and the year will not elapse but that Allah will free him from want by the blessing of *bismillahi'r-rahmani'r-raheem*, in the name of Allah All-Merciful, Most Merciful; and it is said that it is the Mighty name of Allah, and that if a prisoner recites it or it is recited to him for three days, that is a thousand times each night, then Allah, exalted is He, will cause him to be set free; and whoever writes *bismillahi'r-rahmani'r-raheem* and does not omit the *hi* at the end of the *bismillah*, then Allah will write for him (the equivalent of) ten good actions and will remove (the punishment equivalent to) ten bad actions and will raise him ten stations; and whoever writes it well in order to magnify Allah, glorious is He, then He will forgive him; and whoever picks up a piece of paper on which is written *bismillahi'r-rahmani'r-raheem* out of respect for the majesty of the name of Allah – lest it be trod on – then Allah, exalted is He, will record him as being among the *siddiqun* – the truly sincere."

In *Majma' al-Ahbab*, al-Hafidh Abu Nu'aym, may Allah, exalted is He, have mercy on him, has related that Muhammad ibn as-Salt said: "I heard Bishr ibn al-Harith being asked: 'What was the beginning of your affair – for your name is (now) known among people as if it were the name of a prophet?' He replied: 'This is from the overflowing generosity of Allah, glorious is He, – how should I explain it to you? I was a man of ambitious spirit. One day I went out and came across a piece of paper in the road. I picked it up and finding *bismillahi'r-rahmani'r-raheem* written on it, I wiped it (clean) and put it in my pocket. I had two dirhams with me – and I did not possess other than this – and so I went to the perfume sellers and bought a mixture of musk and ambergris with the two dirhams. I then rubbed it on to the paper. After falling asleep that night I dreamt it were as if someone said: "O Bishr ibn al-Harith, You have raised up My name from the road and perfumed it and so I shall certainly perfume your name in this world and the next" – and then what happened (in my life) came to pass.'"

2. One should do *wudu'* in a clean place lest dirt should get onto one's clothes or body – were he to do it in an impure place.

NOTICE: It is not incumbent that one sit while doing *wudu'* although it is recommended.

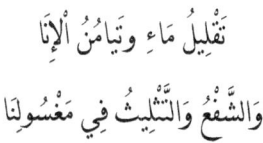

65   using little water, placing the receptacle on the right, washing a second and third time,

Mayyara said:

"3. Using a little water, although this minimum is not specified, for people vary with regard to the amount of water they need." He has also said: "Malik does not restrict the amount and (does not stipulate) that the water used should be copious enough for it to flow on or drop from (the limbs)." He has also said: "Some of the earlier generations used to do *wudu'* with a third of a *mudd*, that is the *mudd* of Hisham." *At-Tawdih*: "His refusal to determine the amount in this way is because no proof exists (as to its amount): even if the water does not 'flow' it still constitutes a 'wiping' without a doubt – this is the opinion of Fadl ibn Musalama. Ibn Mahraz said: 'The most evident meaning of his words is that the amount for the *wudu'* is not determined by its "flowing over" or "dripping".' He said in *at-Tanbeehat*: 'and this differs from the first (opinion), and the well-known (practice) is the *mudd* of Hisham, that is, one and two thirds of the *mudd* of the Prophet, may the peace and blessings of Allah be upon him.'"

USEFUL POINT: he said in *Ghayat al-Ma'ani* that Ibn Naji said: "The most evident meaning of the words of the Shaykh, that is Ibn Abi Zayd, 'and wasting it is an exceeding of proper bounds and a *bid'a*' is that discarding water is forbidden. This is different from the well-known opinion in the *madhhab*, namely that it is permitted to discard the water – (see for example the case of) chicken and rice cut up and marinated in water: the water is discarded afterwards but not the food. Thus the most evident meaning is that it is permitted to pour away the water for no reason. Ibn Harun: 'It is probable that the permissibility of discarding it refers to that about which one has doubts (as to its purity): thus if someone who is normally in contact with impurities, for example, drinks of some water (then the rest may be discarded). However it would be forbidden (to discard it) when no reason exists. Ibn Naji said said: 'There is no incompatibility between the words of the Shaykh and others. Wastefulness is an extravagance and bida.' A person can be (considered) wasteful in his worship because it has been recorded in the *shari'ah* that a little (should be used) in it; but as for pouring water away when not related to the act of worship during purification, then this is permitted if one so chooses, and Allah, exalted is He, knows best.'"

Ibn al-Hattab said, after discussing the matter of the wasting of water: "Know from this that wastefulness is that which is in excess (of what one needs) after having assured oneself of (the performance of) the obligatory, and it is *makruh*, as most of the Shaykhs have pointed out."

4. that one put the receptacle on the right hand side as this facilitates his taking (water) from it (in the best manner).

5. the second and third washing, that is, repeating the washing three times is recommended, and this is the well-known opinion which is evident in *at-Tawdih*. Ibn an-Naji said that each one (of the above) is a separate excellence – and this is also the opinion of Mayyara.

NOTICE: al-Hattab said: "If one is sure that one has not covered (the whole limb) with the first (washing) but the second was (enough to) cover (it), then the third washing is (reckoned) as the second and so one adds a fourth – as is mentioned in the discussion of Naji when he says: 'and is a fourth *makruh*?' Then he says: 'what is meant by three (washings) is that it each (washing) be done fully and properly – (an analogy would be) if one needs two scoops of water to wash a limb, then this would be (counted) as if it were one scoop.'"

بَدْءُ الْمَيَامِنِ سِوَاكٌ وَنُدِبْ

تَرْتِيبُ مَسْنُونِهِ أَوْ مَعْ مَا يَجِبْ

66   beginning with the right (side of one's body), (using the) *miswak*, (keeping to) the order of the sunnas and (within the order of) what is obligatory

6. Beginning with the right, before the left;

7. The *miswak* toothstick: Mayyara said that Ibn al-Hajib said: "(it is correct to do it) even with the fingers if one does not find anything else; and the (fresh) green *siwak* is best for the person who is not fasting" *Tawdih*: "One authority said that one uses the *miswak* before the *wudu'*, then one rinses out the mouth afterwards and ejects the water with any part of the *miswak* that might be in it." Al-Lakhmi said: "He has the choice of whether to do it before the *wudu'* or the *salat*, and if a long time elapses between the *wudu'* and the *salat* it is good to renew it before the *salat*; if another *salat* (time) arrives and he is still in a state of purity, then he should use the *miswak* for this second *salat*; and one can clean (the teeth) with the index and thumb. It is said that it should be done from the right, but it is also said from the left and it should be done gently, not violently."

USEFUL POINT: al-Munawi has mentioned that among the excellent aspects of the *miswak* is that it cleans the mouth, that it is pleasing to the Lord, that it whitens the teeth, that it makes the breath sweet smelling, that it strengthens the gums, that it purifies the character, sharpens the intellect, reduces dampness (in one's constitution), sharpens the sight, it slows down old age, strengthens the back and multiplies one's reward, makes the drawing out of the *ruh* from the body easier and that (the *miswak* itself) makes mention of the *shahada* at the moment of death, and other things besides."

DIGRESSION: among the things which also alleviate the drawing out of the *ruh* is the reading of (Surah) Qaf after the *'Isha salat* – this has been mentioned by al-Mawwaq; and the reading of Ya-Sin to the person in the throes of death, irrespective of whether he himself reads it or it is read in his presence – this has also been mentioned by al-Mawwaq in his commentary on Khalil, as has al-Munawi.

Muhammad ibn al-Hattab said: "It is recommended to apply the *miswak* from side to side and not up and down so as not to cause bleeding of the gums; if the person contravenes this (recommendation) then his brushing with the *miswak* is *makruh*. It is also recommended that he pass the *miswak* gently over the sides of the teeth, the base of the molars and the roof of the palate. It is recommended that he begin with the *miswak* on the right side of the mouth. and there is no harm in the use of someone else's *miswak* with his permission. It is recommended to get children to use it to accustom them to it."

He has also said, affirming Khalil's words 'and (use) the *miswak*) even using the forefinger (if not available)': "The most evident meaning of this is that it applies irrespective of whether the cleaning of the teeth is done with the forefinger during the rinsing with water or without water. As for the first, one authority said : 'It takes the place of the real *miswak* as it is an additional means of cleaning to just the rinsing'; as for the second, an authority has reported that Ibn as-Sabagh has mentioned that there is a difference of opinion regarding it – some of the people of Iraq have said that is the *miswak* (referred to) while others have refuted this!

8. The order of the performance of the sunna is such that the washing of the hands is done before the rinsing of the mouth and the latter before the drawing up water into the nostrils.

9. Adhering to the order of the sunna together with the obligatory elements such that the washing of the hands, rinsing of the mouth, drawing up water into the nostrils and expelling it are done before the washing of the face, and the wiping of the ears is done before the washing of the feet – which is done after the wiping of the head.

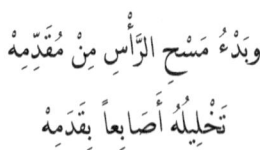

67 and beginning with the wiping of the head from the front, and rubbing in water between the toes of the feet

Al-Mawwaq said that Ibn Yunus said: "Beginning with the front of the head and wiping the nape of the neck is (an aspect of) excellence." Ibn Habib: "… rubbing water (between the toes of the) feet during the *wudu'* is a desirable act, but during the *ghusl*, it is obligatory."

Al-Qarafi has transmitted: "One begins by rubbing water into the little toe of the right foot and then the other toes in sequence, and then the big toe of the left foot and then the other (toes in sequence) – so as to (always ensure that one) starts from the right."

USEFUL POINT: Zarruq said in *an-Naseeha*: "Taking pains to do *wudu'* properly results in ease and expansion for the person – in (an increase in) provision, a protecting love (from Allah) and a lasting protection from acts of disobedience and acts leading to the destruction of oneself and one's deen. It has been narrated that *wudu'* is the weapon of the *mumin* – and this is something tried and proven by experience."

It is recommended to renew it for each *salat* – whether he prays an obligatory or *nafila salat*, according to the most evident meaning of the *Mukhtasar*. The Prophet, may the peace and blessings of Allah be upon him, said: 'Shall I not inform you of that by which Allah will efface wrong action and by which He will raise you stations – doing the *wudu'* properly at times when one has an aversion to doing it, and (taking) many steps to the mosques and waiting for the (next) *salat* after the (previous) *salat* – for this is as a ribat for you' as related by 'Ali ibn 'Abd as-Sadiq, or however the (correct version of the) hadith reads, and this hadith is in Muslim."

Al-Ubbi said in his *Sharh*: "(the words) 'doing the *wudu'* properly' refers to its completion as perfectly as possible and 'when one has an aversion to it' refers to times of intense cold, when one has pain in the body, when it means missing something one likes on account of it, or the difficulty involved in looking for water or having to pay for it and other things. Heating the water to encourage one to worship (by performing the *salat*) does not remove the reward mentioned above. As for 'many steps to the mosque', 'Iyad said that this refers to the distance of the house from the mosque and the frequency one goes there.

In response to the questions of 'Izz ad-Deen I would say: "One should not take the longest way there in order to increase the number of one's steps when one can get there taking a shorter way – for the aim is to reach the mosque. The hadith is an encouragement to the person whose house is far away – in order that he not flag in this matter. Moreover he should not prefer the further of two (possible) mosques to pray in – given the narration which states: 'There is no *salat* for the person living next to a mosque unless he prays in that mosque.' 'A'isha said: may Allah be pleased with her, I said: 'O Messsenger of Allah, I have two neighbours – to which of the two should I give? He replied: 'To the one living closest to (your) house.' An imam of a mosque will not be prevented from receiving what is stipulated as a reward by his repeated going to and from (the mosque), and the Shaykh of the Great Mosque in Tunis whose house was far from the mosque used to say – and he was some eighty years old: This (promised reward) prevented me moving nearer to the mosque': The Bani Salama have transmitted what the Prophet, may the peace and blessings of Allah be upon him said to them when they wanted to move near to the mosque: 'O Bani Salama! Your houses are recording the traces (of your steps to the mosque).' When he says 'Our Shaykh', he is referring to Ibn 'Arafa, just as when Ibn Naji says 'one of our Shaykhs' he is referring to Ibn 'Arafa.

وَكَرِهَ الزَّيْدَ عَلَى الْفَرْضِ لَدَى

مَسْحٍ وَفِي الْغَسْلِ عَلَى مَا حُدِّدَا

68   It is disliked to do more than what is prescribed in the obligatory – when wiping and washing

Ahmad Mayyara said: "Here he is informing us that one should not do more than what has been made obligatory – regarding the wiping the head and ears, that is what has been laid down and determined in the *shari'ah*, namely, the wiping of the head (once), and once for the ears. He interprets the word *fard* 'made obligatory' as that which the *shari'ah* has determined (*taqdir*), just as he has explained in the *Risala* when commenting on the matter of the *zakat al-Fitr*: "The Messenger of Allah imposed it as an obligation (*farada*) – that is determined it(s time and amount) according to one interpretation. Thus what was imposed of the obligation (*farada*) of the washing implies that it is disliked to do more that what has been determined by the Legislator of the *shari'ah*.' Here is clear proof that it is disliked to do it a fourth time. Khalil has also said in *at-Tawdih*: "A similar (text) is (reported) in *al-Muqaddimat*. 'Abd al-Wahhab, al-Lakhmi and al-Mazari (have also said that): 'It is forbidden. It is narrated from one authority that there is a consensus in the *madhhab* as to its interdiction. Its being *makruh* is from the point of view of wastefulness during the *wudu'*, and its being forbidden is from the point of view of the saying of the

Messenger, may the peace and blessings of Allah be upon him, regarding the Bedouin Arab who asked him about the *wudu'*. He showed him how he did it three times saying: 'This is how to do *wudu'*, and whoever does more than this goes beyond the bounds and done (himself) an injustice."

I SAY: "Thus it is (also) disliked to add something in other than the *wudu'*, when the limits of which have been stipulated by the Legislator, such as the doing of more than the thirty three (*suhanallahs, alhamdulillahs* and *Allahu akbars*) after (the *salat*)

وَعَاجِزُ الْفَوْرِ بَنَى مَا لَمْ يَطُلْ

بِيُبْسِ الْأَعْضَا فِي زَمانٍ مُعْتَدِلْ

69 If one is unable to do each element of the *wudu'* consecutively, one should carry on where one left off, as long as the time which elapses is not so long that the limbs – in a moderate temperature – have dried

Ahmad Mayyara said: "He informs (us) that whoever breaks the continuity because he is no longer able (to continue the *wudu'*) then he should carry on where he left off. Thus if his water runs out water, for example, and he does not find any more then his *wudu'* is invalidated if a long time elapses; if a long time has not elapsed and then he finds water, he should carry on where he left off and complete what remains (for him to do). A long time (is defined as that in which) the drying of the limbs (occurs) of a person of moderate stature and temperament in a moderate temperature. Ibn 'Ashir's mentions the limbs but omits 'of moderate stature and temperament.' However this latter is implied by his saying 'in a moderate temperature.' However, it has also been said that the customary practice of the people of the place in question) is to be followed. If he breaks the continuity out of forgetfulness and then remembers, then he should carry on from where he broke off whether the time which has elapsed is great or small – but it should be done with a (renewed) intention."

SECTION: Ibn al-Hattab said that said in *at-Taraz*: "If he remembers a patch of skin untouched by water, or a limb (he has not washed) and he does not find anything to wash these (two places) with, then it is related – in (the discussions dealing with) the elucidation of the finer points (of the deen), from more than one of his Shaykhs – that the judgement in his case is the same as that regarding the person who runs out of water, and that if a long time elapses in his search for water then he should begin the whole of the act of purification from the beginning."

NOTICE: Ibn al-Hattab said that ar-Rajraji said: "If deliberately does not take enough water, then it is not permitted him to carry on where he left off, irrespective of whether the time which has elapsed is long or short – as he has deliberately intended to break the act of purification. This is the most evident meaning (to be understood) from al-Mashdali – for he said in his commentary on *al-Mudawwana's* words 'and his water runs out' that he means 'as long as he has prepared enough for his (*wudu'*)'; and otherwise he should begin again."
I say: "And this is the most evident (of opinions regarding this matter). If however the break is inconsiderable then he is excused beginning again."
I say: "What I have seen in some books of import is that the reason for a person not carrying on where he left off is lack of certainty in his intention."
I say: "Indeed, this it what determines that he cannot carry on where he left off – even if a break does not take place at all, let alone a break of a negligible (character). This, then is in harmony with the words of ar-Rajraji, irrespective of whether the time elapsed is long or short – even though there is a difference of opinion as to the reason. It is also in agreement with the literal meaning of what al-Mashdali says.

ذَاكِرُ فَرْضِهِ بِطُولٍ يَفْعَلُهُ

فَقَطْ وَفِي الْقُرْبِ الْمُوَالِي يُكْمِلُهُ

70 The person who remembers an obligation after a long time has elapsed should do just this; but after a short time, he should complete with continuity;

إِنْ كَانَ صَلَّى بَطَلَتْ وَمَن ذَكَرَ

سُنَّتَهُ يَفْعَلُهَا لِمَا حَضَرْ

71 if he has (already) prayed, then the (*salat*) is invalid, and whoever remembers one of the sunnas should do it when he remembers

He describes the situation in which someone who forgets something of his *wudu'*: this (means) what he has forgotten will either be a *fard* or a sunna. If a *fard* and he only remembers it after a long time has elapsed, then he should do only what he has forgotten and not repeat what comes after it; if after a short time, then he should do what (he has missed) and what comes after it; if he does not remember in both cases until after he prays, then his *salat* is annulled and the obligation to repeat the *salat* remains until he does it as he will have prayed without *wudu'*; if what he has forgotten is a sunna, then he should do just this thing again when the time comes, that is, when he is about to pray with this *wudu'*, and he does not repeat any *salats* he made before making (up) this (sunna of *wudu'*); and no distinction is made in this between a long and short lapse of time, and Allah, exalted is He, knows best."

One understands that something has been missed by way of forgetfulness in both cases, that is, when he says 'the one who remembers' and then 'the one who remembers a sunna' as one only uses the word 'remember' when one has forgotten something. (Whether he may proceed) – if he wants to make it up (something) after a short time or a long time has elapsed (depends on the following): if a long time has elapsed, his *wudu'* is annulled if he has missed out an obligation deliberately – because he has failed to observe the necessary continuity deliberately and consciously; if, however, he wants to make (something) up after a short time has elapsed, then he should proceed like someone who has done something in the wrong order out of forgetfulness, who remembers after a short while and who repeats what he has missed together with (the elements of the *wudu'*) which follow. If he leaves off doing a sunna deliberately and he prays with this (*wudu'*), then it is recommended that he repeat the (*salat*) in the time (allotted for the *salat*), although it has also been said that it is not repeated. A third opinion holds that the obligation on the person to repeat this (*salat*) remains until he (actually) does it and that no distinction is made in this respect between a short and long time, and Allah, exalted is He, knows best:

Whoever misses part of the *fard* of his *wudu'*
  Should repeat it and what follows as long as the time elapsed is not long.
If a long time has elapsed, then he just does what he has missed.
  And he should take care that not to omit to renew the intention for this.
If done deliberately, however, and the time elapsed is long, he should do it again from the beginning –
  Like the person who delays after having knowledge (of an obligation)
And if he has to leave (of doing his *wudu'*) because he has no more water, then he should carry on where he left off (when he has water) -
  If, (that is), the time elapsed is short. However he should begin again if the time elapsed is long,
And he should do the sunnas – if he does not do them
  in their proper place – by doing them (on remembering) as is prescribed.
And it is recommended to repeat the *salat* if he has deliberately missed out

the (sunna elements of the *wudu'*) – so take note!

However it must certainly be repeated in the case of someone who has missed out an obligation of the (*wudu'*).

As for what is considered 'a long time', know it is the (time it takes) for A man's limbs – of average build and temperament

and in average temperature – to dry.

Here end the words of Mayyara.

That Which Breaks Wudu'

نَوَاقِضُ الْوُضُوءِ سِتَّةَ عَشَرْ

بَوْلٌ وَرِيحٌ سَلَسٌ إِذَا نَدَرْ

72   The things which break the *wudu'* are sixteen in number: urinating, breaking wind, incontinence if infrequent

وَغَائِطٌ نَوْمٌ ثَقِيلٌ مَذْيِ

73   and defecating, deep sleep, discharge of *madhy* (thin, pre-seminal fluid)…

AL-MAWWAQ said that the author of *al-Talqeen* said: "The occurrence of physical impurities (*ahdath*) which necessitates *wudu'* are those resulting in the discharge of something from the two orifices in normal (health) – not the (discharge) occurring (as a result of an) uncommon (occurrence) and which is expelled (from the body) because of illness; (they include occasional) incontinence, with respect to excrement or urine, breaking wind, pre-seminal fluid[1], pre-seminal fluid[2]. Not (included among these physical impurities is whatever is emitted) because of (chronic) incontinence, nor (that which may be classed as having no certain existence, being the) result of persistent doubt, nor blood. Al-Lahkmi said (that *wudu'* is not broken by) 'blood from the penis, nor that from the anus.' Ibn al-'Arabi said: '…and likewise air emitted from the penis: *wudu'* is not necessitated if this happens, according to Malik and Abu Hanifa, (the judgement regarding it) being (considered) akin to (that of) belching.' ash-Shafi'i however considers that *wudu'* is necessitated."

Issue – Ibn al-Hattab has raised the question as to what a person should do who – if after urinating and customarily squeezing the base of his penis to

---

1   *Madhy*: a thin, white liquid emitted with sexual pleasure during an erection as a result of foreplay or the thought of foreplay.
2   *Wadyi*: a thick, white liquid emitted immediately after urination.

ensure the last of the urine is expelled – finds that the urine takes so long to stop dripping that both the prescribed time (for the *salat*) as well as the emergency time elapses. Is he commanded to do the *wudu'* and *salat* even if the urine is still dripping from him – that is should he treat it as (chronic) incontinence or should he delay the *salat* until the urine-flow ceases? Moreover, (he asks) what if he is unable through constipation or retention of urine (to free himself completely of faeces or urine) and he fears he will find himself in the same situation (i.e. running out of time) as above – should he pray while in this state of trying to expel faeces or urine, or should he try and remove as much as necessary, even if it means running out of time? With respect to nose bleeding and impurity, they have said that if one fears the time (for the *salat*) will pass one should pray with the impurity (adhering to one). Others have said that if a person fears the time (for the *salat*) will elapse were he to occupy himself with *wudu'* or *ghusl* then he should do *tayammum*. However I do not understand the judgement in this issue as the assumption (in this case) is that (chronic) incontinence is not present. If incontinence is present then the person should do *wudu'* and pray if this is his condition most of the time or it is his condition for the same amount of time as he is free of it. If however, this (incontinence) ceases for the majority of the time then it breaks (the *wudu'*), according to the well-known opinion, – contrary to (the opinion of) the Iraqis, and Allah, exalted is He, knows best.

The Maliki Shaykh of Egypt Shaykh Nasir ad-Deen al-Laqqani, may Allah cause the benefit of his knowledge to last, was asked about this and he replied that the person should delay the *salat* until his urine ceases even if this results in the prescribed and emergency time of the *salat* elapsing – he should not pray when there is urine (still dripping from him) for this invalidates the *wudu'* and annuls it; likewise if he has to occupy himself with cleaning his anus or penis in preparation for the *wudu'* for an obligatory *salat* then he must delay the *salat* if necessary even if it means that the prescribed time passes – he should not pray while in this state for this would invalidate the *salat* and necessitate his repeating it. Abu Nu'aym said: 'If it is not such that it causes one to be occupied during the obligatory (*salat*) then one must pray within the time. It is not permitted to delay the (*salat*) because its performance within the prescribed time is obligatory: one should not abandon this (obligation) in order to attain something (merely) recommended.' This is the most evident (judgement) from the principles of the (Maliki) *madhhab*. This also is what is the most evident in my opinion, and Allah, exalted is He, knows best. The words of Ibn al-Hattab (on the subject) end with Khalil's words '... with the setting of the sun.'"

According to 'Ali ibn 'Abd as-Sadiq his saying 'deep sleep' is irrespective of whether it is short or long – and (with regard to its being short) there is agreement on this and (with regard to its being long) this is the well-known judgement. The signs (of deep sleep) are that the cloth used to tie a person's garment loosens, saliva drips from his mouth, his tasbih for example drops from his hand or someone speaks near him without him hearing anything. If, however, he does wake up on account of this, then his sleep is (considered) light. An-Nafrawi has also mentioned similar things.

NOTICE: He said in *ad-Dakheera* that the author of *at-Taraz* said: "Malik has made a distinction in *al-'Utbiya* between the person who sleeps sitting up and stretches himself out while waiting for the *salat* and the person who is not waiting for it. When someone said to him that he often had dreams (*ru'ya*) he replied: 'They are confused or evil dreams (*hulm*) because the person waiting for the *salat* is not able to have his fill of sleep – unlike someone who is not (waiting for the *salat*). This is something that necessarily happens to people who are waiting for the *salat*. Confused or evil dreams are often from the whisperings of the self which occur during light sleep. (True) dreams, however, occur frequently at the end of the night when one has satisfied one's craving for sleep.'"

BENEFITS: firstly: it is related in *Sahih Muslim*: "Al-Bara' ibn 'Azib related to me that the Messenger of Allah, may the peace and blessings of Allah be upon him, said: 'If you take to your bed then do your *wudu'* as if for the *salat*, lie on your right side and then say: "O Allah I have submitted my self to you and have handed over my affair to you. I seek your refuge for all that is mine out of desire for and fear of You for there is no refuge and no salvation from You except by You. I have iman in Your Book which You have sent down and in Your Messenger which you have sent." Make these your last words and if you die this night then you will die on the *fitra* (of purity)!' – or words to this effect."

Al-Ubbi said that al-'Iyad said: "One should ensure (that one does) *wudu'* before sleeping – then if a person dies, he dies in a state of purity and will be far removed from the deceit and wiles of Shaytan's during his sleep, and out of reach of his attempts to sadden or grieve him. Thus the last action of his in the *dunya* – should he die – will be undertaken in a state of purity and in a state of remembrance (of Allah). However there is a difference of opinion, according to us and others, as to whether such a *wudu'* would permit one to also do the *salat*." The correct opinion is that if he intends by this (making of the *wudu'*) to pass the night in a state of purity then he is also permitted to perform the *salat* and other acts of worship with it. Moreover this *wudu'* is (only) broken by some impurity which comes to pass before he lies down, not after it (that is, while in a state of unawareness, asleep – for his intention to be in a state of purity still holds good).

2. Whoever recites '*Allah bears witness that there is no god but Him as do the angels and the people of knowledge, upholding justice. There is no god but Him, the Almighty, the All-wise*'[1] Allah will create for him seventy thousand angels who will seek forgiveness for him until the Day of Raising Up.

3. Ibn al-Hattab has commented on the *Risala's* explanation of the words 'whoever of you sees something he dislikes in a dream then when he awakes he should spit three times to his left' then he should say: 'O Allah I seek refuge with You from the evil which I have seen lest it harm me in my deen or my *dunya*' with the following: "He should put all the narrations into practice such that if he sees something he dislikes then he should spit to his left saying 'I seek refuge with Allah from the accursed Shaytan and from the evil of this (dream)', turn over on his other side and then pray two *rak'as*; and if he restricts himself to part of this (*du'a*) then it will be enough to remove the evil, by the permission of Allah, exalted is He."

In al-Bukhari it is narrated: "A good dream is from Allah and so if one of you sees something he likes, then he should not speak about it except to someone he likes; if he sees something he dislikes then he should seek refuge with Allah from its evil and from evil of shaytan, and he should spit three times and not speak about it to anyone, and then it will not harm him."

Another hadith on this subject is that narrated of Abu Sa'id al-Khudri, namely that he heard the Messenger of Allah, may the peace and blessings of Allah be upon him, say: "If one of you sees something in a dream which he likes, then it is from Allah and he should praise Allah for it and speak about it; if he sees other then this which he dislikes, then it is from Shaytan and he should seek refuge from its evil and he should not mention it to anyone, and then it will never harm him."

He said in *al-Fath*: "Part of the *adab* of the interpreter (of dreams) is what is related by 'Abd ar-Razzaq from 'Umar, namely, that he wrote to Abu Musa saying: 'If one of you sees something in a dream then he should relate it to his brother and say: "the good is for us and the evil for our enemies"' – and the persons of his (chain of narration) are trustworthy."

He has also said in *al-Fath*: "The gist of what has been mentioned regarding the *adab* of the good dream is three things: that the person should praise Allah,

---

1 Ali 'Imran: 18

exalted is He, for it, should delight in it and speak about it – but only to people he likes, not to people he dislikes. The gist of what has been mentioned of the *adab* of a dream one dislikes are four: that the person seek refuge of Allah, exalted is He, from its evil and from the evil of shaytan, that he spit to his left three times on awakening from his sleep and that he not mention it to anyone."

He has also said: "The way in which one seeks refuge from an evil dream has been related in a *sahih* tradition recorded by Sa'd ibn Mansur, Ibn Abi Shayba and 'Abd ar-Razzaq with *sahih* chains of narration from Ibrahim an-Nakha'i who said: 'If one of you sees something he dislikes in a dream then on awakening he should say: "I seek refuge by that by which the angels of Allah and His Messengers have sought refuge from the evil of this dream of mine lest something which I dislike befall me with respect to my deen and *dunya*."'"

4. Sayyidi 'Abd ar-Rahman ath-Tha'alabi – may Allah benefit us by him – has commented on the words of Allah *'and let him not associate anyone in the worship of his Lord'*[1] saying : "Take note: It has been narrated to us in *Sahih Muslim* from Jabir, may Allah, exalted is He, be pleased with him, that he said: 'I have heard the Prophet may the peace and blessings of Allah be upon him, say: "Surely there is an hour in the night – no Muslim man succeeds in witnessing it and in asking Allah for good but that he will be granted it – and this (applies) every night." If you want to know which is this hour then recite the following words of, exalted is He, before you sleep: *'Those who have iman and do right actions will have the Gardens of Firdaws as hospitality..'*[2] to the end of the surah. (If you do this) you will wake up at this hour insha'Allah, exalted is He, by His overflowing generosity. By whatever means you wake up, however, then make *du'a* for me and for yourself. This is one of the things that Allah glorious and exalted is He, has revealed to me and so take benefit from it. I have only written it down after making *istikhara*.[3] Take care that you do not make a *du'a* against a Muslim during this (hour) – even if he is a tyrant. If you act contrary to my (instructions) then Allah will be your Reckoner and I will be your adversary in from of Him. I desire of you that you let me share in your *du'a* – given that I have accorded you this great benefit – and that I act as your Shaykh in it. Surely the Qur'an contains secrets which Allah reveals to those of His *awliya* He wishes – may Allah, exalted is He, make us of them by His

---

1   al-Kahf – The Cave: 105
2   al-Kahf – The Cave: 102
3   a particular *du'a* taught by the Prophet, may the peace and blessings of Allah be upon him, to his Companions – to be recited after two *rak'ats* before undertaking something one has resolved to do – in order to seek from Allah, exalted is He, the best in it. Ed.

overflowing generosity" Here ends his words, may Allah be pleased with him and benefit us by them.

I say: "And I also desire of you that you permit me to share in your *du'a*."

5. Whoever perseveres in saying *Allahu akbar* thirty four times, and *subhana'llah* thirty three times before he retires to bed will not be struck by incapacity or exhaustion in any matter he undertakes.

6. Al-Munawi said in his *Kabir* that al-'Iraqi said: "It is recommended that one relate a good dream to the person concerned (i.e. the person seen in the dream). It is also recommended that if someone sees something that will make the person (seen in the dream) happy, then he should inform him of it."

7. Ibn Naji said in his *Hashiya 'ala Risala*: "I have seen in the *Sharh Manthouma Ibn al-'Imad*, in (the section regarding) the *adab* of eating, a difference of opinion regarding the superiority of sleep over staying awake when one does not perform any acts of worship. (The author) argues: 'There is a difference of opinion as to whether staying awake – if it is not accompanied by *dhikr* of Allah, exalted is He, – is better or sleep. It is said that it is better as sleep is an imperfect state and it has also been said that sleep is superior as it may be that one sees the Creator, may be glorified and magnified, the Prophets, and the *Salihun*.'"

As for his mention of *madhi* (pre-seminal fluid) – it is a thick, white, fluid which is emitted accompanied by sexual pleasure and an erection when engaged in love-play or recalling (this love-play).

Notice: *Wudu'* is not invalidated by merely looking (at a woman) or having an erection when not accompanied by an emission of pre-seminal fluid. Khalil said: "(It is not invalidated merely) by experiencing sexual pleasure through seeing (a woman), or by having an erection." Ibn al-Hattab said that al-Lakhmi said in his *Tabsira*: "There is a difference of opinion regarding an erection if the person has not touched (his penis). It has been said that he does not have to do *wudu'* unless pre-seminal fluid has been emitted, although it has also been said that he should do *wudu'* as the penis only retracts (from its erection) after an emission of pre-seminal fluid and that an erection is accompanied by desire (*ma'-ikhtiyar*)." I consider that a person should act in accordance with what is usual regarding his own person – if he knows that he does not (usually) have an emission of pre-seminal fluid then he is still in a state of purity. If, however, he usually does have an emission of pre-seminal fluid then this breaks his *wudu'*. If there is no predictable pattern in this respect, then he should do *wudu'*. If after inspecting himself – immediately after (an erection) or after some time (has elapsed) – he does not find anything, then he is still in a state of purity. If his usual constitution is such that when he has an erection during the *salat* he does not have an emission of pre-seminal fluid then he should carry on (with the *salat*). If, however, he is a person who usually has an emission, then he should break off (the *salat*) unless the erection is not significant and he does not fear an emission from it. If his constitution is such that he has an emission of pre-seminal fluid after an erection and he does not fear an emission before completion of the *salat* then he should complete it – unless it becomes clear to him (after the *salat*) that the emission has taken place before (completion of the *salat*), in which case he must make up (the *salat*). If he is in doubt (as to this matter) then there is a difference of opinion as to whether the *salat* is acceptable or not."

سُكْرٌ وَإِغْمَاءٌ جُنُونٌ وَدْيُ

73   intoxication, fainting, madness or discharge of *wadyi* (after urination),

In *Ghayat al-Amani* – with respect to the words of the *Risala* 'or intoxication' – the (author) said: "This applies irrespective of whether it results from something halal like (sour) milk or something haram like wine etc." Indeed this is correct for Ibn al-Qasim said: "Whoever loses his intellect – be it with (sour) milk or fermented drink – then he must do *wudu*'." Ibn 'Umar said: "(This judgement is) other than (in the case of) murder – for if someone kills another, he is not put to death if he is totally intoxicated but rather if he is only slightly tipsy (and is still able to think rationally)." However, it is also said that he is put to death in all circumstances. One of the commentators has explained *nashwan* (tipsy) as the state of someone who is capable of being both mistaken or correct in his judgement.

لَمْسٌ وَقُبْلَةٌ وَذَا إِنْ وُجِدَتْ
لَذَّةُ عَادَةٍ كَذَا إِنْ قُصِدَتْ

74   touching (a woman) and kissing if (sexual) pleasure is experienced, or if intended.

'Ali ibn 'Abd as-Sadiq said in his *Taqreer*: "Kissing other than on the mouth, be it on the vagina, or any where (on the body) invalidates (the *wudu*') in all circumstances – even if the person is coerced or does it inadvertently. However if it is done as a (sign of) farewell or (as an expression of) endearment, it is not invalidated as long as no sexual pleasure is experienced – (that is) in the case of an adult woman who is not a relative (*mahram*). As for relatives, sexual pleasure is not normally associated with this (kind of kissing) – that is except in the case of a corrupt person. As for the cheeks and upper surface of the breasts, this is (considered) as 'touching' (a woman which necessarily breaks *wudu'*) – according to what is contained in Dawud al-Laqqani's commentary on *al-'Ashmawiya*.

Khalil has added to that which annuls *wudu'* saying: "...touching (a woman) if the person normally experiences sexual pleasure, even if it is (touching her) nail, hair or something covering (her skin)." Thus (the interdiction in the *Mudawwana*) has been interpreted (in two ways) – as (applicable after) the lightest (of touches), or in all circumstances, as long as sexual pleasure is intended or experienced (in both cases). When neither of these two is present (*wudu'*) is not (annulled) – except, that is, kissing on the mouth (which annuls it in all cases) even if the person is coerced or does it inadvertently; however all this does not apply if done as a farewell or as a (sign of) endearment.

USEFUL POINT: He said in *Ghayat al-Amani*: "What is meant by 'touching (a woman)' is (actively) seeking (to do it). Allah, exalted is He, said: "*We touched (inna lamasna), as usual, the heaven in search of news but found it filled with fierce guards and meteors*"[1] meaning "*we sought to travel to heaven...*" and in the hadith: "Go and search (*iltamis*) (for something as a dowry) even if it is an iron ring..." . It is true that the two Arabic roots *lamasa* and *massa* are connected in that they can both denote 'touching', 'feeling' or 'holding' but they are also differentiated in that the first can also have the meaning of 'to search after in order to lay hold of' – thus one can refer for example to *tamas al-hajaran* – meaning 'the contact between the two stones' but one would not say *talamas al-hajaran* because two inanimate objects are unable to seek out mutual contact of their own volition. Having then established that 'touching a woman' refers to experiencing sexual pleasure then we know that the meaning of His words '*or touched women*'[2] refers to a touching which intends sexual pleasure and no other meaning."

USEFUL POINT: It is prohibited to kiss the person who is in *wudu'* or to have sexual intercourse with the person who has had a *ghusl* when there is no (further) water available – unless a long time elapses, according to Khalil. Ibn 'Arafa has stipulated that the (interdiction) does not apply in the case of someone (with a bandage around) a head-wound – because of the long time (needed to heal the wound). Al-Mawwaq has also mentioned that Ibn 'Arafa said: "It is also prohibited to have intercourse with the traveller or to kiss him

---

1   al-Jinn – The Jinn:8
2   al-Ma'ida – the Table: 7 and an-Nisa' – Women: 42

if there is not enough (water) for both of the (partners); this (interdiction) does not (however) apply to the person with (a bandage around his) head-wound – the latter may have intercourse because of the length of time (needed to heal his wound) whereas in the former case (of the traveller) he may not because of the short time (which usually elapses before he finds water). But the judgement (regarding these two classes of persons) is reversed when the circumstances of each are reversed[1]. Ibn Rushd said: "This interdiction is a (only) recommendation, and (kissing in such circumstances) has been permitted by Ibn Wahb." In *at-Taraz* he states: "Ibn al-Qasim has prohibited a person in *wudu'* – who finds himself without water – from urinating as long as (the pressure of) retention is insignificant." Ibn Mu'ala said[2] – after mentioning the text of the *Mudawwana* – that Qadi Abu Waleed Ibn Rushd said: "The judgement regarding the traveller differs from the person with (a bandage around his) head wound as the latter takes a (long) time to heal in most cases while the traveller is able to find water close at hand in most cases. However, when the traveller is in a place where he knows he will not find water except after a long (search), then he may have sexual intercourse with his wife if he suffers through the length of waiting." Ibn Habib has also related this from Mutarraf, Ibn Majishun and Asbagh, and as a hadith (of the Prophet, may the peace and blessings of Allah be upon him. If the person with (a bandage around his) head wound is able to heal himself of his head wound within a short time, then he should not have sexual intercourse until his head wound is healed and he is able to wash it. This is clear as the judgements are connected to the meaning (of the situation) not to the (mere) names (of things or occurrences) – unless, that is, the law lays down that the judgement is connected to them explicitly. However, here (in this case) it is completely a matter of choice and (a question of) what is recommended for the person to do, not that each person is obliged to wait. Ibn Wahb has narrated from Layth ibn Sa'd that the traveller may have intercourse with his wife and that if he has no water then he should do *tayammum* and perform the *salat* – and this is the preferred judgement of Ibn Wahb based on the words of, exalted is He, "... *and if you cannot find any water, then do tayammum with pure earth.*'[3]"

Az-Zurqani has commented on Khalil's words 'when water is not available it

---

1 for example a light head wound might take less time to heal than the time it takes to find water in a desert
2 the following paragraph is extremely garbled and I have relied on the version of the text taken from Ibn *Rushd's Tahseel wa Bayan*, vol.1, p. 56-7
3 an-Nisa' – Women: 43

is prohibited to kiss the person who is in *wudu'* or have sexual intercourse with someone who has made a *ghusl*, unless a long time elapses' saying: "(meaning if) he is harmed by this or he fears hardship – not simply out of lust of the self. Thus if a long time elapses he may have intercourse – the exception thus referring to the second (of the two above mentioned cases) as one suffers no hardship by refraining from kissing. (As for the case of intercourse in which) a woman has been in control of her self but the man has imposed himself on her, then she has more right to the means to do the *ghusl* on a journey when there is only enough water for the one of them – as it was he who had intercourse with her despite her unwillingness. Thus he is obliged to provide the water for her to do the *ghusl*. This (latter case) is not based on the same principle as the case mentioned in the *Mukhtasar* where a man – if he fears he would cause himself harm by repeatedly washing his head on account of *janaba* – (simply) wipes over his head: his substituting the latter (instead of properly washing his head) is less of a departure (from the original instruction to wash) than doing *tayammum*."

USEFUL POINT: It is forbidden to kiss a person unrelated to you, that is – as one can surmise – in the case of younger women, not in the case of old women. An-Nafrawi said: "It is also permitted to kiss a child – as is stated in Tawudi's *Hashiya*; it is also permitted to kiss one's wife – examine *al-Jami' as-Saghir* together with al-Munawi's commentary on it, and examine too *adh-Dhahab al-Ibreez fi Manaquib 'Abd al-'Aziz* which contains words to the effect that the various ways one may enjoy the company of one's wife are all recorded in the pages reserved for good deeds."

DIGRESSION: – related to our subject – regarding the basis for some of the judgements regarding kissing and when they may be applied. Al-Wansharisi said in *al-Jami'*- narrating from Qasim al-'Aqbani – that "at-Tirmidhi has related the hadith of az-Zuhri from 'Urwa from "A'isha, may Allah be pleased with her, who said: 'Zayd ibn Haritha came to the house of the Messenger, may the peace and blessings of Allah be upon him, and knocked at the door. The Messenger of Allah rose to (greet) him naked dragging his robe – by Allah I had not seen him naked – neither before this (time) or after it – and he embraced him and kissed him.' The most obvious meaning is that this kiss was on the mouth as is the most obvious sense of the tradition related from 'Abdallah ibn 'Umar, may Allah be pleased with him, namely that 'When he returned from a journey he would kiss (people) as a greeting and he would say that an older man (*Shaykh*) may kiss an older man.' However, some have interpreted this to mean on (a part of the body) other than the mouth like the head, cheeks, between the eyes. Others have interpreted it in its literal sense saying (it refers to) a man kissing his son and the like from among his relations as a sign of love and endearment – like one would kiss a small child. This is different than a man kissing the hand of his master or lord – for abstaining from this is better. If this is (understood as) a greeting then the Messenger, may the peace and blessings of Allah be upon him, would have had more right to it – given he is the Lord of all creation and the Messenger of the Lord of the worlds. As this has not been confirmed in the behaviour of the Companions towards the Prophet, may the peace and blessings of Allah be upon him, imam Malik said: 'Abstaining from it is preferable to me.' Some of the Shafi'is have said: 'If the kissing of someone's hand is done in recognition of his doing-without, his correctness, his knowledge, his nobility, his honourable character or for some other quality of the deen, then it is not disliked. Indeed it is recommended. If however, it is done for his wealth, position and the like then it is disliked in the strongest possible terms.' He added 'and one of them has indicated that it is haram.'"

An-Nafrawi has commented on the words of the *Risala* 'Malik disliked the kissing (of another's) hand' saying: "What may be understood by mention of the 'hand' this is that kissing of the mouth must necessarily be more disliked: there is no licence for one man to kiss another's mouth; but as for kissing his sister, daughter or mother on returning from a journey, there is no harm in this – as Malik has made clear. Likewise, there is no harm in kissing his daughter's cheek; however, it is disliked if his daughter in law or his freed female slave kiss him."

Al-Mawwaq has commented on the words of the *Risala* 'Malik disliked the kissing (of another's) hand' saying: "... it is also said that it is permitted to kiss the head of one's parents, for a brother (to kiss) the cheek of his brother and for the (husband) to kiss his wife on the mouth."

As-Sudani said: "(The judgement regarding) kissing depends on the place kissed – one may kiss the forehead of one's father, the hand of the Amir, the cheek of a brother in Allah, women related to each other may kiss each other on the upper part of their bosoms and a husband may kiss the mouth of his wife."

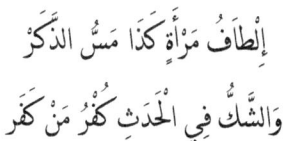

75 a woman touching inside her vagina, a man touching his penis (with his palm), doubt as to whether one has become impure, and becoming a

kafir

Al-Mawwaq said that in *al-Kafi* it states: "They have interpreted touching (on the part of the woman) (*altaf*) as her experiencing sexual pleasure, and Ibn Abi Uways said: 'I asked my uncle Malik as to its meaning and he replied "her putting her hand between the labia of the vagina."'"

Al Mawwaq said referring to Ibn 'Ashir's saying 'touching his penis' that someone said to Malik: "What if he touches his penis over a fine cloth." He replied: "He does not have to do *wudu*' – (and this is) based on a hadith (to this effect)."

Mayyara said: "There is a difference of opinion amongst the followers of Malik with regard to the person who touches his penis and prays without (renewing) his *wudu*'. It is said that he should repeat the *salat* if still within the (prescribed) time' – this is the opinion of Malik and ibn al-Qasim, while it has also been said that he does not have to repeat it, and this is one of two sayings of Malik and Ibn al-Qasim. It is these two opinions which form the basis of this difference of opinion. It has also been said that the *salat* should be repeated in all circumstances, and this is the opinion of Ibn Nafi' and Ibn Dinar. It has also been said that the person who does it deliberately should repeat (the *salat*) in all circumstances, whereas the person who did it out of forgetfulness should repeat it only if the prescribed time has not elapsed – this has been narrated by Ibn al-Habib."

USEFUL POINT: Zarruq said in *an-Naseeha*: "It is prohibited to touch the penis with the right hand." Ibn Zakari has commented on this, saying: "…and it is recorded in *Sahih Muslim*: 'No one should touch his penis with his right hand' and al-Ubbi said that the Dhahiris have said: 'Its prohibition is absolute (i.e. haram) although the *fuqaha* have interpreted it as being (only) *makruh*.' One may understand from the *Mukhtasar* and that it is a general prohibition and not restricted to the time one is washing one's private parts, although the (judgement that it annuls *wudu*') is conditional in the hadith transmitted by Muslim upon the ('touching' taking place when washing one's private parts). The principle (regarding judgements in general) is to set the absolute (judgement) against the conditional (judgement) and so it begs the question as to the rationale regarding what is said in *al-Mukhtasar*. It may be answered by what al-Ubbi mentioned from Taqi ad-Deen namely that setting the absolute against the conditional is the (general) principle in the matter of prohibitions or commands – if this is not done then all the benefit implicit in the conditions will be lost."

As for the matter of being in doubt that a *hadath* – state of impurity – has come about, al-Mawwaq said that Ibn Yunus said: "Whoever is in any doubt as to any part of his *wudu'*, then he should wash that part about which he is in doubt; if he has certainty regarding his *wudu'* (in the first instance), but then he has doubts and he does not know if a state of impurity has come upon him after his *wudu'* or not, then he should repeat his *wudu'* in the same manner as the person who has doubts as to whether he has prayed three or four (*rak'ats*) – this annuls the doubt except in the case of the person who is prone to persistent doubt in which case he does not have to repeat any of his *wudu'* or his *salat*." Ibn al-Habib said: "If he imagines that he has passed wind, then he should not do *wudu'* unless he is certain of this; likewise, if doubt has come upon him as to whether anything has happened and then he remembers the state of impurity (then he should not do *wudu'*)." Then he says: "If he doubts as to whether he has urinated or not, then he should repeat the *wudu'*."[1]

He has also said: "Abu 'Umar said that Malik said: 'Whoever is certain of his *wudu'* but has doubts as to whether a state of impurity has come upon him then he should begin the *wudu'* (again).' However no other (*fuqaha*) follow him in this. Ibn Nafi' opposes him in this saying: 'He does not have to do the *wudu'* again. This is the opinion of the rest of the *fuqaha* and is the *madhhab* of ash-Shafi'i, Ibn Hanbal, ath-Thawri, Ishaq, Abu Thawr and at-Tabari."

Mayyara quotes the following – to complete this theme:
If one accepts that doubt can beset someone (in one matter)
    Then it necessitates – to be fair – (the acceptance of) doubt in a comparable (matter):
Like doubt as to the state of impurity coming upon a person, or in the case of divorce
    Although the difference (between them) is not absolutely and immediately clear
Someone who has investigated (this) said that one should examine
    the doubt at its source, and then the significance will manifest:
If that which he has doubts about is that which
    has caused the doubt to arise, then is taken as the determining factor.
This then is what the judgement – in the case of the person in question – is based on,
    for in the very word 'doubt' is the beginning of knowledge.
Thus if doubt exists regarding the *wudu'* (itself), then this means his doubt

---

1 the text in this section (from 'benefit' onwards) is garbled in several places. An attempt at coherency has been made by resorting to Mayyara (pp.129-30) upon which this text is partially based.

lies in the pre-condition (to the *salat* which is dependent on *wudu'* for its validity), and if this pre-condition is fulfilled, then one has fulfilled (the obligation);

and if there is doubt as to the onset of a state of impurity,

then this (means there) is doubt in something which (if not put right), prevents (the proper fulfilling of the *wudu'*).

In *Ghayat al-Amani* he says that al-Qarafi says in *adh-Dhakheera*: "The rule is that only knowledge is considered in the law. This is based on the words of, exalted is He: '*Do not pursue what you have no knowledge of*'[1]; and also the fact that there is no room for a mistake when knowledge is present. However, because knowledge is difficult to obtain in most instances, the Legislator has permitted one to follow what one surmises (is true) – because this surmising is rarely wrong, indeed is usually right – despite the doubt remaining. But if we have doubt in the means (i.e. purification) then we cannot conclude the effect (i.e. the *salat* – is valid); and, likewise if we doubt in a condition or pre-requisite (to something) we cannot conclude that that which is dependent upon this condition (is valid); and, furthermore, if we have doubts in the case of something which prevents (a judgement from being made) then one cannot extract a judgement. There is a consensus as to this rule and it cannot be rejected. However, there is a difference of opinion between the *'ulama* as to its application. Thus ash-Shafi'i, may Allah be pleased with him, argues: 'Purity is (a matter about which one can be) sure – any doubt about it is invalidated, remaining as a (mere) appendix to it.' Malik, may Allah have mercy on him, said: 'Fulfilling the duty of the *salat* is a matter about which one may have certainty. However this (certainty) stands in need of a means (to its attainment) which frees one (of further obligation). Any doubt in the condition necessitates doubt in the thing dependent upon the condition and so doubt comes about as to (the validity of) the *salat* – because this has been effected after the purification about which one has doubts. Thus this (purification) is the means which frees one (from the dependent duty of the *salat*): that about which one has doubts is invalid and so applies itself to (and invalidates) the fulfilling of the duty."

His saying 'in the case of someone becoming a *kafir*' means that the *wudu'* of someone reneging on his deen is annulled, and this judgement of his is the well-known opinion. Ashhab has a contrary opinion to this, however: he considers that the renegade remains in *wudu'* if he comes back to Islam. Ibn 'Arafa said in the chapter on *Ridda* (Reneging on Islam) may Allah protect us from it! – after discussing (the judgement of) such a person – that 'Iyad said:

1   al-Isra' – The Night Journey: 36

"The principle in all of this is the question as to whether the judgement on him is the same as that of a normal *kafir* – based on the words of Allah, exalted is He: "*If you associate others with Allah, your actions will come to nothing*"[1]. If so then his previous (acts of) obedience are annulled just as (all previous actions) are removed from a *kafir* who becomes Muslim – and this is the opinion of Ibn al-Qasim. However it has also been said that the judgement on him if he returns to Islam is the original judgement on him – that is, as if he had not reneged. Ashhab relies on this (judgement) – and so (he argues) those who are entitled to inherit, inherit from him if he dies at the moment of his rejection (of Islam), and the good name of his wife remains protected.

وَيَجِبُ اسْتِبْرَاءُ الأخْبَثَيْنِ مَعَ

سَلْتٍ وَنَتْرِ ذَكَرٍ وَالشَّدَّ دَعْ

76 It is obligatory to free (the penis and anus) of the (last remains of) urine and excrement, to apply pressure to the penis and shake it but not excessively

Proof of the obligation of *istibra'* – this freeing of the penis and anus of the last remains of impurity – is afforded by the hadith on the subject of the two graves.[2] One should only apply light pressure (the length of the penis) for any strong pressure would do harm to the place in question, loosen the urinary bladder or might even cause malfunction of the erection or weaken it – and this is a right of the wife. However, it does not necessarily entail these three as the temperaments of people differ. Zarruq said: "While urinating, he should pass his two fingers between the anus and base of the penis thereby expelling any urine already in movement and also preventing any further (from rising). He does not have to stand up and sit down or clear his throat saying 'ahem' (to avert people of his presence) although he may do any of these as he sees fit." Al-Lakhmi said: "Whoever usually retains urine but finds he may release it when he gets up, then he must get up and sit down."

He said in *al-Jalab*: "*Istibra'* is freeing the penis and anus from any impurity."

NOTICE: One of the *'ulama* has mentioned that urinating in still water causes forgetfulness and if a person urinates while taking a bath it causes the whispering (of shaytan). He has also said that retaining urine causes cystic calculus, that excessive pulling (of the penis to expel the remaining urine)

---

1 az-Zumar – The Companies: 62
2 al-Bukhari, *Bab al-Wudu'*, 57

causes weakness of judgement and other maladies, that retention of excrement causes colic, spitting in the lavatory causes dental caries and that looking at one's urine or excrement cause the light of one's sight to disappear." This Zarruq said in *Sharh al-Waghleesiya*. Moreover just prior to this he has also said that talking in the lavatory causes deafness.

BRANCH: Know that many people do not do *istibra'* properly and for this reason one should not pray with something worn by someone else as an undergarment unless one is certain as to whether it is clean or not; nor with the clothes of a *kafir*; however the cloth (woven by a *kafir*) is assumed to be pure, as is any (object of) artisanal work (produced by a *kafir*) or the clothing of a breast-feeding mother, or that of a milkmaid or someone churning (milk), or of someone who collects the butter from the leathern bag, or of a female servant who pours out water or a woman serving food or the sieve (she uses to prepare the food) – all of these are assumed to be pure until there is an indication to the contrary which proves to be true.

USEFUL POINT: The author of *Hayat al-Hayawan* said that at-Tirmidhi al-Hakeem has transmitted: "Anyone sitting in the lavatory who finds a louse should not kill it. Rather he should bury it for it has been related that whoever kills a louse while in the lavatory then shaytan will spend the night with him in his hair and will cause him to forget *dhikr* of Allah for forty mornings. It has also been said that whoever kills a louse while in the lavatory, then he will not cease to be anxious."

USEFUL POINT: The author of *al-Jami' as-Saghir* said: "The most likely (reason for a man's) being tormented in the grave is on account of urine." A-Munawi said: "...in other words, because of negligence in freeing himself from it: failure to free oneself from it invalidates the *salat* which is a pillar of the deen and the best of actions and the first thing for which the slave will be taken to account. The torment of the grave is true according to the people of sunna and it is one of the (traditions) which has been narrated in a multiple chain of transmission. It is obligatory to believe in it and to consider *kafir* the one who denies it."

USEFUL POINT: The author of *an-Nurain fi Islah ad-Darain* said: "Among the reasons for torment in the grave is lack of purification from urine, telling lies, backbiting and treachery. Whoever refrains from these things, then his grave will be as a meadow of the Garden and his proximity to it will be like the closeness of the mother to her child."

وَجَازَ الْإِسْتِجْمَارُ مِن بَوْلِ ذَكَرٍ

كَغَائِطٍ لَا مَا كَثِيراً اِنْتَشَرْ

77 It is permitted to use (only) stones to clean urine from the penis, and to clean oneself of excrement (with them) – as long as it has not spread excessively (beyond the anus itself)

This means that it is enough to wipe the penis and anus with stones or the like and that *instinjah* – cleaning with water – is not necessary, even if water is available, according to the well-known opinion, although cleaning oneself with water is better . However, in the case of women, it is not enough that she clean herself only with stones. Rather she must use water. Likewise water must be used to clean oneself if the excrement has spread considerably around the anus and should be used to clean oneself after an emission of semen, after menstruation, after blood lost after birth and pre-seminal fluid.

Al-Mukhtasar does not mention the things which one may overlook – and there is no harm in mentioning them here in order to complete the benefit.

Included among such things is an amount of blood less than the size of a dirham and pus or fluid from a wound. Mayyara said, adding to those things which may be overlooked: "…any amount of blood less than a dirham in all circumstances, and pus or fluid from a wound." Ibn al-Hattab said: "…irrespective of whether the blood is from a person's own body or has got on to his (from someone else)." He said in *at-Tawdih*: "(this is) according to the most evident opinion within the *madhhab*, and one of the Shaykhs is of the opinion that this dispensation is particular to what is from someone's own body."

He has also said: "The most manifest meaning of the words of *al-Mukhtasar* is that this (blood) may be overlooked in all circumstances – in the *salat* and elsewhere, and one is not obliged to wash it off. However there is a difference of opinion as to what is understood by a 'little' – that is, as to whether it may be overlooked in all circumstances and in all cases such that it may be treated as a pure fluid; or whether this dispensation is restricted to the *salat* such that one does not have to break off (the *salat*) if one remembers it during the (*salat*) and one does not repeat the (*salat*); or whether, before the *salat*, one is recommended (but not obliged) to wash it off." He discusses all this *at-Tawdeeh*, and the first is the *madhhab* of the Iraqis. Muhammad ibn 'Abd as-Salam said "this is the most evident (judgement) – like the other impurities which may be overlooked"; and the second is supported by Muhammad ibn 'Abd as-Salam and the *Mukhtasar* from the *Mudawwana* while the author of *at-Taraz* and Ibn 'Arafa have affirmed this from al-Mazani, ascribing it to Ibn al-Habib and likewise an-Naji. The author of *at-Taraaz* said: "...and this is contrary to the manifest opinion of the *madhhab*." Ibn Farhun has transmitted (a judgement) from Ibn Habib like that of the Iraqis. Thus it appears that there are two opinions: it is as if the *Mukhtasar* has relied on the preferred opinion of the author of the *Taraz* while Muhammad ibn 'Abd as-Salam has relied on that of the Iraqis – or it may be that what he intends is (only) to reject the obligatory (nature of the judgement).

He said in *Ghayat al-Amani* that al-Fakihani said: "Blood is classified in three ways, based on the amount: a negligible amount which it is permitted to (have on one's person or clothes when) beginning the *salat* and which do not necessitate a repetition of (the *salat*); blood amounting in size to the area of one's little finger which it is not permitted (to have on one's person when) beginning the *salat* but which does not necessitate that one repeat the *salat* (should one discover its existence afterwards); and finally an amount corresponding to more than (the size of) a dirham which it is not permitted to have on one's clothes at the beginning the *salat* and which necessitates that one repeat the *salat* (should one discover its existence afterwards)."

Also among the things which may be overlooked is that mentioned by Ibn al-Hattab: "The Qadi Abu'l-Walid ibn Rushd, may Allah have mercy on him, during his discussion of the impure states (*al-ahdath*) which may come upon a person and which cause him to suffer the whisperings of shaytan – has included in this category the urine which in all probability splashes on to one's person from (certain) public highways, that is urine whose precise location cannot be determined but whose existence one nevertheless considers highly likely, given that certain stretches of the highway are often used by a large number of people to urinate. In such a case it is not obligatory to wash it from one's clothing or leather socks, nor from one's body – as it cannot be avoided, and Allah, exalted is He, knows best. This has been transmitted by Ibn Farhun."

Ibn 'Arafa said that al-Baji said: "(This includes) any impurities which one fears might splash on to one's person from the road, that is, whose existence one considers most likely but which one cannot ascribe a precise location to, and this (judgement) is accepted by al-Mazari. The most evident conclusion from what he is referring to is that if a man places his foot or leather sock on a road or allows his clothing to touch any part of it when he is aware that in all likelihood urine is to be found there and that it may spray or splash on to him, then he does not have to wash the affected part even if it has got wet."

Among the issues regarding the *salat* discussed by al-Burzuli is the following: "Whoever does *wudu'*, goes out with pattens or wooden clogs on and his foot slips out (of them) while it is still wet and some earth clings to it and he prays, then he does not have to make up (the *salat*)." Al-Burzuli continues by saying, may Allah have mercy on him: "…because the legal principle governing dust (or earth) from the road is that it is (assumed to be) pure."

Also included among the things for which there is a dispensation are polished or shiny swords. Ibn al-Hattab said that in the case of a polished sword and the like, for example a butcher's knife, mirror and anything else which is smooth and shiny made of iron or (semi-) precious stone, then it is enough to wipe it, rather than wash it – as washing might spoil it, although it has also been said that the principle behind the judgement is that any impurity is removed by wiping it. This judgement, however, does not apply to anything affixed to the sword or the like, such as cloth or a mounting.

ISSUE: During his discussion of impurities which may be overlooked Ibn al-Hattab has posed the question as to "whether a little of the impurity of the sort mentioned above may still be overlooked if it mixes with a fluid." He continues: "I have not seen an explicit text on the matter but the most evident judgement is that it may still be excused. Moreover the branches of the *madhhab* point to this (too)."

Muhammad ibn 'Abd as-Salam, may Allah, exalted is He, have mercy on him, during his explanation of the words of Ibn al-Hajib regarding the removal of impurity and other things which may not be overlooked: "If the taste (or trace of it) remains then the (place) is not purified. As for things which may be overlooked, they do not have to be got rid of (completely): if they are (for the large part) removed but the taste or some trace of them remain then they may be excused – for overlooking the whole necessitates overlooking a part."

He has also said in *al-'Arida*: "Our *'ulama* have two opinions regarding whether – if a person who has bleeding in the mouth spits out his saliva such that the blood is removed – this is enough to purify (his mouth) or whether he should wash it with water. The correct opinion is that purity is (only) attained by (washing with) water if there is a lot (of blood); if negligible, then it is excused. Saliva is not capable of purifying anything."

Then, after a discussion, he says that all these traditions indicate that the judgement regarding blood – or some other impurity which may be overlooked – is not altered (when such an impurity comes into contact with) liquid, and Allah, exalted is He, knows best.

That which he has transmitted from *al-'Arida*, namely "that saliva purifies the mouth" is one of the two opinions mentioned by Ibn 'Arafa. In the following text (he also says): "The mouth becomes pure when bleeding stops and after spitting out the (blood). Al-Lakhmi, he says, gives preference to the first judgement, while Ibn al-'Arabi gives preference to the second."

The author has indicated by his words 'but not if it has spread out (around the anus)' that it is not enough to use stones or the like for cleaning and that water must be used in this case – and this is the correct opinion.

Issue al-Hattab said: "(The author) said in the introduction to the section on washing (*ghusl*): 'If the woman is so fat that her hand does not reach to the place of impurity, it is not permitted her to have someone else, like a female slave or any one else, wash it for her. It is not permitted for her to reveal her (private parts) to other than her husband. If her husband is able to do the washing for her, then this is in order and he will be rewarded generously for this. If he declines to do this, then it is not obligatory for him and she should pray with the impurity still on her. No one should see her private parts as covering the private parts is obligatory. There is agreement that this is also not permitted to those related to her. There are four differences of opinion (in her case) as to the removal of impurity in the *salat*, one of them being that its removal is recommended. There is an ease (and licence) regarding things about which there is a difference of opinion – as opposed to things about which there is no difference of opinion (which must be strictly carried out)."

As for a man, if his hand cannot reach this (place of impurity) then he should buy a female slave to do this for him. If his wife is willing to wash him, then he is not obliged to buy a female slave. It is not permitted for him to reveal his private parts to other than the above mentioned. If he is not able to find (a female slave), then his *salat* with this impurity is less of an offence than revealing his private parts. All this is in accordance with the *madhhab* of Malik, may Allah, exalted is He, have mercy on him." Here ends the discussion of al-Hattab regarding Khalil's words 'washing the private parts with water.'

Issue: Ibn al-Hattab has also said that the author of *at-Taraz* – when talking of the *adab* of cleaning oneself with stones – says: "Malik has permitted that he enter the lavatory in possession of a dinar and dirham, even if the name of Allah, exalted is He, is written on it. Ibn al-Qasim has related from him in the *'Utbiya* that: 'He does not esteem it to be such a serious matter if one washes one's private parts while wearing a signet ring although he has also said that: "I prefer that he removes it – there is a licence in this and those of earlier generations were not mindful of this."' Ibn al-Qasim said: 'I wash my private parts while wearing a (ring) on which is mention of Allah, exalted is He.' Ibn Habib said: 'I dislike that in him.'"

He has also said after a while: "There are, in all, three opinions regarding the washing of one's private parts while wearing a signet ring, (firstly) that it is permitted – and this is what is to be understood from the words of Ibn al-Qasim and his practice; (secondly) that it is disliked and this is what is to be understood from the words of Malik in three places in the *'Utbiya*. This (latter) is Ibn Rushd's understanding from the words of al-Lakhmi who said: 'There is a difference of opinion as to whether he should wash his private parts while wearing it on his hand or whether it is better not to do so. This difference is based on the hadith of Anas: "The Messenger of the Prophet, may the peace and blessings of Allah be upon him, would remove his signet ring when entering the lavatory" – as related by at-Tirmidhi – together with that narrated in the *Sahih*, namely that "He prohibited that one touch one's penis with one's right hand." If (he argues) the Messenger, may the peace and blessings of Allah be upon him, kept his right hand from touching his penis then it is all the more fitting that one remove *dhikr* of Allah from it (in the lavatory). Moreover Malik considered it *makruh* to give dirhams with the name of Allah on them to a Jew or Christian and so – by the same token – it is all the more fitting that one remove His name from such a place of impurity.' Al-Fakihani said – after recommending the wearing of a signet ring on the right finger: 'Even though there might be the name of Allah, exalted is He, on it, it is not necessary that one remove it while washing one's private parts for this is (only) recommended in the case of someone who wears his ring on the left hand.' (Thirdly) there are those who consider that it is prohibited (to wear a ring in such a place). This (judgement) may be understood from the discussion in *at-Tawdih*, that of Muhammad ibn 'Abd as-Salam and also from the discussion of Ibn al-'Arabi who says in *al-'Arida* – in the section regarding the *adab* of washing one's private parts: 'The signet ring on which is the name of Allah should be removed for it is not permitted that a Muslim wash his private parts while wearing it on his hand.' Then he gives a complicated explanation on the subject: 'It is narrated from Malik in the *'Utbiya* that there is no harm in washing one's private parts while wearing a signet ring containing mention of Allah. One of my Shaykhs said: "This transmission is invalid, may we seek refuge in Allah that any filth come into contact with His name." I had a signet ring on which was inscribed Muhammad ibn al-'Arabi and I refrained from washing my private parts with it lest I should violate the name of Muhammad. Even though this (name of mine) did not denote the Noble and Generous (Prophet, may the peace and blessings of Allah be upon him) I considered that (my) sharing (his name) was sanction enough to prohibit it (for myself).' Ibn al-'Arabi said in the introduction: 'He should avoid washing his private parts while wearing a signet ring on his hand if there is one of the names of Allah, exalted is He, on it or one of the names of the Prophets, on whom be peace and blessings . It has been narrated from Malik, may Allah have mercy on him, that he has permitted this although this narration has been rejected by the latter generations of this *madhhab*. It is not fitting to incline towards this (judgement) or give it any attention for it is not (possible) to ascribe it to any one of the *'ulama*, let alone imam Malik who had such great respect for the Presence of Allah, exalted is He, and that of the Prophet, may the peace and blessings of Allah be upon him, as is well known. And Allah, exalted is He, knows best.' He has also said in *al-Ishad* when talking on (the subject of) washing one's private parts: '... and that it is done with the left hand. If he is wearing a signet ring on his left hand on which there is mention of Allah, then he should transfer it to his right hand.' Shams ad-Deen at-Tata'i said in his commentary: 'This is an obligation, and Allah knows best.'" Here ends the commentary of al-Hattab on Khalil's words '...if he misses it, then do it during it....'

Ibn al-Hattab continues at the point where Khalil says '...(touching the Qur'an is prohibited) even with a stick...' saying: "In one historical account it is also recorded that Abu Dharr – and the like is recorded about others of the *fuqaha* from al-Andalus – instructed in his testament that one bury with him a collection of traditions he had composed and this was carried out. Another instructed in his will that he be buried with his signet ring on which was written 'There is no god, only Allah and Muhammad is the Messenger of Allah', may the peace and blessings of Allah be upon him, and this was carried out. (The reason for) this (practice) is not difficult to comprehend, in my opinion. It was intended as a reminder to the dead person of how to answer the angels and to gain *baraka*. According to the narration of Ibn al-Qasim it is permitted to wash one's private parts while wearing a (ring)."

In the *Mi'yar*, the author has narrated from one of the *'ulama* who lived at the same time and in the same place as Malik, namely Muhammad ibn Ahmad ibn Muhammad ibn Ahmad ibn Marzouq the following – and it is also recorded in the *'Utbiya*: "I asked Malik regarding a signet ring on which was mention of Allah as to whether one should wear it on one's left (hand) while washing one's private parts. Malik replied: 'I hope that it will be (deemed) insignificant.' This he has transmitted in *an-Nawadir* and from the *'Utbiya*. Ibn al-Qasim said: 'Malik deemed the wearing – while washing one's private parts – of a ring on the left hand on which the word Allah glorious is He, was inscribed as insignificant while Ibn Habib considered it *makruh* to wash one's private parts while wearing one.'"

The gist of these transmissions in the *madhhab* – as to whether one should wash one's private parts while wearing a signet ring on which mention is made of Allah – is that there are two opinions: that it is permitted and disliked. One of the (ulama) said: "…and they are both attested to in the *Mudawwana*: (evidence for) permission is (attested to) from (the incident regarding) the exchange of coins between a Muslim and his Christian slave for the most evident interpretation is that it involved dinars and dirhams on which was inscribed the name of Allah, exalted is He; (evidence) that it is disliked is (attested to) from what he relates in the 'Book of Trade carried out in the Land of the Enemy': '…and do not buy (anything) from them with dinars and dirhams on which is inscribed the name of Allah because of these (people) are impure.'" There are also those who consider that what is related in the Book of Exchange refers to coins which are not inscribed (with His name) – (in which case, they argue) the two opposing views can be reconciled. However, Ibn Yunus said: "Ibn al-Qasim has narrated that it is permitted and the Prophet, may the peace and blessings be upon him wrote: 'In the name of Allah, the All Merciful, the Most Merciful – to Caesar, the Emperor of Rome.'" Moreover in the *Sahih* of al-Bukhari, there is the letter to Heraclius in which he wrote – as well as the *bismillah*: '*Say, "People of the Book!" come to a proposition which is the same for us and you …*[1]'"

If one accepts the opinion of those who argue that it is permitted to write to the (non-Muslims) using a little of the Qur'an, like an *ayat* or the like, then it would also be permitted to exchange coins with them as long as the amount of dinars and dirhams on which is inscribed (the name of Allah) is negligible – that is, by analogy with the case of the person in a state of major ritual impurity who may read an *ayat* or the like but is not permitted to read a lot. As for the attaching of (an amulet of) protection against evil to a *kafir* which contains the name of Allah, exalted is He, there are two opinions; likewise, there are two opinions regarding doing *dhikr* of Allah in the place set aside for the lavatory – and the most evident judgement in this respect being that the prohibition is one of karaha – dislike (rather than total prohibition). Ibn Rushd said in *al-Bayan*: "His saying 'I hope that it will be (deemed) insignificant' – indicates that it is disliked and that removing is better in his eyes." Ibn Rushd has also said: "The practice of Ibn al-Qasim is not good – however it is possible that he did what he did because his ring was tight and it was difficult to transfer it to the other hand whenever he needed to wash his private parts."

1 Ali 'Imran: 63

It is also reported of him in another passage: "The evidence (attesting to the obligation) to avoid impurity in the *salat* is stronger than the argument for avoiding it (when wearing something) with an inscription bearing mention (of His name or when performing *dhikr*). For this reason it has been related: 'Remember Allah in all your states.' This and similar arguments – and Allah knows best – form the evidence of Ibn al-Qasim (namely that) remembrance of the great name and writing it down on something are the same. In other words, expression (of His name) on the tongue or the writing (of it) manually are both signs indicating a meaning which is known to the heart. However the sign is not addressed to Him but rather reverence emanates from Him to Him, and to Allah, may He be glorified belongs absolute perfection, and to Him no imperfection may be ascribed. For this reason *dhikr* is permitted in a place which is not pure although calling for blessings on the Prophet, may the peace and blessing of Allah be upon him, is not permitted in such a place. Thus if it is permitted to make *dhikr* (of Him) in that place, then writing is also permitted in the same (place). However, no one, as far as I know, has permitted the performance of the *salat* with impurity (when one has knowledge of it) from the commencement. Indeed the least that has been said on the matter is that its removal is recommended." Here ends the discussion in *al-Mi'yar* as narrated by Ibn Marzouq.

Issue: It is forbidden to put one's fingers into one's private parts while washing them. Al-Amir said: "It is forbidden to put one's fingers into the anus or vagina except if necessary to remove any filth."

Issue: Ibn 'Arafa said that al-Qarafi said: "that which a (once) married woman washes of her private parts is the same as the virgin because the place of urination is situated in front of the place of virginity or the private parts of a married woman; and when menstruating, the married woman should wash away all that appears from her vagina at the time of sitting; and the virgin what is below her virginity and it is possible to argue that the urine runs over it and so it is to be washed, and the first is more evident."

Issue Ibn al-Hattab said commenting on the words of Khalil 'it is permitted when clean and dry…': "the discussion of dust is included and by it he is giving an explicit judgement regarding robes (which drag in the dust)."

Issue: Mayyara said: "It has been narrated that the Messenger of Allah may the peace and blessings of Allah be upon him went to the place used by the people for disposing of their waste and rubbish and then he urinated while standing – this is narrated by al-Bukhari, Muslim, Abu Dawud and at-Tirmidhi."

However 'A'isha has denied this saying: 'Whoever say that the Messenger of Allah, may the peace and blessings of Allah be upon him, urinated while standing then reject it' and it may well be – and Allah, exalted is He, knows best – that she denied this cause of what he normally did. Mujahid said: 'He only urinated standing a single time' and al-Khatabi said he did this because of an illness he had and he was unable to squat on account of it – and the Arabs (of the time) used to ease the pain in (the small of) the back by this (standing).'"

Issue: Khalil said: "In open country, one seeks cover, that is, it is recommended." Ibn al-Hattab said that Ibn Naji said in his commentary on the *Mudawwana*: "I have not found a text in our *madhhab* which defines the degree of cover" and an-Nawawi said transmitting from their *madhhab* that it is equal to the rear part of a saddle, that is three hand spans and that between him and it there should be three arm spans or less and any more than this is haram – as if he were in an open plain: and what he mentions conforms to our *madhhab* – based on (obligation of) the *sutra* – that erected in front of one during the *salat* – this is transmitted by al-Ubbi also from an-Nawawi in the commentary on Muslim. Then he related he said: "the most evident of the two opinions from our point of view is that if he lets the end of his robe down between him and the *qibla*, then it is enough. Al-Ubbi said: "It is narrated above from Lakhmi that for the latter there is enough justification in that it serves to screen those praying."

I say: "Since al-Lakhmi has mentioned his discussion above regarding the difference of opinion as to the reasoning (behind the judgement) and has lent support to the opinion that it is because of the sanctity of the *qibla*, then it necessary follows with respect to the other opinion that it is permitted the person who lets his robe-end down to urinate."

Benefit: al-Bazzar has narrated from him, may the peace and blessings of Allah be upon him, that "whoever squates to urinate facing the *qibla* but then remembers and turns away from it out of respect for it, then he will not get up from where he is squatting but that he will be forgiven." This is mentioned in *adh-Dhakheera*.

SECTION CONCERNING GHUSL

'Ali ibn 'Abd as-Sadiq said: "The (*ghusl*) acts as a separation between the two states (of purity and impurity), and the Book, sunna and *ijma'* all confirm its obligatory nature – as they do the *wudu'*. There is no difference of opinion as to the obligation – or the preconditions upon which they are both dependent – of both of these within the *umma* and anyone who denies the (*ghusl* or the *wudu'*) is a *kafir*; but not, however, someone who abandons doing it but while believing it (is part of the *'aqida*). The *ghusl* has *fard* obligations, sunnas and recommended aspects. Al-Jazuli said: "One must know them, and whoever does not know them, then his testimony (before a judge) is not permitted, nor is it permitted he be an imam (in a *salat*), and whoever prays behind such a person, then he remains under the obligation to repeat it (until he performs it), as in the case of (someone ignorant of the) *wudu'* and *tayammum*.'"

The most obvious meaning of his saying 'anyone who denies the (*ghusl* or the *wudu'*) is a *kafir*' is that it even applies to an ignorant person. Likewise this applies to anyone who denies any matters of the deen which are known to be necessary and indispensable (*daruri*), like the prohibition of backbiting, fornication, drinking wine and the like. However, strictly speaking, if he denies after (having acquired) knowledge then he is a *kafir* for he would be denying the Messenger of Allah may the peace and blessings of Allah be upon him; if he does not know then he is not a *kafir* except if he acts in disobedience by deliberately not learning what is incumbent upon him – and that is a matter between him and Allah. However, according to the manifest (judgement) of the law, his word is not accepted (if he claims not to know) if he lives in the society of the Muslims and has wide ranging contact with them; if this is not the case then his word is accepted.

There is no harm in relating some of what has been discussed on the subject. Ibn Hajar al-Haytami said in *al-Mathanat*: "What counts as a denial (of the deen) is the refusal to accept what is known as 'the necessary' in the deen of Muhammad, may the peace and blessings of Allah be upon him, that is, things which are known by intuitive or instinctive understanding even by the ordinary masses amongst the Muslims, like for example the oneness of Allah, prophethood, the day of raising up, the reward and the punishment, as well as the obligations, like the *salat*, for example, and the prohibitions, like wine or sexual intercourse with a menstruating woman, and the permitted things, like buying and selling, and marriage, and the recommended acts like the sunnas (of the *salat*). Moreover in the *Rawda* he considers that the prohibition for a person other than the husband of marrying a woman during her idda period is not something which is automatically known as one of the necessary and intuitive matters of the deen." After a while he continues: "... also considered as *kafir* is someone who forbids that about which there is agreement as to its being halal or haram. Thus if you were to say: 'there is no use in stipulating that (a person have) knowledge (of the matter in question) together with stipulating that he must have frequented the society (of Muslims) for as soon as he knows and denies it, then he is guilty of *kufr* – even if he has not frequented (the Muslims); (likewise), if he does not know, he is not treated as a *kafir* even if he has kept the society (of Muslims)' then I would reply: 'This is true. However, the person who keeps company (with Muslims) is not believed on the face of it when he claims ignorance, as opposed to someone who does not (keep company). Moreover, it may well be that a matter has been transmitted in unbroken, multiple chains of transmission, and is known (and practised) as a necessary (part of the deen) with respect to one group of people but not with another, and so one would consider as *kafir* the person who was exposed to this (knowledge and practice) which had been transmitted in an unbroken, multiple chain of relation but not in the case of someone else. As for what is generally agreed upon but which is not known as a necessary and indispensable part of the deen, (there is) for example the right of the daughter of a son (to inherit) a sixth together with the daughter of one's own loins – anyone denying this would not be considered a *kafir*, according to us. However, the Hanafis would consider (such a person as *kafir*) if (such a judgement) is established with certainty or the people of knowledge have declared that it is certain and the person in question continues to refute (its validity) out of disobedience."

The (examples) mentioned (above) are clear and unambiguous with respect to the matter we have mentioned. Among those who have clarified (this matter) and stipulated the above mentioned condition, namely (that one have knowledge of the judgement in question) are Ibn Hajar in *Fath al-Bari*, al-Qastalani, al-'Alqami, ash-Shihab in the commentary on the *Shifa* and Zarruq in *an-Naseeha*. In the *Shifa*, (for example) he says, adding to those acts he considers *kufr*: "... likewise if a person denies (the reality of) Makka or the Sacred House (of the Ka'ba), or the Mosque of the Haram or the form of the hajj – despite affirming that the hajj is an obligation set out in the Qur'an and that facing the direction of the Qibla is likewise (an obligation set out in the Qur'an) – by saying 'I do not know whether the (hajj is to be understood as comprising the) commonly accepted form or some other form, or whether the House, the Haram Mosque and the *qibla* are located in Makka' and by claiming that 'perhaps the transmitters from the Prophet, may the peace and blessings of Allah be upon him, who have understood it in this way, have made a mistake or were deluded (in their understanding) or the like' then there is no doubt that they are to be considered as *kafir*. (All this holds good) as long as it may be supposed that they are aware of the (true teaching) and as long as they frequent the company of the Muslims but not if they have recently entered Islam – in which case they should be told: 'What you should do is ask any of the Muslims if there is something you do not know.'"

He has also said in another place: "Likewise we consider as *kafir* anyone who denies anything stated explicitly (in the Qur'an) – as long as he is aware that it is from the Qur'an to be found with the people (who have memorised it) and in the *mus-hafs* (which are widely available) among the Muslims and he is not ignorant of this (fact)."

As an illustration of this (explicit text) ash-Shihab said: "...like the Day of Raising Up for example." Among those who have stated that one can only consider as *kafir* the person who denies something which is known as being a necessary part of the deen after he has acquired knowledge of the judgemment of what he is denying and is aware that the judgement regarding what he is refusing to accept has been transmitted to him in a unbroken, multiple chain of narration – for then he would be denying the Prophet may the peace and blessings of Allah be upon him – is al-Muhaqqiq Ibn ash-Shat in the *Hashiya al-Farouq*. Al-Qarafi said in *al-Farouq*: "The basis of *kufr* is a specific violation of the sanctity of Lordship either through ignorance of the existence of Allah mighty is He and majestic or His sublime attributes or is (an act of) *kufr* like throwing a *mus-haf* in a place of filth, prostrating to an idol, frequenting the churches of the Christians during their festivals, indulging in their states or denying whatever of the deen may be known necessarily (through intercourse with people or by intuition for example). Our saying 'a specific violation' is in order to distinguish it from the major and minor wrong actions. These latter, it is true, are also violations but they are not (acts of) *kufr* or a denial of what may be known of the deen necessarily and inevitably (through keeping company of the Muslims for example), like denying the *salat* and fasting, for example. Moreover this (judgement) does not only apply to the obligations and supererogatory acts made with the intention of bringing one closer to Allah, exalted is He. Rather anyone who denies things which are inherently licit would also be committing *kufr* – like if the person were to say: 'Allah, exalted is He, has not permitted (the eating) of figs and dates.' However, it would be irrational to claim that the person who denies something about which there is general agreement is always guilty of *kufr*. Rather (for this to hold true), this (matter of) general agreement must be so generally well-known and widespread in (people's) deen that it has become something that will be necessarily (known by them) – for how many a matter about which there is general agreement is not even known by the elite of the *fuqaha*! Thus denying a matter of consensus which is not widely known is not an act of *kufr* – for many a group from amongst the Rafidis and the Khawarij have denied the principle of consensus but, by Allah, I do not know anyone who affirms that they are *kafir* merely because they deny the consensus. The reason for this is they have made efforts to produce proof and evidence (against the consensus) but they have not been successful in the same way as the majority (*jumhur* of the *fuqaha'*) have been. This then is an excuse in their favour. It is like for example someone who has recently become Muslim who comes from the land of *kufr* and spontaneously denies some of the rites of Islam which are well known as necessary elements (of the deen): such a person is not considered a *kafir* because he has the excuse of not having experience (of such things) – even though we would consider as *kafir* someone else who did the same.

It is on this same principle that we would answer the questions: 'Why is it that you consider as *kafir* the person who contradicts matters about which there is a consensus but you do not consider as *kafir* the one who denies the principle of consensus?' and 'how is the branch stronger than the principle?' The answer is that we do not consider someone a *kafir* who denies consensus simply because it is a consensus but rather because of the fact that being so widespread it is necessarily known (by all). Thus whenever the quality of being widely known is added to this consensus, then the person who denies it is (necessarily) guilty of *kufr*. If, however, this quality of being well known is missing then we do not consider someone as a *kafir*. Thus it is on this basis that we do not reckon the branch to be stronger than the principle – for this would necessarily follow if we considered someone as *kafir* merely because there was a consensus (on the matter in question) rather than the fact that it was well known. Thus we do not consider those who deny the legality of the *fard* obligations as *kafir* merely on the basis of the consensus – for how this consensus has been arrived at is only known by elite of the *fuqaha*, not by the rest. Shaykh Abu'l-Hasan al-Ash'ari, may Allah be pleased with him, has even included the (mere) desire (to commit) *kufr* as an act of *kufr* – like wanting to build churches so acts of *kufr* may be carried out."

Ibn ash-Shat has commented on his words 'the basis of *kufr* is a specific violation...' saying: "Kufr is not a violation of lordship but rather an ignorance of lordship. As for the violation of the sanctity of lordship, it does not normally issue from someone who believes in the reality of lordship. As for his words 'as for ignorance of the existence of Allah, exalted is He, and His sublime attributes' I would say that ignorance of this is *kufr* – in particular in the case of someone who does not hold that disobedience is an act of *kufr*. However, as for someone who does hold to this, then *kufr* is either ignorance of Allah, exalted is He, or denying something (about Him); violating His sanctity, may either be with ignorance or with knowledge and may usually be overlooked."

Commenting on his words: 'or the *kufr* takes the form of an action, like throwing a *mus-haf* into a place of filth' Ibn ash-Shat said: "Throwing down a *mus-haf* into a place of filth is either done with the intention of rejecting it and what it contains or without this intention. If done as an act of denial, then this is *kufr*; otherwise it is an act of gross disobedience, but not *kufr*."

Commenting on his words 'prostrating to an idol' he said: "If the prostration to the idol is done while believing that it is a god, then this is *kufr*; if not, then it is not *kufr* but rather an act of gross disobedience even if done without any external coercion. It is permitted if done under coercion."

Commenting on his words 'or frequenting the churches of the Christians during their festivals and indulging in their states' he said: "This too is not *kufr* unless he believes what they believe."

Commenting on his words 'and denying whatever of the deen may be known necessarily (through intercourse with people for example) he said: "This is *kufr* if he denies it after obtaining knowledge – in which case it would be a refusal to accept; otherwise it is ignorance. As for his saying 'so our saying "a specific violation" is in order to distinguish this from the major and minor wrong actions for they are also violations but not (acts of) *kufr*' – a special explanation of this will follow after this."

I SAY: "The major and minor wrong actions are not a violation of the sanctity of the Lord. Opposition to Him is rather an expression of insolence, and this is instigated by the intents and desires (of the self)."

Commenting on his words 'and denying whatever of the deen may be known necessarily (through intercourse with people for example)' to his words 'even though we would consider as *kafir* someone else who did the same' he said: "What he said is correct, except for his restricting the matter with the mere proviso that it be 'well known in the deen' – for not only does it have to be wide-spread but it must also have reached this (particular) person and he must have taken cognisance of it. Only then would he be considered to have refuted Allah, exalted is He, and His Messenger and would be considered a *kafir*. If, however, he is not aware of this matter and it is one of the well known basic tenets of the deen, then he would be guilty of disobedience for having abandoned the means to gain knowledge of this but not a *kafir*."

Commenting on his words 'It is on this same principle that we answer the question...' to his words 'this consensus is only known by elite of the *fuqaha* not by the rest' he said: "What he said here is correct except for the omission of the condition that the person must have knowledge of this well known matter."

Commenting on his words '...and Shaykh Abu'l-Hasan al-Ash'ari, may Allah be pleased with him has also included as *kufr*....' he said: "If the reason for this is a person's conviction of the precedence of *kufr* over Islam then he is guilty of *kufr* and there is no doubt about this. If, however, he has a church built for a *kafir* in order to get on intimate terms with him and towards whom he wanted to show affection by this means then this is an act of disobedience, not *kufr*." Here end the words of Ibn ash-Shat.

'Ali ibn 'Abd as-Sadiq said that the words 'and whoever is not aware of it .....' are contrary to the words of *al-Mukhtasar* 'and a judgement which is known' narrated by the commentator and al-Qubbab; however it corresponds to what al-'Aufi said.

I say: "This judgement is (merely one possible) example to be followed; but as for the judgement regarding his *salat* this judgement is to be found in the *salat* itself – and the correct view is that stated in the *Nawazil* of Ibn Hilal: "... there is the question as to whether the *salat* of the person – whose *wudu'*, *ghusl* and *salat* is as described but who is ignorant of the judgements concerning the *fard* obligations of the sunan or the aspects of excellence – is acceptable or not. If you say that it is not, then what does the person do who has been in this state for a long time – for years as you mentioned? Should he repeat his *salats* (to make up for those past) whenever he prays as soon as he becomes aware of this or not? The answer is that if the person in question comes (to the *salat*) in a state of purity and the *salat* is performed in the well known way and there is nothing (basically) missing from it, then his *salat* is (accepted as) correct. However, he must learn (the rest of the judgements) – but does not have to repeat his *salat* even if he does not know the *fard* obligations of the sunna" His *Nawazil* is one of the books one can rely on, as is the work of Ibn 'Abd al-'Aziz and this is what Zarruq affirms in *Sharh al-Waghliseeya*.

THE FARD OBLIGATIONS OF THE *Ghusl*

فَصْلٌ فُرُوضُ الْغَسْلِ قَصْدٌ يُحْتَضَرْ

فَوْرٌ عُمُومُ الدَّلْكِ تَخْلِيلُ الشَّعَرْ

78 Section: the *fard* obligations of the *ghusl* are: that one's intent be present, that one complete the various elements of the *ghusl* one after each other without interruption, one rub all over (the body) and ensure that water penetrates the hair (to the skin)

'Ali ibn 'Abd as-Sadiq said: "His saying 'one's intent be present' means that he should consciously seek to establish an intention at the beginning of the *ghusl*. This is because what is required is that the intention accompanies that which is intended: if he makes it an inordinately long time before or after then it is not acceptable while if he does it just a little before, then there are two opinions. Proceeding from this (latter difference) is their difference of opinion regarding the person who walks to the place of purification intending to make the *ghusl* of *janaba* but who then forgets his intention when beginning his purification. Ibn al-Qasim said: 'The prior intention is acceptable as that which approximates to a thing also lends its judgement to that thing' while Sahnun said 'This is acceptable of him when done in a river but not in the hammam because of the possible delay in (performing the *ghusl* in the case of) the latter – as mentioned above.' An opinion transmitted by al-Qarafi holds that it is unacceptable in both cases, that is both in the hammam or rivers. This (judgement) has also been indicated by another (of the *fuqaha*).

The form of this (intention) is the same as mentioned above in connection with *wudu'*, namely the intention to remove the state of bodily impurity (*hadath*), in this case a major impurity, or (the intention) to make licit what was (previously) forbidden (during the state of *janaba*) or to make licit a *fard* obligation."

Ahmad Mayyara said: "The place of the intention is at the beginning of the *ghusl*, either when removing the impurity itself – if he begins with this as required – or when beginning with something else, or when washing his hands before removing the impurity itself – depending on whether we argue that washing them beforehand is obligatory for the *ghusl* or that washing them beforehand is a sunna. Thus if one intends the (removal of) *janaba* while washing off the impurity, then one does not need to wash that place (again) as the removal of ritual impurity does not need an intention and is included in the *ghusl* of the *janaba*."

Al-Mawwaq said that Ibn al-Arafa said – regarding his saying 'completion of the various elements of the *ghusl* one after each other without interruption, rubbing all over the body' – that means "ensuring water penetrates the hair (to the skin) is obligatory." Ibn Yunus said: "The correct judgement is that it is obligatory to ensure water penetrates the beard to the skin." Ashhab (has narrated that he) had learnt of this (judgement) while Ibn al-Qasim that it was annulled."

Commenting on the words of the *Risala* 'she does not have to loosen her braids' Ahmad al-Mayyara said that this applies as long as "they are loose and water is able to penetrate them – for if this is not the case then she must loosen them." He then goes on to say: "Ibn Rushd has made a *fatwa* – regarding the person who suffers from some disease afflicting his head which prevents him from washing it but which he is able to wipe over – saying that he may change to doing *tayammum* if he fears that his illness will get worse. Ibn 'Arafa said: 'The most evident judgement is that it should be wiped over, and the same is related by Muhammad ibn 'Abd as-Salam.'"

In *al-Mi'yar* he says: "The Shaykhs are agreed that one should review what Ibn Rushd says critically, and so (judgement on) this (matter) is not restricted to Muhammad ibn 'Abd as-Salam and Ibn 'Arafa as Mayyara has inferred."

An-Nafrawi's comments on the *Risala* saying: "If one fears catching a cold from pouring water onto one's head then one should (first) wash one's body and then wipe over the (head)." Al-Jazuli said: "I have heard it from several Shaykhs such that I have attained certainty in the matter – so much so that if necessary, I would do it myself. However, this practice must be based on one's own personal experience or on the directions of a doctor with insight – not merely based on (an unfounded) fear. (Thus it may only be carried out) as stipulated, (that is), when there is a licit excuse to change from the principle (judgement, namely the washing) to something in its stead (i.e. the wiping). Thus he should not change (from performing the purification with water – (merely) on the basis (of fear) – to doing *tayammum* as this purification is one which should be carried out with water throughout."

He has also said that Abu 'Imran al-Fasi said: "It is permitted as a special licence for the bride to wipe over (her head) for the *wudu'* and *ghusl* for seven days on account of the perfumes on her head; if she has applied them to the rest of the body, then she may do *tayammum* for to remove the perfume would be a waste of money – which is forbidden."

However, at the end of this explanation Ibn al-Hattab said: "This is contrary to the well known judgement in the *madhhab*. I would argue that among the things which indicate that it is contrary to the *madhhab* is that the (*fuqaha* of the *madhhab*) have not permitted the wiping over something which is covering (the hair) in the case of *wudu'* or *ghusl* – except when there is a pressing need. And cosmetics (including perfumes) do not fall in this category."

فَتَابِعِ الْخَفِيَّ مِثْلُ الرُّكْبَتَيْنْ

وَالْإِبْطِ وَالرُّفْغِ وَبَيْنَ الْأَلْيَتَيْنْ

79   and see (that the water reaches) the recesses (of the body) and folds (of the skin), like behind the knees and the armpits, the junction of the thighs and the buttocks

'Ali ibn 'Abd as-Sadiq said: "As long as it does not present too great a difficulty, the person must make sure he reaches the crevices (of the body), folds of fat (of the belly) and any part that is hidden, covering and rubbing all these (places) with water. It is not necessary to remove any filth from nails. Rather, he should clench his fingers into his palms – (simply) washing them all (together) – and that will be enough. He should move any ring, earring or bracelet (up and down to ensure water reaches the skin beneath them), as is recorded in the *Muqaddima* of Ibn Rushd. (Incidentally), implicit in this latter (transmission) is permission to pierce one's ears in order to carry earrings. This (judgement) – which is correct – is also supported (by the fact) that Sara swore she would mutilate Hajar: on the orders of al-Khalil, (Ibrahim) on whom be peace, she then forced her down and pierced her ears[1]. This is narrated by al-Khurshi in his commentary on Khalil."

In the *Sharh ar-Risala*, Zarruq – and others – has mentioned that the piercing of ears is prohibited, saying 'and it has become a widespread custom afflicting the people – however, al-Qarafi and others have exaggerated in their rejection of this.'" Here end the words of 'Ali ibn 'Abd as-Sadiq.

---

1   Ibrahim, on whom be peace, had suggested the 'mutilation' of the ear-piercing as an acceptable way of fulfilling her oath.

In *Ghayat al-Amani* the author said: "Among the widespread customs afflicting the people is the piercing of ears for earrings. Al-Ghazali and others have been quite zealous in their rejection of it. Indeed the *ijma'* is close to claiming that it is prohibited – and this (consensus) has been narrated by Ibn al-Hajj. However imam Ahmad has declared that it is permitted – according to one (*faqih*) we have encountered. This, in fact, is the (correct judgement) to be followed – for any (judgement) other than this would result in a bad opinion of the character of the whole *umma*." A discussion of this has been made above in (the section dealing with) examples of the *makruh*.

ISSUE: Ibn al-Hattab, in the *Hashiya ar-Risala* – at the point where he states 'he must ensure water penetrates to the skin of his beard, his armpits and between his buttocks' – says "He should relax (his body) in order to wash the anus for this is one of the (inaccessible) places of the body where sweat and impurity abound. Examine the words of Ibn Rushd 'he should relax (the body)....' The most evident judgement is that this is obligatory, although it may be argued that this is (only) recommended for the *istinja*' – the washing of the private parts after urination or defecation. However, a distinction may be drawn (between the two matters): the matter regarding (the removal of) an ritual impurity (*najasa*) is of less significance, given that the (ulama) have differed on this (subject) – contrary to the removal (of the state of ritual impurity which comes upon a person with the onset of) a *hadath* (a bodily change necessitating the washing of every part of the body with the *ghusl*), for there is agreement that this is obligatory – reflect upon this."

وَصِلْ لِمَا عَسُرَ بِالمِنْدِيلِ

وَنَحْوِهِ كَالْحَبْلِ وَالتَّوْكِيلِ

80   and reach those parts which are difficult of access with a cloth or the like – for example, a rope – or have someone else do it

'Ali ibn 'Abd as-Sadiq said: "It is not permitted (to perform this cleaning) by means of a wall made of plaster because it would ruin it, nor by means of the wall of the hammam as this cannot be cleaned."

Al-Mawwaq has commented on Khalil's words 'and rub (the water) in (using one's hands) – even after (applying) the water, or using a cloth, or have someone else do it for you; and if one is still unable (to perform the washing), then (the obligation is) removed' saying: "Ibn 'Arafa said: (The obligation to clean) any (part) one cannot reach is annulled. If the person is able to get help from someone or (reach such places) with a cloth then it is obligatory, according to Sahnun, but not obligatory according to Ibn Habib. Ibn Rushd said: 'The correct judgement is that of Ibn Habib – that is, one which takes into consideration the differences of opinion for they may be likened to "the ease in the deen" (stipulated in the *shari'ah*). Then he should continue (if unable to reach any part of his body) by pouring water over the particular (place to be washed) and it will be acceptable.'"

Ahmad Mayyara said: "He should rub with his hand and if his hand cannot reach a part of his body he should rub it with a cloth, a rope or the like or have someone else – whom he is permitted to touch, like his wife or slave girl – rub this place for him. If he is incapable of reaching some (part of the body) other than that between the navel and the knees, he may have someone else rub it for him – other than his wife or slave girl. This is the well known opinion and it is also what Sahnun holds to. However, it has also been said that, with respect to any place he cannot reach with is hand, the obligation to rub is annulled, and this is in *al-Wadiha,* while yet another holds that if the area in question is considerable then he is obliged to do it with a cloth or have someone else do it – as mentioned above – but that if insignificant, then the obligation is annulled, and this is (the opinion) of al-Qadi Abu'l-Hasan. Thus if he has no means whatsoever to rub (the place in question), then the obligation is annulled – that is, if he cannot reach some part of his body with his hand, or with a cloth and he cannot find anyone to do it for him at all or he has found someone, but the place in question lies between his navel and his knees, and the person is other than his wife or slave girl. Ibn al-Hajib said: 'If it is a place which cannot be reached in any circumstances, then (the obligation) is removed; if he can reach it with a cloth or rope or can get someone to help him, (then he must do it, unless the area is small), and he must do it if the (area) is considerable.' The most evident meaning of this is that it is permitted to allow someone else to do it for those parts he is unable to rub himself even when he is able to rub it with a rope or the like – and this is indeed correct, and Allah, exalted is He, knows best."

NOTICE: It is not a condition of the *ghusl* that the rubbing be done with the hand. Rather it is acceptable to do it with any limb, contrary to the *wudu'*, (where it is unacceptable) except when in the case of the feet – which may be rubbed against each other.

An-Nafrawi has commented on the *Risala* saying "It is not stipulated that the rubbing be with the hand, I mean when rubbing the leg, for if one rubs the one against the other it is acceptable – as opposed to some other part of the body like the hands which one must rub with the palm (of the hand) if one is able. This is the rule regarding *wudu'*. As for the *ghusl*, however, it is permitted to rub one limb with another, unconditionally." There is a similar statement in the *Majma'* of al-Amir

Ibn 'Arafa said in his *Mukhtasar*: "The most evident understanding of what Abu 'Umar says is that he does not deny that the act of worship is effected by wiping (one's feet) with one's hands when performing the *wudu'*, but not in the case of the *ghusl*."

ISSUE: Ibn al-Hattab said: "It is not obligatory for a man to rub the parts of his wife's body that she cannot reach herself, nor is it obligatory for her, but it is recommended of them both. Likewise, if she is unable to reach her vagina because of her obesity, then it is not obligatory that he wash it for her, although it is recommended (of him). If he does not do it (for her), then she should pray with the impurity. Likewise, in the case of the man, it is not obligatory for the woman to wash his private parts if he is unable to reach them himself, but rather it is recommended (of her). If she does not do it, he should buy a slave girl if he is able; if unable, then he must pray with the impurity (still on him)."

ISSUE: Ahmad Mayyara said: "It is not stipulated that the rubbing (of the skin) be at the same time as the pouring of the water or the immersing oneself in it (completely), according to the well known opinion – although Ibn al-Hajib has declared it to be 'the most correct view' saying: 'If he rubs (the water in) after immersing himself or pouring (water over himself) then it is accepted of him, according to the most correct view, according to Abu Muhammad. However, the view of Abu'l-Hasan al-Qabisi is contrary to this. It has also been said: 'The difference of opinion revolves around the purity of the limbs – as for the person who has impurity on his body, this is only removed by rubbing at the same time as pouring (the water).'"

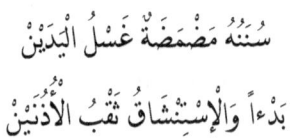

81   Its sunnas are rinsing the mouth, beginning (the *ghusl*) by washing the hands, sniffing up water into the nose and wiping inside one's ear hole

His saying 'rinsing the mouth' means (it should be done) once. His saying 'beginning by washing of the hands' means before commencing anything else – contrary to the *wudu'* for then the (hands are washed) after the washing of the private parts. The judgement as to its being a sunna is dependent upon a condition, namely, his stipulating 'beginning by' – for the actual washing of them (in the *wudu'* itself) is obligatory. Ibn al-Hattab said that Ibn al-Muneer said: "Its sunnas are washing the hands before putting them into the vessel (containing water), pouring water three times over the right hand and then washing it, and then the same with the left."

If (ample) water is available and there is an impurity on his hand, then the judgement in this (matter) is also that mentioned by Ibn al-Hattab, namely: "The author of *al-Muntaqa* said: 'Either the impurity on his hand will alter the water or will not: if it will alter it, then he should not put his hand into it – and this judgement applies to the person for whom (ample) water is not available; if it will not alter the water, he may put his hands in it – and then wash his hands with the water he scoops up and perform the *wudu'* or *ghusl* – for if putting his hand (in the water) does not change the water, then it will not cause it to become impure. However, it is *makruh* for him to do so if other (water) is available, and the judgement applies to a small amount of water in which an impurity dissolves but does not alter it.'

The most evident of the opinions of our fellow (Malikis scholars) is that it is preferable to *tayammum*: according to the judgement of Ibn al-Qasim (for example) he should not put his hand in it but rather do *tayammum*."

The opinion of Ibn al-Qasim he is referring to is that a small amount of water is rendered impure by a small amount of impurity even if it does not alter it, and this is also what the author of the *Risala* holds to.

His saying 'sniffing up water into the nose' means (he should do it) once and refers to drawing it up by means of both the nose and breath. He has not mentioned the blowing out of this water (*al-instinthar*) – which is a sunna of its own, according to Ibn al-Hattab.

His saying 'wiping the ears' means that one should wipe them not wash them. Ibn al-Hattab said: "From the expression in Khalil's *Mukhtasar* it would appear that the washing of the 'cavities of the ears' is sunna, but that is not what is meant for that would injure them."

Zarruq said in *Sharh al-Irshad*: "The washing of the outer and inner fleshy part of the ear is obligatory while the cavity or channel is sunna. However, he should not pour water into them but rather (use) the water clinging to his palms: it will be enough if he moves his fingers in his ears immediately after (washing the ears proper) or at the same time if he can. Thus he has followed the literal meaning of the terms used in the *Mukhtasar* (namely, Khalil's) words 'the washing of the ear channel' – but this is not what is meant."

Al-Mawwaq said that Ibn Bashir said: "Rinsing the mouth and sniffing up water, according to us, are two sunnas of the *ghusl* – as is wiping inside the ears. However, what is meant by 'inside' here is wiping inside the ear channel – for there is no difference of opinion as to the obligatory nature of the outer (parts) of it."

Al-Khurshi said that "One should be mindful of washing both of the (ears) properly" and he excludes the cavities of the ear from (the obligation to wash) the outer parts of the ear which stick out and are adjoined to the head. In the commentary of Ibn al-Hattab, *al-Ajhouri*, he says: "What is meant by the ear cavity is that which it is sunna to wipe, that is, all that part of the (ear) channel into which the end-section of the finger may be introduced, not just what is called the 'tip' of the finger." He said in *at-Taraz*: "As for wiping inside the ears for the (*ghusl* of) *janaba*, this is sunna. It is one of the (parts of the body) which it is not possible to wash or pour water into – because of the harm (this might cause)."

مَنْدُوبُهُ الْبَدْءُ بِغَسْلِهِ الْأَذَى

82   It is recommended to begin by washing away any filth…

What he is referring to here is anything ritually impure which is to be found on his body, that is, after he has completed the washing of his hands. Thus the use of the word 'begin' here is relative – and not like the previous use of the same word, where it is meant literally.

Ahmad Mayyara and Ibn al-Hattab have both said – and the text is taken from the latter: "The author of *at-Tawdih* said: 'What is meant by his words, I mean Ibn al-Hajib's words "if he washes himself with one washing, intending thereby to remove the state of impurity (*hadath*) and in doing so he removes an (actual fleck of) impurity (*najasa*)" is that this is acceptable of him.' The like is transmitted of al-Lakhmi and Muhammad ibn 'Abd as-Salam and others – contrary to what the words of Ibn al-Jilab imply, namely the obligation to remove (the actual spot of impurity) first, as more than one (of the *'ulama*) have understood from his words. Our Shaykh, may Allah have mercy on him, said: 'What Ibn al-Jilab said is true – and one cannot argue with him in this (matter) – for the water will necessarily separate itself from the limb completely (during the washing) and if it has become impure (in the process of this washing) then it would not be possible to claim that purity has been obtained for the person performing this act of purification. It is for this reason then that he must necessarily (first) remove the actual fleck of impurity (*najasa*) before proceeding to purifying himself from the state of impurity (*hadath*).'"

I say: "These words apply to a limb on which (ritually impure) filth is to be found but if there is none on it or only a little dirt, then there is no harm if the water is altered by this (dirt) – let alone any stipulation that this (dirt) be first separated from the (limb) it in order for purification to take place, and Allah knows best."

Zarruq said in the commentary on the *Risala* that Abu 'Umran al-Baja'i said, commenting on the words of Ibn al-Hajib 'and the wiping should not be done over henna and the like': "This indicates that there is no harm in water becoming admixed with something after it has touched the limb" and then goes on to say "...and the first generations used to oil and bind their feet with cloth, and it is clear that the water would be adulterated by its coming into contact with a part of the body (to which oil had been applied)."

Ibn al-Hattab has a long discussion (on the subject) which I would like to record as it has become a matter affecting so many people: "Abu al-Hasan as-Saghir has asked, with respect to the words of the *Mudawwana* 'until he removes it', whether this (removal of impurity) has to be done with water, as one of the Shaykhs said, or whether – and this is the most evident meaning of the text – anything may be used to remove it. The Shaykh goes on to say: '... and whoever says (that it should be done) with water states this "so that the water which one wipes with does not become adulterated – given that as soon as his hand touches (the dirty spot) the water (used) will (necessarily) be adulterated (however slightly)." However this is not correct: most people's limbs are not (absolutely) free of dirt and after water has been poured over the first limb it will necessarily be adulterated (somewhat) when it reaches the next; besides no one has stipulated that the limbs be (absolutely) pure and free of dirt. Moreover, the words of the *Mudawwana* 'and if the (actual) henna (itself) has disappeared but some of it has spread' are an indication of the difference of opinion among some of the Shaykhs (regarding this matter).'"

Ibn Farhun, commenting on the words of Ibn al-Hajib 'and wiping is not done on henna' said that Ibn Harun said: "What he means is that if it is sprinkled on or applied to the head in a solid mass. However, the women of the Companions may Allah be pleased with them, used to apply perfume to their hair and he, on whom be peace and blessings, used to sprinkle perfume on the parting of his hair to cause it to glisten – and so there is no problem in such (cases): no one would argue that the water becomes adulterated when used to wipe over (the hair when treated in this way) for surely that would be ignorance of the sunna and a complete lack of understanding of the deen. This is also explained by the incident mentioned in *al-Bayan*, namely, where the author says – of the woman who makes a concoction of dates and currents and who uses it when combing her hair: 'I do not think there is any harm in this.' Ibn Rushd said: 'It is disliked according to the *Mukhtasar* of Ibn 'Abd al-Hakam, although permitted as a (special) licence. Its being disliked is from the point of view of the interdiction of the two things admixed to it, not from the point of view of it being something covering (the hair) and preventing the (proper) wiping (of the hair). Moreover, here is clear textual evidence for permission to wipe over the (hair). What is prohibited is what is solid (in consistency) and what comes between the hair and the water (used for wiping).'"

Then he transmits the above mentioned words of Zarruq and goes on to say that al-Jazuli said regarding the question of henna: "Al-Faqih said: 'It is not permitted until it is removed with water' while another said 'if she shakes it off.' The (correctness of the) first (opinion) is more evident as (in the case of the second some of) the (henna) would remain and adulterate the water."

I SAY: "Al-Jazuli's saying that it 'is more evident' is that which Abu'l-Hasan Ibn Farhun and others consider weak. The most evident (judgement) is that of Abu'l-Hasan, Ibn Farhun and others which has already been mentioned in the discussion regarding used water – as related from al-Qarafi – namely, that there is no difference of opinion that water is absolutely pure as long as it is still on the limb."

Then he says that Shaykh Yusuf ibn 'Umar said: "One should not wipe over something covering (the hair) except when absolutely necessary. Likewise, if oil has been applied to the head on account of an illness, then one (only) wipes over it because of necessity."

I SAY: "The most evident meaning of the discussion is that one should not wipe over oil if there is no pressing need and this amounts to the same as mentioned by Abu'l-Hasan – as related from one of the Shaykhs – namely, that one should not wipe over henna until it has been washed out with water so as not to adulterate (the water used in the *ghusl*). However, according to the preferred judgement, it is permitted to wipe over it as long as there is not a lot (of henna) and does not become so solid a mass on the hair that it forms a barrier preventing (the water from reaching the hair)."

He has also said: "Ibn Farhun said that Shaykh Abu'l-Hasan said: '...like the pitch that young girls – still in their father's houses – apply to their hair for it is (much) less impenetrable than matted hair (- being closer to a liquid) but despite this can be wiped over.' All this refutes what Abu'l-Hasan has narrated from one of the Shaykhs, namely that the water will be adulterated."

He also comments on Khalil's words 'water already used is disliked' saying:

"Abu'l-Hasan said – relating from Ibn Abi Zamanain – that 'used water' refers to the water which runs off into a large dish, bowl or the like, (for example) or (the water used) when a person – whose body is clean – washes himself in a large basin. Someone else said that 'used water' is that from (the washing performed to remove) the state of impurity (hadath) which drips from the limbs or comes into contact with them during the wudu' or the (ghusl of) janaba as long as (the water left over) from these two (kinds of purification) is free of impurity (nujus) and dirt (wasakh) – for otherwise it would be water in which impurity had dissolved or adulterated water, and would bear the corresponding judgement attached to this (type of water). A judgement similar to this latter (judgement) is contained in at-Tawdeeh and in the discussion of the commentator. What is apparent from all this is that mere contact of the water with the limb causes it to become 'used.' However, this is not what is intended by them for the author of the Dhakheera said: 'Water about which there is a difference of opinion is that which accumulates on the limbs not that which spills over into the vessel after the purification nor what has been used on one of the limbs and which then runs on to another.' He has also said in his Farouq: '...and there is no difference of opinion that the water is pure as long as it remains on the limbs – and this has been explained in this way by more than one (of the 'ulama).' Thus his saying 'or comes into contact with it' may be understood as meaning 'if the person doing the wudu' or ghusl puts his limbs in the water and washes them in it.'"

He has also made a commentary in the (section regarding) burial – after mentioning that the corpse should be rubbed with ground lotus leaf (sidr) and then water should be poured over it – saying: "...what may be understood from this is that if pure water comes into contact with a limb it remains pure – even if then adulterated (by becoming admixed with something on it), it does not adversely affect the water." Ibn 'Arafa has also said on this subject, relating from at-Tunisi: "If water is mixed with ground lotus (preparation), it is (considered as) adulterated (water), but if poured onto a body after the latter has been rubbed with it, then it is not (considered as) adulterated."

He then has a long discussion regarding Khalil's words 'the obligations of the wudu' in which he gives preference to what is given preference to here. The following is taken from this discussion, related from Ibn 'Arafa who heard it from Abu Zayd. It concerns the person who gets into a basin which is ritually impure and who then gets out and washes his hands, scooping up pure water with them. Using his hands, he then washes his face on which there is impure water. Then he returns them (to the water) using them to scoop up some water and washes the rest of his limbs. He said: "I do not see any harm in this and I consider there is an ease in this" and he has also said: "This is what the people have permitted." However, the words of Ibn Rushd are clear in this respect, namely, that it is impure: "If he causes (the water) to become impure by returning his hands to it after having touched his body with them when applying the water to it and washing it, then there is all the more likelihood that the water would become impure by its application and its coming into contact with (his body) – and so it will not be purified at all." The consensus – as to the invalidity of this (view) – also necessarily implies the invalidity of the view of those who say that his purity is rendered impure by this and that the *ghusl* is not accepted of him, and Allah is He who grants success.

... saying the *bismillah*, washing the head three times

There are two opinions as to whether his words 'saying the *bismillah*' mean just this or one should add *ar-rahmanir-raheem* – 'All-Merciful, Most Merciful.' Khalil said "... and the *ghusl*, *tayammum*, eating and drinking are begun with the *bismillah*." Al-Khurshi said "...and when drinking and eating he should add (the words) as (related) in the hadith 'and grant us *baraka* in what you have provided us with', and in the case of milk 'and increase us in it.' It is said aloud in order to remind the careless person and instruct the ignorant person. If the person forgets it at the beginning he should say '*bismillah* in the beginning of it and at the end of it' during the (act he is engaged in), and if he only remembers after he has finished, then he should read Surat *al-Ikhlas* – 'Sincerity'- for it has been narrated 'that will Shaytan will vomit what he has eaten.'" His student, an-Nafrawi, said: "This means he will vomit outside the vessel."

NOTICE: Mention has already been made above – where the author narrates from the *Nawazil* of as-Sijistani on the subject of *wudu'* and the saying of *bismillah* – that the *bismillah* pronounced when drinking wine, engaging in fornication and the like is *kufr*. Examine this (matter) in conjunction with what al-Khurshi says: "...as for forbidden or *makruh* sexual intercourse, there are three opinions: it is said that it is *makruh* to say it and this is what the commentator has restricted himself to as well as the author in *at-Tawdih*; secondly, that it is haram; and finally that it is *makruh* when said during (intercourse which is) *makruh* and haram (when said) for what is haram. Examples of intercourse which are *makruh* are having intercourse with a woman who is in a state of *janaba* – that is, having intercourse a second time with her before she has washed her vagina, or a person having intercourse when this causes him to change (his intention from a *ghusl*) to *tayammum* (a second time)."

After a discussion he goes on to say: "...and the most evident meaning of his words, that is Khalil's, 'and *ghusl*, even if as a result of something haram' (is that one should say the *bismillah*) – and the most evident meaning of his words 'and eating' is that it applies when eating too. However, he has mentioned in *ash-Shamil* 'that the (saying of the *bismillah*) is *makruh* when eating something haram or *makruh*.' The reason he has given is that the name of Allah is (said) for the *baraka* and as an aid to what he wants to do. Thus it has been said: 'So this demands that it be haram with regard to the haram' – and this (argument) is clear. Al-Qarafi has declared that 'saying the *bismillah* over something haram is haram' – this is narrated by Sayyidi as-Siraj. What is contained in the words of at-Tata'i is that it is haram – both when (said over) something haram and *makruh* – and he finds support from this from al-Qarafi, although this is contrary to what others have narrated." Examine too what he has narrated from al-Qarafi together with what is in his *Qawa'id*, namely "The 29th section -'Regarding when one should say the *bismillah* and when one should not commence with the *bismillah*, and when it is *makruh* to say it.' As for the first, (then when performing) the *ghusl*, *wudu'* or *tayammum*, although there is a difference of opinion in these matters, (carrying out the) ritual slaughtering, performing the rites (of hajj), and the recitation of Qur'an. Also included here are the permitted actions which are not acts of worship, like eating, drinking and sexual intercourse. Examples of the second are the *salat*, the *adhan*, hajj, *'umra*, the various *dhikrs* and *du'as*; and of the third, the forbidden things – for the aim in mentioning His name is to obtain *baraka* (increase) in whatever one is doing and if an action is haram or *makruh*, then its increase would not be desirable."

As for his words 'washing the head three times', 'Ali ibn 'Abd as-Sadiq said: "This means covering the whole of the head with each handful of water." 'Isa Ibn Naji said: "This is the most evident meaning of the discussion (on the subject made by) people of the *madhhab*, and the *fatwa* (in this *madhhab*) is on this basis; or it means two handfuls of water – one for each side of the head – and the third for the top of the head, and this corresponds to the most evident meaning of the hadith. Both of these (opinions) have been transmitted by Ibn Harun, and they may both be understood as implied in the words of the author (Ibn 'Ashir) and likewise in the *Mukhtasar* and the *Risala*. At-Tata'i' said, following the judgement of Ibn Naji: "The correct judgement is to believe with certainty in the second of the two judgements – by analogy with the (odd number of) stones used for the cleaning one's private parts after defecation –

according to one of the two judgements on the subject."

He should begin with the washing of the skull, that is the back part of the head, so as to cause the skin of the head to contract and thereby seal the pores through which troublesome illnesses may gain access. The experience of those who have tried this shows that they are not afflicted by any grievous ailments and their sight is not dimmed by (any ill effect of) the water – so understand this benefit!

تَقْدِيمُ أَعْضَاءِ الْوُضُوءِ قِلَّةَ مَا

83   first wash the parts of the body (which one would wash) for the *wudu'*, use a little water...

'Ali ibn 'Abd as-Sadiq said: "The well known judgement is that he should wash the (various limbs) one after the other with the intention of removing the major state of impurity (known as) *janaba*."

His saying 'a little water' is understood as meaning that the precise amount is not stipulated, according to the well known judgement – as in the case of the *wudu'*. Indeed, what is required is the minimum (amount of water) needed to cover (all the body) and to ensure that a proper washing may be carried out – and this varies from person to person. One does not learn from his words the judgement which applies when he uses a lot of water – namely, that it is *makruh*."

Al-Khurshi said, commenting on the words of Khalil 'and a little water without stipulation as to the amount' that: "...the amount of water used is not stipulated as a *mudd* for *wudu'* or a *sa'* (i.e. four *mudds*) for the *ghusl* – contrary to Ibn Sha'ban who defines it in this way and who bases (this judgement) on the practise of the Prophet, may the peace and blessings of Allah be upon him." Then al-Khurshi goes on to say the following – and Ibn al-Hattab says something similar, indeed we are quoting the text from the latter when he says in *al-'Arida*: "...and if were to say that the *wudu'* should be done with a *mudd* and the *ghusl* with a *sa'*, then this means by volume not by weight – as the volume of a *mudd* or *sa'* of water is much greater than when reckoned by weight – so reflect upon this point!"

A brief explanation is contained in *at-Tawdeeh* where he states: "The stipulation of the *mudd* and the *sa'* is by volume not by weight." Zarruq said: "The amount referred to is that corresponding to an ample *mudd* of food – for the amount of a *mudd* of water is small while that of food is several times more. Ibn al-Hattab's mention of the *faqih* who holds a contrary position to the above, namely that the amount must be a *mudd* and that he is known as Abu'l-Ishaq is not disputed – what is not clear, however, is whether this refers to Abu Ishaq ibn Sha'ban – and this is the opinion of one group, among them Khalil in *at-Tawdih* – or to Abu Ishaq at-Tunisi – and this is the view of al-Fakinani."

NOTICE: al-Khurshi said, commenting on Khalil's mention of 'food' and 'water': "…this in order to denote that throwing away water is permitted." The author of *al-Jam'* said commenting on Ibn al-Hajib's assertion 'that throwing away water is permitted': "The most evident meaning of these words is that it is permitted to throw away water without reason. However, the most obvious meaning of Abu Muhammad's words contradict this namely 'wasting it is an exceeding of bounds and an innovation.' Ibn Naji said: "What he says is not in fact contrary to the other for wasting and innovation – for this applies in the case of an act of worship which the *shari'ah* has commanded to be performed using a little (water). However, pouring away water – other than during an act of worship undertaken for the purpose of purification – is permitted, and is up to the individual person to decide (whether he does this or not). And this was the *madhhab* of our Shaykh Burzuli."

'Ayn-Jeem[1] said in his commentary *Tanbeeh* that Ibn al-Harith said: "The ('ulama) are in agreement regarding the improper use of bread and flour and that it is *makruh* to do *wudu'* with either of them – and what is meant (by the latter) is cleaning the hands with either of them (to get rid of any excess filth before immersing one's hands in the water to start the *wudu'* proper), although there is a difference of opinion as to (permissibility of) doing *wudu'* with bran. Al-'Ateeq has mentioned from Sahnun that he regarded it as *makruh* while Ibn Nafi' that there was no harm in it."

Ibn 'Arafa has narrated that Ibn Rushd said: "As for doing the *ghusl* with milk, or a woman combing her hair with liquid impregnated with dates and currants, there are narrations attesting to its being *makruh*, but not that it is prohibited." See also az-Zurqani.

Sayyidi Ahmad Zarruq said: "It is forbidden to regard food with disdain or to throw it in the rubbish." Examine what has been transmitted by az-Zurqani together with what has been narrated by Sayyidi Ahmad Zarruq: it is possible to harmonise the two by understanding the misuse (of food) – which is *makruh* – as referring to its misuse when thrown in the rubbish. Consider, then, whether what is meant by 'rubbish' is anything which *is actually* ritually impure or (merely) that which one *deems* unclean – like spittle, for example which may in fact be pure. The author of the *Risala* said "…and it is *makruh* to

---

1 Shaykh Shinqeeti has not indicated whom these letters refer to.

wash the hands with food or with anything like millet or lentils for example." Al-Aqfahisi said "… *makruh* in the sense that it should be avoided" while Ibn 'Umar states: "It has been said that it is *makruh* while it has also been said that the degree of *karaha* – dislike – is of the order of a prohibition as such (an action would indicate) contempt for food."

Al-Burzuli said: "Ibn al-Hajib has transmitted from one of the *fuqaha'* that it is allowed to burn or set fire to a foodstuff – when (for example) boiling down juice to make syrup, unless there is a dearth of food; likewise the burning of goods containing the name of Allah, exalted is He, (is permitted)."

I say: "The author of *al-Madarik* said that al-Abyani asked Luqman ibn Yusuf about the (medicinal) balm or paste people applied to their legs and he replied that there was no harm in it."

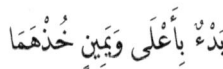

… begin with the top and from the right, so take notice

Ibn al-Hattab said: "Know that the most evident meaning of the texts (of the *'ulama*) is that the top right hand side and top left hand side precede what is below of the right and the left, and the right hand side of both what is above and below precedes anything on the left hand side. The description of Ibn Jama'a is unequivocal – as to the obligation on each individual regarding the way the *ghusl* is done: "The perfect way to do it is that he sit in a pure place and then washes the two orifices (namely the anus and penis) and the area immediately around them. He then does the *wudu'*, making the intention – with his *wudu'* – of removing the major ritual impurity. When he has completed his *wudu'*, he immerses his hands in the water and rubs the water clinging to his hands into the hair on his head. Then he scoops up three handfuls of water into his hands to properly complete the washing of the (hair) – making sure the water penetrates to the skin. After this, he applies the water to his ears, washing (both) the outer and inner part of them, then beneath his chin, to his neck, his upper arms and then beneath his armpits. He should rub water right into his belly button with his finger. Then he scoops the water over his back, using both hands behind his back to rub it in. He washes his right side, then the left, the backs of the knees, the right leg, the left, and then both feet. If he uses a container which has a pipe (attached) to pour (the water) over his body, then this is less likely to lead to a waste (of water)."

Zarruq said in *Sharh ar-Risala*: "He begins with the upper parts of his body and concludes with his chest and his belly – this is what al-Qarafi said and what Ibn Naji has transmitted, may Allah have mercy on him. (Adhering to the order of) all (the above) is recommended." He has also said in *Sharh al-Irshad*: "One of the (*fuqaha*) has mentioned that the chest should be washed after the belly."

$$تَبْدَأُ فِي الْغُسْلِ بِفَرْجٍ ثُمَّ كُفَّ$$
$$عَنْ مَسِّهِ بِبَطْنٍ أَوْ جَنْبِ الْأَكُفِّ$$

84 Begin the *ghusl* by washing the private parts, then avoid touching them with the palm (of the hand) or the sides of (the palms)

$$أَوْ إِصْبَعٍ ثُمَّ إِذَا مَسَسْتَهُ$$
$$أَعِدْ مِنَ الْوُضُوءِ مَا فَعَلْتَهُ$$

85 or the inside of the fingers, and if you do touch them, then repeat that (part of the) *wudu'* you have already done

Mayyara said: "That one should begin with the private parts has already been mentioned by the author as one of the recommended actions. He has repeated it – and Allah knows best – to highlight what follows, namely that the person doing the *ghusl* should refrain from touching their private parts with the inside or side of the palm after having washed them – in order that this washing exempt one from (having to do) the *wudu'* (again). If, however, he does touch his penis with his hand after having completed the *ghusl* or during it, then he has to repeat what he has done of the *wudu'* – as he has indicated with his words 'and if you do touch.....' This judgement not only applies when touching (the penis) but also whenever he breaks the (*wudu'*) – (for some other reason) other than touching. He has mentioned 'touching' in particular because this is what usually occurs. His saying 'avoid touching them' refers to touching the private parts (of a man or woman)."

The most evident understanding of his mentioning the breaking (of the *wudu'*) *specifically through touching* – that is, with the inside or side of the hand or inside or side of the fingers – is that what is being referred to by 'private parts' (*farj*) here is in particular the penis. I am not certain at the present time that annulling (of the *wudu'*) occurs when a woman touches her vagina for this is not immediately evident from his words which refer specifically to 'touching with the palm or side of the hand.' However such a meaning could well be contained in these words, that is, that it also applies to a woman touching her vagina – however she does this. If (the words of the author) refers (only) to the penis, then his mention (of the palm, side of the palm and side of the finger) also have this specific meaning.

مُوجِبُهُ حَيْضٌ نِفَاسٌ إِنْزَالٌ

مَغِيبُ كَمَرَةٍ بِفَرْجٍ إِسْجَالٌ

86 *Ghusl* becomes obligatory because of menstruation, bleeding after childbirth, emission of sperm, the penis penetrating the vagina or penetration whatsoever.

By menstruation is meant blood which comes out of its own accord, even if just a drop. This usually (occurs) before a woman becomes pregnant – from when she is nine years old up to seventy – and does not last for more than fifteen days. It excludes the bleeding after childbirth. As for the bleeding after childbirth, it is the blood which flows out after giving birth, even during the interval between twins. The least amount (of such bleeding) is (reckoned as being) like that of menstruation, even (if it happens) just once and the maximum is sixty days – this has been said by 'Ali ibn 'Abd as-Sadiq.

NOTICE: The author of *Ghayat al-Amani* said: "As for the definition of menstruation according to the *shari'ah*, al-Fakihani said: '…that which comes out of the vagina by itself – in the case of woman who, in normal circumstances, is capable of giving birth – and which does not last longer than fifteen days; not (however the bleeding which occurs) in the case of illness or childbirth. Our saying 'by itself' is to exclude that which comes out as a result of a wound or the like; our saying 'from the vagina' is to exclude that which comes out other than from the vagina, like from the anus; our saying 'in the case of woman who, in normal circumstances, is capable of giving birth' is to exclude a minor, like a girl of seven years or an old woman of seventy years – although fifty has also been stipulated, given that women of that age are not usually capable of becoming pregnant, even though theoretically it might be possible; our saying 'not more than fifteen days' is to exclude anymore than this for then it would be called *istihada* (intermittent post menstrual bleeding), according to the well known opinion; our saying 'not in illness' is to exclude any emission of blood due to illness, other than *istihada* while our saying 'not in childbirth' is to exclude the blood of childbirth.'"

NOTICE: Abu'l-Hasan has also said in *Ghayat al-Amani* – in response to the view that a *ghusl* is not recommended for the bleeding of *istihada*: "This is justified, that is the narrations declaring that no *ghusl* is required, because she is pure – and thus there is no legal reason for the obligation (of *ghusl*) – and because the bleeding is a result of illness or a malaise."

ISSUE: Mayyara said: "If a woman who is usually regular in her menstruation has bleeding which lasts longer than usual or she delays making the *ghusl* after the usual period (to ensure her purity) (*al-istidhhar*), the judgement in her case is that she is pure and if the flow of blood last longer than fifteen days, then the increase over and above her normal period is (reckoned as) *istihada*, otherwise (the judgement of) her normal period is assigned to her – this has been transmitted by al-Qulshani in *Sharh ar-Risala*." Al-Lakhmi has also narrated: "She has made up the fasting (she has missed) and reckons the stopping of the blood at the time of menstruation as a sign that whatever lasts longer than this is *istihada* – and this is clear. If the bleeding stops within fifteen days and a woman has (another) bleeding after this, then she should reckon from the end of the (first) bleeding, i.e. from the (new) judgement assigned to her: thus if her (first) period was eight days for example and this goes on for longer, she makes *istidhhar* for three days and then takes a *ghusl*; if it stops on the thirteenth day and she begins to menstruate again and it carries on, then she bases here reckoning on thirteen and makes istidhhar for two days only, and Allah knows best. His saying 'she has made up the fasting she has missed' refers to the period she fasted from after her normal period and the istidhhar but before the blood stopped flowing, namely the twelfth and thirteenth in the above mentioned example – when it becomes clear she has fasted while she was menstruating. The most evident meaning of the judgement is that she is absolutely pure after the normal period and istidhhar, and that there is no difference between her blood stopping within the fifteen days or after it." And this (judgement) from Mayyara is what al-Khurshi and Ibn 'Abd as-Sadiq have restricted themselves to.

ISSUE: Ibn 'Arafa said: "There are two opinions as to whether the yellowish and brown discharges are (to be considered) as menstruation in all circumstances or only as long as they are not to be found after doing the *ghusl* and before the completion of the purity: the first, that she is pure – according to the author of *at-Talqeen* together with al-Jilab, *al-Mudawwana* and Ibn Majishun, but that *wudu'* is necessary – and al-Baji and al-Mazari consider it the *madhhab*, while al-Lakhmi's view is contrary to the *Mudawwana*."

Al-Mawwaq said: "If the woman sees yellow or brown discharges during her period of menstruation or outside of it, then it is menstruation even if she does not see any blood with it." Al-Baji said: "…even if this is not preceded by blood." Ibn al-Majishun said: "If a woman makes a *ghusl* and then sees a drop of blood – or blood in the water used for the *ghusl* – then she does *wudu'* but does not make a *ghusl* – and this is called *at-tariya*, 'a wetting.' Ibn Yunus has included this as an accepted judgement of *fiqh* and likewise al-Baji who said said: "Any drop of blood – or blood in the water used for washing – which is seen after the purity following childbirth or menstruation, does not necessitate a *ghusl*."

Neither he nor Ibn 'Arafa have explained the preferred judgement although he has explained it after a discussion on the subject: he shows that the view of Ibn al-Majishun is contrary to that preferred (by most) even though al-Baji, Ibn Yunus and al-Mazari (also) restrict themselves to this (judgement).

As for his saying 'emission', Ibn 'Abd as-Sadiq said: "This refers to the emission of seminal fluid, irrespective of whether from the man or woman and irrespective of whether the person is asleep or awake. The most evident meaning of his words is that a woman can have an emission of seminal fluid although there is no support for this view: it is not stipulated with regard the emission of (seminal) fluid from the woman that it be discharged from her vagina – for what usually occurs in the case of a woman is that it is discharged within the womb and from there lends itself to the formation of the child. However it can happen that the womb causes it to be discharged outside (of the womb). She does not have to wait for it to be discharged from the womb and emitted (from the vagina) for the judgement of *janaba* to be applied to her. It has also been said that what is meant by 'emission' is any sensation (on her part that an emission has taken place), or any unusual occurrence (which she experiences) within her."

At-Tawudi said that this is contrary to the preponderant view: "Ibn al-Hattab said: 'The most evident meaning of Khalil is that what renders the *ghusl* obligatory is the emission of seminal fluid, even from a female – contrary to those who say, as al-Qadi has documented, that the (mere) sensation on the part of the woman of its leaving its (usual) location (in the womb) renders the *ghusl* obligatory for her – given that the (fluid) may fall back into her (womb and not result in an actual emission from the vagina)" He has only mentioned the (fluid's) leaving its (usual) place in the case of the woman but despite this, his view is contrary to the well known opinion – (that is) with respect to the (woman). As for the man, the most evident judgement is that he is not under an obligation to take a *ghusl* unless the seminal fluid completely leaves the penis. The author of *al-'Arida* said: "If the seminal fluid is set in movement but does not (actually) appear then he does not have to take a *ghusl*." Ahmad ibn

Hanbal said that he is obliged (to take a *ghusl*) as sexual desire has (clearly) occurred given that the (seminal fluid) has been set in motion. This, however, is a weak judgement for even if it has occurred it has not been completed: (legally speaking) this (sexual desire) is (classed as) a *hadath* (i.e. a physical change which signals ritual impurity but) which only necessitates a purification on his part when it occurs *completely* – as (is the rule with) all the other *ahdath* (physical changes).

Al-Ubbi said in *Sharh Muslim*: "A woman may have a dream during sleep and her body may become exited and appear to be on the point of emitting seminal fluid but it does not (actually) come out of it – or (in the case of a man) it may reach the beginning of the penis or half way into it – but (neither) has to make a *ghusl*. If the seminal fluid of the woman does reach the place that she washes after going to the toilet, namely the parts of her that manifest when she squats to urinate or defecate, then she should make the *ghusl*. In the case of a virgin, however, she does not have to (make a *ghusl*) until her (private parts) protrude for the inside of her vagina is considered as (having the same judgement as) the inside of the penis."

This is a clear and unequivocal statement, namely, that as long as the seminal fluid remains in the penis of vagina and does not appear, then *ghusl* is not obligatory – and the hadith 'If she sees the (seminal) fluid …' confirms this.

Al-Mawwaq said that al-Baji said: "If he engages in sexual foreplay with his wife and experiences 'utmost (sexual) pleasure' without intercourse and without an emission but then after doing *wudu'* and praying does have an emission, then according to Malik in *al-Majmu'a* 'he must make a *ghusl* as the (fluid) has left its usual place on account of the experience of (sexual) pleasure.'" This (example) serves to support the judgement that a *ghusl* is indeed necessary even when no (seminal fluid) appears. Ibn al-Qasim has transmitted that he should repeat the *salat* while al-Asbagh said that he does not have to repeat the *salat*. The transmission of Ibn al-Qasim is regarding someone who sees (in a dream) that he has had a wet dream and has no emission but who then makes *wudu'*, prays and has an emission without experiencing sexual pleasure. The significance of this narration is used as a proof by Ibn al-Mawwaz, namely that he becomes *junub* by the emission of (seminal) fluid – and this (only) *after* the correct performance of the *salat*. Al-Baji said: "In my opinion this is a most manifest proof – given that if he had done the *ghusl* before the emission of the sperm it would not have been accepted of him." 'Abd al-Wahhab said: "The *ghusl* and repetition of the *salat* is a narration of Ibn Wahb. However what is stipulated within the *madhhab* is that *ghusl* and repetition of the *salat* is not necessary because the emission was not accompanied by sexual pleasure."

Ibn al-Hattab said that among the replies given by Ibn Rushd, may Allah have mercy on him, (to people's questions) was one regarding a man who had a sexual dream and was about to have an emission but who then wakes up – or is woken up – and nothing in fact was emitted. However when he gets up and does *wudu'* for the *salat* he has an emission. When asked whether he had to have a *ghusl* or not he replied: "As for the person who has a sexual dream but does not have an emission until after he wakes up – on making *wudu'* for the *salat* – then he must do a *ghusl*; but as for the person who has sexual intercourse but does not have an emission until he has a *ghusl* then he only has to have a *wudu'*." However, it has also been said that he should repeat the *ghusl* – although the former (judgement) is more evident.

His saying the penis 'penetrating the vagina or penetration whatsoever' means irrespective of whether it penetrates the vagina or the anus, and even (penetration in the case) of animals. As for penetration when (the penis is) covered with something, there is a difference of opinion – mentioned by Ibn Naji in his commentary on the *Risala*: thus it has been said that it necessitates *ghusl* in all cases, that it is not necessitated at all and also that, if the covering is insubstantial, he must do it and if not, then not.

وَالْأَوَّلَانِ مَنَعَا الْوَطْءَ إِلَى

87   As for the first two, intercourse is forbidden until the *ghusl* is made...

This is like the words of Khalil who – adding to what is forbidden the menstruating woman – says 'and intercourse in the vagina, even beneath a waist wrap, and even after purity and *tayammum*.' Al-Mawwaq said: "There is the saying of Malik on this (matter), namely: 'The menstruating woman should tighten her waist wrap and his affair is in her upper (body)' that is he may have intercourse with her in her folds of flesh or her armpits or whatever he wishes of her upper body. Malik has also said: "He should not have intercourse with her between her thighs." Ibn Yunus said (by way of explanation): "... in order prevent the means which might lead to (illegal intercourse)." Ibn Habib said: "There is no restriction as long as he avoids the vagina" and this Asbagh has also said.

Al-Mawwaq has also said, commenting on his words 'and even after purification': "Ibn Yunus has commented on Allah ta ala words 'and do not approach them until they have purified themselves. But once they have purified *makruh* for a man to have intercourse with his wife even if there is someone in the room who does not understand or who does not hear, be it a child or someone sleeping: Ibn 'Umar would have the women and slave girls, even infants in the cradle, removed (from the same room). It is also narrated that he even disliked that there should be animals or any living thing with a *ruh* in the same house. This was out of his extreme sense of modesty – for (he argued) if one permitted oneself (the licence) to do it in the presence of a child – on one occasion, then how easily it might be to do it – the next time – in the presence of someone before whom one should have modesty. Thus the judgement of *makruh* is in the sense that one should avoid it (if at all possible). It is a judgement based on clear textual evidence, that is, because the licence to have sexual intercourse is clear and this is the principle of the matter – unless, of course, the private parts or another part of the body between the navel and knees are exposed which (is another judgement in itself and) is forbidden. The term '*makruh*' (with respect to this judgement) has been transmitted from Ibn Abi Zayd who said in *an-Nawadir* from the *Kitab ibn Mawaz*: 'Malik disliked that a man have intercourse with his wife or his slave girl when there was someone in the house who could hear his heavy breathing.' It has also been transmitted from Ibn al-Majishun that he said: 'It is not fitting that there be someone else asleep in the house with him, irrespective of whether it is a child or an adult.' Ibn al-Majishun's use of the words 'it is not fitting' is proof that the judgement of '*makruh*' is made in the sense that 'it should be avoided' – for this is what these words normally imply. Likewise what has been transmitted from Malik, namely, that he considered it *makruh* is also understood to mean that one should avoid it: if there are no accompanying circumstances indicating prohibition, then the (judgement) remains based (in the first instance) on the principle that intercourse is permitted but that – in this situation – it is (also) *makruh* because of the lack of modesty associated with (having intercourse when someone else is present). However, if a man experiences difficulty and hardship in this respect because of the size of his family and the narrowness of the house then he is at liberty (to have intercourse). However, he should make as much effort as he can (to avoid intercourse in such circumstances) but if he finds abstention oppressive then he should put up a curtain and desist from loud breathing. As for what is reported regarding the question from al-Mateeti, the answer is not unequivocal: 'It is not permitted for a man that he have intercourse with his wife or slave girl when there is someone else in the house.' Even if on the face of it such an answer indicates prohibition it is not in fact an explicit prohibition for the words 'it is not permitted' can be understood to mean 'it it disliked':

themselves...'[1] saying 'this means with water.' Ibn Bakeer is of the opinion that it is permitted to have intercourse with her as soon as she notices she is clean – even if she has not taken a *ghusl*. This is because the prohibition is related to and dependent upon her menstruation and any judgement necessarily ceases to be applicable when connected to a reason or justification which no longer exists. Ibn Yunus goes on to say: 'This (latter) is correct by analogy but the former is more prudent and preferable to me.'

A GOOD STORY: Ahmad Bab said in his description of Ibrahim ibn Muhammad al-Madani that his student Ibn Marzouq related the following biography: "He is an imam, the possessor of true knowledge and teacher, the leading figure amongst the *Salihun* and the vigorous men (of Allah) of his time, famous for his miraculous actions, a wali by consensus of the people. Among his miraculous actions is that mentioned by one of his great companions Abu 'Abdallah ibn Jameel who said: 'A question was put to me and I followed the judgement of Asbagh and Ibn Habib rather than the well known opinion – on account of an excuse (I felt was justified in the circumstances). Then I was afflicted by a violent pain and I thought that it was a punishment for my desisting from the well known judgement. While still in pain, I visited the Shaykh who said: "What is the matter with you O such a such a person?" I said: "My wrong actions" and he replied immediately: There can be no wrong action in the case of someone who follows Asbagh and Ibn Habib."'"

USEFUL POINT: The author of *al-Mi'yar* said: "Al-Huffar was asked about a man having intercourse with his wife when there was someone in the house, be it a minor or an adult, asleep or awake – that is, as to whether it was forbidden – which is the obvious meaning of the words of al-Mutayati – or whether it was *makruh* – as is clear from the statements of other Shaykhs; and whether al-Huffar's words, may Allah have mercy on him, were to be understood as a commentary on what others had pronounced earlier on the subject or whether his words were contrary to what they had said; and, if understood as a commentary, whether it was enough to erect a barrier, curtain of linen cloth, canvas or something else after having assured oneself that the person is sleeping – despite the enormous hardship it would clearly represent for poor people of restricted means, in particular during the cold season. Al-Huffar replied: '(The judgement regarding) its being *makruh*, disliked, is in the sense that it should be avoided and is similar to the injunction to cover oneself when going to the toilet out of a sense of shame – for modesty is encouraged in the *shari'ah* and is one of the qualities of iman.' It is for this reason that it is

---

1 al-Baqara – The Cow: 220

(the gist of the phrase is that) both are being enjoined to abstain and it is permitted (within the dictates of correct speech) to use an expression such as 'it is not permitted' to transmit this injunction. This (latter interpretation) is preferable given that it can hardly be understood as meaning the contrary – for what Malik and Ibn al-Majishun have said does not contradict what al-Mateeti said and so does not constitute a difference of opinion. Even if it was indeed said by him, then it should be understood as conjecture but not counted as another judgement."

After mentioning some of the explanation of *al-Mi'yar* Ahmad Bab said – with respect to the words of Khalil 'and their being in the same bed even if no intercourse takes place': "It has been clearly declared to be *makruh* in *al-Kafi* when the author says: 'It is *makruh* for him to sleep between his two wives or slave girls or to have intercourse with one of them such that the other can hear or that someone – be it a child or an adult – can see him or that he speak to one wife about his intimacy with the other wife.'"

I SAY: "It can hardly be that al-Mateeti has understood the narration as indicating prohibition. If you were to say: 'This incites jealousy, causes hostility and only brings evil' I would reply: 'This applies in particular in the case of two wives. It would be difficult to make a more general judgement, that is the prohibition of intercourse when there is a person sleeping in the same room who is not a guest – except for those with ample means.' Shaykh Haloulu said: 'The most evident judgement in my opinion regarding this matter is that it is permitted – (and this is) based on the hadith of Abu Talha in the *Sahih*[1] namely (the hadith which relates how) "he returned from a journey and his wife said to him – referring to his son who had been ill – that 'his breath was quiet.'[2] Abu Talha understanding from this that he was healthy had intercourse with her....." The hadith goes on to narrate how (the next day) he informed the Prophet, may the peace and blessings of Allah be upon him, of what they had done. The fact that he, may the peace and blessings of Allah be upon him did not disapprove of their (having intercourse) as well as the fact that people must have had intercourse every night during the period of the revelation (in similar circumstances, that is, with others present in the same room) demonstrates that it was permitted. Had it been prohibited they would certainly have asked about it – given the difficulty of (always) abstaining from (intercourse when someone else is in the same room) for

---

1 See al-Bukhari *K. al-Adab*, 116, *K. al-Jana'iz*, 40
2 meaning in fact that he had died – but not wanting to upset him at that particular moment, she had told a half truth which lead Abu Talha to believe that he was healthy.

most people. Moreover, if someone had asked, it would surely have been transmitted. The fact that it has not been transmitted – despite the frequency with which it must have occurred – indicates that there was no prohibition. The similar (absence of transmission) affords legal proof that there is no *zakat* on fresh vegetables and honey. Likewise Malik has based his argument against the legality of the prostration of thanks on the fact that there were a great many victories at the time of the Prophet, on whom be peace, and during the Khalifs after him but that this prostration is not narrated of them: if, he argues, it were the practice (of the people) then it would have been narrated (of them) – thus the fact that it has not been narrated is evidence that it was not practised, and Allah knows best.'"

غُسْلٍ وَالْآخَرَانِ قُرْآنًا جَلاَ

... and in the case of the last two, recitation of the Qur'an is forbidden

except, that is, a single *ayat* or the like, when recited in order to seek refuge in Allah, exalted is He, – this is stated by Khalil who says 'and recitation (is forbidden) except the like of an *ayat*, recited in order to seek refuge or similar.' Al-Khurshi affirms what he said saying: "The prohibition applies to other than the *ayat* or two or the like recited in order to seek refuge in a moment of fear or sleeplessness or when seeking to prove an argument by quoting (from the Qur'an); or the like (recited) in case of hardship; or to the eleven *ayats* of the last two (suras) – based on the principle that they are used to seek refuge. However, one should not recite "*Say: 'He is Allah, Absolute Oneness'*"[1] as this is not recited in order to seek refuge contrary to 'the *ayat* of the Footstool' (*ayat al-Kursi*) or any other *ayat* used to seek refuge. He may also combine an *ayat* for seeking refuge with one cited to prove an argument. (Also considered) like (the *ayat* recited for) 'seeking refuge' (and therefore permitted) is replying to or disproving a reciter or any one else (of knowledge) in order to prevent him from doing something forbidden." Then he added, narrating from his Shaykh, '*Ayn-Jeem*: "There is no reward in reciting something to seek protection and the like if one does not make the intention to do it as a *dhikr*. If, however, it is done as a *dhikr*, then the most evident judgement is that he will get the reward – if carried out with this intention, as ash-Shafi'i has mentioned. The most evident judgement is that what one says when mounting one's beast – in order to repel any difficulty on the part of the (animal) when carrying him – may be considered as a *ruqya* (a charm or incantation) as what is intended is one and

---

1 al-Ikhlas – Sincerity: 1

the same."

Al-Mawwaq relates that Ibn Yunus said: "Malik said: 'The person in a state of major ritual impurity should not read more than an *ayat* or two when he retires to bed, or when seeking refuge or protection when frightened or the like – and nor should it be done as mere recitation. As for the woman who is menstruating, however, she may recite as she does not have her purity (from menstruation)' What he means by this is that if she becomes pure (from menstruation) but has not yet taken a *ghusl* with water, then she should not recite as she has her purity (from menstruation and thus the possibility of purifying herself with a *ghusl*)." Ibn Rushd said: "The correct (judgement) is that if a woman begins her menstruation and she is in a state of major impurity, then she may recite the Qur'an – that is, even if she does not make a *ghusl* for the state of major impurity – as the judgement on her with respect to her *janaba* is annulled by the judgement on her resulting from her being in a state of menstruation."

Al-Baqouri said in *Iqtisar Qawa'id al-Qarafi* that Malik said: "As to the question why it is permitted for the menstruating woman to recite what she wishes but it is not permitted for the person in *janaba*, the answer is that the (matter in question) is based on the principle that a case of necessity renders permissible what would elsewhere not be permissible. 'Necessity', according to us, applies (in this particular case) to the menstruating woman – for without such a reason permitting her to recite the Qur'an – she might forget it. However, no such 'necessity' applies in the case of the person in *janaba* as he has the means to put an end to this state preventing him (from recitation – by doing the *ghusl*).

وَالْكُلُّ مَسْجِداً وَسَهْوُ الِاغْتِسَالْ

مِثْلُ وُضُوئِكَ وَلَمْ تُعِدْ مُوَالْ

88 and in the case of all four, entering the mosque is forbidden. And if you have been negligent (and have overlooked a part of the skin when washing), then (make it up immediately) as in the case of the *wudu'*, but you do not have to repeat washing the parts already washed after (what you had omitted)

Regarding his words 'and in the case of all four, entering the mosque is forbidden' al-Khurshi said: "If the person in the state of *janaba* does not find water except from a well or irrigation channel inside the precincts of the mosque, then he should do *tayammum*." One text (I am aware of) is quite definite with respect (to this judgement), while al-Mazari is ambivalent on the matter. (There is no difference of opinion, however, that) this (judgement) applies to the resident person who is in good health. As for those who have an excuse – because of a disease or because they are on a journey – then it is permitted for them to make *tayammum* as they are included in the literal meaning of the words "those ill or on a journey may do *tayammum* for the eclipse of the sun and the moon, and likewise the one who seeks asylum for the night in the mosque or when the place where he spends the night is inside the mosque." There is hardly any difference of opinion regarding the above mentioned. As for the person who becomes junub, he may go out without doing *tayammum* – and there is a consensus that this (judgement) is from the Prophet, may the peace and blessings of Allah be upon him."

Al-Mawwaq said that Ibn Yunus said: "If he remembers in the mosque that he is in a state of *janaba* then he should go out and does not have to make *tayammum* – and there is also a consensus that this is from the Prophet, may the peace and blessings of Allah be upon him."

In the *Mi'yar* from Marzouq from *an-Nawadir* it is stated that "one of our companions who was sleeping in the mosque and who had a wet dream said: 'He should make *tayammum* in order to go out of it.'"

Ibn al-Hattab said that al-Burzouli said: "Whoever comes to the mosque in a state of *janaba* and the bucket (for carrying the water for *wudu'*) is inside the (mosque) then, if the time is short, he does *tayammum* and goes in to get it and if there is time enough, then he should wait until someone brings it out to him."

(As for Ibn 'Ashir's words) 'And if you have been negligent (and have overlooked a part of the skin when washing), then (make it up immediately) as in the case of the *wudu'* means 'as in the case of an omission in the *wudu'*, and the judgement regarding this has been mentioned above – namely, that if you have missed washing a patch of skin or a whole limb then you should make up for it as soon as you remember by washing it with the intention of (removing) the state of *janaba* but if you delay doing it after remembering it, then your *ghusl* is invalidated and any *salat* you have prayed, you should do again. (His words) 'but you do not have to repeat washing the parts already washed after (what you had ommitted)' apply irrespective of whether you remember soon afterwards or sometime afterwards. If, however, what you have missed out is a sunna, then you should make it up whenever you can.

SUPPLEMENTARY REMARKS:

1. Among the things which become prohibited through ritual impurity is touching the Qur'an, even in the case of the minor ritual impurity. Ibn

'Arafa said: "Ritual impurity prohibits one from touching of the *mus-haf* or carrying it even when moved by means of something other (than one's hand) or on a cushion. Ash-Shaykh has narrated from Abu Bakr: 'One should not turn over a page with a stick or something else' and from Ibn 'Umar: 'The *fuqaha* of the major towns are in agreement that only the person in *wudu'* should touch it.' Zay-ya-fa' has surmised something contrary in the words of al-Lakhmi: 'It is said that it is (only) recommended that one is in *wudu'* when touching of the Qur'an.' However this (matter) must be understood in the way al-Mazari has interpreted the words of one of the *fuqaha* who said that the *ghusl* of the woman with *istahadha* before fifteen days is (only) a recommendation – namely that 'It should not be supposed that she is not committing a wrong action if she were to pray without making a *ghusl* – indeed she would be considered to be committing a wrong action, according to the consensus. What is meant by 'recommended' (in this case) is that she has the option of desisting from the *salat*, that is not doing it when she has not done the *ghusl*.'"

I SAY: "The consensus which has been related of Ibn 'Abd al-Barr is (in fact) not necessarily from Ibn 'Abd al-Barr and likewise the interpretation with respect to the words of al-Lakhmi is (likewise) not uncontested. Ibn Fa'ida (for example) has opposed him in this in the *Sharh al-Mukhtasar* and the text is to be found immediately after the words of Ibn 'Arafa: 'the falsity (of the argument) shows up in what al-Lakhmi has transmitted – after transmitting the argument that *wudu'* is (merely) recommended – namely, that the evidence for the obligation of *wudu'* before touching of the Qur'an is contained in the words of Allah, exalted is He, '*No one may touch it except the purified*'[1] when he says: "There is a difference of opinion as to its meaning: some have said that it refers to the angels' touching (of the Qur'an) and this is based on the words of Allah, exalted is He, '*Inscribed on Honoured Pages, exalted, purified by the hands of scribes, noble, virtuous*'[2] while others have said it is a proscription – thus the person who argues for a recommendation relies on the first interpretation.'"

In *al-Mi'yar* the author says: "Ibn Lubb was asked as to whether the copyist of the Qur'an was permitted to abandon the purification given how difficult it would be for him (to remain constantly in *wudu'*) and he replied: 'The copyist of the Qur'an has no licence (to continue copying) when he is not in *wudu'* – except when following the judgement of Ibn Maslama from the people of the *madhhab*, namely that being in *wudu'* before touching the Qur'an

---

1 al-Waqi'a The Occurrence: 82
2 'Abasa: He frowned: 13-16

is recommended and not an obligation.'"

In the commentary of Zarruq on *al-Waghleesiya* he says: "One group are of the opinion that being in *wudu'* before touching the Qur'an is recommended, and this (judgement) is preferred by al-Lakhmi."

I SAY: "It is clear from these transmissions that what Ibn 'Arafa has related from the followers of Ibn 'Abd al-Barr should be used with caution, and Allah knows best who is the best guided in this matter."

2. Al-Khurshi has referred to the words of Khalil 'and the touching of the *mus-haf*' saying: "I came across the following: 'Examine what the judgement would be if the person in a state of ritual impurity touches a Qur'an stand on which is a *mus-haf*, or if he touches a raised shelf on which parts of the Qur'an are lying or places shoes on the place where the Qur'an is deposited – so reflect (on this matter).'" *'Ayn-Jeem* is satisfied with his affirmation of the permissibility of the first two but states in his commentary that: "It is not permitted to treat the *mus-haf* with disrespect, nor to treat even a part of it with disrespect. However it is not prohibited – or considered a sign of disrespect – to carry it in something or to put it on one's shoulders such that it rests against one's back – consider (what would be the judgement) if someone leans with one's back against a wall on which the Qur'an or part of the Qur'an is written."

3. The author of *al-Mi'yar* said: Sayyidi Abu'l-Qasim al-Burzuli was asked about purity from filth (on one's clothes for example) and as to whether such (purity) was stipulated before the touching of the noble *mus-haf* and he replied: 'As for the touching of the *mus-haf* not being conditional upon purity from filth then were anyone to claim a consensus (regarding this judgement) then it would not be going far wrong: Look how the *'ulama* have warned against attaching amulets (in which the Qur'an is written) to animals or to a menstruating woman, against reciting the Qur'an in the highways or filthy places, or making *dhikr* of Allah in the lavatory, against dealing with the Mushrikun with dinars and dirhams on which is inscribed the name of Allah, exalted is He, or against washing oneself (after relieving oneself) while wearing a ring on which mention of Allah is made. Touching the Qur'an is more important that anything mentioned above – and so if it were conditional upon being pure from filth (on one's clothes) they would not have forgotten to mention it."

4. The author of *al-Mi'yar* said: "Abu 'Aziz was asked whether someone who was holding a (*mus-haf*) in his hand when his clothes were ritually impure was permitted to make much *dhikr* of Allah (by reciting) and whether he was permitted to enter a mosque, to touch and read from books of *tafseer*, books dealing with subtle points of the deen or books of instruction and exhortation;

whether he was permitted make the *adhan* in the (mosque) or read the Qur'an, hadith and the like or whether he should wait until he has removed the impurity from himself. He replied: 'If this is the normal place of residence, then it is permitted; if not, then he may make *dhikr* but it would be better if he made a *ghusl*. However, it is not permitted that he enter the mosque with his (clothes in this state) unless he is staying there – in which case he is permitted to enter it and make the *salat* in this (state) but should not stay in the mosque as there would be no hardship involved in his washing it off. He should not take off the clothes on which there is an impurity and then put them in the mosque unless he fears he might lose them. He is permitted to touch and read books of *tafseer* when in a state of *janaba* – likewise books of exhortation and instruction and those concerned with the subtle matters of the deen. He may make the *adhan* and read the Qur'an although it is preferable that he take a *ghusl*. He is also permitted to listen to someone reciting the Qur'an and hadith."

This is how I have found the text in two copies of his (work) although I am not responsible for any incorrect reading of the diacritical points on the part of the copyists: often various copies are to be found with the same corruptions, and it may well be that the author died before correcting his copy.

5. It is recommended that the person in a state of *janaba* make *wudu'* before going to sleep. Ibn Habib said that it is obligatory while al-Ubbi said that the well known judgement is that the *wudu'* of sleep – in the case of the person in a state of *janaba* – is as important as the *wudu'* for the *salat*.

6. Zarruq said in his *Naseeha*: "Delaying the *ghusl* for the *janaba* causes whispering (of shaytan)." Ibn Zakari has mentioned this in his commentary and also with respect to the hadith 'There are three persons which the angels will not approach: the corpse of a *kafir*, the person stained with khulouq¹ and the person in a state of *janaba* until he makes *wudu'*.' 'Iyad said: "The person in a state of *janaba* intended here refers to someone who disdains to do the *ghusl*, who delays until the time of the *salat* is past and persists in this practise – it does not refer to any person in state of *janaba*. (Proof that this is the correct interpretation is) based on the fact that the Messenger, may the peace and blessings of Allah be upon him, would make the round of his wives with one *ghusl*." Then he adds to his words 'it causes the whispering (of shaytan)' saying 'it also causes poverty.' Ibn Zakari said: "He stipulates that this holds true of the person who does not do *wudu'* and makes a habit (of not doing it)."

7. Khalil said: "the *ghusl* does in stead of the *wudu'* even if he realises that he

---

1 a perfume composed of saffron and other things. See an-Nasa'i, vol.5, p.142

is not in fact in a state a *janaba*, and the washing of *wudu'* does instead of the *ghusl* even if he has forgotten his state of *janaba*, like (when making up for) a patch of skin (inadvertently left untouched during the washing), and even if (the patch left uncovered by water is not skin but plaster, for example) in the case of a splint (covering the area)." Al-Mawwaq said, commenting on this point, that al-Lakhmi said: "The intention for the *wudu'* does instead of (that of *ghusl*) and vice versa as both of them are *fard* obligations: if he does the *wudu'* and remembers that he is in a state of *janaba*, then it is acceptable for him to continue, carrying on from what he has already washed during the *wudu'*."

He has also said, commenting on his words 'like a patch (left untouched during the washing)' that Ibn Yunus said: "It is stated in the *Mudawwana* that if the person in a state of *janaba* suffers a fracture or break and water does not cover completely the place being treated with a splint or plaster, then he only has to wash this particular place when it heals – purifying himself in doing so – and to repeat what he prayed during the day of his cure (before discovering he has left a patch unwashed). However, if he purified himself from a *state of janaba* after being healed, then he should repeat what he has prayed after being healed up to his second purifying of himself." Ibn Habib said: "This applies if the cause of his not doing the *ghusl* is out of forgetfulness; when, however, it is out of negligence or deliberately, then he should begin the *ghusl* anew and repeat the *salat*." Ibn al-Qasim said: "If the (patch of skin which has been left unwashed) is on the 'limbs of *wudu'* and then he does *wudu'* after becoming healed, then he must repeat what he prayed after being healed up to the moment of his *wudu'*." Ibn Yunus said: "The washing of the *wudu'* is acceptable in this case – instead of the washing of *janaba* – as what is done in both is identical and they are both *fard* obligations: thus the one does instead of the other."

8. The author of *al-Mi'yar* said: "The two majestic Shaykhs, Abu 'Ali ibn Qadah and Abu'l-Hasan al-Muntasar were asked regarding the person who has leaves a patch (of skin) untouched during the washing of *janaba* and who breaks his state of purity before completing the purification while washing over it with the intention of *wudu'*. Abu 'Ali replied: "If we say that the breaking of the state of purity is only made good on completion of the whole act of purification, then the patch (of skin untouched by the water) is not purified from the state of *janaba*; if we say that each part of the body is purified of its state of impurity when the washing of that particular part is completed, then the state of *janaba* is removed." Abu'l-Hasan replied: "It is purified of the state of *janaba* in all cases as it was washed with the intention of a *fard* obligation."

SECTION REGARDING TAYAMMUM

فَصْلٌ

لِخَوْفِ ضُرٍّ أَوْ عَدَمِ مَا

عَوَّضَ مِنَ الطَّهَارَةِ التَّيَمُّمَا

SECTION

89 If you fear illness or there is a lack of water, then do *tayammum* instead of the (usual purification)

MAYYARA has related that al-Mazari said: "The well known judgement is that one may do *tayammum* if one fears one would become ill, or one's illness would be aggravated or the cure of the illness would be delayed (by doing it)." Ibn Wahb said: "The exceptionally corpulent may do *tayammum* if they are not able to do *wudu'* and likewise the person suffering from sea sickness at sea – even when water is available in both their cases but they are unable to do *wudu'* with it because of their weakness or because the water would harm them." Ibn al-Qusar said: "The healthy person may do *tayammum* if he fears he will catch a cold or get a fever and likewise the sick person who is able to do *wudu'* and pray standing but who when the time for the *salat* arrives is sweating and he fears that if he gets up his sweat will dry and his illness will be extended – and so he does *tayammum* and performs the *salat* towards the *qibla* by gesturing (rather going through all the proper movements). If the time (for the particular *salat* in question) passes before his sweat has dried then he does not make up (his *salat*) – and this is the view of Mutarrif and Asbagh and Ibn al-Majishun." One text reads: "This (opinion) is in accordance with the *madhhab*." Ibn Nafi' has narrated: "The person who has water but fears he would go thirsty (if he used his water for *wudu'*) may do *tayammum*, or (likewise if) he fears death or illness." Al-Mazari said: "Thinking (for example, one will become ill) is as good as knowing (one will become ill)." Ibn Rushd said: "Fear for the sake of others is the same as fear for himself." Ibn Basheer said: "…likewise his fear for animals." Ibn al-Hajib said: "…likewise if he thinks he will go thirsty or those with him will go thirsty, be they animals or humans." The author of *at-Tawdeeh* has narrated details regarding animals from Ibn 'Abd as-Sadiq in which he discriminates between a beast of burden which he is in need of in order to arrive at his destination and animals whose flesh can be eaten. He goes on to say: "The most evident judgement is that if he has a dog or a pig with him, then he should kill them and not leave the water for them."

There is no difference of opinion that the person who fears for his own safety (if he were to go and get the water in his possession nearby) on account of a thief or wild animal should do *tayammum*. As for someone who fears (squandering) his wealth, the well known judgement is that he may do *tayammum* although it has also been said that he may not, and Ibn Basheer thinks it unlikely. Ibn Naji said: "The (judgement which) conforms with the principle of the *madhhab* is that if he needs this money, then he should do *tayammum* in all circumstances and that if he does not – and the amount is small – then he must buy water with it and not do *tayammum*; if this is not the case, then he should do *tayammum*."

Al-Khurshi said, commenting on the words of Khalil 'or if some (animal) worthy of respect (*muhtaram*) with him might go thirsty' that al-Ajhouri said: "With the words 'worthy of respect' is excluded any dog which one has no specific reason to have in one's possession. As for a monkey or bear, however, these are not excluded – even though, in the case of the bear, there is the argument that its meat is prohibited for consumption." Al-Mawwaq said: "He has excluded by what he says any (animal) which is not 'worthy of respect' and the author, in his commentary on Ibn al-Hajib, has mentioned dogs and pigs as examples – because they may be killed." I say: "This is so in the case of animals. It is also possible, however, to provide examples of human beings – such as the person who must be put to death without warning (like the person who has insulted the Prophet, may the peace and blessings be upon him), or someone killed in time of warfare, as long as there is someone present who is authorised to kill them."

If you were to argue "Even if this type (of person or animal) is not 'worthy of respect', then it should not be left to die of thirst as that would amount to torture -which is prohibited' then I would reply: "If it (becomes clear that it) is permitted to kill the first two (animals mentioned above) and if the other two (persons) have been designated for killing, then it is obligatory that they be killed immediately – so as to avoid unnecessary suffering."

What may be understood from his words is that one may do *wudu'* if there is someone authorised to kill or capable of killing these two (above mentioned) persons condemned to be put to death, that is, the imam or someone delegated by him or any other Muslim from the group available when the former two are unable to carry this out; if this is not the case, one should do *tayammum* and give them both to drink – and this is the most obvious meaning (of what he says).

The gist of this is that in the case of creatures who are not 'worthy of respect' one gives priority to using the water for *wudu'*. However, if (use of the water to) do the *wudu'* would lead to their suffering through thirst – irrespective of whether it is person or an animal in question – because they cannot be put to death immediately, either because of a legal constraint preventing one from taking the law into one's own hands and putting to death a renegade or fornicator for example, or for some physical constraint, like one not having the physical strength to kill a dog or pig, (then the water is given them to drink.)

Then he goes on to say, after some discussion, that Ibn al-Hattab said: "Just as one should make sure there is enough water left over to drink, so too one should ensure that there is enough for making bread and cooking – in order to take care of one's bodily needs. This has been clearly explained by al-Qurtubi with respect to cooking – and making bread is all the more important."

I have found the following text: "Examples of person who are not 'worthy of respect' would be the married man who commits fornication, the renegade (from Islam) after the time allotted for his turning in *tawba* (has expired) or the murderer with respect to person who has the right to kill him (as retaliation) – although this (latter) is not an absolute and general (right in all cases) but rather (each case) must be established with evidence, and mere knowledge of the (murder) is not enough. One must examine whether one is instructed to kill all (three categories of person) as soon as one is able or to leave them to die of thirst. Al-Fayshi expresses it in the following manner in *al-Iziyya*: "As for the creature who is 'not worthy of respect', one should use the water (for *wudu'*) and leave the (animal or person) to die of thirst." If it is possible to combine (use of) the water (for *wudu'*) and for drinking, then one should combine it for both purposes – unless one experiences disgust, fearing one might catch an illness if one gives them to drink of one's water (from the same vessel), in which case one should do *tayammum* (and give it all to them to drink)."

Al-Mawwaq said after transmitting the discussion of Ibn Rushd and Ibn Bashir on the words of Mayyara 'His fearing thirst in others is as his fear being thirsty himself': "Likewise his fear in the case of animals...." Ibn 'Arafa said: "If he allows the sale of the (animal) or its meat so cheaply that he may not buy water with it – and there is no need (for him to do this) – then the (*tayammum*) is invalidated."

ISSUE: Ibn al-Hattab said, commenting on Khalil: "Ibn Naji said: 'Ashhab has responded correctly when asked as to whether the sick person should fast or do the *salat* standing when he has the capacity to do so but only with difficulty and exhaustion saying: "He should break his fast and pray sitting and the deen of Allah is ease".'"

ISSUE: Ibn al-Hattab has related in *Hashiya ar-Risala* that al-Aqfahisi said: "If he is able to (do the *wudu'*) with hot water, then he must heat it up. *Tayammum* is not permitted him unless he is unable to touch (water) at all or he cannot not find anyone to heat it up for him and he would experience great difficulty in doing it himself."

NOTICE: There is no harm if the (water) changes (colour) through (contact with) the utensil used to heat it – even if the change is clearly visible – as long as it is made of something from (some material extracted from) the earth like iron or copper. Al-Khurshi said, commenting on Khalil's words 'or it becomes fixed as in the case of salt' saying: "…or iron, copper, irrespective of whether the (water) has (merely) run over these (metals) or the utensils (used) are made of these two (metals) and the (water) has changed by standing in them (for some time) or by being heated in them."

ISSUE: What counts in assessing 'thirst' is a thirst which one fears would cause illness. Ibn al-Hattab said: "In the narration of Ibn al-Qasim from Malik there is the question as to whether the person who has a little water with him should give it to a man – who passing by asks if he can have it to drink – and (as a result must) do *tayammum*. Malik replied: 'This depends: if one fears for the man's life, then one should give him to drink but if one does not fear for his life, then I do not consider (one should give him to drink). It may be that he is only slightly thirsty but if his state is such that one fears for his life, then I consider one should give him to drink.'" Ibn Rushd said: "Fear for someone else's life is the same as fear for oneself" and commentating on a narration from Ashhab in the section on *wudu'* 'If he has enough water to do the *wudu'* but fears he will himself go thirsty, then he should do *tayammum*' he said: "and this is correct."

The most manifest meaning of the words of Ibn Rushd is that it is not permitted him to drink – when there is only a little water – and do *tayammum*. Reflect about this, and Allah, exalted is He, knows best.

ISSUE: ibn al-Hattab has related that al-Qurtubi said in his *tafseer*: "One of the (valid) reasons for doing *tayammum* is if one fears (doing *wudu'*) will (result in a delay and one's) losing one's companions (when the caravan moves off) – and this is clear, and Allah knows best."

ISSUE: The author of *ad-Dakheera* said: "A rule: difficulties which are distinct from the (actual) acts of worship are of three kinds: the extreme kind, like fearing for someone's life, in which case it is obligatory to alleviate (this difficulty before proceeding with) the act of worship, a fear of a less intense kind, like a slight pain in one's finger, in which case completion of the act of worship in full takes priority over removing this difficulty, and the third kind which lies between the two former kinds. Thus in the case of any (difficulty) which approximates to the more intense kind, it is obligatory to ease the burden of the act of worship. That which approximates to the slightest of difficulty does not obligate that the (burden of worship) be alleviated. As for any (difficulty) lying between these (two limits), then there is a difference of opinion. However, as for those difficulties which may not be distinguished from the (actual) acts of worship, these cannot be made alleviated, like taking a *ghusl* in cold weather or fasting during hot weather – as they are prescribed irrespective of such (conditions)."

Mayyara said: "As for (the reason) dependent upon a lack of water – and this is the second reason in the words of the author – if this lack (of water) is ascertained, then one may do *tayammum* without having to look for (water) given that looking for something which one has ascertained to be non existent would be a waste of time. If, however, one has not ascertained that it does not exist – that is if one is aware of its existence or thinks it to be there or has doubts as to whether it exists – then one must look for it. If one looks for it and does not find it, then one does *tayammum*. The matter of searching (for water) differs (according to circumstance) – thinking it does not exist is not the same as doubting its existence, and having doubts is not the same as being under the illusion (of its existence). Thus searching in the first (case) is more justified than the second, and the second more justified than the third. Moreover people are not equal with respect to their physical strength: in general a man is not like a woman (in this respect) nor a young man as an old man. The obligation on each person is that they look (for water) – but without undergoing inordinate difficulty."

Malik said: "There are some people who have difficulty in covering half a mile. (The question poses itself as to) whether, if (such a person) is in the company (of others), he should ask one of them (for water) and whether, if they do not give him any, he should do *tayammum*, or whether he should do *tayammum* without even asking them." There are various ramifications to this matter. Malik, may Allah be pleased with him, said: "If the company (of people) is withholding their water because they themselves only have a little, then he may do *tayammum* without asking (them). Moreover, if this is not the case but there are a lot of people accompanying him, then he does not have to ask them." Malik has added: "He does not have to ask forty men and he does not have to repeat the *salat* (if he prays with *tayammum*). If, however, the number of people accompanying him is small and he does not ask for water from them, then he should repeat the *salat* if its time has not elapsed; and if (only) two men or three, then the obligation to repeat it remains with him – however great the delay." Al-Lakhmi has investigated this matter, so examine the *Tawdih*. If there is (still) no water (available) – irrespective of whether he has looked for it or not – then he must do *tayammum*, if he is a traveller, according to the consensus, and should also do it if resident, like for example a prisoner, according to the well-known view.

Khalil said: "the *tayammum* of the sick person and the traveller – as long as on a journey which is licit (according to the *shari'ah*) – may be done for a *fard* (*salat*) and a *nafila* (*salat*), and in the case of the resident person, for the *janaza salat*, if incumbent on him and the *fard salat* other than the *jumu'a*, but not the sunna, if there is not enough water or he fears – by using the (water) – he will fall ill, aggravate his illness, that his cure will be delayed, or some creature (be it a person or animal which is *mutaram*) 'worthy of respect' will go thirsty or (he fears that) by looking for it, he will waste money or the time of the *salat* will elapse; likewise (he may do *tayammum*) when there is no one to hand him the water (if he is unable to move) or no means (like a bucket) to get it – and there is a difference of opinion as to whether he should do *tayammum* if he fears use of such means will cause him to miss (the time of the *salat*)."

Ibn al-Hattab said, commenting on his words 'and the traveller – as long as on a journey which is licit (according to the *shari'ah*)...': "(If applicable in the case of a journey with a licit – *mubah* – purpose) then it applies all the more to travel which is obligatory or recommended, and if one argues that it refers also to travel which is permitted – *ja'iz* – then this may be inferred from the text which includes such an interpretation. However, (clearly) excluded is any travel (undertaken for a purpose) which is disliked or prohibited."

Then he goes on to say, after a discussion: "Notice: firstly, most of their texts (on the subject) refer to an act of disobedience, that is a journey other than one which is permitted – as Ibn al-Hajib said. However, also implicit is the exclusion of (journeys) which are *makruh* – that is, contrary to what is implied in the text of Khalil's *Mukhtasar*. However, the most manifest interpretation is the first as shortening the *salat* is not (absolutely) forbidden in the case of a journey which is *makruh* but rather is proscribed in a *makruh* sense – as will be described in the section below. They have also said that the *salat* is not repeated if it is shortened, that is, in the light of their stipulation mentioned above that this applies (only in the case of) licit travel, according to the well known opinion – and here it is all the more applicable, so reflect upon this."

("Notice:) secondly, as examples of journeys considered as acts of disobedience Ibn Farhun has mentioned that undertaken by a runaway slave, by a highwayman, by anyone in defiance of (the wishes of) his parents or by the person who goes against his Shaykh when the latter has delegated his affairs to him – according to what one (of the 'ulama) has mentioned on the subject. Such persons are not permitted to do *tayammum* according to the most correct judgement. Rather they must return to whatever they should be doing and if they have a firm resolve to make *tawba*, then they are permitted (to do *tayammum*), and Allah known best."

Al-Khurshi has related that al-Laqqani said: "What is meant by licit (*mubah*) is that which stands opposite to what is prohibited or disliked. Included in what is licit is travel for trade, for example, when the person is able to do without the profit from it or that of the shepherd when his animals are not dependent upon him for their life. Excluded (from the term 'licit') is the prohibited, like travel in a state of disobedience, for example; and the disliked, like travel for distraction and amusement. The judgement regarding the person committing an act of disobedience by his travel is delayed until only (time enough for) one *rak'a* with its two prostrations remains within the *daruri* time and then *tawba* is demanded of him: if he makes *tawba*, then all well and good but if not, then he is put to death. Delaying the (judgement) is done in the hope that he will make *tawba*. If he does makes *tawba*, then he may do *tayammum*. There are two views as to whether his *salat* is acceptable if he does *tayammum* before making *tawba*, that is whether he has to repeat it within the time or whether – as is the judgement of this *madhhab* – he remains under an obligation to repeat it, however great the delay. As for the journey which is disliked then *tayammum* is also disliked, that is, Allah will not reward him for the *tayammum*."

He has also said, commenting on his words 'he does not repeat': "…that is, if the person who is resident and in good health does the *tayammum* and prays and then finds water, then he does not repeat the *salat*, even if his thinking (he would not find water) proves false, according to the well-known opinion."

Ibn al-Hattab has related that al-Lakhmi said: "There are three opinions with respect to the healthy person who is not in a state of imprisonment, who has little time (remaining to do the *salat*) and who – if he were to ask for water – would have no time left (to do the *salat*). Malik has permitted him to do *tayammum* and to pray and (stated that) he does not have to repeat it even if he finds water within the (prescribed) time. However, he has also said: 'He should repeat (the *salat*) if he finds water within the time.' In the *Kitab Muhammad* the author says: 'he should look for water even if the time elapses.'"

It is clear from the words of al-Lakhmi that the healthy person – who, fearing the time will elapse if he looks for water, does *tayammum* and prays, but then finds water within the time – does not have to repeat (his *salat*) if his (finding water) proves contrary to his expectation. The same (judgement) is to be found in *Mudawwana* when he says: "Whoever – whether on a journey or resident – fears that the time (for the *salat*) would elapse if he were to draw up water from a well, then he should do *tayammum* and pray and he does not have to repeat it within the time or outside of the time – when he does *wudu'*." There is also a judgement from Malik regarding the resident of a city, namely, that he should repeat it when he has done *wudu'*.

Al-Khurshi has narrated that al-Ajhouri said: "Also included in the words of the author '(the case when) they do not have (access to) water belonging to others' is (the case when there is both) water (available which is) dedicated for drinking purposes in particular as well as (water) which may be used for *wudu'* but one does not which of the two is which."

Ibn al-Hattab said: "(The question may be posed as to) whether or not the person who finds water belonging to others or water which is dedicated for drinking purposes in particular is to be considered (legally speaking) as someone 'without water' – since what is missing legally is the same as what is missing physically, and this is what the Shafi'is hold to although I have not found a text on this subject. The most evident view is that he should (be reckoned as someone) 'without water', and should do *tayammum*."

He has also said regarding (Khalil's) words 'or the (prescribed) time elapsing': "That is, likewise *tayammum* is licit if they fear that the time will elapse if they look for water."

He said in the *Mudawwana*: "Whoever is resident and fears that the sun will rise if he goes to the Nile to do *wudu'* – when he finds himself on the levees or the banks of Fustat – then he should do *tayammum* and pray, and not go off for water." Also included in his words is the person who fears the time will elapse if he has to occupy himself with raising water from a well – as said in the *Mudawwana*: "Whoever fears – while on a journey or when resident – that the time will elapse if he raises water from a well should do *tayammum*." The author of *al-Talqeen* says: "…thirdly, if he fears that by occupying himself with using the well the time will elapse – either because of the short time remaining, or because of the delay which he will necessary incur in transporting it, or because of the depth of the bucket and well-rope – then he should hold to the judgement of *al-Mukhtasar* regarding the four types of resident person mentioned in *at-Tawdih*: this (case) is included in his discussion of (firstly) 'those who fear the time will elapse if they were to go and seek water', (secondly) 'those who fear it will elapse if they were to raise water from a well', thirdly, 'those who fear the time will elapse because there is no instrument available' and fourthly, 'those who fear that the time will elapse by there (actual) use of the water.' The judgement (in his case) will then be clear from these (four cases). What is meant by 'time' is the '*ikhtiyari*' time. Ibn al-Ghazi has related that Ibn Rushd said: "The view that the person who fears the rising of the sun should do *tayammum* is based on the opinion that the *Subh salat* does not have a '*daruri*' time. If one accepts, however, that it does have a '*daruri*' time and it is approaching the time of dawn, then he should endeavour to seek water as long as he does not fear dawn will break – as anyone who does not find water should transfer to *tayammum* if he fears the '*ikhtiyari*' time will elapse." And what he said is evident.

Al-Lakhmi said: "The time in which one does the *salat* with *tayammum* is the '*ikhtiyari*' time, not the '*daruri*' time: thus any time in which the *salat* may be performed with *wudu'* and when it is not permitted to delay it – as an option – is also the time in which it is done with *tayammum*, and it should not be delayed."

Al-Khurshi said, commenting on his words 'likewise, when there is no one to bring it to him or no means' – after a discussion in which he objects to the argument of al-Hattab: "The gist of the matter is that if there is no one to bring him the water or no means then he (is considered as someone) 'without water' and should do *tayammum* at the beginning of the time – and this is recommended if he holds out no hope (of finding water). If, however, he hopes to find water or knows it will be possible to get water, then he should do *tayammum* at the latest time (possible), as will be explained below. As for the person who finds the means but who fears that the time will elapse if he uses it to raise water, then he is (considered to be) in the same position as the person who fears the time will elapse if he uses the (water)."

Khalil said: "He should seek it for every *salat* and even if he only surmises its (existence), but does not (have to) if he knows of its non-existence for certain – as long as the seeking does not cause undue difficulty; just (as he should seek it from those) in whose company he finds himself if their number is small or from those in his immediate vicinity if their number is great – as long (that is, with respect to the latter) as he is ignorant as to whether they are withholding it for themselves." Al-Mawwaq said that al-Baji said: "He does not have to exert himself (inordinately) when going to look for water: he does not have to go to places he would not normally go to or go off the road more than he would normally do when going to fetch water from springs or streams. If in doing so he would become separated from his companions, then he should do *tayammum*, and there is no limit or restriction to this." Ibn al-Mawaz has related from Malik: "... (he should seek water) as long as he does not fear exhaustion from a half a mile – for some people have difficulty in covering such a distance." Muhammad said: "The interpretation of his words is that he is referring to weak men or women rather than strong men and women."

Commenting on Khalil's words 'if their number accompanying him is small' he said that Ashhab said: "He should ask those persons nearest to him and those he thinks will give it to him. He does not, however, have to enquire of forty men from the group but rather only those close to him and those from whom he hopes will receive (water)." Malik said: "If he knows that they will refuse it him, then he should not ask it of them." Ibn Rushd said: "If he desists from seeking water – from those close to him whom he hopes will have (extra) water available and whom he thinks will not refuse him – and he does *tayammum* and prays, then he remains under the obligation to repeat the *salat*, however great the delay."

Al-Kharshi, commenting on Khalil's words 'likewise, a small number accompanying him', said: "...that is, likewise he should seek it from a small number accompanying him, like four or five, irrespective of whether they are near him or not." 'Abd al-Malik, Ibn 'Abd al-Hakam and Asbagh have said: "If he does not seek it, then he remains under an obligation to repeat it within the time unless there are (only) one or two men or the like, in which case he remains under an obligation to repeat the *salat* however long the delay – as has been indicated in *Sharh as-Sanhouri*."

He said, commenting on his words 'or there are many around him' that as-Sanhouri said in his *Sharh*: "...like forty for example" and the previous Shaykhs have said: "...if he does not do this, then he is committing a wrong action, but he does not repeat." He, however considered the argument that to address a small number of persons is like addressing a large number weak. When someone responded that one can easily imagine that three persons would have water on them – because, being such a small number, they would be unlikely to rely on others (for water) – he replied that if such were the case, one would know of the (availability of water or not) as knowledge about three persons (travelling) in one's company is more likely than knowledge of others (in a much larger company). Al-Lakhmi said: "It has been narrated that if he believes that in all likelihood they will give him water, then he remains under an obligation to repeat the *salat*, however long the *salat*." The like has been reported from Ibn Rushd in his narration from Abu Zayd. Al-Lakhmi has also said: "If the matter is difficult, and he does not seek water, then it is permitted to say that one should repeat the *salat* within the time."

Issue: al-Khurshi said, commenting on Khalil's words 'seeking in such a way as not to incur hardship': "If he knows that they will give some to him merely because they feel embarrassed (by his presence) but that they would not give to him if it were not for this, then the obligation to search is removed. The question remains as to whether, if they were to give him (water) under these circumstances, it would be permitted for him to use it or not, or whether he would be considered as being in the same position (legally speaking) as a person who has taken possession of something unlawfully. The people with the water are under no obligation to hand it over to the person who asks it of them, even if his giving up seeking the (water) would lead him to do the *salat* (with *tayammum*) – as is clear from what follows when he says 'and excess of food and drink to the person in need.'"

Issue: al-Mawwaq has related that Abu 'Umar said: "It is not obligatory to carry water for the *wudu'* (on one's person). Al-Baji said: "It is permitted to undertake a journey using a route even if one knows for certain that there is no water (available on it) – when one undertakes (the journey) to seek wealth or to pasture cattle. It is also permitted him to remain in a place in order to protect his wealth or money even if this leads him to doing the *salat* with *tayammum* – this 'Iyad has stated in *al-Ikmal*."

Ibn al-Hattab has related that Ibn Naji said in his commentary on the words of the *Risala* 'it is disliked to go to sleep before (doing) the (*tayammum*, when in a state of *janaba*)': "What may be understood from the discussion of the Shaykh is that it is disliked that a man go out without water from his house before the time (for the *salat*) to fields which are cultivated over a distance of some miles – when he has doubts as to whether water is available or not. Reflect then, whether he under an obligation to carry water (on him) if it becomes clear (to him) that there is no water. I have seen – with regard to a lesser case – the *fatwa* of our Shaykh ash-Shabeebi in which he instructs (him) to do this, but I do not know if he intended this as an obligation or a recommendation, although I tend to regard it as an obligation."

The most evident judgement is that there is no obligation – based on the saying of the *Mudawwana* 'Whoever leaves one village, making for another – without being in *wudu'* and without being (legally speaking) a traveller – and the sun goes down, then if he hopes to find water before the red disappears from the sky he should go ahead (and look for it); but otherwise, he should do *tayammum* and pray. Shaykh Abu Muhammad has narrated this with the words 'from village to village, over a mile or two.' None of the commentators, however, understands it as applicable after it the onset (of the red in the sky). So reflect on this.

In the *Nawazil al-Qubbab* the author says: "Al-Qubab was asked about a man who excused himself from the hajj saying it would cause him to be without water, to do the *salat* in *tayammum* and to be (at times) with ritual impurity on his (clothes) and he replied: 'As for his excuse that he will need to do *tayammum*, that he will be ritually impure, that he will not find water and he will pray with this (ritual impurity on him), then this has no basis. Moreover, I do not know of any difference of opinion arguing that such (an excuse) is permitted with regard to licit (actions undertaken with a view to) seeking profit and for other (purposes) – so how can such (an excuse be permitted) in the case of worship.'"

ISSUE: Ibn al-Hattab said: "If he finds enough water to wash his face and hands and is able to scoop up what falls from his limbs and complete the *wudu'*, then he should do this – he will be on a par with someone who finds 'used' water and is under an obligation to use it to purify himself when there is nothing else available." This latter has been related by Shaykh Ibn Abi Zayd – and Ibn Yunus and others of the commentators of the *Mudawwana* have narrated this of him during the subject of used water. Indeed Ibn 'Arafa and others have also narrated it during their discussion of the same subject. Ibn Harun said: "The (water) is (considered) 'used (but pure)' in the view of those who argue that each limb becomes pure after this (particular part of the body) has been purified. However, those who say that purity is only achieved when the whole act of purification is finished – and this is the well known opinion – then it is not considered 'used (but pure).' The like has also been narrated of Lam-'ayn-fa. Ibn Naji has narrated it in the *Sharh al-Mudawwana* and al-Barzuli has narrated it in *at-Tahara* where he says: 'If he has (only) enough water with him to wash just his face and arms but is able to scoop up the water which drips (from his body) and wipe his head and wash his feet with it, then he should do this.'"

ISSUE: The husband must supply his wife with water for her *wudu'* and *ghusl* even if from the (water of the) *janaba* of someone other than him. This al-Khurshi said in his *Saghir*, commenting on the words of Khalil 'water is obligatory...' that is, "a husband is under an obligation to supply his wife water to drink and for her *wudu'* and *ghusl*, even if from the (water of) *janaba* from sexual intercourse other than him." In *Kifayat at-Talib*, the author, commenting on the words of the *Risala* 'then they both purify themselves with it together' said: "What may be understood from this is that the husband should supply water to the wife for her to purify herself (of menstruation) or for *wudu'* by buying it or otherwise (if necessary) – and this is the well-known opinion – as it is part of her upkeep." 'Abd al-Baqi has also written on the subject in *Ghayat al-Amani* saying that Ibn Naji has distinguished between (water for) the *janaba* caused by someone other than the (husband), in which case it is not obligatory (on him), and (water for use for the *janaba* caused by him) in which case it is obligatory (on him). He has composed a poem in which he indicates (the judgement of) Ibn Naji with the words 'even if it is ... ':

The commentators of Khalil deem it obligatory for husbands
   to supply their wives with water for *wudu'*, O my friend!
Yes, likewise for the *ghusl*, even (with water of the *janaba* of) intercourse
   with other than her husband – may Allah protect you from harm!
Many people are unaware of this,
   and those who put this into practice are few in number.
Those who do practise (this) must realise
   that while others refuse (this judgment) they also have success –
And must realise that their knowledge and understanding
   is from a man of excellence who has guided this *umma*.

ISSUE: al-Khurshi and al-Mawwaq have said: "Sahnun narrated that two men who had enough water between them for one of them to do *wudu'* contended with each other over the value (of the water). " Ibn Rushd said: "This is correct: when a man must buy water for more than the value (that they acquired their water for), and as long as he himself does not raise the price (to make a profit himself), then he is obliged to contend with his companion as this act of bargaining is (an accepted part of) buying (and selling). If, however, one of them accepts the value (assigned by his companion) without bargaining or before the price (they agree upon) has attained the price of the water which he must buy (given that he has handed his share of water to his companion) and he does *tayammum* and prays, then he remains under the obligation to repeat, however great the delay – as he is not considered to be of the people of *tayammum* because of his capacity to buy water (that is, had he insisted on bargaining with his companion and obtaining the full price for the water he had to buy)."

Al-Mi'yar has added that one of the (*'ulama*) said: "There is a difference of opinion in this. The *'ulama* have also said: 'If a woman leaves off doing the *salat* deliberately until five *rak'ats* remain and then she begins to menstruate, then they are annulled for her. Whoever has water with him which would be enough for his (*wudu'*) but who then spills it or makes it impure, then he has committed an act of disobedience and is considered as a person who may do *tayammum* – in accordance with the *fiqh* regarding anyone who oversteps the bounds or throws precaution to the wind such that he is forced to do *tayammum*: he does *tayammum* but does not have to repeat the *salat*.'"

ISSUE: The author of *al-Mi'yar* as well as al-Khurshi have said – and the text is taken from the former: "Al-Mazari was asked whether there any harm in a woman desisting from (intercourse with) her husband – out of fear she would be harmed by the cold water and because she wanted to maintain the *salat* (with *wudu'*) – or any harm in the husband forcing her (to intercourse) when he knows that she will leave off doing the *salat*. He replied: 'Fear that the (coldness of the) water will cause harm renders *tayammum* licit or (fear) that causing someone to do something that will in turn cause them to transfer from the purification with water (to *tayammum*) is not permitted except in the case of need. Thus her making herself available (for intercourse and her ensuing transfer to *tayammum*), that is, her undertaking of that which will remove the purification by water is not permitted except in case of extreme need on the part of the husband. If he is not in any such need on the part of the husband, then it is not permitted that she make herself available (to him) and he must not force himself on her – if he believes she will abandon the *salat*."

Al-Mi'yar has added to al-Khurshi saying: "Likewise, it is not permitted for the traveller who arrives (home) during the day to have intercourse with his wife when she is under an obligation to fast (that day) – that is in the case of a Muslim (wife). (This is because even) if it is licit for him, it is not for her and to assist her in committing an act of disobedience would be an act of disobedience itself. There is a difference of opinion as to whether it is permitted to have intercourse when the wife is a Christian. Our Shaykhs are of the opinion that the (question as to whether intercourse with them is permitted or not) depends on whether they have been instructed in matters of the deen. This has also been indicated in the *Mudawwana* – in (the section regarding) having intercourse with somebody wounded in the scalp and the traveller. The answer to this and other questions lies in one and the same (principle) indicated (in the *Mudawwana*), namely, the consideration of what constitutes the necessity and need for intercourse (in the case of the husband), based on the length of time (he must wait). For this reason, the author distinguishes between the traveller and the person wounded on the scalp."

Ibn al-Hattab said: "It is not permitted for a person without water to urinate if he is able to retain this urine – as long as this (retention of urine) does not (become so uncomfortable as to) render the *salat* invalid. This is because (refraining from urinating) enables him to avoid doing *tayammum* for the *salat*. There is no difference of opinion, however, that if it does render his *salat* invalid, he should do *tayammum*. Likewise, if he has water with him and the time for *salat* begins and he spills it (deliberately) then – although he is considered to have committed an act of disobedience – he is still permitted to do *tayammum*. This (judgement) is contrary, however, to one of the two opinions of the followers of ash-Shafi'i."

BRANCH: He said in the *Mudawwana*: "If the healthy person fears he will die because of (the effect of) snow or the cold, then he should do *tayammum* for the *janaba*." Abu'l-Hasan has related in the *Kabir* that Abu Muhammad Salih said: "What may be understood from this is that whoever finds himself in a land of ice and snow then he should not have intercourse with his wife if it results in his having to do *tayammum*." Shaykh Abu'l-Hasan said: "This applies in a land where he does not expect to have to wait long (for the snow to disappear and for him to be able to do *wudu'*); if, however, it means his having to wait a long time, then he is permitted to have intercourse with his wife."

وَصَلِّ فَرْضاً وَاحِداً وَإِنْ تَصِلْ

جَنَازَةً وَسُنَّةً بِهِ يَحِلّ

90 and he may pray one *fard salat*, and if performed after this, then the *janaza* and sunna *salats* are permitted also

With this verse begins the second section, namely what (acts of worship) one may perform with the *tayammum*. Thus he says that it is only permitted to pray one of the *fard salats* and that the *janaza* and sunna *salats* are permitted with *tayammum* as long as they follow on immediately after (the *fard*).

$$\text{وَجَازَ لِلنَّفْلِ ابْتَدَا وَيَسْتَبِيحُ}$$
$$\text{الْفَرْضَ لَا الْجُمُعَةَ حَاضِرٌ صَحِيحٌ}$$

91   It is permitted to begin with *nafila salats* (when only *nafila* are performed) as (it is permitted to begin with) the *fard salat*, but not the *jumu'a* for the healthy person who is resident

Ahmad Mayyara said: "Here, he is informing us that the traveller and sick person may perform the *tayammum* for the *nafila salats* — that is for those *salats* other than the *fard salats* — as long as he begins with them and performs them independently such that he makes *tayammum* for them specifically with them in mind. As for performing the *nafila* with the *tayammum* of the *fard* when done *after* the latter, this has been mentioned in the previous verse. His statement regarding the *tayammum* done independently is the well known opinion regarding the right of the sick person and the traveller — as they are mentioned specifically in the text (of the Qur'an). However, the healthy person, who is resident and who has no water, like for example the person in prison, should not do the *tayammum* for the *nafila* independently, but rather he should only do the *tayammum* for the *fard salat* independently, according to the well known opinion. (But, as mentioned above,) if he has done the *tayammum* for the *fard salats*, then it is permitted for him to do the *nafila salats* with that *tayammum*."

Then he has added: "Thus the resident, healthy person should only do the *tayammum* independently for the *fard salats*, but he should not do it for the *jumu'a* or *nafila salats*." And this is indicated by Ibn 'Ashir with his words:

$$\text{الْفَرْضَ لَا الْجُمُعَةَ حَاضِرٌ صَحِيحٌ}$$

...   and the *fard salat* (is permitted), but not the *jumu'a* for the healthy person who is resident

BRANCH: Ibn al-Hattab has related that Malik said: "Only the traveller who does not find water should pray the *janaza salat* with *tayammum*" and then he has added: "There is no harm in him doing *tayammum* in order to touch the *mus-haf* and read a *hizb* from it if he does not find water when he is on a journey."

BRANCH: Ibn al-Hattab said that al-Qurtubi said: "A 'journey' (in this case) is not restricted to a journey during which one is permitted to shorten the *salat* — and this is the *madhhab* of Malik and the majority of the *fuqaha*."

BRANCH: Ibn al-Hattab relates that al-Wanwaghi said that al-'Awfi said: "Consider whether the person in *janaba* who wants to go into a mosque to perform the prescribed *salat* in *jama'a* (with others) and to repeat what he has already prayed on his own has to do *tayammum* in order to enter the mosque and then again for the *salat*. It has been said that this is not permitted as he has no compelling need to so the *salat* in *jama'a* or repeat it (as he has already performed it) – and this is so in the case of the person who is resident and healthy. As for the person who is travelling, however, then it is permitted."

ISSUE: Ibn Hilal said in his *Nawazil*: "Praise belongs to Allah! If the person without water is in good health and resident, then he should not do *tayammum* except for the *fard salat* or a specific *nafila salat*, like the *fajr* (*salat*) – and this is the well known *salat*. As for the teacher, he should not teach children the Qur'an and not have them write it down if he is in *janaba* as he should be able to find water in a short space of time – unless, that is, he and the (children) are far from the town and are unable to find water for days on end, in which case he should do *tayammum* and teach them."

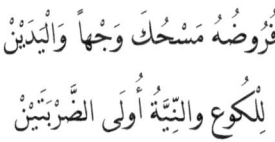

92 The obligatory (aspects of *tayammum*) are to wipe one's face and hands up to the wrists, the intention, the first of two strikings (of the earth)

Al-Khurshi said, commenting on the words of Khalil 'and wipe over the whole of the face and hands up to the wrists': "This means he should cover everything mentioned by Ibn Sha'ban: 'He does not have to rub into the creases or wrinkles of the face but should take care to wipe over the septum of the nose, the eye-bone and brows and between the nether lip and chin if there is no hair on it, and he should wipe over his beard, if long, with his hands, covering whatever he would in the washing, and what is not acceptable in the *wudu'* is not acceptable in the *tayammum*.'"

Ibn al-Hattab said: "If he wipes his face with one finger, then it is acceptable – as Ibn al-Qasim said with respect to the wiping of the head. Ibn Naji said that Ibn Atiyya said: 'This is the well known judgement.'"

Al-Khurshi said, commenting on his words 'and his hands up to his wrists': "If there is a lot of earth, dust or any other particles clinging to his hands, then he should shake them gently in order to avoid disfiguring his face (with dirt) or harming it (in any way). He should not wipe too hard – his (*tayammum*) being invalid if he does, as al-Aqfahisi said. However, Nun-Ta' said: 'I have not seen this judgement other than from him.'"

BRANCH: Mayyara has related: "Ibn al-Hattab said: 'One should remove any rings', and some (ulama) have also said: '…and one should rub between the fingers.' The author of *at-Tawdih* said: 'He has indicated the weakness of the opinion with his words "some (ulama) have said" – and the reason for this weakness is that 'rubbing' does not correspond to the meaning of the term 'wiping' which indicates an action which is lighter in nature (than rubbing).'"

Al-Khurshi said that Zarruq said: "A student mentioned to me that he had heard one of the Shaykhs describing (what was meant by) rubbing in a way which is not generally accepted (by the *'ulama*) – namely wiping the edges of the fingers with the inside of one of the fingers rather than interlocking or interlacing the fingers with each other. The (Shaykh) justified (this method by saying) that the edges of the fingers would not be covered (by wiping over) with earth, only the inner side of them – when doing it any other way."

As for his saying 'and the intention…', this is the third aspect of the obligatory aspects (of *tayammum*). It must be made when striking the ground the first time. The author (Ibn 'Ashir) has not mentioned this fact – and Allah knows best – on account of its obviousness that is, because a characteristic of intention (in general) is that it must be done at the beginning of what is intended. The likelihood that his words 'the intention, the first striking (of the earth when done) twice' mean that 'the intention is to be made in the first of the two strikings' rather than that 'this first (and only the first) striking is one of the obligations of *tayammum* as mentioned at the beginning of the verse' is not great because it would mean omitting an element of the *wudu'* which must be mentioned – and which is expressly mentioned among the proofs for the judgement – and including instead of something which is obvious. Further, when making the intention, one should make the intention to render the *salat* licit by *either* (making this intention for) the state of lesser or for that of the greater impurity. If one forgets that one is in a state of *janaba* and does *tayammum*, then the *tayammum* is unacceptable."

Commenting on Khalil's words 'he makes the intention to render the *salat* licit and the intention (in particular to render) the major impurity licit if he is in a state (of *janaba*) – repeating (the intention and *tayammum* whenever necessary if his *janaba* lasts over several *salats*) – but it does not remove the (actual) state of impurity' Kharshi said: "…similar to the intention made to render the *salat* licit is the intention for the obligation of *tayammum* – as in the *wudu'*, as Ibn Farhun said, narrating from Ibn Daqeeq al-'Eid."

NOTICE: Mayyara said what may be understood from their saying that 'the person doing the *tayammum* makes the intention to render the *salat* licit but that it does not remove the state of impurity' is that this 'rendering licit' has a more general sense than the 'removing of impurity' – or at least a sense equal to it. However a problem arises since what is meant by 'impurity' in this case is the obstacle inherent in the (impurity of) the limbs – but if this obstacle is not removed, then how could it be said that one is rendering the *salat* licit? This would imply the reconciliation of two opposites (which is impossible). However, that the impurity is the obstacle (to the *salat*) and that the (*salat*) may be 'rendered licit' (by the *tayammum*) is recognised by the *ijma'* (as an incontestable the fact). Ibn Rushd has responded (to this apparent contradiction) by saying: 'It is possible to argue that the (state of) *janaba* is a "reason or cause" which is (itself) based on "two further reasons or causes", the first, the (reason for the) obstacle preventing the *salat* and the second the (cause of the) obligation of the *ghusl*. Thus it is that the Legislator has established the *tayammum* as a means of removing one of the two reasons, that is the obstacle preventing the *salat* but has not made it a means of removing the other – which (can only be achieved by) the use of water. Indeed, if water becomes available, the Legislator has commanded that the second 'means' should come into effect, that is, the obligation to do the *ghusl*. Thus there is no contradiction in our saying on the one hand that 'the *tayammum* removes impurity' and fact that 'one is commanded to do the *ghusl* (when water becomes available) in the future.' This, on my life, is what the Shaykhs meant by saying that 'the *tayammum* does not remove impurity' – that is, it does not remove all the causes of the impurity. Thus any problem which arises is from people's limited understanding of the matter, so reflect upon this matter for it is an exceptionally good explanation."

Khalil: "There is in fact no difference of opinion in the matter because what is meant by those who say that *tayammum* does remove impurity is that it removes one of the causes, that is the obstacle preventing the *salat* while what is meant by those who say that *tayammum* does not remove impurity is that it does not remove one of the reasons of this impurity, that is, the obligation of *ghusl* – and so the negation and the assertion come to the same."

Notice Ibn 'Arafa said: "The person who makes the intention to render the *salat* licit does not (actually) remove the impurity, according to the well known opinion."

$$\text{ثُمَّ الْمُوَالَاةُ صَعِيدٌ طَهُرَا}$$

$$\text{وَوَصْلُهَا بِهِ وَوَقْتٌ حَضَرَا}$$

93 (also obligatory is) performing the actions (of the *tayammum*) consecutively without interruption, using pure earth, performing the (*tayammum*) immediately before (the *salat*) and within the time (of the *salat*)

Mayyara said: "Fifthly, as for 'consecutively and without interruption' it says in the *Mudawwana*: '*Tayammum* (done) before is only acceptable as long as it is done shortly before (the *salat*). Whoever does it a long time before should begin the *tayammum* again.'" He has also said : "Performing its various elements in the wrong order is like performing the *wudu'* in the wrong order."

Then he says: "Sixth, 'pure earth' – Ibn al-'Arabi said: 'What may be understood from the root meaning of the word *sa'eed* is that it refers to the surface of the earth and as such, to any surface, be it of sand, rock, clay or earth.'"

Al-Khurshi has related that an-Nawawi said: "Also included in the word *turab* – 'earth, dust' – is *bat-ha* – that is, the soft earth left after a flood. Al-Azhari, however, said that 'our fellow *'ulama* from Iraq have said that it refers to two things – either the earth left in a valley after a flash flood and which dries and hardens, or to (any) hard earth.'"

BRANCH: an-Nafrawi said: "*Tayammum* on stone is valid even if there is no earth on it, and even on flagstones which have been specially shaped with an adz or (stone) transported from one place to another, as long, that is, as it has not been baked. Anything may have been done to the stone used in *tayammum* except baking. For this reason, it is permitted on the flagstones of a mosque or on other stones, like the upper or lower grind stones, irrespective of whether they are broken or not; and likewise it is valid on the earth of the mosque, although one *'alim* has prohibited it, arguing that it would lead to the (floor of the mosque) being impaired."

Al-Khurshi and the author of *al-Mi'yar* have said – and here the text of the former is being used – that Ibn Naji said: "Our Shaykh ash-Shabeebi made a *fatwa* and maintained it right up to his death, namely, that it is prohibited to do *tayammum* on a grind stone which had not been broken, although our Shaykh before him had given a *fatwa* that it was permitted, even if it was broken, as its being specifically a *grindstone* only holds good when used as such; otherwise its nature as a stone is predominant."

Mayyara said: "Seventhly, also included as one of the obligations is that the *salat* is directly connected to the (*tayammum*). Ibn al-Jilab said: 'He should not do *tayammum* for the *salat* before its time, nor at the beginning of its time and then delay doing the *salat*: one of the conditions of *tayammum* is that it is directly linked to the *salat*.' Ibn at-Talamsani said: 'Ibn Sha'ban has a contrary opinion in two matters.'"

BRANCH: Ibn al-Hattab has related that al-Burzuli said: "As-Sayouri was asked whether the person who had done *tayammum* and begun a *fard salat* but then had broken it off after being afflicted by doubt as to whether he had said the *Allahu akbar* at the beginning of the *salat* had to do the *tayammum* again. He replied: 'He does not have to do the *tayammum* again.' Al-Burzuli said: 'This applies when he does not delay – if he delays, then his (first) *tayammum* is annulled.'"

NOTICE: from this it may be ascertained that there is no harm in doing the *tayammum* before the *iqama*, and Allah, exalted is He, knows best. Indeed, this is what is required – for the *iqama* of the person in a state of impurity is *makruh* (disliked).

Commenting on his saying 'within the time (of the *salat*)' Mayyara said: "Eighth: the time for the *salat* must have commenced for it is not valid to do the *tayammum* before this time. Khalil's said 'and its performance in the time.' 'Ali ibn 'Abd as-Sadiq said: 'This is particular to the *fard salats*' and Ibn al-Hattab said: 'The time for the above mentioned (*salat*) must have begun.'" Mayyara has also said that Ibn 'Arafa said: "A condition of *tayammum* with regard to the *fard* (*salat*) is that the time (of the *salat* has commenced)."

$$\text{آخِرُهُ لِلرَّاجِ آيِسٌ فَقَطْ}$$

$$\text{أَوَّلُهُ وَالْمُتَرَدِّدُ الْوَسَطْ}$$

94 One should delay it, if one hopes (to find water) and do it at the beginning (of the time) only if one has given up hope of finding it. If one finds oneself wavering between the two (states), then (perform it) in the middle (of the prescribed time for the *salat*).

Mayyara said[1]: "There are three types of person with regard to the *tayammum*:

---

[1] The following section is garbled in the Shinqueeti edition. The translation has been made from Mayyara's text.

the person who does *tayammum* at the beginning of the *ikhtiyari*[1] time, and this refers to the person who has given up hope of finding water within the *ikhtiyari* time. Among those who (legally speaking) share this state with him are those who think that there is no likelihood of finding water. This is because, in many legal matters, those who think something is improbable are considered as those who have certainty (regarding it); others include the sick person who is unable to tolerate contact with water – as long as he is aware of his lack of tolerance (in the *ikhtiyari* time). It is to such persons that he is referring with his words 'at the beginning, only if one has given up hope of finding it' – excluding with his words 'if one hopes' and 'the person who wavers' – and the like, not those persons who think that there is little probability of finding water or the sick person who is unable to touch water as they are included in the meaning of the term 'if one has given up hope' as mentioned above. Therefore what is required is that they be included. There is also the category of persons who do the *tayammum* 'in the middle' of the time – that is, those who are in doubt as to whether they will be able to obtain water or whether it even exists, and these he has indicated with his words 'those who waver, in the middle.' He said in *at-Tawdih*: "Also included in the section of 'those who waver' is the person who fears (attack) from wild animals and the like, or the sick person who does not find anyone to hand him the water – and so they both perform the *salat* at the middle of the time."

Then he said: "Finally, those who pray at the end of the time are those who are certain of finding water within the time, or those who think they will in all probability. Such a person is called 'the one who entertains hopes' as his belief that he will in all probability (find water) is considered to be on a par with certainty. He has indicated this category with his words 'one should delay it if one hopes.' Thus, if the person who entertains hopes (is allowed to) delay, then it is all the more logical that a person who is certain should do so."

NOTICE: delaying in the case of the person with certainty until the latest time is recommended, although it has also been said that it is obligatory. The author of *Ghayat al-Amani*, commenting on the words of the *Risala* 'if the traveller is certain of the existence of water within the time then he should delay (the performance of the *salat*)' said: "This (delay) is understood as something which is recommended according to Ibn al-Qasim and as something obligatory according to Ibn al-Habib."

Al-Khurshi said, commenting on the words of Khalil 'and in this (regard),

---

1   Time for the *salat* has been categorised by the Maliki *'ulama* as either *ikhtiyari* (optional) or *daruri* (necessary). The *daruri* time for the *Dhuhr salat* can extend up to shortly before *Maghrib*.

one may delay the (prescribed *salat* time of) sunset to the appearance of the red (in the sky)' has mentioned that as-Sinhouri said in his commentary: "It could be said that the matter of delay is in consideration of the opinion that the (person in question) may extend the range of what is possible for him. However, it should not be taken has the establishment on his part of an (extra) ramification (of the *shari'ah*) – in opposition to the well known opinion. Rather, it is an exception to the words 'the one who entertains hopes may delay to the end of the time' – this (latter opinion) has been stated by one of the *'ulama*. It resembles what another said, namely: "One should not interpret what the author has transmitted from the *Mudawwana* in the sense that the time of *Maghrib* may be extended – nor that the person 'who entertains hopes' should delay (his *salat*) into last part of *daruri* time."

The like has also been transmitted from Ibn al-Hattab: "One could say that the matter of delay on his part is out of consideration for the difference of opinion regarding the strength of the judgement which argues for the (possibility of) prolongation. However, this does not mean that doing this constitutes a ramification of the *shari'ah* which is contrary to the well known opinion but rather we would argue that it is a branch of the well known opinion and that in this particular case, it is an exception to their saying 'the person who entertains hope should delay to the last possible time within the *ikhtiyari* period' – that is except the *Maghrib salat* and this is evident for those who reflect upon it."

Al-Mawwaq, commenting on the words of Khalil 'the person who hopes (to find water) but who does the *tayammum* before the final possible time..' said: "(Regarding the person who) is certain of finding water in the last possible time, Ibn al-Qasim said: 'If he makes *tayammum* at the beginning of the time and prays, then he must repeat the *salat* if he finds water within the time, but if he does not, then he does not have to make up (the *salat*).' Ibn Yunus said: 'This is because when the time for the *salat* began, he was obliged to perform it but because he was without water he found himself (under the judgement contained) in the words of Allah, exalted is He: "...*and you cannot find any water, then do tayammum with pure earth.*"[1] Moreover, he is instructed to repeat the *salat* as a recommended act when it is still within the time.'"

He has also said: "I have found the following text: 'This distinction between the person who has given up hope and other than him applies during the *ikhtiyari* time but if he remembers during the *daruri* time, then he must do *tayammum* without distinguishing between whether he has given up hope or

---

1 al-Ma'ida – The Table:6

not.'"

$$\text{سُنَّتُهُ مَسْحُهُمَا لِلْمَرْفِقِ}$$

$$\text{وَضَرْبَةُ الْيَدَيْنِ تَرْتِيبٌ بَقِي}$$

95 Its sunnas are wiping (ones forearms) up to the elbows, striking twice with the hands and observing the order

$$\text{مَنْدُوبُهُ تَسْمِيَةٌ وَصْفٌ حَمِيدٌ}$$

96 it is recommended to say the *bismillah* and (to wipe one's hands) in the praiseworthy manner

Mayyara said: "He then informs us of the sunnas of *tayammum*. Firstly, wiping the arms from the wrists to the elbows, secondly, the second striking (of the earth) in order to wipe them (again) and thirdly, the order – such that he first wipes the face and then wipes the hands. However, if he does it the other way round and prays, then it is acceptable."

"Then he mentions what is recommended, namely the saying of the *bismillah* and the 'praiseworthy manner', that is, the recommended manner of wiping the hands. He has not explained it due to its being well-known."

NOTICE: the author, that is Khalil, does not mention a fourth sunna, that is, removing whatever (excess earth and dust) is clinging to the hands. (Note too that) if he wipes over something before wiping over his face and hands his *tayammum* is valid, according to the most evident interpretation – and this is stated *at-Tawdih*

$$\text{نَاقِضُهُ مِثْلُ الْوُضُوءِ وَيَزِيدُ}$$

... that which breaks the (*tayammum*) is the same (as that which breaks the) *wudu'* – with the additional (condition of)

$$\text{وُجُودُ مَاءٍ قَبْلَ أَنْ صَلَّى وَإِنْ}$$

$$\text{بَعْدُ يَجِدْ يُعِدْ بِوَقْتٍ إِنْ يَكُنْ}$$

97 the availability of water before doing the *salat*. If one finds (water) afterwards, then one repeats (the *salat*) within the time – [if one's state is]

$$\text{كَخَائِفِ اللِّصِّ وَرَاجٍ قَدَّمَا}$$

$$\text{وَزَمِنٍ مُنَاوِلاً قَدْ عَدِمَا}$$

98 like the person who fears (attack by) a thief, or entertains hopes (of finding water) but who nevertheless (does *tayammum*) before the final time (and then finds water), or the person who is physically incapable and who has no one to hand him (the water)

Mayyara said: "Here he informs us that whenever the *wudu'* is broken by the onset of a state of physical impurity (*hadath*) or for whatever reason, then this (same *hadath*) breaks the *tayammum*. His saying 'with the additional (condition of) the availability of water before doing the *salat*' is clear. The author of *at-Talqeen* said: 'Whoever does *tayammum* and finds water before doing the *salat* must use the water and his *tayammum* is rendered invalid – unless the time remaining is so short that he would miss the *salat* if he were to occupy himself with this (*wudu'*), in which case he does not have to use the (water) and his *tayammum* is not rendered invalid, according to the valid judgement within the *madhhab*.'"

NOTICE: al-Khurshi said: "If a group of people see water after doing the *tayammum* and one of them makes for it, then only his *tayammum* is invalidated, and likewise if the others accord this (water) to him of their free own will – according to the most correct judgement." Ibn al-Hajib said: 'If he gives if to one of them and he does not touch it (himself), and if that person (in turn) gives it to another, then the *tayammum* of the person to whom it is given is not broken if there are a great number of people, like a troop of soldiers or a great crowd of people. If, however, they are few, like three in number, and they give it to one of them, then the *tayammum* of the person to whom it is given is broken. Moreover if he says: "This water is for you" – irrespective of whether they are a few or a lot – like ten thousand, for example – then only the *tayammum* of the person to whom it is given is invalidated. This (latter) is the opinion of Sahnun. Ibn al-Hajib goes on to say: 'His saying "this is for one of you" is not the same as his saying "this is for (all of) you people" for the latter would clearly mean that each person must get his share – which would necessarily be insufficient to do *wudu'* with (in the case of each individual person). Moreover if he gives his portion (to another), then his (*tayammum*) is not invalidated.'"

The author of *at-Tawdih* said: "What may be understood from Ibn 'Ashir's saying '(the availability of water) before doing the *salat*' is that the existence of water during the *salat* or after it does not break the *tayammum*, and this is so in general. Thus if he finds it during the (*salat*), then he carries on and his *salat* is valid – unless, that is, he has forgotten the (water he has stored) in his pannier bag but remembers during the *salat*, in which case he should break off doing the *salat*. It is stated in the *Mudawwana*: 'If he remembers the water in his saddle bag and he is in (the middle of) a *salat*, then he must break off (the *salat*), but if a man catches sight of water during the *salat*, he should carry on and his *salat* is valid.' Ibn Yunus said: 'This is because the person who remembers water in his saddle bag after having begun the *salat* is considered (legally speaking) to be someone who has found water and in possession of it: that is, when his possession of this (water) and knowledge of the (existence of water) are combined during the state of *salat*, then his (*tayammum*) is invalidated – as he has become capable of obtaining water before completing the (*salat*) and was in possession of it when beginning the *salat*. (This state of his) is different from that of the person who catches sight of water during the *salat* – for the latter is not considered as someone who has found water and in possession of it, having entered upon the *salat* in accordance with what is commanded of him and having carried it out through one of the two means of purification (Allah, exalted is He, has made available to him). Thus he is obliged not to break off (his *salat*) – in accordance with the words of Allah, exalted is He: '*Do not make your actions of no worth.*'"[1]

If he finds water after finishing the *salat*, his *salat* is valid. However, there are various matters to be considered regarding the question as to whether one has to repeat the *salat* within the time – and these (matters) are dependent on the diversity of (states of) those doing *tayammum*. There are those who repeat, whether they prayed during the time they have been instructed to (do the *salat* in, according to the *shari'ah*) or whether they are actually performing the *salat* or not; and there are those who do not repeat unless they have done the *salat* before the time prescribed and they were in *tayammum*. The author has indicated some of these details with the words 'and if he finds (water) afterwards.'"

SEAL: Mayyara said[2]: "The author said nothing about wiping over *khuffs* and wiping over splints or bandages. As for wiping over splints, then one should first wipe over the wound if one is able to. If, however, a person fears harm (will afflict him) if he were to wipe then he should wipe over the splint and the like – as he would do in the case of *tayammum*; likewise, he should wipe

---

1 Muhammad: 34
2 my edition of Shinqueeti is again garbled and the original from Mayyara has been used.

over any medicinal preparation covering his nails and any (medical dressing made of) paper placed on the temples; and if he has a ligature, dressing or bandage, then he should wipe over it even if covers an area beyond the place of (immediate) pain. If, however, there are a great many dressings and it is possible to wipe beneath them, then it is not acceptable that the person wipe over them. He should also wipe over any bandage covering a place punctured for the purpose of bloodletting – and any other wound he fears (will get worse if) if he washes it." Then Ibn 'Arafa said: "He should wipe over his turban if it is difficult for him to wipe his head, and should wipe over his head during the washing for *janaba*. However, the *fatwa* of Ibn Rushd that the person who fears harm will come to himself if he washes his head should do *tayammum* has been criticised. One should wipe (just) once over splints – as in the case of *khuffs*. However if harm would occur by wiping over the wound[1] – and the splint has not been attached tightly to the wound or it lies atop a soft, fleshy part of the body or it cannot be attached properly, like in the case of a wound to the eyebrows and the wound is situated on a part of the body wiped for the *tayammum* – then he should leave it untouched and wash around it. If it is situated on a part (of the body) other (than that wiped during the *tayammum*) then it is said he should do *tayammum* so as to ensure the purification is complete and perfect (that is, by means of one kind of purification, not a combination of two). However, it has also been said that he should wash what is healthy and leave out (washing) the place of the splint as *tayammum* may only be done when there is no water. Thirdly, he should do *tayammum* if (the splint) extends over a large area. This is because the larger area takes precedence over a small area. Fourthly, he combines the *wudu'* and the *tayammum*, doing the *wudu'* first."

The author of *Ghayat al-Amani*: "If he cannot tighten or fasten the bandage except by including (part of) the healthy place, then he should wipe over it and wash the area beyond it. Included in the meaning of 'bandage' is a turban on the head which is worn as a bandage for a wound. Khalil said: 'and if he is unable to wipe over it and the place is on one of the parts wiped over for the *tayammum*, then he should leave it and do *wudu*'; if not, he – thirdly – does *tayammum* if the sick part is more than the healthy part; and – fourthly – combines the two.'"

Al-Khurshi said: "What he means by 'if he is unable to wipe it and it is an area of the body wiped over during the *tayammum*' and in particular 'if he is unable to...' is that (if unable) for whatever reason, that is, unable, either with water or with earth, then he should leave it and do *wudu'* as doing (the

---

1 here the original text of Mayyara has been used as that of *Kitab al-Mufeed* is garbled.

purification) with water even imperfectly is better than doing it with earth imperfectly. If, however, he is able to wipe it with earth and not with water, then he should transfer to *tayammum* for doing it perfectly with earth is better than imperfectly with water – and this al-Awfi said, relating from 'Abd al-Haqq. He is not instructed, however, to wash anything other than this limb and he should do it with water imperfectly."

I have found the following text: "If he is able to wipe over a wound with water – when there is something covering it – but is unable to wipe over the wound with earth, then water is preferable. In other words, what is understood from 'if unable to wipe over it' is that if able to wipe over it with earth, then he should do *tayammum* over it even if it is over something covering it."

I say: "Reflect why in this case they have given an unequivocal judgement with regard to his doing *tayammum* if he is able to wipe over with earth, how they have justified it arguing that a purification with earth which is perfect is preferable to a purification with water which is imperfect and how they have narrated four opinions regarding the case when the wound is not situated on a part of the body wiped over during the *tayammum*. The analogy (applied in these cases) is based on the fact that the two matters resemble each other, the cause or reason being the same in both – that is, that a perfect purification with earth is preferable to one done with water which is lacking or vice versa. Khalil said: 'and if it is removed for medication or falls off during the *salat* then one breaks off the *salat* and puts it back and does the wiping (again).'"

Al-Khurshi said: "There is no harm in turning (the splint or bandage) around on the limb and he does not have to have a doctor to heal the limb (for the conditions of *tayammum* to apply), even if this goes on a long time."

After a discussion, he then goes on to state that as-Sanhouri said: "He said in *al-'Utbiyya*, narrating from Sahnun from the 'Book of Purification', 'Issue: if a splint which covers a part (of the body) that is washed during the *wudu'*, falls off after a man has made *wudu'*, wiped over this splint and begun the *salat*, then he must break off what he is doing, put the splint back, wipe over it and then begin the *salat* again. The same applies if he has done *tayammum* and has wiped over the splint – thus if he has prayed one *rak'a* or two and then the splint falls off, then he must put it back, wipe over it and begin the *salat* again."

Ibn Rushd said: "What he said is correct as wiping over the splint does instead of the washing or wiping of that place during the *wudu'* and the *tayammum*: if it falls off during the *salat* then the purity is invalidated with respect to that place."

I say: "What may be understood from the above mentioned narration together with the words of Ibn Rushd is that wiping over the splint is not particular to the purification by water only but rather includes purification by earth also. This is also contained in the words of the author above: 'and if unable to wipe over it – and it is on part (of the body which is) wiped over during the *tayammum* – then he should leave it and do *wudu'*.' This is because what one understands from this is that if he is able to wipe over it, he should not leave it but rather wipe over it – that is, in every case described above, although some of what is described applies to the obligations of the *ghusl* and some to the obligations of *tayammum*. Furthermore in the above mentioned case narrated from as-Sayouri they have not stipulated whether the wound is on a part of the body wiped over during the *tayammum* or not – that is, it is not permitted for the person who is stung by a scorpion and is in such pain that he cannot take his hand out from under his clothes to do *tayammum* above his clothes. The judgement in this case is the same as the person who is 'without water' and 'without pure earth.' However, al-Burzuli's interpretation of his *tayammum* as being in accordance with (the example) narrated of al-Qabisi from *al-Ima'* and his analogy with a part of the body which is in pain during the *wudu'* disregard this narration – and so reflect about this and ponder on it and your Lord is more aware of those who are rightly guided."

An-Nafrawi, commenting on the words of the *Risala* 'then they both purify themselves with it together' said: "…but if he is able to do *tayammum*, even over something covering (the skin), then it is obligatory on him and the (obligation of) *salat* is not removed from him." Commenting on the words 'and he should pray it as much as he is able' he goes on to say: "…and he has not mentioned the purification (assuming that) one is aware that it is necessary, even in the case of someone who is incapacitated, even (if it has to be performed) over a covering and even (if it has to be performed) with the help of another. If he is incapacitated in all senses, then the (obligation to) pray is removed from him, according to the *madhhab* of Malik – both his obligation to do it now or to do it later. This is because with regard to the person who is incapacitated – irrespective of whether this incapacity is with respect to the purification with water or with earth – the same judgement is applied to him as the person 'without water or pure earth.'

The Book of Salat

THE BOOK OF SALAT

Know that the *salat* is obligatory according to the Book, the sunna and the *ijma'* and anyone who contests this (judgement) is a *kafir*. There are two opinions as to whether someone who abandons the *salat* is a *kafir* or not – the preferred being the latter, (namely, that he is not). Ibn Hajar al-Haytami said: "the argument that a person who abandons the *salat* is a *kafir* is very weak."

Issue: Ibn al-Hattab has related that al-Burzuli said: "Ibn Abi Zayd was asked as to whether a man – notorious for not doing the *salat*, who was then rebuked and was addressed in such a way as to invoke fear of Allah in him and who then prayed a day or two but subsequently returned to his habit of not doing it and when addressed yet again said 'Allah is Merciful Compassionate and I am a wrongdoer' and who then dies in this state – could lead the *salat*, whether testimony should be accepted of him, whether the *salat* should be made over him when he dies, whether he should be greeted when met, whether one should accept and use any present from him and whether one should have him separate from his wife; (he was also asked as to the judgement) when his wife (rather than him) was in this state and whether (any such judgement made with regard to her state) should also be applied to the husband. (To these questions) he replied: 'The [funeral] *salat* is made over him, any present from him may be accepted and used and he is not made to separate from his wife. As to whether any judgement regarding his wife – if it is she who is in such a state – may also be applied to him, the *salat* is made over him, presents may be accepted from him and he is not made to separate from his wife but one should not pray behind him and his testimony is not permitted. It is (however) recommended that he separate himself from his wife if such is her state.' He was also asked regarding a man who pecks at the *salat* most of the time, who does not do the bowing or prostration properly, who when rebuked for this desisted (from such negligence) but then returned to it (afterwards). He replied: 'His testimony is not permitted, nor is it permitted that he lead the *salat*, but one should greet him.'"

ISSUE: It is recommended to command children to do the *salat* in order to get them used to doing it for when they become of age. Khalil said: "Command the child to it when seven (years old) and strike him when ten" and the author of the *Risala* said: "It has been narrated that they are to be commanded to the *salat* when seven years old, that they should be beaten when they are ten (if they do not do it) and that they should sleep in separate beds." Ibn al-Hattab has related from al-Mawwaq who has transmitted that al-Lakhmi said, quoting Ibn al-Habib: "If they reach ten years, then none should undress with either of their parents or with their brothers or any other person unless each has his own outer wrap – although this is not advisable, and I am of the opinion that they should be separated completely, irrespective of whether they are males or females, and if done when they are seven, then all the better. If delayed until they are ten, then there is a licence in this, but as for punishing them, then after they are ten years old." Al- Mawwaq said that Ibn 'Arafa has narrated – on the subject of discipline – that it should be done by admonishment and spanking, but not by insults. However, if words are of no use, then he should be struck with a whip, one to three times, but only so as to cause him pain (and not to inflict any wound). During Ibn 'Arafa's discussion in *al-Ijara* on the subject of instructing children he says: "He should rebuke the children if they are negligent in learning (the Qur'an) off by heart by admonishing them and spanking them but not by abusing or insulting them – as do some teachers who say to the child 'O monkey', or 'Ifrit.'"

The author of *Ghayat al-Amani* said: "Beating them when ten years old – this is the judgement of Ibn al-Qasim, based on the most evident meaning of the hadith. It is not stipulated how (many times) – rather, enough to act as a deterrent (to further bad behaviour), although it should not cause injury. Some have said that it should be three lashes, but not on the back and done over clothes or on the soles of the naked feet. Anything additional to this which goes beyond what is normal, then there is a retribution (to be paid) in the case of someone other than the parents. There is a difference of opinion regarding the moment when children should be separated from each other (when sleeping). Ibn al-Qasim said 'when they reach seven years old' while Ibn Wahb said 'when they reach ten' and this (latter) is based on the most evident meaning of the hadith. Likewise, a child is separated from his father and mother when he reaches ten, irrespective of whether male or female. What is meant in this (discussion) is (that children be separated by) a sheet, even if they are under one bed-cover."

BENEFITS: 1. in *al-Jami' as-Saghir* it is stated: "Whoever abandons the *salat* will meet Allah and He will be angry." The author has commented on this saying, "that is, (abandoning) the five (daily *salats*) deliberately, while aware that he has no excuse, that is, that, he is deserving of the punishment of '*those with anger on them*'[1] and that if He wills, He will accept him and act leniently with him, and if He wills, He will torment him and withhold His mercy from him." At-Tayyibi said: "If Allah is described by the term 'anger', then this is to be understood in the utmost degree, that is revenge. Thus, abandoning a *fard* obligation and neglecting to do it on time without excuse are major wrong actions. If someone persists in abandoning it and dies in this state, then he will be (raised up) amongst the 'wretched losers' unless he obtains the forgiveness of Allah." Al-Qasriyy said: "Those who abandon the *salat* will be raised in the company of Fir'awn and Haman, as has been narrated in a hadith."

2. al-Khurshi said: "The hadith of Abu Hurayra 'Whoever treats the *salat* with contempt, then Allah will punish him with fifteen kinds (of punishment), six (of which will be) in this world, namely, removal of *baraka* from his provision, removal of it from his life, removal of the sign of the *Salihun* from his face, his not being included (as one of those accepted) in the *du'a'* of the *Salihun*, his not being rewarded for any good action he undertakes and his own *du'a* not being raised to the heaven ..." — as at-Tatari has narrated — is a hadith rejected (as untrustworthy), while the author of *al-Mizan* said that it is invalid, and the text is clearly invalid."

---

1   Al-Fatiha: 7

Obligations of the Salat

فَرَائِضُ الصَّلاَةِ سِتَّ عَشَرَةَ

شُرُوطُهَا أَرْبَعَةٌ مُفْتَقَرَةٌ

99   There are sixteen *fard* obligations of the *salat* and carrying them out is conditional upon four things which must be complied with

تَكْبِيرَةُ الْإِحْرَامُ وَالْقِيَامْ

لَهَا وَنِيَّةٌ بِهَا تُرَامْ

100 the saying of *Allahu akbar* (which marks entry into the *salat* and) its sanctity (by which all other actions but the *salat* are excluded), the standing for the (*salat*) and the intention

MAYYARA said: "The first of these is the *takbirat al-ihram*, that is, the saying of *Allahu akbar* by which one enters into the inviolable sanctity of the *salat*. The mention of the *Allahu akbar* together with (the term) '*ihram*' – sanctity – indicates that the one is distinct from the other as it would not be permitted, grammatically speaking, to annex one word to another of the same meaning. Indeed this is so as the saying of the *Allahu akbar* is distinct from what is intended by 'the sanctity of the *salat*.' This *takbirat al-ihram* is obligatory on the imam, on the person performing alone and the person praying behind the imam. It cannot be said in any other form than *Allahu akbar*. It is not permitted (for example) to say *akbar*, prolonging the 'a' sound of the *ba'* for it would result in a change of meaning – and this has been clearly stated in an authoritative text." The author of *ad-Dhakheera* said: "As for (the practice of) the common people who say *Allahu wakbar*, there is room for licence in this as it is permitted to change the *hamza* to a *waw* if followed by a *dhamma*. As for the person who is unable to speak at all, the intention is enough, but as for the person who is incapable because of his ignorance of the

(Arabic) language, then al-Abhouri said 'the intention is enough' while Abu'l-Faraj said 'he enters the *salat* with that which he entered Islam with' and one of the Shaykhs of 'Abd al-Wahhab said 'he enters the *salat* with the equivalent – in his language – to the saying of *Allahu akbar* although there is agreement that he should not substitute the recitation (of the Qur'an following the *Allahu akbar*) with his language as the miracle (of the Book) is in the Arabic.'"

'Ali ibn 'Abd as-Sadiq has related: "''Ayn-jeem said: 'There must be a natural elongation when pronouncing the majestic name: if it is left out, then his *salat* is unacceptable just as the person remembering (Allah) would not in fact be remembering Him if he were to leave out (His name).' Likewise, if he leaves out one letter it is also unacceptable, although if he substitutes the *hamza* for a *waw* and he says it as the common people say, or he combines the *hamza* and the *waw* and he says *wa'akbar*, it is not invalidated."

Ibn al-Hattab has related that Ibn al-Muneer said: "By the saying of the *Allahu akbar*, he should intend the *'ihram'* (that is, entering into the sanctity of the *salat*) and one should beware of making an elongation between the (initial) *hamza* – 'A' – (of the word *Allahu*) and the *lam* – 'l' – such that a question might be construed from this (form of pronunciation)¹ or that he lengthen between the *ba'* – 'b' – and the *ra'* -'r' -changing the meaning in doing so, or that one prolong the *dhamma* – 'u' – vowel of the *ha'* – 'h' -such that a (long) *waw* – 'uw' – results or that one lingers on the *ra'* rolling it emphatically. All of these count as mispronunciations and one should beware lest the *salat* be invalidated (through them)."

Al-Munawi said: "Leaving out the *alif* of the majestic name is a mispronunciation and invalidates the *salat* – on account of the lack of meaning arising from the omission of part of what should be pronounced."

I say: "Ibn al-Hattab said, with respect to the *adhan*, that omitting the *alif* from the word 'Allah' is prohibited and that increasing (still further) the natural prolongation of it is disliked."

Notice: al-Fakihani said: "The meaning of *Allahu akbar* is 'Allah is greater' (that is, too far removed from any other form or concept such) that one could attribute partners with Him or that He should be mentioned without praise and glorification. It has also been said that its meaning is 'Allah is greater than all things', and it is said its meaning is 'Allah is the Great.'"

As for (Ibn 'Ashir's) saying 'standing', Ibn Yunus said: "Among the *fard* obligations of the *salat* about which there is agreement is the *takbirat al-ihram* and the 'standing for this (*takbirat al-ihram*)' that is, (it is obligatory) for the

---

1 An *alif* and *hamza* at the beginning of the sentence makes it interrogative

person who prays alone, the imam, as well as the person behind the imam." In this regard Malik said: "If the person behind the imam says *Allahu akbar* for the bowing – but with the intention (that he is saying it) for the *takbirat al-ihram* – then it is acceptable." Ibn Yunus said: "This is correct as long as he says *Allahu akbar* (just before going) into the bowing while he is still standing, although it has also been said that it is acceptable even if he says *Allahu akbar* when he is already in the bowing (position)." Ibn Bashir said: "…and this latter is the *madhhab* of the *Mudawwana*; and the reasoning behind this is that the standing is necessary for the recitation (of the *Allahu akbar*) but the person behind the imam does not have to make the recitation."

BRANCH: Mayyara said: "The imam should wait until the lines are straight, for if he says *Allahu akbar* too and the persons behind him are still occupied with straightening the lines, then they will miss some of the *salat*, and whoever misses the Fatiha has missed something of great benefit; and if the lines are not straightened, then those praying have missed out on the excellence (and reward) for straightening the lines."

Commenting on Ibn 'Ashir's words 'and the intention…' al-Mawwaq has related that Ibn Rushd said: "Among the *fard* obligations of the *salat* about which there is agreement is the intention. Its complete form is that the one making the intention should be conscious of iman – a complete trust – in his heart and that he accompany this with a belief that the obligation of the particular *salat* he is about to perform is an act of *qurba* (bringing him closer to Allah). This implies four intentions: belief that it is an act of *qurba*, belief that it is an obligation, belief that his aim is to perform (the *salat*) and his specifying one particular *salat*. Thus if he pronounces the *takbirat al-ihram* and his intention is made in this manner, then he has entered into the *ihram* – the sanctity – of the *salat* in the most perfect state. However, the (intention) is also acceptable if it just consists of specifying one *salat* in particular for this latter contains within it the obligation, the *qurba* and (aim to) perform it. Likewise, if he lacks this consciousness of iman in his heart at the moment he says the *Allahu akbar*, it does not render this *takbirat al-ihram* invalid – given that (at some time) previous (to this moment) he must have been conscious of this iman (in Allah by his being a Muslim) and because he is described in terms of this quality (of iman) both in his remembering or forgetting it. People have invented a lot of things with respect to the intention – so much so that one man of sixty years of age came asking if he had to repeat the fast of Ramadan (believing) he had fasted it without the (correct) intention after someone said to him: 'you have omitted the "aim" of the intention.' But reflect on (this matter and how – if this were so – one intention would need another intention and how in turn the intention of the intention would also need an intention. What is, however, imaginable is that a person might commence his fasting without a (correct) intention if he is unaware of the (precise day when) the month (of Ramadan commences)."

Mayyara said: "The third obligation is the intention which is made for the purpose of the *salat*, that is, one makes the (*salat*) one's aim, and there is no doubt that it is acceptable if accompanied simultaneously by the *takbir*. If, however, it is delayed until after the *takbirat al-ihram*, then there is agreement that it is unacceptable. If it precedes it by a long time, then there is agreement that it is not acceptable; and if by a little, then there are two opinions: the most evident (judgement) in the *madhhab* is that it is acceptable because none of the (*fuqaha*) has stipulated (so rigorous) a simultaneity that might lead to persistent doubt – which would be reprehensible both in the *shari'ah* and in the natural order of things. Rather what is meant by the stipulation that the (intention) should 'accompany it simultaneously' – for those who hold to this (judgement) – is that it is not permitted to *separate* the intention from the *takbir* – and al-Mazari has indicated this."

Abu 'Umar said: "The final teaching (regarding this matter) within the *madhhab* of Malik is that there is no harm in the intention being removed (from one's mind for a time) after one has made it one's purpose to go to the mosque for a specific *salat*. However, it is not enough that one make the intention for a *salat* in general but rather the person must specify the *Dhuhr* (*salat*) or *'Asr* (*salat*), for example, and it is preferable that this specifying (of one's intent) be done in the heart, not by saying anything (out loud). Nevertheless if one does say something and it is different to one's intention, then what counts is one's intention rather than anything (else) pronounced without intention."

Al-Khurshi said, commenting on the words of Khalil '... and it is invalidated if it precedes it by a long time; if not (preceded by a long time), then there is a difference of opinion...': "(Here Khalil is) drawing attention to a minor separation (of the intention from the *takbir*), that is, when he makes an intention at home and then becomes unaware of it when he says the *Allahu akbar* for (this intention) in the mosque. This is contained in the words of Ibn 'Abd al-Barr: 'The final teaching (regarding this matter) within the *madhhab* of Malik is that there is no harm in the intention being removed (from one's mind for a time) after one has made it one's purpose to go to the mosque- as long as he does not change this (intention) for something else.' The distance in question here is the distance from the furthest house to the mosque in Madina – as the imam is talking about his town."

ISSUE: al-Khurshi said also: "There is agreement that the intention does not last for an indefinite period."

Al-Hattab also has a similar statement: "There is agreement that an intention should not be made (for an indefinite) period (ahead)" – and this statement of al-Hattab is more forceful.

ISSUE: al-Mawwaq has related that al-Lakhmi said: "Ashhab has permitted that someone enter into (a *salat*) with the imam when ignorant of whether the latter is (performing the *salat* of) Friday or Thursday or that he intends what the imam has intended when ignorant as to whether the latter is shortening the *salat* or performing it in full." Ibn Rushd both permits it and affirms that it is acceptable saying: "There is agreement on this." Al-Mazari and Ibn Bashir have said: "There are two opinions as to whether an intention to do a (specific) number of *rak'ats* is necessary. Ibn Yunus has a different point of view arguing that the (*salat*) is acceptable even if, when he enters the *salat*, he does not know whether the imam is praying Jumu'a or *Dhuhr* as long as he intends to perform the *salat* behind the imam and what he intends and what the imam actually does concur with each other. Ibn Rushd said: "…and the proof of this is that 'Ali ibn Abi Talib and Abu Musa al-Ash'ari, may Allah be pleased with both of them, went to the Messenger of Allah, may the peace and blessings of Allah be upon him, on the occasion of the final pilgrimage while both in a state of *ihram*. The Messenger of Allah may the peace and blessings of Allah be upon him, asked them: 'How did you enter into the state of *ihram*?' They both answered: '*Labbayk*' – at your service – 'by saying the *labbayk* of the Prophet, may the peace and blessings be upon him' and he approved of what they had done."

ISSUE: the author of *al-Mi'yar* said: "Sayyidi Qasim al-Uqbani was asked: 'Some of your students have narrated from you that "Whoever forgets the *Subh salat*, or sleeps through it, then remembers it or wakes up and does not know if the time has passed or not should begin the *salat* without an intention." He replied: "I no longer remember what has been narrated from me. However, the reason for this (judgement) is clear: what is meant by *al-ada* – the proper performance of the *salat* – is that the person performing the act of worship knows that he is doing it in the time prescribed for it in the first instance; and by *al-qada* – making it up afterwards – is that he is aware that he is doing it in the time prescribed for it in the second instance. However, if he has no knowledge of either matter – as he is in doubt as to whether the time for carrying it out has passed or not – then he should do it, despite his doubt, in the manner mentioned above. This is because deciding between (these two possibilities) is preferable than delaying the performance (of the *salat*) until one becomes certain that it is *qada* time – for doing it when uncertain as to whether the time has passed or not is (counted) a (praiseworthy) action 'undertaken with haste with the intent of obtaining benefit', (especially as it) includes the possibility that it is in fact being performed in its proper time. Delaying it would be (indicative of) 'a lack of haste in seeking to obtain benefit' together with the certainty that one would be making it up after its time. Moreover the validity of the performance (of the *salat*) is not dependent upon the intention being made for *ada* or *qada*."

Ibn al-Hattab said, commenting on the words of Khalil 'as if he had not thought it': "If a person sets about doing a *nafila salat* when in fact a *fard salat* is incumbent on him, then his *salat* is still valid and his *salat* with the intention of *nafila* is acceptable." Ibn al-Jilab and others have clearly stated that this is so, and Allah knows best. Ibn Rushd has mentioned two opinions. An example of this is that if he intends to pray *Dhuhr* but then forgets and thinks he is in *'Asr* and prays two *rak'ats*, and Allah knows best."

NOTICE: Ibn Farhun said in *Sharh Ibn al-Hajib*: "As for the person who does this deliberately, intending by doing so to annul and reject an obligatory *salat*, then it is invalidated. If, however, he does not intend to reject it, then it is not incompatible as *nafila salats* are desired by the Legislator. While there exists an absolute requirement in the case of an obligation, any (further) intention (made for a) *nafila* is (considered) an affirmation of this not a particularity of it."

فَاتِحَةٌ مَعَ الْقِيَامِ وَالرُّكُوعُ

وَالرَّفْعُ مِنْهُ وَالسُّجُودُ بِالْخُضُوعُ

101 (also obligatory is) the Fatiha done while standing and the bowing, the return to standing position after it, and prostration with submissiveness

Mayyara said: "Fourthly, also among the *fard* obligations is the reciting of the Fatiha. It is necessary for the imam and the person praying alone, but not the person praying behind the imam, although Ibn al-'Arabi considered it necessary when not done aloud. This is the judgement in the case of the *fard salat* but as for its recitation for the *nafila*, it is a sunna according to the well known opinion."

'Ali ibn 'Abd as-Sadiq has related that Zarruq said in *Sharh al-Qurtubiya*: "Its recitation is not acceptable when done according to one of the rare or irregular recitations (*shadhdh*), and the reciter is under an obligation to repeat it however great the delay (if this occurs)."

If you were to say 'What is the definition of the "irregular" in your opinion?' then the reply would be that of al-Wanshareesi who has related in *Ikhtisar Nawazil al-Burzuli* that Ibn 'Arafa said: "What is meant by an 'irregular' reading is that it is not one of the seven (accepted) readings at all. This (term) is also applied to any (way of recitation) which is not employed by those who recite in accordance with the well known methods of the reciters who pronounce the 'a' like 'e' or 'i' (*imala*) or the use the accepted vowelling and the like. The former (way) is that which is used, according to the most evident judgement, by the people of *usul* and the *fuqaha* while the latter, according to the most evident judgement, is what is used by the reciters. Moreover, according the former, it does not exist in the *mus-haf* of 'Uthman while according to the latter, it does. Furthermore, the *salat* according to the former is not permitted. Al-Mazari has narrated in *Sharh al-Burhan* that this is (a matter which is) agreed upon." The author of *Sharh at-Talqeen* said that "al-Lakhmi has taught that one does not have to repeat the *salat* if one prays with such (a recitation), and this has also been narrated by our Shaykh Ain-Seen from Abu 'Umar ibn 'Abd al-Barr in a narration beginning with Malik. As for using such recitation on an occasion other than the *salat*, then there are two ways (of viewing the matter) according to the Shaykhs." Makki and al-Qadi Isma'il have said, narrating from al-imam al-Abyani in his commentary on *al-Burhan*: "Most are of the opinion that it is prohibited." 'Iyad said: "The *fuqaha* of Badhdad are agreed that anyone who uses such a recitation should be required to do *tawba*. "As for the second way (of viewing the matter), it is that of Abu 'Umar ibn 'Abd al-Barr in *at-Tamheed* in which he states that there are two opinions: Ibn Wahb has narrated that al-Abyani has permitted it in his commentary on *al-Burhan*, although the well known view in the *madhhab* is that it is not permitted. On the basis of this latter judgement, then, it would be disliked if one were to start off by reciting with it in the *salat*. If, however, someone nevertheless does use (this mode of recitation), then the *salat* is acceptable. Al-Qadi Isma'il, al-Abyani and others have also said this. Moreover it is Qur'an and it does not follow that it cannot be called Qur'an just because the imam does not permit it in the *salat*, and Allah knows best."

There is no difference of opinion that it is permitted to recite it outside of the *salat* although there is a difference of opinion as to the form it takes in the *mus-haf* of 'Uthman. Al-Burzuli said: "The people of Granada asked our Shaykh, the imam, about it after the Ustadh Abu Sa'd Ibn Lubb had said that the exceptional and rare readings were not (part of the) Qur'an and a reciter read the following words of Allah, exalted is He, in the surah *al-An'am – The Livestock* – during the *Tarawih* (*salat* of Ramadan): *'date clusters hanging down, and gardens of grapes'*,[1] reciting the (nominative) vowel (sign) 'un' in the word *jannatun* (instead of *jannatin*). When the above mentioned Ustadh responded (by correcting him during the *salat*) the reciter was unable to hear him because of his deafness. Despite repeating it several times, he was still unable to hear it and so (the Ustadh and others) went (after the *salat*) into the *mihrab* with him and were then able to make themselves heard. Following this (incident) most of the students started discussing the matter, (some of them) supporting their argument with evidence that Mujahid and others had narrated it as *jannatun* from Asim, that al-'Amash had recited it in this way as well as others of the Imams. (Our Shaykh,) Ibn 'Arafa replied by saying: "The correct judgement is that if only he had desisted from (correcting the imam) and not exposing himself to the like of such (a discussion regarding) the *salat* given the existence of conflicting judgements (on the matter) – and especially as the (*Tarawih*) is a *nafila salat*."

USEFUL POINT: Ibn al-Hattab said, commenting on the section 'An *'alim*'s examination of the states of his people' in *al-Madkhal*: "One of the most important things and one which should be most emphasised is an examination of the recitation (of the people). It is of three kinds: obligatory, sunna and that which has aspects of excellence. As for what is obligatory, it is an obligation upon every person who performs the *salat* to recite the Umm al-Qur'an (that is, the Fatiha) with all its letters, vowelling and *tashdid* markings (that is, a doubling of a letter) – for whoever does not master these, then his *salat* is invalidated, unless he is behind the imam. As for the sunna, it is to read a surah with it. As for the aspect of excellence, it is the recitation on other occasions, I mean other than when performing (a *salat*) which is *fard*. One should teach this (knowledge of recitation) to one's children, slave boys and girls, unless they are non-Arab and are unable to pronounce the (reading) properly – in which case there is no objection (to his not teaching them)."

I SAY: "Compare what Ibn al-Hattab has narrated from *al-Madkhal* regarding the invalidation of the *salat* in the case of someone who has not mastered its letters and vowels with what follows, namely that the preferred judgement in the case of the *salat* performed behind someone who mispronounces is correct – and thus the *salat* of the former, in comparison, should be all the more acceptable."

As for his saying 'together with the standing', Mayyara has related that Ibn

---

1 al-An'am – Liverstock: 100

Yunus said: "The standing – in the case of the imam and the person praying alone for the duration of the Umm al-Qur'an – is one of the *fard* obligations about which there is agreement." Al-Mawwaq has related that Ibn 'Arafa said: "The standing for the *takbirat al-ihram* and the recitation of what is obligatory is obligatory." One of the Shaykhs said: "…and the *witr* and the two *rak'ats* of *fajr* also[are *fard*] – because of their saying 'these two (*salats*) are not prayed in the Hijr.¹'"

BRANCH: The author of the *Risala* said: "If the sick person is unable to pray standing he should pray sitting cross-legged, and if not, then as he is able." An-Nafrawi said in his *Sharh*: "Know that the person who prays the *fard salat* sitting is the one who cannot stand in general or who fears illness from standing or fears it will be aggravated – as in (the conditions of) *tayammum*. As for the person who experiences extremely difficulty in (performing) it but is not actually sick, then the most evident judgement is that the matter rests on whether he is healthy, in which case it is not valid that he sit; or sick, in which case he may sit in whatever fashion is possible for him – as is specified in the explanation of 'Ali ibn 'Abd as-Sadiq, in opposition to his student Ibn 'Arafa for the most evident interpretation of his words is that the *salat* (with respect to the above mentioned case) is valid when done sitting."

ISSUE: an-Nafrawi said: "The person doing the *salat* lying down should indicate (the movements)." However, he does not tell us if he should indicate with all his limbs or just some of them. What may be understood from one of the Shaykhs is that he should indicate with his head, and if unable to indicate with his head, then with his eye and his heart, and if he cannot do this, then (merely) with his finger.

'Ayn Jeem said: "The most evident judgement is that the order of the (degrees of) indication mentioned above is obligatory."

As for Ibn 'Ashir's words 'and the bowing', Mayyara said: "The minimum (movement required) is that he incline such that he places his palms close to his knees. It is recommended that his knees be straight, that he place his palms over them, that he ensure there is a space between his elbows (and his thighs), that he not hang his head to the ground and that his back be straight."

As for his words 'and straightening up from it', Mayyara said: "…and if he fails to do this, then it is necessary to repeat the (*salat*), according to the well-known judgement. In Ibn 'Arafa's words: 'What is required is that he straighten up after the bowing and that he stay straight for a moment (*al-i'tidal*)

---

1 The Hijr is the semi-circular walled area outside the Ka'ba at one end of it. *Fard salats* may not be prayed there as it is considered to be inside the Ka'ba.

after raising (his body from the bowing).' Ibn al-Qasim has transmitted that 'whoever goes down into *sajda* after the bowing should not count this (as a valid movement), and I prefer that he should carry on (the *salat* until the end) and then repeat the *salat*.'"

Ibn al-Mawaz: "If he does it out of negligence and straightens up (while still in a) bent (position inclined) towards bowing, that is, he does not return to stand straight, then he should repeat his *salat* (and this is acceptable) but if he does straighten up in a hunched over fashion – meaning that later he raises himself – he should prostrate after the *salam* and his *salat* is valid. If he returns to a straight position but with his back hunched then he should make a prostration (of negligence) after saying the *salam* and his *salat* is acceptable. If he is following the imam (who makes this mistake) then the imam bears the responsibility for the *sajda* of negligence." Ibn al-Qasim said: "…and if he raises his head after his bowing but does not straighten up for a moment before making the *sajda*, then his *salat* is acceptable and he should seek forgiveness of Allah." Ibn Yunus has related that Ashhab said: "His *salat* is not acceptable." Abu Ishaq said: "…and this is deemed correct by al-Qubbab and is indeed correct." The author of *at-Talqeen* said: "Among the *fard* obligations of the *salat* is straightening up after the bowing although there is a difference of opinion as to whether one must pause a moment while standing (*al-i'tidal*). However, the preferred judgement is that it is obligatory to do whatever approximates to (the term) 'standing', and likewise with regard to the term 'sitting' between the two prostrations.

His saying 'prostration with submissiveness' means on both the forehead and nose but does not specify the duration. However, if he makes *sajda* (only) on his forehead but not his nose, then his *salat* is valid although he should repeat the (*salat*) if still within the *ikhtiyari* time. If he makes *sajda* on his nose but not his forehead, then his *salat* is rendered invalid – and this has been stated by 'Ali ibn 'Abd as-Sadiq. What is connected to his saying 'with submissiveness' will be discussed at the point where the author says 'the heart (is distracted by) thinking about what is incompatible with submissiveness.'

ISSUE: Ibn al-Hattab said: "The author of *al-Bayan* said: 'There is no harm in doing the *salat* on a bed. In my opinion, this refers to a mattress placed on the floor for a sick person.' Al-Qadi said: '…and what he said is correct. There is no difference of opinion in this (matter) for (performing) the *salat* on a bed is like (performing) the *salat* in a room or on a flat roof or terrace, and I seek help of Allah.' Ibn 'Arafa said that Ibn al-Qasim has transmitted that 'There is no harm in doing it on top of a bed.' Ibn Rushd said: 'This is because it is like a room.'"

ISSUE: Ibn al-Hattab has also related that Ibn Farhun said: "It is not permitted to do the *salat* on a mattress which is raised above the floor. If it is difficult for the sick person to get down from his mattress to do the *salat* on the floor and he is unable to do the prostration on account of the pain of his illness, then he should pray on his mattress. If it is not pure, then he should throw a thick, clean sheet over it. If the sick person is someone who is able to do the prostration on the floor, then he should get down onto the floor and pray doing the *sajda* on the floor."

BRANCH: He should get down onto the ground from a bed made of wood but not from one made out of strips of woven fabric and the like. Ibn Hattab also says something similar.

An-Nafrawi gives a further explanation saying: "Just as the sick person is allowed to do the *salat* riding on a beast, so he is also allowed to do the *salat* on a bed which is made of strips (of cloth) and the like – that is, not made of wood or stone – as long as he is unable to get down on to the ground. If he is able to get down, then his *salat* is not valid on this (bed). (Likewise) if he obliged (to perform the *salat*) by indication (because he is sick) and he indicates towards the bed (then this is not valid. However, if he indicates towards the earth, then his *salat* is valid just as it would be valid on a beast if he were in this state. 'Alama Bahram said – regarding beds made of wood: 'There is no difference of opinion that it is permissible to do the *salat* on them as they are (considered) analogous to roofs or terraces.'"

وَالرَّفْعُ مِنْهُ وَالسَّلَامُ وَالْجُلُوسُ

لَهُ وَتَرْتِيبُ أَدَاءٍ فِي الْأُسُوسِ

102 and (also obligatory is) raising (one's hands from the ground), saying the *salam*, sitting for this (*salam*), and the order of the *fard* elements when performing these obligations

Al-Mawwaq said: "This second section concerns the pillars of the *salat* between the two prostrations. Sahnun said: 'One of our companions said: "Whoever does not raise his hands from (the ground after) the prostration, then his (*salat*) is not acceptable, although another of our companions has deemed this of lesser importance."

As for his words 'saying the *salam*', (note what) Khalil said: "...(the pronouncing of the final) *salam* must be with the *alif* and *lam* (i.e. *as-salamu*...

rather than just *salamu*...), and there is a difference of opinion as to whether one should make a (specific) intention in order to conclude the *salat*." Ibn Rushd said: "Just as one cannot enter the *salat* without the *Allahu akbar* – by which one both makes the intention to enter the *salat* and to commit oneself to a state of *ihram* (sanctity) (in which all else is forbidden the worshipper for the duration of the *salat*) so one cannot leave the *salat* except by saying the *as-salam* – by which one both makes the intention to leave the *salat* and to enter the state of *tahallul* (by which things, other than the *salat*, become permitted again). If, however, he does say the *salam* at the end of the *salat* without making this intention, then it is accepted of him – because of the intention he has made previously and because he does not have to renew the state of *ihram* for every one of the pillars of the *salat*. If he forgets the first saying of the *salam* then the second does not (make the *salat*) acceptable." Ibn al-Majishun said: "It is necessary that he renew the intention in order to leave the *salat*." Ibn al-'Arabi said: "What is well known in the *madhhab* is contrary to this."

Mayyara said: "If he pronounces the *salam* in such a manner as to sound half way between *as-salam* and *salam* then according to Ibn 'Arafa 'This is not reckoned as serious (a mistake) as mispronouncing something in the Fatiha.'"

His saying 'and the sitting for this (saying of *as-salam 'alaikum*)' means sitting for as long as it takes to say it without rushing. Any further (sitting) in addition to this is a sunna.

Mayyara, commenting on his words 'the order when performing the obligations' said: "What is meant is that he should not perform any one (of the obligations) before its proper place and that if he does, then his *salat* is not accepted – this is stated by al-Qubbab, according to the consensus."

وَالْاِعْتِدَالُ مُطْمَئِنّاً بِالْتِزَامْ

تَابَعُ مَأْمُومٍ بِإِحْرَامٍ سَلَامْ

103 standing straight for a moment while relaxing (the limbs) at the same time; those behind the imam must perform the *takbirat al-ihram* and the *salam* after him

Mayyara said: "The thirteenth (obligation) is standing straight, the fourteenth is being relaxed or at ease. However, as there is no automatic connection between the two – as one can stand straight without relaxing the limbs and one can relax the limbs without standing straight – Ibn 'Ashir, fearing that one might imagine that these two things may be performed separately, has added 'and at the same time' in order to remove any doubt, and Allah knows best."

Al-Mawwaq has related that al-Jilab said: "A moment of relaxation or ease is obligatory in all the pillars of the *salat*, that is, in the standing, bowing, raising the head from it, in the prostration and between the prostrations. What this means is that the bowing, the standing straight after the bowing or the prostration, or the sitting between the prostrations are not acceptable unless one is relaxed and at ease for a moment during (each movements of) bowing, standing, prostrating or sitting. This is the correct opinion which has been transmitted in the traditions, and this is the view of the majority of the *'ulama* and the people of discernment."

The author of *al-Istidhkar* has added: "There is a straightening up (*i'tidal*) when lifting up the hands (from the ground) after the prostration. This straightening up is an obligation – on account of the Prophet's command, on whom be blessings, to do it and his saying 'Allah does not look upon the person who does not straighten his back in his bowing and prostration.' There is no difference of opinion as to what constitutes 'straightening up' although there is with regard to the moment of relaxation of the limbs (*at-tuma'neena*) after this straightening up (*al-i'tidal*)."

Ibn Shas said: "If we say that 'straightening up' is obligatory, then being at ease and relaxed for a moment is also obligatory – although it has also been said that it is not obligatory." Prior to this (Ibn Shas) has also related that Abu Muhammad said: "What is obligatory is to stand as straight as possible." Ibn al-Qasim has narrated that: "Whoever raises his head from the bowing and the prostration and does not stand straight or sit straight before doing the prostration, then he should seek forgiveness of Allah – but does not have to repeat the (*salat*)."

Issue: the author of *al-Mi'yar* has related that Ibn Farhun said: "Our *'ulama* have recorded that Malik said 'If a group prays on a ship with their heads bent beneath its roof, then their *salat* is acceptable.' Shaykh Abu'l-Hasan as-Saghir said: '… when in a tent or awning the (judgement) is like that regarding a ship, and the (judgement) is less strict with regard to the *nawafil salats*.' I asked the *faqih* Abu 'Abdallah Ibn 'Arafa (on this matter) and he replied: 'The (judgement regarding) the *nawafil salats* is less strict in these circumstances' but when I asked him about the obligatory *salats*, he did not say anything about them."

Ibn al-Hattab said with regard to the words of Khalil '(that one must) straighten up is the most correct (view), although most (ulama) reject this (view)': "What most people hold to is the most evident position of the *madhhab* of the *Mudawwana*." He has also said in the chapter '*Salat* on a Ship': "Their praying on board separately is more preferable to me than their praying in a group with their heads bent beneath its roof." Ibn Basheer said: "This (judgement) must be understood (as applicable) when they have to bend (their bodies) a lot. If, however, the (bending) is only slight, then it is preferable to do it in a group, and the tent is (considered to fall under) the same judgement as the ship."

USEFUL POINT: Sayyidi Zarruq said in *Sharh ar-Risala*: "...(as to whether) it is obligatory to instruct the ignorant person before he asks (about a matter) or whether it is only obligatory to call his attention to something – such that if he asks, he should be informed, but if he does not, then he should be left alone – at-Tartushi prefers the former (response). However, the latter (response) is the one (usually) relied on and this is because the Messenger, may the peace and blessings of Allah be upon him, said to a Arab Bedouin 'You have not prayed' but did not (offer to) teach him (how it should be done) until, that is, the (Bedouin) said: 'I do not know other than this – so teach me O Messenger of Allah!'"

I SAY: "What he is referring to by the 'Arab Bedouin' was an Arab Bedouin who had not performed his *salat* properly: the Messenger, may the peace and blessings of Allah be upon him, said to him 'Go back and pray for you have not prayed' – or whatever the exact words of the Prophet, may the peace and blessings of Allah be upon him, were."

Commenting on his words 'those behind the imam must perform the *takbirat al-ihram* and the *salam* after him', Mayyara said: "The fifteenth (obligation): If he performs them simultaneously with the imam, then they are both invalidate (the *salat*). (That the *salat* is invalidated) is all the more true, therefore, if he precedes the imam. He should repeat the *takbir* if he precedes him or does it simultaneously and the *salat* is rendered invalid if he says the as-*as-salamu 'alaykum* before him or simultaneously." Khalil said: "He must follow after the imam in saying the *takbirat al-ihram* and the as-*as-salamu 'alaykum*. Doing them simultaneously, even if the person behind the imam only has doubts (as to whether these two were simultaneous) invalidates (the *salat*), but not if it is *immediately* after; likewise (the *salat* is not invalidated in the case of) other than the two (above mentioned, namely the *takbir* and *salam*, like the bowing, prostration, etc) as long as he does not precede the imam (deliberately – that is he may begin before him in these movements but then must follow him, finishing them after him; if however he completes these acts before him the *salat* is nullified but if he does not (precede the imam but rather does it simultaneously), this is only disliked." Al-Mawwaq said, commenting on his word 'simultaneously' that Sahnun had heard from Ibn al-Qasim: "Whoever says the *takbirat al-ihram* with the imam, then his (*salat*) is acceptable, but doing it after him is more correct." Ibn Rushd said: "…and it has also been said that it is not acceptable, and this is the opinion of Malik, Asbagh and Ibn Habib, and this is the most evident meaning of the hadith 'If he says *Allahu akbar*, then (all of) you say *Allahu akbar*' – as the (word) 'then' necessitates (one understand) succession. This difference of opinion is when he begins the *takbirat al-ihram* with him and finishes it with him or after him. The legal judgement regarding the *as-salamu* is the same as that of the *takbir*." Sahnun said: "If one man prays behind another in *salat* and he has doubts as to the *tashahhud* of the imam – and says the *salam* with him simultaneously – then there is a difference of opinion as to whether it is accepted because of the simularity (between their two states), but if he says it after him then the *salat* of the second only is acceptable."

Mayyara has also said, commenting on his words 'but not if it is *immediately* after' that Ibn Shas said: "Among the conditions of praying behind the imam is that one follows immediately after him, but not simultaneously or before him." Ibn Rushd said: "…and if he begins after he has begun the *takbir*, then it is correct." Mayyara said: "If he completes it with him or before him it is invalidated and if he completes it after him then there is a consensus (that it is acceptable)." Ibn 'Arafa said: "Following the imam in other than the *takbirat al-ihram* and the *salam* is better."

Mayyara has commented on his words 'but if he does not (precede the imam but rather does it simultaneously), then this is (only) disliked' by saying that al-Baji said: "It is disliked that the person praying behind the imam pronounce the words which form part of the *salat* – that is those words other than the *takbirat al-ihram* and the *salam* – before the imam, although it does not render the *salat* invalid. As for the actions of the *salat*, however, if he does them after the imam and *keeps up with* him, then this is the sunna of the *salat*; if he begins an action after the imam has finished it, then this is prohibited if he does it deliberately; if he does it with him – going down into the bowing when he goes down and straightening up when he straightens up, then this is prohibited in general."

In Ibn al-Hattab said: "(Take note of) a beneficial point transmitted in the hadith: 'May the person who raises his head before the imam fear lest Allah turn his head into that of a donkey.' Ad-Dameeri said in the commentary on the *Sunan* of Ibn Majah that Shaykh Taqi du-Deen said: 'This transformation either refers to a physical transformation, or it must be interpreted as having a metaphorical meaning – in the sense that stupidity is attributed to a donkey and this quality may also be applied to a person who is ignorant of what is incumbent on him, with respect to (performance of) the excellent (aspects) of the *salat* and following the imam. It is perhaps preferable to interpret this metaphorically as a transformation in the outward does not in fact happen despite the fact that persons praying behind the imam often raise their heads before him, – this is what ad-Dameeri has stated. It has also been said that what is meant is that the transformation of his form will take place on the Day of Raising Up. However, it is not impossible that this could actually take place in this world. Shaykh Shihab ad-Deen Fadlallah has transmitted in *Sharh al-Masabih* that one of the 'ulama did this to prove (the truth of it) and Allah transformed his head into that of a donkey. As a result he would sit behind a curtain so as not to be visible to people, and he would give *fatwas* from behind a screen."

I SAY: "This is the sunna of Allah with respect to those who make a mockery of the pure law. Commenting on the hadith 'If one of you wakes up from his sleep, then he should not put his hand into the vessel (of water) until he has washed it three times for surely none of you knows where his hand has been during the night' – or whatever the exact text of the hadith is, al-Munawi said, transmitting in his own words what Muhammad ibn Fadl at-Tamimi had mentioned in his commentary on *Muslim*: 'When he heard this hadith, one of the innovators said in ridicule: "I know where my hand was during the night in bed." When he awoke (the following day) he found his hand and arm in his anus.' Ibn Tahir said: 'So one should take care not to make fun of the sunnas and any (warnings which are supported by) clear textual evidence lest the evil of his action befall him swiftly.' An-Nawawi said: 'Something similar happened in our time. The incident, narrated by a great number of persons, has also been affirmed as correct by certain judges: a man in a village around Basra in AH 665 had a bad opinion of the people (whom Allah had blessed) with goodness (and special gifts). His son, however, believed in them. (One day) his son came to his (father) from a right acting Shaykh bearing a written petition and the father said in derision: "Your Shaykh has given you this petition" and he took it and inserted it in his anus out of contempt for it. Some time passed and then the man who had inserted the (piece of paper bearing) the petition into his anus gave birth to a puppy which had a resemblance to a fish. The man then killed it and died immediately, or after two days (according to another report).'"

He has also said in another place in his *Sharh* that ar-Rahawi and at-Tabarani and others had narrated from Zakariya as-Sahi: "We were walking quickly in an alley of Basra to one of the Muhaddiths when a man said in jest 'Lift your feet lest the angels' wings be broken (underfoot)' and he remained rooted to the spot, his feet started to tremble and then fell off. Ar-Rahawi has commented: '(Believe it) as if you had witnessed it as the people who narrated it are trustworthy and well known!'"

Ibn al-Hattab and Zarruq have said – and the text is taken from the latter's commentary on the *Risala*: "Whoever deliberately raises his head before the imam after having done the bowing with him and paused for a moment to relax, then he has done an evil action. If he does not keep up with the imam in the bowing, that is, he does it before him, straightens up before him and does not do the bowing with him as he is obliged to do, then he (is counted) as having missed it."

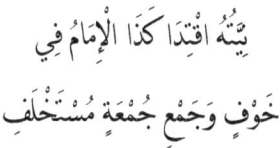

104 One should make an intention to perform (the *salat*) following (the imam); just as the imam should make an intention in the 'fear' (*salat*), in joining (the two *salats*), in the *jumu'a*; and whenever standing in (for the imam)

This is like the words of Khalil: "and the condition for following the imam in the *salat* is making first of all the intention (to follow him), as opposed to the imam (who does not have to make an intention to be imam), even for the *janaza salat*; excepted are the *jumu'a salat*, joining two *salats* (of Maghrib and *'Isha*) in a mosque on a rainy (night), the *salat* of fear (in the presence of the enemy) and when someone stands in (for the imam – where the imam must make the intention as all four *must* be done in a *jama'a*); analogous (to the four above cases is the imam's making the intention to perform the *salat* in a group in order) to acquire the merit (of his imamate of the *jama'a*)." Mawwaq has related that Ibn 'Arafa said: "The validity of the *salat* of the person behind the imam is conditional in all cases upon his making the intention to follow his imam, as opposed to the imam himself – for there is no harm in your following an imam who does not make the intention of being the imam for you, even in the case of the *janaza salat*." Ibn Shas said: "The *janaza salat* is not conditional upon it being done in a group." Ibn Rushd said: "The validity of the *janaza salat* is dependent upon there being an imam, like the *jumu'a salat*." Ibn 'Arafa said: "(Ibn Rushd's) mention of the *janaza* (*salat*) together with that of the *jumu'a* is based on the obligation, (in his view), to perform both in a group, and the connection between the two is to be found in the intention of the imam; likewise when joining (two *salats*) if it is raining."

Then al-Mawwaq has mentioned what (Qadi 'Abd al-Wahhab) said in *at-Talqeen*: "It is not necessary for the imam to make the intention to be the imam except for the *jumu'a* and the fear *salat*. However al-Mazari has added (to the discussion) the case in which someone stands in for the imam (who has to abandon the *salat*)." Ibn 'Arafa said: "There is a point of difference with Ibn Basheer over his saying 'standing in for the imam.' This is based on the fact that the person taken as an imam (after the original imam leaves) initiates the *salat* and as such (is required to make an intention for) their *salat* to be valid." Musa has transmitted that an imam began the *salat* for a man and women but then became ritually impure and left the *salat*. Although the man (behind him) did not step in for him, the women (carried on and) finished the *salat*. Ibn al-Qasim said: "The *salat* of the women is acceptable *if* he had made the intention of being their imam in the *salat*. For this reason if he leads women, then their *salat* is complete as long as he had intended to serve as their imam." Ibn Rushd: "His stipulating – with respect to a man leading women in the *salat* – that he should intend to be their imam is contrary to what is in the *Mudawwana*, namely that 'there is no harm if one follows an imam who has not intended to lead you (in *salat*).'"

Commenting on his words 'joining (two *salats*) al-Mawwaq has related that 'Iyad said: "Whenever a *salat* is prayed before its time because of the joining (two *salats*) it is necessary that the imam make the intention of being the imam and of joining the *salats*." Al-Qubab said: "This refers, in particular, to the time when it is raining."

Commenting on his words 'likewise, with respect to the merit of praying in a group', he has related that al-Mazari said: "If the imam makes the intention to lead the *salat*, then he receives (the reward for) the excellence of the group – for otherwise he does not get the (reward)." Ibn 'Arafa said: "to be valid, the person being followed as an imam who has not made this intention to pray in a group (i.e. when the original imam leaves and another steps in) must repeat the (*salat*)." Ibn 'Allaf said: "I do not think that anyone would say to him that he should repeat it in the group or that he should examine the saying of the *fuqaha*: 'a man is not rewarded for doing a *fard kifaya*[1] unless he makes the intention of coming closer (to Allah, exalted is He).'"

ISSUE: Mayyara has related that 'Ali ibn 'Abd as-Sadiq said: "One of our

---

1 (an obligation of a communal nature which if performed by one person relieves the others of this burden)

Shaykhs said, regarding the intention to be made when following the imam: 'This condition must be met although it is not necessary to make any overt sign that one is fulfilling it. Indeed there is already an indication of adherence to this (condition) by the very fact that the person doing the *salat* behind the imam waits for the *takbir* of the imam; furthermore if he were to be asked the reason for his waiting, he would reply that he is praying behind the imam – and what he said is evident.'"

ISSUE: the author of *al-Mi'yar* said: "I asked him, may Allah have mercy on him, that is, al-Qouri, about the person who persisted in staying away from the group *salats* of *Maghrib* and *'Isha* but when rain fell he would hasten to the mosque in order to seize the opportunity to pray the two *salats* together. (He replied:) 'His (*salat*) is correct and he is not making any mistake (by doing this) and he does not have to repeat (the *salats*). It would follow – if (one were to argue that) the joining (in his particular case) was not valid – that (there existed a judgement to the effect that) there was only excellence in the *salat* in the group for those who had *not* made it their custom to (only) pray when the (two *salats* of *Maghrib* and *'Isha*) were joined.'"

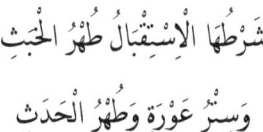

105 Its conditions are: facing the *qibla*, being clean of filth, covering up the private parts and purification from an impure state (*hadath*)

Mayyara said: "If you were to ask whether someone who is ignorant of (the science of ascertaining) the *qibla* from the signs (in the cosmos) would be guilty of disobedience if he set off on a journey (in this state) the reply would be: 'If his journey takes him via villages which are connected to one another (by a definite path or track) and in which there are *mihrabs* (indicating the direction of *qibla*) or there is someone accompanying him on the road who has knowledge of the signs (in the sky or on the land) which would indicate the *qibla* and whose uprightness and knowledge can be relied upon and whom one could thus follow (with impunity), then he would not be guilty of disobedience. However, if none of these (conditions) are fulfilled, then he would be (guilty of an act of disobedience) as he would be exposing himself to the obligation of facing the *qibla* without affording himself (the means of obtaining) any knowledge of it.'"

Mayyara has also said: "Branch: If the obligation falls on a person who is able to practice *ijtihad* and *taqlid* is prohibited for him and this person has the ability to ascertain the (direction of the) roads which may be used as an indication for finding out the *qibla* then he must inform himself of them. Thus the (*ulama*) have said that it is forbidden for someone who is not knowledgeable (of the direction of the roads) but who nevertheless has the capacity to find it out to make *taqlid* (of another in this respect)."

BRANCH: Ibn Zakari has related in *Sharh an-Naseeha* that al-Qarafi said: "As for the difference between what one is under an obligation to find out with respect to the stars and what one is not under an obligation to find out, the most evident argument of our fellow '*ulama* is that it is not permitted to follow someone else with respect to the direction of the Ka'ba when one has the capacity to come to a judgement oneself. They have stated explicitly that the person who is capable of obtaining knowledge is obliged to find this (knowledge) out and *taqlid* of someone else is not permitted him. Most of the indications regarding the *qibla* are to be found in (observation of) the planets. Thus it is obligatory to know those by which the *qibla* is known, like the two bright stars of the Ursa Minor, the North Star and any (other stars) which serve, like them, to finding out the *qibla*. The most evident meaning of their discussions (on this subject) is that it is an obligation on each and every person to learn about such (matters). The author of *al-Muqaddimat* said: 'One should learn the laws governing the celestial bodies which serve to indicate the direction of the *qibla*, as well as the watches of the night and whatever may be deduced from these, and the changes which come about over the land and sea during the darkness of the night – if the positions of these bodies cannot be ascertained (merely) from the sphere of the sky; also their celestial orbits and the times of their ascendence and setting, and all this is recommended from the words of Allah, exalted is He: "*It is He Who has appointed the stars for you so you might be guided by them in the darkness of the land and the sea.*"[1]'"

I SAY: "What may be deduced from the principles (of the science of *fiqh*) is that (knowledge of) the (cosmic signs) from which the times of the *salat* may be ascertained is a *kifaya* obligation. This is because it is permitted to make *taqlid* with regard to the times (of the *salat*). The author of *at-Taraz* said: 'It is permitted to make *taqlid* with regard to the times of the *salat*, except regarding the *zawal* – the moment of inclination of the sun from the zenith – for this is an obvious matter which is necessarily known to all and so renders *taqlid* unnecessary. For this reason it is not an obligation on each and every individual, but rather an obligation of a communal nature: given that knowledge of the times of the *salat*

---

1 Livestock – al-An'am: 98

are obligatory then it follows that (knowledge of the signs) by which these times are known is obligatory on the community as a whole. As for the times when (the judgement regarding this knowledge) is one of recommendation (rather than obligation), it is when undertaking journeys – in order that travellers may safeguard themselves from the darkness of the land and sea."

The author of *al-Mi'yar* related from Ibn Siraj that Ibn Qusar stated: "The *mihrab* is that which is known to have been erected by the leader of the Muslims or those that the people of the land have agreed by consensus to establish – that is both the *'ulama* and the common people who take it by *taqleed*, and I do not know of anyone who has contradicted Ibn Qusar in this matter. Moreover, he is of the view that (in the absence of such *mihrabs*) one should (only arrive at a decision after) seeking to ascertain the zenith or compass point – so what about others who (only) seek the (general) direction?"

Ibn al-Bana said: "The mosques which have been built in varying directions – based on different computations of the zenith[1] – are correct (in their alignment). It is not permitted to change them for they are in accordance with *ijtihad*, that is, their being built in a particular direction is the fulfilment of a (legitimate) judgement in accordance with *ijtihad* and so cannot be annulled. All (leading *fuqaha*) are in accord that there is no further difference of opinion in this – being both based on (the principles of *fiqh*) and a correct legal judgement. Moreover it indicates how past generations came to an assessment of where the direction lay and this (assessment) then became a kind of (legally binding) consensus.

Ibn Siraj has also related that Ahmad ibn Khalid said of the saying of 'Umar 'Whatever is between the east and the west is *qibla*': "There is a licence and ease for all people in this." When someone said: "Do you (people) say this in Madina?" He replied: "We and the (people of Madina) are alike (in following this judgement) and this ease and licence with (respect to assessing) the *qibla* is meant for all people," and then he added: "those in the east have no knowledge of this ease with relation to the *qibla*."

Issue: an-Nafrawi said: "There is a difference of opinion in the signs and indications of the *qibla*. Ibn al-Qasim said: 'The indication of the *qibla* during the day is that you stand facing your shadow before it starts to extend – and

---

1 *sumout* (sing.: *samt*, from *samata* meaning to follow a right course, or a good direction) is legally speaking the precise computation of the direction of the *qibla* by means of the zenith, the stars, mental reflection and the use of mechanical instruments such as the astrolabe. *Jiha* (literally, direction, from *wajaha*, to face) denotes a more general meaning than *samt* – indicating a more approximate direction with regard to the *qibla*.

this (direction) is your *qibla*.' One of the *'ulama* has related that Ibn al-Qasim said: 'This does not apply to all times.' 'Ayn Jeem said: 'In the case of the person who does not have the capacity for *ijtihad*, who does not find anyone he can follow and does not find a correct *mihrab*, then the person intending to do the *salat* must stand with the place where the sun sets behind his back and with the place where it rises in front of him and then his *salat* will be correct at any time. If there is any deviation (from the *qibla*) in his case, then it will only be slight, and this does not harm (the validity of his *salat*) according to us.'"

Al-Khurshi related that Ibn al-Qusar said: "As for the settled areas in which the *salat* has been said repeatedly (for generations) and it is known that the imams of the muslims have erected the *mihrabs* and that people of the land, as a community, have set them up, then both the *'alim* and the common people should follow (the direction of) these (*mihrabs*). This is because it is recognised that they could only have been built after the *'ulama* had made *ijtihad* in the matter. As for land which is deserted or abandoned in which no one is to be found, then the *mujtahid* should not make *taqlid* of any *mihrabs* he may find there. It may be that such 'abandoned or deserted lands' may be interpreted – as at-Tajouri maintains – as applying to any land which one is unfamiliar with, that is, when one does not know who has set up its *mihrabs*. As for those which are familiar, like (those of) Baghdad and Alexandria, then there is no obstacle to following their *mihrabs* – as long as they are all facing one direction."

ISSUE: Ibn al-Hattab has related that the author of *al-'Arida* said: "The aim of the person who faces the *qibla* and who can see the House with his own eyes and the person who cannot see it is the same. One of our *'ulama* said: 'It is necessary to seek for the source.' However, this is completely invalid for no one is able to do this and whatever is impossible, then it cannot be a duty. What is possible, however, is to look for the direction: each person should aim for this direction in accordance with what he thinks (is in all probability correct) – if he is of the people of *ijtihad*; if not, then he should follow the people of *ijtihad*." Then he goes on to say: "The common person prays in every mosque and prays behind every person but the *mujtahid* seeks to find the correct judgement with regard to mosques (he suspects of being) built in the wrong direction. If necessary, he should pray in a direction which deviates from the *mihrab* – as long as he can be sure that he will be spared people speaking ill of him and safe from the threat of punishment. If he is not safe from such (a threat), then he should pray in the (mosque in question) and repeat (the *salat*) in his house or another mosque, according to the correct judgement."

NOTICE: Know that ignorance has become widespread and people in general have become like those – described by our Master Muhammad, may the peace and blessings of Allah be upon him, from whom knowledge, at the end of time, would be removed. Thus it is that many people in our time believe that the *qibla* is the Rawda[1] of the Prophet, may the peace and blessings of Allah be upon him; others who know that the *qibla* is the Ka'ba but who think that the Ka'ba is the Black Stone. The *'ulama* are agreed that the *salat* of the former is invalid. As for the judgement of the latter, reflect upon the matter! Such people should know that the *qibla* is the Ka'ba, that the Ka'ba is the whole of the Bait al-Haram, that the Black Stone is (only) part of it and that anyone who prays to other than the Ka'ba – deliberately or in ignorance of the judgement – then his *salat* is invalid, and there is no difference of opinion in this.

Al-Khurshi said: "USEFUL POINT: the height of the Ka'ba is twenty five cubits, although it has also been said that it is twenty seven, and this (latter, I consider) to be correct. Its width is twenty cubits on all sides. The Ka'ba is the Bait al-Haram, the Sacred House which Allah has bestowed with honour, and it is the name of the Ancient House."

Commenting on the words of Khalil 'there is a difference of opinion as to whether the person who forgets remains under an obligation to repeat the *salat*, however great the delay' al-Khurshi said: "The person who is ignorant of the direction of the *qibla* is considered (to fall under the same category) as the person who forgets. As for the person who is ignorant of the obligation to face the *qibla*, he must repeat (his *salat*), however great the delay – and there is no difference of opinion in this."

I SAY: "What may be understood from his words is that ignorance of the obligation to face the *qibla* is not *kufr* – for if it were he would not be under an obligation to repeat the *salat* later, however long the delay, and Allah, exalted is He, knows best."

Commenting on Ibn 'Ashir's saying 'being clean of filth', 'Ali ibn 'Abd as-Sadiq said: "…that is, anything which is ritually unclean (*najis*), be it (discovered) at the commencement (of the *salat*) or at any time one remembers it (irrespective of whether the time for the *salat* has elapsed or not) and (as soon as one is) capable (of removing it). What is meant here is (the removal of any filth) from one's clothing, from the place (of *salat*) or the exterior of the body; and included in the judgement is (removal of impurity from) inside the mouth, from the nose and ears even if these places are internal and not part of

---

1 The tomb of the Prophet, may the peace and blessings of Allah be upon him, in Madina al-Munawwara.

the purification necessary when one's state of purity is broken."

ISSUE: More than one of the *'ulama* have narrated from Qadi 'Abd al-Wahhab a (judgement about which there is) consensus, namely, that it is an offence to pray with ritual impurity (on one's body or clothing) when done deliberately although they have questioned (the degree of the offence) arguing that the sunna (does not bear this out). Ibn 'Arafa said in his *Mukhtasar*: "Al-Mazari has expressed surprise at what has been narrated from the Qadi – namely, that someone who does this deliberately is considered guilty of a wrong action by consensus – because it contradicts the argument from the sunna. One of his Shaykhs – as well as others – has concurred with his reply arguing that the difference of opinion is over whether or not it is an obligation according to the Book and sunna. Al-Mazari said: 'The (argument) is based on a rejection of the view that one can deem someone who leaves off doing a sunna guilty of a wrong action – for to do this would be to assume that such an action were obligatory (as only the abandoning of the obligatory will be punished by Allah, exalted is He, not the sunnas).'

The author of *Ghayat al-Amani* has related that al-Fakihani said: 'It is curious that the Qadi Abu Muhammad should relate a consensus that any one who deliberately prays with this (impurity on him) is guilty of an offence when any such consensus could only apply to what is obligatory – given that an offence can only result from an obligation (not a sunna).' He continued, saying: 'I asked one of my Shaykhs about this but he refrained from giving a reply, and when I asked another he replied that the matter had to seen as a difference of interpretation.'"

ISSUE: al-Mawwaq has related that Ibn Habib said "What has to be taken into account (also) is the place of his standing, sitting and prostration, and the place where he puts his hands; moreover, there is no harm in doing the *salat* in front of the wall of a toilet as long as the actual place (where he is praying) is clean; and whoever prays on a place of filth which has dried, then he should repeat within the time irrespective of whether it lay beneath his forehead or nose or another (part of his body)." 'Iyad said: "If the hem of his clothing falls onto filth which is dry – other than where (he is actually praying) – it is of insignificance." Al-Abyani said: "It is permitted for someone (performing the *salat*) to remove his sandals and stand on them – for it is analogous to (praying on) the surface of a reed mat."

An-Nafrawi said, commenting on the words of the *Risala* 'There is no harm in performing the *salat* on the clean part of some matting when another part of it is unclean': "From this (example) we may deduce the validity of *salat* on fur which is ritually impure on the inside – even if it is the skin of a dog, pig, or a sheep which has died without being ritually slaughtered, as long as the fur or wool is covering the skin. It cannot be said that the wool is adjacent to the filth and so rendered filthy (by this connection) for we would argue that the filthy part is (indeed attached to) the underneath of the skin but does not extend to what is outside and, as it were, 'additional' to it. This then is comparable to the example of the matting which is ritually unclean on the underside."

Commenting on Khalil's words 'and it is better that the person alone do (the *salat*) at the beginning (of its time)' Ibn al-Hattab said in the 'Chapter regarding the Time of the *Salat*': "(However) sometimes delaying it may be better or obligatory, like in the case of someone who has no water and hopes to find it during the last possible time – as has been mentioned above in the 'Chapter on Tayammum'; likewise, in the case of the menstruating woman, if she becomes free of here menstruation but there is a delay in the appearance of white liquid marking the (definitive) end of the menstruation; and, in my opinion, anyone who has an impurity on himself or clothing and entertains hope of finding water within the time is (to be considered as one of) those for whom it is an obligation to delay; likewise, in the case of someone who has an excuse which prevents him from standing and hopes that it will go away in the time – so reflect upon this, and Allah, exalted is He, knows best."

ISSUE: Khalil said: "If she is in doubt as to whether her clothing has been stained (with blood), then she must sprinkle it with water. If she does not do this, then she must repeat the *salat*, as well as washing (away the blood)." Al-Amir said: "The view of Ibn Habib is in accordance with this, although it is weak." Ibn al-Qasim, Sahnun and 'Isa have said: "She should repeat within the time in all circumstances because there is no hardship in this." Al-Qarinan and Ibn al-Majishun have said that there is no necessity to repeat at all while Ibn 'Arafa has stated: "(only) if she had forgotten to sprinkle (the bloodstain), otherwise she remains under an obligation (to repeat the *salat*) however great the delay – according to 'Isa, Sahnun and Ibn al-Qasim, together with what Musa has transmitted from his Shaykh with respect to someone who has a wet dream and who does not see the (stain before the *salat*). Al-Qarinan, Ibn al-Majishun, Ibn Najeeb and Ibn Rushd have also transmitted from Ibn Nafi' that the person who has a wet dream but who does not see it (before the *salat*) does not have to repeat (it)."

Ibn al-Hattab said: "In *al-Wadiha*, Ibn Habib's judgement that both the ignorant person and the person who does it deliberately are under an obligation to repeat (the *salat*) however long the delay is conditional upon whether he has doubts as to whether his clothing has been stained by the emission of sperm or by some other impurity. As for someone who finds (a stain) after a wet dream and who washes and rinses out whatever is visible to him but is unaware that he should sprinkle over any other place (he suspects of being stained but which) is not clearly visible to him and then prays – he does not have to repeat the *salat* after he has prayed but he does have to sprinkle his clothes with water for any *salat* after this." The author of *al-Mi'yar* has transmitted from al-Mawwaq: "Any impurity which is (merely) imagined is not taken into consideration (at all), and (even) any impurity about which one has doubts carries far less weight that what is actually found (on one's clothes) according to the principles of our *madhhab* – and for this reason Ashhab, Ibn al-Majishun Ibn Nafi' have said: 'There is no obligation to repeat for the person who does not sprinkle.'"

Ibn al-Hattab said: "His thinking (something is so) is (legally speaking) the same as his doubting as long as he does not think that *in all likelihood* something is indeed impure – such that his 'thinking' resembles certainty. The most evident judgement is that washing (out the stain) is indeed obligatory as the judgements of the *shari'ah* are based on one's thinking something is so in all likelihood."

ISSUE: al-Mawwaq said that the author *al-'Arida* said: "If an impurity is mixed with a lot of water, then any judgement applies to the water not to the impurity. Thus a handful of water, being greater (in volume) than a spot of pre-seminal fluid (is considered to be water when admixed to it). A similar (judgement) may be found at the beginning of Ibn 'Abd al-Barr's *al-Kafi*."

ISSUE: al-Wansharisi said in the *Ikhtisar Nawazil al-Burzuli*: "The Prophet, may the peace and blessings of Allah be upon him, sometimes used to wear a striped yellow garment from Yemen – a garment which was produced by dyeing with urine. It is said that it is not permitted. Al-Burzuli said: 'What may be understood from this is that it is permitted to dye with shed blood.'"

ISSUE: an-Nafrawi has mentioned: "It is *makruh* to make the *salat* on a mattress over which children walk, and on anything else which cannot be protected from becoming impure. However it is not necessary that one repeat the *salat* for one of the conditions for repeating is that one be either sure of the impurity or – in the case where there is a lack of certainty of purity – one assumes impurity to exist in all likelihood, that is, in the case of dung hills, slaughtering places and the like."

At the end of the 'Chapter on the Times of the *Salat*', Ibn al-Hattab, speaking of the places in which it is disliked to do the *salat*, said: "The author of *an-Nawadir* has related that Ibn Habib said: 'I do not like *salat* done in a house where people do not shun wine and urine. If, however, someone does (do the *salat* in such a house) then he should repeat it, however long the delay. It is also disliked to do the *salat* on matting or carpeting which is in everyday use – that is, upon which children or servants or anyone who is not used to taking care (of purity) walk. A man should reserve a place in his house which is maintained (specially) for the *salat* or use a clean mat (specially for the *salat*). However, if he does not do this and prays wherever he wishes in his house then he does not have to repeat – as long as he is not certain of any impurity.'"

ISSUE: 'Ayn-Jeem said in *Hashiyat ar-Risala*: "If a child clings to his father during the *salat* and the latter thinks that in all likelihood the child's clothes are pure, then he has nothing to make up; if, however, he is certain of their impurity and does the prostration on some part of the child's clothes or sits on part of them, then his *salat* is invalidated – otherwise it is not."

ISSUE: If a person prays in clean clothing but touches the clothing of someone else which is impure, then it does not affect his (*salat* adversely) – unless he prostrates on this (other clothing) or sits on it. A judgement similar to this is to be found in *Ghayatu'l-Amani* from al-Burzuli.

ISSUE: the author of *al-Mi'yar* has related that al-Mawwaq said in *an-Nawadir*: "It is recorded that Sahnun said: 'An injured person may use the bones of animals which have been ritually slaughtered to (assist in) his healing but should not use wine as a cure, the bones of people, of pigs or the bones of anything which has died without being ritually slaughtered; nor dung or whatever is not permitted to eat. If he finds an old bone and does not know if it is the bone of a sheep, human being or pig, then there is no harm in (using) it, unless it is from a battle field which is known to contain a lot of human bones or from a place known to contain a lot of pig bones; in which case, it is not suitable for use unless the various (types of bone) may be distinguished from each other. If one is ignorant as to whether some bones have (come from an animal which has) been ritually slaughtered then he does not have to desist from using them as long as he thinks they have been ritually slaughtered. It has been said the Prophet, may the peace and blessings of Allah be upon him, treated his (injured) face with an old bone at the battle of Uhud.' The use of such a bone – which was in all probability impure – is a proof that it is also permissible to use the paper of the Europeans, despite the probability of it being impure. One should also not lose sight of the basic principle (in *fiqh*), namely, that things are (assumed to be) pure even when one knows for certain that their purity is (only) probable, and Allah knows best."

Commenting on Ibn 'Ashir's saying 'covering up the private parts' Ibn 'Abd as-Sadiq said: "(that is) with something thick, and even if with some (item of clothing) lent (from another), or when one is alone in a room, both at the beginning (of the *salat*) and throughout (the *salat*), although it has also been said that it is necessary without condition and without restriction. Both (judgements) are well known. With regard to the first (judgement), his *salat* is not valid if he prays exposing his private parts, and with regard to the second (i.e. if he performs the *salat*, naked, alone in a room), it is valid although (considered to have been) done in a state of disobedience, and it must be repeated within the time."

BRANCH: al-Khurshi has related that Ibn 'Arafa said: "According to Ibn Basheer and Ibn al-Hajib, (the wearing of) transparent (clothing) is deemed on a par with nakedness; and what is so fine as to be insubstantial is disliked, although, according to al-Baji, both (the transparent and the insubstantial) are deemed the same – that is, one must repeat (the *salat*) within the time. Al-Laqqani said: '(Al-Baji) distinguishes between a thick covering and something through which the private parts *are visible without looking attentively* – and this is what is meant by those who say transparent (clothing) is 'deemed on a par with nakedness.' As for transparent cloth through which the private parts may not be discerned except by looking attentively, then this is what is meant by those who say that the *salat* is valid in 'transparent' clothing. In this way one may harmonise the different views of Ibn 'Arafa and Ibn al-Hajib.'"

An-Nafrawi said: "The 'transparent' refers to that through which the colour of the body may be seen – and may be discerned to be either white or black." His Shaykh, al-Khurshi, has a similar statement.

In *Ghayat al-Amani* it is stated that the author of *al-Jawahir* said: "Those with a responsibility (to do the *salat*) are of two kinds: men and women. Women, in turn, are of two types: free woman and slaves. As for

1. The *umma* is of a consensus that the 'two pudenda', namely the external parts of the vagina and the anus, are both private parts." I said: "…and this has also been related by al-Lakhmi." The author of *at-Tawdih* said: "He has does not attribute it back (to the original relater or to the Prophet, may the peace and blessings be upon him) nor do I think that it may be attributed to them." The author of *al-Lubab* said: "…however, this is the manifest meaning of the words of Asbagh: 'If a man prays with his thigh uncovered, he does not have to repeat (the *salat*).'"

2. The *'awra* (the greater area considered as 'private parts') is between and including the navel and the knee.

3. It has also been defined as above but *not* including the two (the navel

and the knee themselves). This is stated in *at-Tawdih* from al-Baji, and is the *madhhab* of the majority of our fellow scholars. The author of *al-Irshad* said in *al-Mu'tamad*: "This is the well known view."

4. In al-Jilab's work it is stated: "The private parts of a man include the private parts, the anus and his thighs." Ibn al-Hajib, after relating the (above mentioned) three opinions, said: "It has also been said that it is obligatory to cover the whole of the body." In *at-Tawdih* it is stated: "...that is, covering everything that is (normally) covered by a robe – but the head and the like is not intended." However, the person who said this does not mean that the whole of the body is (considered as) 'private parts.' Abu'l-Faraj has taken this opinion from a judgement of Malik regarding the *kaffara*[1] – if one clothes a poor person then it should be cubit of cloth and a veil for a woman, and a robe for a man, that is, the minimum required for the *salat*. Al-Mazari has responded by saying that this (measure) is what *may* (be given as *kaffara*), arguing that what Malik intended to indicate was the minimum amount acceptable as an act of generosity (intended as a *kaffara*) gift." Ibn Naji has related that there are six opinions with regard to the *'awra* of a man, four of which have been mentioned.

5. The thighs are considered as *'awra*, although not (in such a strict manner) as the actual 'private parts' – and this is stated by Abu Muhammad in the chapter on 'Fitra.'

6. The private parts and the anus are (considered) the coarsest, rudest part of the *'awra* while (the area between) the navel and the knees is the least (shameful) part – this has been stated by al-Baji. The proofs (upon which this judgement is made) – within the *madhhab* – are well known: it has been narrated from the Prophet, may the peace and blessings of Allah be upon him that he did bare his knees on occasion; and Abu Hurayra asked Hasan that he bare the place that the Prophet, may the peace and blessings of Allah be upon him, had kissed and Hasan bared his navel and Abu Hurayra kissed it. Our Shaykh said: "If you were to argue that it does not necessary follow that if a part of the body is bared on one occasion then it cannot be considered part of the *'awra* – with respect to the Messenger of Allah, may the peace and blessings of Allah be upon him, baring his thigh one day – then any proof formulated on this basis would not be sufficient."

I say: "The principle which may be deduced from this baring (of part of the body) is that it is not *'awra*. As for the issue of the thigh, this is excluded from the principle on account of what has been recorded with (specific) regard to

---

1 Literally: 'that which covers' i.e. compensation paid (to the poor) to make up for a minor wrong action

the (thigh). Thus the proof is established. As for the proof above – namely, that the navel and the thigh are not part of the *'awra* – this applies between men, and even if the same has been reported of women, there is no ambiguity. However if an analogy is made between a woman and a man, then the difference is evident. The author of *adh-Dhawahir* goes on to say: 'All of the body of a woman is *'awra* except for her face and palms, and a similar judgement is recorded in Ibn al-Hajib.' It states in *at-Tawdih*: '…and this is with relation to men who are not closely related to her, but as for the judgement regarding a woman's *'awra* with respect to other women, then the well known judgement is that it is the same as a man with another man.'"

BRANCH: Mayyara said that 'Izz ad-Deen was asked whether it was permitted for a man to go to a *hammam* who – although he used to sit apart from other people – was known for exposing the part of the body which was *'awra*. He answered: "It is permitted for him to come to the *hammam*. However, if possible, he should be censured – and anyone doing this would be rewarded for it (by Allah, exalted is He,). If one is incapable of censuring him, then one should condemn it with one's heart – and one would also be rewarded for such censure. One should protect one's gaze from his *'awra* as far as possible. It would only be necessary to censure him with respect to showing his (actual) private parts or anus as the *'ulama* differ as to the extent of the *'awra*. Some of them have said that it is only the (actual) private parts and the anus and so it would not be permitted to censure those persons following the judgements of the *'ulama* (who deemed the *'awra* to be restricted to these parts if they were only exposing their thighs) – unless, that is, the person who is actually exposing himself believed that it (what he was exposing) was forbidden. And there are still (a number of) people who follow the controversial judgements of (certain) *'ulama* and they are not censured for this. Ibn 'Arafa was asked about the two 'offensive parts' and he replied: 'they extend from the front of the penis and the testicles and from the anus and between the buttocks.'"

His saying 'purification from impurity' refers to the *ghusl*, the *wudu'* and *tayammum* as mentioned above.

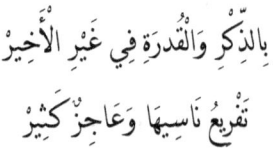

106 (All these conditions are necessary only) when remembered and when one is capable – other than in the last condition (i.e. purification from

an impure state which must be fulfilled in all cases). As for the various (judgements) applicable in the case of someone who forgets or who is incapable – they are many in number.

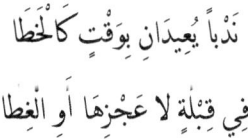

107 It is preferable in these two cases that the *salat* is repeated when within the time, similarly whenever one is mistaken in the direction of the *qibla*, but not in the case of incapacity or failing to cover one's private parts

'Ali ibn 'Abd as-Sadiq said: "(These conditions apply) from the commencement and throughout (the *salat* and he has also indicated) with his words 'with awareness and capacity' that awareness and capacity must be present in all (three) except in the case of 'purification from impurity', for this latter is absolutely necessary, without condition. There are many ramifications to this as the author Ibn 'Ashir has stated with his words 'they are many in number.' Thus 'the one who forgets' is with reference to the first three conditions which are dependent upon awareness and capacity; the ramifications with regard to the person who is incapable are also many. The author has indicated the details of both cases with his words 'it is preferable in these two cases that the *salat* be repeated' that is, the person who forgets should always repeat, however long the delay, while the person who is incapable in certain circumstances, that is, if he is incapable of purifying himself from filth then, it is recommended that he too repeat (the *salat*) – as in the case of the person who forgets – within the time, that is when the sun turns dark yellow just before *Maghrib*, or before the end of the night. If he is incapable of covering his private parts or of facing the *qibla*, then he does not have to repeat the *salat*, as is mentioned in the following words (of the author) 'like in the case of some one who makes a mistake in the direction of the *qibla*' – although he should repeat in the *ikhtiyari* time."

Then he goes on to say with respect to his words 'but not in the case of incapacity': "…that is, there is no need to repeat with respect to (a mistaken) *qibla* on account of illness and the like; likewise, in the case of the person who does not cover his private parts."

$$\text{وَمَا عَدَا وَجْهِهِ وَكَفِّ الْحُرَّةِ}$$

$$\text{يَجِبُ سَتْرُهُ كَمَا فِي الْعَوْرَةِ}$$

108 All of (the body of) a free woman must be covered, as the private parts, except the face and the palms.

$$\text{لَكِنْ لَدَى كَشْفٍ لِصَدْرٍ أَوْ شَعَرٍ}$$

$$\text{أَوْ طَرَفٍ تُعِيدُ فِي الْوَقْتِ الْمُقَرِّ}$$

109 If the breast, the hair or another part of her body is uncovered, then she should repeat the *salat* in the prescribed time.

'Ali ibn 'Abd as-Sadiq said: "This refers to the time extending from *Dhuhr* to the paling of the sun towards sunset, and all of the night from *Maghrib* until just before dawn, according to the *madhhab* of the *Mudawwana*, and the most evident interpretation is that this is irrespective of whether the person does it deliberately, out of forgetfulness or out of ignorance – and this judgement is correct (in my view). One may also understand from this that if she reveals more than this, like her belly (for example), then she remains under an obligation to repeat the *salat* however great the delay; and that if a slave girl prays revealing her breast or other parts, like her hair and feet, then she does not have to repeat. Indeed this is correct, according to the well known view, as her *'awra* is (considered to be the area) between her navel and her knees, like (that of) a man. The same applies in the case of an old woman turning grey, who no longer awakens desire and who is free, although if she prays with her thigh exposed, then she should repeat within the time – contrary to a man for the thigh is not (considered to be) the same as the private parts themselves in his case. As to whether it is forbidden to look at it or not, there are two opinions: the *'awra* in the case of the slave girl is (considered) ruder, more shameful than his. The gist of it all is that the *'awra* of the man and the slave girl with respect to the *salat* is between the navel and the knee, and in the case of the free woman with respect to the *salat*, everything except for the face and the palms – as most of the authors have stated – but as for (the matter of) looking (at someone's *'awra*) this varies according to circumstances: the *'awra* is between the navel and the knee in the case of a man with another man, the slave girl – even in the case of a woman who no longer awakens desire – with another woman or a man, and in the case of a free woman with another woman, even if she is a mushrik, although it has also been said that it is not permitted for her to expose any of her body in front of a mushrik woman unless she is a slave woman of hers – and this is the view of our Shaykh. Another of the *'ulama* has related that there is agreement in this; it also corresponds to what Sayyidi Abu 'Abdallah ibn al-Hajj said: '…and the *'awra* of the free woman, when in the presence of a man unrelated to her, is (all of her body) other than the face and the palms; and with a person closely related to her, (everything) except her face and the extremities of her body; and she may see of a person who is unrelated to her (the same parts of the body) as he may see of a person who is closely related to him (like a sister or aunt, for example); and of a person who is not related to her, everything other than the *'awra*, that is, between the navel and the knee, as in the case of a man with a man.'"

His words 'the *'awra* of the free woman with (respect to) an unrelated man is (everything) other than the face and the palms' is (the same judgement) given by Khalil, Ibn 'Arafa and others. However, al-Mawwaq, as well as the author of *al-Mi'yar*, has rejected this, saying: "…in response to those who claim that a woman's face and the palms are not to be considered as *'awra*, then it is clear that they are not *'awra* – if you mean with respect to the *salat*; if you refer to an unrelated male person – unrelated to her – looking at these two (parts of the body), then we do not accept that they are not (to be considered as) *'awra* or that it is permitted for an unrelated male person to look at these two (parts of the body) – for the *madhhab*, or (at least) the well known opinion within it, is contrary to the (judgement permitting an unrelated man to look at her). The author of the *Risala* said: 'There is no wrong in the first glance, when not deliberate, nor in looking at a woman who no longer awakens desire or a young girl when there exists an excuse (for identifying her) in the case of testimony required of her and the like, and it is also permitted (to look at her) when seeking her in marriage.'"

He has also said in another place: "A man should not be alone with a woman who is unrelated (to the degree that marriage between them would be prohibited), but there is no harm in looking at her for the purpose of examining her (prior to marriage) or the like; but as for a woman who no longer awakens desire, then he may see her face whatever the circumstances." His saying that one may look at the face of a woman who no longer awakens desire is proof that it is forbidden to look at that of a young girl – for otherwise one would be making both a negation and assertion (of something, which is illogical). What is meant is that a second, deliberate, look at a young girl –

without a valid reason – would be molesting (her), and molesting someone is haram. This is also the view of Ibn al-Jilab: "in the section on 'Closely Related Persons', beginning 'there is no harm in a man looking at the face of the wife of his father ... to the end of the section' there is proof that it is not permitted to look at the face of other that those mentioned (in this passage)." In the *Jami' al-Muqaddimat* it is stated: "...and it is not permitted to look at a young girl without a legitimate reason, (such as, when needing her) testimony, treating her, or wanting to marry her."

ISSUE: the author of *al-Mi'yar* has related from al-Mawwaq that the latter objected to the words of 'Ali ibn 'Abd as Sadiq '...whenever it is permitted looking at him it is also permitted to touch him' saying: "...as for being permitted to look without being permitted to touch – examples of this would be the touching of a *mus-haf* in the case of a person in a state of ritual impurity; likewise, (entry into) a mosque in the case of a person in a state of *janaba*; or (the touching of) filthy unclean matter; or when upright, honourable men of the community (on behalf of the judge) inspect the private parts of people (suspected) of fornication with a view to charging them with the crime; or the inspection of the private parts of a hermaphrodite; or (the examination) of the urine from either of them; or (examination of) private parts of a minor – for Ibn Yunus has mentioned in the section 'Inheritance Shares of the Hermaphrodite' that it is permitted to inspect the private parts when testimony as to his (gender) is required, and that likewise it is permitted to inspect parts of the body (of a slave – normally prohibited from being seen -) for imperfections but that it is not permitted to touch them."

NOTICE: Just as it is obligatory for a woman to cover herself in front of a person not closely related to her, so it is also obligatory for her to cover up between her navel and her knees in front of any *mahram*, other than her husband, even a woman. As for Sahnun's words 'there is no *'awra* when two (persons of) like (status with regard to their *mahram* degree), this is not adhered to in practice, or it is interpreted (in other than its literal meaning)', they are referred to in *Mufeed al-Hukkam*: "Ahmad ibn Khalid said that Malik and his followers are of a consensus, as far as I know, in the case of a man who takes his newly-wed bride to bed and then claims that she is afflicted with a vaginal hernia or that her vagina is closed and the wife denies this, refusing to allow women to examine her: (they say that) Sahnun makes an exception in this case for he says in the book of his son: 'Women should examine her, although this is not practised. Ahmad said the meaning of Sahnun's words 'women should examine her' is that two women should sit behind the woman with a mirror placed in front of her vagina. After her thighs and the lips of her vagina have been parted, the women then inspect her by means of the mirror. In this way nothing is hidden from them within the vagina, and this is a good means (of discovering the validity of her claim) – so recognise its (value). I have composed the following, and I seek forgiveness of Allah the Vast:

It is obligatory on women to cover themselves
   Except for their faces and their palms – so know this! –
In the presence of a man not closely related. The author of *al-Mi'yar*
   deems this obligatory – and it is the preferred judgement.
He considers the slave, the servant
   and the nobleman alike (in this matter) – so understand O friend!
He treats equally a woman of low birth
   and of high birth;
And uncovering the *'awra* between people of like (status) with regard to their *mahram* degree
   The perspicacious regard as a part of error.
They have made an interpretation of the (literal) words of Sahnun – who strives so strenuously –
   And this is reported of them in *Mufeed al-Hukkam*
So leave off, may Allah guide you! looking at the haram
   For how many, how many it has removed from Islam!
So we ask the All-Merciful by the Qur'an
   For success and firm establishment in Iman.

With his words 'and this is the preferred judgement', he is indicating the preferred judgement of 'the Malik of his time and his place', Muhammad ibn Marzouq, that is, the obligation of a woman to cover her face and her hands in the presence of a man not closely related to her.

Know that Ibn Marzouq's adorning him with the title of 'the Malik of his time and place' has its origin in the 'Section on Sales' in al-Wansharisi's *al-Mi'yar*; with his words 'interpreted the words of Sahnun', he has indicated what is stated in *Mufeed al-Hukkam* mentioned above; with 'how many have left Islam' he has indicated those who have died outside the pale of Islam because of their looking what is haram – as related by Ibn Zakari in *Sharh an-Naseeha*.

NOTICE: It is obligatory for the husband to prevent his wife from going out with her limbs exposed. His honour and good name is adversely affected if she does so. In *an-Nawazil*, it is stated that the author of *al-Mi'yar* relates the case of a man whose wife used go out with her face and the extremities of her body exposed; she would concern herself with securing brides and organising feasts attended by men and women at which the women would dance and the men would stand round looking at them. The question was raised as to whether the honour and good name of the man whose wife did this was adversely affected and he replied: "Praise belongs to Allah, exalted is He, and Allah glorious is He, is the possessor of success by His generosity! The answer is to be found in the *fatwa* given by Shaykh Abu Mansur ibn Ahmad ash-Shadhili regarding the man whose wife would go out and conduct her business with the extremities of her body and her face exposed – just as the people of the desert are accustomed to do. (He declared that) 'he is not permitted to lead the *salat*, that his testimony is not accepted, that even if he is in need, it is not permitted to give him *zakat* and that Allah's anger remains upon him for as long as she continues to do this.' Abu 'Abdallah az-Zawwawi said: 'If he is able to prevent her (behaving in this manner) but does not in fact prevent her, then what Abu 'Ali has mentioned is correct.' Abu 'Abdallah Muhammad ibn Marzouq said: 'If he is able to prevent her from being seen by those who are not permitted to see her but does not do so, then this will adversely affect his good name. If, however, he is not able, then his (honour) is unaffected.'"

Issue: the Shaikhs have denigrated those about whom you asked – no behaviour is more outrageous than that to be found amongst those (women) who go out and go about their business with their faces and limbs exposed. If they have given a *fatwa* affirming the adverse effect of a wife's behaviour on the good honour of the husband then the flawing of his good name in the case of this particular wife he is responsible for is all the more pertinent – given the additional details mentioned in the question, namely, her consorting and dancing in front of men who are quite unrelated to her. There is no doubt as to the harm in mixing in such corrupt company.

Zarruq said in *Sharh ar-Risala*: "As for woman who go out wearing ostentatious clothes, then (know that) any woman who ostentatiously adorns herself is haram: the Prophet, may the peace and blessings of Allah be upon him, has spoken of 'those woman who are dressed, but who are nevertheless as if naked, who incline from side to side, attracting the attention of otherss will not enter the Garden and will not find its fragrance'; he has also said, on whom be peace and blessings: 'Many a woman dressed in this world will be naked on the Day of Raising Up.'"

Thus it is an obligation on woman not to go out attired in clothes which would attract the attention of men; rather in ordinary clothes worn out through use, or a woollen over-shirt and trousers which would not even attract the attention of a dog if thrown in front of it. However, today their state is such that they only go out in their best clothes, even borrowing from their neighbours; they use perfume when going out and adopt coquettish airs when walking – attired so outrageously that were such attire on a wooden stick, people would be attracted to it. By such (behaviour) she is exposing herself to the hate of Allah and His anger – as is her husband or anyone else who affirms such (behaviour) in her, and Allah is the One Who brings success.

In *al-Jami' as-Saghir*: "There are three persons who will not enter the Garden, the one who disobeys his parents, a contented cuckold who panders to his own wife, and a woman who affects to be like a man."

Al-Munawi al-Kabir said of this latter that this refers to matters of gait and dress, not to her (imitating men in their) capacity for knowledge – for this is a praiseworthy characteristic.

The author of *al-Mi'yar* said: "Among the acts of innovation is women adorning themselves with various kinds of ornaments which are visible (when they go out), being proud and self conceited in their gait, using ostentatious perfumes and displaying themselves in a seductive fashion. Such (women) should be prevented from going out in this state. It says in *al-Ikmal*: 'The *'ulama* have stipulated that women should be inconspicuous when going out – not ostentatiously adorned with perfume in a manner likely to arouse men; neither should young girls lest they arouse men's passions.' Ibn Musalama said: 'It is well known that a young and beautiful girl should be prevented (from going out).'"

One of the Shaykhs said: "(the meaning of the prohibition of) 'perfume' implies too (the prohibition of the use of excess) wrappings and beautiful clothes."

An-Nawawi said: "One may add to these conditions that there should not exist on (public) highways any fear of corruption or evil." 'Iyad said: "If woman have been discouraged from going to the mosque, then all the more reason to discourage them from going to other places." He also gave a *fatwa* forbidding them from going to places where people gathered for knowledge, for *dhikr* and instruction in the deen – even if they were separated from the men. The author of *al-Mi'yar* said: "This has been transmitted with respect to the *salat* – and this is correct, especially in this time." However, on another occasion he says: "Al-Mawwaq was asked – regarding the seventh day (of remembrance) held after a person's death, to which reciters and other men come and which is attended by women who sit near the men: 'Should one instruct them not to come or tell them to sit at a distance from the men – may Allah raise you amongst those who will receive His reward?' He replied: 'Ibn Siraj, may Allah, exalted is He, have mercy on him, used to say that it is a misguided innovation to make a judgement within the *shari'ah* which is not applicable or appropriate – such that no distinction is made between those who say, of something licit, that it is 'recommended' or 'obligatory' or those who say that something is 'disliked' or 'haram.' All success is dependent upon keeping to the limits of Allah: "*Those who overstep Allah's limits are wrongdoers.*"[1] What has been described (above) is licit – based on the evidence of the Messenger of Allah, may the peace and blessings of Allah be upon him, who instructed emancipated slave women, those menstruating, and (young girls) usually kept in seclusion to go out on the occasion of the 'Eid al-Fitr and al-Adha – as recorded in *Sahih Muslim*. However those women who are menstruating must keep at a distance away from the *salat* but are able to witness the benefit (contained in the *salat*) and the supplications of the Muslims.'"

NOTICE: Al-Ubbi said, commenting on (*Sahih*) Muslim, that al-Qadi Abu 'Abdallah ibn al-Murabit has related: "If a woman has trouble covering what she has been commanded to cover, namely, her wrists, legs and upper part of her chest, then this (obligation) may be overlooked in case of pressing need."

Ash-Shihab said in *Sharh ash-Shifa*: "Ibn al-Murabit is Ibn Mus'ab and he is one of the most illustrious of the Maliki Imams of the *Maghrib* and of great excellence."

شَرْطُ وُجُوبِهَا النَّقَا مِنَ الدَّم

بِقَصَّةٍ أَوِ الْجُفُوفِ فَاعْلَم

110 A condition of it being obligatory is her being free of menstrual blood or of the whitish fluid (which marks the end of the cycle), or becoming dry

Ibn 'Abd as-Sadiq has related that 'Iyad said: "The whitish fluid indicates that the womb has become free of blood. Dryness is determined by inserting a cloth or piece of cotton into the vagina and (ascertaining that) it remains dry, devoid of any moisture." The most evident meaning of 'Iyad's words is that both (indications) are equally (valid in determining the end of the menstruation), and this is the view of ad-Da'udi and 'Abd al-Wahhab. When any one of the two (signs) become visible, one should act accordingly, without delay. However, Ibn al-Qasim said: "The whiteness is more decisive proof – both in the case of a woman who is accustomed to seeing only this (whiteness)

---

1 al-Baqara – The Cow: 227

and in the case of the woman who is accustomed to seeing both indications. As for the woman who is accustomed to experiencing (only) dryness (rather than the whitish fluid), then she should for wait for it until the end of the *ikhtiyari* time." Ibn 'Abd al-Hakam said: "Dryness alone is more of a telling sign both in the case of the woman who is used to (determining the end of her cycle) by it and in the case of the woman who is used to telling the end of the cycle by both (signs)." The gist of the matter is that they are both signs of purification – by common agreement, according to Ibn al-Qasim, Ibn 'Abd al-Hakam and others. However, they have differed as to which of the two constitutes the stronger proof. Moreover, there are two views as to whether the sight of the whitish fluid is the stronger (of the two) indications in the case of a young woman who has just started having her periods. It is *makruh* for a woman to examine herself to ascertain if she has become clean before *fajr* although it is obligatory before going to sleep and at the time of the *Subh salat*.

However his statement – mentioned above – that the woman who is used to dryness (as a sign of the end of her period) should wait until the end of the *ikhtiyari* time is contrary to the opinion about which there is common agreement, namely that she does not have to wait for it. Mayyara has composed the following:

As for the woman who is accustomed to observing just one (of the two signs which indicate the end of menstruation),

then this (one sign) is enough – as soon as she observes it – according to the agreed narration.

As for his saying 'there are two opinions as to the whiteness being a stronger indication in the case of the young woman who has just begun to have her periods', there is also the question of her examining herself – but it is not correct: al-Mawwaq has related that al-Baji has narrated from Malik: "A woman does not have to inspect herself to see if she has become pure during the night – and I dislike this (practice); people did not have lamps; rather she must do this if she wants to go to sleep or after she has got up for the *Subh salat*; women must inspect themselves at the times of the *salat*." A similar judgement is recorded from Ibn al-Qasim who added: "and this is not part of the practice of the people." Ibn al-Qasim said: "What has been arrived at by analogy is that she must inspect herself earlier enough – just before *fajr* – such that should she find herself clean, she would have enough time to make *ghusl* and pray the *Maghrib* and *'Isha* before the beginning of *fajr* – for there is no difference of opinion that the *salat* becomes obligatory at the end of the time but that the obligation (to do it) is removed from her in the case of difficulty. If she wakes after the *fajr* and finds herself clean but does not know whether she became pure during the night, then she should consider the *salat* subject to her state at the moment she went to sleep and so she does not have to make it up the *salat* of the night – unless, that is, she is certain that she became clean before the *fajr*. In Ramadan, however, she is commanded to fast that day – as a precaution."

USEFUL POINT: The Muhaqqaq Muhammad ibn 'Abd al-Qadir al-Fasi said in his commentary on *Husn al-Haseen*: "In the *Hilyat al-Adhkar* it is stated: 'The *'ulama* are of a consensus that it is permitted for the person in a state of both minor and major ritual impurity, for the menstruating woman and for the woman after childbirth to make *dhikr* with the heart and on the tongue, that is, *dhikr* by way of *subhana'llah*, the saying of *al-hamdulillah, la ilahah illa'llah, Allahu akbar*, the sending of peace and blessings on the Messenger of Allah, may the peace and blessings of Allah be upon him, making *du'a'* and any other *dhikrs* beside these. The reciting of Qur'an is haram for the person in *janaba*, the menstruating woman and the woman after childbirth.' He goes on to give a long explanation of the various branches and judgements – which it is not the place to elucidate here – together with an explanation of the differences of opinion and cases of agreement. However, the well known opinion of the *madhhab* of Malik is that it is forbidden for the person in a state of *janaba*, but not for the menstruating woman. Al-Baji said has related that 'Our fellow (jurists) have said: "She may recite – even after she has become pure, before her *ghusl*".' Ibn 'Arafa said: 'Their reasoning is based on there being no means of making *ghusl*.' 'Abd al-Haqq said: 'She should not recite and should not sleep until she has made *wudu*' – as in the case of the person in *janaba*.' Al-Hattab said: 'in *at-Tawdih*, it is restricted to the second – where the author says: "The difference of opinion as to the recitation of the menstruating woman is with regard to her state before she has become pure; (there is no difference of opinion) regarding her state after becoming pure of blood – namely, that she is considered (subject to the same judgement) as the person in *janaba*."' Ibn Farhun and others have also restricted it in this way, and this is the most evident judgement – and Allah knows best." His being ascribed the title of Muhaqqiq originates from Sayyidi Ahmad ibn 'Abd al-'Aziz al-Hilali in *Sharh at-Tayyiba*.

USEFUL POINT: the author of *Ghayat al-Amani* said, commenting on the words of the *Risala* 'and likewise if she observes dryness, then she is (considered) pure on account of its apparition': "Al-Aqfahisi said: 'The meaning of this is that she is considered clean; but as for the *ghusl*, if time is short, then she has to purify herself immediately unless there is something preventing her (from doing so); but if there is ample time, then she does not have to do it immediately, unless her husband is in need of (having intercourse with) her – in which case she should make *ghusl*. *Ghusl* (in this particular case) takes precedence over performing a good act for one's parents if she is asked to do something for them – because a good action performed for the sake of her husband is done in return for something whereas a good action undertaken for her parents is without compensation; and *ghusl* for the sake of her husband is given preference over repayment of debts and the returning of deposits – because she may delegate this (obligation) to another.'"

ISSUE: the author of *Ghayat al-Amani* said: "The proof that the longest period of blood is fifteen days is furnished by the words of the Messenger, may the peace and blessings of Allah be upon him, on the occasion of dispraise of women: 'One of you may remain half of her time not praying.' The hadith is an indication that the maximum duration of the menstruation is fifteen days – because his words are meant as an exaggeration, and if he had meant anything else he would have explained it (in more detail). However 'Ali ibn 'Abd as-Sadiq said that *'Ayn-Jeem* said: 'This hadith is invalid and has no basis – as is (demonstrated) in *al-Maqasid*.'"

ISSUE: 'Ali ibn 'Abd as-Sadiq said: "It is obligatory for a woman to ask about anything she is ignorant about – with regard to whatever is necessary of the judgements, that is, regarding the menstruation and other things; likewise for a man, although it is more particularly binding on a woman as menstruation is particular to women. (If she is ignorant about a matter), she should first ask her husband, and he is obliged to teach her or to enable her to learn; indeed, it is her right on him; and that he command her to it. If he does not do any of these things, he becomes partner to her offence – that is, if he aids and abets her in this. He is guilty of this offence if he refuses (to assist) her after she has asked him (to teach her or let her acquire the knowledge elsewhere). Nowadays people only regard women – as well as children and slaves – as a means to fulfilling their needs in this world. This is clearly evident in the case of many people, especially the people of the desert. They do not seek of women anything beyond this. They do not embody the words of Allah ta'la 'You who have iman! safeguard yourselves and your families'[1] and the saying of the Prophet, peace and blessings of Allah be upon him: 'Each one of you is a guardian and each one of you is responsible for whatever he is guarding: a man is a guardian over the family of his house.' It is strange that a person becomes angry at a woman who wastes her money but does not become angry with her for losing her deen. We ask Allah to be spared this trial. The *'ulama* have said

---

1 at-Tahrim - The Prohibition: 6

it is obligatory upon the person who wants to marry a woman to ask her about the attributes of iman and what it is necessary to hold to regarding matters of *'aqida*. If she is able to reply, then all well and good; otherwise, he should leave her. If the marriage does take place and she is ignorant – of those things which if ignorant of, one becomes guilty of *kufr* – then she should inform herself (of them) from him. This I have seen in a *fatwa*, and the like from Ibn Farhun in his *fatwas*. And we ask Allah for forgiveness and pardon."

This is all extremely pertinent – except his words 'it is obligatory upon the person who wants to marry a woman…' for this is contrary to the *fatwa* of the great *'alim* of his time and place, al-Mawwaq, as is stated in *al-Mi'yar*: "He was asked – regarding the *fatwa* of a man who claimed to have studied (*fiqh*), namely, his *fatwa* that every person is obliged to ask his wife regarding her *'aqida* and that if he finds her holding to something that is impossible of Allah, exalted is He, like for example, His having a direction (or place in space), then he must separate himself from her as she is a mushrik – 'O Sayyidi, is the *fatwa* he gave an obligatory judgement or not?' and what is the judgement regarding the person who is ignorant and who only holds to *la ilaha illa'llah Muhammad ar-rasulallah*, may the peace and blessings of Allah be upon him, as is the case with most people?'

He replied: 'This is nonsense and whenever such things are said in front of the ordinary people it creates chaos. People should not be stirred up and provoked in matters of *'aqida*. The two *shahadas* are enough, as imam Abu Hamid said, and this has also been transmitted in the *sahih* hadith. If it were obligatory to ask people about this after marrying, then it would also be obligatory before it – but a woman is not first subjected to an examination of her *'aqida* before being permitted to bear witness that there is no god, only Allah and that Muhammad is his Messenger; one of their principles being that anything (contrary to the deen) which suddenly appears should be removed as soon as it occurs and if already present (in the matter in hand) should be rejected (before dealing with the matter). Indeed, if an evil belief manifests in a wife – without one actively enquiring after it – one should examine it with regard to the judgement it is subject to for such (problems of *'aqida*) are often not addressed with precision, and Allah is the One Who brings success by his overflowing generosity, and He glorious is He, knows best.'"

In *al-Mi'yar* he also states: "Abu 'Abdallah al-Abdousi was asked whether a man who had married a woman and had found aspects of her *'aqida* which were corrupt had to separate from her. He replied: 'There are three kinds of corruption regarding *'aqida*, one is *kufr* according to the *ijma'*, another is innovation and renders the *'aqida* invalid – but is not considered *kufr*, and the third is that about which there is a difference of opinion as to whether it is *kufr* or not.'"

As for an aspect of belief which is *kufr*, according to the consensus, then the judgement on the person who holds to it is the same as that of the Zoroastrians and it is not permitted to marry a woman (who holds to such a belief); however, if a man does in fact marry her and is not aware of this (in her), learning of it after (the marriage), then he must separate from her. Separation is annulment without divorce and is established (legally) either by evidence which one comes to know of through (conversation with) her while being engaged to her or by way of her own open avowal – as long as there is corroboration on behalf of her husband. If he does not affirm this in her, then her word is not accepted – for then she is suspected of wanting to separate from him by means of this claim (of belief in something contrary to the correct *'aqida*). It is recommended (whatever the circumstances) that he separate from her in order to distance himself from (impurity of belief), for reasons of scrupulousness and as a protection from what is dubious – (as the Prophet, may the peace and blessings of Allah be upon him, said, evil action is that which 'causes the heart to waver – even if people give you *fatwa* after *fatwa* (to try and reassure you that something is alright).'

As for aspects of belief (in her) which are not considered *kufr*, (although reprehensible), according to the consensus, it is not necessary to separate from her; rather he is obliged to instruct her and afford her right guidance or order to correct her *'aqida* – if there is no other close relative, or anyone else who is can do this.

As for aspects of belief about which there is a difference of opinion as to whether they are *kufr* or not, then one should examine the state of the man and wife: if they both agree that the judgement (in the case of such beliefs) is that they are not considered as *kufr*, then they may stay together. If, however, they follow the judgement that such beliefs are to be deemed *kufr*, then they must separate. This is likewise the case if only the husband holds to this judgement – as the right to revoke the bond of marriage is in his hands. If the man holds to the view that a certain belief is not to be deemed as *kufr* but the woman does, then the *qadi* must resolve the difference between them: if he decides that such a belief is to be regarded as *kufr*, then they must separate; if not, then she must stay with him, and his judgement puts an end to their difference of opinion."

The reply of 'Abd 'Abdallah al-Abdousi – when asked whether a man should test his wife regarding her *'aqida* – is also relevant to this subject: "As for the correctness of the deen of Muslim women, they are judged according to their outward (behaviour) and one should desist from prying into their secrets for this matter is between them and Allah glorious is He. However if the husband thinks that her *'aqida* is in all probability corrupt, then he should question her in this regard, and he must teach her anything she does not know. Some *'ulama* – whom people used to follow (in matters of the deen) – used to instruct that those witnessing the contract of marriage should test the *'aqida* (of the bride) before concluding the contract (of marriage) – on account of the corruption dominating women's *'aqida*. Thus it was that this practice (of examining the women) came into being, and as a result, a great nation of women was guided to the true *'aqida*."

فَلَا قَضَا أَيَّامَهُ ثُمَّ دُخُولْ

وَقْتٍ فَأَدِّهَا بِهِ حَتْمًا أَقُولْ

111   She does not have to make up her days (of menstruation). The next (and final condition) is that the time for the *salat* has arrived – in which case I say: 'Be sure to perform it within this [time]'.

The author has not explained the times of the *salat*. This Khalil has done with his words "the *ikhtiyar* time of *Dhuhr* is from when the sun inclines from its zenith to when the shadow of an object reaches it maximum length not counting the shadow of the zenith (which varies from place to place); and this point also marks the beginning of the time of *'Asr* which lasts until the colour (of the sky) turns to a deeper yellow (towards sunset). The *salats* (of *Dhuhr* and *'Asr*) have in common a length of time corresponding to the time of one of the two *salats*; there is a difference of opinion as to whether it refers to the last time – when the shadow of an object has reached its maximum length, or to the moment during the first part of the doubling of its length."'

Al-Mawwaq said that Ibn Abu Uways has narrated from Malik that the *salat* of *Dhuhr* at the time of the zenith is the *salat* of the Khawarij.

Khalil said: "The time of *Maghrib* is after the sun has gone down for a duration of time which permits the performance (of the three *rak'ats*) after having fulfilled its conditions (of *wudu'*, etc)." Al-Mawwaq said: "The time of *Maghrib* is after the setting of the sun and it is not to be delayed." Ibn Rushd said: "…except if one has an excuse – like when the *salats* are joined in the case of a sick person, or person compelled (by circumstances) and the traveller; and there is a consensus that it is more excellent to hasten to perform the *Maghrib* immediately after the setting of the sun."

Ibn al-Hattab related that Ibn 'Arafa said: "One must take into consideration any extra time one may need to wash for the *salat* given that this (washing) only becomes obligatory after the time (of the *salat* has begun) but not before. The consensus is that there can be no obligation of responsibility (for an act of worship) fixed for a particular time when their is not enough time (to fulfil the necessary conditions of that act of worship). This same sense may be understood in the words of al-Mazari: 'Both the person who performs the *salat* immediately after the sunset and the person who delays a little are considered to be doing it within the proper time.' This has been narrated by Ibn al-'Arabi who defines the delay (permitted) as the amount of time it takes for the *adhan*, the *iqama* and the putting on of one's clothes.'"

The gist of this is that – according to those who say that the time of *Maghrib* is quite specific and cannot be extended (like the other *salats*) – one must take into account an amount of time which will permit the making of the *ghusl* (if necessary), *wudu'*, the putting on of one's clothes, the *adhan*, *iqama* and the three *rak'ats*, with respect to each person who is praying. Anyone who is needs to do any of these things, then it is better that he do them in time for *Maghrib*. If, however, he delays the *salat* a little in order to fulfil its conditions – that is just enough to do these things properly – then he is not committing a wrong action and is considered to be carrying it out in its *ikhtiyari* time; whoever does not need to do any of these things, then the matter is clear (namely, that he should pray as soon as possible after sunset).

I have said: "One should add to such considerations the amount of time it takes to do the *istibra'* properly – for this is also obligatory."

Al-Khurshi said: "The discussion of the author is based on the beginning of the time. As for extension of its time, there is agreement among the *'ulama* that it is permitted to extend it to the disappearance of the red in the sky; and in the *Muwatta'*, it is narrated of the Prophet, may the peace and blessings of Allah be upon him, that "at *Maghrib* he recited the sura, *at-Tur* – 'The Mount' and *al-Mursalat* – 'Those Sent Forth', and this affords support to the view that the *ikhtiyar* time may be extended right up to the time when the redness disappears (from the sky). It is not permitted to extend the recitation until after the disappearance of the redness, according to the *ijma'*, while it is permitted as long as the redness remains, according to the *ijma'*; and if this period (of redness) did not constitute *ikhtiyari* time, then it would also not have been permitted, like the period after the redness."

USEFUL POINT: he has related in *Kitab at-Tashawwuq* that Abu'l-Hasan ibn

Harazim said: "My father advised me to kiss the hands of Ibn an-Nahawi every time I met him. One day, I came to him after *Maghrib* and he gave the *adhan* and the *iqama*; when he was about to say the *takbir*, the robe on his shoulders shook from his intense fear; and when he said the *salam*, he made a *du'a* for me. Then I left to go back to my father. I said to him: 'He prayed before the time of the people of the land.' He replied: 'Do not speak ill of a *wali* of Allah – the *Maghrib salat* does not have any other time but the time he performed in – it is the others who have innovated in this matter by delaying it.'"

Khalil said: "*'Isha* is from when the redness disappears up to the end of the first third of the night." He said in the *Risala*: "It is *makruh* to sleep before this or to engage in conversation of no serious purpose after it. However, if the conversation is of benefit, then there it is not disliked, even if about matters of this world."

Al-Haytami said, giving examples of what should not be talked about after *'Isha*: "….matters which have no benefit in the deen, which do not have Allah and His Prophet, may the peace and blessings of Allah be upon him, as their subject matter, which do not contain knowledge, which are not concerned with commanding to the good and forbidding evil in the realm of knowledge or with setting things right between people; or speaking without striving to raise the tone of the conversation and or without speaking well of people. The most excellent of words are those spoken in front of someone whose authority one fears; or words of persistence and apositeness – when talking with one's wife or a guest, or regarding matters of the *dunya* – that is about things of an essential and necessary nature to man or about anything to his benefit."

Al-Khurshi said: "Al-Baji has related from one of the companions of Malik that 'it is permitted for a man to sleep at night – even if it means he will sleep beyond the *ikhtiyari* time for one does not have to leave off doing something which is permitted on account of something that is not (yet) obligatory.' His saying 'even if it means…' contains within it both the preferred (*rajih*) judgement and the preponderant (*marjuh*) judgements. If, however, he sleeps after the time has begun, knowing or thinking that he will (certainly) remain asleep until after the time is over, then he is not permitted to sleep." Lam-'ayn-sad has also said something similar, adding: "What may be understood from this is that someone who is aware that his wife would leave off doing the *salat* because she is in a state of *janaba*, then it is not permitted the husband to compel her to have intercourse after the time for the *salat* has begun; he can, however, before it; and if he is aware that she will not perform the *salat* but he commands her to it, then he will not be guilty of a wrong action. It is permitted to sleep after the *adhan* of *Subh* in the last sixth of the night."

An-Nafrawi said: "Whoever knows that his wife will not do the *ghusl* until the following day if he has intercourse with her during the night but he is only able to have intercourse with her during the night, then he may have intercourse with her as long as he instructs her to do the *ghusl* during the night; if she refuses to do this, then he (at least) has carried out what is obligatory upon him. As to whether he is permitted to have intercourse with her or he must he divorce her – if he is aware that she does not take a *ghusl* when he has intercourse with her, the well known opinion is that it is permitted although he should command her to do the *ghusl*, even strike her – if he thinks it will be of use; if she does not do it, then she is guilty of disobedience but it is not necessary to divorce her; although some hold a contrary opinion. Indeed, it is only recommended to separate from her – as is recommended in the case of the woman guilty of fornication or any woman guilty of innovation which is forbidden."

Al-Ubbi said in *Sharh al-Muslim*: "The Shaykh, that is Ibn 'Arafa, used to say: 'The husband whose wife leaves off doing the *salat* is not guilty himself of any wrong as long as he forbids her from acting in this way. If she does not desist, he does not have to divorce her however; nor does he have to take the matter to the *qadi* – for she might well follow his instructions (for a while) but then (later) return to what she had been used to doing, and it would be difficult to take the matter to him every time she left off doing the *salat*.'"

Khalil said: "*Subh* is from the time of the true dawn until the light manifests clearly." Al-Khurshi has related from '*Ayn-Jeem* that as-Sanhouri said: "(what is meant by) 'the light manifests clearly' is that one can clearly recognise the person sitting besides one." Abu'l-Hasan said: "This light is such that people can see each other's faces."

I say: "The most evident judgement is that this is according to average sight in a place without a roof, and without any curtain or veil. The author's mention above of the last part of the *ikhtiyari* time is based on the narration of Ibn al-Qasim, Ibn 'Abd al-Hakam and the judgement contained in the *Mudawwana*. It is said that it is the actual rising of the sun – and this is the narration of Ibn Wahb, as well as being the view of most *'ulama*; and according to the judgement of Ibn al-Hajib, also the well known view."

The author of *at-Tawdih* said: "This is not so, rather the first is the *madhhab* of the *Mudawwana*. 'Ali ibn 'Abd as-Sadiq said that this is the well known view. Indeed what Ibn al-Hajib said corresponds to what Ibn al-'Arabi said: 'The correct view from Malik is that the *ikhtiyari* time is up to the rising of the *Subh* and anything narrated from him contrary to this is not correct.' Ibn 'Ata'illah said: 'If there is a means of resorting to an interpretation of the (literal text of the) *Mudawwana*, then there is no problem – otherwise how could one say that the *madhhab* of *al-Mudawwana* is not correct?'"

I SAY: Ash-Shadhili said in his *Sharh ar-Risala*: "The view that the *ikhtiyari* time lasts up to sunrise is that of Ibn al-Habib as is stated in *at-Tawdih*, although an-Naji has attributed it to the narration of Ibn Wahb in *al-Mudawwana* and to most of the *'ulama*; 'Iyad, however, has attributed it to all of the *'ulama* and imams of *fatwa*, saying: 'this is the well known view of Malik; and Ibn 'Abd al-Barr said: 'and this is the practice of the people.'"

NOTICE

1. Ahmad Zarruq said in *Sharh ar-Risala*: "It has been narrated in *Tahdheeb at-Talib* from more than one of his Shaykhs that one is considered to have caught the *ikhtiyari* time if one does just the *takbirat al-ihram* (within the time); what Ibn Rushd and 'Ali ibn 'Abd as-Sadiq have understood, however, from the discussion of Ibn al-Hajib is that it is only attained by performing the complete *salat*; Khalil has understood from it that one does one *rak'a* within the *ikhtiyari* time one has attained it the *salat* if he does, and this has also been said by Ibn Harun. Examine this matter for it is important."

2. Zarruq has also said in *Sharh ar-Risala*: "Ibn al-Qasim narrated hearing of the person who forbade the delaying of the *salat* until the sun had passed its zenith – forbade him delaying it as long as its time had not passed. Ibn Rushd said: 'This refers to the *ikhtiyari* time, although it has also been said it refers to an *ikhtiyari* time which is shared with the following *salat*.' The most evident judgement regarding what ibn Qasim has narrated is regarding the *Maghrib* is that it goes on as long as dawn has not broken. 'Ali ibn 'Abd as-Sadiq has also narrated something similar."

3. There is a difference of opinion as to whether it is haram or *makruh* to deliberately delay the *salat* to the *daruri* time. The former is the judgement of Khalil who says: "One is guilty of a wrong action unless one has an excuse – (for example), being in a state of *kufr*, apostasy, or being not yet of age, fainting, madness, sleep, being unaware or negligent (without intent), in the case of the menstruating woman or the like (after childbirth), but not the person who is drunk. All these are excused, except the person who was a *kafir* and (becomes Muslim again) who is capable of purifying himself."

Ibn 'Arafa said: "Also (included among those considered to be) without excuse is anyone who delays the *salat* to the *daruri* time. Ibn Muhriz said: 'It has been narrated of Ibn al-Qasim that he considered it *makruh* while at-Tunisi considered it a wrong action if performed (thus). Ashhab, Ibn Wahb and ad-Da'udi have also interpreted the hadith 'Whoever misses the *'Asr salat*, it is as if he has brought harm and loss to his family' in this way. Sahnun, al-Aseeli and al-Baji have interpreted it as referring to delaying the *salat*. Ibn Marzuq said: 'Consider whether the first implies that the person who delays is committing a wrong action while the latter that he is not committing a wrong action.' I am not aware that what Ibn al-Hajib has related from Ibn al-Qussar – regarding the person who delays it to the *daruri* time – means that the person is guilty of disobedience. Indeed, Al-Mazari has narrated from Ibn al-Qussar that the threat of punishment does not apply to him but rather that he is committing a minor wrong action – and this is closer to the meaning of *makruh*."

NOTICE: al-Khurshi said, commenting on the words of Khalil 'in a state of *kufr*, apostasy': "The *'ulama* have deemed *kufr* an excuse under all circumstances – given that when one becomes Muslim one does so out of desire for Islam and one cuts oneself off from what has gone before."

USEFUL POINT: 1. Zarruq said in his *Naseeha*: "Among the things which blight the *salat* is delaying it to the middle of the *ikhtiyari* time or to the end of it, delaying it to the *daruri* time without an excuse or rushing to perform it." Ibn Zakari said in his commentary: "He has described delaying it as a blight because it is an indication of a lack of care in safeguarding the *salat* – which is commanded by Allah, exalted is He: 'Safeguard the *salat* – especially the middle one.'[1]

The *'ulama* have said that safeguarding it is performing it at the beginning of its time. In one hadith it is stated: 'The best of actions is the *salat* at the beginning of its time' and in another 'The beginning of the time is the contentment of Allah.' He has excluded, with his words 'without an excuse', those who have an excuse – it is preferred, for example, that those who have an impurity on their clothes and who entertain the hope of finding water within the time should delay the *salat*. His saying 'rushing to perform it' refer to someone who endeavours to do it on time but then has doubts as to whether it is indeed the time after having (thought he had) ascertained it: it is recommended a person delay the performance of the *salat* slightly until it is perfectly clear that the time has come and that any doubt or uncertainty (as to the time) is inconceivable."

2. Al-Khurshi has related from our Shaykh ar-Ramli in *Sharh al-Minhaj*: "It is sunna to wake up someone who is sleeping especially when the time is short. If he is acting in disobedience by deliberately sleeping, then the person who is aware of his state is under an obligation to wake him. Likewise, it is

---

1 al-Baqara – the Cow: 226

recommended to wake up a person sleeping in front of someone doing the *salat*, or in the front row, in the *mihrab*, on the roof; also after sunrise and before sunrise – as the earth cries out to Allah on account of his sleep; or after the *'Asr salat*; or someone who isolated and withdrawn alone in a house – for this is *makruh*; also to awaken a woman if she is lying down sleeping with her face facing the sky – according to al-Haleemi, or a man sleeping face downwards – which is a position hated by Allah, exalted is He."

The author of *al-Jami' as-Saghir* has stated: "Whoever sleeps after *'Asr* and his intellect becomes blocked, then he should not blame anyone but himself." Al-Munawi said in his *Sharh* that it is related in *al-Mizan* from Marwan at-Tatari: "I said to Laith ibn Sa'd: 'Do you sleep, O Abu'l-Harith, after *'Asr*? when Ibn Lahee'a has narrated to us from Aqeel and Makhoul from the Prophet, may the peace and blessings of Allah be upon him: "Whoever sleeps after *'Asr*...".' Then he replied: 'I would not abandon something in the hadith of Ibn Lahee'a from Aqeel which would be of benefit to me.'"

3. Ibn al-Hattab has related that al-Qarafi said "The legality of the 'fear *salat*' proves that the exigency of the *ikhtiyari* time is greater than the requirements to fully accomplish the pillars, to acquire a state of humility or to face the *qibla* – for otherwise the Legislator would permit delaying the *salat* for reasons of safety; and this, despite the fact that we are quite unaware of the exigencies of time, or of the elevated and noble nature of such exigencies. Similar to this is doing the *salat* with *tayammum* – which is proof that the exigency of the *ikhtiyari* time is greater than the requirement of purification with water."

I SAY: "It would appear that his mention of *ikhtiyari* time is support for Shaykh Khalil's (legal) preference expressed in his words: 'and delay until the latest time of *ikhtiyari* time and pray by gesture' and Allah knows best."

سُنَّتُها السُّورَةُ بَعْدَ الْوَاقِيَةِ

112 Its sunna are the sura after al-Waqiya (the Fatiha) – the Shield ...

Mayyara said: "About twenty-two sunnas are contained in these lines:

1. Reading a sura after reciting the Fatiha of the first and second *rak'a* in all the *salats*. This applies to the imam and the person doing the *salat* alone. As for the person behind the imam, if his *salat* is aloud, then the sunna is that he should listen – as mentioned below; if not, then it is recommended he recite – as mentioned below. The author of *at-Tawdih* said: 'The most evident judgement is that the recitation of a complete sura is either an aspect of excellence or a sunna of less intensity (than other sunnas) – the (basic) sunna being the

recitation of any part (of the Qur'an) with the Fatiha.' 'Ali ibn 'Abd as-Sadiq said: 'His saying "its sunnas" refers to the *fard salats* which are prescribed at specific times – as long as there is ample time. He excludes, by his words "*fard salats*", the *nawafil salats* – for this (recitation) is not a sunna in them but rather a recommendation; by his words 'prescribed at specific times', the *janaza salat* for it has no specific time; by his words 'ample time', the *salat* of a person whose time is short: it is forbidden him to recite (other than the Fatiha) if this would cause him to make the *salat* outside of its time.'"

BRANCH: Ibn al-Hattab said: "If a person knows with certainty that the time would elapse were he to recite a sura in a *rak'a*, then he must leave off reciting a sura; likewise if he thinks (this would occur) in all probability. Now another question remains to be examined: if a person is sure or thinks in all probability that part of the *salat* would fall outside of the time if he were to recite a sura in a *rak'a* then should he recite it – given that (strictly speaking) he has 'caught' the *salat* by the fact that he has caught a (single) *rak'a*? It has been said that he is obliged to desist from (reciting) the sura and restrict himself to reciting the Fatiha because performance of part of the *salat* outside of the time is not permitted. (A discussion of) this will come in the section on *witr*: if only enough time for two *rak'ats* remains before sunrise and he has not prayed the *witr*, then he must pray the *Subh salat* and leave off doing the *witr*, according to the most well known opinion; and this, despite the fact that sunnas are prescribed in all circumstances. However, if he performs one *rak'a* within the time and the time elapses, then he may recite a sura in the second *rak'a* – irrespective of whether he has read a sura in the first *rak'a* or not. This is the most evident judgement in my view, and Allah knows best."

Al-Mawwaq has related that Ibn Rushd said: "If he has read a sura silently to himself with the imam, then he may recite another, if he wishes or he may remain silent and make a *du'a* – and there is a licence in this."

ISSUE: al-Mawwaq has related – from Ibn 'Arafa – a narration of Ibn al-Qasim: "There is no prostration of negligence if one leaves off doing it in the *witr*", and Ibn Nafi' has narrated that there is no harm in just reciting 'the Mother of the Qur'an' (i.e. the Fatiha) in the *nafila salat*. I am not aware of what Ibn Shas and his followers have said." He has also related that Ibn Rushd said: "If a person fears thieves and so leaves off doing the *tashahhud* and two surahs, then he has committed an infringement, but his *salat* is accepted."

ISSUE: Ibn 'Arafa has related that al-Baji said: "It is *makruh* to recite a sura in the second (*rak'a*) whose position (in the Qur'an) occurs before that of the one recited in the first." 'Iyad said: "There is no difference of opinion that it is permitted but that it is *makruh* within one *rak'a*." Ibn al-Qasim has narrated: "This is part of the practice of the people, and this (practice within the one *rak'a*) and adherence to the order (of the Qur'an) are of equal weight." Ibn Habib, Ibn 'Abd al-Hakam and Mutarrif: "Adherence to the order is better." Ibn Rushd: "By my life, there is good in this for it is the practice of the people."

USEFUL POINT: al-Khurshi has related that the author of *al-Bayan* said: "Malik disliked pronunciation of the *hamza* in the recitation during the *salat*, and he preferred the 'easy reading' that is the recitation of Warsh. Al-Qarafi has narrated that he also disliked the *tarqeeq* – thinning the pronunciation with half closed mouth, the *tarkheem* – truncating the termination of a word, the *rawma* – the half pronounced vowel sound, the *ishmam* – giving a consonant a slight shade of a vowel sound after it, and other ways of recitation. The author of *Sharh al-Ajhouri* says: "Supplement: Inversion of the order of one (sura) is forbidden in one *rak'a*, or in one time, and the recitation of two or more suras out of order is *makruh* in the *salat*; or on other occasions – this is, if he intends it as recitation – but if he intends it only as *dhikr*, then the (judgement) is other than the former, and this has been mentioned by al-Wansharisi."

مَعَ الْقِيَامِ أَوَّلاً وَالثَّانِيَةُ

... together with the standing both for the first and the second

Mayyara said: "Secondly, the standing for the recitation of the first and second suras – here he is referring to the imam and the person doing the *salat* alone also; as for the person behind the imam, he is obliged to follow the imam. Ibn al-Hajib and the Shaykh have followed Khalil regarding (the judgement) when standing for a sunna sura[1]; and al-Mawwaq has narrated from al-Lakhmi and Ibn Rushd that the person who is incapable of standing for the sura should do *ruku'* immediately after the Fatiha. Ibn 'Arafa said: "... the standing for the sura for the person reciting it is *fard*, just as the *wudu'* is *fard* with respect to the *nafila salat*, – not a sunna as they have designated – otherwise he should sit and recite it."

جَهْرٌ وَسِرٌّ بِمَحَلِّ لَهُمَا

تَكْبِيرُهُ إِلاَّ الَّذِي تَقَدَّمَا

---

1   here there is a mistake in the text and the original of Mayyara has been referred to (*ad-Durr ath-Thameen*, p. 197)

113 (reciting) out loud or to oneself – in accordance with the particular *salat*, the saying of the *takbir* except that mentioned above,

Ibn 'Arafa said: "He is able to hear his own voice when saying it aloud, and others (near him can hear him) a little; the woman can be heard less than him – although she can hear herself."

NOTICE: 1. Muhammad ibn 'Abd al-Qadir said in *Sharh Hisn al-Haseen*: "See whether she is an old woman – in which case there would be no danger of seduction and the hearts would not incline to her. The most manifest judgement in her case is that she is (permitted to recite out loud) – which is the logical conclusion from his reasoning, and Allah knows best."

2. There is a difference of opinion as to whether someone who leaves off doing the sunnas deliberately invalidates the *salat* or not. Mayyara said: "There is a difference of opinion as to whether the person who leaves off doing a sunna deliberately (invalidates the *salat*) or not; and whether there is a prostration (of negligence)." Ibn al-Hattab said: "The manifest judgement is that the difference of opinion is in regard to the person performing the *salat* alone and the imam; as for the person behind the imam, the imam takes on this responsibility for him – for he said in *an-Nawadir*: 'It is stated in *Kitab Ibn al-Mawaz*: "The imam is not responsible for the *takbirat al-ihram*, the *salam*, the prostration or bowing but assumes responsibility for all the other *takbirs* and for any negligence, forgetfulness – or a sunna left out deliberately in which case he is committing a minor offence."

Mayyara said: "Fifth, the *takbirs* other than the *takbirat al-ihram* are sunna – as this latter is a *fard*, as mentioned above."

كُلُّ تَشَهُّدٍ جُلُوسٌ أَوَّلُ

وَالثَّانِي لَا مَا لِلسَّلَامِ يَحْصُلُ

114 each *tashahhud*, the first and second sitting – except for the part of it in which the *salam* is said (which is *fard*)

Mayyara said: "Sixth and seventh, the first and second *tashahhuds* (are sunnas) in whatever form they are said; as for the specific form of the sending of greetings to Allah (in the *tashahhud*) it is another sunna."

Eighth and ninth, the first sitting and the second – except for an amount of time in which the *salam* may be said for this part is the *fard*.

BRANCH: al-Mawwaq said: "...and in the *'Utbiyya* of Ibn al-Qasim, Malik said: 'Whoever forgets to do the *tashahhud* and the imam says the *salam*, then he should do the *tashahhud* but not do any *du'a* afterwards and should himself say the *salam*."

$$\text{وَسَمِعَ اللَّهُ لِمَنْ حَمِدَهُ}$$
$$\text{فِي الرَّفْعِ مِنْ رُكُوعِهِ أَوْرَدَهُ}$$

115 and the saying *sami'Allahu liman hamida* (Allah hears him who praises Him) on rising from the bowing – all of the above are (*mu'akkad*) sunnas

$$\text{الْفَذُّ وَالْإِمَامُ هَذَا أُكِّدَا}$$
$$\text{وَالْبَاقِ كَالْمَنْدُوبِ فِي الْحُكْمِ بَدَا}$$

116 of particular importance, that is for the person praying alone and the imam, while the following sunnas are (only) *mandoub* – recommended, and as such their judgement (does not require a prostration of negligence if omitted)

What is being indicated here is that these are the sunnas to which a particular importance are attached – for which one does a prostration of negligence if one leaves off doing them; as for any other sunnas which do not have this degree of importance, the judgement regarding the person who leaves off doing them is as the person who leaves off doing a recommended act: he does not have to compensate in any way.

$$\text{إِقَامَةٌ سُجُودُهُ عَلَى الْيَدَيْنْ}$$
$$\text{وَطَرَفِ الرِّجْلَيْنِ مِثْلُ الرُّكْبَتَيْنْ}$$

117 (namely) the *iqama*, prostrating on both hands and on the ends of the feet and on the knees

Mayyara said: "The eleventh (sunna), the *iqama* for the *salat*: it is a sunna for each *fard* irrespective of whether it is for a *salat* done on time or after its time, that is, in the case of a man; as for a woman, if she does the *iqama* to herself, then this is appropriate. It is permitted for someone who has not said the *adhan* to say the *iqama*, and the saying it to oneself – in the case of the person praying alone – is appropriate."

BRANCH: Ibn al-Qasim has narrated: "No one should do the *iqama* to himself after the *iqama* has been said and whoever does it has acted contrary to the sunna."

Khalil said: "If the woman says the *iqama* to herself, then this is appropriate." Al-Khurshi said: "What he means is not that doing it aloud is appropriate but rather that it is inappropriate and *makruh*, that is, contrary to what he said."

He has mentioned two opinions regarding the *adhan* of the woman: that is it prohibited and that it is disliked. The first is from the author of *al-Qawanin* and from ash-Shabeebi's commentary on the *Risala*, and the second is based on *ash-Shamil* in which it is stated: "Saying the *adhan* is disliked in the case of a woman", and this is also affirmed by another source: "The most evident judgement of the *madhhab* is that it is disliked that a woman say the *adhan*." Then he goes on to say: "…and the reasoning in the *madhhab* is that it is disliked for a woman to raise her voice when there is no need – for raising her voice may lead to corruption or a lack of modesty. The woman should say it so that only she herself and those directly near her can hear it – that is, when it should be said aloud, both for her *salat* and her saying *labbayk* (on the Hajj) and this has been narrated by al-Qarafi who has accepted its validity." Al-Hattab said: "It would be better to understand that its 'being disliked' is of the order of a prohibition."

Issue: Ibn al-Hattab said: "There is no harm in drinking water after the *iqama* and before the *salat*."

Useful point: Ibn al-Hattab said: "The author of *al-Bayan* has related that Malik said: 'The following has reached my notice: a man went on Hajj and sat down beside Saʻd ibn al-Musayyab. The muʻadhhin called the *adhan*. He then made to go out of the mosque, finding the wait for the *salat* too long but Saʻd said to him "Do not go out for it has reached my notice that whoever goes out after the *adhan* not intending to come back will be afflicted by something evil." Then the man sat down again. However, he still found waiting for the *iqama* too long and said: "I just feel he is imprisoning me." Then he went out and got on his mount but was thrown to the ground and broke his bones. News of this reached Ibn al-Musayyab who commented: "I thought that something hateful to him would afflict him."' Ibn Rushd said: 'Saʻd's saying "it has reached my notice" means that he has heard it from the Messenger of Allah, may the peace and blessings of Allah be upon him, for he would not have used this term when it was a matter of an opinion. What befell him was the punishment in this world: the person who goes out after the *adhan* from the mosque with the intention of not returning is giving preference to his needs in the *dunya* over the *salat* – for which the *adhan* has been made and for which the time has come for. If, however, he goes out not desiring it and refusing to do it, then he is a *munafiq.*' Sa'd Ibn al-Musayyab has also said: 'It has come to my notice that no one goes out from the mosque after the call to the *salat* but that he is either someone who wants to return or he is a *munafiq.*'"

The author of *at-Tamheed* has mentioned one the narrations of Malik from Abu Hurayra – how he saw a man who passed through a mosque and left it after the *adhan*: "This person is committing an act of disobedience – and is acting against (the judgement of) Abu'-Qasim." Abu 'Umar ibn 'Abd al-Barr said: "The *'ulama* are of a consensus that this hadith may be used as proof against the person who does not do the *salat* – when he is (already) in a state of purity; likewise, the person who prays alone – except in the case of those *salats* which are not repeated (like the *nafila*): thus it is not permitted that he leave the mosque, according to the *ijma'*, except if he goes out to do the *wudu'* and intends to return."

I SAY: "His saying 'it is not permitted – *la yahillu*' means it is *makruh* for him to go out – for the *makruh* is what is not halal, the halal being what is licit – *mubah*. The most manifest meaning of the hadith is prohibition; likewise, his saying 'he is acting against (the judgement of) Abu'-Qasim.' However, this is not so – for it is prohibited to leave after the *iqama* has started, but before it, it is permitted."

ISSUE: Ibn al-Hattab has related in the work *Masajid al-Qaba'il* from a narration of Ibn al-Qasim from the 'Book of the *Salat*': "Malik was asked about two men who entered a mosque and remained at the back: while the *iqama* for the *salat* was being said, they were still at the back, facing the imam; and when the imam said the takbirat'ul-*ihram*, they were talking. He replied: 'I consider that they should leave off talking when the imam says the *takbir*.' Ibn Rushd said: '... what he said is correct for their talking when the imam is performing the *salat* – when they themselves are in the mosque, approaching the *salat* – is clearly a disliked act: it is acting frivolously towards and shunning the *salat* intended.'"

I SAY: "Even worse than this is when they are talking while standing in the *salat* line – after the imam said the *Allahu akbar*; indeed, this is prohibited, if it confuses those doing the *salat* next to them. There is no doubt about this, and Allah knows best."

The author of *an-Nawadir* said that Malik said in *al-Mukhtasar*: "If the imam says the *takbirat al-ihram*, then no one should talk any more."

Mayyara said: "The twelfth is making the prostration on both hands, on the knees and on the tips of the feet. Ibn al-Hajib said: 'As for the hands, Sahnun said: "There are two opinions regarding (the judgement) if he does not raise them from the ground between the two (prostrations).'" In *at-Tawdih* it is stated that: 'On the basis of the judgement that not raising them invalidates (the *salat*), then prostration on them is an obligation; otherwise, it is not.' 'Ali ibn 'Abd as-Sadiq said: 'and the meaning of this is clear. Moreover, it is unlikely that anyone would argue that it does invalidate (the *salat*) for keeping one's hands on the ground would be contrary to 'relaxing a moment (*i'tidal*) in the sitting position' – thus any (judgement of) invalidity would be because of this absence of 'relaxing a moment in the sitting position', not because of the obligation to make the prostration on one's hands; and it is 'unlikely' in the sense that this is what comes to mind in the first instance – so be aware of this."

إِنْصَاتُ مُقْتَدٍ بِجَهْرٍ ثُمَّ رَدٌّ

عَلَى الْإِمَامِ وَالْيَسَارِ إِنْ أَحَدٌ

118 the person following (the imam) should listen to what (is recited) aloud, then answer (silently) the (*salam* of the) imam, and the person to the left if there is someone (there),

بِهِ وَزَائِدُ سُكُونٍ لِلْحُضُورِ

سُتْرَةُ غَيْرِ مُقْتَدٍ خَافَ الْمُرُورُ

119 prolonging the 'sitting still a moment' in order to be present, placing a *sutra* – in the case of someone not following (the imam), if he fears someone will pass in front of him

The thirteenth sunna: this refers to those following the imam listening to the recitation of the imam in *every salat* done aloud, that is, listening to the Fatiha and another sura – both those who can hear the imam and those who cannot, and irrespective of whether the imam leading the *salat* is someone who remains silent between the *takbir* and the Fatiha – like the Shafi'is – or not.

The fourteenth sunna: the person behind the imam should return the *salam* of the imam although the presence of the imam is not stipulated – if the person behind the imam arrives late, joining the *salat* after it has started, he says the *salam* even after the imam has left. Ibn Sa'dan said: "If the person following the imam is (actually standing) ahead of the imam, then he says the *salam* to the imam in the position he is in, directing his intention – in saying it – to the imam, but he should not turn to him.

What is to be understood from his saying 'then he returns the *salam* to the imam' is that this judgement applies in the case of the person behind the imam who catches one *rak'a* or more; otherwise he does not return it.

The fifteenth sunna: the person behind the imam should return the *salam* to the person to his left if there is someone (to his left); and if not, then he does not.

The sixteenth sunna: any prolonging of what is termed *tuma'neena* – being relaxed and at ease for a moment – is described in *at-Tawdih*: "The most evident judgement in the *madhhab* is that this *tuma'neena* is obligatory. What is obligatory is to remain still for a minimum period of time; there is a difference of opinion as to the person who extends the duration of this moment of stillness – as to whether it may be termed an obligation or an excellence.

This he has indicated with his words 'if one prolongs the sitting still a moment in order to be present' – that is, adds to the minimum amount (of time) necessary for the limbs to relax: this is the *tuma'neena*, as mentioned above, although I have not seen anyone else who has justified it by arguing it is to obtain 'presence of the heart' as Ibn 'Ashir said, may Allah have mercy on him.

His words 'placing a *sutra*' refer to an object blocking off the space in front of the person doing the *salat* – as long as he is not behind the imam – if he fears someone will pass in front of him.'

Mayyara said: "The seventeenth sunna applies to the imam or the person doing the *salat* alone."

Khalil said: "The *sutra* is for the imam or the person doing the *salat* alone if they fear someone will pass in front of them. It should be any clean, stable object – as long as it is not a distraction; of the width of a spear or length of an arm; but not an animal and not a single stone or a line (draw on the ground); nor a woman who is not closely related, and in the case of a *mahram* – who *is* closely related and whom it is not permitted to marry – there are two judgements. Anyone who passes in front of the person performing the *salat* is committing an offence if there is enough room for him to pass elsewhere; likewise, the person doing the *salat* who exposes himself (to such passers by and does not put up a *sutra*)." It is stated in the hadith: "The person doing the *salat* should place in front of him a *sutra* similar (in height) to the rear part of a saddle." It is narrated of Malik: "It should be the length of the bone of the forearm" and he has added "…and I prefer it be of a width common to most spears and lances" Ibn Sayyidihi said: "(The length of) an arm is considered to be the length of an average arm – between the elbow and the ends of the fingers."

Ibn al-Hattab has related that an-Naji said: "What he has mentioned in the book is the well-known judgement." Ibn al-Habib said: "It is permitted even if (the *sutra* is) lower in height than the rear part of a saddle or (thinner than) the thickness of a spear – this has been related by Ibn Rushd and Ibn Harun." There is no difference of opinion regarding al-Lakhmi words "it is permitted using (a *sutra* whose length is) the span of a hand" as this (length) approximates to the length of he bone of the forearm. Ibn 'Attab's words 'the length of the arm' – which he has related from Malik – probably refer to the length of the bone of the forearm; and the length narrated by others from Malik is of this order.

Then he goes on to relate that an-Naji said: "Our Shaykhs, that is Ibn 'Arafa and Abu Mahdi, have decided that the curtain normally used to cover a door may be used as a *sutra* – given that the cover afforded by this (curtain) is greater than that afforded by the length of the bone of the forearm; and likewise plants or fodder if they are amassed in a pile. What they have said regarding plants or fodder is clear but as for the curtain and the like, the most manifest judgement is that it is contrary (to the well-known judgement) because of its thinness."

Al-Mawwaq has related, commenting on his words 'and not an animal' that Ibn Rushd said: "If he uses a horse, mule or donkey as a *sutra* then he is committing an offence although the person who passes behind them is not guilty of a wrong action. However, there is no harm in a camel." It appears that he considered the cow and sheep as having the same judgement as the camel – but not the horse on account of its impurity.

Also on this subject is that related from Malik: "There is no harm if someone does his *salat* in front of the wall of a toilet or graveyard as long as the place (of his *salat*) is pure."

Al-Mawwaq has also said, commenting on his words 'a single stone', "Ibn 'Arafa said: 'It is disliked with a single stone.' Ibn Bashir said: 'If the *sutra* is a single object like a stone or stick then one should place it to the right side lest it appear as an idol – if the Prophet, may the peace and blessings of Allah be upon him, made his *salat* in front of such a object, he would place it to his right or left and not turn towards it.' Also connected to this subject (is the judgement): "There is no good in placing a *mus-haf* in the direction of the *qibla*."

Among the excellent aspects (of this sunna), according to 'Iyad, is the close proximity of the *sutra*. It is recorded in the *Sahih* that between the place where the Prophet, may the peace and blessings of Allah be upon him, was praying and a wall was a space through which a sheep could pass. Al-Qubab has defined this as "a space such that the person performing the *salat* may ward off the person passing in front of him with this hand."

Commenting on Khalil's words '...a woman who is not closely related, and there are two opinions in the case of the woman who is a *mahram*', al-Mawwaq has related that al-Jilab said: "A man should not take a woman as a *sutra* unless she is a *mahram* in relation to him, but there is no harm in taking a child as a *sutra* if he keeps still and stays in one place, not moving from it." Ash-Shaykh has narrated: "A wadi – a river gully – water or fire should not be taken as sutras." 'Ali has narrated: "... nor a person who is sleeping or people sitting in a circle." Ibn al-Qasim said: "There is no harm in making the *salat* towards a man's back but not that of a woman who is not closely related to him." Ibn Qasim has also narrated: "It is permitted to make the *salat* in an elevated place as long as the heads of the people are not visible; if not he must place a *sutra*, although Malik prefers there be a *sutra* in any case." There is no harm if a person, intending to make up (part of the *salat*) after the imam said the *salam*, moves to a nearby column in front of him – or to the right, to the left, or moves back a little – in order to take it as a *sutra* as long as it is nearby; if some distance away, he should get up and warn any passers by (of his intention) if he can." Ibn Nafi' has narrated that this should be done "with courtesy" and relates how on one occasion "a man broke the nose of another and 'Uthman said to him: 'If you had left him alone it would have been better.'" Ibn Sha'ban said: "The compensation to be paid in such an incident is due from the tribe and family of the person who did it." Ashhab said: "...even after he has indicated (his intention to the person passing in front of him)." Ibn 'Arafa said: "Ashhab's judgement has found acceptance among the (ulama)." Ibn al-'Arabi said: "The person doing the *salat* is entitled to a space enabling him to bow and prostrate." The author of *al-Majmu'a* said: "If the imam takes a spear as a *sutra* and it falls down, then he should set it up again if it is light (and easy to restore to its former position). If, however, it would interfere with his *salat*, then he should leave it." Malik said: "Nothing passing in front of the person doing the *salat* breaks his *salat*, neither a menstruating woman, a donkey, a black dog or anything else." Malik has also said: "It is not disliked that a man pass along the rows while the imam is leading the *salat* for the imam stands as the *sutra* for them even if they are not (standing) as close (as normally required) to the *sutra*." Again, Malik said: "If there is a man standing to the right and one to the left of the person doing the *salat*, and the one on the right wants to hand an article of clothing to the one on his left (by passing) in front of him, then it would not be right for him to do so." Ibn al-Qasim said: "He should also not speak to him."

Al-Ubbi related in *Sharh Muslim* – at the point where he says 'and his companions were talking' – that 'Iyad said: "Their talking in the presence of someone performing the *salat* other than in a mosque (is permitted) as long as those talking are not standing on either side of him (i.e. one to his right and one to his left)." An-Nawawi said: "… and this is only (permitted) as long as they do not disturb him."

In the *Mudawwana* he says: "The person standing to the right of the person doing the *salat* should not pass (anything) to someone to the left of the person performing the *salat*."

Ibn al-Hattab said: "In the *Masa'il Ibn Qudah* he states: "If the person doing the *salat* is distracted by something in front of him which prevents him from making the prostration he should remove it, and if it is to his right, he should move it away – but not push it away to the left of him as it would be like a 'person passing' in front of him."

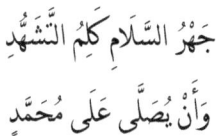

120 saying the *salam* aloud, the (particular) wording of the *tashahhud*, and the *salat* on Muhammad,

Az-Zurqani, commenting on Khalil words 'Saying out loud the final *salam* of *tahlil* (marking the end of the state of '*ihram*' of the *salat*') only' said that his saying 'only' excludes the saying (aloud) of any other *salam* (to his left) – which may be done, as a sunna, by the person behind the imam. Rather, it is not to be said aloud, but to himself – as is stated in (the work of) al-Hattab. Likewise, it is recommended that all the *takbirs* of the *salat* – in the case of the person performing it alone or behind the imam – be done silently; but not in the case of the imam – for, as al-Lakhmi says, it is recommended that he say them aloud, as well as the *sami' allahu liman hamida* so as those behind may follow in the bowing and prostration. It is also recommended that every person doing the *salat* should do the *takbirat al-ihram* aloud."

The nineteenth sunna is the '*tashahhud*' which refers to the text beginning with *at-tahiyyatu lillah*…., although it has also been said that it is recommended (rather than a sunna).

NOTICE: The author of *Ghayat al-Amani* said: "One of the commentators said that the ordinary people often pronounce it *at-tahiyatu lillah* – with an extra *alif* after the initial *ta'* and with only one *y* rather than two, and the shafi'is have clearly stated that the *salat* is rendered invalid through such (mispronunciation) – although we have not found any such texts from the scholars of this *madhhab* – so examine this."

I say: "One of my contemporaries said: 'The people of the *madhhab* have clearly prescribed what is required for the validity of the *salat* and have stated that, according to the preferred judgement, mispronunciation in the recitation does not invalidate it, even if it is during the Fatiha. They have also stated that a mispronunciation of the '*salam*' is of the same order as one made during the Fatiha and that mispronouncing any of the words of *dhikr* do not invalidate the *salat*." Examine what he said equitably – for surely being equitable is the business of the noble; and envy is a well known quality of the rabble; and the overflowing generosity of Allah is wide: often real victory is granted by Allah not to the one who overcomes but to the one who is overcome.

USEFUL POINT: The author of *Ghayat al-Amani* said, commenting on the words of the *Risala* 'and I seek refuge with You from the trial during life and after death, from the ordeal of the grave, the ordeal of the Massih ad-Dajjal': "Al-Aqfahisi said: 'The trial during this life is *kufr*.' However, it is also said to refer to a change of one's state (from being a Muslim to a *kafir*) at death. The ordeal of the grave refers to the questioning of the two angels, that is, the ordeal of being unable to answer with certainty when questioned by the two angels. We have mentioned this in the knowledge that those killed *shaheed* are not interrogated in their graves. The ordeal of the Masih ad-Dajjal will be a tremendous affair: he will claim lordship and all provision will be in his hands; those who follow him will be *kuffar*; he will travel all over the world, except to Makka and Madina and he will remain in the world forty days."

Mayyara said: "The twentieth sunna is the sending of peace and blessings on the Prophet, may the peace and blessings of Allah be upon him, in the last *tashahhud*, although it has also been said that it is (only) recommended, like the text of the *tashahhud*."

The Adhan

سُنَّ الْأَذَانُ لِجَمَاعَةٍ أَتَتْ

فَرْضاً بِوَقْتِهِ وَغَيْراً طَلَبَتْ

121 the *adhan* for the *fard salat* performed in the *jama'a* – in order to call others to it – is a(nother) sunna, when the time comes,

MAYYARA said[1]: "The twenty first sunna: He excludes the single person with his words 'in a *jama'a*' for it is not a sunna for him unless he is travelling – in which case it is recommended that he call the *adhan* if he is in open country. This (sunna) is based on the hadith of Abu Sa'id al-Khudri who related that the Prophet, may the peace and blessings of Allah be upon him, said to 'Abdallah ibn Zayd: 'If you are with your sheep and goats in your pasture land and you call the *adhan* for the *salat*, then raise your voice, for no man or jinn hears the call from a distance but that he will bear witness (to his action) for him on the Day of Raising Up.' Abu Sa'd: 'I have heard this (directly) from the Messenger of Allah, may the peace and blessing of Allah be upon him.' Ibn 'Arafa has related that Ibn Habib said: 'The person who is by himself and resident, and the isolated group do not have to call the *adhan*.' Malik said: 'If, however, they do call the *adhan*, then this is a praiseworthy action.' Abu 'Umar has narrated: 'I dislike that the person who is alone leaves off doing it.' Ibn Habib considered that it was a recommended action for the person alone, while Malik that it was recommended for the person alone on a journey and anyone else in open country – based on the narration to this effect. Ibn Bashir and Ibn al-Hajib considered the *adhan* to be recommended for the person who is travelling alone and anyone in open country for the benefit of those lagging behind. With his words 'to call others to it' he is specifying those who have not been called to it. Ibn al-Hajib said that if they do not intend to call them to the *salat*, then both 'they should not call the *adhan*' as

---

1 There are numerous mistakes in this text – recourse has been had to the original of Mayyara.

well as 'if they call the *adhan*, it is a good action' has been recorded. It has been said by some that there is a difference of opinion while others have asserted that there is no difference of opinion. That there is a difference of opinion is manifest – and this is attributed to al-Lakhmi and al-Mazari; and that there is agreement is attributed to Ibn Bashir who said: 'Rejection of it is understood as a rejection of its being a sunna of particular importance not a rejection of it as being a good action for Ibn 'Arafa has mentioned that al-Lakhmi has narrated from Ibn Habib: "Whoever makes the *salat* in his house and leads a group for the *salat* which is not in the mosque, then they do not have to call an *adhan*; but as for the cities, and places of settlement, if a *janaza* takes place and the *salat* is about to be done, then the *adhan* and the *iqama* is called." The gist of what Ibn 'Arafa has narrated is that the *adhan* is recommended for anyone in open country, irrespective of whether alone or in a group, or whether travelling or not, and Allah knows best.'"

Commenting on the words of Khalil '...the *adhan* of the person alone if travelling', al-Khurshi said: "The meaning of this is that the *adhan* is recommended for the person who is alone if travelling from where he is resident, that is, if he is in open country. This is based on a narration from al-Bukhari from Abu Sa'd who said to 'Abdallah ibn 'Abd ar-Rahman ibn Sa'sa'a: 'I see that you like sheep and goats and the countryside: if you are amongst your sheep and goats or in your pasture land in the countryside and you call the *adhan* for the *salat*, then raise your voice when calling for no jinn, man or anything else hears the voice of the *mu'adhdhin* – however great the distance – but that they bear witness for him on the Day of Raising Up.' Abu Sa'd also added: 'I heard this from the Messenger of Allah, may the peace and blessings of Allah be upon him.' It is also based on the narration of the *Muwatta*' from Sa'd ibn al-Musayyab who used to say: 'Whoever does the *salat* in open countryside, then an angel prays to his right and another to his left, and when he calls the *adhan*, makes the *iqama* and does the *salat*, then angels equal in vastness to the mountains pray behind him.' Our mentioning that the text 'I see that you love sheep and goats and the open countryside...' is part of the narration of Abu Sa'd to 'Abdallah ibn 'Abd ar-Rahman ibn Sa'sa'a is correct, as Ibn as-Salah, an-Nawawi and others have affirmed this. Those who have imagined it as a hadith of the Prophet, may the peace and blessings of Allah be upon him, have attributed it to Abu Sa'd (– rather than via Ibn Sa'sa'a)."

'Ali ibn 'Abd as-Sadiq said: "It is only valid from a Muslim not a *kafir*; as to whether it is valid when there is a Muslim with him, our Shaykh has declared the first (to be true); he should be of sound mind, not mad; male not female;

of age, not a child, although there is a difference of opinion in this; and it is recommended that he be in a state of purity, and in the case of the person in *janaba*, there is a difference of opinion: it has been said both that he may and he may not; Abu Muhammad ash-Shabeebi has given a *fatwa* affirming the first while 'Isa ibn Naji has disapproved of this saying: '…as it is *dhikr*, and there is agreement that no kind of *dhikr* can be prohibited (when in this state) other than the Qur'an.'"

Khalil has added to what is recommended saying: "…(the person hearing the *adhan*) should repeat (after the *mu'adhdhin*) up to the end of the double declaration of the *shahadas* (in a low voice) – even if he is doing a *nafila salat*, but not for the *fard*." Al-Khurshi said: "…he should not repeat during this (*fard*); and it is permitted to speak during the *adhan*: the Companions used to speak during the *adhan* and imam Malik would speak with his companions on the day of *jumu'a* while the imam was sitting on the minbar prior to the *adhan* and would only stop when the imam began his *khutba*, and Allah knows best."

I say: "The meaning of his words 'and it is permitted to speak during the *adhan*' is that it is permitted for someone other than the *mu'adhdhin* while the latter is making the *adhan* – not that it is permitted for the *mu'adhdhin* to speak while making the call, and Allah knows best."

Branch: Ibn al-Hattab said: "As for the *adhan* of the person who is mounted, it is permitted, and this is stated in the *Mudawwana*, as his status is understood to be the same as the person standing – this is stated by Ibn Farhun; indeed, he is in a higher position and may be more easily heard."

Useful point

1. Mayyara and Ibn al-Hattab have said: "Some *mu'adhdhins* emphasise certain places (in the *adhan*), for example, they lengthen the *ba'* of *akbar* such that it becomes *akbaar* and *akbaar* is the plural of *kabar*, meaning a drum, resulting in a phrase amounting to *kufr*; another example, is that they extend the beginning of the *shahada* so that it resembles the interrogative form[1] – when what is required is a statement of fact, not a petition; and some also do this when saying the divine name;[2] or they pause over the *la ilaha*, and this is a mistake; also some of them do not elide the nunation at the end of Muhammad into a *ra'*, and this is counted as a minor mispronunciation by those conversant with the rules of recitation; also some do not pronounce the *ha'* in *hayya 'ala's-salat* nor the *ha'* in *hayya 'ala'l-falah* resulting in a sound whose meaning approximates to 'burn in the Fire' in the case of the first, and to a phrase without meaning in the

1   Meaning *aashhadu* rather than *ashhadu*, the former meaning "Do I witness?" Ed.
2   Thus *Aallahu akbar* means "Is Allah greater?" Ed.

second." Zarruq added: "…the elongation of the *hamza* or the pronunciation of it with a *sukun* (of vowellessness) in *akbar* and pronouncing the nun of *an la-ilaha illa'llah* with an 'a' (that, is the vowel sign *fatha*, rendering it *ana la-ilaha*…); and extending the *ha'* of *ilaha* and pronouncing it with a *sukun* or nunation, or pronouncing an extra *ha'* after the *ha'* of *ilah*; or saying Muhammad with a *u* (- *Muhummad* -), and lengthening the *hayya* or pronouncing only one *y* (*haya*); or changing the *hamza* of *akbar* into a *waw* (*wakbar*) – although they have deemed it a minor fault in the *takbirat al-ihram* and so here it must be counted even less of a fault." I say: "One thing remains which has not been pointed out as far I can see, namely the *ishba'* – the prolonging of the vowel sound at the point of connection of two words (*al-wasl*); however, if one pauses over it at the end of the *adhan* and the *iqama*, then the prolongation (*madd*) is permitted because of the conjunction of two vowelless consonants. Indeed Ibn Jazari in the *Bab al-madd wa'l-qasr* has mentioned that 'the Arabs customarily pronounce the madd when making *du'a*, when seeking help of Allah (*istighatha*) and when exaggerating negation of anything; indeed they introduce the madd on other occasions for other than this reason. I have seen in the *Kitab al-Mawaqeet* that the shortening of the *alif* in the name Allah is not permitted, except in poetry and that exaggeration of its madd is *makruh*, that is a violation of the limits of the *madd*.'"

2. Al-Munawi said, commenting on the words 'If the *adhan* is said in a town, then Allah will protect it from affliction that day': "Imam ar-Razi said in *al-Israr* that the water (of the Tigris) at Baghdad increased so much that it threatened to flood. Then he saw one of the *Salihun* and it was as if he were standing at the side of the river saying 'There is no power, no strength except by Allah, may Baghdad be flooded.' Two people came and one said to the man: 'What did you command should happen?' He replied: 'that Baghdad be flooded but then I negated the command.' He said: 'Why?' The man replied: 'The angels have transmitted that yesterday seven hundred vaginas were deflowered through haram relations and that Allah became angry and commanded it to be flooded. However the angels then transmitted that seven hundred *adhans* and *iqamas* had been made on the morning of that day and Allah forgave the first (seven hundred violations) for the second (seven hundred good actions).'"

3. The author of *al-Jami' as-Saghir* said: "If the *mu'adhdhin* begins the *adhan*, the Lord places His hand on his head, keeping it there until he finishes his *adhan*. He then forgives him to the extent of the reach of his voice. When he has finished, the Lord says: 'My slave has spoken the truth and has borne witness with the witnessing of truth – so receive the good news.'"

Al-Munawi said: "The 'hand' is a metaphor for the generous bestowal of mercy, pure goodness and *baraka*. Thus is mentioned in the *Muhtasib*. It should be understood as having general validity, and the overflowing generosity of Allah is vast."

Ibn al-Hattab said: "The meaning of this is that if his wrong actions were of physical proportion, then an amount equal to the distance between him and the reach of his voice would be forgiven him. It has also been said that mercy will extend to him as great as the extent of his *adhan*. Al-Khatabi said: 'It means that the forgiveness of Allah, exalted is He, will be total (in his case) if he raises his voice as much as possible, in other words the greater he raises his voice, the greater will be his forgiveness.'"

4. Ibn al-Hattab has related that the author of *al-Masa'il al-Malquta* said: "The purified *salih*, the truthful *faqih*, the most sufficient, the *mujtahid*, the neighbour of the Sacred Mosque, the divested one, the man of the earth, Sadr ad-Deen ibn ash-Shaykh as-Salih Baha' ad-Deen 'Uthman ibn 'Ali al-Farsi, may Allah protect him, said: 'I met the Shaykh, the noted scholar of Islamic sciences, the *mufassir*, the *muhaddith* who is famed for his excellence of character, Nur ad-Deen al-Khurasani in the town of Shiraz. I was with him at the time of the *adhan*. When he heard the *mu'adhdhin* say 'I bear witness that Muhammad is the Messenger of Allah', the Shaykh kissed the thumbs of his hands and wiped once over his eyebrows with his nails at each saying of the *shahada*, starting from the inner corner of the eye and ending with the outer corner of the eye at the temples. I asked him about this and he replied: "I used to do it – although this practice of mine was not based on any hadith. However, when I left off doing it, my eyes became afflicted by illness. Then I saw the Messenger of Allah, may the peace and blessings of Allah be upon him, in my sleep and he said: 'Why have you left off wiping over your eyes when remembering me at the time of the *adhan*? if you want your eyes to get better, then start wiping them again' – or words to this effect. On awaking, I wiped them and my eyes got better, and the illness has never returned to this day."'"

5. In the *Sahih* of al-Bukhari it is narrated that the Messenger of Allah, may the peace and blessings of Allah be upon him, said: "Whoever, when hearing the *adhan*, says:

اَللَّهُمَّ رَبَّ هَذِهِ الدَّعْوَةِ التَّامَّةِ وَالصَّلَاةِ الْقَائِمَةِ ءَاتِ مُحَمَّداً الْوَسِيلَةَ وَالْفَضِيلَةَ

وَابْعَثْهُ مَقَاماً مَحْمُوداً الَّذِي وَعَدتَّهُ

Allahumma rabba hadhihi'd-da'wati't-tammati wa's-salati'l-qa'ima ati Muhammadun al-waseela wa'l-fadeela wa'b'ath-hu maqaman mahmoudan alladhi wa'adtahu – 'O Allah, the Lord of this perfect call and of this salat which is being established, give Muhammad the means and grant him excellence and raise him to the al-Maqam al-Mahmud as You have promised him' – then my interceding for him will be assured on the Day of Raising Up.

Ibn Hajar said: "'Iyad has related from one of his Shaykhs that this applies in particular to someone who expressly remembers and wishes for the exalted presence of the Prophet, may the peace and blessings of Allah be upon him – not to someone who merely does it for the reward or the like. However, this is an arbitrary, unsatisfactory judgement. If he had excluded, for example, the negligent, the frivolous, then it would have been more fitting."

6. The author of *as-Sira al-Halabiya* said: "As-Suyuti was asked, may Allah have mercy on him, whether it has been transmitted that Bilal, may Allah be pleased with him, or any others, had made the *adhan* in Makka before the hijra and he answered, may Allah have mercy on him, that it had, albeit via weak, unreliable chains of transmission. The well known view – which is considered as correct by most of the *'ulama* and which is corroborated by *sahih hadith* – is that the *adhan* was instigated after the hijra and that neither Bilal nor any other person called the *adhan* before this. Ibn Hajar has also affirmed this, mentioning that in fact there are no traditions of a *sahih* rank indicating that the *adhan* was first called in Makka before the hijra."

7. The author of *as-Sira al-Halabiya* also said: "It is transmitted from Abbas, may Allah be pleased with him, who said there was a man from the Jews, a trader – although another transmission from as-Suddi reports him as being from the Christians – in Madina who heard the *mu'adhdhins* say 'I bear witness that Muhammad is the Messenger of Allah, may the peace and blessings of Allah be upon him, may Allah requite the one who lies' and in another report '…may Allah burn the one who lies.' Then his servant entered with a lighted brand while he was asleep and a spark fell and set fire to the house and burnt the people in it."

8. al-Fakihani said in *al-'Umda* that 'Iyad said: "Know that the *adhan* is an all-encompassing expression of *'aqida* and iman, comprising both an intellectual affirmation and an acceptance of transmitted knowledge: initially, it is an affirmation of the Essence and this necessarily implies, in turn, an affirmation of His beauty and goodness, and also of *tanzih*, that is, a disassociating of Him from the opposite (of these two things) – and this (is achieved), by means of pronouncing *'Allahu akbar'* for this expression, despite its brevity, indicates all we have mentioned. Then the person (calling the *adhan*) affirms the absolute Oneness of Allah, and rejects the opposite of this, that is any possibility of

His being associated with another. This is the pillar of Iman and *tawhid* and precedes all other duties in the deen. Then he declares his affirmation of Prophethood, bearing witness to his submission to our Prophet, may the peace and blessings of Allah be upon him. This is a principle of great import – after the bearing witness to His unity: it is said after the declaration of *tawhid* as it is one of the actions which is possible (rather then inevitably necessary). The declaration of *tawhid*, however, is only concerned with necessary fundamentals (with respect to Him); there then follow the additional principles of *'aqida* arrived at by means of the intellect – regarding what is obligatory, what is impossible and what is permitted of Allah, exalted is He. Then the *adhan* calls to the act of worship, the *salat*, and makes mention of it after the affirmation of Prophethood as knowledge of the obligatory nature (of the *salat*) comes from the Prophet, may the peace and blessing of Allah be upon him, not from the intellect. Then the *adhan* calls to success (*hayya 'ala'l-falah*), and this is the last part of the *'aqida* with respect to iman. This is then repeated with the saying of the *iqama* in order to make known that the *salat* is starting. This repetition also implies a further affirmation of Iman, and a confirmation with the heart, tongue and hand at the outset of the worship so that the person performing the *salat* enters upon the act of worship fully aware of its implications, with insight as to his own Iman, and conscious of the enormity of what he is embarking on, of the vastness of the Real which is the object of his worship and of the generous reward he may expect."

وَقَصْرُ مَنْ سَافَرَ أَرْبَعَ بُرُدْ

ظُهْراً عِشاً عَصْراً إِلَى حِينَ يَعُدْ

122 Shortening the *salat* for the traveller for a distance of four *bareeds*,[1] for Dhuhr, 'Isha and 'Asr until he returns

مِمَّا وَرَى السُّكْنَى إِلَيْهِ إِنْ قَدِمْ

مُقِيمُ أَرْبَعَةِ أَيَّامٍ يُتِمّْ

123 to within (the confines of) a settled place as long as he does not intend to stay somewhere (on his journey) for more than four days, in which

---

1 A *bareed* is twelve Arab miles. Each 'Arab' mile is 1973 metres; 48 miles would be 93,703 kilometres.

case he does the *salat* in full

Mayyara said: "The twenty second sunna: the shortening of the *salats* of four *rak'ats*, that is, those of *Dhuhr*, *'Asr*, and *'Isha* is for the person travelling at least four *bareeds*, in which case he prays two *rak'ats* and continues to do the shortened *salat* until he returns from his journey – as long as he does not intend to take up residence for four complete days; if he does, then he should do it in full. The shortening of the *salat* begins from after the settled areas and it ends on one's return to them after one's journey. Note that in the (Arabic text the) *mimma* indicates the beginning point of one's destination and *wara'* the end point of the destination."

Then he goes on to say: "The narrations which speak of 'two days' or 'a day and a night' are based on these four *bareeds*, according to the people who know." Then he continues: "(The *salat* of travelling) is conditional upon the journey having already started – as the principle (in *fiqh*) states that intention alone does not bring about a change to the basic judgement (governing an act of worship – in this case the full *salat* of four *rak'ats*) unless accompanied by a (corresponding) action."

Ibn al-Hattab said that the author of *at-Taraz* said: "If the traveller – after travelling some distance away from his family – makes an intention to return after starting out but then subsequently makes another intention to set out on the journey, then he should not do the shortened *salat* until he has departed from the place he is in." The author of *al-Mawaziya* said: "This is clear – for he begins the journey (afresh) from where he is."

He has also said, regarding the person who sees off travellers – and who is then asked by them to be the imam and who makes the intention to travel before doing the *takbirat al-ihram*: "He should pray the *salat* of a resident with them."

'Ali ibn 'Abd as-Sadiq, confirming the words of the author said: "Four *bareeds* constitutes the distance for the traveller and permits him to shorten (the *salat*). A *bareed* is four farsakhs and a farsakh is three miles: one *bareed* is therefore twelve miles and four *bareeds* is sixteen farsakhs or forty eight miles. There are two views on this matter: either that it is a (fixed) limit – and this is what is the most evident judgement of the *Mudawwana* – or it is an approximate reckoning – and this is the opinion of "Ta-ta". A mile is a thousand fathoms (*ba'a*) and a fathom is the distance between outstretched arms. Al-Baji said: 'This has been said by some although it has also been said that it is three thousand five hundred cubits – this has been narrated by our Shaykh from *'Ayn-Jeem*.' Ibn 'Abd al-Barr said: 'This is the most correct that has been said about it.' Then he goes on to say, commenting on his words 'until his return': '...that is, he continues to shorten the *salat* until he returns from his journey and reaches the place he started from.' The like has also been said by Ibn al-Hajib and in *al-Mukhtasar*. Muhammad ibn 'Abd as-Salam said: 'It is the best, although weak — even if it is the preferred judgement of these Shaykhs. The *madhhab* holds that he should continue to shorten the *salat* until he enters inside the walls of the town, that is, amongst the houses of a settled area or within less than a mile, according to the most evident judgement of the *Mudawwana* and the *Risala*, as Shaykh Salim as-Sanhouri and others have said; and this is also accepted by our Shaykh.'"

BRANCH: an-Nafrawi said, commenting on the words of the *Risala* '... he should continue to shorten the *salat* until he reaches the houses of the settled area or within less than a mile': "What is evident from this is that this includes entering orchards where people are living or any area covered by this judgement, like entering a settled region or being near it. This is because one would not consider such (areas) separate from it — according with what is accepted by Ibn Naji. However this is contrary to his Shaykh who reckons being 'near to it' does constitute a separation or a distance. When giving his class, 'Ayn-Jeem would insist that the correct judgement was that of Ibn Naji, arguing that there is no sense in reckoning it as separate while stipulating that one must cross over it for the shortening of the *salat* to be permitted: to stipulate that one must go beyond it would be treating it not as a separate distance between the town proper and the beginning of the highway but as part of the town."

BRANCH: Mayyara has related that al-Mawwaq said: "Examine the case of the *kafir* who intends to travel four *bareeds* and then becomes Muslim, having travelled half of the distance. Ibn 'Arafa has related from as-Sulaymaniya that he should not shorten the *salat*. Al-Lakhmi said: 'The same applies in the case of the person who reaches puberty.' He has also said: '...and in the case of the menstruating woman, there is a difference of opinion.'

Examine too a similar incident about which there is a difference of opinion amongst the Shaykhs of our time, namely, regarding a group who travel and shorten the *salat* and who see the new moon of the month of Ramadan when they are still twenty four miles from their destination on the return journey to their town (just before sunrise). It appears to me that they should not fast (the coming day) since if shortening the *salat* is permitted so is breaking the fast. The reason for their shortening is their travelling at night and for this (reason alone) they should not fast the following morning. However, (it is argued), strictly speaking, they should still fast if the distance remaining to be covered to their town (on sighting the moon) is less, as in this case, than the distance for which it is permitted to shorten the *salat*."

'Ali ibn 'Abd as-Sadiq has related from al-Khudayri that the judgement of the menstruating woman is certainly the same as that of the child (who attains to puberty) and the *kafir* (who becomes Muslim).

NOTICE: an-Nafrawi said: "It appears that puberty does not constitute a reason for shortening the *salat* as no one has recorded a clear statement to this effect. Rather there has been a discussion amongst some of the Shaykhs on this matter. What is apparent, however, is that shortening the *salat* is permitted in the case of children as the licence (to shorten) has been granted (by Allah) as an alleviation (of the difficulty) for the traveller – and the child who is travelling should be the first to benefit from such a dispensation, over and above the person who has just reached puberty (and is now of age); moreover the four-*rak'a salats* obligatory on the adult are reduced by a half (through this dispensation) and it would be hard to comprehend how one could reduce by half an obligation but not do likewise in the case of the *salat* of the child which is only recommended. Al-Qarafi said: 'It is true that children are not addressed by the obligations (of the *salat*) and the things which are haram. However, if it is said that the dispensation is particular to the person who is of age, then judgement that it is licit to eat carrion when there is a pressing need would contradict this: as far as we know, no one has argued that this (meat) is haram for the person who is under age when he has a pressing need (to eat) – and so the judgement is clear.'"

ISSUE: Khalil said: "(The shortening of the *salat*) ends when re-entering his land or (entering) the place where only his wife, with whom he had consummated the marriage, resides – even if constrained (to enter) because of the force of the wind (driving the boat), as long, that is, as one has the intention to enter it and as long as the distance between this (place where he makes the intention) and the place (he intends to enter) does not constitute the (legal) distance (necessitating the shortening of the *salat*)." Ibn al-Hattab said that the author of *at-Tawdih* said: "The journey is interrupted by entering one's place of permanent residence as long as one actually enters it or has the intention to enter it; but not if one is crossing it."

He has also said, commenting on his words 'when one has the intention to enter it – as long as the distance between this (place where he makes the intention) and the place (he intends to enter) does not constitute the (legal) distance (necessitating the shortening of the *salat*)': "If this distance amounts to four *bareeds* he shortens the *salat*, otherwise he does not. Four scenarios may be imagined: he shortens the *salat* before it and after it – if the distance before it is the legal distance necessitating this shortening; the opposite, when the distance does not constitute the legal distance permitting the shortening; shortening before but not after, when the distance is such that it permits the shortening before but not after; and the opposite of this latter – and this is clear, and Allah knows best."

The author of *al-Irshad* said: "If, in the course of this distance, he passes by his people, then what is taken into consideration is the distance (he will travel) when continuing on beyond (the place) his family (resides). Al-Buhairi said in his commentary: '…that is, if the distance he will travel after (seeing) them is four *bareeds*, then he should shorten (the *salat*); if less, then he does not.' What the author means by 'passing by them' is that he goes in to visit them for just passing by them would not in itself annul the judgement of (shortening the *salat* when) travelling; rather, what interrupts it is stopping over with them – and the author of *al-Muqaddimat* and others have also indicated this. Indeed, the intention of going in to visit them annuls the judgement of travelling even if this intention is made during the journey – unless between him and them is still a distance permitting the shortening of the *salat*. His words 'even if this intention is made during the journey' is contrary to what has been mentioned from Ibn al-Hattab; al-Khurshi has narrated two judgements – so examine them in his Kabir."

The author of *al-Mi'yar* has related from al-Mawwaq that 'Ali said – with regard to a woman who travelled to a place and shortened the *salat* to it: "If she has not resolved to remain there and her husband goes out to stay with her, then they should shorten (the *salat*) as it is not there permanent home and they do not intend to stay."

Issue: It is also stated in *al-Mi'yar* from Ibn Lubb: "As for the matter of the traveller coming to the end of his shortening of the *salat* I have said: 'He should do his *salat* in full if he is in doubt as to the length of his stay there: effectively he has come to the end of his journey and the return is a renewed journeying. This is different than when he is in the middle of his journey and has doubts as to the length of his stay – in this case he should continue with the shortening of the *salat* as this is his intention. This is stated explicitly in the discussion of al-Lakhmi and others." He has also said in another place: "Ibn Siraj was asked as to whether the traveller who stays in a place not knowing how long he will remain there should keep to his shortening of the *salat* and he replied: 'If the place is situated on the same path as his journey, then he should shorten for the period of his stay; if it is the end of his journey, then he should do it in full.'"

I say: "..and there is a difference of opinion regarding this reply. What has been stated explicitly is that he should not interrupt his shortening of the *salat* unless he makes the intention to stay for four days – examine Ibn Yunus, al-Jilab and *at-Talqeen*."

I SAY: "Al-Mawwaq, commenting on Khalil's words '...and if his journeying is delayed' said: "Ibn 'Arafa and al-Lakhmi have both transmitted what corresponds to the *fatwa* of Ibn Lubb and Ibn Siraj."

ISSUE: al-Mawwaq, commenting on the words of Khalil 'when on the outward journey' said: "Ibn 'Arafa said: 'The return is not taken into consideration when calculating the length of this (journey)'; al-Lakhmi said: 'What is taken into account is the distance to (a place) but the return is not added to it (when reckoning the distance)'; Malik said: 'Whoever goes out and travels around different villages and this amounts to four *bareeds* then he should shorten'; al-Lakhmi said: 'What he means by this is that the 'return home' is not reckoned (as part of total distance)'; Ibn 'Arafa said: 'Sanad is presented as having a difference of opinion: "the person who 'travels around' is the same as the one who goes directly (to a place).""""

He also said, commenting on Khalil's words 'making directly for a specific destination': "Malik said: 'Whoever goes out to seek a runaway slave or for some (other) matter – and it is said to him "the thing you are after is in front of you a *bareed* away" and he walks for days like this not knowing when the end of his journey will be – should pray in full on the outward journey and shorten it on the return journey, as long as it amounts to four *bareed* or more.' Ibn Junus said: 'Our companions differ regarding the person who goes out to look for a runaway slave and covers a distance of four *bareeds* and then wants to return but someone says to him 'What you are looking for is at a *bareed*'s distance away in front of you, or to your right or to your left' and he says 'I'll get to that place and then I'll carry on to my house whatever happens, irrespective of whether I find him or not.' One of our companions is of the opinion that he should not shorten the *salat* until he returns from the place where he was told the slave could be found – as the journey to a place is not added to the return from it (in the calculation) – and he had declared: 'I am about to set out and go to the place where I have been told the slave is to be found.' Thus he is considered as someone who is returning – and is included in the same judgement as the person who takes that particular way because of the difficulty of the terrain or on account of some matter other than the runaway slave – for such a person is considered as beginning his journey from that place. As for the person who wants to travel in the direction of the *qibla* of his area and then some matter (needing to be attended to) is mentioned to him at a distance of two *bareeds* beyond this region of his (in the opposite direction to the *qibla*) and he says 'I will go out to (see to) the matter beyond this area of mine and then I will return to the way I first had in mind – but without entering my town – and then I will continue to the completion of my journey', he should shorten the *salat* from the moment he goes out from his village. Likewise, the person who covers exactly four *bareeds* and who says 'I will go out from such-and-such a place and then I will continue from there to my house' – there is no difference between them. Ibn 'Arafa said: 'This is speculation and is refuted by the narration of ash-Shaykh: "Whoever travels for two *bareeds* and then returns by another way should shorten; if he passes by his house but does not want to stop by at his house, he should do the full *salat* on the return journey until he crosses it." Examine his words 'and he passes by his house' for he discriminates between this and Ibn Junus' words 'I shall return to my way and I will not enter my town'[1]. Consider too that it appears – from what Ibn 'Arafa says – that the person who makes a roundabout journey is classed in the same manner as the one who goes straight (to his destination), that is, he does not consider him to be 'making a roundabout journey.'"

ISSUE: Ibn Mawwaq has related: 'Al-Lakhmi has also said: 'It is correct for him to engage in the *salat* on the basis that he choose between adhering to the four *rak'ats* or shortening them to two.' Al-Mazari said: 'This is based on (the judgement that the number of) *rak'ats* is not binding.'"

Mayyara said further on: "As for the person who deliberately leaves off making the intention either to shorten the *salat* or to do it in full, or (merely) avoids (making this intention), then there are two opinions as to the validity of his *salat*, irrespective of whether he does it in full or shortens it." This is the difference of opinion mentioned by al-Khurshi, commenting on the words of Khalil 'there is uncertainty (as to the judgement regarding) abandoning making the intention of shortening or doing it in full': "According to one view, it is valid if he does it in full" – examine what he says in his *Kabir*.

ISSUE: al-Mawwaq has related that al-Baji said: "If travellers and people who are resident come together, then it is better that one of the travellers becomes the imam for the travellers and one of the people who are resident leads the *salat* for those resident; if one of them leads the *salat* for all of them, then it is better that one of the travellers is their imam as the *salat* does not change in character for those behind him. Malik considered it *makruh* for the traveller to do the *salat* behind the resident because his performing all (four *rak'ats* of) the *salat* alters his *salat* (as a traveller) – except if there is something preventing

---

1 The text appears to be garbled as these words do not correspond to those of his above.

him (from shortening it), in which case he does not have to repeat (the *salat*) if he prays (the full *salat*) behind a resident. Ibn Rushd said: '...and this is because the excellence of the sunna in the shortening is more certain that the excellence of the (*salat* in a)jam'a. However, Malik deemed it less of an infraction if a group of travellers has someone who is resident be their imam when he is advanced in years and man of excellence – given how desirable it is pray behind such a person; or in the case of the head of a household – given that his desisting from being their imam would constitute a disregard for his right to lead the *salat*.' Al-Lakhmi said: 'The most evident judgement from these (latter) words of Malik is that the group is more excellent than the act of shortening: although a sunna, the *jama'a* is also a sunna and the reward is increased through it – and this is the view of Abu 'Umar.'"

COMPLEMENTARY REMARKS: The author said nothing about joining (the *salats*). Khalil has stated the following: "It is permitted (for the traveller) to join the *Dhuhr* and *'Asr salats* when on land and even if the (journey) is short (and does not amount to four *bareeds*); moreover, (this licence) is not conditional upon the (traveller) having to make haste: it is not disapproved of (to make use of this dispensation although it is more praiseworthy to travel in less time) – although with regard to this matter the (*Mudawwana*) stipulates that the traveller should hasten to arrive at (their destination if) the reason (for their travel is of importance). It is permitted to join the *salats* at the place where the caravan stops at a watering place – when the sun declines from the meridian if the person has the intention of making a stop after sunset (when the *daruri* time of the afternoon would be past); however, if before the deep yellow (of late afternoon), the *salat* of midday should be done immediately and the *'Asr* should be done later; if (the stop is to be made) after the sky has become deep yellow (but before the sunset proper), then he has the choice with regard to joining or not."

Al-Mawwaq said in his commentary: "It is narrated from Malik: 'The traveller should not join (the *salats*) unless he is travelling with haste and fears he will not arrive in time to attend to the matter (he is travelling for).' It has been narrated of Ibn al-Qasim: 'I disapprove of the joining of the two *salats* for the journey, although in the case of women (the degree of disapproval) is less.' Ibn Rushd said: 'Malik's disapproval of joining when travelling refers to the traveller who is not in haste – and this corresponds to the words of the *Mudawwana*: "(The disapproval is) deemed less severe in the case of women because of the difficulty of their alighting (from the caravan) for every *salat* – given that she must veil herself and given too the fact that it is also permitted in the case of men, even if they are not in a hurry when journeying."' Ibn Habib is also of this opinion. Moreover, in the *Muwatta'* there is the hadith regarding the military expedition of Tabuk: 'The Messenger of Allah, may the peace and blessings of Allah be upon him, joined *Dhuhr* with *'Asr*, and *Maghrib* with *'Isha*.' Abu 'Umar said: 'This hadith indicates a licence to join when travelling even if one is not hastening on the journey.' This is also the view of Ibn Habib who pointed out that 'the Messenger of Allah, may the peace and blessings of Allah be upon him, joined (the *salats*) when he had come to a stop and was no longer travelling: indeed from his tent or canopy he would go out and establish the *salat* and then return to his tent. In this there is a clear proof negating the argument of those who stipulate that one should be travelling with haste.'"

Then, commenting on his words 'stopping in a watering place, if the sun has declined from the meridian' he said: "Ibn 'Arafa said: 'If the sun has declined from its zenith at the stopping place and he intends to make the next stop after *Maghrib*, then he should join (the *salats*).' Abu 'Umar said: 'Abu Faraj has related from Malik: "He should join when he wants, although it is preferred at the beginning of the time, or to delay the second (of the two *salats*) or at the middle of the time (when the times of the two *salats* overlap)." He justifies this with an explanation and then after this he goes on to say: "It has been narrated from Malik from Ibn Shihab who said: 'I asked Salim ibn 'Abdallah whether one should join between *Dhuhr* and *'Asr* when travelling and he replied: "Yes, there is no harm in this: Have you not seed the people at 'Arafa?"' This reply of Salim is a sound principle for those able to understand its good sense – over zealous concern for a matter leads one to obduracy and it is well known that joining the *salats* in the case of the traveller is a licence (from Allah) and an ease. If joining is as Ibn al-Qasim has stated, then it would also be permitted to join *'Asr* and *Maghrib* and *'Isha* and *Subh*. Ibn 'Arafa said: 'If he sets out before the sun has declined from its zenith and intends to halt after the sky has become deep yellow and before sunset, then al-Lakhmi said: "It is permitted to delay and join (the *salats*)".' This has also been stated by Ibn Musalama. Ibn Rushd said: 'He should join them in the time common to them both and if he joins them just after the sun has inclined from its zenith, then there is a narration to the effect that he should repeat the *salats*.'"

Al-Mawwaq has related from *al-Mi'yar* – after the discussion refuting those who claim that joining is not permitted on a journey except in the case of a long journey where it would be permitted to shorten the *salats* he says: "Ibn Sirin is of the opinion that it is permitted to join when resident without excuse; and Ashhab, according to one of his judgements, that it is permitted when the need is there, or for a valid reason as long as this does not become a habit. The like of this is recorded from 'Abd al-Malik with regard to *Dhuhr* and *'Asr* in *al-Ikmal* where he says: 'If, according to them, it is permitted in all circumstances when resident or with a valid reason, then how could it not be permitted during a short journey like this?' All this indicates that this matter is of less importance than shortening the *salat* and it does not necessary follow from the judgement that it is permitted (to join) during a short journey that it is also permitted to shorten during it – because of the clear difference (between the two cases). It has come to my notice that our Shaykh, Ibn 'Arafa – and my overriding belief is that I heard it (directly) from him – said: 'One of my Shaykhs – and he named him but I forgot it – said: "If he wanted to enter the hammam he would join *Dhuhr* and *'Asr* after the sun had reached its zenith – in accordance with what he narrated from Ashhab – because of the length of time he stayed in it." If he joined the *salat* with this excuse, then what is your view regarding (the stipulation that one) hurry when travelling in the case of a short journey!'"

ISSUE: al-Mawwaq said: "'Ali has narrated: 'The person who wants to embark on a journey by sea after the sun has past its zenith and fears that he will not be able to stand for the *'Asr* because he knows he will be seasick should join the two (*salats*) on land and do them standing.' Ibn Bashir said: 'Whoever knows from his state (of health) that if he embarks upon a boat he will become seasick and will miss the *salats* at their proper time, then he should not embark according to what has been clearly stated in the *madhhab* – even if it is for hajj or *jihad*; and if he knows from his state (of health) that he will not be able to do it except by missing out one of the *fard* obligations and by doing something in its stead, then the judgement in his regard is the same as someone who knows that he will not be able to pray standing: if he finds an alternative then he should not embark; if not, then there is a difference of opinion regarding the standing based on the judgement of indulgence, or special permission. Those who admit of an analogy permit embarkation as they would permit him to change from purification with water to purification with earth in the desert – even if his embarkation is to seek after something of this world; those who do not, prohibit embarkation if it leads to his missing out one of the *fard* obligations. If he is not sure as to whether he will be sea sick or not, then they have said that it is disliked but not prohibited – for the principle (underlying the judgement) is that health (is assumed).'"

TWO BENEFITS: the first: an-Nafrawi said: "The judgement regarding travel is that it is licit; indeed, under circumstances it may be obligatory, like the hajj for the person who is able, or like travel in a military expedition in the case of the male who is able; sometimes it is recommended, like travel to visit a Salih[1] or to seek knowledge which is not obligatory; sometimes it is haram, like travel to commit highway robbery; sometimes *makruh*, like travel to go fishing merely for sport; and sometimes (merely) allowed like travel to acquire profit in order to increase one's wealth but undertaken as an act of worship bringing one closer to Allah, exalted is He. All these latter are in the case of travel undertaken to seek after something; as for travel undertaken in order to flee, for example, from a land where the haram is widespread and from which no one living there can avoid, or like travel from a country where a man of excellence is treated with disrespect, or where the Companions are insulted, or for other reasons, then the judgement is that it is obligatory."

2. Al-Wansharisi said in his *Mi'yar* during his discussion with those persons who prohibit the placing of a silk cover over the dead woman on the bier: "Rejection of this argument necessitates supposing that those who argue for it base the legality of adorning women with gold and silver and pure silk on their being actually receptive for copulation – and this would be an (example of) reasoning based on the wisdom (inherent in adornment). However, there is a difference of opinion amongst those expert in the principles (of the law); al-Ghazali and al-Fakhr have differed as to the signs or indications (necessary in determining a judgement in this case) and a group of those expert in these principles have prohibited using it as a reason (underlying a judgement); it has been reported of ash-Shareef and is ascribed to him in *al-Mahsoul*, and a group of those expert in the principles have accepted the permissibility of using it as a reason (for establishing a judgement). The aim inherent in the terminology of the legalists is to arrive at confirmation or negation of a judgement by way of the wisdom (or reason) underlying (the case) – like, for example, difficulty is the 'cause' for the (permissibility of) shortening (the *salat*) or breaking one's fast when travelling. The word 'supposed cause' (*madhanna*) is a term applied to a physical act (of worship) in which one assumes a 'wisdom' (or cause) which has been intended by the Legislator – in this particular case, the assumption of difficulty reveals the wisdom contained in the permission (to shorten the *salat* or break the fast). However, it should be noted that the Legislator, may the peace and blessings of Allah be upon him, established travel as a reason for permission to break the fast and to shorten (the *salat*) – 'difficulty' (in itself) which gives rise to the (two) judgements (through our assumption of an underlying wisdom or reason) is not (of its nature) clearly

---

1 a man who acts with the right action at the right time

defined but rather differs in accordance with the different (natures of) people and with different times and circumstances: an amir or someone of financial means is not subject to the same difficulties undergone by others who do not enjoy the means at their disposal; likewise, the difficulties experienced in one season are not the same as in another; it varies too according to the incidents occurring on a particularly journey – dependent upon the difficulty of the road or otherwise. If the Legislator, may the peace and blessings of Allah be upon him, has established (mere) 'difficulty' as the reason for the permission to break the fast or shorten (the *salat*) controversy would have increased and the reasons and principles (underlying other judgements) would have been brought into disarray. Thus 'difficulty' as a reason has not been explicitly stated (by the Legislator) as it does not lend itself – as we have seen above – as a reason in a general sense. However, in the case of a long journey, the reason (underlying the judgement) is manifest and the 'difficulty' which is the 'reason' underlying the shortening (of the *salat*) and breaking of the fast is present to all intents and purposes – and so it is that (in the case of a long journey) the Legislator, may the peace and blessings of Allah be upon him, (may be said) to have made the (two judgements) conditional upon the (reason)." I have corrected the mistakes in one manuscript by comparison with a second.

مَنْدُوبُهَا تَيَامُنٌ مَعَ السَّلَامْ

تَأْمِينُ مَنْ صَلَّى عَدَا جَهْرَ الْإِمَامْ

124 It is recommended to turn the head to the right when saying the (final) *salam*; and for the person performing the *salat* to say amin (silently) but not for the imam (after) reciting (the Fatiha) aloud;

وَقَوْلُ رَبَّنَا لَكَ الْحَمْدُ عَدَا

مَنْ أَمَّ وَالْقُنُوتُ فِي الصُّبْحِ بَدَا

125 and the saying *rabbana laka'l-hamd*, but not for the imam; and the *qunut* for the *salat* of Subh;

رِداً وَتَسْبِيحُ السُّجُودِ وَالرُّكُوعْ

126 the wearing of a cloak; the saying of '*subhana'llah*' during the prostration and the bowing...

Mayyara, after having finished describing the sunnas, follows them with the recommended aspects, that is, the excellent aspects: the first: "As for 'turning to the right when saying the *salam*' Ibn 'Arafa said: 'The saying of the *salam* – in the case of other than the person following the imam – is done by turning slightly to his right; as to whether in the case of the *salam* of the person following the imam it is also so, or whether the beginning (of it) is to the right, there are two views.' Abu Muhammad Salih said: 'The turning to the right should take place when pronouncing the *kaf* and the *mim* of *alaykum*.'

2. "The saying of *amin* is at the end of the Fatiha in the case of the person performing the *salat* alone – irrespective of whether he has recited it aloud or silently; and in the case of the person behind the imam, after his reciting (the Fatiha) to himself silently and after the recitation aloud of his imam; and in the case of the imam, after his own reading silently – but not aloud."

USEFUL POINT: Ibn Wahb has recording in his *Musannaf*, in a narration from Bahr ibn Nasr from Abu Hurayra, may Allah be pleased with him: "I heard the Messenger of Allah, may the peace and blessings of Allah be upon him, say: 'When the imam says *amin*, then say the *amin* too – for the angels say the *amin* and whoever says it at the same time as the angels, then both his past and future wrong actions will be forgiven.'"

3. As for the supplication known as the *qunut* in the *Subh salat*, 'Iyad said: "Among the excellent aspects of the *salat*, and those which are recommended is the *qunut* during the *Subh salat*. There is a licence in it to do it before or after the bowing although what I hold to is doing it before the bowing. There is no *qunut* during the *witr* during the last half of Ramadan."

BRANCH: The author of *al-'Utbiyya* said: "Whoever catches the second *rak'a* of *Subh* should not do the *qunut* in the *rak'a* he makes up – in the case of the person following the judgement that one should make up both the words and movements (of the *salat*); and in the case of the person following the judgement that one should make up the words only, then he only has to make up the words of the first *rak'a* – and there is no *qunut* in this; and in the case of someone applying the judgement that one should carry on doing (the *salat*) from where one had left off (*al-bana'*), then one should always do the *qunut*."

USEFUL POINT: The author of *Ghayat al-Amani* said, commenting on the words of the *Risala* about the *qunut* 'We desist from the company of those who deny You': Ibn Naji said: "This means 'desisting from the deen of those who deny You.' This does not contradict the licence to marry a woman from the people of the Book for marrying her does not imply that we take on her deen. Rather, marriage is a contract and classed as one of the legal acts of buying and selling. What is intended is that one express hate for any other deen (than Islam)."

I SAY: "Ibn Naji has also stated in his book *Ma'alim al-Iman 'ala rijal al-Qayrawan* – after relating the story of al-Bahlul ibn Rashid – that he returned a present of oil made to him by a Christian and the messenger said to him: 'Why are you returning the gift from him?' He replied: 'I remembered the saying of Allah, exalted is He, "*You will not find people who have iman in Allah and the Last Day having love for anyone who opposes Allah and His Messenger*"[1] and I feared lest I eat of the oil of the Christian and find love in my heart (for him) and that I be reckoned as one of those having love for those who oppose Allah and His Messenger – all for the sake of this object of insignificance from the *dunya*.'" I said: "..and this (attitude) of al-Bahlul is the result of his intense scrupulousness – for (in fact) the love mentioned in the *ayat* refers to love in the deen; as for the love relating to acts undertaken in the world, this is not referred to in the *ayat*: proof of this is afforded by the licence to marry a woman of the Book – for there is no doubt that if one were to marry such a woman, then one would incline to her and have love for her."

Mayyara said:

"5. The cloak. Ibn Rushd and 'Iyad have said: 'Wearing a cloak for the *salat* is recommended' and others have added: 'There is no difference in this between the imam and others.'"

6. The saying of *subhana'llah*… during the *sajda* and the *ruku'*.

USEFUL POINT: al-Mawwaq has narrated (from Malik) – at least in some copies – regarding this matter: "'I am not aware of (the practice) of the people who say: *subhana rabbiya'l-'adheem* and in the prostration *subhana rabbiya'l-a'la*.' Thus he disapproved of it but did not specify (his reasons) any further – nor did he mention any particular *du'a*. Ibn Rushd has transmitted this narration saying: '..this is not to say that he considers leaving off saying it better than doing it for it is one of the sunnas which it is recommended to act upon according to all (the *fuqaha*).' Then he goes on to interpret the dislike of Malik in the same manner as Ibn Bashir has interpreted Malik's dislike of the *adhan* made by the person who is alone saying: 'The *adhan* is a *dhikr* and *dhikr* of Allah is not prohibited for anyone who wants to do it – especially if it is of the kind which is specified explicitly by the *shari'ah*.' Commenting on this, Ibn al-'Arabi has narrated the text of at-Tirmidhi: 'Most of the *'ulama* esteem that the permission to make the prostration of thanks should be acted upon, except for Malik, for this is not his judgement.' Ibn al-'Arabi said: 'Even if Malik does not

---

[1] al-Mujadila – The Disputer: 21

consider this (should be acted upon), prostration to Allah is always incumbent on a person – in the sense that if one finds the least excuse for doing it, one should seize the opportunity.' Malik was asked about recitation of the sura Ya-Sin from the Qur'an after a person has died and he replied: 'I have not heard this and it is not part of the practice of the people.'"

Ibn Yunus said: 'Why does he have Malik refute this but then interpret his words 'and this is not part of the practice of the people.' Likewise, Malik has rejected (the practice as sunna) of washing one's hands before the meal saying that 'it is not (part of) the practice' and considers that one should desist from it. Ibn Rushd said by 'practice' he indicates that is not part of what is obligatory and would not be punished if left out. It has been narrated of the Prophet, may the peace and blessing of Allah be upon him, that he said: 'Making *wudu'* before eating repulses poverty.' Moreover, there is a consensus amongst the *'ulama* that the cleanliness stipulated by the *shari'ah* indicates such (a practice) and that the Prophet, may the peace and blessing of Allah be upon him – when instructing the person doing the *wudu'* to wash his hands before immersing them in (the vessel containing) the water – was also indicating this same thing. Malik said: 'It is not the practice of the people to give *sadaqa* (of silver) equal in weight to the hair (shorn) from a new-born child.' Ibn Rushd said: 'It is a recommended practice' and al-Baji said: 'This is a practice (of the people).' Thus they both interpret the words of Malik. Malik said: 'The words of a person sacrificing (an animal) "O Allah, by You and to You" is an innovation.' Ibn Rushd said: 'There is no objection to someone who says this and it will be rewarded if Allah wills.' Thus he has also interpreted the words of Malik. As for the words of Malik 'the saying of the *qunut* in the last half of Ramadan is not a practice (among the people)' al-Baji said: 'It is a praiseworthy action although it is a new matter which has been introduced (later).' He then goes on to interpret the words of Malik. There is a similar narration from Abu 'Umar ibn 'Abd al-Barr who says: '...and it is not at the lowest level of what is licit (- i.e. it is certainly licit). However, Malik denied that it was part of the body of knowledge that people talked about – when a more important matter was also being addressed.' As for the phrase 'O Allah, (I worship) with iman in You', Ibn Rushd said: 'This is a praiseworthy saying although Malik considers it *makruh* for anyone to say it' – and then he goes on to interpret the rejection of Malik and examine the words of Abu 'Umar 'and it is not at the lowest level of what is licit' – (what he is referring to here is that) the ('*ulama*) have stated explicitly that any difference of opinion regarding the legality of something is only with regard to matters of more import than merely the licit. However, 'Izz ad-Deen said in his *Qawa'id*: 'If there is a difference of opinion as to whether something it stipulated in the *shari'ah*, then doing it is more excellent. Thus if one of the imams have deemed something *makruh* while another has judged it to be otherwise, then doing it is more excellent, like in the case of raising one's arms (when making the *takbirat al-ihram*). We have stated this as the *shari'ah* encompasses the recommended actions as it does the obligatory actions.'"

The author of *al-Masalik* said: "As for our *madhhab*, Malik has stated in the *Muwatta'* that one does not have to fulfil a vow (of the type) which is (merely) licit – as opposed to other (types of vow) which he esteemed to be *makruh* and which other (*fuqaha*) esteemed to be recommended: such vows should be fulfilled. Malik held it to be *makruh* to make a vow to sacrifice a defective animal or to sacrifice an animal without (first) making a vow. He held it to be *makruh* to reward someone for doing the hajj but has also stated that (such a vow once made) should nevertheless be carried out; and that (in the case of the example of the defective) sacrificial animal (the fact that the vow must be fulfilled) does not affirm (in any way that such an animal should be slaughtered). Thus this is a judgement about which there is a difference of opinion as to its legality. As for their agreement as to the prohibition of something, Abu 'Umar said in more that one place: 'If there is mention of a prohibition in the Qur'an and sunna with respect to something you own, then it is a prohibition which is intended as advice, as an indication of the best way of acting or as an instruction meant to guide: this is because it is your property and you may dispose of it as you wish as long as this property is not a living creature for the Qur'an and sunna prohibit one from disposing of (such property) in *any* way one wishes. Examples of such prohibitions are the turning a (water)skin inside out (and drinking from it), or cleaning oneself (after defecating) with the right hand or eating with the left and the like from Ibn Rushd; likewise, the prohibition of the Prophet, may the peace and blessings of Allah be upon him, against walking in one sandal is a prohibition of the order of a piece of advice: that is, if one were to walk in one sandal, one would not be guilty of an act of disobedience, according to the majority (of the '*ulama*), even if he was aware of the interdiction."

He has also said: "A prohibition from the Legislator is not said to be a prohibition of an absolute kind (*nahyi tahreem*) unless the prohibition is accompanied by the threat of punishment." He goes on to say: "If the prohibition is transmitted unconditionally, then it is understood as an educative instruction unless there is something associated with it which indicates (leaving it) would be of benefit to the body or one's wealth, in which case the prohibition would have the force of being *makruh*, not of being (totally) prohibited." Ibn Rushd said on more than one occasion: "Matters about which they have differed as to whether they are halal or haram are (as a general rule) *makruh*." He has also said: "It is not permitted for a *mujtahid* who considers something haram for him to declare that it is absolutely haram when someone else opposes him in this." As to whether it is permitted to say 'it is haram according to me', and 'in my opinion', such (expressions) are rejected by those who judge strictly according to the principle that the truth, of its nature, is one; however, in the case of those who hold that such (expressions are not absolute but rather) express approbation or what is correct in all probability, then they are permitted – examine the *Jami' al-'Utbiya* regarding this matter."

'Izz ad-Deen said: "It is strange that people give absolute judgements regarding things which about which there is a difference of opinion – saying, for example, it is haram. They are unaware that this is a denial of Allah and amounts to making false claims about him – as there is no difference between making something which is halal haram and something haram halal: Allah, exalted is He, said: '*Do not say about what your lying tongues describe: "This is halal and this is haram", inventing lies against Allah.*'"[1]

Ibn al-'Arabi said: "The subject of 'forbidden things' is vast. That which is forbidden by the sunna is not the same as that which is forbidden by the Qur'an – and for this reason Ibn al-Qasim said: 'Whoever marries both a woman and her aunt on her father's side and is aware of the prohibition escapes the *hadd* punishment as the prohibition issues from the sunna; as opposed to whoever marries both a woman and her sister for he is given the *hadd* punishment as the prohibition is from the Qur'an; likewise, the prohibition of any wild animal with fangs is not of the order of carrion forbidden in the Qur'an.' 'Iyad has transmitted that 'one should only declare 'haram' what Allah and his Messenger has made haram – but as for that about which there is difference of opinion amongst the *'ulama* as to whether it is halal or haram one should not say of it "it is haram".'"

Ibn al-'Arabi said: "There is no obligation but that it issues from one of the following three things: Qur'an, sunna or the *ijma'* – consensus." Abu 'Umar said on more than one occasion: "An obligation is not established unless there exists a consensus – without any difference of opinion – and a proof to which there is no refutation." Ibn al-'Arabi has also said: "Beware of the confusion that is current in the expressions of our companions from the *Maghrib* when they say 'the *salat* becomes the enemy of the one who leaves off doing the sunna

---

1   an-Nahl – The Bee: 116

as there is no difference between the sunna and the Qur'an – except that one must accept (the whole of the Qur'an) and may leave out (certain sunnas).'"

He has mentioned on another occasion the *rak'a* of *witr* and stressed its being a sunna. He has also mentioned the words of Sahnun: "Whoever leaves off doing the *witr* is disciplined" but that Sahnun has added: "This is from Asad ibn al-Furat – and this, by Allah, is salty not sweet! – for surely the back of the *mumin* is inviolable and not subject to punishment, except if guilty of disobedience."

Abu 'Umar said in his *Tamheed*: "Do you not see that the Companions, may Allah be pleased with them differed amongst each other – and they are the models (to be followed): none of them blamed the other for his difference of opinion and harboured any misgivings against him. If one has a complaint it must be taken to Allah, and He is the Helper of his *umma*. We are from its midst and any difficult matters can be resolved between us."

He has narrated with his chain of narration to ath-Thawri that he said: "Knowledge is a licence from an man of knowledge; as for being severe this is condemned by all." He has also has reported with his own chain of narration: "The *'alim* should win over the people by making it easy for them and allowing them a licence as long as offences are not trivialised by his doing this." He has also added: "… as long as neither Allah nor His Prophet has forbidden it and there is no consensus against it, in which case the (first and principle) judgement (in *fiqh*) – namely that a thing is assumed to be licit – still governs the matter in question." Then he has transmitted – with his own chain of transmission to Usama ibn Shareek: "I witnessed the tribes of nomad Arabs ask the Messenger of Allah, may the peace and blessings of Allah be upon him: 'Is there any harm in such-and-such a thing?' and he replied: 'Slaves of Allah, Allah has removed all harm except for that which befalls a man who speaks evil of his brother in some manner (behind his back) – for this will cause harm and bring about his destruction.'"

I have mentioned above 'in one of the copies' as the copies differ and some contain things that the others do not. However, all of it is correct and can be relied on insha'Allah.

سَدْلُ يَدٍ تَكْبِيرُهُ مَعَ الشُّرُوعِ

> ... letting one's arms hang by one's side, saying *Allahu akbar* when beginning (the movements of the *salat*)

$$\text{وَبَعْدَ أَنْ يَقُومَ مِنْ وُسْطَاهُ}$$

$$\text{وَعَقْدُهُ الثَّلَاثَ مِنْ يُمْنَاهُ}$$

127 but after getting up from the middle (sitting, after the second *rak'a*), clenching the three smaller fingers of his right hand

$$\text{لَدَى التَّشَهُّدِ وَبَسْطُ مَا خَلَاهُ}$$

$$\text{تَحْرِيكُ سَبَّابَتِهَا حِينَ تَلَاهُ}$$

128 when saying the *tashahhud* while letting the other (two fingers) remain straight, and moving one's index finger while saying (the *tashahhud*)

Mayyara said:

"7. 'letting one's arms hang by one's side' refers to this being recommended in the *fard salat*.

8. Saying the *Allahu akbar* when beginning any movement of the *salat* except when standing up from the sitting position, in which case one should not say the *Allahu akbar* until one has reached the fully straight position. The person behind the imam should not get up for the third (*rak'a*) of the imam until after the imam himself has got up and is straight, as is mentioned in the *Risala*.

9. Clenching together the three last fingers of the right hand during the *tashahhud*, that is the middle, little and ring finger, and allowing the thumb and index to remain straight. Ibn Bashir said: 'He should allow the index finger to be straight its (right) side facing upwards and stretch out the thumb.' Al-Mawwaq said: '…so as to form the number thirteen in Arabic.' Ibn al-Hajib said: '…to form the number twenty-nine in Arabic' although another narration has fifty-three.' Ibn Bundoud said: 'First one should clench the little finger tightly into the palm, then the ring- and middle finger likewise, pressing the little finger against the flesh at the base of the thumb with the other two fingers against it while extending the thumb and forefinger out together, bending the latter inwards.'

10. Moving the index finger throughout the saying of the *tashahhud*:

Ibn Mawwaq said that Ibn al-Qasim has narrated: 'He should indicate with his two fingers during the *tashahhud*', and that the narration emphasises the importance of moving them. Ibn Rushd said: 'This is the sunna.' Ibn al-'Arabi said: 'Beware of moving (your fingers) during the *tashahhud* and do not pay any attention to the narration of *al-'Utbiya* for it is corrupt.' Our companion the *faqih*, Abu 'Abdallah az-Za'rouri has composed the following for us:

Indicate with it and move it pointing its end towards the front, and a difference of opinion has been ascribed to this matter

$$وَالبُطَنَ مِنْ فَخْذٍ رِجَالٌ يُبْعِدُونْ$$

$$وَمَرْفِقاً مِنْ رُكْبَةٍ إِذْ يَسْجُدُونْ$$

129 the belly should not touch the thigh of a man, nor the elbow his knee when prostrating;

$$وَصِفَةُ الْجُلُوسِ تَمْكِينُ الْيَدِ$$

$$مِنْ رُكْبَتَيْهِ فِي الرُّكُوعِ وَزِدِ$$

130 the specific way of sitting (for the *tashahhud*); placing the hands firmly on the knees for the *ruku'*; and also

$$نَصْبُهُمَا قِرَاءَةُ الْمَأْمُومِ فِي$$

131 his knees should be straight (during the bowing) …

11. That he keep a distance between his belly and thighs and between his elbows and knees;

12. The way to sit for the two *tashahhuds* and between the two *sajdas*: Al-Mawwaq has related that Malik said: '…the sitting between the two prostrations and in the *tashahhud* irrespective of whether the two sides of the buttocks are touching the ground.' Abu 'Umar said: 'His left buttock should touch the ground and he should prop up his right foot on the front part of the sole with the underside of the big toe resting on the ground.' Al-Qubab said: 'As for the right hand buttock, it is raised above the ground.'

The author of the *Risala* said: 'Do not sit on your left foot but rather it must be allowed to rest on the side of the left buttock.' Abu 'Umar said: 'He places his left foot beneath his right shin.'

13. [In the Arabic] he only mentions that one should firmly place one's *hand* (on the ground) – in the singular. However, he is in fact indicating *both* hands as it is a generic term.'

14. That he keep the knees straight during the *ruku'*.

$$\text{سِرِّيَّةٍ وَضْعُ الْيَدَيْنِ فَاقْتَفِي}$$

... the person behind the imam reciting (to himself) whenever (the imam recites) silently, placing the hands

$$\text{لَدَى السُّجُودِ حَذْوَا أُذُنٍ وَكَذَا}$$

$$\text{رَفْعُ الْيَدَيْنِ عِنْدَ الْإِحْرَامِ خُذَا}$$

132 level with the ears in the prostration, and likewise, raising the hands for the *takbirat al-ihram*

15. That the person behind the imam recites the Fatiha and another sura to himself;
16. That he place his hands level with his ears while prostrating;
17. That he raise his hands for the *takbirat al-ihram*;

$$\text{تَطْوِيلُهُ صُبْحاً وَظُهْراً سُورَتَيْنْ}$$

$$\text{تَوَسُّطُ الْعِشَا وَفَضْلُ الْبَاقِيَيْنْ}$$

133 He should recite two long suras in the *Subh* and *dhuhr salats*, medium length ones at *'Isha*, and shorter ones for the two other *salats*

$$\text{كَالسُّورَةِ الْأُخْرَى كَذَا الْوُسْطَى اسْتُحِبّ}$$

$$\text{سَبْقُ يَدٍ وَضْعاً وَفِي الرَّفْعِ الرُّكَبْ}$$

134 likewise, recite a shorter sura in the second *rak'a*; it is recommended, too, to shorten the sitting in the middle (of the *salat*), and to put one's hands on the ground first (going into *sajda*) but to first raise the knees when rising

18. He should recite long suras in the first and second *rak'ats* of the *Subh* and *Dhuhr salats*, middle size ones for *'Isha* and shorter ones for *'Asr* and *Maghrib*;
19. In the second *rak'a*, he should recite a shorter sura than the one in the first – for every *salat*. Al-Mawwaq has related that Ibn al-Qasim said: 'It is still the practice of the people to recite Surat ash-Shams – The Sun – in the first *rak'a* and al-Balad – The City – in the second;

20. He should make the first sitting shorter (than the second). Ibn Rushd said: 'Shortening the first sitting is an aspect of excellence.'

21. Placing the hands – before the knees – in the air (when moving) towards the prostration, and raising them after the knees when getting up."

CONCLUSION

Mayyara said: "Ibn 'Ashir has not mentioned that making *dhikr* is recommended after the *salat*, and it is reported of the Messenger of Allah, may the peace and blessings of Allah be upon him, that after the *salam* he would say:

أَسْتَغْفِرُ اللَّهَ (٣)

اَللَّهُمَّ أَنْتَ السَّلَامُ وَمِنْكَ السَّلَامُ وَإِلَيْكَ يَعُودُ السَّلَامُ حَيِّنَا رَبَّنَا بِالسَّلَامِ، تَبَارَكْتَ يَا ذَا الْجَلَالِ وَالْإِكْرَامِ، لَا إِلَهَ إِلَّا اللَّهُ وَحْدَهُ لَا شَرِيكَ لَهُ، لَهُ الْمُلْكُ وَلَهُ الْحَمْدُ وَهُوَ عَلَى كُلِّ شَيْءٍ قَدِيرٌ، اَللَّهُمَّ لَا مَانِعَ لِمَا أَعْطَيْتَ وَلَا مُعْطِيَ لِمَا مَنَعْتَ وَلَا يَنْفَعُ ذَا الْجَدِّ مِنْكَ الْجَدُّ

astaghfirullah (3)

allahumma anta's-salam, wa minka's-salam, wa ilayka ya'oudu's-salam, hayyana rabbana bi's-salam, tabarakta ya dha'l-jallali wa'l-ikram. la ilaha illa'llah wahdahu la sharika lah, lahu'l-mulku wa lahu'-hamd, wa huwa 'ala kulli shay'in qadir. allahumma la mani'a lima 'atayt, wa la mu'tiya lima mana't, wa la yanfa'u dha'l-jidd minka'l-jidd – O Allah, You are peace, and from You is peace, and to You peace returns, our Lord bring us to life with peace, blessed are You, Possessor of majesty and generosity, there is no god except Allah, alone without partner, to Him belongs the kingdom and to Him belongs all praise, and He has power over all things. O Allah, none can prevent what You give and none can give what You prevent, and the good worldly of those who possess it does not benefit them with You."

I SAY: The author of *al-Jami' as-Saghir* said: "Whoever seeks forgiveness of Allah at the end of each *salat* three times and then says:

أَسْتَغْفِرُ اللَّهَ الَّذِي لَا إِلَهَ إِلَّا هُوَ الْحَيُّ الْقَيُّومُ وَأَتُوبُ إِلَيْهِ

astafirullaha'lladhi la ilaha illa huwa'l-hayyu'l-qayyum wa atoubu ilayh – 'I seek forgiveness of Allah the One Whom there is no god but He, the Living, the Self-Subsistent and I turn to Him in repentance' – then his wrong actions will be forgiven him even if he had fled from an army[1]."

The following narration is pertinent: "Whoever begins his day with good and ends it with good, then Allah will say to the angels: 'Do not write down the wrong actions between this time'" – or whatever the exact form of the narration is. Al-Munawi said: "…that is, the minor wrong actions – as is apparent from a comparison of similar (narrations), although it may also be understood to include all wrong actions in general, and the overflowing generosity of Allah is vast."

His saying 'with good' refers to *salat*, *dhikr*, the reciting of *subhana'llah*, *al-hamdulillah* and *la ilaha illa'llah*, giving *sadaqa* and commanding to the good and forbidding evil, and the like.

Makruh Acts in the Salat

وَكَرِهُوا بَسْمَلَةً تَعَوُّذَا

فِي الْفَرْضِ وَالسُّجُودَ فِي الثَّوْبِ كَذَا

135 and they have deemed *makruh* the *bismillah*, saying *a'oudhu billahi* – 'I seek refuge' – in the *fard salat*, and prostrating on cloth

'Ali ibn 'Abd as-Sadiq said, commenting on his words 'the *bismillah*': "He means *bismillahi'r-rahmani'r-raheem*, irrespective of whether for the Fatiha or for the (following) sura, whether (recited) by the imam or other than the imam."

Mayyara said: "Having finished with the obligations, sunnas and the recommended aspects, he begins to speak of that which is *makruh*: the first and second of these is the *bismillah* and the *ta'awwudh* – the seeking refuge from Allah – for the *fard* (salat), but not for the *nafila* – for there is no harm in saying the *bismillah* in them."

Al-Hattab said that in the *Mudawwana* it states: "It is *makruh* to prostrate on velvet-like carpet, carpets of fur or (camel) hair, leather, cotton or linen cloth or saddle blankets: one should not place one's hands on such (things) but there is nothing to make up if one does pray on these things. There is no harm if one stands or sits on the above mentioned (things) as long as one places one's face and hands on the ground – and all this the author indicates with his words 'as is prostrating on cloth.'"

NOTICE: prostration on cloth is of four kinds:

---

1 One of the major wrong actions, according to the *shari'ah*

1. That he prostrates on his own clothing, and the judgement in this case is that it is *makruh*. This is mentioned in Ibn 'Ashir's words below 'on part of the sleeve.'

2. That he rolls out his clothing and prays on it and prostrates on it, and this is also *makruh*. This is what is meant here by his words 'as is prostrating on cloth' and is also indicated by Khalil words 'and it is *makruh* to prostrate on cloth.' This, as mentioned above, is also the view of al-Hattab, as well as al-Mawwaq.

3. That he stand and sit on the cloth while placing his forehead and hands on the ground. This is permitted – being stated explicitly in the *Mudawwana* as al-Hattab and al-Mawwaq and others have mentioned. This is also what is to be understood from the words of Khalil 'and it is *makruh* to prostrate on cloth' as what may be implied by 'prostration' is prostration on the face and hands and what may be implied from 'standing and sitting' is that it is not *makruh* on the ground.

4. The opposite of the third, namely, that he prostrate on the cloth of his turban while standing or sitting on the ground – although neither Khalil nor the author explains this. Az-Zurqani has mentioned that there are two judgements on the matter, one that it is invalid and the other that it is valid.

$$كَوْرُ عِمَامَةٍ وَبَعْضُ كُمِّهِ$$

136 the fold of the turban or part of the sleeve...

Al-Mawwaq said: "Malik said in the *Mudawwana*: 'Whoever prays while wearing his turban, then what I prefer is that he raise it from part of his forehead such that part of his forehead touches the ground; and if he prays on the fold of his turban, then I dislike it, although he does not have to repeat (the *salat*).'" Ibn Habib said: "This (holds true) if the (cloth) is only two layers (thick) but if it is thicker (than this) then he should repeat (the *salat*)." At-Tunisi said: "The words of Ibn Habib are an interpretation (of his rather than a judgement)."

Mayyara has related that Ibn Maslama said: "He should not prostrate on the clothing he is wearing nor with his hands in his sleeve." Al-Mazari said: "It is recommended that the hands be uncovered." Ibn Habib's words – that it is recommended that one touch the ground directly with one's face and hands – has already been mentioned above, the original of this being from al-Mawwaq.

$$وَحَمْلُ شَيْءٍ فِيهِ أَوْ فِي فَمِهِ$$

... or carrying something in it or one's mouth

Mayyara has related from the *Mudawwana*: "Malik disliked that a person pray with a dirham or dinar in his mouth, or anything else" Ibn al-Qasim said: "If he does, however, then he does not have to make the (*salat*) up, and Malik also disliked that a person pray with his mouth full of bread or something else." Ibn Yunus said: "Malik disliked it because it distracted the person from his *salat*."

قِرَاءَةٌ لَدَى السُّجُودِ وَالرُّكُوعِ

137 reciting during the prostration or the bowing ...

Al-Mawwaq said: "In the *Sahih* it states 'I have been prohibited from reciting the Qur'an while in *ruku'* or prostrating.' 'Iyad said: 'The prohibition of reciting during the bowing or prostration is the *madhhab* of the *fuqaha* of the major cities although some of the earlier generations allowed it.'"

تَفَكُّرُ الْقَلْبِ بِمَا نَافَى الْخُشُوعُ

... allowing the heart to think about anything which negates humility

'Ali ibn 'Abd as-Sadiq said: "...that is, thinking about the affairs of the *dunya*, although the *salat* is not rendered invalid by such (thoughts) even if the person spends a long time thinking – as long, that is, as he carries out his *salat* properly for otherwise it would invalidate his *salat* – this our Shaykh said."

It is recorded in the *Sahih* from 'A'isha, may Allah be pleased with her, who said: "I asked the Prophet, may the peace and blessings of Allah be upon him, about being distracted in the *salat* and he replied: 'It is Shaytan stealing from your *salat* under false pretences.'"

Ibn Abi Jamra said, may Allah be pleased with him, commenting on this hadith: "As for whether physical or spiritual distraction is meant – or a combination of the two – the most evident meaning of the hadith is that it is physical, and if it is physical, then the spiritual necessarily accompanies it. There still remains the question as to what is meant by the spiritual: if we examine the words of the Prophet, may the peace and blessings of Allah be upon him: 'Allah does not accept the *salat* of a man until his heart is with his limbs', then the spiritual distraction is the same as that of the physical. What we mean by 'spiritual' is anything in the heart which distracts from what it is engaged in at the moment (of the *salat*). This is the judgement of a group of *'ulama* who say that one has to be present throughout the *salat* – and that means not being distracted. However, and the majority are of the view that (being present) 'throughout' (the *salat*) is (merely) a prerequisite for perfection (in the *salat*) and that the obligation in the first instance is the act."

As for his saying that 'Allah does not accept the *salat* of a man…', I have not been able to ascertain if this is the actual text of the hadith and I have transmitted it from a corrupt manuscript. However, even if it were sound, it would not be permitted for us to rely on the soundness of the text without a chain of narration. Sayyidi 'Abdallah al-'Alawi said:

A Muslim does not say "The Prophet said…" without a chain of narration – for fear of transmitting a lie

In *adh-Dhahab al-Ibreez* the author comments: "In short, allowing the *nafs* – the self – free rein with its thoughts is harmful. However, when they attack the slave spontaneously and he defends himself and opposes his *nafs*, and when the shaytan associated with his *nafs* is also present, then this is not harmful. Indeed, it is rewarded as this (struggle on his part) represents something more that what is required of him. Allah, exalted is He, says: '*Allah does not impose on a self any more than it can stand*'[1]; moreover, a man cannot completely free himself of thoughts of the *dunya* during the *salat*."

In *Ikhtisar Hawi as-Suyuti* he states: "Reflecting – when pronouncing the words of the Qur'an – about how they were revealed does not negate fear of Allah for this is part of worship and the deen; what does negate this fear of Allah is thinking about affairs of this world. Nothing has been stated to the effect that affairs of the deen or the next world (are harmful)."

Mayyara has related that "Zarruq, commenting on the words of the *Risala* 'He should carry out the bowing and prostration with a sincere and fearful humility (*khushu'*)' said: '(what he intends by his words is to) encourage this humility.' 'Iyad has reckoned it as one of the obligations of the *salat*, and Ibn Rushd said it is one of the *fard* obligations of the *salat* which, however, does not annul the *salat* if missing. Some of the Sufis have said: 'Anyone who does not have humility in the *salat* is close to punishment.' One of the *'ulama* who has abridged the *Ihya'* said: 'The presence of the heart in the *salat* is necessary according to the consensus although it is not necessary throughout *all* of it according to the consensus – rather it is obligatory for part of it: one should have it for the *takbirat al-ihram*. The well known opinion is that thinking about matters of the *dunya* is *makruh*.'"

In Ibn Hajar's commentary on al-Bukhari, an-Nawawi has related that there is a consensus that this state of humility is not an obligation. The words of al-Qadi Husayn are not a refutation of him when he says: "There is a point when – striving to suppress one's urine and faeces – sincere humility (necessarily)

---

1   al-Baqara – the Cow: 285

disappears and the *salat* is rendered invalid." Abu Zayd al-Marouzi has also affirmed this saying that this (judgement) is possible over and beyond the above mentioned consensus (that humility is not obligatory) and that what is meant by 'consensus' is that no one has explicitly stated that this 'humility' is an obligation – and both cases refer to the judgement regarding this striving to retain urine and faeces and a lack of humility."

Then he goes on to say: "As for the words of Ibn Battal: 'If someone were to say that "Fearful humility is an obligation in the *salat*" then one should reply: "It is enough for a person that he enter upon the *salat* with his heart and intention – wanting the face of Allah. However, he has no power in the face of the thoughts which come to him."' The gist of his words is that this fearful humility is necessary to the extent he has mentioned. Other follow what is manifest from the narrations and these vary: if it appears (from one narration) that it is haram for one of the obligatory aspects of the *salat* to be missing and that fearful humility is one of these obligatory aspects (then they consider it must be present); otherwise they do not."

USEFUL POINT: the author of the *Dhahab al-Ibreez* said: "Ash-Sha'rani said in *al-Kibreet al-Ahmar*: 'The man of intellect is the person who comes to the *salat* 'perfectly' – that is, with the whole of his being – so that Allah accepts it of him completely. Any imperfections in the *fard salat* necessitate that he recite the Fatiha in the *nawafil salats*. If he does not do this, then he should complete his reading of it with a presence of heart at times other then the *salat*.'"

$$\text{وَعَبَثٌ وَالْاِلْتِفَاتُ وَالدُّعَا}$$

$$\text{أَثْنَا قِرَاءَةٍ كَذَا إِنْ رَكَعَا}$$

138 and (absent minded) play, turning (away from the *qibla*) and making *du'a* during the recitation, and likewise in the bowing

'Ali ibn 'Abd as-Sadiq said affirming him: "…playing absent mindedly with his beard during the *salat* may lead to an absence of this 'fearful humility'; it may also result lead to his pulling out a hair with some of its flesh at the root and so to his having something which is ritually impure on him – unless it is extremely small in quantity and size." Az-Zurqani has delineated it in *al-Izziya* saying "two or three hairs are excused as long as it is not more than this – for this would annul the *salat*." He has also said: "..and there is a similar (judgement) in this matter regarding the dead body of a lice which is impure according to the well-known opinion; and likewise the flea, according to Ibn al-Qussar; and it is said to be the judgement of most of the *fuqaha*; Ibn Fa'ida has preferred this (judgement) in his commentary on the *Mukhtasar* although the well known judgement is that it is pure, that is, when dead; likewise ticks – the difference between them being that lice live on man."

A DIGRESSION: Sayyidi Ahmad Bab said, commenting on the words of Khalil regarding what is licit '…insects and vermin of the earth': "Abu'l-Hasan said: 'the term "insects" refers to creatures who have no flowing blood.' Ibn al-Hajib said: '…and insects may be eaten and sacrificed like locusts' and 'there is no harm in eating the insects and vermin of the earth.'"

Then he goes on to say that al-Qalshani said that Ibn Bashir has mentioned that the eating of insects without sacrificing them is permitted, according to one of the latter *fuqaha*; and Ibn Rushd has understood it in accordance with the judgement of the *Mudawwana*: "The (matter or liquid) into which insects (fall and) die is not rendered impure."

Then he goes on to say: "Insects and vermin – like, for example, locusts, scorpions, scarab beetles, grasshoppers, hornets, drones, bees, woodworms, mites, worms and caterpillars, gnats and mosquitoes, and flies."

As for his saying 'distraction', Ibn al-Hattab said: "The most evident meaning of the words of the author of *at-Taraz* is that brushing (away) something is permitted even when not absolutely necessary – although this must be an error for what he means is when 'absolutely necessary.' Cases of non-necessity would be termed 'distractions.' However, distraction is of different kinds: Brushing (something off) one's cheek is less of a distraction than off one's neck and in my opinion (brushing off something from) one's nose less (of a distraction) than from one's chest."

Then he goes on to say: "It states in the *Mudawwana* that someone said to Ibn al-Qasim: 'What if one gets distracted by the whole of one's body?' and he replied: 'I have not asked Malik about this although (in may opinion) it is all the same.' Al-Buradha'i has expressed this concisely saying: 'The person performing the *salat* should not be distracted but if he is, then this does not break his *salat* even if this involves the whole of his body.' Al-Hassan said: '…unless he turns his back on the *qibla*.' Abu'l-Hasan as-*Saghir* said: '…to his words "even if he looks at the whole of his body" he has added in *al-Umm* "…and his legs are facing the *qibla*."' As for his saying: '…Abu'l-Hasan said: "unless he turns his back on the *qibla*" this refers to his turning eastwards or westwards (depending on his position with regard to the *qibla*) – and this is his interpretation.'"

As for Ibn 'Ashir's words 'making *du'a*', it states in *al-Mi'yar* it in a narration from Abu Muhammad that the making of *du'a* is permitted in the *salat* when standing, sitting and prostrating but not when bowing; that one may make *du'a* if one remembers – but not for too long such that it violates the rules of the *salat*. When he was asked as to whether there was any harm in reciting an *ayat* about the threat of punishment during the *salat* and saying things like: "Do You see yourself punishing me when I have got to know You! You are the beloved of my heart and the coolness of my eye! You are too sublime that You would gather me together with my enemies in the Fire! I do not think this (could possibly happen) for You will forgive the *muminun*!" he replied: "It is not fitting that he say any of this in the *salat*, and it is *makruh* at other times. What is recommended is *du'a* from the Qur'an – *allahumma rabbana*… and the like. However, it has also been said that the most manifest judgement from the *'Utbiya* is that this is (only) permitted when the (imam) recites '*Say He is Allah, Absolute Oneness*'[1] and the person following the imam responds: 'such is Allah' – for the (author of the *'Utbiya*) said: 'There is no harm in this or if he makes a *du'a* accompanying it with the words "Allah will cause it to be".' The hadith which talks of the person making the *salat* '…such that whenever he recites an *ayat* about punishment, he seeks forgiveness from such (punishment) and whenever he recites an *ayat* about mercy, he asks Allah (to grant him mercy) from His generosity…" indicates also that it is permitted." I cannot guarantee that there are no mistakes in the manuscript – although (even if there are) it does not prevent one from understanding what is meant.

Al-Mawwaq said, commenting on *Sharh Khalil*: "The author of *al-Kafi* said: 'Recitation of the Qur'an does not corrupt his *salat* nor *du'a* or any kind of supplication (to Allah).'"

USEFUL POINT: Ibn al-Hattab said, commenting on the words of Khalil 'and if he were to say: "O such a such a person, may Allah do such-and-such a thing to you" it would not render the *salat* invalid': "Malik said in the *Mudawwana*: 'There is no harm in making a *du'a* to Allah against a oppressor.' Ibn Naji said: "What he means by his saying 'there is no harm' is that he is declaring it licit." This appears to mean – even if the person (against whom the *du'a* is being made) is not oppressing him (personally) but rather someone else. This (judgement) is correct, according to the agreement (of the *fuqaha*). It also appears that he may make a *du'a* for him to die other than on the deen of Islam – and this is the view of one of our Shaykhs and our own Shaykh approved of it and made a *fatwa* using this (judgement) – although what is correct, in my opinion, is that it is forbidden."

1   al Ikhlas – Sincerity: 1

In al-Bukhari it is recorded that a man insulted Sa'd ibn Abi Waqqas, may Allah be pleased with him, and Sa'd made a *du'a* against him, saying "O Allah, if this slave of yours is lying, if he did it to show off and for his reputation, then lengthen his life and his poverty and expose him to trial and affliction." Afterwards when the man was asked (about it) he would reply: "I am advanced in years and have been subjected to trial and affliction for I have been struck by the *du'a* of Sa'd." 'Abd al-Malik said: "I saw him after his when his eyebrows had fallen over his eyes from old age and had become an object of ridicule for the slave girls."

In his commentary on what may be understood from the hadith, Ibn Hajar said: "It contains permission to make a *du'a* against someone who commits an injustice – and all that this implies of imperfection in his deen. However, this does not mean one seeks to have him commit an act of disobedience but rather that the person who has committed the injustice be subject to calamity and that he be punished for his (injustice). Similar to this is the legality of requesting that someone make the *shahada* – even if it means a *kafir* will learn that someone is a Muslim and get the better of him. One of the first words of Musa, on whom be peace was: '*Our Lord, obliterate the wealth (of Pharoah and his ruling circle) and harden their hearts.*[1]'"

Another benefit: al-Mawwaq said, commenting on the words of Khalil '(it is *makruh* to make) a special *du'a* (restricted in nature – given that Allah is vast and generous) and when in a language other than in Arabic if he is able to do it in Arabic': "Malik disliked that a man say the *takbirat al-ihram* in a language other than Arabic, that he make a *du'a* in it or make an oath in it or in any form that might prevent him from comprehending that the oath he is making is by Allah. 'Umar, may Allah be pleased with him, prohibited *ritana* – speaking or mumbling in foreign and barbarous languages – saying: 'It is a way of concealing and deceit.' Ibn al-Qasim has reported the question put to Malik about a non-Arab, unable to speak Arabic properly, who makes a *du'a* in his *salat* in his own language and he replied: '*Allah does not impose on any self any more than it can stand*'[2] – as if it was of little consequence. Ibn Yunus said: 'Umar prohibited *ritana*, that is, in mosques.' It has also been said, however, that this (rule only applies when) in the presence of someone who does not understand (this foreign tongue) – in which case it would fall under the judgement which prohibits two persons from excluding a third (from their conversation by talking in a language he does not understand)."

1 Yunus – Jonah : 88
2 al-Baqara – The Cow: 285

The author of *Ghayat al-Amani* said in the section *Tanbeehat*: "...ritana – that is, speaking in their language (other than Arabic)."

USEFUL POINT: Muhammad ibn 'Abd al-Qadir al-Fasi said in his commentary on the *salat* performed for a particular need in *Hisn al-Haseen*: "Beware of the foolish knowing of it lest they make a *du'a* with it to their Lord and He answers them" – after transmitting the narration of Wuhayb: "Do not teach it to the foolish amongst you lest they seek help by way of it to commit acts of disobedience of Allah, mighty and majestic is He." What may be understood from this is that the *du'a* of the foolish are answered – and this is indeed correct: if he has Iman in Allah and His Messenger, may the peace and blessings of Allah be upon him, then any act of obedience on his part will not go unrewarded – and his *du'a* is one of these acts of obedience.

The author of *Nawadir al-Usul* said: "Allah has singled out this *umma* (for His particular favour) by accepting *du'as* without first stipulating that those making them be free of wrong actions – as was the case regarding people from other (religions). For this reason He said: '*Call on Me and I will answer you.*'[1]"

Du'as are only acts of obedience if the person asks for something which is permitted – not if they lead to wrong actions. Thus *du'as* are not prohibited unless one asks for something which is haram – and this is what is implied by his words 'beware of the foolish...' This is also clear from the above mentioned narration of Wuhayb where he says: "Do not teach it to the foolish amongst you lest they ask for help by means of it in order to commit an act of disobedience against Allah, mighty and majestic is He." However, this (statement of Wuhayb) implies too that He will accept *du'as* even if they entail acts of disobedience – and so poses the problem that it contradicts the hadith: "The slave will continue to have his *du'as* answered as long as he does not ask for something involving a wrong action or his breaking off relations with his family"; also the fact that making a *du'a* for something permitted is a correct and beneficial act of obedience but making one for something haram is an act of disobedience. How, then, could one say that such *du'as* are accepted and answered? One may reply by saying that 'absolute acceptance' is not what is intended here – but rather 'an answer' in a more general sense. Thus what may be understood by the hadith "The slave will continue to have his *du'as* answered..." is an answer in general: that a *du'a* in this case will surely be accepted, that the reward will be granted and that the specific thing being asked for will be obtained. As for the former case, what is intended is that the person making the *du'a* will obtain only the specific thing he asked for,

---

1 Ghafir – Forgiver: 60

not the reward. This resembles the *du'a* of the *kafir* who has been wronged – for it has been recorded that it will be answered even though his *du'a* is not an act of worship at all and no reward will be granted him. This is because Iman – a prerequisite of an act of worship – is absent. Thus his being granted what he requests is on a par with his being granted the provision and similar blessings of this world which will be a proof against him – and which will have evil consequences for him – in the next world. It has also been said there is nothing to prevent a disobedient *mumin* from being rewarded for his *salat* and for any other recitation or *dhikr* he does with it. There are two distinct matters involved here, one involving obedience and the other disobedience. If he were to make a *du'a* for something haram after finishing the *salat*, then this would not invalidate the *salat*; likewise, seeking – in his heart – after something prohibited during the *salat*. The most manifest judgement is that he has committed an act of disobedience but the *salat* is valid. Likewise, if he were to look at something haram (during the *salat*)." Here end the words of Muhammad ibn 'Abd al-Qadir, although I cannot guarantee that there are no mistakes in the text.

تَشْبِيكٌ أَوْ فَرْقَعَةُ الْأَصَابِعِ

تَخَصُّرُ تَغْمِيضُ عَيْنٍ تَابِعٌ

139 interlocking or cracking the fingers, placing one's hands on the hip (when standing), closing one's eyes

Mayyara said: "Ibn al-Qasim has narrated that there is no harm in interlocking one's fingers in mosques when not during the *salat*, but it is *makruh* during the *salat*. In the *Mudawwana* it is stated that Malik disliked the cracking of fingers during the *salat*. Ibn Yunus said that it is disliked because it distracts from the *salat*."

Mayyara said:

"15. Placing one's hand on the waist is one of the disliked actions of the *salat*, and it is one of the actions of the Jews."

Then he goes on to say: "Sixteen: shutting one's eyes is disliked lest people imagine that it is desirable in the *salat* – that is, as long as one is not distracted by opening one's eyes, in which case it is preferable to close them."

CONCLUSION

This includes some important matters:

1. al-Mawwaq said, commenting on the words of Khalil '...adorning the

(*mihrab* indicating the direction) of the *qibla*': "Malik has narrated what was done to embellish the *qibla* of the Mosque in Madina saying: 'The people disliked it when it was done as it distracted them from their *salat*.' Ibn al-Qasim said: '... giving away *sadaqa* instead of using it to buy incense to be burnt in the mosque or to (buy) perfume for it is preferable to me than burning incense in the mosque and perfuming it.' 'Iyad said: 'his words "perfuming it" means with clay impregnated with saffron.' He has interpreted his saying 'preferable to me...' by comparing it to the judgement mentioned by Ibn Rushd with regard to the texts indicating that it is *makruh* to bequeath something to a *kafir* saying 'Malik said: "Whoever makes a vow to do so should fulfil it."' Ibn Rushd said: '.. it is true that there is a reward in all cases for bequeathing something to a *dhimmi kafir*. However, the judgement that it is *makruh* arises from giving preference to a *dhimmi* over a Muslim – not the act of bequeathing to a *dhimmi* in itself.'

2. Alif-lam-mim-sad has not mentioned that it is disliked to speak after the *Subh salat*. Khalil, however, has mentioned this, saying 'speech after the *Subh* as sunrise approaches.' Az-Zurqani said: 'It would appear that 'approaching' means in the sense commonly understood by people – although it is recommended to recite Qur'an and perform *dhikr*.' Ibn al-Musayyab was asked: 'Which is best at the above mentioned time, Qur'an or *dhikr*?' and he replied: 'The recitation of Qur'an, although the earlier generations have transmitted that *dhikr* (is better).' The acquisition of knowledge (would also be included) – according to what Ibn Naji esteems to be correct – because of the great degree of ignorance and lack of true knowledge. The author's deeming speech to be *makruh* indicates the opposite (judgement applies) when one is silent – and this is indeed the case. This, however, contradicts (the judgement of) the Iraqis who hold that desisting from speaking is not rewarded – a reward being made only when *dhikr* is performed. The judgement of the *Risala* appears to confirm the author, that is, that the *makruh* judgement is also removed by means of sleep after the *Subh* (*salat*) – when one sleeps with the intention of desisting from speech, that is, he is rewarded for silence and sleeping if he intends obedience (to the instruction of the *shari'ah*), even though sleep at this time is proscribed on account of the narration 'Sleeping after the *Subh salat* prevents provision.' However, it has also been said that this means that it prevents 'ample' provision or that it refers to his experiencing difficulty in acquiring provision. Speech without *dhikr* of Allah and without knowledge is *makruh* in mosques. It is recommended to make extended *dhikr* and seek forgiveness of Allah when the sky turns to deep yellow before the *Maghrib*.

3. It is proscribed to do the *salat* at the bottom of a river valley. Ibn al-Hattab: 'Tenth, the places mentioned in *al-Jawahir* where it is *makruh* to do the *salat*: that is, in the bottom of a river valley, as river valleys are the refuge of shaytan.' Ibn 'Abd al-Barr said in *at-Tamheed*, explaining the forty-third hadith of Zayd ibn Aslam: 'The preferred judgement with us on this subject is that the river valley (mentioned in the hadith) and any other are all places where it is permitted to pray as long as one is sure there is nothing impure in them to prevent this. There is no sense in purporting that the place where one goes to sleep and misses the *salat* is a place of Shaytan and an accursed place and that one should no longer perform the *salat* in it – given that we know of no place which is free of the presence of Shaytan and no place where Shaytan does not go.'

'Ayn-Qaf said: 'I am not aware of the transmission regarding the river valley and Ibn al-Hajib's relating it as part of the *madhhab*.'

In *at-Tawdih* it is said that that the author is alone in transmitting this. I say: 'Ibn Shas has mentioned it when discussing the places where it is *makruh* to perform the *salat*, and also in his discussion of the conditions of the *salat* – and this has been related from him by the author of *adh-Dhakeera* who affirmed it (as correct).'"

Fard 'Ayn and Fard Kifaya Salats

فَصْلٌ

وَخَمْسُ صَلَوَاتٍ فَرْضُ عَيْنٍ

Section:

140 and the five *salats* are an individual *fard* obligation, …

that is, they are an obligation on every sane adult. This is a part of the deen which is known (by all) of necessity and whoever disputes its obligatory nature and the obligation of its prostration or bowing and the like is a *kafir*.

وَهِيَ كِفَايَةٌ لِمَيْتٍ دُونَ مَيْنٍ

… and (the *salat*) over the dead person is a communal responsibility, without doubt

Al-Fakihani has stated that this is the judgement of most (of the *'ulama*) and al-Jazuli said: "This is correct, although it has also been said that it is a sunna

– and this is the judgement of Ibn al-Qasim and Asbagh. It is also stated by Sanad – as long that is as there is someone to perform it, for if not, it becomes a responsibility on each and every person (*fard ain*)."

USEFUL POINT: ash-Sha'rani said in al-*Yawaqeet wa'l-Jawahir* from Shaykh Muhyi'd-deen: "Know that Allah, exalted is He, has only made it an obligation on us to perform the *salat* over the dead person so that our intercession will be accepted in it and in order to make known to us that our asking during it is accepted and that Allah, exalted is He, is content with this of us – for the command to do something necessarily entails that the Legislator is content with it. Some of the Mu'tazilis say that the person who kills himself is in the Fire – that it is assumed he is a *kafir* and that he died on his (act of) *kufr* or is classed as one of those for whom the *janaza salat* is not done. For this reason we say that *salat* over the person who kills himself is obligatory and that our *salat* over him is of benefit to him and prevents him from remaining for ever in the Fire – despite their claims. The judgement of the people of sunna and *jama'a* is that neither a *mumin* or a person of *tawhid* remains for ever in the Fire. There is also the hadith: 'Make the *salat* over the person who says *la ilaha illa'llah*.' Even the people of innovation who do not deny their innovation are included in this (hadith) as the Messenger, may the peace and blessings of Allah be upon him, did not discriminate or exclude anyone but rather made a general statement with his words 'the person' and referred thereby to any person. The Legislator has only commanded us to make the *salat* over those who say *la ilaha illa'llah* in order to extend His mercy to such persons, either by not having them enter the Fire at all or by having him leave it after having subjected them to a degree of punishment (befitting them)."

USEFUL POINT: al-Munawi said in his commentary on the hadith 'There is no Muslim who dies and forty men – who do not associate partners in any way with Allah – do the *salat* over him but that He accepts their intercession for him': "Ibn al-'Arabi said: 'Take pains – if someone amongst you dies – that forty men or more perform the *salat* over him for they can intercede for him, according to the text of the hadith: "…an Arab passed by a *janaza* at which a large number of people were taking part and he said: 'He is one of the people of the Garden.' Someone asked 'Why?' and he replied: 'Which generous person would refuse the intercession of a large group of people who came to him for the sake of a single person? by Allah, he would never refuse them! – so how must it be in the case of Him, the most Generous and most Merciful of all – surely they only have to make a *du'a* for their intercession to be accepted of them.'"

USEFUL POINT: 'Ayn said in his gloss on the *Risala* that Ibn 'Umar said: "Presence at the *janaza* is for three reasons: out of desire, out of fear and out of an expectation of requital – and the reward is for the first not the others."

I SAY: "As to whether or not a person who attends both on account of his desire and for the reward, or out of fear or for the reward will have the above mentioned reward, the words of Ibn 'Umar imply that he will not – for it is (a kind of) *shirk*; likewise, if a person attends out of desire and fear. There remains a further possibility: namely, if he attends out of fear for himself. In this case, he is considered to have done what is obligatory on him and will be rewarded for it. But how, then, does this accord with the words of Ibn 'Umar – that the reward is granted in the case of the first and not the two others? There is no contradiction in this as what is meant is that he will get the reward in the last two cases mentioned by the author – but this does not exclude that he will receive another reward. Al-Burzuli also has given a contrary view to Ibn 'Umar, regarding the requital mentioned by; likewise what is stated by al-Quyyoumi in *Sharh at-Taghreeb wa't-tarheeb*: 'Branch: nothing whatsoever of the reward will be denied the person behind the *janaza* if he is only there because it is one of his relations – for this is commanded of him and is not classed as showing off on his part, as one person has claimed. We have narrated from *al-Hilya* of Abu Nu'aym from Ibn Sirin who was asked about this and he replied: "This is (classed as) maintaining ties with relations, be they alive or dead – indeed the reward is even greater (in this case).""'

In the *Matla' al-badrayn fi man yu'ti ajrahu marratayn* of Hafidh as-Suyuti there is also something which corresponds to this: "Ibn Abu Dunya has related in *Kitab dhikr al-mawt* from Ibn 'Ateeq who said: 'I asked Muhammad ibn Sirin as to whether a man who follows a *janaza* – not out of expectation of a reward (in the next world) but in order to see his relations – would get a reward and he replied: "Just one reward! Indeed he will get two: his praying over his brother and the reward of maintaining good relations with the living.""'

I SAY: "One of the people of this time have said: 'As to his words at the beginning regarding whether he attends out of fear or for requital – examine them and study them equitably.'"

ISSUE: az-Zurqani said, commenting on the words of Khalil regarding various recommended aspects ''…and the standing of the imam between the middle and the shoulders of the woman, with the head of the dead woman to his right': "This is recommended when the *salat* is being said in other than the noble *rawda* (of the Prophet's tomb, may the peace and blessing of Allah be upon him) in which case one should have the head of the dead person to the left so that the feet do not point in the direction of his noble grave."

I SAY: "Examine whether one may extrapolate from this that one should not stretch out one's feet towards the *mus-haf* of the Qur'an – given that a single letter of the Qur'an is better than the Prophet, may the peace and blessings of Allah be upon him, as one of the *'ulama* said. However, I saw something from the *Sharh al-Burda* of Ibn Marzouq after this showing there is a difference of opinion in the matter: 'As to whether the degree (of excellence of the Prophet, may the peace and blessings of Allah be upon him,) corresponds to his *'ayats'* – his signs or miracles, this matter is disputed: one of the commentators has mentioned an objection to Alif-Lam-Sad's saying that one of the miracles of the Prophet, may the peace and blessings of Allah be upon him, was of greater excellence than the Qur'an – namely that this *ayat* of his was in fact the Qur'an itself. However, he did not accept it saying: "We do not accept this for he is better than the spoken word which was revealed on him".' Then he goes on to transmit something from another commentator affirming the first but does not give an answer to what he says. Thus it is as if the matter is not one of the essential matters in his view, so examine it in the place mentioned. Muhammad 'Abd al-Baqi has mentioned in *Maqasid al-Hasana* that the hadith which speaks of the superiority of a letter of the Qur'an over the Prophet, may the peace and blessings of Allah be upon, him, is weak and invalid."

Al-Mawwaq has related that Abu 'Umar said: "There are differences in the traditions as to where the imam should stand in relation to the *janaza*, and there is no binding rule from the Book and the sunna. However, there is no harm in anything that has been transmitted from the earlier generations."

ISSUE: al-Mawwaq has related from Abu 'Umar that Malik and others have said: "Whoever does not catch the *salat* over the *janaza*, then he should not do the *salat* over the dead person, nor at his grave." Ibn Wahb and others have said: "He should pray at his grave." Abu 'Umar said: "The *salat* over his grave or wherever he makes the *salat* is licit as neither Allah nor His Messenger have proscribed it. Moreover, there is no agreement as to its being *makruh*. One should not prevent anyone from doing something good except when incontrovertible proof exists." In *al-Masalik* – regarding the *salat* of the Prophet, may the peace and blessings of Allah be upon him, for the Negus (of Abysinnia) – there is proof that he made the *salat* for a dead person whose body was not physically present. The Malikis argue that this (practice) applied only to Muhammad, may the peace and blessings of Allah be upon him. We have said: "What Muhammad did, may the peace and blessings of Allah be upon him, the *umma* does after him. If someone were to ask whether the Negus was in fact present at the *janaza* we would reply that our Lord blessed is He and exalted, has the power to do this and that our Prophet, may the peace and blessings of Allah be upon him, would be worthy of such (a miracle)."

THE FARD OF JANAZA

$$فُرُوضُهَا التَّكْبِيرُ أَرْبَعاً دُعَا$$

$$وَنِيَّةُ سَلَامُ سِرٍّ تَبَعَا$$

141 Its *fard* obligations are the *takbir* four times, the *du'a*, the intention, and saying the *salam* silently

$$وَكَالصَّلَاةِ الْغُسْلُ دَفْنٌ وَكَفَنْ$$

142 and like the *salat*, the *ghusl*, burial and enshrouding the corpse [are communal responsibilities] ...

'Ali ibn 'Abd as-Sadiq said: "His words 'like the *salat*' means 'like the judgement of the *salat* over the dead with all that it implies of the difference of opinion as to whether it is sunna or obligatory. The well known judgement -which we have restricted ourselves to – is that it is a communal obligation."

Al-Mawwaq has related that Ibn Rushd said: "It is recommended that the first washing be with clear water, the second with water and the lotus tree leaves, and the third with water and camphor."

Two useful lessons: firstly, as-Suyuti has related the hadith in which the Prophet, may the peace and blessings of Allah be upon him, said: "Whoever cuts down a lotus tree, then Allah will bend his head down into the Fire" and noted that it has been reported by Abu Dawud, that ad-Diya' esteemed it as *sahih* in *al-Mukhtar*, and that at-Tabarani has related it in *al-Awsat* – who added ".... of the lotus trees of the Haram (in Makka)."

I SAY: "I am of the opinion that it is to be understood as referring to the lotus trees of the Haram as occurs in the narration of at-Tabarani. Ibn al-Athir said in *an-Nihaya*: "It is said that what is being referred to is the lotus trees of the open country which the travellers and animals use for shade; or those in private property which are mistreated and cut down by someone without the right to do so. Whatever the truth of the matter, the hadith is defective in its chain of narration. Most of the *'ulama* follow what has been narrated from 'Urwa ibn az-Zubayr, may Allah be pleased with him, who would cut down lotus trees and would make doors from them. The people of knowledge are agreed that cutting them down is licit."

2. Al-'Alqami said in his commentary on *al-Jami' as-Saghir*: "It is recommended that the washer be a trustworthy person and that if he sees something good, then he should mention it and if he sees something bad, he should not disclose it – unless there is some benefit in this, like for example, if the person was a person of open innovation and he reveals what he sees to prevent others (from such innovation); or if he was openly unjust."

Al-Munawi said: "An-Nawawi said: 'If the person washing the dead person sees something he approves of like light in his face or (smells) a pleasant perfume, then it is sunna that he speak about it to people; if he sees something he dislikes like a blackening of the face, malodour, malformation or alteration of the limbs, then it is forbidden for him to talk about it."

Issue: Khalil said, adding to what is recommended "the person washing him also should take a *ghusl* himself." Al-Mawwaq has related that Ibn Rushd said: "The most evident meaning of what Ibn al-Qasim reports having heard is that the person washing the dead person is obliged to take a *ghusl* himself (afterwards)." Ibn al-Qasim said: "This is the best of what I have heard." The most evident judgement in my view is that he approves of the judgement that taking a *ghusl* is obligatory, like his narration from Malik. Ibn Abi Zayd has understood the words of Ibn al-Qasim 'that he recommends *ghusl*' as being "like the saying of Malik in *al-Mukhtasar*." It has also been said that he does not have to take a *ghusl*. Malik said in *al-Wadiha*: "This is what the majority hold to – and this is something that has been arrived at by examination and analogy as the washing of the dead person in itself is not something which brings about physical impurity."

As for his saying 'burial', he said in *Ghayat al-Amani*: "It is recommended that he be placed on his right side facing the *qibla* and that the earth be placed in front and behind him so that he does not roll over. The name of Allah ta*barakallah* should be mentioned when placing him in the grave and the words *bismillah wa 'ala millatil-rasullullah* – in the name of Allah and the nation of the Messenger of Allah, may the peace and blessings of Allah be upon him. One should make *du'a* but not so long as to cause hardship to people."

Branch: al-Mawwaq said that Ibn al-Habib said: "It is recommended that the grave not be dug too deeply, rather a forearm's length, and this is accepted by Ibn Abi Zayd." Al-Baji said: "…that is, the hole for the niche in the lateral wall for the grave itself will be bigger." Ibn 'Aat said: "Those who are of the opinion that the depth should be the length of a man or twice this are referring to (burial in) open countryside, or when the likelihood of desecration exists."

Issue: al-Mawwaq has related that Ibn 'Arafa has also said: "The husband has the most right to place his wife in the grave; and if he is not present, then her nearest relative." Ibn al-Qasim said: "...and if she has no relatives, then someone from the people of excellence." Sahnun said: "If there are no close relatives of hers, then a woman, and if no (woman), then someone from the people of excellence." Ibn al-Qasim said: "The husband has more right than the father or the son." Ibn Rushd said: "This is correct." Ibn al-Habib said: "When raising her, the husband may get help from a close relative, but if no one is available, then a person of excellence should raise her and the husband should lower her."

Al-Mawwaq said that a person may also be buried at night. Mutarrif said: "There is no harm in performing the *salat* over the dead at night or burying them at night. Ibn Shihab is of this view as well as Ibn Abi Hazim. As-Saddeeq was buried at night as well as Fatima and 'A'isha, may Allah be pleased with both of them. and it is also permitted to kiss the dead: Abu Bakr kissed the Prophet, may the peace and blessings of Allah be upon him, and the Prophet, may the peace and blessings of Allah be upon him, kissed Ibn Madh'oun."

Issue: Ibn al-Hattab has related that al-Aqfahisi said: "It is permitted for someone to prepare a shroud and grave for his own death but then use it for someone else if the need arises." What he is referring to is a grave on land that he himself owns. As for the burial sites belonging to the Muslims in general, then it would not be permitted – as has been stated in *al-Madkhal* and *at-Tawdih*.

Issue: al-Mawwaq has related that Ibn Habib said: "There is no harm in placing one stone at the end of the grave to ensure that the (precise) position (of the grace) is not forgotten when the marks of the (fresh earth) are effaced." Ibn 'Arafa has related that al-Hakim said: "It is not a practice based on the hadith to prohibit the setting up of something to mark the grave and the making of an inscription on it for the graves of the Imams from the East to the West have been erected with inscriptions – and this is a practice which the later generations adopted from the earlier ones."

Issue: al-Mawwaq has related that al-Mazari said: "According to us, it is permitted to sit at graves. What is being referred to in the prohibition of sitting on them is the act of defecating and urinating – this is how Malik interpreted it and it has also been narrated that this is how the Prophet, may the peace and blessings of Allah be upon him, understood the matter. Moreover, 'Ali used to use the graves to recline and sit on." Ibn Habib said: "There is no harm in walking over them if their traces have been effaced. As for a vaulted grave with a path going under it, I do not like (people walking there) as this would be a violation (of the burial area encompassed by) the arch." Ibn 'Abd al-Ghafur said: "The graveyard may be ploughed up after ten years if there is a shortage of space for burial." Another *'alim* said: "It is not permitted to take the stones of disused graveyards if there is a shortage of burial space – even years after they have fallen into disuse." Yet another said: "It is not permitted to take the stones of graveyards whose marks have been effaced even if it to use them to build bridges or mosques – the judgement that it is not permitted to plough over them is based on this." Then he goes on to say: "If it is (nevertheless put to another use), then the rent from it should be given towards helping in the burial of the poor." Ibn Rushd said: "As for the building of a mosque on a graveyard whose marks have been effaced, this is not disliked as the graveyard and mosque are both waqfs for use by the Muslims: if it cannot be used to bury the dead and is needed to build a mosque, then there is no harm in this. This is because there is no harm in using what belongs to Allah for something else also dedicated to Him when the benefit from the latter is greater and the people are in more need of it."

One of the *'ulama* has given a *fatwa* regarding walking over grave-mounds arguing that the Messenger, may the peace and blessings of Allah be upon him, would cross graveyards by going *over* the grave-mounds not between them. Another said that walking over graveyards is permitted when necessary and when one has a grave there (to attend to). He has also indicated that one should take care not to destroy them – and noted that what is deemed 'necessary' is subject to specific rules.

The author of *al-Mi'yar* said that the Prophet on whom be peace said: "If the grave is coated or daubed with clay, then the person buried there will not hear the *adhan* or *du'as* and will not know who visits him – so do not daub the graves of your dead with clay. Make *du'as* for them for they can hear *dhikr*, and the earth of the grave continues to glorify Allah ten times a day until the person buried is forgiven – as long as the grave has not been coated with clay."

As for his saying 'enshrouding', al-Mawwaq has related that Ibn 'Arafa said: "When enshrouding the dead person, one should cover the whole of the corpse." Al-Mazari said: "Enshrouding is obligatory according to us."

Issue: al-Mawwaq said: "It is recommended that only the most excellent and best – in guidance and in speech – of his family sit with him when he is dying and that they do a lot of *du'as* for him for the angels are present with him and they will bear witness to the *du'as* of the people present."

Issue: Ibn al-Hattab said: "Do not be grieved that the dead person does not respond to what is said to him for he is witnessing what they are not witnessing."

Al-Qarafi said: "If a person's tongue becomes dumb, his intellect goes, he does not declare the two *shahadas*, he does not respond with Iman in his heart and he dies in this state, then he dies as a *mumin* . His lack of iman at the actual moment of his death does not harm him – for just as the *kafir* – when death comes and his tongue is dumb and his intellect goes – has become incapable of *kufr* so he too is physically incapable of this (expression of Iman). However, the *kafir*'s incapacity to express his *kufr* at this moment is of no benefit to him and the judgement of him with Allah is the same as those who actually manifest *kufr* in this moment. What is taken into account is the *kufr* or iman which preceded this moment."

Issue: al-Mawwaq has related that Ibn Habib said: "There is no harm in carrying the dead person from the country to the town or from one place to another." When Sa'd ibn Zayd and Sa'd ibn Abi Waqqas, may Allah be pleased with them, died, they were carried to Madina."

Issue: al-Mawwaq related that Malik disliked that anyone should cry out aloud in the mosque in order to announce a *janaza,* saying: "There is no good in it. However, I do not see any harm if someone goes round the circles of people and lets people know without raising his voice." Ibn Rushd said: "Calling out in the mosque for the *janaza* is not permitted because it is *makruh* to raise one's voice in mosques. Malik considered this to be the same as the judgement prohibiting people from declaring the death of someone in a mosque and from calling people to witness his *janaza*. As for letting people know without calling out, this is permitted, according to the consensus."

Issue: al-Mawwaq related that Ibn al-Qasim and Ashhab narrated: "Recitation (over the dead person) and burning incense are not part of the practice." Ibn Rushd said: "Ibn Habib said 'It is recommended' and has related the hadith of the Prophet, may the peace and blessings of Allah be upon him: 'Whoever recites Ya-Sin – or it is recited to him – when he is in the throes of death, then Allah sends an angel to the angel of death commanding that "death should be made easier for my slave."'" He has also said: "Malik disliked that it be done as a sunna." Something similar has been related of Ibn Yunus. Ibn Habib said: "When someone is on the point of death, it is recommended that sweet smelling incense be brought close to him, or some other perfume, and there is no harm in reciting Ya-Sin at his shoulder. When Malik was asked about it, he replied that he did not dislike it but that he disliked that it be taken as a sunna."

Useful point: al-Munawi said – commenting on the hadith 'Prompt those of you who are dying to say *la ilaha illa'llah*': "If someone were to argue:

'Whoever dies as a *mumin* will enter the Garden without doubt and whoever is not (destined to be) spared the Fire will certainly enter it – so what is the use of saying this to him?' – that Ibn al-'Arabi said: "If you repeat (*la ilaha illa'llah*) to him and he does not say it (after you) and he says only *la* – 'no!' – then do not despair of him. I know of someone in Tunis who was asked to repeat this as he was in the throes of death. His eyes glazed and he said *la* – 'no!' He was a *salih* and people were afraid for him. They all agreed that he had answered (no!) to them. However, afterwards he was able to tell them: 'Shaytan came to me in the form of various persons from among my forefathers saying "Beware of Islam! die as a Jew or a Christian! – for there is more salvation in this for you" and I would say to them *la* – 'no!', and Allah protected me.'"

USEFUL POINT: al-Munawi has also related that Ibn al-'Arabi said: "I was with someone from amongst you who was dying and the people (there) recited Ya-Sin in his presence. I became ill and fainted, and I was considered as one of the dead. I saw a group of people like a shower of rain who wanted to injure me. Then I saw a beautiful, perfumed and powerful person who kept pushing them away from me until he overpowered them. I asked him: 'Who are you?' and he replied: 'Sura Ya-Sin' and then I woke up and there was my father at the head of my bed crying. He was reading Ya-Sin and had just finished it."

Benefit al-Buhayri has related in *Sharh al-Irshad* that Ibn al-'Arabi said: "Allah has created man with love for the *dunya* and hate for the next world. If this results in his relying on the *dunya*, having love for it or preferring it, then he will have lasting misery; if it results in fear for his wrong actions and a desire to do good actions which will save him, then he will have good news, forgiveness and blessings. If he feels embarrassed before Allah, exalted is He, for the wrong actions he has committed, then Allah, exalted is He, will have even more embarrassment than he: this sense is also transmitted in the hadith *qudsi* of the Prophet, may the peace and blessings of Allah be upon him: 'If My slave longs to meet Me, I long to meet him, and if My slave does not want to meet Me, I do not want to meet him.'"

USEFUL POINT: With regard to the hadith in al-Bukhari: "If four people bear witness to the good of a Muslim, Allah will cause him to enter the Garden. I said: 'and what about three, Messenger of Allah?' and he replied: 'and three' and we asked: 'and two?' and he replied: 'and two' and we did not ask him about one", Jasousi has related that *'Ayn-Jeem* said: "The fulfilment (of the sense of this hadith) is conditional upon the praise being said by a just and good person who is worthy of making this testimony of good character. The character (of the person), however, does not necessarily have to correspond to their testimony – as some have claimed. Rather this (hadith) is an indication of what Allah, exalted is He, has in store for his slave in return for the testimony of a man of truth." This has also been stated by as-Suyuti.

There is also the hadith: "If the slave dies and Allah is aware of something evil in him but the people speak good (of him), then Allah will say to the angels: 'I have accepted the testimony of my slaves about my slave and I have forgiven my slave despite my knowledge (of him)'" – and this supports what Suyuti has mentioned, namely, that the praise of those who speak well of a person will be evidence in support of his entry to the Garden and that any bad said of him will not be taken into account – unless it corresponds to the reality.

USEFUL POINT: al-Munawi said, commenting on the hadith 'The *mumin* dies with the sweat on his brow...' – or whatever the exact text of the hadith is: "The sweat on his brow at the moment of death is a sign of iman for if the good news comes to him and he has done something repugnant, then he will feel shame and ignominy and his brow will sweat. What is below (i.e. the rest of his body) dies but the strength of life remains (for a moment) at the top (of his body): the sense of shame remains in his eyes. All this occurs at the time of the good news and the lifting of the veil – but a *kafir* is blind to this."

USEFUL POINT: it is stated in *al-Mi'yar*: "Ahmad ibn Bakout was asked as to whether the people's practice of carrying off the earth of graveyards for its blessing was permitted. He replied: 'It is permitted as long as the people are seeking blessing at the graveyards of the *'ulama*, the *shaheeds* and the right acting persons. People used to carry off the earth of Sayyidi Hamza ibn 'Abd al-Muttalib, may Allah be pleased with him, a long time ago. It could hardly be that the *'ulama* of Madina have conspired to keep silent about this were it a forbidden innovation – that is surely far from the truth.'"

I SAY: "This is like the practice of the common people of carrying of earth from the tombs of Shaykh Abu Ya'za and Shaykh Abu Ghalib as-Saryawi in order to seek a cure by it from difficult sores and ulcers."

I SAY: "Ahmad Zarruq, in his commentary on the *Risala*, has stated that it is forbidden."

USEFUL POINT: al-Munawi, commenting on the hadith 'If three of a Muslim's children die before committing any crime they will meet him at the eight gates of the Garden and he will enter by any he wishes' said: "There are various benefits associated with the death of children: they will be a shield from the fire, as is stated in a number of narrations, they will cause the scales to weigh heavily in favour (of his parents), they will intercede for them regarding entry to the Garden, they will give their (fore)fathers to drink of the drink of the

Garden on the 'Day of Great Thirst', and they will alleviate the agony of death for their parents: they will remember their (children) who were a coolness for their eyes and who preceded them (in death), and other things besides."

USEFUL POINT: al-Munawi, commenting on the hadith 'Whoever remembers some misfortune – even if it happened some time before and who again says *inna lillahi wa inna ilayhi raji'un – surely we belong to Allah and surely we are returning to Him*,[1] then Allah will write for him a reward the like of the day the misfortune first struck' said: "Useful point: in a *marfu'* hadith it states that what nullifies the reward for misfortune is a man clapping his right hand in his left; and his saying '*and beauty lies in showing steadfastness*'[2] or 'contentment with what the Majestic King has decreed.'"

Al-Munawi has also said, commenting on the hadith: 'Whoever is struck by misfortune – with regard to his wealth or body – but conceals it and does not complain to people, then Allah will take it upon Himself to forgive him': "This does not contradict the saying of the Prophet, may the peace and blessings of Allah be upon him, during his illness: 'O my head!' for this was said to let people know – not as a complaint. Thus if a person were to say '*al-hamdulillah*' and then let others know about his illness, this is not a complaint – whereas in the case of someone who speaks about it in a state of ill temper and anger it is. The mere saying of one word (of praise or complaint) will result in his being rewarded or punished according to his intention."

USEFUL POINT: there is a difference of opinion as to whether or not deeming *kafir* those who are struck by affliction for their wrong actions is conditional upon their being steadfast and patient. The preferred of two judgements is that indeed they can only be deemed *kafir* if they are not patient (and if they complain inordinately). Examine this at the point where Alif-lam-sad speaks of *tasawwuf* and 'patience and steadfastness.'

I SAY: "The opposite of steadfastness is being anxious, concerned and impatient: in the *Sahih* of al-Bukhari, Muhammad ibn Ka'b has defined it as 'speaking evil and thinking evil'; Ibn Hajar said: 'what is meant by this is any (state which) arouses sadness, anxiety and despair (and the belief) that Allah will not change the misfortune in this world for something of more benefit. It also means thinking it unlikely that the reward promised (by Allah) for his steadfastness will be granted.'

Those holding to the view that displaying steadfastness is stipulated (for the Muslim) in the face of afflictions differ as to whether these afflictions only

---

1   al-Baqara: 156
2   Yusuf: 18

atone for one's wrong actions but contain no reward in them (for the person afflicted) – and this is what al-Qarafi holds to, or whether they both atone for wrong actions and also bring a reward – and this is what Ibn ash-Shat holds firmly to. Ibn ash-Shat refutes al-Qarafi's words, and this is also the unequivocal view of Ibn Hajar in *Fath al-Bari* who esteems the words of al-Qarafi as weak.

USEFUL POINT: Ibn al-Hattab has related that the author of *al-'Arida* said: "As for the person killed by thieves, there is no difference of opinion that he is a *shaheed*, although he is still taken to account for his wrong actions; likewise, whoever is killed unjustly defending his money or his self, whoever drowns or is killed as a result of highway robbery, then they are considered *shuhada'* but are still taken to account for their wrong actions. Not everyone who dies as a result of an act of disobedience is *not* a *shaheed* – whoever dies while committing a wrong action but for one of the (well-known) reasons associated with dying *shaheed* then he will have the reward for his dying *shaheed*. Likewise, if someone fights (in *jihad*) on a horse which he has taken wrongfully, or the (roof of a) house falls in upon a group of people committing an act of disobedience, then they die *shaheed* – but are still taken to account for their wrong actions."

SUNNA SALATS: WITR, ECLIPSE AND SALATS FOR RAIN

وِتْرُ كُسُوفٍ عِيدٍ اِسْتِسْقَا سُنَنْ

... while the *witr*, eclipse, 'Eid and rain *salat* are sunnas

Al-Mawwaq has related that Ibn Yunus said: "The *witr* is a sunna of special emphasis and no one can afford to leave off doing it." Sahnun said: "One should challenge or take formal exception to the person who leaves off doing it." Ibn 'Arafa said: "One of the *'ulama* has argued – in support of challenging someone who leaves off doing it – that it is a sign of belittling certain aspects of the deen." Asbagh said: "He should be rebuked." Al-Mazari said: "...because of his belittling the sunna." Likewise Khuwayz Mundad said: "The one who leaves off doing the sunna is a corrupt person." Mention has already been made of Ibn al-'Arabi's difficulty (with this judgement). I say: "This refers to Ibn al-'Arabi's comment on Khalil's words 'and his saying *subhana'llah*... while bowing' when he says: "...and beware of ....' I have mentioned this at the point where Ibn 'Ashir says 'the saying of *subhana'llah*.. during the prostration and bowing' – so examine it if you wish. As for other judgements regarding the *witr*, they are famous amongst students of *fiqh*, but this commentary does not deal with the well known matters (of *fiqh*)."

As for his mention of the 'eclipse', al-Mawwaq said: "This refers to the eclipse of either the sun or the moon, or a partial eclipse. The *salat* for the eclipse of the sun is a sunna of special importance. Malik said: '…a sunna which one should not leave off doing.' Ibn al-Qasim said: 'According to the judgement of Malik, the people of the villages and towns should pray it and those travelling should also perform it and do it together – unless they are actually travelling, in which case then each person should do it alone. A woman should perform it in her house although there is no harm in an older woman – not liable to distract the attention of men – from coming out (to perform it).' Ibn Habib said: 'Slaves should also pray it.' Ibn Yunus said: 'Everyone should pray it – (this judgement is) based on his saying: "If you see the (eclipse) of these two (i.e. the sun or moon), then make haste to the *salat*".' Ibn al-Qasim has narrated that he had heard: 'If those (who are not obliged to pray the *jumu'a*) do the *salat* of the eclipse in the open country voluntarily, then there is no harm in this.' Ibn Rushd said: 'As for those who are obliged to pray the *jumu'a*, they have no licence to leave off doing the *salat* of the eclipse in a *jama'a*.' Ash-Shaykh said from Ashhab: 'Whoever is not able to do it because of weakness – or in the case of a woman – should pray it alone.' It is also narrated that it is not made up (after the event)."

As for his mention of the ''Eid', al-Mawwaq said, commenting on the words of Khalil 'it is sunna to pray two *rak'ats* for the 'Eid for those who are obliged to do the *jumu'a* – from the time (after sunrise) when it is permitted to do *nafila* to the zenith': "The author of the *Talqeen* said: 'its time is from when the sun rises.' Al-Lakhmi said: 'Its time is when the sun has risen, has turned white and the redness has disappeared.' In *an-Nisa''a* it is reported from the Messenger of Allah, may the peace and blessings of Allah be upon him, that it is during the time that the *nafila* is permitted, that is, when the sun is shining fully and has risen the height of a spear – and here he is referring to the spear common among the Arabs. Ibn Basheer said: 'It is recommended to perform this *salat* after the sun has risen and has become white, and it should not be delayed beyond this.' Ibn Sha'ban has related from Malik: 'The imam should make haste to come out quickly for the 'Eid al-Adha and make the *salat* less long than he would for the 'Eid al-Fitr *salat* because the people will be occupied with their sacrificial animals and with returning to their families in the highlands.'

Issue: As for his words 'and doing it in the case of those not commanded to do it', 'Isa heard from Ashhab regarding the people of the villages who were not required to do the *jumu'a* that 'they do not perform the 'Eid-*salat*.' Ibn al-Qasim heard that 'there is no harm in there gathering and doing the 'Eid *salat* without a *khutba* – although if a *khutba* is made, then all well and good.' Ibn Rushd said: 'There is a difference of opinion in the narration regarding this matter in the *Mudawwana*: examine the text where talks about "those commanded to do the *jumu'a*".' Ibn Yunus has related from Ibn Habib: 'The *salat* of the 'Eid is binding on every Muslim: it is obligatory on women, slaves, travellers – and whoever is commanded to do the *salat* (in general) is also commanded to this (*salat*). If they do not do in a *jama'a*, then they should perform two *rak'ats* wherever they are and follow its sunna regarding the *takbirs* and the recitation, and this is the opinion of Malik and a group of his companions.' Abu 'Umar said: 'It is narrated from Malik in the *Mudawwana* that it is not incumbent on women; rather it is recommended in their case.'"

ISSUE: Ibn al-Hattab said in *al-Masa'il al-Malquta* that an-Nuhas said: "Abu Ja'far and others have said: 'There is agreement as to it being *makruh* for one man to say to another: "May Allah extend your life."' One of them said: 'This is the greeting of the atheists.' Ibn 'Abd al-Barr has related in *al-Isti'ab* that 'Umar said to 'Ali, may Allah be pleased with him: 'You have spoken the truth, may Allah extend your life.' If this is true then his words regarding what they are agreed upon is annulled."

BRANCH: The author of *at-Taraz* said: "No one denies that the young men may practice sports with their weapons during the two 'Eids and that one may watch them; likewise, that young boys may beat drums and the like." Then he has mentioned the playing of the Abyssinians saying: "This has also been mentioned by Malik who disliked their playing in the mosque: (in this regard) he has related the hadith describing how Sayyida 'A'isha, may Allah be pleased with her, was in a mosque, watching them."

As for his words 'the rain *salat*', al-Mawwaq has related that Ibn 'Arafa said: "Ibn 'Abd al-Hakam has related that the rain *salat* is sunna." Al-Lakhmi said: "He means 'at a time of drought or for drinking – even if performed for animals in the desert, or on a ship, or when people who are resident have taken in their crops and need more water." Al-Lakhmi has also said: "Performing the rain *salat* to increase fertility is licit, and is recommended if drought afflicts others – (given the evidence in the *ayat*:) '*help each other to goodness*'[1] and the two *hadith*: 'Whoever of you is able to benefit his brother, then let him do it' and 'The *du'a* of the Muslim for his absent brother is answered.' Al-Mazari has responded to this by saying: 'This refers to making a *du'a*, not to the sunna of the *salat*.'"

---

1 al-Ma'ida – The Table: 2

Al-Mawwaq has also related: "Abu Mus'ab said, relating from Malik, that one should only go out to perform the rain *salat* in extreme drought."

NOTICE: Khalil said: "It is recommended to do the *khutba* standing on the ground (not on a mimbar), to fast for three days before it,[1] to give *sadaqa* – although the imam should not command (people) to do these two things but should command (them only to turn in) *tawba* – and to seek to ward off Allah's punishment." 'Ayn-Qaf said, confirming his words, that is, 'turning in *tawba* from wrong action': "This means regret for acts of disobedience considered disgraceful by the *shari'ah* – even though he might not see any harm in them from a purely selfish point of view."

QADA' OF FAJR AND SUBH

فَجْرٌ رَغِيبَةٌ وَتُقْضَى لِلزَّوَالُ

وَالْفَرْضُ يُقْضَى أَبَداً وِبِالتَّوَالُ

143 *fajr* is a (particularly) desired (sunna) and can be made up right up to the sun's zenith. However, the obligatory must be made up however long the delay, and in its order

An intention is needed (for this *salat*) according to the well-known view, and it is not permitted to pray this (sunna) before the dawn.

ISSUE: Ibn al-Hattab said, commenting on Khalil's words 'the *salat* is not acceptable if it becomes clear the *takbirat al-ihram* was done before *fajr*, even if one had made an effort to find out the time': "What may be understood by the words of the author is that it is not permitted to make the two *rak'ats* – despite having tried to ascertain the time – unless he *thinks* that the dawn has broken. This is in fact correct: in the *Mudawwana* Sanad said: '…if he ascertains the time of *fajr*, then he is prohibited from doing (any further) *nafila salats*, and if he does the two *rak'ats* of *fajr* (at this moment), then he does them when there is a certain expansiveness with regard to the timing – as opposed to the *fard* which may only be prayed when one is *sure* the time has come.'"

ISSUE: al-Mawwaq has related that Ibn al-Qasim had heard: "Whoever finds the imam doing the *tashahhud* for the *Subh salat* when he has not yet done the *fajr salat*, then I consider that he should make the *Allahu akbar* and join in the *salat* with him." Ibn Rushd said: "This is better than sitting with him until he says the *salam* and then doing the *salat* of *fajr* – because of the command to

---

1 Here the text of Khalil is defective.

do the *salat* of greeting before *sitting* in the mosque. It has also been narrated that whoever catches the sitting (of the imam) has caught the excellence of doing the *salat* in a group." Ibn 'Allaf said: "Based on this latter judgement, he should (stand up and) complete the *salat* and not count it as merely a *nafila salat* although he may repeat it with (another) group."

USEFUL POINT: I have found the following extraordinary piece of knowledge which is only to be found in a few books: It is reported from Sayyidi 'Abd al-Wahhab ash-Sha'rani from 'Ali al-Khawwas from Sayyidina Dawud, may the peace and blessings of Allah be on him and our Prophet, that he said: "Whoever says three times morning and night:

سُبْحَانَ الدَّائِمِ الْقَائِمِ، سُبْحَانَ اللَّهِ الدَّائِمِ الْقَائِمِ، سُبْحَانَ الْحَيِّ الْقَيُّومِ، سُبْحَانَ اللَّهِ وَبِحَمْدِهِ سُبْحَانَ اللَّهِ الْعَظِيمِ، سُبْحَانَ الْمَلِكِ الْقُدُّوسِ سُبْحَانَ اللَّهِ رَبِّ الْمَلَائِكَةِ وَالرُّوحِ

subhana'd-Da'im al-Qa'im, subhana'llah al-Qa'im ad-Da'im, subhana al-Hayyu'l-Qayyum, subhana'llah wa bihamdihi subhanallahi'l-'adheem, subhana'l-Malik al-Qudduus, subhana'llah rabbi'l-mala'ikati war-ruh – *subhana* to the Everlasting, the Self-Subsisting, *subhana* to the Self-Subsisting to the Everlasting, *subhana* to the Living, the Sustainer, *subhana* to Allah and by Praise of Him, *subhana* to the Vast, *subhana* to the King, the Pure, *subhana* to the Lord of the Angels and the Ruh) then he will die on Islam without doubt, and there will be no hesitation or wavering."

However, the well-known view among people (who know) is what I have mentioned above at the author's words 'iman with certainty', namely, that there are six phrases not seven, and that they should be said between *fajr* and *Subh* only – so examine this matter at the point where he says 'iman with certainty.'

As for his saying 'and the obligatory…', 'Ali ibn 'Abd as-Sadiq said: "This means that the obligation to do it is not removed however much time elapses and that making it up must be done in accordance with what was missed – that is, shortened (if he had shortened the *salat*) or in full (if full), silently or aloud. He should also stand and make the *qunut* in the case of the *salat* of *Subh*, according to the most evident meaning of the *Risala*. He should make up (this *fard salat* irrespective of the time –) at sunrise or sunset or during the *khutba* of the *jumu'a* – that is, at any time during the night or day, irrespective of whether he omitted to do it deliberately, out of negligence or ignorance."

ISSUE: Zarruq said, commenting on the words of the *Risala* 'at sunrise and sunset, and however it is best for him': "That is, irrespective of whether he has a few (to make up, that is less than five), or a great number – as long as it is not too excessive, although this cannot be strictly defined. Rather he should strive as he is able, as Ibn Rushd said, while seeking to maintain the upkeep of his family. Something similar has been related by Ibn al-'Arabi from Abu Muhammad Salih: 'If he makes up two days (worth of *salat*) every day, then this is not excessive, and five (days) has also been mentioned. As for making up just one *salat* every *salat*, this is next to nothing as the common people would say – whoever is only able to do this, should not leave off doing it for it may be that one evil act is less significant than another and he has been prohibited from doing *nafila salats* altogether (until the others have been made up). One of the Shaykhs has made a *fatwa* saying: "If he (for any reason he does) leave off making them all up, then he should not leave off doing the *nafila*, and if he does make up a *fard*, then he should not perform the *nafila*."'"

Al-Ubbi has related that Ibn Naji said: "The most evident judgement in the *Mudawwana* is that making up (a *salat*) should be done immediately and that it is not permitted to delay it if one is able – and this is correct, according to the well known judgement. However, it has also been said that it may be delayed, and also that he should make up two days (*salats*) every day."

Ibn 'Arafa said in his *Mukhtasar*: "It is stated in the *Mudawwana* that whoever remembers that he has a small number of *salats* to make up should pray them there and then; if a great number, then he should pray them as he is able – while going about to settle what he needs, and when he has seen to these (needs), he should carry on praying until he finishes them." According to the first of the replies of Ibn Rushd (on this matter) he said: "Making up what one has forgotten or left off doing deliberately or left off doing through compelling circumstances becomes obligatory as soon as one remembers and is able. It may not be delayed after this, according to the consensus." In the other reply, he has stated: "There is no obligatory time although one is instructed to make up what one has missed as soon as possible lest death come upon one unawares: he may delay it as long as he thinks that in all probability he will be able to carry it out (before his death). Thus it is obligatory when remembered but not immediately, and the person who has to (make up) such (*salats*) should not do the *nafila*."

Muhammad al-Bannani has related that Ibn Rushd said in *al-Bayan*: "The time for making up) the forgotten (*salats*) is not restricted – thus it is not permitted to delay them (when remembered) under any circumstances, even if the sun is setting in the case of *'Asr* or is rising in the case of the *Subh*."

ISSUE: Zarruq said: "Doubt which is not based on any clear evidence is considered merely as a minor infraction for it is (caused by) the whispering (of shaytan). One does not have to make up (any *salat* about which one has doubts) except when there is a real basis for the doubt. Many of those given to correctness are obsessed with making up past *salats* missed without their having in fact missed them – as thinking or suspecting they have missed them is the same for them as actually having missed them. They call this 'the *salat* of a lifetime' and they consider that it is a perfecting (of their *salats* as a whole). Indeed some only want to do it so as not to have to pray the *nafila* at all: instead of each *nafila* they make up a 'missed' *salat*, arguing that perhaps there was some imperfection in it, or something missing, or that something had been done in it out of ignorance. However, this is far from the practice of the earlier generations. It amounts to an abandonment of the recommended *salats* and to getting caught up in something (i.e. doubt) which is endless (in nature). I have heard our Shaykh, Abu 'Abdallah Muhammad ibn Yusuf as-Sanusi mention that this has been prohibited in a clear text. I asked him about this and he replied: 'Al-Qarafi clearly stated this in the *Dhakheera*' – although I have not been able to find it there. Indeed, I have seen the opposite to this from Sayyidi 'Abdallah al-Balali in *Ikhtisar al-Ihya*' so examine this for it is important: practice in accordance with knowledge contains only good, and the opposite only bad."

I say: "In *Ma'alim al-Iman fi Ta'reef Rijal al-Qayrawan* by Ibn Naji there is a similar statement from al-Balali: 'Abu Bakr al-Maliki said: "He should give *sadaqa* of a third of his wealth and make an intention to fulfil any obligation he still has towards other persons – even though he is longer aware of who exactly they are: it is better to make this particular intention beforehand than merely giving away *sadaqa* without this (intention)." Abu'l-Hasan said: "…and likewise in the case of someone who wants to do the *nafila salat*: he should perform the *salats* of a complete day but in doing so make an (additional) intention to perform five *salats* missed (in the past), or to perform (more scrupulously) a *salat* which previously he had performed in a superficial manner and which would not have been accepted of him, or to make up a *salat* he had forgotten."'"

Nafila Salats: greeting the mosque, Duha and Tarawih

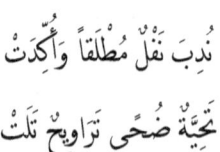

144 It is recommended to do the *nafila* at all times, although particular

importance is attached to the *salat* of greeting, the mid-morning *salat* and the *Tarawih*

Mayyara said: "The author, may Allah have mercy on him, has informed us that the *nafila* is recommended and by his words 'at all times' he means that there is no limit to the number of *nafila*; rather, that it is recommended to do as much (*nafila salats*) as he is able at any time of the night or day, that is, except when it is prohibited. Among the particularly recommended kinds (of *nafila*) is 'the greeting of the mosque' for it says in the two *Sahihs*: 'If one of you enters a mosque, then he should do (two) *rak'ats* before sitting down.' Abu Mus'ab said: '…except if he enters the mosque a lot, in which case the first (two) *rak'ats* are enough.' It is stated in *at-Tawdih*: 'If one were to speak of the sunna of the greeting (rather than *nawafil*) it would not be far from the truth. Our *'ulama* have said: "The two *rak'ats* are not in themselves desired but rather the point is that in performing them one distinguishes between the mosque and other houses." For this reason, if one prays the *fard salat* (immediately), then it is enough: only those intending to sit (immediately) are addressed (in the hadith) as requiring to make the (two) *rak'a* (of greeting).' As for the person (who is merely) passing by (the mosque) Malik said: 'It is permitted for him to leave off doing the (two) *rak'ats*.'"

Al-Mawwaq said that 'Iyad related: "The greeting of the mosque is a *salat* of excellence." Malik said: "It is praiseworthy but not obligatory." Abu 'Umar said: "…and this is the view of the *fuqaha* as a whole." Al-Qasim would enter the mosque and sit and not do any *salat* – and this is what Ibn 'Umar did, may Allah be pleased with him☐ and his son Salim. Abu 'Umar said: "Al-Ghazi ibn Qays travelled to Madina in order to hear from Malik, and Ibn Abi Dhi'b entered the Mosque of the Prophet, may the peace and blessings of Allah be upon him, and he sat down without praying two *rak'ats*. Al-Ghazi then said to him: 'Stand up and do (two) *rak'ats* for your sitting without performing them is a sign of your ignorance of the sunna…' and more words of this stern and course nature. So Ibn Abi Dhi'b got up and did the (two) *rak'ats* and then he prayed his *Dhuhr*. Then the people formed a circle around him and when al-Ghazi ibn Qays saw this he became embarrassed and regretted (what he had said). When he asked who it was he was told: 'It is Ibn Abi Dhi'b, one of the *fuqaha* of Madina and one of its most noble people' and so he got up and started to excuse himself. Ibn Abi Dhi'b said: 'O brother, there is no blame on you – all you did was to command me to good and we obeyed you.'"

'Iyad has recounted a similar story involving excellence of character about the Qadi al-Jama'a, Ibn as-Saleem: "He was present one day in a mosque on the outskirts of Qurtuba waiting for a *janaza*. Then the time for *'Asr* came and he made a sign to a man from amongst the ordinary people indicating that he should call an *adhan*. The man's face changed at his words and he said: 'Do you not see someone who is more impure than I among the people gathered here.' The Qadi smiled, sought forgiveness of Allah and then went out himself and called the *adhan*. On returning he said to the man: 'I have found someone more impure than you, may Allah turn in mercy to us and you.'"

Ibn al-Hattab said: "Branch: Ibn Naji in *Sharh al-Mudawwana* in the *Kitab al-Qadhf* has posed the question as to whether one should repeat (the two *rak'ats*) if one first prays the *salat* of greeting, goes out for something one needs and then returns soon afterwards. He goes on to say: '...all this is different to the saying of *as-salamu alaykum* for I do not see a difference of opinion in this matter: a person should say the *salam* to anyone he meets even if they have no social relations with each other. This is what the earlier generations used to do and this was accepted by our Shaykh, Abu Muhammad 'Abdallah ash-Shabeebi. He gave a *fatwa* to this effect – and this is correct because the nature of the *salam* is that it is for all time and all occasions."

As for his saying 'mid-morning *salat*' al-Mawwaq said: "The *Talqeen* and the *Risala* state that that the *salat* of the mid-morning *salat* – ad-Duha – is a *nafila*." Abu 'Umar said: "It is a *salat* of excellence and consists of eight *rak'ats*, although it has also been counted as a sunna." It has been transmitted in *at-Tawdih* from Ibn Rushd: "Most (of the reports are that) the *Duha salat* is comprised of eight *rak'ats*. Among the benefits of this *salat* is that it does instead of the *sadaqa* that is owing each morning from the three hundred and sixty joints in a man – as has been recorded by Muslim. It has also been said – regarding this same matter – that it suffices if he does two *rak'ats* of Duha." Al-Hafidh Abu'l-Fadl az-Zayn al-'Iraqi has related that "a rumour has spread amongst the ordinary people that whoever interrupts doing it will go blind and so many have left off (starting) doing it for this very reason. However, what they say has no basis. Indeed it appears that this is (the influence of) Shaytan insinuating things amongst the speech of the common people so as to prevent them from a great good – and in particular (preventing them from) giving in full this *sadaqa* demanded of them." Al-Hakim has related that the Messenger of Allah, may he peace and blessings of Allah be upon him, has commanded us to perform the *Duha salat* using (particular) suras, amongst them wa'sh-shamsi wa duhaha[1] and wa'd-Duha[2] – and the fittingness is clear here.

1 ash-Shams – The Sun: 1
2 wa'd-Duha – The Morning Brightness: 1

GOOD NEWS: Adam ibn Abi Iyas narrated in *Kitab ath-Thawab* from 'Ali ibn Abi Talib, may Allah be pleased with him: "The Messenger of Allah, may the peace and blessings of Allah be upon him, said: 'Whoever prays two *rak'ats* of *Duha* with iman and trusting that Allah will reward him what is his due, then Allah will record a reward equal to two hundred good actions for him, will remove two hundred wrong actions from his record, will raise him two hundred degrees and will forgive him all his minor wrong actions both those past and those to come – except in cases of requital and retaliation.'" In the *Sunan* of at-Tirmidhi and Ibn Majah it is recorded from the hadith of Abu Hurayra, may Allah be pleased with him, that the Messenger of Allah, may the peace and blessings of Allah be upon him, said: "Whoever persists in doing multiples of two *rak'ats* for *Duha*, then his wrong actions will be forgiven even if they are as great as the foam of the sea."

'Ali ibn 'Abd as-Sadiq said: "Its first time is when the sun shines white, the last time is when it is at its zenith and its best time is when a length (of time has elapsed since *Subh* which is) similar (to the length of time) between *'Asr* and *Maghrib*."

Al-Mawwaq said that Ibn al-'Arabi has related: "Whoever performs it is counted as one of the *Awabun* – those who turn frequently in praise and *salat* to Allah, and three hundred and sixty bones (of his) will be protected from the Fire."

As for his saying '*Tarawih*', 'Ali ibn 'Abd as-Sadiq said: "…that is, praying the well known pairs of *rak'ats* in Ramadan." In the *Risala* it states: "If one recites the Qur'an as best as one can, one has the right to expect a reward (from Allah) and to expect that one's wrong actions will be forgiven." In the hadith of 'A'isha, may Allah be pleased with her, it states: "The Messenger of Allah, may the peace and blessings of Allah be upon him, did not do any more than twelve *rak'ats* followed by the *witr*." Malik said: "This is what I hold to myself – because of his practice, may the peace and blessings of Allah be upon him." Ibn Sha'ban said: "The (*Tarawih*) has been recorded from the Prophet, may the peace and blessings of Allah be upon him, and so no one with intellect should miss it – even if he only recites the Umm al-Qur'an in every *rak'a* between *'Isha* and *fajr*." It is recommended to recite the whole of the Qur'an during it although a sura is enough. It is permitted to perform it alone in one's house as long as the mosques are not empty. Its time is after the *salat* of *'Isha*. (It may be said that) in general, there is a great excellence spending the night standing in *salat* and the best time for it is at the end of the night because of the hadith in which it is stated that our Lord – that is, His command and mercy – descends at this time and because of the hadith: "Whoever recites two *ayats* from the end of surat al-Baqara – the Cow – in the night, then they will be enough for him." Whoever perseveres in this standing in *salat* during the night will necessarily be present at the *Laylat al-Qadr* – the Night of Power – for Allah has granted it to us and has ensured the gift of its sweetness to us for ever, and surely He is the Bestower of blessings and the Noble and Generous. It is recorded in a *Sahih* hadith that whoever stands for it with iman and in expectation of Allah's reward, then he will be forgiven his past wrong actions. Let it be enough for any man to realise that in leaving off doing it, the slave is depriving himself of the divine gift and support which descends on those who are awake – for surely there is no night but that help and support descends from the heaven and is granted to those who are awake. Those asleep are necessarily deprived of it. Al-'Arif ash-Sha'rani said that Shaykh al-Islam Zakariya, may Allah have mercy on him, has related: "We have found out from experience that in order to rid oneself of an illness which the doctors are unable to cure a person should pray as many *rak'ats* as he is able at the end of the night and then ask Allah for (the help) he needs: He will cure him speedily." He also used to say that the breeze just before dawn heals the sick.

NOTICE: al-Munawi said, commenting on the hadith 'Whoever recites the last two *ayats* from Surat al-Baqara – The Cow – during the night, they will be enough for him...': "There is a similar tradition in the narration of al-Bukhari but with an addition to the text indicating '...if one *perseveres* in it.' This refers to the *ayat* beginning: '*The Messenger has* iman ..' to the end of the sura.[1] His saying 'it will be enough for him' means that it will save him having to spend the whole of that night standing reciting the Qur'an; or that he will rewarded for any recitation of the Qur'an – irrespective of whether it is recited in a *salat* or at another time; or that they contain enough (for anyone) with respect to the *'aqida* and the action mentioned in them (if held to and applied); or that they will protect a person from all evil and every disliked thing; or that they will protect him from the evil of shaytan, or from blight and disease; or that they will ward off the evil of men and the jinn; or that what one obtains from reciting them will be enough of a reward in itself – such that one will not have to seek anything else; or that they dispense with the need to recite *ayat al-Kursi* – about which it is narrated that if one recites it before retiring to bed then Allah will keep one's house safe."

NAFILA SALATS: WITR, BEFORE DHUHR AND 'ASR, AFTER MAGHRIB

---

1 al-Baqara -The Cow: 284-5

and Dhuhr

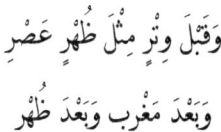

145 (*nafila salats* are performed) before the *Witr*, before *Dhuhr* and *Asr*, and after *Maghrib* and after *Dhuhr*

Al-Mawwaq said, commenting on the words of the *Risala* 'It is recommended to recite the *nafila salats* of the night aloud and those of the day silently but there is a licence in this if one does the *nafila* aloud during the day': "Ashhab heard [Malik say] that there is no harm in raising one's voice when reciting in one's *salat* when alone in one's house for it may well be that it stimulates one (to recite more). They used to do this in Madina, and the travellers used to agree to meet at specific times in the night to stand in *salat* with the Qur'an reciters." Ibn al-Qasim heard [Malik say] that it is recommended. Ibn Rushd said: "This is when someone has a clear intention to (recite aloud) so he may be taken as a model – in which case he will obtain the reward of being followed by others." Ashhab has narrated that 'Umar ibn 'Abd al-'Aziz – who had a fine voice – would go out at the end of the night and recite. Then Ibn al-Musayyab said to Burd: "Get rid of this reciter for me" and he replied: "The mosque does not belong to us – it belongs to the people." When 'Umar heard this, he took hold of his sandals and retired. Ibn Rushd said: "What Sa'id meant when ordering him to drive the reciter away from him was away from his immediate vicinity: the person who feels he is being molested has the right to forbid the person from molesting him. If a man raises his voice while reciting the Qur'an from his house, then his neighbour may forbid him from doing it." This judgement is based on what has been reported from Ibn al-'Arabi in his *Masalik*, namely, the words of the Messenger of Allah, may the peace and blessings of Allah be upon him, to 'Umar: 'Lower your voice a little' – and this narration has been transmitted from Ibn al-Musayyab. Then Ibn al-'Arabi goes on to say: "Reciting aloud is better for the person whose intention is to recite aloud, and the best of people are those who bring benefit to others and he himself benefits from the speech of Allah: in it he makes it reach his ears and awaken his heart to reflect on the speech and understand the meanings. All this is only possible when it is recited aloud. Another benefit one might also expect is that anyone asleep will wake up and will remember Allah. His (recitation aloud) will be helping this person to perform a praiseworthy action and to (increasing his) *taqwa*. Thus in this one action, there might be ten intentions – and the person performing this action will have a reward equal to ten good actions."

The author of *al-'Arida* said: "There is no doubt that reciting the Qur'an aloud or saying (hadith or *dhikr*) aloud is better (than silently) – as long as it is devoid of showing off. Allah has expressed His contentment with this on the tongue of His Messenger, may the peace and blessings of Allah be upon him, when He says, 'Whoever remembers Me in himself, I will remember him in Myself, and whoever remembers Me in a company of people, I will remember him in a company better than his.'"

Ibn 'Arafa said: "(It is recommended) to raise one's voice when making a *du'a* and *dhikr* in a mosque at the end of the night – when done with a praiseworthy intention of coming closer to Allah; and it is permitted at the darkest part of the night after the first half has past, although it has also been prohibited. That it is permitted, is recorded by Ibn Sahl, Ibn 'Attab and al-Musayli, and that it is prohibited, by Ibn Dahoun and Ibn Hazm. Examine the last quarter or fifth of *Nawazil Ibn Sahl* where there is a long discussion of the matter. Criticism is made of the person making supplications out loud to Allah in the middle of the night. Part of the response of Ibn 'Attab was that it is not permitted to disapprove of this: it was *dhikr* of Allah by which the hearts are expanded and by which the hearts of the people of iman are made tranquil. Since when, he argued, has making *du'as* and seeking forgiveness of Allah obliged anyone to reject or justify such practices? Have not those who disapprove heard the words of Allah, glorious and exalted is He: '*Do not chase away those who call on their Lord...*'[1]? Then he goes on to provide a proof (for his argument) by quoting the words of Malik – namely, that the people of the earlier generations would agree to meet at a certain time just before dawn to stand for recitation of the Qur'an. Al-Musayli said: 'Whenever a person calls to this, it is a praiseworthy action and one is commanded to it. It is a desirable action and a long established practice of the *Salihun*: 'Urwa would stand in the night and cry out on the road urging the people (to remember Allah). He would be in a state of fear, reciting: "*Do the people of the cities feel secure against Our violent force coming down on them in the day while they are playing games.*"[2]' 'Iyad said: 'Ibn 'Attab is the Shaykh of the muftis, a *hafidh*, a man of insight, he obtained his *fiqh* from the people of Andalusia – from the most illustrious of the *fuqaha*, in accordance with the practice of the people of excellence. He was possessed of a discriminating intellect and lived in accord with the people of the earlier generations.' It

1   al-An'am – Livestock: 52
2   al-A'raf – The Ramparts: 97

is recorded in at-Tirmidhi – who considered it a *sahih* tradition – that the Prophet, may the peace and blessings of Allah be upon him, would stand and say 'O people remember Allah!' when a third of the night had passed."

As for his saying 'before *Dhuhr* and *'Asr*', Mayyara said: "Doing *nafila salats* before the (*fard*) *salat* and after is recommended because of the saying of the Prophet, may the peace and blessings of Allah be upon him: 'Whoever perseveres in doing the four *rak'ats* before *Dhuhr* and after it, then Allah will forbid the Fire from (touching) his bones' – and this has been narrated by Abu Dawud. It is recorded in the *Muwatta'* and in the *Sahih* of Muslim that the Prophet, may the peace and blessings of Allah be upon him, said: 'Allah will have mercy on a man who prays four *rak'ats* before *'Asr*.' The Prophet has also said, may the peace and blessings of Allah be upon him: "Whoever prays six (*rak'ats*) after the *Maghrib* and does not utter any evil speech between them, then they will be equivalent for him to the worship of twelve years.'"

I SAY: "I cannot guarantee the exact wording of the hadith, that is, that there are no extra or missing words." Sayyidi 'Abdallah Abu'l-Hajj Ibrahim al-'Alawi said, may Allah bring coolness to his grave:

A MUSLIM DOES NOT SAY 'THE PROPHET SAID...' WITHOUT A CHAIN OF NARRATION LEST HE FALSELY ASCRIBE SOMETHING TO HIM

Al-Munawi, commenting on the hadith 'Whoever makes up a hadith of mine, aware that it is a lie, then he will be reckoned amongst the liars' said: "So the narrator of a hadith should not say 'The Messenger, may the peace and blessings of Allah be upon him, said...' unless he knows that this is so, or that he say, regarding a weak hadith, 'It has been narrated...' or 'It has reached me...' If he narrates what he knows or thinks is a false hadith – without acknowledging this – then he will classed as one of the liars: his broadcasting these falsities is effectively helping those who (deliberately) impute things to the Prophet. Thus he will share in their wrong actions to the same degree as someone who helps a person commit injustice. For this reason one of the *Tabi'un* would fear ascribing something to the Prophet, preferring to have the chain of narration stop before (explicitly declaring that he had said it). Instead he would say: 'It is less of a responsibility to ascribe a falsity to a companion.'"

Mayyara said: "It is not stated in the *Mudawwana* whether Malik prescribed specific *rak'ats* before the *salat* or after it. That this was done in the time (before and after the *salat*) has been stated by the people of Iraq. Ash-Shaykh said: 'It is recommended to perform the *nafila* after *Dhuhr* by praying four *rak'ats* and say the *salam* after each pair of *rak'ats*; and likewise before *Dhuhr*, before *'Asr*. After

Maghrib, two *rak'ats* (should be performed).' However, the author of the *Risala* says: 'If he does the *nafila* with six, then this is praiseworthy.' Al-Jilab said: 'Two *rak'ats* after *Maghrib* are recommended, as are the two *rak'ats* of *fajr*.'"

NOTICE: Ibn al-Hattab, commenting on the words of Khalil 'and follow the (*'Isha*) with pairs of (*rak'ats*), sealing each with a *salam*' said: "Branch: Ibn al-Hajib said – and is commented on in *at-Tawdih*: 'There are two opinions as to whether one should specifically make an intention for the (pair) preceding (the *witr*) or whether it is enough to do any two *rak'ats*.'"

Ibn Bashir said: "The correct view is that he has a choice: if he wishes he may do two *rak'ats* and specify them, or he may just do them as an (ordinary) *nafila*."

Ibn al-Hattab said: "Whoever does a *nafila salat* after *'Isha* and does not do the *witr* and then he does pray a single *rak'a* after the *fajr* then he is doing this single *rak'a* alone, (unaccompanied by a pair) according to the strongest of two judgements which are mentioned by Ibn 'Arafa in response to the narration of Ibn Rushd to the effect that there was agreement in this matter."

Prostrations for Forgetfulness

لِنَقْصِ سُنَّةٍ سَهْواً يُسَنّ

قَبْلَ السَّلَامِ سَجْدَتَانِ أَوْ سُنَنْ

146 When one or more sunnas are missed out of negligence, two prostrations should be made before the *salam* (*alaykum*)

إِنْ أُكِّدَتْ وَمَنْ يَزِدْ سَهْواً سَجَدْ

بَعْدُ كَذَا وَالنَّقْصُ غَلَبْ إِنْ وَرَدْ

147 in the case of *mu'akkad* sunnas; anyone who does something extra, should prostrate after this; if he misses something (and does something extra), it is his missing something which counts;

وَاسْتَدْرِكِ الْقَبْلِيَّ مَعْ قُرْبِ السَّلَامْ

وَاسْتَدْرِكِ الْبَعْدِيَّ وَلَوْ مِنْ بَعْدِ عَامْ

148 if one forgets to do a prostration of negligence owing before (the *salam*), it is made good (afterwards) – if little time has elapsed after saying the *salam*; if one forgets such a prostration after (the *salam*), then it is to be made good even after a year.

عَنْ مُقْتَدٍ يَحْمِلُ هَذَيْنِ الْإِمَامْ

وَبَطَلَتْ بَعَمْدِ نَفْخٍ أَوْ كَلَامْ

149 The imam bears the responsibility for both of these (i.e. for what has been missed or any addition) – and not those following him; and the *salat* is invalidated for blowing out (air excessively) or speaking

Mayyara said: "The author, may Allah have mercy on him, has informed us about the case when someone – out of negligence – misses *one* sunna to which a special importance has been attached (*mu'akkada*) in his *salat*, like for example, if he recites silently instead of aloud in a *fard salat*; and (the case) when, by leaving out the sura after the Umm al-Qur'an in the *fard salat*, he misses out the various sunnas attached to such a sura – that is, the (sunnas of its) recitation, of the mode in which it is recited – whether aloud or silently, and of the standing (to recite it). In both these case, he says, it is a sunna, that is, it is required of him for a reason based on (a judgement within) the sunna, that he perform two prostrations *before* saying the *salam*, that is, after finishing the *tashahhud*, according to the well known judgement. However, it is also said that he does not have to repeat the *tashahhud*. Then the author goes on to inform us that whoever is negligent by performing something extra, like reciting aloud when it should be done silently in the *fard salat*, then it is a sunna in his case to also perform two prostrations *after* the *salam*, that is, to do the *takbirat al-ihram* (once) for them both, go down into prostration, do the *tashahhud* and then make the final *as-salam alaykum* aloud. In the case where – out of negligence – he both adds something additional *and* misses something out, like for example, he misses out a sura of the *fard* but then gets up to do a fifth *rak'a*, then what he has missed dominates (regarding the judgement) and so he makes his prostrations before saying the *salam*. If someone (has missed something) necessitating that he do the prostrations (of negligence) *before* (saying the *salam*) but then he forgets to do them until after he said the *salam* – and then remembers a short time after saying the *salam* – then he should prostrate there and then. What is implied here is that if a long time elapses, then he cannot make them up and they are considered irrevocable – and this is indeed the case. If, however, these prostrations were necessary for his having left out *three* sunnas and a long time elapses (before he remembers), then his *salat* is invalidated, according to the well known judgement; if, however, they were due for anything *less* than this, then he does not have to do any prostration and his *salat* is valid. If any one is owing prostrations after the *salam*, then he should prostrate whenever he remembers them, even after a year. The imam bears responsibility for anything extra or lacking in his *salat*; if, however, someone following him in the *salat* – and not the imam – makes a mistake, then he does not have to make any (extra) prostrations."

BRANCH: an-Nafrawi said in his *Sharh ar-Risala*: "As for any addition to the spoken elements of the *salat*, there is no prostration for negligence in this matter and the *salat* is not invalidated even if done deliberately – like, for example, if someone were to repeat a sura or an *Allahu akbar*. This is not, however, the case if the spoken elements in question constitute a *fard* obligation, in which case one should prostrate for any negligence regarding it — like, for example, if he were to repeat the Fatiha out of negligence, even if it is within one *rak'a*. However, there is a difference of opinion in this matter, some saying that the *salat* is invalidated by repeating these (elements) deliberately — although the judgement relied upon (in the *madhhab*) — and to which al-Ajhouri restricts himself — is that it is not invalidated."

BRANCH: an-Nafrawi said: "Whoever mistakenly says the *salam* after only two *rak'ats* but then remembers and goes on to complete the *salat*, he should prostrate after the (final) *salam*. Al-Burzuli said: 'Our Shaykh, the imam, gave a *fatwa* that he should do a *takbirat al-ihram* before prostrating, although I have also heard in discussions that he does not have to prostrate or make the *takbirat al-ihram* as the word *as-Salam* is one of the names of Allah, exalted is He.'"

ISSUE: Ibn al-Hattab said, commenting on the words of Khalil 'and the (sunna) which is not *mu'akkad* like the *tashahhud*...': "Ibn Yunus has related that Malik said: 'Whoever makes a mistake in the fourth (*rak'a*) by going on to a fifth (*rak'a*) immediately after sitting for part of the *tashahhud* should return to his sitting (position), make the *tashahhud* and prostrate for his negligence — and his *salat* is (considered) complete. If he has forgotten the last *tashahhud* (completely) and has made the sitting and the (final) *salam*, then if (he remembers) a short time afterwards, he should do the *tashahhud* and then prostrate after the *salam*; if a long time has elapsed, then he does not have to make up anything, if he makes *dhikr* of Allah — and not all people know the *tashahhud*.'"

ISSUE: Ibn al-Hattab has related that al-Mashdali said: "There are two matters to be examined here: the first is that the Shaykhs have differed as to whether the *salat* of the person who catches the *salat* of the imam as he does the prostration (of negligence) after the final *salam* — that is, who makes the *takbirat al-ihram* and sits with the imam until he has done the *salam* and then stands to make up (his own *salat*) — is valid or not. It has been said that it is not valid given that the words ('the prostration ....after') imply he did not actually join the imam for the *salat* proper. However, it has also been said that it is valid given that the words 'he catches the *salat* of the imam' imply he did."

I SAY: "Similar to this difference of opinion is that which 'Isa reports as having heard: "If the person who comes late for the *salat* does not catch anything — but out of ignorance follows the imam when the latter does the prostration of negligence afterwards and then gets up to make up his own *salat*, then this is valid according to Ibn al-Qasim who bases his judgement on the words of Sa'd.

However, it is invalid according to 'Isa. Ibn Rushd said: 'This (judgement) is based on analogy as he has counted something as part of the *salat* which is not actually part of it.'"

"The second matter to be examined is whether — in the case where the person coming late only catches the prostration of negligence made afterwards and then, when he gets up to make up (his own *salat*), another joins him taking him as his imam — the *salat* of the person following him is valid. One of he *'ulama* said that it is not valid." I say: "However, what is customarily accepted, based on the principle of the *madhhab*, is that it is valid as he is considered to have the status of a single person (praying along) — like the (judgement regarding the) person repeating a *salat* with others in a *jama'a*. Moreover, It would appear that the prostration of negligence done afterwards is something 'additional' to the *salat* (and as such not actually part of it) — so reflect about this and Allah knows best."

BLOWING OUT OR SPEAKING

وَبَطَلَتْ بِعَمْدِ نَفْخٍ أَوْ كَلَامٍ

… it is invalidated if one deliberately blows out (breath) or speaks

لِغَيْرِ إِصْلَاحٍ

150 for a reason other than to correct (the imam) …

Mayyara said: "Here, may Allah have mercy on him, Ibn 'Ashir is informing us that the *salat* is invalidated for various reasons. Among them is deliberately blowing out one's breath or speaking deliberately without intending to correct (the imam's recitation during the) *salat*. The author of the *Risala* said: 'Blowing out breath is the same as speaking, and anyone who does so deliberately, invalidates his *salat*.' Ibn al-Qasim said: '…and if done out of negligence, then he should prostrate for this negligence.' Ibn Shas said: 'Whoever is compelled to speak, then his *salat* is also invalidated.' Al-Mazari said: '…even if he speaks intentionally in order to prevent a blind person from having a serious accident, his *salat* is invalidated, that is, even if his speech is absolutely necessary.'"

Mayyara has also said: "What may also be understood from his words 'speaks for a reason other than to correct (the imam)' is that whoever speaks deliberately in order to amend the *salat* does not invalidate it."

'Ali ibn 'Abd as-Sadiq said: "What is implied by 'deliberately blows out (breath)…' is that it does not invalidate the *salat* when done out of negligence – however, the judgement in this case is that he should prostrate after the *salam* if the amount (of blowing) is negligible, but the *salat* is invalidated if considerable."

Ibn al-Hattab said: "Shaykh Abu'l-Hasan said, commenting on his words 'blowing out (breath) in the *salat* is like speaking': 'Ibn al-Majishun said: "Blowing out breath, clearing one's throat and belching are all like speaking".' Ibn al-Qasim and Asbagh have also said this and 'Abd al-Haqq has mentioned it in his book *Min hashiyatin yushkar*."

Al-Mawwaq said: "Malik said on the matter: 'Whoever says the *salam* after (only) two *rak'ats* out of negligence, and turns and speaks, then he should carry on doing the *salat* where he left off and make the prostration for his negligence – if it is something insignificant; if, however, the interval is considerable and his sitting and speaking go on for some time, then he should begin the *salat* again – and there is no specific limit in this. However, if he has already left the mosque, then he should repeat the *salat*. The Prophet, may the peace and blessings of Allah be upon him, spoke out of negligence but carried on with the *salat* where he had left off – by saying the *takbir* for what remained to be done and prostrating for the negligence after the *salam*.'"

'Isa reported that he had heard that the imam may ask one of the people behind him whether he had completed the *salat* or not.

Ibn Rushd said: "It might appear that this means he asked them before saying the *salam*. However, this is unlikely as the imam has no need to ask, before the *salam*, whether he has completed the *salat* or not because even if in doubt, he must carry on and assume certainty – unless, that is, someone says '*subhana'llah*' to him (indicating a mistake has been made), in which case he should amend what he has done wrong. If, nevertheless, he does ask them before saying the *salam* and makes the *salam* while in a state of doubt, then he has invalidated his *salat*; he may ask them if he makes the *salam* in a state of certainty, and then has doubts. This is different from the case where a person steps in for the imam (who has to leave the *salat*) and questions (them), on entering the *salat* because he is unaware of what the imam has already prayed – for this is permitted if he cannot understand by someone indicating to him."

BRANCH: Zarruq said, in confirmation of the words of the *Risala* 'Whoever speaks out of negligence should prostrate after the *salam*': "…irrespective of whether (he forgets) he is in the *salat* or (does not realise) he is speaking. However, if the words uttered were of the kind specific to the *salat* and of an inconsiderable amount, then he does not have to do any (extra) prostration –

irrespective of whether they were uttered deliberately or out of negligence."

ISSUE: al-Mawwaq has related that Malik did not consider it *makruh* for someone to say *as-salam alaykum* to a person praying for he said: "Whoever says *as-salam alaykum* to someone while he is praying a *fard* or *nafila salat*, then he should return the (greeting), indicating with his hand or his head." Ibn al-Qasim has also said in this regard: "There is no harm in making a light gesture – during the *salat* – to a man who needs something: Malik permitted him to answer his (greeting) by making a sign to him – and this is similar; and there is no harm in shaking hands during the *salat*."

ISSUE: Khalil said, adding to the (list of things done in the *salat*) for which no (extra) prostration is due and which do not invalidate (the *salat*): "...and scratching his body." The author of *al-Mi'yar* said: "Abu 'Abdallah al-Abdousi was asked as to whether a man who had an itch during the *salat* and who scratched himself a lot because of it – but who did not omit any of the words or actions of the *salat* – had to repeat his *salat* or not. He replied: 'As for an itch during the *salat*, if he scratches it out of necessity – that is, he is unable to wait (until after the *salat*) because the pain would completely preoccupy him if he were not to scratch it – then this is permitted as long as it does not impair the *salat* in any way and he does not spend an inordinate amount of time scratching himself, and as long as it does not occupy him to such an extent that he does not know what he has prayed, in which case it does invalidate the *salat*. If, however, it is not done out of necessity and he scratches himself on account of the pleasure he derives from it, then this is *makruh*. It has been reported in a tradition: '(There are) six (things) from Shaytan' – that is, which are caused by Shaytan – and scratching is mentioned (among them). If he spends an inordinate amount of time occupied (with this) or it preoccupies him such that he no longer knows what (exactly) he has prayed, then he should repeat (the *salat*); if this is not the case, then he does not have to."

ISSUE: Khalil has also said, adding to the (list of) things for which the prostration (of negligence) is not necessary and which does not invalidate (the *salat*): "...killing a scorpion which intends (to attack) him." Ibn al-Hattab said: "As for any creature other than a scorpion or a snake – birds, wild animals, worms, bees and mosquitoes, for example, there is no difference of opinion that killing any of these during the *salat* is *makruh* and that it should not be done. However, if someone does (kill one of them), then it does not invalidate the *salat* unless the person becomes inordinately preoccupied with this (action)."

Al-Burzuli said: "It is stated in *Masa'il Ibn Qudah* that if he fears lest a lamp or light (fall over), then there is no harm in seeing to it during the *salat*."

ISSUE: Ibn al-Hattab related that al-Burzuli said: "At the end of *Masa'il Ibn Qudah*, there is the matter of clearing one's throat and spitting out where the author says: 'O brother, if someone does it out of necessary, then he does not have to make anything up; if not done out of necessity but rather merely for others to hear him, then there is a difference of opinion as to whether the *salat* is invalidated or not. The correct judgement (in my opinion) is that it does not,' I said: 'Our Shaykh, the imam gave a *fatwa* in support of the judgement of Ibn 'Abd al-Hakam who deemed it invalid, irrespective of whether done out of ignorance or deliberately.' He responded: 'This is intended as a censure to the common people for their excessive (clearing of their throats) in the main Zaitouna mosque during the *Qunut* in the morning, merely to draw attention to themselves, and Allah is the Bringer of Success.'" The author of *Masa'il al-Ifriqiyeen* said: "There are two views as to whether the *salat* is invalidated if a person clears his throat in order to indicate something to another. Al-Lakhmi was asked about clearing one's throat during the *salat* and he replied: "If the *mukallaf* swallows any phlegm collecting in the throat, then this does not invalidate the *salat* or the fast – even if he is able to suppress it – that is, as long as it has not come out of his throat and reached the soft palate (of his mouth). There are two opinions as to whether one should repeat the *salat* or fast if it reaches his mouth and then one swallows it again, that is a difference of opinion as to whether the judgement (in this case) should be the same as (if he had swallowed) food – given that this (phlegm) is not the same as food. What he means by 'as long as it has not come out of his throat and reached the soft palate (of his mouth)' is when it happens by itself – without his having to actively clear his throat."

Commenting on the words of Khalil 'blowing (spit) on one's clothes when necessary', Ibn al-Hattab has related that Al-Ubbi, in the chapter entitled 'The prohibition of spitting in the direction of the *qibla*', has commented on the hadith '...if he does not find (anything to spit in), then he should do this and spit in his clothes' saying: "This shows it is permitted to spit during the *salat* if necessary, and to exhale a little as long it is not done out of frivolity and no spit comes out."

ISSUE: Khalil said, adding to those things for which no prostration of negligence is necessary and which do not invalidate the *salat*: "...moving forward two rows to take (the column of the mosque, for example, as) a *sutra*, (if he arrives late for the *salat* of the imam), or filling up a gap." Al-Mawwaq said in his commentary: "Ibn Yunus said: 'This refers to gaps in the *salat*: if he sees one in front, or to the right or left, while praying and he is able to fill it, then he should go forward to fill it, and there is no harm if he gently parts the row (in front) in order to reach it.' Ibn Nafi' has related: 'Whoever gets up from bowing and sees a gap should move (forward) to fill it if it is nearby.' Ibn Habib said: 'If it is far away, then he should wait until he has prostrated and has got up.' Ibn al-Qasim has reported that he heard: 'He should make his way through to it (even) if there are two rows between him and the (gap).' Ibn Rushd said: 'The Prophet said, may the peace and blessings of Allah be upon him: "Whoever fills the gap in a row, then Allah will raise him a rank for it and will build a house for him in the Garden."' Ibn al-Qasim said 'I consider that the person doing the *salat* should indicate to the person at his side that he should straighten the row as long as it is only slightly (bent). He should not, however, concern himself with it if it is (very) crooked.' Ibn Rushd said: 'This is because he should concern himself with his own *salat* – rather than seeing that the row is straight.'"

Distractions

... وَبِالْمُشْغِلِ عَنْ

فَرْضٍ وَفِي الْوَقْتِ أَعِدْ إِذَا يُسَنُّ

... and anything (like colic for example) which distracts from performing the *fard* (aspects invalidates the *salat*); and if from (one of) the sunna (aspects), one should repeat it, if still within the time.

This is easy to understand. Ibn al-Ghazi said, commenting on Khalil's words 'and anything which distracts one from performing the *fard*...': "It is stated in the 'Book of Purification' in the *Mudawwana*: 'Whoever is afflicted by retention of urine or faeces, or by a rumbling of the stomach, then he should pray if (the pain is) inconsiderable; if, however, it is such that it distracts him, or causes him to hurry the (*salat*), then he should not pray until he relieved himself; and if he does nevertheless pray in this state, then it is recommended that he repeat the *salat* however long the delay.' Ibn al-Qasim has not reported anything regarding nausea, while 'Iyad is of the view that it is recommended to repeat the *salat* (in the case of nausea). Al-Baji has reported from one of his contemporaries: 'If (the distress is) inconsiderable, then he should pray in this state but if he has to compress his stomach with his thighs because of the nausea, then he should break off doing the *salat*; if he carries on (despite this), then he should repeat the (*salat*) if still within the time; if, however, it distracts from the *salat* or causes him to hurry it, then he should repeat it however long the delay.' Al-Lakhmi said: 'As for this nausea (in the stomach) or anything else troubling him, if the (distress) is inconsiderable, then it is recommended that he relieve himself of it before the *salat*; if he does nevertheless pray, then the *salat* is accepted of him; if it causes him to hurry (the *salat*) and distracts his heart somewhat, then he should repeat it within the time; but if he no longer knows whether he did the *salat* properly or not, then he should repeat it, irrespective of how much time passes.' Ibn 'Arafa has restricted himself to these reports. Ibn Basheer said: 'If it distracts him from the *fard* aspects (of the *salat*), then he must repeat it later, however long the delay; and if he allows himself to be deliberately distracted from the sunna aspects, then within the time – although the *salat* is deemed acceptable if the sunnas or the aspects of excellence are left out deliberately and he has nothing to make up.' Muhammad ibn 'Abd as-Salam said: 'There is nothing wrong in what he says, regarding the *fiqh* of the question; and this is what *alif-lam-mim-sad* relies on.'"

Al-Fakihani has stated in the *'Umda*, commenting on the tradition 'If the *iqama* has been said for the *'Isha salat* and the evening meal is ready, then begin with the evening meal' – or whatever the exact wording of the tradition: "Al-Lakhmi said: 'There are four aspects regarding the *salat* when food is ready: if a person's *nafs* is not yearning after it, then it is permitted to begin with the *salat*; if his *nafs* is yearning for it, but it will not result in his doing the *salat* quickly as a result, then it is recommended that he begin with the food – although if he does not do this, then there is no harm in it; if it would result in him hurrying the *salat* – then it is recommended that he begin with the food but (if he does not eat and) it results in his hurrying, then it is recommended that he repeat the *salat* within the time; and if his thoughts become preoccupied with it and he does not know how many (*rak'ats*), he has prayed, then he should repeat (the *salat*) even if the time is past.'" The author of *al-Bayan wa Taqreeb* said: "This applies in all probability to the person whose thoughts are distracted (by the food) for most of the *salat*."

Then he goes on to say: "Whoever is affected by something which preoccupies him, which distracts his heart and overwhelms his very being, then – if he thinks that in all likelihood it will pass before the time (for the *salat*) elapses – he should delay the *salat* until it goes, as long as the time does not actually elapse; if he thinks, however, that in all likelihood he will continue to be affected by it until the time has passed, then he should resist (thinking about) it as much as he can and make the *salat* in this state; if he does the *salat* but his distress disappears within the time, then it is recommended for him to repeat.

This latter judgement is based on the analogy of the person who performs the *salat* on a riding beast for fear of wild beasts and then when he is safe again (repeats it) – and this is not the same as in the case where he fears the enemy (in which case he does not have to repeat it). However, it should be noted that the hadith specifically applies to circumstances in which there is ample time for them both, that is the food and the *salat* – for otherwise where there is a conflict of interest, then one must pray the *salat*."

Voiding Wudu', Forgetting, Laughing or Eating and Drinking Deliberately

وَحَدَثٍ وَسَهْوِ زَيْدِ الْمِثْلِ

قَهْقَهَةٍ وَعَمْدِ شُرْبٍ أَكْلِ

151   if his purity is broken in any way, or he inadvertently makes an addition of (a further two *rak'ats*) the like (of which he has already performed – i.e. for the *Subh*), or he guffaws or deliberately eats or drinks (something)

Mayyara said: "Amongst the things which also invalidate the *salat* is when a physical change (like urination) breaks his state of purity – whatever its nature, that is whether inadvertently, deliberately or it overcomes him, despite himself. Also classed as one of these things is his inadvertently making an addition to the *salat* of something he has already performed. Khalil said: 'by the addition to the four (or doing more than four, in the case of three *rak'a salats*), likewise doing two extra *rak'ats* for a *salat* demanding only two.' However, this is conditional upon the person being certain that this addition has been made – not merely in case of doubt. Al-Mawwaq has related that Ibn Rushd said: 'If – with regard to the movements of the *salat* – he has doubts as to whether the addition is considerable or not, then it is enough that he do the prostration of negligence, according to the agreement of the *'ulama*, although this is not the case for the person who is certain he has made the addition.'"

Also among the other things which invalidate (the *salat*) is laughing out loud boisterously. Al-Mawwaq said: "It has been reported from Malik: 'If the person praying guffaws, then he should break off the *salat* and begin again; if behind the imam, he should carry on until the imam has finished and then repeat the *salat*.'" Sahnun said: "If the imam laughs out of forgetfulness, he should do the prostration of negligence if insignificant; if it was deliberate or done out of ignorance, then his *salat* is invalidated as well as the *salat* of those behind him."

Ibn Habib related: "Whoever laughs out loud deliberately, out of forgetfulness or is overcome by this laughter, then his *salat* is invalidated: if he is alone, he should break off the *salat*; if behind the imam, then he should carry on and repeat it afterwards; if he is the imam, then he should have someone else take his *salat*, in the case of negligence and when overcome by laughter, but he should begin again if done deliberately." Ibn Yunus said: "What Sahnun said is based on analogy that it is like speech – because the *'ulama* consider blowing out one's breath to be analogous to speech; indeed this (laughter) is even more similar. Ibn Habib's judgement on the other hand is one by way of precaution."

I say: "What he attributed to Ibn Habib is attributed to Ibn al-Qasim."

Notice: It is stated in *Ghayat al-Amani*: "Al-Qarafi said, commenting on *Sharh al-Jilab*: 'Malik, ash-Shafi'i and Abu Hanifa are agreed that smiling does not invalidate the *salat* when doing the (*salat*) alone, nor when one is the imam or following the imam.'" Ibn al-Qasim said: "…irrespective of whether done in negligence or deliberately – because there is no sound, only the movement of the corners of the mouth."

Then he goes on to say: "Al-Fakhani said: 'If he has doubts as to whether his smile was accompanied by a laugh or not, Asbagh said: "What I prefer is that (it is an obligation to) repeat (the *salat*), if done deliberately, and that it is recommended, if done out of negligence." This is his *madhhab* when laughing does actually occur. It is as if the judgement here is that of precaution and that he has treated it as if it is (the same as) laughter. This judgement of precaution should be applied – according to the teaching of this book – as it is safer.'"

Useful point: al-Ubbi said, commenting on the tradition reported in Muslim 'They were talking and laughing and he, may the peace and blessings of Allah be upon him, was smiling': "This (tradition) contains permission to talk about past nations, and permission to laugh. However, laughing a lot is *makruh* as it causes the heart to die and it is a quality of the idle. What is praiseworthy and befits the people of excellence is smiling, and the most pronounced laugh of the Prophet, may the peace and blessings be upon him, was (like the) smile (of other people)."

Another benefit: It is stated in *al-Jami' as-Saghir* that the Prophet, may the peace and blessings of Allah be upon him, said: "If you knew what I knew, you would laugh little and weep a lot and you would hardly be able to stomach your food and drink."

Also: "If you knew what I knew, you would weep a lot, laugh little and you would go out to the highways and raise your voice to Allah seeking His help – while ignorant as to whether you will be saved or not."

Also in *al-Jami' as-Saghir*: "If you knew what you are going to meet after death, you would no longer eat any food out of desire, you would no longer drink anything out of desire, you would not enter a house to seek shade in it, and you would wander to the highways, beat your breasts and would weep for yourselves."

وَسَجْدَةٍ قَيْءٍ وَذِكْرِ فَرْضٍ

أَقَلَّ مِنْ سِتٍّ كَذِكْرِ الْبَعْضِ

152 or does an (extra) prostration (deliberately), or vomits (and deliberately swallows his vomit again) or remembers missed *fard* (*salats* as long as they amount to) less than six, or part (of a *salat* – all invalidate the current *salat*),

Mayyara said: "Among the things that invalidate (the *salat*) is the addition of a prostration and the like – although more appropriate would be to say: 'the deliberate addition of a *rak'a* and the like.' Ibn 'Arafa said: 'A small action of this kind done deliberately (invalidates), even if it is (just a) prostration, but if done inadvertently, then a prostration of negligence will make up for it.'"

NOTICE: He does not mention a deliberate sitting after one (*rak'a*), the 'sitting of relaxation' as it is called, for this invalidates the *salat*. As to whether he should do the prostration of negligence or not, there are various aspects to the matter. Ibn 'Arafa said: "Sitting after (just) one (*rak'a*) for the length of time it would take to do the *tashahhud* is reckoned as negligence, and one should prostrate for it (after the *salam*); as for whether he should prostrate for something less than this when he only sat to still himself a moment, there are two opinions. This difference of opinion is based on two corresponding sources of proof: from Ibn al-Qasim, (on one side) and Ibn Kinana, Ibn Abi Hazm, and the two reports of Ibn Wahb and Ibn Abi Uways (on the other). Ibn Rushd said. 'The imam who has doubts and who (remains) sitting to wait and see what the people (behind him do) does not have to make the prostration of negligence.'"

Zarruq said, commenting on the words of the *Risala* '(After doing the second prostration) he should get up (directly, pushing up with his hands) without going into a sitting position again (before getting up)': "The teaching of the *madhhab* is that whoever does nevertheless return deliberately to a sitting position (before getting up), then he does not have to make up anything; however, if done in negligence, and he remains for a length of time equal to the time of the *tashahhud*, then he should do the prostration (of negligence); if less than this, then Ashhab said: 'He should prostrate' while Ibn Kinana and Ibn Abi Hazam together with the two narrations of Ibn Wahb and Ibn Abi Uways: 'He does not have to make it up with any prostration." As to whether it is merely licit or recommended to push up with one's hands (when getting up), it is recorded as a (practice confirmed with) evidence by Ibn al-Qasim and that it is *makruh* not to do it – in accordance with what Ashhab has reported as hearing. Ibn Rushd too approved of it.'

Mayyara said: "Also among the things which invalidate (the *salat*) is vomiting deliberately. Ibn Rushd said: 'The well known opinion is that whoever is overcome by vomiting or who eructs but does not swallow it again, then he does not have to make anything up in his *salat* or his fasting; if he does swallow it deliberately and he is able to spit it out, then one should not dispute the fact that his fasting and *salat* are invalidated; if he swallows it out of forgetfulness or is overcome, then two opinions are recorded from Ibn al-Qasim.'"

Also among the things (which invalidate the *salat*) is remembering missed *salats* during his *salat*, if less than six. However, the well known opinion, followed by Mayyara, is that this invalidation is conditional upon his remembering a *salat* which is still within the time – for he only has to repeat others he remembers after he has completed his present *salat*: "When remembered, they should be done in order, as long, that is, as they are still within the time, and those missed (before the time the person is still in) and any others missed can be done on another occasion, although a small number can be done after completion of the *salat* still current, even if their time has past – as to whether this can be four or five, there is a difference of opinion. If one does not (immediately) make up a (*salat*) missed deliberately, then one should do it in the *daruri* time. There is a difference of opinion as to repeating a *salat* made behind the imam."

Also one of the things which invalidates is remembering part of a (previous) *salat* while doing the present one, like for example if one is performing the *salat* of *'Asr* and one remembers a *rak'a* or a prostration of *Dhuhr*, that is, when a considerable time has elapsed between the thing missed out at *Dhuhr* and the *'Asr salat* one is now engaged in – considerable in the sense that one has left the mosque, or a long time has elapsed. This matter is mentioned by Ibn 'Ashir in the following line:

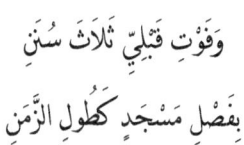

153 or (recalling) omitting a prostration (of negligence) which one should have done before the *salam* (of a previous *salat*) to make good three missed sunnas – if one has left the mosque or a long time has elapsed

Mayyara said: "Also among the things which invalidate (the *salat*) is remembering – during the *salat* – a prostration he should have made before the *salam* (in a previous *salat*) and which was owing because he missed out three sunnas. Ibn 'Ashir also means that both the *salat* – which he remembers he has not done the necessary prostration for – *and* the one he is currently engaged are invalidated: the first because of the absence of this prostration, that is, because he has omitted to do it when the time which has elapsed is still inconsiderable, and the second, that is, the current one during which he remembers the (missed) prostration, because this is (classed as) 'remembering one *salat* during another.'

The same applies if he remembers this outside of the *salat*, and the time between his remembering it and the *salat* which he omitted doing the prostration for is considerable. In short, these two issues are connected to the one before, that is, 'remembering one *salat* during another.'"

Ibn Mawwaq said: "If he neglects to do a prostration of negligence which should be done before saying the *salam*, then he should prostrate if the time elapsed is not considerable; if considerable, al-Lakhmi has narrated from the *Mudawwana*: 'It is invalidated.' Ibn Basheer said: 'This is the well known judgement.' Ibn Rushd said: 'It is not invalidated, unless it was based on (missing out) three sunnas.' Ibn Yunus said: 'There is a difference of opinion regarding the judgement of Ibn al-Qasim – that is, the obligation to repeat (the *salat*) when three *Allahu akbars* or three spoken elements of the *salat* (*tasmee'at*) are left out and one remembers this after a time has elapsed. Asbagh does not consider that it should be repeated, and this is also my opinion. This is not the case, however, when the first sitting is omitted. Abu 'Umar said: 'All of he *fuqaha* are agreed that whoever misses other than the *takbirat al-ihram* does not have to make anything up.' It is reported from 'Ikrima: 'I did the *salat* behind a Shaykh who said '*Allahu akbar*' twenty two times, so I said to Ibn 'Abbas: "He is stupid", and he replied: "May your mother be bereaved of you! A sunna of Abi'l-Qasim, may the peace and blessings of Allah be upon him." 'Umar ibn 'Abd al-'Aziz, al-Qasim, Salim and Ibn Jubayr did not complete the *takbirs*. Someone said to 'Umar ibn Abdal Aziz: "You do not complete the *takbirs* but your governor does" and he replied: "That is the most preferred *salat*."' Ibn Abi Shayba has mentioned that 'the Messenger of Allah, may the peace and blessings of Allah be upon him, did not complete the *takbirs*, and Ibn 'Umar did not use to make the *takbir* if he performed the *salat* alone.' Abu 'Umar said: 'The proof of those who consider that the person who leaves out any other *takbir* than the *takbirat al-ihram* has nothing to make up is this tradition from the Messenger, may the peace and blessings of Allah be upon him, and (the reports) from a group of the Companions to the effect that they would leave out doing the *takbirs* – and did not criticise each other for this.'"

As for his saying 'as long as he has not left the mosque', al-Mawwaq said: "Whoever says the *salam* after doing (only) two (*rak'ats*) out of negligence, and turns (to someone) and speaks, then if a short time has elapsed he should carry on with his *salat* from where he has left off and make a prostration of negligence; but if a long time elapses and he goes on sitting and talking, then he should do the *salat* from the beginning again – and there is no precise limit to this. However, if he goes out of the mosque, then he should repeat the *salat*. Ashhab said: 'If the (*salat* is performed) in the desert (that is, prayed in a *jama'a*, but not in a proper mosque), he should make up from where he left off as long as he has not gone so far from the rows (of the *salat* line) that he would no longer be permitted to pray in their *salat*.'"

BRANCH: Ibn al-Hattab has related: "Al-Hawari said, regarding the person who separates himself from the *salat*: 'Anyone who arrives after the *salat* (in the mosque has begun), who catches the last *rak'a* of a four-*rak'a salat* or of *Maghrib* but neglects to make up the first sitting he missed, then he is (considered) as the person who has forgotten the sitting in a two *rak'a salat*. However, if he forgets the prostration of negligence and a long time elapses, then he does not have to repeat the *salat* if he suddenly remembers – because of the difference of opinion in all respects in this matter; on the other hand, if he *deliberately* misses out the prostration of negligence, then he should make the *salat* again – out of consideration for this difference of opinion. I cannot however find an explicit text on the matter."

وَاسْتَدْرِكِ الرُّكْنَ فَإِنْ حَالَ الرُّكُوعُ

فَأَلْغِ ذَاتَ السَّهْوِ وَالْبِناَ يَطُوعُ

154 (If one remembers missing) any obligatory part (of the *salat* one is currently performing), one should put it right there and then, but if one has already gone into the bowing, then one treats as annulled the *rak'a* containing the omission and carries on (the rest of the *salat*) basing it on what one has done previous to this (annulled *rak'a*)

$$\text{كَفِعْلِ مَنْ سَلَّمَ لَكِنْ يُحْرِمُ}$$
$$\text{لِلْبَاقِي وَالطُّولُ الْفَسَادَ مُلْزِمُ}$$

155 Anyone who (remembers only after) making the *salam* should do likewise, although he must say *Allahu akbar* for the rest; but if a long time has elapsed, then this invalidates (his *salat*)

Mayyara said: "The author, may Allah have mercy on him, has informed us that anyone who forgets a pillar of the *salat*, that is one of its *fard* obligations, like the bowing or prostration and then remembers it, should put it right there and then. If, however, he does not remember it until after he has begun the bowing, that is he has inclined to the bowing of the *rak'a* which follows the *rak'a* in which something is missing, if the thing omitted is either a bowing or – in the case where it is other than this, like a prostration, for example and the bowing intervenes between it and between the putting right of what has been omitted – a (mere) raising of the head, then he should consider the *rak'a* containing the negligence annulled, that is, the *rak'a* in which he was negligent for part of it, and then continue, based on what he had done before this. However, all this only applies as long as the act of negligence occurs in other than the last *rak'a* – and this is what the author is indicating in the first line. If the mistake was made in the last *rak'a*, then he should make good what he neglected to do – by annulling this (current) *rak'a* of which some of it was omitted and carrying on from before this. However, if he does not remember until after he makes the *salam*, then he must make the *Allahu akbar* for the remaining part of the *salat* – which consists of making up for the invalid *rak'a*. If he says the *as-salamu alaykum* but does not say the *Allahu akbar* until after a long time has elapsed, then his *salat* is invalidated – and this is what the author is indicating in the second line. Thus that which prevents the (immediate) performance of what has been omitted – if that which has been omitted occurs in other than the last *rak'a* – is the bowing in the *rak'a* which follows; if it does occur in the last, then the thing that prevents (this immediate rectification) is the *salam*. For example, if one recites in a *rak'a* and prostrates but forgets the bowing, then if he remembers while prostrating or while sitting between the two prostrations or in the *tashahhud*, then Malik said: 'He should return to the standing position and then do the bowing, and it is recommended that he recite (once more) before bowing.' If he remembers while still standing in the following *rak'a*, then he does the bowing, straightening up and prostration and this takes the place of the bowing he had left out. If he remembers while bowing in the following *rak'a*, then imam Abu 'Abdallah al-Mazari said: 'The Shaykhs have differed over this: one of them said "he should raise his head with the intention of putting right the first" while another said "he should carry on with this *rak'a* and the first is invalidated" – and this second opinion is the well known opinion.'"

Ibn al-Hattab said: "Ibn 'Arafa has related that al-Mazari said: 'and if he remembers while bowing in the second *rak'a*, then one of the *'ulama* said "he should raise his head with the intention of the first" and this is correct, although others have rejected this as his bowing his head was (made with the intention) of the second; one said: "he should raise his head for this one but bow for the first and then rise again."' Ibn 'Arafa said: 'It is reported that Ashhab would carry on from the second (*rak'a*).'"

He has also said, commenting on the words of Khalil 'or two prostrations': "and if he remembers two prostrations while sitting, or omits the bowing for the second *rak'a*, goes down for its prostrations and then remembers the two prostrations of the first while he is in a state of prostration, then 'Abd al-Haqq has stated that he should return to the standing position – so as to go down to the two prostrations from the position of standing; if he does not do this and does the two prostrations from where he is, that is, from the sitting position or the prostration, then his going down (from the standing position) will have been omitted – in which case he should make the prostration before saying the *salam*, if he had omitted this out of negligence."

BRANCH: in *at-Tawdih* it is stated that al-Mazari said: "If he does not remember until he is bowing in the second, there is a difference of opinion as to whether he should raise his head so as to go down in the prostrations from the standing position. This difference is based on their difference as to whether it is the movements (of the *salat*) which are intended (or the positions themselves)."

Ibn 'Arafa said: "If he remembers a prostration while going down to the bowing, then he should 'carry on down (to prostrate immediately)', according to one report, or 'perform it after straightening up' according to another. Al-Lakhmi gives preference to the second. The first is from *Sama' al-Qarinayn*. The author of *at-Ta'qeeb fi kitab at-Tahdheeb* has stated that if he forgets the two prostrations of the first (*rak'a*) and then remembers (them) while he is bowing in the second, then he should raise his head with the intention of making good the first (*rak'a*) and then go down for the two prostrations from the standing position. There is no harm in this raising of his head in the second – but he does not count it (as a *rak'a*) as he raised his head with the intention of putting right the first. If he does not do this – and is still negligent in this regard, going down for the two prostrations directly from the bowing position – then he should prostrate before the *salam* to make up for the omission of not 'standing.'"

Ibn Mawwaq said: "Malik has stated on this matter: 'Whoever performs a *rak'a* and forgets its prostrations but then remembers them while standing in the second before the bowing, then he should pray two prostrations.' What he means is that he should go down (directly) into the two prostrations and not sit and then prostrate. He then goes on to say: 'Then he stands up and begins the recitation for the second *rak'a*. If he has forgotten a prostration from the first, and he remembers it before he does the bowing in the second – or after the bowing, but has not raised his head from it – then he should return and do the prostration which is still due from him.' What he means is that he should sits, then prostrate – as he has to make a separation between the two prostrations by means of the sitting, which is not the case when a person has forgotten the two prostrations. Malik then says: 'So if he has prostrated, then he should stand up and begin the recitation for the second *rak'a*. If he remembers either of these two (that is, the omission of either one or two prostrations) after raising his head from the *rak'a*, then he should carry on if he is at the beginning of his *salat*: he considers the first *rak'a* annulled and should make the prostrations after the *salam* to make up for either of them.' Malik has stated: 'The act of bowing is (reckoned as completed with) the raising of the head from this (position).' 'Abd al-Malik said in *al-Majmou'a*: 'Likewise, if the person behind the imam is in the standing position in the second, and he remembers a prostration from the first or he has doubts (as to whether he has done it) then he should return to the sitting position and do the prostration – unless he fears that the imam will rise from the bowing in the second (*rak'a*) with the result that he will do it after the imam and have to make up a *rak'a*.'"

مَنْ شَكَّ فِي رُكْنٍ بَنَى عَلَى الْيَقِينْ

وَلْيَسْجُدُوا الْبُعْدِيَّ لَكِنْ قَدْ يَبِينْ

156 Whoever has doubts regarding an obligation should resume from where he is certain, and then prostrate after the *salam*; and if an imperfection occurs

$$\text{لِأَنْ بَنَوْا فِي فِعْلِهِمْ وَالْقَوْلِي}$$

$$\text{نَقْصٌ بِفَوْتِ سُورَةٍ فَالْقَبْلِي}$$

157 because he omits the sura after the Umm al-Qur'an when resuming from the actions and spoken elements (of the *salat* which he knows) to be correct then he should do the prostration before the *salam*

Mayyara said: "Ibn 'Ashir is informing us that whoever has doubts regarding an obligation of the *salat* should carry on from what he is certain of – meaning, he should do (again) what he has doubts about and then prostrate after the *salam*. There is a difference of opinion, however, as to whether 'thinking in all likelihood' (*ghalabata'dh-dhann*) he has done something is more similar to 'doubting' he has done it or more similar to 'being certain' he has done it. Those who hold that it is like 'doubting', say that he should annul what he 'thinks he has in all likelihood done' and carry on based on what he is actually certain of and make the prostrations after the *salam*; those who think it is like 'being certain', say that he should assume that he has in fact done whatever he 'thinks he has in all likelihood done' and should not prostrate after the *salam*. Al-Lakhmi has mentioned these two opinions.

Ibn 'Ashir's words, beginning with the 'however' indicate that it may be that he does in fact miss out something despite his carrying on from where he is certain – that is, he carries on from the movements and spoken elements which he assumes to be correct but in doing so misses out the sura following the Fatiha, in which case he should make the prostrations (of negligence) before the *salam*. The judgement in his case is like the person who has come late for the *salat*, that is, he makes up what he has missed of the spoken elements of the *salat* and carries on from what he has missed regarding the actions."

NOTICE: an-Nafrawi said: "What may be understood from the author's words is that all this applies when he knows the obligation missed out is either a prostration or a bowing. If, however, he has forgotten an obligation but does not know whether it is a prostration, a bowing or some other obligation, then he should make the *takbirat al-ihram* together with the intention but without interrupting (the actual *salat*) or uttering anything. This is because he is in a state of uncertainty regarding the *salat* (as a whole) – so he should do the whole of the *salat* and prostrate after the *salam*. If, however, he is certain that he has only done the *takbirat al-ihram* or something else in addition to it, then he should resume from what he is certain he has done: if he has done the takbiratu'il *ihram* and the Fatiha, for example, then he should carry on based on having done these two and only perform what follows these two things. Thus anything he has doubts about he places after that which he is certain of: if someone certain of having done only the *takbirat al-ihram*, then he assumes he has forgotten the Fatiha and so on. This does not mean one can argue 'the making a *takbirat al-ihram* accompanied by an intention necessarily implies that the first is annulled completely – so why does one prostrate after the *salam*?' – for what we are saying is that the making of the (first) *takbirat al-ihram* remains valid throughout the *salat* as it has not been interrupted by the *salam* or by speaking. What is intended by the saying of the second *takbir* is the establishing of certainty (regarding this matter). It does not invalidate the first, as we have mentioned above: indeed (it may be assumed that) in all probability his *takbirat al-ihram* was done and nothing has happened to invalidate it – and so this (second) *ihram* is purely additional."

Issue Ibn al-Hattab said: "Abu Muhammad was asked as to whether the person who is subject to persistent doubt in the *salat* and who makes an additional *rak'a* to annul the doubt has to make a prostration on account of this addition, or whether this addition invalidates his *salat*, or whether simply he does not have to make anything up because of his state of persistent doubt. He replied: 'If he is ignorant and thinks that the addition makes up for a defect then his *salat* is correct.' I said: 'and what if he is a man of knowledge?' He replied: 'Such a person cannot be a man of knowledge but is rather someone with deficient knowledge, and the judgement in his respect is as we have mentioned to you. (Anyone in) this state of persistent doubt is alleviated, legally speaking, (of responsibility for his doubts) and such an addition does not lead to the *salat* being invalidated – rather, he should make a prostration after the *salam*.' I said 'but why not before the *salam* as his doubts were with regard to a omission (rather than an addition)?' He replied: 'He did not omit anything but rather *thought* there was an omission.' I said: 'If this applies in the case of someone subject to doubts *in general*, then this is as the Shaykh has already mentioned and the judgement is as above. If, however, the doubts occur to him regarding an omission of one of the *rak'ats* and these doubts recur, then the correct judgement is that it is not said of such a person that he 'makes an addition (of the missing *rak'a*) deliberately' – for it would be necessary to say this of him if it were not for his state of persistent doubt. It may well be that this matter should be classed along with the judgement regarding the person who repeatedly has to do the *salat* again on account of the great number of incidents of negligence on his part and his not being in a state of humility – or other states of this nature. Moreover, the people of the Qayrawan differ as to whether this matter is a praiseworthy condition or whether it results from seeking to deepen one's knowledge of the deen.'"

كَذَاكِرِ الْوُسْطَى وَالْأَيْدِي قَدْ رَفَعْ

وَرُكَّاً لَا قَبْلَ ذَا لَكِنْ رَجَعْ

158 likewise, the person who has already raised his hands and knees and remembers (having omitted) the middle (sitting and does not return to the sitting position should prostrate before the *salam*), but does not (prostrate) if he returns (to the sitting position) before (raising his hands and knees)

This is like the words of Khalil: "The person who has omitted the first sitting should return to it as long as his hands and knees have not left the ground, in which case there is no prostration to be made; if they have (left the ground), then (there is a prostration to be made before the *salam*) but he should not (return to the sitting position); however the *salat* is not invalidated if he does return (to the sitting position) even if he has got up and is standing." Al-Mawwaq said in his commentary: "Malik said in this regard: 'Whoever forgets the sitting in the two *rak'ats* such that he moves away from the ground and stands up, then he should carry on and not return but should prostrate before the *salam*.' Ibn 'Arafa said: ''Iyad has approved of the *tafseer* of ash-Shaykh "... as long as he has raised his hands and knees".' Ibn al-Qasim said in *al-Majmu'a* from Malik: 'If he has left the ground but has not yet come to a still and stable standing position, then he should not return but should prostrate before the *salam*; if, however, he does return, then he should prostrate after the *salam*.' Ashhab said: 'If he has come to a still and stable standing position and returns, then he should prostrate before the *salam*.' Ibn Yunus said: '...because being in the standing position, he must carry on, and the making up the omission remains a responsibility for him; by returning however, he effectively makes an addition and so becomes someone who has made both an omission and an addition, requiring that he prostrate before the *salam*.' It is reported from Sahnun: 'His *salat* is invalidated – except if he returns out of negligence.' Al-Mazari said: 'According to the well known opinion, his *salat* is not invalidated, even if he returns unaware (of the judgement), because the prohibition of returning after having come to the still and stable standing position is not such that it affords absolute proof against him or that one cannot "interpret" it (as being in fact valid). Indeed, if he returns after having come to a standing position, then he has acted correctly according to Ibn Hanbal and others, and it does not invalidate his *salat*.'"

Ibn Rushd has related: "Ibn 'Abd al-Hakam and 'Isa have said: 'His *salat* is invalidated, and this is the judgement of Sahnun.' Malik said: 'He should prostrate after the *salam*' and Ashhab and 'Ali have said: 'He should prostrate after the *salam* because of the addition of the standing.' Based on this judgement, he should carry on the sitting until he completes it. It is also said that he should prostrate before the *salam* because it amounts to an addition and an omission – and based on this judgement he does not have to carry on with the sitting which he returns to for he makes up for sitting he had omitted with the prostration before the *salam*: one cannot do something again which has been already made up for."

Issue: al-Mawwaq and al-Hattab have said: "Ibn al-Qasim has reported that someone completed the sitting with the imam in the two *rak'ats*, then fell asleep. He did not wake up until the people had stood up whereupon he himself stood up without doing the *tashahhud*.' Ibn Rushd said: 'This is as he said because the *tashahhud* has been missed by his being asleep: its time and place has passed (irrevocably) and there is nothing for him to make up – this (deficiency) is something which is born by the imam. Moreover his *wudu'* is not broken by this amount (of sleep) as it is insignificant.'"

Issue: Ibn al-Hattab said, commenting on the words of Khalil 'and with the *salam*': "Whoever begins to say the *salam* after the *salam* of the imam but then leaves off doing the rest of the *salam* at the moment when the imam says *Allahu akbar* for the 'Eid after this *salam* and says it instead after the imam said the three *takbirs*, then he should repeat the *salat*, however long the delay."

I say: "What he means is that it is invalidated because he has spoken with the words *salam* out of ignorance before the completion of the *salat*. If he had said the *Allahu akbar* with him before saying anything of the *salam*, then it would have been valid, although *makruh* – being in this case an addition and classed under the heading of 'delaying the *salam* after the *salam* of the imam', as Ibn 'Abd al-Hakam said. Likewise, if he is occupied with the *tashahhud* after the *salam* of the imam, this is also *makruh* but his *salat* is valid."

Laws Governing the Jumuʿa

Laws Governing the Jumu'a

The Khutbah

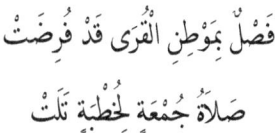

159 Section: The *salat* of *jumu'a* following a *khutba* is obligatory in towns and settlements

THE meaning of this is clear and I do not need to give any lengthy explanation of it given the existence of commentaries amongst the people (of knowledge).

USEFUL POINT: The author of *al-Jami' as-Saghir* said: "There is no more excellent *salat* than that of *fajr* on the day of *jumu'a* when done in a *jama'a*, and I consider that anyone taking part in it will be forgiven," – or whatever his exact words were. Al-Munawi said: "The fires of Jahannam are not lit on the day of *jumu'a* and its doors are closed, the violence of the Fire is not the same as on other days. If (the life of) a slave is taken on this day, it is proof that he will have a happy end as the *jumu'a* is the day when the Final Hour occurs and when Allah discriminates between His friends and enemies. The *jumu'a* is the day He will invite them to visit Him in the Abode of Eden. The life of no *mumin* will be taken on this day – when His vast and boundless mercy overflows – but that happiness and mastery will be written for him and he will be protected from the trials of the grave."

A FURTHER BENEFIT: The author of *Majma' al-Ahbab* has related: "Ad-Darani said: "If tears flow from the eye of someone setting out for *jumu'a* – even if a single tear – then Allah, blessed and exalted is He, will command the angel on his left side 'roll up the page of My slave and do not record any wrong actions on it until the following *jumu'a*!'" Abu Sulayman said: "I met Abu Sahl as-Safar in Basra and I questioned him about the hadith. He said: 'Abu Sulayman, if all that he has from his weeping is that his page is rolled up from one *jumu'a* to the next, then he has nothing.'"

USEFUL POINT: it has become widespread practice in our district not to give the offspring of animals any milk from their mothers on the night of the *jumu'a*, some students even saying that it should not be given until the sun rises the following morning. However, I have not seen anyone discuss this matter in the accepted books, neither in a positive or negative manner, except one *'alim* of our time who has composed a work and written that this (practice) is forbidden saying: "The day of *jumu'a* is as the other days." I said: "Moreover, none of the commentators of the *Mukhtasar* – that is, available here – have stipulated anything (to the contrary). One of the men of knowledge said: 'Their milk is permitted night after night as long as it does not harm their offspring.' It is also said that it bears witness to what he says, and Allah knows best."

NOTICE: they that if it *does* harm the offspring it is forbidden – even if one merely suspects it (may harm them). Some have also referred to the prohibition in the *shari'ah* of burdening a slave or an animal with more that he or it can bear. The author of *al-Mi'yar* said: "Any such action is considered to be an evil act (*munkar*) which should be stopped (by the person witnessing it)." However, al-Munawi, in his greater commentary on the *al-Jami' as-Saghir*, said that this is conditional upon this act going on for a considerable time (and that it is not a one-off, spontaneous act). He goes on to say: "'The third (mounted) on an animal is cursed' – meaning, if a person mounts an animal when there are already two on it and it cannot bear him, then he is cursed, that is, proscribed from the stations of the *Abrar* – the good – until he has been purified by the Fire." His saying "on an animal" is from the narrator and not from the completion of the hadith, and if only the compiler had made that clear it would have been more appropriate. Moreover, he said, "That was about three returning from a journey on this animal," and this is a specific case and refers to a specific animal: it does not necessarily follow that three persons on any animal is always forbidden. If the beast is able to bear three or more because of its strength, the lightness of those it is carrying or the shortness of the distance (to be covered) then it is permitted – as an-Nawawi and others have said. Indeed, this is our *madhhab* and the *madhhab* of everyone, and the narration of 'Iyad that some have prohibited it is invalid. I would also like to point out that the *fuqaha* have declared that a master may sometimes burden his slave with what he can only manage with great difficulty as long as he does not always burden him in this way. What he says is based on this (declaration), and I have not seen any objection to this.

USEFUL POINT: the author of *al-Jami' as-Saghir* said: "There is nothing more beloved to Allah than a young man who turns in *tawba*, there is nothing more hated by Allah, exalted is He, than an old man who persists in his acts of disobedience, there is no good action more beloved to Allah, exalted is He, than one undertaken during the night or day of *jumu'a* and there is no wrong action more hated by Allah than one committed during the night or day of *jumu'a*."

USEFUL POINT: it is *makruh* to leave off one's work on the day of *jumu'a*, and it is prohibited to consider some days as being unlucky or to believe what the astrologers say. In the *Kabir* – after a long discussion of the words of *al-Jami' as-Saghir* 'the last Wednesday of the month is one of continuous misfortune' al-Munawi states: "In short, seeking protection from Wednesdays in the belief that they are unlucky and believing in what the astrologers say is prohibited in the strongest possible terms – for there is no harm and no intrinsic benefit in these days as such. It follows that one cannot proscribe (any particular day). Whoever does seek to see an omen (in a day) is contesting this reality. Whoever is certain that no harm or benefit can occur but by Allah, then none of this (belief) has any effect on him anyway."

He continued after a while by commenting on the words of the author of *al-Hidaya* 'Anything begun on the Wednesday will be completed', Burhan al-Islam said in *Ta'leem al-Muta'allim*: "For this reason, a group of the *'ulama* would strive to have their lessons on this day – knowledge is light and displaying such knowledge on the day light was created is fitting for it helps to bring it to completion. Some consider it is recommended to plant trees on this day on account of the *marfu'* tradition of Ibn Hibban and ad-Daylami: 'Whoever plants (something) on Wednesday should say "*Subhana*, O You who cause all to be raised up and You who will inherit everything, cause it to bear fruit for people to eat."' Others have said that when the Caesar of Rome sent a letter to al-Mu'tasim warning him, the latter wrote on the back of it 'The reply is as you see not what you hear *"and the kafir will soon know who has the Ultimate Abode."*[1] He then stood up and left immediately (to fight) – and the day was a Wednesday. He did not even enter his house. The astrologers had prohibited him from doing so saying "it is a ill fated omen" but he had replied "for them not for us!" Thus he started out on a campaign on this day during which sixty thousand captives were taken and sixty thousand were killed. It was a battle in which Allah helped Islam and the people of Islam."

Hafidh Ibn Hajar said: "(One day,) the Sultan was angry at al-Kamal al-Barizi, the private secretary, but then (soon afterwards) became content with him and so rewarded him on Wednesday 14th of the month of *Rabia Awwal* in

---

1   ar-Ra'd – Thunder: 43

844 AH: al-Kamal rode in the (Sultan's) cavalcade the like of which had never ridden in before. Five fours coincided on this day – the 800 also contains twice times four."

In *Tadhkirat al-'Ilm*, al-Balqeeni narrates from one of the *'ulama*: "It is clear from experience – and it never fails to prove true – that anything undertaken on a Sunday which coincides with the fourteenth of the lunar month will not be completed. This happened to Nasir Faraj – as it has happened to others: he set out on a journey at the beginning of the year, saying "If I travel in (the month of) *Muharram*, then I should be in a state of *Ihram* but if I travel in the month of *Safar*,[1] then I fear that my hands will turn yellow." So he delayed the journey to the month of *Rabi'* (*al-Awwal*) but on setting out he became ill. Having accomplished nothing he remarked: "I thought it was the *Rabi'*[2] of delight and ease but in fact it is the *Rabi'* of illness and blight." In another proverb it states: "Do not have enmity to the days lest they have enmity towards you."

USEFUL POINT: the author of *Ghayat al-Amani* has narrated that Ibn Zarqoun said: "The *'ulama* are of a consensus that whoever abandons performing a *jumu'a* without a valid excuse is not a *kafir* unless he does it out of disobedience."

As for Ibn 'Ashir's saying in 'in towns and settlements', Mayyara has commented: "Ibn Basheer said: 'One of the conditions for performing the *jumu'a* is that the place be inhabited. The well known judgement is that it is not stipulated that it be a city but rather that it be performed in all towns as long as they are inhabited continuously, are self-sufficient and the splendour of Islam is manifest through their *jama'a*. This may apply to shanty towns but not to tent settlements.' In the commentary of Shaykh al-Jazuli it states: 'Any buildings where a lot of people live – but not isolated buildings in which just one or three persons live – may be termed 'a village or settlement (*qarya*)' as long as they are able to remain there (continuously) and can obtain everything necessary to live. If the number of inhabitants reaches 400 and the settlement is composed of a series of interconnected separate areas, then it is called a town (*madina*) – which in Arabic comes from the word *tadween* and which implies a place of coming together; if contiguous and the various communities are densely packed one against the other, then it is called a city (*misr*), irrespective of whether it is surrounded by a wall or not. The word *qarya* may apply to all of them in the sense that they are all settlements. Whatever has a wall around it is called a *hisn*, a fortified city.'"

As for his words 'with a *khutba*', Mayyara noted: "Khalil said in *al-Mukhtasa*r

---

1   the root meaning of *Safar* is yellow
2   one of the meanings of *rabi'* is 'spring'

'with two *khutbas* – of the kind known to the Arabs as *khutbas* – before the *salat*, and which are attended by the *jama'a*.' Ibn al-Qasim said: 'The minimum that may be pronounced in a *khutba* is *al-hamdulillah*, the sending of peace and blessings on the Prophet, a warning and a giving of good news and Qur'an.'"

BRANCH: it is forbidden to speak during the *khutba*. Khalil said, comparing it to his words '(travel) is forbidden after the time of the zenith': "...also forbidden is speaking during or between the two *khutbas* [of the imam after he has stood] – and even for those not listening (who do not understand his words), unless [the *khateeb*] is speaking about something other than the *khutba*, according to the preferred judgement."

Al-Mawwaq said, commenting on his words 'likewise speaking': "Ibn 'Arafa said: 'One must listen to the two *khutbas* and be quiet during and between them, even if one does not hear them and even those outside the mosque. And most are of this opinion.'" Ibn al-Harith said: "There is a consensus (in this)." He has also said, commenting on his words 'even those not listening': "Ibn al-Qasim said: 'I have seen how Malik would speak with his companions on the day of *jumu'a*, even after the imam had entered (the mosque), and continue right up to the end of the *adhan*; only when the imam had got up and had begun speaking would he and his companion turn to face the imam.'" Commenting on his words 'unless the *khateeb* is speaking about something other than the *khutba*, according to the preferred judgement', al-Lakhmi said: "It is not permitted to move anything that makes a sound during the *khutba*, like a door or even new clothing, for this would distract those listening." Malik said: "One should not speak even if the imam has starting uttering something he is not permitted to utter, like cursing or reviling someone whom he is not permitted to abuse or to praising someone he is not permitted to praise." Ibn Habib said: "If the imam erroneously speaks about something which does not concern the people, then the people do not have to listen attentively or even face him. This was the practice of Ibn al-Musayyab." Al-Lakhmi said: "This is correct."

THE JAMI'

بِجَامِعٍ عَلَى مُقِيمٍ مَا اعْتُذِرْ

حُرٍّ قَرِيبٍ بِكَفَرْسَخٍ ذُكِرْ

160 in a *jami'* mosque. It is obligatory for the resident without a valid excuse,

who is free, and who lives nearby – that is, within three miles,[1] and who is male;

Khalil said: "...in a (large) *jami'* mosque built exclusively as a mosque, and (if more than one, then,) in the oldest." Al-Mawwaq has related that al-Baji said, commenting on his words 'built exclusively...': "One of the conditions regarding the mosque is that it be constructed in the way mosques are normally built. (On one occasion) the people of a town made a *fatwa*, after having demolished their mosque, to pray four *rak'ats* as it had no roof and the day of *jumu'a* arrived before they had (had time to) rebuild it. Ibn Rushd said: 'This is an unlikely (judgement) for even if a mosque has been demolished it still remains known as a mosque and the legal judgement (as to its being a mosque) remains in force. However it would not be correct to name the site designated for the building of a mosque a mosque before it is built – being mere space.'"

He has also said, commenting on his words, 'exclusively...': "Al-Jilab said: 'The *jumu'a* should not be performed in one city in two mosques. If the people do nevertheless (perform it twice), then the valid *salat* is that performed in the oldest mosque.' Abu Muhammad has related from Ibn Yunus: 'If there are two *jami'* mosques in one area, then the *jumu'a* is that of the oldest mosque whether the imam prays in the oldest or the newest.' Ibn 'Abd al-Hakam said: '...except in the great cities like (Cairo in) Egypt or in Baghdad for there is no harm in performing two *jumu'as* if necessary. This was practised when there were many people and they did not object.'"

As for his saying 'there is no harm in performing two *jumu'as*, if necessary', the like is reported of the Shafi'is who base their judgement on the saying of the Prophet, may the peace and blessings of Allah be upon him: "There is to be no harming and no reciprocating harm." Many important benefits have been derived from this hadith, among them this one. We shall mention, insha'Allah, the discussion of Ibn Hajar al-Haytami regarding the hadith even though the greater part of it is not about this specific matter. We shall make this digression on account of the above mentioned matter, because of the terms he uses and because of the benefits contained in it – which no student can do without. After speaking about the hadith itself, he goes on to speak about what our imams have derived from it, namely the well known principle 'harm should be removed': "Many aspects of *fiqh* are based on it, and one of them is the judgement of ash-Shafi'i, may Allah be content with him: 'If a matter becomes constricted and difficult, then it should be expanded and made easier.' He uttered these

---

1 *farsakh*: twelve thousand cubits, corresponding roughly to three miles

words as an answer to the problem of a woman who loses her guardian during a journey and who hands over her affair to a man who subsequently marries her, and regarding the judgement in the case where a fly lands on excrement and then on one's clothing. However, the *ulama* also recognise (on occasion) the opposite of this, namely, if a matter is (too) 'expanded', then it should be constricted, like for example making a lot of unnecessary movements in the *salat* would not be tolerated whereas a little – if necessary – is. This (latter judgement) is also connected to the principle that 'harm should be removed.'"

The following principles, however, must be taken into account:

1. Compelling or harmful circumstances may render proscribed things licit on condition that the (overall) harm ensuing is attenuated. Thus it is permitted, for the person in compelling circumstances, to eat carrion, to take a thread which does not belong to him in order to stitch a serious wound, or (in certain circumstances) to criticise the good name of an honoured person, to utter an expression of *kufr*, to spend money or wealth extravagantly when compelled to do so, and to ward off an assailant even if this leads to his death. If the haram is so widespread in a region (or community) that hardly anything halal exists, then it would be permitted to use what one has need of – even, (on occasion), when such use is not purely out of need, as long as it does not lead to an abuse or the enjoyment (of the haram). Ibn 'Abd as-Salam has narrated from 'Izz ad-Deen ash-Shafi'i: "...this applies when the owner of the wealth is known; otherwise, it is considered as *fay'*-booty to be used for the public good. In general, any wealth whose owner is unknown belongs to the *bayt al-mal*. However, the dead body of the Prophet, may the peace and blessings of Allah be upon him, would be excluded from the (above) judgement for it would be forbidden to regard this as 'carrion' even if a person's life were threatened. This is because its prohibition within the *shari'ah* is of more import than saving someone whose life is threatened. Likewise, fornication and killing do not become 'licit' – even in compelling circumstances – as the evil of these two acts would be equal in odiousness to any compelling threat to the person's own life, or indeed would be greater.

2. What is considered licit for the person who is in compelling need is subject to specific limits: thus he should not eat more carrion than he needs to survive. It would not be licit for anyone who is able to stop someone such as a suitor by indicating with his eye to state it openly and explicitly. If a woman is bleeding (from her arm), then she must not uncover her arm except when absolutely necessary, and then only the particular place where it is bleeding. It is permitted to have more than one *jumu'a* when it is difficult for everyone to

gather in one place.

What is implied by his saying that it is not permitted for the person in compelling need to eat the dead body of the Prophet, may the peace and blessings of Allah be upon him, is that one may eat the dead bodies of other people. However, the well known judgement in our *madhhab* is that the dead body of a person is not to be eaten at all. Moreover, his saying that one may only eat an amount of carrion which ensure one's survival is contrary to the well known judgement of our *madhhab* – even though the author of the *Mukhtasar* holds to it. As for the question of the woman who loses her guardian while on a journey, something which concurs with it from one of the followers of Malik is stated in *al-Mi'yar* although I do not know if the judgement put forward is the predominant judgement or it is a weaker view.

As for his saying 'no valid excuse', al-Mawwaq has related that Ibn Rushd said: "Among the conditions of *jumu'a* – without which a *jumu'a* is not obligatory, although acceptable when performed without them – is that those attending be male, free and resident. It is not obligatory upon a slave, traveller or a woman. In *at-Talqeen* it states: 'It is an obligation on the person who lives outside of the major city to come to it – that is, up to three miles away or thereabouts. 'Ali has narrated that this condition is reckoned from the minaret.' Ibn Yunus said: 'This is not the case, however, in a major city for the people of the large city must strive to come even if it is five or six miles away.'"

Khalil said: "…a valid excuse to leave off doing the (*jumu'a*) – and the *jama'a* (in general) – is (that the place is) excessively muddy and rainy, or (a person is) afflicted by elephantiasis or leprosy, illness, or must look after a sick person or a close relative or the like, that one fears for one's property, that one might be imprisoned or beaten – according to the most evident judgement (of Ibn Rushd) and the most correct (of al-Lakhmi), that a debtor fears being imprisoned (by a creditor), when a nude (person is unable to obtain clothes), when someone – who hopes to be pardoned – will escape from (an act of) retaliation (by not attending), when having eaten garlic, during a stormy night (in the case of the *jama'a* of *Maghrib* and *'Isha* in general); but not on account of a wedding, blindness or having attended the 'Eid (earlier in the day, if on a Friday) even if the imam has given his permission."

In his commentary al-Mawwaq has related that al-Lakhmi said: "Among the valid reasons for not attending the *jumu'a* is an illness which makes it difficult to get there or a sickness which makes it impossible for the person afflicted to remain in the *jami'* mosque and results in his *jumu'a* being invalidated; that his wife, daughter or one of his parents have become gravely ill, are in the throes of death or have died; also if a person fears that the Sultan might take his wealth if he attends, or that someone will steal from his house or the goods belonging to someone else might burn." Ibn Basheer said: "…and likewise his fearing for the wealth of others." Al-Lakhmi said: "Whoever eats garlic, onions or leeks should use something to get rid of the odour." Ibn Sha'ban said: "The person whose breath smells of garlic should use the courtyard of the mosque not the inner area." Al-Baji said: "Our contemporaries have stated explicitly that it is *makruh* to enter the mosque when smelling of garlic, and in my opinion also the place used for praying the two 'Eids and the *janaza salats*." Ibn Wahb said: "It is stated in *al-Mabsout*: 'I do not consider that that the person who has to do the *jumu'a* and who has eaten garlic that day should attend the *jumu'a* – neither in the mosque itself or in the courtyards. As to whether it is permitted for a person who has eaten garlic to enter when there is no one there, the most evident judgement in my opinion is that it is not permitted.'"

He has commented on his words 'a stormy night' saying: "It is reported in the *Muwatta'* that Ibn 'Umar, may Allah be pleased with him, made the *adhan* for the *salat* during a cold and windy night saying: 'Make the *salat* in your tents and wherever you are' – the Messenger of Allah, may the peace and blessings of Allah be upon him, would also command the *mu'adhdhin* to say 'Make the *salat* in your tents and wherever you are' if the night was cold and rainy.'" Al-Baji said: "Ibn 'Umar has made a analogy between the wind and the rain. The underlying rationale connecting the two is the 'difficulty' present in both. It may well be, indeed it is most likely, that his words 'make the *salat* in your tents and wherever you are' were uttered after the completion of the *adhan*."

Abu 'Umar said: "Included in the *fiqh* (of this subject) is permission not to go to the *jama'a* on a rainy night or when the wind is violent; also implied is anything which causes difficulty and which provides a valid reason preventing one (from going). If it is permitted not to attend the *jama'a* for the *'Isha* (on a stormy night), or on account of eating garlic, then this (excuse of 'difficulty' is all the more reasonable)."

ISSUE: it is stated in *Nawazil al-Qubbab*: "Al-Qubab was asked about a man who – whenever going to the *jama'a* – could not help getting involved in speaking behind people's backs or in excessively indiscreet conversation or in clever, (but fruitless), conversation and the like. He replied: 'If this is true, then we should examine the state of the man in question: if it is known that by going to the *jama'a* he will inevitably get involved in the haram, either by backbiting himself or listening to others backbiting, and that this will occur as a result of his own desire and interest in it and that he will not condemn it, either openly or in his heart, then it is not permitted for him to go out – even for a *nafila salat* if it means his getting involved in an act of disobedience. However, if while merely listening to such talk, he himself feels aversion to it and manifests his disapproval of it if he is able, then it is not a wrong action and so he is not prohibited (from going).'"

The (above discussion concerns) one of the aspects of excellence. However, (using the argument that backbiting is inevitable) may also be one of the tricks of Shaytan in order to divert someone from the excellence of the *jama'a*. If useless or superficial discussion is not forbidden, then it is *makruh* – in which case the excellence of the *jama'a* is something of greater importance. As for people 'embellishing their language', if it means someone having the capacity to express himself eloquently, then this is permitted; but if it leads to an embellishment of the language on the part of those whose business is the deen and scrupulous behaviour, then this is showing off. I am not sure in this case what he is referring to. However, what is meant is (clear, namely) that whenever he knows that he will fall into the forbidden, then it is not permitted for him to go out; and if he does not (know with this degree of certainty), then he may go out but must strive to ward off such things. There are mistakes in the manuscript but the overall meaning is clear insha'Allah.

Hastening to the Jumu'ah

وَأَجْزَأَتْ غَيْراً نَعَمْ قَدْ تُنْدَبُ

عِنْدَ النِّدَا السَّعْىُ إِلَيْهَا يَجِبُ

161 If, however, other than these (persons who are under an obligation to) perform it, then it is accepted of them (and counts instead of *Dhuhr*), indeed it is recommended. And when the call is made, one must make haste to it.

In other words, if the traveller, slave, child, any person living further than three miles from it or a woman perform it, then it is accepted of them.

As for his words 'when the call is made one must make hasten to it', it is stated in *at-Tawdih*: "Know that there are two aspects regarding the people for whom it is obligatory to make the *jumu'a*: either they live far away or near by. In the case of the person living far away, he must make haste before the call such that he will be able to get there in time, and this is agreed upon. Al-Baji and the author of *al-Muqaddimat* have said: 'There is a difference of opinion as to when a person should set out for it: it has been said: "...when the sun has begun to go past the zenith" although it has also been said: "...when the *mu'adhdhin* calls the *adhan*." The difference of opinion is based on their dispute as to whether it is obligatory to be present at the *khutba*: those who deem it obligatory on each and every person, consider it obligatory for a man to go to it immediately after the sun has past its zenith – in order to get to it on time; those who do not deem it obligatory that each and every person be present consider that it is only obligatory to leave on hearing the *adhan* – for it is clear that if a person does not set out until the *adhan* is made he will miss the *khutba* or part of it.' Likewise, there is a difference of opinion as to whether the person living at some distance (from the mosque) should make haste in order to catch the *salat* or the *khutba* – and their differences correspond to the distance involved."

THE GHUSL

وَسُنَّ غَسْلٌ بِالرَّوَاحِ اتَّصَلَا
وَنُدِبَ تَهْجِيرٌ وَحَالٌ جَمُلَا

162 It is a sunna to make a *ghusl* and to make it immediately before leaving (for the mosque). It is recommended to set out in the midday heat, to be well-groomed and neat of appearance.

It is a sunna to delay the *ghusl* for the *jumu'a salat* as much as possible prior to the moment of departure. Ibn 'Arafa said: "The *ghusl* is required for it and its form and the (amount of) water to be used is the same as that of the *janaba*. It is accepted that it is a sunna for all who go to it – even someone who does not have to go, and likewise in the case of the two 'Eids. The well known judgement is that it should be done immediately before the setting out although an insignificant interval is excused. However, it is not acceptable before *fajr*, contrary to the opinion of al-Awza'i; and not after the *fajr*, that is immediately following it, contrary to Ibn Wahb. Abu 'Umar said: 'I am not aware of anyone who has deemed the *ghusl* of *jumu'a* to be a *fard* obligation, except the Dhahiris.'"

Khalil said: "(It is sunna to) repeat the *ghusl* if one eats or sleeps out of his own choosing." Al-Mawwaq said that Malik has recorded: "If one makes the *ghusl* for the *jumu'a* and then sets off for the mosque and then becomes ritually impure, then this does not break his *ghusl*; nor if he goes out and then does *wudu'* and returns. If he sleeps and does *wudu'* after his *ghusl*, then he should repeat it so that his *ghusl* is 'joined to', that is, immediately precedes his going to the mosque." Ibn Habib said: "This applies if the matter goes on for a long time, but if not, then he does not have to repeat it."

As for his words 'and well-groomed and neat of appearance', al-Mawwaq has related: "'Iyad said: 'Among the recommended aspects of the *jumu'a salat* are the *fitra* acts of trimming one's moustache, plucking the hair from under one's arms, shaving off the hair of the pubes and cutting one's nails.' Ibn Habib has also mentioned the *miswak*."

The Jama'a

بِجُمْعَةٍ جَمَاعَةٌ قَدْ وَجَبَتْ

سُنَّتْ بِفَرْضٍ وَبِرَكْعَةٍ رَسَتْ

163 It is obligatory to have a *jama'a* for the *jumu'a* whereas it is (only) a sunna for the *fard salat*, and the (excellence of this *jama'a*) is assured by catching (at least) one *rak'a*.

وَنُدِبَتْ إِعَادَةُ الْفَذِّ بِهَا

لَا مَغْرِبًا كَذَا عِشَا مُوتِرُهَا

164 It is recommended that the person who has prayed alone (at home) repeat (the *salat*) with the *jama'a*, but not in the case of *Maghrib* or *'Isha* – when followed by its *witr*.

Al-Khurshi said, commenting on the words of Khalil 'The *jama'a* for the *fard salat* other than the *jumu'a* is sunna': "This means: the formation of a *jama'a* for a *fard salat* which is incumbent on each and every person – both that whose time is still current or any other still to be made up from the past – is a sunna.' Ibn Shas said: 'It is a *mu'akkad* sunna.' Then he goes on to say: 'It is not obligatory except in the case of the *jumu'a*.' imam Abu 'Abdallah and the two Qadis, Abu'l-Walid [ibn Rushd] and Abu Bakr [ibn al-'Arabi], have related from one of the people of the *madhhab* that it is a communal *fard*. Al-Jazuli said in his commentary on the *Risala*: 'It is an aspect of excellence.' The most evident meaning of his words and those of others is that it is a sunna in the *jumu'a*, and in every mosque and applies to every person who prays – even to the individual person who is alone: that is, it is a sunna in his regard to search for a *jama'a*. The evidence for this is that it is *recommended* for the person who performs the *salat* alone to seek a *jama'a*: so what is implied is that, in his regard, it is a sunna not to do the *salat* alone, contrary to the judgement of Ibn Rushd – who harmonises between the (different) judgements arguing that it is a *fard* in general, a sunna in every mosque and an aspect of excellence from the point of view of an individual person. The most evident meaning of the words of Ibn 'Arafa is that this judgement of Ibn Rushd is contrary to that of the majority, and this is what as-Sanusi understands in his commentary on the words of the author. Ibn 'Arafa said: 'Most Shaykhs say that the *jama'a* of the five (daily) *salats* is a *mu'akkad* sunna.' He then goes on to say: 'It is narrated from Ibn Rushd that it is recommended for a man with respect to himself in particular, a *fard* obligation in general and a sunna in every mosque.'"

In accordance with the method employed by Ibn Rushd in arriving at his judgement, the words of the author may be understood to mean that the *jama'a* is to be established in every mosque rather than in the area as a whole – a man being obliged to perform his *salat* in a *jama'a*. If you were to argue: "If the establishing of the *jama'a* in a particular area as a whole is a communal obligation and it is a communal sunna in every mosque, then how can it be recommended for a man to establish his *salat* in a *jama'a* – given that a part of the sunna or part of the obligation cannot be (merely) recommended?" I said: "It may be possible to interpret it as referring to a man who performs his *salat* in a *jama'a* which takes place after the establishing of a *fard* or sunna *jama'a* – that is, after the *jama'a* which is established for the area as a whole and after that of every other mosque in the area."

I SAY: "Al-Ubbi said in the *Sharh Muslim*: 'The most pertinent opinion and the one closest to the truth is that mentioned by Ibn Rushd.'"

As for his saying 'a *jama'a* for the *jumu'a*', Mayyara said: "He is informing us that the *jama'a* is obligatory for the *jumu'a*, meaning that the performance for other than the *jumu'a* in a *jama'a* is sunna. His words 'whereas it is (only) a sunna for the *fard salat*' confirm this. His words 'and the (excellence of this *jama'a*) is obtained by catching (at least) one complete *rak'a* means together with its two prostrations. Then he states that if someone prays alone, it is recommended that he repeat (the *salat*) with the *jama'a*, except in the case of *Maghrib* and *'Isha* – where the latter is prayed with the *witr salat*; however, if *'Isha* is prayed alone, then he should repeat it with the *jama'a*. As for the judgement of performing the *salat* in the *jama'a*, Ibn 'Arafa said: 'For most of the Shaykhs, performing the five *salats* in *jama'a* is a *mu'akkad* sunna. Ibn Rushd said a general *fard* obligation, a sunna in every mosque and it is recommended for every man in particular.'"

I SAY: The preference of al-Ubbi for the argument of Ibn Rushd has been mentioned above. Khalil said: "the merit of it is obtained with (just one) *rak'a*." Al-Khurshi said in his declaration on the matter: "The promised excellence of the *jama'a* understood from the hadith, 'The *salat* in the *jama'a* is twenty-five times better then the *salat* of one of you alone', and in another narration its rank is 'twenty-seven' times better, is only obtained by catching one complete *rak'a*. Catching a *rak'a* is determined by having placed one's hands firmly on one's knees before the imam straightens up (from the bowing position) even if one is not able to relax a moment (*tuma'neena*) until after straightening up. Moreover it is not stipulated that one 'remain firm and still' before the straightening up as the words of Ibn 'Arafa imply; nor should one be deceived by the words of Ibn al-Hajib."

Al-Mawwaq said in his commentary: "Ibn Yunus has related that Ibn Rushd said: 'The excellence of the *jama'a* is even obtained by catching just a portion of the *salat* before the *salam* (of the imam).' Ibn 'Arafa said: 'One does not legally catch it with less than a *rak'a*.' Ibn al-Qasim has reported: '(Catching it) is defined as being able to place one's hands on one's knees before the imam straightens up from the bowing.'"

BRANCH: Mayyara said: "Muhammad ibn 'Abd as-Salam said that if the person behind the imam does in fact place his hands on his knees after the imam has straightened up then: '...strictly speaking he should straighten up in accordance with the imam, although one of my Shaykhs said he should stay in the bowing position until the imam goes down into the prostration — and then go down into prostration (directly) from the bowing and not straighten up. This is because the raising of the head from the bowing position marks the completing of the bowing: were he to raise his head it would mean performing this (movement) in the middle of that of the imam. Such practice is regarded as weak because it entails a movement other than that of the imam; and in fact, he can only be said to have 'completed' (the *rak'a*) and in harmony with the imam if this straightening up from the bowing had been valid in the first place. This (judgement) also applies if something similar happens during the prostration. Shaykh Zarruq said in his commentary on the *Risala*: 'He should not straighten up, for straightening up — either in ignorance or deliberately — invalidates the *salat*.'"

BRANCH: Mayyara has also said: "The author of *an-Nawadir* has narrated from the audition of 'Isa that Ibn al-Qasim said: 'The imam should not make those praying behind him wait if he thinks that someone is coming (late for the *salat*).' Ibn Habib said: 'If he is bowing, then he should not extend his bowing', and al-Lakhmi has likewise said: 'Those behind him have more right than someone coming (late).' Sahnun however has permitted him to extend (his bowing), and this is also what 'Iyad prefers. Evidence for this (latter) judgement is provided by (other legal examples, namely, where) the imam waits to pray with the other half (of *mujahideen*) in the 'fear *salat*', or when he, may Allah bless him and grant him peace, shortened the *salat* because of the crying of a child. It is the chosen position of Ibn 'Arafa when it occurs in the last *rak'a*. imam Abu 'Abdallah al-Ubbi said: 'If the Shaykh and imam of the Great Jami' Mosque in Tunis thought it had begun to rain, he would shorten (the recitation of) the *salat* out of consideration for those praying outside (the mosque)."

BRANCH: al-Mawwaq said: "At-Tunisi said: 'The follower does not repeat it for forgetting his having broken his *wudu'* in order to obtain the ruling of [attending] the *jama'ah* because of its being sound for him as a *jumu'ah*, and concerning the imam repeating it in the contrary situation there are some views.' Al-Maziri said, 'There are no views concerning it, but on the contrary, it and its contrary are the same.' Ibn 'Arafa said, 'On the contrary the views are confirmed.'" The words of al-Mawwaq.

BRANCH: al-Mawwaq has also said, commenting on Khalil's words 'after the *iqama* has been said, another *salat* should not begin (in the mosque)': "Ibn 'Arafa said: 'If the *iqama* for the *salat* has been called in a place, then it is prohibited to begin another or to remain sitting in it: those who have not prayed it or who have done it alone should join it – as long as it is one of the *salats* which may be repeated.' Ash-Shaykh said: 'Whoever is sitting with a group of people and they call the *iqama*, then he is commanded to join them, according to the hadith.'"

ISSUE: an-Nafrawi said, confirming the words of the *Risala* 'and whoever only catches the *tashahhud* and the sitting may repeat in a *jama'a*': "…that is, whoever only catches the *tashahhud*, i.e. and then carries on to complete his *salat*, and we only said, 'and carries on to complete his *salat*,' to indicate that anyone who catches less than a *rak'a* with the imam may interrupt and join another *jama'a* if he entertains any hope of finding another; only if he does not hold out any hope of a *jama'a* should he complete his *salat* and not interrupt it since he does not have the intention to repeat it in order to obtain the excellence of the *jama'a*. As for the person who does intend to repeat it but does not catch a complete *rak'a*, then he should – as a recommended act – make a pair of *rak'ats* and treat them as a *nafila salat* before going on to 'repeat.' This is stated in al-Jilab's work."

This is contrary to what is reported in *al-Mi'yar* from the Shaykh of Shaykhs Ibn Lubb: "As for the person who joins the *salat* of the imam who is doing the final *tashahhud*, then he is under an obligation to complete the *fard salat* which he has done the *takbirat al-ihram* for; if he then finds a *jama'a*, he should repeat with them if he wishes – as long as the *salat* is one which may be repeated. This is what is stated in *al-'Utbiyya* and other works, and the *'ulama* have not reported any difference of opinion in this matter – neither regarding the interruption of one's *salat*, nor changing to a *nafila*. Moreover it is a clear judgement as it is laid down in the *shari'ah* (that one must complete) the *fard* and one cannot invalidate it on account of something which is (merely) a sunna. Do you not see that if someone praying alone stands up and forgets the middle sitting, he does not return to the sitting as his standing is a *fard* and his sitting is a sunna. However, the person who joins the *salat* of the imam may choose between breaking off the *salat* and changing to a *nafila* if he is repeating a *salat* which he has *already prayed alone*. It is easy to confuse these two matters is one is not familiar with them and to choose when one should not choose."

USEFUL POINT: ash-Shatibi said in *al-Muwafaqat*: "A principle: if things of necessity or of (simple) human need and convenience entail other matters which are unacceptable according to the *shari'ah*, then striving after such things of benefit is (only) valid on condition that one protect oneself (from anything contrary to the *shari'ah*) as much as possible – as long as this does not cause undue hardship. An example of this would be marriage: it entails having to seek provision for one's family along with the constriction of the halal and the great expansion of routes to the haram and doubtful matters; often it leads to earning for them from things that are not permitted. However, this may be disregarded if committing something doubtful allows one to avoid committing something which is contrary to one of the obligations of the deen (namely marriage). If one were take (every doubtful or unlawful aspect associated with gaining one's livelihood) when married in these times, then it would lead to the principle of marriage being invalidated – and this is not correct. Likewise, in the case of seeking after knowledge: it would not be correct to stop travelling on the path of knowledge merely because one expected to encounter evil matters on it; or stop going to *janazas* and carrying out the duties demanded in the *shari'ah* – merely because one might get involved in things which are (normally) unacceptable. Such things should not deflect one from one's purpose – when it concerns a principle of the deen or a (social) benefit of a fundamental nature. This is what is understood by the (expression) 'aims and goals of the legislator, may the peace and blessings of Allah be upon him.' They must be understood in a proper manner for they can provoke differences of opinion and controversies. Anything which has been transmitted from the first generations of upright men of the deen which is contrary to these matters (like marriage, discussed above) is the clearest source (for making a judgement) and does not require any other proof."

ANOTHER USEFUL POINT: Zarruq said in his *Naseeha*: "One of the *'ulama* reported from a certain jailer that he asked those delivered to him about 'these two *salats*', that is *'Isha* and *Subh*. However, for a period of forty years he did not find anyone who came into (the jail) who had prayed these (*salats*) in *jama'a* that night. I have asked a lot of people who have been afflicted by calamities and found them to squander the two (*salats*) and I have never found anyone at all who has been afflicted by a major calamity who has (persevered in) praying these two *salats*. If I miss out just one *rak'a* of these two (*salats*), then I see the effect during the (following) day, may Allah give me success in being able to do them by His great generosity."

USEFUL POINT: al-Mawwaq said: "'Iyad, having been introduced to Ibn Yasin al-Jazuli, councillor to the Murabitun *Dawla*, said: 'He was characterised by knowledge and goodness, and persisted in championing the cause of Allah and in putting a stop to evils.' He has also mentioned that 'he had Ibn 'Umar lashed – who was Amir of the Murabitun at that time – for some matter that he personally was responsible for. All were obedient to him: he would insist that everyone do the *salat* in a *jama'a* and he would punish those who came late for it with ten lashes for every *rak'a* that he had missed – for he was amongst those who deemed that a person's *salat* was only valid when behind an imam, because of the people's ignorance in recitation and the *salat* at that time.'"

USEFUL POINT: Mayyara said at the end of his *ash-Sharh al-Kabir*: "If a person seeks knowledge or the ability to recite but does not strive in earnest to be at the *iqama* of the *fard salats*, then this is proof that he is not seeking the face of Allah, exalted is He. Someone in the service of knowledge is also in the service of Allah, may His majesty be exalted, but if he does not follow His instructions, then he is merely serving his whims. For example, if someone delays the beginning of the *salat* and is content to catch the end of it – anyone who leaves off doing the beginning of the *jama'a* out of choice does not in fact obtain the reward of the *salat* in *jama'a*. There is difficulty in understanding the words of Malik narrated by Ibn Wahb 'what you have stood up for is not more important than what you have stood up from' if this standing up is with regard to the *salat* of the *jama'a*; if, however, [he stood because of the arrival of] the time and there was plenty of time [before the *jama'a*] – or it is for another *jama'a* – then there is no problem. One must take account of the precise nature of the case in hand, just as in the case of the person who immediately makes for the writing board and the book after the *salat* and who has no desire to obtaining the excellence of saying the *subhana'llah*, *al-hamdulillah* and *Allahu akbar*."

It states in *Tanbih al-Ghafil*: "It is reported from 'Umar, may Allah be pleased with him, that he saw a man who immediately started doing the *nafila* after the *salam*. So he got up, went up to him and threw him to the ground saying: 'Those before you were only destroyed because they made no separation between their *fard* and *nafila salats*.' Then the Messenger, may the peace and blessings of Allah be upon him, saw him and said: 'Allah has established what is correct through you, Ibn al-Khattab!' Reflect about this matter for it is a supererogatory act connected with the *salat* – and what is the importance of such things as writing boards and books in comparison! Tell me what does the person who does the *salam* and then immediately starts the prattling that we hear so much of nowadays gain – in comparison with the person who does the above mentioned *dhikr*? The '*ulama* have stated that the minimum (amount of *dhikr*) required is the recitation of the *ayat al-Kursi*, and the saying of *subhana'llah*, *al-hamdulillah* and *Allahu akbar* ten times each. Every student of knowledge who is true to himself should have a *dhikr* he does every day – even if it is (only) asking blessings for the Prophet, may the peace and blessings of Allah be upon him, a hundred times, – in order to help him purify his intention. Seeking knowledge is the most excellent of actions and likewise those *rak'ats* accompanying the *fard salat* which are especially emphasised, like the two *rak'ats* of *Maghrib* – for it is narrated that they are raised up (to heaven) with the action of the day."

His declaration that the person who leaves off doing the first part of the *salat* in *jama'a* out of choice will not obtain the excellence of the *jama'a* is in accordance with what al-Hafeed[1] Ibn Rushd has stipulated. Al-Khurshi said: "The explanation of Abu'l-Hasan in the *Sharh ar-Risala* was what he relied on." Al-Laqqani said: "The stipulation of al-Hafeed is contrary to the apparent meanings of the narrations. However he has a penetrating insight, and the most evident judgement of the author resembles what is evident from the narrations." The end of what al-Khurshi said. The origin of the words of

---

1 Hafeed means 'the grandson', i.e. the *qadi*, philosopher and author of *Bidayat al-Mujtahid* who was the grandson of Abu'l-Walid ibn Rushd al-Jadd – the grandfather, the author of a number of core works. Ed.

Mayyara and what has been narrated of Malik from Ibn Wahb, et al, is to be found in the *Madarik* of 'Iyad: "Ibn Wahb said: 'I was writing while with Malik and the *iqama* was called' – and in another narration 'and the *mu'adhdhin* called the *adhan*. I had books spread out in front of me and so I immediately started to gather them together. Then he said to me: "Be at ease, that which you are standing up for is not more excellent than that which you are standing up from – if the intention is correct."''''

NOTICES

1. Al-Khurshi has related: "*'Ayn-Jeem* said: 'It is prohibited for a person to pray alone in his house when his intention is to come to the *jama'a* because by attending the *jama'a* he is repeating the first *salat* and the Messenger, may the peace and blessings of Allah be upon him, prohibited the making of one *salat* twice in a day. If this were permitted he would have mentioned it when urging people to attend the *jama'a*, that is, that it were permitted for someone to say he will pray (alone) and then wait (for the *jama'a*). However, it is permitted in compelling circumstances: it is stated in *al-Umm*: 'Malik informed me from al-Qasim ibn Muhammad – at the time when the Umayyads used to delay the *salat* – that he would pray in his house and then come to the mosque to pray with the (*jama'a*). When asked about this, he replied, "That I pray twice is preferable to me than not praying at all" – that is, not in its time.' The Faqih Sanad said: 'He is referring both to the prohibition of praying twice – for the Prophet, may the peace and blessings of Allah be upon him, said: "Do not make the *salat* twice in a day" in a narration of Abu Dawud – and also to his prohibition of leaving off doing the *salat* in its time. When two prohibitions coincide, then performing two *salats* is a lesser evil than not doing the *salat* (on time).'"

2. Al-Khurshi said, commenting on the words of Khalil 'and it is recommended that the one who has not obtained this excellence [of *salat* in *jama'a*], like for example, the person who has prayed with a child – but not if he has prayed with a woman – should repeat the *salat* behind the imam, committing his affair to Allah (and trusting that he has acted correctly in one of the two)': "*'Ayn-Jeem* said: 'The words of the author refer to a person who spontaneously formulates the intention of repeating a *salat* as a *fard salat* and at the same time commits his affair (to Allah) – *after* he has made the intention to perform the *fard salat*, irrespective of whether this occurs to him during the *salat* or after it. If, however, this occurs to him while making the first intention, then this is not acceptable because of his lack of certainty and resolve regarding the intention to repeat *as a fard*, and our Shaykh Karim ad-Deen has referred to

The imam

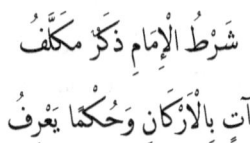

165 An imam must fulfil the conditions of being male and *mukallaf* (that is, of age and sane), be (physically) capable of performing the *fard* aspects of the *salat* and know the judgements (pertaining to the *salat*)

This is clear. Al-Mawwaq said: "If something happens to the imam which prevents him from standing, then he should appoint someone in his place to pray with the people and he should join one of the rows and pray with the (new) imam. Ibn 'Arafa said: 'Being imam is conditional upon his being capable: he is prohibited from being an imam if he is unable to perform the bowing and prostration, or the Fatiha, as in the case of the dumb or the 'illiterate' person (who is incapable of recitation).'"

Ibn al-Hattab said, commenting on the words of Khalil 'it is *makruh* for the person whose arm has been cut off or paralysed': "Branch: al-Burzuli said, after mentioning the difference of opinion regarding the imam who has lost an arm, or who has paralysis (in his limb) or is subject to incontinence and other things: 'Included here is the question regarding an (imam) who, on account of his age, is so bent that he resembles a person bowing, or almost resembling this state, and whose standing may hardly (be termed) standing. Such (a person) existed – and we are basing what we say on actual experience: our Shaykh permitted it in this specific instance and used to pray behind this imam because of his advanced age, his excellence of character and his having gone away in earlier years to seek knowledge.'"

Al-Khurshi said: "Abu 'Abdallah al-Quri has given a *fatwa* saying that the *salat* of a man whose back is bent is valid for those who are not afflicted in the same way. However, his Shaykh Abu 'Abdallah al-'Abdusi has given a *fatwa* saying that his *salat* is invalid as he is in a state of bowing and not standing straight."

Al-Mawwaq said: "The *fatwa* of al-Quri is the correct one as people would normally consider him to be standing: you would say 'the Shaykh stood' or 'the Shaykh sat' (in ordinary speech). Thus the *salat* behind him is valid even if his back is bent so much it is like he is bowing."

As for his saying 'and know the judgements', al-Mawwaq related: "'Iyad said:

'Among the obligatory attributes of the imam is that he be an *'alim* and a *faqih* regarding what he needs to know of the *salat*.' Al-Qubbab said: 'and al-Mazari may be quoted here for he considered that one of the things preventing someone being the imam was a lack of sufficient knowledge of the recitation and the *fiqh* of the *salat* needed to ensure the validity of the *salat*. By *fiqh*, however, he did not mean knowledge of the rules of the prostrations of negligence, for the *salat* of the person who is ignorant of these rules is nevertheless valid if his *salat* is free of that which invalidates it. Rather, the validity of the *salat* is dependent upon a knowledge of the way to do the *ghusl* and *wudu'*; it is not stipulated that one be able to specify all the necessary details of the sunnas and aspects of excellence.' Ibn Abi Yahya said: 'Whoever is not aware of the difference between the *fard* aspects and other aspects but he performs the *salat* as it should be done, then it is valid – as Abu Muhammad has mentioned. Ibn Rushd has noted that Jibril, on whom be peace, did the *Dhuhr salat* with the Prophet, may the peace and blessings of Allah be upon – with all its *fard* aspects and excellence – and then the Messenger of Allah, may the peace and blessings of Allah be upon him, said: "Pray as you have seen me pray" and that he only commanded them to do what they could see.'"

NOTICE: Alif-lam-mim-sad has not mentioned the condition that he be Muslim and this is taken up by Khalil with his words: "and it [the *jama'a*] is invalid in the case of someone who is clearly a *kafir*." Al-Khurshi has related that *'Ayn-Jeem* said: "It does not automatically follow that he is a Muslim merely from the fact that he does the *salat*, even if it is in a mosque – contrary to (the opinion of) Abu Hanifa who argues that if he is in a mosque, then one may assume he is a Muslim as this is one of the obvious marks of Islam. However, this (assuming that he is not a Muslim, even if in the mosque) only applies if he does not call the *iqama* for the *salat* or within it [the *iqama*] he doesn't articulate the declaration of the two *shahadas*. Otherwise, he is a Muslim just as he would be if he called the *adhan*. Furthermore, one may formulate the judgement that anyone who performs the *salat* a lot possesses iman. The author of *al-Muqaddimat* said: 'The *'ulama* have arrived at a consensus regarding the *salat* – and they have not arrived at such a (strong) consensus regarding any other matters of the *shari'ah* – that anyone who was known for his *kufr* but was seen doing the *salats* in their time, even performing a considerable number of *salats* in their proper time, then one adjudges him to possess iman – even if they are not aware that he has (formally) confirmed *tawhid* with his tongue.' However, one may infer from this that one may not assume the same thing of someone who does the fast in Ramadan, goes on Hajj and pays the Zakat – even repeatedly."

وَغَيْرُ ذِى فِسْقٍ وَلَحْنٍ وَاقْتِدَا

فِي جُمْعَةٍ حُرٌّ مُقِيمٌ عُدِّدَا

166 and must not be corrupt, or someone who mispronounces, nor (himself) be following (another imam in front of him); and regarding the *jumu'a*, be free and resident.

'Ali ibn 'Abd as-Sadiq said, commenting on his words 'must not be corrupt': "The most evident meaning of this is that it encompasses physical corruption, such as drinking wine and the like together with any corruption of his *'aqida*, like the Qadiriyyas and any other sects holding false beliefs. The commentator said: 'This is correct, so whoever prays behind a person who is corrupt with respect to these two aspects should repeat the *salat* – however great the delay.'"

In *al-Mukhtasar* there are details regarding the difference between physical corruption – which invalidates (the *salat*) – and corrupt *'aqida* – which necessitates repeating (the *salat*) within the time. The commentator of this work, ad-Dawudi said: "This is the well-known judgement and is the *madhhab* of Ibn al-Qasim in the *Mudawwana*. It is also the most evident meaning of his words, irrespective of whether this refers to a governor who must be obeyed or not." Our Shaykh said: "Also included (as corrupt) would be an unjust officer, whoever takes a salary from the official tax revenues, whoever gives his wife money to go to the *hammam* and the man whose wife goes out to a wedding – for *salat* behind such people is invalid, as is their bearing witness (before a judge). However, even if the invalidity (of the *salat*) behind the corrupt person is the preferred judgement of Ibn 'Ashir – and likewise the *Mukhtasar* and it has been declared by Ibn Bazeeza – what is relied upon (in practice) is the opposite of this, as Abu'l-'Abbas al-Qubbab has mentioned, based on what has been transmitted by *'Ayn-Jeem* who said: 'The most just of *madhhabs* is that one should not (actively) propose a corrupt person to mediate or be the imam but that the person who prays behind him does not have to repeat [the *salat*] if he has fulfilled the necessary requirements of the *salat*.' This is what is accepted by at-Tunisi, al-Lakhmi, Ibn Yunus and has been declared by Ibn Rushd. Shaykh 'Abd al-Baqi said: 'This is what is relied on in practice and it is not fitting that the author diverge from what such Imams have accepted and propagate the view of Ibn Bazeeza. The Prophet, may the peace and blessings of Allah be upon him, said: "Make the *salat* behind every upright and every corrupt person." What he meant by corrupt person is the Muslim who is disobedient, not the *kafir*.' 'Abdallah ibn 'Umar, may Allah be pleased with him prayed behind al-Hajjaj – and may he suffice as an example of a corrupt person. The most one can say is that it is *makruh*, as is mentioned in *al-Yawaqeet* from Shaykh Muhyi'd-Deen."

It is stated in *al-Mi'yar*: "Ibn Siraj was asked whether it is permitted to make the *salat* behind someone who is involved in the financial matters of the treasury and whether the person praying behind him should repeat the *salat* – that is, if we assume it is prohibited. He replied: 'As for someone being an imam who serves as an official witness in financial matters to the government, then the correct (judgement) is that this is permitted if the imam can be trusted regarding matters connected to the *salat*, namely the purification, its preconditions and other things which are necessary and which would impair the validity (of the *salat*) if left out. Thus if he leads the *salat*, then this is permitted. If, however, he is someone given to indulgence and insolent behaviour – such that he would not give a second thought to contravening (the *shari'ah*) and could not be trusted to perform (the *salat*) with the proper purification and intention, in short someone of fraudulent character – then if one knows this to be true of him or even suspects it, then it is not permitted for him to be the imam. The person who does nevertheless pray behind him should repeat the *salat*. If, on the other hand, a person does indeed do things which are unacceptable but he at the same time applies himself to the deen and holds to what is necessary in the *salat*, then it is permitted for him to be the imam: if one were only to pray behind someone about whom nothing detrimental had ever been said, one would never be able to pray behind anyone. It has been reported in a hadith that when an imam whose state is unacceptable because of the wrong he commits begins the *salat*, his wrong actions are removed from him and that the *salat* of the *muminun* behind him is purified; but that when he leaves off being the imam his wrong actions return to him before his very eyes – just as they were before he was the imam."

Al-Bannani said: "As for the *salat* of the corrupt person, know that there is agreement that if the validity of the *salat* is in doubt – or in all likelihood thought to be in doubt because of something preventing the *salat* from being valid – then the *salat* is indeed invalidated behind him. If, however, one only suspects this to be the case, then according to the judgement of Ibn 'Arafa it is valid – although, according to al-Qubbab, invalid."

Zarruq reported from *Junnat al-Murid*: "There is a consensus amongst the people that the *salat* is valid behind every upright person and every corrupt person."

It is stated in *al-Mi'yar*: "Al-Mawwaq was asked whether one accepted the *tawba* of someone who killed (another) and he replied: 'The *madhhab* of the people of sunna and the *jama'a* is to accept Allah's words, exalted is He: *"Allah does not forgive anything being associated with Him but He forgives whoever He wills for anything other than this"*[1] – which apply even without this *tawba*. When *tawba* is made, then *kufr* and other actions involving disobedience (of Allah, exalted is He,) can disappear by the mercy of Allah. He has also said, glorious and exalted is He: "*Say to those who are kafir that if they stop they will be forgiven what is past.*"[2] The *'ulama* have said: "Turning in *tawba* from wrong actions is more to be hoped for than turning in *tawba* from *kufr*. It is not permitted to revile someone who turns in *tawba* from *kufr* or disobedience, that is, from his state before Islam or from his state of disobedience." Someone who becomes Muslim or who turns in *tawba* from a major act of disobedience may lead the *salat* if his (present) state is acceptable – in particular, if in the case of the person who had killed someone, he did it in self-defence or to protect his wealth: a man asked the Messenger of Allah may the peace and blessings of Allah be upon him: "What is your judgement regarding a man who comes to take my wealth?" and he replied: "Do not give him your wealth." He then asked: "And if he fights me for it? and he replied: "Fight him." He again asked: "What if I kill him?" and he said: "Then he is in the Fire.""'

In his commentary on *al-Mukhtasar* he has related: "Ibn Basheer said: 'The difference of opinion as to the validity of a corrupt person being the imam is based on a difference of opinion regarding his state – if he is someone who is critical and insolent regarding the deen such that he might leave out doing what he is entrusted to do of the *fard* aspects, like the intention and the purification, then his being the imam is not valid. If he is someone who in all likelihood commits major wrong actions but does not criticise the deen and is not insolent, then he may be the imam – and this may be known according to the circumstances.' Al-Lakhmi said: 'I consider that the *salat* is acceptable if his corruption is such that it is not connected to the *salat*, like fornication, taking things unlawfully or murder. Despite the things which may be observed in (the behaviour of) the Sultans they often take care to uphold the *salat*. Something similar has been said by Abu Ishaq.'"

'Alaq, however, has refused to accept al-Lakhmi's statement that killing is not one of the things which would impair the *salat* – that *salat* behind a

---

1 an-Nisa' – Women: 47
2 al-Anfal – Booty: 38

murderer who is corrupt would be valid. It has also been reported of Malik that it is not permitted for someone to be the imam even if he has turned in *tawba* although another report of Malik indicates that he did indeed accept the *tawba* of the killer.

Al-Qubbab said: "The most equitable of the *madhhabs* is that a corrupt person is not put forward for mediation or as an imam, but that whoever makes the *salat* behind him does not have to repeat it as long as the person upholds the obligations of the *salat*." He has also said: "And this is what at-Tunisi, al-Lakhmi and Ibn Yunus accept." Ibn al-'Arabi said: "*Salat* in the *jama'a* is the very meaning of the deen." Then he goes on to say: "Imperfections and flaws may penetrate into it through the corruption of the imams. However, it is not possible for the common people to absent themselves from (the *salat* of) such imams – indeed they have no reason to find them unacceptable as they themselves are no different from such imams; only the person who is more excellent will demand what is more excellent. If your imam is like you and you say: 'I will not do the *salat* behind him', then you will not be able to do the *salat* yourself for what you censure in him you will have to censure in yourself; in effect, his *salat* is only valid if your *salat* is valid. If only the just and upright were to be proposed for the post of imam, then '*monasteries, churches, synagogues and mosques where Allah's name is mentioned much, would have been pulled down and destroyed.*'[1]"

As for his saying 'someone who mispronounces', 'Ali ibn 'Abd as-Sadiq said: "...that is, during his recitation – in which case the *salat* is not valid behind him. There are two opinions as to whether this applies generally, that is, both in the case of the Fatiha and other [*suras* and *ayas*] than the Fatiha, or just to the Fatiha. As to a mispronunciation in which there is no discrimination between the *dhad* and the *dha'*, the gist of what our Shaykh has mentioned is that there is agreement that if it is deliberate, then his *salat* is invalidated; if out of forgetfulness, there is agreement that it is valid; if the person is incapable, then there is agreement that it is valid – with regard to the present or future; if, however, it is now – not in the future – and time allows, and there is someone to teach him, then there is a difference of opinion, and this (difference) he has indicated in *al-Mukhtasar*."

Ash-Shabrakheeti said in *Sharh al-'Ashmawiyya*: "There is a difference of opinion regarding someone who cannot distinguish between the *dhad* and the *dha'* being the imam – that is, he pronounces the first instead of the second or vice versa, like many of the people from *Sham* or non-Arabic speakers. Ibn Abi

---

1   al-Hajj – The Pilgrimage: 40

Zayd and al-Qabisi have stated the *salat* of the person behind him is invalidated but his own *salat* is valid as long as he does not do it deliberately when he has the capacity to pronounce (properly). Ibn Rushd has related that there is agreement that the *salat* is valid behind him, although *makruh*."

I SAY: "This is what 'Ali ibn 'Abd as-Sadiq holds to and what al-Bannani and at-Tawudi prefer, but it is contrary to al-Hattab and those who follow him. The discussion in *al-Mukhtasar* indicating this is the following: 'There is a difference of opinion as to whether mispronunciation applies absolutely or just to the Fatiha, and whether it applies in the case of a lack of discrimination between the *dhad* and the *dha'*.' Al-Mawwaq has related that Ibn al-Lubad said: "Whoever makes the *salat* behind someone who mispronounces the Fatiha should repeat the *salat* unless his capacity (for recitation) is equal to that of the imam, and this is the view of al-Qabisi, who together with Abu Muhammad have said: '…and likewise the person who does not discriminate between the *dhad* and the *dha'* in the Fatiha.' Abu Muhammad, Ibn al-Lubad and Ibn Shabloun have all mentioned that 'if he mispronounces in other than the Fatiha, then the *salat* behind him is accepted.' Al-Qabisi said 'It is not accepted' and he bases his view on the most evident meaning of the words of Malik regarding someone who is "not good at the Qur'an" and "who does not distinguish between the Fatiha and other suras."' He goes on to say: 'and this (judgement of Malik) is more correct and resembles (the judgement regarding) someone who leaves out reading a sura deliberately.'"

Ibn Rushd said: "The meaning of the words 'he is not good at the Qur'an' as narrated in *al-Mudawwana* and *Kitab Ibn al-Muwwaz* is that he cannot recite any of it off by heart and does not know it. One of the later *'ulama* said that it is not permitted to make the *salat* behind someone who mispronounces, even if he does not mispronounce the Fatiha. He bases his judgement on what is implied by the words 'who is not good at the Qur'an' in the *Mudawwana* – that is, he understands this to mean someone who is not good at reciting the Qur'an and who does not distinguish between the Fatiha and other suras. Ibn Rushd said: 'This is an interpretation on his part which is improbable as a judgement.' Ibn al-Qussar and 'Abd al-Wahhab have both said: 'The *salat* behind the person who mispronounces is invalid if it alters the meaning, like saying *iyyaki* instead of *iyyaka* and saying *an'amtu* instead of *an'amta*; but is permitted if it does not alter the meaning, like saying *al-hamdi* instead of *al-hamdu*, or saying *lillahu* instead of *lillahi*. It is also said that the *salat* is *makruh* when begun with such a person, but that if it does nevertheless take place it is not obligatory to repeat it.' Ibn Rushd said: 'and this is the correct judgement from among the various judgements as the reciter does not intend what he actually says when he mispronounces and he believes the same as someone who recites it without mispronunciation.' This is also what Ibn Habib holds to: he bases his judgement on what has been reported from the Messenger of Allah, may the peace and blessings of Allah be upon him, when he passed by some client slaves (*mawali*) who were mispronouncing what they were reciting and he said: 'Fine indeed what you are reciting!' When he then passed by some Arabs who were reciting without mispronouncing, he said: 'This is how it was revealed.' Al-Lakhmi said: 'The best judgement is that it is prohibited to do the *salat* behind someone who mispronounces if another person can be found. If he does nevertheless lead it, then those behind him do not have to repeat and his mispronunciation does not render it something "other than Qur'an" – as long as he does not intend to deliberately mispronounce like this. If he restricts himself to that which he is able to recite free of mispronunciation, then this *salat* is acceptable. Related to this subject is the case of someone who divorces (his wife) in a non-Arabic language: two just and upright persons who know his language must be present when he bears witness (to his intent). Ibn Khallikan, in his biography of Ibn al-A'rabi, the author of *al-Lugha*, said: 'He took from Tha'lab and Ibn as-Sikkeet – and al-Asma'i and Abu 'Ubayda were mistaken (in what they said of him).' He goes on: '...and he would permit the *dhad* instead of the *dha'* and vice versa in Arabic usage – and it is probable that what he meant by this is a considerable softening of the *tarqeeq* – the pronouncing with half closed mouth in order to make the sound finer, of the *taghleedh* – the deliberate emphasis of certain sounds, and a softening of the precise articulation of all the letters, because over-preoccupation with such things distracts one (from the *salat*)."'

Ibn 'Arafa has mentioned in his *Mukhtasar*: "...2. al-Lakhmi has permitted the *salat* of the person who mispronounces; 3. (it is permitted) if it occurs in a sura other than the Fatiha; 4. according to the Qadi and Ibn al-Qussar, if it does not alter the meaning, although it is better to prohibit it or to find someone else to lead it. If he does nevertheless lead it, then those behind him do not have to repeat. Al-Mazari attributes the second to al-Qabisi and asserts that, according to al-Lakhmi, the *salat* is not valid behind such a person. As-Saqqali has also reported of him: 'as long as they are not equal in their capacities (for recitation).' He attributes the third to Ibn al-Lubad, Shaykh as-Saqqali, and Ibn Shabloun. Al-Mazari said: 'al-Lakhmi has transmitted that he was not aware that it was permitted in all circumstances.' Ibn Rushd has attributed it to Ibn Habib, and this is what as-Saqqali has preferred from ash-Shaykh and al-Qabisi – regarding whoever does not distinguish between the *dhad* and the *dhal*.' 'Abd al-Haqq said: 'Al-Qabisi has based his judgement on that of Malik – "whoever is not good at the Qur'an and who does not distinguish between the Fatiha and other suras."' Ibn Rushd said: 'He has come to this judgement based on his understanding of these words "someone who is not good at recitation" – but such (an interpretation) is unlikely and incorrect.'"

Ibn al-Hattab said – after a long discussion in which he transmits what we have mentioned from al-Mawwaq and Ibn 'Arafa: "He has mentioned in *an-Nawadir* that Ibn Habib said: 'It is *makruh* for a person who mispronounces to be the imam if there is someone who can recite better than he can. If there is no one who is acceptable (from the point of view of his character), then the person who mispronounces or pronounces incorrectly, or the 'illiterate person' who just has enough Qur'an to do the *salat* is preferable to a reciter who is not acceptable. Abu Bakr ibn Muhammad, that is, Ibn al-Lubad has told us that anyone who prays behind someone who mispronounces the Fatiha, must repeat (the *salat*) – and what he meant was – unless their capacity (for recitation) is equal.'"

Then he said: "Third notice, if someone doing the *salat* mispronounces something, then it is either out of negligence or otherwise; if out of negligence, there is no doubt that it does not render the *salat* invalid, irrespective of whether it occurs in the Fatiha or outside it, irrespective of whether it alters the meaning or not. The worst that could be said is that it is on a par with someone who speaks inadvertently during the *salat* – and this does not invalidate the *salat* for, as has been mentioned above, whoever leaves out an *ayat* from the *salat* should make the prostration of negligence and his *salat* is not invalidated. So how could the (judgement) be otherwise in the case of (the mispronunciation of) two or three words, that is, someone who is not in fact 'leaving out' anything? If, however, the mispronunciation which occurs in the *salat* is not out of negligence, but rather deliberate and the person has the capacity to pronounce it correctly, then there is no doubt that both the *salat* of this person and that of those behind him is invalid for he has deliberately uttered something other than Qur'an or words of *dhikr* during the *salat* – and just one word is enough to invalidate the *salat*. If the mispronunciation issues from an incapacity to do it correctly, then if it is an incapacity to learn and this incapacity, as in the case of some non-Arab speakers, some of the courser Bedouin Arabs and many of the slaves and slave girls is absolute, or comes about because time has been too short to learn – and there is no possibility of having someone lead who does not mispronounce because he cannot be trusted either because he is physically corrupt or his beliefs are corrupt – then there is no doubt as to the validity of the *salat* in such cases. The judgement in such cases is the same as someone with a speech impediment, although there is a difference of opinion, as mentioned above, regarding the person who prays behind him. If, however, there does exist a capacity to learn, that is, the capacity both (of the imam) and that of those following him, then there is a difference of opinion as to the validity of the *salat* when someone is incapable of reciting the Fatiha but capable of leading the *salat* – as mentioned above there are two opinions, and that the most evident in the *madhhab* is that it is invalidated."

There is something similar from al-Khurshi, except he does not mention 'as in the case of some non-Arab speakers and some of the courser Bedouin Arabs (whose incapacity) is absolute' – so examine the matter if you wish. Al-Hattab said after a discussion: "There is no objection to the validity of the *salat* in the case of someone who does not distinguish between the *dhad* and the *dha'*, according to the preferred opinion, that is, as to the validity of the *salat* of the person following him; and also according to the judgement of al-Qabisi and Ibn Abi Zayd, based on a judgement of Ibn Yunus as mentioned above – except if the capacity (of the imam and one of those behind him for recitation) is equal *and* when following (the imam in question) would clearly and without doubt be invalid. However, in the case where he does have this capacity, then the above mentioned difference of opinion holds. The most evident judgement in this matter is that all this applies in the case of a minor mispronunciation, and that it does not invalidate the *salat* – except when it is done deliberately and when one has the capacity (for proper recitation), as has been discussed above, and Allah knows best."

Al-Khurshi has related that 'Ayn-jeem said: "Third: it is *makruh* to follow someone with a minor mispronunciation, like pronouncing the *nun* and the *nunation* in a normal manner when they are followed by a *waw*, *ya*, *mim* or *nun* (for these latter cause the *nun* to be assimilated, for example) for such pronunciation is contrary to the consensus. and represents a reading which is not practised."

I say: "The same applies for all the other rules of recitation which should be respected. As for making a short sound long or an elongated sound short, this is a form of mispronunciation about which there is a difference of opinion – as is clear from the discussion of Zarruq who says: 'I have seen from Mayyara words to the effect that it is *makruh* to follow an imam who mispronounces slightly, that is, who mispronounces but who nevertheless remains within the accepted limits of recitation (*hay'at al-ada'*).'"

Ibn al-Hattab said: "Al-Qadi Abu Hafs said: 'I asked Abu 'Ali al-Jalouli about the *salat* behind someone who pronounces the simple *nun* or the nunation which are followed by a *ya'* and a *waw* in the normal manner (without converting to a nasal sound) and he replied: "*Salat* behind him is *makruh* as it is contrary to the consensus and is a recitation which no one adheres to."' Shaykh Abu Muhammad 'Abd al-Haqq has told us: 'One of the people of knowledge is of the opinion that the *salat* behind a reciter who mispronounces something which is not permitted, like pronouncing the simple *nun* and the *nunation* followed by a *ya'* or a *waw* in a normal manner (without assimilation to the following letter), or substituting the *dha'* for a *dhad* and vice versa and the like, is permitted – as long as it is not during the Fatiha.'" He said also said: "Qadi Abu'l-Hasan al-Qabisi has prohibited *salat* behind him even if his mispronunciation is in other than the Qur'an. Shaykh Abu Muhammad said: 'This is correct because if he changes the Qur'an, (the judgement) is the same as if he had spoken during the *salat* – and this is how it is in a correct manuscript as far as I remember (in the section:) "Regarding the *salat* when the words of Allah have not been mispronounced" for what he has uttered is not the speech of Allah but rather his own speech, so he is considered like someone who deliberately said something during the *salat*."

Al-Bannani differs in two ways from what is contained in the discussion of Ibn al-Hattab, in his stipulating that what the author said is subject to what has been mentioned above and his discriminating between the manifest and more subtle aspects of mispronunciation: "The gist of the matter is that there is agreement that if the mispronunciation of the person who mispronounces is deliberate, then his *salat* as well as the *salat* of those behind him is rendered invalid; if out of negligence, then there is agreement that it is valid; if he is physically incapable and cannot be taught, then it is valid as he is (considered on a par with) someone with a speech impediment; if he is ignorant, but he can be taught, then there is a difference of opinion about him, irrespective of whether it is feasible to teach him or not and irrespective of whether it is feasible that he follow someone who does not mispronounce or not: the preferred opinion in the matter is that the *salat* of those behind him is valid – and so his *salat* is all the more likely to be valid. As for the legal judgement regarding following someone who mispronounces: if done deliberately, it is haram; in the case of someone who speaks with an impediment, it is *ja'iz* (permitted); and in the case of the person who is ignorant, it is *makruh* if one cannot find someone (else) to lead the *salat*, and if someone may be found, it is forbidden – as the transmitted reports indicate. There is no difference between the manifest and the more subtle forms of mispronunciation with regard to all that has been mentioned above – and this is what Abu 'Ali said."

At-Tawudi said, after a long discussion: "If one accepts this, then the *salat* of the reciter behind someone who is 'not good at the Qur'an' is invalid if his not being good at it means he does not know the Fatiha off by heart — and this is what the *'ulama* (usually) mean by 'an illiterate person'; and likewise his own *salat*, according to the most evident judgement of the *madhhab*. If his 'not being good' at it means that he mispronounces during it, like for example someone who does not know the exact place of articulation of each letter, then the *salat* of the person following is valid and permitted if he is on a par with him or less good than him; even if he is better than him, or there is someone else of similar capacity — but who is not asked to lead the *salat*, and they pray behind the person who mispronounces, their *salat* is valid and they do not have to repeat, although it is *makruh* for them to initiate the *salat* with such a person. This is the preferred judgement and the one on the basis of which a *fatwa* is to be made — and applies irrespective of whether the imam is capable of learning or not."

Ibn al-Hattab said: "Notice: the author has not mentioned the judgement that the *salat* of the person following the person who mispronounces is generally valid, despite al-Lakhmi and Ibn Rushd having preferred this judgement, saying: 'It is the most correct judgement and it is apparent from the discussion of more than one of the Shaykhs that it is preferred.'" Then he goes on to say: "and the most preferable, that is of the judgements, and Allah knows best, is that of Ibn Rushd and al-Lakhmi."

NOTICE: al-Khurshi said: "His saying 'with someone who mispronounces' refers to someone's recitation, not the saying of the *takbir* or *sami' allahu liman hamida* and the like."

USEFUL POINT: There is no dispute that mispronunciation which alters the meaning or adds or leaves out a letter is forbidden in the *salat*, and at other times. In the commentary of al-Munawi, he says: "There is not one of us who can afford to be content with his (recitation of the) Qur'an but as long as one does not alter the words, does not violate the order or add any words, and does not omit any letter it is acceptable; however, if one does make any of these mistakes, then it is forbidden, according to the consensus."

He has commentated on the words '…there is an angel charged with the Qur'an and whoever does not recite it properly — whether non-Arab or Arab — then the angel will cause him to recite it properly and will raise him by correcting him' saying: "What is being referred to here is someone who corrupts the recitation or mispronounces it such that it alters the meaning but who does not do so deliberately: if such a person corrupts the recitation, then it is not (considered a corruption of the) Qur'an."

Al-Khurshi said, commenting on the words of Khalil 'and recitation with mispronunciation': "Al-Mawardi said in *al-Hawi*: 'If recitation with mispronunciation is such that the expression of the Qur'an is deformed by the addition or omission of vowel sounds or by shortening a sign of elongation or elongating what should be recited as short or by excessively lengthening such that the word is obscured and the meaning of the word is lost, then this is forbidden: the reciter becomes a deviant (*fasiq*), and the person listening (behind) is guilty of a wrong action, as he has deviated from the correct way to what is crooked.'"

Commenting on the tradition 'The Messenger of Allah came out to us, may the peace and blessings of Allah be upon him, while we were reciting the Qur'an and there were Arabs and non-Arabs amongst us and he said: "(All of you) recite! for all of it is good!" – or whatever his exact words were' and on the tradition '(all of you) recite the Qur'an in accordance with the difference of your tongues!' al-'Alqami said: "One must adhere to the correct articulation of the letters although this compliance varies according to the degree of skill in eloquence and good speech: do you not see that some of the Bedouin Arabs pronounce the letters clearly, some pronounce indistinctly and still others are between the two. Some, for example, can fully articulate the *qaf* while others cannot. It may well be that this is what is meant by 'the difference of your tongues' or by 'mispronunciation which does not alter the meaning' – for this is permitted although *makruh*. As for the person who mispronounces and alters the meaning, then he should not recite more than the Fatiha, as the Imam of the Haramayn (al-Juwayni) said – for he would be uttering something which is not Qur'an when not absolutely necessary. As-Subki has supported him in this. By our saying 'more than the Fatiha', we mean 'during the *salat*.'"

NOTICE: Ibn 'Arafa said in his *Mukhtasar* in the 'Chapter on the Shahada': "Ibn Sha'ban has mentioned the difference of opinion in rejecting the testimony of the reciter of the Qur'an with an incorrect pronunciation. It may well be that he refers to the mispronunciation of someone who corrupts the text of the Qur'an and disregards the place of articulation of the letters – for he cannot be referring to someone who intones the Qur'an or recites it with a beautiful voice: the Messenger of Allah, may the peace and blessings of Allah be upon him, heard the recitation of Abu Musa al-Ash'ari and said: 'You have been given one of the flutes of the family of Dawud.' Before Shaykh Ibn Abi Zayd transmitted the words of Ibn Sha'ban, he also said: 'It is *makruh* to recite in such away such that one mispronounces and it resembles singing' although I do not reject the testimony of someone who does this.'"

USEFUL POINT: The author of *ash-Shifa* said, adding to the consensus of the *umma* regarding what is *kufr*: "…likewise, the person who rejects the Qur'an or a single letter of it, who alters anything of it or adds to it, as the esotericists (*Batinis*) and the Isma'ilis do, or someone who claims that the Qur'an is not proof of (the reality of) the Prophet, may the peace and blessings of Allah be upon him."

He has also said: "The Muslims are of a consensus that the Qur'an as it is recited in all parts of the earth and written out in the *mus-hafs* amongst the Muslims, that is, everything between the covers from the *al-hamdu lillahi rabbi'l-alameen* to the *qul a'oudhu bi-rabbi'n-nas* is the word of Allah and His revelation which came down upon the Prophet Muhammad, may the peace and blessings of Allah be upon him, and that everything in it is true, and that anyone who deliberately leaves out even a single letter of it, who changes it for another or who adds to it a letter which is not contained in the *mus-haf* of the Qur'an – about which they are of a consensus that it is not part of the Qur'an – is a *kafir*."

Ash-Shihab said, commenting on his words '…what is not from the Qur'an, that is, whatever is added, even if one single letter…': "What he means by 'exchanging one letter for another' is exchanging it and believing that it is Qur'an. However, this does not include the person who uses a translation of the Qur'an in the *salat* on account of his incapacity to speak in Arabic – as is indicated in the narration from Abu Hanifa – for the person using the translation does not claim that his words are the Qur'an or the word of Allah." There is something similar in *Kitab al-Barakat* where, adding to what constitutes apostasy, he says: "..someone who says that the Qur'an is not a miracle, who contests the truth of an *ayat* of it – about which there is a consensus, or who adds a word to it, believing that it is part of it."

USEFUL POINT: Ibn al-Hattab said: "Ibn Bashkuwal has mentioned – with his own chain of narration to Muhammad ibn 'Umar ibn Yunus who said: 'I was in Sana' when I saw a man around whom the people were gathered and I enquired: "What is the matter?" Someone replied: "Its a man who was a *mumin* in the month of Ramadan and who could recite the Qur'an with a beautiful voice but when he reached '*Allah and His angels call down blessings on the Prophet*'[1] he recited instead 'Allah and His angels call down blessings on 'Ali, the Prophet. You who have iman! call down blessings on him and ask for complete peace and safety for him' and was struck dumb, was afflicted with

1 al-Ahzab – The Confederates: 56

leprosy and blindness and remained rooted to the spot where he was sitting." Praise belongs to Allah who has spared me from the affliction of the person who said that and Who has preferred me over many others whom He has created – with may aspects of excellence.'"

USEFUL POINT: it is permitted to mispronounce in other than the Qur'an and in the hadith. It states in *al-Madarik* that Rabi'a, when asked "How are you?" replied "*bikhayran*" – instead of "*bikharin*" ("well"), which is the correct form of the word.

ANOTHER USEFUL POINT: it is also stated in *al-Madarik* in the biography of ad-Darwardi al-Kufi: "He is a trustworthy person although he would mispronounce in an ugly fashion."

Also in *al-Madarik*, az-Zubayr ibn Bakar said: "When ad-Darwardi recited to al-Mughira and began to mispronounce in an ugly and distasteful fashion, he said to him: 'Woe to you, Darwardi! your pronunciation before you sought this position was clearer.'" He also said: "Abu Mus'ab said: 'Malik considered him trustworthy.'"

Commenting on Ibn 'Ashir's saying 'who is not following (another imam in front of him)' Mayyara said: "The seventh condition for someone being an imam is that he must not be following another: the *salat* of whoever follows someone who himself is following an imam is invalid. As for his saying that 'he be free and resident', this means that for the *jumu'a* there are two extra conditions, the first that he be free – thus for a slave to be the imam for the *jumu'a* would not be valid, and the second, that he be resident – thus the *jumu'a* behind the traveller would not be valid unless he has made the intention to stay for four days or more."

THINGS MAKRUH IN THE IMAM SUCH AS INCONTINENCE

ويُكْرَهُ السَّلَسُ والقُرُوحُ مَعْ

بَادٍ لِغَيْرِهِمْ وَمَنْ يُكْرَهُ دَعْ

167 It is *makruh* in the case of someone with incontinence, or with sores, or when a Bedouin serves as an imam for others, and desist from (praying behind) someone if people dislike him (as imam)

Al-Mawwaq has narrated that Ibn Bashir said: "There is a difference of opinion if the *wudu'* is spoiled because of an emission (of urine) in exceptional circumstances (like incontinence). Is it to be considered a licence, that is, something which may be overlooked, with respect to the particular person in question, and something which does not affect others? or does the spoiling of that render the emission as if it were nothing? There are two opinions on this matter – and a corresponding difference of opinion as to whether he may be an imam for others. Likewise, the judgement regarding someone from whom an impurity exudes and which he cannot do anything about, like someone who has a wound or sore: there are two judgements as to whether he is permitted to be an imam. It has been reported that 'Umar was afflicted in this way while being an imam but he did not leave (the *salat*). Ibn Yunus has noted: 'The Prophet, may the peace and blessings of Allah be upon him, commanded (the person) to do *wudu'* in the case of (an emission of) pre-seminal fluid and to wash his penis.' Ibn Wahb narrated: 'Umar ibn al-Khattab, may Allah be pleased with him, said: "(Sometimes) I feel it rolling down my thigh in droplets during the *salat* but I do not leave (to clean it) until I have carried out my *salat*" – that is he was vigorous and subject to loss of pre-seminal fluid at the end of his life.' 'Iyad said, narrating from one of his Shaykhs and Sahnun: 'His leaving his imamate is better, except in the case of someone of exceptional uprightness.'"

As for his saying 'a Bedouin being an imam for others,' al-Mawwaq said: "It is reported of Malik: 'A Bedouin Arab should not lead (the *salat*), neither as a resident nor a traveller, even if he is better at reciting than the others (present).' Ibn Habib said: 'This is because of their ignorance of the behaviour of other people, because of the imperfection that may be imputed to them in their not having to attend the *jumu'a* or strive after the excellence of the *jama'a*.' Ash-Shaykh said: 'If one of them does nevertheless lead the *salat*, then their *salat* is acceptable, as in the case of a person with only *tayammum* leading those who have purified themselves with *wudu'*. Malik disapproved of this but Ibn Maslama did not disapprove of it.'"

As for his saying 'and desist from (praying behind) someone if people dislike him (as imam)', al-Mawwaq said: "'Iyad said with respect to the attributes which are disliked in a person who is the imam: 'when he takes a salary for being the imam, when the people of his *jama'a* do not like him or one of the *jama'a* (behind him) desires himself to be the imam.' Ibn Rushd said: 'Whoever is aware that those present recognise that he has more right to lead the *salat* does not need to ask their permission. If, however, he fears that someone dislikes his being the imam, then he should ask their permission: if most of the *jama'a* dislike (his being the imam) or the best of them, then it is obligatory that he step back; if only a few, then it is recommended, and the state of someone who is received by a *jama'a* is nonsense.'"

Ibn al-Hattab said: "The author of *al-Madkhal* said: 'If he fears that there is someone in the *jama'a* who dislikes his being the imam, then leaving it there and then is better for him – on condition that the dislike is based on the dictates of the *shari'ah*, that is, this excludes dislike of his being imam for some worldly or selfish reason or the like. If however, the dislike is based on the *shari'ah*, then he should not put himself forward (as imam) because it has been reported in the hadith that the Prophet, may the peace and blessings be upon him, cursed three (kinds of) people: 'a man who leads a people (in *salat*) when they dislike him, a woman who passes the night with her husband displeased with her and a man who hears *hayya 'ala'l-falah* (- "come to success" – in the *adhan*) and does not respond.'"

'Ali ibn 'Abd as-Sadiq said: "And on account of the hadith: 'Five people do not obtain the (reward of the) *salat*: a woman with whom her husband is displeased, a slave running away from his master – until he returns, a person who stops talking to his brother for more than three days, a man addicted to wine and an imam who leads the people in *salat* when they dislike him.' This is reported by as-Samarqandi in his *Tanbih al-Ghafileen*." He then goes on to say after this: "This dislike on behalf of the people may be of two kinds. On the one hand it may be on account of some corruption in him or because he mispronounces some of the recitation – in which case they can find someone else, or because there is someone who is more knowledgeable than him in the *jama'a* – and it is this very person who dislikes him and dislikes him leading them in the *salat*; on the other hand, their dislike may be because he commands to what is good and so they hate him or it is because of envy – and there is no one in the *jama'a* who is more knowledgeable than him – then their dislike is null and void, and he should lead them despite them."

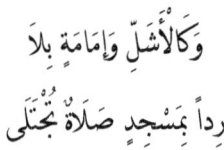

168 likewise, a person whose arm is paralysed (or amputated), or not wearing a cloak when imam in a mosque, or when a (row of the) *salat* is...

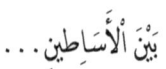

169 interrupted by columns ...

Al-Mawwaq said, commenting on the words of Khalil 'and it is *makruh* for a person whose arm is cut off or paralysed': "Al-Mazari said: 'The majority of our companions hold to the narration of Ibn Nafi' from Malik, namely, that there is no harm in someone whose arm is cut off or paralysed being the imam, even in the *jumu'a* and the 'Eids.' Al-Mazari goes on to say: '...as it is a limb which does not prevent him from fulfilling the *fard* aspects of the *salat*: thus his being the imam is permitted when it is missing, as in the case of someone who is blind.' Malik said: 'Defects are in matters of the deen, not in matters of the body.' Zounan has related from Ibn Wahb: 'I do not consider that the person whose hand has been cut off should lead the *salat* – nor the person whose arm is paralysed and who is unable to put his hand on the ground.' Ibn Rushd said: 'He means it is *makruh*.' The gist of all this corresponds to the judgement of Malik 'there is no harm in his being the imam, and it is the judgement of the majority, except for Ibn Wahb who disliked it – and so to restrict oneself to the judgement of Ibn Wahb would be difficult (to justify)."

As for his saying 'or not wearing a cloak when imam in a mosque', al-Mawwaq said: "It is reported of Malik: 'I dislike this in the case of imams of mosques, and when a person is travelling or at home, I prefer him to drape a turban over his shoulders.'"

As for his words 'the *salat* which is interrupted by the columns', al-Mawwaq said: "It has been narrated of Malik: 'There is no harm in having rows between the columns if the mosque is small.' Ibn Yunus said: 'There is no harm in the rows joining with the columns and this is not what is meant by interrupting the rows – which is prohibited.' Ibn Mas'ud considered it *makruh* to pray between the pillars – and what he was referring to was if the mosque was spacious. Ibn 'Arafa said: 'What may be understood from the *Mudawwana* is that if the mosque is spacious, then it is *makruh* to pray between the columns.' The author of *al-Mabsut* said: 'It is not *makruh*.'"

... وَقُدَّامَ الْإِمَامُ

جَمَاعَةٌ بَعْدَ صَلَاةِ ذِي الْتِزَامْ

... or (standing) in front of the imam, or performing another *jama'a* after the regular *jama'a*

Al-Mawwaq said, commenting on the words of Khalil 'or in front of the imam, when not necessary': "It has been recorded from Malik: 'There is no harm in performing the *salat* in a closed room with the *salat* of the imam – other than the *jumu'a* – if they can see what the imam and the people are doing from a window or from a stall (in the mosque) as long as they are able to hear his *takbirs*, in which case they say the *takbir* with him, they do the bowing with his bowing and they prostrate when he prostrates. This is permitted. The wives of the Prophet, may the peace and blessings of Allah be upon him, prayed in their rooms with the *salat* of the imam.' Malik has also said: 'If the rooms or houses are in front of the imam, then this is *makruh*; but if they nevertheless do the *salat* (in front of him), then it is complete (and accepted).'"

As for his saying 'another *jama'a*....', al-Mawwaq said: "It has been reported from Malik: 'The same *salat* should not be performed twice in a mosque unless in a mosque where there is no appointed imam, in which case anyone may make another *jama'a* in it.' Ibn Yunus said: 'Another *jama'a* is not made because of the enmity it might cause between imams, and also so that the people of *bid'a* are prevented from putting forward one of their imams.' Ibn al-Qasim has reported: 'If there is a mosque where one does a second *jama'a* sometimes but not at others, then I consider that one should not do a second *jama'a* in it, neither at a time when it is not (usually) done nor at a time when it is (usually) done.' Ashhab has reported: 'There should not be a second *jama'a* on board a ship.' Ibn Rushd said: 'This does not contradict their judgement that it is permitted to perform a *salat* above deck with one imam, and another below with another imam – as they are two (separate) places.'"

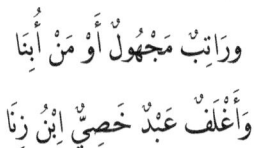

170 (likewise) appointing a regular imam who is (as yet) unknown or someone who is blameworthy, uncircumcised, a slave, a eunuch, or a bastard

Al-Mawwaq said: "Ibn Habib has related from Ashhab and Ibn Nafi' and Asbagh and Ibn 'Abd al-Hakam: 'It is not fitting that someone unknown lead the *salat* other than the officially appointed imam (who is known).' Ibn 'Arafa said: 'If someone is appointed over a mosque but does not perform the *salat* in it because of some other matter which is more preferable according to the *shari'ah*, then one should not perform the *salat* behind another officially appointed imam until the people have got to know him – and this is the practice of those I met.'"

As for his saying 'or blameworthy', it does not mean that he is necessarily referring to someone you don't go to because he is the lowest type of deviant. Rather, what it probably refers to is someone, blamed in the past, who then turned in *tawba* and made good his *tawba* – but about whom people persisted in talking, on account of what he had done in the past. It may also mean 'suspect' which meaning is supported in the Arabic language, for in al-Bukhari it states: 'We did not *suspect* him of using charms.'"

As for his saying 'an uncircumcised man', Ibn al-Qasim has reported: "An uncircumcised person should not lead the *salat*." Sahnun said: "…but the person who does nevertheless follow him, does not have to repeat the *salat*."

As for his saying 'a eunuch', Ibn al-Mawwaq said: "Al-Mazari said: '(There is no harm in) a physical imperfection if it has no bearing on the *salat*, but if it means his appearance resembles that of a female, as in the case of eunuchs, then Malik has deemed it *makruh* for him to be an officially appointed imam for the *fard salats*.'"

As for his saying 'a bastard', al-Mawwaq said: "Malik has reported: 'I dislike that a bastard be taken as an officially appointed imam.' Abu 'Umar said: '…lest he expose himself to people's evil talk – as being an imam is a position of esteem and honour and people strive after it and are envious of it.'"

USEFUL POINT: al-Munawi said, commenting on the words of *al-Jami' as-Saghir* 'None of his parent's guilt falls on the bastard': "It appears that this is the full version of the hadith, but that is not the case and the rest (of the narration) as is mentioned in *al-Mustadrak* is: '*No person bears the burden of another*'. As for the tradition 'the bastard is the worst of three', it is understood as referring to someone who does exactly what his parents did – so that the meaning accords with the (apparently contrary) meaning of the tradition.'"

He has also said, commenting on the words 'a bastard is the worst of three': "This refers to him and his parents since the *hadd* punishment has been meted out to the two of them and this annuls their wrong action – (and he is left alone and) does not know what will be done with him (in the afterlife). However, it has also been said that it referred to a particular person who had been marked out by evil and hypocrisy; or to someone to whom his mother says: 'You are not the real son of your father' and he kills her; or to a person who acts like his parents acted."

مُجَذَّمٌ خَفَّ وَهَذَا الْمُمْكِنُ

171 It is permitted in the case of an impotent man, a blind man, someone with a speech impediment or afflicted by leprosy, as long as it is slight – and this is enough (for our purposes here).

Al-Mawwaq said: "'Isa and Ibn al-Majishun have said: 'There is no harm in someone who is impotent being the imam.'"

As for his saying 'a blind man', al-Mawwaq said: "Malik said: 'There is no harm in taking a blind person as an officially appointed imam.'"

As for his words 'someone with a speech impediment', al-Mawwaq said: "Ibn Rushd said: 'The person with a speech impediment is someone whose recitation is unclear. The person with a lisp cannot pronounce some of the letters and is like the non-Arab speaker who cannot distinguish between the *dha'* and the *dhad* or between the *seen* and the *sad* and the like. There is no dispute (amongst the *'ulama*) that the person who follows such an imam does not have to repeat, even though it would be *makruh* if he did follow him – unless, that is, there is no one other than him who is acceptable.' Al-Mazari said: 'Qadi Abu Muhammad regarded that it was correct for someone to lead the *salat* if he spoke 'thickly' and was unable to pronounce the *ra'* correctly as there is no alteration of the meaning but it is rather an imperfection of the articulation of the letters.'"

As for his saying 'afflicted by leprosy, as long as it is slight', al-Mawwaq said, commenting on the words of Khalil 'a person afflicted with leprosy unless the illness is in advance stages': "There is no difference of opinion (amongst the *'ulama*) that someone with leprosy may be the imam unless his illness is particularly repellent and it is known from his neighbours that they feel repugnance at keeping his company – in which case he should withdraw from being the imam."

As for his words 'and this is enough', Ibn 'Arafa said: "This means 'this is what is fitting for this book' – which has been composed for the beginner.'"

NOTICE: the author has not mentioned the judgement regarding someone who differs in the derivative rulings being the imam. Al-Mawwaq said in his commentary: "Al-Mazari has transmitted a consensus as to the validity of following someone who differs in the derivative rulings of the deen which are a matter of opinion. The author of *al-Madarik* said: 'Abu'l-Ma'ali al-Juwayni proposed 'Abd al-Haqq as-Siqali (as imam) and made the *salat* with him saying to him "the part is encompassed by the whole" – alluding to the question of wiping over the head (for the *wudu'*) as Abu'l-Ma'ali was a ash-Shafi'i.'"

It is also recorded in *al-Madarik*: "Abu Bakr al-Abhari was the imam of his time. When asked to take over the judgeship of Baghdad, he refused and he indicated ar-Razi. The latter also refused and indicated al-Abhari. When he again refused, someone else took it over. Ar-Razi held to the *madhhab* of Abu Hanifa. It is also reported that Sulayman ibn 'Imran said: 'Sahnun said to me: "You have put me to the test. By Allah, I will put you to the test" and he made me responsible for the judgeship.' Sulayman held to the *madhhab* of the Iraqis."

He has also commented on the words of Khalil 'and a *mujtahid* does not follow someone else': "Abu 'Umar said in his *Tamheed*: 'Ahmad ibn Hanbal was asked about a man who made the *salat* while wearing (something of) leather (from an) animal (which had not been ritually slaughtered) and he replied: "There is no harm in making the *salat* behind him if he is someone who has made an interpretation." Someone said: "So you consider it is clean?" He said: "No." Someone then said: "But how can one make the *salat* behind him when he is doing something wrong?" He replied: "The person who makes an interpretation is not the same as someone who does not practice interpretation. Anyone who interprets something from the Messenger of Allah, may the peace and blessings of Allah be upon him, in a different manner than us and makes this his practice, then there is no harm in making the *salat* behind him."'"

An important digression of benefit

Al-Munawi said, commenting on the words in *al-Jami'* 'the differences of my *umma* are a mercy':

"The person who is not a *mujtahid* should follow a specific *madhhab*. However, the correct judgement according to ash-Shafi'i is that it is permitted to transfer from one *madhhab* to another in the light of the hadith 'differences (among the *'ulama* of my *umma*) are a mercy' – although it is not permitted to follow the Companions or one of the *Tabi'un*, according to Imam al-Haramayn, that is, in the case of anyone who has not set down his *madhhab* (in a formal manner). Thus it would be prohibited to follow other than the four (Imams) regarding the matter of judgements and *fatwas* because the four *madhhabs* have spread (throughout the *umma*), their general principles have been defined and their details have been categorised – whereas the others have died out and no longer have any followers. Imam ar-Razi has also transmitted a consensus of the *'ulama* of 'knowledge and practice', saying that it is not permitted for the ordinary people to follow any of the leading figures from amongst the Companions.

"However, someone who is not one of the common people, who is one of the *fuqaha'* who models himself (on one of the four Imams) may model himself on someone other than the four with respect to an action particular to him if he is aware of this person's connection to one of the Imams who may be taken as models and if he fulfils all the conditions (of trustworthiness) stipulated by this Imam – on condition that he not make this a pretext to merely adopt everything which is easier from the *madhhabs* and thereby remove all responsibility from his shoulders, in which case it would not be permitted, contrary to the view of Ibn 'Abd as-Salam who permits it in all cases, but one may also understand his words to mean that one may only follow (someone other than the four Imams) when it does not lead to the above mentioned relaxation. Ibn al-Hajib said, as did al-Amidi, 'If a practice with respect to a certain matter is not acceptable according to the judgement of one Imam, but which another has declared is "a practice about which there is agreement", then this 'agreement' and their argument pertaining to it stands and remains valid if it is one which has been reached on behalf of the *'ulama* of *usul* – the roots of the deen; if this is not the case, then it is rejected. One would not for example make *taqlid* of ash-Shafi'i in wiping over part of the head (for *wudu'*) while at the same time following Malik in deeming the dog pure, with respect to the same *salat* – as each judgement is particular to each Imam: it would be prohibited to make *taqlid* of another (imam) in these *particular* examples, but not necessarily in the case of other similar matters. For example, if a *fatwa* is made that someone should separate from his wife while waiting to see (if in fact the divorce will actually happen) but in the meantime he marries her sister and then another *fatwa* is made to the effect that no separation is necessary, then he may not return to the first (wife) without this separation; or, for example, if one holds to the neighbour's right of pre-emption, following the Hanafi judgement, it would be prohibited to then follow ash-Shafi'i in rejecting this right if this right of pre-emption is indeed demanded of him – as this judgement is not common to both the Imams. If, however, he were to buy another piece of land and he makes *taqlid* of ash-Shafi'i in holding that the neighbour has no right of pre-emption, he would not be prohibited from following him – as occurred in the above case – and so he may refuse to hand over the second piece of land. However, al-Amidi and Ibn al-Hajib – and whoever follows these two, like al-Mahalli – have said that it is prohibited in this case: for them, it is not permitted, as a general rule, (to change to another Imam) after having acted according to a particular practice in first place – and to claim that there is agreement is invalid.'

"Az-Zarakhshi has related: '...that the Qadi Abu Tayyib called the *iqama* for the *jumu'a salat*. Just as they were about to do the *takbir*, a bird dropped its excrement on him and he said: "I am Hanbali!" and he then made the *takbir*. His *madhhab* does not prohibit him from following something contrary (to his school) in case of necessity – and anything which is similar to this, according to as-Subki.' He then goes on to say: 'Changing from one *madhhab* to another has different aspects:

"'1. That he believes that the other *madhhab* has preponderance (in this matter), in which case it is permitted to act according to what he thinks is the preferred judgement;

"'2. That he does not believe that there is a preponderant judgement in which case it is also permitted;

"'3. That by his *taqlid* of this (judgement) he intends (to avail himself of) the licence or ease in it – and he is in need of it because of something that has befallen or afflicted him – in which case it is permitted;

"'4. That he only intends (to avail himself of the) licence and ease – in which case it is prohibited as it is out of selfish desire not for the sake of the deen;

"'5. That he does this a lot and following this licence becomes his custom – in which case it is prohibited for the reason above, and because a great amount would be regarded as corrupt (anyway);

"'6. That there arises as a result of that 'a compound reality' which is prohibited according to the consensus, and so is prohibited;

"'7. That he is aware, in the case of his first *taqlid*, as a Hanafi for example, that the claim of pre-emption on behalf of a neighbour is acceptable, and he holds to this, but when this right of pre-emption is enacted against him, he wants (to change *madhhab*) and make *taqlid* of ash-Shafi'i – and this is prohibited because his responsibility (remains constant) both in first and second instance – he being a single individual and *mukallaf*, that is, responsible and answerable (in both cases). The discussion of al-Amidi and Ibn al-Hattab apply to him.'

"Al-Balqeeni was asked about *taqlid* in the Surayji case and he replied: "I do not give a *fatwa* on the soundness of the dwellings but nevertheless when he acts in emulation (*taqlid*) of the one whose verdict is that there is no divorce that is sufficient. Allah does not take anyone to task (if they make *taqlid* which is incorrect) as there is no censure or punishment with regard to *taqlid* of the derivative rulings arrived at by *ijtihad*. In other words, he is of the view that *taqlid* of the less weighty judgement (*marjuh*) is permitted. Another of the 'ulama said: 'Those who have prohibited making use of the licence (afforded by another *madhhab*) do so when this is done for a reason other than for the deen. Otherwise this (practice) is not prohibited – like, for example, the sale of something that has not been inspected (or actually seen): as-Subki has given a *fatwa* saying that it is better to make *taqlid* of ash-Shafi'i in this matter because people often need to (buy things to) eat and drink (but buy them on order, rather than being present for the actual sale), and because (such practice would be permitted in line with his judgement that) if something becomes difficult and constricted, then it should be made easier and expanded. Thus it is preferable to make *taqlid* of ash-Shafi'i rather than Malik, in accordance with the *fatwa* of al-Mateeti, whereas the Hanafis hold that it is prohibited to change from one *madhhab* to another in all circumstances. The author of *Fath al-Qadir* said: 'The person who moves from one *madhhab* to another is guilty of an offence and punishable with corporal punishment – even if he does this with *ijtihad* and with proof; doing this without such *ijtihad* or proofs is more unacceptable. However 'moving (from one to the other)' only really applies with regard to the judgement of a *specific* issue – which he makes *taqlid* of and practices accordingly – for otherwise his saying 'I have made *taqlid* of Abu Hanifa regarding the matters he has made a *fatwa* for' or 'I practice in accordance with him in general' – when he is not aware of the nature of the various (individual) judgements – is not in fact *taqlid*. His undertaking to act – although it appears that he is acting in accordance with *his* judgement regarding the matter that is confronted with – is not proof in itself that he is bound by obligation to follow the *mujtahid*; rather, the proof afforded by the judgement of the *mujtahid*, with regard to the particular matter of concern to him, requires that one act upon it because of the words of Allah, exalted is He: '*Ask the people of reminder if you do not know*'[1] – and a question, by it nature, only arises whenever something 'happens' to the person. This commitment (to the *mujtahid* – to follow what he decides in a particular situation) usually spares the people (the danger of) following judgements based on mere licence and ease. This is not the case, however, when a Qadi (whom the people often tend to take as an example) holds only to the declarations of a *mujtahid* who delivers the easiest of judgements and who is unaware that this is prohibited – both from the point of view of transmitted knowledge and by way of the intellect."

"The Malikis are of the view that it is permitted to transfer to another *madhhab* when the necessary conditions are met. It is stated in the *Tanqeeh* of al-Qarafi, as reported from az-Zanati: "It is permitted under three conditions: that one does not arrive at a harmonisation of two (conflicting judgements) such that it is contrary to the consensus, like for example (a judgement permitting someone) to marry without a dowry, a guardian or witnesses – for no one holds to this; on condition that, in making *taqlid* of another, one is convinced

---

[1] al-Anbiya' – Prophets: 7

that one is following the better judgement; and on condition that one should not merely seek after the examples of licence from the different *madhhabs*." Another (of the Maliki *madhhab*, other than al-Qarafi) said: "It is permitted as long as it does not invalidate the decision of the judge and it is contrary to the consensus, the general principles or clear analogy; and something has been transmitted from the Hanbalis which indicates that it is permitted." The end of al-Munawi's words.

وَالْمُقْتَدِي الْإِمَامَ يَتْبَعُ خَلَا

زِيَادَةً قَدْ حُقِّقَتْ عَنْهَا لَا

172 The person behind (the imam) must imitate the imam except if the latter makes an addition – and the person following him is certain of this – in which case he does not do it.

Mayyara said: "He informed us that the person imitating, that is, following the imam must follow him in all his actions of the *salat* except if the imam makes a definite addition to the *salat* and the person behind is convinced that it is not in accordance with what is demanded (in the *salat*), in which case the person behind the imam desists from doing it and does not follow the imam in it. What may also be understood from his words is that the person following him must not perform any actions of the *salat before* the imam, and this is correct. Indeed, it is not fitting that he do them simultaneously with him, but rather after each movement of the imam – for this is the meaning of 'to follow.'"

Al-Mawwaq said: "Al-Baji said: 'It is *makruh* with respect to the spoken aspects of the *salat* – other than the *takbirat al-ihram* and the saying of the final *salam* – for the person behind the imam to utter them before him, although it does not invalidate his *salat*; but as for the movements of the *salat*, if he begins them after the imam but then catches him up while performing them, this is the sunna of the *salat*; if he enters into a movement after the imam has left it, then this is prohibited if done deliberately.'"

Al-Khurshi said, commenting on the words of Khalil 'but preceding the (imam) is prohibited, otherwise, (if simultaneous), it is *makruh*': "similar to the prohibition of 'preceding him' is that of his delaying one of the movements of the *salat* such that the imam finishes (before he begins), as al-Mawwaq has reported from al-Baji. The most evident interpretation of this is that it depends on whether the movement is one of the *fard* aspects (of the *salat*) or not: to delay the second prostration in the last *rak'a* until after the imam has pronounced the final *salam* would be forbidden but to raise one's head before the *salam* of the imam would not be forbidden."

Mayyara said: "What he has indicated with these words, and Allah knows best, is that if the imam adds something (to the *salat*), then the judgement in this case is that those behind him may be classed in two ways: firstly those who are certain that something unacceptable has been done according to the *fiqh* (of the *salat*). Al-Hattab said: '...because he knows that both his *salat* and that of the imam has been completed; what is meant by his being "certain" here is certain belief. If such is the case then, then they must remain sitting and say out loud "*subhana'llah!*" (to avert him). If he still does not realise (his mistake), then one of them should speak to him: this does not invalidate the *salat* as speaking is excused if done in order to correct the *salat* – as long as it is not excessive.'"

Then he goes on to say after a discussion: "The second type are those who are not certain that something unacceptable has been done according to the *fiqh*. This is a more general classification than the former for it comprises those who perceive that something unacceptable has been done according to the *fiqh* (of the *salat*) – as well as those who merely think, suspect or imagine that the imam has, (for example), stood up for a fifth *rak'a* because one of the four others was invalid. These people must follow the imam in his standing up for the fifth (*rak'a*): whoever deliberately remains sitting, then his *salat* is invalidated because he is (considered to be) acting contrary to what he has been commanded to do; if, however, this is done out of negligence, then it does not invalidate (his *salat*) but he must do another *rak'a* instead of the one which is invalid."

BRANCH: Ibn al-Hattab said, commenting on the words of Khalil 'and if the imam makes (just) one prostration and stands up, he does not follow...': "The gist of this matter – in the case where the imam misses out doing the second prostration, stands up and those (behind him) say *subhana'llah* to indicate this (mistake on his part) but he does not return – is whether they themselves should prostrate and whether this *rak'a* is then accepted of them; or whether (it is also accepted of them in the case where) they do not follow the imam in this – even if he does return and make this prostration. (That it is acceptable) is the judgement of Ibn Mawaz, and it is correct according to what al-Lakhmi and al-Mazari have transmitted. It is also the judgement of Ibn al-Qasim – except that he recommends that it be prayed again. The *madhhab* of Sahnun is that they should not make this prostration but that if they do nevertheless do it, then they should not count it and when the imam does this prostration they should follow him in it. What is clear from this is that their deliberately doing this prostration does not prejudice (their *salat*): it is as if this is on account of the difference of opinion in this matter. There is also a dispute (among the *fuqaha*) as to whether this difference of opinion is of general application, that is, irrespective of whether only the imam misses it out, or whether both he and one of those behind him miss it out – and this is the most evident meaning of the words of al-Lakhmi and al-Mazari and what the understanding of the author is based on – or whether difference of opinion is based only on the imam missing it out and one of those behind him. If, however, only he misses it out, then they should not follow him in this – but rather they should prostrate for it and this is accepted of them. If they follow the imam in not doing the (prostration), then their *salat* is invalidated, according to the agreement (of the *fuqaha*), and this is what Ibn Rushd holds to. The most evident interpretation of the words of the author is that they correspond to the judgement of Sahnun and that the author has understood that the difference is applicable in both cases – so reflect upon this, and Allah, exalted is He, knows best."

BRANCH: al-Mawwaq said: "Ibn al-Qasim has related the following in this regard: 'What I consider – and hold to – regarding someone who falls asleep behind the imam in the first *rak'a* is that he should not count it and should not follow the imam in it – even if he 'catches up' with the imam before he raises (his head from) its prostration; but he should prostrate with the imam and make it up after the *salam* of the imam. Al-Mazari said: '…as the person who does not 'catch' a (full) *rak'a*, has not fulfilled (any of) it and it is not licit for him to make it up before having finished the *salat*; rather, he is considered as someone who has missed something before joining the *salat* (late).' Ibn al-Qasim said: '…and if he falls asleep after completing the first (*rak'a*) – in the second, third or fourth – then he follows the imam as long as the latter has not raised (his head) after the prostration.'"

Al-Mazari said: "…because whoever completes a *rak'a* (by catching a part of it) has fulfilled (all of) it and is thus considered to have 'caught' the *salat*, and whoever has 'caught' the *salat* makes up afterwards for what he has missed with the imam."

Then he goes on to say, commenting on the words of Khalil 'if someone following is prevented from doing the *rak'a* because of the sheer numbers of people, or because of sleep or the like, then he should follow the imam – in other than the first *rak'a* – as long as he has not raised (his head) from the prostration of this (*rak'a*)': "There are three matters (to be considered):

firstly, the case where he falls asleep after the *takbirat al-ihram* but before the bowing, and this is mentioned above; secondly, where he falls asleep after raising his head from the bowing but before the prostration, in which case he follows the imam as long as he has not raised his head from the *rak'a* which follows it; thirdly, where he falls asleep after placing his hands on his knees but before raising his head, in which case – in accordance with the judgement that the completion of the *rak'a* is (marked by) the raising of the head from it – he is considered as someone who has fallen asleep before the bowing."

وَأَحْرَمَ الْمَسْبُوقُ فَوْراً وَدَخَلْ

مَعَ الْإِمَامِ كَيْفَمَا كَانَ الْعَمَلْ

173 The person who arrives late (for the *jama'a*) should make the *takbirat al-ihram* immediately and join the *salat* with the imam – whatever his position or movement -

مُكَبِّراً إِنْ سَاجِداً أَوْ رَاكِعًا

أَلْفَاهُ لَا فِي جَلْسَةٍ وَتَابَعَا

174 saying '*Allahu akbar*', if joining him in the act of prostration or bowing, but not in the sitting, and should then follow (the imam).

إِنْ سَلَّمَ الْإِمَامُ قَامَ قَاضِيَا

أَقْوَالَهُ وَفِي الْأَفْعَالِ بَانِيَا

175 When the imam says the (final) *salam*, he must get up to make up for the spoken aspects (of the *salat*) but must carry on with the movements from where he joined (the *jama'a*).

كَبَّرَ إِنْ حَصَّلَ شَفْعاً أَوْ أَقَلّْ

مِنْ رَكْعَةٍ وَالسَّهْوَ إِذْ ذَاكَ احْتُمِلْ

176 He must say the *Allahu akbar* (when standing up after the imam's *salam*) if he has completed a pair (of *rak'ats*) or less than a *rak'a* (with him); and in the case of (the ma'mum's) negligence (while behind) the imam (then the latter) is responsible.

With respect to these lines of Ibn 'Ashir, Mayyara has mentioned some of the judgements connected with the person arriving late for the *jama'a*. He informs us that if such a person finds the imam performing the *salat*, then he must make the *takbirat al-ihram* immediately, that is, at the moment of joining (the *jama'a*) and then join the imam in whatever position he finds him, be it standing, bowing, prostrating, or sitting. This is what is being indicated in the first line. If he finds him when bowing or prostrating, he makes another *takbir* for the bowing or prostration, and if he finds him sitting or standing, then he does not make the *takbir* – only the initial *takbirat al-ihram*, and this is indicated in the second line."

By his words 'and should then follow (the imam)' at the end of the line, he is indicating that the person arriving late (for the *salat*) must imitate whatever the imam is doing at the moment of joining him – irrespective of whether this (movement) 'counts' for this person, such as the bowing, or it does not 'count', like the prostration. His saying 'and should then follow (the imam)' is thus connected in meaning to the *takbirat al-ihram*. He then informs us that the person arriving late (for the *salat*) who wants to do what he has missed before joining the imam – that is, after the imam said the *salam* – must make up the spoken elements (of the *salat* he has missed) and carry on the movements (based on those already done before him by the imam). As for the spoken elements, he makes them up in the manner he has missed them: thus what he 'catches' and performs with the imam is (in effect) *the end of his salat* – and he makes up the first part (he has missed); as for the movements, he carries on (from the point at which he joins the imam) 'basing' his movements on what the imam has already done (as if he had done them with him): thus (what he has missed) he treats as 'the first part of his *salat*', and then adds to it the last part. This the author has indicated with the line beginning 'if the imam says the (final) *salam*.' There are various aspects to be considered when determining whether a person who arrives late should say the *takbir* when standing up after the imam said the final *salam*: if the person who arrives late performs two *rak'ats*, then the sitting of the imam – which the latter concludes with the saying of the *salam* – precedes the third *rak'a* of this person, that is, he has caught the third and fourth *rak'ats* of a four-*rak'a salat* or the second of *Maghrib*, and so he should stand up saying the *takbir* – for this is the judgement of the person who gets up for the third *rak'a*; likewise, if he catches less than a *rak'a* with the imam, that is, he catches it after the imam straightens up from the bowing in the last *rak'a*, then he also stands up with a *takbir* – for (the judgement in his case) is like the person who is beginning the *salat*. This the author has indicated with his words 'He must say the *'Allahu akbar'* if he completes a pair (of *rak'ats*) or less than a *rak'a.*' What may also be deduced from this is that if he completes a *rak'a* or more – not a pair, but rather an odd number, namely, three or one – when he catches the second or the fourth of a four-*rak'a salat*, the third of a three-*rak'a salat* or the second of a two *rak'a salat*, then he gets up without saying the *takbir*. This is because the *takbir* which he 'stands up with' he has in fact said when sitting down to join the imam. He is on a par with someone who makes the *takbir* in order to stand but who is then prevented by something (from doing the standing immediately): (thus, after the *salam* of the imam, he is) then able to stand but does not have to make another *takbir*. With his words 'and in the case of negligence, the imam bears the responsibility', Ibn 'Ashir is informing us that if the person behind the imam makes a mistake when following him, then the imam covers for him. What may be deduced from this is that if the person arriving late makes a mistake after the *salam* of the imam, then the latter is not responsible for this, for in this case he is like the person performing the *salat* alone – and this has already been mentioned by Ibn 'Ashir in the section on 'prostration of negligence.'

ISSUE: Ibn al-Hattab said: "There is another (related) issue mentioned by al-Burzuli: 'When the imam has to do a prostration of negligence after the *salam* and he does it in its place (i.e. after the *salam*) but those following him do it before his *salam* and then do their *salam*, then it is reported of al-Lakhmi that their *salat* is valid.' He is like the person who does a prostration of negligence which should be done after the *salam* before the *salam*. If the imam does the prostration of negligence which should be done before the *salam* afterwards, then our Shaykh, the imam, may Allah have mercy on him, said: 'Those behind him should do it before the *salam* – especially if it is for something which invalidates the *salat* when not done, like for example in the case of a *fard* aspect (of the *salat*). The most evident judgement of other *fuqaha* is that they should follow him in the *salam* and prostration as this (following of the imam) is enough for them (and removes the responsibility for the prostration before the *salam* from them), and this (judgement) resembles what has been mentioned above."

Then he goes on to say: "Branch: as to whether the person who arrives late should get up to make up for what he has missed immediately after the *salam* of the imam or after the imam has finished the prostration of negligence or whether he may choose in this matter in this regard, all three (judgements) have been narrated, and Ibn al-Qasim has opted for the first in the *Mudawwana*."

$$\text{وَيَسْجُدُ الْمَسْبُوقُ قَبْلِيَّ الْإِمَامِ}$$

$$\text{مَعَهُ وَبَعْدِيّاً قَضَى بَعْدَ السَّلَامْ}$$

177 The person who joins (the *salat*) late should make the (prostration of negligence) which has to be done before the *salam* with the imam; that to be done after, he should make up after the *salam*,

$$\text{أَدْرَكَ ذَاكَ السَّهْوَ أَوْلاَ قَيَّدُوا}$$

$$\text{مَنْ لَمْ يُحَصِّلْ رَكْعَةً لاَ يَسْجُدُ}$$

178 irrespective of whether he was present if (the imam) was negligent, although the (*fuqaha*) have stipulated that if he did not catch a (single) *rak'a*, then he does not do any prostration (of negligence with the imam).

Al-Mawwaq said: "Whoever completes a *rak'a* with the imam and the imam has to perform a prostration of negligence, then – if it is one to be done before the *salam* – he should prostrate with him before (standing to) make up (what he has missed), and this is enough on his part: he does not have to repeat it before his saying of the *salam* for himself. If, however, it is to be done after the *salam*, then he should not make the prostration with him until he has done what he has to make up: the person behind the imam may begin making up (what he has missed) – if he wishes – when the imam says the *salam* at the end of the *salat*, or after the prostration. If the person behind the imam remains sitting until the imam says the *salam* after his prostration of negligence, he should not say the *tashahhud* but rather make *dhikr* of Allah. Ibn al-Qasim said: 'What I prefer is that he gets up after the imam's *salam* as this marks the end of the imam's *salat*: even if the imam were to become impure after the *salam* (but before completing his prostrations of negligence) this would not effect the person behind him. Thus he goes on to make up (what he has to make up) and then does the prostration (of negligence), as his imam has done – irrespective of whether the imam had made his mistake while the person (arriving late) was already behind him or not.' However, in *al-Mustakhrajah*, Ibn al-Qasim is also reported as having stated the opposite of this, saying '...as he gets up alone while the imam is prostrating...' Ibn al-Qasim also said: '...and if he (joins the imam and) has to make up for a mistake which he himself has (also) made, then – if it is something he has missed out – he should make the prostration *before* the *salam* both for the negligence on his part and that the imam. This is because (in the case of a combination of) an addition (on behalf of the imam) and something missing (on his part, a prostration is made before). If, however he (also) makes an addition, then he makes the prostration for it after the *salam*; if the prostrations of the imam are before the *salam* and he himself makes a mistake while making up, then if it is something which he *leaves out* he should make the prostrations before the *salam* but if it is something (unnecessary) which he *adds* then he should make the prostrations after the *salam*.'"

Notice that if this person who comes late is ignorant (of the rules of the *salat*) and he makes the prostrations of negligence with the imam *after* the *salam* and then stands up and makes up (what he has to make up), then his *salat* is valid, according to what has been narrated from Ibn al-Qasim: "… and it is preferable to me that he repeat them both after the *salam*, and that he repeat them whenever he remembers." Ibn Rushd said: "Ibn al-Qasim has excused him on account of his ignorance and has judged him in accordance with the person who forgets – in accordance with the judgement of Sufyan in the *Mudawwana*: 'The reason for the judgement of Sufyan is that if the two prostrations are after the *salam*, then they constitute part of what is necessary for the completion of the *salat* of the imam: by joining the *salat* of the imam, he must not do anything contrary to the imam with respect to this (*salat*).'"

Ibn al-Qasim has reported hearing that "If the imam does not do the prostrations of negligence he should do, then those behind him should do them." Ibn Rushd said: "If the prostration if for something which invalidates the *salat* when not done and the imam does not return to do the prostration soon afterwards, then his *salat* is invalidated. However, their *salat* is valid as his omitting to do the prostration of negligence is not negligence on their part – for they have done it, and this is the principle (of the matter)."

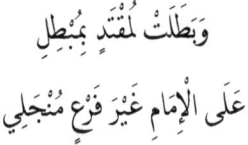

179 The *salat* is invalidated for those behind the imam when that of the latter is invalidated, other than in one obvious case:

مَنْ ذَكَرَ الْحَدَثَ أَوْ بِهِ غُلِبَ

$$\text{إِنْ بَادَرَ الْخُرُوجَ مِنْهَا وَنُدِبْ}$$

180 if the imam remembers that he is in a state of ritual impurity or is overcome by ritual impurity (during the *salat*) – as long as he leaves the *salat* immediately. In this case it is recommended

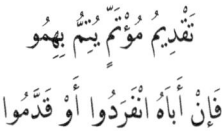

$$\text{فَإِنْ أَبَاهُ انْفَرَدُوا أَوْ قَدَّمُوا}$$

181 that he designate one of those following him to complete the *salat* for them; if he refuses, then they may complete it individually or may themselves put someone forward (to lead the *salat*).

Mayyara said: "Here he is informing us that the *salat* of the person following the imam is invalidated when that of the imam is invalidated, that is, if the *salat* of the imam is invalidated, this invalidity is also applicable to those behind him because of the connection of their *salat* to his – except in one manifest aspect – as manifest as the bride on her bridal throne – that is, when the imam remembers he is ritually impure during the *salat* or he is overcome by ritual impurity. In reality, they constitute two cases (not one) and so the matter is easy (to understand). Ibn 'Ashir is referring to the judgement of the *fuqaha*: 'Whenever the *salat* of the imam is invalidated so too is that of those following him, except when remembering one is in a state of ritual impurity or is overcome by this state.' However one may question why they have restricted themselves to merely these two cases. Then he goes on to stipulate that the validity of the *salat* of those behind – with respect to these two exceptional cases – is conditional upon the imam immediately leaving the *salat*. What is meant is that if he remembers that he is ritually impure or this state overpowers him (during the *salat*) and he does not immediately resolve to leave the *salat*, then the *salat* is invalidated for those behind also because they are following someone who is in a state of ritual impurity deliberately. Then Ibn 'Ashir goes on to mention that it is recommended for the imam to designate that one of those praying behind him should complete the *salat* with them, that is, he appoints someone (to lead) for the rest of the *salat*. If the imam declines to do this and he leaves without appointing anyone over them, then they have the option of either completing it individually – that is, other than in the *jumu'a* which is only valid when done in the *jama'a*, in which case they *must* appoint someone to lead them if the imam does not do this – or designate someone from amongst them to lead them to the end of the *salat*. It is also clear from his words that the imam should not designate someone who has not taken part in the *salat* behind him, nor someone who has come late and who has joined with the imam after he has realised that he is in a state of ritual impurity and can no longer continue. This is because such a person is considered 'not to belong' (*ajnabi*) and inappropriate to be the imam."

Al-Mawwaq said, commenting on the words of Khalil '(it is invalidated) if (behind an imam) in a state of impurity, or if he deliberately (carries on, after remembering he is) in a state of impurity or those behind him realise this': "Malik said: 'If anything happens to an imam such that his *salat* is annulled and he carries on leading them, then their *salat* is also annulled and they must repeat when they know this. Moreover, if someone behind him becomes aware of his state of *janaba* while the imam has forgotten it and carries on leading them, then the *salat* of this (person) is invalid. Yahya ibn al-Qasim reported hearing that if someone – who sees impurity on the clothes of the imam – is able to point this out to him, then he should do so. However, if he is unable, and he does the *salat* with him, then the (imam) should repeat the *salat* however long afterwards (he realises this) as anyone who deliberately performs the *salat* with impurity on his clothes is obliged to repeat the *salat* both within the time and after it; on the other hand, the *salat* of the person who does the *salat* aware of the impurity of his imam's clothes is acceptable even if he only repeats it within the time. Ibn Rushd said, commenting on Yahya ibn al-Qasim's words, 'if he is able to point this out to him': '...so the imam leaves after designating another and (the person who had seen the impurity) carries on his own *salat* with the newly designated person unless he has done anything of the *salat* with the first imam *after* seeing the impurity and *before* pointing it out to him, in which case he has invalidated his *salat* and should interrupt and begin again.' His saying that his *salat* is acceptable even if he only repeats within the time is based on the judgement of those who argue that the *salat* of those following the imam is not of the same level as their imam – although there is a difference of opinion regarding the principle of this matter: Ashhab has related that someone who deliberately does the *salat* when his clothing is impure does not have to repeat, and this is the most evident meaning of the *Mudawwana* regarding someone who touches a spot (on his body) which has been cupped (and blood exudes); Ibn al-'Arabi held to the *madhhab* of Ashhab arguing that if two men deliberately (pray with impurity on them) – one of them praying within the time, when aware (of this) and capable of changing (into other clothes), the other delaying it, when aware of this (impurity), until after the time and then praying in pure clothes – then their two states are not equal, indeed are not even similar to each other."

NOTE: that what he has ascribed to Ibn al-'Arabi, the author of *al-Mi'yar* has ascribed to Ibn al-Mu'adhdhal – after a discussion in which he explains that not everything which one is prohibited from doing *when embarking upon* an act of worship is actually taken into account if one does nevertheless (embark upon the act of worship) and does whatever it is one should not be doing. The discussion is to be found where he says "…and based on this Ibn al-Mu'adhdhal says: 'If two men….'", as reported by al-Mawwaq. Then he goes on to say: "as for the person who deliberately performs the *salat* in the time (aware of) the impurity on him, the people are of a consensus that he is not the same as the person who delays it until outside the time, and is not even similar to him, despite the transmission of the consensus from more than one Shaykh that it is obligatory to avoid impurity during the *salat* – among them al-Lakhmi and al-Mazari, and al-Baji has confirmed this as correct. This is also stated by 'Abd al-Wahhab in his *Talqeen*." In his *Kabir* and his *Takmila al-Minhaj*, Mayyara has composed a poem enumerating the various differences of opinion[1]:

The *salat* of the imam is invalidated – but not that of those following him if he leaves immediately and they carry on – when he remembers his state of impurity which happened before (the *salat*); when something impure exudes from him; when his private parts are uncovered; when he fails to do the prostrations of negligence for missing three (sunnas);

or if he fears for his self or property; when he changes his intention during the *salat* from that of a traveller to that of a resident; or he thinks he has a nose bleed, irrespective of how little; or when overcome by a guffaw, or through forgetfulness; or when he remembers a small number of *salats* missed; when he leaves out a prostration and stands up and those behind him try to avert him by saying 'subhana'llah' but he does not return (for the prostration).

However, the well-known judgement is that if the imam guffaws, or as a traveller, (changes his intention) or remembers previous missed out *salats*, it invalidates in all cases and designating another is not valid.

TWO BENEFITS AS A SEAL: the author of *al-Jami' as-Saghir* said: "The imam and the *mu'adhdhin* have the reward of those that pray with them."

USEFUL POINT: Ibn al-Hattab said "According to the *madhhab* of the *Mudawwana* it is *makruh* to take a salary for being the imam in the *fard* and *nafila*. The words of Khalil may be understood as being of general application

---

1   There are mistakes in the text; the correct text may be found in *ad-Durr ath-Thameen*.

regarding the *fard* and the *nafila*. However, in the *Kitab al-Ijara* Ibn Yunus said: 'Ibn al-Qasim said: "In my opinion this is particularly disliked with regard to the five daily *salats*".' Ibn Rushd has ascribed this – in his *Rasm as-Salat ath-Thani min Sama' Ashhab* – to the *Mudawwana*. The reason for this is that even if the *fard* is not incumbent on *him specifically* in the mosque, it is incumbent on him to maintain its times and its limits: if it is feared that he would neglect the *fard* (in the mosque) and not hold to the *nafila* at all – without a salary – then according to him a salary is a lesser evil. Moreover giving a salary for something that one is *not obliged* to give a salary for is permitted and even if being an imam is an act of worship undertaken in order to come closer to Allah, the principle of the matter remains the same as the *adhan* and the building of a mosque."

The Book of Zakat

The Book of Zakat

Mayyara said: "The *sadaqa* of one's wealth is called *zakat* because it produces *baraka* and increase in the wealth from which it has been taken. It has also been said: '…because the amount given is purified and made to increase by Allah – as is stated in the hadith: "A slave does not give out in *sadaqa* of the good things he has earned – and Allah only accepts what is good – but that it is as if he places it in the hand of the Most-Merciful who then takes care of it for him just as carefully as one of you would take care of a foal or young camel in your possession until it is as great as a mountain."' It has also been said: 'The person who pays (the *zakat*) will himself be purified in the eyes of Allah – as Allah, exalted is He, said: *"Take from their wealth to purify and cleanse them."*'[1] As for its being one of the five pillars, this is a matter which is known and accepted (by all Muslims). The proofs from the Book, the sunna and the *ijma'* are well known and so we will not linger on this matter. Whoever denies that it is an obligation is a renegade from Islam (*murtadd*). For three days, he is asked to turn in *tawba*: if he does not turn in *tawba*, then he is put to death as a *kafir* on account of his denial of what is known of the deen necessarily (by all Muslims); if he confirms that it is an obligation but refuses to pay it, then it is taken from him by force, even if he has to be fought for it, and he is punished for refusing to give it, but (once given), then it is accepted of him (by the Muslims and Allah, exalted is He), according to the well known opinion."

Ibn al-Hattab related: "Ibn 'Arafa said: 'Knowledge of its obligation for other than those who are new to Islam is imperative. Ibn Rushd said: 'Anyone who denies it is a *kafir*.'" I said: "…he is referring to are those who are not new to Islam and is indicating that the judgement of Ibn Habib, namely 'that the one who (merely) abandons it is a *kafir*' is invalid."

Ibn al-Hajar al-Haytami said in his *Sharh al-Arba'in*: 'Among those who refused the *zakat* – that is at the time of Abu Bakr, may Allah be pleased with him – were those who denied its obligation and the necessity of paying it to

---

1   At-Tawba – Repentance: 104

the imam. In reality they are *ahl al-baghy* – those who commit gross violations of the *shari'ah*.' After a while he goes on to say: 'One is not saying (in this instance) that a denial of the *fard* obligation of *zakat* is *kufr*. How is it then, one might ask, that I can maintain that they are *ahl baghy*? This is because we are saying this in the light of our present (society) for which the (matter of *zakat*) is something necessarily known and accepted by all as imperative: whenever this is the case, then denying the (*zakat*) is an act of *kufr* – as opposed to those times, given how recently they had accepted Islam, and how ignorant they were of the laws and given the possibility of abrogation; unless the denial of what is necessarily well known and accepted is on behalf of someone (from our present day society) who has recently accepted Islam or someone who does not mix with Muslims, in which case he is not a *kafir*. This (understanding of the judgement) is more applicable and fitting than the (absolute) judgement of Qadi 'Iyad, namely, that the person who denies its obligation is considered to belong to the same category as a *murtadd*."

USEFUL POINT: the following is recorded in the *Sahih al-Bukhari*: "(On the Last Day) camels will come to their owner in a better state of health than they ever had in this world and if he has not paid the *zakat* on them in this world, then they will trample over him with their feet; and sheep will come to their owner in a better state of health they ever had in this world and if he has not paid *zakat* on them, they will trample over him with their hooves and gore him with their horns." The Prophet, may the peace and blessings of Allah be upon him, said: "One of their rights is that they should be milked while water is kept in front of them. I do not want any one of you to come to me on the Day of Raising Up carrying a bleating sheep about his neck and saying: 'O Muhammad (please intercede for me)' for I will say to him: 'I cannot help you for I have conveyed (Allah's message to you).' I do not want anyone of you to come to me carrying a braying camel about his neck saying: 'O Muhammad (please intercede for me)' for I will say to him: 'I cannot help you for I have conveyed (Allah's message to you).'" It is also recorded in al-Bukhari that the Prophet, may the peace and blessings of Allah be upon him, said: "By Him in whose hand is my self!" or "By Him with whom there is no other god!" – in whatever the exact form of his oath – "There is no man who has camels, cows or sheep and goats and who does not pay the *zakat* on them but that they will be brought (before him) on the Day of Raising Up bigger and fatter than they had ever been and they will trample over him with their feet and hooves and will gore him with their horns. (These animals will form a circle): when the last has had its turn, the first will start again, and this punishment will go on until Allah has finished judging the people." It is also recorded in al-Bukhari's *Sahih* that the Messenger of Allah may the peace and blessings of Allah be upon him said: "Whoever is given wealth by Allah, exalted is He, and does not pay the *zakat* of his wealth, then on the Day of Raising Up his wealth will be make to resemble a bald-headed, poisonous, black male snake with two black spots like raisins over his eyes. The snake will encircle his neck and bite his cheeks saying: 'I am your wealth! I am your treasure.' Then the Prophet, may the peace and blessings of Allah be upon him, recited: '*Those who are tight fisted with the bounty Allah has given them should not suppose that it is better for them.*'"[1]

Ibn Hajar said: "His saying 'in a better state of health than they ever had in this world' means they will be bigger, fatter and more numerous: their health and strength would have varied while in his possession but (on the Last Day) they will be brought (before him) in the most perfect of states so that they are all the more able to inflict injury on him. His words 'the two black spots like raisins' refer to certain black spots on his jawbones or at the corner of his mouth. Al-Qurtubi said: '"bald" means "white headed" from the poison.'"

USEFUL POINT: Ibn Hajar, commenting on the hadith 'Mu'adh ibn Jabal was sent to the Yemen with the words: "Inform them that Allah has made the five *salats* each day and night obligatory for them, and if they obey you in this then inform them that Allah has imposed the obligation of the *zakat* on them"': "The wisdom in mentioning the *zakat* after the *salat* is that anyone who claims *tawhid* but who denies the *salat* is in fact rejecting (*tawhid*): his wealth (automatically) becomes booty and his *zakat* is of no use."

فُرِضَتِ الزَّكَاةُ فِيمَا يُرْتَسَمْ

عَيْنٍ وَحَبٍّ وَثِمَارٍ وَنَعَمْ

182 *Zakat* is a *fard* obligation on everything which has been laid down (in the *shari'ah*): gold and silver, grains and fruit, and grazing livestock.

Mayyara said: "Here he has informed us that *zakat* is taken on three types of things: the first is *'ayn* which is gold and silver and the second, *hubub wa thimar*, refers to grains and fruits – and here Ibn 'Ashir is indicating, like Ibn al-Hajib, Shaykh Abu Muhammad and others, *harth*, that is, agricultural produce. Al-Jazuli said: '*harth* indicates any of the various kinds of grains and fruits which are used as staple, storable foods; another (*'alim*) has used the term *mi'sharat*,

---

[1] Ali 'Imran – The Family of 'Imran. 180

that is, a tithe or tenth part, as mentioned in *al-Jawahir*. The third is *na'am*, that is, camels, cows, sheep and goats."

$$\text{فِى الْعَيْنِ وَالْأَنْعَامِ حَقَّتْ كُلَّ عَامْ}$$

$$\text{يَكْمُلُ وَالْحَبُّ بِالْإِفْرَاكِ يُرَامْ}$$

183 It becomes due on gold and silver and livestock after a full year, on grains when they become firm and may be separated from the ears,

$$\text{وَالتَّمْرُ وَالزَّبِيبُ بِالطِّيبِ وَفِي}$$

$$\text{ذِي الزَّيْتِ مِنْ زَيْتِهِ وَالْحَبُّ يَفِي}$$

184 on dates and raisins when they ripen, and on the oil from oil-bearing seeds – if they amount to the *nisab* (minimum legal amount)

Mayyara said: "Here he has informed us that *zakat* on gold and silver is due, that is obligatory, for every full (lunar) year which passes, that is, the obligation on these two is conditional upon the elapsing of the year but that the obligation of the passing of a year with respect to the *zakat* of grains is not stipulated – rather it becomes obligatory on grains when they begin to become firm. As for oil-bearing seeds, *zakat* is paid on the oil if the grains amount to the *nisab* – the legal minimum measure."

NOTICE: the question is often raised as to what a person should do if he does not know (whether a full) year (has passed), and whether he should pay the *zakat* before he is certain that the full year has in fact passed. I shall transmit for you the discussion of al-Hattab – which is also contained in *al-Mi'yar* – on this subject: commenting on the words of Khalil regarding the *zakat* of gold and silver 'and if two (consecutive profits, for example one in Muharram and the other in Rajab) fall short (of the minimum...)' he said: "It is possible that what Khalil is referring to when he goes on to say 'if the person is in doubt as to which one of the two it belongs to' is that he has doubts as to which *hawl* (computation of the full lunar year) the first profit belongs and whether it was acquired in the first or second *hawl*. The most evident judgement is that – if understood in this manner as obligatory – then, it is placed along with the second year. I have not however found an explicit text on the matter, and Allah, exalted is He, knows best."

After a long discussion, he goes on to say: "If he trades with two sums (of money) and he makes a profit of six dinars but does not know which of the two they belong to, then he should pay *zakat* based on the second (month). He should not pay it when any doubt exists for he would be paying his *zakat* on the first sum before the year was up."

In *al-Mi'yar* it is stated: "Our Shaykh Abu 'Abdallah ibn al-'Abbas, may Allah have mercy on him, was asked about the commentary of Muhammad ibn 'Abd as-Salam on the words of Ibn al-Hajib 'if he has five from Muharram and five from Rajab': "If someone trades with one lot of five and it becomes twenty but then he does not know whether they were from Muharram or Rajab, then he should pay the *zakat* for the latter (month): if he were to be ordered to pay the *zakat* for the former, then he might be paying the *zakat* before its *hawl* – before the full year had elapsed on the sum – for it is quite possible that the sum used was from the latter month. However, it could also be argued that by ordering him to pay the *zakat* for the second *hawl*, he would be delaying the *zakat* from payment in its proper time – as it is also quite possible that it was the first sum (from Muharram). Why, one might ask, have you given preference to one of the two possibilities over the over? Is it that delaying (payment) to the second *hawl* is the lesser of two evils as the harm inflicted on the person – whose money it is – by his paying it before the *hawl* is greater than that caused by delaying its distribution to the poor people, and this for more than one reason?." Abu 'Abdallah then replied: "What you have indicated in the matter – both in what you suggest as the preferred judgement and your reason for this – is correct: Ibn al-Hajib is stating that one should delay the *zakat* past its time and Muhammad ibn 'Abd as-Salam is justifying this – so his words actually contain the answer."

Then he has also added, after a discussion: "Anything other than this would lead to the possibility that the *zakat* be paid before its proper time, and whatever leads to this is rejected and not practised."

After a while, he then he goes on to say: "Abu'l-'Abbas Sayyidi Ahmad ibn Zaghou has answered this matter of *fiqh*, saying: 'Praise belongs to Allah! the answer to the matter is that *zakat* is not obligatory on wealth of the type which is assessed from *hawl* to *hawl* unless one is certain that the full year has elapsed – and in fact there can be no certainty until the second *hawl* has actually arrived. (In this case) he cannot be certain with regard to the first *hawl* because of the possibility that some part of it still remains.' This answer is based on the famous principle that any doubt with regard to a condition necessarily entails doubt with regard to the matter governed by the condition. Thus doubt as to whether the year has actually elapsed necessarily entails doubt as to the obligation of *zakat*. Indeed, it is on a par with doubt as to whether the time for the *salat* has arrived, in which case *salat* is not permitted."

The *faqih* of Algeria, 'Ali ibn Muhammad al-Halabi has answered by saying: "As for his saying 'by ordering him to pay the *zakat* for the second year he is delaying the *zakat* from payment at its proper time', we argue that in (the case of) of profits of this kind (i.e. with regard to these two months), the obligation of paying *zakat* on them is dependent upon the passing of a full year – and all that this judgement entails. Doubt as to which sum the five dinars were taken from leads to doubt as to the presence of the necessary condition for the obligation of this *zakat* – that is, the (condition of) time. Doubt as to the fulfilment of any necessary condition means the annulling of the requirement itself. Moreover, it is not said of any legally binding demand – which *not yet* become obligatory – that it has been 'delayed from its proper time', and praise belongs to Allah and He is enough for us."

NOTICE: (in the case of agricultural produce) a person must pay the *zakat* on grains when they become saleable, that is, after they have become firm in their ears.

ISSUE: 'Ali ibn 'Abd as-Sadiq said: "Anything gleaned – which is permitted when it has been left (by the owner) who has no intention to return to (collect) it – is not reckoned. It is like what is eaten by the birds. But as for what is picked up or gleaned immediately after the harvest this is part of the reward of the harvester and it is reckoned and *zakat* is payable on it. Anything eaten by an animal during the threshing is not reckoned because of the difficulty of assesssing this (in the calculation). However, our Shaykh has stipulated this is only permitted as long as it is not done deliberately; otherwise, it should be taken into account. There is no *zakat* on anything lost through some natural calamity like a drought or crop failure – this, as-Sudani has stated."

I SAY: "It is stated in *al-Mi'yar*: 'Abu't-Teeb was asked about a people whose crop was estimated for them but who were prevented from having access to it until they paid dirhams in cash – how is *zakat* applied in their case? He replied: "One reckons up everything that has been paid of the crop in dirhams and this is deducted from the worth of the crop and then *zakat* is paid on the rest."' He has also replied: 'As for the dirhams which were paid to the financial authorities (*al-makhzan*), they are only taken into account for the (specific crop) intended – not on anything else which was not paid for in dirhams. This deduction is made from the day payment (is actually made).' As for the payment demanded by the Sultan on the basis of an estimate of the crop, Ibn Muhriz said: 'The strongest judgement in my opinion is that he should pay *zakat* on all of it and that no allowance is made for the payment made. However, those who argue that he should deduct the amount paid in cash, say that he should see what is harvested on the day of threshing and then deduct the amount of cash paid from the worth (of the crop) *on that day*, not on the day of its estimation.' It has been said that the preferred judgement of Ibn 'Arafa, may Allah, exalted is He, have mercy on him, is that payment of the *zakat* is obligatory under all circumstances – comparing payment of the *zakat* to the payment for general costs (of hiring people, for example) incurred in producing the crop (which cannot be deducted from the zakatable amount) – even if great, and he has taken this judgement from the *Mudawwana*. What I prefer is that if his particular crop fails, then he does not take into account what has (already) been paid (as a tax); if the crop failure is general, then it is taken into account – and this judgement is based on the analogy of what applies in the case of (ground) rents (which one may deduct from the zakatable amount).¹"

Ibn al-Hattab said: "Shaykh Nasir ad-Deen al-Laqani was asked as to whether – when some of the goods which arrive in Jedda from India, for example, are sold in order to pay the (non-*shari'ah* customs) duties with the sum paid for them – the owners of the goods must pay Zakat on this sum or not. He replied: 'As for the goods one was forced to sell to pay the taxes, *zakat* must still be paid on them – and the reward for the person from whom the taxes were unjustly demanded is with Allah..'"

I was asked as to the judgement with regard to their taking goods in payment of a tithe tax.

I replied: "If they take goods, then one does not have to estimate the value of them. If, however, he is compelled to sell the goods – and to pay the price he receives for these goods to them – then he does have to pay *zakat* on this (transaction), and Allah knows best."

ISSUE: Abu'l-Hasan said in *Ghayat al-Amani*: "...the third of the *fard* obligations of the *zakat* is that it is paid when it becomes due and it is not delayed beyond its time of obligation. However, if it is nevertheless delayed, then it is accepted of him – although his doing this is prohibited."

ISSUE: az-Zurqani said in his commentary on Khalil: "If he sells dates after they are ripe and grains after they have become firm as an unspecified amount, that is, en bloc (*juzafan*), merely bought as seen (in a heap, for example,) then the *zakat* is paid on them by informing the buyer of their amount – for he is entrusted with this, and this is the most efficient way. If, however, he is a

---

1 There are marked differences between the text of the *Mi'yar* in Shaykh Shinqeeti's work and the *Mi'yar* itself (see: *al Mi'yar*, vol.1, p. 363ff.)

corrupt person or a *kafir*, then the amount is estimated. Examine at-Tatari (in this regard). The words of the author are a clear indication that payment of *zakat* on crops must be taken from the crop itself, and Ibn Jama'a has also stated this explicitly. It is permitted to stipulate that the buyer must pay it – if he is a trustworthy person and there is no doubt that he will pay it."

ISSUE: az-Zurqani said: "Sanad has also said: 'If what has been stipulated (on the buyer) is with regard to foodstuffs, that is, the obligation to pay the *zakat* on five *wasqs*[1] for example, then the (zakatable amount) should be set aside and not sold on; if nevertheless he does sell it, he must pay a like amount instead but the sale is not invalidated as *zakat* is governed by the same judgement as debts: it is permitted for a person to dispose of something as long as he guarantees the same in its stead, like borrowing from something deposited on trust, or borrowing from the inheritance of a minor who is not yet permitted to dispose of his wealth."

ISSUE: after a discussion of the rule governing the wealth of a child, Ibn al-Hattab said: "The gist of this is that if the *madhhab* of the executor is that *zakat* is obligatory on the wealth of a child – either by his own *ijtihad*, if he is a *mujtahid*, or by *taqlid* of someone who holds that it is an obligation – then it is obligatory on him to pay it. The *madhhab* of the father of the child is not taken into account as the wealth has been transferred from him; nor that of the child as he is not legally of age. Moreover the child is not consulted about it. Thus if there is no judge in the area who rules that no *zakat* is to be paid, then the executor or legal guardian must pay it, and it is not necessary to bring the matter before the judge. Rather, he should bear testimony to having paid it – but is believed even if he does not give testimony – if he is a trustworthy person. As to whether he must pay an indemnity (*gharam*) or swear an oath when he is not a trustworthy person, I have no specific text on the issue. If, however, there is a judge in the area who considers that the *zakat* does not have to be paid on the wealth of a child but the executor is of the conviction that it should, then he must pay it, and he does not have to mention this to the child after he becomes of age – and this may be understood by their words above; if, however, he does not think that it should be paid, then if there are a number of judges in the area – one of them considering that *zakat* is obligatory while others that it is not – then what appears from their discussion is that he must bring the matter before the judge who considers that *zakat* is obligatory, just as he would also have to do in the case where he finds wine in the inheritance and

---

1 a measure of volume equal to sixty *sa's*, each *sa'* equal to four *mudd*, each *mudd* a double-handed scoop

he considers that it is obligatory to break (the bottles of) wine. This is what appears from the discussion of Ibn Bashir above. Thus the judge may order him to pay it, making a judgement to this effect. He may not bring the matter before the judge who considers that it does not need to be paid. If, in the area, there is only one judge and he thinks that it does not need to be paid, then the most evident interpretation of their discussion is that he does not have to bring the matter before him and that it is not obligatory on him; rather he should delay its payment until the child becomes of age. If, when the child in question becomes of age, he makes *taqlid* of someone who holds that *zakat* on the wealth of a child is not to be paid, then he does not have to pay anything – and this is clear. If he makes *taqlid* of someone who holds that it is obligatory to pay *zakat* on the wealth of a child, then he must pay it – and this is what the author of *an-Nawadir* states. It is reported in *al-Majmou'a* that Ibn al-Qasim said: 'Zakat on the wealth of the mad person is paid like that of the child. If the executor of the wealth of an orphan has not paid the *zakat* on his wealth, then the orphan should pay it when he takes possession of it for the years passed. If the executor had borrowed it for years, then he only pays *zakat* on it for one year – from the day that the executor became responsible for it.' If the executor brings the matter to the judge who is of the persuasion that no *zakat* is to be paid on the wealth of minors and who judges that it should not be paid but then the child comes of age and makes *taqlid* of someone who considers that it is obligatory, then the most manifest judgement is that the obligation to pay *zakat* is not removed from him – so reflect on this."

وَهِىَ فِي الثِّمَارِ وَالْحَبِّ الْعُشْرُ

أَوْ نِصْفُهُ إِنْ آلَةَ السَّقْيِ يَجُرّ

185 There is a tenth to pay on fruit and grains, or the half of this if a means of irrigation has been employed.

خَمْسَةُ أَوْسُقٍ نِصَابٌ فِيهِمَا

فِى فِضَّةٍ قُلْ مِائَتَانِ دِرْهَمَا

186 The *nisab* – the legal zakatable amount – is five *wasqs*, on silver at least two hundred dirhams.

عِشْرُونَ دِينَاراً نِصَابٌ فِي الذَّهَبْ

وَرُبُعُ الْعُشُرِ فِيهِمَا وَجَبْ

187 The *nisab* for gold is twenty dinars – of which a quarter of a tenth (2½%) is due on both (gold and silver)

Mayyara said: "It is called '*nisab*' as one of the meanings of (the Arabic root) *nasaba* is 'to direct or aim' and so it is fixed as a (marker) flag before which there is no *zakat*. Allah, exalted is He, says: '*The Day they will emerge swiftly from their graves as if rushing to rally to the flag (nusub)*'[1]; or it is derived from the word *naseeb* – portion or share – as the destitute do not have to pay anything of their wealth when it is below this portion or minimum."

Ibn al-Hattab said: "*Nisab* also has the meaning of 'source or root' and in the *shari'ah*, the meaning of 'portion' or 'minimum amount.' If this amount is reached, then the *zakat* must be paid on it – and Malik has explained it in this manner. It is called '*nisab*' as it is like a flag marking the obligation of *zakat*; or because, if wealth reaches this (amount), then it is 'aimed at' (*nusiba ilayhi*) by the sending of *zakat* assessors who incur the difficulty (*nasb*) (of collecting it); or because it means portion (*naseeb*) – as the destitute will have their portion from it."

NOTICE: there is a difference of opinion as to whether owning the *nisab* is a 'cause' or 'condition' (of *zakat*). Ibn al-Hattab said, commenting on the words of Khalil in the section *Zakat al-'ayn* '…if the ownership is full': "He has made ownership a 'condition' for the *nisab* – and likewise Ibn al-Hajib and Ibn 'Arafa and others. However, what is most evident is that it is the 'cause', as al-Qarafi said – as it is the full ownership which actually makes the *nisab* a reality, and therefore is the true 'cause' of it whereas this is not the case when regarded as a 'condition.' Even if cause and condition – within the framework of the *shari'ah* – resemble each other in that absence of either entails absence (of the *zakat*) and that the existence of either does not necessarily entail either the existence or non-existence (of *zakat*) in itself, they differ, as al-Qarafi said, in that the cause is inherent in the (zakatable) thing itself whereas the condition is inherent in other than it: thus ownership of the *nisab* implies (enjoyment of the) riches and blessings of the thing possessed *in itself* (and as such is a cause) whereas the *hawl* – the passing of the full year – is not like this (and as such is a condition), but rather is that which perfects the ownership and which permits

---

1 al-Ma'arij – The Ascending Steps: 43

the growth (of the thing owned) throughout the year."

USEFUL POINT: it is obligatory that that which is paid in *zakat* is of good quality – as Allah does only accepts what is good. Ibn Hajar al-Haytami said, commenting on the hadith 'Allah is good and only accept what is good': "He only rewards for what He knows is good, that is, whatever is purified of any corrupt motive, like (something given) to show off or in vanity, and which is halal. This is best illustrated, according to us, in the example of the person who gives something thinking it is halal while in fact it is haram within – for the person is nevertheless rewarded for his intention of obeying (the command of Allah, exalted is He,). Allah, exalted is He, does not accept anything paid which is haram for the person paying any such *zakat* would be disposing of something which is haram – for example, his disposing of something belonging to someone else. Acceptance of this from him would mean, in effect, that he was being both commanded to something and being forbidden from something (by Allah) simultaneously, and this is impossible. All this may be understood from what is implied by the discussion, namely that what is good in itself and acceptable is incompatible with what is not good and which is unacceptable – and the two cannot be reconciled. Disposing of wealth (as *sadaqa* or *zakat*) may be prohibited in itself as it has been acquired illegally – and this is what is being referred to in many of the hadith in this regard – and therefore not accepted of him, in which case he not only receives no reward for it but is also punished for it, according to all (the *fuqaha*), and this has been transmitted from Ibn al-Musayyab. As for disposing of wealth which cannot be returned to its rightful owner or to the person who should inherit it, then this is permitted according to most of the *'ulama*. The (rightful owner) will benefit from the reward (for such disposal) in the next world as he was unable to benefit from it in this world. Al-Fadeel Ibn 'Iyad said: 'As for wealth or property which is inviolable because the owners are not known, it is thrown into the sea.' However, this is an unlikely judgement. ash-Shafi'i said, may Allah be pleased with him: 'It is kept until the person who has a right to it appears – as long as there is hope of his reappearing.' I cannot guarantee that the manuscript is without mistakes."

NOTICES

1. Ibn al-Hattab said: "It is stated in the *Mudawwana*: 'Whoever hires out Kharaj land to someone who uses it for agricultural purposes, then the *zakat* on what the earth produces is the responsibility of the person who hires it out and the *kharaj* tax on the land is not counted towards the *zakat* for the crop produced, irrespective of whether the land is his or belongs to another.' Al-Qarafi said: 'There are two types of *kharaj* tax, the first of them, that exacted

by 'Umar, may Allah be pleased with him, on the territory of Iraq: he had conquered it by force and had divided it amongst the Muslims but then he decided that they should give it up lest it go to ruin while people were involved in *jihad* or lest they themselves became preoccupied with it to the detriment of the *jihad*. Thus he took it back from them, compensating some but not others, and then he imposed the *kharaj* tax on it and made it a *waqf* for the Muslims.' Sanad said: 'This is counted as a rent according to Malik and ash-Shafi'i, and for this reason Malik has prohibited the right of pre-emption on it. However, it has also been said that he bought it from the dhimmis for a price to be paid in instalments each year, and this is the *kharaj*.'"

2. Mayyara said: "Al-Burzuli said in his *Nawazil*: 'Whoever irrigates his crop and pays a tenth thinking this is the rate (rather than a half of this), then he is not permitted to deduct this from the next crop which he has not yet paid for. He must pay the tenth in full for the next crop. However, if he finds what he has paid out from the first still in the hands of the poor, he should take it back. This is analogous to someone who – out of ignorance – gives someone something in return for giving him *zakat*, or someone who despite being free of any obligation to pay the bloodwit pays it unaware that it should in fact be paid by the body of relations or comrades who are legally responsible for its payment.' 'Ali ibn 'Abd as-Sadiq has also transmitted this and added: '…also in the case where someone pays the *zakat* or *kaffara* to someone who does not have a right to it.'"

3. Mayyara said: "Ibn al-Hajib said: 'There is no *zakat* on the partner until his portion reaches the *nisab* – with respect to gold and silver, agricultural produce or animals. Likewise, if the portion of one of the inheritors is below the *nisab* then he does not have to pay the *zakat*.'"

Issue: al-Wansharisi said: "One of the *fuqaha* of North Africa was asked about an incident in which a man who, when requested (for a share of the *zakat* on a crop), promised the person who had requested it that he would give it to him at the time when the (other) people were given their measure. The person did not however come at this time and so the man gave it to another. Then the person who had made the request came to demand it of him. He replied: 'He is not obliged to give anything as (the promise) was only valid if he came (in person) to take possession of it. He gave him a time to collect but he had not set aside a specific share for him.'"

Also on this subject, al-Qabisi was asked about an unjust Sultan who used to take a tenth (of the crop) and use it (for himself) and who used to wrongly impose taxes on people. The Sultan would store this wealth with a man who only accepted it of him because he feared the consequences if he did not. He replied: "If he forced him to store it and the man could see no alternative but to accept, then he is under no liability for it. However, residing in a land where there is no escape from such practice is not good."

وَالْعَرْضُ ذُو التَّجْرِ وَدَيْنُ مَنْ أَدَارَ

قِيمَتُهَا كَالْعَيْنِ ثُمَّ ذُو احْتِكَارْ

188 and on goods for trade, and on a credit incurred (as capital) to buy and sell (on a daily basis), and the amount due is the same as gold and silver; it is also due on anything stocked (for sale later, when market conditions are favourable).

زُكِّى لِقَبْضِ ثَمَنٍ أَو دَيْنْ

عَيْناً بِشَرْطِ الْحَوْلِ لِلْأَصْلَيْنْ

189 The *zakat* is paid in gold or silver when taking possession of the price (for the sale of the goods), or of the credit incurred as capital, on condition that the year has elapsed on the two.

Mayyara said: "In these two lines the author has mentioned the *zakat* of goods and credit. He has informed us that both the value of the goods for trade and the amount of credit at the disposal of the manager (of the business) are assessed in gold and silver and then the *zakat* is paid on the assessed value. What is meant by 'goods for trade' are the goods from one of the two types of trade, that is *idara* – the management (of a business by buying and selling on a daily basis) – in which case the manager assesses the worth of the goods of the business at a particular moment at the end of the *hawl*, customarily selling them for gold and silver, and then paying the *zakat* on the price released, in according with the conditions of assessment governing both types (of currency), and an explanation together with the manner of the assessment is to follow below, insha'Allah. As for long-term trade with stock, he pays the *zakat* on receiving the price for his goods; as for the credit, at the moment of repossession of the credit from the revenue of the credit together with the price of the goods in gold and silver – as long as the *hawl* has elapsed on the original goods and the credit. There are various aspects to the judgement of goods: if they are intended to be kept (for personal use), then there is no difference of opinion that there is no *zakat* on them. Ibn Bashir said: 'This the *umma* has understood from his saying, may the peace and blessings of Allah be upon him, "a Muslim does not have to pay *zakat* on his horse and his slave".' If, however, they are for trade, then *zakat* is paid on them, according to the majority of the *'ulama*, although not according to the Dhahiris."

Trade is of two kinds: the management of a business through buying and selling on a daily basis (*idara*) and the withholding of stock from immediate sale in order to wait for favourable market conditions (*ihtikar*). In the case of *idara*, the money and goods do not remain in his hands (for very long) but rather he sells whenever he sees a profit, however great or small, sometimes even selling for no profit. This (type of trade) is exemplified by shop keepers and those who import goods from other countries. In the case of *ihtikar*, on the other hand, the trader buys goods and then observes the markets. He withholds them (from sale) until he sees a large profit to be made – even if this means their remaining with him for years. Then if the goods are such that they are zakatable by payment in kind, like the *nisab* of animals, then the *zakat* is paid each year, irrespective of whether it is for one's own use or for trade, and likewise for the *nisab* of fruit and grains. But if the *zakat* does not have to be paid in kind, as in the case of all other goods such as clothing and slaves – and included in this is anything which falls short of the *nisab* in the case of grains and fruit and livestock – then the application of *zakat* to them is dependent as a whole on various conditions, the first of them being that he be in possession of its equivalence (in gold and silver) for there is no *zakat* on inherited land or on a gift until it is sold and a year has elapsed on the price released.

Second of the two is that he intends to trade with the goods (in question) for if he does not intend trade with them, then there is no *zakat* until he sells them and a year has elapsed on the price released, irrespective of whether he had intended to keep them as his own possessions or he had made no such intention as the 'principle' governing all goods is (the quality of) possession.

3. that the origin of these goods for trade is that they were paid for either in gold or silver; if, however, they were originally acquired in return for other goods, then there is no *zakat* payable until he sells them and a year has elapsed on the price released, although Ibn al-Hajib has narrated two judgements on this. If these conditions are fulfilled, then the *zakat* is obligatory in which case the owner of these goods makes the following distinction: if he is a 'manager' (*mudir*), he assesses his goods at the end of the *hawl* for each year and then pays the *zakat* for the amount he assesses, reckoning the start of the *hawl* from the moment of the first cash transaction, not the moment when he undertakes the

buying and selling – a judgement which differs from that of Ashhab. Thus if he takes possession of a thousand (dinars) in Muharram and then he conducts a business with them by (buying and selling) goods in Rajab, then the first full *hawl* is reckoned from Muharram – while Ashhab said it is Rajab. The (*fuqaha*) have said: 'He assesses each kind (of goods) on the basis of what he usually sells them for during this time, that is on the basis of an average price in normal selling conditions – not when compelled (to sell for more or less in special circumstances). Thus brocade and the like, slaves, land and buildings are assessed in gold and thick cloth, clothing and the like, in silver."

Issue: Ibn al-Hattab has related: "Ibn Juzayy said, after discussing the (definition of the) manager (*mudir*) and the person who sells by withholding stock (*muhtakir*): branch: 'Whoever sells goods for goods and does not come into the possession of cash, then he does not have to pay *zakat* unless he does this in order to escape payment of *zakat*, in which case this obligation is not removed from him.' And this applies to both the *mudir* and the *muhtakir*, and this is the most evident judgement, and Allah knows best."

Zakat of Livestock

في كُلِّ خَمْسَةِ جِمَالٍ جَذَعَةٌ

مِنْ غَنَمٍ بِنْتُ الْمَخَاضِ مُقْنِعَةٌ

190 On every five camels, a sheep or goat of two years (is to be paid); a she-camel in its second year

فِي الْخَمْسِ وَالْعِشْرِينَ وَابْنَةُ اللَّبُونِ

فِي سِتَّةٍ مَعَ الثَّلَاثِينَ تَكُونُ

191 is enough on twenty-five camels; on thirty six camels, one she-camel in its third year;

سِتًّا وَأَرْبَعِينَ حِقَّةٌ كَفَتْ

جَذْعَةٌ إِحْدَى وَسِتِّينَ وَفَتْ

192 on forty-six, a she-camel of four years is enough; on sixty-one, a she-camel of five years;

بِنْتَا لَبُونٍ سِتَّةً وَسَبْعِينَ

وَحِقَّتَانِ وَاحِداً وَتِسْعِينَ

193 on seventy-six, two she-camels of three years old; on ninety-one, two she-camels of four years old;

$$\text{وَمَعْ ثَلَاثِينَ ثَلَاثٌ أَيْ بَنَاتُ}$$

$$\text{لَبُونٍ أَوْ خُذْ حِقَّتَيْنِ بِأَقْتِيَاتٍ}$$

194 on every thirty over a hundred, three she-camels of three years or two she-camels of four years, according to the assessment [of the tax-collector].

$$\text{إِذَا الثَّلَاثِينَ تَلَتْهَا الْمِائَةُ}$$

$$\text{فِي كُلِّ خَمْسِينَ كَمَالًا حِقَّةُ}$$

195 This is only if the total is one hundred and thirty; on every fifty (over a hundred), a she-camel of four years;

$$\text{وَكُلُّ أَرْبَعِينَ بِنْتُ لَبُونٍ}$$

$$\text{وَهَكَذَا مَا زَادَ أَمْرُهُ يَهُونُ}$$

196 on every forty, a she-camel of three years, and so on.

Mayyara said: "Ibn 'Ashir has begun his discussion of *zakat* as others have done with the *zakat* of camels and has informed us that on every five camels, a sheep or goat of two years (is paid), and that this rate remains valid until they number twenty four after which, as he says, a camel of two years is to be paid on twenty five. The 'sheep or goat of two years' is a *jadh'a*, i.e. which has past one year, according to Ashhab and Ibn Nafi.' It is stated in *at-Tawdih*: 'This is what is widely accepted, according to some of the copies of Ibn al-Hajib.' The author of *al-Jawahir* said: 'This is what is stated in the *Risala*', and has added: 'The *jadh'a* is an animal of one year.' It has also been said that it refers to an 'animal of eight months', while others have said 'of ten months.'"

Ibn 'Ashir then goes on to say that if the number reaches twenty-five, then payment in kind is obligatory, i.e. a camel of two years. Then he informs us that one continues to pay this until the number reaches thirty five, after which a female camel of three years is to be paid. One continues to pay this up to forty five but when the number reaches forty six, a camel of four years is to be paid. One continues to pay this up to sixty. When the number reaches sixty one, a camel of five years is paid. One continues to pay this amount up to seventy five but when it reaches seventy six, two camels of three years are paid. One continues to pay this amount up to ninety but when it reaches ninety one, then two of four years are paid. One continues to pay this up to one hundred and twenty but when the number reaches one hundred and twenty one, three camels of three or two of four are paid. Any further information should be sought from another commentator as only the necessary information is given here, and no commentary is given."

BRANCH: al-Mawwaq said: "'Abd al-Mun'im said: 'If he pays a camel instead of sheep which is equal to them in worth, then it is acceptable.' Ibn al-'Arabi and al-Baji have said: 'It is not acceptable.' Ibn 'Arafa said: 'Al-Mazari's deeming payment of the price or value (of the livestock, instead of payment in kind) acceptable is improbable as assessment is made on the basis of payment in kind.' Muhammad Ibn 'Abd as-Salam has deemed the judgement of 'Abd al-Mun'im to be correct."

At-Hattab has transmitted these (words of al-Mawwaq's) and added: "One may question his saying 'this is improbable' as what he means is not the actual 'value' but rather that it is classed in this manner (i.e. payment of the sheep is not in kind but in the form of a camel of like value). Do you not see that the *fuqaha* have said (something similar) in the chapter on 'Distribution of the Zakat', namely, that it is not permitted to pay by 'value or worth' such that one pays in goods instead of in gold and silver."

NOTICE: there is a difference of opinion regarding the (payment of *zakat*) according to value. It has been said that it is not acceptable, and this is what Khalil holds to when he says '…or (payment of) the value is not acceptable.' This is what al-Hattab restricts himself to with regard to Khalil's words 'and the most correct (view, i.e. that of 'Abd al-Mun'im and Ibn 'Abd as-Salam, rather than al-Baji's and Ibn al-'Arabi's), is that a camel is acceptable (in payment for sheep or goats when the latter are not available)' saying: "…that is, as long as he only pays it instead of (the one) sheep which is due on the five (camels), and he does not (pay four such camels) on twenty four – for then it would clearly represent a payment based on value, and this is not permitted."

Al-Mawwaq said: "'Isa has reported from Ibn al-Qasim: 'If the slaughter of a sheep is his *zakat*, then it is acceptable, but not if he divides it up, in which case he should substitute it for another.' Ibn Rushd said: 'Ibn Habib has also transmitted something similar to this and this is the most evident judgement for if the value of it when slaughtered is less than when alive then he would (in effect) be paying for it with 'merchandise' ('*ard*) rather than in kind, and this is not acceptable according to Ibn al-Qasim.' Al-Baji said: 'The well known judgement it that it is not acceptable to make the payment on gold and silver in other than gold and silver.'"

Ibn al-Hattab said: "Branch: if a three year old she-camel is due and none is available then a four year old male camel may not be taken, whereas a three year old male camel may be taken for a two year old female; if a four year old female is due and two she-camels of three years are paid it is not acceptable, although it is for ash-Shafi'i – and this is stated in *adh-Dhakhira*."

His saying 'it is not acceptable' is based on the judgement that (a corresponding) value is not acceptable. Abu'l-Hasan said in *Ghayat al-Amani*: "He said in *at-Tawdih*: 'If a two year old she-camel and a three year old male camel are (both) available, then he should take only the she-camel as the latter forms the basis of the judgement: the owner of the camels must not give a three year old male camel and the *zakat* collector must not coerce him to give one.' However, there is a difference of opinion if they both accept that it should be taken. Ibn al-Qasim said in the *Mudawwana* that 'it is acceptable' while Ashhab has prohibited it. Al-Lakhmi said: 'the first judgement is more correct for it may well be that his (decision to) accept it (in payment) was taken out of consideration for the poor – either because (when sold) it would be worth more, or because if slaughtered, it would provide more meat as it is a bigger (animal).'" Payment in value is not permitted, but if it nevertheless happens, it is acceptable – this is the clear judgement of al-Hattab who comments on the words of Khalil 'and on one hundred and twenty one to (one hundred and) twenty nine, two she-camels of four years old (are due)' saying: "If the *zakat* collector takes better than is due but returns (some of) its value (in money as compensation) or he takes less (than is due) and takes (some extra money as compensation for the lack), then this is not permitted. However, if it nevertheless happens, then the well known judgement is that it is accepted; and likewise taking (all of) the value (in money) is not permitted but if it nevertheless happens, then the well known opinion is that it is accepted."

I say: "His judgement that taking some extra (payment) for what is lacking or returning (part of the value) for anything extra is accepted – although not permitted -is different from what Ibn 'Arafa holds to. The latter has mentioned three judgements in this regard, none of which correspond to this – if the copy (in my possession) is correct: 'There is a judgement that it is permitted and one that it is *makruh* if he pays better (than is due) or less and then takes something to compensate for what is better or makes up something (in the case of a lack); the third judgement, that it is not accepted, belongs to Malik, Ibn al-Qasim, together with Ashhab and Asbagh.'"

Ibn al-Hattab, commenting on Khalil's words 'it is permitted to pay gold for silver and vice versa' has also said: "It is stated in *an-Nawadir* in an explanation of how much *zakat* is given that 'there is no harm in putting together smelted lumps of gold with dinars or paying (the *zakat*) on dirhams (with smelted lumps) if there is a great need for the (dirhams); but if they pay the *zakat* on the dirhams, they should not pay it by exchanging them into dinars, or exchanging them into copper coins (*flous*) because of a great need (for the dirhams) amongst them; they may, however, put the smelted lumps together with the dirhams if they wish, and if they pay the (*zakat*) for them in copper, then this is wrong, but (the *zakat*) is accepted.'"

What he says with respect to the gold is contrary to the well-known judgement, while his words regarding the copper coins are in accordance with the well known judgement, namely that whoever pays according to the value (rather than in kind) is incorrect but nevertheless accepted – as more than one have declared. What is transmitted in *at-Tawdih* is different from what may be understood from the words of the Khalil at the end of the section: '(it is not accepted) if paid willingly (that is without opposition) to a ruler who is unjust in distributing it, or if paid willingly in value (rather than kind, i.e. something other than gold or silver)."

However, his saying that such (a transaction) 'is wrong' can be understood as prohibition, and this is what he holds to; and it is also possible that it indicates that it is *makruh* and this is expressed in the third judgement – and this is most likely as he has attributed it to *at-Tawdih* and what is mentioned in *at-Tawdih* is that it is *makruh*, as you will see shortly insha'Allah.

As for the third judgement, namely, that payment in value is *makruh*, al-Bannani said: "Shaykh Abu'l-Hasan has objected to what Khalil has mentioned, namely, that (the *zakat*) is unacceptable when paid willingly in value (rather than kind), arguing in this manner because he has followed Ibn al-Hajib and Ibn Bashir in this – and likewise the judgement of Ibn 'Arafa that the payment of goods instead of gold or silver is not satisfactory according to the well known judgement – since the author of *at-Tawdih* has also objected to it on the grounds that it is contrary to the *Mudawwana* saying: 'The well known opinion regarding paying according to value (rather than kind) is that it is *makruh* but not haram.' It is stated in the *Mudawwana*: 'and he should not pay for the *zakat* he owes on goods or foodstuffs (in money), and it is *makruh* for a man to buy (back) what he has given.'"

Thus he has classified this (transaction with the same judgement) as someone who buys back his *zakat*, and the well known judgement is that it is *makruh* not haram. He has mentioned this in order to object to the words of Ibn al-Hajib. Moreover, the words of Khalil 'and (it is not acceptable when paid) in value' is contrary to what the author of *at-Tawdih* holds to. Shaykh Sayyidi Abu'l-Hasan said: 'The most evident interpretation of his words is that what is contained in *at-Tawdih* and (in the discussion of) Muhammad ibn 'Abd as-Salam is the preferred judgement, and this is also supported by the fact that it is the preferred judgement of Ibn Rushd who says that "its being accepted is the most evident of the judgements" and by the fact that Ibn Yunus affirms him – as narrated by Shaykh Ahmad Shaykh Abu'l-Hasan.' As for the various (judgements) of Ibn 'Arafa, I have not seen them mentioned by anyone else."

Al-Mawwaq has related, commenting on the words of Khalil 'and (it is not acceptable when paid) in value', that Ibn al-Qasim said: "I do not like it if someone 'buys' what he gives (in *zakat*) even if it is after the agent (collecting it) has taken possession of it, but if he does nevertheless do it, then I do not see any harm in it." Ibn Rushd said: "Paying the value to the agent is *makruh* for two reasons: because it amounts to the 'return' of the *zakat* and because it might be worth less than paying (in kind) – and this would mean a loss with regard to the right of the poor (to it); as for the buying of the *zakat* from the agent after having handed it over to him, this is less *makruh* as it is only reprehensible on account of one (rather than two) reasons, namely it amounts to a 'return' of the *zakat*. However, it does not in fact truly amount to 'a return of the *zakat*' unless he were to buy it back from the poor to whom it was given; (one must also take into account that) the hadith (upon which this judgement is based) refers to something given (by 'Umar, may Allah be content with him,) voluntarily (in charity, rather than as obligatory *zakat*)"[1].

USEFUL POINT: Ibn Rihal has mentioned in the *Hashiya Mayyara 'ala't-Tuhfa*, when discussing 'the taking possession of the *zakat*': "It is not permitted, according to the latter generation of *'ulama*, meaning it is haram."

NOTICE: giving 'the value' is not justified by giving something better, like giving a two year old female cow for a two year old male cow, or in the case where a two year of she-camel is due, one better than it – this is stated by al-Hattab and al-Mawwaq. However, Muhammad said: "It is permitted for a female to be taken for a male cow if its owner is willing, and 'Isa has recorded hearing from Ibn al-Qasim that the Prophet, may the peace and blessings of Allah be upon him, sent a man out to collect *zakat*. The man came to someone who had to pay a two year old she-camel but the latter said to him: 'By Allah, I shall not be the first to give an animal that cannot be milked or cannot be

---

1   See al-Bukhari, *Bab az-Zakat*, p.331, no.567.

ridden' and he gave him a larger camel. The Prophet, may the peace and blessings of Allah be upon him, then ordered him to accept it and made a *du'a* for him that he be blessed in his camels and (as a result) they grew (strong) and multiplied. He said: 'To this day, he is known as "the man for whose camels the Prophet, may the peace and blessings of Allah be upon him, made a *du'a*"'"

Ibn Rushd said: "The age of the animals is (used in) defining the amount (to be paid) and any (animal) older (than what is due) is not taken unless the owner willingly accepts. This matter is not like the number of *rak'ats* of the *salat* – the age or number (of the animals) cannot be added to, and there is no difference of opinion in this."

BRANCH: al-Mawwaq said, commenting on the words of Khalil 'for every five camels, a female sheep': "One may understand from this that a *female* sheep is stipulated as payment for the *zakat* on camels, and likewise, a female sheep as payment for the *zakat* of sheep and goats. However, mention will be made below that *a male or female* may be taken, according to Khalil, and this is the *madhhab* of Ibn al-Qasim and Ashhab, while Ibn al-Qussar has stipulated a female in both cases; as for discriminating between the two kinds (of livestock, i.e. between camels and sheep and goats, I have not come across this (judgement)."

ISSUE: Ibn al-Hattab has also said, commenting on Khalil on this subject: "If the two types (of livestock, i.e. sheep and goats) are not to be found in one area, then Ibn 'Arafa has transmitted from one of the Shaykhs of al-Mazari that 'it is demanded that they be acquired from the area in the immediate vicinity.' The most evident judgement is that one takes into account the most prevalent livestock of this (neighbouring area) just as one would in the area in question (i.e. taking payment in sheep if sheep are the norm, and goats if they are the norm) – as discussed above – and Allah knows best."

ISSUE: Ibn al-Hattab has also said: "If the collector assesses the livestock and then they are all lost – either by a natural calamity from Allah, or seized unlawfully – and there is no *zakat* to pay on the amount remaining, then Ibn Yunus said: 'Their owner has nothing to pay as they were no longer his responsibility and he did not cause their loss – and this is what Abu Umran has stated. However, it has also been said that the *zakat* on what the *zakat* collector has assessed must be paid and if they were lost through some natural calamity from Allah, exalted is He, then he takes it from what remains – even if nothing (of any considerable amount) remains. It has also been said, regarding gold and silver (the major part of which) is lost or destroyed that the poor have a right to a tenth of what remains as they 'owned a share' with him with respect to what was lost. Thus what remains is to be divided (according to this), and it also makes sense to apply this (judgement) to livestock. However, the first (judgement) is more correct as they are not 'partners' in the true sense of the word, and so this indicates that they do not have a share in it."

ISSUE: al-Hattab said: "Ibn 'Arafa said: 'As for livestock which has been seized illegally and which is returned after (several) years, then according to Ibn al-Qasim, *zakat* is paid on it for one year only. However, he also has another judgement, along with Ashhab, to the effect that it should be paid for each year and al-Lakhmi has explained this by arguing that the first (judgement) is based on the case where the yield or returns (of the livestock) have not been returned as well; in another interpretation he has also inferred that this refers to the case where he will (pay *zakat*) on the gold or silver he receives for the future sale (of this livestock). Zakat is paid on date palms seized illegally when they are returned with their produce – as long as *zakat* has not already been paid on them."

عِجْلٌ تَبِيعٌ فِي ثَلَاثِينَ بَقَرْ

مُسِنَّةٌ فِي أَرْبَعِينَ تُسْتَطَرْ

197 on thirty cows, a two year old cow (is paid), on forty a three year old,

وَهَكَذَا مَا ارْتَفَعَتْ...

198 and so on ...

Mayyara said: "Ibn 'Ashir has informed us that on thirty cows, a calf of two years is paid, and this rate remains the same up to thirty nine. When forty is reached, a three year old is to be paid. The rate remains the same for more than this: for every thirty more, a two year old is paid, and for every forty more, a three year old."

Al-Mawwaq has related: "Ibn Bashir said: 'There is a difference of opinion as to the age of the calf to be paid on thirty: it is said it is two years old, while it is also said that it refers to one which has completed two and begun its third year. Ibn Yunus has ascribed the first judgement to Ibn Habib and the second to Ibn Nafi.' Al-Lakhmi said: 'The judgement of Ibn Habib is more correct and this is the well known opinion according to those knowledgeable of the Arabic language.'"

Then he goes on to say, commenting on the words of Khalil 'on forty, a cow of three years': "Ibn Yunus has reported from Ibn Habib: '...a cow entering its fourth year.' Al-Lakhmi has related from Abu Sha'ban: 'one which has completed two years (and has begun its third year', and this is correct. Ibn Yunus has ascribed this (latter judgement) to Ibn Nafi' while al-Baji has ascribed it to al-Qadi (Ibn Rushd)."

ثُمَّ الْغَنَمْ

شَاةٌ لِأَرْبَعِينَ مَعَ أُخْرَى تُضَمّ

... As for sheep or goats, one sheep or goat is paid on forty, and then another is added

فِي وَاحِدٍ عِشْرِينَ يَتْلُو وَمِئَةْ

وَمَعْ ثَمَانِينَ ثَلَاثٌ مُجْزِئَةْ

199 when one hundred and twenty one is reached; three is enough with eighty more (i.e. on two hundred and one upwards);

وَأَرْبَعاً خُذْ مِنْ مِئِينَ أَرْبَعْ

شَاةٌ لِكُلِّ مِائَةٍ إِنْ تُرْفَعْ

200 take four on four hundred, and then one sheep for every hundred from then on.

Mayyara said: "He has informed us that there is no *zakat* on less than forty sheep and that when forty is reached, then a male or female yearling is to be paid, according to the well known view. The *lam* in the words *li-arba'in* indicates a point or limit, namely the 'limit of forty', as in the phrase *li-yawm il-qiyama* ('on the Day..') in the words of, exalted is He: '*We will set up the Just Balance on the Day of Rising*'[1]; in the same manner as the *lam* – here translated as 'of' – in His words: 'Those who are *kafir* say of those who have iman "*if there was any good in it they would not have beaten us to it*"[2] for the 'of' (*lam*) specifies and delineates them in particular. Thus he continues to pay one sheep up to a hundred and twenty but when the number reaches a hundred and twenty one he pays two sheep on them."

1   al-Anbiya – The Prophets: 47.
2   al-Ahqaf – The Sand Dunes: 10

NOTICE: Ibn 'Arafa said: "The (*zakat* collector) should only take a yearling sheep or goat. Ibn Habib said 'a sheep which has completed one year (and is entering its second).' Ibn Wahb said 'ten months old.' Another said 'eight months' and yet another 'six months.'" Al-Buhayri said in *Sharh al-Irshad*: "There is a difference of opinion regarding the (age of the) sheep to be paid on sheep or goats, and camels. Ibn al-Qasim and Ashhab have said 'a one or two year old, male or female sheep or goat is acceptable.' This latter is stated in *al-Jawahir* and is the well known opinion." The well known opinion is that it should have completed its first year (*jadh'*), although one which has completed it second year (*thiny*) may also be given.

ISSUE: Ibn al-Hattab said, commenting on the words of Khalil about the transactions of association (*khalta*) 'as long as (each of those associated with the transaction) have made the intention (to join with each other): "ISSUE: at the beginning of the section on the 'Zakat of Livestock' in the *Utbiyya* the author said: 'He was asked about a man who gave his son a gift of some of his sheep but who kept them for him (with his own sheep) and branded them: if he reckoned them together with his own sheep, then he would have to pay two sheep (in *zakat*) but if he kept them separate, then he would only have to pay one. He replied: "He should not put them together with his sheep." He was then asked: "What if he does put them together with his own and he tells the *zakat* collector when he comes 'I have only such-and-such a number and the rest I have given to my son' should the *zakat* collector believe him?" He replied: "He should believe him if there is evidence that he has indeed given them (to his son).""' Ibn Rushd said: "What he means is that he should believe (him when he says) that he has allotted them (to his son) if he sees evidence of his having given (them to his son) – even if he has not yet (physically) allotted them." The most manifest meaning of the judgement of Sahnun is that he should believe what he says even if he supplies him with no proof at all, and this (judgement of Sahnun's) is (based on the legal principle of discretionary opinion, that is) his juristic preference (*istihsan*) – not on analogy – as the (father) was affirming the sheep (now) belonged to his (son) and (as a consequence) was claiming that *zakat* was no longer payable on them.

ISSUE: al-Hattab said: "Sahnun was asked about someone who grants a man a thousand dirhams but (only) sets them aside (for him): years go by without the person to whom he gave them taking possession of them. He replied: 'If he does (finally) take possession of them, then he must wait until a year has elapsed before paying (*zakat* on them), and he does not have to pay anything for the years which have passed; if he does not take possession of them at all, then they are returned to their owner and he pays the *zakat* on them for however many years have passed.' Ibn Rushd said in *an-Nawadir* relating from Ibn al-Qasim from a narration of Sahnun from the latter: 'If the person to whom they have been given takes possession of them, then *he* must wait for a year to elapse on them and the obligation to pay the *zakat* (for the years passed) is not removed from him.' The reason for Sahnun's judgement is that when the person gave the dinars and the person to whom he had given them did not take possession of them, then (the validity of) this *sadaqa* remains conditional upon his taking possession of it. Thus when he takes possession of it, ownership of it is transferred from the possession of the person who has given it *from the day he gave it*, and he does not have to pay the *zakat* on it (for the years passed). The reason for the judgement of Ibn al-Qasim is that the person to whom the dinars have been given may either except or decline – what the person giving them had made an obligation upon himself to give: if he does accept them, then it becomes an (immediate) obligation for the donor to hand them over to him. Just as *zakat* must be paid only on receipt, so ownership of the property is *only* transferred from him by this acceptance (and actual receipt of the money).' He then goes on to say: 'If what is given is such that there is a yield on it (in the case of animals), then the yield according to the judgement of Ibn al-Qasim belongs to the person giving it up to the day when the other accepts (and takes physical possession of it) – if he accepts; and according to the judgement of Sahnun, it belongs to the person he gives it to – if he accepts.'"

وَحَوْلُ الْأَرْبَاحِ وَنَسْلٍ كَالْأُصُولْ
وَالطَّارِي لَا عَمَّا يُزَكَّى أَنْ يَحُولْ

201 The *hawl* (elapsing of the year) on any profit or offspring is as the original (capital or livestock), but the 'year' has to elapse on anything suddenly acquired (as a gift, sale or inheritance, if – when added to other wealth in one's possession below the *nisab* – the total amounts to the *nisab*) – although if *zakat* is already due on what (is in one's possession as the *nisab* has been reached and some sudden acquisition is added to it) then no (further) elapsing of a year (is necessary).

Mayyara said: "He has mentioned three matters in this line: the first, the elapse of the year on the *profit* of wealth corresponds to the elapse of year on the original wealth. Profit, as Ibn 'Arafa said, 'is an increase in the value of the article sold through trade with respect to the original price.' His saying 'an increase in the value' indicates an increase in the price not an increase in the thing sold itself – for example it does not apply (in the case of animals whose value increases) as they grow. His mention of the words 'trade' excludes any profit on the price of something owned for personal use; in this case he must wait a year to elapse on the thing – after its coming into his possession – before paying *zakat*. Thus he excludes it here, even if it is called 'profit' (when sold for a higher price.) An example of this is when someone buys something for personal use for ten dinars and then sells it for fifteen – and this (judgement) applies irrespective of whether the original (value of the thing which is sold) for a profit constitutes a *nisab* or not. An example of when it does constitute a *nisab* would be when someone who has twenty dinars in his possession for ten months then buys something with it and this thing remains with him for two months and then he sells it for thirty dinars: in this case he pays *zakat* on the original, namely the twenty – and this is clear – but he also pays *zakat* on the profit, namely the ten, as the elapse of the year is reckoned in accordance with the original, namely, the twenty for the profit is assumed to be 'hidden' as a potential in the original from the beginning of the year in question. This judgement is based on the assumption that something as yet non-existent is in fact existent. An example where the *nisab* is lacking would be in the case of someone who has a dinar which has been in his possession for part of the year in question. The person then buys something with it and sells it when the full year has elapsed for twenty dinars – and so he pays *zakat*. Again one assumes that the profit, namely the nineteen dinars, was potential in it, that is 'hidden' in the original from the beginning of the year.

Issue: the second matter mentioned in this line is that the year which elapses on the offspring of livestock corresponds to the year of the livestock itself, that is, the mother animals in question. Thus whoever has thirty sheep or goats for example, as the elapse of the year approaches, and they have offspring and they become forty in number – even if just one day before the year has elapsed, or after the completion of the year but before the coming of the *zakat* collector by a day – then the *zakat* must be paid on them. Again, the elapse of the year for the offspring corresponds to the elapse of the year of the mother and so the judgement in this case is the same as in the case of the profit – i.e. *zakat* is paid on that which was not existent but potential. So if a person has eighty (head) and they give birth just before the elapse of the year and they become one hundred and twenty one in all, then the *zakat* is obligatory – and two sheep are to be paid. Thus the elapse of the year with regard to the offspring is the same as that of the mothers, irrespective of whether the mothers had constituted a *nisab* or not – and the same applies to cows and camels. The author of the *Risala* said: 'The elapse of the year on the profit of wealth corresponds to that of the wealth itself, and likewise that of the offspring of livestock corresponds to that of their mothers.'"

NOTICE: Reflect as to whether one may also infer – from his examples where the *nisab* is reached before the elapse of the year – that he does not have to pay *zakat* if the *nisab* is not reached until *after* the year has elapsed. 'Abd al-Baqi (az-Zurqani) and Ibn al-'Amash have differed regarding this matter. The unequivocal judgement of az-Zurqani – and that which his commentators also accept, given their silence on the matter – is that *zakat* is not obligatory unless the year has elapsed. Thus, on this basis, whoever comes into possession of thirty sheep in Ramadan, for example, and then the year elapses on them and their number is the same but then in Shawwal they have offspring and become forty in number, then he does not have to pay the *zakat* until the next Ramadan. Ibn al-'Amash is of a different opinion saying he does have to pay *zakat* at this juncture. The wording of az-Zurqani's judgement corresponds to that of Khalil who says '…likewise, (if a new *hawl* begins when the *zakat* collector) passes (in order to take the *zakat*) from the (animals – but he finds) they do not constitute a *nisab* and then he returns and find the *nisab* has been reached (on account of offspring or an acquisition, then the *hawl* is reckoned from the first day he passed not the second).' Az-Zurqani's mention of *istiqbal* – 'waiting for the elapse of the year to receive payment of the *zakat*' is similar in meaning to Khalil's 'likewise when the *zakat* collector passes…' that is, when he returns to find the *nisab*, which had been lacking, has now been reached by the addition of the birth of offspring or the exchange of some of his livestock for another kind such that the *nisab* is reached, say in camels, or by the acquisition (of additional animals) through a gift, charity or purchase. In this latter case, according to the agreement (of the *'ulama*), he should wait until the year has elapsed basing his reckoning on the livestock he first had and on the day the *zakat* collector first passed – for this is in effect the beginning of the 'year' – not from the day he returned or from the day when the *nisab* is completed after the new offspring or acquisition and the original livestock have been put together. This is because the completing of the *nisab* by way of the offspring (or acquisition) is after the elapse of the year and after they have been added (to the original), even if they were few in number and this occurs just before the elapse of the year. His mention of 'after they have been added (to the original)' refers to what Khalil has also indicated with his words '… and (if this *nisab* is reached) by his adding any (eventual) profit (through the increase of the number of livestock) before the end of the year, even by one single day – although this addition is not calculated if added to a number of animals below the minimum *nisab*.'

The gist of his words is that the adding of offspring to (a number of livestock which constitutes) less than the *nisab* is conditional upon the offspring having arrived before the elapse of the year; if they arrived after the elapse of the year on the mothers and they are less than the *nisab*, then *zakat* is not paid on them until the year has elapsed on them in the future.

Commenting on his saying 'and anything suddenly acquired (as a gift or inheritance for example), then the year does not have to elapse on it if *zakat* is due on the (other wealth in one's possession)', Mayyara said: "This is the third matter contained in the above mentioned line of Ibn 'Ashir's – after mention of the judgement regarding an increase (in livestock) by the arrival of offspring and of the reckoning of the elapse of the year with that of their mothers, irrespective of whether the mothers constitute a *nisab* or not. Here he is explaining the judgement whereby he unexpectedly acquires (livestock) other than by offspring, either by gift or inheritance. Thus he informs us that *zakat* must be paid on any livestock unexpectedly acquired in addition to what was (originally) non zakatable as it was less than the *nisab* – that is, *zakat* is paid on the addition and on what he already had, but on condition that the year elapses on the whole taken together. Thus he waits for the year to pass on it all – both on what he had and what was unexpectedly acquired – from the moment that the *nisab* was completed.

The author of al-Buhayri, commenting on the words of *al-Irshad* 'anyone who suddenly acquires extra livestock of the same kind which constitutes the *nisab* or less then he should wait until the year has elapsed' said: "…that is, anyone who possesses livestock and then acquires more of the same kind, irrespective of whether this is acquired through inheritance, a gift or purchase, irrespective of whether it constitutes a *nisab* or below it, then he adds the second (lot) to the first, and he pays *zakat* on the whole according to the elapse of the first year even if his coming into possession of the second lot occurred just one day before the elapse of the first year or before the arrival of the *zakat* collector – on condition that the original (lot with him) constituted a *nisab*." It is stated in the *Mudawwana*: "If the first is less than a *nisab*, then he should await until a year has elapsed for all of it – from the day he took possession of the second, additional amount.."

If one were to point out a certain inconsistency with what has been mentioned above regarding the acquisition of something additional with respect to gold and silver and ask what is the difference between taking possession of an additional amount of gold and silver which constitutes a *nisab* and then taking possession of an addition which does not constitute a *nisab* – given that each addition is reckoned according to its own particular 'year' and the second is not put with the first – then one might answer by saying that the *'ulama* have distinguished between the two in three ways, as mentioned by Khalil in his *Tawdih*: the first – and I shall restrict myself to it for fear of tiring the reader – is that if each addition (in the case) of livestock is reckoned in accordance with its own particular 'year', then this would necessarily lead to a contradicting of the *nisab* which has been stipulated by the Prophet, may the peace and blessings of Allah be upon him. An example of this would be where someone who has forty sheep or goats and half of the year has elapsed, then acquires an additional forty – and then a further forty: if each addition were to be reckoned in accordance with its own particular year, then he would pay three sheep on one hundred and twenty and this is contrary to what the Prophet has declared, may the peace and blessings of Allah be upon him.

ISSUE: Ibn al-Hattab said, commenting on the words of Khalil '(a first profit) which is below (the *nisab*) is added (even after completion of the *nisab*, to the second)': "If he has less than the *nisab* in his possession and the year elapses, and then he buys goods with it and sells them after a day or a month or two, then he must pay *zakat* on all of it on the day he sells and its 'year' is reckoned from that day (of selling); but if he already has the *nisab* and the year elapses and he does not pay *zakat* on it and then he buys goods with it and then sells them after the elapse of the year – by just a day or by two months – then he pays *zakat* on the wealth on which the year has elapsed and he does not pay *zakat* on the profit except after the elapse of the year from the day that *zakat* became obligatory on the original – this has been recorded in the *Sama' Ibn al-Qasim* in the 'Book of Zakat' and Allah knows best."

He also goes on to say after discussing the matter of *fawa'id* (profits): "If the 'year' arrives on the first – and it is below the *nisab* – but then the *nisab* is reached with the profit on it before the 'year' has passed on the second, then the judgement in this regard is that *zakat* is paid on the first when the *nisab* is reached and its 'year' is reckoned from that day; and the second is reckoned according to its own 'year.'"

I SAY: "Some of the *'ulama* of our time have said these two matters correspond to the two contradictory judgements mentioned by az-Zurqani namely that 'the judgement regarding the putting together of the offspring of livestock with the original (livestock) – which is below the *nisab* – applies when this occurs *before* the elapse of the year, although some have argued that this is contrary to the judgement regarding profit on wealth.'"

وَلَا يُزَكَّى وَقَصٌ مِنَ النَّعَمْ

كَذَاكَ مَا دُونَ النِّصَابِ وَلْيَعُمَّ

202 No (extra) *zakat* is paid on amounts which (are above one rate but which) fall short of the (next) rate of livestock, nor on anything below the *nisab* in general,

وَعَسَلٌ فَاكِهَةٌ مَعَ الْخُضَرْ

إِذْ هِيَ فِي الْمُقْتَاتِ مِمَّا يُدَّخَرْ

203 nor on honey, soft fruit and vegetables – for *zakat* is paid on storable, basic commodities.

Mayyara said: "Ibn 'Ashir has informed us that no *zakat* is payable on amounts which fall between the set rates and that it is not due on less than the *nisab* with respect to everything zakatable, that is, on gold and silver, on agricultural produce and livestock – and this he has referred to by 'in general'; and that it is not payable on honey, soft fruit or vegetables as *zakat* is paid on grains and fruit which are storable and constitute staple foods, and the latter are not of this kind. There is agreement that no *zakat* is payable for an amount falling between the set rates in all cases other than 'transactions based on association' (*khalta*), and Allah knows best." Then he goes on to say after a discussion: "Non-payment of *zakat* on amounts which fall between the set rates only apply in the case of livestock, as Ibn 'Ashir has stated, but as for the *zakat* of gold and silver, and agricultural produce, this (judgement) does not apply; indeed (payment is made on) anything over the *nisab*. There is agreement (as to the above-mentioned judgements) regarding gold and silver, agricultural produce, and livestock – in other than cases of 'transactions in association.' That no *zakat* is payable in the case of non-staple and non-storable basic foodstuffs, like vegetables or fruit which is not stored at all, like apples and the like, or which are stored, like walnuts and pomegranates, or which are stored as staples, but only rarely, like figs, is the well known judgement. Thus his saying 'storable' is conditional upon its also being a 'staple' (honey, for example, being storable but not a staple): it is, therefore not obligatory on honey, fruit and vegetables because the obligation applies only to what is staple and storable, that is basic foodstuffs in common use."

NOTICE: Mayyara has here mentioned the restrictions and stipulations regarding the *zakat* of 'transactions undertaken in association' – which are common set down in the registers of the people (engaged in such activity). Although this commentary is not intended for (the elaboration of) such (detail) – and for this reason we have avoided talking about it – we shall nevertheless deal with a part of this (subject), if Allah wishes and concentrate on the most important matters, not those which are by nature obvious. Khalil said: "People associated in a transaction involving livestock are considered as one single owner with regard to the amount on which the *zakat* becomes obligatory – that is with regard to the age of the animal to be taken (as payment) and to it kind – on condition that each of those involved in the association have formed the intention to come together, that each is a free man, Muslim, that each possesses at least the minimum zakatable *nisab*, that the year has elapsed, that the two or more (associates) enjoy together the possession or use of the major part of the following five: the place where the animals shelter (during the day), the water (supply for the livestock), the place where they spend the night, the pasture as long as both associates permit its use for the other, the male animal used as a stud (for the whole flock or herd). As for these associates from whose livestock the *zakat* is taken, the one pays in association with the other, that is, each pays in proportion to what each possesses of the joint *nisab* – even if one of them has livestock whose number falls between the set amounts. One proceeds in like manner (with regard to reckoning the *zakat*) when the *zakat* collector interprets the rules of his *madhhab* such that the *zakat* becomes due from both only when the animals have reached the *nisab after the conclusion of the association*; or he interprets that *zakat* should be taken from the *nisab* of them both *before the association* – even if the livestock of none of the two reaches the *nisab* (individually); or he judges it should be taken from the *nisab* of just one of them – and then increases the number or value of the animals to be paid because of this association. However, all this is invalid (on his part) if he imposes this (assessment) unjustly, or by coercion, or if the *nisab* has not in fact been reached for both of them. Thus if the owner of eighty sheep or goats enters in association with someone who has himself eighty and is in association with two others who each possess forty, or with someone who possesses eighty but who only holds forty (of the eighty) in association with one other person, then in the first case, he pays one sheep, and in the second a half of the value." Ibn al-Mawwaq has related, commenting on Khalil's words 'people associated in a transaction involving livestock': "Ibn Yunus said that 'associate', with regard to sheep and goats, refers to the person who does not join his companion in watching over the animals but co-operates with him in assembling (the flock) and on other occasions." Malik said: "… the sheep and goats may be distinguished from those of his companion (in the case of a *khalta* association) but a partner (in a partnership) does take a part in watching over them and his sheep and goats cannot be distinguished from those of his partner."

Al-Mawwaq has also said, commenting on Khalil's words 'and that the year has elapsed': "'Isa has reported hearing from Ibn al-Qasim: 'Whoever pays *zakat* on his sheep and goats and forms an association with another man six months after paying this *zakat* and then the *zakat* collector comes in this month in which he had formed an association with his sheep and goats – and *zakat* is obligatory on those of his associate – then *zakat* is payable on the sheep and goats of his associate but he does not have to pay the *zakat* until the year has elapsed from the day his associate had paid the *zakat*; unless, that is, he removes his sheep and goats from the (association) before this, in which case he would be on a par with someone who had made an acquisition of sheep and goats or purchased them and they had remained in his possession for several months before the arrival of the *zakat* collector – for there would be no *zakat* payable until he returns the following year."

Ibn Rushd said: "This is as he said: two men who have formed an association do not have to pay the *zakat* of the association until a year has elapsed on the livestock of each of them: thus if the livestock of one of them is one hundred and the year elapses on them, and the other livestock are fifty in number, but the year has not elapsed on them and the *zakat* collector takes two sheep from them both together, then – if he has taken the two from the person with the hundred – he is due nothing from his associate with the fifty as one (of the two) he had to pay anyway and (payment of) the second (is considered to have been) imposed unjustly on him; if, however, both have been taken from the sheep and goats of his associate with the fifty, then the latter has recourse for one (of the animals) from his associate with the hundred and the second (is considered to have been) imposed unjustly on him; if one has been taken from the person with the hundred and one from the person with fifty, then the person with the fifty has no recourse to his associate with the hundred regarding the one taken from him as its payment has been imposed unjustly and cannot be reclaimed, and there is no difference of opinion in this, other than in the case where *zakat* is paid on the basis of an association but the livestock of one of them is below the *nisab*."

He has also said, commenting on his words 'this is invalid if he has imposed this unjustly or by coercion': "Ibn Bashir said: 'If one of them has the *nisab* but the other does not and the *zakat* collector acts contrary to the rules and takes from them both – claiming that they each may have recourse to the other (if they are not content with the assessment) – then the person whose sheep or goats have been taken is regarded as having been afflicted by loss (*museeba*) (beyond his control) – if the tax collector *intended* to act unjustly or by coercion in this instance. Commenting on Khalil's words 'and if the *nisab* has not been reached for both of them' Ibn Bashir said: 'If they come together and neither of them has a *nisab* and the total resulting from their coming together (for the association) also does not constitute a *nisab*, then it would be a completely illegal for the *zakat* collector to take (any payment) and it is to be regarded as a loss which has afflicted them (which is beyond their control).'"

The author of *al-Irshad* said: "If the *zakat* is taken from the *nisab* of what (is assessed after the portions of both associates) have been placed together on the basis of what (the collector) infers (is the payment to be made on the total *nisab* without distinguishing between the proportional assessment of each associate), then they should restitute to each other what is due in accordance with what they possess." Al-Buhayri said in his commentary: "An example of this is if four people have forty sheep, each possessing ten, then if the *zakat* collector takes payment from them (but without exacting a sheep from each, rather taking them as he finds them) – basing his action on *taqlid* of the *madhhab* of those who hold to such (practice) or because he himself is among the people of *ijtihad* (and has judged this practice valid) – then his (assessment) has the force of law and is on a par with a judgement made by a ruler in matters of *ijtihad* which cannot be annulled." He said in *al-Irshad*: "If he does not hold to such a practice then payment is (only exacted) in proportion to what each possesses." Al-Buhayri said in his commentary: "that is, if the *zakat* collector is not making *taqlid* – with respect to the two (above mentioned) matters – of one of the Imams and he himself is not of the people of *ijtihad*, then any sheep which are not legally obligated are regarded as having been seized unlawfully. However, there is no recourse for recovering them; rather their seizure is regarded as a loss afflicting the associate in question over which he has no control." What is meant by 'the two matters' is the *zakat* collector's interpreting the judgement (of assessment) as permission to take from the *nisab* of both of them or from one of them and to increase payment in the case of association.

The gist of the discussion of the above *'ulama* is that what is meant by the 'inference' of the *zakat* collector is that he is one of the people of *ijtihad* and the action he takes is the result of his *ijtihad* or the result of his making *taqlid* of someone from among the people of *ijtihad*; otherwise he would be acting unjustly and his action would be regarded as an illegal seizure – in which case this (payment) is regarded as a loss to be borne by the person from whom it was taken – and he is not owed anything by his associate. This then constitutes a clear rejection of those among the *'ulama* of our time who argue that if the *zakat* collector takes a sheep or camel or anything else illegally, then the associate must (also) contribute – or indeed that his tribe or family is legally obligated. This is clearly incorrect and one must make *tawba* from this, and success is by Allah.

NOTICE: The *zakat* of an association is conditional upon the 'year' of both (associates) being the same. If their two 'years' differ, then each of them pays his *zakat* separately. Ibn Shas has stated this in *al-Jawahir* as is also mentioned in *Hashiya at-Tawudi*, in the works of al-Hattab and al-Khurshi, in Abu'l-Hasan's *Ghayat al-Amani* and the work of ad-Dardir – may Allah benefit us by them. Moreover this (judgement) is accepted by ad-Dasouqi, Shaykh al-Amir and al-Khurshi and others. We had initially misunderstood the matter and misinterpreted the import of the above-mentioned discussion of al-Mawwaq, and Allah knows best.

NOTICE: Alif-lam-mim-sad has made no mention of the *zakat* of *waqf* but Khalil has mentioned it saying: 'Zakat is paid on gold and silver which has been set aside as a *waqf* for making loans, likewise on vegetables (grains and fruit designated as a *waqf* (to be distributed), or animals (for their milk or wool or as transport) or on their offspring – either for the benefit of a mosque (for example) or for persons who have not been specified explicitly; it is also payable by the person who owns the *waqf* if he is managing the distribution of its proceeds; in the case of individuals (within the *waqf*), they pay when each has a *nisab*.' Al-Mawwaq has noted, commenting on his words '*zakat* is paid on gold and silver which has been set aside as a *waqf* for making loans': "Ibn Rushd said: 'As for *zakat* which has become obligatory on camels, cows, sheep and goats and on dinars, dirhams, gold or silver ore or nuggets, then there is no difference of opinion that *zakat* is due on all of it, each year, that is, on *waqf* property whose profit or produce has been designated for any good purpose, irrespective of whether it is held in *waqf* for specific persons or for the poor or travellers (in general)." Malik said in this respect: "Whoever sets aside a hundred dinars (as a fund to be used) for the purpose of loans or donates a camel to be used in the way of Allah either as transport and (as a means of income from the sale of) its offspring, then *zakat* has to be paid." Al-Lakhmi said: "As for dirhams which have been given as a *waqf* in order to make loans, *zakat* is not paid on them if they are loaned out and exist (in effect only as) a debt (owing to the *waqf*) until possession of them is taken again, that is if possession of their *nisab* is taken – irrespective of whether the *waqf* is for specific persons or unknown persons. The person who borrows them must pay *zakat* as long as the (return of the loan) remains his responsibility and he has enough to discharge his obligation – as with all debts; and if possession is taken of it (from the borrower), then *zakat* is paid on the basis of it being in the property of the *waqf* for one year."

He has also said, commenting on his words 'likewise on vegetables (grains and fruit designated as a *waqf* (to be distributed), or animals (for their milk and wool, or as transport) or on their offspring – either for the benefit of a mosque (for example) or for persons who have not been specified explicitly': "As for designating vegetables a *waqf* for the poor, for specific persons or for people who are not specified, then Malik said in this regard: 'Zakat is paid on gardens which have been set aside as *waqf* in the way of Allah or for a specific (group of) people.' Sahnun said: 'Those specified and those not specified are alike – for if five *wasqs* are produced, then *zakat* is payable.' Ibn Yunus said: 'This is the most evident judgement of the *Mudawwana* and the reason for this is that those for whom the *waqf* has been made own the use of the gardens but do not own it such that they may sell or bequeath it; and the reward for it (with Allah) continues for the person who made the *waqf* and so it is *as if* the *zakat* is on his property.' Ibn Rushd said: 'If date gardens and vineyards have been made *waqf* for persons who have not been specified – like "the poor" or Bani Zahra or Bani Tameem – then there is no difference of opinion that *zakat* is paid by the "owner" of the *waqf* on the fruit produced and that the *zakat* is due on the produce if the whole of it reaches the minimum necessary zakatable amount.' There is a difference of opinion however if it has been made a *waqf* for specific persons. Ibn al-Qasim said in the *Mudawwana*: 'Zakat is also paid on it by the owner of the *waqf* and this (judgement) is based on the principle outlined in the "Book of Waqf", namely, that whoever dies from among those for whom the *waqf* has been made – before the fruit has ripened – then those who would normally inherit from him do not receive his share and it returns to its owners.' Ibn Yunus and Ibn Rushd do not stipulate here that the owner is responsible for distributing (the benefits or produce of the *waqf*). As for designating animals or their offspring as *waqf*, this has been already been mentioned above regarding the passage in the *Mudawwana* which speaks of the person who gives a camel in the way of Allah. Al-Lakhmi said: 'If the *waqf* consists of camels or a sheep, that is the use of their milk or wool, then *zakat* is payable on all of them by the owner of what has been given in *waqf* as long as they reach the *nisab*, irrespective of whether the *waqf* is for a specific group or one what is not named.'"

He has further said, commenting on the words of Khalil 'if the owner is responsible for distributing (the produce or benefit of) it': "It has already been pointed out above that according to Ibn Yunus the most evident judgement in the *Mudawwana* – and the statement to this effect is recorded by Ibn Rushd – is that there is no difference between making a *waqf* of a garden for a specific (group of people) or for an unspecified (group), and that making a *waqf* for someone specific has not been stipulated as a condition (of *waqf*). Al-Lakhmi said: 'If a garden has been made a *waqf* for a specific group of people and they themselves irrigate it and are responsible for it, then anyone whose portion reaches the *nisab* of five *wasqs* must pay *zakat*; anyone whose portion does not amount to this does not pay; but if the owner of the garden irrigates and is responsible for it and he divides the produce (himself), then *zakat* is paid if the whole of it amounts to five *wasqs*. If someone makes forty sheep a *waqf* for four other persons, each being assigned ten, then *zakat* is still payable as he has made over (only) the use of them while the sheep themselves still belong to him. This is other than in the case of the *waqf* of date palms for there is no *zakat* payable on the palms themselves, rather the *zakat* is on the fruit – and this is what has been given. Thus it is correct to assert that *zakat* is paid on the "ownership" of the fruit while *zakat* is paid on the sheep themselves as they remain *waqf* property and have not been given away as such. If a garden has been made a *waqf* for a mosque or mosques and the produce amounts in all to five *wasqs*, then *zakat* is paid even if each mosque only receives one *wasq* as its share – although Tawus and al-Makhoul have said that no *zakat* is payable on whatever has been made a *waqf* for the mosque. Their judgement is one based on analogy: either by arguing that that the (produce) remains the property of the person who made the *waqf* in which case no *zakat* is due as a dead person does not have to pay *zakat*; or that his property has been transferred from him, in which case *zakat* is also not payable as mosques are not required to pay *zakat*.' Ibn 'Arafa said: 'Al-Baji has stated clearly that the *waqf* remains the property of the person who made it and so *zakat* must be paid on gardens given as waqfs by the person who made the *waqf*.' Al-Lakhmi's statement that 'the action of making something a *waqf* removes its ownership from the person who made the *waqf*' is incorrect."

$$\text{وَيَحْصُلُ النِّصَابُ مِنْ صِنْفَيْنِ}$$

$$\text{كَذَهَبٍ وَفِضَّةٍ مِنْ عَيْنٍ}$$

204 The *nisab* may be reached by (putting together) two kinds (of zakatable items), like gold and silver in the case of money,

$$\text{وَالضَّأْنُ لِلْمِعْزِ وَيُحْتُّ لِلْعِرَابِ}$$

$$\text{وَبَقَرٌ إِلَى الْجَوَامِيسِ اصْطِحَابُ}$$

205 or (putting) sheep with goats, Bactrian with Arabian camels, cows with water buffalo,

$$\text{وَالْقَمْحُ لِلشَّعِيرِ لِلسُّلْتِ يُصَارُ}$$

$$\text{كَذَا الْقَطَانِي وَالزَّبِيبُ وَالثِّمَارُ}$$

206 wheat and barley with spelt, likewise pulses with legumes and currents with fruit.

Mayyara said: "He has informed us that the reaching of the *nisab* is not conditional upon it being of one kind or many kinds. Thus regarding the *zakat* of money, there is no difference between it being of one kind, like twenty dinars, or two hundred dirhams, or it being made up of both of them, that is, an (actual) portion (taken) from each (kind) rather than (a portion of each) based on (proportional) value. What is meant by a 'portion of each' is that each dinar is reckoned at a rate of ten dirhams even if the value (of a dinar) at any given time is less (than ten) or more – for example someone who has ten dinars and one hundred dirhams, or one hundred and fifty dirhams and five dinars, or fifty dirhams and fifteen dinars. The gist of this is that if he has half of the *nisab* from one kind of currency, then the existence of the *nisab* is conditional upon having the half from the other currency. With respect to the *zakat* of livestock, no distinction is made as to its being a *nisab* entirely composed of sheep, or all of goats, or of a mixture of them both." Examine the end of his discussion (for more details) – such matters are clear and unambiguous and not as such the subject of this work.

NOTICE: the author's judgement with respect to wheat and barley being 'of one kind' is the well known judgement within the *madhhab*, although as-Sayouri and 'Abd al-Hamid have differed with him in this; just as Ibn Lubaba has differed with respect to sheep and goats, arguing they constitute two kinds and that they may not be placed together for (the purposes of) *zakat*, as is stated in *al-Mi'yar* and other works.

His mention of 'pulses and legumes....' is clear. Khalil said: "pulses and legumes are put together and wheat and barley are put with spelt. If in a region, one of them is sown before the harvest of the other, then the middle (harvest) is added to either of the other two, not the first to the third." Ibn al-Hattab said in his confirmation of this: "that is, if the (crop) to be added to the other (in reckoning the *nisab*) is the second sowing before the harvest of the first — and the growing is in three periods and the third sowing takes place before the harvest of the first and second — then a portion of the third is added to each (of the two harvests); and if the sowing of the second is before the harvest of the first and the third is after the harvest of the first but before the harvest of the second, then the middle (harvest) is put with each of the other two individually: if the *nisab* is reached by this addition, then *zakat* is paid and if not, then it is not. Thus if two *wasqs* are harvested from the first and three *wasqs* from the second, he puts them together and pays *zakat*; and if two *wasqs* are harvested from the third, he also pays *zakat* on the third as the *nisab* is reached when this is added to the middle harvest. As for the *zakat* on the middle (harvest), this he had paid with the second. If each of the three yields two *wasqs*, then *zakat* is not due on the whole. If the first yields three *wasqs*, the second two *wasqs* and the third three, then it is due on the second and the third but not on the first."

Then he goes on to say: "Ibn Rushd said: 'If two *wasqs* are yielded on the first and three on the second — and we hold that they should be put together — then one must examine what happens to the first, that is, whether it remain or is it spent. If it remains (in storage), then *zakat* is paid on all of it and if it is spent or sold, then *zakat* is not paid — according to the *madhhab* of Ibn al-Qasim with regard to (the judgement of) two sets of profit — until the year has elapsed on the first of the harvests. Likewise, if two *wasqs* are produced from the third — and we say that it should be added to the middle harvest — then no *zakat* is payable, according to the *madhhab* of Ibn al-Qasim, as the middle does not constitute a *nisab* — after the *zakat* has been taken from the three *wasqs*: that is there is not enough to constitute a *nisab* when put with the third — so reflect on this and Allah knows best.'"

Then he goes on to say: "It is stated in *at-Taraz* that if grapes and olives are harvested at the same time or contiguous to each other, then they are put together; if one is harvested in winter and the other in summer, then they are not put together."

مَصْرِفُهَا الْفَقِيرُ وَالْمِسْكِينُ

غَازٍ وَعِتْقٌ عَامِلٌ مَدِينُ

207 It is distributed to the poor and the destitute, the ghazi warrior, in order to set (slaves) free, to the (zakat) agents and those in debt,

مُؤَلَّفُ الْقَلْبِ وَمُحْتَاجٌ غَرِيبٌ

أَحْرَارُ إِسْلَامٍ وَلَمْ يَقْبَلْ مُرِيبٌ

208 to those whose hearts may be brought closer (to Islam), the stranger in need, that is as long as they are free, Muslim and there is no doubt as to their state.

Mayyara said: "Abu 'Umar said: 'The poor person (*faqir*) is the person who does not have enough to live on, and the destitute (*miskeen*) is the person who has nothing at all. With respect to the poor and the destitute there are four conditions: firstly, that they are free: if given to someone who is not free, it is not accepted (as *zakat*); secondly, that they are Muslims.' It is stated in *at-Tawdih*: 'There is a difference of opinion as to whether it may be given to the people of sectarian beliefs – Ibn al-Qasim has permitted this, while Asbagh prohibited it; and likewise in the case of someone who has abandoned the *salat*, and it may well be that the differences are based on the difference of opinion regarding the judgement as to whether they are to be treated as *kafir* or not.'"

Then he goes on to say after a discussion: "The third condition is that the living expenses of the (poor or destitute person in question) is not (already) the obligatory responsibility of a person of means – irrespective of whether this is a personal responsibility undertaken willingly or a legal one which is binding (through blood ties for example), and irrespective of whether it is the person (of means responsible for their upkeep who is) giving the *zakat* or another: thus *zakat* is not to be given to a poor woman who has a rich husband, nor to a poor man or woman who both have a rich son."

I say: "…nor to a minor who is poor but whose father is of means, as the obligation for payment of his upkeep is his father's – because he is of means.

The author has not explained this possibility and has restricted himself to mention of the poor – but mention of it has priority given the difficulty of comprehending such details from the general principles. In *at-Tawdih* Ibn 'Abd as-Salam has related from another the following: 'Poverty with respect to a father – or anyone standing in for him, legally speaking – is of two kinds, the first, when his means are constricted and he is in need, but not such that the need is extreme, in which case it is permitted to give him *zakat* and the son does not have to pay for his upkeep; rather no obligation exists (on behalf of the son) – just as no obligation existed before his means were constricted; secondly, when he has a pressing need and his poverty is extreme, in which case his son has an obligation to pay for his upkeep, in which case it is not permitted to give the *zakat* to him.' Likewise, it is not given to someone whose upkeep and clothing expenses are the legal responsibility of a person of means – but this does not apply in the case where he has taken on this responsibility willingly, like for example, responsibility for the upkeep of a step daughter or step-mother and the like (for he is not legally bound for their upkeep). It is stated in *at-Tawdih* that this refers to any person who is legally responsible for upkeep and clothing, irrespective of whether his responsibility is manifest (by his responsibility towards someone who is living as part of the family) or because of the state (of poverty of the person in question) and irrespective of whether they are related to him or not. This has been stated by Ibn 'Abd as-Salam. Moreover, if provision for the upkeep and clothing of someone – which is someone's obligation, either through a personal commitment or because it is legally binding on him – is interrupted, then it is permitted make a payment for the costs of upkeep or clothing of the (poor person) which have been withheld from him – and there is no harm (in giving him *zakat*) even if both have been withheld. However, with respect to someone who voluntarily expends on another, Ibn 'Arafa said: 'Shaykh Mutarrif said: "(Zakat) should not be given to anyone in the family who is in no need of his upkeep, irrespective of whether the person is related or not; but if it is nevertheless given, then this is something which is not correct, but it is accepted (as *zakat*) from the (person who gave it) as long as he continues to pay upkeep".' Ibn Habib said: 'If the person (who has voluntary undertaken to provide upkeep for someone) interrupts (his payment) because *zakat* has been paid (instead), this (*zakat*) is not accepted.' This (judgement) is transmitted by al-Baji only with respect to someone who is unrelated, and he does not stipulate that the giving (of *zakat*) is permitted only when the donor is unaware (that the person in question is normally being provided for.)"

Then he goes on to say, after a discussion: "The fourth condition is that the person not be of the family of the Prophet, may the peace and blessings of Allah be upon him for it is not permitted to give (them anything) from obligatory *zakat* or from *sadaqa* – and this is the judgement of Asbagh, Mutarrif, Ibn al-Majishun and Ibn Nafi' and is the well known judgement. Ibn 'Abd as-Salam said: 'This is because they are treated in the same manner as him, on whom be peace and blessings, (with respect to this prohibition).' It has also been said that *sadaqa* may be given, but not the obligatory *zakat* – and this is (in accordance with) the judgement of Ibn al-Qasim. Again it has been said that they may be given of the *zakat* and *sadaqa*, and this is (in accordance with the judgement) of al-Abhari who argues that this is because their right to a portion from the bayt al-mal has been denied them in our time and that if it were not permitted for them to take *sadaqa*, then the poor amongst them would be deprived."

I shall continue to relate a little of what others have said regarding the author's discussion of the conditions. 'Ali ibn 'Abd as-Sadiq said: "What may be understood from the author's words is that it is not given to a person of means – and this is correct – except if this would be of benefit for the Muslims (in general) as is clear from the discussion of Sayyidi Muhammad al-Janan al-Fasi in his gloss on the *Mukhtasar*: 'It is stated in the book of Ibn Rushd, the grandson: "It is permitted to give *zakat* to the *'ulama* even if they are of means, and likewise to those (whose activity is) of benefit to the Muslims, like judges, muftis, teachers and *mu'adhdhins*."' Al-Lakhmi said: 'The *'ulama* have more right to the *zakat*, even if they are of means.'"

At-Tawudi said in the gloss of az-Zurqani: "The Shaykh of our Shaykh, the vast *'alim*, the Guide, Sayyidi al-Hassan al-Yousi has commented on the words of al-Janan saying: "His mention of giving it to the *'ulama* even if they are of means, in accordance with what is reported in the book of Ibn Rushd, the grandson, is not part of the *madhhab*, and it is not permitted to give a *fatwa* to this effect – for those to whom the *zakat* is given are the eight categories and the *ayat* (mentioning them) is a *muhkama ayat*, that is, one which is clear and unambiguous, according to the consensus. *'ulama*, judges and the like are given from the bayt al-mal and they have no claim to the *zakat*. If there is no bayt al-mal or (payment from it is for any reason) impossible or unfeasible, then they may be given (from the *zakat*). Allah will call to reckoning those who occupy themselves with pages upon pages of *fatwas* regarding the deen of Allah but who do not take their knowledge (directly) from those who know: they are amongst those who are astray and who lead others astray, and we ask Allah to be spared (being afflicted by their ignorance."

NOTICE: The author of *al-Mi'yar* said: "Sayyidi Abu 'Abdallah az-Zawawi was asked whether or not someone who had land which yielded no profit for him – and who would be reduced to a state of deprivation for ever if he were (compelled) to sell it – may be given of the *zakat* as long as he is in need? He replied: 'He may be given of the *zakat* and Allah knows best.'"

This is with regard to the words of the author. As for the conditions, then I would say – and by Allah, may I engage in the matter by Your strength: "Al-Mawwaq said, commenting on the words of Khalil 'as long as he is a Muslim and is free' saying: 'Ibn 'Arafa said: "(*zakat* for the) poor or destitute is conditional upon their being Muslim and their being free. Ibn al-Qasim has reported that the people of sectarian beliefs may be given if in need and that they are (considered to be) among the Muslims." Ibn Rushd said: "If one fears that their erroneous beliefs may have influence (over others), like their preferring 'Ali over the two Shaykhs (for example), then the person who prays has priority over others although the person who is not praying is given if he has a clear need.".'"

Al-Ubbi said in the *Sharh Muslim* that 'Iyad said: "Distributing *zakat* to the people given to committing acts of disobedience is *makruh*. Rather it is recommended to take care of (the needs of) the people of modesty and good behaviour. As to whether the obligation to pay the *zakat* (is fulfilled by giving it people of dubious character), there is no doubt that *zakat* given to those guilty of stealing and fornication is accepted – if they are in need; there is a difference of opinion regarding those who are not in need, like people of means, slaves or those who are not permitted to take it, but who are nevertheless given of it because the person giving it to them is unaware (that they are not entitled to it): Malik and ash-Shafi'i have said it is not accepted, while Abu Hanifa, ash-Shafi'i and Ibn al-Qasim – in one of his two judgements – have said that it is accepted. One of our contemporaries said: 'It is taken (back) from them if it still exists, and their is a difference of opinion as to whether they should be made to compensate if they have already used it; if they had deceived the person who gave it (to them), then it is taken from them; if the person who gave it to them was aware of their state, then it is permitted for them (to retain it) but compensation for it is to be paid to the destitute.'"

Ibn al-Hattab said: "It is stated in *an-Nawadir*: 'Ibn Habib does not permit it be given to someone who has abandoned the *salat* and said it is not accepted of the person who gives it.' However, he alone holds to this judgement, and even if there are others who have more priority (than they), there is no harm in giving it to them if there is a clear need amongst them.'"

It is stated in *al-Mi'yar*: "Muhammad ibn 'Abd al-Hakam was asked: 'Should a man give his *zakat* to someone he knows does not do the *salat* and who neglects the *wudu'*?' and he replied: 'If he affirms Islam, then there is no harm in his being given the *zakat*.'"

Also on the subject it is stated: "'Abd ar-Rahman al-Waghleesi was asked whether *zakat* given by someone – who is ignorant of the basic beliefs of Islam – to a person as (ignorant as) himself is accepted of him if he then makes *tawba* and becomes acquainted with the judgements (of the deen). He replied: 'It is accepted, and Allah knows best.'"

All this is related to the discussion of Mayyara regarding the first two conditions. As for the third, there is nothing to add to what he transmitted. As for the fourth, namely, that it is not to be given to the Bani Hashim, it is transmitted in *al-Mi'yar*, from the *'alim* of his time, Ibn Marzouq: "The preferred judgement in this time is that it may be given (to them) – and sometimes giving it to them is better than giving it to others, and Allah knows best."

USEFUL POINT: It is stated in *al-Jami' as-Saghir* that: "Whoever extends his hand to any of my family, then his reward will be (assured) on the Day of Rising." Al-Munawi said: "Here is evidence of the manifest and obvious solicitude of Allah and His Messenger for them – and so congratulations to the one who relieves them of any distress or who extends an invitation to them or who obtains something for them! The declarations (of the Messenger, may the peace and blessings of Allah be upon him) which testify to this are countless in number, and whoever wants to study this matter further then he should read *Tawtheeq 'Ara'l-Iman* of al-Barizi and the works of Ibn al-Jawzi."

NOTICE: 'Ali ibn 'Abd as-Sadiq said: "It is stated in *al-Akhdari al-Kabir*: "NOTICE: The owners of (zakatable) wealth are obliged to refrain from giving their *zakat* to other than the eight categories." He then goes on to say: "…and his going on a journey in order to give (*zakat* to someone not included in the eight categories) is considered as an journey undertaken in disobedience (to the *shari'ah*), according to the statements of the *'ulama*, and it is not accepted of him if he is aware of the (prohibition of doing this). He must likewise avoid doing what some of the ignorant of our time do, that is, giving *zakat* to the *mu'adhdhins* and reciters of Qur'an as a salary. Some people talk about this openly while others (only) allude to it – but the result is that it has become a widespread custom amongst the Bedouins of the desert. However, it is a manifest mistake and a violation of the *shari'ah*, and we ask Allah, exalted is He, to be spared such (ignorance)."

I SAY: "This is also widespread amongst the townspeople, especially in this time, and this (practice) is not only prevalent amongst the *mu'adhdhins* and the reciters, but in all activities – as we have often witnessed. Someone hires a shepherd or someone to harvest (their crop), for example and he states the wage (he is prepared to pay). If the person to be hired is not content, he says to him 'We will give you (something) from the *zakat*' and so he is content. However, this is incorrect and any (*zakat*) given in this manner is not accepted of him, and we ask Allah that we be free of such practice."

Ibn Zakari said in *Sharh an-Naseeha*: It is stated in '*Udda al-Murid*: "Among the incorrect practices which are widespread in some areas is the custom of persistently giving *zakat* to those who are praised or denigrated, or in order to acquire esteem and rank in this way; or it is used to pay fines or damages, and this is a disgraceful and ignominious act."

He said in *al-Ihya'*: "Among the things the people of wealth do is to require of the poor that they serve them and they desist from seeing to their needs until they themselves need them in the future; or they give only to those from whom they themselves require something in particular; or to those who pay attention to them – only in order to parade their importance and to increase their rank as people of position in society. All such (practices) corrupt the intention (which is a necessary prerequisite for payment of the *zakat*), and reduce the value of the action to nothing. Those guilty of such (action) are deluding themselves while imagining that they are obeying Allah."

NOTICE: Ibn al-Hattab said: "If he gives it to someone who he believes to be of means but then it turns out that he is poor, then it is accepted of him – although there is no reward for him as it is a wrong action."

ISSUE: Ibn al-Hattab has also said: "Al-Burzuli has related that al-Mughira said: 'It is not to be given to orphans.' Al-Burzuli then goes on to comment: 'We would point out, however – as we have learned from our Shaykh – that this refers to paying it to them in clothing or foodstuffs for this would be giving the value of what was due rather than the thing in kind. If, however, the commodity itself (taken in *zakat*, like gold and silver, for example) is given to them, then it would be correct.'"

ISSUE: Khalil said: "There is a difference of opinion as to the permissibility of giving it to a debtor and then taking it from him (immediately)." Al-Mawwaq has reported: "Ibn 'Arafa said: 'The most manifest meaning is that if he takes it after giving it with the willing consent of the poor person – without having stipulated that it be returned to him immediately – then it is accepted of him, and even if given unwillingly, it is also accepted if he has something to cover himself and feed himself for several days; otherwise, it is not permitted; and if given on condition (that it be handed back), then it is as if he has not given it.'"

His saying 'the Ghazi warrior' refers to someone fighting in the way of Allah.

As for his words 'to set (slaves) free', al-Mawwaq said, commenting on the words of Khalil 'and a believing slave...': "Examine whether it is permitted to free a slave from one's house on the understanding that he will be a 'client of the Muslims' (as it was the *zakat* of the Muslims which freed him) for there is a difference of opinion in this (matter)."

As for his saying 'to the (*zakat*) agents', more details may be found on this in Khalil's *Mukhtasar* and the commentaries.

His saying 'those in debt' refers to the words of Allah '*and the debtors al-(gharimeen)*[1].' Khalil said: "and (it may be given to) the debtor, even (to pay his debts) if he has died; but on condition that it is a debt for which one may be imprisoned and not a debt incurred for some corrupt activity (like buying wine) or (acquiring something merely to become indebted) in order to be able to take the *zakat* – unless he makes *tawba*, in which case. according to the best opinion, (he may be given of the *zakat*) as long as he has handed over any gold or silver in his possession or anything else (of value towards the debt)." Al-Qalshani, commenting on the words of *Sharh ar-Risala* 'the correct judgement is that this condition – that is, his saying "as long as he has given any gold or silver in his possession..." – is not stipulated': "... as to whether it is stipulated – when giving (some) of the *zakat* to the debtor – that he hand over any gold and silver he possesses and anything else which is not absolutely necessary (for his survival), the correct judgement is that this is not stipulated. This is because any such demand would represent a violation of the honour of the poor or indebted person. Al-Baji said: '... the giving (some) of the *zakat* to him is conditional upon the effect it would have on his (social) state: if, for example, he has land which he farms, or assets with which he trades and his being in debt would compel him to sell them – leading to a (radical) change in his (social) state – then giving it to him is permitted.'"

'Ali ibn 'Abd as-Sadiq said: "Our Shaykh said: 'If the debtor has a house or garden but selling them would reduce him in rank and status, then he may be given of the *zakat* – in which case he should not sell his house or garden for there would be no benefit in this. (The same judgement applies to) a Bedouin's tent – or whatever (apparel) is customarily carried on the camel by the Bedouin – for it is on a par with the house of a town resident of a town. There is a difference of opinion – amongst the latter *'ulama* – as to whether he should return any (such *zakat*) if he is no longer in need of it – just before his

---

1 at-Tawba – Repentance: 60

death (for example).'"

His saying '...to those whose hearts may be brought closer (to Islam)' refers to what is contained in the *ayat* about *mu'alafati qulubuhum*.[1]

Khalil said: "'those whose hearts may be brought closer' refers to the *kuffar* – in order that they may become Muslim, and the judgement (based on this *ayat*) remains in force (and has not been abrogated)." Al-Mawwaq said: "There is a difference of opinion as to whom this refers to: it is said they are various kinds of *kuffar* who are given of the *zakat* in order to bring them closer to Islam; and it is also said that it refers (specifically) to a people who have become Muslim in the outward but (in whose hearts) Islam has not yet taken root and so they are given (of the *zakat*) in order to strengthen their hearts in their Islam; again it is said that it refers to the followers of *mushrikun* leaders – who (themselves) have become Muslim: the followers are given *zakat* in order to also bring them to Islam. These opinions may appear different but the point of all of them is to give to those who are unable to accept Islam fully without some (financial) incentive, and so it may be classed as a kind of *jihad*."

His words 'the stranger in need' refers to the words of Allah, exalted is He: '*and travellers*.'[2] Khalil said: "The stranger in need (is given of the *zakat*) in order that he may return to his home, as long as he is not travelling illegally, and as long as he finds no one to make him the (necessary) loan – if he is of means in his country. His saying (that he is in need) is accepted, but if he remains (and does not return), then (what has been given) is taken back from him – as in the case of the ghazi warrior (who is given of the *zakat*, but does not go to war). As for the debtor – who after having been given becomes of means, there is a difference of opinion (as to whether it should be taken back from him)."

His saying 'and there is no doubt as to his state' corresponds to the saying of Khalil 'and the (poor and the destitute) are believed, except in case of doubt.' Al-Mawwaq said: "Ibn al-Qasim has reported that the claim of the poor person should be believed." Al-Lakhmi said: "...as long as he is not known to be of means and when it would be difficult to prove his lack (of means). If he claims poverty from having to sustain a large family, then the person who has been afflicted by a sudden stroke of misfortune is believed."

CONCLUSION: this section contains important matters of benefit, insha'Allah, which the author has not mentioned:

1. The intention is obligatory for the *zakat*. Khalil said: "and making the intention for (paying) it is obligatory." Al-Mawwaq said: "Ibn Mawwaz's

---

[1] at-Tawba – Repentance: 60
[2] at-Tawba – Repentance: 60

statement has been mentioned above, namely, that whoever gives it as *sadaqa*, then it is not counted as his *zakat* – for either he had made the intention of giving *sadaqa* voluntarily or he gave it without making any intention at all." Ibn Bashir said: "If we argue that the destitute have a legal share in the *zakat* and that the (judgement) is analogous to (the judgement governing) the return of something which has been kept for safe keeping or (that governing) the repayment of debts, then no intention is needed; but if, on the other hand, we are of the conviction that the judgement in effect here corresponds to (the judgement governing all) acts of worship, then an intention is needed (as in all acts of worship). However, there is no difference of opinion within the *madhhab* that if the Amir takes it from those – on whom it is obligation – then it is accepted, and this is clear, if one is of the view that no intention is needed in this case. However, if one argues that an intention is needed – and this is the judgement of Ibn Qussar – then the 'intention' could be assumed to be present if the Amir takes the *zakat aware* of who must pay; but if he takes it while being ignorant of who is obligated, then al-Lakhmi argues that the judgement here is subject to the same difference of opinion as freeing someone as an act of expiation – *kaffara* – (on behalf of someone else) without his permission (or without his knowing it), or the slaughter of animals designated for slaughter without the permission of the owner." Ibn Rushd said: "The most evident judgement is that *zakat* taken from someone by compulsion is not accepted – as *zakat* is imposed on each particular person according (to his wealth and not as a general poll-tax). However, if it nevertheless happens, then it is accepted (as *zakat*) from the person from whom it is taken, just as *zakat* would be accepted when exacted from the wealth of a minor or a mad person even though the correct intention is clearly not present in their case."

Az-Zurqani said, confirming the words of Khalil 'and making the intention for (paying) it is obligatory': "…when setting it aside or paying it to the poor, irrespective of whether the latter knows it is *zakat* or not – this is stated in *at-Tawdih* in one place, and is the most manifest meaning of the words of the Khalil. However, the author of *at-Tawdih* has stipulated in another place – as is stated in *al-Jawahir* – that it is conditional upon informing the poor person. One of the Shaykhs of al-Burzuli has given a *fatwa* to this effect and this is also what Sad-ra' has declared. Thus anyone who wants to pay *zakat* without fulfilling the above condition would be following those *'ulama* who do not stipulate it. Commenting on his words 'and its distribution to the poor…', our Shaykh said, according to what has been transmitted by his student: 'It is *makruh* to inform him that it is from the *zakat* or that Allah has determined it (for the poor) as this may offend his heart.'" Examine what he has reported regarding its being *makruh* for this is of more particular application than the two previous transmissions – thus if he pays it without an intention, it is not accepted except when paid by someone he has delegated (for this purpose), as is indicated by his words: "if he (himself) is not the person who (actually) pays." However, this case is also subject to the judgement regarding the details of slaughtering (animals belonging to someone else without their permission), as al-Qarafi has explained. It is not permitted to steal *zakat* from someone from whom it is due as there no intention would have been made (by person from whom it is taken); and even if the owner of property which is stolen makes an intention to the effect that it should be considered as *zakat*, then this intention is not accepted of him as one of the conditions of designating (something as) *zakat* is that it be paid (according to the conditions) mentioned above. However, it is more fitting to regard (stealing) it as permitted when it is known that he will not pay it under any circumstances or when there is no governor in the area who can compel him to pay it or when the owner of the (zakatable) wealth employs trickery to prevent it from being taken; for in such cases, his being relieved of it (by force) is better for him – according to one judgement – than it staying in his possession (and) as such, an on-going responsibility (until payment is made).

NOTICE: Ibn al-Hattab has related: "Ibn 'Arafa said: 'as for any delay (in payment of the *zakat*) on wealth – over which a year has elapsed but whose owner is absent – then *zakat* should be paid from the place when he is situated. There are two narrations as to whether he should pay it immediately in the case where no objection or excuse is offered on his part or where he is able to find someone to pay the money in advance.' Al-Lakhmi has stipulated that this difference of opinion applies to someone who expected to return before the (zakatable) year on the wealth in question had elapsed – for otherwise he should have appointed someone in his place; if he had refused (to do this) then his responsibility (to pay) comes into immediate effect and he must pay there and then, according to one of the two judgements of Malik – which is based on (the principle that *zakat* should be paid from) the place the owner finds himself in. However, based on (the principle) of 'relocation' (*naql*), that is, that it is permitted (for the goods to be brought to him or for him to return to the goods), and according to the judgement of Sahnun, then (payment) is delayed." This latter (judgement) is based on the location of the wealth (rather than the location of the owner).

Al-Mawwaq said, commenting on the words of Khalil 'the traveller pays *zakat* on what he has with him (in the land he finds himself in) and what he has at home – as long as the latter has not been already paid, and as long as his paying it while travelling would not cause hardship': "Al-Lakhmi said: 'There is a difference of opinion on the *zakat* of the traveller, as long as he is absent from his land. Malik said: "He pays *zakat* unless he is need himself and he has no provision with him. Thus he may delay payment until someone can be found to lend him the amount payable" – he means he pays the *zakat* by borrowing what he needs.' He has also said: 'he delays (payment of) his *zakat* until he is able to distribute it in his (own) land – and this is clear if the poor people there are more entitled to the *zakat* of his wealth. Moreover, *zakat* is connected to the (zakatable) things themselves (except in the case of goods for trade) and the owner may not pay (the value of them instead, as in the case of livestock, for example).'"

It is stated in the *Mudawwana*: "If the year elapses while the person is absent from his country, then he pays the *zakat* on what he has with him and what he has left behind in his country – likewise if he has left all of his wealth behind – unless he fears that he will be left in need and will not find someone to lend him (the amount due), in which case he should delay its payment until he returns; and if he finds someone to lend him the money and he pays his *zakat*, then this is what I prefer." However, he also said on another occasion: "He should distribute it in his country." Al-Lakhmi said: "The person who wants to travel should delegate someone to pay it for him when the year elapses if he knows that he will not return until after the 'year.'"

I SAY: "Ibn 'Arafa's words and those of al-Mawwaq regarding the person on his journey are based on the person being absent from his wealth. If, however, the wealth is removed from him, then al-Hattab has addressed this issue by saying: 'NOTICE: if the year elapses and his camels are travelling, then neither the *zakat* collector nor the owner should pay *zakat* on them until they return; and if they die, then he owes nothing on them, even if he knows that the year has elapsed.'" Ibn Rushd said: "He does not pay *zakat* on them as he does not know what will happen to them; and if they die, then he does not owe anything as he has not been negligent in this and he only has to pay *zakat* on them (when alive.)"

His saying 'should not pay *zakat* on them' means that he does not have to pay it there and then – and this is stated clearly in *al-'Utbiyya*. This is because he is prohibited from paying *zakat* on them – and this may also be understood from what Ibn al-Hattab said.

Also with regard to this subject, Ibn Rushd said: "It has been reported of Sahnun: 'if the mudir-trader expedites goods and the month for paying the *zakat* on them arrives, then he should pay the *zakat* along with whatever else he has to pay the *zakat* on – as long as he knows their (exact) amount or his people are aware of it; otherwise, he should wait until the person entrusted with them returns, in which case he must pay for the years which have passed – in accordance with the information supplied to him by the person in whose hands the goods had been entrusted. I know of no difference of opinion in this – for the goods are his property and he is responsible for them. Moreover the profit on them belongs to him and the obligation to pay *zakat* on them (for the years passed) is not removed in the case of loss or ruin."

He has also said in another place: "Ashhab said, with regard to a man who allots a portion of his wealth before the year has elapsed on it and sends it with someone to Egypt so that he may buy food with it – which he himself wants to eat and which he does not want to sell: 'I think *zakat* must only be paid by him as *zakat* is payable on the commodity itself and the obligation to pay the *zakat* is not removed by his intention to buy essential foodstuffs with it.' In the last section of what has been reported of Asbagh, it is stated: 'Whoever sends dinars (with someone) in order to buy clothes for his family and he acquires them, then he does not have to pay *zakat* on them, irrespective of whether he swears to this or not, as this is between him and Allah; and if he does not have the intention to acquire them, then he must pay the *zakat* on the (gold or silver) as they remain in his property."

It has been recorded with regard to the *mudir*-trader that if he sends money (with someone to trade with), then he should pay *zakat* on it if he knows its amount and knows whether or not it has been spent (on goods) or not; otherwise he should delay (its payment) and pay the *zakat* for every year (it has been away from him). It is stated in ash-Shamil: "If he sends money in order to buy clothing for himself and his family and the year elapses before it has been bought, then he should pay *zakat* on it" – that is, if he knows the amount and that it has not been spent, and Allah knows best.

In *al-Mi'yar* it is stated: "Sayyidi 'Isa al-Ghabareeni was asked about the kinds (of persons entitled to the *zakat*) and whether one takes into account the place of the owner or the place of the crop if there is a distance between them. He replied: "The place of the (zakatable) wealth is taken into account that is, the crop or the livestock, if there is a distance between them which makes transport impracticable; if the distance is negligible, then no (actual) separation exists (between the two), and Allah knows best."

3. Ibn al-Hattab said: "Ibn Rushd said at the end of the *Sama' Ashhab*: 'The Amir of each region has to take the *zakat* of his region and no other Amir may

collect it. The *zakat* collectors of Madina should not take from someone whose home is in Iraq. Sahnun said, with regard to a man who has forty sheep in four regions, that each Amir should take a quarter of a sheep if this is his due, and if each Amir takes money to the value to a quarter (of a sheep instead), then this is accepted; if he has five *wasqs* (of dates), that is, a *wasq* in each region, then he pays each Amir the *zakat* of a *wasq*; but if the governors are not just, then he should pay what he owes in the manner we have mentioned.'"

USEFUL POINT: 'Ali ibn 'Abd as-Sadiq said: "One of the *fuqaha* said: 'When someone receives *sadaqa* or *zakat*, it is either because he has requested it or (he has been simply given it) without asking. As for the first, if he is in need, then it is permitted for him to take it in all circumstances, that is, both from *sadaqa* given voluntarily or (*zakat* given) as an obligation; but if not in need, then it is forbidden him in all circumstances. As for the second, that is when not asked for, if he is in need, then it is permitted in all circumstances and if not in need, then it is permitted for him to take of the *sadaqa* given voluntarily, but not from *zakat* given as an obligation – thus the combinations are eight in number.'"

I SAY: "There is no harm in mentioning a (further) aspect of the judgement with respect to the person who asks (for *zakat* or *sadaqa*). In the *Sahih* the following is recorded: 'The man who persistently asks of people until the Day of Rising comes will have no shred of flesh left on his face.' The Prophet then went on to say: 'The sun will come so close on the day of Rising that the sweat (of the people) will reach up to the middle of their ears. When all the people are in this state, they will ask Adam for help, then Musa and then Muhammad, may the peace and blessings of Allah be upon him.'"

The *'ulama* have differed as to the judgement of the person who asks or begs (things of people). The well-known judgement of the *madhhab* of ash-Shafi'i, as al-Munawi has stated in his *Kabir*, and Ibn Hajar in his *Fath al-Bari*, is that it is permitted They have both stated: "...and the *'ulama* have interpreted the criticism of the person who asks for *zakat* as referring to someone who has no right to it." An-Nawawi said of such (people): "It is haram for them (to ask)." As for the *madhhab* of Malik, there is a difference of opinion amongst his followers. What the Arif, Ibn Abi Jamra has decided upon, may Allah, exalted is He, benefit us by him, as well as Ibn Hilal in his *Nawazil*, is that it is haram. 'Ali ibn 'Abd as-Sadiq and al-Khurshi, in the chapter on *Dhihar* – divorce through repudiation – have concluded that it is *makruh*, and al-Bannani and at-Tatari have not contested this.

It is stated in al-Qarafi's *Dhakheera*: "ISSUE: asking people for something:

'The Author of *al-Qabs* said that if the asking is for something regarding the deen or *dunya* which is necessary, then it is obligatory, according to the *fuqaha*; and in the case of difficulty, but not absolutely necessity, then it is recommended – as he may well be able to bear the difficulty; and in the case of asking for (something, merely on account of) the pleasure (it affords), then it is *makruh*; and if one only asks for (something) very occasionally (and not habitually), then it is licit.'" The words of Ibn 'Abd al-Barr, as transmitted by Ibn al-Hattab, are confused: the text occurs where he discusses the words of Khalil 'and he is in possession of the *nisab*.' "He said in *at-Tamheed*, commenting on the words of the Prophet, may the peace and blessings of Allah be upon him, "Whoever asks and he has an *uqiya*'s weight...": 'This (hadith) contains an indication that it is *makruh* to ask if someone has an ounce of silver – and an *uqiya* is equivalent to forty dirhams, and that whoever asks when he has this amount or (an equivalent) number of dirhams or whatever is equal (in value), then he is considered an importunate and obtrusive person. Imploring (someone) – when not with respect to imploring Allah – is blameworthy for Allah has praised those in the *ayat* "*They do not ask from people insistently.*"[1] For this reason, I have said that asking in the case of someone who possesses this amount is *makruh* and I have not said that it is prohibited, that is, (I have not said) it is not permitted, for what is not permitted is prohibited – whether done with importunity or otherwise. What is prohibited is to become preoccupied with it. It is permitted for him to use whatever comes (to him) from the *zakat* without asking, and there is no difference of opinion as far as I know in this matter. It is not permitted to give *zakat* to a person of means except in five cases. As for giving someone something other than *zakat*, it is permitted – for both those of means and the poor.'"

Commenting on the words of the Prophet, may the peace and blessings of Allah be upon him, '*zakat* is not permitted for those of means except in five cases': "Here the obligatory tax is being referred to; as for that given of one's own free choice (i.e. *sadaqa*), it is not prohibited for anyone to give it, as mentioned above, although to refrain from taking it is better; and there is no harm in accepting it when (given) without asking, although asking for it is not permitted except in the case of someone who is compelled to."

In the *Tabsira* of Ibn Muhriz, Abu'l-Hasan al-Qussar said: "It is not permitted for anyone who possesses the minimum means of subsistence to beg, but if he has nothing then it is permitted for him to ask; and it is permitted to give him (an amount which is) enough to live on for the rest of his life in one go."

1 al-Baqara – The Cow: 273

I SAY: "The (legal) principle (that may be inferred) from the hadith 'whoever asks while possessing an *uqiya* (of silver) is (that it refers to) someone who is importunate in asking' is the prohibition of the Prophet may the peace and blessings of Allah be upon him, of asking when one possesses an *uqiya*. The *zakat* is the obligatory right of every poor person but it is not permitted for the person of means. It is not permitted to give anyone of means who has enough to live on of the *zakat*. However 'being rich' or 'of means' varies from person to person: there are some for whom a little is enough as they have a small family and their daily needs are small; while for others, only a lot will do because they have a large family and a large expenditure on their daily needs. Thus each must be assessed accordingly. It is permitted to give to the poor such that they become 'of means', that is, so that they will have enough or even more than enough (to live on through the *zakat*) because they were poor at *the moment of* taking it and it is permitted to give *zakat* to the poor. There is no well-defined limit in this, in our view and success is with Allah." This has been transmitted by al-Burzuli. It is also stated in *al-Aarida* – in the chapter 'Those for whom the *zakat* is permitted': "Issue, fifthly, asking (for something) can be obligatory or recommended. As for the former, it refers to the person in need; as for the latter, it refers to someone helping another by asking on his behalf – if he himself is too embarrassed to do so or he hopes that the other's speaking on his behalf will be more effective than himself. The Prophet would ask for others, may the peace and blessings of Allah be upon him, as is recorded in many hadith."

He does not discuss Ibn Rushd's interpretation – in *al-Bayan* – of the apparently contradictory aspects of the hadith which are critical of asking (people for things), that is, where he states: "It is narrated of him, may the peace and blessings of Allah be upon him, that he said: 'Whoever asks people when he himself is not in need, then the live coals of jahannam will be increased.' I said: 'Messenger of Allah 'and what does "not in need (refer to)"'? He replied: 'When the person knows that his family have enough for a midday meal and enough for an evening meal.' He has also said: 'Anyone of you who asks while in possession of an *uqiya* of silver or the equivalent, then he is (considered) importunate in his asking.' Again he has also said, may the peace and blessings of Allah be upon him: 'No slave (of Allah) asks for something when not in need but that he will appear with his face disfigured, marked by toil, and covered in scratches on the Day of Rising.' Someone said: 'O Messenger of Allah! and what is his being 'not in need' refer to?' He replied: '(being in possession of) fifty dirhams or the equivalent in gold.' He has also said: 'Whoever asks when he has the equivalent of five *uqiyas* of silver, then he is (considered) importunate in his asking.' This (latter) amount is the amount which should be taken as the basis for the prohibition of asking for charity. The (various) narrations, (although textually different), are not considered incompatible in meaning: rather the one is considered to have abrogated the other. If one understands the hadith in this manner, it is more appropriate to consider the least amount mentioned in the four (hadith) as having been abrogated by the amounts which follow. Thus the least (amount) is abrogated by the greatest amount – which (results in) the easiest (judgement) on people, and the easiest way is from Allah and a mercy."

As for the issue (indicated in the hadith) 'Whoever knows that someone's heart is sound and that he well-disposed (towards you), then there is no harm in asking him' in the commentary of Ibn Hajar on al-Bukhari he says: "It is permitted to ask for a gift from someone if you know he is well-disposed (towards you) and he will respond (to your request)."

There is similar from al-Ubbi in the *Sharh Muslim* in the 'Marks of Iman' as related by Ibn Naji from his uncle: "When the poor gathered at the house of the Salih Shaykh Abu Zayd Yusuf al-Melilly he would instruct me – if I was present – to spend money from my own purse so that we might buy enough doughnuts or other things for them as he knew it would make them happy. Our Shaykh ash-Shabeebi said: 'I witnessed this – and I know of no other man whom I might cite for being so well-disposed.'"

NOTICE: in Qubab's commentary on the words of Ibn Jama'a 'It is permitted for the buyer to ask the seller, after concluding the sale, that he tip the scales (in his favour), just as he may ask him – without any formality to reduce the price for him – (the seller's response being) an expression of generosity and his being well-disposed (towards the buyer)': "Ibn Rushd said: 'As for the question of the weighing (of commodities) which we have taken from *al-'Utbiyya*, his asking the (buyer) to tip the scales (in his favour) is not included in this matter; rather such (practice) is part of the customary behaviour of people (in the market) and it is an expression of kindness and indulgence in selling – which is recommended of the buyer and seller. The Prophet, may the peace and blessings of Allah be upon him, said: "Allah has mercy on a forbearing slave if he shows indulgence when selling and buying, and when he passes judgement – if requested." His asking for a reduction in price after the conclusion of the sale is similar to this.'" It is stated in the *Utbiyya* in the *Sama' Ashhab* from the 'Book of General Sales': "I asked him about the person who buys goods – and who is satisfied (with them and the price) – but who then asks the (seller) for a reduction in price (which he grants and) is also satisfied. He replied: 'I see no harm in this, as long as it continues to be the practice of the people. It is neither the same as a man saying to another: "Lend me your robe, lend me your riding beast" – which I do not see any harm in, nor do I consider it to be in the same (category of judgements) as the kind of asking or begging which is prohibited – as long he asks in a normal manner. As for asking importunately, subserviently or imploringly, however, this I consider *makruh*. As for the person who buys goods and then says – despite his satisfaction (with the goods and price) – "if you do not reduce the price for me, I will argue with you", there is no good in this.' It is stated in the *Sama' Ibn al-Qasim* from the above mentioned book: 'He was asked as to whether it was halal for a man who had bought goods but who then asks the seller to reduce the price for him – despite his satisfaction with the goods. He replied: "It is halal and there is a blessing in it – but the seller is better than him."' Ibn Rushd said: 'What he said is clear, namely that if he asks him for a reduction, despite his being satisfied with the sale, then it is halal for him to reduce the price – although I consider that desisting from (asking is) better. I base this (judgement) on the words of the Prophet, may the peace and blessings of Allah be upon him, who said to 'Umar ibn al-Khattab, may Allah be pleased with him: "The good in any one of you lies in his not taking anything from another" and his saying: "The hand which is uppermost is better than the one below."' However, he does not see any objection to this (asking on his part), or that he is committing a wrong action, nor any interdiction (to this practice) as he does not consider this a prohibited form of asking. Rather, it is as the case mentioned above where (the Shaykh) instructs him to pay (for something out of his own pocket); or (the case) where he compares (the permitted form asking) to borrowing a riding beast or clothing – as long as he does not ask importunately, subserviently or imploringly, for this is *makruh* and is not fitting. This he has stated in *Sama' Ashhab* – and it is correct for if he were to (ask in) this (manner), then he would not be reducing the price for him out of his good will. The Prophet, may the peace and blessings of Allah said: 'The property of a Muslim man is only halal for another when (given) with good will.' As for his saying 'there is no good in the buyer who says: "If you do not reduce the price, I will quarrel with you"', it is clearly not halal for him and is not permitted because the (seller) would be reducing the price out of fear that he will quarrel with him. If the (buyer) does nevertheless do this, then either he must return the (amount of the) reduction, or it may be seized from him, or the (seller) may forego (return of the amount)." I say: "Study this section for this is contrary to the practice of many people who argue and who demonstrate excessive behaviour towards each other. He is encouraging them to come to an amicable settlement and this is halal and better for you than having it resolved through laws. What Ibn Rushd said here is clearly correct for it is not permitted to take something which is granted (by the seller) merely out of fear that a dispute and testimony on oath will ensue – as long, that is, as the (seller) has not become obligated (to the granting of a lower price)."

USEFUL POINT: al-Munawi has related in his *ash-Sharh al-Kabir*: "Al-*Khateeb* has narrated that a stranger came to ad-Daraqutni and asked him to recite (Qur'an) and he refused. Then he asked him to dictate some hadith for him. He dictated them for him from memory in one sitting and there were more than ten narrations in all – including 'The best thing is to make a gift when it is needed', upon which the (stranger) went away and then came back and gave him something. Ad-Daraqutni then had him sit next to him and he dictated from memory some ten hadith to him, including 'If a generous man from a people comes to you then treat him generously.' Ibn al-Jawzi said: 'It is strange that ad-Daraqutni relates two hadith which are completely incorrect but does not comment on them.' Then Ibn al-Jawzi began to explain their invalidity." (Al-*Khateeb*) follows this with a statement of as-Suyuti: "How strange that Ibn al-Jawzi decides to reject well established hadith without basing his judgement on any firm evidence – for the hadith 'If a generous man of a people comes to you then treat him generously' has been reported from more than ten of the Companions, and this is a *mutawatir* hadith narrated with multiple chains of narration – according to those who hold that a multiple chain consists of at least ten narrators." The discussion of al-Munawi concludes with the hadith "The best of things is a gift given when needed." At the beginning of his commentary he has introduced ad-Daraqutni, saying: "He was the Hafidh, the Illustrious, 'Ali ibn 'Umar al-Baghdadi, a ash-Shafi'i (*faqih*), imam of his time and the Lord of the people of his time. When someone asked the ruler: 'Have you see his like?' He replied: 'He himself had never encountered anyone like himself – so how can I be expected to have seen someone like him?'" Al-*Khateeb* then said: "He was the pinnacle of his time, the imam of his age, of sound *'aqida*, knowledgeable of the *madhhab* of the *fuqaha* and of a wide ranging knowledge."

There is also the question mentioned in *al-Mi'yar*: "Shaykh Abu Muhammad ibn Abu Zayd was asked whether he ate the food of someone who does not pay the *zakat* and he replied, on one occasion: 'There is no harm in eating it' while on another occasion he said: 'Transacting with him is permitted while eating his food is *makruh* – if it occurs so frequently that he feels indebted towards him (and obliged to compensate).' He was then asked: 'What if the person eating his food is a poor person or a traveller and they (both) possess nothing' and he replied: 'This is permitted as they are people who have a right to the *zakat*; the matter may also be regarded – not from this point of view – but rather (from the point of view that whatever is eaten is) is to be considered as something owing to the person out of the *zakat*. Those who consider that eating with such a person is the same as with any other person argue that (the ongoing, persistent eating of a person's food) is subject to the same (judgement) as "gifts which entail compensation." Those who do not consider that (eating of the food of someone who does not pay *zakat*) is the same as (eating of the food of anyone else) argue that it is better not to eat (of his food). As-Sayouri has mentioned something similar. Those who consider (the eating of his food) as an act of kindness or charity (on his part) are complicating the matter because such acts are the prerogative of those who perform them and as such can only be regarded, legally speaking, from the point of view of "the legal obligation to assist those in need" (*al-mawasat*) – and this matter cannot be categorised in this way.'"

He has also said: "As-Sayouri was also asked whether the *zakat* of those who had seized wealth illegally but who were unable to return it to its rightful owner was accepted of them or not. He replied: 'It is taken from them and given to the people in need if they are unable to return it to its rightful owners – as long as they do not know them and are unable to find out (where they are). Those who are not in need should not take it, nor someone who is being followed (as a *faqih*)[1]. The taking of *zakat* from them is in accordance with the judgement regarding 'those who have become responsible for the something they themselves do not own or who become indebted to someone else indirectly (*mustaghriq adh-dhimam*)'[2]. The most evident judgement of the *Mudawwana* is that *zakat* is taken from them, and this is based on his declaration that '*zakat*, exacted from a person who has seized livestock illegally, is accepted on behalf of its rightful owners' – although it is argued that this applies when they are known, in which case it is as if the person who had seized them is acting as the representative (of the rightful owners), unlike the case where he

---

1   See *al-Mi'yar*, vol. 1, p.394.
2   for example, those who have become responsible for something even though it does not legally belong to them, as in the case of someone who receives payment for illegal taxes – and who turns in *tawba* – but cannot give back the money with him, which he is now responsible for, as he no longer knows where the rightful owners of the money are. The *'ulama* have asked whether – if such a person then pays *zakat* or *sadaqa* – it may be accepted of him (see *al-Mi'yar*, vol 1., p. 382).

does not know them and is unable to find out."

It is also stated in *al-Mi'yar*: "Someone asked about the person who had given his *zakat* to someone who was not entitled to it and whether one could eat of his food or not; and whether the person who has taken on responsibility for seeing to the needs of people, be they travellers or resident, has an obligation to see to the needs of such people, that is, those who have abandoned the *salat* or those who refuse to give *zakat* and any others whose behaviour is corrupt, and whether such a person (responsible for the needs of the people) – who has the money or commodities (due to them from his or other people's *zakat*) handed over to them at the hand of unjust agents and similar characters like bandit-chiefs and people (notorious for) seizing wealth illegally – should be helped in rectifying (and recovering) the unjust payments (to such people) if he as already handed over the *zakat* (for distribution) at their hand. He replied: 'If he hands over the *zakat* and there is no doubt or difference of opinion that this is not permitted, then it is not accepted of him and the judgement on him is the same as the person who has not paid his *zakat* at all; it is *makruh* to eat his food – as long as he has not exceeded all bounds in this matter, and he should be avoided – if he is forbidden from (such practice) and given words of advice (in this respect) but does heed them.'"

I say: "This contradicts somewhat that which has been transmitted above from Ibn Abi Zayd."

Issue: Ibn al-Hattab has related: "Sanad said, during his discussion of those to whom the *zakat* is given: 'Whoever is given *zakat* on the understanding that he dispense it to his people – and he himself is of the family – then it is permitted for him to take a reasonable amount (from it). This (judgement) is clear as the cause of his entitlement is valid, and there is no difference between him and the others who are entitled (to the *zakat*).' Something similar to what he has mentioned from *al-Muwaziya* is to be found in *an-Nawadir* in the 'Book of Zakat' and the 'Second Book of Hajj', namely the judgement that a messenger sent with payment for someone else or with a ransom has no right to any of it unless he himself is destitute, in which case he may (take from it). Commenting on this, he said in *at-Taraz*: '(Cases of) payment of *kaffara* and *zakat* which have been given to a destitute person on the understanding that he distribute it to another destitute person is similar to this – for he may take a reasonable amount for himself.' Abu'l-Hasan as-*Saghir* said: 'What may be understood from this matter is that whoever is given *sadaqa* to distribute to other, then he himself is permitted to take his portion if he is a destitute person. However this is a matter about which there are two judgements. The reason for this (difference of opinion) is the question as to whether the agent is included in the transaction (he has been entrusted with) or not, that is, whether the person instructed with bringing something to someone or conveying news to someone is himself understood as being one of those people addressed by the message or entitled to whatever is sent with the messenger or not. The judgement is analogous to someone who is given water to give to the thirsty, that is, that he himself may drink if he is thirsty.'"

In *Rasam al-Bazz* from *Sama' Ibn al-Qasim* from the 'Book of Goods and Agencies' he said: "The person who is sent with money to a military expedition or to the Hajj – in order to distribute it to others who are absent for a prolonged time – is permitted to take a reasonable amount from it, if he is in need. 'Reasonable' means that he does not favour himself such that he takes more than he gives others. However, it is recommended that he borrow (what he needs) if he is able to find someone who can lend him this (amount) and that he take nothing of the (amount he has been entrusted with). It is recommended, too, that on his return he inform the owner of the (sum entrusted to him) of what he has done, and if the owner is not willing to forego repayment, then he must repay it to him; if he dies and he is unable to inform him, then nothing is held against him as his taking it was permitted, according to the agreement of the *'ulama* – that is as long as the amount (he took for himself) was like that he gave others. It is not permitted that he take more for himself unless the owner of the money knows and he agrees to this."

ISSUE: in *Nawazil al-Qubbab* he says: "What do you say regarding a poor man who travels from his house and *zakat* is distributed in the house while he is absent but he has not delegated anyone: should some of the *zakat* be taken for him or not?" His replied 'If he is known to be in need of it and that he would agree to this being done on his behalf, then it is permitted, and Allah, exalted is He, knows best.'"

Zakat al-Fitr

زَكَاةُ الْفِطْرِ صَاعٌ وَتَجِبُ

عَنْ مُسْلِمٍ وَمَنْ بِرِزْقِهِ طَلَبْ

209 The *zakat al-fitr* is (paid with) a *sa'*, and it is obligatory on every Muslim and anyone else for whose upkeep he is responsible –

مِنْ مُسْلِمٍ بِجُلِّ عَيْشِ الْقَوْمِ

لِتُغْنِ حُرّاً مُسْلِماً فِي الْيَوْمِ

210 if they are Muslim, (that is a *sa'*) of the most widely used foodstuffs of the people – (enough) to feed a free Muslim for a day

MAYYARA said: "In this section he is dealing with the *zakat al-fitr* and informs us that the amount (to pay) is a *sa'*. As mentioned above, a *sa'* is four *mudd* – four double-handed scoops – of the Prophet, may the peace and blessings be upon him, and the judgement as to its (payment) is that it is an obligation on the Muslims, that is, if able to pay it. What may be understood from the specific designation of the obligation *being on the Muslims* is that it is not obligatory on the *kuffar*; and that no discrimination is made between a free person or a slave, between a male or female, an adult or a minor – as long as they are Muslim – and this (understanding) is correct. It is obligatory on the person himself and on any one else whose upkeep he is responsible for, like his wife, parents, children or slaves – if they are Muslim. Anyone who has to pay for someone else – other than himself – should make the payment on their behalf. However, if his wife is of means and she has poor parents, then she should make the necessary payment for them, while her husband pays for her – that is if she and her parents are Muslims. All this is included in the words of Ibn 'Ashir 'on any Muslim and anyone else whose upkeep he is responsible for.' His saying 'the most widely used foodstuffs of the people' refers to the foodstuff of those it must be given to. Then Ibn 'Ashir then indicates the wisdom of the judgement instructing that it is 'in order to feed a free Muslim for a day', that is, the day of the 'Eid al-Fitr. The words *an il-muslim* – refer back to *tajib*, that is, it is obligatory *on* – this use of *'an* in the sense of *'ala, on,* is also to be found in the *ayat* 'But whoever is tight fisted is tight fisted only to himself (*'an nafsihi*).'[1] The words *wa man talaba bi rizqihi*, meaning literally 'and whoever seeks of his provision' – means, as stated above, whoever is dependent on him for his upkeep."

Then he goes on to say: "The amount of a *sa'* is well known as the (valid measure) for all the various kinds of foodstuffs that it may be paid in. Habib said: 'Two *mudds* of wheat are paid, not a *sa'* (i.e. four *mudds*).' Al-Qubab said: 'This *sa'* is according to the measure in use in the city of Fes today.' One of the Shaykhs said: 'It is four double-handed scoops.'"

Al-Mawwaq has also transmitted what al-Qubbab said, saying: "Al-Qubab said: 'This sa corresponds to the measure in use in the city of Fes today.' One of the Shaykhs of Granada said: 'It is four double-handed scoops.'" Ash-Shatibi has also said something similar.

It is stated in *Kifayat al-Muhtaj*: "Ash-Shatibi, may Allah have mercy on him said: 'It is difficult to trust (the authenticity of) the measures which are mentioned in the various narrations because of the great discrepancy between them – as I have discovered (on investigating the matter). The measure according to the *shari'ah*, as transmitted by the Shaykhs of the *madhhab*, is approximately a double-handed scoop made with average sized hands, that is, neither large nor small, and a *sa'* consists of four of them. I have used this (measure with my own hands), and it is correct. This is what people should return to as it is based on the simple, approximate measure of the *shari'ah*. Qubab's assessment of the matter is not required with respect to the *shari'ah*, as it is complicated and artificial.'"

NOTICE: What is meant by the *zakat al-fitr* being 'obligatory on every Muslim' is that it is obligatory on anyone who declares the two *shahadas*, irrespective of whether one knows whether he is aware of what they mean or not. Thus, the mere declaration of the two *shahadas* on the part of a zoroastrian means that he is obliged to pay the *zakat al-fitr* and that the laws and judgements of Islam are applied to him. Some students (of *fiqh*) have made the mistake of claiming

---

[1] Muhammad: 39

that the *zakat al-fitr* is not an obligation on anyone until he is aware of what the (two *shahadas*) refer to and of the evidence (to support them). They have been excessively influenced by some of the *mutakallimun* who argue that anyone who merely imitates (in the sphere of belief, without any understanding) is a *kafir*. Sayyidi 'Abdallah Wuld al-Hajj Ibrahim al-'Alawi has adequately rejected their arguments in his responses so examine them. Ever more erroneous are those who have ruled that the property of the common people may be taken with impunity – when they do not understand what the two *shahadas* refer to – and who have argued that anyone who does not understand the proofs upon which the *shahadas* are based is a *kafir*, and that a *kafir*'s wealth is not protected (from seizure). The arguments of the *mutakallimun* have confused them, and in turn, have confused others, for there is agreement that the laws of Islam – with respect to the outward aspects of the *shari'ah* – are applied to whoever confirms the two *shahadas*. So examine the *Sharh as-Sanusi* and al-Manjouri's *Hashiya al-Kubra*.

Al-Qastalani said in *Sharh al-Bukhari*, after describing the difference of opinion within the *umma* regarding iman: "…all this is with respect to Allah, exalted is He; with respect to us (in the world), however, all that is necessary is affirmation (of the two *shahadas*: there is agreement that if someone affirms (these two), then we assume he has iman."

Al-Haytami, commenting on a hadith in the collection entitled *The Forty* (*hadith*), namely, 'I have been commanded to fight people until they bear witness that there is no god, only Allah and that Muhammad is the Messenger of Allah and that they establish the *salat* and pay the *zakat* and if they do this, then their blood and property is safe from me, except if there is a right to it according to the laws of Islam, and their reckoning is with Allah' – or whatever the exact wording of the text is – said: "(Allah is responsible for) the reckoning of all that is hidden within their (hearts), and their secrets are with Allah as He alone is aware of the (nature of their) iman, *kufr*, hypocrisy or anything else contained in the innermost (reality of their hearts). Whoever has a pure iman, then his reward will be that of the *mukhlisun* (the purified), and those who do not (have this purity), will not (have this reward), rather the laws of the Muslims will be applied to him in this world and in the next, he will be amongst the worst of the *kuffar*."

The author of *Fath al-Bari* said, commenting on the hadith 'whoever changes his deen, then put him to death': "The (*fuqaha*) are of a consensus that the laws of this world are applied according to the outward, and that Allah is responsible for the inner reality of people. The Messenger, may the peace and blessings of Allah be upon him, said to Usama: 'Why did you not split open his belly and find out what his heart contained.'¹"

He has also said, commenting on the above mentioned hadith in al-Bukhari 'I have been commanded to fight people...': "Abu Bakr said: 'By Allah...'² in affirmation of the judgement." Al-Khattabi said, commenting on the (above) hadith: "Whoever openly declares his Islam, then the laws of Islam – regarding the outward – are applied to him, even if he keeps his *kufr* a secret at the same time. The differences of opinion (amongst the *'ulama* in this regard) are based on whether one should accept that a person – who openly claims to have returned to Islam after people had learnt that his *'aqida* was corrupt – has indeed returned to Islam or not; as for the person about whose (true) beliefs one is ignorant, there is no difference of opinion that the outer laws of Islam are applied to him."

DIGRESSION: al-Haytami said, after a discussion: "It has been argued that if the laws of the Muslims are applied to him, on the basis of his declaring (the *shahadas*) on his tongue while he is in fact a *kafir* inwardly – like marrying a Muslim woman or receiving the inheritance of a Muslim relative – but then *kufr* disappears from his heart, then intercourse is in all likelihood permitted (him), as is his receiving (the inheritance), because of his declaration (of the *shahadas*) and the application of the laws of the *shari'ah* on him; however what is more evident and correct is that intercourse is not permitted (him) until after the contract of marriage has been renewed, and that his receiving the inheritance from a Muslim relative is not permitted (until he declares the *shahadas* again). This is because although we did not act in accordance with what was hidden inside (his heart) in the beginning – as this was not manifest to others, we must now judge according to his (former state, based on his present genuine acceptance of Islam) for this change of state is as a manifest sign (of his former *kufr*, and that this first application of the laws to him was invalid).

I SAY: "This (second judgement) is the conclusion of ash-Shihab in the commentary on the *Shifa* and it occurs during his discussion of the hadith of al-Bukhari 'I am granting him a portion of the Fire'³. The gist of it is that when

---

1   *Sahih* Muslim, Iman; Ibn Majah *Kitab al-Fitan*, vol.5, p.268: meaning it would have been no use to do this. This was on the occasion where one of the *mushrikun* had been put to death despite his declaring the *shahada* just before he died. The Messenger went on to say, may the peace and blessings of Allah be upon him, "Then you did not accept what he had declared and you were not aware of what his heart contained."
2   I have not been able to find this in Fath al-Bari, see vol.1, p.94ff.
3   It is also recorded in the *Muwatta'* that the Prophet, may Allah bless him and grant him

the law is applied by the ruler in accordance with the outward (evidence) then it is correct and may be executed, and even if it is contrary to the reality or truth (of the person's heart), what is halal is not rendered haram and what is haram is not rendered halal as we judge according to the outward and Allah is responsible for the inner (reality of people) – and this with respect to property, to the lives of people and to other matters. The law is (only) applied according to the outward and the (reckoning of the) inward remains until the next world."

As for his saying 'of the most widely used foodstuffs of the people', Khalil said: "from those (zakatable) commodities from which a tenth is taken, or (cottage) cheese." However, he does not mean all of those commodities from which a tenth is taken, but rather a particular number of them, namely, wheat and barley, spelt and millet, rice, maize, dates, raisins and ninthly, cottage cheese. If the *alas* variety of small grained wheat is the most widely used food of a people, then it may also be paid with it as is stated in the *Risala* – that is in the absence of another (kind of staple). The gist (of the matter) is that if these foodstuffs are available, then one should see which one is the most widely used; however, even if they are not widely used, then it must be paid in one (of them), if any of them is available; if none of them is available, then one should take from what is most widely used as food.

There is something similar to his saying 'it must be paid in one (of them), if any of them is available' from az-Zurqani. At-Tawudi has objected to it – noting that: "the original statement is from al-Hattab who says that it is the most evident judgement of the *madhhab*. However it is not the most evident, and for this reason al-Mustafa said: 'The most evident meaning of their words is that it is to be paid in other than the nine (mentioned above) if it constitutes their staple food and is available, or constitutes one element of their staple food."

It is stated in the *Mudawwana*: "Ibn al-Qasim said: 'If any kinds of legumes and pulses, like beans, or anything else which we have mentioned above – which are not accepted – are the staple food of the people, then there is no harm in paying (the *zakat*) with it, and it is accepted of them.'"

Abu'l-Hasan said: "The commonly used food of the people refers to what is eaten in times of ease, not in times of famine or drought." Something similar

---

peace, said, "I am but a man to whom you bring your disputes. Perhaps one of you is more eloquent in his proof than the other and so I give judgement according to what I have heard from him. Whatever I decide for him which is part of the right of his brother, he must not take any of it for I am granting him a portion of the Fire." (*Al-Muwatta'*, 36.1, Judgements)

has been stated by Ibn Rushd in *al-Muqaddimat* – however, he has stipulated that its payment in other than the nine is conditional upon its being their staple food in both times of plenty and dearth. Al-Hattab has stated that declaration of the author is by way of a commentary or explanation particular to him and is not to be relied on for it renounces the unequivocal statements of the imams in the *Mudawwana* and Ibn Rushd, al-Lakhmi and others.

Abu'l-Hasan and Ibn Rushd's stipulating a condition with respect to the statement in the *Mudawwana* is also what al-Qussar holds to – this is related by Ibn 'Ashir from him from his *fatwas*, namely that it is not taken from *al-'ushba* plant, also known as *ayar'ee*, a kind of sarsaparilla, although others have mentioned that people do pay with it, in which case this (judgement) would be contrary to the above-mentioned stipulation of the two Shaykhs.

It is stated in the commentary of Jasous on the *Risala*: "What may be understood from the words of Alif-mim-sad 'from wheat...' is that if the people have another kind of staple food – in addition to the (well known) staples – like for example, milk or meat – then they should not pay in them, even if they are the most widely used staples (amongst them). This is the most evident judgement of the *madhhab*, that is, that they should pay in the nine kinds (mentioned). This is contrary to what Khalil said 'unless another kind of staple food is used.' However, if they *only* use something other than these (nine), then it is permitted to pay with it, according to the well known judgement; and the manifest meaning of the declarations of the *'ulama* of the *madhhab* (is that it is also permitted) even when one of the nine kinds is available, contrary to what al-Hattab has stated based on the words of the author. However, if they only use the staples mentioned – and this is what the words of the author are based on – then (it is paid according to) the three categories."

Al-Hattab has related: "Abu'l-Hasan said: the *zakat al-fitr* to be paid is of three kinds, the first kind is made up of wheat, barley and spelt – whereby *zakat al-fitr* is paid from them irrespective of whether they constitute the most widely use foodstuff or not; if the most widely used foodstuff is other than these three, then it may also be paid from (one of) these three and it is accepted, as long as the most expensive of the three is paid and not than the least expensive – when all three are available; as for other than these three, that is the seven remaining foodstuffs of the ten, these are not paid unless they constitute the most widely used foodstuffs of the people of the land; and payment is not made in other than these ten if they do not constitute what is most widely used food – although there two (conflicting) opinions as to whether it should be paid in the latter at all, even if it is the most widely used foodstuff."

NOTICE: al-Hattab said: "Ibn Naji said in *Sharh al-Mudawwana*: 'One of our Shaykhs said: "What the people eat in Ramadan is taken into consideration, not what they eat before it", and our Shaykh accepted this (judgement)' This is correct because the *zakat al-fitr* is a purification for those fasting: what they have eaten during the month is taken into account because it is this (month) which is the justification for the *zakat* and because the (*zakat*) becomes obligatory at the end of this (month). One of our contemporaries have objected to what I have said (in this regard) by pointing to the fact that in a (transaction undertaken by) two associates, one does not take into consideration their coming together or parting company before the elapse of the year. I have replied to him that the reason for (taking into consideration what is eaten is Ramadan) is based on the suspicion that they want to escape payment (of the best food) for the *zakat al-fitr*. There is more justification for suspecting the two (associates) of (seeking to avoid payment) than suspecting the people of a (whole) region (of seeking to avoid payment of the best food for the *zakat al-fitr*). Moreover, Ramadan is justification in itself for the *zakat al-fitr* – not the complete year. In the question of the two associates, the 'justification' or 'principle' (underlying the association) is the completion of the year – not the month in which the association was formed."

I (that is, Ibn al-Hattab) have said: "What he has mentioned from one of his Shaykhs is clear – as is his reply to it. By 'one of his Shaykhs', he is referring to Ibn 'Arafa although I have been unable to find what he has narrated from him in his *Mukhtasar*: it may well be that he heard it from him, or he heard it from his Shaykh, al-Burzuli and transmitted it from him; or he found it in a *fatwa* of his, or elsewhere. One of the *fuqaha* said: 'One takes into account only the day on which it is obligatory.'" I have said: "His saying that the whole year has to be taken into account is contrary to what Ibn Naji has transmitted from Ibn 'Arafa, and the most evident judgement is what Ibn 'Arafa said. As for what he has mentioned from one of the *fuqaha* – namely that the day on which it is obligated is taken into consideration – this is extremely unlikely as it is well known, and a custom, that most people do not eat the same food for the day of the 'Eid as they do for the rest of the year."

Then he goes on to say: notice: "If meat and milk are the staple food of a people, then we say that they should pay in these. Ibn Naji said in his *Sharh al-Mudawwana*: 'If we accept (other judgements) beyond the well known judgement, then (we might accept that) our Shaykh Abu Muhammad ash-Shabeebi could pay in meat and milk and the like to the amount of a sa.' However, our Shaykh, al-Burzuli did not accept this, saying 'the correct judgement is that it must be paid by the measure, like wheat – and this is unlikely (in this case) as meat and the like are not customary (paid or sold) by the measure.' What ash-Shabeebi said is evident and Allah knows best."

I say: "Sayyidi 'Abdallah ibn al-Hajj Ibrahim al-'Alawi has chosen the judgement of al-Burzuli, so examine it in his (book of) responses."

Then al-Hattab goes on to say after a discussion: "Notice: if the people of a land use two or three kinds of staple food equally as much, and there is no one food which is the most widely used, then the most evident judgement is that payment is made from each according to what the person paying uses, although I have not see an explicit text on the subject, and Allah knows best."

Ibn al-Hattab then goes on to say that al-Fakihani said in *Sharh ar-Risala*: "There is a difference of opinion regarding pulses and legumes. Ibn al-Qasim said: 'If it is the most widely used food of a people, then it is accepted of them.' Ibn Habib said: 'It is not accepted.' What is here narrated of Ibn al-Qasim is contrary to what has been transmitted from him in the *Mudawwana*, that is, that he did not hold that it was accepted unless it was their staple food, and he did not say whether it was the food they used most – so reflect on this."

Conclusion: this is comprised of several most important matters. Ibn 'Arafa said: "It is stated in *al-Mudawwana* that the traveller pays the (*zakat*) where he is, and that it is permitted for his people pay it on his behalf. Ibn Rushd said: 'This applies if he has left something for them to pay with on his behalf even if he has not instructed them to pay to it for him – that is, he does not pay it (while on the journey); and if he has not left something for them to pay with, then he must pay it for them.'"

Al-Hattab said: "If he pays for his family, then he should pay with the kind (of food) that they (customarily) eat; if they pay it on his behalf, then if should be with the kind of food that he eats. Al-Aqfahisi said in *Sharh ar-Risala*: 'If the travellers pays for himself, there are two (different) opinions as whether he should take into consideration the kind of food that the people of the land eat or what he himself eats – that is, (whether he should take into consideration) the place where he finds himself or that of his family.'"

I have said: "The most manifest meaning of his words is that he takes into consideration the customary food of the country in which he finds himself in, even if it is meat or milk, in which case it would be permitted for the townsperson, if he is outside of the town, to pay for himself in the food of the place in which he is in, be it meat or milk or anything else, and he does not have to take into consideration that his people are in their country; likewise he has to pay for his family with milk, according to one of the two opinions transmitted by al-Hattab from al-Aqfahisi, that is, what is taken into consideration when paying for his family is the customary food of the place he is in, not the food of the place they are in – so reflect on this equitably for surely being fair is the business of the noble, and being proud and envious is the affair of the people of deviation. Be acquainted with all this but do not rely on it until you see what it is based on, for *fiqh* is based on the traditional transmitted knowledge (of the *fuqaha*, as distinct from the rational sciences based on logic), and Allah is the Granter of Success."

Al-Hattab said, commenting on the words of Khalil 'the traveller pays (where he is) and it is permitted for his people to pay it on his behalf': "He has declared that it is permitted for his family to pay – and this is the unequivocal statement of the *Mudawwana*, mentioned above during the discussion of Ibn 'Arafa. Likewise Ibn al-Hajib said: 'If the family of the traveller pays it for him, then it is accepted.' Abu'l-Hasan said, following after the discussion of the *Mudawwana* above: '…and if his family pays it for him, it is accepted (by Allah, exalted is He,) on his behalf, as long he is aware that his family has paid – (his knowledge being based on the fact) that he had instructed them to pay it, that he had left them something to pay with and that he trusts they will carry out (the payment).'"

It is stated in *at-Tawdih*, following the discussion of Ibn al-Hajib above: "and this is evident, if this is what they customarily do (when he is travelling) or if he has instructed them (to do so); otherwise the most evident judgement is that this is not accepted of him, as no intention is involved."

The author of *at-Taraz* has expressed the judgement – based on juristic preference (rather than analogy) – that it is accepted even if he does not know of it, and even if he has not instructed them to pay for him or even if this has not been their custom (in the past), saying: "If the traveller does not pay it and his people pay it on his behalf, then it is accepted in two instances: firstly, if he had instructed them to pay it or this is what they customarily do, in which case it is accepted of him without doubt, for it is as if he has delegated them (to pay it); secondly, if he had not instructed them (to pay) and it is not his custom to have them pay it, there is a difference of opinion (as to whether is it accepted of him) – (and this difference of opinion is) based on (the same principle governing) the difference of opinion regarding someone who pays the *kaffara* for someone else without his knowing it and without his having giving permission to do this. However, the preferred judgement is that it is accepted of him as this (case) is (an instance of) a financial obligation which is (legitimately) removed from him – when carried out on his behalf – even if he is not aware of it, analogous to the case where (someone else pays his) debt. Moreover, it (is also analogous to the case) where someone finds something (of worth) and pays *zakat* from it on behalf of its owner – for this is permitted, that is, if the (rightful owner) comes to know of this afterwards and accepts (what has been done); otherwise – if *zakat* should not have been paid on it – his right to be compensated takes priority. Likewise, if his people do not let him know that they are sacrificing his animals in order to provide for themselves, they are accepted of him (as legitimate sacrificial animals)."

BRANCH: Ibn al-Hattab said: "Ibn al-Hajib said: 'If you were to ask whether the father's paying the *zakat al-fitr* on behalf of the son – who is of means – is accepted, I would reply: "To answer that it is accepted or rejected in an absolute manner would be wrong. What should be said is that if the son is a minor, it is permitted, and if an adult, then it is not permitted – according to those who argue that an intention is necessary regarding *zakat*, and this is stipulated in the *madhhab*."' What he is referring to, and Allah knows best, is the instance where the father does not let him know of this – and this is the most evident understanding of those who argue that it is not accepted – based on the judgement that *zakat* is conditional upon the intention. So reflect upon this, and Allah knows best. Similar to this is the case where someone voluntarily pays the *zakat al-fitr* for a person who is of means – and a case has been mentioned above (at the beginning of this chapter) – with respect to the wife who wants to pay for her own *zakat* but her husband, who is (also) of means, refuses. The most evident judgement in all of this is that it is accepted, and that the responsibility to pay the *zakat* is removed from those for whom it has been paid – if the person who has paid informs them of this; if he does not, then it is not accepted from him on account of the absence of intention, as mentioned above in the discussion from the *Tawdih*, and Allah knows best."

Just before this al-Hattab had also said, commenting on the words of Khalil 'on every Muslim for whom he provides': "He said in *at-Taraz*: 'If the husband is poor and is unable to provide for the upkeep of his wife, then he does not have to provide upkeep during the period of his (financial) difficulty; and she has the option of staying with him or separating from him: and if she stays with him, then she is responsible for the (day to day expenses of her) upkeep and for likewise the *zakat al-fitr* until his situation becomes easier. If he is able to pay for her upkeep only, she does not have to pay for the *zakat al-fitr* – as she does not have to pay for her upkeep (upon which payment of the *zakat al-fitr* is conditional): this responsibility is removed from her just as his responsibility to pay the *zakat al-fitr* is removed (from him), although this (payment of the *zakat al-fitr*) is recommended on her part. If the woman wants to pay for herself and her husband refuses, and he is of means, then it is not accepted (of her) as he is addressed (for this payment) and not her. There is a difference of opinion in this branch and the previous one – namely regarding the (husband) who is able to pay for (her) upkeep only – as to where the obligation of this (*zakat*) actually lies, that is, as to whether it falls on the person who pays it or on the person who is the 'cause' of his having to pay it. We have already discussed this matter with regard to payment of *zakat* for the slave above.'" The following is what Ibn al-Hattab said: "Having established that the obligation is that of the master, the people of knowledge have then vied with each other to ascertain the principle underlying its obligation, that is, whether it falls on the master and the slave is the 'reason' or 'cause' of its obligation or whether it the obligation falls on the slave but the responsibility (for paying) is borne by the master – and the state of slave-hood and possession is the 'reason' for his bearing it. According to this *madhhab* it is obligatory – as a principle – on the master; the followers of ash-Shafi'i differ, may Allah be pleased with him (over this matter)."

NOTICE: al-Hattab said, commenting on the words of Khalil 'and from each Muslim': "Also included in the discussion of the author is someone who frees (a slave) who is a minor – for he is responsible for his upkeep and for paying the *zakat* (*al-fitr*) on his behalf, and the 'reason' (or principle upon which this judgement is based) is the past (condition of) slave-hood. He said in *Mukhtasar al-Waqar* : 'The *zakat al-fitr* is to be paid on behalf of the breast feeding infant – if he frees him – until he is able to earn for himself and he is no longer responsible for his upkeep.'"

As for those for whom one pays the *zakat al-fitr*, they are those who are free and Muslim and poor. Khalil said: "It is paid for the free, the Muslim, if poor."

As for the time it is to be paid, Khalil said: "(it is permitted) to pay it (a little) before its (obligatory time), like two days (before), and there are two interpretations as to whether (this permission) is absolute, or whether (it is only permitted in the case) of someone who is responsible for distributing it." Ibn al-Hattab said: "Both interpretations are well known judgements, and the most preferred is that it is accepted in both cases as this (more general interpretation) is the most evident meaning of the words of the *Mudawwana*. Shaykh Zarruq said in Sharh al-Irshad: 'This is what is said, and most are of this opinion.'"

The author of *ash-Shamil* said – after mentioning that both judgements are widely accepted: "Most are of the opinion that it is accepted in both cases, and al-Qarafi has also stated this and has considered weak (the argument of) those who understand the text of the *Mudawwana* as only meaning that it is accepted in the case of the person responsible for its distribution."

NOTICE: this difference of opinion is with regard to its being handed over to the poor person before the time of its obligation. Al-Lakhmi said, after mentioning the difference of opinion: "If he knows that it will remain in the hands of the person who has received it – up to the time that it becomes obligatory, then it is accepted. This judgement is unequivocal as the person who gave it, may take it back – if we argue that it is not accepted of him; and if he takes it back, then he would be (considered, legally speaking) as someone who is just about to make the payment – from this moment on. (It is also unequivocal) because the person (he gave it to) has no need to look for his food[1] on the day of the 'Eid – that is because the (donor) knows that it will remain with him until that day, and Allah knows best."

CONCLUSION: al-Mawwaq has related: "Ibn al-Qasim said: 'As for all pulses and legumes or any other related kinds which we have mentioned as not being accepted, there is no harm in paying in them – and it is accepted (as valid *zakat*) – if they are the staple food of a people.' Khalil has included pulses and legumes in the category of (zakatable) agricultural produce on which a tenth is paid – so examine what he meant by his words 'unless their staple food is something else.' It is stated in the *Mudawwana*: 'It is not permitted to pay (the expiation for the) oath of divorce known as *dhihar* in flour, nor the *zakat al-fitr* or *kaffara*.' Ibn Junus said: 'Ibn Habib said: "If he pays the flour in surplus (over and above the precise *mudd* – given that a *mudd* of grain will become more when ground), then it is accepted of him."' Ibn Yunus has also said: 'He does not contradict Ibn al-Qasim in this, insha'Allah – as he has given what he is obliged to give and has ground it (as an extra service) willingly; and just as it would be accepted of him if he had paid it in the form of bread, so it is accepted as flour.'"

Ibn 'Arafa said, regarding *zakat al-fitr*: "It is not permitted to give it as flour. Ibn Habib said: 'It is accepted if given with a surplus, and likewise fine bread.' One of the *'ulama* of the Qayraween have said: 'The judgement of Ibn Habib is an interpretative judgement.' Commenting on the finer points of Ibn Habib, he said: 'He dislikes it to be paid in flour on account of the discrepancy (which arises between a *mudd* of grains and a *mudd* of flour from these grains when ground). However, if someone pays more than the (stipulated) food-measure, then it is accepted of him.' Asbagh said: 'Abd al-Haqq said: "This does not contradict the *Mudawwana,* and likewise (it is accepted) if he pays in bread".' Al-Lahkmi said: 'What he means by saying in the *Mudawwana* that it is not accepted of him – if paid in flour – is if he pays it without giving an additional amount

---

1 one of the 'reasons' behind the *zakat al-fitr* is that the poor are spared the trouble of having to go round looking for their provision that day – *mustaghnin 'an tawafin dhalika'l-yawm.*

(for the disparity between grains and flour); but if he does pay it with this surplus, it is accepted of him, indeed is better as the (recipient) does not have to go to the trouble of grinding it.' Ibn Yunus has also said on another occasion: 'What Ibn Habib says about flour is not contrary to what is in the *Mudawwana*.' One of the *'ulama* of the Qayraween in our area said: 'Malik says about this: "It is not accepted for the *kuffara* of a (broken) oath if it is only enough for the midday meal but not the evening, or only enough for an evening meal but not the morning; and he should give them bread which is already seasoned or accompanied by something."' Ibn Habib said: 'Plain, dry bread is not accepted – rather (it should be) accompanied with oil, meat or milk; and if he pays it with the same amount of plain bread as a measure of food, then it is accepted of him with respect to the *zakat* of fitr and *kaffara* – which has to be paid in cooked food; but as for the (expiation) of the oath of *dhihar* and the ransom to be paid as compensation for (minor) injury, it is not accepted.' At-Tunisi said: 'If he pays a *mudd* of wheat using a *mudd* of the Prophet, may the peace and blessings of Allah be upon him, for the expiation of a (broken) oath, it is accepted of him, likewise in barley or something else; and if he pays in flour, then it must be equivalent to a *mudd* of wheat – just as (it should be the equivalent to a *mudd* of wheat) if he pays in bread without any additional seasoning.'"

I have said: "His saying that a *mudd* of barley is accepted of him for the expiation of a (broken) oath is contrary to the (judgement) he has restricted himself to in the 'Chapter on Oaths', namely, that a *mudd* of barley is not accepted. The gist of the matter may be found where he mentions (this matter) in the (above mentioned) chapter and in the *Mukhtasar* of Ibn 'Arafa, in al-Qalshani's commentary on the *Risala*, and in Ibn Fa'ida's commentary on the *Mukhtasar* – and these four books are considered to be trustworthy books by the people of the *madhhab* – namely, that the *mudd* of wheat was not permitted in Madina according to Malik and Ibn al-Qasim; likewise (the judgement that it is not permitted) according to Ibn al-Qasim is also to be found in other than the *Mudawwana*. Malik said: 'People other than the people of Madina have a staple food which is other than that of the people of Madina so they should pay a little more than the *mudd*.' As for other than wheat, there are two judgements: it is said that one pays the equivalent of a *mudd* of wheat, while it is also said that one pays a little more than the *mudd*. As for what al-Mawwaq said, as related here from at-Tunisi, namely, that a *mudd* of barley and the like is accepted as payment for the expiation of the oath, this is the most evident judgement from the *Risala* and the *Mukhtasar*, and this is what al-Khurshi, ash-Shabrakheeti and Abdal-Baqi hold to, although al-Bannani and at-Tawudi have rejected it. There is no doubt that the trustworthy books mentioned above do not mention this – other than that it is 'well known' according to them, and there is no doubt that 'paying a little more' means 'paying a little more than the *mudd*' according to them. The proof of this is that Malik and Ibn al-Qasim are agreed that the *mudd*, that is a *mudd* of wheat, is (considered) enough in Madina. Malik said: 'People other than our people (in Madina) have staple foods which differ from our staple foods and so they pay a little more than the average *mudd*, that is, (people) other than the (people of Madina) mostly pay in foodstuffs (which have been prepared and ready to eat) and their demands are higher, and so a *mudd* is not accepted.' The authors of the above mentioned books relied upon (in this *madhhab*) have said: 'The difference of opinion is with respect to the *mudd* of wheat and with regard to people other than those of Madina, for other than them pay a little more than a *mudd*.' However examine what they mean by 'a little more' for I do not understand it."

He said in *al-Mi'yar*: "As-Sayouri was asked whether it was accepted that a person – whose basic food and that of his area was either raisins or pulses and legumes, or cottage cheese or milk or millet or rice or lentils – could make payment (of these) for the expiation of an oath, and whether payment of the *kaffara* was accepted if paid in something else, like the equivalent *value* (of the foodstuffs), like *zakat*; and whether – if his food and that of his region is barley – it is accepted of him if he pays in wheat."

He replied: "The various kinds of foodstuffs you have mentioned are accepted if they are their staple foods as the text of the Qur'an encompasses such (an interpretation): *'(The expiation is that you feed...) with the average amount you feed your family.'*[1] The difference of opinion which has arisen regarding the *zakat al-fitr* concerns milk and legumes. I have also discovered a difference of opinion about the dirhams to be paid for the expiation of an oath: (payment of dirhams) is not accepted by us, although it is by others. Whoever pays in wheat – and it is the best of what he usually eats – then it is accepted."

He has also said: "'Abd al-Mun'im has asked: 'How is the expiation of the oath to be paid when some people eat wheat and some barley? He replied: 'Each pays in accordance with what he eats, as Allah, exalted is He, said: "*with the average amount you feed your family, or clothe them*".'[2] It is stated in *al-Madarik*: 'Muhammad Ibn 'Abd al-Hakam said: "Ibn Wahb advised my father to pay two *mudds* for the expiation of an oath while Ibn al-Qasim instructed that one *mudd* should be paid for the expiation."'"

1   al-Ma'ida – The Table: 89
2   al-Ma'ida – The Table: 89

Book of Fasting

Book of Fasting

Mayyara said: "Here the author, may Allah have mercy on him, is commencing his explanation of the fourth pillar of Islam, namely the fast (*sawm*). The root meaning of the word *sawm* is to refrain or abstain from, and the person who refrains from something is expressed in Arabic by *sama 'anhu*. There is also the expression *sam an-nahar* meaning literally 'the day desists from (appearing)' – that is, the sun ceases to move (so quickly), when (it inclines and) the shadows increase (in length); the use of the word in the sense of 'desisting from moving' is understood here in an approximate sense – that is, in the sense of 'slowing up.' There are two judgements as to whether it is permitted to say *ana sa'im* – meaning 'I am desisting from speaking': it is related of an-Nakha'i (that it is permitted); (while others that) it is not permitted because (declaring that he is not speaking) contradicts the perception of the person addressed (- who experiences that he is indeed speaking). In the (language of the) *shari'ah*, it refers to refraining from 'the two appetites' of the stomach and the private parts for a whole day, with the intention of *qurba* – of coming closer to Allah, that is, for His sake – and (with the intention of) fulfilling the legal obligation; this, in order to oppose the desires which are responsible for the appetites of the stomach and private parts, to bring the *nafs* – the self – under control, to polish the mirror of the intellect, to take on the attributes of the angels and to arouse the slave's concern for those who are hungry."

'Ali ibn 'Abd as-Sadiq said: "The (fast) is classified in different ways: for example, it may be an obligation; or may be *makruh*, like for example, (fasting) the day of the Mawlid, the Prophet's birthday, may the peace and blessings of Allah be upon him. This (latter judgement) is recorded from Zarruq from one of the (*'ulama*) who justifies this (judgement by arguing) that it is one of the 'Eid days of the Muslims. Our Shaykh, Abu 'Abdallah al-Qouri, has expressed his juristic preference for this (latter judgement)."

Useful point: The author of *Mukhtasar Hawi as-Suyuti* said: "If you were to ask: 'Is not fasting the day of the Mawlid an expression of gratitude to

Allah – given that it is the best of actions in His eyes and that the Bani Israel fasted on the day of 'Ashura?' one could answer by saying that: 'This day is intended for relaxing, for spending more time with one's family and for taking the opportunity of being with one's children. Do you not see that the (*'ulama*) in the east and west have instructed (the men) to release their wives and children (from any responsibilities on this day), and to sing *qasidas* and songs praising the Prophet – in order that they may appreciate subtle meanings (of the deen) and that their hearts be moved to perform good acts and actions for the next world. As for any other activities associated with this (celebration), however, such as (forms of) singing and amusement which might (normally) be disapproved of, then it should be made clear that there is no harm in joining in whatever is licit and lends to the atmosphere of joy on that day; but that whatever is haram or *makruh* is prohibited. By my life, why would one not (attempt to) put a stop to anything reprehensible?! why would one not want to assist and support the one, may the peace and blessings of Allah be upon him, who was sent to put a stop to such things?! Moreover which other night is greater than this night, the night when the sublime *malakut* was adorned, as the bride is adorned, for the bridegroom of the divine kingdom?!' Al-Hafidh Shams ad-Deen al-Jazari has related that he saw Abu Lahab in a dream and the latter was asked: 'What is your state?' He replied: '(I reside) in the Fire. However, my torment is alleviated a little on Monday nights, and I may sip water from these two fingers of mine, just this amount' – and he indicated the tip of his finger. 'This is because I freed Thuwaiba when she informed me of the good news of the Prophet, may the peace and blessings of Allah be upon him, and because she gave him to suck.' If Abu Lahab, a *kafir* whom the Qur'an has censured, has been given a respite in the Fire – through the joy and happiness of the night of his Mawlid, may the peace and blessings be upon him, then how much greater must be the reward of someone from his *umma*, may the peace and blessings of Allah be upon him – someone who possesses *tawhid*, who is filled with joy by his Mawlid and who strives as much as possible to demonstrate his love for him, may the peace and blessings of Allah be upon him! By my life, his reward will be from the Noble and Generous Lord who will cause him to enter into the Gardens of Blessings."

Al-Bannani in *Hashiya az-Zurqani*, commenting on the prohibition of bequeathing something forbidden – (indicated) in Khalil's words '… and also by (bequeathing something prohibited which is) an act of disobedience' – he said: "The (*fuqaha*) have given the example of (bequeathing) wine to someone who drinks it (himself) or to someone who (as a result of becoming inebriated) kills someone else. However, no Muslim would make a will to this effect. Rather, a more fitting example would have been someone who, in his will, instructs that a dome be built over his own (grave) when he is not someone worthy of such (a memorial); or who (instructs that) a celebration of the night of the Mawlid be held in a manner which has become customary in these times, that is, where the men and woman mix freely with each other, where one may look at people who are *mahram* – that is, whom they are forbidden to look at as they are unrelated to them – and other reprehensible activities; or who instructs that (a sheet of paper on which is) written the answers to the questions (which each will be asked) in the grave should be placed in his grave and shroud – unless they be inserted in a copper casing (for example) and placed in the walls of the grave for the blessing – this has been stated by al-Masnawi."

صِيَامُ شَهْرِ رَمَضَانَ وَجَبَا

211 The fast in the month of Ramadan is obligatory ...

Al-Hattab said: "The *umma* are of a consensus that the fast of Ramadan is an obligation; that anyone who contests that it is obligatory is a renegade; that whoever refuses to fast while affirming its obligation is given the *hadd* punishment, according to the well-known judgement from the *madhhab* of Malik. Ibn 'Arafa said: 'The fast of Ramadan is obligatory and anyone who contests this (judgement) or abandons the (fast) is subject to the same judgement as (someone who contests or abandons) the *salat*.'" He has also said – with regard to *fard al-ain*, (a judgement whereby) the obligation falls on each and every individual: "Anyone who refuses to fast (in accordance with) this (obligation in Ramadan) is put to death, and likewise, anyone who refuses to do the *salat*, the *wudu'* or the *ghusl* of the *janaba* – although only the Sultan in authority can have him put to death. The author of *at-Tawdih* said: 'The judgement of Ibn Habib – with respect to putting to death anyone who abandons the *salat* as a *kafir* – is a sounder argument than that of the fast for there do not exist the same (degree of) proofs for the latter as for the *salat*; and we are not aware of anyone who agrees with him regarding the fast – except the judgement of Ibn 'Uyayna; in contrast to the *salat* for in this he concords with the (general) body of the Companions and the *Tabi'un*.'"

> ... and it is recommended to fast in (the months of) Rajab and Sha'ban

It is clear what Ibn 'Ashir means by these words.

USEFUL POINT: firstly, the author of *al-Jami' as-Saghir* said: "Whoever voluntarily fasts a day without anyone knowing of it, then Allah will not accept that he be granted any reward less than the Garden." Al-Munawi has commented on this saying: "... that is, he will enter it without being subjected to any torture or punishment; or it means (he will enter) with the first group of forerunners; and the most evident judgement is that if he conceals his action (of fasting), but is unable to prevent someone from finding out (that he is fasting), then this will not stop him from attaining the above-mentioned reward – for the reward is attained by someone who fasts for the face of Allah and who is free of any hypocrisy or showing off, and this applies here.'"

2. Ibn Hajar al-Haytami, commenting on the subject of innovation, said: "Ash-Shafi'i said, may Allah be pleased with him: 'Anything innovated which is contrary to the Book, the sunna, *ijma'* or the traditions is a *bid'a dalla* – an innovation which leads astray; any new (judgement) of benefit (to the Muslims) which is not in any way contrary to the (above mentioned sources) is a *bid'a mahmuda* – a praiseworthy innovation.' In short, there is agreement that new (judgements) of benefit (to the Muslims) are recommended – as long as they are in accord with past tradition and are not based on anything proscribed by the *shari'a*. Among such (new judgements are those which) are *fard kafaya* (that is, implying a communal responsibility), for example, the (obligation on a community to make available) works containing the (various) knowledges (of *fiqh*, *tafsir*, etc.,) and the like. Imam Abu Shama said: 'One of the best innovative practices in our time is the annual practice, on the occasion of his Moussem, may the peace and blessings of Allah be upon him, of giving *sadaqa*, doing good deeds, putting on one's best attire and joining in the spirit of joy and happiness for all of these acts, especially acts of kindness towards the poor, are an expression of love for him, may the peace and blessings be upon him; and an expression of reverence and esteem in the hearts of those taking part; and an expression of gratitude to Allah, exalted is He, for his gift of the Messenger of Allah, may the peace and blessings of Allah be upon him, whom He has sent in His generosity "*as a mercy to mankind.*" Reprehensible innovation is anything which is contrary to any of the above, whether it be open and manifest, or by association.' Then he goes on to say: 'Among the reprehensible acts of innovation is the performing (of any special *rak'ats* of) *salat* on the two nights known as *ar-Ragha'ib* – "the nights when things desired may be asked for" – that is, the night of the first *jumu'a* in Rajab and that of

the middle of Shaʻban. They are both blameworthy acts of innovation and the hadith (allegedly referring to them) is fabricated.' Again he goes on to say: 'Any criticism refers to the celebration of these two nights in particular – that is, in the manner now popular amongst the ordinary people – but it in no way invalidates what has been (correctly) related regarding the night of the middle of Shaʻban, for example in the narration: "On this night Allah, exalted is He, will forgive more (wrong actions) than the number of hairs on a sheepdog."' After a further discussion he says: 'Al-Baihaqi has reported that he, may the peace and blessings of Allah be upon him, made an (extra) *salat* on (this night) saying: "On this night each birth and death of mankind is recorded, and during this (night) their actions are raised up and their provision is brought down (to them)."' Al-Baihaqi has added: 'There is someone whose (trustworthiness is) unknown in the chains of narrations of both, but their (validity) is strengthened somewhat if assessed together.'" However, they cannot stand as evidence (here) – even if their (validity) is indeed somewhat strengthened (by considering them together) – as there is no mention that the *salat* in question was of a special character; moreover *qiyam al-layl*, 'standing the night in *salat*', is a sunna of general import and his *salat*, may the peace and blessings of Allah be upon him, on the occasion of these two nights was similar to any other night. Indeed, he would not abandon these (night *salats*), having taken them upon himself as an obligation. Among the other reprehensible kinds of innovation is the lighting of fires for the night of ʻArafa and *Mash'ar al-Haram* (at Muzdalifa); or gathering for the *layali al-khatam* – the final nights marking the end of Ramadan, setting up (special) minbars and holding speeches from them. Such (events) are considered *makruh* – as long as men and women do not mix with each other, that is, as long as there is no physical contact between them; if they do mix with each other, they are forbidden."

3. Al-Hattab said: "Ibn Hajar has related: 'There are no *sahih* hadith which affords proof as to the superiority of Rajab (over other months), or (to the excellence of) fasting any part of it, or to any particular (time) during this (month) when *qiyam al-layl* – standing the night in *salat* – is recommended. Imam al-Harawi al-Hafidh has already given a definitive statement about this before me. Everything we have related from him is based on sound chains of narration, just as we have related (sound transmissions) from others. However, the people of knowledge are well known for indulgence in their interpretations, allowing (certain) hadith to be understood as indicative of the excellence and superiority of these (nights), even if there is a weakness (in the chain of transmission) – as long, that is, as they are not (held to be) fabricated. (If such an interpretation is

accepted), then it should be conditional upon the person acting in accordance (with such a hadith) and upon his being aware that the hadith is weak; and that such (practice) should not be allowed to become (so) popular that people (begin to) act according to a weak hadith, holding something to be legally (binding) when in fact it is not part of the *shari'a* – with the result that the ignorant come to regard it as a sound sunna. Ustadh Abu Muhammad Ibn 'Abd as-Salam and others have warned people from becoming like those referred to by his words, may the peace and blessings of Allah be upon him: 'Whoever relates a hadith as if it were from me while aware that it is a lie, then he (too) will be (considered as) one of the liars.' How, then, could one *act* in accordance with such (hadith) after hearing what the Prophet, may the peace and blessings of Allah be upon him, said about merely *narrating* them)! Moreover, there is no difference between acting in accordance with such hadith in the case of *ahkam* – obligatory laws – and acting in accordance with them in the case of *fada'il* – aspects of excellence – as it is all part of the *shari'a*."

Then he goes on to say: "Al-Hafidh Abu 'Umar ibn as-Salah was asked as to whether fasting the whole of Rajab was a wrong action or was rewarded; and whether the hadith, reported by Ibn Dihya, of the Messenger of Allah, may the peace and blessings of Allah be upon him – 'Jahannam burns from one end of the year to the next for the person who fasts Rajab' – was correct. He replied: 'He would not be doing anything wrong by (fasting) this (month): none of the *'ulama* of the *umma*, as far as I know, would ascribe any wrongdoing to him. (While it is true that) those knowledgeable of the whole corpus of hadith have declared that no hadith regarding fasting in Rajab has been confirmed (as correct), that is, (no hadith has been found which attributes) any particular excellence in its regard, this does not mean one is obliged to desist from fasting in it – given the (other) narrations which establish the excellence of fasting in general. The hadith reported in the *Sunan* of Abu Dawud regarding the sacred months is indication enough of the importance attached to fasting. As for the hadith 'Jahannam burns .... for the person who fasts Rajab', it does not (have the rank of) *sahih* and its chain of narration is not sound.'"

Al-Damiri has recited the following verses:

The completion of the fast of the Deaf One[1] is recommended

    for any one who is able, and if a vow, then it is obligatory.

Ahmad considered it *makruh*, if done alone,

    and the judgement that it is prohibited in all circumstances has also been narrated.

---

1   An epithet for the month of Rajab

Ibn Majah has related that it is forbidden,
   although in the *ad-Dibaja* this (judgement) is considered weak.
Shaykh 'Izz ad-Deen said: "Those who prohibit (people)
   from fasting this (month), forbid it in all circumstances.
And have been severe in their rejection of its validity."
   However, he goes on to say. "One should not heed their *fatwa*
As those who have transmitted (the laws of) the *shari'ah*
   have not mentioned that fasting the whole of it is unacceptable.
Rather, this (fast) has (always) been understood as included in the general exhortation to fast,
   and as such, all objections are removed."
Ibn as-Salah said: "The narration that the person who fasts in Rajab
   will necessarily incur punishment
Is not sound, and it is not permitted to attribute it
   to the Messenger of Allah. Those narrating it are astray.
The general application (of the judgement regarding) the excellence of fasting
   is also proof that fasting at particular (times) is recommended."

كَتِسْعِ حِجَّةٍ وَأُخْرَى الْآخِرْ

كَذَا الْمُحَرَّمُ وَأُخْرَى الْعَاشِرْ

212 (Fasting is also recommended) during the (first) nine days of Dhu'l-Hijja, and in particular on the last (of these nine days); likewise (all of) Muharram, and in particular on the tenth, that is 'Ashura.

Al-Mawwaq said: "Ibn al-Habib said: 'It is narrated that one is particularly exhorted to fast the (first) nine days (of Dhu'l-Hijja), the *yawm at-tarwiya*[1], and the day of 'Arafa, and that fasting any of the nine days is equivalent to fasting two months at another time; and that the fasting of the *yawm at-tarwiya* is the equivalent to one year while that of 'Arafa is equivalent to two, although Ashhab, Ibn Wahb and Ibn Habib have said that it is better for the person making hajj not to fast – so that he will have more strength for the *du'a*.'"

As for Ibn 'Ashir's saying 'likewise (all of) of Muharram…', al-Mawwaq and Ibn 'Arafa have said: "The narration about the day of 'Ashura refers to the tenth of Muharram." Ibn Yunus said: "Section: the fast of 'Ashura is desirable

---

[1] 'The day of providing water' – the eighth day of Dhu'l-Hijja when the hajjis take a provision of water for Mina; or when Ibrahim reflected upon the sacrifice of his son

but not necessary. On this day the covering is put over the Ka'ba every year. It has been ascribed a special quality, namely, that even if a person has not made the intention to fast the previous night, and morning comes, then he may still fast it – and even continue fasting the rest of the day if he has eaten. This is narrated of the Messenger, may the peace and blessings of Allah be upon him, and from more than one (of the people) of the first generations. Ibn 'Abbas would continue the fast for two days for fear of missing it, and he would also fast it when on a journey, as Ibn Shihab would do. Reports urging one to spend on one's family have also been narrated – that the Messenger of Allah, may the peace and blessings of Allah be upon him, said: 'Whoever is generous to his family on the day of 'Ashura, then Allah will be generous to him for the rest of the year'; also that the people of Makka and Madina would treat it almost as if it were an 'Eid." Ibn Yunus has also narrated that Ibn al-'Arabi said in his *Masalik*: "As for spending on the day of 'Ashura and being generous, there is agreement that it will be compensated for – for Allah will reward every dirham given with ten like it.' I have seen the following lines from Ibn Habib:

Do not forget – may the All-Merciful not forget you – 'Ashura.
    Remember Him, you will be remembered (by Him) among the living.
The Messenger said, may the *salat* of Allah encompass him,
    A word upon which we found the truth and light.
Be generous with your wealth on 'Ashura for there is
    excellence in this and we have found it reported in the narrations.
Whoever is generous on the night of 'Ashura,
    then he will have ease for the rest of the year."

My Shaykh Ustadh Abu 'Abdallah al-Manouri, may Allah renew His mercy on him, recited to me: al-Khateeb Abu Bakr ibn Harb recited (it) to me on the day of 'Ashura: al-Khateeb Abu 'Ali al-Qurashi recited (it) to me on the day of 'Ashura': 'al-Khateeb Abu 'Abdallah Ibn Rushd recited (it) to me on the day of 'Ashura and he had composed it on the day of 'Ashura:

The fast of 'Ashura which is recommended
    as a sunna is well established without a doubt.
The Prophet, Mustafa, may the peace and blessings of Allah be upon him, said that
    it makes up for the wrong actions of the previous year,
And that whoever is generous on this day, then he will continue
    to enjoy ease in his life for the rest of the year."

USEFUL POINT: al-Bayjuri said in *Sharh ash-Shama'il*: "Using henna, kohl, oiling oneself, cooking grains and other practices which have become prevalent are all spurious inventions – so much so that one of the (men of knowledge) said: 'The use of kohl is an innovation of those who killed Husayn, may Allah be pleased with him.'"

Another benefit: al-Bayjuri has also said in *Sharh ash-Shama'il*: "In his book *as-Sirat al-Mustaqeem*: Ibn 'Arafa said – regarding the special qualities of (the words) *bismillahi'r-rahmani'r-raheem*: 'Whoever writes the *bismillah* one hundred and thirteen times on a piece of paper on the first day of Muharram and carries it on him, then neither he nor his family will be afflicted by any adversity for the rest of their life; and whoever writes ar-Rahman fifty times and goes into the presence of an unjust ruler while carrying it on him, then he will be protected from his injustices.'"

وَيَثْبُتُ الشَّهْرُ بِرُؤْيَةِ الْهِلَالْ

أَوْ بِثَلَاثِينَ قُبَيْلاً فِي كَمَالْ

213 The (beginning of the month) is ascertained by the sighting of the new moon or the completion of thirty days of the previous month.

Mayyara said: "Here he is informing us that the beginning of Ramadan is ascertained by establishing one of two things, either the sighting of the new moon or the (elapse of the) thirty days (of the previous month), that is Sha'ban, and is thus alluding to the words of Ibn al-Hajib and others of the people of the *madhhab*: 'The beginning of Ramadan is known in one of two ways, the first, the sighting of the new moon and the second, the completion of the thirty days of Sha'ban.' As for the sighting of the new moon, it is confirmed in relation to the person who (actually) saw it, but as for anyone other than this person, then it is confirmed for him in two ways: either by means of news of it spreading (amongst the people) such that he obtains (certain) knowledge of it or thinks this (news to be true) such that it almost has the force of (certain) knowledge[1]; or by way of a testimony according to the (required) conditions, that is, the testimony of two just, free men – and this is the well known judgement.' Ibn Musalama said: 'It is established by the testimony of one man and two women' while Ashhab said by '…one man and one woman.' It is stated in *at-Tawdih*: '… the validity of such a testimony from just one man and one woman is improbable, and this is likewise (improbable) in the case of the 'Eid al-Fitr and the celebratory days like 'Arafa and 'Ashura – nothing is confirmed except by

---

1   Ie. News of the sighting comes from various independent persons such that it is impossible that they could have colluded in relaying false information.

means of two just men or by news which has spread amongst (the people).' However, there is a difference of opinion whether fasting may begin on the testimony of just one person who informs that he has sighted it himself: Malik has prohibited that one fast (merely) on his testimony, while Ibn al-Majishun has permitted it – although this (only) applies where there is a Qadi and a *jama'a* of Muslims who maintain the laws of the shar'iat and the times of worship, that is, his testimony only may not be considered if these conditions apply; if there is no imam at all, or there is one but he does not act correctly regarding (the sighting of) the new moon and has no concern for it, then it is enough to hear of it from a trustworthy person or by sighting it himself. Thus he may fast on the strength of these (two sources of information) and may break the fast on the strength of these; and those who follow him may act in this way too – this is narrated by al-Baji and others from 'Abd al-Malik. This judgement refers to the region where these conditions apply – in the manner mentioned above. If this (news) is transmitted to another region, then this may happen in one of four ways: news is brought from a person who himself heard it from another, in which case those whom the news reaches, must perform the fast and make it up (if necessary); or by means of the testimony of someone who has heard the news from another; or via someone who has heard the news from the testimony of another; or by means of a testimony based on another testimony[1] – and the judgement is the same in (all four) if the testimony which is transmitted has been confirmed (as credible) by the person in highest authority, that is the Khalif, or if it has been confirmed by a particular (local) person in authority, and this is the well known judgement – although 'Abd al-Malik said that this is only binding for those (people) under his authority. There are two different opinions, as to whether it is enough that the transmission be from one person from the imam or by way of (general) news which spreads (through the people). Al-Baji said: 'If the sighting of the new moon is established by the imam and he issues the judgement on this (basis, namely that fasting should begin) and news of this is brought to someone by a just person or news of it comes from another region, then Ahmad Ibn Muyassar al-Iskandari said: "You are obliged to fast as (the judgement in this case) is the same as (the judgement governing) 'the (obligation to) accept the news from one just person', and is not classed in the category of a testimony."' Shaykh Abu Muhammad said: 'The judgement of Ibn Muyassar is correct and resembles (the judgement regarding) a man transmitting the news to his family or his young daughter[2] – for this (news) obliges them to fast the next day.' It has

---

1   The text of Mayyara is defective in the text of Shaykh Shinqeeti
2   Literally his virgin daughter (according to the original text of Mayyara) – perhaps what

also been transmitted that Abu Umran al-Fasi said: '(The obligation to fast) is not established by this.' However, this difference of opinion applies to informing (persons) other than one's family; as for news transmitted to one's family from one person – and anyone who follows them in this – there is agreement that it should be accepted, as reported before from Abu Muhammad."

In *al-Mi'yar* it is stated: "Ibn as-Siraj was asked about fasting and breaking the fast merely on (the basis of) hearing news and he replied: 'No one should rely – for starting or breaking his fast – on someone whose uprightness and probity is unknown. However, if he breaks the fast (when it is not in fact the end of the fast), he does not have to pay *kaffara* as he would be subject to the judgement of a *mutawwil* – that is, someone who breaks his fast on the basis that he himself believed it legitimate to do so. As for villages or towns where there is no *qadi* and no one who takes the trouble to watch for the new moon, then he should rely on the person who informs him if amongst the upright, that is, if he hears it from him personally, even if it is only one person, irrespective of whether he is from the town or from elsewhere – for news from one upright person is also enough if a sighting is made, according to the required conditions, in another town.'"

NOTICE: It is also stated in *al-Mi'yar*: "…among the issues discussed by al-Qafasi and an-Nakha'i is the following: 'The validity of a testimony made on receiving news (from others) is not conditional upon the probity and uprightness of the people (in question): even if they are Christians or people whose reputation is not wholly sound, then the (testimony) is valid.' 'Abd al-Jalal ar-Rub'i, responding to this said: 'Whoever thinks that information through multiple channels has to be transmitted by people of uprightness and of probity has not fully understood the matter under discussion for even if the transmission by multiple chains of narration is via *kuffar*, this news counts as (certain) knowledge – and this is the *ijma'* of the people of sunna, as well as others from amongst the people of innovation.'"

In the *Sharh at-Tayibiya* from Ibn 'Abd al-'Aziz it is stated: "As for the minimum number of persons needed to constitute *at-tawatir* – news based on multiple source and channels – what counts is (not so much the number of persons) but rather whether or not certainty regarding the ruling has been obtained and whether or not uncertainty has been removed. Although some stipulate five (persons) – while others twelve, twenty or forty – there is no evidence that certainty can only be obtained by a particular minimum number of persons relaying (the information)."

---

is meant is that she is still a minor, although the significance of this is unclear.

TWO BENEFITS: firstly, al-Munawi said in *Sharh al-Jami'*: "Shaykh al-Islam Zakariya was asked about a man who claimed to have seen the Prophet, may the peace and blessings of Allah be upon him, and that he had said to him: 'Instruct my *umma* to fast three days, to celebrate an 'Eid after these (three days) and to make a *khutba*' — he was asked whether such a fast would be obligatory, recommended, permitted or forbidden; and whether it would it be *makruh* for him to say to someone 'the Prophet may the peace and blessings of Allah has instructed you to fast three days'; and whether it would (still) be (considered as) relating untruths about him, (may the peace and blessings of Allah be upon him), if he based what he said on a dream which he had heard from someone other than the person who had actually had the dream, or from the person himself; and whether it is possible for Iblis, may Allah curse him, to use the name of the Prophet, may the peace and blessings of Allah be upon him, to claim he is the Prophet, and to command a person to obey him only in order to cause him to disobey; and whether it is possible for him to take on the noble form of the Prophet, may the peace and blessings of Allah be upon him; and in what manner the genuine vision of him, may the peace and blessings of Allah be upon him, differs from the spurious; and whether there are any judgements in the *shari'ah* regarding seeing (him) in dreams; and whether it is he himself who is seen or his *ruh*, may the peace and blessings of Allah be upon him, or its likeness? He replied: 'No one is obliged to fast, and none of the other judgements mentioned above apply. It is not recommended, rather it is *makruh* or prohibited; however if a person is convinced that the vision is genuine, then he should do what is indicated in it as long as the law of the *shari'ah* is not affected by it. There is nothing in the judgements (of the *shari'ah*) to doubt the accuracy of the one who sees a vision. However, it is prohibited for someone to say 'The Prophet, may the peace and blessings of Allah be upon him, has commanded you to...' as mentioned above or to back up what he has to say with evidence from the dream. There is no rational reason why Iblis, may the curse of Allah be upon him, could not use the name of the Prophet, may the peace and blessings of Allah be upon him, and tell the person sleeping that he was the Prophet, may the peace and blessings of Allah be upon him; or that he command him to do something which (appears) to be an act of obedience. A genuine dream is one which is free of *adhghath* – '*the jumbled mass (of mixed up dreams)*.'[1] These latter may be of different kinds. Firstly, they may occur when shaytan plays tricks on the person having a dream: he causes him to despair by making it appear, for example, that his head has been cut off;

---

[1] Yusuf – 44

secondly, when the person dreaming sees one of the prophets command him to something forbidden or impossible; thirdly, when Iblis causes a person's *nafs* – his self – to insinuate something to him in a waking state such that a wish or desire is realised and the person sees the Prophet as if in a dream. Having a vision of Mustafa, may the peace and blessings of Allah be upon him, in his well known form, is to perceive him himself; seeing him in other than this form is perceiving the likeness of him. The former does not need to be interpreted while the latter does. This also corresponds to the words of an-Nawawi: 'The correct (judgement) is that he is actually seen, whether in his well known form or otherwise.'"

SECOND BENEFIT: al-Hattab has related: "al-Dameeri said: 'It is recommended, when sighting the new moon, to recite *"Blessed be He who has the Kingdom in His hand!"*[1] as it has been transmitted that it is a salvation and a protection.' Ash-Shaykh Taqi ad-Deen as-Subki said: 'This is because its thirty *ayats* are the same number as the days of a month; and because tranquillity descends when reciting it; and because he, may the peace and blessings of Allah, would recite it before sleeping.'"

فَرْضُ الصِّيَامِ نِيَّةٌ بِلَيْلِهِ
وَتَرْكُ وَطْءٍ شُرْبِهِ وَأَكْلِهِ

214 The obligations of the fast are: making an intention in the (first) night, abstaining from intercourse, drinking and eating,

وَالْقَيْءِ مَعْ إِيصَالِ شَىْءٍ لِلْمَعِدْ
مِنْ أُذُنٍ أَوْ عَيْنٍ أَوْ أَنْفٍ قَدْ وَرَدْ

215 not (deliberately) vomiting and ensuring that nothing reaches the stomach entering via the ear, nose, or eye.

وَقْتَ طُلُوعِ فَجْرِهِ إِلَى الْغُرُوبْ
وَالْعَقْلُ فِي أَوَّلِهِ شَرْطُ الْوُجُوبْ

216 The time (of the fast) is from the appearance of dawn to sunset. Being

---

1 i.e. Sura al-Mulk – The Kingdom, 1-30

of sane mind at the beginning (of the fast) is a condition for its being obligatory.

وَلْيَقْضِ فَاقِدُهُ...

217 any person deprived of this (sanity) must make it up...

His saying 'The obligation of the fast is making an intention' resembles the words of Khalil 'its validity is wholly dependent on making the intention the night before.' Ibn al-Hattab said, commenting on *fard al-'ain* – an obligation of an individual (rather than communal nature): "The form of the intention is that it be made the night before – whether for an obligatory or voluntary (fast), or a (fast undertaken as a) vow or (for) *kaffara* – or that it be made just before dawn, and that it be done with a certainty of resolve, without hesitation, and that an intention is made to carry out the obligation of (the whole of) Ramadan." Ibn Juzayy said: "This 'certainty of resolve' excludes any hesitation – and so making the intention in Ramadan to fast the 'day of doubt' the next day is not acceptable on account of the lack of certainty. However, there is no harm in doubt or wavering after thinking (the fast has begun) on (hearing) a testimony, or (after thinking it has finished because) it is close to the end (of the month) of Ramadan, or in the case of someone made captive (by *kuffar* who has lost track of time and) who forms a judgement (based on calculation)."

The author of *an-Nawadir* in the 'Book of Fasting' has related that Malik said: "Making the intention the night before means having the resolve to fast before the appearance of dawn. It may be that he abandons this resolve just before *fajr*. If the dawn appears, then his intent is based on the last state of his resolve – that is whether he had resolved fast or not to fast."

USEFUL POINT: voluntary fasting is one of those (acts of worship) whose (completion) become binding once started. Ibn al-Hattab said in *Fasl al-Jama'a*: "These (acts of worship) comprise the *salat*, fasting, *i'tikaf*, hajj, 'umra, taking an imam (in the *salat*) and *tawaf*. One of the *'ulama* has formulated them in verse saying:

The *salat*, the fast, then the hajj and *'umra*,
   followed by the *tawaf*, the *i'tikaf* and the taking of an imam (in the *salat*)
All should be repeated if they are interrupted deliberately,
   and the repeating (of these acts) in an obligation which is binding.

Examine his statement that one must repeat 'taking an imam' for the most evident judgement is that this is not binding. This is correct, that is, the intention is necessary at the beginning on joining (the *salat*) behind an imam and it is not permitted for him to abandon it; however, if he ceases (to follow an imam), he does not have to repeat it with another imam, and Allah, exalted is He, knows best."

Zarruq said in *Sharh al-Irshad*: "The principle of the *madhhab* is that for each act of worship, the first (part) of it is dependant upon the last (part) of it, and that each act must be completed (in its entirety). The principle (on which this judgement is based) is the hajj – which must be completed – and (the same applies in the case of) the *'umra*, the *salat*, the fast, the *i'tikaf* and the *tawaf*, unlike the *wudu'*, recitation, *dhikr* and the like." Examine *adh-Dhakheera*, chapter 15, regarding the *nafila salat*. Among the things discussed in this (work) is (the following): "Our companion has declared that if someone (who is already in a state of *wudu'*) refreshes his *wudu'*, then he does not have to do it again if he breaks off (halfway through doing it); likewise beginning an act of *sadaqa*, of recitation or *dhikr* or any other act (undertaken in order) to come closer to Allah (does not have to be made up if interrupted)." After mentioning these seven (acts of worship) in the 'Book of Fasting' of *adh-Dhakheera*, he goes on to say: "…unlike *wudu'*, *sadaqa*, *waqf*, travel for the purpose of *jihad* and other matters."

Al-Mawwaq, after commenting on the Khalil's words 'the person intending it should make his intention on entering it' regarding *i'tikaf* said: "*Dhikr* and recitation do not have to be completed merely because they have been begun – for *dhikr* is something which may be done in parts, and anything undertaken (but not completed) may validly be considered as worship, as in the case of recitation."

Ibn 'Ashir's saying 'abstaining from intercourse' is like Khalil's '…by refraining from intercourse.' Al-Mawwaq, commenting on Khalil's additional words 'and emission of semen or pre-seminal fluid' said: "As for the emission of pre-seminal fluid, Ibn 'Arafa said: 'An emission which occurs as a result of recalling something (sensual) breaks (the fast) as does looking (at a woman) without deliberately seeking sensual stimulation – if he persists in his looking or recalling. If he looks without intention or recalls something (stimulating) and has an emission, but does not persist in this looking or remembering, then it has been said that he has to make it up; and what has been reported of Ibn al-Qasim is with regard to looking at or remembering (something sexually stimulating) which he is compelled to (by circumstance and over which he has no control). However, it has also been said that he does not have to make it up unless he persists in it. Ibn al-Qasim has related this judgement from Malik (specifically) with regard to 'remembering' – although 'looking' may also be understood in this context. Indeed there is (essentially) no difference between the two statements. This judgement is evident as a fast does not have to be made up for (an emission of) pre-seminal fluid according to ash-Shafi'i, Abu Hanifa and most of the people of knowledge, and the Baghdadis have said: 'The (judgement that a) person who kisses and has an emission has to make up (his fast) is (only a) recommendation in the *madhhab* of Malik.'"

Ibn 'Arafa said: "Ibn Rushd has related: 'If he intends (obtaining) sensual pleasure by looking or recalling something (sensual), or when touching (a woman), kissing or bodily contact (prior to sexual intercourse), but remains free (of any emission), then he has nothing to make up; if he has an erection, but does not have an emission, his fast is only broken in the case of the third (kind of action mentioned above), namely though bodily contact (prior to sexual intercourse) – according to the transmission of Ibn al-Qasim and the narrations from Ashhab and Ibn al-Qasim. Sahnun, however, has rejected it.' Al-Baji said that Ibn Wahb has related: 'He does not have to make it up.' Ibn al-Qasim has related in the transmission of 'Isa: 'Bodily contact (*mubashara*) is the same as any other (contact).' 'Iyad said: 'There are two opinions as to the obligation of making up (the fast) if one has an erection when kissing or as a result of bodily contact. It is said that this difference is based on (the difference between) having an erection in the (above) two cases and having one as a result of seeing (something stimulating) or touching (a woman) inadvertently.' Ibn Rushd said: 'If he intends this and has an emission, then he has to make up (the fast).'"

'Ayn-Jeem – and those who follow him – has preferred the judgement that he does not have to make it up when having an erection. Examine az-Zurqani or 'Ali ibn 'Abd as-Sadiq (in this respect). Ibn 'Arafa said: "'Iyad has related – in his discussion of the obligation or recommendation to make it up after a pre-seminal emission: '... thirdly, if (emission is a result of) touching, kissing or bodily contact (prior to intercourse) or deliberately looking, not if he does not intend to look – according to most of the Shaykhs; however, one of them, as well as Ibn Habib and al-Mughira have said: "There is no making up for a pre-seminal emission, even from touching."'"

Ibn 'Ashir's saying '(abstaining) from drinking or eating' is clear and the judgement is even clearer.

As for his saying 'not vomiting', the author of the *Risala* said: "If he tries to vomit and succeeds, he must make it up." Ibn al-Fa'ida said in *Sharh al-Mukhtasar*: "Ibn 'Arafa said: 'It is obligatory to make it up after vomiting deliberately, and it is recommended (to make it up) – in the case of an obligatory or voluntary fast – when done mistakenly.' Al-Lakhmi has adopted the judgement of Ibn al-Qasim '(vomiting) does not interrupt the continuity of the fast (of Ramadan, for example)'; and, according to the relation of Ibn Habib and Ibn al-Majishun, 'swallowing back – if one is able to spit it out – is (considered) the same as eating.'"

As for Ibn 'Ashir's saying 'and ensuring that nothing reaches the stomach....'" Mayyara said: "... fifthly, among the obligations of the fast is preventing anything from reaching the stomach, whether via the ear, the eye or the nose or any other way – from the appearance of the dawn to sunset. It is not enough simply to prevent something from reaching the stomach by refraining from eating or drinking; rather, injections or enemas may also not be administered. Moreover, anything which enters the throat annuls the fast, even if it does not reach the stomach, just as anything which reaches the stomach annuls it also, even if it does not pass by the throat – if it enters via the anus, for example, when the enema is liquid. If, however, something is introduced which is not liquid, like a cord or plaited tampon, or something is introduced via the opening of the penis – where the urine comes out – then he does not have to make anything up. In the *Mudawwana* it is stated that Malik disliked the use of an enema when fasting and that if employed during the obligatory (fast) – and something reaches the stomach – then the fast must be made up, although *kaffara* does not have to be paid."

'Ali ibn 'Abd as-Sadiq said, commenting on Ibn 'Ashir's words 'the time (of the fast) is from the appearance of dawn to sunset': "this (also) indicates the period during which the making up (of a fast) may become obligatory, that is, any time during the day when something reaches the stomach from the eye, nose or ear; if, however, he takes or applies something at night and it descends (into his stomach) during the day, then he does not have to make anything up – as this occurs within his body and 'descends', as it were naturally, from the top to the bottom."

Mayyara said: "He said in *adh-Dhakheera*: 'Whoever applies kohl at night, then there is no harm if it descends into his stomach during the day. Whoever knows that kohl and the like does not usually reach his throat, then he does not have to make anything up' – this Al-Lakhmi has stated. What (is to be noted is that) he is referring to this when done at night, and Allah knows best. Ash-Shaykh Abu'l-Hasan as-*Saghir* said: 'This is also the principle (to be applied) regarding anything applied to the head, like henna, oil or anything else.' He said in *Tahdheeb at-Talib* from as-Sulaymaniya – regarding someone who breathes in vapour or smoke as a medicine and finds the taste of the vapour in his throat: 'He should make up (the fast) in the same way as someone who applies kohl or oil to his head and then notices (the taste of) it in his throat would make (it) up.' Abu Muhammad said: 'One of our companions has informed me that Ibn Lubaba said that anyone who breathes in smoke or vapour does not break the fast, and that he considered it *makruh* for him (to breath in vapour while fasting).' It is stated in one of the commentaries on the *Mudawwana* – after narrating the above from as-Sulaymaniya – that 'the fast should also be made up if one breathes in the vapour from a cooking pot – as it is composed of tiny particles; but not in the case of the (extremely) fine perfume (composed of musk and amber) known as *ghalia*.' Ibn al-Hajib said: '...unlike the application of oil to the head, that is, the fast does not have to be made up.' It has also been said: '...unless he gets a taste of it.' Muhammad Ibn 'Abd as-Salam said: 'The difference of opinion is based on a difference of state.' He said in *at-Tawdih*: 'I do not accept the first judgement.' 'Iyad considered application of oil to the head as *makruh* in his *Qawa'id*.' Al-Qubab said: 'It is not permitted according to the well-known opinion, that is, if he applies henna or something else to his head, knowing that it will reach his throat; and it is *makruh* according to the judgement of Abu Mus'ab, and this is also what he holds to in his *Qawa'id*. Sanad said: 'If he scratches the bottom of his leg with colocynth and then finds the taste of it in his mouth, or he picks up snow or ice with his hand and then feels a coldness in his stomach, then he does not have to make anything up.'" As for smelling perfumes, the author of the *Mi'yar* has transmitted that Imam Abu'l-Qasim al-Aqbani said: "I do not know of anyone who holds that it breaks the fast, although it is *makruh* according to the *madhhab* of one of the people of knowledge."

ISSUE: az-Zurqani has related: "Ibn al-Hattab has narrated from al-Burzuli: 'Whoever has a nose bleed, squeezes his nose and blood comes out of his mouth, but does not let it reach his throat, then he does not have to make anything up.' This is because it comes out of the nose and reaches the mouth but not the stomach – and as long as it does not reach the stomach, he has nothing to make up."

'Ali ibn 'Abd as-Sadiq goes on to say: "What is to be inferred from his saying 'and if it does not reach his throat, then he does not have to make anything up' is that if it does reach his throat, then he has broken his fast – and this corresponds to what has been confirmed (above), namely, that any liquid reaching the throat breaks a person's fast. What is to be inferred from his saying 'as long as it does not reach the stomach...' is that if it only reaches the throat, it does not break his fast. However, it may well be that his former judgement should be acted upon."

I have said: "Likewise, his fast is not broken by rinsing his mouth with water when thirsty, or swallowing his spittle after the taste of the water has disappeared or, in the case of a sore in his mouth, swallowing his spittle after bleeding has ceased – according to what Ibn al-Quhah has recorded. Ibn al-Hattab said, commenting on the words of Khalil 'rising the mouth when thirsty': 'Ibn 'Arafa said that Ibn al-Qasim stated that swallowing his spittle (is permitted).' Al-Baji said: 'What he means is after the taste of the water has disappeared.' In the *Majha'* the author has deemed it *makruh* for the person fasting to immerse his head under water."

'Izz ad-Deen was asked as to whether the fast of someone who spits out blood from a mouth sore but does not rinse out (his mouth) is annulled if he swallows his impure spittle and he replied: "It is not permitted for the person who is fasting to swallow his impure spittle, and his fasting is annulled if he does this. The licence (to swallow) is (only) in the case of spittle which is permitted (because it is pure, and because to spit it out continually) would be very difficult. Thus swallowing it (in this case) while fasting – and at other times – is forbidden, and his fasting is invalidated because the licence for swallowing it has been removed (by the presence of the blood)." Al-Mashdali said: "This is clear if the bleeding does not stop. If it does stop, then there is no harm (in swallowing), as stated above, for any impurity remaining is of a theoretical, secondary nature (*hukmiya*), not one based on the actual source of impurity." As for the (judgement) reported by 'Abd al-Haqq, namely, that a bucket which has been (waterproofed by) the application of oil and which is used to wash (the private parts) after going to the toilet renders all the water impure, obliges one to conclude that all (spittle) in the mouth is impure even if the bleeding has stopped – until, that is, he has washed out his mouth with water – as the Shaykh said. Ibn Qudah said: "in this case, the (mouth) is purified with a liquid other than water (i.e. its spittle)." The well known judgement is that it is not accepted in the *salat*, but there is no harm with regard to eating as the *source* of the impurity itself has disappeared.

As for his saying "being of sane mind at the beginning (of the fast) is a condition for its being obligatory" Mayyara commented: "Here he is informing us that being of sane mind at the beginning of the fast, that is, at the appearance of dawn, is a prerequisite for the obligation of the fasting, that is, for the validity and correctness of its performance – as Ibn Rushd has explained. It follows then that, in the case of insanity, the fasting is not an obligation and that it is not valid or correct (if performed); but that it is still an obligation on him, that is, whoever loses his intellect at the appearance of dawn must make it up later."

Then he goes on to say after a discussion: "This judgement applies to someone who loses his intellect through insanity; but as for (losing it) through sleep, Ibn al-Hajib said: 'There is agreement that sleep does not affect (the validity of the fast), even if it goes on throughout the day – for it veils the intellect but does not cause it to disappear' – and is therefore not referred to in the words of the author 'and that he make up any fast he has missed', and Allah knows best."

$$... وَالْحَيْضُ مَنَعَ$$

$$صَوْماً وَتَقْضِي الْفَرْضَ إِنْ بِهِ ارْتَفَعْ$$

... menstruation prevents fasting, and the woman must make up the obligatory (fast) when it stops.

Mayyara said: "Having spoken of the obligations and its conditions, he now goes on to discuss what prevents (a person from fasting). Thus he informs us that menstruation is one such obstacle, whether the fasting is obligatory or not; and for this reason he says 'fasting' (rather than the fast of Ramadan)." Then Mayyara goes on to say that "a woman must make up any obligation, that is any obligatory fast, if the obligation is (temporarily) removed because of the menstruation" – although his words may also mean – "if the obligation is annulled." He then says: "What is to be concluded from his words 'she must make up the obligatory (fast)' is that if she makes a fast which is not obligatory, then she does not make it up – and this is correct."

He then goes on to say: "If a woman is in doubt as to whether she has become pure before the dawn or after it, she must fast because of the possibility that she was indeed pure *before*; and she has to make it up afterwards because of the possibility that she became pure *afterwards*. It is stated in *at-Tawdih*: 'Ibn Rushd said: "and this is contrary to the *salat*, for it is not incumbent on her to make up the (*salat*) as long as she is in doubt as to whether she is pure during the (time prescribed for the *salat*) or not, and this is obvious for menstruation is something which prevents both the carrying out of the *salat* and making it up, and what requires *qada* (that is, having to make up the *salat* in general) – namely her becoming pure again – (this is non-existent) on account of the doubt (about whether she is in fact pure). But as for the fast, menstruation only prevents one carrying it out, but does not prevent one from making it up. Thus it is that it is necessary to make up the fast, but not the *salat*."'"

$$\text{وَيُكْرَهُ اللَّمْسُ وَفِكْرٌ سَلِمَا}$$

$$\text{دَأْبًا مِنَ الْمَذْيِ وَإِلَّا حَرُمَا}$$

218 It is *makruh* to touch (a woman) or allow thoughts (of a sexual nature) – that is, as long as one remains free (of any emission) of pre-seminal fluid; otherwise such (things) are forbidden.

Mayyara said: "He has informed us that it is *makruh* for the person fasting to touch (a woman) or have thoughts (of a sexually stimulating nature) if he is not subject to emissions of pre-seminal fluid or – and this is even more obvious – of semen; if he is sometimes subject to (such emissions), then it is forbidden for him (to touch women or deliberately persist in such thoughts). Moreover this judgement is not restricted to 'touching (women)' or '(sexual) thoughts'; rather it applies to other (activities) besides these two, such as any kind of foreplay, looking at, kissing, or caressing each other and having bodily contact. The difference between 'touching' (*al-lams*) and 'bodily contact' (*mubashara*) is that the former is with the hand and the latter is with the body. It is stated in *at-Tawdih*: 'There are three different judgements regarding the activity prior to intercourse. If the person knows that he will remain free of (any emission of) pre-seminal fluid and semen, then it is not forbidden, although the (*'ulama*) have deemed it *makruh*, according to the well known judgement. The degree of dislike has been categorised into different degrees of severity, and the *'ulama* have adopted what Ibn al-Hajib said (on the subject), namely – in order of ascending severity – thoughts (of a sexual nature), then looking, then kissing, then bodily contact, then mutual caressing. If, however, the person knows that he will be subject to an emission of sperm or pre-seminal fluid, then it is forbidden. If he has doubts as to whether he will be subject (to them or not), then there are two judgements, the most evident of them, that it is forbidden – as a precautionary measure – prior to any act of worship. However, it is also said that it is not prohibited – (and this is based on the) the principle (that everything) is licit (before proved to be otherwise).' Al-Lakhmi said: 'If the person is subject to an emission on one occasion but not on another, then it is forbidden.'"

Al-Mawwaq said, commenting on the words of Khalil '… foreplay (ordinarily leading to intercourse), like kissing or having (sexual) thoughts (is permitted) – if one knows one will be free of any emission; otherwise it is forbidden': "Ibn al-Qasim said: 'Malik is strict regarding kissing when fasting, with respect to both the obligatory and voluntary fasts.' Ashhab said: 'touching with the hand is less (reprehensible) than kissing, kissing is less (reprehensible) than bodily contact, and bodily contact is less (reprehensible) than caressing the private parts or any other part of the body, and I prefer that one desist from any of this. Malik is stricter regarding kissing during the obligatory fast than kissing during the voluntary fast in which one does not have to make up for kissing or touching even if one has an erection and an emission of pre-seminal fluid. The men of excellence would avoid going into their houses during the day in Ramadan fearing for themselves – lest, as a result, something *makruh* happened to them.'

Al-Lakhmi said: 'Kissing, bodily contact and hand contact are not prohibited in themselves, and they may be variously licit, forbidden or disliked, depending on what is involved. Whoever knows that he will not have any emission of sperm or pre-seminal fluid, then such things are licit for him, while anyone who knows that he will certainly have an emission (of sperm) or that on occasion he will have one and on another he will not, then they are prohibited him – and it is in this light that Malik's judgement, (recorded) in the *Mudawwana*, may be understood – "Whoever gives his wife one kiss in Ramadan and has an emission, then he should make up (a day) and pay the *kaffara*." If he is subject to emissions of pre-seminal fluid, then there is a difference of opinion: those who consider that it invalidates the fast, (hold that) it is obligatory to desist from whatever it is that causes such (an emission); while those who do not, (hold that) it is (merely) recommended to desist from that (which causes the emission). And the judgement that pre-seminal fluid does not invalidate (the fast) is the better (of the two); moreover in the Qur'an it is stated that one should desist from whatever annuls the *major* purity, not the *minor* (purity) – if it were necessary to make up for what invalidates the minor purity, then the fast would be invalidated merely by kissing, bodily contact or touching hands, even without an emission of pre-seminal fluid. All agree that *kaffara* is not rendered obligatory when done deliberately and that it does not interrupt the (obligation to fast) consecutive days if the fast has been undertaken for (the expiation of the oath of divorce known as) *dhihar*, or for the (unintentional) killing of someone.' Abu 'Umar said in his *Tamheed*, regarding the Prophet's kissing his wives, may the peace and blessing of Allah be upon him, while fasting: 'If a person is not subject (to any emission), then he may (kiss); if someone fears for the *umma* of Muhammad, may the peace and blessings of Allah be upon him, more than what the Prophet himself feared for it, then he is guilty of a clear aberration and excessive strictness. Even if it is recommended to be steadfast and patient (when fasting), it is impossible that the (hadith) referred only to him, may the peace and blessings of Allah be upon him, and that he said nothing about (its particularity to him).[1]"

ISSUE: among the disliked things is fasting six days of Shawwal – lest they be (considered) joined to Ramadan. Khalil said: "(fasting the three days is recommended) but fasting (the three) 'white' days (of the full moon in the middle of the month, i.e. 13th, 14th, and 15th) is disliked (if one believes it must be these three in particular), as is (fasting) the six days of Shawwal (when considered an integral part of Ramadan)." Al-Hattab, commenting on these (words of Khalil) said: "Muslim has related (the hadith) '...whoever fasts Ramadan and follows it with six from Shawwal' (but) Malik considered it recommended to fast in other than (the six days following Ramadan) lest they be taken as part of Ramadan by the ignorant – for the law has designated this (fast) in Shawwal as it is easier to (continue) fasting immediately after the fast (of Ramadan). However, what (is indicated in the hadith) may be fulfilled (by fasting) other than these (days) – and so the law also instructs that it be delayed in order to attain the benefit (of fasting) and that (of avoiding the risk of considering it part of Ramadan)." Then he goes on to say: "Ash-Shabeebi said: 'Malik disliked this lest it be seen to constitute part of Ramadan, but as for individual instances, then it is not *makruh* for a man to fast it.' It is also recommended that one fast it in other than (the first six days of) Shawwal in order to multiply these (six) and those of Ramadan until the required number – mentioned by the Prophet, may the peace and blessings of Allah be upon him, when he said 'Whoever fasts Ramadan and follows it with six of Shawwal, then it is as if he has fasted all the time' – is attained. In other words, fasting of the month of Ramadan becomes the equivalent of ten months[2] and the fasting of the six days of Shawwal becomes the equivalent of two months making a whole year – in all. Its being designated in Shawwal is in order to make it easier for the person – who has become accustomed to fasting (in Ramadan) – and not because the time (of Shawwal), as such, is of particular importance. If he were to fast in the first ten days of Dhu'l-Hijja, then it would also serve to attain the number of days intended, as mentioned above."

Ibn ash-Shat said in his *Hashiya* on *al-Furuq*: "His saying that Shawwal, in particular, has been appointed out of concern (to make it easier) on the *mukallaf*, and (that the six days are better fasted at another time) to avoid the possibility

---

1 see (al-Mawwaq), *Mawahib al-Jalil*, p. 416, vol.2 where al-Mawwaq's text is clearer than the text of the translation.

2 Based on the hadith that a good act is rewarded ten times over.

that it leads (the ignorant into supposing that they are part of Ramadan) is not a well founded judgement."

وَكَرِهُوا ذَوْقَ كَقِدْرٍ وَهَذَرْ

219 They considered it *makruh* to taste (something) like (food from) a cooking pot and (to engage in) idle talk;

Mayyara said: "He has informed us that the people of the *madhhab* consider it *makruh* for the fasting person to taste what is cooking to see if it is salty (enough). He uses the Arabic letter *kaf* meaning 'like…' to indicated that this also refers to other things like tasting honey, chewing gum or chewing food to give to infants. The (*fuqaha*) also consider idle talk to be *makruh*, and 'idle talk' means 'talking a lot without benefit.'"

USEFUL POINT: in *al-Jami' as-Saghir* he said: "Most people guilty of wrong actions on the Day of Rising will be those who get involved in what does not concern them. Al-Munawi said: 'that is, occupying himself with something which brings no benefit to him in the next world – the more someone speaks the more (likelihood) there is that it will consist of worthless prattle; or that one will utter outrageous things, errors and mistakes; or that one will not reflect about (what one is saying) – and that his wrong actions will multiply without him realising it. In the hadith of Mu'adh is related: "and will anything else propel people into the Fire on their noses (so surely) as the harvests of their tongues." In the narration of at-Tirmidhi it is related that a man died and someone addressed him saying: "Receive the good news of the Garden" but then al-Mustafa – the Chosen One said, may the peace and blessings of Allah be upon him: "Do you not realise that he may well have spoken about things which did not concern him, or that he has been niggardly with something which was of no benefit for him to retain." The people[1] consider that excessive speech about what does not concern one or being mean issues from the selfish desires of the *nafs*, and the sicknesses of the hearts. Such (habits) are cured by (carrying out) the individual obligations (of the *shari'ah*); and healed by becoming aware that one's time is one's most precious commodity and that it should be filled with the most precious of activities, namely *dhikr*. They have also indicated that remembering the Day of Rising should also remind one that any afflictions or sicknesses which occur as a result of such evil habits are not (like other afflictions) such that they will expiate other wrong actions.'"

Yunus ibn 'Ubayd said: "All goodness may be corrupted or spoilt except that

---

1 i.e. the Sufis

which issues from guarding the tongue – for it is part of goodness (itself) and cannot be spoilt by anything. This is because a man can increase his fasting, but then break it with what is haram, he can rise in the night (to stand in *salat*) but then make mistakes (in the day), or engage in idle prattle, or bear false witness; but if he guards his tongue, then I can only hope that all his action will be good."

NOTICE: Ibn Hajar al-Haytami said, commenting on the words, 'whoever believes in Allah and the Last Day, should speak well or not say anything': "As for not speaking on any occasion or holding to the belief that it is an act of *qurba* – coming closer to Allah, exalted is He, – in general, or that speech is prohibited during certain acts of worship, for example during the fast and hajj, then the narration of Abu Dawud (should be considered): 'One should not remain the (whole) day up until the night without speaking.' Al-Isma'ili has related that this prohibition refers to the *i'tikaf*, although this is also related with regard to the fast (in general). The words *yasmut* ('he should not speak') are used (in the hadith) rather than *yaskut* ('he should remain silent') as the former has a more specific meaning, that is 'remaining silent when one has the capacity to speak' – and this is what is intended; as for remaining silent when incapable – because the instrument of speech is defective, that is when dumb, or impaired, or when speech is rendered incomprehensible through stammering – there is no particular excellence in not speaking in this instance."

Ibn Hajar said in *Fath al-Bari*, commenting on the hadith 'Abu Bakr as-Siddiq went in to see a woman from Ahmas...', after his discussion of the prohibition of not speaking throughout the day until nightfall: "Ar-Rouyani said: 'Branch: people have taken on the custom of not speaking in Ramadan, but it has no basis in the law of those who were before us and it is resolved as a disagreement over the case.' The silence which is forbidden is to forgo speaking up for the truth in the case of someone who is able to do so, and similarly [the silence that] is permissible is where both alternatives are equal."

I have said: "The two Ibn Hajars are Shafi'is and the one from amongst the people of our *madhhab*, the one who knows it in its entirety, Muhammad ibn Rushd in *al-Bayan* said: 'If one of the men from among them wanted to (particularly) exert himself, he would desist from speaking just as he would from eating, although he would not desist from making *dhikr* of Allah – but this is (now) abrogated in our *shari'ah*, and its prohibition is based on the Prophet's prohibition, may the peace and blessings of Allah be upon him, (of such practice).'"

غَالِبُ قَيْءٍ وذُبَابٍ مُغْتَفَرْ

being overcome by vomiting or (swallowing) a fly may be overlooked,

غُبَارُ صَانِعٍ وَطُرْقٍ وَسِوَاكُ

يَابِسٍ إِصْبَاحُ جَنَابَةٍ كَذَاكُ

220 as can the dust from (the work of) craftsmen and from streets, or (the use of) a dry *miswak*; and likewise, if one awakes in a state of *janaba*

Mayyara said: "He has informed us that if the fasting person vomits involuntarily, or if a fly enters his mouth, then this (may be overlooked and) is forgiven, and it is not necessary to make up (the fast) in either case; nor in the case of some other (analogous matter) because the dust (arising) from (artisans') workshops is considered on a par with the dust (arising) from flour with respect to the grinder (which may be overlooked); and likewise in the case of (dust arising off) roads, and using a dry *miswak* – as long as it does not break up and dissolve (during use); or waking up in the morning in a state of *janaba* such that one only makes the *ghusl* after sunrise – for all (these instances) are considered (in the same category) as the dust or the fly (swallowed) involuntarily and which may be overlooked."

Al-Mawwaq said, commenting on the words of Khalil 'there is nothing to be made up when overcome by vomiting': "As for the question of vomit which comes out (of the mouth involuntarily), Malik said: 'Whoever is overcome by vomiting in Ramadan does not have to make up anything, but if he vomits (deliberately), then he does.' Ibn Rushd said: 'It is reported from Ibn al-Qasim that the obligatory and the voluntary fast are (considered) the same in this respect.' Ibn Yunus said: 'Our fellow (*fuqaha*) have justified this by arguing that when someone vomits involuntarily nothing can get back into his throat because it comes out in one go, and also that he has no control over it – and so it resembles having a wet dream; contrary to the person who deliberately encourages himself to vomit.' Again Ibn Yunus said: 'If he makes himself vomit in jest, not being ill and with no excuse and something gets back into his throat, then he must pay *kaffara*; otherwise he (just) makes it up.' Al-Baji said: 'The most evident judgement of Malik and his followers is that he has no *kaffara* to pay, and he is considered as someone who takes water into his mouth and it reaches his throat involuntarily – and so he should make it up, but does not pay *kaffara.*'"

Al-Mawwaq also said, commenting on the words of Khalil 'the *miswak* (tooth-stick) is permitted the whole day': "Malik said: 'There is no harm in (using) the *miswak* at the beginning and end of the day as long as the stick is dry, even if it is moistened with water, but I dislike a fresh stick to be used lest (part of) it dissolve (into particles).' Ibn Habib said: '...except in the case of an *'alim.*'"

He has also said, commenting on his words 'the *miswak* is permitted the whole day': "Malik said that if a fly enters the throat of a person who is fasting or a fragment of a grain or the like gets (lodged) between his teeth which he then swallows with his spittle, then there is nothing against him, and if this occurs during his *salat*, then it does not invalidate it."

NOTICES

1. Al-Mawwaq said: "Al-Lakhmi has related: 'There is no harm in phlegm if it descends to the throat if he is able to spit it out.' Al-Qubab said: 'Someone who had not heard this (judgement) felt they must get rid of the phlegm however difficult this may be, but this became extremely irksome in the case where it kept coming back.' In the words of al-Lakhmi there is a clear statement that as long as it does not reach the uvula (i.e. the pendant fleshy part of the soft palate), there is no difference of opinion, even if he is capable of spitting it out. Al-Lakhmi said: 'There is a difference of opinion if it reaches the uvula and then returns.' Ibn Habib said: 'He (is considered to) have done something incorrect, but does not have to make up anything' – and the expression is that of Ibn Yunus. Ibn Habib said: 'Whoever clears his throat and then swallows his phlegm from in front of the uvula or after it has reached the base of the tongue, then he does not have to make anything up – although he has done something incorrect – as phlegm is not food or drink, and it arises in the head.' Al-Baji said: 'The basis of Ibn Habib's judgement is that the person is not retrieving it from the earth but rather that it forms in his mouth – in the usual manner like spittle; however it is *makruh* to swallow it because one does have the possibility of expelling it, unlike spittle (which would be too irksome to get rid of constantly).' Ibn Rushd said: 'Asbagh has related from Ibn al-Qasim that there is nothing for him to make up if phlegm is swallowed deliberately.' Al-Qubab said: 'and in his *Qawa'id* 'Iyad holds to what Ibn Habib said, and this is the preferred judgement.'"

What may be concluded from the above is that the Shaykhs give preference to the judgement of Ibn Habib – that he has nothing to make up in the case of swallowing phlegm even if he is able to spit it out, but that it is incorrect to do so; and al-Qubbab has given preference to this judgement and it is the one which 'Iyad has restricted himself to in his *Qawa'id*; and Ibn Rushd ascribed it to Asbagh from Ibn al-Qasim, and this ought to be the basis of the *fatwa*.

2. Ibn 'Arafa said: "Ibn Shas said: 'Swallowing blood issuing from a tooth is (considered) negligent if it happens involuntarily; and if done deliberately, then there are two judgements as to whether one should make up (the fast).'"

Issue: Ibn al-Hattab said: "Among the disliked things regarding fasting is continuously fasting, going to see one's wives or looking at them, foolish talk, putting anything wet or moist into the mouth if it has taste and sleeping a lot during the day."

وَنِيَّةٌ تَكْفِي لِمَا تَتَابَعُهُ

يَجِبُ إِلَّا إِنْ نَفَاهُ مَانِعُهُ

221 Making the intention just once is enough for the obligation (to fast) consecutive (days) except if interrupted by something which prevents this (fasting consecutively)

Mayyara said: "He has informed us, regarding the obligation to fast on consecutive days – for example in Ramadan in the case of the resident (person) who is (also) healthy, in the case of the two months (undertaken) as *kaffara* for the oath of *dhihar* or the *kaffara* to be paid when deliberately breaking the fast of Ramadan and the like, that it is enough to make one intention at the beginning for the whole of it, unless something occurs to prevent this obligation to fast consecutive days, as in the case of illness, travel or menstruation, in which case one must renew it; and that (the intention must also be renewed) if one continues (to fast) when it is no longer obligatory – despite the licence to interrupt this obligation to fast consecutive days, for example, with respect to the traveller when he fasts on his journey or the sick person if he takes on the fast. Thus in these two cases they must renew the intention each night even if they have not broken the fast – as continuing the fast in both their cases is no longer obligatory, and this is the judgement of Malik in *al-'Utbiyya*; although it is also recorded from Malik in *al-Mabsout*[1] that: 'It is not necessary to renew it, and that the (intention) is still valid – (if someone with a valid excuse nevertheless fasts) – despite the (the possibility of an) interruption (with respect to the judgement of obligation regarding) the consecutiveness of

---

1 of Qadi Isma'il, of Baghdad, whose work is no longer extant, except via secondary sources

the days, as in the case of menstruating women, travellers or the sick; however, the intention to fast must be renewed if the traveller returns home or the sick person gets better, in which case one (single) intention is enough for them for the rest of the fast.' If the fasting of the traveller is done on the journey and the fasting of the sick person during his illness, then they must both renew it each night until the reason for the absence of any obligation of consecutiveness is removed, namely illness and travel, as has just been mentioned from the *Utbiyya*. These particulars (regarding the judgement of fasting) apply generally with respect to Ramadan; in the case of the obligatory *kaffara*, they apply in the case of sick persons if they break the fast, but not in the case of travellers for if the latter break the fast, they interrupt the consecutiveness and should begin the fast from the beginning – and renewal of the intention for the rest of the fast is not possible."

نُدِبَ تَعْجِيلٌ لِفِطْرٍ رَفَعَهُ

كَذَاكَ تَأْخِيرُ سُحُورٍ تَبَعَهُ

222 It is recommended to be quick in making the *iftar* after the fast, and likewise to delay the *suhur* (pre-dawn meal) prior to the fast

In these lines, he is alluding to the words of the *Risala*: "Part of the sunna is to hurry to break the fast and to delay the *suhur*." '*Sahur*', with an *a* on the *seen* is a name for that which one has for *suhur*, and with a *u* it is a name for the act. The source for what he mentioned is the words of the Prophet, may the peace and blessings of Allah be upon him: "Good will remain with people as long as they are quick to break the fast and they delay the *suhur*" – for breaking the fast quickly strengthens (the body) for the *salat* and delaying the *suhur* strengthens it for the fast." It is also recorded in the *Sahih*: "Take the pre-dawn meal for there is a blessing in the *suhur*."

NOTICE: Ibn al-Hattab said: "Ibn Naji has related in *Sharh ar-Risala* that al-Baji said: 'Being quick to break the fast means not excessively delaying the *iftar* after the sunset – nor holding to the belief that it is not permitted to make the *iftar* at sunset, as the Jews hold. However, anyone who delays it because something (unexpected) occurs or by his choosing – while still holding that the fast has been completed at sunset, then this is not *makruh* – and this has been narrated by Ibn Nafi' in *al-Majmou'a*.'"

USEFUL POINT: 'Ali ibn 'Abd as-Sadiq said: "Regarding the words of Allah, exalted is He, '*then you will be asked that Day about the pleasures you enjoyed*'[1] al-Hafidh Abu Nu'aym has narrated in *al-Hilya* that Mujahid said: 'This refers to every thing you have enjoyed of this world.' Hasan ibn 'Atiya said that he said: "There are three whose food will not be reckoned: the person fasting when he takes his *iftar*, the person about to fast when he takes his *suhur* and the left-over food of the guest eaten by the host." He has also said: "When the slave says 'O Allah make this a wholesome provision for me' over his food, then he will not be asked to account for it, and no reckoning will be made for it – for he will have fulfilled his (duty) to express his gratitude (to Allah, exalted is He)" – this is taken from the work entitled *al-'Ulum al-Fakhira*. Likewise, *'Ayn-Jeem* has composed the following regarding eating with one's brothers:

It has been transmitted that there is no account for (food) eaten at the *suhur*, likewise (none when taken) together with one's brothers, or (when) taking the *iftar*

And add to this: eating the leftovers of the guest for one of the *'ulama* has declared that this has been narrated.

مَنْ أَفْطَرَ الْفَرْضَ قَضَاهُ وَلْيَزِدْ

كَفَّارَةً فِي رَمَضَانَ إِنْ عَمَدْ

223 Whoever breaks an obligatory fast must make it up and, in addition, pay *kaffara* in Ramadan, if done deliberately

لِأَكْلٍ أَوْ شُرْبٍ فَمٍ أَوْ لِلْمَنِي

وَلَوْ بِفِكْرٍ أَوْ لِرَفْضِ مَا بُنِي

224 by eating, drinking or having an emission of sperm – even if this was (only) as a result of thoughts (of a sexual nature), or by abandoning the (intention) upon which the (fast) is based –

بِلَا تَأَوُّلٍ قَرِيبٍ وَيُبَاحُ

لِضُرٍّ أَوْ سَفَرِ قَصْرٍ أَيْ مُبَاحُ

225 without a plausible interpretation; and it is licit (to break it) if it harms

---

[1] at-Takathur – Competition: 8

(one's health), or when on a journey – for a licit purpose – during which one would shorten the *salat*

Ibn 'Ashir's saying "whoever breaks an obligatory fast" resembles Khalil's words "he must make up in the case of an obligatory fast in all circumstances." Al-Mawwaq said in his commentary: "Malik said about this: 'Whoever eats in Ramadan and has doubts as to whether he has eaten before dawn or after has to make it up.' Ibn Yunus said: '…because an obligation is not annulled by something which is uncertain.' Ibn al-'Arabi said: 'Just as the sunna is to be quick in having the *iftar*, likewise the sunna is to stop eating a little before (the dawn). This is because "proximity to the dawn" is (considered to be) one of the "proscribed matters" of the fast, and also because of his saying, on whom be blessings and peace: "Eat and drink until Ibn Umm Maktoum calls (the *adhan*)" – he was a blind man and would not call (the *adhan*) until someone told him that morning had come. And our *'ulama* have interpreted this referring to when "the time of the morning is close."'"

As for his saying 'and in addition the *kaffara*', Mayyara said: "The meaning of this is that the *kaffara* is to be made in addition to the obligation to make up (the fast), and the commentary on this will be made below together with (the commentary on) the next two lines (of Ibn 'Ashir), that is, those which deal with (the judgement of those who) deliberate eat or drink in Ramadan; or who deliberately cause an emission of sperm through intercourse, kissing or bodily contact – even by having thoughts (of a sensual nature); or those who deliberately omit the intention, without any plausible interpretation."

Then he goes on to say after a long discussion: "We have added to the conditions of the *kaffara*: being free of ignorance – that is to exclude the case where someone breaks the fast deliberately out of ignorance – for there is no *kaffara* owing on his part. Al-Lakhmi said: 'The well known judgement of the *madhhab* is that the judgement regarding the ignorant person is the same as (that of) the person with a plausible interpretation – and included here is the person who has recently become Muslim and who thinks that fasting is restricted to not eating food, in which case he is excused (if he has intercourse).'"

The judgement within the *madhhab*, according to Mayyara, is based on (deliberate) violation (of the fast) – so (the excuse of) someone (who is ignorant but who) comes seeking counsel and information (about what is correct) is accepted, and he does not have to pay *kaffara*; as is (that of) anyone discovered (breaking the fast) as long as it is plausible, while (payment of the *kaffara*) is incumbent on him if he has no plausible excuse.

Ibn al-Hattab said, commenting on the words of Khalil 'he must pay *kaffara*, if he has no plausible interpretation and is not ignorant, when having intercourse – (although this) only (applies) in Ramadan (and not for a *qada* fast for example)': "... if one were to ask what is the difference between the person who is ignorant and the person who has a (plausible) interpretation – for the latter is also ignorant of the judgement – and why the (*fuqaha*) have distinguished between a plausible and inplausible interpretation, then the reply would be that there is in fact no difference between the two – unless one understands the 'ignorant person' as referring to someone who has just become Muslim and who is ignorant of the obligation of Ramadan or some of the well known matters which are prohibited in Ramadan while one understands the 'person who has a plausible interpretation' as referring to the person who breaks the fast for a reason about which the judgement is unknown. Some of the *'ulama* have said that it is permitted to break the fast for such a reason. The gist of what al-Lakhmi said is that there is no difference (of judgement) between 'the person with a plausible excuse' and 'the ignorant person', and that there is no *kaffara* to be paid by either of them as the *kaffara* is only to be paid by someone who (deliberately) violates (the fast). Thus anyone who does not violate it and claims to have a reason (for not fasting) which excuses him, or who comes wanting to know the correct judgement, then this is accepted of him. Whoever comes across another (breaking the fast) should examine his excuse: if it resembles that of those who would normally be considered to be ignorant (of the laws), then he is believed; if the excuse is an unlikely one, then he is not believed."

NOTICE: the author has not mentioned examples of 'plausible interpretation' while Khalil has done so: "(the *kaffara* is) not (due) from whoever breaks the fast out of forgetfulness, or does not do the *ghusl* until after the dawn, or has the *suhur* near to the dawn, or arrives (after a journey) at night (and does not fast the following day, believing it not to be obligatory), or who undertakes a journey of a length which does not necessitate shortening the *salat* (believing that he does not have to fast), or who sees the new moon of Shawwal (and supposes the fast to have ended the previous night) during the daylight hours (of the last day) of ramadan – for in the above (instances) they all believe it is licit to break the fast." Ibn al-Hattab said: "As for the 'plausible interpretation' there are two matters (to be taken into consideration): the first, whoever is fasting in the morning, then embarks on a journey and breaks his fast without any other excuse but that he considers the journey (itself) permits the breaking of the fast, and secondly, whoever is fasting in the morning, then resolves to travel and who breaks the fast before setting out thinking that his resolve to travel makes it licit for him to break the fast – then the most evident judgement of Khalil is that he does not have to pay *kaffara*, even if he breaks it deliberately."

Then he goes on to say after a discussion: "Notice: wherever we have mentioned (above) that there is no *kaffara* to be paid – because each (of the persons in question) thought that it was licit (to break the fast) – then the most evident judgement is that he has also not committed any wrong action as he has not intended to commit anything prohibited. Ibn Rushd said at the end of the *Sama'* 'Isa in the 'Book of Fasting' regarding the issue (entitled) 'whoever is fasting in the morning, then resolves to travel and breaks the fast before setting out' and the issue (entitled) 'Whoever breaks his fast after setting out believing that he has a plausible excuse': 'The most evident judgement amongst the (various) judgements is that he does not have to pay *kaffara* as *kaffara* is paid to make amends for a wrong action; but whoever believes he has a plausible excuse, then he has not done anything wrong; and if he is mistaken in his understanding (of the grounds for his excuse), then (it should be remembered that) Allah, exalted is He, has pardoned the *umma* of his Prophet, may the peace and blessings of Allah be upon him, their mistakes and anything done out of forgetfulness. Those who consider that *kaffara* must be paid in any of the above, justify their judgement by saying that ignorance is not a valid excuse – arguing that there exists no licence to be ignorant of such matters and that if he was unsure, then he should have refrained (from breaking the fast) until he had asked (someone who knew). If he does not do this, (they claim), then his going ahead (and breaking the fast) before asking, necessitates his paying the *kaffara* – basing (their judgement) on the words of Allah, exalted is He, "ask the People of the Reminder if you do not know."'"[1]

ISSUE: In the *Ajwiba* al-Qubbab, on being asked "What do you say regarding the man who has doubts as to his fasting and does not know if he has broken it deliberately or not?" he replied: "the principle (underlying this case) is (that the person is considered) exempt from any obligation – and no *kaffara* is owing because of doubt; (the principle underlying any instance where one seeks to) be cautious or scrupulous is (that the person is considered) exempt from any obligation and (that such caution is employed to) free oneself of any doubt if one is able – as long, that is, as it does not distract one from what one is certain of."

NOTICE: the author does not mention examples of "far fetched interpretations" (that is excuses based on implausible reasoning) while Khalil has mentioned them saying: "... contrary to far(fetched) interpretation (– for example in

---

1 an-Nahl – The Bee: 43

the case of someone who has sighted the new moon but his (attestation) is unacceptable; or someone who breaks the fast, believing he has fever (which he has not) – even if he is (later) afflicted by fever; or likewise, if a woman supposes her menstruation to have started, based on her customary cycle, whereas in fact it has not – even if later it does appear; or in the case of cupping; or in the case of someone who speaks behind someone's back." Ibn al-Mawwaq said: "Ibn al-Qasim said: 'Whoever has himself cupped in Ramadan and considers this reason enough to break the fast and so eats, then he only owes the making up of the fast of that day.' Ibn Rushd said: 'Ibn Habib, however, considers that it is obligatory for him to pay *kaffara*. This is analogous to someone resident, who is fasting in a morning of Ramadan. Then it occurs to him to travel and he is of the opinion that this is reason enough for him to break the fast and so he eats before setting out. Then he sets out and travels – and there is a difference of opinion in this.' Ibn al-Qasim said: 'I consider that he only has to make up a day as he was acting according to his own particular understanding' – and this is the most evident of the judgements because *kaffara* is an expiation of a wrong action and the person interpreting (a situation according to his own understanding) is not guilty of a wrong action."

USEFUL POINT: Ibn al-Hattab has related that Al-Qastallani said in *Sharh al-Bukhari*: "The majority consider that lying, backbiting and talking behind people's backs do not invalidate the fast" and then he goes on to mention what the author of *al-Ihya* has related from Sufyan and Mujahid. Then he says: "The well known judgement from Mujahid is that if one protects oneself from two bad qualities – namely backbiting and lying – then his fast will be sound, and this is narrated by Ibn Abi Shayba." Then he has transmitted from as-Subki: "Acts of disobedience prevent the attainment of the reward for the fast, according to the *ijma'* – although this (judgement) is disputed given the difficulty of avoiding (every wrong action). It applies (if wrong actions) are numerous."

I SAY: "Subki's words are supported by the hadith of al-Bukhari: 'Whoever does not leave off bearing false witness and acting in accordance with such (false witness), then Allah has no need that of his leaving off eating and drinking.'"

He said: "There is no harm if a man says I am fasting – as an excuse (not to do something, for example) but he must not say it merely for something to say or to extol himself."

As for his saying 'or by abandoning the (intention) upon which the (fast) is based' 'Ali ibn 'Abd as-Sadiq said: "… this is in accordance with the well-known judgement that the fast is broken. The most evident meaning of the text of the *Mukhtasar* is that there is no harm in this unless this abandoning of the intention occurs during the actual fast, that is, between dawn to sunset – but not after this time because he then goes on to say 'or if the intention is abandoned during the day.'"

Al-Mawwaq said: "As for the case where someone deliberately abandons the intention during the day, Malik has commented on this saying: 'Whoever begins the morning with the intention of breaking the fast during Ramadan but he does not eat or drink, then he should make up (a day) and pay *kaffara*, and if he had made the intention to fast before the sunrise, then this is of no avail to him unless he does not eat or drink.' Thus Malik – at the end of his statement regarding (having the intention to) break the fast after the morning has begun (in Ramadan) – has added: 'unless he does not eat or drink.' Malik said something (else) in this regard but I do not know if he said 'he is to make it up with the *kaffara*' or 'without the *kaffara*.' However, what I prefer is that he pay the *kaffara* (too). In the work entitled *an-Nukat*, more than one of our Shaykhs said: 'Whoever renounces or denies his *salat* or his fast, then he has indeed abandoned it, contrary to someone who renounces his *ihram* or his *wudu'* after completing it or during it. Our companions differ regarding something of less significance than this, like when someone changes his intention to that of a *nafila* (act) when in (the middle of) an obligatory act – that is, when he does this out of negligence; for anyone who does this deliberately or in jest, then there is no difference of opinion that he invalidates what he is doing.' Examine *an-Nukat* (for further discussion). Ibn Yunus said: 'As for Ashhab's words "there is no *kaffara* to be paid by the person who intends to break the fast", it may be that he is referring to the person who has already made the intention to fast and then he intends to break it – for this does not break the first intention he had made, unless he actually breaks it.'

Al-Lakhmi said: 'There is a difference of opinion whether breaking the fast can happen by intention if the fast has already been effected correctly (i.e., has actually commenced). According to the *Mudawwana*, he is deemed to have broken the fast, and this is the best judgement as desisting (from food and drink) is not an act of qurba unless accompanied by an intention for Allah. Thus if he makes a new intention to the effect that he is desisting (from food and drink) for the rest of his day but not for the sake of Allah, exalted is He, then he is on a par with someone who does two *rak'ats* of the *salat*, then makes the intention to complete it on the basis that he is not doing the rest of the *salat* for the sake of Allah – as long as he is in a state of awareness, not forgetfulness, of what he is engaging in; or he washes part of his body during the *ghusl* with the intention of purifying himself but then does the rest with the intention of cooling himself – for neither of these are permitted in any circumstances. If he makes the intention to break the fast by eating or drinking or otherwise, but then changes his mind and completes it in accordance with his first intention, then his fast is accepted. This is not the same as the first example for there he made the intention to desist from (food and drink for example) but not to do it for the sake of Allah while the other intends to do something which will break his fast but does not in fact do it and so he remains with the (first) intention which was made for the sake of Allah.'"

Ibn 'Arafa said something similar: "Abandoning the intention before putting it into effect (by fasting) prevents the (fast being accepted) and, it is recommended he make up for this invalidation (of the intention by undertaking another day's fast). Al-Lakhmi said: 'This is unlike the intention – which occurs to him while still retaining the intention of (fasting) for the sake of Allah – to invalidate it by eating food for this (new intention) was absent at the beginning (of the fast).' Ibn Abdous has related: 'As for the traveller who fasts in Ramadan, who becomes thirsty and who is told – after his table cloth has been laid out for him to break the fast and just as he is reaching out for it – 'you have no water with you' – and who thus desists (from breaking the fast), I prefer that he make up (a day).' Al-Lakhmi considered that he did not have to be made up." I say: "The recommendation (to make it up) is mentioned by Ibn Abi Zayd from a narration of Ibn Abi Ashras, although he also said: 'and I know of a narration (confirming) that he does not have to make anything up' and this (latter) is the most dominant judgement of his.'"

As for Ibn 'Ashir's saying 'and it is licit (to break it) if it harms (one's health)' Mayyara said: "As for permission to break the fast in case of harm (to one's health), this applies when he fears that the harm will continue or increase, or will cause another illness. If, however, fasting would lead to death or life-threatening impairment (of health), then it is prohibited and he must break the fast."

Ibn al-Mawwaq said: "Ibn Yunus said that Abu Muhammad has related: 'Amongst the judgements of our companions is that if a sick person fears that by fasting a day, his illness would be increased, his sight weakened or he will be beset by some other affliction, then he should break the fast.'"

Ibn 'Arafa said: "Al-Lakhmi said: 'Fasting in the case of a sick person is obligatory if it is not burdensome for him; and if it is, then he may choose (whether to break it or not). If he fears that it will cause the illness to be prolonged or cause another illness, then it is prohibited – although if he does fast, then it is accepted of him. (The judgement regarding) weakness – in the case of a healthy person or an old person who intends (to fast) – is (considered) the same as that of a sick person.'"

It is related of the Baghdadis that breaking the fast when one fears that the illness will be intensified or that recovery will be delayed is permitted, not obligatory. Ibn 'Arafa said: "Asbagh has heard from Ibn al-Qasim that if the person fasting fears death from the heat or thirst then he should break the fast. Ibn Rushd said: 'There is agreement in the case of (fear of) death, and there exist two judgements in the case of illness.'"

He has also said: "The fast of the pregnant woman is obligatory if it is not burdensome for her; and if she fears it will cause harm to herself or baby, then it is prohibited; otherwise she has the option."

Mayyara has transmitted this judgement of his regarding the pregnant woman and has added a further point of benefit saying: "Al-Lakhmi said: 'The fast of the pregnant woman is obligatory if she does not find it troublesome while it is prohibited if she fears it will cause harm to her or her baby; and if the fasting exhausts her but she has no fear (of harming herself or child) if she fasts part of the (month), then she has the option of fasting or breaking the fast. What Malik deduces in the *Mudawwana* is that if she breaks the fast for one of the reasons which permit her to break it, then she must make it up, but does not have to (make the expiation of) feeding (the poor) as she is (considered as) a sick person.' Al-Mawwaq said: 'Examine the nature of the *fuqaha*'s discussion of this (matter), namely that refers to her being ill – so there still remains the question as to what (is the judgement) if she begins fasting in the morning and is healthy. I have been asked about this when I was in al-Bayazeen – so examine this!'"

Ibn al-Fa'ida said in *Sharh al-Mukhtasar*: "As for the judgement of Ibn Bashir that it is forbidden for the sick person to fast if it causes him great harm or if it is very troublesome to him, (this means that) if it is difficult for him, but does not lead to his harm or injury, then it is not forbidden, but he can break the fast if he fears death or the prolongation or exacerbation of his illness – and this is what Ibn 'Arafa holds to. There is no contradiction as the (judgement to break the fast) becomes obligatory when one thinks that (harm) will in all likelihood (result from fasting) while the (judgement) becomes one of choice when doubt (exists). What this means is that if he thinks that it will result in all likelihood in this (harm), then it is forbidden for him to fast; and that if it is burdensome for him, but in all likelihood will not result in this (harm) as far as he assesses – although he still harbours fears based on his doubts, then it is not forbidden and he may choose. So reflect on this, and by my life what he said suggests itself as the most convincing argument."

'Ayn-Jeem said in his *Hashiya ar-Risala*: "The gist of what Ibn 'Arafa has mentioned is that if the breast feeding mother – according to the conditions particular to her case – together with the pregnant woman fear the onset of illness for themselves or for their babies, then they must break the fast; and that if they find it burdensome, then they have the choice of breaking it or not. Thus he does not consider them as (subject to the same judgement as) the healthy for he has also said that if the healthy person fears the onset of illness, then there is a difference of opinion as to whether he should break it (or not); and that he should not break it merely because he finds it burdensome; but that the sick person who finds the fast burdensome may break the fast. Ibn 'Umar said: 'and if the sick person finds it burdensome but does not fear that his illness will increase nor that its cure will be delayed, then the judgement in his case is that he has the option.' What may be concluded from this is that if it is burdensome on the pregnant, breast feeding or sick person, then they may break the fast even if they do not fear the onset of illness or that it will be increased; as for the healthy person, he may not break the fast just because he experiences difficulty in fasting – and there are two judgements as to whether he may break the fast if he becomes ill, the most evident interpretation being (in the case of the judgement permitting him to break the fast) that this applies whatever the illness. It is clear that what is being referred to by 'burdensome' – which makes breaking the fast licit for him – is some difficulty in addition to that which he would experience were he healthy."

Ibn Fa'ida said in *Sharh al-Mukhtasar* – and it is one of the books to be relied on: "The sick person has four states: when slightly (ill) during which fasting is not difficult for him, in which case he (is considered) as the healthy person; when it is difficult but he does not fear that it will get worse, in which case he has the option of fasting or not; when he fears that the illness will be prolonged or that another sickness will appear, in which case he does not have to fast but if he does nevertheless fast, then it is accepted of him; and when a healthy person has a weak constitution, in which case he is considered the same (as the latter): if the fast does not exhaust him, then he must fast, while if it does – and nothing more serious results – then he has the option, while if he fears the onset of illness, he may not fast. The same applies in the case of an old man or someone who experiences thirst: if they find fasting burdensome, they may break the fast during the heat only and should make up in the cooler season; and if they are unable (to fast both) in the cooler season and in the summer, then they do not have to make anything up – except in the case where one day (the find) they are able to make it up, in which case it becomes binding upon them. The pregnant woman has three states: she is either at the beginning of her pregnancy and has no difficulty in fasting during this period, in which case fasting is an obligation on her; or she fears the onset of an illness for her baby or for herself through fasting, in which case it is obligatory for her to break the fast; or when she finds it burdensome to fast although she does not fear anything (untoward will result), in which case she has the option. The breast feeding mother has eight states, four of which necessitate that she make the fast, namely: when fasting would not be harmful to her or her baby; or when it would be harmful but the baby has (inherited) wealth which is used to hire a woman to breast feed it, or the father has money, or the mother has money – on condition that the baby accepts another (wet-nurse). There are three which necessitate breaking the fast namely: when the fast is harmful to her or her baby; when the baby does not accept other (than its mother), or does accept but there is no one available; or there is one available but no money to hire one. There is a difference of opinion regarding the eighth state, namely when fasting is burdensome for her and she does not fear for herself or for her baby but it does not accept other than its mother."

Issue: al-Hattab said: "It is stated in *al-Majmu'a* from Ashhab: 'As for the sick person who, if he has to fast, is capable of it, or if he has to pray, is able to stand for it, but only with difficulty and exertion, then he should break the fast and pray sitting, and the deen of Allah is ease.' Malik said: 'I have seen Rabi'a breaking the fast when ill and if it had been other than him I would have said that he should have been encouraged to fast – surely this (matter) is (to be decided) in accordance with the capacity of people.'"

As for Ibn 'Ashir's saying 'or when on a journey where one shortens the *salat*', Khalil said: "as for his breaking the fast, (it is licit) for a journey begun before dawn, or for whoever has not formed the intention (the previous night) while on this journey; if he has (made the intention), he must make it up, even a voluntary fast, but no *kaffara* is to made, unless during travel (in Ramadan), he did form the intention (during the night) to fast (but then broke it)." Ibn al-Fa'ida said: "As long as the traveller shortens the *salat*, he has the option of fasting or breaking the fast after the day of his setting out; and if he set out before *fajr* on the day of setting out, then he also has the option; if after *fajr*, then he should complete his fast for that day; and if he breaks the fast after setting out or before and he has resolved (to travel), then he must make it up; and there is a difference of opinion as to the *kaffara*, that is, if he breaks the fast without an excuse, but as for thirst, and the like, there is no *kaffara*."

'Ali ibn 'Abd as-Sadiq said: "As-Sanhouri was asked whether it was licit for the cultivator or harvester who became thirsty during the daylight hours of Ramadan to break the fast and he replied: 'As for the cultivator, it is permitted for him to break the fast without any doubt and it is also permitted for those labourers (absolutely) necessary to bring in the harvest; but it is *makruh* for those who are not needed. However, none of them should have the intention not to fast during the night previous to the fast; rather all should have the intention to fast – and then if any are afflicted by thirst, they may break the fast and then make it up when they are able.'"

NOTICE: according to the well known opinion there is no need for the person who is compelled (to break the fast) to desist (from food) even when whatever has compelled him is removed. Ibn al-Hattab said, commenting on the words of Khalil, 'like the person who is compelled': "that is, anyone who begins the morning fasting and is then compelled to break the fast because of hunger or thirst may continue to break the fast for the rest of the day – even by having intercourse. Sahnun has permitted this, and Ibn Habib said: 'He should only satisfy his compelling need.' Al-Lakhmi said: 'The first (judgement) is logically more consistent as he has broken his fast for a licit reason. It is analogous to the person who experiences (intense) thirst and knows that he will not be able to fulfil the fast unless he drinks (at least) once during the day: despite this (need to drink only once), he should make the intention the previous night that he will break the fast and he may eat (normally) and have intercourse with his wife (if he wishes); likewise, if he is ill and needs a little to drink during the day (in order to be able to fast), then he is not commanded to fast or to desist from other than that this absolute minimum. The difference of opinion in this is like the difference in the case of the person who is compelled to eat carrion. The author of *at-Tawdih* said: 'If we argue that he may eat his fill and take provision from it – and this is the well known opinion, then it is permitted for him to carry on (breaking the fast) in this case; if we accept the judgement of Ibn Habib that he should eat (only) as much as will ensure he stays alive, then in the (above mentioned) case (of fasting), he should only satisfy his pressing need.' Al-Burzuli said: 'The well known judgement in the case of carrion is that he may eat his fill and take provision from it, and so likewise in this case – he may drink and eat his fill, and have intercourse if he wishes.' This he has mentioned after the question put to Ibn Rushd as to whether the person who is afflicted by a great thirst and who drinks may (continue to) eat and have intercourse after this during the rest of the day. He replied: 'There is a difference of opinion in this (matter), and the correct judgement is that he has to make up and pay *kaffara* unless he interprets (his action as being excusable) and considers that it was permitted.' Al-Burzuli said: 'The judgement he has chosen is that of Ibn Habib, and (is based) in particular on the case of carrion, namely, that he may eat (only) what is enough to keep him alive, although the well known opinion is that he may eat his fill and take provision from it – and (in the case of fasting) may eat, drink and have intercourse as he wishes. In the *Mudawwana* (the case mentioned) of someone who needs to ride the beast he is taking to sacrifice (in Makka) and who mounts it (is analogous) for he does not have to dismount when he has recovered his strength. Likewise if it is licit for him to marry his slave girl on two conditions,[1] then the well known judgement is that it is also fitting for him to marry her; and likewise if someone makes an oath to divorce a (slavegirl) he has been married to for years, but fears fornication,[2] then his oath is annulled as what has been licit for him once (again becomes licit).'"

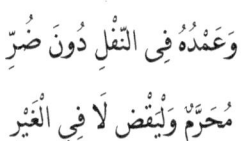

226 It is prohibited to break a *nafila* fast deliberately without illness. (If it is broken, however), he must make it up; but not on account of something else (i.e. for forgetfulness).

Mayyara said: "Having discussed the judgement regarding breaking an obligatory fast either out of forgetfulness or deliberately – and that it must make it up in all cases, with the addition of the *kaffara* according to the above mentioned conditions – he talks here about the judgement of the person who breaks a *nafila* fast either out of forgetfulness or deliberately. He has informed us that deliberately breaking a *nafila* fast is prohibited if the person fasting is not ill – and this is the judgement regarding breaking such a fast *prior* to embarking on it; if, however, it is broken, then he must make it up, and Ibn 'Ashir has indicated this obligation above. What may be understood from his words 'deliberately' and 'without illness' is that breaking the voluntary fast out

---

1   See Ibn Juzayy on an-Nisa' 25: "The *madhhab* of Malik and most of his followers is that it is not permitted for a free man to marry a slavegirl except on two conditions: firstly, he does not have the means (to marry a free woman), secondly, that he fears he will commit fornication, as mentioned at the end of this *ayat*; Ibn al-Qasim, however, permits it."
2   an-Nisa' – Women: 25. Allah, exalted is He, says: "*If any of you do not have the means to marry free women who are muminun, you may marry slavegirls who are muminun … This is for those who are afraid of committing fornication.*"

of forgetfulness or (even) deliberately – when some pressing need afflicts the person fasting – is not forbidden, and this (judgement) is correct. Moreover he does not have to make up the (fast) in either of these two instances, informing us of this with his words 'but not on account of something else' – i.e. in the case of forgetfulness or deliberately, but on account of some pressing need. Ibn al-Hajib said: 'It is obligatory to make up the *nafila* if broken deliberately or if broken when it is specifically forbidden. His saying 'if broken deliberately' excludes forgetfulness, and his words 'specifically forbidden' exclude breaking the fast for some pressing need – for it does not have to be made up in both these cases. Mention has already been made above – when Ibn 'Ashir says 'SECTION: the obligations of the *wudu'*...' – that there are (certain) matters in our *madhhab* which once undertaken, become binding (although the judgement remains that of '*nafila*' before their commencement). One such (matter) is when someone interrupts a (a *nafila* act of worship) without a pressing need, in which case he must repeat it – and (*nafila*) fasting would be included here. The author of *at-Tawdih* said: 'It is stated in *al-Wadiha* that Ibn Habib said: "It is not fitting that he break his fast on account of an invitation to eat at a celebration or another occasion. Ibn 'Umar was asked about this and he replied: 'That is someone who is taking his fast in jest.'" Malik was asked and he was still stricter in what he said. Mutarrif said – when asked whether it was permitted for a man fasting outside of Ramadan to break his fast when invited to do so just as he sets foot in his own house: 'He should not accept and should resolve not to break it; and if the (host) makes an oath to divorce his wife (if his guest does not eat and break his fast), or to leave or to set free a slave, then the (fasting person) should induce him to perjury rather than break the fast – unless there is another (valid) reason for this; and likewise if the (host) swears by Allah (to do such-and-such a thing) with respect to the (fasting person), the latter should let him break his oath rather than break his fast; and the person who has made the oath pays *kaffara* for it – for even if the person fasting had sworn by Allah to break the fast, then I consider that he should not break it, and that he pay *kaffara*; and that he reject (the invitation of anyone) except his father and mother for I prefer that he obey them both – even if they do not make an oath to the effect that he should break his fast, as long as this (invitation of theirs) is (made) out of their concern for him because of his continual fasting or the like.' Mutarrif has also told me: 'I have heard Malik say this regarding someone who fasted a lot or persisted in fasting (regularly) over a long period and who was instructed by his mother to break it.' Malik has also said: 'I have been told about men from amongst the people of knowledge who have been instructed by their mothers to break the fast and they have done so.'

Ibn Ghulab said: 'and if his Shaykh prohibits him from fasting then it has the same force as if his parents had prohibited him from doing so. This is because of the contract (of allegiance he has made with his Shaykh which) prohibits him from disobeying him and or from undertaking anything without his instruction; and so obedience on his part becomes an obligation on account of the words of Allah, exalted is He: "*fulfil your contracts!*"'[1]

Al-Khurshi said commenting on the words of Khalil 'like a father or a Shaykh': "What is being referred to by the word 'Shaykh' is the instance where someone has a contract (of allegiance to him) and has taken upon himself not to disobey him – and this has been stated by Ibn Ghulab. One of the (men of knowedge) said: 'It may be he is referring to a Sufi (Shaykh).' Ibn Naji said: 'The most evident judgement of the *madhhab* is that the Shaykh from whom he takes knowledge does not have the same status as the father although one of the (ulama) I have met has attributed (the same status) to him.'" Then he goes on to say: "One of them said: 'The teacher of knowledge has the same import as that of the father or is of even greater import.' Ibn Rislan said: '... so much so that one of our companions said: "Disobeying one's parents is forgiven when *tawba* is made – unlike disobedience to the Shaykh of instruction (which is not forgiven).""" Something similar to what al-Khurshi has narrated has been transmitted in *Ghayat al-Amani* from Ibn Naji.

It is also stated in *Ghayat al-Amani*, in a commentary on the words of the *Risala*: 'O Allah forgive me and my parents and our imams': "Ibn Naji said: 'What he means by the Imams are all the Imams and the Amirs and in my opinion the words of the Shaykh are an indication that whoever wants his *du'as* to be accepted should begin with (mention of) his parents followed by (mention of) those whom he has learnt from – that is, that he should give precedence to those to whom he is related, although one of the *'ulama* of a previous generation would give precedence in his *du'as* to those who had instructed him over his parents. He justified this by saying that his teacher had given him life in the next life while his parents had (only) given him life in this world.' The truth (of the matter) in my opinion lies in the first (judgement). Moreover, one of the (*fuqaha*) I have met gave a *fatwa* to this effect basing his judgement on the fact that this is also indicated by the *shari'ah*. Do you not see that the upkeep of one's parents, if poor, is an obligation on the son who is capable of supporting them – while none of the people of knowledge, as far as I am aware, have stated that this is obligatory with respect to one's teacher."

1 al-Ma'ida – The Table: 1

BRANCH: Mayyara said: "Al-Lakhmi said: 'Whoever takes the *suhur* breakfast before a voluntary fast and then realises the dawn has (already) broken should desist (from eating, drinking and intercourse) for the rest of the day if he had had made the intention to fast (that day) the previous night.' He said in the *Mudawwana*: 'but he does not have to make it up; and if, his intention from the beginning of the night was to get up and take the *suhur*, and he indeed embarks upon the fast after the *suhur*, (but then realises dawn has broken), then he may eat for the rest of the day and he does not have to make it up; likewise, if he has not made the intention to fast from the start of his day.'"

Examine this for what may be understood from these words is that the person who makes the *suhur* after the dawn mistakenly is considered on a par with the person who eats out of forgetfulness, and for this reason he must desist from (eating, drinking or intercourse) if he had the intention of fasting the previous night. However, whoever has the intention the night before of making up a fast missed in Ramadan and who takes the *suhur* after the dawn by mistake, then he does not have to desist (from eating, drinking or intercourse) for that day – and this is like someone who breaks the fast while making up a day for Ramadan out of forgetfulness for it is not forbidden for him to eat again, and Allah knows best.

I have composed the following lines on these two matters:
Whoever makes the *suhur* for a *nafila* fast or to make up a fast,
   and it becomes clear to him that dawn has broken,
Then – with regard to the first – it is forbidden to break the fast
   if he had the intention of fasting the previous night, although he does not have to make it up (if he does);
With regard to the second, there is no explicit text from the *fuqaha*,
   although it appears that it is permitted to carry on eating after breaking the fast –
Like someone who breaks the fast out of forgetfulness when making up a fast:
   he is not prohibited from breaking the fast, although it has been reported that it is disliked.
Then I have found a text in the *Tahdheeb*
   similar to the (judgement) which sanctions (breaking the fast).

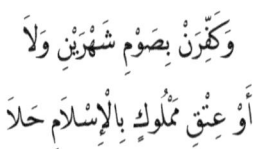

227 and *kaffara* is paid by fasting two consecutive months or freeing a Muslim slave

His saying 'by fasting two months' refers to two full months if one has not begun (fasting) with the new moon, otherwise from the new moon to the next, whether it is a full month or not.

وَفَضَّلُوا إِطْعَامَ سِتِّينَ فَقِيرْ

مُدّاً لِسْكِينٍ مِنَ الْعَيْشِ الْكَثِيرْ

228 (The *fuqaha*) have preferred that one feed sixty poor people, (that is) a *mudd* of the most widely used food to each destitute person

He has not mentioned that this is conditional upon their being Muslims as he has already mentioned this in the section on Zakat al-Fitr – and the fact that the two chapters are connected (in meaning demonstrates that this condition is also applicable here). His use of the word 'destitute' has a more general meaning than the word 'poor people' and so the latter is not strictly speaking a legal condition (as it is subsumed by the first). The *mudd* is (to be given) to each of the sixty using the *mudd* (measure) of the Prophet, may the peace and blessings be upon him and this has been stated by 'Ali ibn 'Abd as-Sadiq and the like is also related from Mayyara and al-Mawwaq – (basing their judgement on the fact) that all *kaffara* is paid with this (particular *mudd*), except the expiation of the *dhihar* oath of divorce. His words 'the most widely used food' refers to the staple food of the region in which the person paying the *kaffara* finds himself in, although it is also been said that it refers to *his* staple food (that is, the staple food of the person it is being given to); and it must be from one kind (of food). Being able to choose (one of the two other forms of *kaffara*, namely fasting two months or freeing a slave) must be in the form of a choice of substitute for it is not acceptable if two or more forms (of *kaffara*) are combined such that he feeds thirty and fasts a month, or he frees half of a slave – according to the well known judgement – as the choice is between one of the three above mentioned options, not the option to take a part (of the fasting option, a part of the feeding option…) and combine it with another part; likewise it is not accepted to participate in two kaffaras such that that each portion for each destitute person is taken from (the combined) one hundred and twenty (*mudds*). 'Ayn-Jeem said: "It is not (considered to be) 'combining' (and therefore not considered prohibited) to feed thirty destitute people with wheat and then thirty with dates or barley if circumstances necessitate this; or to feed thirty with cooked food and to give (thirty) *mudds* (of dry food) to thirty others. Such combinations are accepted (in the *shari'ah*): feeding thirty with cooked food and thirty others with dry food is not (considered to fall under the prohibition of) 'combining' (various forms of *kaffara*); rather it is permitted, according to the most evident judgement." He then goes on to say: "(as to the question) as to whether the *kaffara* is obligatory immediately or whether there may be a delay, the first is the most evident (of the two judgements) – and this has been stated by al-Khurshi."

In the name of Allah, All Merciful, Most Merciful
Praise be to Allah, the Lord of all the worlds
O Allah send blessings and peace on our Master Muhammad
and on his Family and Companions – equal in number to the
blessings sent to him by all His creatures from the beginning
of creation to the end of time – that is, all blessings which are
encompassed by Your knowledge

The Book of Hajj

The Book of Hajj

From the *Murshid al-Mu'een 'ala'd-Daruri min 'Ulum ad-Deen*

THE commentator, (Shaykh Ahmad ibn al-Basheer al-Qalawi ash-Shinqeeti), has not made a commentary on the lines (of Ibn 'Ashir referring to the) hajj and he has not offered any explanation for this absence of commentary although he has made a commentary on the text in the *Risala* referring (to the laws of) hajj entitled *Mawarid an-Najah wa Masadir al-Falah*. He himself went on hajj with a large group of people from the town of Shinqeet. It may be that he had been influenced by the practice of the *'ulama* of al-Andalus and the whole of the Maghrib, that is, their prohibiting the hajj and their considering its obligation to be annulled for the people of all these countries from the sixth century hijri – because of the lack of negotiable highways, the lack of means and the lack of security for persons and their property.

Al-Hattab has mentioned from al-Mazari that Shaykh Abu'l-Walid issued a *fatwa* declaring the obligation to make hajj had been removed from the people of al-Andalus and that at-Tartushi had made a *fatwa* declaring that it was haram for the people of the Maghrib. Moreover, Ibn Rushd al-Hafeed has mentioned – after his completing (the chapter on) the laws of hajj in his *Bidayat al-Muhjtahid* – that he added the book of Hajj to the (work) after more than twenty years (had elapsed). He has also mentioned that he did not intend to discuss the hajj when composing the (work) but does not give any reason (why he changed his mind).

Al-Hattab said: "Shaykh Zarruq said in *al-Irshad*: 'The laws of hajj are numerous, its branches are also complex, and consideration of them is slight today, particularly in the lands of the Maghrib because of the absence of any need for them.'"

I say: "The lack of need for them is on account of the *'ulama*'s prohibition of the hajj for the people of these lands. Thus they have abandoned learning its laws because of the lack of need for them. However now that all the obstacles have been removed, all kinds of transport are available and all who desire to get there are able to do so with ease and safety – and given that the missing text (of Ibn 'Ashir) regarding the hajj contain the laws of hajj in a complete and comprehensive manner, as well as a complete explanation in clear and correct terms of the *'umra* and the visit to the tomb of the Prophet, may the peace and blessings of Allah be upon him – we have decided to include the text of the Book of Hajj from the *Murshid al-Mu'een*. In fact, it has no need of explanation on account of its clarity. However, we shall attempt to gather what is possible of the statements of the *'ulama* on the subject and to establish the benefits, the uncommon matters, particularities and exceptions in accordance with the manner of the commentator, our grandfather, may Allah have mercy on him – that is in the light of his words regarding the nature of his commentary when he says: 'Know that the intention of the commentary, may Allah accept it by His overflowing generosity and by the rank of Muhammad, the Prophet, may the peace and blessings of Allah be upon him and on his Family, is to elucidate the hidden or confusing aspects and to resolve the unfamiliar issues – not to transmit what is familiar and well known, except what pertains to matters of *'aqida*.' I ask Allah glorious and exalted is He, for the same as our grandfather, the commentator, asked Him for, that is, success, acceptance, help, solicitude and protection from mistakes; and for a correct intention and for an acceptance purely for His sake, glorious is He, wa ta'ala, Amin – for He it is who has the means to grant all this and who has the capacity to grant this. May Allah bless and grant peace on Muhammad and on his Family and Companions. Glory be to your Lord, the Lord of might, beyond anything they describe. and peace be upon the Messengers. and praise be to Allah, the Lord of all the worlds.

This has been written and compiled by the grandson of the author, the *qadi* Muhammad ibn Ahmad ibn 'Abdallah ibn Ahmad ibn Basheer al-Qalawi ash-Shinqeeti, the head of the Supreme Court for the Islamic Sharia and former Public Prosecutor for the Islamic Republic of Mauritania.

Nouakchott, end of Rajab, 1418, corresponding to November 1997.

Ibn 'Ashir said:

$$\text{اَلْحَجُّ فَرْضٌ مَرَّةً فِي الْعُمُرِ}$$
$$\text{أَرْكَانُهُ إِنْ تُرِكَتْ لَمْ تُجْبَرِ}$$

229 The hajj is a *fard* obligation once in a lifetime; if any of its pillars are left out, it cannot be made good. (These pillars are:)

$$\text{اَلْإِحْرَامُ وَالسَّعْيُ وُقُوفُ عَرَفَهْ}$$
$$\text{لَيْلَةَ الْأَضْحَى وَالطَّوَافُ رِدْفَهْ}$$

230 entering *ihram*, the *sa'y* between Safa and Marwa, standing on 'Arafa the night before the Day of Sacrifice followed by the *tawaf*.

$$\text{وَالْوَاجِبَاتُ غَيْرُ الْأَرْكَانِ بِدَمْ}$$
$$\text{قَدْ جُبِرَتْ مِنْهَا طَوَافُ مَنْ قَدِمْ}$$

231 The obligations other than the pillars are made good by a sacrifice – among them the *tawaf* made on arrival,

$$\text{وَوَصْلُهُ بِالسَّعْيِ مَشْيٌ فِيهِمَا}$$
$$\text{وَرَكْعَةُ الطَّوَافِ إِنْ تَحَتَّمَا}$$

232 and joining it immediately to the *sa'y*, walking in both, the two *rak'ats* of the *tawaf* if (the *tawaf* is of the kind which is) incumbent (i.e. *tawaf al-qudum* and *al-ifada*),

$$\text{نُزُولُ مُزْدَلِفٍ فِي رُجُوعِنَا}$$
$$\text{مَبِيتُ لَيْلَاتٍ ثَلَاثٍ بِمِنَى}$$

233 staying at Muzdalifa on the return, spending three nights at Mina (after 'Arafa),

$$\text{إِحْرَامُ مِيقَاتٍ فَذُو الْحُلَيْفَهْ}$$
$$\text{لِطَيْبَ لِلشَّامِ وَمِصْرَ الْجُحْفَهْ}$$

234 entering the *ihram* via the appointed places at Dhu'l-Hulayfa for (the people of) Tayb, at al-Juhfa for Sham (Greater Syria), Egypt (and the West),

$$\text{قَرْنٌ لِنَجْدٍ ذَاتُ عِرْقٍ لِلْعِرَاقْ}$$

$$\text{يَلَمْلَمُ الْيَمَنَ آتِيهَا وِفَاقْ}$$

235 at Qarn for the (highlands of) Najd (of the Arabian Peninsula), at Dhat al-ʿIrq for Iraq (Fars and the east), Yalamyam for the Yemen (and India) and whoever arrives via these (*miqat*, even not of these regions) should do as (those of these regions),

$$\text{تَجَرُّدٌ مِنَ الْمَخِيطِ تَلْبِيَةٌ}$$

$$\text{وَالْحَلْقُ مَعْ رَمْيِ الْجِمَارِ تَوْفِيَةٌ}$$

236 not wearing anything sewn, declaring *labbayk, Allahumma labbayk* …, shaving (the head) and stoning (the shaytans).

$$\text{وَإِنْ تُرِدْ تَرْتِيبَ حَجِّكَ اسْمَعَا}$$

$$\text{بَيَانَهُ وَالذِّهْنَ مِنْكَ اسْتَجْمِعَا}$$

237 And if you wish (to adhere to) the order (of the acts) of your hajj, then listen to an explanation (of it) and concentrate your thoughts:

$$\text{إِنْ جِئْتَ رَابِغاً تَنَظَّفْ وَاغْتَسِلْ}$$

$$\text{كَوَاجِبٍ وَبِالشُّرُوعِ يَتَّصِلْ}$$

238 if you arrive at (the village called) Rabigh (on the east coast of the Red Sea), then clean yourself (by shaving the pubes, plucking the armpits and trimming the moustache and nails) and make a *ghusl* like the obligatory (one before *jumuʿa*) just before beginning (the *ihram*);

$$\text{وَالْبَسْ رِداً وَأُزْرَةً نَعْلَيْنِ}$$

$$\text{وَاسْتَصْحِبِ الْهَدْيَ وَرَكْعَتَيْنِ}$$

239 wear (two pieces of seamless cloth), one about the torso and one about

the waist and a pair of sandals, accompany the sacrificial animal and make two *rak'ats*

بِالْكَافِرُونَ ثُمَّ الْإِخْلَاصُ هُمَا

فَإِنْ رَكِبْتَ أَوْ مَشَيْتَ أَحْرِمَا

240 reciting (surat) al-Kafirun – The Rejectors and then al-Ikhlas – Sincerity; enter into the *ihram* whether you are mounted or walking,

بِنِيَّةٍ تَصْحَبُ قَوْلاً أَوْ عَمَلْ

كَمَشْيٍ أَوْ تَلْبِيَةٍ مِمَّا اتَّصَلْ

241 with the intention, accompanied by the words associated with it – namely the *talbiya* and the *takbir*, or the action (associated with it) – like (setting out to) walk (towards the places of the rites) immediately before the (entering the) *ihram*;

وَجَدِّدَنْهَا كُلَّمَا تَجَدَّدَتْ

حَالٌ وَإِنْ صَلَّيْتَ ثُمَّ إِنْ دَنَتْ

242 and this (*talbiya*) is to be repeated every time there is a change of state (like standing, sitting or mounting) or after the *salat*. When you near –

مَكَّةَ فَاغْتَسِلْ بِذِي طُوىً بِلَا

دَلْكٍ وَمِنْ كُدَا الثَّنِيَّةِ ادْخُلَا

243 Makka, make a *ghusl* at Dhu Tuwa without rubbing (excessively lest one remove some hair) and enter by (the narrow pass between the two mountains called) Kuda ath-Thaniya.

إِذَا وَصَلْتَ لِلْبُيُوتِ فَاتْرُكَا

تَلْبِيَةً وَكُلَّ شُغْلٍ وَاسْلُكَا

244 When you reach the houses (of Makka) then leave off the invocation of the *talbiya* and all other activity, and go

لِلْبَيْتِ مِنْ بَابِ السَّلَامِ وَاسْتَلِمْ

الْحَجَرَ الْأَسْوَدَ كَبِّرْ وَأَتِمَّ

245 to the House from the Gate of Peace, kiss the Black Stone, say *Allahu akbar* and perform

سَبْعَةَ أَشْوَاطٍ بِهِ وَقَدْ يَسَرْ

وَكَبِّرَنْ مُقَبِّلاً ذَاكَ الْحَجَرِ

246 seven circuits of the House – with the House on your left, and say *Allahu akbar* when kissing that stone

مَتَى تُحَاذِيهِ كَذَا الْيَمَانِي

لَكِنَّ ذَا بِالْيَدِ خُذْ بَيَانِي

247 whenever passing by it; likewise the Yemeni corner (before it) – however, (greet) this (by touching it) with your hand (and then place it on your mouth), and accept this explanation!

إِنْ لَمْ تَصِلْ لِلْحَجَرِ الْمَسْ بِالْيَدِ

وَضَعْ عَلَى الْفَمِ وَكَبِّرْ تَقْتَدِ

248 If you do not reach the Black Stone (on the second circuits), then touch it with the hand, place it on your mouth and say *Allahu akbar*, thereby following (the sunna).

وَارْمُلْ ثَلَاثاً وَامْشِ بَعْدُ أَرْبَعَا

خَلْفَ الْمَقَامِ رَكْعَتَيْنِ أَوْقِعَا

249 Walk briskly the (first) three circuits and then walk the last four (at a

normal pace). Then perform two *rak'ats* behind the Station (of Ibrahim).

وَادْعُ بِمَا شِئْتَ لَدَى الْمُلْتَزِمْ
وَالْحَجَرِ الْأَسْوَدَ بَعْدُ اسْتَلِمْ

250 Make (as many) *du'as* as you wish at (the space in the wall of the Ka'ba known as) al-Multazim and then kiss the Black Stone.

وَاخْرُجْ إِلَى الصَّفَا وَقِفْ مُسْتَقْبِلَا
عَلَيْهِ ثُمَّ كَبِّرَنْ وَهَلِّلَا

251 Then go out to Safa and stand facing the (Ka'ba), exclaim *Allahu akbar* and (the words of) the *labbayk*.

وَاسْعَ لِمَرْوَةٍ فَقِفْ مِثْلَ الصَّفَا
وَخُبَّ فِي بَطْنِ الْمَسِيلِ ذَا اقْتِفَا

252 Then make the *sa'y* to Marwa and stand (there) like at Safa and make great haste – for this is following (the sunna) – in Batn al-Maseel (between the two green markers),

أَرْبَعَ وَقَفَاتٍ بِكُلٍّ مِنْهُمَا
تَقِفْ وَالْأَشْوَاطَ سَبْعاً تَمِّمَا

253 standing four times at each of the two and complete the seven going to and fro.

وَادْعُ بِمَا شِئْتَ بِسَعْيِي وَطَوَافْ
وَبِالصَّفَا وَمَرْوَةٍ مَعَ اعْتِرَافْ

254 Make *du'a* as (much as) you wish during the *sa'y* and *tawaf*, and at Safa and Marwa, in a state of recognition (of your wrong actions).

وَيَجِبُ الطُّهْرَانِ وَالسِّتْرُ عَلَى

مَنْ طَافَ نَدْبُهَا بِسَعْيٍ يُجْتَلَى

255 It is obligatory for the person doing the *tawaf* to be free of impurity (both on oneself and one's clothes), to be in a state of ritual purity and to cover (one's private parts); and it is recommended for the *sa'y* as a particular mark of excellence.

وَعُدْ فَلَبِّ لِمُصَلَّى عَرَفَةٍ

وَخُطْبَةُ السَّابِعِ تَأْتِي لِلصِّفَةِ

256 Resume the saying of the *talbiya* until (reaching) the *musalla* of 'Arafa; and (attend) the *khutba* of the seventh day (of Dhu'l-Hijja) – this is a description (of what is correct)!

We shall begin the discussion of the hajj by transmitting (a description of) his hajj, may the peace and blessings of Allah be upon him, in order to acquire the blessing and good fortune of it and because of his saying, may the peace and blessings of Allah be upon him: "Take your rites from me." This hajj of his provides a detailed description of the general instruction (afforded by the hadith). O Allah grant peace and blessings on our Master Muhammad and on his Family and Companions.

A DESCRIPTION OF HIS HAJJ, MAY THE PEACE AND BLESSINGS OF ALLAH BE UPON HIM, FROM ZAD AL-MA'AD FI HADY KHAYR IL-'IBAD OF IBN AL-QAYIM AL-JAWZI

(Ibn Jawzi stated that) "there is no difference of opinion that after his hijra to Madina he, may the peace and blessing of Allah be upon him, did not perform any hajj other than the 'Farewell Hajj.' At-Tirmidhi narrated from Jabir ibn 'Abdallah, may Allah be pleased with both of them, that the Prophet, may the peace and blessings of Allah be upon him, performed hajj three times, twice before the hijra and once afterwards – together with an 'umra." Then (Ibn Jawzi) goes on to say, after a discussion, that the hadith is not secure from doubt (as to its authenticity).

"He, may the peace and blessings of Allah be upon him, went out during the day after making the *Dhuhr salat* six days before the end of Dhu'l-Qa'da on a Saturday. He performed the *'Asr salat* in the shortened form at Dhu'l-Hulayfa, and *Maghrib*, *'Isha*, *Subh* and *Dhuhr*. After he had applied oil and perfumes, the musk could be seen glistening in the parting of his hair, may the peace and blessings of Allah be upon him. He put on a waist wrapping and then a wrapping around his torso, and entered the *ihram* for hajj after making the *salat* of *Dhuhr*. There is no transmission from him that he made two *rak'ats* for (entering into the state of) *ihram*. He then proceeded until he came to rest at Dhu Tuwan where he spent the night of Sunday, that is four days before the end of Dhu'l-Hijja, and made a *ghusl*. On entering the mosque, he made for the House. He did not, however, make the (two) *rak'ats* of greeting (which is normally a sunna on entering) a mosque as the greeting is (contained in) the *tawaf*. When he came alongside the Black Stone, he touched it with his stick. Every time he came to the Black Stone he would say *Allahu akbar*. It is also confirmed that he would salute it with his hand – placing his hand on it and then kissing his hand; also that he would touch it with his stick; and also that he would kiss the (Stone). It is narrated of him that he would place his lips on it for a long time and weep. Whenever he greeted it he would say *bismillah wa'llahu akbar*. The well known opinion is that he was mounted. When he had finished his *tawaf* – after walking briskly three times and walking at a normal pace four times – he took his upper wrapping under the right arm and threw it over one shoulder, leaving his other exposed, and then stretched out his hands and shoulders. When he had finished he came to the Station (of Ibrahim) and recited: '*Take the Maqam of Ibrahim as a place of salat*'[1] and made two *rak'ats*, reciting al-Ikhlas – Sincerity – twice. Then he greeted the Black Stone. Then he went out to Safa and recited '*Safa and Marwa are among the Landmarks of Allah*'[2] saying 'Let us begin with what Allah has begun with.' Then he went up on (to the mount of) Safa until he could see the House and turning to face it, he exclaimed words of *tawhid* and *takbir* and said:

لَا إِلَهَ إِلَّا اللَّهُ وَحْدَهُ لَا شَرِيكَ لَهُ، لَهُ الْمُلْكُ وَلَهُ الْحَمْدُ، وَهُوَ عَلَى كُلِّ شَيْءٍ قَدِيرٌ، لَا إِلَهَ إِلَّا اللَّهُ وَحْدَهُ لَا شَرِيكَ لَهُ، لَهُ الْمُلْكُ وَلَهُ الْحَمْدُ، وَهُوَ عَلَى كُلِّ شَيْءٍ قَدِيرٌ، لَا إِلَهَ إِلَّا اللَّهُ وَحْدَهُ أَنْجَزَ وَعْدَهُ وَنَصَرَ عَبْدَهُ وَهَزَمَ الْأَحْزَابَ وَحْدَهُ

---

1 al-Baqara – The Cow: 124
2 al-Baqara – The Cow: 157

"*La ilaha illa'llah wahadahu la sharika lah, lahu'l-mulku wa lahu'l-hamd wa huwa ala kulli shay'in qadir, la ilaha illa'llah wahadahu anjaza wa'adahu wa nasara abdahu wa hazama al-ahzab wahdahu* – there is no god but Allah, Alone without partner, to Him belongs the kingdom and to Him belongs all praise and He has power over everything. There is no god but Allah alone without partner, to Him belongs the kingdom and to Him belongs all praise and He has power over everything. There is no god but Allah alone, He has completed His promise and aided his slave to victory and He alone has brought defeat to all the (other) parties."

He walked very quickly throughout all his *sa'y* -from the moment he stepped down into the river valley until the moment he left it by walking upwards.

On the Thursday, he, may the peace and blessings of Allah be upon him, made for Mina and spent the night of the *jumu'a* there. After sunrise, he proceeded from there to Arafa where he found its summit had been marked out (as the area, known) as Namira, (where the *masjid namira* came to be built) – in accordance with his orders. He dismounted and remained there until the sun had passed its zenith. Then he departed on his she-camel Qaswa until it came to the bottom of the river valley situated in the Ard Arina, the wide open space extending from Makka. He delivered the famous *khutba* to the people – a single *khutba* – and then commanded Bilal to make the *adhan*. After the *iqama*, he performed *Dhuhr* with two *rak'ats*, (reciting) silently in both. Then he rose and prayed (a further) two *rak'ats* (for *'Asr*). Then he mounted (his she-camel and rode) until he came to a halt at the end of the mountain at the Sakharat (rocks). Facing the *qibla*, he began to occupy himself with *du'as* and recitation while still mounted – until the sun had set. Most of his *du'as* consisted of:

لَا إِلَهَ إِلَّا اللَّهُ وَحْدَهُ لَا شَرِيكَ لَهُ، لَهُ الْمُلْكُ وَلَهُ الْحَمْدُ، بِيَدِهِ الْخَيْرُ، وَهُوَ عَلَى كُلِّ شَيْءٍ قَدِيرٌ

"*La ilaha illa'llah wahdahu la shareeka lah, lahu'l-mulk wa lahu'l-hamd, bi-yadihi al-khair, wa huwa 'ala kulli shay'in qadir* – There is no god but Allah, to Him belongs the kingdom and to Him belongs all praise, in His hand is all good and He has power over all things."

Al-Baihaqi has mentioned the hadith in which it is recorded that he, may the peace and blessings of Allah be upon him, said: 'My most frequent *du'a* and that of the Prophets before me at 'Arafa is the saying of the:

لَا إِلَهَ إِلَّا اللَّهُ وَحْدَهُ لَا شَرِيكَ لَهُ، لَهُ الْمُلْكُ وَلَهُ الْحَمْدُ، وَهُوَ عَلَى كُلِّ شَيْءٍ قَدِيرٌ

la ilaha illa'llah wahdahu la shareeka lah, lahu'l-mulk was lahu'l-hamd wa huwa 'ala kulli shay'in qadir.

It was here that the *ayat 'Today I have completed your deen for you and completed My blessing upon you and I am pleased with Islam as a deen for you'*[1] was revealed to him.

When the sun had set and the sunset was well passed – such that the yellow had disappeared – he left 'Arafa. He would say the *talbiya* on his way without interruption. He alighted on his way, poured himself some water and made a light *wudu'*. Usama was sitting behind him on his mount up to Muzdalifa. Then he made *wudu'* for the *salat* and joined two *salats* together with one *adhan* and two *iqamas*; he did not pray between them, although it has also been related that he prayed them with two *adhans* and two *iqamas*. Then he slept until dawn – without spending the night in *salat*. There is no truth in reports that he spent the two nights of the 'Eids in *salat*. He stayed standing where he was thereby demonstrating to people that all Muzdalifa is considered a *mawqif* – a place of standing. Then he prayed the *Subh salat* at the beginning of its time with an *adhan* and *iqama* and stood at the Mash'ar al-Haram (the station at Muzdalifa, east of Makka) until the day had broken completely.

He then had al-Fadl behind him on his mount and he declared the *talbiya* while proceeding on their way. He commanded Ibn 'Abbas to collect seven pebbles for him for stoning the shaytan and stoned the *Jamrat* al-'Aqaba with seven pebbles saying *Allahu akbar* with each pebble. He left without making any *du'a*. He slaughtered a camel. Mu'ammar ibn 'Abdallah shaved him, standing over his head with a razor, and he, may the peace and blessings of Allah be upon him looked into his face saying: 'O Mu'ammar! the Messenger of Allah has given you access to the lobe of his ear and you have a razor in your hand!' and Mu'ammar replied: 'By Allah, O Messenger of Allah, may the peace and blessings of Allah be upon him, this is one of Allah's blessings on me.' Then he went on to Makka and made the *tawaf al-ifada*. It is reported of Ibn 'Umar that he returned and prayed *Dhuhr* at Mina.

In *Sahih* Muslim it is recorded that he prayed *Dhuhr* at Makka, then returned to Mina, stayed there for the nights of the days of *Tashriq*, and would stone the *jamras* after the sun had passed its zenith saying *Allahu akbar* with each pebble. He would also make *du'a* after each of the first two *jamaras* – equal in length to surat al-Baqara – but would not make *du'a* at the last one. He left on the third day after *Dhuhr* to al-Muhassib (the road between the plain of Makka

---

1 al-Ma'ida – The Table: 2

and the village of Mina), that is, al-Abtah, the wide (water) course (full of pebbles) at the Khayf Bani Kanana (the part of the valley that rises a little from the channel in which the water flows). Then he prayed *Dhuhr* and *'Asr*, and *Maghrib* and *'Isha*, after which he lay down to rest for a while. He then proceed to Makka, making the *tawaf al-ifada* at night, just before dawn; and he did not walk briskly in this *tawaf*. He gave permission to 'A'isha to make *'umra* from at-Tan'eem in the company of her brother 'Abd ar-Rahman and when she arrived he, may the peace and blessings of Allah be upon him, gave permission to leave with the caravan to Madina."

Hajj

AL-HATTAB said: "The meaning of the word hajj is 'to make for'; it has also been said that it also implies 'performing it repeatedly'; in the *Qamus* (dictionary) it states that the hajj is 'making for, desisting from, arrival, great dispute, hesitation and a making for Makka to perform the rites.' A consensus has been related from more than one (of the *fuqaha*) that it is an obligation at least once in a lifetime; from another that it is obligatory every year; and yet another once every five years, based on what is related from him, may the peace and blessings of Allah be upon him: 'It is incumbent on every Muslim to come to the Sacred House of Allah once every five years.'"

Ibn al-'Arabi objected to it saying: "It is prohibited to relate this hadith for it is fabricated – so how can one possibly establish a legal judgement from it?" He also said in *al-Qabas*: "It is mentioned from one person that it is obligatory every five years, based on the hadith that has been narrated on this matter. However this (hadith) is weak." Thus it is not to be taken into consideration because of its irregularity (*shudhudh*)[1]. An-Nawawi said: "This (hadith) is contrary to the consensus and anyone holding to it is contradicted by the consensus against it; if, however, its narration is accepted (as correct), then it is to be understood in the sense of being recommended, that one is exhorted to go (at least once) during this period – just as the *'ulama* have interpreted the *sahih* hadith (below)."

Ibn Abi Shayba and Ibn Hibban, in his *Sahih,* have narrated from Abu Sa'id al-Khudri, may Allah be pleased with him, that the Messenger of Allah, may the peace and blessings of Allah be upon him, said: "Allah, exalted is He, said: 'I have given health to the body of a slave, I have granted him ample means and five years passes and he does not go to the Sacred Places!'" Ibn Farhun said in his *Manasik*: "The *'ulama* have said: 'This is to be understood in the sense

---

1 The *shadhdh* (irregular hadith) is that which a trustworthy narrator or an utterly truthful person narrates which is contrary to someone weightier than him because he pays extra attention to detail or because of the greater number [of narrations] or some other factor which causes [his narration] to be weightier. (*Qawa'id fi 'ulum al-hadith*, Zafar Ahmad al-'Uthmani at-Tahanawi)

of being recommended and to emphasise (the importance of going) within a period of time like this.'"

Its obligation is stated in the Book where Allah, exalted is He, says: "*Hajj to the House is a duty owed to Allah by all mankind – those who can find a way to do it.*"[1] Its obligation is also recorded in the sunna, namely in al-Bukhari, in his saying in the *sahih* hadith: "Islam is built on five things..." and among the (pillars) mentioned is "the hajj to the House for those who can find a way to do it." It is also an obligation once in a lifetime, according to the consensus, if one is able, based on the hadith of Muslim whose chain of narration is from Abu Hurayra, may Allah be pleased with him: "The Messenger of Allah, may the peace and blessings of Allah be upon him, addressed us saying: 'People! the hajj has been made a *fard* obligation on you – so go on hajj.' A man asked him: 'Every year, Messenger of Allah?' He remained silent until he had repeated it three times and then replied: 'If I were to say "yes" then I would be making it obligatory and you would not able (to fulfil this obligation).' Then he went on to say: 'Leave me as long as I leave you. Surely those before you perished by their excessive questioning and their differences with their prophets.'"

The pillars of Hajj

The pillars of Hajj are four in number. If they are missing or one of them is missing, then the hajj is invalidated and cannot be made good by sacrifice – contrary to other obligations. They are the *ihram*, the *sa'y* between Safa and Marwa, the standing at 'Arafa on the night (before the day) of sacrifice and the final *tawaf*. As for these four not being made good by sacrifice or anything else, there is clear textual evidence from more than one (of the *fuqaha*).

These (four pillars whose absence invalidates the hajj) are classified in three ways. One type is when the hajj is lost by leaving the (particular pillar in question) out, although nothing becomes due (as compensation) when it is left out. This (type) is (represented by) the *ihram*, that is, when it is either left out entirely or when the intention or the *talbiya* – which are the constituent elements of the *ihram* – are left out, in which case the hajj remains an obligation on the *mukallaf*. Another type (of pillar) – whereby the hajj is lost by missing it out and whereby the person making the hajj is commanded to do an *'umra* and to make it up next year – is the standing at 'Arafa, according to the agreement (of the *fuqaha*). Finally there is the type (of pillar) whereby the hajj is not lost and whereby one is not released from the state of *ihram* back to the normal state except by its performance – even

---

1 Ali 'Imran – The Family of 'Imran: 97

if he were to go to the furthest corners of the east and west and were to return to Makka to perform it – namely (the performance of) the final *tawaf*, according to the agreement of the *fuqaha*, and the *sa'y*, according to the well known opinion. This has been stated by al-Hattab in his *Manasik*. There is an unusual (*shadhdh*) narration from Malik to the effect that a person does not have to return for a *sa'y* (which has not been performed) and that it may be made good by sacrifice.

Khalil said: "The hajj has been made a *fard* obligation and the *'umra* a sunna (once in a lifetime); however, there is a difference of opinion as to (the obligation of) its immediate performance and to (whether it is permitted to) delay it if one fears that it will be missed. Its *fard* obligation as well as its actual performance is conditional upon one being free and a *mukallaf*. This condition should be met at the moment of entering into *ihram*, (together with an intention based on its obligatory nature) not with the intention of performing a *nafila* act."

Al-Hattab said: "The hajj and *'umra* are conditional upon the person being a Muslim; and the hajj is valid in the case of someone who has no sense of discrimination (e.g. due to his youth or his being retarded) or the mad person – in which case the person in charge of them should make the *ihram* in their stead, freeing them thereby (of this obligation, and thus assuming all responsibilities of the hajj upon himself), make the intention (for them), but does not say the *talbiya* for them. As for children who are almost of age and who are obedient when instructed (to do something), they should enter the *ihram* at the *miqats*, according to Malik; then there are the very young children, of seven or eight years old – these should only enter the *ihram* near the hajj; and the custodian of someone is counted as the father, even if there is no specific instruction from a relation or anyone else."

It is stated in the *Mudawwana* that there is no harm in a male minor entering the *ihram* wearing ankle rings around his legs and bracelets around his arms, although Malik disliked underage boys adorning themselves with gold.

Al-Hattab has also said: "*Ihram* is made on behalf of the *mutbaq* but not the person who has fainted. The *mutbaq* is defined as someone in a permanent state of mild catatonia, capable of understanding when spoken to, but who cannot reply properly – as long as he can distinguish the earth from the sky and a person from a horse." The legal judgement of the mad person who is also *mutbaq* is that of the child, as is stated in the *Mudawwana*.

Again al-Hattab said: "As for the minor who is incapable of discriminating in matters of purity and who cannot follow when instructed (to do something), his *tawaf* is not invalidated when his ritual purity is broken by the onset of a minor impurity."

Al-Hattab said commenting on Khalil's words '(hajj should not be performed) by means of taking on a debt or receiving the means as a gift': "There is agreement that whoever does not have the capacity to pay back a loan contracted on account of the hajj does not have to contract this loan; nor that he (is under any obligation to) accept (a gift of) money for the hajj or for getting to Makka – and the most evident judgement from (the work of Sanad ibn 'Inan al-Misri entitled) *at-Taraz* is that there is agreement about this because it might entail a feeling of indebtedness to someone: he is under no obligation to accept a gift on account of the hajj, or a loan, or to ask; moreover, anyone who has a workshop or industry of some kind from which he is able to save up enough to go on hajj is under no obligation to do so, and can give away any extra (profit rather than save it up). There are many possibilities of this nature, but a person is not obliged to entertain any of them on account of hajj. One such scenario is when someone goes to another in order to make the hajj with him and in so doing takes upon himself what is not incumbent upon him, and then finds himself bound by a feeling of gratitude; and there are those who ask (help) to go on hajj from someone who is unjust. One of the *'ulama* has even forbidden his student from taking a loan from someone who loves him and from whom he does not fear any reproach (for favours received) saying that either he will (in fact end up) reproaching him (for not paying it back) or his (own) child will begrudge (his father having given it to him) or (one of) the people of the land (will begrudge it him). You are under no obligation to make any request of this nature."

Likewise, if someone possesses dirhams which he uses as a means (of investment), living from the profit he makes, then he does not have to do the hajj with them if he fears he will perish (by using them up). Likewise regarding the question as to whether or not the person who has goods but only enough to (ensure a steady) turnover – that is the profit and the proceeds from the returns is only just enough for him to live on – has to sell them and make the hajj with (the money released by) their (sale) such that he would return as a poor person and would not be able to earn his living properly: in such a case he does not have to do this. This is also what Abu Hanifa said and one of the Tabi'un. All this is included or implied by what the author (Khalil) said. As for someone who hires the services of someone, he may prevent him from going on hajj.

And Imam Ibn 'Arafa bought a hajj for the Sultan of Ifriqiyyah. This is from al-Hattab.

Al-Hattab also stated: "Useful point: the threefold aspects of hajj are:
There are:

Three aspects to the *ihram*: hajj, *'umra* and *qiran*;

Three *ghusls*: for the *ihram*, on entering Makka and the day of 'Arafa;

Three [pairs of] *rak'ats*: for the *ihram*, the *tawaf al-qudum* and for the *tawaf al-ifada*;

Three aspects to the joining between the area outside *al-Haram* (*al-hill*) and *al-Haram*: with respect to the person doing the hajj, the person doing the *'umra* and hunting;

Three occasions for walking with great haste: for the *tawaf*, the *sa'y* and in the Batn Mahsir (of the bare plain tract);

There are three *khutbas*;

Three places of stoning the *jamras*;

The days of *Tashriq* are three in number, as are the number of days of sacrifice;

And those who pass the *miqat* are three in number: the person wanting to perform the rites, the person who does not intend to perform them and the person who intends to go to Makka;

Those in *ihram* are of three kinds regarding the shaving (of the hair): those who must cut their hair – that is those with matted hair, short hair or (those who are subject to this judgement but) who in fact have no hair, those who have to (merely) clip it as in the case of adult women, and those who are permitted to do the one or the other, although shaving is better – that is, other than those mentioned;

And the sacrificial animal is of three kinds: camels, cows or sheep and goats;

And its marks are three, the garlanding, the making known (*ish'ar*) and the returning to the normal state after the *ihram* (*tahlil*)."

Zarruq said: "All the actions of hajj demand that one walk, other than the standing at 'Arafa, at the Mash'ar al-Haram and the stoning of the Jamrat al-'Aqaba."

The *ihlal* and the *talbiya* (of *labbayk*...) on the hajj from the time of the *miqat*

It is narrated from Ibn 'Umar that he said: "At this (mount called) Bayda' of yours, you are denying (the practice of) the Messenger of Allah, may the peace and blessings of Allah be upon him: he did not say the *ihlal* except at the Mosque, that is, the mosque of Dhul-Hulayfa" – there is agreement about this.

It is related from Anas, that the Prophet, may the peace and blessings of Allah be upon him, prayed *Dhuhr*, then mounted his riding beast and declared the *ihlal* when ascending the mount known as al-Bayda' – this is narrated by Abu Dawud.

It is related from Jabir that the saying of *ihlal* by the Prophet, may the peace and blessings of Allah be upon him, was from Dhu'l-Hulayfa from the moment when his riding beast drew level with it – this is narrated by al-Bukhari who states that it was narrated by Anas and Ibn 'Abbas.

It is narrated from Ibn 'Umar that the Prophet, may the peace and blessings of Allah be upon him, would declare the *ihlal* when his riding beast drew level, standing, at the Mosque of Dhu'l-Hulayfa by saying:

لَبَّيْكَ اللَّهُمَّ لَبَّيْكَ، لَبَّيْكَ لَا شَرِيكَ لَكَ لَبَّيْكَ، إِنَّ الْحَمْدَ وَالنِّعْمَةَ لَكَ وَالْمُلْكَ، لَا شَرِيكَ لَكَ

"*Labbayk allahumma labbayk, labbayk la shareeka laka labbayk, inna'l-hamda wa'n-ni'mata laka wa'l-mulk, la shareeka lak* – At Your service! O Allah, at Your service! At Your service! You have no partner. At Your service! The praise and blessing are Yours and the kingdom. You have no partner" and 'Abdallah would add here:

لَبَّيْكَ لَبَّيْكَ وَسَعْدَيْكَ، وَالْخَيْرُ بِيَدَيْكَ، وَالرَّغْبَاءُ إِلَيْكَ وَالْعَمَلُ

"*Labbayk, labbayk wa-sa'dayk wa'l-khayru biyadayk, wa'r-raghba'u ilayka wa'l-'amal* – At Your service! At Your service! At Your service and at Your call. Good is in Your hands, and I am at Your service. Our desire is for You, and our action." – agreed upon (by al-Bukhari and Muslim).

It is narrated from Jabir that the Messenger of Allah, may the peace and blessings of Allah be upon him, would make the *ihlal* and declare the (same form of the) *talbiya* as in the hadith of Ibn 'Umar. Jabir then said: "and people added '*dha'l-ma'arij* (Lord of the Ascending Steps) and similar phrases and the Prophet, may the peace and blessings of Allah be upon him, who was listening, did not say anything to them (to indicate that they should not do so)." The same meaning (although with different wording) is related by Ahmad, Abu Dawud and Muslim.

It is narrated from Abu Hurayra that the Prophet, may the peace and blessings of Allah be upon him, said in his *talbiya*:

لَبَّيْكَ إِلَهَ الْحَقِّ لَبَّيْكَ

"*Labbayka ilaha'l-haqq labbayk* – At Your service, God of the Truth, at Your service!" – and this is narrated by Ahmad, Ibn Majah and an-Nasa'i.

It is narrated from Ibn 'Umar that the Messenger of Allah, may the peace and blessings of Allah be upon him, said: "The people of Madina say the *ihlal* from Dhu'l-Hulayfa; the people of Sham from al-Juhfa and the people of Najd from Qarn", and Ibn 'Umar added: "This was said to me but I did not hear the Messenger of Allah, may the peace and blessings of Allah be on him, say that "the place of the *ihlal* for the people of Yemen is from Yalamlam" – there is agreement as to this.

It is narrated that Sa'id ibn Jubayr said: "I remarked to Ibn 'Abbas how strange it was that there was a difference of opinion amongst the Companions of the Messenger, may the peace and blessings of Allah be upon him, regarding his making the *ihlal* and he replied: 'I am the most knowledgeable of people in this (matter). There was (only) one hajj performed by him with this (*ihlal*): after his *ruku's* (of *salat*) in the mosque, he imposed it as an obligation when sitting there and he declared the *ihlal* for the hajj. When his she-camel rose he (again) said the *ihlal* and then proceeded. When he ascended the mount of al-Bayda', he made the *ihlal* –everything in accordance with what had been learned from those who narrated it'" – and I relate this in an abbreviated form. This has been narrated by Ahmad and Abu Dawud. The other five have narrated this from him in an abbreviated form – (and) that the Prophet, may the peace and blessings of Allah be upon him, made the *ihlal* after each *salat* – and there is agreement as to the authenticity of this relation.

Khalil said: "…and the sunna is to do the *ghusl* immediately before (the *ihram*), although there is no sacrifice (to be made if this is not done), and it is recommended in Madina for the person who intends *ihram* from Dhu'l-Hulayfa, and for the entry to Makka, at Tuwa, but not (in the case of) a woman who is menstruating. It is also (a sunna) to then make two *rak'ats* (before the *ihram*), although a *fard salat* is acceptable (instead of a sunna before the *ihram*). The person mounted should enter the *ihram* on moving off after positioning himself (on the saddle), and in the case of the person walking, at the moment he sets out walking." Khalil has also said: "As for the *tawaf*, (the sunna) is to perform it walking, and whoever is able (to perform it walking but has nevertheless performed it mounted or carried in stretcher by others) and has not repeated it (afterwards when he is able while still in Makka), then he should make a sacrifice." Again Khalil said: "The (*ihram*) is established by means of the intention even if the formulation employed does not correspond to the (particular type of hajj he goes on to make), in which case no sacrifice (to make up for this contradiction) is necessary. (The *ihram* is effected by means of the intention) – even if sexual intercourse takes place – when accompanied by the words (*labbayka allahumma…*) or the act (of divesting oneself of one's

ordinary sewn clothes) when both the former are undertaken in conjunction with this (*ihram*), and (is effective) whether he has specified (having taken the *ihram*, for the hajj or the *'umra*, or for both), or he has not specified. (If he has not specified it, it is recommended) to apply this (intention) to (the 'separate') hajj (known as *ifrad*, if he has entered the *ihram* during the month of hajj, or prior to the *tawaf* of arrival, after which the application to the hajj is obligatory) -although analogy requires that this be applied to the *qiran* (type of hajj because the (non-specific intention naturally comprises the two). If the person (entering into *ihram* has specified that this be for the *ifrad* type of hajj, for the *'umrah* or for *qiran*, but) then forgets which form he has stipulated, he should do the *qiran* (as a precaution), and make a new intention for the hajj: he fulfils all the rites of the *qiran* and thus fulfils only the obligation of this hajj not that of *'umrah* (by virtue of his renewed intention), which he should perform thereafter. This is like the case – not identical but analogous – where he doubts having formed the intention for the separate rite of *ifrad* or the *tamattu'*...."
Khalil also says: "and to repudiate the (hajj) is null and void after entering the haram or during it. However, there is uncertainty as to whether entering the haram with the words 'I intend to take the *ihram* like Zayd or such-and-such a person has taken it' – without knowing which kind of hajj this latter had intended – is correct or not."

It is narrated that Ibn 'Abbas, may Allah be pleased with them both, said: "The Messenger of Allah made Dhu'l-Hulayfa the *miqat* for the people of Madina, al-Juhfa for the people of Sham, Qarin al-Manazil for the people of Najd and Yalamlam for the people of Yemen. These places are for them and for those entering via these places who are not resident of these places but who intend the hajj and the *'umra*. Those who live this side of the (above mentioned places), then there place (of *ihram*) is from the (place of) the people (in question) – and so on up to the people of Makka who enter (the *ihram*) from there."

It is narrated that Sufyan ibn 'Uyayna said: "A man said to Malik ibn Anas: 'From where should I enter the *ihram*?' He replied: 'Enter the *ihram* from where the Messenger of Allah entered it, may the peace and blessings of Allah be upon him', and he repeated this to him several times. Then the (man) said: 'and if I were to add to it' and Malik replied: 'Do not do this for a I fear trial and affliction for you.' He said: 'What is there of trial and affliction in it? (The *miqat* are) only markers to which I am adding (something)!' Malik replied: 'Allah, exalted is He, said: "*Those who oppose his command should beware of a testing trial coming to them or a painful punishment striking them.*[1]" He said: 'What testing trial is in it?' He replied: 'What trial is greater than your considering yourself superior to (him) and refraining from (accepting) him, may the peace and blessings of Allah be upon him, or you considering your choice for yourself in this matter better than the choice of Allah for you or that of the Messenger of Allah, may the peace and blessings of Allah be upon him.'" It is said that the Messenger of Allah, may the peace and blessings of Allah be upon him, made Dhat al-'Irq the place for the people of Iraq and 'Umar's designating it a *miqat* was by his (own) sanction as he was unaware of the hadith and the fact that it had been appointed as a *miqat* by the Messenger of Allah, may the peace and blessings of Allah be upon him. The (above hadith) has the rank of *sahih* according to Muslim, Abu Dawud, and an-Nasa'i, al-Hattab said. And it is correct.

It is said that the reason for the *miqats* is that the Black Stone possessed a light which extended up to the actual *miqats*. Thus the place (of the *miqats*) is by a particular (divine) designation (*tawqeefan*). He said that the angels would watch over Adam, on whom be peace, at the House. The (*miqats*) represented the limits of their surveillance and also the site of landmarks and sacred places. The reason for the limits of the Prophetic haram are similar: the Angels would guard over it to ward off the plague and the Dajjal and so the limits of its inviolability coincided with the extent of their surveillance of it; or (these limits are defined) by the lights of the day of his arrival (after the hijrah) or by his physical contact with this place, may the peace and blessings of Allah be upon him. The *miqat* of Dhul-Hulayfa possesses a particular excellence from its being situated in the haram of Madina al-Munawwara and its being the place where he put on the *ihram*, may the peace and blessings of Allah be upon him. The author of *at-Taraz* said: "These *miqats* have a validity specific to the actual places not to the names: thus if a *miqat* is a village which falls into ruin and its buildings and name are transferred to another place, then it is still the original place that counts (as the *miqat*) as the legal judgement is connected to this (place and not the name)." *Hashiya al-Madani 'Ali Kanun 'ala Khalil.*

Al-Hattab said: "Whoever crosses the *miqat* out of ignorance without entering the (the state of) *ihram* should return and enter the *ihram*, and he does not have to sacrifice an animal" – this he has related from Malik – "and whoever is in Makka and leaves it with the intent of returning, who had made the *'umra* there but then interrupts (his *ihram*) while maintaining the intention to perform the hajj (afterwards), and goes out for some necessity with the

1   an-Nur – the Light: 61

intent of returning, then he does not have to renew his *ihram*. If, however, he goes out without intending to return but then does in fact return, he does have to re-enter *ihram*. Whoever goes (to Makka) without intending the rites and then it occurs to him to do the rites after having passed the *miqats* should enter the *ihram* from where it occurred to him to perform them, and he does not have to sacrifice an animal. Whoever enters *ihram* having passed the *miqat*, then his *miqat* is from where he entered the *ihram*."

He has also said: "Whoever travels by sea, then he should enter *ihram* when in line with (the *miqat*) or facing it, contrary to Sanad who said he should wait until he reaches land and enter the *ihram* from there when he proceeds with the caravan (after disembarking). Khalil has mentioned this is *at-Tawdih*, as well as al-Qirafi, at-Tadali, Ibn 'Arafa and Ibn Farhun, and they have not commented that this is contrary to the most evident judgement of the *madhhab*; indeed the most evident meaning of their statements is that they accept it, subject to the statement of Malik. This then is the most obvious meaning (of the issue) and the statement of the author must also be subject to this (judgement).

As for Khalil's words 'and the condition of the sacrifice is that he is not resident in Makka or Dhu Tuwa at the time of doing either *qiran* and *tamattu'*, al-Mawwaq has related that Malik said: "because he would be (considered as) a resident of the Masjid al-Haram in which case no sacrificial animal is required of him, nor fasting; and likewise anyone who makes the *'umra* in the months of hajj and returns to his country or one equally distant to it owes nothing."

Commenting on Khalil's words '(Whoever stays in Makka or Dhu Tuwa does not have to sacrifice) even if he is staying there because he has been hindered from leaving' Ibn al-Hajjib said: "The person who is hindered from leaving is considered as the resident there, just as the person who is hindered from leaving another place and the person who enters without the intention of becoming a resident are considered as non-residents."

If he has resort to the inhabitants of Makka (for pasture or forage) in other than the months of hajj and then makes *'umra* in the months of hajj followed by hajj in the same year, then he does not have to sacrifice as he has made *'umra* after setting foot in the (Haram and after taking up temporary residence there).

As for Khalil's words 'or he goes out for some need' Ibn al-Hattab said: "that is, whoever spends all one's time there such that he becomes resident and then goes out for some need – even if he stays a long time in another place – then he does not have to make a sacrifice as long as he does not deny that this is his place of residence, irrespective of whether there are any of his people there or not." As for Khalil's words 'not if he spends all his time in other than it' he said: "that is, whoever separates himself from the people of Makka and denies it as his place of residence, then he is no longer subject to the judgement of being one of its inhabitants and he must sacrifice for the *tamattu'*, if he makes the (hajj of) *tamattu'*."

There is a difference of opinion regarding the judgement of the *talbiya* ash-Shafi'i and Ahmad have said that it is sunna. Ibn Abi Hurayra said that it is obligatory, and this Ibn Qudama has related from one of the Malikis while al-Khattabi has related it from Malik and Abu Hanifa.

Ash-Shawkani, the author of *Nayl al-Awtar*, said: "These (imams) have differed as to the obligation of making a sacrifice if the (*talbiya*) is left out: Ibn Shas from among the Malikis and the author of the *Hidaya* (of al-Marghinani) from the Hanafis have said that it is obligatory but that an action, connected to the hajj, like setting out on the way, may stand in its stead. Ibn 'Abd al-Barr has related from ath-Thawri, and Abu Hanifa, Ibn Habib from the Malikis, the author of the *Bidaya* from the Hanafis, az-Zubayri from the Shafi'is and the Dhahiris have all said that it is a pillar of *ihram* and that the latter is not established without it. Ibn Sa'd has transmitted from 'Ata' with a *sahih* chain of narration that it is *fard*, and this is also related by Ibn al-Mundhir from Ibn 'Umar, Tawus and 'Ikrima.

Mention may be made here of the fact that the Companions of the Prophet, may the peace and blessings of Allah be upon him, would raise their voices until they became hoarse. It is also related that the Prophet, may the peace and blessings of Allah be upon him, said: "Jibril came to me and commanded me to command my Companions to raise their voices when uttering the *ihlal* and the *talbiya*." This is related by the five narrators, and is considered *sahih* by Tirmidhi. He said in *Nayl al-Awtar*: "...thus he has excluded women by the fact he said 'my *Companions*' – for women do not say it aloud, but rather restrict themselves to saying it such that only they can hear themselves. Ar-Ruyani said: 'It is not forbidden for her to raise her voice as her voice is not considered '*awra* – i.e. forbidden for others to hear – according to the correct judgement, but rather is *makruh*.' Something similar has also been said by Abu't-Tayyib and Ibn ar-Ruf'a. Dawud, however, is of the opinion that it is obligatory for her to raise her voice, and this is the most evident meaning of his words 'and he commanded me to command my Companions' especially given the fact the actions and spoken elements of the hajj elucidate the general obligation (for both men and women) contained in the words of Allah ta'ala: '*Hajj to the*

House is a duty owed to Allah by all mankind'[1] and his saying, may the peace and blessings of Allah be upon him: 'Take your rites from me!'"

There is agreement among the *'ulama* that the form of the *talbiya* of the Messenger of Allah, may the peace and blessings of Allah be upon him, was:

لَبَّيْكَ اللَّهُمَّ لَبَّيْكَ، لَبَّيْكَ لَا شَرِيكَ لَكَ لَبَّيْكَ، إِنَّ الْحَمْدَ وَالنِّعْمَةَ لَكَ وَالْمُلْكَ، لَا شَرِيكَ لَكَ

"*Labbayk allahumma labbayk, labbayk la shareeka laka labbayk, inna'l-hamda wa'n-ni'mata laka wa'l-mulk, la shareeka lak* – At Your service! O Allah, at Your service! At Your service! You have no partner. At Your service! The praise and blessing are Yours and the kingdom. You have no partner"

Malik said: "The *talbiya* is to be said until Makka or the Masjid al-Haram and then is to be resumed after it. One should not raise one's voice in the mosques which have a jama'a, but rather it is enough that the person beside him hears it, except in the Masjid al-Haram and Masjid Mina, where one should raise one's voice. It is recommended that a company of people raise their voices when members of the company meet each other, and when looking out from the top of an elevation. The people of knowledge are agreed that the *talbiya* of the woman is such that she (only) may hear herself." This is related by Abu 'Umar and is recorded in the *Bidayat al-Mujtahid*.

The saying of the *talbiya* is interrupted when the sun begins to decline on the day of 'Arafa, and this is a narration from 'Ali, may Allah ennoble his face. Malik said: "and this is still the practice of the people of knowledge in our city."

Ibn Shihab said: "The Imams, Abu Bakr, 'Umar, 'Uthman and 'Ali would interrupt the *talbiya* when the sun declined on the day of 'Arafa."

The majority of the *fuqaha* of the major cities, the people of hadith, Abu Hanifa ash-Shafi'i, Thawri, Ahmad, Ishaq and others have said that the *talbiya* is not to be interrupted until the stoning of the last *jamrat* al-'Aqaba. In a *sahih* hadith from al-Fadl – who was riding behind the Prophet, may the peace and blessings of Allah be upon him, on the Day of Sacrifice – it is narrated that "the Prophet kept on saying the *talbiya* until he stoned the *jamrat* al-'Aqaba" – and this is recorded in al-Bukhari by a group of narrators.

Khalil said: "and the *talbiya* is renewed whenever changing one's state and at the end of the *salat*, and there is a difference of opinion as to whether it is to be done (right up to entry) into Makka or (should be interrupted) for the tawwaf (of arrival)." He has also said: "and repeat it after the *sa'y*, even in the mosque (of Masjid al-Haram or Mina) up to the time of arrival at the *musalla* of 'Arafa."

---

1 Ali 'Imran – The Family of 'Imran 97)

Ar-Rahwani, in his commentary on az-Zurqani, has related that Malik said: "There is no harm in someone who has made the *ghusl* in Madina wearing his (normal) clothes until Dhu'l-Hulayfa and then removing them when he enters the *ihram*." He has also narrated from Ibn al-Majishun and Sahnun that "If you want to leave Madina, then come to the grave and first make the greeting on entering, then make a *ghusl*, put on the two cloths of your *ihram* and pronounce the *labbayk* after your (two) *rak'ats* at Dhu'l-Hulayfa.

The kinds of ihram of the hajj

1. Ifrad

The *ifrad* hajj is taking on the hajj alone, that is not the *qiran* or the *tamattu'* hajj. According to Malik, may Allah be pleased with him, it is the best as this is the hajj that the Messenger, may the peace and blessings of Allah be upon him, entered the *ihram* for, according to the narration of Jabir ibn 'Abdallah, may Allah be pleased with them both. 'A'isha said, may Allah be pleased with her: "We went out with the Messenger of Allah, may the peace and blessings of Allah be upon him, in the year of the farewell hajj and there were those of us who undertook to do the hajj and *'umra* while the Messenger undertook to do (only) the hajj." It has also been narrated from 'A'isha in many chains of narration and from al-Qasim from her that the Prophet, may the peace and blessings of Allah be upon him, did only the *ifrad* hajj. A group of narrators has narrated this except al-Bukhari – and this is recorded in *Muntaqa al-Akhbar* (of Ibn Taymiyya al-Jadd (the grandfather)).

It is narrated from Nafi' that Ibn 'Umar said: "We embarked upon the hajj alone (*ifrad*) together with the Messenger of Allah, may the peace and blessings of Allah be upon him" and this is narrated by Ahmad. It is recorded by Muslim that the Prophet, may the peace and blessings of Allah be upon him, entered upon the *ifrad* hajj. This is stated in *Nayl al-Awtar*, a commentary on *al-Muntaqa*, and this is also the judgement of Abu Bakr, 'Umar, 'Uthman, 'A'isha and Jabir, may Allah be pleased with them; and (this is affirmed) because the Khulafa ar-Rashidun performed the *ifrad* hajj and kept to it – and if it were not the best form, they would not have persisted in it; and because the *ifrad* does not necessitate a sacrifice. An-Nawawi said: "This is the consensus – on account of the (*ifrad*) being complete (and without imperfection) whereas in the case of the *tamattu'* and *qiran*, one has to make good (the imperfection of not having re-entered) by the *miqat*, and what does not have to be made good is (as a general rule always) better."

The *umma* are in agreement as to the permissibility of making *ifrad*, and that it is not *makruh*. 'Umar and 'Uthman and others considered *tamattu'* *makruh*. Abu 'Umar ibn 'Abd al-Barr said: "The *ifrad* has been related from the Prophet, may the peace and blessings of Allah be upon him, via Jabir ibn 'Abdallah by multiple, *sahih* chains of narration, and is the judgement of Abu Bakr, 'Umar, 'Uthman, 'A'isha and Jabir."

Those who consider that the *ifrad* is best argue that the *qiran* and *tamattu'* are (permitted as) a licence (but do not constitute the normal form), and for this reason a sacrifice is obligatory for them both. 'A'isha, may Allah be pleased with her, performed the *ifrad* hajj, in the ninth year, and 'Attab ibn Asyad made the *ifrad* hajj in the eighth year when the hajj was established for the first time in Islam. 'Abd ar-Rahman made the *ifrad* in the year of the *Ridda* (reneging from Islam of many Arab tribes) and as-Siddeeq made the *ifrad* in the following year. Amir al-Mumineen 'Umar ibn al-Khattab, may Allah be pleased with him, performed the *ifrad* for ten years (running) the Amir al-Mumineen, 'Uthman ibn Affan, may Allah be pleased with him, for thirteen years. This is what the practice of the people of Madina – that is the Imams and leaders, the *'ulama* and the ordinary people – is based on, and how can one abstain from (acting upon) this! The latter (statement) is taken from ar-Rahouni who relates from az-Zurqani in his commentary on Khalil.

Being prevented from making the Hajj

It is stated in the *Bidayat al-Mujtahid*: "There are two instances of being prevented: because of the enemy or because of illness. The majority are agreed that if a person is prevented by the enemy, then he is to return to his normal state (from *ihram*) at the point he is being prevented. Malik said: 'He is not obliged to make a sacrifice, nor to repeat it.' As for the person prevented by illness, he may only leave the state of *ihram* by performing the *tawaf* and the *sa'y* between Safa and Marwa, and he has to make a sacrifice; and the (*fuqaha*) are of a consensus that he is obliged to perform it again. Anyone who misses the hajj by miscalculating the number of days, or who was unable to see the new moon (at the beginning of Dhu'l-Hijja) or for any other excuse, then he is subject to the same judgement as the person who is prevented through illness, according to Malik; the person of Makka who is prevented through illness is (subject to) the same (judgement) as someone from elsewhere, according to Malik, that is, he should leave (the state of *ihram* of hajj) by performing (only what is necessary for) the *'umra*, and he has to make a sacrifice and repeat the hajj.

"As for the proof of Malik regarding being prevented by the enemy, it is that the Prophet, may the peace and blessings of Allah be upon him, and his Companions left the state of *ihram* on the occasion of al-Hudaybiya and then slaughtered camels and shaved: they returned to the normal state and released themselves from all restriction of the *ihram* before doing the *tawaf* of the House. There is no evidence that the Messenger, may the peace and blessings of Allah be upon him, instructed any of the Companions, or anyone else with him, to make up anything or repeat any of it. The proof of those who deem it obligatory to repeat it is that the Messenger of Allah, may the peace and blessings of Allah be upon him, made the *'umra* in the year after the year of al-Hudaybiya in order to make up that (previous) *'umra*, and for this reason it is called the *'umra al-qada* (the *'umra* which was made up); and also the consensus (of the *'ulama*) that the person prevented through illness and the like must make it up.

"As for the person prevented through illness, he may only (leave the *ihram*) and return to his normal state by performing a *tawaf* of the House and the *sa'y* between Safa and Marwa – in short he may only return to his normal state by doing the *'umra*, and this is the *madhhab* of Ibn 'Umar, 'A'isha and Ibn 'Abbas. The people of Iraq differ with them arguing that he must leave the *ihram* and return to the normal state on the spot, and that he is subject to the same judgement as the person who is prevented by the enemy. The principle underlying the *madhhab* of Malik is that (strictly speaking) the person who is prevented by illness remains in the state of *ihram* until the following year until he performs the hajj to make up for that (of the previous year), and so he does not have to make a sacrifice.

"Those who maintain that the *ayat* applies to the person prevented by illness have argued that *al-muhsar* means, according to its verbal form, 'to be prevented by illness' and that this form is not used (in Arabic) to refer to someone besieged by the enemy. The form used to express 'prevention by the enemy' is the form *hasara*, in which case one would say *hasarahu al-'aduww* (the enemy prevented him) while *ahsarahu al-marad* would mean: 'he is prevented by disease'. It has also been reported in a hadith: 'Whoever breaks a limb or becomes lame, then he leaves the state of *ihram* and he owes another hajj.'

"There is no difference of opinion amongst the Muslims regarding the prohibition of killing game in the Haram – 'the inviolable area', although they do differ as to the *kaffara* – expiation – to be paid. There is a consensus among the *'ulama* that if the person in *ihram* kills game, then he must pay compensation – based on the clear textual evidence for this. They differ regarding the person who is not in *ihram* who kills game. The majority of the *'ulama* of the major cities have said that he has to pay compensation while Dawud [adh-Dhahiri] and his followers have said that he does not. They have differed as to whether compensation is to be paid or not if game is killed mistakenly. The majority are of the opinion that it is to be paid while the Dhahiris have said that there is no compensation to be paid by the person (responsible). Malik said: 'If a group of people in *ihram* kill game, then each has to pay full compensation', and this is also the opinion of ath-Thawri and a group of the *fuqaha*; while ash-Shafi'i said: 'One of them (only) has to pay it.'" Here ends the section from *al-Bidaya*.

Khalil said: "If he is prevented by the enemy, civil unrest or wrongful imprisonment while on hajj or *'umra*, then he must leave *ihram* and return to his normal state as long as he did not know (of this impediment beforehand) and holds out no hope of the (impediment) being lifted before the time of the hajj has passed. He does not have to make an (extra minor) sacrifice (to make up for his missing the hajj because of the hindrance). (He leaves *ihram*) by the slaughter of the *hady* animal (which he has brought with him) and by shaving (the head) but he does not have to make an (additional minor) sacrifice if he delays leaving the state of *ihram*."

2. Tamattu'

The *tamattu'* is the uttering of the *ihlal* and the entering into the state of *ihram* for the hajj in the months of hajj, then invalidating it by making *'umra*, then re-entering the *ihram* for the hajj in its time within the same year, without returning to one's country or to a place equal in distance. (There is a difference of opinion as to whether the person from Makka may be considered as someone performing the *tamattu'*; (those who consider he may, are in agreement that) he does not have to sacrifice a *hady* animal.

The *tamattu'* is the best (form of hajj) according to Ahmad, the majority of the *'ulama* and the *ahl al-hadith* (people of hadith) – basing (their judgement) on the saying of his, may the peace and blessings of Allah be upon him: "If I had not brought the *hady* animal with me, I would have made it an *'umra*." Ahmad said: "There is no doubt that the Prophet, may the peace and blessings of Allah be upon him, was doing the *qiran* hajj, and *tamattu'* is what I prefer" – taking his proof from his saying, may the peace and blessings of Allah be upon him: "Had I known what I know now, I would not have brought the *hady* and I would have made it an *'umra*."

3. QIRAN

The *qiran* is when one enters into both rites together or one enters into the *'umra* in the months of hajj, then follows it with the hajj. Each of the different kinds of hajj has valid proofs and (is based on) clear traditions – all of which have their legal foundation in his saying, may the peace and blessings of Allah be upon him: "Take your rites from me!" This has been extracted from the *Bidaya* of Ibn Rushd al-Hafeed (the grandson).

Entry into Makka without Ihram

Muslim and an-Nasa'i have narrated from Jabir, may Allah be pleased with him "that the Prophet, may the peace and blessings of Allah be upon him, entered (Makka) 'the Day of the Opening of Makka [to Islam]', wearing a black turban, and he was not in *ihram*."

It is related from Malik from Ibn Shihab from Anas that the Prophet, may the peace and blessings of Allah be upon him "entered Makka in the Year of the Opening [of Makka to Islam] wearing a protective helmet of mail over his head and neck." He also said at the end (of the hadith): "Malik said: 'The Messenger of Allah, may the peace and blessings of Allah be upon him, was not in *ihram* on that day.'" This is narrated by Ahmad and al-Bukhari.

Ash-Shawkani said in *Nayl al-Awtar* – after a discussion about his entry into Makka: "...one may point out that this (above mentioned) hadith refers specifically to fighting with him, may the peace and blessings of Allah be upon him, but is not intended to indicate permission to pass into (Makka intending hajj) with other than the *ihram* – and his *umma* is an exemplar of his actions. It is related from Ibn 'Umar and an-Nasir – and constitutes (the basis for) the last of the two judgements of ash-Shafi'i and one of the two opinions of Abu Abbas – that entering into the *ihram* is only obligatory for the person who enters (with the intention of performing) one of the two rites (of *'umra* or hajj), not for the person who only wants to enter (Makka)." He then goes on to say: "The Muslims at his time, may the peace and blessings of Allah be upon him, would come and go to Makka according to their needs, and there is no report that he ever instructed any of them to put on the *ihram* – neither in the instance of al-Hujjaj ibn Ulat, or that of Abu Qatada when he killed a wild donkey within the *miqat* while not in *ihram*: he had been sent on some errand before the hajj and had passed through the *miqat* without the intention of hajj or *'umra*. He, may the peace and blessings of Allah be upon him, affirmed his act (of killing the wild donkey) and in doing so necessarily (affirmed the principle) that one retains the normal state of freedom (from the constraints of *ihram*) – by virtue of the absence of any obligation – until there is reason (for assuming) that this (state of freedom or release from restriction) has been removed (by some restriction). The hadith of Ibn 'Abbas – 'no one enters Makka without the *ihram* other than wood carriers, workers and those with some (trading) interests there' – has been objected to: Talha ibn 'Amr is to be found in his chain of narration and he is (considered) weak. Some of the latter (*muhaddithun*) have avoided use of the hadith of Ibn 'Abbas as its chain of narration is interrupted before reaching the Prophet, may the peace and blessings of Allah be upon him."

Ihram

Khalil said: "(The *ihram*) is established by the intention even if the formulation employed does not correspond to the (particular type of hajj the person goes on to make)." The Messenger, may the peace and blessings of Allah be upon him, said: "Surely actions are by intentions" – and there is agreement on this.

In the *Bidayat al-Mujtahid* of Ibn Rushd al-Hafeed al-Maliki it states: "The *ihram* has conditions, the first of which is the time and place. As for the place, this is what is known as the *mawaqeet al-hajj*, the *miqats* of hajj, and the majority of the *'ulama* are of the opinion that whoever misses the *miqat* with the intention of entering *ihram* and does not put on the *ihram* until he has gone past it has to make a (minor) sacrifice. There are those among the (*fuqaha*), amongst them ash-Shafi'i, who say that if he returns to the *miqat* and enters the *ihram* from it, then the obligation to make a minor sacrifice is removed from him; others, that the obligation to make the minor sacrifice is not removed from him even if he does return, and among them is Malik. There is a difference of opinion as to whether the best is to enter the *ihram* from one's house (if it is nearer Makka than the *miqat*) or from the *miqats*, if his home is outside of these. One group have said that the best for him is from his residence and the *ihram* from the (*miqats*) is (merely) a licence, and this is the opinion of ash-Shafi'i, Abu Hanifa, ath-Thawri and a group of the *fuqaha*. Malik as well as Ishaq and Ahmad have said that his entering the *ihram* is best from the *miqats*, and the *ihram* of the people of Makka is from the low-lying tract of ground (called) Jawf Makka. However, it is also reported of Malik that it is from the Mosque and that they should embark on it at the sighting of the moon or with the people on the day of *Tarwiya* (the day of providing water – the eighth day of Dhu'l-Hijja – when the Makkan hajjis provide themselves with water for the visit to Mina)."

THE PERIOD OF THE MIQAT

It comprises the month of Shawwal, Dhu'l-Qa'da and the nine days of Dhu'l-Hijja. Khalil said: "And the pillar of both of them (the hajj and *umra*) is the *ihram* and the time for the hajj is Shawwal until the end of (the hajj in) Dhu'l-Hijja. It is *makruh* to enter into *ihram* before this, just as it is *makruh* to enter it before arriving at the place (stipulated, that is, depending on where one is coming from)." Khalil has also said: "It is contracted by formulation of the intention, together with the words (*labbayka'llahumma...*) and the deed (of divesting oneself of one's ordinary sewn clothes) when both the former are undertaken in (direct) conjunction with this (*ihram*), and (is effective) whether he has specified (having taken the *ihram* for the hajj or the *'umra* or for both) or he has not specified. If he has not specified, it is recommended to apply this (intention) to (the separate) hajj (known as *ifrad*) if he has entered the *ihram* during the month of hajj, or prior to the *tawaf* of arrival, after which the application to the hajj is obligatory, although by analogy it requires that it be applied to the *qiran* (type of hajj) because this (non-specifying) comprises the two. If the person entering into *ihram* has specified that this be for the *ifrad* (type of hajj), or for the *'umra*, or for *qiran*, but then forgets which form he has stipulated, he should perform the *qiran*, as a precaution, and make a new intention for the hajj and is (thus) released from this (obligation of hajj).[1]"

The *fuqaha* are in agreement that the *ihram* is not established without the intention but they differ as to whether the intention is accepted without the *talbiya*. Malik and ash-Shafi'i have said that the intention alone – without the *talbiya* – is accepted. Khalil said: "The (*ihram* is contracted) even if the formulation (of the type of hajj) differs from what (one actually goes on to perform)" and he has also said: "or he omits to stipulate which (type of hajj)." Al-Hattab said: "Refraining from expressing in words the rite one intends and restricting oneself to the intention (only) is better according to Malik." Abu Hanifa said: "The *talbiya* in the hajj is like the *takbiratu'l-ihram* for the *salat*, except that it is acceptable in any formulation." In the *Mawarid an-Najah* of our grandfather Ahmad ibn al-Basheer, may Allah have mercy on him, he states that Abu'l-Hasan said in *Sharh at-Tahdheeb*: "The saying of the *talbiya* once is enough." Khalil said: "And if it is left out at the beginning (of the *ihram*), then a minor sacrifice (*dam*) is to be paid."

From al-Qurtubi it is related: "What is narrated from 'Ali ibn Abi Talib – and what 'Imran ibn Husayn actually put into practice – about the assuming of the *ihram* before the *miqats* established by the Messenger of Allah, may the

---

1 This instance is also discussed below in more detail.

peace and blessings of Allah be upon him, is what 'Abdallah ibn Mas'ud holds to together with a group of the *salaf*. It is also confirmed that 'Umar assumed the *ihram* at Iliya' while al-Aswad, 'Abd ar-Rahman and Abu Ishaq assumed the *ihram* from their houses – which is accepted as a concession by ash-Shafi'i."

Abu Dawud and ad-Daraqutni have narrated that Umm Salama said: "The Messenger of Allah may the peace and blessings of Allah be upon him, said: 'Whoever assumes the *ihram* from the Bayt al-Muqaddas for the hajj or the *'umra*, then he has no more wrong actions than the day his mother gave birth to him.'" In another narration it reads "he is forgiven the wrong actions of his past life and those to come" and this is related by Abu Dawud. In these (two narrations) there is permission to assume the *ihram* before the *miqat*. This and what follows is also narrated by al-Qurtubi.

Malik considered it *makruh*, may Allah have mercy on him, for someone to assume the *ihram* before the *miqat* and what he, may the peace and blessings of Allah be upon him, did is better, namely he assumed the *ihram* from the *miqats*. The Companions who had assumed the *ihram* before the *miqats* understood that the actions of the Messenger of Allah, may the peace and blessings of Allah be upon him, were performed to afford ease (to the *umma*, and as such could be interpreted as containing a certain licence to assume the *ihram* a little before the *miqats*).

He has also said in his *tafseer*: "The people of knowledge are of a consensus that anyone who assumes the *ihram* before arriving at the *miqat* is a *muhrim* (i.e. is in fact in a valid state of *ihram*), and all of them consider he has become subject to (the conditions of the) *ihram* if he does this – arguing that he has (merely) done something extra rather than missed something out."

The *ihram* is valid even when ritually impure or dirty cloths are donned. Malik said: "I have cloths which I used for the *ihram* of (several) hajjs and I have not washed them, and I do not see any harm in this; likewise the *ihram* is valid with (sperm from) *janaba*, or from (blood from) menstruation and from urine and faeces – so much so that the Companions have said: 'If someone does not find anything to remove perfume from his cloths with, then he should remove it with urine and then assume the *ihram*.' He should not assume the *ihram* with cloths smelling of musk until the smell disappears, although if he does, then there is no compensation to be paid. *Ihram* in other than white is not recommended."

Tawaf

It is stated in the *Bidayat al-Mujtahid* of Ibn Rushd al-Hafeed: "There are three kinds of *tawaf*: the *tawaf al-qudum* when arriving in Makka, the *tawaf ifada* and the *tawaf al-wada'*. The majority of the *'ulama* are of a consensus that the form of each *tawaf* – whether of an obligatory nature or not – is that one begins at the Black Stone and that one should kiss it if one is able, or touch it and then place one's hand on one's mouth (if one is not able); that, with the House to one's left, one go round seven times, walking briskly (*ramal*) in the first three (circuits) and normally in the last four – that is, for the *tawaf al-qudum*, when arriving at Makka, for the person on hajj or *'umra*, but not for the person doing *tamattu'*; and that women do not have to walk briskly. They differ regarding the judgement that one should walk briskly the first three times as to whether it is a sunna or a mark of excellence. They are of a consensus that the person who assumes the *ihram* from Makka and who is not of its people does not have to walk briskly."

They are in agreement that one of the sunnas of the *tawaf* is the greeting of the corner of the Black Stone and the Yemeni corner, in the case of both men and women, but they differ as to greeting the two remaining corners. Mu'awiya, may Allah have mercy on him, said "There is nothing of the House that is left out", and it is also narrated of Mu'awiya, Jabir Ibn Zubayr al-Hasan, al-Husain, Anas and 'Urwa that they all touched them both. They are also of a consensus that the 'obligatory' *tawaf* – which if left out means one loses the hajj – is the *tawaf al-ifada*, that is, the one performed after the stoning of the *jamrat* al-'Aqaba on the Day of Sacrifice and that missing it out cannot be made good by a minor sacrifice.

The majority of the *'ulama* are of the opinion that by doing *tawaf al-wada'* one may do without the *tawaf al-ifada*, if one has not already done the *tawaf al-ifada*. The majority of the *'ulama* hold that the *tawaf al-qudum* does not do instead of the *tawaf al-ifada* given that it is before the Day of Sacrifice. A group of the followers of Malik have said that it does do instead of it.

They are also in consensus that the person from Makka only has to perform the *tawaf al-ifada* and that the person doing the *'umra* only has to do the *tawaf al-qudum*. They are of a consensus that the person doing the *tamattu'* has to do two *tawafs*: the *tawaf* for the *'umra* and that of the hajj.

The person doing the *ifrad* only has to do one *tawaf*, and for the person doing the *qiran*, according to Malik, ash-Shafi'i, Ahmad and Abu Thawr, it is acceptable that he do one *tawaf* and one *sa'y*.

They differ as to the time of the *tawaf*. There are those who permit it after *Subh* and after *'Asr*, and who have prohibited it at the time of sunrise and sunset, and this is the opinion of Malik and his followers; while the followers of ash-

Shafi'i consider that it may be made at any time.

It is stated in *al-Mughni* of Ibn Qudama al-Hanbali that the mode of wearing the upper cloth is to place the middle part of it under one's right shoulder and to place the end over the left shoulder leaving the right shoulder bare.

Abu Dawud and Ibn Majah have related that the Messenger of Allah, may the peace and blessings of Allah be upon him, did the *tawaf* wearing his cloth in this way and it is narrated from Ibn 'Abbas that the Prophet, may the peace and blessings of Allah be upon him, and his Companions performed the *'umra* from al-Ji'rana, that they walked briskly around the House and that they wore cloths beneath their arms which they threw over their left shoulders.

This is what ash-Shafi'i holds to and many of the people of knowledge. Malik said: "This mode (known as *idtiba'*) of wearing the cloth is not sunna" and he has also said: "I have not heard any of the people of knowledge of this city of ours mentioning that *idtiba'* is a sunna."

If one finishes the *tawaf*, one should adjust the cloth (to cover the shoulder) as making *idtiba'* is not recommended in the *salat*. Whoever misses out doing the *ramal* (walking briskly) in the first three circuits does not have to make them up in the remaining circuits.

Khalil said: "Then the *tawaf* (is performed) for both (the *'umra* and hajj) in a state of ritual purity and (having ensured) one's body and clothes are clean, and (the private parts are) covered – for it is invalidated by impurity and cannot be continued from where one has left off. It should be interrupted for a *fard salat*. It is permitted to perform the *tawaf* under the covered portions if the (area around the House) is very crowded, otherwise (if done for another reason, like to avoid the cold) it must be repeated (if he is still in Makka). (If however he has left), he does not have to return to do it again, nor is any minor sacrifice to be made."

Al-Hattab said: "That is, one of the conditions of the *tawaf* is that it take place in the Mosque – if he does it outside, then it is not accepted."

Ibn Rushd said: "There is no difference of opinion about this." Al-Hattab said: "and similar to this, and Allah knows best, is when someone performs the *tawaf* on the roof of the Mosque – and (that) this (is also not accepted) is the most evident judgement, although I have not seen any specific text on the subject."

The Shafi'is and the Hanafis, however, have declared that it is permitted to make the *tawaf* on the roof of the Mosque, while the Hanbalis have not objected to it, and Allah knows best. One should make the two *rak'ats* of *tawaf* outside of the House, and not on the roof and not in the *hijr* (the space between the north wall of the Ka'ba and the low circular wall to the north of it, including that wall itself). He said in the *Mudawwana*: "One should not pray any *fard salat* in the *hijr* (of the Ka'ba) or in the Ka'ba (itself), nor the two obligatory *rak'ats* for the *tawaf*, nor the *witr*, nor the two *rak'ats* of *fajr*, but any other than these of the (*nafila*) *rak'ats* of *tawaf*, then there is no harm in them."

As for the *tawaf* inside the Mosque, one should take care when performing it that one's head and arms do not enter the space of the Shadhirwan (the buttressed base of the Ka'ba wall) for one's *tawaf*, in this manner would be not valid. Khalil said: "He should kiss (the Black Stone and ensure) his body is upright inside the Mosque", that is, he must not perform the *tawaf* with his head inclined such that his whole body is outside of the House, the *hijr* and the Shadhirwan. When kissing the Black Stone, his two feet must be kept firm on the ground, and then he should return to an upright position and continue the *tawaf* upright.

Al-Qubbab said: "One of the later *fuqaha* instructed people to be cautious at the Shadhirwan", and then al-Qubbab goes on to say: "but if it is as they claim, then the upright men of the earlier generations would have warned against something – which given the potential for such a practice – must have occurred often. However, the fact that it is not mentioned is proof that such (practice) may be overlooked and forgiven." This is taken from the *Hashiyat al-Madani* on *ar-Rahouni's* commentary. Then he goes on to say: "and one should take care to avoid it – but that it invalidates the hajj is unlikely!"

Al-Muhibb at-Tabari has stated that occupying oneself with the *tawaf* is better than the *'umra* and that if one tires, then one should pray two *rak'ats*, sit down and look at the House for looking at the House is an act of worship. It is stated in the *Mudawwana*: Ibn al-Qasim said: "I prefer the *tawaf* for the people who are from outside Makka to the *salat*, but not for the people of Makka for it is recommended that they increase their *nafila salats*." It is recommended for the people of Makka and those who are resident in it that they refrain from performing the *tawaf* during the days of the hajj to make it easier for the hajjis. Al-Hattab said: "It is not necessary to make a minor sacrifice if the *tawaf al-ifada* has been delayed until the end of Dhu'l-Hijja."

It has also been said that it is (a kind of) deprivation for someone who is resident in Makka when a day goes by without his performing the *tawaf* – for it has been reported that there is a great excellence in it: it is narrated that Ibn 'Umar, may Allah be pleased with them both, said: "I heard the Messenger of Allah, may the peace and blessings of Allah be upon him, say: 'Whoever makes *tawaf* of this House, reckoning (the times he does it), then for each step the (reward of) one good action is written for him, one bad action is removed from his (record), he is raised in station and he will have (a reward) equal to (freeing) a slave.'"

It is narrated from Jabir ibn 'Abdallah, may Allah be pleased with them both, that the Prophet, may the peace and blessings of Allah be upon him, said: "Whoever performs the *tawaf* of the House seven times, prays two *rak'ats* behind the Maqam and drinks of the water of Zamzam, then Allah will forgive him all his wrong actions however great they are" – this has been narrated by Abu Sa'id al-Jundi. Whoever assumes the *ihram* from Makka for the *ifrad* hajj, then he should do the *sa'y* after the *tawaf al-ifada*. If he does not do it until he returns to his people, then he must make a (minor) sacrifice – and this is taken from al-Hattab, who relates from Malik.

The person who enters the *ihram* from Makka does not do the (obligatory) *tawaf* or *sa'y*. It is recommended that he make a *ghusl*, take off any sewn clothes, make the (*nafila*) *tawaf* seven times, perform (two) *rak'ats* (after seven circuits) and then enter the *ihram* following this. If he performs the *tawaf* and the *sa'y* (immediately) after the *ihram* for hajj, it is not accepted in place of the obligatory (*tawaf* and) *sa'y*, according to Malik, while ash-Shafi'i said that it is accepted and was done by Ibn Zubayr, and this is the *madhhab* of Ahmad.

The *murahiq* designates the person who fears he will miss the standing at 'Arafa and so leaves off doing the *tawaf* and *sa'y* – he should do the *sa'y* immediately after doing the *tawaf al-ifada*, although if he does it before, it is accepted, as stated by al-Mawwaq. He must pray the two *rak'ats* of the *tawaf* after the prescribed *salats* – for the latter do not stand instead of these two. This is what Malik and the people of *ra'y* hold to – contrary to the Hanbalis. There is no harm if he prays the two *rak'ats* without a *sutra* while men and women are doing *tawaf* in front of him, for the Prophet, may the peace and blessings of Allah be upon him, prayed them while the people were doing the *tawaf* in front of him – and there was nothing between him and them.

Ibn Zubayr would pray while people were doing *tawaf* in front of him. When a woman passed in front of him, he waited until she had raised her foot and then he prostrated. This holds for all the *salats* in Makka: they are not done with a *sutra* – and this is taken from (the work of) Ibn Qudama al-Hanbali.

(As for the practice of marking the passing of each seven circuits with the performance of two *rak'ats*) there is no harm in joining the (total number of) seven (circuits) and making two *rak'ats* for each seven (at the end of the total). This is what 'A'isha did, may Allah be pleased with her, and al-Miswar ibn Makhrama, may Allah be pleased with him; some of the *'ulama* also hold to this. Ibn 'Umar, al-Hasan, az-Zuhri, Malik and Abu Hanifa considered it *makruh*. From Ibn Qudama.

In the *Bidayat al-Mujtahid* it is stated: "One of the *salaf* has permitted not separating the seven circuits – that one does not separate them from each other by *rak'ats*. Then later he should make two *rak'ats* for each seven circuits. It is recommended to perform a lot of *tawaf* of the House although it is narrated from Malik that one should not do *nafila tawaf* after the *tawaf al-qudum* until after the completion of the hajj. It is also related from him that *tawaf* of the House is better than *nafila salat* in the case of people from distant lands (and not of Makka), and this is the practice adhered to."

USEFUL POINT: a woman differs from a man in ten points with regard to the hajj: covering the head, shaving, wearing sewn clothes, wearing leather socks, not raising her voice for the *talbiya*, not walking apace in the *tawaf* or walking quickly in the *sa'y*, the standing at 'Arafa – for it is best that she sit, keeping at a distance from the House during the *tawaf*, the ascent of Safa and Marwa, and she does not cover her face except to veil herself (temporarily) from any (passing) men who do not show respect.

In the work of Ibn al-Mawaz, there is (mention of the) permission to pick one's teeth with a stick in the case of men, and that the most likely judgement regarding the wearing of a ring in the case of men is that there is no compensation to be paid.

THE TIME OF THE TAWAF

He said in *Bidayat al-Mujtahid*: "As for the time when the (*tawaf*) is permitted, the (*fuqaha*) have three differing opinions:

The first, that the *tawaf* is permitted after the *Subh* and *'Asr* and prohibited at sunrise and sunset, and this is the *madhhab* of 'Umar ibn al-Khattab, Abu Sa'id al-Khudri, may Allah be pleased with them both, and is also the opinion of Malik and his followers and a group of the *fuqaha*;

The second, that it is *makruh* after *Subh* and *'Asr* and that it is prohibited at sunset and sunrise, and this is the opinion of Sa'id ibn Jubayr, Mujahid and a group of the *fuqaha*;

The third, that it is licit at all these times, and this is the opinion of ash-Shafi'i and a group of the *fuqaha*. They differ as to whether the *tawaf* is permitted without being in a state of ritual purity, although they are of a consensus that being in a state of purity is among its sunnas. Malik and ash-Shafi'i have said: 'Tawaf without this ritual purity is not accepted, neither when done deliberately or out of negligence.'

Abu Hanifa said. 'It is not accepted; he has to make a minor sacrifice and it is recommended that he repeat it.' Abu Thawr said: 'If he does the *tawaf* when not in *wudu'*, his *tawaf* is accepted of him if he is unaware of this, but it is not accepted if he is.' The Shafi'is stipulate that the clothing worn by the person doing the *tawaf* must be pure, just as it is stipulated for anyone performing the *salat*.

The proof of ash-Shafi'i that it is permitted to do the *tawaf* and *salat* during it (after every seven *rak'ats*) at all times is the hadith related by ash-Shafi'i, namely: 'O Bani Manaf or O Bani 'Abd al-Mutallib, if you take on responsibility in any way for this matter, then do not prevent anyone from making the *tawaf* of this House or from making *salat* in it at any time of the night or the day he wishes.'"

It is stated in *Nayl al-Awtar* that it is *makruh* to make the *tawaf* mounted, for although his *tawaf*, may the peace and blessings of Allah be upon him and that of Umm Salama, (was mounted), it took place before the Mosque was walled off; when it was walled off, entry was prohibited (to animals) – for there was no ensuring that it would not become polluted (by their presence). Thus it was not permitted after its being walled off – as opposed to before this, when it was not forbidden and when it was exposed to pollution; and the same applies to the *sa'y*.

Khalil said: "It is recommended that the person who has two families, (one in Makka and one elsewhere, make a sacrifice for the *qiran* or *tamattu'*); however, there are two interpretations as to whether this applies in all cases or whether one should only take into account the place where the person usually stays." Al-Hattab said: "There is a difference of opinion amongst the Shaykhs of the *Mudawwana* in understanding this: it is also said that it is recommended in all cases, even if he does stay in one of them more than the other; also that if he stays in one of them more, then this is the deciding factor – such that if he stays in Makka, then he is Makkan and does not have to make a minor sacrifice, whereas if he stays in Makka less (than the other place), then he is counted as a non-Makkan."

Al-Mawwaq: (It is stated by) al-Kafi: "Malik is undecided in this matter saying that it is one of the matters that is problematic and I prefer that he make the minor sacrifice of the *tamattu'* if he is performing the *'umra* and then going on to the hajj."

It is also related from al-Hattab, from Ibn Yunus and al-Barada'i that Malik said: "Whoever has family in Makka and family in another region and who comes to Makka for an *'umra* in the month of hajj and then makes the hajj in the same year, then this is an ambiguous matter, and as a precautionary measure he should sacrifice a *hady*."

Al-Qurtubi said in his *tafsir*: "The *'ulama* are of a consensus that if he moves from Makka with his family and then returns in the months of hajj, intending to do the *'umra*, and stays there until hajj in the same year, then he is in a state of *tamattu'*. They are also of a consensus that if the person of Makka comes from beyond the *miqat* in a state of *ihram* for the *'umra* and embarks upon the hajj from Makka, then he does not have to make the minor sacrifice if his family is in Makka and they do not live elsewhere."

People have differed as to (what is meant by the term in the Qur'an) *hadir al-Masjid al-Haram* ('*whose family lives near the masjid al-Haram*')[1] although they are of a consensus that the people of Makka and those adjacent to it are considered as those '*whose families live near to the Masjid al-Haram*.' One of the *'ulama* said it refers to those for whom attendance of the *jumu'a* is obligatory and not for those for whom it is not an obligation. Malik and his followers have said that it refers to "those who have family in Makka or the adjacent areas."

The Sa'y between Safa and Marwa

The author of the *Bidayat al-Mujtahid* said: "The *sa'y* between Safa and Marwa is an obligatory pillar, according to Malik and ash-Shafi'i, and whoever does not fulfil it must perform a hajj the following year; and this is also the judgement of Ahmad and Ishaq; the *'ulama* of Kufa have said that it is a sunna and that if he returns to his country without having done the *sa'y*, then he has to make a minor sacrifice; one of the (*fuqaha*) said that it is voluntary and he has nothing to make up if he does not do it."

The form (of the *sa'y*) is that the person begins in Safa and finishes at Marwa, (walking between them) seven times and that he walk in the manner termed *ramal* – briskly – in each of them from the moment he reaches the Batn al-Maseel until he passes the boundary mark or the two green markers; and so if he begins with Marwa, then this course is annulled. They are of a consensus that there is no restriction to what is said (while performing it), and that it is the place of saying *du'a*. They are in agreement that one of the conditions is that women be free of menstruation; but there is no difference of opinion between them that ritual purity does not constitute one of its conditions – other than al-Hasan, for he has likened it to the *tawaf*. Again they are in agreement that the *sa'y* can only take place after the *tawaf* and that whoever does it before the *tawaf* must repeat it, even if he is outside of Makka. If he is unaware (of this order) and (later) has intercourse with a woman while still on the *'umra* or hajj, then he has to make a minor sacrifice, and make the *'umra* or hajj (again) the next year. Abu Hanifa said that if he leaves Makka, he does not have to

---

[1] Surat al-Baqara: 196

return although he must make a minor sacrifice. Ath-Thawri said that he owes nothing. This latter is also extracted from the *Bidaya*.

Khalil said: "Its validity is (assured) by its being done before the *tawaf* and by making the intention to perform it as a *fard*, otherwise he must make a (minor) sacrifice." Al-Mawwaq has related from the *Mudawwana*: "The *sa'y* is only permitted after the *tawaf* and the intention of performing a *fard* obligation must be made." Abu 'Umar said: "It is only permitted to make the *sa'y* between Safa and Marwa with an intention to do it as part of the hajj or the *'umra*, and only after the *tawaf ad-dakhoul* or after the *tawaf al-ifada*. However, if his *sa'y* is not linked to one of these two *tawafs* such that he returns to his country, his *sa'y* is (still) accepted although he has to make a minor sacrifice."

Al-Hattab said: "The *tawaf al-qudum* has also been designated as a *fard*, and this is common within the basic (teaching) of the *madhhab*, that is, that the terms '*wajib*' or '*fard*' are synonyms." He has also said: "There is no harm in making a slight interruption between the *sa'y* and the *tawaf*, or during the *sa'y* itself in order to (perform some of) the *tawaf* (if one is in doubt as to having performed it properly)." Malik said: "Whoever makes the *tawaf* at night and delays the *sa'y* until the morning, then there is no harm in this, if done in the same state of ritual purity. If, however, he had slept and had broken his *wudu'*, then he should repeat it – and this is reprehensible! – and he should repeat the *tawaf*, the *sa'y* and the shaving a second time if still in Makka; if he has left, he should make the *hady* sacrifice and this will be accepted of him. If he speaks a little, buys and sells, is afflicted by colic or becomes *junub*, then he should go out, purify himself and carry on from where he has left off. If a woman has her menstruation after the two *rak'ats* of *tawaf*, she should complete her *sa'y*. If someone completes it in a state of *janaba*, then it is accepted of him."

At-Tunisi said: "It is not stipulated that his *tawaf* be considered obligatory", and in was his opinion that all the obligatory aspects of any matter of hajj which are undertaken as voluntary aspects will be accepted in their stead."The author of *Mawarid an-Najah* said: "Ash-Shawkani said in his *Nayl al-Awtar*: 'This hadith contains the recommendation to walk briskly (*sa'y*) from Batn al-Wadi (bottom of the valley) until starting the ascent, and then to walk the rest of the distance to Marwa. This *sa'y* – walking briskly – is recommended each of the seven times in this valley, as is the walking in the (area) before and after this. If, however, he (merely) walks, or he walks briskly (*sa'a*) in *all* areas of it, then this is accepted of him but he will not have gained the excellence (and corresponding extra reward) of it – and this is the opinion of ash-Shafi'i and those who are in agreement with him. Malik said that the person who leaves out doing the brisk walking in its place must repeat it, although there is another narration from him which is in agreement with the judgement of ash-Shafi'i.'"

$$\text{وَثَامِنَ الشَّهْرِ اخْرُجَنَّ لِمِنَى}$$

$$\text{بِعَرَفَاتٍ نَاسِعاً نُزُولَنَا}$$

257 On the eighth of the month go out to Mina and dismount at 'Arafa on the ninth.

$$\text{وَاغْتَسِلَنْ قُرْبَ الزَّوَالِ وَاحْضُرَا}$$

$$\text{الْخُطْبَتَيْنِ وَاجْمَعَنْ وَقَصِّرَا}$$

258 Take a *ghusl* just after the sun has past its zenith, attend the two *khutbas*, and join and shorten the *salats*

$$\text{ظُهْرَيْكَ ثُمَّ الْجَبَلَ اصْعَدْ رَاكِبَا}$$

$$\text{عَلَى وُضُوءٍ ثُمَّ كُنْ مُوَاظِبَا}$$

259 of *Dhuhr* and *'Asr*. Then ascend the mount, (preferably) mounted (on one's riding beast), and in a state of *wudu'*, then persevere in

$$\text{عَلَى الدُّعَا مُهَلِّلاً مُبْتَهِلاً}$$

$$\text{مُصَلِّياً عَلَى النَّبِيِّ مُسْتَقْبِلاً}$$

260 making *du'a*, saying *la ilaha illa'llah*, humbly supplicating, sending blessings on the Prophet while facing the *qibla*.

$$\text{هُنَيْهَةً بَعْدَ غُرُوبِهَا تَقِفْ}$$

$$\text{وَانْفِرْ لِمُزْدَلِفَةٍ وَتَنْصَرِفْ}$$

261 Stand a little while after the sunset, then hasten to Muzdalifa making your way

$$\text{فِي الْمَأْزِمَيْنِ الْعَلَمَيْنِ نَكِبْ}$$

$$\text{وَقَصِّرْ بِهَا وَاجْمَعْ عِشاً لِمَغْرِبْ}$$

262 between the two mountains (called the) Ma'zamayn avoiding (other than this way), and then shorten and join *Maghrib* and *'Isha* in (Muzdalifa).

$$\text{وَاحْطُطْ وَبِتْ بِهَا وَأَحْيِ لَيْلَتَكْ}$$

$$\text{وَصَلِّ صُبْحَكَ وَغَلِّسْ رِحْلَتَكْ}$$

263 Dismount (with your saddles and belongings) and spend the night there (in Muzdalifa) filling it with *dhikr* and *salat*. Perform your *Subh salat* and then move off as light starts to break.

$$\text{قِفْ وَادْعُ بِالْمَشْعَرِ لِلْأَسْفَارِ}$$

$$\text{وَأَسْرِعَنْ فِي بَطْنِ وَادِي النَّارِ}$$

264 Stand and make *du'a* at the Mash'ar (at Muzdalifa) before sunrise and make haste at the bottom of Wadi an-Nar (also known as Batn al-Muhassir).

$$\text{وَسِرْ كَمَا تَكُونُ لِلْعَقَبَةِ}$$

$$\text{فَارْمِ لَدَيْهَا بِحِجَارٍ سَبْعَةِ}$$

265 Go as you are (either mounted or walking) to the (*jamrat*) al-'Aqaba and throw the seven pebbles there

$$\text{مِنْ أَسْفَلٍ تُسَاقُ مِنْ مُزْدَلِفَةِ}$$

$$\text{كَالْفُولِ وَانْحَرْ هَدْياً إِنْ بِعَرَفَةِ}$$

266 from below, having brought them along with you from Muzdalifa, (the pebbles being) about the size of beans. Sacrifice the *hady* if at 'Arafa

أَوْقَفْتَهُ وَاحْلِقْ وَسِرْ لِلْبَيْتِ

فَطُفْ وَصَلِّ مِثْلَ ذَاكَ النَّعْتِ

267 you had stopped with it, then shave, continue to the House and perform the *tawaf* (*al-ifada*), praying (two *rak'ats*) as described (before).

وَارْجِعْ فَصَلِّ الظُّهْرَ فِي مِنًى وَبِتْ

إِثْرَ زَوَالِ غَدِهِ أَرْمِ لَا نُفِتْ

268 Then return and pray *Dhuhr* at Mina (the day of the 'Eid) and remain (three) nights (if possible). Immediately after the sun passes its zenith, you must go and stone the

ثَلَاثَ جَمَرَاتٍ بِسَبْعِ حَصَيَاتٍ

لِكُلِّ جَمْرَةٍ وَقِفْ لِلدَّعَوَاتِ

269 the three *jamras*, each with seven pebbles and stand – making *du'a* -

طَوِيلًا إِثْرَ الْأَوَّلَيْنِ أَخِّرَا

عَقَبَةً وَكُلَّ رَمْيٍ كَبِّرَا

270 for a considerable time after the first two; then finish with the *jamrat al-'Aqaba* (that is, after the one next to the mosque of Mina and the middle *jamra*); and for each stoning say *Allahu akbar*.

وَافْعَلْ كَذَاكَ ثَالِثَ النَّحْرِ وَزِدْ

إِنْ شِئْتَ رَابِعًا وَتَمَّ مَا قُصِدْ

271 Do likewise on the third day and add if you wish a fourth (day), and what was intended is now complete.

These lines are clear and do not need to be explained: what has been mentioned is what is customarily done by all the hajjis, and all the books and commentaries in current use adequately describe (all) this (in more detail). This is not, however, the intent of the present author.

Despite this, we shall try to summarise as far as possible the laws, (particular points of) benefit and narrations connected with the subject, both from within the *madhhab* and outside of it.

The Day of Tarwiya (watering) and 'Arafa

The person performing the hajj goes out on the eighth day of Dhu'l-Hijja to Mina, that is, on the *Yawm at-Tarwiya*. As for the seventh day, this is called the *Yawm az-Zina*, the day of embellishment, that is the day when the noble Ka'ba is adorned. It is stated in the *Bidayat al-Mujtahid*: "They are of a consensus that the validity of hajj – in the case of the person whose time is short – is not conditional upon staying the night in Mina and performing the *salats* there." Khalil said: "His going out to Mina is for as long as (is necessary) to pray *Dhuhr* in its time and to spend the night there." It is *makruh* to leave for there before the *Yawm at-Tarwiya*. Malik considered it *makruh* for him to go out before this (day) or (to go out) before the ninth to 'Arafa.

On the day of the ninth, that is, the day of 'Arafa, the person on hajj walks to 'Arafa and stands there. He said, may the peace and blessings of Allah be upon him: "Hajj is 'Arafa – whoever comes before the *salat* of *fajr*, during the night, has fulfilled the hajj." This is narrated by Abu Dawud and Ibn Majah.

Khalil said: "Hajj is being present at 'Arafa for a time during the night prior to the Day of Sacrifice, even if only passing, that is, as long as it is done with the intention (of being present). He should be in a state of *wudu'* when standing or mounted – and remain standing (a while) unless tired."

"They are of a consensus that being present at 'Arafa is one of the pillars of hajj and that whoever misses it must make the sacrifice of the *hady* and perform the hajj the following year." *Bidayat al-Mujtahid*.

They are also of a consensus that whoever stands at 'Arafa before the sun inclines from the zenith and leaves before the sun inclines has not carried out the (obligation of) standing – if he does not return after the sun begins to decline or that night before the dawn, then he has missed the hajj. This is based on the hadith "Hajj is 'Arafa and whoever reaches 'Arafa before the dawn has fulfilled this (particular obligation)".

There is a difference of opinion regarding someone who stands at 'Arafa after the sun has passed its zenith and who departs from there before the *Maghrib*: Malik said: 'He must do the hajj the following year unless he returns before dawn.' On the whole, the validity of the standing there, according to Malik, is dependent upon his standing (at least a little while) during the night.

The majority of the *'ulama* have said that whoever stands at 'Arafa *after* the sun has passed its zenith has (nevertheless) fulfilled (the obligation of) hajj, even if he departs before the *Maghrib*, although they differ as to whether he must make a minor sacrifice because of this (delay).

The form of the standing according to Malik is that he stand at the end of the day and not leave until it is certain that the sun has fully set. If he leaves before the sunset, then his hajj is valid according to the majority of the *'ulama*, except for Malik. Ibn 'Abd al-Barr said: 'We are not aware of any of the *fuqaha* of the major cities who hold to the judgement of Malik.'"

It is also stated in *al-Bidaya* that they differ regarding someone who stands at (the place called Batn) 'Urana at 'Arafa. Malik said: "His hajj is complete but he must sacrifice a *hady*." Ash-Shafi'i said: "He has no hajj."

The *salat* of *Dhuhr* and *'Asr* are joined with the two *adhans* and the two *iqamas*, according to Malik, while according to Abu Hanifa, ash-Shafi'i and a group (of the *'ulama*) it is with one *adhan* and two *iqamas*.

It is stated in *al-Mughni* of Ibn Qudama al-Hanbali: "Jabir said: 'He only misses the hajj (if he has not stood there) when the dawn breaks of the night of *Jam'*.[1] Abu az-Zubayr said: 'I said to him: "Did the Messenger of Allah say that, may the peace and blessings of Allah be upon him?" and he replied: "Yes".' This has been narrated from al-Athram.

"The Messenger of Allah, may the peace and blessings of Allah be upon him, on being asked by some people of Najd 'Messenger of Allah, how is the hajj?' replied: 'Hajj is 'Arafa. Whoever arrives before the *salat* of *fajr* of the night of the Day of Gathering has fulfilled his hajj.' This is narrated from Abu Dawud and Ibn Majah. Muhammad ibn Yahya said: 'I have not seen a hadith from ath-Thawri which is more genuine than this.'" Ibn Qudama.

In the gloss of ar-Rahuni on az-Zurqani's commentary on Khalil he said: "The author of *al-Muntaqa* stated: 'Abu Hanifa and ash-Shafi'i said: 'The standing during the day on Yawm al-'Arafa is reckoned from the time the sun has passed its zenith to the *Maghrib* – and the standing during (at least a little of) the night is (considered) a consequent (but subservient) adjunct to it (*taba'*): thus whoever stands part of the day, then it is accepted of him, and whoever stands a portion of the night, it is also accepted of him; however, they have also said that whoever stands in the day but not the night, then he must make the minor sacrifice while whoever stands a part of the night but not the day does not.'

"It is stated in the *Ahkam* of Ibn al-'Arabi: 'The Malikis have said that the *fard* is

---

1   *Jam'* without *al* is another name for Muzdalifa.

the standing at night; while ash-Shafi'i and Abu Hanifa have said that the *fard* is standing during the day; and Ahmad that it is both at night and during the day.'

"'I say: "It is clear that there is a problematic point in our *madhhab*, namely, why is it obligatory to make a minor sacrifice for leaving out something which is (only) an adjunct (*taba'*) while this (obligation) is absent with regard to something which is *fard* in itself? – so reflect upon this with equity, and Allah knows best!"'" The gloss of ar-Rahuni on az-Zurqani's commentary on Khalil, and the person who says "I say," is Ibn al-'Arabi.

It is stated in the *Hashiya of* al-Madani on *Ganun* on *Khalil*: "He said in *an-Nawadir*, relating from Malik: 'I do not like anyone standing (alone) on the Mounts of 'Arafa but rather (he should stand together) with people, and there is no place which is more excellent (that others) – as long as he stands with the people.'"

He said in *al-Jilab*: "It is *makruh* to stand on Mount 'Arafa." He then goes on to say after a discussion: "The gist of the matter is that standing on Mount 'Arafa is *makruh*, as is distancing oneself from people; it is recommended to stand with people, and this does not contradict the recommendation that one should stand (as) near (as possible) to his place of standing, may the peace and blessings of Allah be upon him, namely, by the large rocks covering the *Ruwabi as-Sighar* side – the side of the lesser ridges – which is at the foot of the mountain situated in the middle of 'Arafat." Al-Hattab.

Ibn al-Jama'a said: "That it is preferred to stand on the Mount of Mercy (*jabal ar-rahma*) has become a widespread belief amongst the common people – they light candles and men mix with women in the ascent and descent, but this is a mistake. It is done out of ignorance and is an ugly innovation which appeared after the disappearance of the first upright generations."

Khalil said: "(The standing is also valid) if the multitude make a mistake (in observing the moon) such that the standing is done on the tenth (of Dhu'l-Hijja); but not if the (solitary) ignorant person (makes a mistake)."

Al-Hattab also said: "If the people taking part in the gathering make a mistake and they stand on the tenth, then their standing is accepted, as opposed to the eighth for this is not accepted of them, although it has both been said that it is accepted in both cases and that it is not accepted." Ibn al-Hajib has related the three opinions and Ibn al-Katib is of the opinion that that there is agreement within the *madhhab* that it is accepted on the tenth.

Sahnun and Ibn al-'Arabi deemed the judgement of Ibn al-Qasim correct that the standing is valid even if (the day) is mistaken – as is stated in *al-Jawahir*.

Al-Hattab also said: "Al-Muhibb at-Tabari said in *al-Qurba* that it is recommended to climb up (the Mount) and he used the word 'being present (at 'Arafa)' to indicate that what is meant by 'standing' is being at 'Arafa in a state of composure – in whatever manner it may be, be it standing, sitting or reclining, with the exception of merely passing by, in which case there are specific stipulations (for this to be valid). Sanad said: 'None of the *'ulama* has stipulated that the 'standing' must be actually performed standing but rather (only) that it takes place at 'Arafa and that it is acceptable in any manner, be it standing or sitting, walking or mounted, in fact in any manner one can possibly imagine.'"

He then goes on to say: "What is obligatory in the standing is being there in whatever manner; what is recommended is that one stand straight or be mounted on one's camel facing the *qibla*."

Ibn 'Abd as-Salam said: "The word *wuquf* (standing) is not meant literally, but rather being in a state of composure at 'Arafa. If (one accepts the judgement of) those who hold that someone (merely) passing is enough, then he has to make the (minor) sacrifice (to compensate) – this has been related by Ibn Farhun."

Commenting on Khalil's words '(and it is also valid) in the case of fainting before the sun passes its zenith', al-Hattab said: "that is, if someone faints before the sun has passed its zenith – having assumed the *ihram* before this for the hajj – and his companions perform the standing at 'Arafa, then this is accepted, according to Ibn al-Qasim who has also narrated that he does not have to make the minor sacrifice (to make good this defect). Sanad said: 'This is because fainting does not invalidate the *ihram* if he had already entered it with the intention of *ihram*.'"

Again al-Hattab stated:

"Branch: Sanad said: 'If he proceeds to 'Arafa while asleep on his litter – and remains asleep until the people move off and he is with them (all the time) – then this is accepted as his standing.'

"Branch: I have not seen a definitive text with specific reference to the case of someone drinking an intoxicating liquor such that he loses his intellect – whether out of choice or because of something he has eaten unaware (that it is intoxicating) or when he is given food by someone which intoxicates him – and he misses the standing. However, the most evident judgement is that if this occurs and he is not to blame, then he is considered as (subject to the same judgement as) someone who faints or is mad; if, however, he has deliberately (become intoxicated), then it is not accepted of him, and (the case is) analogous to that of the person who is ignorant, indeed it is (much) more likely to be accepted of this latter, and Allah knows best."

Al-Mawwaq, commenting on the matter, said: "Malik said: 'Whoever faints before he arrives at 'Arafa but people stand by him while he is unconscious until moving off from there, then it is accepted of him, and he does not have to make any sacrifice (to make up for this).'"

Commenting on Khalil's words '(The standing is also valid) if the multitude make a mistake (in observing the moon) such that the standing is done on the tenth', Ibn Shas said: "If the person on hajj (i.e. all the people) stands on the tenth, having made a mistake in the sighting of the new moon, then the hajj is accepted of them, and they do not have to make it up: they should proceed with what they are doing even if this (mistake) becomes apparent to them and is confirmed during the rest of the day or afterwards. Their state in this regard throughout all of it is as if they had not made a mistake, and al-Mawwaq has also stated something similar."

Al-Hattab said: "What one may conclude from the discussion of al-Lakhmi and Ibn 'Abd as-Salam is that whoever enters 'Arafa before *fajr* and remains there until dawn breaks – that is *fajr* arrives before he leaves (on the tenth) – then his standing is accepted and his hajj is valid: the validity of his standing is not conditional upon his leaving 'Arafa before *fajr*. However, standing at 'Arafa during the day is *wajib* – obligatory – and whoever leaves off doing this must sacrifice (to make up for it).

"If he is constrained to leave 'Arafa before *Maghrib*, then it is accepted, in principle, according to the *madhhab*. However its validity is subject (only) to the difference of opinion regarding (the case of) those who move off before sunset but who do not leave (the plain of) 'Arafa until the sun has set: (some hold) that it is accepted but that he must make a sacrifice (to make up the defect) as he had set off with the intention of leaving before the *Maghrib*."

He said in *al-Bayan*: "What most of the people of knowledge hold to is that if the people on hajj are mistaken as to (the day of) 'Arafa, then their hajj is not accepted – and this is the judgement of Malik, Layth, al-Awza'i, Abu Hanifa, Abu Yusuf, Muhammad Ibn al-Hasan, 'Uthman al-Butti and a group besides them." This is stated in *Mawarid an-Najah*, a commentary on the *Risala*.

Ath-Thawri was asked when the people were leaving 'Arafa towards Muzdalifa as to which people were most in loss – and the questioner was making an allusion to those guilty of injustices and tyrants – and he replied: "The person most in loss is someone who thinks that Allah will not forgive such people."

Someone also mentioned that one of the hajjis saw an angel addressing another angel saying: "This year six hundred thousand people have made hajj, but only six of them have been accepted. However Allah has caused each of the six who had been accepted to intercede for one hundred thousand and so has accepted all of the hajjis on account of these six" – Allah is Possessor of vast generosity.

Muzdalifa is *Jum'* with a u on the *jeem*.[1] He, exalted is He, said: "*Remember Allah at the Sacred Landmark (al-Mash'ar al-Haram, between 'Arafa and Mina). Remember Him because He has guided you.*"[2]

Commenting on Khalil's words 'If he does not dismount, then he must make a sacrifice (to make up for it)' al-Hattab said: "Sanad said: 'Dismounting is obligatory and is effected by putting one's saddle and effects on the ground and remaining a while. It is likewise (effected) if one remains a while without putting down one's saddle and effects.'" Al-Hattab also said, after a long discussion: "and the gist of what he says is that whoever does not dismount before dawn breaks and has no valid excuse (for not doing so) must make a sacrifice (to compensate), according to Ibn al-Qasim; whoever leaves off doing it for a valid reason does not have to (make a sacrifice) even if he arrives after the sunrise."

It is stated in *Bidayat al-Mujtahid*: "They are of a consensus that whoever spends the night in Muzdalifa on the night (prior to the) sacrifice and joins the *Maghrib* and *'Isha* with the imam and stands after the *salat* of *Subh* until the first light after the standing at 'Arafa, then his hajj is complete.

"Al-Awza'i and a group of the *Tabi'un* have said: 'It is one of the *fard* elements of the hajj and whoever misses it, has missed the hajj and has to do the hajj the following year.' However, the *fuqaha* of the major cities consider that it is not one of the *fard* aspects of the hajj and that whoever misses the standing there and the spending the night (there) must (only) perform a sacrifice (to make up for this deficiency).

"In the hadith of 'Urwa ibn Mudarras, one of the *Tabi'un* – and it is a hadith about which there is agreement as to soundness – it is narrated: 'Whoever performs this *salat* with us, that is, the *salat* of *Subh* at *Jam'* (Muzdalifa) – having arrived at 'Arafa before this, whether during the day or the night, then he has completed his hajj, and so should trim his nails, hair and beard.' However, there is a consensus amongst the Muslims that one does not have to act in accordance with anything that is indicated in the hadith – that is, most of them hold that the hajj of those who stand at Muzdalifa at night but who move off from there before the *Subh* then their hajj is complete; and likewise in the case of someone who spends the night there and sleeps through the

---

1 I cannot find the spelling *Jum'* in Lane's Lexicon but find instead *Jam'* without *al*. Ed.
2 al-Baqara – The Cow: 198

salat. They are also of a consensus that his hajj is also complete if he stands at Muzdalifa without making *dhikr* of Allah – although this diminishes the force of the argument (as to the necessity of *dhikr*) afforded by the *ayat*: 'When you pour down from 'Arafa, remember Allah at the Sacred Landmark.'[1]

"The sunna of Hajj is that the people spend the night there, joining the *Maghrib* and *'Isha salats* at the beginning of the time of *'Isha*, and then move off after *Subh* when the light begins to penetrate the darkness." *Bidayat al-Mujtahid* by Ibn Rushd al-Hafeed (the grandson).

Al-Hattab said: "The *salats* of *Maghrib* and *'Isha* should only be done at Muzdalifa – if done before it, then they should be repeated." Al-Jazuli said: "The well known (judgement) is that if he misses the joining (of the *salats* with the people), then he should not join them alone – and this is an unusual (judgement)."

It is stated in *al-Afsah* by Wazir ibn Hubayra al-Hanbali: "They are in agreement that it is permissible to move off from Muzdalifa after midnight of the night (prior to) the sacrifice – except Abu Hanifa who said: 'It is not permitted until dawn has broken, otherwise one must sacrifice'; they are also in agreement that the standing at the Mash'ar al-Haram is part of what has been laid down (in the practice) while they differ as to whether it is an obligation. Malik, ash-Shafi'i – in one of his two judgements, and Ahmad – in one of his two narrations, have said: 'It is obligatory and if not performed, then a sacrifice must be made.' Abu Hanifa said: 'If he is there after the *fajr* and before the sunrise, then he does not owe any (sacrifice).'"

The Mash'ar al-Haram (the Sacred Landmark) is one of the names of Muzdalifa. It is stated in al-Mughni: "If he prays the *Maghrib* before coming to Muzdalifa and does not join (it with *'Isha*), he has contravened the sunna but his *salat* is valid" – and this he has attributed it to all (the *'ulama*) other than Abu Hanifa and ath-Thawri.

Again it is stated in *al-Mughni* of Ibn Qudama: "It is not permitted to move on from Muzdalifa before midnight. Malik said: 'If he passes by it and does not dismount, then he has to make a sacrifice; if he does, then he does not have to make one – irrespective of when he moves off.'"

Al-Hattab said: "Dismounting is obligatory and is effected by setting down one's saddle and effects, and remaining settled a while. The most evident judgement is that it is not enough to have the camel kneel down only but rather the saddle and effects must also be put down." This is indeed the most evident judgement if one does not remain a while. If one does, however, and one does

---

[1] al-Baqara – The Cow: 198

not put one's saddle down, then the most evident judgement is that this is acceptable.

Moving off from Muzdalifa, that is, Jamʻ the 'Place of Gathering', and the Mashʻar al-Haram

It is stated in *Bidayat al-Mujtahid*: "They are in agreement that the Prophet, may the peace and blessings of Allah be upon him, stopped at the Mashʻar al-Haram, namely, at Muzdalifa after having prayed the *fajr*, that he then moved on from there before sunrise to Mina and that on this day, namely, the Day of Sacrifice, he stoned the *jamrat* al-ʻAqaba after sunrise.

"The Muslims are of a consensus that whoever stones it after sunrise (or at any time) up to the moment the sun passes its zenith on this same day has stoned it within the (proper) time; they are of a consensus that he, may the peace and blessings of Allah be upon him, did not stone any other (*jamra*) on the Day of Sacrifice although they have differed as to whether it may be stoned before the moment of *fajr*: Malik – as well as Abu Hanifa, Ahmad and Sufyan – said: 'He should repeat the stoning' while ash-Shafiʻi said: 'There is no harm in this.'

"The proof of Malik and those who agree with him, is his (actual) practice, may the peace and blessings of Allah be upon him, while the proof of the others is the hadith of Umm Salama, narrated by Abu Dawud and others, to the effect that it was stoned before *fajr* together with the hadith of Asma, the daughter of Abu Bakr, may Allah be pleased with them both, who added: 'We used to do it (at night) when the Messenger of Allah was still alive, may the peace and blessings of Allah be upon him.'

"There is a consensus among the *ʻulama* that the recommended time for stoning of *jamrat* al-ʻAqaba is from the time of the sunrise to the time when it has passed its zenith but that if stoned before *Maghrib* on the Day of the Sacrifice, it is accepted of him, and he does not have to make a sacrifice – except for Malik who deems it recommended to make a sacrifice.

"There is a difference of opinion regarding the stoning at night or the next morning. Malik said: 'He must make a sacrifice' while Abu Hanifa said: 'If he does the stoning during the night, then he does not have to make a sacrifice, but if he delays it to the next morning, he does.'"

Khalil said: "He should return to Mina, above al-ʻAqaba, and stay for three nights, and if he fails to remain for most of one night (of the three), then he must make a sacrifice (to make up for this); or (it is permitted to stay) two nights, if he is in a hurry." Al-Hattab said, commenting on this: "The person who is going down (from 'Arafa after the *tawaf al-ifada*) returns to Mina and does not wait for the *salat* in the mosque, even if it is the *jumu'a salat*, unless the *iqama* is said while he is there; and he should not perform one or two *tawafs*, contrary to what is said. The best for him is to make *salats* at Mina and remain there following his practice, may the peace and blessings of Allah be upon him."

Khalil said: "He makes the two night *salats* (of *Maghrib* and *'Isha*) at Muzdalifa and stays the night (of the tenth day) there. Whoever does not dismount, must make up for it with a sacrifice. The *salats* are joined and shortened (for those who stop) at Mina and 'Arafa, except for residents there; and if he is unable (to join the other hajjis), then he should join the *salat* after the redness of early evening if he had gone out with the imam (but had been left behind); if he has not (done the standing at 'Arafa with the imam), he (does not join them but) makes each (separately) in its time. If the two (*salats* of *Maghrib* and *'Isha*) have been performed before (the descent to Muzdalifa), then he should repeat them; (it is recommended that) he depart (from Muzdalifa) after the *Subh salat* at the end of the night, at first light; he should stop at the Mash'ar al-Haram (at the mosque near Mina, between the two mounts of Muzdalifa and Quzah), repeating *Allahu akbar* and making *du'a* until the first light, facing the *qibla*. There is no standing after this (time), and not before the *Subh*. He should make haste in Batn Muhassir (a *wadi* between Muzdalifa and Mina). Immediately on arriving at (Mina), he must stone the (*jamra*) al-'Aqaba even if mounted (that is, without waiting to dismount); but in the other (stoning of *jamrat* al-'Aqaba, that is, on the Day of Sacrifice) he should walk, and on (completing) this (stoning), he returns to the state of *hill* (i.e. of normality, after the state of *ihram*), except with regard to (sexual relations with) women and hunting; and it is (still) *makruh* to wear perfume (at this juncture)."

Commmenting on this, al-Hattab said: "The Mash'ar al-Haram is the name of the building at Muzdalifa and it denotes the whole of it. It was built by Qusayy ibn Kilab in order that those on hajj might find their way. Standing in any part of Muzdalifa is accepted although it is best at the building itself.

"This first stage of coming out of *ihram* into the state of *hill* is effected by stoning the *jamrat* al-'Aqaba, or by the fact that the time for performing this has passed. Ibn 'Arafa said: 'Missing the stoning of the 'Aqaba because the time has passed is the same as (actually) performing it.'"

Again Khalil said: "The stoning of the 'Aqaba extends from immediately after the sunrise up to immediately after the sun has passed its zenith but before *Dhuhr*. His standing takes place following (the stoning of) the first two (*jamra*s, not the third) and lasts for the amount of time it would take to read Surat al-Baqara quickly – with the left (side of the House in front of him, that is, to his right, according to ad-Dasuqi) in the case of the second."

He goes on to say: "Then he shaves, (and this removal of hair is acceptable) even if it is by means of a depilatory, and it should be done to the whole of the head, although trimming is accepted, and this is the sunna in the case of women – that she trim an amount equal in length to the finger tips – while men should cut back near to the root of the hair. Then he performs the *tawaf al-ifada* and with this (*tawaf*), he returns (from the state of *ihram*) to the state of *ihlal* (in which the remaining prohibited things become licit for him)."

Al-Hattab said: "Making haste or delaying are equal in excellence, except that in the case of the person who makes haste it is conditional upon his leaving Mina before the sunset, otherwise he should delay (leaving) until he does the stoning on the third day. Abu Hanifa said: 'He may leave as long as dawn of the third day has not broken. Ishaq and those of legal judgements (*ashab ar-ra'y*) have given licence to make the stoning on the day of moving off before the sun has passed its zenith, although they should not move off before the sun has passed its zenith.' The like is related of Ahmad, and 'Ikrima has also granted licence in this. Tawus said: 'He should perform the stoning before the sun has passed the zenith and also move off before it'" – this is taken from Ibn Qudama al-Hanbali.

A female minor may shave or trim her hair, and in the hadith it states: "Women have only to trim (their hair)" – this 'Umar and his son have stated, and there is nothing contrary to this (statement of theirs).

Al-Mawwaq said: "He said in *az-Zahi*: 'He should not go and perform voluntary *tawaf* during the days of Mina but rather remain in the Mosque of Khayf in order to perform the *salats* in it, and this is the best.'" Al-Hattab said: "It is recommended for the *muhrim* if he leaves the *ihram* and returns to *ihlal* – his normal state – that he distinguish between the two states of *ihram* and *ihlal* by trimming his beard more than usual and paring his nails; also that he make the *tawaf al-ifada* (while still) in the *ihram* clothing. He should interrupt declaring the *talbiya*, according to Ahmad, when stoning the *jamrat* al-'Aqaba. This is based on the hadith narrated by al-Fadl, who had been sitting mounted behind him, may the peace and blessings of Allah be upon him: '... that he continued to say the *talbiya* until he stoned the *jamrat* al-'Aqaba' – this is narrated by the group of the scholars of hadith."

Malik said: "He stops saying the *talbiya* when proceeding to the mosque of 'Arafa; afterwards he stones the *jamrat* al-'Aqaba, performs the sacrifice, shaves or trims (his hair)" – and then, according to Malik, may Allah be pleased with him, what had been haram for him becomes halal, except for women and hunting, and perfume remains *makruh*; and according to Ahmad everything becomes halal except women.

The stoning is done with pebbles taken from any place – that is, anything that may be termed a pebble, irrespective of its colour. Malik said: "Picking them up (off the ground) is preferable to me than breaking up (a larger stone into pebble size bits), and he does not have to wash them; if he does need to break them, however, then there is no harm in this" – and this is extracted from al-Hattab.

Abu Hanifa said: "It is permitted to perform the stoning with clay, (hard) mud and anything from the earth." It is also narrated from Ahmad that it is recommended to wash the (clay), although this is not the practice (adhered to). If he makes the stoning with an impure stone, it is accepted; and the best is that the pebble be the size of a slingshot stone, although if he throws something bigger it is accepted. Ibn 'Umar, may Allah be pleased with them both, threw the dung of sheep and goats, and it is also permitted with marble, alabaster, quartz or flint and whetstone.

Khalil said: "It is *makruh* to throw with what has already been thrown." Sheen said: "that is, whether he himself has thrown it or someone else." Al-Lakhmi said: "If the throwing is done more than once with one stone it is not accepted, although Ibn 'Arafa has disputed this judgement of his, and Allah knows best." From al-Hattab.

If the throwing is repeated seven times with one pebble, it is not accepted. Abu Ishaq said: "He must repeat the (throwing) as long as he has not left during the days of Mina; however, if he has left, then he does not have to make anything up" and so has deemed the matter of (performing it with only) one pebble of insignificance.

Ash-Shaykh said: "The most evident meaning of the words of Abu Ishaq is that they are contrary to those of al-Lakhmi as the latter did not command the stoning to be repeated" – this is taken *from Mawarid an-Najah*, a commentary on the *Risala*.

It is also stated in the *Bidayat al-Mujtahid*: "They are of a consensus that whoever does not stone the *jamras* during the days known as *at-Tashriq* until the sun sets on the last of them, does not have to stone them afterwards.

"They differed as to the obligation of the *kaffara*. Malik said: 'Whoever leaves off doing the stoning, whether all or some of it – even (if he misses out) just one pebble – has then to make it up with a sacrifice.' Abu Hanifa said: 'There is a sacrifice to be made if the (stoning is) left out.' Ash-Shafi'i said: 'He has to pay a *mudd* of food for one pebble, two *mudds* for two, while for three, he has to sacrifice.'

A party of the *Tabi'un* granted licence with regard to (missing out) one pebble – based on the hadith of Sa'd, may Allah be pleased with him: 'Some of us say that the stoning was with six (pebbles) while others among us that it was done with seven but none of us found fault with the other.' The majority of the *'ulama* hold that the *jamrat* al-'Aqaba is not one of the fundamental pillars of the hajj."

It is stated in the *Mughni* of Ibn Qudama al-Hanbali: "If the pebbles are thrown all at once, then only one is accepted, according to Malik, Ahmad, ash-Shafi'i and the *ashab ar-ra'y* – although 'Ata said that it is accepted – and he should say *Allahu akbar* for each pebble."

They are of a consensus that he should repeat when he has doubts as to whether he has hit the (*jamra*) or not and that on the first day he should only stone the *jamrat* al-'Aqaba with the seven (pebbles) but that during the days known as *Tashriq*, (he should stone) three *jamras* with twenty-one pebbles, seven for each *jamra*; that he should perform the throwing for two days and then move off on the third; that he should make *du'a* after the first two *jamras*, but not the 'Aqaba for that there is no *du'a* after it; that he does not perform the stoning during the days of *Tashriq* until after the sun has passed its zenith; that the time for performing the stoning of the *jamrat* al-'Aqaba is the Day of the Sacrifice from the break of dawn to the *Maghrib*; that the time of *qada* – making it up (after missing it) – is after sunset each day up to the sunset of the fourth day, and that any time after this (period of four days) is also (considered) *qada* but that there is an obligation to sacrifice a *hady* if there is a delay (after these four days) in 'making up', according to the well known opinion" – this is extracted from Mayyara.

The stoning on the first day is conditional upon the observance of the order of the *jamras*; it is also recommended that the one be stoned immediately after the other and that each pebble be thrown immediately after the other.

Observance of the order regarding the *jamras* is obligatory and if they are done in the wrong order then they should be repeated – this is the opinion of Malik and ash-Shafi'i while al-Hasan and 'Ata have said that the order is not obligatory. This latter is also the judgement of Abu Hanifa for he said: "If he does the stoning in the wrong order, he should repeat, but if he does not (repeat) then it is accepted of him."

Some of them have based their argument on what is related of the Prophet, may the peace and blessings of Allah be upon him, who said: "There is no harm in someone performing one rite before another", and it is narrated of Sakeena the daughter of al-Husayn, the son of 'Ali, may Allah be pleased with them, that she was missing a pebble and so threw her ring.

If he leaves out the standing and *du'a* at the *jamras*, he has left out a sunna but he has nothing to make up – the Prophet, may the peace and blessings of Allah be upon him, performed (all the) obligatory and recommended acts (but discriminated between the two kinds of rite for the sake of the rest of the *umma*).

Ishaq and the *ashab ar-ra'y* – those of legal judgements (rather than *ahl al-hadith*) – have granted a licence regarding the stoning on the day of departure *before* the sun has reached its zenith – as long, that is, as one does not *move off* before the sun has passed its zenith. Something similar is reported from Ahmad, and 'Ikrima has granted licence in this also. Tawus, however, said: "He should throw before the sun has passed its zenith and also move off before it" – and this is taken from *al-Mughni* of Ibn Qudama.

Ibn Rushd said in *al-Bayan*: "Whoever hastens [and only stones on three days rather than four] and leaves Mina for Makkah, and he had alighted whenever he had passed by Mina, or he had returned for some necessity and the sun had set while he was there, then there is no difference of opinion that he carries on and that he does not have to remain until he throws [his pebbles]."[1]

It is stated in *al-Mughni* of Ibn Qudama that Ibn 'Abbas said: "No one should remain the night above (and beyond) the 'Aqaba of Mina, and this is the judgement of 'Urwa, Ibrahim, Mujahid and 'Ata and is also related from 'Umar ibn al-Khattab, may Allah be pleased with him; it is also the judgement of Malik and ash-Shafi'i."

Commenting on Khalil's words '…above (and beyond) the 'Aqaba…', Ibn al-'Arabi said: "Anyone who does not pass the night there [at Mina] must make a minor sacrifice. However, it is related from Ahmad that if someone does not pass the night at Mina, then he has nothing to make up, although he has not acted correctly. This is the judgement of *ashab ar-ra'y* – the people of legal judgement, namely that nothing is required to be made up in this matter by the *shari'ah*."

---

1 He had stoned on the first day, then done his *tawaf al-ifada* in Makka and returned to Mina and performed the stoning for two more days but not intending to remain for the fourth day, which is optional. Then having departed, he had returned to Mina for some reason and was there while the sun set. He is not, in these circumstances obliged to remain for the fourth day and perform the stoning. Ed.

In the *Kitab al-Ifsah* of Wazir Ibn Hubayra al-Hanbali it is stated: "They differ with respect to spending the specified nights in Mina. Abu Hanifa said: 'Whoever does not (spend the nights there) has nothing to make up'; while Malik said: 'He has to make a minor sacrifice if he does not spend most of each of the nights in Mina'; and from ash-Shafi'i there is a narration that a sacrifice is required; from Ahmad there is one narration that a sacrifice must be made and that he has acted incorrectly, although it is also reported of him that no sacrifice is due, while in another narration, that he should spend a dirham and a half in *sadaqa* for each day (as compensation)."

Ibn Qayyim al-Jawziyyah said in his *Zad al-Ma'ad*: "The Prophet, may the peace and blessings of Allah be upon him, granted a special licence for people who were responsible for providing water and for those who took care of the animals to spend the night outside of Mina. Thus whoever has money or property and fears that it will be lost, or is ill and fears he will not be able to stay there, then (the obligation to spend the night) is also removed from him."

It is also stated in *al-Mughni*: "If he delays the stoning on one day to the day after or delays the whole of the stoning to the end of the days of *Tashriq*, then he has abandoned the sunna and there is nothing due from him other than that he must make the intention to perform the stoning for the first day before proceeding with the intention for the second, and then likewise for the third – and this is what ash-Shafi'i and Abu Thawr said. The order is respected when making the (single) intention for the whole group (of *jamras*), just as (one would make one intention for) two *salats* (performed) together or (for a number of) missed *salats*."

It is also stated in *al-Mughni*: "It is preferable that there not be less than seven pebbles but if one or two are missing, then there is no harm in this."

Ibn 'Umar used to say: "I am not sure if I have thrown six or seven." Abu Hayya – who was one of those of Badr – said: "It is not of great significance (how many) pebbles a man throws." 'Abdullah ibn 'Umar said, "Abu Hayya has told the truth."

The Qadi said, as stated in the work of Ibn Qudama al-Hanbali: "His throwing on the second day (rather than the first) is not *qada* – i.e. an act of making up after the proper time has passed – as the (whole rite of stoning) is (considered as) one single span of time: the judgement regarding any delay in the stoning of the *jamras* of al-'Aqaba is like that with respect to stoning during the days of *Tashriq* – that if it is not stoned on the Day of Sacrifice, it is done the following day."

Khalil said: "...(and whoever delays his) throwing of any pebble until the night (rather than doing it during the day, owes a minor sacrifice); (and the obligation to make a sacrifice applies not only to adults but) also to a minor who cannot throw properly or to someone who does not have the strength (to throw) when another does it in his stead."

Malik said: "The *hady* is to be sacrificed when the throwing of a pebble, or all (seven pebbles), is delayed until the night; or – in the case of a minor who cannot throw properly – if his guardian does not throw for him (in time); or – in the case of an incapacitated person – if he does not get someone to throw for him; or – in the case of a healthy person who throws before the *Maghrib* – if he gets someone to do it for him, then he must sacrifice the *hady*."

If he repeats the throwing seven times with one (single) pebble, it is not accepted. Abu Ishaq said: "He should repeat (the stoning) as long as he has not left during the days of Mina; but if he has left, then no (sacrifice) is due of him" – and so he has deemed throwing with one single stone of little consequence.

Ash-Shaykh said: "The most evident meaning of the words of Abu Ishaq is that they contradict the words of al-Lakhmi as the latter has not commanded (the stoning) to be repeated" – and this is taken from Shinqeeti's commentary *Mawarid an-Najah* on the *Risala*.

Commenting on Khalil's words '…and the *tawaf al-wada'* – the farewell *tawaf*), al-Kafi said: "No one should leave for his country until he has made his farewell (circuits of) the House seven times, and it is one of the rites, and a sunna. This (obligation) is only removed in the case of a menstruating woman. This rite is (only) recommended according to Malik. It is the last act of the hajji in Makka al-Mukarrama, and it is called the *tawaf al-wada'* and also the *tawaf as-sadr*" – this is stated by al-Mawwaq.

Khalil said: "(the merit of the *tawaf* of farewell) is annulled if he stops (in Makka), even for only part of a day; although it is not annulled if one is delayed for some insignificant matter." Qadi 'Iyad said in *at-Tanbihat*: "The days known as *Tashriq* include the Day of Sacrifice and the three days after it. Malik said in the *Muwatta'* – and others too – that the days of *Tashriq* are the days termed *al-ma'dudat* ('the numbered days' as mentioned in the Qur'an), that is, the three after the Day of Sacrifice. Malik disliked them being called 'the days of *Tashriq*'; the women used to say *Allahu akbar* aloud during the nights of *Tashriq* following the time of Ibn 'Uthman and 'Umar ibn 'Abd al-'Aziz."

Khalil said: "It is *makruh* to throw with (a pebble which has) already been thrown, just (as it is *makruh*) to call the *ifada tawaf* the *tawaf az-ziyara* (the *tawaf* of visiting), or (to say) 'we have visited his tomb', may the peace and blessings of Allah be upon him." Malik reckoned the use of the phrase "We have visited the Prophet, may the peace and blessing of Allah be upon him", or "We have visited the House of Allah ta'ala" to be something immense, justifying the dislike of these (phrases) by saying that these terms are only used between equals and on the occasion of going to something that is not obligatory. It cannot be that the person visiting esteems himself superior to the person he has visited (if it is an obligation). Thus the person who goes to the Sultan to seek his right would not say: "I have visited the Sultan." Likewise with the Messenger of Allah, may the peace and blessings of Allah be upon him, and the *salat* in his Mosque – they only seek mercy and overflowing bounty from Allah by way of these acts and are not literally visitors. This has been extracted from al-Hattab's work.

From al-Madani 'Ali Ganun (in his *Hashiya 'ala az-Zurqani*): "(Khalil) said in *at-Tawdih*: 'Our Shaykh used to say: "It may be said that Malik disliked (their saying) such (things) as he feared they would indulge in vaunting (the excellence of) their worship and their reputation – as it has been related: 'Whoever visits me when I am dead, then it is as if he visited me when alive', and Allah knows best."'"

$$\text{وَمَنَعَ الإِحْرَامُ صَيْدَ البَرِّ}$$

$$\text{فِي قَتْلِهِ الْجَزَاءُ لَا كَالْفَأْرِ}$$

272 The (state of) *ihram* prohibits hunting on land, and compensation has to be made if (game is) killed, but not (creatures) like mice (or rats),

$$\text{وَعَقْرَبٍ مَعَ الْحِدَا كَلْبٍ عَقُورْ}$$

$$\text{وَحَيَّةٍ مَعَ الْغُرَابِ إِذْ يَجُورْ}$$

273 scorpions, vultures (or kites), wild beasts (like lions, tigers or wolves), snakes, or crows (and ravens) if (any of these) are causing harm.

$$\text{وَمَنَعَ الْمَخِيطَ بِالْعُضْوِ وَلَوْ}$$

$$\text{بِنَسْجٍ أَوْ عَقْدٍ كَخَاتَمٍ حَكَوْا}$$

274 It also proscribes the wearing of clothing which are (fashioned and) sewn to (cover the form of the limbs), or something woven which is fixed with a button or clasp, or (the wearing of) a ring;

$$\text{وَالسَّتْرُ لِلْوَجْهِ أَوِ الرَّأْسِ بِمَا}$$

$$\text{يُعَدُّ سَاتِراً وَلٰكِنْ إِنَّمَا}$$

275 or covering the face or head with anything which may be (properly) termed a covering; but it only

$$\text{تَمْنَعُ الْأُنْثَى لُبْسَ قُفَّازٍ كَذَا}$$

$$\text{سَتْرُ لِوَجْهِ لَا لِسَتْرٍ أُخِذَا}$$

276 prohibits a woman from wearing gloves (*quffaz*) – in addition to covering her face, but not if she takes a veil (to protect her from the importune gazes of men);

$$\text{وَمَنَعَ الطِّيبَ وَدُهْناً وَضَرَرْ}$$

$$\text{قَمْلٍ وَإِلْقَا وَسَخَ ظُفْرٍ شَعَرْ}$$

277 prohibited also is (the wearing of) perfume and oil (in the hair or beard), killing (and removing) lice, or removing dirt, nails or hair –

$$\text{وَيَفْتَدِي لِفِعْلِ بَعْضِ مَا ذُكِرْ}$$

$$\text{مِنَ الْمُخِيطِ لَهُنَا وَإِنْ عُذِرْ}$$

278 and compensation (*fidya*) must be paid if any of the above mentioned occurs, from sewed clothing right up to here, even if he has a valid excuse;

$$\text{وَمَنَعَ النِّسَا وَأَفْسَدَ الْجِمَاعُ}$$

$$\text{إِلَى الْإِفَاضَةِ يَبْقَى الْامْتِنَاعُ}$$

279 also prohibited is (having any sexual contact with) women (including marriage), and intercourse invalidates (the hajj), and this prohibition lasts until the (*tawaf*) *al-ifada*;

$$\text{كَالصَّيْدِ ثُمَّ بَاقِي مَا قَدْ مُنِعَا}$$

$$\text{بِالْجَمْرَةِ الْأُولَى يَحِلُّ فَاسْمَعَا}$$

280 as is hunting (prohibited), then the other things which are prohibited for him, these are rendered halal at the stoning of the *jamra ul-ula* (the first *jamra*) – so heed (these instructions!

$$\text{وَجَازَ الِاسْتِظْلَالُ بِالْمُرْتَفِع}$$

$$\text{لَا فِي الْمَحَامِلِ وَشُقْدُفٍ فَع}$$

281 It is permitted to shade oneself with something raised (of a fixed nature, above one's head), but not (by means of the roof of) a litter or a *shuqduf* sedan – so take note!

The *'ulama* are of a consensus that the *fidya* compensation is to be paid for removing something noxious out of necessity, although they differ as to whether this obligation is dependent upon someone doing it deliberately, and whether the person who does it deliberately and the one who does it out of forgetfulness are (to be considered in) the same (way).

Malik, Abu Hanifa and ath-Thawri hold (that they are subject to the same judgement) while ash-Shafi'i, in one of his two judgements, and the Dhahiris have said that there is no compensation to be paid for someone who forgets. They are in agreement that it is obligatory on the person who is compelled to shave his head because of illness or when some creature (like lice infests his hair and) causes irritation to his head. The majority hold that if someone in *ihram* indulges in something which has been prohibited him, then he has to pay the *fidya*.

One group have said that there is nothing to pay for paring one's nails, and from Abu Hanifa, in one of his two judgements, that there is nothing to pay unless he trims all his nails. According to Malik, the '*fidya*' in this case, refers to a sacrifice which is carried out by the person owing the *fidya* wherever he wishes and it is not a *hady* sacrifice which may only be made in Makka or Mina. Ash-Shafi'i said that making it good with a (minor) sacrifice (*dam*) or feeding (poor people) is only done in Makka, whereas the fast is done wherever he wishes. The feeding, according to Malik, ash-Shafi'i and Abu Hanifa and their followers is carried out with two *mudds* for each destitute person, according to the *mudd* of the Prophet, may the peace and blessings of Allah be upon him.

This is taken from the *Bidayat al-Mujtahid* of Ibn Rushd al-Hafeed.

The commentator Mayyara said: "The person in *ihram* may not kill wasps or bees, contrary to (the judgement of) Qadi 'Abd al-Wahhab, nor bugs, flies, gnats or fleas, and if he does, then he should feed (people) as he is able – nor (may) lizards (be killed)."

Again the same commentator said: "Notice: first, the gist of Ibn 'Ashir's words is that the prohibited things in *ihram* are six in number, of which the first five may be made good – the first of them by the *jaza'* compensation (for game) and the remaining four by the *fidya* compensation; the sixth is the case of sexual relations with women, and it also invalidates (the hajj), as mentioned above, although if foreplay (only) occurred, then it is made good with a *hady* sacrifice, conditional, that is, upon the specific nature of what occurred, as mentioned earlier; if (this contact occurred) subsequent to a marriage contract, then no *hady* sacrifice is due, nor any *fidya*, but rather only forgiveness from Allah must be sought."

The gist of this and his previous words 'and the obligations which are not (considered) pillars and which may be made good by a minor sacrifice', is that the person who has to make good (some imperfection of the hajj) – either because of omitting something which is not a pillar or doing something which he is demanded to desist from and which does not invalidate (the hajj) is categorised in three ways: the *hady*, the compensation for (killing) game, and the *fidya*. The *fidya* is what becomes due from (wearing) clothing (which is not allowed), from the use of perfume or oil or removing dirt, nails or hair or killing lice. This, in turn, is of three types, the first, the sacrifice (*nusuk*) of a sheep or any (larger animal): Allah, exalted is He, said: *"(the expiation is fasting) or sadaqa or sacrifice (nusuk)."*[1] *Nusuk* is anything (sacrificed) in order to bring one close to Allah, exalted is He, and part of its meaning is thus obedience; secondly, the feeding of sixty destitute people, each with two *mudds*, according to the *mudd* of the Prophet, may the peace and blessings of Allah be upon him; thirdly, fasting three days. He may perform whichever of the three he wishes, whether he is rich or poor, and this (*fidya*) is not specific to a particular time or place – except when he intends the first of the three, namely the *hady*, in which case it is subject to (all) the judgements governing the *hady* other than that he may not eat of it.

Ibn 'Arafa said: "There is a choice in (kind of) compensation to be paid for *fidya* (for removing) something noxious: he may either fast, or feed (the destitute), or may make a sacrifice wherever he wishes with respect to all

---

1 al-Baqara – The Cow: 196

(kinds of noxious things): Allah, exalted is He, has not made specific mention of the location of the *fidya* compensation – and has designated it as a *nusuk*, not a *hady* – and so wherever one performs the sacrifice it is accepted."

Al-Hattab, commenting on the words of Khalil '(it is also prohibited) to cover her face, other than (using a head-covering to) hide it from importune men as long as it is not fixed (with pins or knots)' said: "A woman may cover her face from men, but not (merely) because of the heat or cold; and if she raises the gathered seam of her veil and throws it over her head, she has nothing to make up, as covering her head and wearing sewn clothing (only) necessitates that a *fidya* be paid when this is done for a considerable time and when using clothing to protect (the head or face) from the heat and cold and the like, and there is no harm in allowing the folds of her cloak to drop over her face; however, as for the basket-like device made of woven palm fronds which women attach to their faces and over which they then hang a cloth – the most evident judgement is that *fidya* must be paid for (wearing) it."

Khalil said: "…(*fidya* is not paid) for girding oneself or for carrying (something) out of need or out of poverty, but not for trade." The author of *Mukhtasar al-Wiqar* said (explaining the above): "There is no harm in tightening a cloth around his waist above his waist wrapper if he wants to do something (requiring greater freedom of movement) as long as he does not tie it with a knot – but he should not carry (something merely) out of reluctance to discard it, and if he does, he must pay a *fidya*. What is prohibited in this respect is anything which is not connected to a need arising from the movements involved in *ihram*; and there is no blame attached to anything done out of necessity but the *fidya* remains. There is no harm in his carrying his belongings on his head or placing a rope around them and carrying them on his back, pulling with the rope down over his breast."

Khalil said: "(It is licit to) change his clothing or to sell it, although not to wash it, except if it is ritually impure, in which case (it is washed) with water only."

Al-Mawwaq said: "There is no harm in changing the clothing with which he assumed the *ihram*, or selling it on account of lice which are molesting him or something else."

It is stated in the work of al-Hattab: "Washing it on account of dirt is the same as washing it because of a ritual impurity; and the *muhrim* may use a *miswak* even when full of sap."

Commenting on Khalil's words '(it is licit) to attach to the skin (below the waist wrap) a belt for his money (for his own personal expenses) or to add the (money for the) expenses of another (for safekeeping)' al-Hattab said that it is stated in *at-Tawdih*: "The most likely judgement is that no *fidya* is due as the expenses of the other are part and parcel of his; however, if he attaches the (belt) to his waist wrapper, then the *fidya* is due; and likewise if he attaches it over his waist wrapper when it contains the expenses of another" – and this is taken from al-Mawwaq.

Khalil said: "(and it is licit) to cut open a wound (to extract the pus)... but *fidya* is due for the application of a bandage or dressing the size of a dirham." Khalil then goes on to say: "...(*fidya* is also due for) putting cotton in one's ears or placing card or paper on the temples (as a remedy against headaches)... and it is *makruh* to attach money for one's expenses to one's arm or thigh, or to rest one's head (face down) on a pillow." Al-Jazuli said: "Sleeping on one's face is the sleep of *kuffar*, tyrants and shaytans, and the most evident judgement is that it is prohibited."

Khalil said: "...and cupping without an excuse (is also *makruh*)." Sahnun said: "It is permitted if no hair falls from one's head on account of it." Al-Hattab said: "It is permitted with a valid excuse, and if no hair falls on account of it and no lice are killed, then nothing is due, but otherwise he has to pay the *fidya*. Ibn Basheer, however, has mentioned a judgement to the effect that the *fidya* is indeed due – although the (author) said in *at-Tawdih*: 'but it is an obscure (judgement).' If he kills a lot of lice, then he must pay the *fidya*, otherwise he must feed (someone) with a handful of foodstuff."

Commenting on Khalil's words 'immersing the head (is *makruh*)...' al-Hattab said: "(that is,) for whoever has lice in his hair, otherwise it is not *makruh* for him; and it is permitted for him to wash his head in order to cool it, although it is related of Malik that this is *makruh*, except when absolutely necessary."

Commenting on Khalil's words '(it is also *makruh*) to dry it vigorously (lest one kill lice, etc)' he has also said: "the 'it' here refers to the head, although there is a grammatical mistake (in the text), the pronoun (in Arabic) here being feminine while the word for head is masculine; but (rubbing) elsewhere is not (*makruh*)."

He has also said: "but (it is not *makruh*) to wash one's hands using something to get rid of dirt (i.e. with non-perfumed soap, for example)."

Sheen said that it is stated in *at-Taraz*: "He may wash his hands with hot or cold water, with potash, alkali or soap, or with anything which clears tar and removes its smell; but should avoid anything like fragrant herbs and sweet smelling fruit."

Khalil said: "(It is prohibited to oil the body) like the palm of the hand and the (sole of) the foot." Sheen said: "Whoever oils his foot or palm (using an oil) which does not contain perfume for a valid reason, then there are two (different) judgements as to the obligation to pay the *fidya*." Then he goes on to say: "If he oils his feet or hands because of splits (in the skin), then he does not have to pay (any *fidya*)." Khalil said: "likewise (*fidya* is also due) if someone covers his face when sleeping." However, al-Mawwaq said: "If the *muhrim* pulls a blanket or cover over his face while asleep, but then pulls it off immediately on waking, he does not have to pay compensation – even if it lay (over his face) for a considerable time; likewise, if he sleeps and a man covers his head or puts perfume on it, but then he pulls it off or removes the perfume (on waking), then he does not have to pay compensation – but *fidya* is due from the person who did this."

Commenting on Khalil's words 'If a *muhrim* shaves the head of someone who is not in *ihram*, he should give food (to the poor)' Sheen said: "unless he is making sure that there are no lice, in which case he does not have to pay any food." However, it is stated in al-Hattab: "Ibn al-Qasim said: 'I consider that he should give some food away as a *sadaqa*.'"

Khalil said: "and cutting a nail (merely for aesthetic reasons) – but not for removing something harmful (from one's finger, like a broken nail) – there is a handful of food (to pay)." Ibn al-Qasim said: "I have not heard of any amount more than a handful of (food)stuff – for doing something less serious than removing something injurious" and he has also said, regarding (killing) one or more lice, (that) a handful (of food is to be paid), and a handful (*hafnah*) refers to one hand(ful), (unlike the *mudd* which is two handfuls) – and this is taken from al-Mawwaq.

Commenting on Khalil's words 'likewise, (a handful of food is to be paid) if a *muhrim* shaves a companion (*muhrim*) at the site of cupping, unless the person (doing the shaving) ascertains that no lice are to be found in this (particular place on the body)' Sheen said: "Al-Mawwaq stated regarding this matter: 'If the *muhrim* is compelled to have cupping done, then it is permitted for another *muhrim* to shave the place to be cupped and to cup him if he ascertains that he will not kill lice, otherwise it is not (permitted), and the *fidya* is to be paid by the person who has it done to him.'" Khalil also said: "the *fidya* is paid when something is done merely as a act of embellishment or vanity or when something troublesome or annoying is removed (like trimming one's moustache) ... and (if many *fidyas* are due), there is only one to pay as long as the person was under the impression it was permitted and as long as he did the various things demanding a *fidya* immediately after each other (perfuming himself and cutting his nails, for example, such that it appears as one act)."

Al-Mawwaq, commenting on the words of Khalil said: "If he does (various) things necessitating that the *fidya* be paid, for example, he puts on (normal sewn clothes), perfumes or shaves and trims his nails, then if these (actions) occurred on the same occasion or soon after each other, then there is (just) one *fidya* to pay – as stated (by Khalil)."

It is stated in the work of al-Hattab: "Branch: what makes the *fidya* (count as) one (single *fidya*) is his intention to do *all* the things necessitating the payment of a *fidya* he needs to do (in one go) – and this has been stated by al-Lakhmi."

Commenting on Khalil's words '(only one *fidya* is to be paid too) if he intends to repeat such (actions after a while)' al-Hattab said: "that is, if anyone does any of the prohibited things while in *ihram* and makes the intention to do it (again) after this – and indeed repeats it – then the *fidya* is one (and the same) for this, even if a (considerable) time elapses after the first."

Commenting on Khalil's words '(paying the *fidya* for) wearing (normal) clothes is conditional upon one deriving some benefit (like protection from) the heat or the cold' al-Hattab said: "The things or actions necessitating the *fidya* are conditional upon the *muhrim* acquiring some benefit from them; and benefit is only to be had from some of these things when they are done for a considerable time (like wearing) clothing (for example) – for no *fidya* is to be paid unless there is benefit (to be gained by protection) from the heat and cold (and this can only happen if the person keeps them on his person)." Al-Hattab said: "(*fidya* is to be paid) if the (action) lasts (some time), like a day, (for example)." Ibn al-Hattab goes on to say: "Notice: if he wears (clothes) and does not acquire benefit (through protection from) the heat or cold and his wearing these (clothes) does not last a day or near a day, then he has no *fidya* to pay" – and there is no doubt that 'almost a day' should be considered the same as 'a day.'"

Commenting on Khalil's statement 'but he has not committed a wrong action if he does it with a valid excuse' al-Mawwaq said: "It is stated by al-Kafi: 'No one should do anything which he has been commanded to avoid without some pressing need – just because he finds (paying) the *fidya* easy – for a licence only exists in the case of pressing need.'" It is stated in the work of al-Hattab: "that is, the reason for the obligation to pay the *fidya* is not that a wrong action has been committed but that some benefit has been had; however, sometimes he has a valid excuse and may derive benefit (from the thing in question) and sometimes he is prohibited (from enjoying this benefit) – that is, in the case of someone who has no valid excuse, and Allah knows best."

Al-Hattab said: "There is no objection to the *muhrim* slaughtering any (sacrificial animal including) sheep, cattle or camels – this is transmitted by Ibn Farhun and others. The author of *at-Taraz* said: 'Abu Qurra has narrated from Malik, regarding the *hady* animal, that if he slaughters – *dhabaha* (a sheep or cow) or slaughters – *nahara* – (a camel), in the Haram, then (either) is accepted of him, and this is also transmitted by Abu'l-Hasan.'"

Malik was asked as to whether a *muhrim* may scratch his boils so much that blood comes out and he replied "Yes, there is no harm in this." Muhammad ibn Rushd said: "as far as I know, there is no difference of opinion that this is permitted." Khalil said: "(it is permitted to) open up a boil and scratch what one cannot see (on one's back, for example) as long as done gently."

Our noble lady 'A'isha, may Allah be pleased with her, was asked as to whether the *muhrim* may scratch himself and she replied: "Yes, he may scratch and may do it vigorously" – she also added: "If my hands were bound and I could only do it with my feet, then I would do so" – this is extracted from *Mawarid an-Najah*, a commentary on the *Risala*. It is also stated: "given that such a need often occurs and cannot be avoided, then it may be overlooked on account of this need, and the obligation to pay the *fidya* is removed."

I say: "This is an important principle. Related to this principle is permission for the *muhrim* to pour water over his head and feet on account of the heat, or for (some other reason) other than the heat. It is related in the transmission of Abu Uways that Malik granted the *muhrim* licence to raise something above his head as protection from the cold and for him to clean dirt from beneath his nails – (that is) he does not have to pay a *fidya*. However, it is *makruh* for the *muhrim* to enter the public baths (*hammam*) for this would imply he is going to clean himself and remove dirt (from all over his body). If he does nevertheless enter – and if he rubs himself down and cleans himself of the dirt – then he has to pay the *fidya*. Also included here is shaving one's moustache, trimming one's nails, shaving the pubic hairs and plucking one's armpits."

The *fidya* is the "sacrifice of a sheep or a larger animal, or the feeding of six destitute people, each with two *mudds* (as in the case of the *mudd* payable for the *kaffara*), or fasting three days, even the days of Mina, and this (*fidya*) is not specific to time or place."

Khalil stated: "(It is *makruh* for the *muhrim* to lie) face down into the pillow, to wear dyed clothes if (the person in question is of such rank that he is) followed (by others), or to smell (aromatic plants) like basil… and to look at oneself in the mirror; and it is prohibited to remove nails, hair or dirt – except when washing the hands with something like soap."

Khalil said: "(no *fidya* is due) when locusts are covering everywhere as long as the *muhrim* tries his best to avoid killing them; otherwise, (if the locusts are not everywhere, or he has not taken care to avoid killing them), he must pay the compensatory value (in foodstuffs to be decided by the Qadi, that is, if more than ten), while if one (to ten in number), a handful (of foodstuffs), and (the *muhrim* must also pay even if he has killed one while turning over) in his sleep; likewise, a handful (of foodstuffs) is due (for the killing) of worms (and ants and the like). The compensation is obligatory for killing such (animals) even if this is done out of extreme hunger, or out of ignorance, forgetfulness (of being in *ihram*) – and the reparation is to be paid each time such an act is repeated."

It is stated in the work of al-Mawwaq: "Ibn al-Hajib said: 'If the locusts cover the road or path, then the obligation to pay compensation is removed if one tries one's best to avoid killing them.' This detail is not mentioned by Ibn 'Arafa. Also related (to this subject is the judgement that) any locusts found in the Haram are not to be hunted – neither by someone who is permitted to hunt nor by someone who is not. Ibn al-Hajib also said: 'Locusts should not be caught in the Haram of Madina. If however the *muhrim* cannot avoid (treading on) them because of their great number, then Ibn Wahb narrated from Malik that no compensation is to be made. Malik also said on an occasion before this: "If someone steps on a fly, he should pay compensation by feeding people, even if he was unable to avoid doing it, and likewise in the case of ants and worms and other such creatures." The compensation is to be paid in the case of killing them, and even if done out of hunger, then he is still responsible for paying compensation for them.'"

Ibn al-Hajib said: "(whether done out of) ignorance, intentionally, neglect or need, it is all the same regarding the *fidya*, and the person who forgets is like the person who does it intentionally with regard to the obligation to pay the compensation, but not regarding the fact that it is (essentially a) wrong action – for in his case (i.e. the person who forgets) it is not held against him."

Commenting on Khalil's words 'and sexual intercourse and its foreplay (invalidates the hajj in all cases)' Sheen said: "It is clear what is meant here." It is related from al-Mawwaq that "If the *muhrim* reneges (on his deen), then he invalidates his *ihram* and does not need to make it up later. Khalil said: 'It is also invalidated in all cases if one deliberately causes ejaculation of sperm, even if by way of looking (a while at a woman) – that is, it invalidates it in all cases before the standing at 'Arafa – if it occurs before the *tawaf al-ifada* or after it or before it on the Day of Sacrifice; otherwise, he has (only) the *hady* to sacrifice.' Malik said: 'If the *muhrim* looks (at a woman) – intending to experience sexual pleasure in doing so – such that sperm is ejaculated, then his hajj is invalidated; but if he does not look with excessive intent and does not prolong his (regard) but nevertheless has an ejaculation, then his hajj is complete and he owes a *hady*.' If sexual relations occur after the standing on the Day of Sacrifice, but he has not performed the stoning and he has not done the *tawaf al-ifada*, then the well known judgement is that it invalidates (the hajj); and whoever has intercourse after the Day of Sacrifice before he performs the stoning and the *tawaf al-ifada*, his hajj is not invalidated and he must do the '*umra* and sacrifice two *hadys*. The person who has sexual relations after the stoning and before the *tawaf al-ifada* has to make a *hady* sacrifice and perform the '*umra*."

Al-Hattab said: "He said in the *Mudawwana*: 'If the *muhrim* deliberately persists in recalling (something sexually) stimulating such that he has an ejaculation, or he plays with his penis and has an ejaculation, or he touches (a woman), kisses (her) or has body contact (with her), or persists in looking (at her) until he has an ejaculation, then he invalidates his hajj; likewise in the case of a female *muhrim* if she does what the worst kind of women do who play with themselves such that she has an emission.'"

USEFUL POINT: it is stated in the work of al-Hattab: "Some of the later ('*ulama*) have concluded from this that masturbating with the hand is haram" – and then he goes on to say: "There is no doubt as to its being prohibited."

Ibn 'Arafa also said on this matter: "Deliberately causing an ejaculation is considered the same as sexual intercourse while wet dreams are disregarded." Khalil said: "likewise (a *hady* is also due) for an emission of pre-seminal fluid, or by kissing (on the mouth) – pre-seminal fluid and kissing both necessitate the sacrifice of a *hady* just as extended foreplay and excessive bodily contact both necessitate the *hady*; however, a minimum of (contact) – other than kissing – as long as there is no emission of pre-seminal fluid, does not (necessitate the *hady*), although it is (considered) a wrong action."

Mayyara said: "Know that the three types of (minor) sacrifices of the hajj – the *hady*, the voluntary sacrifice and the one made because of a vow – may be classified into four types depending on whether the person giving it may eat of it after slaughter or whether he is forbidden from eating of it:

1. As for any *hady* which becomes obligatory because of some defect in the hajj or '*umra* as well as any *hady* made on account of a vow for which he has become liable – as long as he has not named the destitute (as the recipients) or has not made an intention (to give it) to them – then he may eat of these two types before or after (the official place of sacrifice at Mina);

2. Whatever has been named for the destitute or intended for them is not to

be eaten, neither before (the place of sacrifice) or after;

3. That which may be eaten of before (the place of sacrifice), not after – that is, the compensatory (sacrifice) made for the hunting and the *fidya* (sacrifice) made (for killing or removing something) injurious or troublesome, if it is paid as a *hady* or (the sacrifice) one has become liable for on account of a vow (undertaken) for the benefit of the destitute if named specifically for them or intended;

4. That which may be eaten of after (the place of sacrifice) but not before it, that is, the voluntary *hady*, the *hady* on account of a vow with a *specific* (sacrificial) animal in mind – as long as it has not been named explicitly for (the benefit of) the destitute or by way of an intention."

In the *Mawarid an-Najah*, the commentary on the *Risala*, it states: "He said in the *'Utbiya*: 'He was asked about a woman who, intending (to perform) the *'umra*, was prescribed a (medicinal) drink to delay her menstruation – which she then drank' and he replied: "This is not correct" and he considered it *makruh*. Ibn Rushd said: "He disliked it for fear she would suffer some bodily harm from it; however, Allah will excuse her if she has a valid excuse and will give her (a reward) if she has a (sincere) intention – for whoever intends a good action and is prevented from it by an excuse acceptable to Allah, exalted is He, then Allah will record the corresponding reward for him, Allah willing." The smelling of perfumes in general is prohibited although there is no *fidya* to pay on 'masculine' perfumes (which emit a scent but do not leave any trace on the person who touches them), like basil, rose and jasmine, nor in smelling the 'feminine' perfumes (which do leave a trace), like musk, camphor, saffron and the (essence extracted from the yellow flower known) as *wars*.'" This has been extracted from al-Mawwaq.

Commenting on Khalil's words 'It is forbidden to cut what is growing', al-Hattab said: "It is forbidden to cut what is growing in the Haram, that is, those (plants) which grow by themselves – and even those cultivated by people, like the cultivation of wild greens and vegetables, acacias and the like. The most evident meaning of the general import of the words of the author (Khalil) is that the gathering of fodder in the Haram is forbidden; although it has been declared *makruh* in the *Mudawwana*, he has also said in the latter (work) that it is permitted to pasture (animals) on the grass and trees in the Harams of Makka and Madina but that it is *makruh* to gather fodder in the Haram, whether in *ihram* or not, for fear that one might kill the creatures (to be found in the grass); and likewise in the case of the *muhrim* out of *ihram*. However, if there is no danger of killing these creatures, then they do not have to pay any compensation. As for gathering fresh herbage or prodding trees or shrubs with a stick to bring down leaves and broken branches, the most likely judgement is that it is so disliked as to be forbidden."

It is also stated in the work of al-Hattab:

"NOTICE:

1. Sanad said: 'As for the cutting of grass, we do not forbid it for the animals (themselves), but for other than (animals) we do – that is, when (people) store it and clear the land of it;

2. What may be understood from his words 'clear the land of it' is that it is forbidden, that is, if there is no specific benefit in it; however if one wishes to build in a place or plant something there, this is permitted.' At-Tadali said: 'There is a difference of opinion concerning some of the exceptions to the general (prohibitions associated with the Haram): (the medicinal plant known as) *idhkhir*, senna leaves, the bush used as a *miswak*, (using a) staff to prod (trees or bushes), cutting down (plants) to build, cutting down to repair a wall' – and these have been mentioned by Ibn Farhun in his *Manasik*';

3. It may be understood from the above that picking the fruit of the trees which grow by themselves is permitted;

4. It may be understood by the author's words 'those (plants) which grow by themselves' that it is forbidden to cut them even if they have been cultivated (by man) – as al-Baji has explained. The author of *al-Jawahir* and Ibn al-Hajib have mentioned that this is the (judgement of the) *madhhab*, and this is how we have understood (Sanad's) first point – and for this reason the author, (Ibn Farhun), said in his *Manasik*: 'likewise, if it has been planted, even if it is not cared for (afterwards).'"

Our grandfather, Ahmad ibn al-Basheer ash-Shinqeeti said in *Mawarid an-Najah wa Masadir al-Falah 'ala ar-Risala*: "He has included in his *Manasik*, as Ibn Mu'alla has done, the prohibition of removing any of the earth from the two Harams – as well as their stones, plants, bushes, branches or pots made of their clay – and depositing them elsewhere. Whoever takes any of these things is obliged to return them." His following (the judgements of) Ibn as-Salah and Ibn Farhun in this show that he is acting in accordance with the principles of the *madhhab*. However, there is a need to harmonise (apparent inconsistencies regarding certain judgements) – and among the matters about which there is uncertainty is taking Zamzam water to other countries. It has been transmitted that he, may the peace and blessings of Allah be upon him, asked 'Umar ibn Suhayl for some Zamzam water and he sent him some of it. Another matter (of apparent inconsistency is) that they consider it *makruh* to bring in earth and stones from anywhere outside of the haram into the haram – although most of the stones of the Ka'ba are from outside the Haram; moreover Malik approved the purchase of the *kiswa* (cloth covering the Ka'ba – from outside of Makka). Another such matter of ambiguity is the reply of Malik to the person who had asked whether he should return the stones – which he had taken from the Mosque of the Messenger of Allah, may the peace and blessings of Allah be upon him, and become attached to – back to the mosque. He replied: "No, and I would permit (you) to throw them away." Then someone asked: "Abu 'Abdallah! People say that they cry out when removed from it (and continue doing so) until they are returned to it" and he replied: "Let them cry out until their throats are gasping for air." Then he asked: "Do they have throats" and he said: "How else could they cry out?" – and so he was obliged to consider what he had mentioned about their crying out as invalid. It is also narrated that a man brought pebbles from Makka to the Maghrib and that they would cry out during the night, preventing him from sleeping, until he returned them. Again it is related that when Amir al-Qarmati – who had commanded that the Black Stone be taken out (of the Ka'ba) and carried off – died, the earth would cast him out every time they tried to bury him and that only when they had returned the Stone to the Noble Ka'ba could he be buried undisturbed – this is stated *in Mawarid al-Hajj*.

There are thirteen creatures in all that the *muhrim* is permitted to kill in the haram: six may be sacrificed for food and seven may be killed if they are causing harm or injury.

As for those which are slaughtered for food, they consist of three (classes of) animals, namely camels, cows and sheep/goats, and three birds, namely, ducks, geese and chickens.

As for those which are killed to prevent them causing harm or injury, they consisit of three (kinds) which fly, namely, crows, vultures (/kites) and wasps (/hornets) – although there is a difference of opinion regarding this latter (type); and three which are to be found on land, namely scorpions, snakes and mice (/rats). There is also one (type of creature) which fits either category, namely, wild dogs: if killed to prevent them causing harm or injury, then this is permitted, but if killed merely because one considers they may be killed with impunity, then a *fidya* must be killed. This has been taken from al-Hattab.

Khalil said: "If someone other than the person who owes the garlanded sacrificial animal slaughters it, then it is accepted, even if he makes the intention to slaughter it for himself, that is, only when done out of error." It is stated in the work of al-Hattab: "If someone else slaughters the *hady*, then it is accepted of the person he is doing it for, if done out of error, but if done for himself in contravention of what he was supposed to do, then it is not accepted, irrespective of whether the other person entrusted him to do it or not. However, Abu Qurra related from Malik that such (a *hady*) is accepted of the person who slaughters although he has to pay the price of it in compensation." The *madhhab* of the *Mudawwana* is that in the case of companions (on a journey) who make a mistake – one person slaughtering the *hady* of another and vice versa – then any such (*hady* slaughtered in this way) is accepted of the person, even if it is without his permission – and this is stated by Ibn al-Hajib. It is stated also in the work of al-Hattab that: "something similar is stated in the *Mudawwana*: if he slaughters the *hady* of someone other than his companion it is accepted of him, even if it is without his permission." Khalil, too, said in *at-Tawdih*: "and something similar is stated in the *Mudawwana*." Ibn al-Hattab also said: "Branch: there is no harm in the *muhrim* slaughtering any (of the above mentioned) animals – this has been transmitted by Ibn Farhun and others."

UMRA

وَسُنَّةَ الْعُمْرَةِ فَافْعَلْهَا كَمَا

حَجّ وَفِي التَّنْعِيمِ نَدْباً أَحْرِمَا

282 Perform the sunna of the *'umra* as the (first part of the) hajj. It is recommended to put on the *ihram* at at-Tan'eem.

وَإِثْرَ سَعْيِكَ احْلِقَنْ وَقَصِّرَا

تَحِلُّ مِنْهَا وَالطَّوَافَ كَثِّرَا

283 Immediately following your *sa'y*, shave (your head) or trim (your hair), leave the state of *ihram* and perform the *tawaf* frequently

مَا دُمْتَ فِي مَكَّةَ وَارْعَ الْحُرْمَةَ

لِجَانِبِ الْبَيْتِ وَزِدْ فِي الْخِدْمَةَ

284 as long as you are in Makka. Take care to observe the sanctity (of Makka) as well as the House, increase your (acts of) service (to Allah ta'ala)

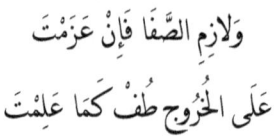

285 and maintain the *salat* in *jama'a*. When you are resolved to leave, make the *tawaf* (in the same manner) as you have learned of above.

These lines do not need any explanation as they are clear.

Mayyara said in his commentary: "Here he is informing us, may Allah have mercy on him, that the *'umra* is a sunna *mu'akkada* (i.e. on which particular emphasis is placed) once in a lifetime – and this is indeed the well known judgement; and that it is recommended that the *ihram* for it take place at-Tan'eem. This is based on his ordering, may the peace and blessings of Allah be upon him, 'Abd ar-Rahman Ibn Abi Bakr to go to 'A'isha, the wife of the Prophet, may the peace and blessings of Allah be upon him, and have her make the *ihram* at at-Tan'eem for the *'umra*."

(Mayyara) has described the two *miqats* – i.e. the *miqat* of location and that of time – and has stated that the form of this *ihram* and the actions associated with it are the same as the hajj – up to where he says: "Know that the required actions in the *'umra* are of three types: pillars which cannot be made up (if not done), obligations which can be made good and sunnas for which nothing is due if left out. The pillars are the *ihram*, the *tawaf* and the *sa'y*; the obligations are made good with the making of a minor sacrifice, as on the hajj."

(Ibn Rushd) stated in the *Bidaya*: "Ibn 'Umar narrated that his father said: 'A Bedouin Arab with a fair face and (dressed in) white clothes came into the presence of the Messenger of Allah, may the peace and blessings of Allah be upon him, and asked: "What is Islam, Messenger of Allah?", may the peace and blessings of Allah be upon him, and he replied: "that you bear witness that there is no god but Allah and that Muhammad is the Messenger of Allah, that you establish the *salat* and pay the *zakat*, that you fast Ramadan, that you perform the hajj and *'umra* and that you make the *ghusl* (to purify yourself) from the state of *janaba*."'" As for the obligation of the *'umra*, 'Ali, may Allah ennoble his face, Ibn 'Umar and Ibn 'Abbas affirmed it. Ad-Daraqutni narrated – that 'Abdallah ibn 'Umar used to say: "There is no one from the creation of Allah for whom the hajj and *'umra* are not obligatory – when they are able to find the means to get there, and whoever does anything extra, then this is of benefit for him, and (rewarded as) a voluntary act."

Among those who hold that it is an obligation from amongst the Tabi'un are 'Ata, Tawus, Mujahid, al-Hasan, Ibn Sirin, ash-Sha'bi, Sa'id ibn Jubayr, Abu Barda, Masruq, 'Abdallah ibn Shaddad, ash-Shafi'i, Ahmad, Ishaq, Abu 'Ubayd, and Ibn Jahm from the Malikis.

Malik considered it *makruh* to repeat it in the same year as he, may the peace and blessings of Allah be up on him, did not repeat it in one year, and it was also considered *makruh* by a group of the early generations. Malik said: "The *'umra* is a sunna *mu'akkada* (upon which particular emphasis is laid) but it is not a *fard* obligation like the hajj." Indeed more emphasis is laid on this (sunna) than the *witr salat*, and the person who begins it, is commanded to complete it, although it is permitted (to leave off doing it) according to Mutarrif and Ibn al-Majishun. Ibn Habib said: "There is no harm in doing it once a month" while Abu'l-Hasan and others have said: "'A'isha, may Allah be pleased with her, neglected to do the *'umra* for seven years, then she made up (all of) them in one year."

It is narrated from 'Ali, may Allah ennoble his face, and may Allah be pleased with him that (it may be done) once a month. It is narrated of Ibn 'Umar that he made one thousand *'umras*, performed sixty hajjs, mounted (fighters) on a thousand horses in the way of Allah and that he freed a thousand slaves.

Al-Lakhmi said: "I do not consider that anyone can be prevented from performing any act of worship which brings him closer to Allah, or from making a good (action) more frequently somewhere when there is no text forbidding it."

Malik said: "There is no harm in performing the *'umra* before the hajj, and whoever does the *'umra* with the hajj, then there is no harm in his doing the *'umra* at the beginning of the year."

It is stated in *al-Muwatta'* from 'Uthman, may Allah be pleased with him, that if he did the *'umra* he would not dismount from his saddle until he returned (to Madina), and Allah knows best.[1]

In a hadith he said, may the peace and blessings of Allah be upon him: "The hajj is an act of strenuous exertion (*jihad*) and the *'umra* is a voluntary act" – this is related by at-Tirmidhi who considered it a *hasan* hadith, while in other narrations it is considered *hasan sahih*, although an-Nawawi questioned whether it is *sahih*.

It is stated in *Sahih Muslim* from Sa'id ibn al-Musayyab who said: "When 'Uthman and 'Ali met at 'Usfan and 'Uthman prohibited the *tamattu'* (hajj), and the *'umra* (that is, the hajj and *'umra* together), 'Ali, may Allah ennoble his face said: 'What do you mean about a matter which the the Messenger of Allah

---

1 *al-Muwatta'* 786, p. 327, az-Zurqani, vol.2, where the text reads "he would sometimes not dismount."

performed, may the peace and blessings of Allah be upon him; do you prohibit it?' and 'Uthman replied: 'Leave us in this matter' and he said: 'I cannot leave you.' Thus when 'Ali saw this he embarked upon both (the *'umra* and hajj)."

It is also narrated that Mutarrif related that 'Imran ibn Husayn said: "I will relate a hadith to you for it may well be that Allah will grant you benefit by it – that the Messenger of Allah, may the peace and blessings of Allah be upon him, combined the hajj and the *'umra*. He did not prohibit it right up to his death, and nothing in the Qur'an was revealed about this."

It is narrated in a *marfu* hadith from 'Ata from Ibn 'Abbas that he would stop saying the *talbiya* on the *'umra* when greeting the Black Stone – this is related by at-Tirmidhi who considered it *sahih*, and is stated in *Muntaqa al-Akhbar*.

In the *tafsir* of al-Qurtubi it is stated: "It is related in a *marfu* hadith from Muhammad Ibn Sirin from Zayd ibn Thabit that the Messenger of Allah, may the peace and blessings of Allah be upon him, said: 'The hajj and *'umra* are two *fard* obligations, and there is no harm in starting by whichever you wish.'"

Malik used to say: "The *'umra* is a sunna and we do no know anyone who has given licence to abandon it", and this is the judgement of an-Nakha'i and the *ashab ar-ra'y* – as related by Ibn al-Mundhir.

Some of the people of Qazwin and the Baghdadis related that Abu Hanifa considered it an obligation like the hajj and that it was a sunna *thabita* – an obligatory sunna.

Ad-Daraqutni related from Jabir ibn 'Abdallah who said: "A man asked the Messenger of Allah, may the peace and blessings of Allah be upon him, as to whether the *salat*, the *zakat*, and the hajj were obligatory and he replied: 'Yes.' Then he asked him about the *'umra* and whether it was obligatory and he replied: 'No, but if you do the *'umra*, then there is benefit (in it) for you.'" Mention of this occurs where he comments on the words of Allah, exalted is He: "*and perform the hajj and 'umra for Allah.*"[1]

He said: "Part of the perfection of its performance is that one assumes the *ihram* from the localities where your family (reside). This has been related from 'Ali, may Allah ennoble his face, from 'Umar ibn al-Khattab, may Allah be pleased with him, Sa'd ibn Abi Waqqas. What has been related by 'Ali ibn Abi Talib and also performed by 'Imran ibn Husayn – with respect to entering *ihram* before the *miqats* established by the Messenger of Allah, may the peace and blessings of Allah be upon him, was also held to by 'Abdallah ibn Mas'ud and a group of the early generation. It has been established that 'Umar assumed the *ihram* from Ilya while al-Aswad, 'Alqama, 'Abd ar-Rahman and Abu Ishaq

---

1 al-Baqara – The Cow: 197

assumed the *ihram* from their houses. Ash-Shafi'i also granted a licence in this."

The Messenger of Allah, may the peace and blessings of Allah be upon him, said: "One *'umra* to the next is *kaffara* – an expiation – for any (wrong action committed) between them and the only reward for a hajj which is performed properly is the Garden."

He, may the peace and blessings of Allah be upon him, made *'umra* four times: the *'umra* of Hudaybiyya in Dhu'l-Qa'da, the *'umra* in the following year, the *'umra* of Ji'rana and the *'umra* combined with his hajj; and a single hajj.

It is recorded in al-Bukhari that he, may the peace and blessings of Allah be upon him, said to a woman of the Ansar: "When Ramadan comes, perform the *'umra* during it – for the *'umra* in Ramadan is a hajj" – or words to this effect.

He said in *al-Fath* that Muslim has narrated that: "An *'umra* in (Ramadan) is equal to a hajj."

He has also said in *al-Fath*, narrating from Ibn 'Abbas, that the Messenger of Allah, may the peace and blessings of Allah be upon him, said: "Umm Saleem, an *'umra* in Ramadan equals a hajj with me." Ibn Kathir said in his *tafsir* that he, may the peace and blessings of Allah be upon him, said to Umm Hani': "An *'umra* in Ramadan is equal to a hajj with me."

Further, he said in *Fath al-Bari*: "The point of the matter is that he is letting her know that the *'umra* in Ramadan is equal in reward to the hajj – not that it stands instead of it or that the obligation (to perform it) is removed – for there is a consensus that the performance of the *'umra* is not accepted as a substitute of the *fard* obligation of hajj."

At-Tirmidhi has transmitted from Ishaq ibn Rahway that the meaning of the hadith is similar to what has been transmitted regarding (Sura) Ikhlas – Sincerity (which begins with the words) "Say: 'He is Allah, Absolute Oneness'" – namely that this (sura) equals a third of the Qur'an.

Ibn al-'Arabi said that "The hadith regarding the *'umra* is *sahih*. It is a (special) gift from Allah and a blessing: the *'umra* attains the rank of hajj when joined to Ramadan."

Ibn al-Jawzi said: "The reward for an action increases in proportion to the increase in the excellence of the (particular moment or) time, just as it is increased by the presence of the heart and by the sincerity of one's intention" – this he has stated after mentioning the most likely interpretations of the hadith and that the most evident judgement is that it may be understood in a general sense.

BRANCH: he, may the peace and blessings of Allah be upon him, only performed the *'umra* during the months of hajj (i.e. Shawwal, Dhu'l-Qa'da and the first ten days of Dhu'l-Hijja), although the excellence of *'umra* in Ramadan is well established. (It is) most excellent for others – rather than the Prophet, may the peace and blessings of Allah be upon him, although what he did, may the peace and blessings of Allah be upon him, was most excellent for him. The author of *al-Huda* said: "His being preoccupied, may the peace and blessings of Allah be upon him, with other than the *'umra* in Ramadan was out of his concern to avoid hardship for his *umma* – if he had performed the *'umra* in Ramadan, then the people would have endeavoured to do it (too) – despite the difficulty associated with joining the *'umra* with the fast. Sometimes he would desist from doing certain actions, despite wanting to perform them – out of fear that they would be regarded as *fard* obligations for his *umma* and an (added) hardship for them."

Al-Qarafi said in his *Faruq*: "Giving preference to one act of worship over another is by virtue of the *totality* of what is contained in it – for it may be that that which is surpassed in excellence (by another act of worship) is itself characterised by something of excellence which is not to be found in the latter. The *jihad*, for example, contains the special reward of the *shahada* (the witnessing to Allah, exalted is He, in death) while the *salat* – which is superior to it (as a whole) – is not endowed with this (special reward). Indeed, hajj is superior to the military expedition (raiding parties); moreover, the hajj contains *kaffara* – an obliteration of both major and minor wrong actions. It has been narrated in the hadith that: 'Whoever performs the hajj of this House, who does not (violate it) by having sexual intercourse and who does not do anything to corrupt it, then he will emerge (freed) of his wrong actions as the day his mother gave birth to him.' Thus it (has the characteristic of being able to) remove all wrong actions and the evil consequences of one's wrong actions whereas the *salat* does not possess this characteristic – despite its being superior (in general) to the hajj. This is because it is possible for one (act of worship) which is surpassed in superiority (by another) to contain some (characteristic) which is not to be found in that which is superior to it (in its totality)." Ibn al-'Aziz and others have mentioned that there is an *ijma'* to the effect that the major wrong actions can only be expiated by *tawba*. However, the most manifest meaning of what has been transmitted is that the contrary is indicated – in particular the hadith: "Surely Allah, glorious is He, has forgiven the people of 'Arafa and has Himself taken over responsibility for the consequences (of their wrong actions)" – and this is a *sahih* hadith. Thus the *'ulama* have interpreted it as having a particular meaning for a particular occasion. This is stated in *Mawarid an-Najah*.

It is stated in al-Madani 'Ali Ganun's commentary that: "it is recommended that whoever intends the *'umra* should leave by his *miqat* – and this is based on what is stated in *an-Nawadir* and (by what) al-Jilab said, namely: 'When performing the *'umra* from the *miqat*, it is better (to perform it) from the *miqats* of al-Ji'rana and at-Tan'eem.'"

Al-Ji'rana was the nickname of Lareeta bint Sa'd, and it is she who is referred to in the words of Allah, exalted is He: "*do not be like a woman who spoils the thread she has spun (by unravelling it after it is strong).*"[1] Al-Qurtubi commented on this *ayat* saying that she was stupid and that she would unravel it every time she had spun it.

At-Tan'eem is a well known place outside of Makka at a distance of four (Arabic) miles in the direction of Madina al-Munawwara. It is in the middle of the area outside of the haram. It is termed 'Tan'eem' as the mountain to the right of the entrance is called Na'im, the one to the left is called Mun'im and the Wadi (there) is called Nu'man.

---

1 an-Nahl – The Bee: 92

In the name of Allah, All-Merciful, Most Merciful
O Allah May the peace and blessings be on our Lord, Muhammad and on his Family and Companions.

Visiting our Chief and Master, Muhammad ibn 'Abdallah, the Messenger of Allah

may the peace and blessings of Allah be upon him

Ibn 'Ashir said:

وَسِرْ لِقَبْرِ الْمُصْطَفَى بِأَدَبْ

وَنِيَّةٍ تَجِبْ لِكُلِّ مَطْلَبْ

286 Go to the tomb of Mustafa, the Chosen One, with *adab* and (a clear) intention and your every request will be answered.

سَلِّمْ عَلَيْهِ ثُمَّ زِدْ لِلصِّدِّيقْ

ثُمَّ إِلَى عُمَرَ نِلْتَ التَّوْفِيقْ

287 Greet him, and then go to (Abu Bakr) as-Siddiq, then to 'Umar, and you will have success!

وَاعْلَمْ بِأَنَّ ذَا الْمَقَامَ يُسْتَجَابْ

فِيهِ الدُّعَا فَلَا تَمَلَّ مِنْ طِلَابْ

288 Know that *du'as* are answered at this station, and so do not tire from asking.

$$\text{وَسَلْ شَفَاعَةً وَخَتْماً حَسَنَا}$$

$$\text{وَعَجِّلِ الْأَوْبَةَ إِذْ نِلْتَ الْمُنَا}$$

289 Ask for intercession and a good seal (on death), and hurry to return since you have obtained your desire.

$$\text{وَادْخُلْ ضُحىً وَاصْحَبْ هَدِيَّةَ السُّرُورْ}$$

$$\text{إِلَى الْأَقَارِبِ وَمَنْ بِكَ يَدُورْ}$$

290 Make your arrival in the morning and bring gifts to (gladden the hearts of) relatives and those living around you.

Mayyara said: "It is recommended that when the person on hajj leaves Makka he leave by Kuda and that his intention, destination and all his purpose be to pay him a visit, may the peace and blessings of Allah be upon him, and to visit his mosque and the adjacent area; that (the intention be) purely for him, without combining it (with any other motive) – for it is he, may the peace and blessings of Allah be upon him, who is followed (by all) and who is not a follower himself, and it is he who is the very summit of the whole purpose (of creation). Visiting him, may the peace and blessings of Allah be upon him, is a sunna about which there is unanimous agreement and is an (aspect of) excellence which is desirable (for all).

The person paying the visit should increase his saying of the *salat* on the Prophet, may the peace and blessings of Allah be upon him, on the way there and should declare *'Allahu akbar'* when reaching the top of any elevation and send further blessings on him. He should purify himself, wear his best clothes, apply perfume and renew his *tawba*. Then he should walk on foot and on reaching the mosque, begin by making the (two) *rak'ats* if the time for such is permitted; otherwise he should begin by visiting the noble tomb, may the best blessings and peace be on the one lying there. His *rak'ats* should be made in the *mihrab* of the Prophet, may the peace and blessings of Allah be upon him, if he is able, or in the Rawda or some other place. Then he should approach the noble tomb and assume the qualities of humility, tranquillity, submission, poverty and need. He should feel that he is actually standing in front of him, may the peace and blessings of Allah be upon him – for there is no difference (in the reality of his presence) between (the time) he was alive and (that) after his death. He should begin by greeting him with *salams*, may the peace and blessings be upon him." Malik said: "He should say:

السَّلَامُ عَلَيْكَ أَيُّهَا النَّبِيِّ وَرَحْمَةُ اللَّهِ وَبَرَكَاتُهُ

as-salamu, alayka ayyuha'n-nabiyyi wa rahmatullahi wa barakatuhu – peace be upon you O Prophet! and the mercy of Allah and his baraka be upon you also ...

Then he should say:

صَلَّى اللَّهُ عَلَيْكَ وَ عَلَى أَزْوَاجِكَ وَذُرِّيَّتِكَ وَعَلَى أَهْلِكَ أَجْمَعِينَ كَمَا صَلَّى عَلَى إِبْرَاهِيمَ وَءَالِ إِبْرَاهِيمَ وَبَارِكْ عَلَيْكَ وَعَلَى أَزْوَاجِكَ وَذُرِّيَّتِكَ وَأَهْلِكَ كَمَا بَارَكَ عَلَى إِبْرَاهِيمَ وَءَالِ إِبْرَاهِيمَ فِي الْعَالَمِينَ إِنَّكَ حَمِيدٌ مَجِيدٌ. فَقَدْ بَلَّغْتَ الرِّسَالَةَ وَعَدَيْتَ الْأَمَانَةَ وَعَبَدتَّ رَبَّكَ وَجَاهَدتَّ فِي سَبِيلِهِ وَنَصَحْتَ لِعِبَادِهِ صَابِراً مُحْتَسِباً حَتَّى أَتَاكَ الْيَقِينُ وَأَكْمَلْتَ الدِّينَ بِالنَّصْرِ وَالْفَتْحِ الْمُبِينِ صَلَّى اللَّهُ عَلَيْهِ وَسَلَّمَ أَفْضَلَ الصَّلَاةِ وَأَتَمَّهَا وَأَطْيَبَهَا وَأَزْكَاهَا وَجَازَاكَ عَنْ أُمَّتِكَ أَفْضَلَ مَا يُجَازَى بِهِ نَبِيٌّ عَنْ عَنْ أُمَّتِهِ.

Salla 'alayka wa 'ala azwajika wa dhurriyatika wa 'ala ahlika ajma'een kama salla 'ala Ibrahim wa ali Ibrahim wa baraka 'alayka wa 'ala azwajika wa dhurriyatika wa ahlika kama baraka 'ala Ibrahim wa ali Ibrahima fi'l-'alameen innaka hameed majeed, faqad ballaghta ar-risala wa 'adayta'l-amana wa 'abadta rabbaka wa jahadta fi sabeelihi wa nasahta li'ibadihi sabiran muhtasiban hatta ataka'l-yaqeen wa akmalta'd-deen bi'n-nasr wa'l-fath al-mubeen, salla'llahu 'alayhi wa sallama afdal as-salati wa atammaha wa atyabaha wa azkaha wa jazaka 'an ummatika afdal ma yujaza bihi nabiyyun a'n ummatihi – may Allah bless you and your wives, progeny and all your people just as He blessed Ibrahim and the family of Ibrahim, and may He bless you with baraka and your wives, progeny and your people, just as he Ibrahim and the family of Ibrahim with baraka in all the worlds, and surely You are worthy of praise and illustrious. You delivered the message and handed over what has been entrusted to you, you worshipped your Lord, you fought in His way and you gave advice and counsel to His slaves, with patience, consciously performing everything as it should be done until the certainty (of death) came. You have perfected the deen with the aid and the clear victory (of Allah), may the most excellent, perfect, pleasant and most pure blessings be on you, and may you receive a reward on behalf of your umma which is the best any prophet has ever received on behalf of his umma.

Then he should step aside to the right about an arm's length and say:

السَّلَامُ عَلَيْكَ يَا أَبَا بَكْرٍ الصِّدِّيقِ وَرَحْمَةُ اللَّهِ وَبَرَكَاتُهُ صَفِيِّ رَسُولِ اللَّهِ صَلَّى اللَّهُ عَلَيْهِ وَسَلَّمَ وَثَانِيهِ فِي الْغَارِ جَزَاكَ اللَّهُ عَنْ أُمَّةِ سَيِّدِنَا مُحَمَّدٍ رَسُولِ اللَّهِ صَلَّى اللَّهُ عَلَيْهِ وَسَلَّمَ خَيْرًا

as-salamu 'alayka ya Aba Bakr as-Siddiq wa rahmatullahi wa barakatuhu safiyyi rasulillahi salla'llahu 'alayhi wa sallama wa thanihi fi'l-ghar, jazaka'llahu 'an ummati sayyidina Muhammad salla'lla 'alayhi wa sallam khayran – peace be on you Abu Bakr as-Siddiq! and the mercy of Allah and His blessings – a sincere friend of the Messenger of Allah, may the peace and blessings of Allah be upon him, and the second person in the cave, may Allah reward you on behalf of the umma of our Master Muhammad, may the peace and blessings of Allah be upon him, with the best of rewards.

Then he should move to the right – also another arm's length – and say:

السَّلَامُ عَلَيْكَ يَا أَبَا حَفْصٍ الْفَارُوقِ وَرَحْمَةُ اللَّهِ تَعَالَى وَبَرَكَاتُهُ، جَزَاكَ اللَّهُ عَنْ أُمَّةِ سَيِّدِنَا مُحَمَّدٍ رَسُولِ اللَّهِ صَلَّى اللَّهُ عَلَيْهِ وَسَلَّمَ خَيْرًا

as-salam 'alayka ya Aba Hafs al-Farouq wa rahmatullahi ta'ala wa barakatuuhu jazaka'llahu an ummati sayyidina Muhammad rasulla sallallah alayhi was sallim khayran – Peace be upon you Abu Hafs al-Farouq! and the mercy of Allah, exalted is He, and His blessings, and may Allah reward you on behalf of the umma of our Master Muhammad, may the peace and blessings of Allah be upon him, with the best of rewards.

It is recommended that the person who extends his stay visit Quba', and make the *salat* in its mosque, that he visit the *shaheeds* of Uhud, and ask for mercy for them and pay particular attention to his paternal uncle Hamza, may Allah be pleased with him, by making *du'a*; that he make a visit to Baqi (graveyard) and the famous Companions there together with the members of his Family, may Allah grant mercy and *baraka* to them; that he make *wudu'* from the well Bi'r Arees and drink of its water.

Ibn Abi Jamra, may Allah have mercy on him, has reported that when he entered his mosque, may the peace and blessings of Allah be upon him, he did not sit there except for the sitting of the *salat*. He (just) kept standing there until his caravan left. He said: "I have not gone out to Baqi or anywhere else, and I have not seen anyone other than the Prophet, may the peace and blessings of Allah be upon him. It occurred to me that I should go out to Baqi but then I said (to myself): 'Where am I going – this (here) is the gate of Allah and is open to those who ask and request, those who are humble, in need, to those in poverty and who are destitute. There is no one else one could possibly go to visit who is like him, may the peace and blessings be upon him – in nobility, generosity, grandeur and vastness.'

"O Allah we ask of You by the sublimity of his rank and position with You! Forgive us the wrong actions we have committed in the past, those we will commit in the future, those we have hidden and those we have done openly, and surely You are more aware of them than us. O our Lord give us good in this world and give us good in the next world, and protect us from the torment of the Fire. O Allah forgive us, our fathers and mothers, our Shaykhs, our wives and children, and cause us and them by Your goodness and generosity to attain the goal – with respect to the acquisition of knowledge and performing actions; and (cause) our companions, friends and all those who have a right over us from amongst our brothers and companions (to attain this goal), as well as all the Muslims; and cause us and them to die on the words *la ilaha illa'llah sayyidina Muhammad rasulu'llah*, may the peace and blessings of Allah be upon him, in a state of *tawba* without trial; and accept us and them by your sheer generosity, by your pleasure and your *ihsan*, O You, Possessor of Vast Generosity, *ihsan*, goodness, and Bestower of Gifts, surely You are the good and generous – with an overflowing generosity. If we are not able to attain to Your mercy, then Your mercy is able to attain to us. You have enabled us to make *du'a* in order that You may answer us – and You are the Most Generous of those who have fulfil what they have promised."

O Allah send blessings on our Master Muhammad, Your slave and Your unlettered Prophet, may the peace and blessings of Allah be upon him, and on his Family and Companions and grant peace.

The author's placing the *ziyara* of his (tomb), may the peace and blessings of Allah be upon him, at the end does not mean that it should be understood as having the least rank or the least excellence amongst the rites, or that it is the least act (of devotion) required of a Muslim who possesses sincere iman. No, this is not the case – and what has been transmitted on the subject is mentioned in its usual place – given the circumstances. People would set off on the hajj from far off regions – within the hajj months – but only arrive at the *miqats* just before (the end of the hajj). As time was short, they had to begin with the rites of hajj and then after (their completion) they would go to visit (the tomb of the Prophet, may Allah bless him and grant him peace). Some of the early generations maintained that the (hajj) should be begun in Madina al-Munawwara – and this has been stated by Ibn 'Atiyya in his writings.

It is also narrated from 'Alqama, al-Aswad and 'Amr ibn Maymun that they began with Madina before Makka despite Ahmad ibn Hanbal's *fatwa* that one should do the *fard* hajj before the visit – as a precaution, although it is also related from him that he granted a licence to start with Madina. The *ziyara* of his (tomb), may the peace and blessings of Allah be upon him, is an act of kindness and blessing from Allah to His believing slaves – just as He granted them the gift of the Messenger by sending him amongst them. Allah, exalted is He, said: "*Allah showed great kindness to the muminun when He sent a Messenger to them from among themselves*"□; likewise, Allah bestowed a gift of vast and overflowing proportions on him, may the peace and blessings of Allah be upon him – Allah, exalted is He, said: "*Allah's favour to you is indeed immense*"[1]; and one of His one mercies, exalted is He, to all creatures – Allah, exalted is He, said: "*We have only sent you as a mercy to all the worlds*"[2]; and which mercy is greater that the acceptance of a Lord who is Most Merciful and ever-Returning of every wrong doer who comes to him, may the peace and blessings of Allah be upon him, seeking forgiveness and turning in *tawba* – "*If only when they wronged themselves they had come to you and asked Allah's forgiveness.*"[3]

Surely this (*ziyara*) is an action which has the most hope of being accepted, the strongest likelihood of success – for every one with hope and expectation – given that Allah has promised His slaves who have wronged themselves and who come to their Prophet in a state of *tawba* seeking forgiveness in his presence from Him for their wrong actions, mercy and forgiveness and His turning (to them); and this, unconditionally and not restricted to any time or place. Moreover *ihram* is unnecessary and there are no pillars which render the whole invalid if they are missed out; nor any obligations to be fulfilled and made good (if missed out); not is their any inconvenience or (the obligation to put up with) getting dirty and dishevelled. Rather all it involves is standing before him, may the peace and blessings of Allah be upon him, and even if this standing is repeated several times or lasts the whole day (there is no great hardship involved and one may undertake it) in any state or condition.

1   Ali 'Imran – The Family of 'Imran: 164
2   an-Nisa' – the Women: 112
3   al-Anbiya' – the Prophets: 106

O Allah, send peace and blessings on our Master Muhammad and on his Family and Companions.

Despite this there are still some who criticise the Muslims and those who visit the haram of the Prophet, may he who lies there be granted peace and blessings. They criticise the very act of visiting him, may the peace and blessings of Allah be upon him; of standing facing him, as if in his presence, making *du'a* in front of him and raising one's hands while making *du'a*; of seeking access (to Allah) by means of him, and believing that he can be of benefit (and influence) after his death, peace and blessings be upon him.

The following may be given as an answer to the above objections: visiting him is a sunna (sanctioned) by him (and performed by the Companions and *Tabi'un*), may the peace and blessings of Allah be upon him, which is to be imitated; as for the standing in front of him, and facing him as if in his presence, may the peace and blessings of Allah be upon him, facing him while making *du'a* and raising one's hands, this has been transmitted in the *Shifa* through a relation of Ibn Wahb who said that Malik said: "If one greets the Prophet, may the peace and blessings of Allah be upon him, or makes *du'a*, then one should stand facing his tomb and not towards the *qibla*." It is also related that the Amir al-*muminun*, Abu Ja'far al-Mansur said to Imam Malik: "Abu 'Abdallah" – while he was in the mosque of the Prophet, may Allah bless him and grant him peace: "Should I face the *qibla* while making *du'a* or face the Messenger of Allah, may the peace and blessings of Allah be upon him", and imam Malik replied to him: "and why would you turn your face from him when he is your means (to Allah), just as he was the means of Adam (to Allah) – so face him and seek his intercession and Allah will make him and intercessor on your behalf."

It is also narrated from one of the (men of knowledge) that: "I saw Anas ibn Malik come to the grave of the Prophet, may the peace and blessings of Allah be upon him, and he raised his hands in such a way that I thought he intended to begin the *salat*. He then greeted the Prophet, may the peace and blessings of Allah be upon him, and left."

As for seeking his mediation, may the peace and blessings of Allah be upon him, both when living and dead, a *sahih* hadith – according to the standard of al-Bukhari and Muslim – has been transmitted on the matter. Its text is to be found in the annotated commentary of 'Allama ash-Shaykh Muhammad al-Hafid al-Masri on *al-Awrad at-Tijaniya* where he says that Ibn Khaythama said in his *Tarikh*: "Muslim ibn Ibrahim has narrated to us, Hammad ibn Salama has narrated to us, Abu Ja'far al-Khatami has informed us from 'Ammara ibn Khuzayma from 'Uthman ibn Haneef that a blind man came to the Prophet, may the peace and blessings of Allah be upon him, saying: 'My eyes have been afflicted – call on Allah for me!' and he said: 'Go and make *wudu*', perform two *rak'ats* and then say:

اَللَّهُمَّ إِنِّي أَسْأَلُكَ وَأَتَوَجَّهُ إِلَيْكَ بِنَبِيِّي مُحَمَّدٍ نَبِيِّ الرَّحْمَةِ يَا مُحَمَّدُ أَسْتَشْفِعُ بِكَ عَلَى رَبِّي فِي رَدِّ بَصَرِي. اَللَّهُمَّ فَاشْفِعْنِي فِي نَفْسِي وَ شَفِّعْ نَبِيِّي فِي رَدِّ بَصَرِي

Allahumma inni as'aluka wa atawajjahu ilayka binabiyyi Muhammadin nabi ar-rahma ya Muhammad astashfi'u bika 'ala rabbi fi raddi basari. Allahumma fashfi'ni fi nafsi wa shaffi' nabiyyi fi raddi basari – O Allah, I ask of You and I turn to you by my Prophet Muhammad, the Prophet of mercy. O Muhammad I seek your intercession by my Lord in the return of my sight. O Allah, make me an intercessor for my self and cause my Prophet to intercede for the return of my sight

and if you have any (other) need, then do likewise', and Allah returned his sight to him."

This has also been narrated by an-Nasa'i in his *Sunan*, at-Tirmidhi in his *Sahih*, and Ibn Majah and others – (for example) where mention is made in *Kitab al-Fawz wa'n-Najah*. At-Tabarani has also related it in his *al-Mu'jam as-Saghir* through one of his Shaykhs known as Tahir saying: "Tahir ibn 'Isa ibn Quraysh al-Masri al-Maqarri has narrated to us, Asbagh ibn al-Faraj has narrated to us, Ibn Wahb, that is 'Abdallah has narrated to us from Abu Sa'id al-Makki, that is, Shabeeb ibn Sa'id from Ruh ibn al-Qasim from Abu Ja'far al-Khatmi al-Madani from Abu Imama ibn Sahl ibn Haneef from his paternal uncle 'Uthman ibn Haneef that a man persisted in seeking something he needed from 'Uthman ibn Affan, may Allah be pleased with him, but 'Uthman did not turn to him or pay any attention to his need. He then met Ibn Haneef and complained to him about it. 'Uthman ibn Haneef said to him: 'Go to the place of *wudu*' and make *wudu*', go to the mosque and pray two *rak'ats* and then say:

اَللَّهُمَّ إِنِّي أَسْأَلُكَ وَأَتَوَجَّهُ إِلَيْكَ بِنَبِيِّنَا مُحَمَّدٍ نَبِيِّ الرَّحْمَةِ، يَا مُحَمَّدُ إِنِّي أَتَوَجَّهُ بِكَ إِلَى رَبِّي فَيَقْضِي حَاجَتِي

Allahumma inni as'aluka wa atawajjahu ilayka binabiyyina Muhammadin nabiyyi ar-rahma ya Muhammadun inni atawajjahu bika ila rabbi fa-yaqdi hajati – I ask You and turn to You by our Prophet, Muhammad, the prophet of mercy. O Muhammad I turn by you to my Lord, so that He will take care of my need and make mention of your need. Leave now so I may leave also. The man went off and did what he had told him and then he came to the door of 'Uthman ibn Affan, may Allah be pleased with him. The doorman came to him, took him by the hand and brought him to 'Uthman ibn Affan who (honoured him by) having him sit on a fine carpet and said: "What do you need?" and he told him what he needed and ('Uthman) took care of it for him saying "I did not remember your need until now" and then added: "and if you should need anything (else) tell me."'

Then the man left his house and met 'Uthman ibn Haneef and said to him: "May Allah reward you with the best of rewards – he did not see to my need and took no notice of me until you spoke to him." Then 'Uthman ibn Haneef said: "By Allah, I did not speak to him but I did see the Messenger of Allah, may the peace and blessings of Allah be upon him – a blind man came to him and complained that his sight had left him and the Prophet, may the peace and blessings of Allah be upon him, said: 'Can you not be patient?' and he said: 'Messenger of Allah, I have no one to guide me (when walking).' This grieved the Messenger, may the peace and blessings of Allah be upon him, and he said: 'Go to the place of *wudu'* and make *wudu'*, pray two *rak'ats* and then make a *du'a* with these *du'as*.' Abu Haneef said: 'By Allah we had not yet separated from each other and were still talking, when the man came back to us and it was as if there had never been anything wrong with him at all.'"

At-Tabarani said of the hadith that it is *sahih* and mentioned that 'Uthman ibn 'Umar alone had related it from Shu'ba. Shaykh Ibn Taymiyya said: "At-Tabarani mentioned that he alone had transmitted it in accordance with his knowledge (at the time) and that he was not aware of the narration of Rawh ibn 'Ubada from Shu'ba, and this is (also) a *sahih* chain of narration" – and it is clear from this that 'Uthman ibn 'Umar was not alone in relating it.

Thus it has been clearly established in our eyes that the hadith is *sahih* according to the standard of al-Bukhari and Muslim. Moreover al-Hakim has narrated it in his *Mustadrak 'ala's-Sahihayn* and has narrated it with a chain of narration which complies with the standard of the two Shaykhs. Al-Hafidh adh-Dhahabi said that it complies with the standard of both, and al-Bayhaqi has narrated it by way of al-Hakim and has confirmed that it is *sahih*. This (hadith) provides an explicit text (specifically) to do with seeking his help and mediation, and benefitting by him both when living and dead, may the peace and blessings of Allah be upon him and his Family.

His very words, exalted is He, *'We have only sent you as a mercy to all the worlds'*[1]

---

1 an-Nisa' – the Women: 63 *"We sent no Messenger except to be obeyed by Allah's permission. If*

demonstrate that his mercy to the worlds continues both when alive and dead, and as a benefit to each and every person according to his need. It is narrated in a *sahih* hadith that "Allah grants (blessing) and I divide (and dispose of the blessings)" – or whatever the exact words he used.[1] So how could it possibly be that those to whom such blessings have been granted should not derive benefit from the one who is responsible for disposing of these (blessings)? (and how could they not benefit from) all the blessings and provision he has been accorded by his Lord? Have we, the communities of the *umma* of Muhammad, not benefited from the intervention of Musa, may Allah grant him and our Prophet peace and blessings, regarding the obligation of the *salat*, that is, when he persisted in requesting our Messenger, may the peace and blessings of Allah be upon him, to return to his Lord in order to reduce the (number of) *salats* from fifty – until it was finally reduced to five? (and this occurred) when Musa had already died, may the peace of Allah be upon on him, while our Prophet, may the peace and blessings of Allah be upon him, was still alive, when his *umma* was still flourishing – and would continue to do so after him in the future.

He said, may the peace and blessings of Allah be upon him: "O Allah, do not make my grave an idol which is worshipped after me" and: "Allah's anger was intense against the people who took the graves of their Prophets as mosques." Allah, exalted is He, says: *"Has the time not arrived for the hearts of those who have iman to yield to the remembrance of Allah?"*[2] One may rest assured that the Messenger of Allah, may the peace and blessings of Allah be upon him, has never been and will never be worshipped instead of Allah, exalted is He, and that neither his grave nor his mosque has ever or will ever be taken as an idol – for Allah has answered his *du'a* and has honoured and ennobled him by (having his *umma*) worship with a pure worship. It has been transmitted from Abu Hurayra in a *sahih* hadith that "My *umma* will divide into seventy three groups: seventy two will be in the Fire, and one will be in the Garden" but since his mission as a Prophet and his death, may the peace and blessings of Allah be upon him, that is, more than fourteen hundred years ago, history has demonstrated that none of these groups – neither individuals from amongst them or communities as a whole – have taken him, may the peace and blessings

---

only when they wronged themselves they had come to you and asked Allah's forgiveness and the Messenger had asked forgiveness for them they would have found Allah ever-Returning, Most Merciful."

1 al-Anbiya' – the Prophets: 107
2 al-Bukhari 1: 27, "I am only one who divides up, and Allah [is the One Who] gives." It is a part of the famous hadith of Mu'awiya, may Allah be pleased with him, "For whomever Allah wishes good He gives discrimination (*fiqh*) in the deen."

of Allah be upon him, as a Lord, or an idol or have associated him with Allah in any way; and none have taken his grave as an idol or an object of worship after his death.

The histories of these groups and sects, their false claims and erroneous, ignorant beliefs do not indicate – not even a single letter (of their writings) – that anything of this kind has occurred, that is, any such erroneous beliefs have existed with respect to him, may the peace and blessings of Allah be upon him, or regarding his grave. Allah, exalted is He, said: "*Say: 'If the All-Merciful had a son; I would be the first to worship him.'*"[1]

Rather, what has been recorded of the *umma* since Allah has established it for mankind as the best *umma* is that good has remained in it by virtue of its *tawhid* of its Lord, exalted is He, by its distancing itself from associating anything with Allah, by its firm belief that His Messenger, may the peace and blessings of Allah be upon him, our Master, Muhammad ibn 'Abdallah is His slave and Messenger and that he has no command in the matter, and that the command of the affair is with Allah, and that He is the One Who has the power to harm and to give benefit; and by virtue of their (correctly) recognising that the Messenger, may the peace and blessings of Allah be upon him, disposes of the gifts and blessings of Allah and that he intercedes and is the accepted mediator – with whom Allah is content. Allah, exalted is He, has made His forgiveness and mercy dependent upon belief in him and has promised that whoever comes to him – while he is living or dead – will receive His forgiveness and mercy and that he will find Him Oft-returning and Merciful.

Visiting (him) is required and is a mercy and forgiveness (promised by Allah, exalted is He,); and making *du'as* before him is recommended, as is extending one's hands to him, submissive to Allah, in a state of tranquillity and acceptance. He, may the peace and blessings of Allah be upon him, is the *qibla* of (all) *du'as* and of the answer to the *du'a* – not the *qibla* of the *salat* which is the Ka'ba. Al-Bazzar has narrated with a *sahih* chain of narration from him, on whom be peace and blessings, that: "My life is a blessing and benefit for you: you narrate things and things are brought about for you; and when I am dead, my death will also be of great benefit to you: your actions will be revealed to me – if I see good, then I will praise Allah, and if I see evil, then I will seek forgiveness for you." Al-Munawi considered it as *sahih* in *ash-Sharh al-Kabir 'ala'l-Jami' as-Saghir*, as did al-Hafidh Nur ad-Deen al-Haytami in *az-Zawa'id*. Again he said: "My life is a great benefit for you and my death will be a great benefit to you." Then they asked: "Messenger of Allah! We realise that

1   al-Hadid – Iron: 15

your life is a great benefit for us but how will your death be of benefit to us?" He replied: "As for my life, every time you do something bad, then Allah will create a way out of it by means of me, and when I am dead, I will continue to call from my grave and for the sake of my *umma* until the trumpet is blown (on the Last Day)."

In his *tafsir*, al-Qurtubi has mentioned at the *ayat* where Allah, exalted is He, says *'If only when they wronged themselves they had come to you and asked Allah's forgiveness for them they would have found Allah Ever-Returning, Most Merciful'*[1]: "It has been recorded that Imam 'Ali, may Allah be pleased with him, said: 'A Bedouin Arab came to us three days after the Prophet of Allah, may the peace and blessings be upon him, had been buried. He threw himself on the grave of the Messenger of Allah, may the peace and blessings of Allah be upon him, and strew dust on his head saying: "O Messenger of Allah we have heard your words and we have heeded Allah, mighty is He and majestic, and you! Amongst the *ayats* which were revealed to you was *'if only when they wronged themselves they had come to you and asked Allah's forgiveness for them, they would have found Allah Ever-Returning, Most Merciful.'* I have wronged myself and I have come to you in order that you might seek forgiveness on my behalf." Then a call came from the grave saying: "You have been forgiven."'" More than one (narrator), both of past and later generations, has mentioned this with good chains of narration, amongst them Qadi 'Iyad in the *Shifa* and 'Allama Hibatallah in his book *Tawtheeq 'Ury al-'Alim*.

In his *tafseer*, Ibn Kathir has mentioned at the above mentioned *ayat* that al-'Utbi – who was one of the Shaykhs of ash-Shafi'i, namely, Abu 'Abd ar-Rahman Muhammad ibn 'Abdallah ibn 'Umar – said: "I was sitting at the grave of the Messenger of Allah, may the peace and blessings of Allah be upon him, and a Bedouin Arab came and said:

'As-salam 'alaykum Messenger of Allah, may the peace and blessings of Allah be upon him, I have heard the words of Allah: *"if only when they wronged themselves they had come to you and asked Allah's forgiveness for them they would have found Allah Ever-Returning, Most Merciful"* and I have come to you seeking forgiveness for my wrong actions and seeking your intercession with my Lord' and then he composed the following lines:

O you who are the best of those whose bones are buried in the plains!
   both the plains and the mountains have become fragrant by their fragrance
My self is the ransom for the grave in which you reside,
   for in it is all virtue, liberality and nobility

---

1 az-Zukhruf – The Gold Ornaments: 81

Al-'Utbi then said: "My eyes overwhelmed me (and I slept) and then I saw the Messenger of Allah, may the peace and blessings of Allah be upon him, who said: ''Utbi! catch up with the Bedouin Arab and give him the good news that Allah has forgiven him.'" Many of the *'ulama* have mentioned this event, among them, Ibn 'Asakir in his *Tarikh*, Abu'l-Faraj al-Jawzi and Abu Zakariya Yahya ibn Sharaf an-Nawawi. Moreover on both of these occasions, neither of the Bedouin Arabs were required to turn their back on the Messenger and face the *qibla*.

Shaykh Yusuf ad-Dajawi was asked about seeking help from a prophet or *wali* in order to attain to something from Allah, exalted is He and glorified, on the basis just as valid as any other means from the world of cause and effect and he replied: "Mediation is permitted and is effective – in the widest sense of the word – and it does not contradict the intellect or the gathered body of knowledge (of mankind). Indeed it is of the same order as (the world of) cause and effect. The whole of the world is based on means and causes, and Allah has created people in different ranks and states subject to a divine ordering and in accordance with sublime secrets – so there are rich and poor people, strong and weak, the knowledgeable and the ignorant; there are those who lead and those who are led, and there are kings and subjects. So it follows that the person of a high rank must possess something which the person of lesser rank does not have – and that fact that a person of lesser standing should resort to someone of greater standing is something quite natural. It was for this reason that all these (people of varying ranks) were created – in other words, it is by the will of the Real, the True, that He created people with different capacities, blessings and gifts."

As for *shirk* – associating something or someone with Allah, (it can manifest when) one requests (something) of someone other than Allah (while believing) that he is a god alongside Allah who has the capacity to grant or withhold (things) without His permission. While one cannot imagine that such beliefs originate from any of the *muminun*, there is (of course) no objection to anyone requesting (something) from someone else as long as they believe that he will only do something by the permission of Allah, and that he does not dispose (of anything) except by His power, his permission and His will. And there is no power and no strength except by Allah.

In His wisdom, Allah has rendered His slaves in need of each another. Even if a person is not immediately able to see to the need of another who requests help of him, the capacity to do so may be latent in him – in accordance with the reality of *la ilaha illa'llah*. This is why we learn of the existence of the *muqarrabun* – those who are close or intimate with Allah, exalted is He, whose intercession for others He accepts; the Great Intercessor being the Messenger, may the peace and blessings of Allah be upon him, and then after him the prophets, the *awliya* and the *'ulama*, as has been transmitted in the sunna.

As for what has been transmitted regarding criticism of sons who follow their fathers and forefathers, who exalt idols and believe in gods other than Allah, this refers to the *kuffar* and the heretics – for the Muslims imitate their forefathers with respect to their *tawhid* and they follow in their footsteps with regard to the sunna. Allah, exalted is He, said: "*I hold fast to the creed of my forefathers,*"¹ and also: "*…the religion of your forefather Ibrahim,*"² and also: "*Those you call upon apart from Him possess no power of intercession – only those who bore witness to the truth*"³ – that is, with the words *la ilaha illa' llah*.

So what is there to prevent one from seeking something from such (*awliya*) when it is Allah Who has granted them (whatever power they have)? What is however prohibited is to seek intercession from an idol which does not possess anything.

THE SUPERIORITY OF MADINA AL-MUNAWWARA OVER EVERY CITY IN EVERY OTHER LAND, MAY THE BEST BLESSINGS AND PEACE BE ON THE ONE WHO RESIDES THERE

"O Allah they have evicted me from the place which is most beloved to me, so cause me to reside in the place which is most beloved to You." The Qadi 'Abd al-Wahhab ibn 'Ali ibn Nasr al-Baghdadi al-Maliki said in his book *al-Ishraf 'ala'l-Masa'il*: "Madina is superior to Makka, contrary to the opinion of Abu Hanifa and ash-Shafi'i, because of what 'Amra has narrated from Nafi' – that the Messenger of Allah, may the peace and blessings of Allah be upon him, said: 'Madina is better than Makka', and because he did not say anything similar of any other place; and also because of his saying: 'No one is patient during its times of difficulty and distress but that I will be an intercessor and witness for him on the Day of Rising,' and he has not said this with respect to any other city; and because of his saying: 'No one leaves this (city of Madina) shunning it but that Allah will give it in his place someone better than him'; and his saying: 'O Allah they have caused me to leave the place which is most beloved to me, so cause me to reside in the place which is most beloved to You.' All this is clear and explicit textual evidence which we cannot ignore.

---

1   an-Nisa' – The Women: 64
2   Yusuf: 38
3   al-Hajj – The Pilgrimage: 76

(Madina is also superior) because of his saying: 'I have been commanded to a city which consumes (other) cities and which drives out dross from people just as the bellows drives out dross from iron.' There can be no other meaning to 'consumes cities' than that it is superior to them; and his saying: 'Surely iman resorts to Madina just as the snake resorts to its hole'; and his saying: 'O Allah cause us to love Madina like our love for Makka or even greater than it' – for it would not be permitted for someone to ask his Lord to cause him to love something inferior more than something superior, and there are many narrations to this effect.

And because 'Umar, may Allah be pleased with him, refused to acknowledge 'Abdallah ibn 'Ayyash's saying: 'Makka is better than Madina.' Three times he rejected him, exclaiming 'You are the one who says that Makka is better than Madina!' – and nowhere else is there mention of his rejecting anything as intensely as his rejection of 'Abdallah's words. (Again, Madina is superior) because the Prophet, may the peace and blessings of Allah be upon him, was a man who was formed from its earth and he was the best of mankind, and his grave is the best earth, may the peace and blessings of Allah be upon him; and because hijra to it was made a *fard* obligation, and as such meant just being there became an act of *qurba* – an act of drawing closer (to Allah) – and obedience. All this indicates its superiority over other places." From *al-Ishraq*.

In *Wafa' al-Wafa'* by 'Allama as-Samhudi it is stated: "'There is no place on the earth where I would more like my grave to be situated' that is, Madina – and he repeated this three times; and in another narration: 'Death only comes to a prophet in the place he loves most.' It is also related from Malik and al-Bukhari that 'Umar ibn al-Khattab, may Allah be pleased with him, said: 'O Allah grant me *shahada* in Your way and cause my death to be in the place of Your Messenger.' 'Abd ar-Razzaq said: 'The Companions of the Messenger of Allah, may the peace and blessings of Allah be upon him, would make the hajj and *'umra* and then return, and would not leave (Madina).' There is no doubt that residence in Madina during his lifetime, may the peace and blessings of Allah be upon him, was more excellent (than other cities), according to the *ijma'*, and this (excellence) carries on after his death until there is an *ijma'* reliably established that removes it.

"Malik said, may Allah be pleased with him: 'No grave of a prophet, other than that of Muhammad, may the peace and blessings of Allah be upon him, is known today on earth. One should realise the superiority of the people of the place where the grave is located over other people.' This, Malik addressed to Mahdi the Abbasid Khalif when he visited Madina – who consequently acted upon Malik's instruction to be aware of their superiority and to treat them with kindness."

It is related in a hadith: "By the One in whose hand is my self, there is surely a cure from all illness in its dust." The narrator has also added: "and I think he also mentioned 'elephantiasis and leprosy.'" It is also stated in a hadith: "Fasting Ramadan in Madina is like a thousand months of fasting in another city, and the *jumu'a salat* in Madina is like a thousand *salats* in another (city)" – and this applies likewise to all other good actions in it.

There is also the hadith that the Prophet, may the peace and blessings of Allah be upon him, made *du'as* for it six times more than Ibrahim, may peace and blessings be on him and our Prophet, made for Makka al-Mukarrama.

Its sanctity is like that of Makka until the Last Day, and neither the Dajjal or the pest will enter there. It has also been narrated in a hadith that: "The dust of its earth is a cure for all illnesses" – and this has been affirmed by the experience of the earlier generations of its curative power. In another hadith it states: "Uhud is on one of the terraces of the Garden"; and: "Uhud is a mountain which loves us and we love it"; and: "Surely (the area of) Bat-han is on one of the terraces of the Garden" – and may it be enough for us (to realise) that it is the earth which sustained the best and most noble of creation, that it contains his most illustrious tomb, that it is the land of the hijra and the place where he lived, died, carried out his mission and gathered his community.

Malik used to say: "It is the abode of the *hijra* and the sunna, and is surrounded by *shuhada*, by the best of people after the Messenger of Allah, may the peace and blessings of Allah be upon him, and the best people of the best *umma* that has been produced before mankind."

USEFUL POINT: there are two different opinions as to the reason for the stoning of the *jamras* – and they are mentioned in *al-Muqaddimat*, as stated by al-Hattab: firstly, when Ibrahim commanded that the House be built the Sakina (tranquillity) shaded him and then came to rest over the place of the House. Then Ibrahim left with Jibril and passed by al-'Aqaba where Shaytan confronted him and he (Jibril) commanded him to stone him. He then confronted him at each *jamra* and stoned him – and so this was the reason for (the rite of the) *ramy*. It is also narrated that when he was commanded to slaughter his son, may peace be on them both, he released his son and went after the ram, only managing to get hold of it at the first *jamra* where he had thrown seven stones at it – but it escaped at this point and so he had to repeat this at the second and third (*jamras*). He then took it to the place of slaughter and slaughtered it.

In the *tafseer* of al-Qurtubi on the words of Allah, exalted is He, '*My son, I* saw in a dream that I must sacrifice you. What do you think about this'[1] he states: "Ibn 'Abbas said: 'The dreams of the prophets are revelation, and he was told in his dream: "You have made a vow so fulfil your vow."' It is said that in the night prior to at-Tarwiya, Ibrahim, on whom be peace, saw what appeared to be someone telling him 'Allah commands you to sacrifice your son.' When morning came, he reflected as to whether this was a judgement from Allah or (the whisperings) of Shaytan. For this reason, it was called the day of at-Tarwiya (the day of reflection – from the Arabic *rawiya*: to reflect). During the second night, he saw the same thing and his vow was (again) mentioned. When morning came he realised (Arabic: *'arafa*) that it was from Allah and so it was called the Day of 'Arafa. During the third night, he again saw the same thing and understood that he had to slaughter (an animal), and so it was called the Day of Sacrifice. It has been related that when he slaughtered the (ram) Jibril declared: '*Allahu akbar, Allahu akbar*' and the sacrificial victim uttered: '*la ilah illa'llah wallahu akbar* – there is no god but Allah and Allah is greater.' Then Ibrahim said: '*Allahu akbar wa'l-hamdu lillah* – Allah is greater and praise belongs to Allah' and so these (words) have remained the sunna (to this day)."

Al-Qurtubi also said, regarding the reason for the stoning, that when Ibrahim wanted to slaughter his son, Shaytan came to his mother and said to her: "Do you know where Ibrahim is going with your son?" She replied: "No." He said: "He wants to slaughter him and claims that Allah has commanded him to this." Then she said: "It is good that he obeys his Lord." Then he came to the son saying: "Do you know where your father is taking you?" He replied: "No." He said: "He wants to slaughter you." He said: "and why?" He said: "He claims that his Lord has commanded him to do this." He said: "Then may he do what Allah has commanded him to do in all obedience." Then he came to Ibrahim and said: "Where are you going? By Allah I fear that Shaytan has come to you in your sleep and has commanded you to slaughter your son." Then Ibrahim recognised who he was and said: "Get away from me, enemy of Allah, by Allah I am going to carry out the command of my Lord."

Ibn 'Abbas said: "When Ibrahim was commanded to slaughter his son, Shaytan appeared to him at the *jamrat al-'Aqaba*, and Ibrahim stoned him with seven pebbles and then left; then Shaytan appeared to him at the *jamra al-wusta* (the middle *jamra*), and he stoned him with the seven pebbles and then left; then at *jamra al-ukhra* (the last *jamra*), and he stoned him with seven pebbles and then left; and then Ibrahim proceeded to carry out the command of Allah."

There is a difference of opinion as to the place of the slaughter: it has been

---

1 az-Zukhruf – The Gold Ornaments; 86

said that it was at the Maqam in Makka; it is also said it was at the place of slaughter in Mina, at the site of the *jamras*, where he stoned Iblis, may Allah curse him; it is also said that it was at the Sakra which is at the foot of Thabeer at Mina; while Ibn Jurayj said: "It is in Sham two (Arabic) miles from the Bayt al-Maqdis" – and most are of the first (view). From the *tafsir* of al-Qurtubi.

It has also been narrated that the son said to Ibrahim, on whom be peace, when the latter wanted to slaughter him: "Father, make the rope (binding me) tight so that I do not tremble and fold back your robe so that none of my blood sprinkles on it, lest my mother see it and become saddened. Be quick with the knife at my throat so that it is easier for me (to bear), and have me lie face down so that I am not looking in your face, lest you feel compassion for me, and so that I cannot see the blade lest I become scared. When you see my mother, convey my *salams* to her." When Ibrahim, on whom be peace, drew the knife, Allah caused a sheet of copper to appear in front of it, and the knife was rendered ineffective. From al-Qurtubi.

There is a difference of opinion as to whether Ishaq or Isma'il was the intended sacrifice – and there is evidence for both (opinions). Al-Asma'i said: "I asked Abu 'Amr ibn al-'Ala about the sacrifice and he said: 'O Asma'i, where is your intellect? When was Ishaq ever in Makka? Isma'il was in Makka, and he was the one who built the House with his father, and the place of sacrifice was in Makka.'"

It is also narrated from the Prophet, may the peace and blessings of Allah be upon him, that Isma'il was the intended sacrifice. Allah, exalted is He, said: "*We ransomed him with a mighty sacrifice*"[1] and in the *ayat*, there is an indication that the sacrifice by means of the animal was better. Ibn 'Abbas said: "It was the ram which Habil (Abel) gave as a *qurba* offering to Allah and the (same ram which) was grazing in the Garden before Allah ransomed Ibrahim with it." Al-Hasan said: "Isma'il was only ransomed with a billy goat which had been brought down from Thabeer before being slaughtered by Ibrahim." Abu Ishaq az-Zujjaj: "It is also said that he was ransomed with a mountain goat (*wa'l*)." From al-Qurtubi.

The sacrifice is not obligatory but is a sunna and is well known. 'Ikrima said: "Ibn 'Abbas sent me with two dirhams on the Day of Sacrifice in order to buy some meat for him saying: 'Whoever you meet, then say this is the sacrifice of Ibn 'Abbas.'" Abu 'Umar said: "The gist of all this is contained in what been related of Abu Bakr and 'Umar, according to the people of knowledge, namely, that (the reason) they did not slaughter was to prevent people considering it

---

1 as-Saffat – Those in Ranks: 102

was an obligation." From al-Qurtubi.

Al-Qurtubi also relates the hadith: "There is no action more beloved to Allah on the Day of Sacrifice than the shedding of blood. Surely the (sacrificial victim) will appear on the Day of Rising with its horns, its hair and hooves, and its blood will have a place with Allah before it even falls to the ground – so (perform the sacrifice) with delight" – and this hadith is ranked as *hasan*. From al-Qurtubi.

The Messenger of Allah, may the peace and blessings of Allah be upon him, sacrificed a horned ram. He laid it on its side saying: "In the name of Allah, O Allah accept this from Muhammad, from the family of Muhammad and from the *umma* of Muhammad." From al-Qurtubi.

The person making the sacrifice can share his victim if the price is shared. Khalil said: "It is not to be shared except when the price has been shared. This (is permitted even) if (the number of persons sharing) is more than seven, as long as those (sharing with him) live with him, or are related to him – and even if one (person) donates a share to the other free."

It is stated in the dictionary (of place names) that Mina is a settlement in Makka, and is declinable (grammatically). It is called Mina because blood is spilled there (from the Arabic root *imna*). Ibn 'Abbas said: "(The reason is) because Jibril, may the blessings of Allah be upon him, when about to part company with Adam, may the peace of Allah be upon him and our Prophet, said *tamann!* – wish for something! – and he replied: 'I wish – *atamanna* – for the Garden' and so it was called 'Mina' from this wish (*munya*) of Adam." It is also said that his wish was for Allah to join him with Hawa' (Eve) there; it is also said that is was because of Ibrahim's desire (*tamannin*), may the peace and blessings of Allah be upon him and our Prophet, that Allah annul (the obligation) He had imposed on him to slaughter his son, and Allah knows best. – This is stated in al-Madani 'Ali Ganun's gloss of Khalil.

One point of benefit of a most extraordinary nature is the following: Ibn Khallikan has mentioned in his *Wafayat* that the Qaramita (Carmathians) extracted the Black Stone (from the Ka'ba) and carried it off to Hajar. In the first book of *Wafayat al-A'yan*, pp.148-9, he said: "On the day known as at-Tarwiya the Qaramita, under the leadership of Abu Tahir al-Qaramiti, plundered the wealth of the hajj and killed the hajjis – even in the Masjid al-Haram and in the House itself. When a man from among them climbed up to remove the guttering, he fell to his death. When they (began) tearing off the door of the Ka'ba, the Amir of Makka went out to confront them with a group of nobles and engaged them in battle but the (Qaramita) slaughtered them all and threw (some of) their corpses into the well of Zamzam; the rest they buried in the Masjid al-Haram without shrouding them. When news of this reached al-Mahdi 'Ubaydallah, the ruler of Ifriqiya, he wrote to him condemning what he had done. He commanded him to restore the Black Stone and the wealth they had stolen from the hajjis. He (then) returned the Stone on one weak camel – whereas when they had taken it, they had dispersed its great weight under three strong camels. They took the (Black) Stone in 317 AH, and it remained with them twenty-two years in Hajar. When they returned the Stone, they carried it to Kufa and attached it to the main Jami' mosque for the people to see and then they transported it to Makka al-Mukarrama."

One thing can remind one of something else – just as Allah protected the *muminun* from the evil of those who had violated the sanctity of the House of Allah, and returned the Stone to His House, so Allah also protected them from the evil – and exacted revenge on – those who desired to violate the sanctity of the Messenger of Allah, may the peace and blessings of Allah be upon him, and *"Allah is Almighty, Exactor of Revenge."*[1] O Allah, grant peace and blessings on our Master Muhammad and on his Family and Companions.

Another interesting point of benefit is also to be found in the work *Wafa' al-Wafa' fi Akhbar Dar al-Mustafa* of Samhudi, may Allah, exalted is He, have mercy on him. One day, in 557 AH, the king, Nur ad-Deen ash-Shaheed, who was a just and right acting man, said: "I have seen the Prophet, may the peace and blessings of Allah be upon him, in my sleep and he addressed me saying: 'Save the Haram of the Prophet from those two men' – and he indicated two men. So I made *wudu'*, performed the *salat* and fell asleep, and then saw him (once more) and he repeated the same words to me; so I made *wudu'*, performed the *salat* and slept, and again saw him. He repeated the same words to me and then I woke up as he was saying this." Then he departed quickly for Madina al-Munawwara in the company of twenty horsemen. When he arrived, he called together its inhabitants, and they received the gifts (the king had brought for them). However, he could not see the two men whom the Prophet, may the peace and blessings of Allah be upon him, had indicated. Thus he requested that the rest of the residents should come to take the gifts (they had brought for them) and the people said: "There is no one else except for two rich men from the *Maghrib*, and if it were not for their *sadaqa* and kind support of the people of Madina, the latter would have perished in this year of drought" – and they proceeded to praise them for a multitude of good actions on their part, for their performance of the *salat* and for their visits to the places of significance

---

1 as-Saffat – Those in Ranks: 107

(in the deen). Then he requested that they come and when he caught sight of them, he saw the same features (in their faces) he had seen in his dream. On searching their homes, he could not find any evidence against them, but after a further investigation, he discovered a underground passage beyond the tomb of the Prophet, may Allah bless him and grant him peace, leading to their homes. He called them to him again and after threatening them, they admitted that they were agents from Europe intent on carrying off the noble body (of the Prophet, may Allah bless him and grant him peace) to Europe. He then had them put to death and their corpses burned. He then returned immediately to his place of governance in Iraq. Ibn Athir has declared that there was no one to equal this king after 'Umar ibn 'Abd al-'Aziz – with respect to the correctness of his actions and praiseworthy behaviour.

In the second book, p. 652, as-Samhudi then goes on to mention that one of the heretics suggested to al-Hakim al-'Ubaydi, the ruler of Egypt, that the body of the Noble Prophet should be transported to Egypt. Al-Hakim approved of his suggestion and so had a splendidly ornate building built for the purpose of housing the noble remains. Then one of his officers set off to carry out the plan. However, when he arrived at Madina al-Munawwara, he attended a meeting and someone recited: *"If they break their oaths after making their treaty and defame your deen, then fight the leaders of kufr – their oaths mean nothing – so that hopefully they will stop. Will you not fight a people who have broken their oaths and resolved to expel the Messenger, and who initiated hostilities against you in the first place? Is it them you fear? Allah has more right to your fear if you are muminun."*[1] The people then rose up in uproar and almost killed the person charged with carrying out the plan. His name was Abu'l-Futuh and he said: "(Let us forget all this!) You have more reason to fear Allah. By Allah, if I could have escaped with my life from al-Hakim, I would not have taken up this task." He then became intensely anxious as to how he could resolve his dilemma. The day had not come to a close before Allah sent a wind so strong that the earth almost began to shake, and camels and horses – together with their loads and saddles – fell over and rolled like so many balls over the ground. Most of them perished, and many people too. However, Abu'l-Futuh's heart was alleviated as – through this event – he now had an excuse to present to al-Hakim al-Ubaydi.

It is also stated in the second volume of *Wafayat al-A'yan*, p.662, that the event occurred after 400 AH. O Allah, grant peace and blessings to our Master Muhammad and on his Family and Companions.

He then follows this with an account of another event: a group of people

---

[1] Ali 'Imran – The Family of 'Imran: 4

came from Aleppo and presented a great many gifts to the Amir of Madina al-Munawwara, requesting of him that he allow them to open the tomb of the Prophet, may the best peace and blessings be upon him, so that they might remove (the tombs of) Abu Bakr as-Siddiq, may Allah be pleased with him, and 'Umar al-Khattab may Allah be pleased with him. The Amir granted their request and so requested of the Shaykh of the servants of the Haram of the Prophet – whose name was Sawab – that he see to the needs of these conspirators saying: "They will knock at the door of the Haram for you at night, so open it for them. Leave them to do what they want and do not oppose them." The servant began to weep and took refuge in the Haram of the Prophet where he made *tawaf* of the illustrious tomb. At the end of the night, there was a knocking at the door of the mosque of the Prophet and on opening it, forty men came in one after the other carrying measures, baskets, candles, picks and shovels. They made for the noble tomb, and by Allah, they had not reached the minbar but the earth swallowed them all up – together with all their tools and instruments leaving no trace of them. The author then goes on to say: "The Amir had grown impatient waiting for news of them and so he called me saying: 'O Sawwab, did not the people come to you.' I said: 'Indeed, but such-and-such a thing happened to them.' He said: 'Be careful what you say.' I said: 'It is so – come and see if there is any one of them left or any trace of them.' He then said: 'You must be making this up – if it turns out that it is all your invention, then I will have your head cut off.'" Here ends the account of as-Samhudi – and he has related it with various unbroken chains of narration which are mutually consistent and which, together, lend veracity to the story and demonstrate the trustworthiness of the narrators. O Allah grant peace and blessings on our Master Muhammad and on his Family and Companions.

We have now completed the composition we had in mind, and we ask Allah glorious and exalted is He, that He make it of benefit for everyone, and that he accept it as something undertaken solely for His face glorious and exalted is He, that He forgive us, our parents, our Shaykhs, our children and all our brothers – both for past wrong actions and any committed in the future, both those committed in open and those in secret, and that He grant us well-being in the deen and the *dunya*, with respect both to our persons and our wealth, our words and our actions, and that he cause us to die on the Muhammadan sunna, and to travel on its straight path – for surely He it is who has the power to make all this possible. Amin, "*Glory be to your Lord, the Lord of Might, beyond anything they describe. And peace be upon the Messengers. And praise be to Allah, the*

Lord of all the worlds!"[1] O Allah bless our Master Muhammad, and on his Family and Companions.

Nouakshott, Mauritania 21st Rajab 1418

---

1 at-Tawba – Repentance: 12

Appendix Consisting of Forty Hadith Regarding the Hajj

In the name of Allah, the All-Merciful, the Most Merciful

I am undertaking this in the hope of being able to preserve them for people and to attain to the favour (of the reward promised) for preserving them. Even if the hadith which speaks of 'the excellence of someone who preserves forty hadith for my *umma*' is weak, this does not preclude one from obtaining this favour from Allah and from His Messenger, may the peace and blessings of Allah be upon him.

The Talbiya

1. It is narrated from Jabir that: "The Messenger of Allah entered into the state of *ihram*," and he mentioned the (words of the) *talbiya* the same as contained in the hadith of Ibn 'Umar who said: "...and (some) people added the words *Dhu'l-Ma'arij* – the Lord of the Ascending Steps – and other similar words, and the Prophet, may the peace and blessings of Allah be upon him, did not object to their (saying this)" – (and similar narrations are) recorded by Ahmad, Abu Dawud and Muslim with the same meaning.

2. It is narrated from Abu Hurayra that the Prophet, may the peace and blessings of Allah be upon him: "...declared *Labbayk ilaha'l-haqq labbayk* – at Your service, God of the Truth, at Your service! in the *talbiya*" – and this is narrated by Ahmad, Ibn Majah and an-Nasa'i.

The time of his entering the ihram, may the peace and blessings of Allah be upon him

3. It is related from Ibn 'Umar who said: "As for this (place) of yours (known as) Bayda', you wrongly claim it as the place where the Messenger of Allah, may Allah bless him and grant him peace, entered the *ihram* – for the Messenger of Allah, may Allah bless him and grant him peace, only performed it at the Mosque, that is, the mosque of Dhu'l Hulayfa."

4. It is related from Anas that the Prophet, may the peace and blessings of Allah be upon him, "performed *Dhuhr*, then got on his mount and on reaching the top of mount Bayda' he would enter the *ihram* (with the *talbiya*)" – this is narrated by Abu Dawud.

5. It is narrated from Jabir that the Messenger of Allah, may the peace and blessings of Allah be upon him "entered the *ihram* at Dhu'l-Hulayfa when his mount came up level with it." This is narrated by al-Bukhari who said that it has been related by Anas and Ibn 'Abbas.

6. It is narrated that Sa'id ibn Jubayr said: "I said to Ibn 'Abbas, 'It is surprising how the Companions of the Prophet, may the peace and blessings of Allah be upon him, differed regarding his entering the *ihram*.' He said: 'I am the most knowledgeable person about this – he performed one hajj, and after making the *rak'ats* in the mosque he made it incumbent there and then, declaring the *talbiya* and embarking upon the *ihram* for the hajj while sitting (after the *salat*), and he did the same as soon as his she-camel was carrying him. Then he moved off and when he reached the top of al-Bayda' he again made the *talbiya* and everyone narrates what he heard.'" Ahmad and Abu Dawud narrate it, and the rest of the five in an abridged form from him that the Prophet, may the peace and blessings of Allah be upon him, embarked upon the hajj following the *salat*. I have abbreviated some of the repetitious phrases of the (above) hadith.

Chapter regarding the choice between the Tamattu', the Ifrad and the Qiran forms of hajj and which is the most excellent

7. It is related that 'A'isha, may Allah be pleased with her, said: "We left with the Messenger of Allah, may the peace and blessings of Allah be upon him, and then he said: 'Whoever of you wants to embark on the hajj and the *'umra* should do so, whoever wants to embark on the hajj (only) should do so, and whoever wants to embark on the *'umra* (only) should do so.'" 'A'isha said, may Allah be pleased with her: "So the Messenger of Allah, may the peace and blessings of Allah be upon him, embarked on the hajj and others embarked on it along with him, and others embarked on the *'umra* and hajj, while yet others embarked on the *'umra* – and I was among those who embarked on the *'umra*."

8. It is narrated from Ibn 'Abbas who said: "The Prophet, may the peace and blessings of Allah be upon him, embarked on the *'umra*, and the Companions with him embarked on the hajj, and neither he, may the peace and blessings of Allah be upon him, nor those of his Companions who had brought the *hady* sacrifices along with them left the state of *ihram* – whereas the rest did" – this is narrated by Ahmad and Muslim.

There is also a narration which states that "The Messenger of Allah, may the peace and blessings of Allah be upon him, made the *tamattu'* (hajj) as did Abu Bakr, 'Umar and 'Uthman – and the first to prohibit it was Mu'awiya" – this is narrated by Ahmad and at-Tirmidhi.

9. It is narrated from Hafsa, the Mother of the *muminun*, she said: "I asked the Prophet, may the peace and blessings of Allah be upon him: 'What is the matter with the people that they came out of their state of *ihram*, when you had not left (the state of *ihram*) on your *'umra*?' He replied: 'I had garlanded the *hady* and flattened down my hair (with oil), and so I did not leave my state of *ihram* until I had left the state of *ihram* of the hajj'" – this has been narrated from a group (of narrators) except at-Tirmidhi.

10. It is narrated from al-Qasim from 'A'isha that the Prophet, may the peace and blessings of Allah be upon him, made the *ifrad* hajj, and this has been narrated by a group (of the narrators) except al-Bukhari.

11. It is narrated from Nafi' from Ibn 'Umar who said: "We embarked on the *ihram* with the Messenger of Allah, may the peace and blessings of Allah be upon him, for the *ifrad* hajj" – this is narrated by Ahmad and Muslim; and it is also narrated by Muslim that the Prophet, may the peace and blessings of Allah be upon him, embarked on the *ifrad* hajj.

12. It is narrated by Bakr al-Muzani from Anas who said: "I heard the Messenger of Allah, may the peace and blessings of Allah be upon him, make the *talbiya* for the hajj and the *'umra* together saying *labbayk 'umratan wa hajjan* – at Your service for an *'umra* and hajj." Agreed upon (by al-Bukhari and Muslim).

13. It is also related from Anas that he said: "We went out exclaiming (the *talbiya*) for hajj and when we reached Makka, the Messenger of Allah, may the peace and blessings of Allah be upon him, commanded us to make it into an *'umra* saying: 'If I had known what I now know, I would have made it an *'umra*, but I have brought the *hady* along and have joined between the hajj and the *'umra*'" – and this has been narrated by Ahmad.

14. It has been narrated by 'Umar ibn al-Khattab who said: "I have heard the Messenger of Allah, may the peace and blessings of Allah be upon him, say while he was in the *wadi* known as al-'Ateeq: 'An angel came to me during the night from my Lord saying: "Make the *salat* in this blessed *wadi* and exchange the *'umra* for a hajj!"'" – this has been narrated by Ahmad, al-Bukhari, Ibn Majah, Abu Dawud, and in the relation of al-Bukhari it reads " and he turned the *'umra* into a hajj."

15. It is narrated from Suraqa ibn Malik: "I heard the Prophet, may the peace and blessings of Allah be upon him, say: "I have included the *'umra* in the hajj (and this remains valid) until the Day of Rising." He has also said: "and the

Messenger of Allah joined (the hajj and 'umra in qiran) on the final hajj" – this is related by Ahmad.

16. It is narrated by Anas that the Prophet, may the peace and blessings of Allah be upon him, spent the night in Dhu Hulayfa until the morning. Then he embarked upon the hajj and 'umra, and the people also embarked on them both. After proceeding, he instructed the people to leave their state of *ihram* until the day known as at-Tarwiya arrived – when they embarked on the hajj. He said: "and the Prophet, may the peace and blessings of Allah be upon him, sacrificed seven camels with his own hand while standing and he slaughtered two spotted rams in Madina" – this is narrated by Ahmad, al-Bukhari and Abu Dawud.

Cupping

17. It is narrated from 'Abdallah ibn Buhayna: "The Prophet, may the peace and blessings of Allah be upon him, had cupping done on the middle of his head while he was in the state of *ihram* at Lahyi Jamal on the way to Makka." This is agreed upon (by al-Bukhari and Muslim). Lahyi Jamal is a place on the way to Makka.

Marriage while in a state of ihram

18. It is narrated from 'Uthman ibn Affan that the Messenger of Allah, may the peace and blessings of Allah be upon him, said: "The person in a state of *ihram* should not marry or be married or propose marriage" – this is narrated by the group (of the narrators) except al-Bukhari, and in the relation of at-Tirmidhi there is no mention of 'or propose marriage.'

The obligation to perform the hajj immediately (it becomes possible)

19. It is narrated from Ibn 'Abbas from the Prophet, may the peace and blessings of Allah be upon him: "Make haste to perform the hajj," meaning the *fard* obligation, "for none of you knows what may happen to him" – this is narrated by Ahmad.

Having someone else perform the hajj

20. It is narrated from Ibn 'Abbas, may Allah be pleased with both of them, that a woman from Khath'am said: "Messenger of Allah, may the peace and blessings of Allah be upon him, the *fard* obligation of the hajj has now become incumbent on my father but he is an old man who is unable to sit upright on the

back of his camel…" and he said: "Then make the hajj instead of him" – this is related by the group (of the narrators).

FULFILLING ONE'S PROMISE TO A PERSON WHO HAS DIED

21. It is narrated from Ibn 'Abbas, may Allah be pleased with them both, that a woman from Juhayna came to the Prophet, may the peace and blessings of Allah be upon him, and said: "My mother made a vow to perform the hajj but she did not perform it before she died, so should I do it on her behalf?" He replied: "Yes, make the hajj on her behalf – have you not considered (what you would do) if your mother had a debt – would you not pay it for her? Pay Allah because Allah has more right to payment in full" – this is narrated by al-Bukhari, and by an-Nasa'i with the same meaning (but different text).

THE CAPACITY TO PERFORM IT: PROVISION AND THE MOUNT

22. It is narrated from the Prophet, may the peace and blessings of Allah be upon him, that he said, commenting on the words of Allah '*for those who can find a way to do it*'[1]: "this refers to provision and a mount" – this is narrated by ad-Daraqutni, and al-Hakim has also narrated it, saying it has the rank of *sahih*, according to the conditions of both (Muslim and al-Bukhari).

A WOMAN JOURNEYING WITHOUT A MAHRAM (THAT IS, SOMEONE CLOSELY RELATED TO HER)

23. It is narrated from Ibn 'Umar: "The Messenger of Allah, may the peace and blessings of Allah be upon him, said: 'A woman should not travel for three (days and nights) except with a *mahram*'" – agreed upon (by al-Bukhari and Muslim).

WHOEVER MAKES THE HAJJ ON BEHALF OF SOMEONE ELSE WHEN HE HIMSELF HAS NOT PERFORMED IT

24. It is related from Ibn 'Abbas that the Prophet, may the peace and blessings of Allah be upon him, heard a man saying: ("At Your service on behalf of Shubruma!")[2] He asked: "Who is Shubruma?" replied: "A brother of mine" or "a relative of mine." The other then asked: "Have you made the hajj yourself?" He replied: "No." He said: "Perform it yourself, then make it for Shubruma" – this is narrated by Abu Dawud and Ibn Majah.

---

1   Ali 'Imran – The family of 'Imran: 97
2   Our text was missing the words in brackets which are in the narration of Abu Dawud.

The hajj in the case of a minor

25. It is narrated from Ibn 'Abbas that the Prophet, may the peace and blessings of Allah be upon him, met a group of riders at Ruha and he asked: "Who is this group of people?" They replied: "Muslims." Then one of them said: "Who are you?" He replied: "The Messenger of Allah" and then a woman held up a boy to him saying: "Does he have a hajj?" He replied: "Yes, and you will have a reward!" – this is narrated by Ahmad, Muslim, Abu Dawud and an-Nasa'i.

26. It is narrated from Ibn 'Umar that the Messenger of Allah, may the peace and blessings of Allah be upon him, said: "The people of Madina embark on the *ihram* at Dhu'l-Hulayfa, the people of Sham at al-Juhfa, and the people of Najd at Qarn." Then Ibn 'Umar added: "Someone mentioned to me – and I did not hear it (directly) – that the Messenger of Allah, may the peace and blessings of Allah be upon him, said: 'The people of Yemen embark on the *ihram* from Yalamlam'" – agreed upon (by al-Bukhari and Muslim).

His entering ihram, may the peace and blessings of Allah be upon him

27. It is related from Ibn 'Umar that the Prophet, may the peace and blessings of Allah be upon him, would embark on the *ihram* as his mount came to stand level with the mosque at Dhu'l-Hulayfa and that he would say:

لَبَّيْكَ اللَّهُمَّ لَبَّيْكَ، لَبَّيْكَ لَا شَرِيكَ لَكَ لَبَّيْكَ، إِنَّ الْحَمْدَ وَالنِّعْمَةَ لَكَ وَالْمُلْكَ، لَا شَرِيكَ لَكَ

"*Labbayk allahumma labbayk, labbayk la shareeka laka labbayk, inna'l-hamda wa'n-ni'mata laka wa'l-mulk, la shareeka lak* – At Your service! O Allah, at Your service! At Your service! You have no partner. At Your service! The praise and blessing are Yours and the kingdom. You have no partner" and 'Abdallah would add here:

لَبَّيْكَ لَبَّيْكَ وَسَعْدَيْكَ، وَالْخَيْرُ بِيَدَيْكَ، وَالرَّغْبَاءُ إِلَيْكَ وَالْعَمَلُ

"*Labbayk, labbayk wa-sa'dayk wa'l-khayru biyadayk, wa'r-raghba'u ilayka wa'l-'amal* – At Your service! At Your service! At Your service and at Your call. Good is in Your hands, and I am at Your service. Our desire is for You, and our action" – agreed upon (by al-Bukhari and Muslim).

His 'umra, may the peace and blessings of Allah be upon him

28. It is narrated from Anas that, "the Prophet, may the peace and blessings

of Allah be upon him, made four *'umras* in Dhu'l-Qa'da – apart from the *'umra* with his hajj – his *'umra* from al-Hudaybiyya, an *'umra* the following year, and (finally) the one from al-Ji'rana where he divided the booty of Hunayn" – agreed upon (by al-Bukhari and Muslim).

29. It is related from Umm Salama: "I heard the Prophet, may the peace and blessings of Allah be upon him, say: 'Whoever enters the *ihram* for the *'umra* or hajj from the mosque of al-Aqsa, then he will be forgiven the wrong actions of his past'" – this is narrated by Ahmad, Abu Dawud, and something similar is mentioned by Ibn Majah although without mention of the hajj.

Permission to perform the *'umra* the whole year

30. It is narrated from Ibn 'Abbas from the Prophet, may the peace and blessings of Allah be upon him, who said: "An *'umra* in Ramadan is equal to a hajj" – this is narrated by the group (of the narrators), except at-Tirmidhi; and from 'Ali, may Allah be pleased with him, it is related: "There is an *'umra* in each month" – this is narrated by ash-Shafi'i.

WHAT THE PERSON WHO INTENDS TO ENTER THE STATE OF IHRAM SHOULD DO

31. Ibn 'Abbas has narrated – and he ascribes the hadith directly to the Prophet, may the peace and blessings of Allah be upon him – that "women with post-natal bleeding and those who have their menstruation should make a *ghusl*, enter the *ihram* and carry out all the rites other than the *tawaf* of the House" – this is narrated by Abu Dawud and at-Tirmidhi.

32.[1] It is narrated from 'A'isha: "I would apply perfume to the Prophet, may Allah bless him and grant him peace, while he was embarking on the *ihram* and I would use the best perfume I could find" – and in another narration "when the Prophet, may Allah bless him and grant him peace, wanted to enter *ihram*, he would apply the best perfume he could find" – "and I could see the oil glistening in his hair and beard after that" – al-Bukhari and Muslim have narrated both (narrations).

33. It is narrated from Ibn 'Umar in a hadith of his from the Prophet, may the peace and blessings of Allah be upon him: "Each one of you should enter the *ihram* in his waist wrapping, the wrapper covering his torso and two sandals; and if you do not find two sandals, then two leather socks, and cut them beneath the ankles" – this Ahmad has related.

---

1 This is not numbered in the edition.

Greeting the Black Stone and kissing it

34. Ibn 'Abbas has narrated: "The Prophet, may the peace and blessings of Allah be upon him, made the *tawaf* during the 'Farewell Hajj' on a camel, and he saluted the Corner with his hooked stick" – agreed upon (by al-Bukhari and Muslim).

35. It is narrated from Abu Tufayl 'Amir ibn Wathila: "I saw the Messenger of Allah, may the peace and blessings of Allah be upon him, making the *tawaf* of the House, saluting the Black Stone with his crooked stick and then kissing the stick" – this is narrated by Muslim, Abu Dawud, and Ibn Majah.

36. Ibn 'Amr was asked about saluting the Black Stone and he replied: "I saw the Messenger of Allah may the peace and blessings of Allah be upon him, saluting it and kissing it" – this is narrated by al-Bukhari.

37. It is narrated from 'Umar that he would kiss the Stone saying: "I know that you are (only) a stone which can cause no harm or benefit – and if I had not seen the Messenger of Allah, may the peace and blessings of Allah be upon him, kiss you, I would not have kissed you" – the group narrated it.

38. It is related from Ibn 'Abbas: "The Messenger of Allah, may the peace and blessings of Allah be upon him, said: 'This Stone will come on the Day of Rising with two eyes with which it will be able to see, with a tongue with which it will speak and it will bear witness to those who have truly saluted it'" – this is narrated by Ahmad, Ibn Majah and at-Tirmidhi.

39. In al-Bukhari, in the chapter entitled 'The destruction of the Ka'ba' 'A'isha related, may Allah be pleased with her: "The Prophet said, may the peace and blessings of Allah be upon him: "…it was as if I was looking at him, a black person with thin legs tearing out the stones (of the Ka'ba) one by one."

40. It is related from Abu Hurayra, may Allah be pleased with him, that "the Messenger of Allah, may the peace and blessings of Allah be upon him, said: 'A man from Ethiopia with thin legs will demolish the Ka'ba'" – this too is from al-Bukhari.

It is related in *Fath al-Bari* from 'Ali who said: "Increase your making of the *tawaf* of this House before you are prevented from doing so. It is as if I can see a bald (*asla'*) man from Ethiopia" – or he may have said "insolent (*asma'*)" – "with thin legs who is sitting on it while it was being destroyed" – then the author of *Fath al-Bari* said: "Yahya al-Hamdani related it in another *marfu'* chain of narration of his from 'Ali."

Then he mentioned how the Qaramita (Carmathians) carried the Stone to their country and then returned it after a long time.

O Allah grant peace and blessings on Muhammad and on his Family and Companions.

Praise be to Allah, the Lord of all the worlds, the All-Merciful, the Most Merciful, the King of the Day of Judgement. You alone we worship. You alone we ask for help.

Guide us on the Straight Path, the Path of those whom You have blessed, not of those with anger on them, nor of the misguided.

O Allah we ask You for the intercession of Your Prophet, the Chosen One, and of his Family and Companions the people of sincerity who are true to their word, and that you accept this *du'a* of us; that You forgive us, have mercy on us, overlook our mistakes and the wrong we have done deliberately; that You forgive us, our parents, Shaykhs, our children, our brothers and all the Muslim men and women; and that You remove from us the evil consequences (of our wrong actions) and that You make up for them from the treasures of Your overflowing generosity and goodness; that You cause us to die on Your pure sunna and raise us with Your rightly guided slaves and Awliya whom You have brought near to You; that you shade us with the shade of Your Throne; that You give us the record of our actions in our right hand; that You cause all of us to live within the protection of the deen and the well-being of the *dunya*, with a sound *ruh* and body – for surely You are capable of any thing. How glorious is Allah, the Vast, and all praise belongs to Him! I bear witness that there is no god but Allah alone and without partner, and I bear witness that Muhammad is His slave and his Messenger, may the peace and blessings of Allah be upon him and on his Family and Companions.

Glory be to your Lord, the Lord of might, beyond anything they describe and peace be upon the Messengers. and praise be to Allah, the Lord of all the worlds. Amin.

The Principles of Tasawwuf and the Guides to Realisation

The Principles of Tasawwuf and the Guides to Realisation

وَتَوْبَةٌ مِنْ كُلِّ ذَنْبٍ يُجْتَرَمْ

تَجِبُ فَوْراً مُطْلَقاً وَهِيَ النَّدَمْ

291 It is obligatory to turn in *tawba* immediately and absolutely from all wrong action committed, and this means regret –

بِشَرْطِ الْإِقْلَاعِ وَنَفْيِ الْإِصْرَارْ

وَلْيَتْلَافَ مُمْكِناً ذَا اسْتِغْفَارْ

292 conditional upon eliminating this (wrong action from one's behaviour) and not persevering in it; and one possible way of making redress is through seeking forgiveness

'Ali ibn 'Abd as-Sadiq said: "The word *al-israr* 'persevere' means either to continue the wrong action or to have the intention to return to it. Mayyara said: 'What is meant here is the second of the two – that is, (a *tawba*) conditional upon him eliminating this (wrong action) from his behaviour and not intending to return to it. Thus the latter (meaning) is of a more general import than the former, and had he just mentioned the latter, it would have been enough.' What he intends by this is to state clearly and explicitly that this is obligatory for those specific persons (who have committed the wrong actions)."

Mention must be made here of some sections, even if it means a lengthy discussion, for they are contained insha'Allah in his counsel.

First Section

It must be done immediately – for he did not state that it might be done later. If it were to be done later, then it would (also) be necessary to turn in *tawba* (from this delay) – although turning in *tawba* from one wrong action while remaining with another (wrong action) is valid. Perfection, however, lies in turning in *tawba* from all wrong action. *Tawba* is to abandon wrong actions – both for the sake of Allah and on account of what Allah has threatened (as punishment) on account of such (wrong actions). Ibn Zakari said, commenting on his words (that it is obligatory) 'on those specific persons (who have committed the wrong actions)': "Al-Jazuli said: 'The principle in this (judgement) is the Book, the sunna and the consensus. As for the Book, it is the words of Allah: "*Turn to Allah every one of you, muminun, so that hopefully you will have success*"[1], and His words, exalted is He: "*You who have iman! make tawba to Allah. It may be that your Lord will erase your bad actions from you…*"[2] – and Allah intends (the words) 'hopefully' and 'it may be that' as an obligation; as for the sunna, it is his words, may the peace and blessings of Allah be upon him: "Make *tawba* – for I turn to Allah in *tawba* every day[3] seventy times" while in other narrations it reads "a hundred times" and his saying: "The person who turns in *tawba* from a wrong action is as someone who has no wrong action"; as for the consensus, it is that it is obligatory.'"

He has also said, commenting on his saying 'his exhortation that it must be done immediately – for he did not state that it might be done later. If it were to be done later, then it would (also) be necessary to turn in *tawba* (from this delay)': "Al-Jazuli said: 'So whoever delays it is acting in disobedience and *tawba* is obligatory for him for his delay – and whoever does not (turn in *tawba*), then it is counted as a further wrong action.'"

He has also said, commenting on his words '*Tawba* is to abandon wrong actions – both for the sake of Allah…': "Abandoning wrong actions may either be with respect to the wrong action itself – and this occurs at the time of committing it or immediately following it, or it may be with respect to having chosen this (course of action) or having inclined to such (action) – and this occurs after some (considerable) time has passed since having committed (the wrong action). Thus the *tawba* of an old man is valid even if at the moment of making *tawba* from fornication or banditry (for example) committed earlier (in his life) he is no longer physically capable of such (wrong actions)."

---

1 an-Nur – The Light: 31
2 at-Tahrim – The Prohibition: 8
3 The text has *marrah* – time – but what is well known is that it is *yawm* – day.

Ibn Zakari has also said, commenting on his words 'for the sake of Allah': "that is, out of respect for Him, glorious is He, to demonstrate that this *tawba* is in obedience to His command."

Commenting on his words 'and on account of what Allah has threatened (as punishment) on account of such (wrong actions)' he said: "(As for those) who turn in *tawba* in order to expiate their wrong actions and (to be) raised in stations – he is indicating by this that abandoning wrong actions for a reason connected to the next world, like for example on account of a desire to obtain the reward or out of fear for the punishment, does not preclude someone from being (considered) as being in a state of *tawba*, even though it is less meritorious than doing it (purely) to honour and glorify the majesty (of Allah)." The words of Ibn Zakari.

As-Sanusi said in *Sharh al-Qaseed*: "Know that the reality of *tawba* in the law is regret for the act of disobedience and recognition of it as wrong; and if you wish you might say that it is regret for a wrong action because of its abominable nature with regard to the *shari'ah*. Regret for a wrong action because of the physical harm it might have caused or because it has brought shame to one's good name, honour or the like is not *tawba*. At-Taftazani said: 'There is uncertainty (amongst certain *fuqaha*) as to whether *tawba* based on fear of the Fire or out of desire for the Garden is actually *tawba*. This uncertainty stems from doubt as to whether or not this regret is based on its loathsomeness (in the eyes of the law) and its being an act of disobedience; there is also uncertainty as to whether *tawba* based on its abominable nature when combined with another aim (is actually *tawba*). The truth of the matter is that if this aspect of repugnance is such that it produces regret of itself (i.e. when stripped of any other aim), then this *tawba* is valid; otherwise it is not. Likewise, there is uncertainty regarding *tawba* made during a dreadful illness, that is, as to whether this *tawba* stems from an abhorrence of the wrong action (itself) or rather from fear as it would be in the next world from looking directly at the Fire. The most evident meaning of the words of the Prophet, may the peace and blessings of Allah be upon him, is that *tawba* is accepted as long as the signs of death (marking the last moments of life) have not appeared in the person. The meaning of regret is a sense of sorrow and pain at what one has done and a wishing that one had not done it.' Shaykh Ibn 'Arafa described it as the state where the *nafs* is pained because of the abhorrence of what one has done. At-Taftazani said: 'Another condition has been added to *tawba* and that is the resolve to desist from returning to the (action) in the future.' This (condition) has been objected to (by some who argue) that committing a wrong action in the future would not occur to someone who is confused, mad or the like, or to someone who is incapable of committing such a thing when afflicted by something like dumbness – in the case of unsubstantiated accusations of sexual infidelity, or paralysis – in the case of stealing, or castration – in the case of fornication. Thus one cannot imagine, (they argue), that someone would resolve to desist from (such wrong actions) given that such (a resolve) implies the capacity to undertake and freely choose (to commit these wrong actions). He has answered by saying: 'What is (obviously) meant is desisting from something which one *thinks* one is capable of doing – such that if that capability were to be removed, then the resolve to desist from something would not be stipulated.' The words of Imam al-Haramayn may also be understood in this manner."

Ibn Abi Jamra said, commenting on the words (of the hadith) 'Whoever intends a wrong action but desists from it, then (the reward for) a good action is written for him': "As for our saying 'the manner of desisting which is for Allah' – (what we mean by) 'the manner ...' is that nothing stops him from committing the wrong action which he intended to commit but fear of Allah, exalted is He, because of His punishment, or shame before Him such as He is worthy of being shown, or desire for His promised reward – mentioned when He says: "*as for him who forbade the self its whims, the Garden will be his refuge.*"[1]

The author of *al-Jawahir wa'l-Yawaqeet* said: "The strongest proof of the obligation to make *tawba* immediately is the words of Allah, exalted is He: '*Turn to Allah every one of you, muminun, so that hopefully you will have success.*'[2] If making *tawba* does not come about for us, then we are obliged to make *tawba* for abandoning *tawba*, and if we have no authentic *tawba* for having abandoned *tawba* then we are obliged to turn in *tawba* for having persisted in abandoning *tawba* – and this for as long as we are alive. However, there is no disease but that there is also a cure for it and so if we do not manage to turn in *tawba* at all, then there is always the special mercy of Allah which He bestows on those of the Muslims who die persisting (in wrong action or lack of *tawba*)."

Know that the reality of *tawba* is recognition that Allah, exalted is He, is the One Who determined and decreed the wrong action for the slave (in the first place) before it came into being; and that the meaning of the hadith: "If the slave commits a wrong action, then know that he has a Lord who forgives wrong actions and punishes him for them ... Do whatever you like for I have forgiven you" is indeed "commit any kind of wrong action you wish and seek forgiveness of Me for I will forgive you"! but that there is no benefit

---

1 an-Nazi'at – The Pluckers: 40
2 an-Nur – The Light: 31

in this knowledge – that he has a Lord who forgives wrong actions – *without an expression of (genuine) regret*, so realise this! This is what is accessible of words on its definition and its ruling.

As for the excellence of *tawba*, many narrations have been recorded. In the *Sahih* of Muslim it is stated: "Allah is more overjoyed at the *tawba* of his believing slave than the man with his riding beast – which is bearing his food and drink – in a dangerous desert who goes to sleep and when he awakes, finds it gone. He then looks for it until he is overcome by thirst and says to himself 'I shall return to the place I started from and will go to sleep and die there.' So he places his head on his forearm to lay down and die but then wakes up to find his mount with his provision, food and drink in front of him – Allah is more overjoyed with the *tawba* of the believing slave than this man at (the sight of) his riding beast and provision." – or whatever the exact words of Muslim are.

It is also related in al-Bukhari from 'A'isha, may Allah be pleased with her, that the Messenger of Allah, may the peace and blessings of Allah be upon him, said: "If the slave admits his wrong action and turns to Allah in *tawba*. then Allah will turn to him (in forgiveness)."

It is also related that: "Allah is more overjoyed at the *tawba* of His slave than one of you who comes across his camel which he had lost in the desert."

Likewise it is narrated in *al-Jami' al-Kabir*: "Allah is more overjoyed with the *tawba* of His slave than the man incapable of fathering a child who then becomes a father, than the person who loses his riding beast and then finds it again, and than the thirsty person who arrives at the watering hole." There is also the narration in the same work: "Whoever turns in *tawba* before the sun rises again after having set, then Allah will turn to him." Al-Munawi said: "that is, He will accept his *tawba*, will be content with it and will look with kindness and mercy on him. This is because when the slave comes seeking forgiveness and renouncing (his wrong action), as best as he is able, then Allah will accept this of him and treat him with forgiveness and indulgence. The hadith is also a comfort to the slaves, an encouragement to them to make *tawba* and prevents them from despairing; and an indication that even if the wrong actions are great, then His forgiveness is even greater and His Generosity vaster. His saying 'He will turn to him (in forgiveness)' is a metaphor for His acceptance of the *tawba*. There is also another condition, namely that it occurs before the death rattle."

It is related in *Majma' al-Ahbab* from Wahb ibn Munabbih at the end of the *Zabur* of Dawud: "Listen to me! for I am telling the truth: if one of My slaves commits crimes so great (in number) that they fill the whole world from the east to the west and then he regrets some minor wrong action and turns to Me in forgiveness just once, and I feel that it comes from his heart and that he will not commit it again, then I will remove the (wrong actions) from him more quickly than the rain falling from the sky to the earth."

It is also related in *al-Jami' as-Saghir* that: "Whoever turns in *tawba* to Allah before the death rattle sets in, then Allah will accept his *tawba* of him" – or whatever his exact words were. Al-Munawi said: "If someone's *tawba* is accepted, then he will never suffer torment." Al-Kalabadhi said: "It is clear that at this moment (before death), he cannot make good the past – *tawba* on his part must be (sincere, that is made) from the heart and accompanied by a seeking forgiveness of Him on the tongue; at the moment of the death rattle, however, his *tawba* will not be accepted."

He said in *Fath al-Bari*, commenting on the hadith 'Whoever drinks wine in this world and then later (*thumma*) does not make *tawba* for it will be prohibited (from drinking) it in the next world': "What may be understood from his words 'and then later does not make *tawba* for it' is that *tawba* is permitted throughout one's life as long as the death rattle has not set in – as the 'then later' (in Arabic: *thumma*) indicates a certain delay: acceptance of one's *tawba* is not conditional upon one making it immediately (after the wrong action), and Allah knows best."

Second section

On the judgement regarding 'the making good of criminal or unjust acts (done to other people)' (*radd al-madhalim*), and (the question) as to whether the validity of the *tawba* is conditional upon this restoration (of the right of the wrong person) and related matters – Sheen said: "It is stated in *Sharh al-Wusta*, after Taftazani's discussion of *radd al-madhalim*: '... it must also be realised that this additional aspect is another obligation independent of the definition of *tawba*. The Imam al-Haramayn, may Allah have mercy on him, said that if a killer regrets (his crime) but does not submit himself (to those who have the right to take his life as requital), then his *tawba* is valid, and that his refusal to submit to those with the right of requital is another wrong action, but that it does not impair in any way his *tawba* with respect to the homicide.' Then he goes on to say: 'However sometimes the *tawba* is not valid without fulfilling the right of the (wronged) slave, like for example in the case of unlawful seizure of property – for regret for one's action is not valid if one still has the thing seized in one's possession, and so there is a difference between killing and unlawful seizure of something.'"

He said in *Sharh al-Qaseed*, commenting on his words 'and likewise he must make good any injustice done to someone and not delay': "Regret – if understood in the sense of *tawba* – implies the immediate abandoning (of the wrong action in question), like *tawba* in the case of someone actually in the act of the unlawful seizing something, or the person actually drinking wine. If by *madhalim* the author is referring to the *actual* property unlawfully seized – and not something which he must pay back in kind or money – then *tawba* from this unlawful seizure is conditional upon the return of this (property); if however, he means some (article of property) which has been destroyed or is no longer available, then the validity of the *tawba* in (this case of) seizure is not dependent upon the return of some compensatory thing or sum, according to the majority (of the *fuqaha*), but rather it is another (separate) obligation, independent (of this act of *tawba*)."

There are four kinds of *madhalim*: those related to wealth or property, those related to honour, those related to the sanctity (of one's womenfolk) and those relating to one's person. Zarruq said: "As for that related to wealth or property, there exists a consensus that it is obligatory to restore it." Ibn Zakari said: "that is, if he is able." It is stated in *Manahij al-'Abidin*: "If he is unable to return the property because of poverty or because the thing in question is not available, then he is released from this obligation; and if he is unable to return it because the man (to whom it is to be restored) is absent or has died and he is able to give (a similar amount in) *sadaqa* then he should do so; if not, then he should increase his good actions (towards others) and return to Allah in humility and devotion in the hope that He will fulfil the (wronged person's claim against him) on the Day of Rising."

Zarruq said: "as for what is related to honour, there is a well known difference of opinion regarding the obligation to seek the forgiveness of the person wronged." Ibn Zakari said: "that which is related to honour is of two kinds: the first, when injury has been caused through speech, like calumniation, slander or bearing witness against someone in a disparaging manner. Zarruq said: 'It is obligatory for you to deny or to withdraw what you have said in front of the person to whom you said it, and to withdraw your testimony if you bore false witness; and to seek that he overlook what you said and to demonstrate that you no longer hold to what you said or related.'

The second is backbiting or alluding to someone behind their backs with some disparaging remark but not causing any actual harm or injury, in which case one must either seek to absolve oneself from it or one should praise the person to compensate (for what one said), seek forgiveness (of Allah) and render service – for these are all acknowledged acts (in such a situation). However, it has been said that seeking to be released from it is not obligatory just as granting a release is not obligatory; and it has also been said that this applies in the case of some insignificant matter; and it has also been said that mere mention of it (again) creates a (further) calumny, especially when it is stipulated that one must specify (the wrong action) and describe it (in detail). So fulfil your contracts (with people), renew your sense of obligation and responsibility, increase your seeking of forgiveness (from Allah), and maintain your striving – then Allah will be the first to grant forgiveness in the matter.'"

It is stated in *Minhaj al-'Abidin*: "If regarding a matter of honour, you fear you will anger the person and inflame his passion yet more (by seeking forgiveness of him), then one should have recourse to Allah – seeking that He satisfy the (claim of the injured) person's (pride) in your stead – and should seek forgiveness on behalf of the (injured) person."

USEFUL POINT: al-Baquri has mentioned in the abridgement of *al-Furuq* – as well as Ibn 'Arafa and the author of *Fath al-Bari*: "There is a difference of opinion regarding the *tawba* for *qadhf* – unsubstantiated accusations of sexual infidelity,[1] that is, as to whether it is required to deny what one said. Ash-Shafi'i said that it is stipulated, while Malik that it is not." In *Fath al-Bari*, commenting on al-Bukhari's words 'and how is his *tawba* recognised', that is the slanderer, and it is as if he is indicating the difference of opinion in this: "most of the early generations have narrated that one must deny what one said, and this is the judgement of ash-Shafi'i, and an explanation of this has already been given above from ash-Sha'bi and others; and Ibn Abi Shayba has related something similar from Tawus. It is related from Malik that it is enough for him to increase his good actions and that it is not conditional upon his denying what he said – for it is possible that he was telling the truth in the matter; and the author inclines to this (judgement) too." The end of Ibn Hajar's words.

Zarruq said: "There must be no seeking – of the woman whose good name has been violated – that she release (him) from the (false) accusation." Ibn Zakari said: "The author stated: 'and anything which might bring shame on the female involved, like (seeking her forgiveness) in the case of (accusation of) fornication, even if just once, would be a (further potential) affliction and tribulation. You should seek pardon from Allah (rather than the woman involved); what is obligatory for you is to resolve to renounce and disavow this (violation of her sanctity) – for to manifest (it once more) would be a

---

1 *Qadhf* means an unsubstantiated accusation of sexual infidelity, i.e. it comprises anything less than four utterly reputable witnesses directly witnessing illegal sexual intercourse. Ed.

slandering of the female with whom the fornication was (allegedly) committed and a (further) degradation for oneself in being associated with her crime – that is, an exposing oneself to offence and grievance if one remains silent, and to belittlement if one seeks to get to the truth of the matter but the (fornication) is not proven. All this is forbidden and a violation of (the social) order. Moreover, there is a difference of opinion regarding fornication, that is, as to whether it is a 'right of Allah' or 'a right of man'; and as for the owner's right to or claim over the vagina of the slave girl, it is the same as the right over a wife and the *sariya* slave girl taken in marriage – any other than this is the right of Allah, and it is not possible to seek to absolve oneself of the offence to the injured party for fear of affliction, strife and discord (resulting from this), although Abu Hamid said: "If he is able then it is obligatory." But I would say that this capacity of his would involve another wrong action, namely slander of the woman, and exposure of the person whose right has been violated to innuendo because of the obscenity involved. All of this would amount to disobedience (of the law) and would be an evil action, so examine the (matter)!' – and this he has related from Abu Hamid and recorded in *Minhaj al-'Abidin*.

"He also said in *al-Ihya*: 'If the crime against someone is such that were he to mention it or make it known, he would suffer harm and injury and be ill treated and wronged by its becoming known, as in the case of his fornicating with his slave girl or (members of) his family – that is, people would associated him with this shameful act when talking about it and this would increase his injury, however much he tried to explain – then it is not valid for him to seek to absolve himself. Rather, he should only do so in secret. However, the injustice on his part remains and he must make it good by performing good actions, just as he would make good an injustice done to a person (now) dead or absent. Thus mentioning it and making it known would be another wrong action in itself – from which it would be necessary to seek to absolve oneself from (anew).'" All this is from the words of Ibn Zakari.

It is stated in (the work of) al-Munawi: "Among the conditions of *tawba* is that one should seek release or exemption from the man legally married to the woman with whom fornication has been committed. However this (judgement) is weak; and the correct judgement is that he may be forgiven (for foregoing) this – because of the evil consequences of disclosing it."

THIRD SECTION

As to whether an absolute release or exemption – that is, where one does not specify to the person who has been wronged the nature of the injustice – is enough, or whether it is necessary to stipulate (the injustice), the gist of what he has mentioned (on the matter) is that there are three judgements: firstly, that this absolute exemption is not enough and that there has to be a specifying of the injustice; secondly, that it is enough; and thirdly that the matter depends on the circumstances. The following is a small portion of what they have said on the matter.

It is narrated in al-Bukhari – in the chapter regarding 'whether the person who has committed an injustice towards another man and who seeks release from him for it should explain the nature of his injustice (to him in detail)' – that the Messenger, may the peace and blessings of Allah be upon him, said: "Whoever has committed an injustice against his brother – with respect to his honour or anything else – then he should beg him to forgive him before the Day of Rising when there will no longer be any dinars or dirhams (to compensate for wrong actions). If he has some good actions, they will be taken from him according to the amount of the injustice he has committed and if he has no good actions, then the wrong actions of the wronged person will be loaded on him instead."

At-Tawudi has affirmed this in his *Hashiya 'ala'l-Bukhari*, saying that "he does this by declaring 'I have absolved you from it,' that is, 'I declare you are free of any guilt.' As for whether he should specify the nature of the injustice and whether it is necessary that he describe it in order for his exemption to be valid, the well known judgement of the *madhhab* of ash-Shafi'i is that he does, although the unconditional nature of the hadith indicates the opposite and that it is valid to grant release from some unknown (injustice). It is related from at-Tirmidhi that (this unconditional nature of the exemption applies in the case of an injustice regarding his) honour or wealth, or something connected with his (honour), like his wife, relative or slave."

Ibn Hajar also said in *al-Fath* that his statement clarifies this possible difference of opinion as to the validity of declaring (another) free (from any injustice) in the case of an unknown (injustice) and demonstrates that the unconditional nature of the hadith strengthens the judgement of those who hold that it is valid. He also goes on to comment in the following chapter on the instance where the person absolves him but does not define to what degree – and in this there is also an indication (that it is legitimate) to declare someone free from any claim in the case of some unknown injustice. Ibn Batl, however, has claimed that in the hadith (mentioned) in this chapter, there is evidence for stipulating that the (injustice) must indeed be specified as the word 'injustice' which is referred to (in the hadith) necessarily implies that the extent (and seriousness) of it be known and that nothing be hidden. Ibn al-Muneer said: "The specifying of the extent (of the injustice) does exist in the hadith as (it is necessarily implied by the fact that) the person who has been wronged will require a fulfilment of his claim – which corresponds to the extent of the injustice – against the person who has committed the injustice to, and there is agreement about this. The difference of opinion (only) lies in the case where the wronged person renounces his claim in this world – that is, as to whether his (renouncing it) is conditional upon his being aware of the extent of the (injustice committed), and this is not specified in the hadith. There is an *ijma'* as to the validity of the release from a claim which is known and specific: if the specific thing (which has been seized illegally for example) is existent, then it is valid to release any claim to it (in this world) although this (release) does not mean an exemption (from the blame associated with the injustice committed)."

As to his saying 'with respect to his honour or anything else', it refers to any other thing, including money or property in whatever form, and injury, such as striking someone with one's hand and the like.

It is also related in al-Bukhari in the chapter 'If he releases him from an injustice then he has no right to rescind (his release of him)': "It is related from 'A'isha, may Allah be pleased with her, with respect to the *ayat* '*If a woman fears cruelty or aversion on her husband's part there is nothing wrong in the couple becoming reconciled*':[1] 'A man may dislike his wife and intend to divorce her, so she says to him I give up my rights so do not divorce me – and this *ayat* was revealed for this.'"

Ibn Hajar said: "His saying 'If the wronged person forgives the person who committed the injustice, he has no right to rescind (his release of him)' means – from something known, in the case of those (*'ulama*) who stipulate that it be known; or from something unknown, in the case of those who permit this – and there is agreement up to this point. As for what follows, there is a difference of opinion:

Dawudi said: 'This explanation does not correspond to the hadith although Ibn Muneer has justified the explanation by arguing that it is dealing with the case where a claim is dropped regarding an injustice which is over and done with while the meaning of the *ayat* refers to the dropping of any future claim – such that the non-fulfilment (of this claim) would not constitute an injustice as the right to it has been renounced.' Ibn Muneer said: 'But it is clear that al-Bukhari was subtle in using it as proof – as if he is arguing that should the

---

1 an Nisa' Women: 128

renunciation of any claim expected (in the future) occur, then the renunciation of any claim which has already come into being is all the more appropriate.'"

Ibn Mu'alla said in his *Mansik*: "Notice: An-Nawawi said, may Allah have mercy on him: 'The person who backbites must make *tawba* and must seek forgiveness from the person he has spoken about and it is imperative that he request the (wronged person) to release him (from any claim for requital or compensation). As to whether it is enough that he say: "I have spoken behind your back – so release me" (from any claim you have for requital) or whether he must describe what exactly he said of him behind his back, there are two opinions recorded of the followers of ash-Shafi'i, may Allah have mercy on him, the first, that this (exemption) is conditional upon his explaining (exactly what he said) and that if he releases him (from the injustice committed) without describing (what he said), then it is not valid – just as (it would not be valid) if he had released him from some (amount of) money or (article of) property which was unspecified; secondly, that this (exemption) is not bound by any such condition as (backbiting) is something which may be overlooked and excused, and (precise) knowledge of what (was said) is not stipulated – contrary to the case where money is involved.' He has further said, may Allah have mercy on him: 'The first is more evident as a person may well forgive one wrong action but not another.'" The words of Ibn al-Mu'alla, and the like has also been related in Suyuti's *al-Hawi*.

I say: "This (judgement regarding unconditional release) is sufficient, in our judgement, and there can be no further argument about it. This is because in the case of money or wealth, an unconditional release from any claim, in our judgement, is (also) sufficient. Khalil said: 'and if he releases him from something with respect to some past (injustice), or from any claim (whatsoever), or declares him exempt, then he is released unconditionally – also from slander and theft.' He has also said regarding *wakala* (agency), adding (another condition to) the acceptable (conditions regarding) delegating authority: 'and setting free (from claims), even if he is not aware of (the nature of) these three (conditions of *wakala*)'; he also said regarding gifts: '...and even if it is unspecified.' This acceptance of unconditional release is what an-Nafrawi declares (valid) in his commentary on the *Risala*: 'Backbiting has two aspects: the first, the actual committing of it, and the second, the injury to the person who is backbitten. In the first, *tawba* alone is of benefit and in the second, there must be – as well as the *tawba* – a seeking of forgiveness from the person who has been backbitten, even if this is by means of an unconditional release (on the part of the latter) from an injustice, the precise nature of which is only known to us; and in the case of one of the aspects, according to ash-Shafi'i. According to the Hanafis, however, the backbiting must be specifically described to the person backbitten if he came to hear of it in a particularly shameful manner."

What is ascribed to the Hanafis is what Sa'd ad-Deen at-Taftazani has deemed correct in his *Maqasid* when he says: "a precise description of what he said when backbiting is not necessary except if he heard of it in a particularly shameful way." This has also been related by as-Sanusi in *Sharh al-Qaseed* and *al-Wusta* and he does not mention any other (judgement). It is related from Ibn Abi Jamra, may Allah benefit us by him, that the precise nature (of the backbiting) must be specified, and likewise from al-Mu'alla in his *Mansik* from Ibn Abi Zayd.

After recording this, however, I came across an issue ascribed to Malik (which changed my opinion): in al-Baseeli it is stated – at the point where (he mentions) the words of Allah *'and He knows what they do'*: "Malik said in *al-'Utbiya* regarding someone who says to a man on his death 'Release me from any claim (you might have over me)' that this is not accepted of him until he specifies the nature of the injustice he should free him from." Something similar to what al-Baseeli has related from *al-'Utbiya* from Malik has also been narrated from ar-Rahouni in *al-Wasaya*. (It concerns the case of) a man – responsible for the inheritance of orphans – who, after their coming of age, told them that he had used some of their wealth (for himself) and asked them to release him from any claim on their part. When he asked Malik whether there was any good in their releasing him (from any claim), he replied: "No! unless he specifies the amount that they should exempt him from." The argument of those who have used Khalil's judgement regarding gifts (whose donor is) unknown, as evidence – or a similar judgement in *al-Bayan* – has been rejected by ar-Rahouni with many explicit texts, the gist of which is that a gift from someone unknown is valid although it has no legally binding or irrevocable quality, according to Ibn al-Qasim – contrary to Ibn 'Abd al-Hakam. This, then, clarifies the invalidity of what I have said above – beginning with my words 'I have said...' to 'whose (donor is) unknown', and praise belongs to Allah.

USEFUL POINT: al-Ubbi has related that al-'Iyad said, commenting on the words of Muslim 'No one kills another person but that the first son of Adam (i.e. Qabil (Cain), who committed the first murder) will be held responsible for part of the (crime)': "This he has explained, may the peace and blessings of Allah be upon him, with his words: 'Whoever initiates a good sunna will have its reward and the reward of those who put it into practice until the Day of Rising, and whoever initiates an evil sunna will bear the burden of it and the burden of those who put it into practice until the Day of Rising.' This hadith is cited in *Qawaʿid al-Islam* (as evidence) that whoever initiates something evil, then he will bear the burden (of guilt) of whoever else puts it into practice." I have said: "This applies when the second acts being aware of the first, but if he acts without knowledge of the first, then the Shaykh, that is, Ibn ʿArafa would say: 'There is no (further burden of blame) on the first, and the judgement in the case of the second is the same as that of someone who has initiated an evil act. One should not say of the hadith that it represents "a punishment (of one person) because of the action of another" but rather it demonstrates how the person acting is himself punished – for by initiating (a crime) and causing (others to follow him), then it is as if he himself had committed (the later crimes).' Al-Qurtubi said: 'By analogy to this Iblis shares in the burden of guilt of those who abandon prostration as this was the first way in which he disobeyed his lord. This (principle applies) as long as the first (person) does not make *tawba* from the (initial) act of disobedience: Adam, on whom be peace, was the first to disobey but they are in agreement that he does not share in the burden (of guilt) of those (coming after him) who violate a prohibition (of the *shariʿa*) as he, (Adam), turned in *tawba* and Allah turned (in forgiveness) to him. Thus it was as if he had not committed any crime at all – "for the person who turns in *tawba* is as someone who has no wrong action (to his name).""

I SAY: "The Shaykh used to say: 'It does indeed affect the first, even if he makes *tawba* – for even if his *tawba* from wrong action is valid, it does not mean that he is freed of the burden of guilt if he is aware (of the import of his crime in the future); and the (above mentioned) case of Adam, on whom be peace, applies, although it has also been said that (the case of) Adam has been excluded by consensus, and that it is of particular (restricted) import.'"

I SAY: "Abu Jamra, may Allah benefit us by him, holds (a judgement) which corresponds to (that of) Ibn ʿArafa and Ibn Hajar, while al-Munawi holds one which corresponds to (that of) al-Qurtubi. The author of *Fath al-Bari*, commenting on the hadith 'No one kills another person but that the first son of Adam will be held responsible for part of the (crime)': "that is, whoever initiates something, then it is recorded for him or against him, and this is the principle (underlying the judgement) which states 'that (the act of) aiding and abetting something which is not permitted is (itself) prohibited.' As for the hadith of Jarir recorded by Muslim 'Whoever instigates a beneficial sunna in Islam, then he will have its reward and the reward of those who act by it until the Day of Rising and whoever instigates in Islam an evil sunna, then he will bear its burden and the burden of those who act according to it to the Day of

Rising' this is understood as applying to someone who does not turn in *tawba* from the wrong action in question."

It is stated in the work of al-Munawi, in a comment on the tradition 'Whoever calls to a misguided action, then his burden (of guilt) will amount to (the combined guilt) of those who follow him in it – none of the burden of their guilt will be removed from him!': "If a person calls a group (of people) to a misguided action and they respond to it, then it – that is the (initial call) – is counted as one single wrong action despite there being many wrong actions (involved)." I have said: "If one were to ask: 'How can one make *tawba* from something that is brought into being afterwards and which is not (directly) from one's (own) action?' or someone argues 'a person can only turn in *tawba* from what he has willingly and consciously undertaken (himself), then one might reply by saying that this (kind of *tawba*) is expressed by regretting (one's actions) and by trying to prevent others from committing such actions if possible." Sayyidi 'Abdallah al-'Alawi composed the following:

Whoever turns in *tawba* after having assumed responsibility for his action,
   then he has done what is incumbent on him –
Even if the evil (consequences) of his action remain, he is similar in case to someone who refrains
   from any further propagation of a innovation in which he is followed;
Or someone who turns in *tawba* at the moment of leaving the place from which he had unlawfully seized something,
   or who turns in *tawba* immediately on throwing (something) before it hits (the person intended).

USEFUL POINT: The *'ulama* differ as to whether releasing someone from a claim one has over them is better than claiming one's right or vice versa; or whether one must discriminate (that is, the matter must be judged according to each individual case). The gist of what Zarruq has mentioned in his writings is that there are three judgements in the matter: the first, that claiming one's right is better, and this is the judgement of Ibn Sirin; the second, that one should discriminate between a claim or right in which no injustice is involved – in which case releasing (the other party) from the claim is better – and between a right or claim in which an injustice is involved – in which case claiming one's right is better, and he said that this is the judgement of Malik; and the third that releasing (the other) from one's right over him is better in all cases, and he said that this is the preferred judgement and the one which is practised.

I SAY: And this is the one practised by Ahmad Ibn Hanbal and al-Bahlul ibn

Rashid, and it has also been narrated of Malik that he followed this in the case of the person who beat him. It is stated in *Majmuʻ al-Ahbab*: "Al-Hafidh Ibn Nuʻaym said: 'It is related from Muhammad ibn Ziyad: "Ibn Hani' informed me saying: 'I was with Ahmad Ibn Hanbal and a man said to him: "O Abu 'Abdallah! I have said something about you behind your back so (please) release me from any claim (you have) over me" and he responded: "You are released as long as you do not repeat it." Then I said to him: "Why did you release him from any obligation when he had backbitten you?" and he replied: "Have you not seen how I imposed a condition on him?""""

It is stated in *al-Madarik*: "Abu Zarjuna said: 'I was caught unawares one *jumuʻa* night and was hit over the head. I informed al-Bahlul ibn Rashid of this the next morning and he then kept on at me, insisting that I should release the person responsible from any claim on my part. I said: 'They did such-and-such to me and they did such-and-such to me! Why should I release them from my right?' But he kept on at me until I released them from any obligation." The words of *al-Madarik*.

It is also stated by him that the person who beat al-Bahlul – and who was the cause of his (subsequent) death – asked him to grant him release (from any claim) for his having beat him and he replied: "I sought forgiveness for you, O you poor and miserable creature every time the whip was raised (from having struck me)!" It is also narrated: "You had not untied my hands before I acquitted you." It is also narrated that Malik released the person who had hit him from any obligation.

I SAY: "Al-Bahlul is one of the great and most excellent companions of Malik – reflect on what ʻIyad has transmitted about him in *al-Madarik* and about Malik – that is, about their both forgiving those who had beaten them – together with what Zarruq has transmitted from Malik."

It is also stated in *Siraj al-Mulouk* by at-Tartushi – one of the masters of the Malikis, according to al-Qarafi: "… that forgiveness is better; indeed what Zarruq said is correct, and the principle on which it is based is from the Hafidh of the Madhhab (Ibn Rushd) in *al-Bayan wa't-Tahseel*."

ISSUE: It is correct that *tawba* is not accepted after the sun rises from the west – neither from a *mumin* or *kafir*. What is mentioned by ʻAli ibn ʻAbd as-Sadiq, where he comments on the words of Khalil '… except by way of *tawba* when the injustice committed is (first) put right' has been rejected by at-Tawudi – and it is fitting that it be rejected. More than one (of the *'ulama*) have declared this, among them al-Qalshani, namely, that it is not accepted from anyone after the sun has risen from the west and al-Qalshani has declared this in his commentary on the *Risala* as has Abu'l-Hasan in *Ghayat al-Amani*, narrating from al-Mashdouli, and many others. Ibn Hajar has transmitted in *Fath al-Bari* hadith which also point to this where he says: "Abu Dawud and an-Nasa'i have transmitted the hadith of Mu'awiya in a *marfu'* chain of transmission: '*Tawba* continues to be accepted until the sun rises from the west. However, when it has risen, the heart will be sealed with what is in it, and people will have had enough action.' Ahmad, ad-Darimi and 'Abd ibn Humayd have related: '*Tawba* is not cut off until the sun rises from the west,' In the hadith of Safwan and Ibn 'Abbas, it is stated: 'I heard the Messenger of Allah, may the peace and blessings of Allah be upon him, say: "In the west there is a door open for *tawba* – so wide that it would take seventy years to traverse it – and it does not close until the sun rises from the west"', – and the like has been narrated by at-Tirmidhi who said that it is a *hasan sahih* hadith. It has also been recorded by an-Nasa'i and Ibn Majah; and Ibn Khuzayma and Ibn Hibban considered it *sahih*. In the hadith of Ibn 'Abbas, there is a similar transmission, as recorded by Ibn Mardawayh in which there is: 'So when the sun rises from the west, the two hinges of the gate are pushed back and then brought together again: when it is closed, then no more *tawba* is accepted after this and no good action is of benefit except from the one who had performed a good action before it – for they will (only) be rewarded for what preceded this.' It is transmitted by Na'eem ibn Humayd from 'Abdallah ibn 'Umar, may Allah be pleased with him, who said: '… the (people) will not have to wait long after Yajuj and Majuj before the sun rises from the west and someone will call out "You who have iman, your (actions) have been accepted of you!" and "You who are guilty of *kufr*, the door of *tawba* has been closed on you, and the pens are dry and the pages have been rolled up."'"

It has been narrated by way of Yazid ibn Shurayh and Kathir ibn Murra that: "When the sun rises from the west, the hearts will be sealed with what is in them and the recording angels will move away and the angels will be commanded that no (further) actions be recorded." 'Abd ibn Humayd and at-Tabarani have recorded with a *sahih* chain of narration by way of 'Amir ash-Sha'bi from 'A'isha that: "…when the first of the signs (of the Last Day) manifests, the pens will be set aside, the pages will be laid down, the recording angels will cease (to record) and the bodies will bear witness to their actions" – and even if it is *mawquf* (a statement of 'A'isha), nevertheless the judgement on it is that it is *marfu'* (i.e. ascribed to the Prophet, may Allah bless him and grant him peace). There is also a similar hadith by way of al-'Awfi from Ibn 'Abbas, and by way of Ibn Mas'ud who said: "The sign by which the actions will be sealed is the rising of the sun from the west."

I SAY: "Examine whether one may understand some of these hadith as indicating the same meaning as that mentioned in *al-Jawahir* from Shaykh Muhyiddeen, namely that no *mumin* will renege (on Islam) after the sun has risen in the west when he says: 'If you were to ask whether the *tawba* may continue during the (final) states that accompany one until (just before) death, then the reply would be "Yes – *tawba* remains valid as long as the slave is able to be addressed – until, that is, the sun rises from the west, when the door of *tawba* will be closed and a person's iman – and all the good he has earned by means of this iman – will be of no further use to him."' Shaykh Muhyiddeen added: 'It is clear that no door will be closed on the *mumin* preventing him from making *tawba* but rather the door will close so that his iman may not exit from his heart. How could it (be said to) close on him to the exclusion of this (*tawba*) when the *mumin* has already gone beyond this (stage of) *tawba*, has left it behind him by iman becoming firmly established in his heart. Thus he is happy at the closing of this door on his iman – happy that it will no longer be able to leave after its having entered. So no *mumin* will ever renege (on Islam) after this as there is no door by which iman may leave. Thus he realises that the closing of the door of *tawba* is a mercy for the *muminun* and a misfortune for the *kafirun*.'" Here ends the discussion of ash-Sha'rani.

I SAY: "and there is also, in my opinion, an indication in this of what 'Abd al-Baqi said in my presence, and Allah knows best."

USEFUL POINT: The gist of the discussion contained in *al-Fath* and that of al-Qastallani is that no one knows how much of the *dunya* has passed and how much remains except Allah. Al-Qastallani has refuted the author of *al-Kashf*, that is as-Suyuti saying: "The author of *al-Kashf* has based his argument on weak *hadith* as is his custom. He has relied on two of them to assert that the duration of the *dunya* is seven thousand years and that the Prophet, may the peace and blessings of Allah be upon him, has been sent at the end of the sixth part (of the seven thousand) – among them the hadith of ad-Dahhak al-Juhni who said: "I had a dream which I related to the Messenger of Allah, may the peace and blessings of Allah be upon him," – the hadith in which he relates: "I was with you, Messenger of Allah on the minbar which had seven steps and you were on the top step." The Messenger of Allah then said: "as for the minbar you saw with the seven steps and the top step upon which I was (sitting), (it represents) the *dunya* with its seven thousand years and I am at the end of it in terms of thousands."' This has been related by al-Bayhaqi in his *Dala'il*.

"His saying, 'and I am at the end of it in terms of thousands' i.e. (at the end of) the greater part of the seven thousand, so that it should correspond to the fact that his being sent, may Allah bless him and grant him peace, was at the end of the sixth thousand. If he had been sent at the beginning of the seventh thousand, then the greater (signs of the Hour) such as the Dajjal would have existed more than a hundred years before the Day, and so the Hour would rise upon completion of the thousand, and none of that exists, which shows that what remains of the seventh thousand is more than three hundred years."

Hafidh Ibn Hajar said: "The chain of narration of this hadith is extremely weak and it is recorded by Ibn as-Sakan in *as-Sahaba*: 'Its chain of narration is unknown, and Ibn Raml is not known amongst the Companions'; (and it is related) in Ibn al-Qutayba's *Ghareeb al-Hadith*, that is among the rare, unaccepted hadith.' Ibn al-Jawzi has included it in the fabricated hadith. Ibn al-Athir said: 'The wordings used are fabricated.' Ma'mar has recorded in *al-Jami'* from Ibn Najih from Mujahid that: 'I have been informed from 'Ikrima regarding the words of, exalted is He, '*In a day whose length is fifty thousand years*'[1]: "No one knows how much time has passed nor how much remains except Allah, exalted is He."'"

CONCLUSION: We ask Allah for the best of what (is mentioned in this section) – and it includes matters of great benefit:

1. Zarruq said in *Sharh al-Waghlisiya*: "If for example someone turns in *tawba* from the drinking of wine and he was drinking in company, then his *tawba* must be from three things: the drinking of wine, his being in company and his not condemning it to them. If he does not turn in *tawba* from all these, then he has not turned in *tawba* at all. Thus if his abandoning (drinking) is necessary for his *tawba*, he must observe this rule."

2. Al-Ubbi, in his commentary on Muslim one the hadith known as 'The Calumny (*al-ifk*)', that is, at the point when he said, may the peace and blessings of Allah be upon him: "'A'isha, I have been informed of such-and-such: if you are innocent, then Allah will establish your innocence and if you have committed a wrong action, then seek forgiveness of Allah and turn in *tawba* to Him for if the slave acknowledges his wrong action and then turns in *tawba* then Allah will turn to him' (then al-Ubbi) said: "Qadi 'Iyad said: 'ad-Dawudi said: "This proves that his wives, may the peace and blessings of Allah be upon him, had an obligation to admit what they had done and that it was not permitted for the Prophet, may the peace and blessings of Allah be upon him, to prevent them from doing so. Thus they were different from other women in this respect for he commanded other women to conceal (what they had done)."

1   al-Ma'arij – The Ascending Steps: 4

However, this is not so, for in the hadith he commands her to admit it and to seek forgiveness and turn in *tawba* – but this is between her and Allah, exalted is He. Likewise his saying "if the slave acknowledges his wrong action..." is not a justification for commanding her to openly admit it, but rather to admit it to Allah, exalted is He.' I say: His (particular) understanding of 'this asking for an admission (on her part)' is doubtful – for there is nothing in the hadith which indicates that, as the Qadi has mentioned.""' The words of al-Ubbi.

3. As for the person who finds *tawba* difficult, he must have recourse to Allah, humbly entreat Him and not despair of the mercy of Allah. Jasous – commenting on the words of the *Risala* 'and if any of the *fard* obligations have not been done, then he should do them immediately, desire of Allah that He accept them and should make *tawba* to Him for having omitted them; and he should have recourse to Allah when he finds it difficult to rein in his *nafs* and when trying to set the matter right; and (he should do all this) believing, with a certainty of belief, that He is the Owner of his affair and that He is the One Who guarantees its right course, its success and completion and should not let go of this (belief) irrespective of whether the (action) he is (engaged) in good or evil' – said: "By my life, with respect to the author's instruction to all those who incline to the realm of the desires, all those whose lower selves are unable to free themselves from such (desires), and all those who are overcome (in the struggle), these are extraordinary words! They should be written in gold ink and ruby for they perfectly describe the states of the like of us and clearly indicate what is our best course of action to cure ourselves. And 'May Allah cause us to act by them by His good grace and generosity' as Shaykh Zarruq said. There is a similar statement to that of the author's in the work of Imam ash-Shadhili." The words of Jussous.

It may be that the discussion he is referring to is that of Zarruq in *Jannat al-Mureed* where he says: "Shaykh Abu'l-Hasan ash-Shadhili, may Allah be pleased with him, said, concerning correcting one's manner of worship: 'Whoever inclines to the realm of desires and follows his whims and his self is unable to free itself or to overcome his lack of control, then his state of worship should be of two kinds, firstly a recognition of the blessing of Allah, exalted is He, in His granting him iman and *tawhid* and His causing his heart to love these (qualities) and be attracted to them, and that His causing him to find *kufr*, corruption and disobedience hateful. (In such a state) He should say:

يَا رَبِّ أَنْعَمْتَ عَلَيَّ بِهَذَا وَسَمَّيْتَنِي رَاشِداً فَكَيْفَ أَيْأَسُ مِنْكَ أَنْ تَمُدَّنِي بِفَضْلِكَ، وَإِنْ كُنْتُ

$$\text{مُتَخَلِّقاً فَأَرْجُو أَنْ تُقِيلَنِي وَإِنْ كُنْتُ زَائِفاً فَأَرْجُو أَنْ تَجْعَلَنِي خَالِصاً}$$

"Ya Rabbi an'amta 'alayya bihadha wa sammaytani rashidan, fa kayfa ay'asu minka an tamaddani fi fadlika, wa in kunta mutakhallifan fa arjou an tuqeelani, wa in kunta za'ifan fa arjou an taj'alani khalisan — O Lord You have blessed me with this (state of gratitude) and You have designated me as someone who is rightly guided (by this blessing of Yours) — so how should I despair of You extending Your help to me by Your grace. If I should be negligent (in my worship), then I hope that You will exempt me (from Your punishment) and if I should be insincere, then I hope that You will render me sincere."

2. he must have recourse to and recognise his need in Allah at all times. He must say:

$$\text{يَا رَبِّ سَلِّمْ سَلِّمْ وَقِنِي وَأَنْقِذْنِي}$$

"O Allah grant me safety, grant me safety, and protect me, and save me."

There is no escape for someone who has been overcome by the dictates of destiny and who has been cut him off by them from a pure worship of Allah, exalted is He, except by applying these two (instructions). If he fails to keep to them, then misery will be his lot and distance (from Allah, exalted is He,) will be necessarily his (fate) too. We seek refuge with Allah, exalted is He, and it is of Allah that we must ask for success and guidance for (only) He can grant them from His generosity.'" And more on the same subject will follow insha'Allah.

$$\text{وَحَاصِلُ التَّقْوَى اجْتِنَابٌ وَامْتِثَالْ}$$

$$\text{فِي ظَاهِرٍ وَبَاطِنٍ بِذَا تُنَالْ}$$

293 The outcome of *taqwa* is avoidance of (wrong action) and compliance (with what has been commanded) in the outward and in the inward (with respect to both the 'avoiding' and 'the following'); by that it is obtained!

$$\text{فَجَاءَتِ الأَقْسَامُ حَقّاً أَرْبَعَةْ}$$

$$\text{وَهِيَ لِلسَّالِكِ سُبُلُ الْمَنْفَعَةْ}$$

294 and so this amounts to four kinds (of means in all), and for the person travelling on the Path they represent the means and access to benefit

Ahmad Mayyara said: "Know that *taqwa* in the terminology of the law is a person's protecting himself from what harms him in the next world. The person of *taqwa* – that is, who protects himself, is the person of extreme caution and prudence. Such people are of three ranks: The first, those who protect themselves from the eternal Fire by freeing themselves of *shirk*, and this is referred to in the words of, exalted is He: '*and bound them to the expression of taqwa*'[1]; secondly, those who avoid anything blameworthy, whether by (avoiding the) action (themselves) or by omitting to do something (they should be doing), and this is referred to in the words of, exalted is He: '*If only the people of the cities had had* iman *and taqwa...*'[2]; thirdly, those who distance themselves from whatever distracts their secret from the Real, the True, and who devote themselves with all their spiritual and physical faculties – and this is *taqwa* demanded by Allah, exalted is He, when he says: '*You who have* iman! *Have taqwa of Allah with the taqwa due to Him.*'[3]"

USEFUL POINT: the most effective means to attaining the goal is *tawba*, humbling oneself to Allah and devotion to Him – whatever your state. Ibn Abi Jamra, after discussing this matter, said: "and in it there is an indication of the way of the People (of *tasawwuf*) for they say 'return to your Lord whatever state you are in and You will find that He will deal mercifully with you.' One of the (people of this science) said: 'Make your heart the repository of your secret and your Lord the place of your complaint.' Something similar has been narrated in the story of Yunus, on whom be peace, when he was in the belly of the whale: Allah, exalted is He, caused him to hear the voice of Qarun[4] who had been (condemned to) sink into the earth until the Day of Rising without any stability on it. Allah, exalted is He, then caused Qarun to hear Dhu'n-Nun (Yunus), on whom be peace, and he asked the guardian angels responsible for tormenting him if they could give him respite until he could speak with him. So they gave him permission and he called him and Yunus responded. He requested him (to tell) his story and Yunus informed him. He then said to him: "Go back to your Lord – you will find Him as soon as you set out for Him." Dhu'n-Nun, on whom be peace, then said to him: "and why did you not go back to Him?" He replied: "My *tawba* was delegated to my maternal

1   al-Fath – The Victory: 26
2   al-A'raf – The Ramparts: 96
3   Ali 'Imran – The Family of 'Imran: 102
4   Korah, who was proverbial for his wealth and avarice.

uncle Musa and he did not accept it" – or whatever the exact wording of the narration was. Then Dhu'n-Nun exclaimed: *"There is no god but You! Glory be to You! Truly I have been one of the wrongdoers."*[1] Thus Allah caused him to come out (of the fish) by His overflowing generosity and mercy. For this reason one of the *'ulama* said: "Your *taqwa* is a support for your hope and your hope is a support for your *taqwa*, and if you are devoid of both, then look to your Lord, look to your Lord!" that is the end of the words of Ibn Abi Jamra, and it is similar to what we have seen previously from Zarruq and Jussous. And it is said that the outcome of *taqwa* is:

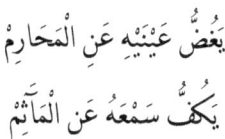

295 One lowers one's eyes before the haram, and seals off one's hearing from any blameworthy matter

Know that there are many things that are haram to look at. He said in *al-Waghlisiya*: "Among the organs of the body that it is obligatory to protect is the eye – so do not look at anything which is not permitted, that is, at the beauty of a woman or a youth with the eye of lasciviousness, or at anyone screened off in a household; nor at anyone else (without good reason) as this is (considered) spying and is a violation of a Muslim's (private sphere); nor at the rich with awe, or at the poor disparagingly; nor should one look askance at a Muslim without a (valid) reason. As for looking at one's own private parts, there is one judgement that it is forbidden. Whoever persists in looking at (what is not permitted) when not absolutely necessary will be tempted into committing fornication – this has been mentioned by Hakeem at-Tirmidhi in his 'Book of the *Salat*.'"

He has also said, commenting on his saying 'except for her face…': "… that is, it is not permitted for a man who is unrelated to her to see any of her other than what has been mentioned – if he wants to be secure from temptation; and it is not permitted for him to linger when looking at the beauty of her face unless he is seeking her hand in marriage; and it is permitted for him after he has informed her (of his intention), according to the well known view, although it is also said (it is permitted) even if he does not." He has also said, commenting on his words 'As for the *mahram* (who is related), it is permitted from the neck to the (top of the) head': "that is, that it is permitted for him to

---

1 al-Anbiya' – The Prophets: 86

see the top of the shoulders, the throat and neck, the hair, but not the breasts and below — for this has a particularly strong effect on the lower self."

As for his saying 'and the ends of the arms and feet', this includes whatever is adjacent to them, like the elbows or the middle of the shanks (of the legs), but not the knees, and the like. He also said, commenting on his words 'as for other than this': "Any other place is (also) liable to evoke sexual feelings and so one must not look at them unless one has no choice in the matter, and only someone with no deen or sense of honour would look intently (at other parts of the body)." Commenting on his words 'except in the case of an old woman, a black woman or the like' he said: "that is, ignoble women who are paid no attention — there is no harm in looking at such (women); but as for an older woman who is better looking than a young woman, or a black woman who arouses more sexual longing than a fairish woman, then it is not permitted to look at either of them."

Al-Ubbi said in *Ikmal al-Ikmal*: "The *'ulama* have said that it is not obligatory for a woman to cover her face when in the street; rather, that it is only recommended, and that it is obligatory for men to lower their eyes (when encountering women in the street)."

He also said: "There is no difference of opinion that the obligation to cover the face is one of the things particular to the wives of the Prophet, may the peace and blessings of Allah be upon him."

USEFUL POINT: as-Sanusi said in *Sharh al-Qaseed*: "It is narrated from him, on whom be peace and blessings, that he said: 'Looking at the beauty of a woman is one of the poisoned arrows of Iblis.' This either causes the death (of the person) or its wound remains until his death — or (at least for) an extremely long time. The *mumin* should always be mindful to protect this noble organ (of sight) from what should be of no concern to it, that is, if he entertains any hope that Allah, exalted is He, by His overflowing generosity, will afford — by means of this organ of sight — a vision of His supreme essence in the next world. One must hope that this aspect of excellence will be attained — for this excellence is part of the reality of the organ (of sight) above which there is no higher excellence — and this is (attained) by preserving and protecting it in every way possible from demeaning it, that is by preventing it from wandering aimlessly and from looking at (things) which are displeasing to the Lord blessed is He and exalted."

He said in *an-Naseeha*: "Also among the forbidden things is looking at tyrants with the eye of esteem and satisfaction at their state." Ibn Zakari said in his Commentary: "... as this is contrary to what has been established in the law, that is, that one should avoid them, sever all contact with them, frown at them and hate with the hate of Allah, as they are unjust." Ibn Shahin has narrated in *al-Ifrad* from a hadith of 'Abdallah ibn Mas'ud, may Allah be pleased with him: "Come closer to Allah by hating the people of disobedience; and look sullenly and gravely at them; and seek after the satisfaction of Allah by being angry at them; and come closer to Allah by distancing yourself from them." By his mention of 'eye of esteem' he has excluded (too the possibility of) looking at them with the eye of belittlement and rejection – that is, in the case of those who are in a position to look in this manner. This is to warn such people from doing this out of pride and conceit, or from a feeling of pleasure at being able to demonstrate their superiority, or from (a feeling of self-satisfaction) when indicating a better way (of behaviour to the tyrants).

Sayyidi Ibn 'Abbad, may Allah benefit us by him, said: "Many of the tyrannical and corrupt and many of those who seek an excessive portion of the delights of this world and its corrupting distractions act humbly and servilely towards those characterised by their knowledge and reformatory fervour; they consider such people to be a thousand times better than they; indeed they do not consider that they have any relation to them at all (being so immersed in this world). However, the greater their submissiveness and humility towards such people (of supposed knowledge) and the more they consider these people superior to them, the prouder and more arrogant these people (of knowledge) become: they begin to look at them disparagingly and to consider that they do not merit (in any way) the mercy of the All-Merciful and the Forgiver. In truth, the one group is not superior to the other – neither on account of their disparaging both this world and the next in the case of the one, nor on account of their entertaining hope in them both in the case of the other. Rather, the whole is from the overflowing bounty of the Most Merciful and Generous and part of His justice, the Wise and the All-Knowing. Take note of the story of al-Khali', which is mentioned in the *Sharh al-Hikam* when Ibn 'Ata'illah says 'An act of disobedience which causes you to become submissive and humble is better than an act of obedience which causes you to become arrogant and haughty': 'Amongst the Bani Isra'il was a man known as *al-Khali' Bani Isra'il* (the depraved one of the Bani Isra'il) on account of his excessive corruption. One day he passed by a man known as *'Abid Bani Isra'il* (the devotee from amongst the Bani Isra'il). Above the devotee there was a cloud which was shading him. Al-Khali' said to himself: "I am the depraved one of Bani Isra'il and that is the devotee of Bani Isra'il – if I sit with him it may well be that Allah, exalted is He, will benefit me by (means of) him" and so he sat next to him. And the devotee said to himself: "I am the devotee of Bani Isra'il and that is the depraved one of Bani Isra'il who is sitting himself down next to me" and despising him out of high-mindedness, he then said: "Leave me alone." Allah, exalted is He, then revealed to the prophet of that time what had occurred to them both, (saying:) "They should revise (their conception of how) the actions (of this world are judged) for I have forgiven the depraved one and have caused the actions of the devotee to be brought to nothing."" In another hadith it is related that the cloud moved over above the head of al-Khali'.

As for his saying 'He should protect...', he said in (the work of) al-Waghlisi: "among the limbs and organs that he must protect is his hearing: he should not listen to what is not permitted, like depraved speech, or any other speech involving backbiting and slander, or anything like singing and sounds from musical instruments and drums when not permitted – in short, anything which is not permitted to listen to or to cause others to hear." He said in his *Sharh*: "(among the faculties) which one is under an obligation to protect is that of hearing. Allah, exalted is He, said: '*Hearing, sight and hearts will all be questioned.*'[1] And he, on whom be peace and blessings said: 'The person who listens to slander is (counted as) one of the slanderers.' Thus the person who listens takes an active role along with the speaker, that is, in the case where he acquiesces to what he is saying or is able to refute it but does not do so." His saying 'He should not listen' refers to listening to the voices of women and experiencing sexual pleasure in doing so. According to a group (of *'ulama*), one should not (even) listen to their conversation. Also included in the term 'speech which is not permitted to listen to' is poetry made in praise of or in denigration (of someone): it has been reported that 'Whoever fills his belly with poetry, then Allah will fill it with vomit and pus' – that is, if delivered in this manner; for otherwise it is of benefit – and poetry used to be recited in front of the Prophet, may the peace and blessings of Allah be upon him."

As for his mention of 'singing', meaning that which is haram; it refers to that which stimulates sexually and leads to corruption and depravity. His mention of 'musical instruments' means that this (prohibition of sexually arousing music) applies whether or not an instrument is being used whether it be a horn, pipes or drums of any nature and description – for one may not listen to any such (music) deliberately."

His saying 'and drums when not permitted' refers to times other than (the celebration of) marriage – when it is licit in order to announce the marriage – as long as there is no reprehensible aspects to it.

---

1 al-Isra' – the Night Journey: 36

As for his saying 'and anything else which it is not permitted to listen to or cause others to hear', the rule in this case is (analogous to the principle) that when it is not permitted to express something it is also not permitted to let others hear such a thing – except, that is, when absolutely necessity, in which case it is *makruh*. Thus when it is not permitted to listen to something it is also not permitted to let others hear it: it is not permitted for a woman to allow her voice to be heard by someone she knows will be aroused by it, nor is it permitted for a man. This is the gist of what Zarruq intended by his discussion and we have omitted some of it.

It is related in al-Bukhari from Ibn 'Abbas, may Allah be pleased with them both, from the Prophet, may the peace and blessings of Allah be upon him: "Whoever claims to have had a dream which he did not in fact have will be ordered to make a knot between two barley grains which he will not be able to do; and if someone listens to a conversation of a group of people who do not want him to hear, or they distance themselves from him (in order not to be heard, and he still tries to overhear), then lead will be poured into his ears on the Day of Rising; and whoever makes an image will be punished (on the Day of Rising) and will be charged with blowing life into it which he will not be able to do." Ibn Abi Jamra has questioned, may Allah benefit us by him, whether His saying, may the peace and blessings of Allah be upon him, 'whoever listens to the conversation of a group of people and they do not want him to hear' is to be understood in a general way, that is, applicable in all cases or whether it is only of particular import. The most evident judgement is that it has a particular application for if it were of general import, it would be more than any of us could bear and our Lord, glorious is He, has shown kindness and favour to us and has not charged us with anything (we cannot bear). Likewise, with regard (to the requirement of) knowing that they do not want us to hear (their conversation): if it were always required of us that we be aware (whether or not someone wants us to hear them), then it would unbearable (for many of us). Rather we have (only) been charged with being aware of the (general) circumstances of the situation – which might indicate an aversion on their part to our listening to the conversation. Thus the 'listening' (being referred to in the hadith) applies to a particular case rather than a general one. For example, if you were to (deliberately try and) overhear people conversing in their homes, you would be subject to (the judgement implicit in) this hadith – for this (instance) must be considered in accordance with the circumstances of the situation – which is their being in their homes and their having closed their doors on you. This alone indicates that they want to keep the conversation to themselves and exclude you and anyone else outside their door. Likewise, if someone goes off with another or with a group without you, then (this too indicates) they do not want you to hear their conversation. If (despite this indication) you were to (try and) overhear them, then you would be subject to (the judgement implicit in) this hadith.

Then he goes on to say: "If, however, they speak in front of you openly and are averse in their hearts to your hearing their conversation, then this does not render you responsible in any way: you are not required to know of their dislike of your hearing their conversation." Here his discussion ends, and may Allah, glorious and exalted is He, benefit us by him and his like.

$$\text{كَغِيبَةٍ نَمِيمَةٍ زُورٍ كَذِبْ}$$

$$\text{لِسَانُهُ أَحْرَى بِتَرْكِ مَا جُلِبْ}$$

296 as, for example, backbiting, slander, bearing false witness or lying, and more importantly one's tongue should avoid saying anything just mentioned

He said in *al-Fath*: "Backbiting is mention of a person in terms he would dislike, whether regarding the physical form of the person or his deen, his (activity in the) world, his genealogy, his wealth, his children, parents, wife, servants, clothes or movements, (even the fact that he is) cheerful or sad – or anything else."

He also said: "It is to say something about your brother which he would dislike if he were to hear it – irrespective of whether it is true or not, or whether it is regarding his physical form, his wealth, children or parents. His saying 'his deen or his (activity in the) world' refers even to (mention of) his clothes, cloak or riding beast or anything connected to him – even your saying 'his sleeve is wide' or 'his robe hangs low', irrespective of whether it is a clear, unambiguous statement, or by way of indication or gesture" – and a similar statement is to be found in Zarruq's *Sharh al-Waghlisiya*.[1]

I SAY: "based on this, whoever backbites a man who has many children then he has backbitten all of them; likewise whoever backbites someone who has two children, then he has backbitten all of them; again, whoever backbites a slave having (various) masters, then he has backbitten all of them. This (backbiting)

---

1 The author says that the *Sharh* is by someone whom he indicates by the letters *Lam-dal*, but the only commentary we have come across is by Zarruq, whom the author indicates by *Dal*. Ed.

is one of the greatest of calamities – how much disaster and misfortune striking the Muslims (in general) has come from it!"

The commentator also related something even more alarming from Shaykh al-Jazuli: "An example of backbiting is: 'The Samarani[1] did such-and-such' because the whole of his tribe would hate that."

Mayyara also said: "It is forbidden in the Book, the sunna and by *ijma'*: as for the Book, (the prohibition is) in His words, exalted is He: '*and do not backbite one another. Would any of you like to eat his brother's dead flesh? No, you would hate it.*'[2] It is said that the comparison being made here is based on the fact that a corpse cannot defend itself. As for the sunna, (the prohibition is) in his words, may the peace and blessings of Allah be upon him: 'Beware of backbiting for it is worse than fornication.' In another narration it reads: '… worse than fornication thirty times in Islam.' He also said, may the peace and blessings of Allah be upon him: 'Whoever would like to divide up his good actions to the left and the right should backbite people.' He also said, may the peace and blessings of Allah be upon him: 'Backbiting consumes good actions just as fire consumes thin twigs.' Again he said: 'Do you know who is the bankrupt person in my *umma*?' They replied: 'The person who is bankrupt is he who has no dirhams or property.' Then he said: 'The bankrupt person of my *umma* is the one who comes on the Day of Rising with the *salat*, the fasting and the *zakat* but has insulted so-and-so, has wrongly spent the wealth of another, has spilt the blood of another, has hit this or that person – with the result that his good actions are made over to (the reckoning of) so-and-so, and if his good actions are used up before he has compensated (for all he has done), then their wrong actions are taken and thrown on him and he is thrown in the Fire.' This has been narrated by Muslim from Abu Hurayra. He also said, may the peace and blessings of Allah be upon him: 'If one's brother is backbitten in one's presence and one defends him, then Allah will defend him in this world and the next, and if he does not defend him, then Allah will bring him low in this world and the next.'"

In the *Madarik* of 'Iyad he states: "Husayn ibn 'Asim said: 'I was with Ibn Wahb and a beggar stopped by the gathering and asked: "O Abu Muhammad, the dirham you gave me yesterday was counterfeit." Then he replied: "O so-and-so (and he named the person), it was only a loan." The beggar who had addressed him became angry and said: "May Allah grant peace upon Muhammad, this is the age he used to speak about, the age when only the hypocrites of this *umma*

---

1 Possibly from a tribe called Samaran. Ed.
2 al-Hujurat – The Private Quarters: 12

will administer the *sadaqa*." Then a man from Iraq got up and slapped the beggar with such force that he fell down in front of him and started to cry out "O Muhammad, O Imam of the Muslims how can such a thing happen in your company?" Ibn Wahb then said: "Who did this?" The man from Iraq said: "I did, may Allah guide you aright! and I did it on account of the hadith that you related to us, that the Prophet, may the peace and blessings of Allah be upon him, said: 'Whoever protects the flesh of his brother from a hypocrite who backbites him then Allah will protect his flesh from the Fire.'"''

It is stated in *al-Jami' as-Saghir* that: "Whoever criticises someone by describing him with an attribute which he does not in fact possess, then Allah will imprison him in the Fire of Jahannam until he makes what he said to become a reality." It is also narrated that: "Whoever defends the honour of his brother, then he will be shielded from the Fire" — or whatever the exact wording of this narration is.

NOTICE:

1. Al-Ubbi said: "Part of backbiting is writing, for writing is one of the two 'tongues.'" The author then mentioned someone whose speech was satirised in writing, saying that it amounted to backbiting unless accompanied by valid reasons for mentioning (the criticism).

2. It is forbidden to poke fun at the reputation of someone even if it is common knowledge that he is a corrupt person, that is, to backbite him without a specific, legal reason — for example, when warning (him against doing something). Thus (it would be forbidden to mock him merely) because one takes a delight (in this) or (merely) to vent one's anger on him. The *'ulama* have thus stipulated that the narration stating that it is permissible to speak about someone notorious for his corruption is conditional upon this (notoriety) being in fact merited, and that this licence is to be understood to apply only when said as a warning, and that it is only permitted as long as the person in question is not pained by what is said of him.

Ibn Abi Jamra said, may Allah benefit us by him: "There are three conditions regarding speaking ill of someone whose corruption is common knowledge: that he himself manifests his corruption; and that he desires that news of it spread, in which case it is not considered backbiting, although there are some *'ulama* who argue that this only applies when one intends to mention his corrupt state to someone who is in a position to bring about a change in him, or to help him or warn him; if this is not the case, then they have prohibited it and have interpreted the hadith (on this subject) as meaning 'Do not backbite a corrupt person.'" Here his discussion ends, may Allah be pleased with us and with him. Al-Buhairi said in *Sharh al-Irshad*: "The meaning of (the hadith) 'There is no backbiting in the case of a corrupt person' (is not that 'backbiting does not apply in the case of such a person' but) that 'no backbiting is permitted in the case of a corrupt person'" and among those who have also interpreted it in this way is Ibn Naji in *Ma'alim al-Iman*, and he has not narrated any difference of opinion on the matter. Also among those who have stated this (same judgement) is 'Ayn-Jeem in his *Hashiya 'ala'r-Risala* where he says, commenting on the words of the *Risala* 'Breaking with someone is permissible': "Breaking off ties with someone who commits an innovation, or breaking with him because of some major wrong action (on his part) – which he is unable to have him punished for, which he is unable to admonish him about and about which the person in question would not accept (admonishment anyway), and backbiting, as long as (what is said is restricted) to mention of their state, is permitted in the case of these two (classes of persons). Abu'l-Hasan al-Mujahir said: 'The person who is well known (to be corrupt) is (subject to) the same (judgement) as the (corrupt) person who is proud of what he does, whether he hides his (corruption) or does it openly.' This however implies that backbiting in the case of the person who is guilty (of what he is accused of) but suffers from people associating such (behaviour) with him and who is unhappy with his (own behaviour) is permitted – however this is not the case. Rather, it is permitted to talk ill of a corrupt person who is content with the ascription to himself of that which people backbite him for." Among those who have stated this and have not spoken of any difference of opinion in the matter is the Shaykh, the Wali Sayyid al-Mukhtar. Ibn Hajar al-Haytami said in *Sharh al-Arba'in*: "and likewise it is not forbidden to talk ill of someone who deliberately separates himself from (one's company) and who is well known (to be corrupt), who does not care what he does – however evil, and does not mind what people say of him."

Al-Munawi also said: "It is forbidden to break off ties with someone who enjoys the right of inviolability, even if it is a *dhimmi*, and even if justified, (and it is forbidden) even if by way of innuendo – as Imam ar-Rafi'i declared – and even if he is guilty of something which renders his testimony invalid; however, as for the person (whose life and property is) not inviolable, like the enemy or someone who has reneged (on the deen of Islam), then it is not forbidden; likewise it is permitted to break off ties with a Muslim who has effectively isolated himself by his immoral behaviour – as long as it is only for the same reason that has brought about his isolation and with the intent of censuring him."

He also said, commenting on the words of *al-Jami'* 'Have you taken into consideration those who mention the immoral person in order that people may know who he is (saying) "Mention the immoral person and his behaviour so that people may be warned against him"': "His saying 'in order that people may be warned against him' is an indication that it is legally permissible to mention him in this connection as long as it is undertaken with a view to holding him to account, with the intention of giving good counsel or in order to protect people from the danger of falling foul of his ways and the like; however, whoever mentions someone of this nature in order to satisfy his anger, as an act of revenge, in order to belittle him or despise him or for any reason prompted by some selfish motive, then one would be oneself guilty of a wrong action."

Al-Mawwaq said in *Sunan al-Muhtadeen*: "(Defaming someone's) honour is wrongdoing that Allah will not let go even if the person slandered[1] is unjust or corrupt: if the person who undertakes it is called to give evidence or is someone in authority in the land, then (the *'ulama*) have said that it is not licit for him to mention the reputation of this person except in so far as is necessary to bring about a change in him; they have also said that 'Allah is a just judge: not only will He take (the tyrant) al-Hajjaj to task, but He will also take others to task for the sake of al-Hajjaj' — and so mocking the reputation of the corrupt person is forbidden according to the *ijma'*."

It is stated in *Siraj al-Mulouk*: "A man said: 'I was sitting with 'Umar ibn 'Abd al-'Aziz, may Allah be pleased with him, when he mentioned Hujjaj and I reviled and insulted the latter. Then he said, may Allah be pleased with him: 'A man commits an act of injustice and the person who has suffered the injustice continues to revile and insult the one guilty of the injustice until he has made good his claim over him — at which point the person guilty of the injustice gains superiority over him.'"

NOTICE: In his *Hashiya ar-Risala*, Ibn al-Hattab has spoken of the question — mentioned in 'The Book of *Ayman*' in the *Mudawwana* — regarding knowledge shared by two men about a third: "Whoever makes an oath to a man that if he (i.e. the one making the oath) were to come to know such and such a thing, then he will inform the other of it but they come to know of it both together, then he would only be keeping to his oath if he does indeed inform him. Ibn Naji said: 'Abu 'Imran has understood this according to its literal, most evident meaning.' Al-Lakhmi said: 'What he is referring to is the case

---

1 *al-mughtaab* is both the active and the passive participle of the verb and is thus both the slanderer and the slandered, but in this case it refers to the person slandered. Ed.

where the person making the oath is not aware of the knowledge of the person to whom the oath was made; if however he knows that he knows, then he would not be breaking his oath except in a strictly literal sense. From this one may deduce the interpretation of Abu 'Imran, namely that if two men are both aware of some piece of slander about a (third) man, then they should not speak about it, indeed that it is forbidden them to do so although there are two (other) judgements (on the matter) – one that it is (only) recommended (not to do so), and a second, that there is no particular recommendation not to do so.' The most evident judgement, and that which corresponds to al-Lakhmi's interpretation is that it is permitted[1] – and this is also in accordance with the *fatwa* of our Shaykh. Ibn Rushd has clearly formulated this saying: 'Backbiting is informing someone of something they were not aware of – (and so if the other is aware of it, it is not backbiting)."' This matter has also been transmitted by al-Qarafi in *al-Farouq*. Al-Hattab transmitted it.

Zarruq said in *Sharh al-Waghlisiya*: "Al-Bilali, may Allah have mercy on him, has discussed the difference of opinion regarding a man mentioning something he has discovered about another (man) to a friend. 'Priority (he says) in every case must be given to preventing the possibility of backbiting for surely it is the scourge of the deen and rarely is a person's deen sound when he is lax in this (matter).'"

Issue: Zarruq said in *Sharh al-Waghlisiya*: "They have differed as to whether backbiting is (considered) a major or a minor wrong action. Al-Qarafi has narrated a consensus that it is a major wrong action, while as-Subki cited that it is a minor wrong action – as long, that is, as it happens (just) once for if someone persists in a minor wrong action, it becomes a major wrong action, and there is agreement on this. The well-known judgement is that one must seek forgiveness (from the person backbitten) and that it is permitted for the other to grant forgiveness – indeed recommended as long as this does not lead to the other becoming emboldened (to repeat his backbiting). Al-Hasan said: 'It is enough to seek forgiveness, that is – and Allah knows best – for the person who has been wronged, or for the person guilty of the injustice or for both, and this is the best.' Ibn Sirin, in reply to someone who sought his forgiveness, said: 'It is not up to Ibn Sirin to forgive something that Allah has forbidden!' The hadith of Abu Dhamdham has already been mentioned namely (the narration in which) he, may the peace and blessings of Allah be upon him, said: 'Is any one of you incapable of being like Abu Dhamdham? – in the morning he would say: "O Allah, I have given my good reputation, dignity

---

[1] the text is clearly garbled at this point

and honour as *sadaqa* to the Muslims!'" The *'ulama* have said: 'This is (only to be understood) with regard to what has (already) happened. As for what has not yet happened, it is not permitted for anyone to say such a thing and Allah knows best.'"

USEFUL POINT: It is stated in *Siraj al-Mulouk*: "Abu Yusuf Ibn Asbat has related that one of the disciples (of the Masih, 'Isa, on whom be peace) died. The followers, noticing that he had experienced violent grief (on dying) expressed their deep concern about this to the Masih, on whom be peace. So the (Masih) stood at his grave and made a *du'a* for him. Allah then caused him to come back to life, and on his feet were sandals of fire. When 'Isa asked him about this he replied: "By Allah, I have not committed any act of disobedience other than that I once passed by someone who was being wronged and did not help him. I would counsel you: 'If you do anything abhorrent to anyone, then make *du'a* to Allah for him, just as Musa did, on whom be peace, after he had wronged Harun by seizing hold of his beard and head saying: "*My Lord, forgive me and my brother and admit us into Your mercy. You are the Most Merciful of the merciful*"[1]; that is, after (Allah) had showed him that Harun was innocent, and that Bani Isra'il had overwhelmed him and had persisted in worshipping the Calf.'"

USEFUL POINT: Zarruq said in his *Naseeha*: "One of the *'ulama* has mentioned certain people who, at the end of each *salat*, sought forgiveness five times for those they had wronged – seeking forgiveness for any right or claim (they have been denied) and for (any violation of) their honour." Ibn Zakari, commenting on his terminology, said in one of his books: "This is with regard to backbiting and not with regard to some matter over which he has a (concrete) claim or right and Allah knows best, and the *'alim* he is referring to – as is stated in *al-Hilya* – is Maymun ibn Mihran, one of the men of excellence from amongst the Followers, according to the author himself."

USEFUL POINT: ash-Sha'rani transmitted in *Tabaqat al-Awliya* from one of the great Shaykhs of the people (of *Tasawwuf*): "I saw the Prophet, may the peace and blessings of Allah be upon him, and he told me: 'O my son, backbiting is forbidden, and if one cannot avoid listening to the backbiting of people, then recite *Surat al-Ikhlas* (Sincerity) three times together with the *Mu'awwudhatan* (the two final suras about seeking refuge) and bestow the reward (for their recitation) on the person who has been backbitten – for backbiting and reward (for good actions) inherit from and complement one other.'"

As for Ibn 'Ashir's mention of slander, 'Ali ibn 'Abd as-Sadiq said: "It is to transmit something to another with the intent of corrupting (someone's

---

1 al-A'raf – The Ramparts: 151

reputation). He, on whom be peace and blessings, said: 'The calumniator will not enter the Garden' i.e. the carrier of tales, that is, he will not enter it with the first of the Forerunners – and the original text is to be found in Zarruq's *Naseeha*. Ibn Zakari said in *Sharh an-Naseeha*: 'Al-Ghazali said: "It is disclosing a secret and revealing something the person does not want to be revealed. It is better that a person remain silent about anything he witness of the (blameworthy) states of people – except when there is a benefit for the Muslims in talking about it or (the chance of) preventing an act of disobedience."'"

Zarruq said in *al-Waghlisiya*: "The worst kind (of slander) is spying and calumny, that is deliberately pointing out people's shortcomings to unjust rulers and tyrants."

Ibn 'Ashir's saying 'bearing false witness' – is declaring something (to a third party) about which he has no knowledge. It is stated in al-Bukhari: "The worst of the major wrong actions is associating someone or something with Allah, rebellious disobedience to one's parents, and bearing false witness" (which he said) three times – or (in some narrations) "and making a false statement" – "and he kept repeating it until we said (to ourselves): 'Would that he had remained silent!'"

It is also narrated: "The feet of the person who bears false witness will not depart before it necessitates the Fire for him."

As for Ibn 'Ashir's saying 'lies', Zarruq said in *Sharh al-Waghlisiya*: "This applies in general. However, in certain instances it is licit (to tell lies); and sometimes obligatory: like denying a wrong act which one has committed or someone else has committed when the right of another is not involved, or disavowal of a man whom a tyrant is looking for – in which case he may swear by Allah on this (lie), and in the case of *jihad* in order to sow disorder among the *kuffar*, or when bringing about reconciliation between two people, or in order to set the heart of one's wife or son at ease, and in other instances (to prevent) conflict or mistrust from arising. (Lying) is not however permitted under any circumstances in order to obtain some benefit for oneself. And the worst of lies is lying about him, may the peace and blessings of Allah be upon him, by claiming to have seen him in a dream (for example) or (telling some) other (lie about him) because of his saying, may the peace and blessings of Allah be upon him: 'Whoever tells a deliberate lie about me, then let him prepare a place for himself in the Fire.' One of the *'ulama* said: 'This indicates that whoever lies about him, may the peace and blessings of Allah be upon him, does not die as a Muslim.'"

Commenting on the hadith 'Whoever tells a deliberate lie about me, then let him prepare a place for himself in the Fire', the author of *Fath al-Bari* – transmitting from another source – said: "If one says that lying is a wrong action except when done in order to set things right – or in other (similar) instances, and that Allah has threatened wrongdoers with the Fire, then what is the difference between lying about the Messenger of Allah, may the peace and blessings of Allah be upon him, and the threat to those who (simply) lie about someone else? The answer has two aspects: first, there is no doubt that lying about him to make something haram appear halal, for example, is 'deeming something halal when it is in fact is forbidden' or 'deeming it halal to declare something halal', and deeming the haram to be halal is *kufr* – and imputing *kufr* (to his words) is itself *kufr*." He goes on to say: "However, it is clear that there is room in what he said for further examination of the matter. The majority are of the opinion that anyone (guilty of this) is not deemed a *kafir* unless he himself holds that the matter is indeed rendered halal (by such a fabrication). Secondly, lying about him is a major wrong action while lying about someone else is a minor wrong action – and so there is a difference between the two. It therefore does not follow that since the threat to the person who lies about him and the threat to the person who lies about another is (ostensibly) one and the same that their place (in the Fire) or the time they remain there is the same."

The worst kind of slander is an unsubstantiated accusation of sexual infidelity (*qadhf*): Zarruq said in *Sharh al-Wahlisiya*: "That is, accusing a *mumin* of fornication or sodomy, or rejecting his genealogy (and claiming he is not the son of who he says he is) and the like. And there is agreement that it is a major wrong action – as Allah, exalted is He, has stipulated that the punishment for it is eighty lashes; and it has degrees, the worst unsubstantiated accusation of sexual infidelity is rejecting that the child of a married woman is of an honourable union."

I SAY: "Included here is the statement of a man 'I found such-and-such a man with such-and-such a woman under one sheet' – examine what al-Khurshi says regarding Khalil's words: 'I found her with a man under one sheet.'"

Zarruq said in *Sharh al-Waghlisiya*: "It is not (considered to be) lying when a statement is (blatantly) improbable like when someone says, for example, 'I came to see you a thousand times today' and the like. Rather, lying applies to something which is probable like your saying: 'I came to see you ten times today' and the like. Among the expressions by innuendo or allusion which are not (strictly speaking) true but which are alternatives to lying is that, for example, of the man who used to instruct his family to say to people who came to see him at his home: '(Tell them to) look for him in the mosque'; while another would say to his servant: 'Make a circle (on the ground) and say (to the people who come to the door) "He is not here."' All such (expressions) are permitted as long as it does not lead to dishonour or humiliation – so be aware of this."

USEFUL POINT: It is stated in *al-Jami' as-Saghir*: "The worst of wrong actions is a lying tongue."

It is also in it that: "If the slave tells a lie, (his guardian) angel will distance itself a mile from him because of the foul smell emanating (from his mouth)."

In *Majma' al-Ahbab*, 'Abd ar-Rahman ibn Mahdi said: "What worse quality could there be in the *mumin* – besides denying Allah, exalted is He – than lying: it is the root of hypocrisy upon which all of hypocrisy is based, and hypocrisy is worse than abandoning the *salat*."

As for Ibn 'Ashir's words 'one's tongue should avoid saying anything which offends', the (following point of) benefit (is to be noted): "It is stated in a hadith: 'Whoever remains silent saves himself.' Al-Ghazali said: 'Al-Munawi said: "Whoever is aware categorically of the sicknesses of the tongue will realise that this hadith is of penetrating import: the Chosen One, may the peace and blessings of Allah be upon him, was given all (knowledge) of language and the very essence of wisdom, and no one can comprehend the oceans of meanings hidden beneath his sayings but the elite.'

Ibn Hajar said: "The *hadith* which speak of the excellence of silence, like 'He who remains silent saves himself' or the hadith of Ibn Abi'd-Dunya – with its *isnad* of trustworthy men – 'The easiest of worship is silence' do not contradict the hadith of Ibn 'Abbas – about which ash-Shaykh is unequivocal as to its validity – namely, regarding 'the prohibition of remaining silent throughout the day up to the night.' This is because each applies to different circumstances: silence which is desirable is desisting from worthless speech; likewise from speech which is licit but which leads to worthless speech; the silence which is prohibited is abstaining from saying something in defence of someone's right or claim when able to do so; likewise abstaining from licit speech when (the claim of) both parties is of equal merit." Al-Ghazali said: "The cure for a person's desire to know that which he has no need to is (remembering) that death is in front of him, that he is responsible for every word he utters, that his every breath is his capital, that his tongue is like a net with which he is able to catch the houris of the Garden and that if he neglects it and does not put it to good use, then it would mean a clear loss (on his part) – this is the cure with respect to knowledge; his cure with respect to action is withdrawal (from company) and silence."

$$\text{يَحْفَظُ بَطْنَهُ مِنَ الْحَرَامِ}$$

$$\text{يَتْرُكُ مَا شُبِّهَ بِاهْتِمَامٍ}$$

297 He should guard his belly from what is haram and be assiduous in avoiding what is doubtful

Mayyara said: "Protecting the stomach from what is haram necessarily implies eating what is halal and this is obligatory according to the Book, the sunna and the *ijma'*. As for the Book, the words of, exalted is He: '*Eat what is good and lawful on the earth*'[1] and also His words: '*You who have iman! Eat of the good things We have provided for you*'[2] and His saying: '*Messengers, eat of the good things and act rightly.*'[3] Ibn 'Abbas said: 'Allah has commanded the *muminun* to the same thing as he has commanded the Messengers and has preceded the (obligation to) eat halal food before right action – indicating thereby that the benefit of actions cannot be obtained unless one's provision is purified and the way of obtaining it is halal.' For this reason one of the men of wisdom said: 'Whoever eats halal food, obeys Allah whether he wishes to or not and whoever eats haram food, disobeys Allah whether he wishes or not – because when he eats what is halal, his veins draw from it and his worship is invigorated and when he eats of the haram his veins draw from it and his worship becomes slack.'

As for the sunna, his words, may the peace and blessings of Allah be upon him: 'Seeking the halal is a *fard* obligation on every Muslim' and his saying: 'Surely Allah has an angel on the Bayt al-Maqdis who calls out every day: "Whoever eats of the haram, then no compensation and no retaliation will be accepted of him."' Abu Hamid said that 'compensation' here refers to optional (*nafila*) acts of worship and 'retaliation' to the *fard* obligations. He has also said: 'Whoever eats of the halal for forty days, then Allah will illuminate his heart and will cause wisdom to flow from his heart.' In another narration it reads 'will cause him to do without in the *dunya*.' Again he said: 'Whoever buys an article of clothing for ten dirhams, one of which is haram, then Allah will not accept (worship of) him as long as he is wearing it.' Again he said: 'All flesh which grows from the haram, then the Fire has more right to it.' Ibn 'Umar said: 'We would desist from forty kinds of halal (actions or

---

1 al-Baqara – The Cow: 167
2 al-Baqara – The Cow: 171
3 al-Muminun – The Believers: 52

things) out of fear we might engage in something suspected of being haram' – for scrupulousness is with respect to (avoiding) things that are halal, but as for the haram, it is obligatory to leave it.' It has been said that whoever spends of the haram, intending to discharge an act of obedience for Allah, then he is like the person who washes his clothes with urine. It is stated in *at-Tawriya*: 'Whoever has no concern about the provenance of his food, then Allah will have no concern as to which of the doors of the Fire He will cause him to enter by.'

The consensus – *ijma'* – is that seeking the halal is an obligation on each and every person who is *mukallaf* – of age and fully responsible."

There is something in *Sharh as-Sanusi 'ala'l-Jaza'iri* which is stricter than this. Al-Muhasibi has stated that the person who consumes things of doubtful origin will be raised on the Day of Rising in a stinking state, and that the filthiest kind of haram act is that of usury – *riba* for it has been established (in the *hadith*) that it consists of seventy (kinds of) crimes – the least severe being like fornicating with one's own mother in Islam – and that a dirham of usury is worse than committing fornication thirty odd times in Islam. He has also said: "Allah will give permission to the both the right acting and immoral person (to rise from the grave) on the Day of Rising – except for those who have consumed *riba* for they will not rise *'except as someone driven mad by Shaytan's touch.'*[1]"

Immediately after this he goes on to say: "There is a difference of opinion as to whether the halal (still) exists or not: it is said that it exists but that the number who seek it are few; it is also said that it is like the lost camel – and this is based on the hadith (regarding knowledge in general); and that the halal may not be distinguished from the haram except by way of knowledge. Ash-Shaykh said: 'It is better that a person not search too much after wealth lest some of it be obtained from the haram.' It is obligatory for the *mukallaf* to desist from the haram in all instances and to what is halal by *ijma'*. If he does not find it, then he must follow the (general) agreement in the *madhhab*; however, if he does not find this (in the *madhhab*), he may follow a difference of opinion within the *madhhab*; and if he does not find this, then he may follow a difference of opinion outside of the *madhhab*. If he does not find this, then it is as Abu'l-Qasim said: 'If the *dunya* were all haram, then we would never be able to obtain anything to live on – so whoever is able to obtain something good and wholesome, having found the proper means to buy his provision, should make every attempt to do so: if he expends himself in doing so, then he will find insha'Allah something with which he will feel at ease (when eating). If he is unable to find out its

---

1 al-Baqara – The Cow: 274

source, then buying bread is better than buying flour, buying flour is better than buying imported crops and buying imported crops is preferable to buying crops which are near.'" Here ends the discussion of Mayyara.

Al-Hattab said: "Notice: if someone does not find a specific text on a matter from the *madhhab* (of Malik) at hand nor can he find anyone who knows how to find out, then the most evident judgement is that he enquire about it from another *madhhab* and that he act in accordance with it – rather than acting merely out of ignorance."

The severity of the (*'ulama*) with regard to the haram and doubtful matters is clear for those who read their books. Al-Ghazali said – and as-Sanusi has narrated of him: "The actions of the person who eats what is of doubtful (provenance) are rejected and not accepted. However, a person must find something to feed himself and his family with. Justifying (consumption of something) by (claiming) ignorance (of the provenance) or by arguing one 'thinks' it correct to do so is not an excuse when seeking to obtain (one's provision) – even if this accords with (a judgement of) one of the *'ulama*; however, a person would be excused if he relies on their judgements, however weak, when he is compelled to (eat something of dubious provenance) or in times of great need." We would thus like to mention certain things (in this respect) – given that alleviating the difficulty of the *mumin* is an (action of) excellence whose merit is well known, and (we hope) his heart will be set at ease (by these comments):

1. al-Qastallani said, commenting on the hadith 'If any of this wealth comes to you – and you are not responsible (for its distribution) and you did not ask for it – then take it and spend it; otherwise do not seek after it yourself': "Salim has added in a narration: 'It was on account of this that Ibn 'Umar would not ask anyone for anything and would not reject anything he was given.' He said in *al-Fath*: 'and this is understood in a general sense: it is evident that he would not reject anything even if of doubtful provenance. It has been established (in a valid narration) that he would accept the gifts of al-Mukhtar ibn Abi 'Ubayd ath-Thaqafi who had conquered Kufa, expelled the governor of 'Abdallah ibn az-Zubayr and who stayed as an amir over it – for a time – without allegiance to the Khalifa. Mukhtar would use the wealth he had obtained from (conquering Kufa) as he wished, but despite this Ibn 'Umar, may Allah be pleased with him, would still accept his gifts. He justified this (by arguing) that he had a right to the *bayt al-mal* and that he would not incur any harm from it however it came to him. He also considered that the consequences (of any wrongful seizure of wealth only applied) to the

first person who took the (wealth); and that Mukhtar possessed other wealth besides this – which he had a right to – and so his giving of this (wealth) willingly without distinguishing (between the different kinds of wealth in his possession) means the (gift) is subject to (the judgement contained in) his words "What comes to you from this wealth – without your asking for it or being responsible (for its redistribution) – then take it." Thus he considered that only (wealth) which is utterly haram would not be included in this judgement.'" This discussion is to be found in the commentary on the 'Chapter Regarding Provision from Rulers.'

In al-Munawi's work, commenting on the narration 'If Allah causes any of this wealth to come to someone without his having to ask for it, then it is provision that Allah has bestowed upon him' it is related that Ibn Jarir said: "Whoever is given of what it is permitted to give, whether it be from a Sultan or otherwise, and whether the (donor) be just or corrupt, then there is no harm in accepting it." Then he has related – with his own (direct) chain of narration – that "'Abd al-'Aziz ibn Marwan wrote to Ibn 'Umar saying: 'Let me know what you need' and he replied to him: 'I have not requested anything of you. However, I also do not refuse whatever Allah might provide me with from you' – then he sent him one thousand dinars and he accepted them."

Al-Mawwaq said: "Ibn Batal has narrated from at-Tabari: 'Whoever from amongst the people of Islam has some money in his possession and does not know whether it has been obtained from the haram or the halal, then it is not (considered) haram for him to have accepted it – as long as he was not aware that it was *entirely* haram' – and the like has been stated by Imams from amongst the Companions and the Followers; (a thing is only considered) haram when it is manifestly and without a doubt haram and so whoever desists from it altogether, then he would be following the (better) path of scrupulousness and the avoidance of what is doubtful. Abu 'Umar has also stated something similar in his *Tamheed*."

2. Al-Wanshareesi said, in his abridgment of al-Burzuli's collection of novel occurrences on which *fatwas* were given, what is explicitly set out hereunder:

"At the end of the response given by Shaykh Muhammad ibn Abi Zayd (al-Qayrawani) relating to the issue of the ruler, we come across the following: Whoever comes upon some property is not permitted to hand it to the amir, since the inequity of such amir is known for sure as a verified fact. Likewise, if it happens that some of the property in the hands of such an unfair amir becomes such a man's acquisition (and thus falls into his possession), he is not allowed to return it to the amir if such property can be hidden away from the amir, due to the fact that no halal property is known to be owned by such amir, all his assets and usurped properties being intertwined in an undifferentiated (haram) mass. The asset that has fallen into such man's hands, in fact, does not belong to the amir, and is nothing but the property of the poor and the destitute".

Al-Burzuli quoted the following from ('Abdu'l-Hamid Abu Muhammad) [Ibn] as-Sa'igh:

"If a person whose property is not known to contain any halal asset [all his properties and usurped possessions being intermingled in one undifferentiated mass] were to deposit some asset with another person, and some of such deposited property is capable of being hidden away from the said depositor, the one with whom it has been deposited is lawfully entitled to take such concealable portion of the deposited property into his possession, and hand it to the poor, so long as he is capable of doing so."

He further said: "A further ramification of the said ruling is that, if people were to take part in a maritime battle, fighting on a boat, and were to seize some booty, and one such fighter knew for certain that he would not be able in the normal course of things to obtain his rightful share of such booty, he would be entitled to circuitously acquire for himself the extent of such rightful share in the booty (and no more than that), and no objection could be legitimately levelled at him in that respect."

It is stated in *al-Mi'yar* at the beginning of *Nawazil al-Ankiha*: "Examine the case of the poor person who has access to wealth or money for which no one can claim responsibility because it was taken in an assault or stolen – Shaykh Abu Muhammad ash-Shabeebi permits (disposal of it in) this case and permits the poor to take possession of wealth (issuing from an act) of injustice, however it happens. Shaykh Abu 'Abdallah ibn Arafa prohibited this at first out of fear of the consequences for the person involved – should what he did come to light, but then he changed his view and permitted it", and there is something similar from al-Hattab and as-Sanhouri in the commentary on Khalil's words: 'if she becomes irrevocably divorced, she should not adorn herself for this is *makruh*' and al-Mawwaq's commentary on Khalil's words '... for the debtor.'

3. Ibn Zakari said in *Sharh an-Naseeha* – and the original, I think, is in the *Mi'yar* or the work of al-Mazari: "al-Mawwaq was asked: 'Is it permitted for someone to eat of the marriage feast if he knows that most of the wealth of the person putting on the feast has been gained unlawfully and is unaware that he has any capital which is halal? and is it permitted for him to eat and then to give away in *sadaqa* an amount equal to what he ate – given the fact

The Book of the Principles of Tasawwuf and the Guide to Realisation 881

that if he were to desist from eating, the organiser of the feast would insinuate (he was snubbing him) or would bear him a grudge, and given the fact that the *faqih* could not abstain from (the proceedings anyway) as the whole affair customarily gets under way by means of his arrival?' He replied: 'The food of the feast is (considered to) belong (legally) to the organiser of the feast as the food itself is not the thing which (is considered) to be possessed unlawfully. The same (principle applies) in the case of dirhams and dinars which have been seized unlawfully: they (are considered) his property and his responsibility such that if he buys a portion of some property with them, then it is permitted for his partner to take this (portion) by the right of pre-emption – unlike for example if he had bought it with (rolls of) silk which had been taken illegally for the owner of the silk which had been seized illegally would retain the right to choice (whether to take the silk itself back or be compensated in kind or money). Thus based on this principle, if someone who was himself owing others money gave you dirhams or dinars, or cooked food or the like, (to which he had no legal right), then those to whom it should have been given would have no claim over you for these (things). Rather the person guilty of the unjust act would be responsible (before Allah) – except if the person to whom an apple, for example, had been given was aware that it was owed to another, then he must pay back the like of it. However scrupulousness demands that he desist from eating anything from someone whose (financial ruin renders) ownership (of anything in his hands) uncertain; but if he does nevertheless eat it, then it is recommended that he give away (something similar) in *sadaqa*, and this is what I prefer."

He also said on another occasion: "Zarruq said in *Sharh al-Irshad*: 'The *faqih* Abu 'Abdallah ibn Sayyidi Ahmad al-Qouri, may Allah have mercy on him, related that the Sultan Abu'l-Hasan al-Merini called the *fuqaha* of his time to a feast. Among the (guests) were people of knowledge and the deen, and among these, was one who said 'I am fasting', while there was another who only ate sparingly, and yet other who only ate the side dishes (literally 'proceeds'); another ate to his fill; still another said 'Bring me some of the food of the Amir on account of the *baraka* for I am fasting.' The Shaykh asked them about this – I think it was Ibrahim al-A'raj – and the first said: 'as for food of dubious provenance, I have protected myself from it by fasting as has been transmitted'; the second said: 'I only ate an amount which would be considered as (legitimate) *sadaqa* for it was not clear (to me) who the food really belonged to – and the person who partakes of it (fully) would be (subject to the) same (judgement) as a person who takes something illegally; the third said: 'I relied on the judgement that the *proceeds* (of land seized unlawfully) belong to the one who seized them unlawfully, just as land tax and revenue (collected by the Amir) only become due from those who are responsible for the land they are working'; the fourth said: 'the price of any food consumed (normally) becomes the debt of the person who consumed it – but he allowed me to eat of it and so it was permitted me to eat it'; the fifth said: 'the food is the right of the destitute – I was able to "recover" some of it and return it to those it (really) belonged to' (i.e. he considered himself among the destitute)." Zarruq said: "and this is the best solution as he has combined (the demands of) the *fiqh* and scrupulousness. What the fourth person did is also clear from the point of view of *fiqh* and its essence. In general a person must act as a *faqih* for himself when he finds himself in a dubious situation, and whoever has no clear understanding (of the matter), then he must protect himself as best he can. One of the *'ulama* declared unequivocally that the wealth which issues from an act of injustice is haram, while 'Izz ad-Deen ibn 'Abd as-Salam rejected this, arguing that (only his extreme) scrupulousness caused him to hold (to this judgement), and that it would have been better if he had been just as scrupulous regarding the deen of Allah and had declared what the (precise) judgement of Allah was in the matter."

4. In *Nawazil Ibn Hilal* he said: "The people of knowledge differed regarding your question whether it is correct to dispose of their wealth in the form of *zakat* or *sadaqa*: al-Mazari stated, may Allah have mercy on him: 'It is permitted for someone who has more debt than credit (*mustaghriq adh-dhimma*) to give something in *sadaqa* to someone who is entitled to it, according to one judgement, as long as he does what the imam (or Amir) would have done[1] – that is, based on the judgement that the imam distributes it as *sadaqa*.' Ad-Dawudi was asked, may Allah have mercy on him, about someone who, finding himself responsible for property or revenue which had been unjustly acquired but ignorant as to whom this property or revenue belonged, gives it away in *sadaqa*; and whether it would be correct to receive such *sadaqa*. He replied, saying: 'He will get no reward for any *sadaqa* he gives on such (property), and the most prudent course for others is not to accept (any such *sadaqa*). However, if the person who takes it considers himself one of the poor and takes it (only) for this reason, then this reason is in all likelihood valid; if he takes it for some enterprise of (benefit to the) Muslims which he himself is engaged in, and is someone who has a right to take it from the *bayt al-mal* (anyway), then this is

---

1 Legally, the amir or imam is *mustaghriq adh-dhimma* as any wealth he disposes of is not – strictly speaking – his.

(also) a (legitimate) way open to him – for if the (person who had acquired the property illegally) were to turn to Allah for forgiveness he would be obliged to dispose of it for a similar purpose, and there would be no harm in his giving it for such a purpose.' There is a similar statement in *al-Miʿyar* to which he added: 'It is said that his saying "he will get no reward for any *sadaqa* he gives on such (property)" is in accordance with the *madhhab* of the [scholars of] Qayrawan (Kairawan) – namely (the judgement in) his regard is like (that of) someone who has been restrained from freely disposing of his property. For this reason Sayyidi Abu'l-Hasan al-Muntasir would go to Sabala ibn Tahir – who was responsible for works in Tunis – and on seeing how many people were making use of the facilities at a crossroads would say: "The halal (wealth) has fallen to the lot of this man – for him to dispose of it here and increase the reward for its owners!" Those who argue that he is not restricted in how he disposes (of the wealth) and that it is permitted for him to give it away as a gift or in *sadaqa* or in some other way, then his *tawba* is reckoned for him and is accepted of him and Allah knows best. Such wealth is treated as *fay'* booty (which is gained without battle), and the laws applicable to it are wide.'" Here end the words of *al-Miʿyar* – and there are mistakes in the copying which do not however render it incomprehensible, and Allah glorious is He, knows best.

5. The author of *al-Miʿyar*, Ibn al-Hattab and al-Mawwaq said – and the text has been taken from the first in the opening section of *Nawazil al-Ankiha*: "Consider the case of the poor person who finds himself in possession of wealth whose owner is unknown and which has been obtained by assault or theft – consider whether this is permitted him. Shaykh Abu Muhammad ash-Shabeebi permitted it and would permit the poor to take possession of wealth whose provenance issued from an act of injustice – however it came to be his; and Shaykh Abu 'Abdallah Ibn 'Arafa would prohibit this initially, fearing that what he had done might become known and he would suffer harm, although he later came to permit it."

As-Sijistani was asked about an amir who gave part of a irrigation channel for to a man as *sadaqa*. (He was asked what the judgement was in the case where) the amir died and the subsequent (amir) sold the whole of the irrigation channel and he replied: "If the *sadaqa* was given on account of some useful attribute in the person to whom it was given – on account of his knowledge or courage, for example, or the like – then the transaction stands and is binding, and it is not permitted to sell this (part) along with the whole of the irrigation channel, and so the transaction (of the second amir) is not valid; however, if it was not given on account of some useful attribute (in the person), then it is not considered (as *sadaqa*) and the sale (of the second amir) is considered to stand."

I say: "This matter, and Allah knows best, glorious is He, is based on the principle that he is subject to the same judgement as the person who is restricted in how he disposes (of the wealth)."

6. al-Mawwaq said in *Sunan al-Muhtadeen*: "'Izz ad-Deen discussed the question of property or wealth acquired from those whose property or wealth was mostly or usually haram, saying: 'It varies according to the circumstances: firstly, there is no problem when he knows whether what he spends is from the haram or from the halal; secondly, when what he spends is of the kind that has been earned from the haram, then it is *makruh* to take it, and it is also strongly recommended to abstain from it out of scrupulousness; thirdly, when what he spends is not of the kind which has been obtained by way of the haram, then there is no harm in taking it, and if he is in doubt as to whether he has bought something with haram money, then there are no grounds for being (over) scrupulous: one should not judge something to be haram if it appears, in all likelihood, to be halal; however if there is hardly any evidence for it being halal, then it is haram to proceed with (the purchase). What is in question here is that something may either be bought with (money) which itself is haram – and this is rare, or it may be bought on credit and then paid for with haram money (later) – and this is the more common of the two transactions: it is what is customary regarding the financial transactions of unjust kings and governors, of highway robbers and bandits, and of woman singers and prostitutes, and all those who usually obtain wealth in a haram way. It is extraordinary that someone should declare this haram – given that this (declaration) amounts to a rejection of Allah's judgement: they do not realise that it is obligatory to desist from any rejection of Allah's judgement that something is haram or halal – for there is no difference between claiming something haram to be halal or vice versa. All success is dependent on clinging to the limits delineated by Allah, exalted is He. (The judgement of) our *madhhab* is that if a partner buys a share with something that in itself is haram, then you may take it by the right of pre-emption as long as what is haram is (in the form of) dinars or dirhams – and this is not the case (when payment is made) with some other (commodity).'"

7. al-Qastallani said, commenting on the hadith of the utilisation of a charm of Abi Sa'id al-Khudri where he says 'Take it and accord me a portion with you': "This he said in order to put their hearts at ease and by way of exaggeration – (that is, in order to declare) that it is halal without a doubt. He also stated – or Ibn Hajar or both of them – that it is not permitted to take a reward for teaching the Qur'an, and they have contradicted Abu Hanifa in this regard –

although they have not denied that it is permitted to take it for making *ruqya* charms."

8. Mayyara said in *Sharh az-Zuqaqiya:* "Useful point: Our Imams, may Allah, glorious is He, be pleased with them, have stated that if there is no *bayt al-mal* – and what they mean, and Allah knows best, is that there may indeed be one but they have no access to it – then people have an obligation to collect money to establish an army or finance students (of knowledge) – for it is a communal obligation. This has been narrated by al-Mawwaq during his commentary on Khalil's words 'The wronged person may take (back) a like amount from the person who had acted unjustly towards him.' However, even if this is an obligation on people, an obligation is (often) not something that one undertakes willingly. Thus if a student of knowledge, whose knowledge will be of benefit for the Muslims, is able to obtain this (funding) by some correct means – by taking a stipend from a rich person or from those committed to helping such students in return for teaching (others) – then this is permitted, even if it is more than he has a right to, that is more than the usual stipend, and Allah knows best."

"In the above mentioned passage, al-Mawwaq narrated matters which conform to these views, so examine them if you wish. If the person who gives the above mentioned stipend is in debt to the *bayt al-mal*, then his being allowed to give it to him is all the more valid in the case of a student of knowledge." Here end the words of Mayyara, and they are accepted by al-Bannani in *Sharh az-Zaqaqiya* also.

9. 'Ali ibn 'Abd as-Sadiq said: "Zarruq said: 'Whoever takes money from the Sultan and is justified in not repaying it, then it becomes his responsibility: he must make *sadaqa* with it, may eat of it if he is in need, and if bankrupt (*mustaghriq adh-dhimma*) may buy clothes of normal quality (for himself) and anything else in common use when absolutely necessary.'"

Abu Nu'aym narrated in *al-Hilya* from Waki' who said: "We do not know (of the existence of) that which is purely halal nowadays. We see only that one must strive (to discriminate) in the world. There is the halal, the haram and what is of doubtful provenance: the halal is a reckoning, the haram is punishment and what is dubious contains (a measure of) censure. The *dunya* has become as a corpse – so take of it (only enough) to keep you alive. If it is halal, then do with just a little of it; if haram, then take only (enough to) ensure your survival; and if of dubious nature, then you will (only) be subject to a light censure."

10. al-Ubbi said commenting on the hadith 'Do not milk the animal of

another except with his permission' – or whatever the exact words of his were, may the peace and blessings of Allah be upon him: "One cannot argue that this (general) prohibition means that (implicit in it) is a (judgement of) 'particular licence' with regard to stray sheep or goats – for we would argue that the meaning of 'particularity' is that some individual instances are excluded from the general rule. Rather, stray sheep or goats are simply unaffected by this general rule as he, may the peace and blessings of Allah be upon him, declared the right of possession of the owner of such (stray animals) to be null and void. Thus such (animals) are considered to be (items of) property which are not protected by inviolability – and as such analogous to the case of the wealth of someone who has nothing to cover his debts. However, 'Iyad said: 'Any property is inviolable when one knows that the owner would not like it (to be taken); as for someone who is content (for it to be used) – or, according to an-Nawawi – someone whom one thinks will be content, then there is no harm in it.'"

11. Mayyara said – regarding 'the taking of another's property when there exists an indication that it is correct or incorrect to do so': "If one knows that the owner would be happy for this to happen, then it is halal, but if one knows that he would not be, then it is haram; and likewise regarding taking something when one fears blame."

12. the author of *adh-Dhahab al-Ibreez*, commenting on His words, exalted is He, '*You who have iman! Eat of the good things We have provided for you*'[1], said: "The 'ulama differ regarding (eating) the food of Sultans, and accepting rewards from them. It has been said that it is permissible for both the rich person and the poor, unless one knows for sure that it is haram, and that the consequences (arising from consuming anything haram) are borne by the donor; it is also said that it is not permitted unless one knows for sure that it is halal; and that it is permitted only in the case of the poor person. Evidence for permissibility is that he, may the peace and blessings of Allah be upon him, accepted the gift of al-Maqawqas, the king of Alexandria and that he borrowed off the Jews – despite the words of Allah '*(people who) consume ill-gotten gains.*'[2] Moreover some of the Companions, like Abu Hurayra, Ibn 'Abbas, Ibn 'Umar and others, lived during times of corrupt and unjust rulers but nevertheless accepted things from them: in the book *Urf at-Tayyib fi Tarikh al-Khateeb* of al-Maqqari, it is stated that Zayd ibn Thabit who was someone firmly established in knowledge would accept rewards from Mu'awiya and his son Yazeed; and Ibn 'Umar, may

---

1 al-Baqara – The Cow: 171
2 al-Ma'ida – The Table: 42

Allah be pleased with him, despite his excellence and scrupulousness, would accept gifts from al-Mukhtar ibn Abi 'Ubayd – who was related to him by marriage, and would also eat of his food. A man asked Ibn Mas'ud – who was a man of vast knowledge: 'A neighbour of mine who transacts with usury and who does not avoid the haram when trading has asked me to share his food – should I accept?' He replied: 'Yes, you will have the blessing and he will have the evil (of his action) as long as you are not aware that it is haram *in itself*, that is a *specific* item which is clearly and without doubt haram because illegally stolen or seized through some unjust act.' 'Uthman said, may Allah, glorious is He, be content with him, regarding the rewards of Sultans: 'The meat of the gazelle is (also) slaughtered (i.e. halal)'; ash-Sha'bi would accept the gifts and eat the food of 'Abd al-Malik whose children he used to educate. Among those who also accepted their gifts were Malik, ash-Shafi'i, Abu Yusuf, an-Nakha'i and al-Hasan al-Basri – despite his doing without and his scrupulousness – and others of the *'ulama* of Kufa and Basra. Yet others who received such (rewards) were Abu Salama ibn 'Abd ar-Rahman, Aban ibn 'Uthman and the seven *fuqaha* (of Madina) – and these (gifts) amounted to more than what Abu'z-Zinad gained while in office. Sufyan ath-Thawri said: 'Their gifts are preferable to me than the gifts between brothers as the latter can make your feel obliged (by their giving) while the Sultans do not make you feel obliged, and I am not aware that any of the Followers desisted from receiving their gifts out of scrupulousness – except Sa'id ibn al-Musayyab in Madina, Muhammad ibn Sirin in Basra and Ibn Hanbal.' It is stated in the hadith: 'What comes to you without asking, then spend it or invest it.'"

Evidence for the judgement that it is permitted for the poor person only is that if their rewards and gifts are from the *fay'* booty, then the poor have a right to it (anyway), just as the people of knowledge have a right to it. 'Ali, may Allah ennoble his face, said: "Whoever enters Islam in obedience and recites the Qur'an in a state of purity, then he has a right to one hundred dirhams from the *bayt al-mal* of the Muslims every year" – and "one hundred dinars" has also been narrated – and "that if he does not take them in this world he will take them in the next." Among the things which are licit are the eating of fruit and (the drinking of) the milk of sheep and goats in the case of the person who is in need, even if they do not have the permission of their owner"; (it is also reported) that it is also permitted in the case of those who are not in need; and that it is permitted in the case of the milk but not the fruit.

13. al-Qarafi said in *adh-Dhakheera*: "Issue: Imam al-Haramayn said in his book entitled *al-Ghuyathi*: 'If the haram covered the whole earth, then it would

be permitted to use it in accordance with one's need. However, its being licit does not apply to (all daily) needs (in whatever circumstances) lest this lead to a weakening (of the economic state) of the slaves and to *kufr* gaining the upper hand in the land, or it lead to people giving up trades and the production of things. That it is 'licit' does not mean that one may make use of it as freely as in the case of what is (always) licit. Rather what is envisaged here is that this wealth has become part of the *bayt al-mal* and that it is permitted (to make use of it) in the case of need – for if someone in compelling need is permitted to take possession of people's property illegally, that is, if one person (may do this), then how much more fitting is it for all people (to be able to make use of something whose source is haram when the need is compelling). It may well be that this (single person) is corrupt in the eyes of Allah, exalted is He, but a community is usually not without a *wali* or a right acting man of Allah.'"

Al-Haytami has narrated the same when commenting on the hadith 'There should be no causing harm or reciprocating harm' where he says: "If the haram has spread all over the land such that the halal is not to be found except only rarely, then it is permitted to make use of what one is in need of, even if it is more than what one actually needs; however, one should not become lax in this (matter) and consume it merely because one delights in it." Ibn 'Abd as-Salam said – that is 'Izz ad-Deen ash-Shafi'i: "This applies when the owner of the property or wealth is known – otherwise it is (considered as) *fay'* booty to be used for the benefit (of the Muslims) for part of the wealth and property considered to belong to the *bayt al-mal* is that whose owner is unknown." He also said: "ash-Shafi'i said, may Allah be pleased with him: 'If the situation becomes constricted, then one should make it easy on oneself.'"

14. The author *of adh-Dhahab al-Ibreez* said: "al-Fakihani said: 'It is not fitting nowadays that one ask as to the provenance of something, for the origins (of things) have become corrupt and this corruption has taken root (everywhere). Rather one should accept something as it appears (to be). This is preferable to asking about it and finding out that it is haram when one needs it – for then one would be taking it with the knowledge that it is haram or of dubious provenance. This makes it easier for people. The claim of those who declare 'the halal is that whose origin I know' is not valid. What I hold to in this time is that whoever takes an amount in accordance with his need and that of his family – that is, without incurring waste or taking in excess of what he really needs, then he is not (considered to be) consuming anything which is haram or of dubious provenance.' Al-Qasim ibn Muhammad said: 'If the *dunya* were (all) haram, there would be no means of living. What, in fact, is haram is

giving to someone whom one holds to be someone of the deen when this is not in fact so or giving someone something to help him gain knowledge while he is not in fact seeking knowledge – such people are living off the deen and this is prohibited. Permission (for giving to such people) is conditional upon there being nothing hidden (in their hearts) which would cause the donor to withhold giving if were to perceive it. There is no difference between the person who takes (something) claiming *tasawwuf* and *taqwa* when he possesses no such qualities and the person who falsely claims to be of the family of the Prophet, may the peace and blessings of Allah be upon him – for they are both haram, even if a *faqih* gives a *fatwa* that it is halal and bases his judgement on outward appearances.' This Mayyara has narrated where he closes with the words: 'This also applies by analogy to the person who strives to be an imam or to give testimony (before a judge) when he knows in himself that there is a defect (in his character barring him from this), or he strives after making *fatwas*, or testimonies or judgeship when he does not fulfil the conditions of these (activities), and Allah knows best. The present writer does not state this (i.e. 'and Allah knows best') in order to exempt himself from any responsibility but rather to establish Allah's proof, namely that contained in His words "*There is not one of us who does not have a known station*"[1] which indicate that these inner states are veiled from the eyes of the people. O Allah make the best of solutions easy for us!' If Mayyara said this then what must be the state of someone who is only prevented from open *kufr* by sheer excellence and generosity."

15. He [al-Ghazali] said in *al-Ihya'*: "I was asked about the difference between bribery and the giving of presents: each is given willingly and often without ulterior motive but whereas the one is forbidden the other is not. I answered: 'Someone who gives of his money or property never gives it without a purpose. However, the purpose is either with respect to the next world or with respect to this. If with respect to this then it is either in return for money, or for some action which would result in the specific thing intended, or in order to gain access to the heart of the person one gives to so that this person in his turn will reciprocate, or on account of love itself, or in order to gain something beyond this by means of this love – thus there are five divisions to this:

i. As for when the purpose is to gain the reward in the next world, that is, when the person one gives to is in a state of need or is an *'alim* who strives on account of the deen, or a right-acting man of Allah who holds to the deen inwardly, if the person receiving (the gift) knows that he has been given it on account of his need, then it is not permitted him to take it if he is not needy;

1 As-Saffat – Those in Ranks: 164

and if he is aware that he has been given it on account of his noble lineage, then it is not permitted him to take it if he is aware that his claim is false; if someone who is given on account of his knowledge, then it is not permitted for him to receive (anything) unless he possesses knowledge to the degree which the person giving believes he possesses; and if the person gives him something believing him to possess perfection in knowledge, when in fact he does not, then it is not permitted him to take it; and if he is given something on account of his deen and his good actions, then it is not permitted for him to take it, if in fact he is inwardly corrupt and immoral – such that if the donor were to be aware of his (corruption) he would not give anything to him: a man may appear to be right-acting in the outward but were his inward to be revealed, the hearts of others might no longer incline to him. Surely the veil of Allah is beauty, and this is what causes him to be loved by people. The people of scrupulousness would delegate someone unaware of their (standing) to buy for them lest the seller deal indulgently when selling to them – fearing that such indulgence might be considered as 'living off the good name of the deen.' This is a weighty matter and acting with *taqwa* is a subtle thing: it is better to avoid taking anything in the name of the deen as long as one is able.

ii. If a manifest aim is involved, like a poor person giving food to a rich person in return for something of the latter, then the judgement is clear: it is permitted if what is sought after is granted.

iii. As for the intent directed at seeking help for some specific purpose, like in the case where someone – who needs (to see) the Sultan – gives something to the agent of the Sultan, in particular to someone of high office, then such a gift is given in return for something. If it is forbidden (by nature), that is, when striving after something haram, for example, or with the intent to commit an act of injustice against someone or anything else of this order, then it is forbidden to accept such (a gift); just as it is forbidden to receive bribes in return for trumped up testimonies – that is it is forbidden to take anything when there is no doubt that it is forbidden; if, however, it is obligatory, like for example a gift given with the intent of) removing some injustice, then it becomes incumbent on each and every person who is able to remove it; if it is licit, that is it is neither obligatory or forbidden and there is some exertion involved such that if it were a normal, accepted task, it would be permitted to take a reward for it, then whatever he takes is halal – when for the purpose in question. Such (a payment) is considered subject to the same judgement as receiving a wage for a specific job, like for example someone saying 'Have the Sultan informed of such an such a matter' – when the person instructed has to exert himself, has to overcome certain difficulties and take certain steps (to achieve the goal); or he says: 'Suggest to someone that he help me in such a such a matter' or 'that he do me such-and-such a favour' – when in order to carry out his purpose he needs to have a long talk with the person in question. Likewise it would be permitted for someone to accept something for acting as a go-between in a quarrel between two people. All such instances may be known from the circumstances: as long as the intent is praiseworthy and not haram then such (payment) is permitted. But if he only intends to say a word and there is no exertion involved, and what he says or does involves someone of rank and position – like his saying to the doorkeeper 'do not close the door of the Sultan on him' or like his laying the case only before the Sultan himself – then it would be haram for him to take anything as it would amount to payment in return for (the influence of) rank and position; and there is no evidence in the law that this is permitted. Rather there is evidence to the contrary – as will be mentioned below (in the section) regarding 'Gifts to Kings.' Further, if compensation is not permitted for waiving the right to pre-emption, or for returning defective (goods) or for branches encroaching into another's yard – or for other transactions involving concrete instances – then how could (payment) be taken in return for (something so immaterial as) 'rank'; analogous to that would be a doctor taking payment in return for uttering a single word when prescribing a remedy – like naming a plant good for piles or some other (illness), which he alone knows, and which he will only reveal for payment – especially when it turns out to be something of little value like sesame seeds. Payment is not permitted in return for this, nor for knowledge in general when it is such that it is usually transmitted to others and does not remain the property of one single person[1]. However, with regard to those skilled in particular arts or trades, like for example those who polish away blemishes in swords and mirrors, then I do not see any harm in taking compensation for such (knowledge) as a lot of exertion is involved in learning such artisanal work in order to practice professionally: if someone takes payment for his work, then he spares the other much trouble.

iv. This is when something is given with the intention to attract love, that is, from the heart of the donee, that is, when given without a specific purpose but rather out of a (general) desire for intimacy or in order to affirm companionship and to increase affection between the hearts. Such intent is to be found in those of intellect, and is recommended in the law. He, may the peace and blessings of Allah be upon him, said: 'Give each other gifts and show

---

1   The text is garbled at this point.

love for each other.' It is true that in general, a person does not usually intend to manifest his love for another merely for the sake of love. More often than not it is on account of some benefit (he has in mind). However, if he does not have a particular benefit (in mind) and does not harbour any specific intent in his heart – neither for the immediate present or for the future – then (anything he gives) is termed 'a gift', and it is permitted to take it.

v. When something is given in order to seek the intimacy of someone else's heart and to attain to someone else's love – but not purely out of love and intimacy. Rather it is given in order to arrive – by means of his rank or standing – to some end which he has indicated in general but not expressed in detail; such that were it not for his rank and standing, he would not have given him this thing. However, if the person's standing is on account of his knowledge or genealogy, then the matter is less serious; and taking such (a gift) would only (be considered to) be *makruh* – for although a gift according to outward appearances, ambiguity exists as to whether it is indeed a bribe. Further, if the person's rank is that of a judge, governor or officer responsible for *zakat* or taxes or any other of the governmental offices, including even the administration of the *awqaf* for example, then this is (considered as a) bribe made in the form of a gift – that is, were it not for the person's authority, the gift would not have been made. Moreover, there is agreement (among the *fuqaha*) that – if the intent at the time of the request is to get on more intimate terms with him and to win over his affection only to obtain something and that if it cannot be obtained by means of (one of) these authorities, then this 'affection' would disappear and he would turn to another (to achieve his goal) – this is an extremely *makruh* practice, although they have differed as to whether it is haram. The reason for their difference of opinion is the ambiguous nature of the matter: the (judgement with regard to the) 'giving' (in this case) varies in accordance with whether it is to be regarded as a 'pure gift' and a 'deliberate bribe' – made in return for (the influence) of rank; the matter is further complicated when what is sought after is not specified. If a contradiction exists regarding various ambiguous issues which have been resolved by analogy and there are narrations and traditions which support the one over the others, then it is obligatory to incline to the one (supported by the narrations and traditions). And in this case the traditions do indeed indicate the severity of the judgement in this matter: he said, may the peace and blessings of Allah be upon him: 'a time will come upon people when one will seek to make ill-gotten gains halal by giving gifts, to make killing permitted for the purpose of admonition: innocent people will be killed (merely) as an example to the masses.'

Abu Mas'ud was asked, may Allah be pleased with him, about *suht* – ill-gotten gains or illegal things – and he said: 'It is when a man does something for someone and is given a present', that is, when he does it without exerting himself, for example; or voluntarily – without any remuneration in mind – in which case it would no longer be permitted him to take compensation for what he did. Masruq interceded and the person for whom he interceded gave him a slave-girl as a gift and he returned her, saying 'If I had known what was in your heart I would not have spoken about your matter and I shall not speak about the matter still in hand.'

Tawus was asked about gifts to Sultans and he said: '(they are) *suht* – illegal' and 'Umar, may Allah be pleased with him, took away the profit from a *qirad* (profit-sharing) transaction which his two sons had contracted with the *bayt al-mal* saying 'This was given to you on account of your relationship to me' – for he realised that it had been given them on account of the rank and authority (of their father).

The wife of Abu 'Ubayda ibn al-Jarrah gave Khatun, the queen of Rome, a gift of saffron-perfumed oil and the latter rewarded her with a jewel; but 'Umar took it, sold it and gave her the price she had paid for her perfumed oil and returned the rest to the *bayt al-mal* of the Muslims. Jabir and Abu Hurayra have said: 'The gift of kings is fraud and deceit.'

When 'Umar ibn 'Abd al-'Aziz returned a gift someone said to him: 'The Messenger of Allah, may the peace and blessings of Allah be upon him, would accept gifts.' He then replied: 'He received gifts but we receive bribes: they would approach him for his prophethood not for his authority, while we are given on account of authority.'

More general than this is what Abu Humayd as-Sa'di related, namely, that he, on whom be peace and blessings, sent a representative to collect the *zakat* of al-Azd and when he returned to the Messenger of Allah, may the peace and blessings of Allah be upon him, the (representative) took some of the (money and property) he had on him saying: 'This belongs to you and this has been given to me as a gift.' The Prophet, may the peace and blessings of Allah be upon him, said: 'Why did not you stay in your father's and mother's house (i.e. as an ordinary person and not a representative) to see whether you would be given gifts or not – if you are telling the truth.' Then he went on to say: 'What is this! I employ a man and he says: "This is your money and this has been given to me as a gift." Why did he not stay in his father's and mother's home to see whether he will be given gifts or not? By the One in Whose hand is my self none of you takes a thing unlawfully but that he will meet Allah on the Day of

Rising carrying that thing. I do not want to see any of you carrying a foaming braying camel or a mooing cow or a bleating sheep.' Then he raised both his hands until the whiteness of his armpits became visible and said: 'O Allah have I not conveyed the message?' If these strict instructions are understood (literally), then a *qadi* or governor should confine himself to the house of his parents; anything given to him while at the house of his mother – outside of his hours of service – would be permitted for him to accept during his period in office; but whatever is given (specifically) on account of his office would be haram; gifts of an ambiguous nature, like those from friends, should be avoided, even if he given outside his hours of service." Here ends the discussion from *al-Ihya* from the 'Book of the *Halal* and *Haram*.'

He also said in the section '*Adab* of Travel': "If someone who strives after the halal and holds to the path of the next world is compelled to take money from another, then he should declare to him: 'If you are giving it to me because you believe I possess some (good qualities relating to) the deen, then (know that) I am not entitled to it: were Allah to remove His protecting veil, you would no longer see me with the eye of respect, but rather you would hold me for the worst of creation or at least for one of the evil people.' If he nevertheless gives it to him and he takes it, then it may be that Allah will be content with this quality of his, that is his own admission regarding the weakness of his deen and his lack of entitlement to the (gift) he is taking. However, it may be just another trick and deception of the lower self, which he should be aware of: his saying this is to declare he is of comparable (rank) to the *salihun* – that is, with respect to the way in which they disparage their lower self, they belittle it and they see all defects and shortcomings (as issuing from themselves). Thus outwardly, his words have the appearance of censure and rebuke while inwardly they are all praise and panegyric (of himself). How many a person is in fact praising himself while outwardly criticising it! Censure of the self – while alone with one's self – is a praiseworthy attribute but censure of it while in company is nothing but showing off. The exception to this is if he (genuinely) wants to convince those listening that he has committed certain wrong actions and that he acknowledges them: such an admission (is permissible) when the circumstances merit it – just as it is possible to conceal such (defects) if the circumstances do not merit such an admission. The person who is true to himself and Allah, exalted is He, knows that it is impossible to deceive himself and so it is not difficult for him to desist from making such (deceitful admissions) – may Allah benefit us by him."

Al-Qarafi said: "Issue: the author of *al-Bayan* said: 'Malik said: "There is no harm in the people of excellence going themselves to the market to buy. If such people are given preferential treatment because of the excellence (of their character) and (spiritual) state, then there is no harm in this. This is (a natural consequence) of their (character): whatever (preference is given) to them, then (it happens) without their asking." 'Umar ibn al-Khattab, may Allah be pleased with him, would go into the market and Salim ibn Abdallah would say: "Allah, exalted is He, said *'We never sent any Messengers before you who did not eat food and walk in the market-place'*[1] refuting the words of the *mushrikun* who would say: *'What is the matter with this Messenger, that he eats food and walks in the market-place?*[2]*'*"

Ibn Hajar said commenting on the Chapter entitled 'Refusing a present for a specific reason': "Ibn al-'Arabi said: 'Bribery is any money or wealth given to buy help with respect to something which is not permitted from someone of rank and influence.'" In the hadith of 'Abdallah ibn 'Umar it is stated that: "Both the one who gives and the one who accepts a bribe are cursed" – this has been related by at-Tirmidhi who ranked it as *sahih*. The person who gives may either intend (the gift) to win the love of the donee, or he may seek his help or his wealth. The best is the first. The third is permitted as, by giving, he may justifiably expect the donee to be kinder to him. This is particularly recommended when he is in need and when he does not ask the donee for anything explicitly; otherwise it is *makruh*. Thus this (need and the manner in which one deals with it) may be a cause for love and vice versa. As for the second instance, if something is given with an act of disobedience in mind, then it is not permitted and it is (considered to be) bribery; if some act of obedience is involved, then it is recommended; if (for some) permitted (act), then permitted. If the person to whom it is given is not in authority and does not have the power to remove an injustice or invalidate a claim, then it is permitted – although it is recommended for him to desist from taking it; if he is in power, then it is haram.'" – here ends the discussion from *al-Fath*.

16. an-Naji said in *Ma'alim al-iman fi ta'reef rijal al-qayrawan* commenting on the biography of as-Sayouri: "His scrupulousness was so extreme that when the wealth and money of people became mixed with (money and wealth from) corrupt and evil provenance in times of conflict, he would desist from eating meat and would only eat of it when it was certain that its provenance was good and pure; he would only wear fur, sandals or leather socks made from the leather of wild animals and he would only write the reply to an answer (of *fiqh*)

---

1 al-Furqan – Discrimination: 20
2 al-Furqan – Discrimination: 7

on old paper or on leather from wild animals; and he was extremely scrupulous in everything he undertook. 'Iyad said: 'He has commented on certain points in the *Mudawwana* which have been transmitted by his followers.' What he means by this and Allah knows best is that he did not (usually) compile the (teachings) in a book and that his followers recorded what they heard from him during his discourses and lessons – based on what al-Mazari said in his commentary on the *Mudawwana*: 'As-Sayouri has only composed a (short) copy book and no (major) works.' The reason for this is the extreme scrupulousness mentioned above. Indeed, he erected a building to tan leather which he would rent out. Contemporary muftis began to criticise him for this and so he drew on a verdict of Malik from the *madhhab*, arguing "that any increase (i.e. in the form of new-born livestock) are considered to belong to the person who had taken illegal possession of the original livestock, as in the *madhhab* of ash-Shafi'i. By analogy the person who buys sheepskins in order to tan them may be said to be emulating Malik in *taqleed* – in the sense that the (skins) may be considered a legitimate 'increase' (over and above the actual livestock) for the one who has taken possession of the animals illegally. Thus it is legitimate for me to take (payment) from them for the rent of my building as it is licit for them (to make use of these skins) according to the teaching of Malik. What I do would only be haram if what they were doing was haram.'" The gist of his reply is that he is gaining (his livelihood) in accordance with the law, and that he would be scrupulous with regard to his dress and food – in accordance with the *madhhab* of Sahnun. He also possessed twelve thousand olive trees on the coast. He would tend to one of them saying: 'I have a contract to water and tend the trees for a share of the produce.' He would take a half of the (produce of this tree) and use it (raw) for his bread and (for cooking) and the other half, together with the (produce from all the) rest of the olives, he would give away to the poor and destitute. Ahmad ibn Nasr ad-Dawudi said: 'The other way round is preferable, that is, eating in accordance with the law and earning (one's livelihood) with scrupulousness for eating is a necessity which cannot be avoided while one has a choice regarding gaining one's livelihood.'"

17 Ibn Zakari said in *Sharh an-Naseehu*. "There is agreement that it is recommended to resolve or avoid any difference of opinion – as much as one is able, and the differences of the *'ulama* are a mercy. One of our Shaykhs would say: 'May we not leave the realm of difference of opinion!' Shaykh al-Jeeyani, may Allah be content with him would say: 'Gain your livelihood with knowledge and eat with scrupulousness.' This is an extraordinary point (of benefit) and one which alleviates the breast – by adhering to it, one may follow

the way of prudence and precaution."

Ibn al-Hattab, commenting on Khalil's words 'the halal is like a lost stray' said: "So a person should strive to adhere to that about which there is agreement in the *madhhab*; if he does not find it, then he should adhere to the strongest (judgement) from among the differences of opinion; if he does not find this, then the exceptional judgement within the *madhhab*; and if he does not find this, then he should examine the difference of opinion outside of the *madhhab* – and he should not leave the judgements of the *'ulama*. This is what is fitting for every issue."

I have said: "Thus there can be no objection to our transmitting from the Shafi'is in this commentary of ours: very often we transmit from them as we have not found an explicit statement about it in our *madhhab* – even after research."

18. Ibn Zakari said – and the original is I think from *al-Mi'yar* or from al-Mazari in his *Nawazil*: "Ibn Lubb was asked about accepting something owing to someone from the *awqaf* (funds) when he is referred for its collection to a tax collector or to someone whose state is unacceptable (with regard to his earnings) what would be the purest way? He answered: 'As for any salary or wage for which he is referred to the tax collector or the like, there is a difference of opinion in this: the well known opinion is that it is *makruh* (but not haram) to transact with such a person since he only takes what is rightfully his which is halal.' This has been mentioned by Ibn Rushd in *al-Bayan*. The same applies when taking payment for instructing children from people of a similar description."

It is stated in the *Dhakheera* of al-Qarafi regarding a matter: "Ibn Nasr ad-Dawudi said: 'The bequests of Sultans who are well known for their injustice and the bequests of those who have no assets to cover their debts are not permitted: their wealth may not be inherited as whatever they have belongs in fact to those they have wronged, if they are known, and to the Muslims (in general), if they are not known.'"

I say: "The author of *al-Mi'yar* has related from Ibn 'Abdallah at-Tinnisi something which shows this is contrary to the preferred opinion: 'As for the person who inherits inasmuch as the person being inherited is not obliged to separate anything off (from the total sum of the bequest), and that is the case where it is predominantly halal, and similarly when it is predominantly haram according to the *madhhab* of Ibn al-Qasim, and similarly the case of someone who has nothing to cover his debts, according to the judgement that it is indeed permitted to transact with such a person. In such cases, it is more fitting that the inheritor is not obliged to separate off anything from (the total sum of the bequest). As for when the person being inherited from is obliged to separate something off (from the total sum of the bequest) and that is when the major part of the sum inherited is haram, according to the *madhhab* of ibn Wahb; and similarly in the case of inheriting from someone who is bankrupt (and whose property has to be made over to his creditors), according to the judgement that prohibits transactions with such people, there is a difference of opinion regarding the person who inherits: it is said that he should have no qualms about inheriting and that any wrong resides with the testator – and this is the preferred judgement. However it has also been said that the inheritor is on a par with his testator – as long as he is not a poor person or there is no benefit for the Muslims.'"

USEFUL POINT: The filthiest kind of haram is the consumption of *riba*: in *Durr al-Manthur* it is stated that at-Tabarani narrated in *al-Awsat* from al-Bara' ibn 'Azib: "The Messenger of Allah, may the peace and blessings of Allah be upon him, said: '*Riba* has seventy-two classes, the least of which is for a man to have intercourse with his own mother, and the worst form of *riba* is arrogantly violating the honour of one's brother.'"

He also said: "Ahmad (ibn al-Hanbal) and at-Tabarani narrated of 'Abdallah ibn Handhala (who was also known as) *Ghaseel al-Mala'ika* – 'he who has been washed by the angels' – (that is, after dying *shaheed* at Uhud) that the Messenger of Allah, may the peace and blessings of Allah be upon him, said: 'A dirham of *riba* which a man knowingly consumes is worse than thirty-six acts of fornication.'"

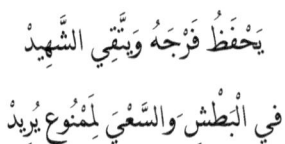

298 He must protect his private parts, and have fearful awareness of the One Who witnesses (him) when he takes (something) or strives for something prohibited which he wants

That fornication is forbidden is a (judgement which is) known necessarily within the *umma*, and anyone who contests it is a *kafir*. Among the *sahih* narrations to this effect is the hadith of the dream of the Prophet, may the peace and blessings of Allah be upon him: "... so we moved off, and we came across something like a *tannur* oven (i.e. a clay-lined pit for baking bread). I think the Prophet said: 'There is much hubbub and voices in it.' We looked into it and saw naked men and women. A flame would extend upwards from below them and whenever it touched them, they would cry out loudly" – according to the text related by al-Bukhari from Samura ibn Jundub. Then he said: "The men and women in this *tannur* are those who have committed fornication."

It is related in *al-Jami' as-Saghir*: "Whoever fornicates has abandoned iman and if he turns in repentance, then Allah will turn in forgiveness to him." It is also related that: "Whoever commits fornication or drinks wine, then Allah will strip him of his iman just as a person strips off his shirt from over his head;" and: "Whoever fornicates will have fornication committed against him even within the walls of his house" – or whatever the exact text is.

Al-Munawi said in his *Sharh*: "This (hadith) indicates that part of the punishment of the fornicator in this world is that fornication will happen to some of the members of his family in a clear and unequivocal manner: and that is because adultery violates honour – and this is in addition to the obligatory *hadd* punishment in this world and his inevitable torment in the next. It is an evil act and the requital for an evil is an evil the like of it, and it is necessary that someone will be given authority over the fornicator who will fornicate with his wife, *and Allah is Almighty, the Exactor of Revenge.*[1]"

Then he goes on to say: "What should also be understood from these hadith is that *anyone* who fornicates will be subject to this punishment, whether he had intercourse with a virgin or a married woman; whether the woman with whom he fornicated is unrelated to him or related so closely that she is *mahram* (and marriage with her is not permitted) – although this would be more of an outrage; whether the woman he had intercourse with is single or married – although the latter is a greater crime. Anything less than actual penetration, like looking at (her), kissing, bodily contact or touching a *mahram* is not termed fornication – for these are wrong actions of lesser import (and may be pardonable)."

It is stated in *al-Jami' as-Saghir*: "… it is better for a man to fornicate with ten women than to fornicate with the wife of his neighbour." Al-Munawi said: "… analogous to this is the slave girl, daughter and sister of his neighbour – for among the rights of one neighbour over another is that he not deceive him or betray his trust with respect to his family. If he does, then the punishment for this (kind of) fornication is equal to ten acts of fornication. Adh-Dhahabi, commenting on this, said: 'Some kinds of fornication are worse than others, the worst being that committed with one's mother, sister, the wife of one's father, a *mahram* woman or the wife of one's neighbour.' Al-Hakim has related

1 Ali 'Imran – The Family of 'Imran: 4

the following which he considers *sahih* – and responsibility lies with him (if it is fabricated): 'Whoever has intercourse with a *mahram* (i.e. someone so closely related to him that it would be forbidden for him to marry her) then kill him.' Thus fornication is a major crime, according to the *ijma'*, and some kinds are more outrageous than others. The most outrageous is that of an old man with his young daughter or sister – especially when he is rich and has lawful wives; or when he compels his neighbour to fornicate with him. There are (many) other similar acts which are (forbidden but) less abhorrent, like an unmarried youth going off alone with an (unmarried) girl and the like – who then regrets what he did and turns to Allah."

It is recorded in the two *Sahihs* that: "Allah has written for the son of Adam his inevitable portion of adultery and fornication whether he is aware of it or not: the adultery of the eye is looking (at something one is not permitted to see), the adultery of the tongue is to utter (what is not permitted to utter) and (adultery of) the lower self is to desire and long after (adultery). The private parts then either confirm what (Allah, exalted is He, has written and make it a reality) or deny it (and refrain from committing this)." Al-'Alqami said commenting on the words 'the private parts either confirm or deny it': "Our Shaykh said: 'The meaning of the hadith is that the son of Adam has had his portion of fornication or adultery prescribed for him: there are those whose 'fornication' becomes a reality by the inter-penetration of the private parts while for others this is metaphorical, that is, it happens only in the sense of 'looking at the haram, etc' as mentioned above – for all these (acts) are metaphorical (rather than real) kinds of fornication. (The application of the *hadd* punishment depends only on) whether the private parts (of the woman) have been penetrated or not; even if penetration has almost taken place, (the *hadd* punishment is not exacted).' Ibn 'Abbas considers the (above mentioned acts) as 'minor wrong actions', interpreting the word *lumam* in the sense used by Allah, exalted is He, when he says: '... *whoever avoids the major wrong actions and indecencies – except for minor lapses (lumam).*¹'"

USEFUL POINT: It is narrated in the hadith that: "Whoever frees a Muslim slave, then for every one of his limbs, Allah will free a limb of his from the Fire – even his private parts for his (the slave's)" – or whatever the exact words of his were, may the peace and blessings of Allah be upon him. Al-Munawi said: "He has mentioned the 'private parts' (*farj*) in particular as they are the cause of the worst of criminal acts after those of *shirk* and murder." Then he goes on to say: "Notice: The 'truthful one' (*as-Sadiq*, i.e. Muhammad, may

1   an-Najm – The Star: 32

the peace and blessings of Allah be upon him) has informed us that Allah, exalted is He, will 'free' the private parts of the person who frees (a slave) by virtue of the reward of the private parts of the person freed. This does not mean that He will free them by virtue of the private parts (of the slave) who has committed acts of fornication and for whom the Fire is the obligatory punishment. However, there are two kinds of fornication: the first, physical contact, either without (contact with) the private parts, or by means of the private parts, but without penetration of the whole of the glans; secondly by penetration. The first is a minor wrong action which is made good by doing meritorious actions, according to the consensus, and the second is among the major crimes, and can only be made good by turning to Allah in *tawba*. The hadith may be understood as referring to the first; and it may imply that setting free a slave has a portion in the weighing (of right and wrong actions) that nothing else has. The apparent meaning is that it renders *kaffara* for the major wrong actions (*kaba'ir*) because it (setting a slave free) is more burdensome than keeping to other acts of worship, like the *salat*."

The author of *al-Fath al-Bari* said: "(Qadi Abu Bakr) Ibn al-'Arabi has seen a difficulty in (a literal interpretation of) his words 'even freeing his private parts for his (the slave's)' as the only crime necessitating the Fire associated with the private parts is fornication: if the hadith is understood as referring to engaging in minor wrong actions, like getting on or between the thighs of one another, then there is no problem in (understanding) how this 'freeing from the Fire' is effected by his freeing (of the slave); however, (there is a problem of interpretation when we consider that full) fornication is a major wrong action and cannot be made good except by turning in *tawba*. Then he (Ibn al-'Arabi) says: 'It is possible that what is meant here is that his (act of) freeing (the slave) is given predominance in the balance, that is, the good actions of the person who sets the slave free outweigh the evil of the fornication.' This does not only apply to the private parts but also to other parts of the body which may benefit from this (act of freeing) – like, for example, the hand of the person who has expropriated something."

USEFUL POINT: Al-Qastallani said: "Al-Ghazali said: 'The lust of the private parts is the strongest of the human passions and the most rebellious – with regard to the intellect – when aroused. Whoever desists from fornication out of fear from Allah when able, when all barriers to it have been lifted and when access to it has been facilitated – in particular when the force of the sexual desire is great, then he will attain to the rank of the *Siddiqun* (i.e. those who are sincere and true).'"

USEFUL POINT: It is related in the *Sahih* from Abu Hurayra, may Allah be pleased with him, that the Messenger of Allah, may the peace and blessings of Allah be upon him, said: "As a dog was encircling a well, almost dying from thirst, one of the prostitutes of the Bani Isra'il saw it and, taking off her boot, (filled it with water) and gave it to the (dog) to drink. She was forgiven on account of it" – or whatever the exact text of the hadith is.

As for Ibn 'Ashir's saying 'and have fearful awareness (*taqwa*) of the One Who witnesses...' Zarruq said in *Sharh al-Waghlisiya*: "Among such (actions of *taqwa*) is restraining one's (feet) from walking where it is not permitted for one to walk, that is, from going to stand near houses of ill-repute and places suspected of criminal activity, or from (going to places) where acts are being committed in disobedience (to the command of Allah), like places where people are fighting without justification – for whoever lends support to a group of people then he is counted as being one of them. Among the acts of disobedience is that a man flee from an advancing army, or that he go somewhere with the intent to commit some wrong action, like when seeking after wine or when conveying evil news of the corrupt to other corrupt persons with the result that they would be strengthened in their corruption. A Muslim (should also restrain his feet) from running (for example) when not absolutely necessary or from extending his foot into someone's beard (when both are lying down); and, according to the Hanafis, from extending both feet towards the *qibla* when this is understood in any way as belittling. As for stretching out one's legs in the mosque in some direction other than that of the *qibla*, this has been confirmed as something which he would do, may the peace and blessings of Allah be upon him."

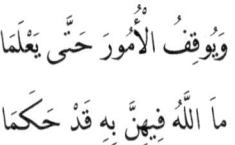

299 He should desist from matters until he knows what judgement Allah has ruled for them

Mayyara said: "His desisting from matters and not engaging upon them (immediately) – when he is unaware of the judgement in their regard – means (desisting) until he knows, that is, until he thinks (he knows) what, in all likelihood, Allah has decreed for him with regard to these matters; and (he comes to know this) by examining the evidence (available to him), or the books of knowledge – if he is someone versed (in such knowledge), or by asking the people of knowledge – in accordance with the words of Allah, exalted is He: 'Ask the People of the Reminder if you do not know'[1]; in which case, he either proceeds to do it or he desists from doing it. (Desisting in this manner) is also obligatory according to the words of the Prophet, may the peace and blessings of Allah be upon him: 'It is not permitted for someone to proceed in a matter until he knows the judgement of Allah in it.' Moreover what is being referred to here is not the same as (the judgement in *fiqh* designated as) 'desisting from acts about which there is doubt' – for 'doubtful matters' (in this context) are those about which the *'ulama* have differed, or those where the evidence for something being halal or haram are esteemed to have equal weight. Someone subject to such a matter usually has an idea of the judgements involved and so his desisting from it is rather by way of scrupulousness (than lack of knowledge). But the matter (in question here) involves someone who has no idea at all of the judgement – and so it is obligatory (in his case), according to the *fiqh*, to refrain until he knows the judgement. In other words his desisting is not (simply) out of scrupulousness, and Allah, exalted is He, knows best."

Examine what he and others have mentioned regarding the *'ulama's* differences with respect to matters of doubt in comparison with what al-Fakihani has stated in *Sharh al-'Umda* – for the latter concludes that (acting upon) such (differences) is licit. The (relevant) text occurs during his commentary on the hadith 'The halal is clear and the haram is clear': "Whoever embarks upon a matter in accordance with one of two judgements on the matter, or in accordance with one of several judgements, then this is licit for him, in particular if the judgement (he chooses) is the predominant one." There is also a similar statement from al-Mawwaq: "Ibn 'Abd al-Barr said in *at-Tamheed*: 'If Allah or the Messenger have not prohibited him from (doing) something, and the people (of *fiqh*) have not reached agreement about it, then the judgement that it is 'licit' remains valid and may be applied (to the matter in question)."

I have said: "It may well be that what al-Fakihani and al-Mawwaq have mentioned applies to judgements other than those which are (considered) weak – for many of the *'ulama* of the *ijma'* have related that it is prohibited to act upon a weak judgement, that is, for (a judge to deliver) a judgement (based on it); likewise in the case of *fatwas*, except in the case of extreme need; however, regarding (a private matter) between him and Allah, then what they say necessarily implies that it would be permissible to act upon such (a judgement) when the need arises – although this is conditional upon the need being of an extreme kind, and Allah knows best."

1 al-Anbiya' – The Prophets: 7

$$\text{يُطَهِّرُ الْقَلْبَ مِنَ الرِّيَاءِ}$$
$$\text{وَحَسَدٍ عُجْبٍ وَكُلِّ دَاءٍ}$$

300 He must purify his heart from showing off, from envy, conceit and every (other) sickness

Al-Munawi[1] said: "Those who have experience (in this subject) have said that worship is of three ranks:

1. That you worship Allah seeking after the reward and fleeing from punishment – and this is contemptible in the extreme as his object of worship in reality is this reward;

2. That you worship Allah in order to feel honoured by worship of Him and by your relation to Him – this is higher (than the first) but not (entirely) pure as the intent in essence is other than Allah;

3. That you worship him for His being God and for your being His slave – and this is the highest of these (three ranks)."

Al-Ubbi said in *Ikmal al-Ikmal*: "Worship (performed) in order to enter the Garden is permitted. However, this is the preferred judgement (only) with regard to those who worship Allah, deeming worship (of Him) necessary, and who believe that He glorious and exalted is He, is a fitting object of worship. Others have gone further, declaring that it is not permitted."

I say: "And in *adh-Dhahab al-Ibreez* of ad-Dabbagh – may Allah benefit us by him – he says words to the effect that 'if he performs with the intention (of obtaining) the reward (*thawab*) only, or with the intention of the reward together with (the intention of acting in) obedience (to what has been commanded) – although this intention to (act in) obedience is such that were there no reward, he would not perform (the act of worship) – then he will have no reward (*ajr*); if he performs it only with the intention of obedience – or with the intention of obedience but accompanied by the intention of reward, being aware that this intention of reward is a consequence of it and secondary to it, such that if there were no reward, he would nevertheless perform the (act of obedience) and so follow the command of his Lord only – then this is rewarded, praiseworthy and commendable." This then is the gist of his words in brief, although not

---

1 The text below in brackets is taken from the older manuscript while in another copy it reads: "This is the judgement of the *'Arif* of Allah, exalted is He, Sayyidi Abdal-'Aziz ad-Dabbagh as stated in *adh-Dhahab al-Ibreez*, which was written about his memorable qualities, who said: 'Performing acts of worship (merely) in order to attain to the reward (prescribed for it) is forbidden, and the person will be punished in the Fire of Jahannam.'" Abridged.

the exact text. However, this is contrary to what ash-Shatibi declared in his *al-Muwafaqat,* for he said: "This is the station of the elite of the elite, and to demand of oneself (or another) that one take this (station) on is something which is almost unbearable."

Moreover, Abu'l-Hasan, commenting on the words of the *Risala* 'Whoever performs Ramadan with iman, carefully observing (what is prescribed) and anticipating the promised reward, will be forgiven', said in *Ghayat al-Ma'ani*: "His mention of 'with iman' means 'with a conscious affirmation of the promised reward'; his saying 'carefully observing (what is prescribed) ...' means 'aware that his reward is with Allah and is stored up in the next world' – that is, he does not perform it to show off or for reputation. This is the *madhhab* of the *fuqaha*, namely that he worships Allah desirous of the Garden and out of fear of the Fire. It has also been narrated that ash-Shafi'i, may Allah be pleased with him, said: 'If there were no desire for the Garden or fear of the Fire, He would not have been worshipped.' (... and he holds that he should worship out of love of Him not out of desire for His Garden or fear of His Fire).[1]

He said in *Sharh ar-Risala*: 'and it is obligatory on him that he know how to perform the *wudu'* (properly), that is, how it is performed purely for Allah – free of any showing off and not for reputation. The *fuqaha* have said that this (state, known as) *ihtisab,* is doing something only for Allah, exalted is He, while being desirous of His Garden and fearing His Fire. The Sufis have said: "*Ihtisab* is performing an action purely for Allah in response to His command, being aware that (only) He is worthy of worship, and out of love for Him, without any desire for His Garden or fear of His Fire." Ibn al-'Arabi said: "... but what the *fuqaha* have said is better as the law (*ash-shar'*) has mentioned this (in these terms). Moreover, were it not for the fear of His Fire or the desire for His Garden, no one would have worshipped Him. (Such an elevated state) may only be witnessed in someone to whom Allah has granted success in his worship of Him, whom Allah has rendered worthy of such (worship) and whom Allah has inspired with the certainty that the Garden has been determined for him. Thus he is probably not referring to people in general for if he were, it would not be correct (to assert this).""

NOTICE:

1. Jasous said in *Sharh ar-Risala*: "Know that al-Ghazali considers that there is no difference between showing off and the other (bad attributes) particular to

---

[1] What is in brackets is omitted in one copy and there is something missing before the words 'he holds that...' – it may be that what is missing is the words 'one of the Sufis' (i.e. one of the Sufis holds that) as it corresponds to a saying of Rabi'a al-'Adawiyya.

the lower self and that the judgement regarding them all is one and the same. Others, however, like Hafidh Ibn Rajab and Ibn Hajar al-Haytami in their commentaries on the *Forty Hadith* of an-Nawawi, al-Qarafi in his *al-Farouq*, al-Bayqouri in his *Ikhtisar* and Ibn ash-Shat in his *Hashiya* consider that both aspects of showing off invalidate worship, while (worship) free of showing off (but blemished by other attributes of the lower self) is not invalidated, although the reward has diminished."

I say: "Ibn al-Hattab, commenting in *Sharh al-Mukhtasar* on al-Ghazali and those of Jasous's words 'both aspects of showing off...', said: 'the meaning is the same, whether the motive of showing off is dominant or the motive of sincerity and purity of intention is uppermost (but still tainted by showing off).'"

I say: "He has differed with al-Ghazali in this, the latter holding that the worship is valid if the motive of sincerity is uppermost – although of less merit than worship which contains no portion (of the self); and that if the motive of showing off is dominant, then it invalidates (the worship) – although it is less evil than someone whose sole intent is to show off – and this (judgement) is based on His words: '*Whoever does an atom's weight of good will see it. Whoever does an atom's weight of evil will see it.*[1]'" He has also said: "If they are of equal intensity, then they will contend with each other and the (act of worship) will be (reckoned) neither for him or against him."

2. Zarruq said in *Sharh al-Waghlisiya*: "It has been said that action accompanied by showing off is better than not acting for fear of this (showing off)."

'Envy' referred to in Ibn 'Ashir's saying 'and envy...' denotes an aversion to blessings and the desire that they be removed from the person who has been granted them. If, however, one wishes similar (blessings) for oneself without disliking them or desiring that they come to an end (for another), then this is *ghibta* – un-envious emulation – which is not haram. This has been stated by 'Ali ibn 'Abd as-Sadiq. Al-Baqouri said: "It is (even) recommended if it involves something meritorious – according to his words, on whom be peace and blessings: 'There is only envy on account of two instances: (a person whom Allah has given wealth and he is given power to use it for for the Truth; the second, a person whom Allah has given wisdom and he decides according to it and teaches it.)'" Commenting on his words – 'there are three things which this *umma* will not be free of: envy, having a bad opinion of people and evil augury – shall I not tell you of the way to avoid these?' They said: 'Tell us, Messenger of Allah', may the peace and blessings of Allah be upon him. He

1 az-Zilzala – The Earthquake: 8-9

said: 'If you think something, then do not affirm it as a certainty, if you are envious, then do not seek after it and if you take a bad omen (from something), then go ahead (and do whatever you are doing) – al-Munawi said: "His saying 'do not seek after it' means if you find some (desire) in your heart, then do not act in accordance with it, for envy will befall the lower self. This is because the latter has been created, as it were, with this (characteristic and so it is unavoidable); and this is why it may be excused. If one becomes too lax and allows the lower self free rein to listen to the whisperings of this (envy) or to act (in accordance with its dictates), then these (whisperings and subsequent actions) will lead to (the person committing) outrage. The person struck by envy must realise that depriving it (of attention) causes it to diminish; if he strives with himself (and contains) this (envy), then the envied person will (cease to be envied): he will instead be regarded as fortunate and there will no longer be any desire to remove this fortune from him; envy (on the other hand) brings only harm and no benefit."

Al-Ghazali said, may Allah be pleased with him: "If a person despairs of attaining to a blessing similar (to that of someone else) and is unhappy that it does not fall to his lot, then it is inevitable that he will want to put a stop to the absence of this (blessing), that is, it is inevitable that this lack can only come to end if he obtains something like it or the blessing of the envied person is removed. (The result of this is that) if one of these two possibilities is blocked, then his heart will be unable to rid itself of the desire for the other (possibility)." Al-Qastallani has also said something similar – as well as Ibn Hajar – when he says: "Envy denotes the desire to remove a blessing from someone who has a right to it. It is a term which is more general than (the consequence of envy, namely) the active striving to remove (a blessing); if he does strive to remove it, then he would be guilty of a blatant injustice. If he does not try to (remove it), does not manifest (his envy) and does not affirm the motives of this dislike (of his for someone else's blessings) – motives which are (anyway) prohibited for a Muslim with regard to the right of another – then one should examine (the circumstances): if his not attempting (to remove the blessing) is merely through his own incapacity to do so – such that were he able (to remove it), he would indeed do so – then he is still blameworthy; but if his not doing this issues from his *taqwa*, then he is excused – for he cannot completely rid himself of the thoughts that afflict the self. It is enough that he strive against them, that he not act in accordance with them and that he not resolve to put them into practice."

Ibn Zakari said in *Sharh an-Naseeha*: "It may be that your lower self will not obey you in treating your friend and your enemy equally. Rather (by its nature) it dislikes inflicting harm on a friend but not on an enemy. However, you are not charged with what you cannot bear – and if you are not able to (control your lower self completely), then you can free yourself of any wrongdoing in two ways: firstly, by not manifesting your envy on the tongue or limbs or any of your actions over which you have control – rather strive to resist anything which might arouse this envy; secondly, by having an active aversion to your lower self and its desire to remove a blessing from one of the slaves of Allah. However, in most cases it is impossible to establish an aversion as a motive to change one's inborn character. An indication (that one has been successful in implanting) this aversion is that if one has the capacity to remove the blessing, one does not nevertheless go ahead and remove it – despite wanting to; and (a further sign) is that if one is in a position to help the person to keep hold of the blessing or to increase him in it, one would do so – despite one's not in fact wanting to. If this is the case, then one is not guilty of any wrong action with regard to the instinctive demands of the nature (of the lower self): (eventually) this nature will disappear (of its own accord through opposition to it) – that is, when one is wholly abandoned to Allah and has ceased to look at the *dunya* and creation."

Ibn Hajar al-Haytami said: "If envy is so firmly implanted in the nature of a man that he cannot bear anyone else to be superior to him, with regard to any aspect of excellence, then it can assume various forms: there are those who strive with their tongue and through their actions to transfer the blessing which they are envious of to themselves; or who strive to remove it altogether (from them both), and this is the worst of the two and the ugliest; and there are yet others who do not act in accordance with their envy and do not strive against the person envied with their tongue or actions. It is recorded from al-Hasan that this latter is not a wrongdoer. The most evident interpretation (of this judgement) is that this refers to someone who is unable to remove the (envy) from his lower self and so he struggles against the lower self in order to desist from it as much as he is able; unlike the person who willingly permits a discourse between this (envy) and his lower self and who simultaneously desires that the blessing be removed from the person he envies – for there is no doubt that in this he is a wrongdoer, indeed guilty of gross corruption."

USEFUL POINT: al-Munawi said, commenting on the tradition 'Envy consumes good actions like fire consumes firewood': "This is because (envy) amounts to an objection to Allah, exalted is He, with regard to something over which the slave has no influence (anyway) and which he is not harmed by

– that is, the blessing granted by Allah to (one of His) slaves. Allah does not do something without a purpose – and thus it is as if he is attributing ignorance and stupidity to the Lord; and as if he is not content with His decree and is looking for another Lord. The envier is punished in this world with eternal (divine) anger and in the next world by seeing his actions come to nothing – and in this respect it is also one of the major wrong actions (*kaba'ir*). The Qadi said: 'those who hold to this view are those who hold that acts of obedience are brought to nothing by acts of disobedience – like the Mu'tazilis. I would respond by asserting that what is meant here is that his good actions are brought to nothing and are deducted from his (account with Allah) because an amount equal to all his good actions is required in compensation for the damage to the property and for the ruin of the reputation of the person he envied.'"

At-Teebi said: "(the term) 'consume' (in the above hadith) is a metaphor for lack of acceptance: his good actions are rejected and are not recorded in the register of his actions, so that they come to nothing."

As for Ibn 'Ashir's mention of 'conceit', Zarruq stated in *Sharh al-Waghlisiya*: "Conceit or vanity is to assume superior qualities in one's speech, actions and in one's state even if this is not directly stated to others, and it is one of the worst states of disobedience with respect to the heart; however it has been said that conceit is something decreed (by Allah, exalted is He). The way to free oneself from conceit is to see the grace and favour of Allah, glorious and exalted is He, in whatever (quality one is being conceited about) and to see (the reality of) your poverty, incapacity and need with respect to everything; and realise that if any real power resided in you, you would determine (the manner of) the necessary (bodily functions) like urinating and even do away with such functions altogether. However, this is impossible, and is rather an indication that such (natural capacities) are blessings from Allah over which you have no control."

Ibn 'Ashir's saying 'and every sickness' refers to (sicknesses) like for example rancour, spite or malice. Zarruq said: "in other words, to harbour a grudge or enmity in one's heart while merely giving the impression that there is no such (sickness) there – rather then (attempting to conceal one's state by) showing the opposite of it (i.e love). Protection from this is by acting in a kind and generous manner towards the person you have a grudge against, and secretly making *du'a* for him – for Shaytan will despair if you do this. As for *hiqd*, resentment, it refers to harbouring feelings (of hatred and malice) in one's heart which then turn into anger – and which can either manifest or be kept hidden. It is repelled by *ihsan*, that is by acting well towards the person you hold enmity towards, by exaggerating one's generosity towards him and actively rejecting what is inside one's heart – the blameworthy aspect of one's ill intent may be eliminated by acting well, and Shaytan will despair of ensnaring you when you do this."

As for pride, Zarruq said: "that is, a person believing that he is better than others in the world with respect to the deen or the *dunya* – to the point that he despises those below him. It has been said: 'Whoever thinks that he is better than a dog then the dog is better than him.'"

Then he said, "Getting rid of pride is by returning to the source of the matter, that is, by realising that you are unworthy of any (of the blessings) surrounding you; that any good (aspect) in your life is from Allah, and that just as He has granted this (aspect of) good to you, so He can also deprive you of it and instead grant the person whom you regarded with pride something (of even) greater (good) than this. Our Shaykh Abu'l-'Abbas al-Hadhrami, may Allah be pleased with him, said: 'How can you feel pride regarding someone when you can never be sure that in the eyes of Allah you are better than him – for you do not know and no one knows what Allah will do with him or anyone else.'"

His Shaykh, as-Sanusi, said in *Sharh al-Qaseed*: "Its (pride's) reality is seeing the self's having some increase in comparison with some aspect of creation of Allah, exalted is He, even if it be a dog, excrement or the like. For this reason they have said: 'Anyone who does not accept the truth irrespective of whether this (truth is imparted) by means of a noble or a mean person, and persists in seeing others as being worse than himself, then he is in a state of absolute pride; whoever hears a statement of truth which does not accord with his desire or whim, and he rejects it, then he has rejected Allah, exalted is He; if he humbles himself, but is still conscious that he has humbled himself, then he remains full of pride – for his being aware of his own humility is proof that he is aware of some superiority of his *nafs* but it also indicates that he has fallen from this high station by this very claim (of humility)." As-Sanusi's words.

Al-Fudail ibn 'Iyad also said: "Whoever persists in seeing anything of worth in his *nafs*, then he has no portion of humility." When asked about humility he replied: "a person who yields to the truth, submits to it and accepts it from whoever expresses it."

He (as-Sanusi) then goes on to say after a long discussion: "The cure for pride, in a legal sense, is reminding the person afflicted by pride of the punishment of Allah, exalted is He, for the proud, reminding him of His hatred and that He will deprive the proud of all good in this world and the next. The most sublime cure, however, is his being aware that all possible creational realities are equal (that is, each and every thing is alike in that – potentially speaking – it may or may not come into being). Thus contingent attributes which the lowest of created forms may assume, may also be taken on by the highest of forms and so (strictly speaking), there is no superiority of one thing over another with regard to its essence. Moreover our Lord, exalted is He, may grant whatever He wills to whatever He wills – without it deserving whatever blessing it was that He bestowed on it. He, glorious is He, has the power to change the lowest of creational forms to the highest and the highest to the lowest – as so often happens in the world of forms: how many a *mumin* becomes a *kafir* one day and how many a *kafir* becomes *mumin*; and how many a person of insignificance becomes powerful and how many a powerful person becomes of insignificance, and how many a rich person becomes poor and how many a poor person becomes rich."

Then he goes on to say after a discussion: "For this reason they have said: 'There is no such thing as a person of intellect who is full of pride – neither before the revelation or after it.'" Again he goes on to say: "If you were to argue that if it is the slave's duty to see no extra merit in himself, even if it be over a *kafir* or a dog, indeed that he see no one worse than himself, then even this – despite attaining to the station of humility and sincerity – is one of the sicknesses of pride: it leads to an even greater sickness, and one of the most pernicious, namely to a denial of blessings. This occurs when he (simply) does not see these blessings.

"I say: It is obvious to the person of intellect that the state of pride is one which denies gratitude, that the station of humility drives one towards it (gratitude) and requires one to take on the attributes (of humility). The more pride descends upon the heart, the less gratitude exists, and the more humility a person has, the greater his gratitude. The reason for this is that when a person full of pride harbours the illusion of perfection with respect to his *nafs* while at the same time seeing it as possessing some extra merit, then whenever he sees some blessing, he attributes it to the perfection which he imagines belongs to his *nafs*. Thus he considers the *nafs* worthy (of this blessing) by virtue of its perfection: he sees, for example, an increase in his capacity for acquiring knowledge and so attributes it to what he imagines to be the acuteness of his intelligence, or to his exerting himself in study, or to staying awake at night to study, or to travelling to meet Shaykhs and such (illusions) as are often witnessed amongst the people of (false) claim and idiotic pretensions – both those who devote themselves to knowledge or who are engaged in other matters. How can there be gratitude for the blessings of Allah in someone like this in any real way? Rather it is the very reason for their lack of gratitude for such (blessings).

This is analogous to what Allah has related about the *kafir* when He says: '*But if We let him taste mercy from Us after he has suffered hardship, then he says, 'This is my due,'*[1] – believing that it is on account of his own merit. As for the person of humility who does not regard his *nafs* as having any extra merit not even in comparison to inert objects, filth or dung and the like – because (he is aware that) all things which are 'possible of existence' are equal with respect to the general all-pervading power of Allah and His will – then whenever he sees the least form of blessing, he realises that its existence is by the overflowing generosity of Allah, exalted is He, and by the beauty of His generosity and excellence; he realises that this (blessing) does not owe its existence to the merit of the thing or person (upon which is it bestowed) in any way; he realises that when something takes on (the characteristics of) this (blessing), then it does so because it is the locus (determined by Allah) for such (blessings) to be; that the opposite qualities (may also come into being) – as is the case for all things which are possible of existence, whether (it is the attribute of *kufr* in) the *kuffar*, (solidity and inertia in) objects, (life in) animals or anything else (of creation); he realises too that none of the things that are 'possible of existence' are worse than him because he is more worthy of perfection than that thing that may possibly exist. This realisation on behalf of the person of humility is an inner gratitude, indeed the highest kind of gratitude. It is absent in the person of pride – and when this occurs in the realm of *'aqida*, he will be a *kafir*, and when absent through negligence or forgetfulness, he will be corrupt and astray." The end of as-Sanusi's words.

In *Fath al-Bari* it is stated: "It is related in the *Sahih Muslim* that the Prophet, may the peace and blessings of Allah be upon him, said: 'No one who has an atom's weight of pride will enter the Garden.' Someone then said 'a man may like wearing beautiful clothes and fine sandals?' He replied: 'Pride is disregard for the truth and treating people disparagingly.'" Then he goes on to say: "'Abd Ibn Humaid related a hadith of Ibn 'Abbas: 'Pride is insolence regarding the truth and holding people in contempt' and then Ibn 'Abbas goes on to relate that he then said 'Messenger of Allah, what is insolence?' He replied: 'It is when you are owed a right by a man but he denies it, so then (another) man tells him to have *taqwa* of Allah but he refuses.' 'Holding people in contempt' is for example not greeting people (one considers) of insignificant rank and worth, or not sitting with them because one despises them." Ibn Hajar.

I say: "One of the strongest cures in my opinion is to remind oneself of the final moment (of death), for whoever reflects upon this moment of death will

---

[1] Fussilat – Made Plain: 50.

not regard his *nafs* as being intrinsically superior to any of the creations of Allah: he can never know (for sure) whether he will die as a *kafir* – in which case dung, a dog or a pig would be better than him, as would any *kafir* or shaytan because they had followed their desires during their time on earth – or as a *mumin* in which case his excellence (by virtue of his iman) will then be by Allah not from himself, even if he is unaware of this, and Allah knows best."

USEFUL POINT: al-Qurtubi said, commenting on 'and no one humbles himself for the sake of Allah but that Allah will raise him': "Humility necessarily implies there be someone to whom one submits. If this is Allah or someone whom Allah has commanded people to submit to, like the Messenger, may the peace and blessings of Allah be upon him, or the imam/leader, or the judge, or one's father or an *'alim*, then this is the obligatory and praiseworthy humility (spoken of in the hadith) by virtue of which Allah will raise a person in this world and the next. As for submitting in humility to the rest of creation, the most excellent kind (of humility) is the praiseworthy, recommended and desirable (kind which exists) if one intends by it the face of Allah: whoever has this kind (of humility), then Allah will raise him in esteem, will cause his name to be mentioned amongst people and will raise his rank in the next world. However, submitting in humility to the people of the *dunya* or to those who are tyrannical or unjust is mere degradation: it is sheer humiliation, devoid of any honour or esteem; it is the cause of disgrace in the next world and brings only loss."

USEFUL POINT: al-Ghazali said: "and whoever claims that he is superior to one of the slaves of Allah, then he brings all his actions to nothing by his ignorance. It means he has no fear of what Allah might devise (being hopelessly lost in ignorance): '*No one feels secure against Allah's devising except for those who are lost.*[1]'"

وَاعْلَمْ بِأَنَّ أَصْلَ ذِي الْآفَاتِ

حُبُّ الرِّيَاسَةِ وَطَرْحُ الْآتِي

301 Know that the root of all blight is love of leadership (rank, praise, honour and ease in this world) and rejection of (the life) to come;

رَأْسُ الْخَطَايَا هُوَ حُبُّ الْعَاجِلَةِ

---

1 Al-A'raf – The Ramparts: 99

$$\text{لَيْسَ الدَّوَا إِلَّا فِي الِاضْطِرَارِ لَهُ}$$

302 that the chief of all faults is love of this world, and that there is no cure but to be in need of Him.

I am not the right person to speak about this station. Indeed from here to the end of the book, it would almost be haram for me to speak about this. If I were to speak about it merely in accordance with my whim and desire, then I myself would be astray and I would also be leading others astray; if I were to speak about it in accordance with the reality (of my state), then I would be a hypocrite, for my words would contradict my actions. Therefore you should read the books of the people (of this science), like al-Ghazali and others, and Mayyara. As this book has been composed with the intention of explaining obscure and unfamiliar matters, I shall now – up to the end of the book – indicate a few points which are not commonly found in the usual books (on this science). As for the evidence and proof upon which the two lines (above) are based, you should study what 'Abd as-Sadiq said in their regard; as for what they indicate, then I say, embarking (on the matter) in the name of Allah:

It is stated in *al-Jami' as-Saghir*: "… is there anyone who can walk in water without getting his feet wet? The person of this world is in a similar situation for he cannot avoid committing wrong actions." Al-Munawi said: "This (statement) inspires an intense dread of the world; it urges one to do without in it and to prefer the next world over it. May it be enough to realise that this (world) is the reason why the poor enter the Garden five hundred years before the rich."

It is state in *Majma' al-Ahbab*: "Wahb ibn Munabbih said: 'The easiest way to behave with respect to the deen and the *dunya* is the way of those who do without in the world; the quickest way to bring on sickness is to follow one's whims and desires – for whoever follows his desires will love wealth and rank, and whoever loves wealth and rank will violate what is forbidden or sacred, and whoever violates what is forbidden, then Allah, glorious and exalted is He, will become angry, and there is no withstanding the anger of Allah exalted is He.'"

It is also stated in it: "Tawus said: 'The sweetness of the *dunya* is the bitterness of the next world, and the bitterness of this world is the sweetness of the next.' Again he said: 'Bishr al-Hafi said, may Allah be pleased with him: "He who loves fame has no *taqwa* of Allah."' Ibn Hajar al-Haytami said in *Sharh al-Arba'in*: 'Whoever makes the next world his concern, then Allah will increase his strength (to this end), will fill his heart with riches (making him independent of the world) and the world will come (to him) despite the world's unwillingness to come; whoever makes this world his (only) concern, then Allah will increase his strength (to this end), will make his poverty appear before his very eyes and only that (portion) of the *dunya* will come to him which has been decreed for him.' This has been narrated by at-Tirmidhi, Ahmad and Ibn Majah. In the narration of at-Tirmidhi it states: 'If the world, in the eyes of Allah, were equal to the wing of a gnat, He would not have given a single drink of water to a *kafir*.' However, know that among the people of doing-without in this world are also those who obtain some of the overflowing superfluity of this world: they take hold of it in order to come closer to Allah by it. It is in this light that Abu Sulayman said: 'Uthman and 'Abd ar-Rahman ibn 'Awf, may Allah be pleased with them, were two of the treasure houses of Allah on His earth: they would spend in obedience to Him, and their transactions (with people) were for the sake of Allah, exalted is He, in their hearts. There are others (who have the opportunity to attain to riches but) who voluntarily do not keep hold of it, or do not keep hold of it, with some struggle with their *nafs*. Ibn as-Samak and al-Junayd preferred the first, that is (the *zuhd* of) those (who spend freely) because of the ascertainment of his certaintyof both the station of generosity and that of doing-without; while Ibn 'Ata' preferred the second, that is because he has to work and struggle (with himself). There are also those who do not attain to anything of the superfluity (of the world), and such a person is a *zahid* in what he attains to whether he is capable or not, although the first, (i.e. the one who has the capacity to attain to something) is better. For this reason many of those of the first generations have said that 'Umar ibn 'Abd al-'Aziz was more of a *zahid* than Uwais. The *'ulama* have differed as to whether is it better to seek the (*dunya*) in order to do good or to desist from it; a party preferred the former and another party preferred the latter."

Al-Haytami also said – before the above mentioned discussion: "Many of the *salaf* have divided 'doing without' into three types: the doing without which is obligatory, namely guarding against major *shirk* (that is idol-worship); then guarding against minor *shirk*, that is, that one intends other than Allah, exalted is He, by anything of knowledge, whether in word or deed; then being on one's guard against any act of disobedience (that is the haram). According to az-Zuhri, Ibn 'Uyayna and others, only a person who is *zahid* with respect to the haram may be called *zahid*, although it has also been said he is only called such if two other qualities of *zuhd* are added to this *zuhd*, namely desisting from anything doubtful immediately, and from any superfluity of the halal. In this light one of them said: 'There is no *zuhd* nowadays, given the absence of anything which is purely licit (i.e. everything has become tainted with the haram).' Abu Sulayman ad-Darani combined all the kinds of *zuhd* into one saying: 'It is leaving what distracts you from Allah, exalted is He. Know that the disparagement of the *dunya* in the Book and sunna does not however refer to its (dimension of) time – that is, night and day – for Allah made, *"night and day succeed each other for those who want to pay heed or to give thanks"*[1], nor to the physical locus – that is the earth, because Allah ...[2] but rather it refers to being distracted with what is in it from what we have been created for, namely worship of Him, exalted is He.' Then there are those amongst the sons of Adam who deny the raising of the dead: they are (usually) those who seek enjoyment in this world although among them are those that command to *zuhd* in this world. However, it has been related that a great deal of it necessarily afflicts one with grief and worry. In this light our colleagues say: The person delivering the *khutba* should not content himself with urging to *taqwa* and should not be content merely to disparage the *dunya* – for disparagement and censure of the *dunya* is well known to all, even to those who reject the Day of Rising. The rest of them affirm the Day of Rising but they may be categorised in three ways: those who do injustice to themselves, those who are of average (disposition in this matter) and those who are the forerunners in performing good actions. The first, and they are the majority, are those that linger over the flower of the world: they take it and use it for what it was not meant for such that it becomes their overriding concern. These are the people of entertainment and sport, superficial adornment, bragging and competing with each other over the amounts of their possessions. None of them are aware of the purpose of the *dunya*, nor are they aware that they are here on a brief journey in order that they may take provision from it for the Abode of Eternal Life – despite their belief as a whole (in this afterlife). The second group take it for what it is meant for but they indulge in all that is licit and enjoy all its permitted sensual delights; although they will not be punished, their station will be reduced in the next world in proportion to their indulgence in the *dunya*. It has been reported from Ibn 'Umar in a *sahih* tradition, may Allah be pleased with him,[3] 'No one receives a portion of the *dunya* but that his rank will

---

1 al- Furqan – Discrimination: 62
2 Here there is a lacuna.
3 In the older manuscript it states 'from 'Umar'.

be reduced with Allah in the next world (in proportion to his indulgence in it)[1] even if he is honoured by Allah.' At-Tirmidhi has narrated: 'If Allah, glorious and exalted is He, loves a slave, then He will protect him from the *dunya* just as any one of you would continually protect a sick person from water.'" The purpose of al-Haytami's discussion is contained in the above but examine the rest of what he says (if necessary).

USEFUL POINT: Al-Munawi said, commenting on the narration 'part of the *fiqh* of a man is that he make sure that his livelihood is correct; and it is not a part of (love) of the world to seek what puts you aright': "this refers to providing for one's means, for the needs of one's family, one's servants and the like – for these are necessary things which one cannot do without, and seeking after them is not (considered to be the same as) seeking after the *dunya,* which is prohibited."

He (al-Haytami) said in *Majma' al-Ahbab*: "Wahb ibn Munabbih said: 'The person who is most abstinent with respect to this world – even if he is devoted to it and greedy for it – is he who is only content with good and halal earnings; the person most desirous for it is he who does not care from where he acquires it, whether it is halal or haram.'"

Al-Munawi said, commenting on the tradition 'the greedy person is he who seeks to earn without it being halal': "'Ali, may Allah be pleased with him, said: 'If a man were to take everything on the face of the earth intending by it the face of Allah, then he would be called a *zahid,* but if he were to leave everything in it without intending the face of Allah, exalted is He, he would not be called *zahid* and he would not be worshipping Allah despite (leaving everything in it). So whatever you take and whatever you leave, let it be for Allah alone, not for anything else.'"

يَصْحَبُ شَيْخاً عَارِفَ الْمَسَالِكْ

يَقِيهِ فِي طَرِيقِهِ الْمَهَالِكْ

303 He must keep the company of a Shaykh who has knowledge of the ways and who will protect him on his path from dangers;

The present commentator and others have refrained from speaking about this, given that it is not permitted, (at least) for me, to speak on this subject or the like of what is mentioned in these two lines – as I have already made clear above: I am a stranger to the (people of this science) and neither one of the

---

[1] This is additional in the older copy.

men of their group, nor one of their students. May Allah benefit us by them, cause us to die on their sunna and raise us in their company.

However, here is the portion I am permitted to mention. Al-Munawi said: "The question has been raised as to whether a *murid* may sit in the company of someone other than his Shaykh when it involves this (matter of *tasawwuf*)? One of the (people of this science) said: 'Yes, if it appears to the *murid* that the other Shaykh is worthy of imitation, then he may do this'; others have said: 'No, no more than the *mukallaf* – the sane, adult person charged with responsibility – would be bound to two Messengers with two different *shari'ahs*, or a woman be shared by two men.' This holds true if he intends a rank; but if what he intends is keeping company for the *baraka*, then there is no harm in it as he would not be under their jurisdiction, but would merely be in their company on the same path."

USEFUL POINT: Ibn Zakari said in *Risala al-Qusayri*, may Allah benefit us by him: "I have heard Ustadh Abu 'Ali ad-Daqqaq, may Allah have mercy on him, say: 'The beginning of every sect is opposition, that is the opposition of someone to his Shaykh and his not clinging to his ways – the connection between them will then be broken, even if they are both in the same place.'" He also said: 'Whoever keeps the company of a Shaykh and then opposes him – even if only with his heart – breaks the contract of keeping company and must make *tawba*.' They said: 'There is no *tawba* for rebellious disobedience to the teacher.'"

Shaykh Zakari said in commentary on it: "This does not mean that it is such an (abominable) act of disobedience that Allah will not turn in forgiveness to this person – for He accepts the *tawba* of his slaves for *kufr* and (even) for any lesser wrong action. Rather, the Shaykh should not pardon him without rebuking him at all."

And, with respect to the author's words "It is prohibited to break a *nafila* fast..." (229) we have previously looked at something on this matter.

USEFUL POINT: Muhammad ibn 'Abd al-Qadir said in *Sharh al-Hisn*: "The Shaykh of our Shaykh, Abu 'Abdallah Muhammad al-'Arabi said: 'The Shaykhs have said, may Allah be pleased with them: 'Whoever does not find a Shaykh of instruction, then sending peace and blessings on the Prophet, may the peace and blessings on him, may do instead.'""

Something similar is stated in *Matali' al-Masarrat fi Sharh Dala'il al-Khayrat*, and also by Ibn Zakari in *Sharh an-Naseeha*.

يُذَكِّرُهُ اللَّهَ إِذَا رَآهُ

$$\text{وَيُوصِلُ الْعَبْدَ إِلَى مَوْلَاهُ}$$

304 He reminds him of Allah when he sees him, and he brings the slave to His Lord.

Examine what the commentators have said about this line for I am not equipped to speak here, may Allah be kind to me and my like.

$$\text{يُحَاسِبُ النَّفْسَ عَلَى الْأَنْفَاسِ}$$

$$\text{وَيَزِنُ الْخَاطِرَ بِالْقِسْطَاسِ}$$

305 He takes the self to account for every breath and weighs his thoughts and feelings in the balance

As for his saying 'He takes the self to account for every breath', al-Ghazali and others have spoken at length on the subject of accounting (for everything one does) and you should read him. Moreover, I am not equipped to speak of the path of the pure.

The 'thoughts and feelings' refers to anything which comes to one's consciousness, that is, one's heart, whether one puts them into practice or not. What is meant by the 'balance' is the judgement in the *shari'ah* as al-Jazuli said in *Sharh ar-Risala*: "A person should place a doorkeeper for good counsel over his heart – which is the amir of his body – that is, with regard to what he wants to do or abstain from. This doorkeeper refers to the law, the *shari'ah*. If it occurs to someone to do something or desist from something, then he should subject this (intent) to the requirements of the *shari'ah*: if it commands him to do it, he should do it and if it commands him to leave it, he should leave it."

USEFUL POINT: It is related in *Sahih al-Bukhari* in the section entitled 'Whoever intends a good action or a bad action' from Ibn 'Abbas, may Allah be pleased with both of them, from the Prophet, may the peace and blessings of Allah be upon him, in a hadith *qudsi* from his Lord that He said: "Allah has written the bad actions and the good actions, and then He explained this (saying): 'Whoever intends a good action and does not perform it, then Allah will record it with Him as a complete good action; whoever intends it and also puts it into practice, then Allah will record a reward equal to ten actions up to seven hundred times and up to many more; whoever intends a bad action but does not put it into practice, then Allah will record it with Him as one complete good action while if he intends it and carries it out, then Allah will record it for him as one wrong action.'"

Ibn Hajar said: "Many of the *'ulama*, however, are of the opinion that one is also held to account for what one has firmly resolved to do. Ibn Mubarak asked Sufyan ath-Thawri: 'Is a slave taken to account for what he intends?' He replied: 'If he is (firmly) resolved to do it.' Many of them have taken His words, exalted is He, as (further) proof: *'but He will take you to task for the intention your hearts have made.*[1]"

They interpreted the *marfu' sahih* hadith of Abu Hurayra 'Allah has forgiven my *umma* for what their selves tell them (to do) as long as they do not put this into practice or speak about it' as referring to the *khatirat* – the thoughts and feelings which occur involuntarily to the mind and heart. However, those (who claim this) have then divided, one group saying that the person with such (thoughts) will be punished for them in the *dunya*, that is, through grief and anxiety, another saying that they will be punished on the Day of Raising Up – but through reproof, not with torment.

Ibn Hajar also said: "Whoever intends to commit an act of disobedience, deliberately disparaging what is haram, then he is guilty of disobedience, and whoever intends an act of disobedience, deliberately intending to belittle Allah, then he has committed *kufr*; forgiveness is granted only in the case of those who intend to disobey Allah but without any intent to belittle. This is an appropriate distinction and should be borne in mind when explaining 'The fornicator does not fornicate when he fornicates while he is a *mumin*.'"

He also said, commenting on his words 'and if he intends something but …': "One of the *'ulama* has considered the exception to this to be when the act of disobedience takes place in the Haram of Makka. Ishaq ibn Mansur said: 'I said to Ahmad: "Has anything been narrated to the effect that a bad action is recorded as anything more than *one* bad action?" He replied: "No, except what I have heard regarding Makka – and this, on account of the honour accorded to that place."'[2] The majority are of the opinion that it applies in general to all times and places, although it may vary sometimes according to the degree of wrong."

NOTICE: among those who declared that merely intending to commit an act of disobedience is not in itself an act of disobedience is Ibn ash-Shat in his *Hashiya al-Farouq*; he likewise said that to intend *kufr* is not itself *kufr*. The relevant text has been recorded by al-Qarafi – with added mention of other benefits: "… although we have said it is permitted to curse an unjust person, one should not call down evil upon him by imploring that he commit an act of

---

1 al-Baqara – The Cow: 225
2 In the older copy it states: '…accorded Allah'

disobedience against Allah or that he become *kafir* – as wishing for an act of disobedience (even upon someone else) is itself an act of disobedience, and to want *kufr* is itself *kufr*."

I say: "This generalisation is not correct in my opinion. Rather, if the wish for an act of disobedience is accompanied by actually talking about or putting into practice this act of disobedience, then it would indeed be an act of obedience, otherwise it is not – according to his words, may the peace and blessings of Allah be upon him, 'Allah has forgiven my *umma* for what their selves tell them to do as long as they do not put it into practice or speak about it.' The intention to commit *kufr* would be included in the general import of the hadith, and I am not aware of anything that contradicts this hadith – and so (merely wishing or thinking something) is not *kufr*, and Allah, exalted is He, knows best. All this applies when someone intends to commit an act of disobedience or *kufr* (with respect to Allah); however, if he intends someone else to disobey or someone else to display *kufr*, then his desire for someone else to disobey or someone else to display *kufr* are both wrong actions but not *kufr* in itself, and Allah knows best."

Notice: mention has already been made above – regarding the words of Zarruq on *wudu'* where he says 'the corresponding intention for it...' – that any intention connected to the action of someone else is called an appetite.

Digression: Ibn ash-Shat said in his *Hashiya 'ala'l-Farouq*: "Al-Qarafi said: 'People have asked whether the person who makes a *du'a* saying "O Allah grant him an evil end" (at the moment of his death) – or any other expression indicating (that one wishes) *kufr* (for someone) – is (himself) a *kafir* or not. (They argue that) wanting *kufr* is itself *kufr* and that the seeker wills what he seeks. I would reply by saying that the person making the *du'a* has two states: sometimes he intends *kufr* as an accidental (consequence) not essentially (for itself) and when (what he has asked for) comes to be, in accordance with his (incidental) desire, then he is not a *kafir* – for he said, may the peace and blessings of Allah be upon him: "I would have liked to have been killed in the way of Allah, then to have been revived, then to have been killed, then revived, and then killed once more." The Messenger of Allah, may the peace and blessings of Allah be upon him, sought to be killed in the way of Allah – when (it is well known that) the killing of prophets is *kufr*. However, his will and purpose, on whom be peace, (in saying what he said) was (to attain yet again to) the station of a *shaheed* and what is apart from that (that the person who would kill him would be a *kafir*) was a consequence of his intention and was not what he intended for its own sake – and so there is no harm in the like of this.'" He then goes on to say: "It has been mentioned above that the person who intends *kufr* is not a *kafir* as long as no *kufr* occurs from him, whether this *kufr* is expressed in words or action. If it was in action, then the person who intends something whose necessary consequence is *kufr* is more appropriately not a *kafir*."

Then Ibn ash-Shat said after a discussion: "al-Qarafi said: 'and sometimes he intends *kufr* in an essential way: he is a *kafir* if his intent was to disobey Allah, exalted is He, with *kufr*.'[1] This is not, however, correct: rather if wishes for *kufr* to befall someone else – meaning harm to befall the other person – then it is an act of disobedience but not *kufr*; unless his intent was for the other person's *kufr* in order to benefit him because that *kufr* is preponderant over his iman, in which case it is *kufr*, and Allah, exalted is He, knows best." He has also said: "Likewise, if the intent of this person making *du'a* against someone is that the latter disobey Allah, exalted is He, rather than deny Allah with *kufr* – and this person actually denies Allah by his act of disobedience in accordance with the intent (of the person who has made the *du'a*) – then the (latter) is not a *kafir*." I say: "What he said is correct."

وَيَحْفَظُ الْمَفْرُوضَ رَأْسَ الْمَالِ

وَالنَّفْلَ رِبْحَهُ بِهِ يُوَالِي

306 He must preserve the *fard* obligation which is his capital, just as the *nafila* acts are his profit, by which he befriends[2] (Allah)

This is clear.

وَيُكْثِرُ الذِّكْرَ بِصَفْوِ لُبِّهِ

وَالْعَوْنُ فِي جَمِيعِ ذَا بِرَبِّهِ

307 He increases *dhikr* by means of the purity of his core, and help in all of this is by means of his Lord

'Ali ibn 'Abd as-Sadiq said: "The 'purity' here refers to his being free (of other than Allah) and the 'core' refers to the heart. What he means here, and Allah knows best, is that the person is required to make *dhikr* with presence

---

1   The following passage is garbled in the original.
2   *Yuwali* means to befriend, but also to do something constantly and to follow something else immediately afterwards.

and awareness of the heart – not merely by moving the tongue. This applies when one is able to do this. He should not, however, desist from doing it even when he is in a state of negligence and forgetfulness during this (*dhikr*) – as he said in *al-Hikam*: 'Do not leave off *dhikr* merely because of your lack of presence with Allah for your forgetting to be in a state of *dhikr* is worse than being in a state of forgetfulness while in a state of *dhikr* for it may be that He will raise you from the state of *dhikr* with forgetfulness to a *dhikr* with awareness, and from a *dhikr* with awareness to a *dhikr* with presence, and from a *dhikr* with presence to a *dhikr* without any otherness – until there is only the One Remembered, and this is not difficult for Allah.'

"Abu 'Uthman was asked: 'Why is it that we make *dhikr* but we find no sweetness in our hearts' and he replied: 'Praise Allah for having adorned one of your limbs with obedience of Him glorious is He.'"

Zarruq said in one of his commentaries on the *Hikam*, commenting on 'do not desist from *dhikr*…': "and this is because your (complete) forgetfulness of Him is omission, while your forgetfulness during it (*dhikr*) along with its existence is directing yourself (towards Him) and employing (your tongue in *dhikr*). There are three benefits to this: the first, employing a limb in that which its specific form means, indeed you will gain; the second, adorning the limbs with the obedience to Allah, exalted is He, for which there is no substitute if you abandon it in any state; thirdly, exposing oneself to the breezes of Allah which He bestows by the very first (*dhikr* of Him) – although He is the Bestower of Grace even without this (*dhikr*), and He does not disappoint the action of anyone who acts (for Him). Someone said to one of the (Shaykhs): 'What is the matter with us: we make *dhikr* of Allah with the tongue and the heart is forgetful.' He replied: 'Give thanks to Allah for His enabling you to make *dhikr* with the tongue for if He had made backbiting to take its place what would you do? And Allah, exalted is He, is too noble and too generous not to (eventually) grace the slave with His presence in his heart after granting him the ability to be present with the tongue.'" Then he said, may Allah benefit us by him, after a discussion: "The Messenger of Allah, may the peace and blessings of Allah be upon him, said: 'Allah bestows breezes during your days (on earth) so expose yourselves to the breezes of the mercy of Allah.' A man said: 'Messenger of Allah, the practices of Islam are too many for me – so indicate a practice by which I can make up for what I have missed and be short and concise.' He replied: 'Let your tongue always be moist with *dhikr* of Allah.' He did not command him to do anything than *dhikr* with the tongue – as this lies within the capability of (every) man without a doubt. However, by persisting in this (*dhikr*), the heart will come to be aware of the meanings – in particular when he has a genuine desire to be present by it or in it. For this reason, it is considered of benefit to people both in the beginning and the end, and he commanded people (to do it) in general and they have not defined or placed any limit on the time for it – for this will vary according to the different kinds of people who customarily practice *dhikr* and according to the way in which their states progress. There are many (other) details to this subject which it would be lengthy to enumerate, and success is by Allah."

Muhammad ibn 'Abd al-Qadir said in *Sharh Hisn al-Haseen* about where he says 'and he should reflect upon what he says and use his intellect to ponder its meaning': "that is, the benefit of *dhikr* is (acquired) by being aware of its meanings during the *dhikr* – so that the person doing the *dhikr* will be able to seize hold of the various kinds of *ma'rifa*. *Dhikr* without presence, although of merit, is in general of little benefit – in comparison with the person who does it with presence. In this light may be understood the words of the one who said: 'There is no good in *dhikr* when the heart is forgetful and negligent', and this is how Abu Zayd ath-Tha'alabi and others have understood the (matter). There is likewise the hadith: 'a *du'a* made from a negligent heart is mere play.'"

USEFUL POINT: al-Munawi said, commenting on the narration 'Any group of people who rise from a meeting in which no mention of Allah, exalted is He, is made will rise as if from the carcass of a donkey – and this meeting will be grief and affliction for them on the Day of Rising' – or whatever the exact words of the hadith are: "that is, the disgusting nature of their conversation and their disparaging of the *shari'ah* will be similar to this carcass in that their words will smell foul and be offensive and repugnant. This is because the meeting contained no *dhikr* of Allah, exalted is He, and was thus only filled by (the offensive words) of their conversation – and what is there after the Truth other than misguidance? it is because they did not seal the meeting with some (mention of Allah) to dispel what had preceded it – and so they got up persisting in the (offensive state which had characterised their conversation). As for his words '... grief and affliction for them on the Day of Rising', they refer to their regret for the evil consequence of their words. The (Messenger) has not explained in this hadith above what one should say at the end of it. However, he explained it by actually doing it. Abu Dawud and al-Hakim have related from 'A'isha and others that ...[1] if he wanted to leave a meeting he would say:

سُبْحَانَكَ اللَّهُمَّ وَبِحَمْدِكَ أَشْهَدُ أَنْ لَا إِلَهَ إِلَّا أَنْتَ أَسْتَغْفِرُكَ وَأَتُوبُ إِلَيْكَ

---

1 there is a lacuna at this point

'Subhanaka'llahumma wa bihamdik, ashhadu al-la ilaha illa anta, astaghfiruka wa atubu ilayka – How glorious are You O Allah and in Your praise! I witness that there is no god but You. I seek Your forgiveness and I turn in *tawba* to You.'

Then a man said: 'You have uttered something which you did not utter before' and he replied 'that is expiation for what was in the meeting.'"

About Ibn 'Ashir's saying 'and help in all of this is by means of his Lord' "as-Sanusi said in *Sharh al-Qaseeda*: 'The gist of the matter is that anything you seek after by means of your self or by relying on anything which like yourself is of a contingent nature, then you will not attain to it and you will have no ease in it; while any matter which you seek after by means of your Lord – that is, by Him, Who alone is unique in (holding sway over) creation, relying sincerely on Him, then you will be worthy of success by Him alone, and you will have no difficulty – and Allah, exalted is He, is the One Who brings success.'"

He also said in the chapter on '*Du'a* and humble supplication to Him': "There is no barrier to either (*du'a* or supplication) – whether from a man of right action or someone depraved; their benefit is to be hoped for whether by a *mumin* or *kafir*."

يُجَاهِدُ النَّفْسَ لِرَبِّ الْعَالَمِيْنْ

وَيَتَحَلَّى بِمَقَامَاتِ الْيَقِيْنْ

308 He struggles against the self for the sake of the Lord of the Worlds, and he will be adorned with the stations of certainty:

خَوْفٌ رَجَاً شُكْرٌ وَصَبْرٌ تَوْبَةٌ

زُهْدٌ تَوَكُّلٌ رِضَاً مَحَبَّةٌ

309 fear, hope, gratitude, patience, *tawba*, doing without, reliance, contentment and love.

يَصْدُقُ شَاهِدَهُ فِي الْمُعَامَلَةِ

يَرْضَى بِمَا قَدَّرَهُ الْإِلَهُ لَهْ

310 He is true towards the One Who witnesses in his transactions; and is

content with what his Lord has decreed for him.

I have already said that it is forbidden to me to talk of those who struggle (against their lower self) as I am foreign to this station and am not a man of its people, nor even of its students.

As for fear, it is stated in *al-Jami' as-Saghir*: "Fear and hope have both sworn that neither will be united in a person in this world and that he will then fell the breath of the Fire and neither will be separated in a person and that he will then feel the breath of the Garden."[1] Al-Munawi said in his commentary: "If there were only fear in a person, then this necessarily implies despair while if there were only hope, this necessarily implies one felt safe from the scheming of Allah. So for happiness (to be established in him) they must come together." One of the 'ulama said: "Alternate between fear and hope: make fear dominant at the time of action and hope at the time of death. Fear at the time of action arises for many reasons, among them reliance on the (action), delighting in it and joy at it – without seeing Who has bestowed it and granted it you as a gift. Allah, exalted is He, said: '*Say: "It is the favour of Allah and His mercy that should be the cause of their rejoicing. That is better than anything they can accumulate."*'[2] Likewise, a person fears at the time of action that the action will not be accepted, that it will be taken from him or something else (occurs) which corrupts the intention or renders him unable to fulfil an act of worship. Hope, on the other hand is (more appropriate) when the term of one's life comes to an end and the means (of performing actions) are cut off – and reliance is only on Allah, the Ever-Giving."

NOTICE: al-Baqouri said *in Ikhtisar al-Farouq* in the fifteenth rule in distinguishing the fear of other-than-Allah which is not forbidden from that which is forbidden: "Know that it has been narrated – with respect to praise of someone – that the slave should not fear other than Allah, exalted is He, and it has also been related that it is prohibited to fear people. Allah said: '*and then you should not fear them but rather fear Me*'[3] and He has also said: '*you were fearing people when Allah has more right to your fear.*[4]'

"It is said: 'what is being referred to by this "prohibited kind of fear" is a fear which takes precedence over fear of Allah, exalted is He, – with the result that he leaves off doing what is obligatory and does what is forbidden.' I say:

---

1 If someone has both fear and hope, they will not experience the Fire, but if someone has only one of them they will not experience the Garden. Ed.
2 Yunus: 58
3 al-Baqara – The Cow: 150
4 al-Ahzab – The Confederates: 37

'... although it is not correct to interpret the noble *ayah* in this way out of respect for the Prophet (to whom it was revealed specifically), may the peace and blessings of Allah be upon him. However if it does not lead to this, then there is no fault in someone having fear of other-than-Allah, like fearing lions, snakes, scorpions and darkness.'" And this is accepted by Ibn ash-Shat.

It is related in *Sahih al-Bukhari* from Abu Hurayra, may Allah be pleased with him, who said: "I heard the Messenger of Allah, may the peace and blessings of Allah be upon him, say: 'On the day Allah created mercy, He created it as a hundred mercies and kept ninety-nine of them with Him and sent just one of them to all of creation. If the *kafir* were to become aware of all the mercy with Allah, he would not despair of reaching the Garden and if the *mumin* were aware of all the punishment with Allah, he would not feel safe from the Fire.'" The author of *al-Fath* said: "al-Kirmani said: 'what is intended by the hadith is that the one charged with responsibility (*mukallaf*) should (always) be (in a state) between fear and hope: he should not go to excess in hope and become like the *murji'is* [who hold that along with iman nothing can do any harm, nor should he go to excess in fear like the *khawarij* and the *mu'tazila*]¹ who hold that the person guilty of a major wrong action will be in the Fire if he dies and has not made *tawba* [but on the contrary he should adopt a median position]1 as Allah, exalted is He, said: *"they are hoping for His mercy and fearing His punishment.""*²

As for his saying 'gratitude', he said in *al-Jami' as-Saghir*: "If the slave gives praise to Allah for the blessings He has bestowed on him then this praise will be more excellent than these blessings even if the (latter) were exceedingly great." Al-Munawi said, commenting on this narration: "Useful point: 'Ja'far as-Sadiq lost a female mule of his and so he said: "if Allah returns it to me, I shall praise Him with praises that He will be content with." It was not long before someone brought it to him together with its saddle and reins. He mounted it and as soon as he was sitting upright, he raised his head to the sky saying: "Praise belongs to Allah" – not saying any more than this. Someone then asked him regarding this and he replied: "Have I left out anything, is there anything remaining (to be said)? I have rendered all praise to Allah."'"

NOTICE: Ibn Zakari said in *Sharh an-Naseeha*: "Ibn 'Abbad said: 'Whoever sees the wrong actions he is committing but is unaware of the blessings of Allah, then he will never have success: being negligent of blessings leads to one denying them and denying them leads to their being taken away. Amongst

---

1   The text missing here in the book has been restored from *Fath al-Bari*. Ed.
2   al-Isra – The Night Journey: 57

the blessings which one must be aware of and be grateful for is the success of the slave in his saying *la ilaha ilallah*, in his making *salat* on the Prophet, may the peace and blessings of Allah be upon him, and in his reading an *ayah* of the Qur'an. All these are the result of the blessing (He bestows) on speech, and an indication of His granting the means to this. Likewise, listening to an *ayat* or hadith or any one of the knowledges of benefit which point to Allah, is the result of the blessing of hearing and His having granted the means to this; or, looking at the vastness of the sky and how it is raised up without any support, or at the stars and planets, or at the sea, rivers, plants, trees is one of the blessings of sight – when this is done in awe and reverence. How many a person has been deprived of such (blessings) or have not even been given them. If a person becomes aware of these blessings in all their variety, then it remains for him to recognise their worth; and that they have not been bestowed upon him because of who he is (but rather by the grace of Allah) – only then will he be able to enjoy them.' Sayyidi Abu 'Abdallah ibn 'Abbad also said: 'and the inevitable result of this is that his Lord will have mercy on him and will be indulgent towards him regarding his faults and lapses – that is, when he is in a state of thankfulness from the heart, when he recognises these blessings and he witnesses the despicable nature of his lower self. This is the reality of gratitude: it necessarily brings an increase (from Allah) with it.'" Here ends the discussion of Ibn Zakari, and if you want more on the subject, then you should study the books of the people (of this science) and the scholars of hadith – as mentioned above, (many matters) have not been included here as they are well known matters. As for Ibn 'Ashir's saying 'patience, *tawba*' a discussion of the definition of patience together with its rules and divisions has been given in other famous works.

NOTICE: there is a difference of opinion amongst the *'ulama* as to whether afflictions acting as expiation (*kaffara*) for a person's wrong actions is conditional upon their being patient (with these afflictions) or not, although (the latter judgement) is stronger. Al-Munawi said, commenting on the narration 'If the slave becomes ill for three days, then he will leave his wrong actions behind as the day his mother gave birth to him': "that is, they will be forgiven him and he will have not any wrong actions (to his account): he will thus be as he was the day his mother gave birth to him – free of wrong actions. This is because mercy envelops the sick person despite the upset to his disposition, and just as Allah cures him – may His Power be manifest! – and heals him of what He himself had caused to afflict him, so the mother treats her child. The literal meaning of the narration and other similar (narrations) is that Allah's blotting out (of his wrong actions) is dependent only on the illness which afflicted him, whether or not it is accompanied by patience. Al-Qurtubi's stipulating that he should have this (attribute of patience) is unacceptable as he has no evidence for this: his argument that the (elimination of wrong actions) is conditional upon patience as this has been stipulated in some narrations is not conclusive as those which are of a *sahih* rank mention a *particular* reward which can only be obtain by means of patience – and there is no *sahih* hadith where the unconditional elimination of one's wrong actions is only dependent on an illness which is accompanied by patience. This is according to al-Hafidh al-'Iraqi who said: 'I have assessed the hadith on the matter and have formulated what I have mentioned above.' Al-Qarafi is also decidedly of this opinion, and Ibn ash-Shat accepted it in his *Hashiya*."

NOTICE: al-Qarafi asserted in *al-Farouq* that afflictions do not raise one (in station) nor do they bring about reward, but rather they eliminate wrong actions only – and Ibn ash-Shat opposed him in this.

Al-Qarafi said in *al-Farouq*: "the two hundred and sixty-third distinction to be made is that between the principle governing the elimination of wrong actions and the causes determining what brings reward: know that many people believe that afflictions are a cause for the raising of rank and station, and the attainment of reward. This is not, however, so. Rather the explanation of the difference between them is that causes for reward are conditional upon two things: first, that the reward is something which is earned by the slave and relates to his capacity or some aspect of it – not something which merely happens to him, like injury to part of his body, for there is no reward for this. The basis of this (judgement) is the words of Allah, exalted is He: '*man will have nothing but what he strives for*'[1] which demonstrate that the reward is restricted to what he strives after and earns; and Allah's words: '*you are simply being repaid for what you did*'[2] which demonstrate that the requital is restricted to what we have been able to do, what was possible for us. Second, whatever is acquired must be something which has been commanded – for there is no reward for something which has not been commanded, as for example actions undertaken before the message (of the Prophet, may the peace and blessings of Allah be upon him, was delivered), or the actions of dumb creatures. Therefore it must involved something which is consciously attained to and which is acquired by our having wanted and chosen it – as well as being something which is commanded (in the *shari'ah*). Thus dead people who hear words of exhortation and counsel

---

1 an-Najm – The Star: 39
2 at-Tur – The Mount: 16

from their graves, such as the Qur'an, *dhikr*, the saying of *subhana'llah* and *la ilaha illa'llah* will receive no reward from this – strictly speaking – as they are neither commanded (to do anything) after death nor prohibited (from doing anything): there can be no wrong action and no reward when there is no command. This then is an explanation of the causes of reward."

Ibn ash-Shat said: "What has been said is not correct. Rather, what is correct is that the 'reasons' or 'causes' for the raising of (someone) in rank are not conditional upon these causes being (in the form of actions which are) 'earned' or commanded – there are things which are causal but there are also others which are not. Included in the latter are for example pain, distress and all the (other various) afflictions – for they all indicate this (lack of 'cause'). Moreover, there are many (other) proofs in the law, all supported by the principle of the 'proven preponderance of merit and advantage (*hasanat*).'[1] As for the general meaning of the *ayat* '*man will have nothing but what he strives for*' and Allah's words '*you are simply being repaid for what you did*' and other similar *ayats* and narrations, they must be understood as being of particular application – in order to harmonise between them and the other evidence (mentioned above which is in apparent conflict with them). If someone accepts this but nevertheless argues that – if the 'cause' of someone's being raised in rank is by virtue of (unearned) blessings – then this should not be called 'reward' or 'requital' for these are words which imply the giving of compensation for something, then (we would say) that he is correct and we would not dispute (that) the terms (do not correspond strictly to the matter being discussed). Further, how is it valid to understand the two *ayats* and the like as possessing only a general application when there is a well known *ijma'* as to the validity of delegation in all financial transactions? and in the light of the widely disparate physical capacities (of people) – and what this entails regarding the performance of the *salat*? Thus the two *ayats* and other similar ones must be understood as applying to (a person's striving to increase his) *iman* and to all other 'actions' of the heart." Here the discussion of Ibn ash-Shat ends, and Ibn Hajar has selected it (for inclusion) in *Fath al-Bari*.

Al-Qarafi said: "as for the things which expiate wrong actions (*mukaffirat*), none of this is stipulated in their regard. Indeed, they may well be acquired by way of doing good actions, based on the words of Allah, exalted is He:

---

[1] This appears to mean that Allah's mercy and generosity is so manifestly vast that reward is always much more readily 'available' than punishment – that is, independent of the merit of slave.

'*good actions eradicate bad actions.*'¹ In other instances, however, it is not like this, for in the case of (the execution of the) *hadd* and other punishments, the (corresponding) crimes and evil actions are expiated and all trace of them is eliminated; and of this order are also afflictions and painful (illness or events)." Ibn ash-Shat said: "What he said on this (matter) is correct except his words 'and all trace of them is eliminated' for if by this he means that all trace of them in the Record (of his actions) is effaced, then this is not correct for it would mean (the crimes) would be reduced to nothing, and this is invalid according to the people of sunna."

USEFUL POINT: Ahmad Bab, commenting on Khalil's words 'and the removal of conflicting (views)' said after a discussion: "and the overflowing (knowledge) of this *salih faqih*, the scrupulous *zahid*, 'Umar ar-Rajraji is due to Allah when he says: 'You must study the fundamental principles of al-Qarafi but do not accept any of them except those accepted by Ibn ash-Shat.'" Whoever comprehends (Ibn ash-Shat's) investigations will be aware of the validity of this and its truth, and Allah knows best.

USEFUL POINT: al-Munawi said, commenting on the hadith 'Anything which befalls (*asaba*) a *mumin* which he dislikes is an affliction or calamity (*museeba*): "Allah covers over and expiates the wrong actions he has committed by means of them. So all misfortune and affliction which befall anyone in the *dunya* is a requital from Allah, exalted is He; likewise, whatever befalls the *mumin* in terms of the pain he experiences, like grief or distress, worry and illness and other afflictions."

Ibn 'Ashir's saying '*zuhd* – doing without' has been mentioned above where he says 'the pinnacle of faults' and so it is not fitting that we mention it (again here). So examine what he says, may Allah be pleased with him. Know that the decree and the thing decreed are two different matters: the decree is a property of Allah which is from before endless time and is synonymous with (His) will or close (in meaning) to it. That which is decreed is dependant upon this (decree) and is contingent and in time. Thus all of our states are decreed by Allah, that is, it is He who has willed them. Many are those who express their contentment with the decree when what in fact they mean is the decreed matter or event – that is metaphorically, and Allah knows best. Contentment with the decree is an obligatory matter and forms the root (of '*aqida*) – for whoever is not content with the decree, is a *kafir*. As for being content with the matter decreed, if it is something which has been prohibited, then (being content with it) is prohibited; and if it has not been prohibited,

---

1 Hud: 114

then either it is an obligatory matter, in which case being content with it is also obligatory, or it is it not, in which case it is a perfecting or completing (of the matter). This (latter instance) is a judgement with respect to what the slave 'acquires and chooses' – regarding the matter decreed; as for what the slave 'does not acquire', that is, with respect to anything imposed upon him (against his will), then contentment with this is a perfection (of character) also, indeed it is among the highest stations and the most sublime stages of intimacy. This, then, is the gist of their discussion, and Allah, exalted is He, knows best.

Sayyidi Zarruq has indicated some of this in his commentary on *Waghlisiya*. Commenting on his words 'contentment' he said: "that is, with the decree of Allah given that it is His decree. However, it is not obligatory to be content with the thing decreed, unless it is obligatory; but rather it is a perfection (of state), when it is something that it is permitted to be content with."

He said, commenting on his words 'and anger at the decree and the destiny': "that is, with the matter or event decreed (not the decree itself) for this would be *kufr*, and we seek refuge with Allah."

Al-Qarafi said in *adh-Dhakheera*: "being angry with the decree is haram according to the *ijma'*. The author of *al-Jawahir* said: 'that is, anger directed at the thing decreed as something evil.' However, Those versed in this science have said: 'It is obligatory to be content with the decree, but not with the matter or event which is decreed, to be content with the destiny, but not with the thing or event destined. To formulate this precisely, if a doctor prescribes a bitter medicament for the sick person or cuts off his gangrenous hand and the patient declares: 'what a terrible thing the doctor has prescribed' then this is an expression of his hate and anger at the 'decree' of the doctor; if, however, he says 'what he did was fine although I experienced great pain at the amputation and discomfort from the bitterness of the medicine' then this does not constitute a criticism of the doctor. Rather the former (expression) is a criticism and censure of him. Thus if people are afflicted by illness and feel pain at the illness – that is, to varying degrees, each according to their disposition or temperament – then this is not a lack of contentment with the decree but rather discontent with the thing decreed; but if the (sick) person says 'What have I done (to merit) being afflicted with this?' or 'what have I done wrong? – I do not deserve it' then this is discontent with the decree. Thus we have been commanded to be content with the decree, not with the thing decreed and so reflect on this for it is a fine point."

USEFUL POINT: He said in *al-Ihya*: "One of the *salaf* said: '(An indication of) one of the finest (states of) contentment with the decree of Allah, exalted is He, is when someone refrains from saying 'It is warm today' – in a tone of complaint – in (the middle of) summer; on the other hand, if (he were to say this) in winter, it would be (an indication of) gratitude. Complaint is the opposite of contentment – whatever the circumstances. Further, finding fault with or criticising one's food is contrary to (expressing) contentment with the decree of Allah, exalted is He; and disparaging the creation is disparaging the Creator – and everything is part of the creation of Allah, exalted is He. If someone were to say 'Poverty is a test and trial, (caring for) the family is a worry and exhausting, and gaining one's livelihood brings (only) anxiety and difficulties' then all this detracts from (the perfection of) contentment: it is better (in this case) to hand over the management of affairs to the One Who manages them and the kingdom to its King."

As for Ibn 'Ashir's words 'reliance' and 'love', I do not consider that it is fitting for me to say anything about these two matters. I only consider the people (of this science are worthy of this). As for myself, I am not of them and they are foreign to me.

As for Ibn 'Ashir's saying: 'He is true towards the One Who witnesses in his transactions' 'Ali ibn 'Abd as-Sadiq said: "that is, He Who witnesses the slave, that is, He Who is present with him, Who perceives what is concealed (in his heart). What this means is that Ibn 'Ashir) is demanding that the slave intend the face of Allah by his acts of obedience – as He perceives him and is close to him – and not (perform them merely) to be seen (by others) or for the sake of his reputation. (When) this (is so), then it is the height of sincerity – which itself is the very essence of slave-hood. Slave-hood is to devote oneself to the Real, the True in conscious obedience, to intend by one's acts of obedience the face of Allah and to (strive to) come close to Him – rather than for any other purpose, like affectation, or seeking to have one's (worship) lauded by people or out of love of people's praise." Examine (this further) to the end of his discussion.

As for Ibn 'Ashir's words 'He is content with what his Lord has decreed for him': "'Ali ibn 'Abd as-Sadiq said: 'The meaning of his is that he is obliged to be content with what has been allotted for him in the decree, whether he likes or dislikes it. Rabi'a was asked, may Allah be pleased with her: 'When is the slave in a state of contentment' and she replied: 'When affliction him causes him to be happy, just as blessings cause him to be happy.'"

I say: "His saying 'he is obliged to be content with what has been allotted for him in the decree' is contrary to what has been mentioned above from al-Qarafi.

$$\text{يَصِيرُ عِنْدَ ذَاكَ عَارِفاً بِهِ}$$

$$\text{حُرّاً وَغَيْرُهُ خَلا مِنْ قَلْبِهِ}$$

311   Then he will become a gnostic of Allah, free, and other-than-Allah will leave his heart

This is clear, and whoever wants to further quench his thirst (for such knowledge), should refer to the commentators.

$$\text{فَحَبَّهُ الإِلٰهُ وَاصْطَفَاهُ}$$

$$\text{لِحَضْرَةِ الْقُدُّوسِ وَاجْتَبَاهُ}$$

312   Then Allah will love him, will choose him for the presence of the Sacred and elect him (over others).

That is, will elect him by the perfection of his knowledge – and this is what is meant by the term 'arrival' (*wusul*) by the people (of this science), as the author of *Muhassal al-Maqasid* said:
The meaning of 'entering the Lord's Presence'
   is the attainment of *ma'rifa* of Him in the heart,
And the attainment of perfection in *ma'rifa*
   is what is meant by 'arrival' by the people (of this science),
And the meaning of 'proximity' is the slave's witnessing
   the closeness of his Lord of Tremendous Glory,
And this is the path of *wilaya*
   for those who are concerned (to acquire) its characteristics.

SUPPLEMENTARY POINT: the author of *al-Mi'yar* transmitted something from Ibn 'Abbad, may Allah benefit us by him, throughout which he is addressing someone: "as for your saying: 'if you permit me to explain my state to you with something more pertinent than that, I shall do so' I have given you permission to make this explanation. However, in doing so you would merely be demonstrating the subtleties of your illness to someone who has the same illness and worse. Where would be the benefit? would it help towards the cure you are after? towards your hope of ridding yourself of this? There would be no harm, however – given that we share an illness – in my talking about a particular method (or cure) which I hold to and which I find beneficial for myself and others – so that we might take this path together, with mutual concern and courtesy, and we might profit in finding relief from our debilitation. The (nature of this method) is that we refrain from all discussion of any illness or sickness: instead we should be the sons of the moment and all our efforts and actions should be directed at being aware of the blessings which Allah, exalted is He, has bestowed on us. In this way we will divest ourselves of any power or strength (we imagine we possess) and instead depend only on Allah, and find refuge only in Him. We will come to a realisation that any gratitude on our part is only by His granting the capacity for and inclination towards this (gratitude). We should restrict ourselves to this and make it our duty at every moment. We should not perceive any other (reality) than this, we should not even attempt to see (anything other than these blessings), indeed not desire anything else (but this vision). Thus taking refuge (in Him), being in need, humility and submissiveness are the doors to all good – there are no others. If an act of obedience issues from us, then we can hope for the overflowing bounty of the One Who has granted us the capacity to (perform it); and if an act of disobedience issues from us, we will fear the justice of the One Who has decreed and allotted this for us. The slave can do no better than to cling to the (state of) *'ubudiyya* (slavehood). I know of no other more legitimate goal than this. It is like the bird who puts his head beneath its wing (and trusts that no harm will come to it) – and how good is the state of the one who realises this! We ask Allah, exalted is He, that He grant us mercy, for He is the Granter of generous blessings and the All-Merciful.

"So brother reflect on what I have set out and expounded to you. If this (path) appears to you to be correct and you approve of it, then make it your own, keep firm hold of it, render it (the means to) the gardens of your heart and stick to it in whatever state you are in; otherwise, I have nothing to say to you. The lines of poetry I shall quote (below) are exquisite, and their secret and core are contained in the latter part of the fourth line. Allah is the One Who grants success, there is no Lord other than Him and may Allah grant peace and blessings to our Master Muhammad, his Family and Companions and *as-salamu 'alaykum*. The lines in question are the following:

I used to reckon that Your love was easily won and of little value –
    but the most subtle spirits are consumed by it,
And I thought ignorantly that arrival at You may be purchased
    by generous gifts of wealth and the soul,
Until I saw that You single out and elect whomever
    You choose for Your vast gifts.
I realised that You are not to be obtained by any deceit or stratagem,
    and so I have hidden my head under my wing

And made my residence the nest of infatuation –

from this (vantage) is always my coming and going."

Ibn Abi Jamra said: "and whoever is weak and unable to attain to this *hijrah* (journeying away from worldly causes to the realm of the Divine), should not neglect his self totally. To do this would be a sign of loss. Instead he should deal kindly with his self, and skillfully manage it in his struggle (*jihad*) and the movement towards (the Divine)."

Then he goes on to say after a discussion of the struggle against the self: "however, this can only occur when one has attained to this state of being in need of Allah, exalted is He, and when one seeks assistance from Him at every moment – otherwise there is no benefit in being wary (of this world), of struggling (against the *nafs*) or in moving (to the realm of the Divine)" – may Allah benefit us by him.

ذَا الْقَدْرُ نَظْماً لَا يَفِي بِالْغَايَةِ

وَفِي الَّذِي ذَكَرْتُهُ كِفَايَةٌ

313 Although these lines do not encompass the full spectrum (of this science), there is enough in what I have mentioned (to set about this path)

This commentary – which Allah has granted to me – is now at an end. It is the custom of the *fuqaha* to conclude their compositions with a chapter comprising various matters which are not linked to one single subject. This includes things like 'sincerity', 'showing off', '*tawba*', 'conceit', 'pride', certain matters concerning the sicknesses of the tongue and the excellences associated with (various) actions; it includes too the lives of the leading men of the earlier generations, remarkable stories, the prohibition of squandering wealth, the exhortation to take care of it properly, kindness towards animals, the prohibition against treating them badly, making the greeting with *as-salam*, the seeking of permission from someone, the visiting of the sick person, the calling for mercy on someone who sneezes, omens, auguries, behaving well towards one's parents, incantations and amulets (containing written *du'a* against evil) (*ruqan*), seeking refuge with Allah, tattoos, remembering the states of death, and some matters regarding the states of the *barzakh* (i.e. the interspace before the Raising Up), the Raising Up (of the dead) and the *Sirat* (i.e. the bridge over the Fire leading to the Garden), as well as other matters. Such (chapters) are entitled *kitab al-jami'* (miscellanea). The first person to compose one was Malik and the people of his *madhhab* followed him in this with a few exceptions, like Khalil in his *Mukhtasar*, and I think also Ibn al-Hajib as well as the followers of both of them. We intend to mention some of what they have mentioned in order to complete the benefit (of this work) and in imitation (of Malik), and we shall take their (work) as a base, may Allah be pleased with them. Those who only study Khalil and his followers when studying works of *fiqh* will consider that what we have done is outside of the purpose (of this section) and has no connection with the *fiqh* (here) at all – and he would be excused for this. For this reason, that is, in order to ward off their objections, I am going ahead with this anyway and am assuming that they will have a good opinion (of my intent in this matter). We have gathered a lot of the discussions from the 'miscellanea' chapters of the people of our *madhhab* in this final section, such as (the author of) *al-'Utbiya* and the '*Hafidh* of the *madhhab* of Malik' Muhammad ibn Rushd who has made a commentary on the former – who was the *mujtahid* of his time, and who is without equal in his age amongst the Malikis except for Ibn Daqeeq al-'Eid – and from Ibn Muneer, and al-Qarafi in the 'miscellanea' chapter in his *Dhakheera*, and his work entitled *al-Farouq*; we have also gathered from al-Bukhari, Muslim and their commentators to gain the *baraka* from them. Therefore I will begin this section with the help of Allah, and may (my intention in this) be for Allah – by His overflowing excellence and all-pervading existence.

SEAL: O You the Most Merciful of the merciful, the most Merciful of the merciful, the Most Merciful of the merciful! grant me the good of the two abodes and grant good also to those who make *du'a* for me, O Master of Majesty and Generosity. May Allah grant my parents and all those who live by the Truth the good of the two abodes O You Who are the Living, the Sustainer of the worlds! may He grant it too to all those who have made *du'as* for me, to all those who love me or who have treated me well, and to all the *muminun* and *muminat*. It comprises, insha'Allah, sixty-three points of benefit, equal in number to the age of the Master of creation Muhammad, may the peace and blessings of Allah be upon him. It may well be that in these sixty-three points, there is a tremendous secret and precious benefits.

1. The author of *al-'Utbiya*, when asked about the meaning of what has been related in the hadith 'wasting wealth is disliked' replied: "Have you not considered the words of Allah, exalted is He: '*but do not squander what you have. Squanderers are brothers to the shaytans.*'[1] Squandering is to prevent it reaching those who have a right to it and spending one's wealth on what is not

---

1 al-Isra – The Night Journey: 27

legitimate." Muhammad ibn Rushd said in *al-Bayan*: "the hadith about it being disliked to neglecting property is from al-Mughira ibn Shu'ba who said: 'I have heard the Messenger of Allah, may the peace and blessings of Allah be upon him, say: "Allah dislikes three things in you: idle chatter, neglecting property and asking a lot of questions."' Included in 'neglecting property' is (using it such that) one prevents it from reaching the person who is entitled to it and or he spends it for something which is not legitimate. If, for example, he makes it a *waqf* and does not give the (proceeds) to those who are entitled to it, then he has 'neglected' it. This is because there is no benefit in it for him – neither in this world or the next. It is as if the (*waqf*) is non-existent, indeed worse than this – for he is denying someone their right. Likewise, if he spends it on what is not legitimate, he is also considered to have neglected it as he has used it for something which contains no reward. Furthermore, if he has squandered it by using it for something haram or immoral, then the blame and responsibility is all the greater."

Spending wealth has six aspects, three of which are squandering: one being waste, the second, spending for some extravagance and the third, for something haram. Then there are three with which no loss is associated, that is spending on what is obligatory, spending for the face of Allah with regard to that which is not obligatory and spending for the sake of people out of a desire to gain praise, honour and esteem. One of the men of wisdom said:

The wealth of those who are honoured for their spending does not perish,
    but the wealth of the mean perishes.

It has also been said that the hadith which speaks of 'neglecting property being disliked' refers to one's neglecting wealth or property, that is, abandoning one's responsibility to take good care of something or to keep it in a good state of repair and to save it from ruin, like a house, for example, which one neglects until it falls down, or a vine which one neglects until it withers. (This understanding of 'neglect') can also include an obligation towards another man which one fails to fulfil – with the result that this (obligation) is forgotten; and other matters of this nature. This, in fact, is the most evident meaning of what has been said about the hadith. It could also be understood in a wider sense – to include refraining from (those acts of) spending, which although rewarded when they take place, are nevertheless not considered a cause of rebuke or chastisement when they do not – like (the spending associated with) keeping up good family relations or giving *sadaqa* to them. It could also be understood to include spending on disliked aspects, such as extravagance and the like. One must however interpret (in another way) Malik's commentary on the hadith –

namely his assertion that the (hadith) refers to '... his denying his obligatory duty to act well towards others, like keeping up family relations and the like' – for (one would not normally speak of) something being *disliked* (*makruh*), as stated in the hadith, if it involves the denying of an *obligation* (*wajib*); rather one must understand this (interdiction) as being (one of) proscription (*mahdhur*). Likewise one must interpret Malik's definition (of neglect as) 'spending it on something not legitimate' as referring to aspects of extravagance and prodigality but not as referring to (things which are) corrupt and haram – for one would not say that 'spending on what is corrupt and haram' is 'disliked' (*makruh*), as has been mentioned in the hadith, but rather that it is 'proscribed.' It has also been said that the prohibition with regard to causing loss to wealth or property refers to those 'whom one's right hand possesses', that is, to the obligation to spend on one's slaves and animals, to treat them well, not to neglect them or allow them to perish. However this is not correct as this (aspect) is not contained in what is related in the hadith – for in the hadith the word 'disliked' (*makruh*) is used and what is 'disliked' (*makruh*), legally speaking, is that which is best left undone and which is rewarded when not done, although there is no blame in doing it. However (the judgement in the case of) a man who does not spend on his slaves and animals, such that they perish or are harmed, is one of 'proscription' (*mahdhur*) not one of mere 'dislike' (*makruh*) – because he is responsible for them.

2. He said in *al-'Utbiya*: "Malik said: 'A donkey carrying milk passed by 'Umar ibn al-Khattab, may Allah be pleased with him, and he flung off what he thought was too much, because he considered that the (load) was too heavy.'" Muhammad ibn Rushd said in *al-Bayan*: "in some books it reads 'he thought that it was *killing* it' and the meaning of this is plain as it is *makruh* for us to make it bear an excessive load according to what has been narrated from the Messenger of Allah, may the peace and blessings of Allah be upon him, namely: 'Allah is kind and He loves kindness and is pleased with it. He will assist and support people in (being kind) in a way He will not assist or support violence.' It has also been narrated that he, may the peace and blessings of Allah be upon him, said: 'Surely Allah is kind and He loves kindness in all matters.' Thus it is not permitted for anyone to place loads upon an (animal) such that it weighs it down and kills it. Anyone who does this is guilty of a crime."

3. He said in *al-'Utbiya*: "The Messenger of Allah was asked, may the peace and blessings of Allah be upon him, about slaves and he said: 'Retaliation will be exacted against you on their behalf on the Day of Rising: their wrong actions and your punishment (of them) will be weighed, and retaliation (for the excess of the punishment over their wrong actions) exacted against you on

their behalf.' Someone asked the Messenger of Allah about (the application of this judgement to) children, and he replied in the following manner – or so it seemed according to the narrator: 'The child is not like this: when you can't clothe yourself, they go naked and when you do not have your fill, they go hungry.'" Muhammad ibn Rushd said: "The meaning of this is clear, and praise belongs to Allah."

4. He said in *al-'Utbiya*: "Asbagh said: 'Ibn al-Qasim was asked about a man who used to hit the slaves belonging to his wife. He would order them (to do this) or prohibit them (from doing that) in order to instruct them, although she disliked him doing this. He said: "I consider that this should only be done with the permission of his wife."'" Muhammad ibn Rushd said in *al-Bayan*: "What he means by his words 'to instruct them' is teaching them how they should serve or chastising them for leaving their work (unfinished) or anything of this nature when they are ordered to do something but they disobey. However, with regard to the rights due to Allah, exalted is He, like *wudu'* and *salat*, then he should indeed reproach them if they fail to perform them – (in this respect) he should command or prohibit them accordingly, without the permission of his wife. This is in accordance with the words of Allah, exalted is He: '*Instruct your family to do salat, and be constant in it.*[1]'"

5. He said in *al-Bayan*: "A man should not have his slaves work on the day of the 'Eid al-Fitr or the days of the 'Eid al-Adha except for light service in the house, like drawing water and the like. As for sending them to the fields or harvest and the like, then he should not (demand this of them). They should be informed that these (holidays) are days of eating, drinking and remembering Allah. If they refuse to work at all, then there is no harm in this and success is with Allah, He has no partner and He has power over all things."

6. He said in *al-Bayan*: "Malik has permitted a man to hurry when travelling when the need for him to do so has arisen – even if it means travelling faster than the well established (pace for certain) stretches of road; and he did not see any harm in tiring out his animal to this (end). He bases his evidence on the journey of 'Abdallah ibn 'Umar from Makka to Madina which lasted (only) three days – for it is a distance of ten (daily) stages when journeying at a normal pace; and that Sa'd ibn Abi Hind also did this – who was known for his goodness, for his worship and for his excellence: part of his striving in worship was to sit with his companions in the mosque after the *Subh salat* – they would sit without addressing each other, being preoccupied with *dhikr* of Allah. This (practice) is based on what has been reported from the Messenger

---

[1] Ta Ha: 131

of Allah who said: 'Should I not tell you of one of the moments in the Garden when the shade is extended, when any action is accepted and when mercy in it is all pervading?' They replied: 'Yes, Messenger of Allah!' He said: 'from the *salat* of *Subh* to the sunrise.' If it is permitted for a man to bear discomfort himself when hurrying on a journey, then it is permitted him to have his riding beast bear this too – given that Allah has subdued it for his use and granted a blessing in it for His slaves. He said: *'They carry your loads to lands you would never reach except with great difficulty.'*[1] The hadith 'Surely Allah is kind, He loves kindness, is pleased with it and assists and supports people in being kind' is an indication that it is *makruh* for him to do this when there is no need and that it is permitted him when there is a need."

7. He said in *al-'Utbiya*: "'Isa ibn Dinar has related to us from Ibn Wahb that a man was driving his donkey and it stumbled. He said to it: 'You miserable beast you have fallen!' The recording angel of the right then said: 'I shall not record this as a good action' and the angel of the left said: 'I shall not record it as a bad action' and the angel of the left was called (and a voice said) 'Write! as long as the angel of the right desists from recording.'" Muhammad ibn Rushd said in *al-Bayan*: "The fact that the angel of the right says 'I shall not record it as a good action' while the one on the left says 'I shall not record it as a bad action' is an indication that they only record the good actions and the bad. As for the licit (actions) which are neither good nor bad, neither the angel of the right records them nor the angel of the left. The meaning of what was said to the angel of the left when called – and Allah knows best – is that he should only write when the angel of the right desists from writing, not because he himself considers it a bad action. Thus the angel of the right is the judge with respect to the angel of the left – for it is he who determines whether the latter records it as a wrong action. Cursing the animal which had tripped up is a wrong action if one understands that it was the angel on the right who instructed the one on the left to record what he himself desisted from recording – and Allah is the guarantor of success."

8. Al-Mawwaq said in *Sunan al-Muhtadeen*: "Malik said: 'The person who has been granted knowledge and who has become recognised for this (attribute) – in that people point him out (to others when he passes) – should place dust on his head and hate his (lower) self when he retires (away from people); he should not be elated by his position of eminence, for when he is lying in the grave and the earth is his pillow this will be a cause of grief and affliction.'"

9. In the chapter entitled the 'Sending of the Prophet', may the peace and

---

1 an-Nahl – The Bee: 7

blessings of Allah be upon him, in *Fath al-Bari*, Ibn Hajar has related from Ibn 'Abbas, may Allah be content with them both: "I was playing with the children when the Messenger of Allah came. I hid behind a door and he followed me saying 'Go and call Mu'awiya for me.'" He then goes on to comment, saying: "in this hadith there is permission to leave children to play (alone) – as long as what (they are playing) with is not forbidden; there is also permission to send a child off to call someone or for a similar (errand) like having him carry someone a gift, or having him ask about something one needs, etc.; and it also indicates that it is permitted to send off someone else's child (on an errand). It cannot be argued that this would be exploiting the child as this (permission) is (only granted with respect to) something of insignificance – and the law tolerates this when there is a need and when it is the customary practice of the Muslims, and Allah knows best."

10. An-Nawawi, commenting in *Sharh Muslim* on 'The responsibility of two persons who insult each other for what they said is for the one who started it – unless the person initially wronged oversteps (in returning the insult)', said: "It is only permitted for the person who has been reviled by another to take his revenge on the other to the degree he has been reviled by him – as long as it is not lying about him, slandering or cursing (him). What one might imagine as being permitted is that he take his revenge by saying 'O how unjust you are! O how stupid you are! O you delinquent!' or expressions similar to this, as hardly any person is (entirely) free of such qualities. The *'ulama* have said: 'If the person who has been insulted has taken his revenge, then he is considered to have obtained his requital owing from the injustice, and the (person who) first (insulted him) is freed of what he owes the person (he insulted). What remains, however, is the crime of the initial insult, and the crime before Allah, exalted is He.' It has also been said: 'all the crime of it is removed from him by the act of the other retaliating against him; the person who started is then only left with the blame and censure but not the crime.'"

11. He said in *al-'Utbiya*: "Ibn al-Qasim, when asked as to whether or not it was permitted for a Muslim to take hold of a carcass – which has not been killed in the proper (ritual) manner – and skin it in order to use it replied: 'There is no harm in a Muslim skinning a carcass, and he may only use it when it has been skinned – that is, when purified of all the (meat) clinging to it.'" Muhammad ibn Rushd said in *al-Bayan*: "The meaning of this is clear as the Messenger of Allah, may the peace and blessings of Allah be upon him, said of carrion or a carcass: '… are you not going to use its skin?' – and there is no way to use its skin but by skinning it, and Allah is the one who grants success."

12. He said in *al-'Utbiya*: "Malik said: 'I have been informed that 'A'isha, may Allah be content with her, would enter the house where the tombs of both the Prophet, may the peace and blessings of Allah be upon him, and Abu Bakr lay bare-headed. When 'Umar, may Allah be pleased with him, was buried there she would not enter it unless she had (first) gathered her clothes about her.'" Muhammad ibn Rushd said in *al-Bayan*: "There is nothing problematic in 'Umar, may Allah be pleased with him, seeking permission of 'A'isha to be buried in her house, as it was her house – and had she denied him this, it would have been her right to do so. The reason she did not enter the house bare-headed – since the time 'Umar was buried there – was because of what had been transmitted in the Qur'an, and because of the reports with multiple chains of narration, that the *ruh* of someone does not die with the body: rather (only) the body dies when the *ruh* is taken from it; the *ruh* is the self (*nafs*) and soul (*nasamah*) about which Allah, exalted is He, said: '*Allah takes back people's selves when their death arrives and those who have not yet died, while they are asleep*',[1] and: '*O self at rest and at peace, return to your Lord, well-pleasing and well-pleased!*'[2] Moreover the Prophet said, may the peace and blessings of Allah be upon him: 'The soul of the *mumin* is a bird which hangs from a tree of the garden until Allah causes it to come back to its body on the Day it is raised up' and: 'When one of you dies, then his place will be shown him in the morning and evening: if he is of the people of the Garden, then it will be in the Garden and if of the people of the Fire, then it will be in the Fire. He will be told: "this is your place until Allah raises you up again on the Day of Rising."' It has also been related, regarding the *ruhs*, that they remain in the area of the graves and that they appear at the upper end of them – usually on Thursdays, Fridays and the night of Friday. It was because 'A'isha, may Allah be content with her, could not be sure that the *ruh* of 'Umar ibn al-Khattab was not in the area of the grave at the moment when she entered the house that she would only go in when she had gathered her clothes about her. This demonstrates her utmost scrupulousness and precaution – for it was not strictly speaking necessary: covering oneself, as Allah, exalted is He, has commanded, is only necessary in the presence of people who are alive in this world, but not in the presence of the dead."

13. He said in *al-'Utbiya*: "Malik was asked about a man applying kohl during the day and he replied: 'I do not approve of a man applying kohl during the night or day unless he is afflicted by some illness (of the eye) – and he applies it (specifically for this reason); kohl is a matter for women and I have not seen

1 az-Zumar – The Companies: 39
2 al-Fajr – The Dawn: 28

anyone apply kohl like this except in the case of extreme need. Sometimes I have felt some (pain in my eyes) and applied kohl, but I have stayed at home and not gone out.'" Muhammad ibn Rushd said in *al-Bayan*: "The meaning is clear as the application of kohl is a (practice) resembling (that) of women, and it is *makruh* for men to resemble women or vice versa – according to the narrations on the subject, and success is by Allah."

14. Ash-Shabrakheeti said in *Sharh al-'Ashmawiya*: "It is related that a European Christian came to Egypt, saying: 'I have a doubt and if you remove it, I will become Muslim.' So a meeting was convened for him in al-Kamiliya. The head of the *'ulama* at the time was Shaykh 'Izz ad-Deen ibn 'Abd as-Salam. The Christian said to him: 'Is what there is agreement about better in your eyes than that about which there is disagreement?' Shaykh 'Izz ad-Deen replied: 'that about which there is agreement is better.' Then the Christian said: 'we and you (the Muslims) are in agreement regarding the prophethood of 'Isa although we disagree regarding Muhammad, may the peace and blessings of Allah be upon him. This necessarily entails that 'Isa is better than Muhammad, may the peace and blessings of Allah be upon him, and that you should follow him.' The Shaykh bowed his head and remained silent from the beginning of the day to *Dhuhr*. The people (still) at the meeting became (more and more) agitated. Then the Shaykh raised his head saying: 'Which 'Isa are you referring to? The one who said to the Bani Isra'il: '... *and giving you good news of a Messenger after me whose name is Ahmad*'[1] – for we affirm *his* prophethood. So this necessarily implies that you should follow him, that you follow what he said; it implies that you should believe in the Ahmad that he gave you the good news about. However, if you are referring to any other 'Isa than this, then we cannot recognise him (according to our knowledge).' In this manner he established the (required) proof and the Christian became Muslim."

15. He said in *al-Bayan*: "Malik was asked about reciting (the Qur'an) in the hamam (i.e. the bathroom) and he replied: 'Recitation in every place is good; however, the hamam is not an (appropriate) place for recitation, although there is no harm in the recitation of (a few) *ayats*. Moreover there were no hamams in people's houses formerly.'" Muhammad ibn Rushd then goes on to say: "It is *makruh* to recite in the hamam as they are not usually free of impurities, just as it is *makruh* to recite Qur'an in the markets and the highways for this same reason. I recommend that one avoid recitation of the Qur'an except in places set aside for this – unless it is a small amount. Likewise, it is permitted in the case of the young boy who is learning to recite – as we will mention below."

---

1 as-Saff – The Ranks: 6

He permitted this in all circumstances in one of his two judgements, and he based this (judgement) on that of Abu Musa.

As for myself, I utter the (Qur'an) while I am walking, while mounted – in fact in all circumstances.

16. He said in *adh-Dhakheera*: "Branch: the *'ulama* differ regarding the (kind of) journey which is only permitted a woman when accompanied by a *mahram*. It has been said (a journey of) twelve miles; while it has also been said (a journey lasting) a day and a night; two nights; three days. And there are (various) *hadith* to this effect from the Prophet, may the peace and blessings of Allah be upon him. It has also been said that it is (generally) prohibited unless she is with a *mahram*, even if it is extremely short."

Then I came across the discussion in *al-Bayan* and I realised that what al-Qarafi had mentioned was an abbreviation it from it – namely where he says: "There is a difference of opinion as to what constitutes a journey which is not permitted for a woman to make except with a *mahram*: it has been said twelve miles and more; others have said a day and a night; others two nights; others three days. And for all of these there are narrations from the Prophet, may the peace and blessings of Allah be upon him. It has been related of the Prophet, on whom be peace, from a narration of Abu Hurayra that he said: 'A woman should not travel except with a *mahram*' and so a group of the *'ulama* have stuck to the general import of this hadith arguing that a woman should make neither a short or long journey, except when with a *mahram*, and success is by Allah."

17. He said in *al-'Utbiya*: "Sahnun said: 'I have been informed that 'Urwa ibn az-Zubayr said to his sons: "O my son, nothing raises a people more than their *taqwa* of Allah. A people is also raised by their marriages. Nothing brings a people lower than disobedience of Allah. Marriages may also bring a people down."' Muhammad ibn Rushd said in *al-Bayan*: "The meaning of this is clear. He, exalted is He, said: '*If you have taqwa of Allah, He will give you discrimination*'[1] and '*Have taqwa of Allah so that hopefully you will be successful.*'[2] There are many (*ayats*) similar in meaning in the Qur'an. 'Umar ibn al-Khattab said: 'the nobility of the mumin is his *taqwa*, his deen, his noble descent or the esteem in which he is held.' If *taqwa* can be said to raise (people up), then there is no doubt that acts of disobedience bring (a people) low and that marriages can also raise or bring low – as 'Urwa ibn az-Zubayr said – for if man marries someone who is of a nobler station then he will be ennobled by it, and if he marries someone of low character, he will be deemed as low by the people."

1 al-Anfal – Booty: 29
2 Ali 'Imran – The Family of 'Imran: 130

18. He said in *al-'Utbiya*: "I heard Malik say: 'Sa'd ibn Jubayr used to say: "If someone were only to command to the good and forbid evil on condition no evil remained in him, then no one would command anyone to do anything anymore."'" Commenting on this, Muhammad ibn Rushd said in *al-Bayan*: "The meaning of this is clear, as no one is free from wrong actions and mistakes. Part of the advice of Khidr to Musa, may peace be on them both, was: 'Increase your good actions for surely you will be afflicted by bad actions. Do good for surely you will also do bad' – and he was a Prophet sent (to mankind) so what must be the state of people of a lesser rank!"

19. The author of *al-Fath* and al-Qastallani have divided (the subject of) 'keeping someone's secret' into various kinds: "It may either be licit, or it may be recommended to mention it; it may be *makruh* in the sense that the person concerned dislikes it (to be made known) even if the secret in question concerns praise of his noble and eminent character; and it may be totally *makruh*; it may also be haram when the person in question would be harmed by it or suffer loss; and it may be obligatory to mention it when it concerns a claim of Allah against him."

He said in *Kitab al-Barakat*:[1] "One of the ugliest and most despicable of utterances is when someone intends to swear to something but then desists from saying *wallahi* ('by Allah') (claiming) that he does not want to be false to his oath (by saying something regarding Allah's knowledge – of which he himself has no knowledge), or (claiming) that he would rather protect himself from the (consequences of such an) oath or the like. Thus he says (instead) 'Allah knows best', or 'Allah knew what (actually happened)' and the like. There is a danger in such expressions: if he is endowed with a certainty that the affair was as he said, then there is no harm (in abstaining from the oath). However, if he has any doubt, then it is the most ugliest of things for he is giving the lie to Allah, exalted is He: he said in effect that Allah knows something of which he does not know for certain how it is; and giving the lie about Allah is *kufr*. In it there is a suble point which is even uglier, that he says of Allah that He knows of the matter in a manner which is different to how it actually is. If this is indeed what he means, then it is *kufr*. Similar to this is the instance where someone – who intends to deny something – says: 'Allah has not heard of this.'"

20. He said in *al-Bayan*: "It has been narrated from 'A'isha, may Allah be pleased with her, that women from the people of Sham came to her. She said

---

1   In *al-'Utbiya* 19. However, there is some repetition in it and in the other copy some blank space.

to them: 'I believe you are from the district where the women go into the hamams?' They replied: 'Yes.' She said: 'I have heard the Messenger of Allah, may the peace and blessings of Allah be upon him, say: 'If a woman takes off her clothes in a place other than her house, then she has violated what is between her and Allah.' (What she means is that) she will rend the 'veil' (of modesty) between her and Allah exalted is He, it will be rent because she cannot be certain that a man will not see her with her head or body uncovered. I have put this into the following verse:

Whoever takes her clothes off outside
   of her house which protects her
Then she violates what is between her
   and the Lord of the constellations, Oh woe to the person who violates!
The author of the *al-Bayan* has mentioned this –
   and he is someone of vast knowledge and certainty –
From our mother 'A'isha who related it
   from my Master and the Master of all creation
May Allah bless him as long as there is a group
   still putting the guidance into practice.

21. Ad-Dameeri said in *Hayat al-Hayawan* ('The lives of animals'): "Among the regulations regarding rams is that it is forbidden to have them fight each other – according to what has been related from Abu Dawud and at-Tirmidhi from the hadith of Mujahid from Ibn 'Abbas, may Allah be pleased with them both, namely that the Prophet, may the peace and blessings of Allah be upon him, 'forbade goading animals to fight each other.' This applies to (goading) animals like rams, cocks and other animals (of this nature). (It is also forbidden) because of what is in the *Kamil* of Ibn 'Adi who relates the hadith from Ibn 'Umar, may Allah be pleased with him, namely, that the Prophet, may the peace and blessings of Allah be upon him, said: 'Allah has cursed those who incite animals (to fight each other).' Al-Haleemi said: 'It is forbidden, it is prohibited – none of the *'ulama* have given permission for this: the animals inflict pain on each other and injure each other. Were the animal to try and inflict this on itself when alone, it would be unable to.' Two narrations have been related from Imam Ahmad, one that it is forbidden, the other that it is *makruh*."

22. Ad-Dameeri said: at the beginning of the 'History of Nisapur' of al-Hakim, from Thamama ibn 'Abdallah ibn Anas ibn Malik al-Ansari – and he was one that the entire body (of hadith scholars) narrated from – that: "We went out on one occasion from Khurasan. We were accompanied by a man

who insulted and defamed Abu Bakr and 'Umar ?. We prohibited him from doing this but he did not stop. One day, just as our food came, he went off to the toilet. He was away so long that we sent someone to look for him. When the man came back, he said: 'Go and see your companion.' We went to where he had sat down to urinate in a burrow and found that desert lynxes had stolen up from behind him and had torn his limbs one from the other. As they were gathering together some of his bones, the (lynxes) approached us but did not molest us being busy with scraping (the meat) off his limbs."

23. Ahmad Bab said in *Sharh al-Mukhtasar,* commenting on his words in the section regarding theft 'or when he holds on to the (money) with the excuse that he will pay at a later time': "Ibn al-Qasim said in *al-Kafi*: 'The hand of the person who steals an amount of money equal to what he is owed – from the person who owes him money – is amputated.' The followers of Malik and others have opposed him in this arguing that it is permitted him to take back the money from the person in debt to him in any way he can. This (judgement) is narrated by Ibn Wahb and Ziyad from Malik. Ibn 'Arafa said: 'Ibn Shash has stipulated that it be a small amount, that it is long overdue and that one is impatient to recover it' (citing him) as if this is the (teaching of the) *madhhab*, following al-Ghazali in this. Ibn Marzouq said: 'Issue: if the ruling in this matter is accepted, then it is better to make it conditional upon (the instance where) the debtor has put off the claimant with a promise or excuse (after he has sought permission to take it) – for this is the reason for the permission, i.e. that he has already sought permission to take a debt. The basis of this ruling is the hadith of Hind in the *Sahih* and elsewhere, where she speaks of his 'tenaciously holding on (to his money)': if the person were just and returned what he owed when asked of him – of his own accord – then it would not be permitted to take any of his money or property without asking.'"

24. He said in *al-'Utbiya*: "He said: 'a woman asked him, saying 'I have taken (into my care) an orphan girl and I anticipate a reward in the hereafter (from Allah). Her hand is the same as mine and that of my daughters. I do not skimp in anything for her. Sometimes someone will ask me about her, and give her some dirhams. So I buy (things) for her; sometimes I use these (dirhams) if I myself have nothing to buy (things) with. (What is the judgement in this?)' He replied: 'I will inform you about this: if what the girl receives from you corresponds (in amount) to what you are given for her – or what she receives is more – then there is no harm in this.'" Muhammad ibn Rushd said: "As he has explained it, this is clear – and is in accordance with His words, exalted is He:

'If you mix your property with theirs, they are your brothers.¹'"

25. It is related in (the *Sahih* of) al-Bukhari from Abu Hurayra that he heard the Messenger of Allah, may the peace and blessings of Allah be upon him, say: "A slave of Allah may utter a word without thinking whether it is right or wrong. However, he may fall down into the Fire for a distance equal to that between the east and the west on account of it."

It is stated in *al 'Utbiya*: "Malik said: 'Bilal ibn al-Harith al-Muzani would relate that the Messenger of Allah, may the peace and blessings of Allah be upon him, said: "A man may utter a word which pleases Allah without giving it much importance but Allah will record for him His contentment until the Day he meets Him on account of it. However, a slave (of Allah) may utter a word (carelessly) without thinking of its gravity and it causes Allah to become angry. Allah will then record His anger with Him until the Day he meets Him, on account of it."' Bilal used to say: 'This hadith prevented me from speaking a lot.'" Malik has also said: "Ibn Mas'ud would say: 'Speak about the truth and you will be recognised for this, act in accordance with it and you will be one of its people.'" Muhammad ibn Rushd said in *al-Bayan*: "Malik has mentioned this hadith in the Miscellany section of his *Muwatta'*, and he has mentioned the words of Abu Hurayra at the end of it which are similar in meaning: 'A man may say something without thinking about it and he will be thrown into the Fire on account of it, and a man may say something without thinking about it and Allah will raise him to the Garden on account of it.' It has also been narrated from him in a hadith attributed to the Prophet, may the peace and blessings of Allah be upon him, that the speech which 'either pleases or angers Allah' and which Allah 'records either His contentment with or his anger with the person (who uttered it) until the Day he meets Him' refers *either* to saying something in front of the Sultan which causes the latter to desist from an act of injustice or crime, *or* to something which assists him in this. There is no difference of opinion amongst the people of knowledge in this – for (clear) evidence is to be found in the narrations on the subject indicating this (judgement), and success is by Allah."

'Izz ad-Deen Ibn 'Abd as-Salam said: "It refers to someone saying something not knowing whether it is good or bad – for it is forbidden for someone to speak about something not knowing whether it is good or bad."

26. He said in *Fath al-Bari*, commenting on the hadith of Umm Zar': "al-Mazari said that one of the (men of knowledge) said: 'These women said things about their husbands which they would have disliked. However, it was not

1 al-Baqara – The Cow: 220

backbiting as they did not refer to them personally or by their names.'" Al-Mazari then goes on to say: "someone would use this excuse if he had heard the women speaking in this manner when their husbands were absent and had then affirmed what they were saying. However what actually happened was different: it was 'A'isha who related the story from some women who were both unknown and absent. If a woman had described her husband in terms he would dislike, then it would be backbiting and forbidden – both for the one speaking and the one listening, unless it was on the occasion of a complaint about him to the judge, and this with respect to someone who is specified. As for someone who is unknown, there is no harm in listening to someone talking about him as this would not injure him or cause him distress. However this is not the case if the person speaking realises that the person he is speaking to recognises the person he is speaking about."

Then he goes on to say after a while: "This (hadith) also demonstrates that it is permitted to describe women and their beauty to a man as long as they are unknown (to him); what is prohibited is describing a particular woman in the presence of the man, and (in particular) describing that (part of) her which a man is not permitted to look at." An-Nawawi said, transmitting what the author of *'Aybat al-Nasik* says about the matter: "The (type of) backbiting which is forbidden is someone saying: 'a person did such-and-such a thing' when it is said as a general statement but the person addressed understands that a particular person (is meant) by this."

27. He said in *al-'Utbiya* during a discussion warning against listening to the people of innovation: "Malik said: 'That man said: "Do not allow the (words of the) person whose heart has swerved (from the truth) to reach your ears."'" Muhammad ibn Rushd said in *al-Bayan*: "The meaning of this is clear: he is warning him not to listen to such people's speech lest doubt enter their *'aqida* by the ambiguous and dubious nature of their words."

28. He said in *al-'Utbiya*: "Malik, commenting on the hadith of the Prophet, may the peace and blessings of Allah be upon him, 'If a man says "The people are ruined" then he is the most ruined amongst them' said: "(This means) he is like them and the worst of them." Muhammad ibn Rushd said in *al-Bayan*: "Malik's commentary on the hadith is correct and what it refers to (specifically), according to all the people of knowledge, is when he says this disparagingly about those of his time; if however, he says this out of sadness for the loss of the best of men and out of fear for those people remaining – because of the paucity of such men, then he is not being referred to by the hadith. It is related from Abu ad-Darda' that he said: 'A man has not reached the heights of

fiqh until he hates all of mankind on account of the essence of Allah and then turns to his own lower self and conceives a more intense hate, and success is by Allah.'"

29. He said in *al-'Utbiya*: "'Abdallah ibn 'Amr ibn al-'As said to the people of Iraq that they were the people who most sought after knowledge but also those who were most given to abandoning it, and that the people of Madina were the people quickest to fall into conflict and unrest but the first to desist from it, that the people of Sham were the people most ready to obey creatures, but the most disobedient of the Creator, that the people of Egypt were the most intelligent when young, but the most stupid when old." Muhammad ibn Rushd said in *al-Bayan*: "This he said with respect to their usual, everyday state. However, this does not constitute backbiting as he has not specified anyone of them when describing the whole group, and success is by Allah."

30. He said in *al-'Utbiya*: "Malik said: 'Ibn Mas'ud would say: "Afflictions are dependent upon what one says."'" Muhammad ibn Rushd said in *al-Bayan*: "What he means is that if a man says 'I will not do such-and-such a thing', believing that he will not do it because he possesses the capacity to desist from doing it, then Allah will punish him by causing him to do this thing. An explanation of this interpretation is to be found in another hadith, namely: 'I do not worship this stone, surely affliction is dependent upon what one says.'"

31. He said in *al-Bayan*: "It has been related that Abu Bakr has related that the Messenger of Allah, may the peace and blessings of Allah be upon him, said: 'None of you should say: "I have stood (in *salat*) for the whole of Ramadan."'" It has been related from Ibn al-Hasan that a man said in the company of Ibn Mas'ud: 'I recited the Qur'an yesterday.' He said: 'What did he say?' The people informed him and he said: 'Tell him that his portion in this is that which he spoke about (i.e. mere speech), and success is by Allah.'"

He said in *adh-Dhakheera*: "Ibn Abi Zayd said: 'Branch: someone said to Malik: "(What about) someone who performs *salat* for the sake of Allah but is afflicted by the desire that people should know of his (assiduity) and that they should meet him on the way to the mosque?" He replied: "If (his) first (impulse) in this is for Allah, then there is no harm in this."'"

I say: "That the slave should love people to esteem him is a natural aspect of the temperament (of man); that he should change his behaviour to this end is something that he acquires – and is an alteration of the original (nature) of obedience (to Allah)." Al-Qarafi has also said something similar in the two hundred and sixty-ninth section (of *al-Farouq*) – after quoting the hadith 'Whoever likes people to appear before him standing up should prepare himself for a place in the Fire': "The prohibition against desiring that people stand up for you should be understood in the case of someone who intends this out of haughtiness; as for someone who desires it in order to dissuade people – (by the imposing nature of his presence) – from causing him harm and in order to suppress any (idea of) failing or shortcoming on his part, then he should not be prohibited from this. The desire to repel anything painful is permitted, as long as it is not from reasons of pride or haughtiness; moreover it is also permitted when it occurs because of the love (of the people for him) – and this inclination is a natural sentiment."

32. He said in *al-'Utbiya*: "A man came to see Ibn 'Umar and found him repairing his sandals. He asked him about this and he informed him (of what he was doing). Then he said: 'What on earth are you doing repairing your sandals? Buy another pair!' Ibn 'Umar then said: 'Have you come (just) to tell me this?'" Muhammad ibn Rushd said: "'Abdallah ibn 'Umar censured him by saying: 'Have you come (just) to tell me this?' as that which he said did not concern him. The Messenger of Allah, may the peace and blessings of Allah be upon him, said: 'Part of the fineness of a person's Islam is to leave what does not concern him.'"

33. It is related in (the *Sahih* of) Muslim from Abu Hurayra, may Allah be pleased with him that the Messenger said: "Do you all know what the *muflis* – the insolvent – person is?" They replied: "The insolvent person with us is the person who possesses no dirhams or belongings." Then he said: "The insolvent person from my *umma* is the one who comes on the Day of Rising with *salat*, fasting and *zakat* but who has insulted such-and-such a person, who has slandered another, who has consumed the wealth of another illegally, who has spilt the blood of another or who has hit another. The (first) person (affected) will be given some of the good actions (of the perpetrator), then another will also be given some of his good actions and (so on): if all his good actions are used up before he has compensated for what he must make good, then the wrong actions of the people (concerned) will be taken (from them) and heaped on him, and then he will be thrown in the Fire' – or whatever the exact words were."

34. It is also related in *Sahih Muslim*: "The sanctity of the women of the *mujahideen* to those who have stayed at home (and not fought) is like the sanctity of their (own) mothers. Anyone who stays at home and stands in for a man of the *mujahideen* in (taking care of) his family and then betrays him in respect to them, will be made to stand before him on the Day of Rising and he will take whatever of his actions he wants." Then the Messenger of Allah turned to us

saying: "What do you think?"

35. He said in *al-'Utbiya*: "Malik said: 'People would say that there is good in a person committing a wrong action – for he turns to Allah on account of it.'" Muhammad ibn Rushd said: "The meaning of this is clear: good may bring about evil and evil may bring about good. Allah said, exalted is He: *'It may be that you hate something when it is good for you.'* [1]"

36. He said in *al-'Utbiya*: "Malik said: 'Al-Qasim ibn Muhammad said: "Wrong actions follow those who committed them"' and 'al-Qasim ibn Muhammad would say: "Whoever meets Allah not having taken part in the shedding of the blood of a Muslim, then he will meet Allah with only a slight load on his back."'" He said in *al-Bayan*: "The Messenger of Allah, may the peace and blessings of Allah be upon him, said: 'It may well be that Allah will forgive every wrong action except the person who dies as a *kafir* or who has killed a *mumin* deliberately.' All wrong actions may be effaced, according to the consensus, through *tawba*, except murder – for the people of knowledge from amongst the Companions and the *Tabi'un* after them differed as to whether the *tawba* of the murderer was accepted."

He has also said on another occasion: "All wrong actions are effaced by *tawba* if one makes *tawba* from them before seeing (death) directly, according to the *ijma'*. This is based on the words of Allah, exalted is He: *'You who have* iman! *Make tawba to Allah: It may be that you Lord will erase your bad actions from you.'* [2] The phrase 'it may be' is understood – when said by Allah – as something obligatory, and evidence for this is contained in the words of the Prophet, may the peace and blessings of Allah be upon him: 'The person who turns in *tawba* from wrong action is as the person who has no wrong actions.' If he does not turn in *tawba*, then he will be subject to His words, exalted is He: *'Allah does not forgive anything being associated with him, but He forgives whoever He wills for anything other than that'* [3] – other than the person who kills (someone) deliberately for they have differed – by way of two judgements – as to whether his *tawba* is accepted and whether he will be saved from the threat of punishment."

An-Nawawi, commenting on hadith of his, may the peace and blessings of Allah be upon him, in the chapter entitled 'the acceptance of the *tawba* of the murderer, even if he has killed many people' in his commentary on *Muslim* 'A man killed ninety-nine people and then he killed one more making it a full hundred, and the man of knowledge gave a *fatwa* that he has a *tawba* (which

---

1   al-Baqara – The Cow: 214
2   at-Tahrim – The Prohibition: 8
3   an-Nisa' – Women: 115

he can make and which could be accepted)': "This is the *madhhab* and the consensus of the people of knowledge – that is, as to the validity of the *tawba* of the person who kills (another) deliberately. There is no difference of opinion from anyone other than Ibn 'Abbas, may Allah be pleased with them both. The difference of opinion related from one of the *salaf* is intended to convey both a rebuke and (an exhortation to) *tawba* – not that he believed his *tawba* was invalid. The above hadith is clear proof of this – even if it is from the *shari'a* of those before us and there is a difference of opinion as to whether legally speaking one may base one's argument on it. However, such a difference is not a (real) subject of disagreement. A (real) difference would (only) exist if our law had not afforded any affirmation of or assent to this (judgement). Thus if such (assent) is to be found, then it is (considered part of) our law without a doubt – and this (assent) is indeed to be found in our law in His words: *'those who do not call on any other god together with Allah and do not kill anyone Allah has made inviolate, except with the right to do so, and do not fornicate; anyone who does that will receive an evil punishment and on the Day of Rising his punishment will be doubled and he will be humiliated in it timelessly, for ever, except for those who make tawba ...'*[1] and the words of Allah, exalted is He: *'as for anyone who kills a mumin deliberately, his repayment is Hell, remaining in it timelessly, for ever.'*[2] The correct (interpretation) of this is that the (threatened) requital is Hell – but that sometimes he is punished with it, sometimes with something else, and sometimes he is not punished (at all) and is instead pardoned. If, however, the person kills deliberately, believing it is licit to do so – when he has right to do so and without attenuating circumstances – then he is a *kafir* and a renegade and remains timelessly in the Fire of Hell, according to the consensus; if he does not hold that it is licit, but rather believes it to be forbidden, then he is (judged) to be a person of corruption and disobedience who commits a major crime but who may be forgiven and who may not enter the Fire at all. This then is the correct (interpretation) of this *ayat*."

37. It is stated in *al-Jami' as-Saghir*: "Whoever wards off his own anger, then Allah will ward off His punishment from him, whoever guards his tongue, then Allah will veil his vices and weaknesses." Al-Munawi said: "'whoever guards his tongue' i.e. from attacking people's honour or from speaking about what is haram 'then Allah will veil his vices and weaknesses' from people so that people do not discover his defects."[3]

1 al-Furqan – Discrimination: 68
2 an-Nisa' – Women: 92
3 We have translated directly from *al-Fayd* because there was a mistake in the text. Ed.

38. It is also stated in *al-Jami' as-Saghir*: "Even if a *mumin* were (clinging to) a (single) reed in the sea, then Allah would send him someone to cause him trouble." Al-Munawi said: "... in order to increase his reward and to raise him in stations. One should encounter such (trouble) with contentment and submission, aware that this (trouble) has been inflicted on him for his own good – either to (expiate past) bad actions or to raise him in rank in the next world."

39. It is stated in (the *Sahih* of) Muslim: "No *mumin* is afflicted by chronic illness, exhaustion, sickness or trouble – or even the worries that beset him – but that Allah will expiate his wrong actions by them." Also in *Muslim*: "There is no Muslim who, when afflicted by something, says what Allah has commanded him to say (namely) *'we belong to Allah and to Him we will return'*[1] and 'O Allah reward me for this affliction of mine and grant me good instead of it' (but that his *du'a* will be accepted)." 'Ali ibn as-Sadiq said in *Sharh al-Mukhtasar*: "There are three ways of pronouncing 'O Allah reward me...': with an extension on the *hamza* and a *kasra* on the *jeem* (*Allahumma aajirni* – O Allah reward me), with a *sukun* on (the *hamza*) and a *damma* on the *jeem* (*Allahumma' jurni*) and with a *kasra* on (the *jeem*) or (*Allahumma' jirni*) – so examine the narration (in the light of this.)"

40. It is stated in (the *Sahih* of) Muslim: "The wealth of *sadaqa* does not diminish and no man forgives (someone) a wrong committed against him but that Allah increases him in honour." It is related in (the work of) ash-Sha'rani: "Yahya ibn Mu'adh would say: 'If someone commits an injustice against me and I do not seek requital, then this is preferable to me than desisting from an act of fornication.'" Ka'b al-Ahbar would say: "Whoever is forbearing in the face of trouble or insult on the part of his wife, then Allah will grant him a reward equal to that He gave Ayyub, on whom be peace and blessing; and whoever is forbearing in the face of trouble or insult on behalf of her husband, then Allah will grant her a reward equal to that He gave Asiya, the daughter of Muzahim, may Allah be content with her."

41. There is a chapter in (the *Sahih* of) Muslim entitled "Proof that whoever is content with Allah as his Lord, with Islam as his deen and with Muhammad, may the peace and blessing of Allah be upon him, as his Messenger, then he is a *mumin* – even if he commits acts of disobedience and major wrongdoing."

42. Al-Bayjuri said in *Sharh ash-Shama'il*: "It has been related by Ibn Hibban and al-Hakim – who considered it *sahih* – in a *marfu'* hadith of 'Umar: "Whoever puts on new clothes and says:

[1] al-Baqara – The Cow; 15

اَلْحَمْدُ لِلَّهِ الَّذِي كَسَانِي مَا أُوَارِي بِهِ عَوْرَتِي وَأَتَجَمَّلُ بِهِ فِي حَيَاتِي

'Alhamdulillahi' lladhi kasani ma uwari bihi 'awrati wa atajammalu bihi fi hayati – Praise belongs to Allah who has clothed me, who has enabled me to cover my private parts and adorn myself by means of them in my day-to-day life' and goes and gives away his old clothes, then he will remain under the protection, shelter and cover of Allah – both when alive and dead."

43. Ash-Shabrakheeti said in *Sharh al-'Ashmawiya*: "He, may the peace and blessings of Allah be upon him, said: 'Whenever Allah wants good for someone, then He causes him to causes him to know the *fiqh* of the deen.' There is a subtle secret in this hadith – as (mentioned) in the *fatwas* of Shaykh Wali ad-Deen al-'Iraqi – the gist of which is that if Allah causes someone to 'know the *fiqh*', then it means that He will cause him to die in Islam because he, may the peace and blessings of Allah be upon him, has declared (in the hadith) that Allah 'wants good for him' and (has indicated thereby) that he does not want good for the *kafir*. This he has mentioned in *Tadhkirat al-'Ibad*."

44. He has related in *al-'Utbiya* that Malik said that Yahya ibn Sa'id said: "While in the territory of the Magrib I sought something of the needs of this world and it caused me concern. I made so many *du'as* to Allah on account of these (things) that I became impatient for them. I mentioned this to the Shaykh with whom I kept company and he replied: 'Do not be averse to (feeling like) this, for (and he cited the hadith) "Allah has placed a blessing for the slave in his needs and has permitted him to make *du'a* for them."'" Muhammad ibn Rushd said in *al-Bayan*: "This story is also related in the record made by 'Isa entitled 'acts performed without intention' from the direct audition (*Sama'*) of Ibn al-Qasim – with an additional description of (his state) after the Shaykh had responded to him by saying 'Do not be averse to (feeling like) this' – where he says: 'so I enjoyed this (state), worked at it (by making *du'as*) and exerted myself. Then (the things I needed) appeared after this. I said (to myself): "What if my *du'as* were for something of the next world?" I mentioned this to a Shaykh whom I used to keep company with and he cited the hadith, namely "Allah has placed a blessing for the slave in his needs and has given permission to make *du'a* for them" (and then said:) "The words 'placed a blessing in his needs' means that He has granted him the capacity to make the *du'a* for them and has granted permission (to do so) for all needs – because the making of *du'a* is one of the acts of worship which is rewarded with a great reward,

whether or not his *du'a* is answered or not; and because no one would go to the trouble of making *du'a* who did not possess a correct *iman* and pure intention. Allah will not allow such (*du'as* to be made) to no avail – for He, exalted is He, said: '*Allah would never let your* iman *go to waste.*[1]'" This then is the reason for the *baraka* of this need: the *du'a* (for it) will also bring him benefit in the next world – even if he is deprived of the benefit in this world – and what he will be given (there) will be better than what he is deprived of (here). The hadith 'Anyone who makes *du'a* will have one of three (possible outcomes): either it is answered (immediately), or it is stored up for him, or it is an expiation for him' does not mean that it will *not* 'be stored up for him' or that it will *not* be 'an expiation for him' if it is answered, and success is by Allah."

45. He said in *al-'Utbiya*: "Sufyan said: 'Sincerity is raising one's finger, *du'a* is raising the palms of the hands and devotion is extending one's hands and arms until they are outstretched.'" Muhammad ibn Rushd said in *al-Bayan*: "What he means is that the act of raising his finger in the *shahada* – and bearing witness that Allah is One – is an indication of his sincerity; and that raising his hands – with his palms outstretched (in *du'a*) to Allah – is (an indication of) a state of devotion. All this is clear and there is nothing obscure in it." If there is anything incorrect in the text, then it lies in the source it was related from. It is related in (the *Sahih* of) Muslim from Umm ad-Darda': "If a Muslim makes a *du'a* for his brother in his heart, then it is answered. There is an angel responsible (for *du'as* positioned at his head): every time he makes a *du'a* (calling) for good on his brother, the angel responsible says 'Ameen and the like for you.'"

46. It is narrated in (the *Sahih* of) al-Bukhari from Abu Hurayra, may Allah be pleased with him that the Messenger of Allah, may the peace and blessings of Allah be upon him, said: "A man walking along the road came across a branch of thorns and he put it aside, Allah thanked him for it, and He forgave him." There is also: "A Muslim is brother to a Muslim, he does not do him any injustice, and he does not abandon him; and whoever looks to the need of his brother, then Allah will fulfil his need and whoever relieves a Muslim of his trouble, then Allah will relieve him of one of the troubles of the Day of Rising; and whoever veils a Muslim, then Allah will veil him on the Day of Rising."

It is also related in (the *Sahih* of) Muslim: "I have seen a man going about as he pleased in the Garden on account of a (fallen) tree which he had cut (up) in order to clear it from the way." Also in (the *Sahih* of) Muslim, related from Abu Hurayra: "If you are as you say, then they will be consumed by irritation and frustration, and you will have a supporter from Allah against them as long

---

1   al-Baqara – The Cow; 142

as you conduct yourself like this" – and this he said to a man who had said: "O Messenger of Allah I have relatives and I keep my ties with them, but they break off relations with me; I treat them well, but they treat me badly; I treat them with forbearance and they treat me ignorantly" – or whatever his exact words were, and Allah knows best.

47. Al-Munawi said in his *Kabir*: "In the commentary on the *al-Hikam* (of Ibn 'Ata'illah al-Iskandari) it is stated: 'Someone had a dream in which he was asked: "What has Allah done with you?" He replied: "He has forgiven me and has had mercy on me. The reason for this was that I was passing down a street in Baghdad while it was raining heavily. Then I caught sight of a cat shivering from the cold and felt pity for it so I put it under my clothing."'"

It is also related in the *Kabir* of al-Munawi: "Complementary detail: 'One of the (men of knowledge) said: "One day the Governor of al-Bukhara – who was an unjust tyrant – caught sight of a mangy dog shivering in the cold. He ordered his servants to carry it to his house, place it in a warm place, feed it and give it to drink. Then a voice said to him in his sleep: 'You were a dog and we have caused you to serve a dog.' The following morning he died and was accorded a great funeral cortege on account of his pity for the dog. (Reflect upon) how much higher (the rank of) the Muslim is in relation to the dog – so perform good actions and do not be concerned whether someone deserves it (or not); and seek after excellence where excellence is to be found and leave meaner aspects to where they belong; and treat creation as subordinate (to the Creator); and do not stop to praise this person or to denigrate that person, but give priority to the first (you meet), and then to the next."

He said: "Al-Ghazali was seen in a dream and someone said to him: 'What has Allah done with you?' He replied: 'He caused me to stand before Him. He said: "What have you come to Me with?" I mentioned various acts of obedience and He said: "I have not accepted any of them. However, once while you were sitting writing, a fly alighted on your pen and out of pity for it you allowed it to drink of the ink. Just as you showed mercy to this (fly), I will show mercy to you: go, for I have forgiven you!"'"

48. Ibn Abi Jamra, may Allah benefit us by him, said, commenting on his saying, may the peace and blessings of Allah be upon him, 'There is no contagious disease, nor is there any (reality in seeing) bad omens' saying: "He said, may the peace and blessings of Allah be upon him: 'If you perceive something as a bad omen, then just carry on (with what you are doing), and do not change your intention from what it was before (the omen) for omens do not prevent anything (from coming to be) nor do they bring anything about.'"

Then he goes on to say, commenting on his saying, on whom be peace and blessings, 'an unpropitious omen – if it exists at all – is to be found in the home, a woman or a horse': "These three things (are such that) one may separate oneself from them (if necessary). There is no great difficulty for anyone to do this. However, he, may the peace and blessings of Allah be upon him, did not state that this kind of omen existed for certain, for he added 'if it exists at all' – and this supports the claim (that it is of no effect). (Implied in) his mention of these three (specifically) is a denial that it exists with respect to a son, brother, companion or any relative, or in food or any financial assets or activity. He did not mention these latter in order to ensure that relatives and companions stay together, and so that no one suspects or looks askance at the other (on account of an omen), or becomes envious of someone's wealth. Today one may observe how some people habitually see bad omens in each other. Someone might say for example: 'the business of such a person was only ruined when a son was born to such-and-such a person' – if he dislikes that particular son – and those (listening) will agree with what he claims; the same goes for the way they talk about their companions, or those they meet – when they say, for example: 'I was only deprived (of such-and-such a thing) because I met such-and-such a person.' This is very common amongst people but is contrary to the sunna of the Messenger of Allah, may the peace and blessings of Allah be upon him. It is pure ignorance. May the above mentioned examples of seeing 'unpropitious signs' in people be enough (to illustrate this point). Omens and (belief in the power of) evil are all contrary to the sunna of the Messenger of Allah, may the peace and blessings of Allah be upon him."

Al-Qarafi said in *adh-Dhakheera* and *al-Farouq* – and the text is from the first: "Seeing bad omens in things (*tatayyur*) and portents or forebodings (*tiyra*) (in general) are forbidden because of what is related in the hadith, namely, that he, on whom be peace, liked auguries but disliked omens, and because it is on a par with thinking badly of Allah, exalted is He. Strictly speaking, *tatayyur* is thinking evil of Allah, exalted is He, and *tiyra* is acting upon such (belief). The person who (imagines he) sees an omen in something, hardly ever escapes the omen he sees – if he acts according to it, while others are not touched by it. One of the *'ulama* was asked about this and he replied: 'The person who sees an omen in something believes that Allah will harm him, and indeed He does cause him harm as punishment for his thinking ill of Him; those who do not see omens, do not think ill of Allah, and so He does not take them to account for it.' The basis of this (judgement) is the saying of his, on whom be peace and blessings, in a relation (of a *qudsi* hadith) from Allah: 'I am in my slave's opinion of Me; let him think of Me what he will'; and in another narration: 'and let him think well of Me.' But this station (of knowledge) needs to be examined further: if a person fears he will perish from encountering a wild animal, for example, then it is not forbidden (to think that he will be harmed), according to the consensus. Things (in creation) are usually of two kinds: first, what is normally held to be harmful, like poison, wild animals, people who act with (open) enmity or (hidden) deceit, or eating heavy, indigestible foods and the like: in the case of such things, it is not forbidden to fear (for one's safety and health) – for it is a fear based on what *usually* happens. The author of al-Qabs said: 'One of the *'ulama* said that the hadith regarding 'contagious disease' is interpreted as referring to certain illnesses (only) – based on evidence of (the devastating effect of) the plague.' Second, that which does not usually lead to harm, like (the superstitious belief of some people, preventing them from) passing in among (a flock of) sheep or goats, or buying soap on Saturday and other (ignorant customs). Such (belief) is forbidden as it is groundless and (considered in the same category as) 'thinking ill of Allah, exalted is He.' Amongst the things which almost belong to one of the two kinds without belonging entirely to it are certain contagious diseases. Scrupulousness demands that one desist from having any fear of such (diseases) lest one take it to be an omen."

Then he says after a long discussion: "Notice: at-Tartushi said: 'Seeking auguries from the *mus-haf*, and from striking sand, and from poetry are forbidden: they are (classified) as being the same as *azlam* ('divining arrows', mentioned in the Qur'an) (and so are prohibited), despite the fact that auguries (taken from signs in creation) are considered something good in the sunna. The (difference between the two) is that 'good' auguries are those which manifest without one having to seek after them (by artificial means) – like someone saying to you spontaneously: "O how successful you are" and the like. Making or seeking interpretations of auguries for payment, from a soothsayer) is forbidden' – as at-Tartushi said. The author of *al-Farouq*, after mentioning what is also in *adh-Dhakheera*, although more briefly – that is, up to where he says 'what is customary (in creation) …' then goes on to say: 'The author of *al-Qabs* related that one of the *'ulama* interpreted his words, may the peace and blessings of Allah be upon him, "no contagious disease…" as referring to certain diseases (only), and that proof of this is his warning against the plague (in particular) and against going anywhere where it is to be found. This is true – for if the nature and activity of (some aspect of) Allah's creation, exalted is He, indicates some unvarying causal relationship, (like the effect of the plague), then one is obliged to believe in it as a general rule, (like the fact that water quenches (thirst) and bread satiates, fire burns and cutting off a person's head will kill him. Whoever does not believe that such (rules, based on natural causes and effects, exist), then he is no longer considered to be a normal, sane person endowed with an intellect. The "cause and effect" in these instances is nothing other than a manifestation of *al-'ada ar-rabbaniya* – "the way divine power customarily acts in creation." The case is similar with regard to what *usually* occurs but which is not *always* the rule, like the various kinds of laxatives or other medicines: they can usually be counted on to have such-and-such an effect – on the basis of experience in the majority of cases – although it does not hold true in every case. Thus it would only be correct to forbid the seeing of omens in these latter instances – that is, with regard to *al-'ada ar-rabbaniya* which does not necessarily bring about harm as such. However, if despite this, someone were to see a bad omen (in such an instance), then he will harmed by it (as a punishment).'"

He also said: "The two hundred and sixt-seventh section (from *al-Farouq*): 'The principle underlying portents: auguries which are halal and omens which are haram: "As for taking omens and acting in accordance with them, we have mentioned their nature and the judgements in their regard above; as for auguries, that is thinking that there is good in something, and acting accordingly, they are generally considered to be the (exact) opposite of omens. However, sometimes auguries clearly indicate good and sometimes the indication is ambivalent. An example of an augury which is clearly positive would be a man unintentionally overhearing someone saying to another 'How happy you are!'; or a child or servant boy being addressed with a beautiful name – such that on hearing it, one's heart is filled with joy. Such auguries are good omens and are thus licit – and are what we are referring to here. It is has also been related in the *Sahih* that the Messenger of Allah, may the peace and blessings of Allah be upon him, changed names he disliked to names he found beautiful. These two kinds are both licit auguries. These are the auguries being referred to by those who related that he, on whom be peace and blessings, 'used to like the permitted (kind of) augury'; or when they related that he, on whom be peace and blessing, 'liked good omens.' As for omens which are forbidden, at-Tartushi commented, saying: 'Taking auguries from the *mus-haf*, geomancy, taking lots and plucking hairs (from one's head) – all of these kinds are forbidden as they are a kind of oracle-seeking analogous to 'divining arrows' which were customary in the Jahiliyya. On the one (arrow) was written "do it!", on another "do not do it!" and on a third (what to do is) "undetermined!" The person selected one of them and if he found "do it!", then he would set about the matter he had in mind; if he found "do not do it!", then he would desist from doing it, believing it would be dangerous or evil to do so; if he selected the one with "undetermined!" on it he would repeat the selection. In this way the person would attempt to seek (to find out his) lot or destiny in the unseen from these sticks. (Taking auguries from geomancy etc.) is thus also a kind of oracle-seeking analogous to these "divining arrows", for the person is actively seeking some good sign which he may act upon or some evil sign which he may avoid. Likewise, whoever takes an augury from a *mus-haf* or something else – and follows it up, such that if the (sign) turns out to be good, he acts upon the (intended action) and if bad, he avoids it – then this would also be considered analogous to the practice of "divining arrows", which has been forbidden in the Qur'an; and I have not seen any difference of opinion related about this. The difference between this and the permitted kind of augury mentioned above is that this latter may waver between good and evil (depending on the intent), whereas the first is only associated with a good (intent) and is naturally accompanied by a good opinion of Allah, exalted is He. Thinking well of Allah is necessarily good as it is a means of bringing about good – whereas the other lends itself to thinking ill of Allah, exalted is He, and so is forbidden. Moreover, it is forbidden, and thus classed a *tayra* merely on account of this bad opinion – not usually for a reason particular (to the omen in question). This is the gist of the difference between omens and auguries which are permitted and those which are forbidden.'" Ibn ash-Shat has also accepted this (definition of al-Qarafi).

49. It has been related in *Sahih Muslim*: "Whoever desires the meeting with Allah, then Allah desires to meet him, and whoever dislikes to meet Allah, then Allah will dislike to meet him." 'A'isha, may Allah be pleased with her, said: "Then I asked: 'Prophet of Allah, does this refer to an aversion to death? – when all of us dislike death.' He said: 'It is not like that, for the *mumin* is he who when given the good news of the mercy of Allah, His contentment and His Garden, desires to meet Allah and so Allah desires to meet him; the *kafir*, however, when told of the anger of Allah and His torment will not want to meet Allah and Allah will not want to meet him.'" An-Nawawi said: "The last part of the hadith explains the first – and is also a commentary on the other *hadith* which speak of 'those who desire to meet Allah' and 'those who dislike to meet Him.' The 'aversion' (on the part of the *kafir*) mentioned in the hadith refers to the moment when the *ruh* is being taken from the body, that is, when *tawba* is no longer possible – not to any other time. Thus the hadith is giving

the good news or warning of what awaits every person: the people of success and good fortune will desire death and the meeting with Allah, they will desire what has been promised them and Allah will desire to meet them, that is, (His love will be expressed) by His generosity and magnanimity; the people of misfortune and ruin will not want to meet Him because of their misdeeds and the requital that awaits them, and Allah will not want to see them, that is, the way His dislike of them will manifest is that He will withhold His mercy and welcoming generosity from them."

50. It is stated *in al-Jami' as-Saghir*: "The son of Adam will not encounter an experience more intense – from the time Allah, exalted is He, created him – than death, but then (the experience of) death will be easier for man than anything after it." Al-Munawi said: "that is, the dreadful states (after death), like the terror of the questioning from (the angels) Munkir and Nakeer, the terror of the rising from the graves on the Day of Rising, the terror of the blast of the trumpet (on the Last Day) and the terror of the Standing (in judgement before Allah)."

He also related in *al-Jami' as-Saghir* that: "The treatment meted out by the angel of death will be worse than a thousand strikes of a sword; also, that if a stone as great in mass as seven pregnant camels (*khalifat*) were to be thrown from the edge of Hell, it would descend for seventy years without reaching the bottom, and *khalifat* is the plural of *khalifah* which is a pregnant camel; also that if a bucket of *ghassaq* – the putrid matter flowing from the misfortunate in Hell – were to be poured out into this world, (all of) the people of this world would putrefy from it; also that if a drop from the (fruit of the) *Zaqqoum* tree of Jahannam were to fall into this world, it would poison the earth and all means of subsistence – and how (terrible) the fruit of this tree must be for those who will eat of it."

O you the Most Merciful of the merciful the most Merciful of the merciful, the Most Merciful of the merciful! By Your overflowing generosity, make the agony of death and what comes after it of the states of terror easier to bear for us and for those we love – for surely You possess vast generosity and You do not care what you give or to whom You give.

51. Ash-Shabrakheeti said in *Sharh al-'Ashmawiya*: "It has been related that a young man was close to death but his tongue refused to respond to the people repeating the *shahada* (for him). So they went to the Prophet, may the peace and blessings of Allah be upon him, and informed him of this. He got up, went in to (his room to) see him and began to repeat the *shahada* to him. The man was shaking and trembling but his tongue would not utter anything. The

Prophet, may the peace and blessings of Allah be upon him, asked: 'Did he use to make the *salat*, pay the *zakat*, fast (in Ramadan)' and they answered: 'Indeed, he did all of this.' Then he said: 'Did he disobey his parents or treat them badly?' They replied: 'Yes he did.' He, on whom be peace and blessings said: 'Bring his mother here!' and she came. She was an old woman who was blind in one eye after the young man had hit her. He, on whom be peace and blessings, said to her: 'Have you forgiven him?' She said: 'I cannot forgive him as he hit me and knocked out my eye.' (The Prophet then said): 'Bring wood and fire' and she said 'What are you going to do with the fire?' He replied: 'I will burn him in front of you as a repayment for what he did.' Then she said: 'I forgive him: I have carried him for nine months, fed him at my breast for two years and I now forgive him.' Then his tongue loosened and he said: '*ash-hadu al la ilaha illa'llah wa ash-hadu anna Muhammad rasoulullah*,' may the peace and blessings of Allah be upon him."

52. Sayyidi 'Abd al-Wahhab ash-Sha'rani related that Khidr said: "I asked twenty-four thousand prophets as to whether there was something to protect the slave from having his iman being taken from him and none of them could answer me until I met Muhammad, may the peace and blessings of Allah be upon him. On asking him about it, he replied: 'It is related (to me) from Jibril from Allah that whoever perseveres in reciting the *ayat* of the Footstool[1], the *ayats* "*The Messenger has iman in what has been sent down − to the end of the sura*"[2], the *ayat*: "*Allah bears witness...*" up to His words "*the deen with Allah is Islam*"[3] and "*Say: 'O Allah! Master of the Kingdom!...*'" to His words "*without any reckoning*"[4] and Surat al-Ikhlas, the *al-Mu'awadhatan* (the two final suras of seeking refuge and (finally) the Fatiha at the end of each *salat*, then he will be protected from having his iman being taken from him.'"

It is stated in *Hashiya as-Safti 'ala'l-'Ashmawiya*: "One of our Shaykhs said: 'The most evident judgement is that one should recite Surat al-Ikhlas after the *ayat* of the Footstool.'"

53. Ash-Shabrakheeti said in *Sharh al-'Ashmawiya*: "Al-Asbahani has narrated one of the hadith of Ibn 'Abbas, may Allah be pleased with both of them, who said: 'The Messenger of Allah, may the peace and blessings of Allah be upon him, said: "Whoever makes two *rak'ats* after *Maghrib* on the night before

---

1 al-Baqara – The Cow: 253
2 al-Baqara – The Cow: 284
3 Ali 'Imran – The Family of 'Imran: 18
4 Ali 'Imran – The Family of 'Imran: 26

jumu'a, reciting in each the Fatiha and *'When the earth is convulsed…'*[1] fifteen times, then Allah will ease for him the agony of death, will protect him from the torment of the grave and facilitate his passing over the *Sirat* (bridge over the Fire) on the Day of Rising"- and there is something similar in *Shafa' as-Sadr* of as-Suyuti.'"

54. It is related in (the *Sahih* of) al-Bukhari from Abu Hurayra that the Prophet, may the peace and blessings of Allah be upon him, said: "The first to be called on the Day of Rising will be Adam who will be shown his offspring. Then it will be said to them: 'This is your father, Adam.' Adam will say: '*Labbayk wa sa'dayk*' and will then be told: 'Send out the party of Hell from among your offspring.' Adam will say: 'O Lord how many should I send out?' Allah will say: 'Send out ninety-nine out of every hundred.' They (Prophet's companions) then said: 'Messenger of Allah, if ninety-nine out of every hundred of us are taken away, who of us will remain?' He said: 'My followers in comparison to the other nations are like a white hair on a black ox.'"

55. It is also related in (the *Sahih* of) al-Bukhari: "The people will continue performing the Hajj and Umra to the Ka'ba even after the appearance of Yajuj and Majuj", and in Muslim: "Whoever of you gets to see him, should recite the opening *ayats* of Surat al-Kahf – The Cave" – referring, by this, to the Dajjal.

56. Muhammad ibn Rushd said in *al-Bayan*, commenting on the hadith 'Anyone who has an atom's weight of iman in his heart will come out of the Fire': "This refers to someone with the least degree of iman such that if there were any less a person would return to doubt and *kufr* were any part of his iman to disappear. Its levels of merit are distinguished by the strength of certainty about Him and knowledge of Him and by his immunity to the onset of any doubts. *Iman* is not a physical body so it cannot be expressed in terms of weight. However, in a metaphorical sense it is correct to speak of 'an atom's weight of iman.' It is expressed in these terms as a metaphor to be grasped by the intellect, and success is by Allah."

57. Ibn Zakari said in *Sharh an-Naseeha*: "There are four stations with respect to people's witnessing His intermediary, may the peace and blessings of Allah be upon him: the first, the place of witnessing belonging to the people of His *shari'ah*. This refers to the *muminun* in general …." up to where he says: "… and here a point of benefit should be noted: that every Muslim has taken his portion of the *wilaya* – the proximity and protection – of Allah, in accordance with His words: *'Allah is the Protector (Wali) of those who have* iman.'[2] This is because

---

1 az-Zilzala – The Earthquake: 1
2 al-Baqara – The Cow: 25

anyone who obeys Allah, exalted is He, by submitting to His commands, even if only once in his life, or who desists from an act of disobedience for this same reason, will by it take (a portion) of *tajalli* (divine manifestation), of *takhalli* (by which he frees himself from wrong action) or *tahalli* by which his heart is expanded – and which is granted those who possess (some portion of) *wilaya* of Allah. What this means is that if the remembrance of Allah occurs to him when something happens to him, He manifests Himself to his heart by His mercy and so voids it of any (thought of) disobedience to Him and clothes it in obedience to Him. And it is likely that after this mercy He says, 'Do whatever you want, for I have forgiven you,' and so this is much more likely for someone who remembers Allah, exalted is He, in the great majority of his affairs. This is that which will aid the slave to honour all of the *muminin* and to hold a good opinion of them."

58. It is related in (the *Sahih* of) al-Bukhari from Abu Hurayra, may Allah be pleased with him, that the Prophet, may the peace and blessings of Allah be upon him, said: "The people will sweat so profusely on the Day of Resurrection that their sweat will sink seventy cubits deep into the earth, and it will rise up until it reaches the people's mouths and ears." Al-Qastallani said: "In the *marfu'* hadith of 'Uqba ibn 'Amir related by al-Hakim: "There are those whose sweat will reach their heels, then those whose sweat will reach halfway up their shanks, in the case of others it will reach their knees, for others it will reach their thighs, for others it will reach their waist, for others it will reach their mouths, and still others who will be completely covered by their sweat and they will beat their heads with their hands." The most evident meaning of his saying 'people' is that it refers to people in general, although in the hadith of 'Abdallah ibn 'Amr ibn al-'As he said: "The distress and affliction of the people that day be so great that sweat will reach up to the mouth of the *kafir*. It was said to him: 'So where is the *mumin* ?' He replied: 'on a throne of gold, shaded by clouds.'" Shaykh Abu 'Abdallah ibn Abi *Jamra* said: "It refers to some people in particular even if its literal meaning appears general: excluded are the Prophets, the *shuhada* and anyone Allah wishes (to exclude). The most intense sweating will be on the part of the *kafir*, then on the part of those who have committed major crimes and after them there will be (a number) of the Muslims – but they will be relatively few in comparison with the *kuffar*."

It is related from Sulayman, as recorded by Ibn Abi Shayba in his *Musannaf* – and the text is his, and the chain of narration is good – that Ibn al-Mubarak said: "On the day of Resurrection the sun will give out heat equal to ten years. It will come close to the skulls of people until there remains only a distance of two bows' length and the people will sweat until the sweat reaches a fathom into the earth. Then the (sweat) will rise until it seethes and bubbles over a man." Ibn al-Mubarak then added: "Its heat will not harm the Muslim man or woman."

Those being referred to, as al-Qurtubi has pointed out, are the men and women whose iman is perfect – for it has been recorded that people differ in this in accordance with their actions. In another narration ranked as *sahih* by Ibn Hibban it has been recorded that: "sweat will enter a man's mouth on the Day of Resurrection until he says 'O Lord give me respite, even if it is into the Fire.'"

59. It is narrated in (the *Sahih* of) al-Bukhari that Abu Sa'id al-Khudri said: "The Messenger of Allah, may the peace and blessings of Allah be upon him, said: 'The *muminun* will be saved from the Fire and then they will be stopped on an arched bridge between the Garden and the Fire and each will have the right to retaliation – regarding wrongs committed against one another. After they are cleansed and purified (through the retaliation), they will be admitted into the Garden; and by Him in Whose hand the self of Muhammad is, everyone of them will know his dwelling in the Garden better than he knew his dwelling in this world.'"

Al-Qastallani said, commenting on saying 'between the Garden and the Fire': "It is said that it is another *Sirat* (bridge over the Fire) and that it is on the side flanking the Garden." Al-Qurtubi said: "They are the *muminun* about whom Allah is aware that any demand of retaliation will not (be so great as to) consume their good deeds." The author of *al-Fath* said: "It may well be that the people of 'the Ramparts (*A'raf*)' will be among them, according to the preponderant opinion, and that they will be of two kinds: those who enter the Garden without reckoning and those – among the people of *tawhid* – who will be stopped by their actions: those who will have success (in the reckoning) will be those who, when required to answer for what they have done, will be able to redeem their (bad actions) by their good actions – that is, they will be freed (from the Fire) because their good actions will be either equivalent to the bad or will be more numerous."

60. The author of *Kitab an-Nurayn*: "The means to pass (quickly) over the *Sirat* is to think well of Allah, exalted is He, to say the *salat* of the Messenger, may the peace and blessings of Allah be upon him, to sit facing the *qibla*, except in the toilet, and to say:

أَشْهَدُ أَن لَّا إِلَهَ إِلَّا اللَّهُ وَحْدَهُ لَا شَرِيكَ لَهُ إِلَهاً وَاحِداً وَرَبّاً شَاهِداً وَنَحْنُ لَهُ مُسْلِمُونَ

'ashhadu al-la ilaha illa' llah wahdahu la shareeka lahu, ilahan wahidan wa rabban shahidan wa nahnu lahu muslimun – I witness that there is no god but Allah alone without partner, One God and a Lord Who witnesses and we are submitted (Muslims) to him'

four times after the *fard salat*. Whoever does this, then Allah will make the *Sirat* (only) four cubits (long) by four cubits wide."

61. It is related in (the *Sahih* of) al-Bukhari: "There are two phrases which are light on the tongue, but are heavy in the balance and are beloved of the All Merciful:

$$\text{سُبْحَانَ اللَّهِ وَبِحَمْدِهِ سُبْحَانَ اللَّهِ الْعَظِيمِ}$$

"*subhanallahi wa bihamdihi subhana'llah al-'adheem* – Glorious is Allah and with His praise Glorious is Allah the Vast.'"

Ash-Shabrakheeti said: "*Tasbeeh* is *tanzih* – distancing Allah from anything contingent (in creation): so (saying) '*subhana'llah*' means one is declaring and confirming His distance from anything which is not appropriate (to His attributes). As for the *ba'* of *bihamdihi*, it has been said that it is causal and so means '*on account of* praise of Him.' What is meant by *hamd* is invoking Allah's intervention and support to enable the person to perform the *tasbih* (properly). 'A'isha said, may Allah be pleased with her, on the occasion when she was the subject of a false accusation and then her innocence was revealed: '*bihamdi' llah la bi-hamdi ahad!* – (by the *hamd* of Allah not by the *hamd* of anyone else!). In other words, it happened on account of praise of Allah, that is by His overflowing generosity, by His kindness and grace: generosity, kindness and grace thus result from the *hamd* and are expressed by the *hamd*." This has been stated by Ibn Daqeeq al-'Eid who also said: "The *ba'* means *alif – lam* (the definite article) – and so what is actually being said here is *subhana rabbi'l-'adheem wa'l-hamdu lillahi* – Glorious is Allah the Vast and praise belongs to Allah" – and this is an opinion without parallel.

62. The author of *Fath al-Bari* said: "Reneging on iman – and we seek refuge with Allah from this – seldom occurs: when the joy of iman has filled the heart, it cannot be provoked into anger by anyone."

63. It is related in *Sahih Muslim* as well as in *al-Jami' as-Saghir*: "When the Day of Resurrection arrives Allah will allot every man a man from the *kuffar* saying: 'This is your ransom from the Fire.' I have also seen another (narration) in a correct copy to the effect that 'He will accord every Muslim a ransom from

the Fire by means (of one of) the *kuffar*.' It is related from Abu Musa that the Messenger of Allah, may the peace and blessings of Allah be upon him, said: 'When the Day of Resurrection arrives Allah will hand over to every Muslim a Jew or Christian saying: "This is your means of freeing yourself from the Fire!"'

O Allah, You are the Most Merciful of the merciful, change the evil actions of those who will possess this (work), those who copy it down and those who study it sincerely into good actions, O Master of Majesty and Generosity, O Master of Majesty and Generosity, O Master of Majesty and Generosity; and give me and those who copy, study or possess – or who helped in it or who corrected it – the seal of fortune and happiness (on death), O Living, O Self-Sustaining! Forgive me and them, my parents, my Shaykhs and those I love and whoever studies it assiduously; and treat us with Your kindness and forgive us by Your overflowing bounty and generosity. O Allah grant blessings to Muhammad and the Family of Muhammad, just as You granted blessings to Ibrahim, You are the Praiseworthy, All-Glorious; O Allah, grant *baraka* to Muhammad and his Family just as You granted *baraka* to Ibrahim, You are the Praiseworthy, All-Glorious. O Allah forgive the *muminun* men and women, the Muslim men and women, the living amongst them and the dead. Glory be to your Lord, the Lord of Might, beyond anything they ascribe. Glory belongs to You, O Allah and all Praise. I bear witness that there is no god, only You, I seek forgiveness of You and I turn in *tawba* to You.

This book, entitled *Mufeed al-'Ibad*, is now complete – and praise belongs to Allah – by His good help, His granting of success and His kindness, and there is no power and no might except by Allah, the Most High, the Magnificent. It has been composed at the hand of the author, the slave, the wrongdoer, who errs and who is indulgent with his lower self, the weak, the despicable Muhammad ibn Ahmad in 1272 after the *hijra* of our Master Muhammad, may the peace and blessings of Allah be upon him. O Allah grant peace and blessings to our Master Muhammad and His Family and his Companions by the number of creational realities encompassed by Your knowledge, O Lord! Amin.

O Allah grant blessings to our Master Muhammad, the Liberator of mankind, the Seal of the Prophets, may Allah bless him and his Family in accordance with his great rank and honour, and his Companions and those who follow them with *Ihsan* to the Day of Judgement. Glory be to your Lord, the Lord of Might, beyond anything they ascribe and peace be upon the Messengers. And praise be to Allah, the Lord of all the Worlds!

Index

INDEX

A

ADORNMENT 465, 916
  bracelet 321
  cosmetics 321
  ear piercing 322
  earrings 321
  henna 269, 328
  oil 782
  perfume 275, 321, 327, 349, 423, 487, 493, 496, 692, 754, 774, 776, 782, 784, 787, 804, 833
  perfumes 321
  signet-rings 268
  threads 265
  turbans 266
  wool 265
AFFLICTIONS 30, 500, 698, 929, 930, 931
ALLAH
  absolute independence 71
  al-'adam al-mumkin 100
  al-huduth 95
  Allah's anger 812
  annihilation 95
  as-sifat al-wujudiyya 93
  attributes 9, 19, 21, 40, 45, 47-48, 50-51, 57, 60, 71-74, 76-77, 79-82, 86, 94-95, 104, 106, 111, 113-4, 117-21, 128-32, 134-7, 145, 150-1, 180, 187, 313, 315, 388, 414, 428, 559, 565, 573, 675, 680-1, 868, 883, 894, 905, 910-2, 928, 941 968
  dhikr 153
  essence of Allah 115, 950
  footstool 104
  haadith 94
  hawadith 96
  hearing 76
  His essence 57, 73, 76, 83, 99, 118, 119, 129, 130, 131
  His Speech 82
  huduth 110
  i'dam 100
  independence 119
  knowledge 76
  Oneness 73, 75, 153, 170, 173, 344, 455, 483, 799
  other than Him 9, 74, 76, 80, 95, 127, 133, 150, 152, 184, 222, 935
  power 76
  Pure Presence 934
  qa'im binafsihi 72
  qadeem 94
  qurba 258
  sifa azaliya 90
  sifa nafsiyya 71
  sifa zahir 72
  sight 76
  speech 76
  speech (*kalam*) of Allah 16, 82, 92, 95, 180, 196, 568
  tanzeehan li-qudsihi 74
  throne 104, 115, 591, 966
  timelessness 46, 112, 113, 114, 120, 122, 126, 127, 128, 129, 131, 134, 150
  will 76
ANIMALS
  bees 84, 520, 784
  billy goat 820

calf 235
camels 206, 207, 246, 266, 598, 600, 613, 614, 615, 616, 619, 622, 625, 632, 634, 635, 647, 739, 749, 789, 794, 822, 823, 830, 963
carcass 233, 247, 924, 942
cat 99, 958
cattle 246, 361, 789
cow 234, 445, 618, 620, 621, 789, 893
dead animals 242
dog 9, 259, 352, 353, 411, 422, 446, 580, 901, 909, 910, 911, 912, 958
donkey 203, 241, 401, 445, 446, 752, 924, 939, 941
dung 63, 412, 413, 776, 911, 912
flowing blood 234
fodder 445, 793
fox 107
horse 235, 445, 500, 610, 737, 958
horses 207, 797, 823
killing game 750
lions 781
livestock 164, 246, 599, 600, 610, 615, 619, 620, 624, 625, 626, 627, 628, 629, 630, 635, 647, 648, 655, 896
locusts 239, 482, 790
mice 781
mountain goat 820
neck 241
old bone 241
pasture 361, 449, 450, 629, 744, 793
pig 247, 352, 353, 411, 413, 912
puppy 402
ram 820
rats 781
riding beast 843
scorpions 482, 781, 794, 926
sheep 234
sheep and goats 18, 246, 449, 450, 598, 600, 619, 630, 632, 636, 739, 776, 887
sheep or goats 621
skinned 234
slaughtering 205, 233, 234, 236, 241, 243, 247, 411, 413, 470, 579, 615, 616, 733, 749, 794, 795, 819, 820, 822, 830, 887
snakes 781
stray sheep or goats 885
tigers 781
urine 246
veins 236
wild beasts 524
wild donkey 752
wolves 781
worms 482, 520, 790
'AQIDA 6, 40, 47, 48, 50, 51, 56, 57, 60, 63, 65, 78, 108, 115, 150, 152, 169, 172, 183, 257, 274, 311, 428, 429, 430, 454, 455, 510, 560, 654, 662, 724, 912, 931, 950
absolute proof 102
annihilation 114
Ash'aris 64, 84, 169, 172
contingent nature 108
Decree 167
imperfection 139
incidental occurrence 107
in-time occurrence 108
kalam 46, 62, 126, 169, 170, 171, 173
lawh al-mahfudh 95
muqallid 48, 56, 58, 59, 60
mutakallimun 47, 61, 64, 74, 75, 258, 661
Mu'tazalis 64, 128, 183, 489
non-existence 98
tanzih 87, 454, 968
taqlid 48, 49, 50, 53, 54, 55, 56, 57, 58, 59, 60, 61, 63, 102, 115, 164, 265, 406, 580, 581, 582, 604, 605, 631, 632
tasawwur 71
tawhid 49, 51, 52, 54, 55, 56, 74, 104, 115, 124, 126, 137, 150, 151, 152, 154, 155, 160, 175, 177, 189, 455, 489, 559, 599, 676, 731, 813, 816, 858, 967
ASTROLOGERS 541

B

BEAR 352
BIRDS 184, 520, 602, 794

Index 975

crows 781
feather 243
ravens 781
BODY
  ankles 213, 267, 833
  anus 285, 415
  armpits 66, 241, 321, 322, 334, 340, 726, 789, 893
  arsenic 203
  awra 415, 421
  baldness 260
  beard 141, 260, 261, 265, 272, 320, 322, 367, 481, 772, 775, 782, 833, 872, 902
  belly 335
  bleeding 545
  blood 242, 302
  breaking wind 285
  breasts 292
  buttocks 321
  cheek 260, 262, 295, 482
  chest 335
  ear cavities 271, 325
  elbow 444
  elbows 262
  excrement 231, 234, 237, 245, 247, 248, 285, 300, 301, 545, 580, 910
  eye-brows 377
  eyes 453
  fat 304
  fingers 262, 277
  foetus 234, 235
  folds of fat 261, 321
  foot 242
  forearms 263
  forehead 260, 261, 295, 396, 410, 478
  forelock 264
  genitals 842
  gums 277
  hair 66, 141, 163, 183, 199, 208, 209, 210, 242, 247, 260, 261, 263, 264, 265, 267, 292, 300, 319, 320, 327, 328, 333, 334, 367, 418, 469, 477, 481, 550, 580, 731, 739, 772, 775, 776, 782, 784, 786, 790, 795, 821, 829, 833, 861, 965
  hands 957
  hands and forearms 256, 260, 262, 264, 267
  head 32, 66, 166, 208, 210, 235, 236, 241, 255, 256, 260, 261, 263, 264, 266, 267, 270, 271, 272, 273, 278, 279, 280, 292, 293, 295, 320, 326, 327, 328, 330, 331, 334, 362, 377, 395, 396, 399, 401, 415, 452, 462, 466, 490, 491, 492, 497, 499, 520, 530, 531, 532, 552, 578, 580, 583, 585, 586, 624, 686, 691, 692, 693, 701, 724, 726, 733, 750, 751, 757, 759, 775, 782, 783, 785, 786, 787, 789, 795, 814, 824, 843, 854, 861, 864, 872, 899, 927, 935, 941, 944, 947, 957, 960, 961
  heart 13, 17, 28, 33, 34, 49, 53, 54, 59, 61, 65, 92, 117, 140, 141, 146, 150, 152, 156, 157, 160, 167, 168, 169, 170, 171, 173, 178, 179, 206, 222, 236, 257, 258, 261, 274, 308, 389, 390, 395, 396, 416, 429, 444, 455, 468, 479, 480, 481, 483, 486, 496, 512, 523, 525, 548, 564, 646, 652, 662, 663, 800, 823, 844, 855, 856, 858, 860, 873, 876, 889, 891, 892, 893, 903, 906, 907, 909, 911, 914, 918, 919, 920, 922, 923, 924, 928, 930, 933, 935, 950, 957, 961, 965, 966, 968
  index finger 277
  jaw bones 260
  ligament 265
  limbs 65, 105, 114, 123, 138, 163, 254, 255, 256, 257, 260, 272, 281, 284, 324, 327, 329, 350, 362, 369, 395, 398, 399, 421, 422, 444, 479, 493, 782, 864, 900, 907, 923, 947, 948
  matted hair 328
  menstruation 65, 66, 258, 301, 336, 337, 341, 363, 411, 430, 694, 702, 708, 754, 761, 762, 792, 833
  molars 278
  mucus 242
  nails 263, 268, 269, 321, 377, 453, 550,

726, 772, 775, 782, 783, 784, 788, 789, 790
navel 323, 414
nose 242, 272, 286, 324, 325, 367, 396, 410, 446, 482, 687, 691, 692
nostrils 278
nura 203
palate 278
palm 262, 335
penis 285, 286, 290, 296, 299, 300, 301, 305, 334, 335, 339, 416, 573, 691, 791
private parts 66, 203, 296, 304, 306, 308, 322, 324, 325, 332, 335, 342, 405, 414, 416, 417, 418, 420, 675, 693, 696, 730, 756, 861, 898, 900, 901, 955
puberty 47, 65, 66, 204, 457, 458
pubes 726
pubic hairs 203
recesses 321
saliva 235, 287, 303
scalp 365
shaving 208
shoulder 262
siamese twins 264
skull 264
soles 384
sperm 65, 66, 103, 336, 412, 695, 696, 704, 705, 754, 791
stomach 235, 248, 522, 523, 525, 675, 687, 691, 692, 701, 876
sweat 235, 322
tattoos 266
teeth 66, 105, 277, 278, 701, 759
temples 141, 261, 265, 377, 453, 786
thighs 321, 340, 414, 416
toes 279
upper body 340
urinary bladder 299
urinating 365
urination 285, 308, 322, 524
urine 286, 420
vagina 234, 242, 291, 295, 296, 308, 324, 335, 336, 338, 340, 414, 420, 424, 847

wadyi 285
wounds 124, 246
wrist 262

BUSINESS TRANSACTIONS
advanced Payment 218
agents 637, 643, 656, 823
bankrupt 867, 880, 897
buying and selling 173, 196, 312, 468, 609, 610, 611
contracts 717, 846
debt for a debt 218
delayed payment 218
full lunar year 600
goods 218, 657
hawl 600
invalid transaction 218
investment 738
partnership 619, 630
profits 600, 602, 627
receiving a wage 890
renting 218
returning of deposits 427
taking possession 609, 618, 622, 623, 627
trade 20, 27, 218, 357, 609, 610, 623, 647, 648, 785
trading 752, 886
usury 175

C

CLOTHES 105, 163, 188, 236, 240, 241, 242, 244, 245, 249, 267, 275, 300, 302, 348, 362, 379, 384, 412, 413, 415, 422, 423, 431, 435, 521, 546, 592, 648, 730, 742, 747, 753, 756, 758, 759, 788, 790, 796, 804, 866, 876, 912, 942, 943, 946, 947, 955, 956
button 782
cloak 179, 466, 468, 574, 575, 785, 866
clothing 592
covering the face 782
gloves 782
khuffs 376
leather socks 302

sandals 410, 511, 727, 833, 872, 895, 912, 952
silk 203, 207, 266, 465, 881
transparent 414
turban 162, 172, 260, 377, 478, 575, 751
veil 7, 107, 415, 433, 463, 498, 759, 782, 785, 890, 894, 919, 946, 957
wooden clogs 303
COMPENSATION 259, 415, 427, 446, 616, 640, 655, 671, 736, 750, 755, 759, 779, 781, 782, 783, 784, 785, 787, 790, 793, 795, 850, 891, 892, 909, 930
  fidya 782, 783, 784, 785, 786, 787, 788, 789, 790, 792, 795
CREATION 933
CUPPING 138, 708, 786, 787, 830

D

DEATH 164, 817
  agony of death 180, 499, 963, 964
  bequests 897
  burial 162, 329, 492, 493, 494, 495, 806
  condemned to death 55, 353, 472, 860
  dead body 231
  drowning 19, 165, 179
  funeral 958
  good seal 804
  ground lotus leaf 329
  heirs 204
  human bones 247, 413
  ruh 278
  testament 306
  throes of death 278
  tomb 173, 409, 491, 724, 781, 803, 804, 807, 808, 809, 817, 818, 823, 824
  washing the dead 259, 493
DECREE 77, 78, 81, 84, 100, 101, 121, 183, 184, 206, 908, 931, 932, 933
  al-irada al-azaliya 78
  decreed 77
DEFECATION 322, 332
DHIKR 764
DIVORCE 149
  dhihar 649

DOORS 493
DREAMS 7, 33, 39, 213, 214, 287, 288, 289, 290, 339, 411, 676, 686, 687, 700, 791, 819, 823, 856, 865, 873, 898, 958
  interpretation 214
DRINKING
  drunk 215, 434
  wine 173, 196, 224, 243, 246, 247, 249, 274, 291, 311, 312, 330, 413, 560, 574, 604, 605, 643, 676, 844, 845, 857, 898, 902
DU'AS 729, 813, 937, 956
  supplications 424, 512

E

EATING
  apples 240, 628
  bread 247, 248, 333, 353, 479, 670, 671, 877, 896, 898, 960
  carrion 714
  chicken 276
  crops 502, 604
  currants 333
  dates 164, 240, 247, 314, 328, 333, 600, 603, 649, 663, 719
  disdaining food 333
  dough 263
  figs 314
  fish 23, 234, 239, 402, 861
  flour 239, 333, 670, 671, 700, 877
  food and drink 843
  fruit 192, 541, 599, 605, 610, 628, 632, 633, 634, 635, 787, 793, 887, 963
  grains 164, 599, 600, 602, 603, 605, 610, 628, 632, 633, 670, 671, 682, 865
  grapes 394, 636
  honey 177, 242, 247, 344, 628, 698
  legumes 635, 636, 663, 666, 670, 672
  lentils 334, 672
  meat 236, 240, 241, 242, 243, 246, 352, 353, 458, 616, 664, 665, 666, 671, 821, 876, 887, 895, 942, 948
  milk 247, 291, 300, 330, 333, 540, 632,

633, 634, 664, 665, 666, 671, 672,
    885, 887, 939
millet 334
oil or fat 230
olives 243, 636, 896
raisins 164, 247, 599, 600, 663, 672
rice 276, 663, 672
roasted meat 236
sarsaparilla 664
solid food 247
staple food 663, 664, 665, 666, 670,
    671, 719
syrup 334
vegetables 164, 344, 628, 632, 633, 792
vinegar 244, 245
ECLIPSE 237, 346, 500, 501
EXCHANGE 307

F

FAMILY
    abstention 342
    brothers 7, 384, 704, 807, 824, 835,
        887, 937, 948
    childbirth 336, 338, 426, 434
    children 10, 37, 38, 39, 62, 142, 201,
        202, 204, 208, 223, 224, 278, 367,
        384, 394, 412, 413, 427, 458, 498,
        499, 659, 676, 737, 807, 824, 835,
        866, 887, 897, 939, 941
    disobeying parents 214
    divorce 216
    emission 66, 290, 301, 336, 338, 339,
        412, 573, 689, 690, 695, 696, 704,
        705, 791
    father and mother 384, 716
    foster son 222
    giving birth 336
    husbands 133, 215, 216, 949
    kissing 203, 292, 293, 294, 295, 690,
        695, 696, 728, 731, 757, 791, 833,
        834, 899
    loud breathing 342
    mothers 716
    nafaqa 219
    orphans 642

pregnancy 65, 66, 712
pre-seminal fluid 412, 689, 690, 695,
    696, 791
prostatic fluid 285, 290, 301, 573, 791
relatives 211, 212, 292, 494, 804, 957,
    959
upkeep of parents 717
FASTING 21, 44, 133, 152, 163, 272, 277,
    314, 337, 355, 527, 665, 675, 678,
    679, 680, 681, 682, 684, 685, 688,
    691, 692, 693, 694, 695, 696, 697,
    698, 699, 700, 701, 702, 703, 704,
    705, 711, 715, 718, 719, 744, 784,
    785, 790, 818, 867, 881, 952
    'Ashura 676, 681, 682, 683
    compelled to break the fast 714
    desisting the rest of the day 717
    eating out of forgetfulness 718
    Eid al-Fitr 424, 660, 683
    intentionally breaking the fast 709
    i'tikaf 688
    Laylat al-Qadr 510
    miswak 700
    nafila broken deliberately 716
    Night of Power 510
    Ramadan 389
FATWA 5, 6, 8, 26, 402, 428, 579, 639,
    664, 889, 903, 956
FIQH
    al-hukm ash-shar'i 97
    Arabic language 86, 90, 95, 220, 565,
        620
    legal premise 99
FORGIVENESS 11, 33, 147, 156, 180,
    186, 187, 188, 204, 257, 258, 288,
    385, 396, 399, 421, 428, 453, 476,
    477, 483, 488, 497, 508, 512, 784,
    808, 813, 814, 839, 842, 843, 844,
    845, 846, 850, 852, 854, 857, 858,
    871, 872, 882, 898, 918, 920, 969

G

GENERAL
    advice 13, 141, 470, 656, 805, 945
    affecting kindness 225

Index

angels 11, 16, 36, 48, 54, 59, 166, 167, 182, 184, 187, 207, 214, 216, 251, 288, 306, 347, 349, 403, 448, 450, 452, 467, 477, 495, 498, 571, 675, 743, 855, 860, 898, 963
Angels 167
apostasy 435
arguments 9, 105, 308, 661
astronomer 57
auguries 936, 959, 960, 961, 962
backbiting 300, 311, 545, 547, 708, 845, 850, 851, 864, 866, 867, 868, 869, 871, 872, 949, 950, 951
Bedouin Arabs 566, 567, 570, 815
beggar 867
bells 206, 207
bismillah 9, 10, 180, 274, 307, 330, 331, 374, 477, 493, 683, 731
blind 578
blind man 578, 705, 810, 811
caravan 218
celestial bodies 406
claiming descent 222
company 360
complaint 49, 472, 499, 860, 932, 950
conceit 903
conversation 13, 24, 212, 220, 429, 432, 485, 547, 864, 865, 866, 924
cursing 226
Dajjal 448, 743, 818, 965
Dar al-Harb 218
dearth of food 334
destitute 179, 606, 637, 640, 644, 645, 785, 792, 881
dissimulation 225
dye 209, 244, 269, 412
ease 754
eid 237
envy 903
evil 12, 17, 18, 26, 27, 28, 37, 74, 116, 158, 159, 162, 167, 183, 205, 206, 207, 208, 223, 225, 226, 237, 274, 287, 307, 402, 423, 428, 429, 432, 441, 472, 477, 486, 498, 499, 505, 510, 511, 513, 540, 545, 554, 555, 557, 577, 594, 698, 800, 813, 822, 835, 847, 852, 858, 869, 886, 894, 895, 899, 901, 902, 906, 911, 920, 921, 924, 925, 930, 932, 936, 945, 952, 954, 959, 961, 962, 969
excessive disputation 219
faqir 637
firewood 908
flattery 27, 224, 225
forbearance 925, 928, 929
games 513
Generosity 178, 807, 843, 937, 969
generosity to guest 223
geomancy 960, 961
good behaviour 14, 177, 640
good intention 220
greetings 198, 199, 212, 439
guest 432
guests 223, 224, 881
guidance 31, 57, 144, 184, 204, 238, 429, 495, 859, 947
hammam 319
hand spans 309
hermaphrodite 420
hospitality 215, 223, 224, 289
hunger 714, 790
hypocrites 867
idols 16, 49, 107, 172, 816
ijma' 138
images 74, 210
iman 3, 13, 16, 19, 21, 35, 47, 48, 50, 51, 53, 55, 59, 61, 66, 67, 287, 289, 342, 389, 427, 428, 454, 455, 468, 469, 496, 509, 510, 512, 572, 621, 661, 807, 812, 814, 817, 840, 855, 856, 858, 860, 876, 886, 895, 904, 905, 912, 922, 930, 953, 956, 964, 965, 966, 968
impotent man 578
ingratitude 215
ink 268
intoxication 291
irrigation 605
Jahiliyya 161, 961
laughing 30, 524, 525
leprosy 139
life 6, 11, 15, 26, 34, 49, 55, 61, 76, 77,

97, 104, 120, 128, 129, 144, 150, 153, 162, 175, 176, 177, 178, 179, 189, 199, 225, 354, 357, 369, 385, 448, 476, 484, 498, 502, 539, 545, 554, 573, 651, 676, 683, 710, 711, 717, 754, 813, 814, 823, 840, 841, 844, 858, 865, 869, 872, 910, 912, 916, 926, 956, 965
lying 866
magic 143
misfortune 39, 179, 199, 499, 541, 644, 856, 866, 931, 962
miskeen 637
modesty 341, 342, 441, 640, 946
moon 57, 346, 457, 458, 501, 683, 684, 685, 687, 697, 706, 707, 719, 749, 753, 768, 770
mubah 356
neighbours 226, 280, 423, 453, 511, 578, 580, 581, 886, 899
niyya 258
non-Arabs 52, 67, 570
omen 541, 906, 958, 959, 960, 961, 962
overhearing 961
poetry 864
poor people 341, 601, 647, 719, 784, 815
poor person 19, 415, 637, 638, 642, 644, 645, 651, 655, 670, 738, 880, 883, 886, 887, 898, 911
pork 240
poverty 638
praise 9
pride 220
procurer 214
prostitute 214
public highways 302
ruqya 345, 884
sea 3, 63, 143, 145, 184, 208, 351, 406, 464, 509, 607, 744, 928, 954
shaytan 7, 12, 16, 49, 216, 221, 247, 268, 299, 300, 302, 349, 480, 488, 506, 510, 686, 733, 912
Shaytan 49, 78, 177, 179, 207, 274, 287, 288, 330, 479, 488, 497, 508, 520, 548, 818, 819, 820, 877, 909
slaughtering places 412

snow 365
soap 787, 790, 960
speech impediment 567, 568, 578
spitting 271, 300, 304, 521, 701
squandering 352, 936, 937, 938
suspicion 665
tanning 230
tents 547
thorn 268
toilet 37, 62, 245, 339, 341, 410, 445, 693, 947, 967
torture 352
trials 539
trickery 22, 142, 143, 646
urine 301
vanity 220
vomit 234, 236, 330, 690, 700, 864
vow 819
wadyi 291
waste and rubbish 308
Wastefulness 276
wax 263
weather 355
weep 824
weeping 539
GIFTS 15, 20, 402, 655, 804, 813, 815, 822, 824, 850, 851, 878, 886, 887, 891, 892, 893, 894, 935
GOVERNANCE
allegiance 14, 716, 878
Amir 295
Amirs 717
Bayt al-Mal 545, 878, 882, 884, 885, 887, 888, 893
Caesar 307
Emperor 307
Khalifas 74, 344, 818, 878
king 141
mujtahid 61
Sultan 89, 541, 542, 602, 608, 677, 781, 879, 880, 881, 885, 890, 891, 949
wakeel 890
waqf 164, 253, 608, 632, 633, 634, 689, 938

H

HAJJ 3, 9, 10, 20, 152, 153, 154, 163, 165, 166, 217, 218, 259, 313, 331, 362, 464, 465, 470, 681, 688, 689, 699, 723, 724, 726, 730, 731, 735, 736, 737, 738, 739, 741, 742, 744, 745, 746, 747, 748, 749, 750, 751, 752, 753, 754, 755, 756, 757, 758, 759, 760, 761, 762, 766, 767, 769, 770, 771, 772, 774, 777, 783, 784, 791, 792, 795, 796, 797, 798, 799, 800, 804, 808, 817, 822, 827, 828, 829, 830, 831, 832, 833
al-ifada 725
al-Multazim 729
'Arafat 463, 679, 681, 725, 730, 732, 733, 736, 739, 746, 747, 758, 759, 763, 765, 766, 767, 768, 769, 770, 771, 772, 774, 776, 791, 801, 819
at-Tarwiya 819
Black Stone 409, 728, 729, 731, 743, 755, 757, 794, 798, 821, 822, 833, 834
Day of Sacrifice 755
Dhu'l-Hulayfa 743
'Eid al-Adha 940
garlands 205, 206, 207
hady 750, 751, 761, 762, 765, 766, 767, 777, 780, 784, 785, 789, 791, 792, 795, 829
herbs 787
House of Allah 89, 735, 781, 822
hunting 739, 774, 776, 781, 783, 792
ifrad 742, 747, 748, 753, 755, 828, 829
ihram 10, 736, 754, 755
jamarat 733, 739, 765, 775, 777-9, 818-9, 820
Ka'ba 729, 757, 766, 794, 813, 821, 822, 834
Makka 4, 39, 202, 217, 313, 448, 454, 682, 715, 727, 728, 732, 733, 734, 735, 737, 738, 739, 741, 742, 744, 745, 746, 747, 749, 750, 751, 752, 755, 756, 757, 758, 759, 760, 761, 762, 780, 784, 793, 794, 796, 801, 804, 808, 816, 817, 818, 820, 821, 822, 829, 830, 831, 920, 940
Maqam of Ibrahim 731
Mina 681, 725, 732, 733, 734, 746, 747, 753, 763, 765, 766, 771, 773, 774, 775, 776, 778, 779, 780, 784, 790, 792, 820, 821
miqat 726, 739, 742, 743, 753
muhrim 754, 775, 786, 787, 788, 789, 790, 791, 793, 794, 795
Muzdalifa 679, 725, 733, 764, 771, 772, 773, 774, 775
pebble 733, 776, 777, 778, 780, 781
pillars 724
qiran 739, 742, 744, 747, 748, 751, 753, 756, 760, 828
ramal 755
sacrificial animals 501, 668
sa'y 725, 729, 730, 732, 736, 737, 739, 747, 748, 749, 756, 758, 759, 760, 761, 762, 763, 795, 796
Safa and Marwa 725, 729, 731, 736, 748, 749, 759, 761, 762
springs 220, 360
streams 360
talbiya 727
tamattu' 742, 744, 745, 747, 748, 750, 751, 755, 760, 761, 798, 828, 829
Tashreeq 733, 779
tawaf 259, 688, 689, 725, 728, 729, 730, 731, 733, 734, 736, 737, 738, 739, 741, 742, 748, 749, 753, 755, 756, 757, 758, 759, 760, 762, 765, 774, 775, 776, 778, 780, 781, 783, 791, 795, 796, 824, 833, 834
tawaf al-ifada 733, 739, 755, 757, 758, 762, 774, 775, 776, 778, 783, 791
tawaf al-qudum 725
'umra 218, 331, 688, 689, 724, 730, 734, 736, 737, 739, 742, 744, 747, 749, 750, 751, 752, 753, 754, 755, 756, 757, 760, 761, 762, 791, 792, 795, 796, 797, 798, 799, 800, 801, 817, 828, 829, 830, 833
wuquf 769

HEALTH
  balm 334
  sane mind 65
HUDUD
  adultery 138, 274, 846, 900
  blood money 197
  crimes 843, 852, 877, 901, 930, 955, 966
  false witness 127, 699, 708, 845, 866, 873
  fornication 196, 197, 311, 330, 353, 420, 433, 545, 562, 640, 715, 840, 842, 846, 847, 861, 867, 874, 877, 898, 899, 900, 901, 955
  hadd 154, 471, 577, 677, 899, 900, 930
  murder 291, 353, 562, 844, 851, 900, 953
  perjury 716
  prison 366
  prisoner 275, 356, 372
  punishments 154, 930
  renegade 353
  retaliation 353, 509, 546, 967
  revenge 385, 822, 870, 942
  seized illegally 620
  setting free 850
  slander 845, 847, 850, 864, 866, 871, 872, 873, 874
  slandering 847, 942, 954
  stealing 479, 640, 646, 842
  thief 352

I

ILLNESS 27, 139, 285, 309, 320, 328, 336, 351, 353, 354, 356, 395, 397, 417, 453, 499, 510, 542, 546, 578, 702, 703, 710, 711, 715, 748, 749, 783, 818, 841, 891, 928, 929, 930, 931, 932, 934, 943, 955
  bandages 376
  bloodletting 377
  constipation 286
  dressing 377
  gangrene 237
  grievous ailments 332
  insanity 693, 694
  leprosy 578
  medical 208, 377
  plague 6, 743, 790, 960
  plaster 350
  pus 301
  splints 376
IMITATING MEN
  women 214
INHERITANCE 17, 174, 604, 626, 662, 851
INSECTS 239, 482
  bedbugs 238
  bees 482
  beetles 482
  flea 233
  flies 234, 238, 239, 482, 784
  gnats 238, 482, 784
  grasshoppers 482
  hornets 482, 794
  lice 234, 238, 239, 482, 782, 783, 784, 786, 787, 788
  louse 233, 239, 240, 242, 300
  mosquitoes 482
  scorpion 379
  ticks 238, 239, 482
  vermin 482
ISLAM 3
  absolute command 197
  Ansar 53, 210, 223, 799
  Books 167
  collective 198
  da'wa 66, 67
  deen 3, 4, 7, 13, 17, 18, 20, 21, 22, 23, 24, 26, 32, 38, 48, 49, 50, 51, 52, 53, 54, 55, 56, 57, 59, 63, 64, 65, 115, 119, 133, 136, 142, 144, 147, 154, 165, 167, 168, 170, 171, 172, 173, 179, 180, 182, 183, 191, 198, 210, 212, 220, 223, 225, 237, 249, 279, 281, 288, 289, 295, 298, 300, 311, 312, 313, 314, 315, 323, 349, 354, 364, 423, 455, 467, 468, 480, 484, 488, 489, 500, 534, 548, 554, 555, 561, 562, 563, 575, 578, 580, 581, 597, 639, 641, 650, 661, 676,

713, 733, 791, 805, 823, 824, 835,
851, 862, 866, 869, 871, 881, 882,
888, 889, 890, 894, 897, 909, 914,
945, 955, 956, 964
dhikr 224
disliked 197
fitra 268, 287, 550
fitrat 64
five obligations 163
halal 3
halal and haram 894
haram 3
hijra 454, 730, 743, 817, 818, 969
ijtihad 50, 51, 63, 164, 406, 407, 408,
581, 582, 604, 631, 632
iman 167
individual 198
Ka'ba 169, 313, 406, 409, 682, 965
law 195
legally capable 10, 45, 47, 48
Madina 39, 173, 224, 390, 407, 409,
448, 454, 487, 496, 498, 507, 508,
511, 649, 671, 672, 682, 730, 734,
741, 742, 743, 747, 748, 790, 793,
797, 801, 808, 816, 817, 818, 822,
823, 824, 830, 831, 832, 887, 940,
950, 969
pale of Islam 421
pillars 163
recommended 197
reneging 298
sunna 15, 19, 25, 35, 39, 48, 56, 57, 61,
72, 74, 75, 81, 84, 115, 122, 126,
127, 128, 136, 148, 156, 158, 159,
160, 161, 171, 172, 173, 175, 182,
183, 186, 187, 188, 198, 201, 209,
219, 223, 226, 246, 250, 255, 260,
270, 271, 272, 273, 274, 278, 282,
283, 300, 311, 320, 325, 365, 374,
383, 392, 394, 398, 401, 410, 435,
436, 437, 440, 443, 447, 448, 449,
450, 456, 462, 469, 470, 471, 472,
473, 489, 491, 492, 493, 496, 500,
501, 502, 503, 507, 508, 515, 516,
517, 522, 523, 528, 549, 550, 551,
552, 554, 562, 583, 597, 678, 679,
680, 681, 685, 703, 705, 728, 729,
731, 736, 737, 741, 745, 755, 756,
761, 772, 775, 778, 779, 780, 795,
796, 797, 798, 804, 809, 816, 818,
819, 820, 825, 835, 840, 851, 852,
867, 876, 915, 917, 931, 959, 960
tariqa 40
two *shahadas* 163

J

JIBRIL 87, 91, 166, 167, 168, 171, 190,
198, 559, 745, 818, 819, 821, 964
JIHAD 166, 464, 500, 608, 644, 689,
797, 800, 873
army 224, 477, 884, 902
battleground 247
booty 545, 599, 833, 880, 883, 887, 888
Enemy 307
fighting in the way of Allah 643
fresh herbage 793
ghazi warrior 644
ghazwa 29, 202, 463, 465, 657, 800
raiding parties 800
shaheed 898, 921
shaheeds 498, 806
slingshot stone 776
soldiers 224, 375
spears and lances 444
swords 303, 891
Uhud 413
victories 344
warfare 352

K

KAFFARA 415, 608, 645, 656, 667, 670,
671, 672, 685, 688, 691, 696, 700,
702, 703, 704, 705, 713, 716, 718,
720, 750, 777, 790, 799, 800, 901,
925
expiation 645, 670, 671, 672, 696, 711,
719, 750, 784, 799, 957
KAFIRS 50, 51, 52, 53, 133, 135, 136,
137, 160, 165, 166, 168, 169, 172,
174, 177, 179, 184, 185, 188, 190,
198, 204, 218, 237, 249, 250, 258,

259, 260, 296, 298, 299, 300, 307,
311, 312, 313, 316, 349, 383, 434,
448, 450, 457, 458, 484, 486, 487,
488, 489, 496, 498, 499, 541, 542,
559, 561, 562, 571, 597, 598, 604,
621, 637, 661, 662, 676, 677, 854,
874, 898, 911, 912, 915, 920, 921,
922, 925, 927, 931, 953, 954, 956,
962, 966
 kuffar 52, 53, 64, 101, 107, 136, 145,
158, 159, 160, 169, 183, 189, 204,
448, 644, 659, 661, 685, 688, 786,
816, 912, 966, 968
KUFR 11, 32, 52, 56, 59, 78, 79, 88, 118,
119, 126, 135, 136, 166, 168, 169,
170, 172, 173, 174, 175, 182, 183,
185, 186, 188, 204, 210, 222, 249,
250, 274, 314, 315, 330, 409, 428,
429, 434, 448, 451, 489, 496, 545,
559, 562, 571, 598, 661, 662, 823,
855, 858, 874, 887, 889, 912, 918,
920, 921, 922, 932, 946, 965

L

LAND
 alabaster 776
 clay 142, 370, 487, 495, 776, 793, 898
 copper 354, 617, 677, 820
 cotton 477, 786
 cultivation 23, 792
 date palms 620, 634
 dust 303, 308
 fields 361, 940
 flagstones 370
 flash flood 370
 flax 203
 flint 776
 grass 230, 793
 iron 292, 303, 354, 817
 irrigation device 883
 levees 358
 linen 341, 477
 lotus 329
 marble 776
 mountains 33, 51, 61, 182, 450, 727, 764
 mud 242, 776
 Nile 358
 open countryside 450, 494
 pitch 263
 pool 230
 quartz 776
 quicklime 203
 river beds 230
 rivers 62, 319, 928
 sa'eed 370
 sand 224, 370
 shrubs 793
 soft earth 370
 stone 370
 tamarisk 230
 tar 232
 trees 230, 492, 493, 541, 793, 896, 928
 turab 370
 turf 229
 valley 370
 village 362
 well 230
 whetstone 776
 wood 230
LEAVES 230
LIFE
 ruh 342

M

MARRIAGE
 bridal chambers 104
 bride price 146
 consummated 458
 dowry 149, 218, 219, 292, 582
 feasts 421
 intercourse 258
 kissing 294
 love-play 290
 married woman 899
 sexual intercourse 13, 173, 292, 293,
  294, 312, 330, 331, 342, 690, 742,
  790, 791, 800
MIQAT 743, 748, 752, 754, 761, 796, 801
MI'RAJ
 Night Journey 11, 67, 144, 201, 298,

864, 927, 937
MONEY 500
  coins 307, 617
  creditor 546
  debts 427, 604, 633, 645, 879, 886, 897
  dinars and dirhams 307, 348
  dirhams 23, 275, 305, 602, 605, 617, 622, 632, 633, 635, 650, 652, 672, 738, 821, 848, 867, 876, 880, 881, 884, 887, 948, 952
  gold 142, 164, 200, 268, 465, 599, 600, 606, 608, 609, 610, 611, 615, 616, 617, 619, 620, 626, 627, 628, 632, 635, 642, 643, 648, 652, 737, 858, 966
  loans 632, 633
  mustaghriq adh-dhimma 882, 885
  qirad 893
  silver 164, 268, 465, 469, 599, 600, 605, 606, 608, 609, 610, 611, 615, 616, 617, 619, 620, 627, 628, 632, 635, 642, 643, 648, 650, 651, 652

N

NAFS
  lower self 14, 15, 18, 22, 24, 27, 28, 29, 51, 54, 66, 78, 118, 127, 159, 169, 170, 171, 209, 216, 221, 480, 523, 675, 687, 698, 841, 858, 910, 911, 912, 915, 936
NAQL 87, 646
  gathering narrated evidence 87
NEXT WORLD
  al-Hawd 187
  Day of Rising 11, 30, 38, 621, 641, 649, 651, 698, 816, 821, 830, 834, 845, 848, 851, 852, 860, 865, 867, 877, 893, 916, 924, 939, 943, 952, 954, 957, 963, 964, 965
  Final Hour 74, 539
  Fire 16, 24, 29, 36, 38, 53, 66, 67, 80, 84, 98, 99, 143, 154, 155, 156, 161, 162, 167, 172, 175, 185, 186, 188, 189, 204, 213, 215, 220, 223, 451, 483, 489, 492, 497, 509, 513, 539, 540, 562, 662, 663, 676, 698, 812, 841, 860, 867, 868, 873, 874, 876, 877, 900, 901, 904, 905, 926, 927, 936, 943, 948, 949, 951, 952, 954, 964, 965, 967, 968
  Fountain of the Prophet 167
  Garden 15, 16, 29, 30, 31, 36, 37, 38, 53, 54, 80, 84, 89, 146, 149, 154, 155, 156, 167, 175, 177, 185, 188, 189, 204, 211, 214, 216, 222, 223, 226, 248, 266, 267, 300, 422, 423, 489, 497, 498, 499, 522, 678, 698, 799, 812, 818, 820, 821, 841, 842, 872, 875, 904, 905, 912, 914, 926, 927, 936, 940, 943, 949, 957, 962, 967
  grave 34, 48, 49, 53, 54, 176, 250, 300, 448, 491, 493, 494, 495, 513, 539, 677, 747, 809, 812, 813, 814, 817, 818, 872, 877, 941, 943, 964
  Jahannam 98, 868, 904
  Last Day 963
  Sirat 167, 183, 184, 187, 189, 683, 936, 964, 967, 968
  the Balance 167
  unseen 224

O

OATHS 671
OTHER RELIGIONS
  Christians 49, 66, 207, 243, 305, 307, 364, 468, 497, 944, 968
  dhimmis 608
  Injil 82, 90, 168, 181, 190
  Jews 52, 66, 79, 88, 182, 204, 305, 454, 486, 497, 703, 886, 968
  jizya 204
  Samaritans 79
  Tawrah 82, 89
  Zabur 82, 179, 181, 190, 843
  Zoroastrians 429

P

PARENTS 659
PROPERTY AND POSSESSIONS

adz 370
astrolabe 407
basin 329
basins 104
baskets 824
bed 397
Bedouin's tent 643
bucket 245, 346, 356, 359, 693, 963
candles 824
carpet 811
carpets 104, 477
chimneys 104
cisterns 104
couches 104
courtyards 547
cradle 342
drains 104
earthenware pot 243
grind stone 370
gutter 248
houses 89, 199, 204, 230, 231, 280, 328, 457, 507, 576, 696, 728, 754, 799, 893, 902, 944
ivory 241
jugs 243
knife 303
lamps 425
measures 824
merchandise 615
mirror 790
mother of pearl 208
picks and shovels 824
pipes 104, 864
plaster 322
purse 652
receptacles 232, 243, 245, 246
ring 262
roofs 231
rope 785
saddle 203, 309, 376, 444, 445, 477, 741, 771, 773, 797, 927
saddles 823
sieve 300
signet ring 305
sofas 104
sword 60, 124, 183, 212, 303, 963

tables 104
thread 801
utensils 354
ventilators 104
vessels 243
walls 457
water bag 230
windows 104
wind-towers 104
PROPHETS 687
Adam 35, 73, 181, 190, 509, 649, 743, 809, 821, 851, 852, 900, 916, 963, 965
al-Masih 181
conveyance of the message 138
Hud 84, 144, 181, 190, 911, 930
Ibrahim 181
'Isa 4, 6, 82, 147, 166, 181, 218, 235, 240
Ishaq 6, 166, 181, 245, 297, 562, 746, 752, 761, 775, 778, 797, 799, 820, 920
Isma'il 181, 393, 702, 820
Lut 181, 190
Messengers 167
miracles of the Prophet 491
Muhammad 3
Nuh 181, 190
Salih 181
Shu'ayb 181, 190
sincerity 138
trustworthiness 138
Ya'qub 181, 190

Q

QUR'AN 7, 16, 24, 25, 28, 29, 33, 35, 53, 56, 57, 82, 86, 87, 92, 94, 95, 118, 144, 145, 146, 161, 165, 184, 188, 196, 204, 207, 208, 237, 238, 250, 274, 289, 306, 307, 313, 331, 344, 345, 347, 348, 366, 367, 384, 388, 393, 394, 421, 426, 451, 469, 470, 471, 472, 479, 480, 483, 487, 491, 509, 510, 511, 512, 516, 533, 543, 564, 565, 566, 568, 569, 570, 571,

572, 579, 641, 654, 672, 676, 696,
761, 781, 799, 884, 887, 929, 943,
944, 945, 951, 960, 962
al-lafdh al-muʿjiz 83, 87
Furqan 82, 181, 190, 895, 916, 954
imala 393
mus-haf 82, 250, 274, 313, 315, 347, 348,
366, 393, 420, 445, 491, 571, 960,
962
shadhdh 393
sleeplessness 344

R

RAMADAN
thirty days 683
REMEMBRANCE OF ALLAH 158

S

SADAQA 208, 219, 469, 477, 487, 503,
506, 508, 509, 597, 607, 623, 639,
645, 649, 650, 655, 656, 678, 689,
779, 784, 787, 823, 845, 867, 880,
881, 882, 883, 885, 938, 955
SALAT 163
a cloth 322
adhan 9, 10, 274, 331, 349, 388, 431,
441, 449, 450, 451, 452, 453, 454,
455, 468, 495, 508, 543, 547, 549,
557, 559, 574, 594, 705, 732, 733,
767
al-ada' 391
al-i'tidal 396, 399, 443
al-qada' 391
arriving late 443
'asr 185
bowing 392, 395
clean of filth 405
columns 575
daruri 357, 434
dawn 418, 433, 503, 510, 512, 687, 688,
691, 693, 694, 703, 705, 706, 708,
713, 717, 718, 733, 734, 767, 770,
771, 772, 775, 777
dhuhr 390, 418, 430, 455, 456, 462, 463,
464, 475, 507, 511, 513, 514, 527,

559, 734
Eid prayer 502
elapse of time 359
fajr 178, 196, 395, 425, 503, 504, 514,
539, 549, 688, 713, 757, 766, 767,
770, 772, 773
fard 11, 20, 258, 280, 282, 283, 311, 315,
316, 319, 350, 365, 371, 385, 387,
388, 389, 392, 394, 396, 404, 439,
440, 449, 451, 464, 473, 477, 480,
481, 488, 489, 492, 503, 505, 507,
513, 516, 517, 520, 522, 523, 526,
530, 549, 550, 551, 552, 554, 555,
556, 557, 558, 559, 562, 575, 577,
583, 588, 594, 598, 599, 603, 677,
678, 688, 736, 737, 741, 745, 756,
757, 762, 768, 771, 797, 798, 799,
800, 808, 817, 830, 858, 876, 922,
968
fard salat 392, 449, 473, 477, 481, 505,
507, 516, 551, 554, 556, 557, 756
fear (*salat*) 403, 404, 436, 553
finding water 372
forgetfulness 283
ghusl 230, 242, 258, 261, 268, 279, 286,
292, 294, 304, 311, 316, 319, 322,
323, 324, 332, 333, 334, 335, 337,
338, 339, 340, 345, 349, 355, 369,
379, 416, 425, 431, 433, 492, 493,
549, 550, 559, 677, 700, 706, 709,
726, 727, 731, 741, 747, 758, 763,
796, 833
hadath 297, 319, 322, 326, 339, 375
healthy 343, 351, 357, 358, 365, 366,
377, 395, 702, 710, 711, 712, 780
ikhtiyari 359, 372, 430
imam 259
impure water 229
impurity 241
instinja' 301
intention 387
inviolable sanctity 387
iqama 431, 440, 441, 450, 452, 455, 523,
553, 557, 580, 732, 733
'isha 166, 403, 731, 734, 764, 771, 772,
774

istibra' 299, 300
Jami' mosque 543
jama'a 539
janaba 119, 254, 255, 259, 294, 319, 326, 332, 338, 345, 346, 349, 350, 361, 363, 365, 367, 369, 377, 420, 426, 432, 451, 549, 592, 677, 700, 754, 762, 797
janaza 356, 365, 366, 403, 437, 450, 489, 490, 491, 492, 496, 508, 547
joining *salats* 403
judgement of travelling 459
jumu'a 539, 732, 761, 774
khutba 451, 502, 503, 505, 539, 542, 543, 549, 686, 730, 732, 916
kifaya 404, 406
knees 395
last possible time 373
latest time 359
maghrib 734, 771
middle prayer 250
mihrabs 407
minbar 451
mistaken *qibla* 417
miswak 277
mosques 279
mu'adhdhin 450, 451, 452, 547, 549, 557
nafila 279, 356, 366, 392, 394, 437, 438, 442, 451, 477, 501, 503, 504, 505, 506, 507, 508, 511, 513, 514, 520, 548, 554, 556, 594, 689, 709, 715, 716, 737, 757, 758, 759, 876, 922
najasa 322
night prayers 679
obesity 324
on board a ship 400
paralysed 574
patch of unwashed skin 263
penetration of water 319
praying alone 440
prescribed time 371
prostrating 440
prostration 392
purification 15, 17, 145, 165, 250, 259, 273, 276, 281, 298, 300, 340, 346, 347, 350, 351, 362, 364, 376, 379, 405, 410, 416, 417, 425, 436, 464, 561, 562, 665
purification 229
qibla 405, 482, 493
qiyam al-layl 679
Qunut 466, 521
rain prayer 500, 502, 503
raising hands from grouind 397
rak'ats 964
redness in sky 362
relaxing 398
return to standing 392
ritual impurity 119, 307, 320, 322, 326, 334, 339, 345, 346, 348, 362, 410, 420, 426, 591, 592, 786
roofs 397
rubbing in water 253, 322
ruku' 438
sajda 396, 397, 468
salat riding 397
shortening the prayer 217, 706
sitting 397
siwak 180
standing in for imam 404
standing straight 398
stones 301
straightening up 395
subh prayer 437, 487, 733, 764
sunnas of *ghusl* 326
sutra 309, 443, 444, 445, 446, 521, 758
takbir 9, 390, 400, 405, 432, 438, 443, 492, 519, 528, 529, 534, 569, 576, 580, 587, 588, 727
takbiratu'l-Ihram 387
Tarawih 394, 507
tashahhud 439
tayammum 286, 293, 294, 311, 320, 325, 340, 346, 351, 353, 354, 355, 357, 358, 362, 364, 367, 368, 370, 371, 373, 377, 395, 416, 436, 573
tent 400
terraces 397
the standing 387
tuma'neena 399
used water 362
water 229

within the time 358, 417, 522
witr 395, 437
wudu' 253
zenith 407
SHARI'A
  law 9
  minors 605
  mukallaf 10, 47, 48, 49, 50, 52, 53, 57, 124, 152, 195, 196, 197, 259, 521, 558, 581, 697, 736, 737, 877, 917, 927
SHIRK 27, 56, 107, 124, 159, 160, 490, 815, 860, 900, 915
SICKNESS 3, 23, 50, 351, 546, 903, 909, 911, 914, 934, 955
  contagious disease 958, 960
  fainting 291, 434, 769
  fever 351, 707
  madness 138, 291, 434
  vomiting 526, 527, 687, 690, 691, 700
SLAVES
  client 643
  client slaves 565
  freeing (the slave) 901
  runaway slave 215, 224, 249, 357, 460
  slave 73

T

TASAWWUF 4, 21, 75, 499, 860, 888, 917
  awliya' of Allah 177
  content 925
  doing without 925
  fear 925
  free 933
  gnostic 933
  gratitude 925
  hope 925
  ihsan 61, 191, 807, 909
  inner truths 63
  killing of our selves 23
  love 925
  ma'rifa 924, 934
  path 917
  proximity 18, 934, 965

  reliance 925
  science 936
  sciences of unveiling 149
  Shaykh 716, 917
  spiritual light 65
  wayfarer 40
  wilaya 934, 965
TAWBA 925
TAXES 603, 608, 655, 892
TRADES AND PROFESSIONS
  artisanal work 300
  artisans 700
  carpenter 105
  doctor 378
  doctors 510
  fortune teller 224
  highwayman 357
  milkmaid 300
  shepherd 222, 357, 642
  soothsayer 960
  workshops 700

U

ULCEROUS SORE 246
UMM AL-QUR'AN
  Fatiha 178, 385, 389, 392, 394, 398, 436, 437, 438, 443, 448, 467, 475, 481, 517, 533, 534, 558, 563, 564, 565, 566, 567, 568, 569, 570, 964
UNSEEN
  tablet of forms 87

V

VIRGIN 308, 339, 684, 899
VOWS 470

W

WAR 644
WOMEN 52, 62, 65, 158, 201, 208, 209, 210, 214, 215, 216, 218, 239, 262, 263, 266, 267, 268, 292, 294, 295, 301, 327, 336, 342, 360, 404, 414, 416, 420, 422, 424, 425, 427, 429, 462, 465, 502, 679, 683, 695, 702, 715, 739, 745, 746, 755, 758, 761,

768, 774, 775, 776, 781, 783, 784, 785, 791, 833, 835, 857, 862, 864, 898, 899, 943, 946, 949, 950, 952, 966
breast feed 713
females 66, 208, 384
free woman 419
istidhhaar 337
istihada 336
journey 217
mahram 216, 217, 218, 219, 239, 292, 420, 421, 444, 446, 677, 831, 861, 899, 944, 945
menstrual blood 424
nushuz 215
plaits 265
whitish fluid 424
womb 424

zakat al-fitr 672
zakat of trade 164

Y

YAJUJ AND MAJUJ 67, 855, 965

Z

ZAKAT 15, 23, 154, 163, 164, 165, 259, 280, 344, 422, 597, 598, 599, 600, 601, 602, 603, 604, 605, 606, 607, 608, 609, 610, 611, 614, 615, 616, 617, 618, 619, 620, 621, 622, 623, 624, 625, 626, 627, 628, 629, 630, 631, 632, 633, 634, 635, 636, 637, 638, 639, 640, 641, 642, 643, 644, 645, 646, 647, 648, 649, 650, 651, 654, 655, 656, 657, 659, 660, 661, 663, 664, 665, 666, 668, 669, 670, 671, 672, 796, 798, 867, 882, 892, 893, 952, 963
barley 164, 635, 636, 663, 664, 671, 672, 719, 865
debtors 643
mu'allafati qulubuhum 644
nisab 600, 605
sa' 659
upkeep 659
wasqs 605
wheat 164

www.ingramcontent.com/pod-product-compliance
Lightning Source LLC
Chambersburg PA
CBHW070752300426
44111CB00014B/2376